INTRODUCTION
TO
COMPARATIVE LAW

BY

KONRAD ZWEIGERT

Emeritus Professor, University of Hamburg
Emeritus Director, Max Planck Institute for Foreign and International Private Law

AND

HEIN KÖTZ

M.C.L. (Mich.)
Professor, University of Hamburg
Director, Max Planck Institute for Foreign and International Private Law

Second Revised Edition

translated from the German by
TONY WEIR
Fellow of Trinity College, Cambridge

CLARENDON PRESS · OXFORD

Oxford University Press, Walton Street, Oxford OX2 6DP

Oxford New York Toronto
Delhi Bombay Calcutta Madras Karachi
Kuala Lumpur Singapore Hong Kong Tokyo
Nairobi Dar es Salaam Cape Town
Melbourne Auckland Madrid

and associated companies in
Berlin Ibadan

Oxford is a trade mark of Oxford University Press

Published in the United States by
Oxford University Press Inc., New York

First edition published 1977 © North-Holland Pub. Co.
This edition published 1987 © Oxford University Press and J. C. B. Mohr (Paul Siebeck)
Printed in one volume new as paperback 1992

British Library Cataloguing in Publication Data
Zweigert, K.
An introduction to comparative law.—2nd ed.
1. Comparative law
ISBN 0–19–825778–3

Library of Congress Cataloging in Publication Data
Zweigert, Konrad, 1911–
[Einführung in die Rechtsvergleichung auf dem Gebiete des
Privatrechts. English]
Introduction to comparative law / by Konrad Zweigert and Hein Kötz;
translated from the German by Tony Weir.—2nd rev. ed.
Translation of: Einführung in die Rechtsvergleichung auf dem
Gebiete des Privatrechts.
Includes bibliographical references and index.
1. Comparative law. 2. Civil law. I. Kötz, Hein, 1935–
II. Title.
K583.Z813   1992   340'.2—dc20   [342]   92–246
ISBN 0–19–825778–3

5 7 9 10 8 6 4

Printed and bound in Great Britain by
Biddles Ltd, Guildford and King's Lynn

Preface to the Second Edition

Auf Vergleichen lässt sich wohl alles Erkennen, Wissen zurückführen.

*Novalis**

A generous and elevated mind is distinguished by nothing more certainly than an eminent degree of curiosity; nor is that curiosity ever more agreeably or usefully employed, than in examining the laws and customs of foreign nations.

*Samuel Johnson***

On its first appearance (Vol. I, 1971; Vol. II, 1969) our *Introduction to Comparative Private Law* met with a very friendly reception, not only from specialists at home and abroad, to whom thanks are due for helpful suggestions, but also from those for whom it was primarily designed—those who were finding the study of law rather a provincial matter when confined to their home system and were keen to take advantage of the wider juristic perspectives offered by comparative law. The book was translated into Japanese by MASAO OKI (Vol. I, University of Tokyo Press, 1974) and into English by TONY WEIR (Vols. I and II, North Holland Publishing Co., 1977), but it has been out of print in Germany for several years. A new edition has therefore been planned for some time.

This proved unexpectedly troublesome. Volume I, on the 'Framework', discusses the nature of comparative law, its function, aims, methods and history, and then surveys the great legal families of the world. Elementary though such a work may be, developments in the last dozen years nevertheless necessitated a great many alterations and additions. To give just a few examples, more has been said on the relationship between comparative law and legal sociology (pp. 10–12) and new sections have been added on the legal profession in France (Ch. 9 III), on the law of Israel (Ch. 18 VII) and on the characteristic features of the civil law trial in England and the United States (Ch. 20 V).

Volume Two, 'The Institutions of Private Law', has also seen much amendment. It considers selected aspects of Contract, Tort and Unjust Enrichment, with the aim of demonstrating how comparative research in law is actually done, of providing basic information on the structures and solutions of foreign systems, and of evaluating the present stance of German law and its possible development. Even this volume can do no more than give the skeleton of comparative law, presenting only the major features of the

* Works III (ed. Minor, Jena 1907) 45, fragment 229.
** Boswell's Life of Johnson I (ed. Hill and Powell, Oxford 1934) 89.

great legal institutions. Rather than answering questions it poses them, and it seeks to stimulate further research, not to replace it. Even so, intervening legal developments in many areas have been such that it was not enough just to update the bibliographies and cite the recent cases. At many points the text had to be amended or extended. Thus there are new sections on standard terms in contracts (Ch. 1 III), on strict liability for products (Ch. 19 V) and on the movement from liability to insurance (Ch. 19 VI). How to include the new material without increasing the size of the book was a difficult question, but we finally decided to omit those passages in Volume One which dealt with a legal institution typical of the style of each of the great legal families— illegitimacy in the Romanistic family, the German doctrine of the abstract real contract and the Anglo-American trust. Despite this drastic step, the book is longer than before.

One point made in the Preface to the First Edition bears repetition. We are fully conscious that this book is neither comprehensive nor conclusive: it is not intended to be. If, as RABEL hinted, there are any 'natives with arrows' lying in wait for comparatists who venture into the thickets of their law, the password is: 'every student serves the truth'.

Finally, a word about this translation. We have been told by many English and American friends that Tony Weir's version of the first edition was fine. Indeed, one American professor of law who is fluent as a native in both German and English went so far as to say that the translation was better than the original, rare though that is, and acceptable, he was kind enough to add, though the original in this case was.

Hamburg, February 1984   KONRAD ZWEIGERT
                                                              HEIN KÖTZ

Translator's Foreword

I was particularly pleased to be allowed to try my hand at translating the *Einführung in die Rechtsvergleichung* by Zweigert and Kötz because on first reading it I had been afraid that so excellent a work, without counterpart in English, might remain inaccessible to those with no German. The enjoyable process of translation, much facilitated by the remarkable lucidity of the original, has left me with an enhanced regard for its merits, deep gratitude for the great helpfulness of its authors and a realisation that nevertheless I have been unable quite to reproduce its calm authority.

Trinity College, Cambridge   TONY WEIR
December 1976
March 1987

Contents
PART I

PART II

Abbreviations

* For decisions from Common Law jurisdictions two citations are sometimes given in the text: the second of such citations is generally easier to follow up, and it is the only one here explained.

App. Cas.	Law Reports, Appeal Cases (1875–90)
ArchbürgR	*Archiv für bürgerliches Recht*
Ark. L. Rev.	*Arkansas Law Review* (from 1946)
ARSP	*Archiv für Rechts- und Sozialphilosophie*
AWD	*Aussenwirtschaftsdienst des Betriebs-Beraters*
BAG	Bundesarbeitsgericht
BAGE	Decisions of the West German Federal Labour Court (Bundesarbeitsgericht)
Bank Arch.	*Bankarchiv*
Basler jur. Mitt.	*Basler juristische Mitteilungen* (from 1954)
BB	*Der Betriebsberater* (from 1946)
BBl.	*Bundesblatt der Schweizerischen Eidgenossenschaft*
BGB	(West) German Civil Code
BGBl.	*Bundesgesetzblatt*
BGE	Decisions of the Swiss Federal Court (Bundesgericht)
BGHZ	Decisions of the West German Federal Supreme Court (Bundesgerichtshof) in civil matters
BlZüRspr.	*Blätter für Zürcherische Rechtsprechung*
Bol. Inst. Méx.	*Boletin del Instituto de derecho comparado de México*
Bol. Mex. der. comp. NS	*Boletín mexicano de derecho comparado* (from 1968)
Bost. Ind. Com. L. Rev.	*Boston College Industrial and Commercial Law Review*
Brit. YB Int. L.	*The British Year Book of International Law*
Bull. civ.	Bulletin des arrêts de la Cour de cassation, chambres civiles
Bull. Soc. lég. comp.	*Bulletin de la Société de législation comparée* (1873–1948, then *Revue internationale de droit comparé*)
BUL Rev.	*Boston University Law Review* (from 1921)
BVerfG	Bundesverfassungsgericht
BVerfGG	Statute of the West German Constitutional Court (Bundesverfassungsgerichtsgesetz)
BVerwGE	Decisions of the West German Federal Administrative Court (Bundesverwaltungsgericht)
BW	Dutch Civil Code (Burgerlijk Wetboek)
Calif. L. Rev.	*California Law Review*
Camb. LJ	*The Cambridge Law Journal*
can.	canon
Can. Bar Rev.	*The Canadian Bar Review*
Cass.	Supreme Court of Cassation (Italy)
Ch.	Law Reports, Chancery Division (from 1891)
Ch. D.	Law Reports, Chancery Division (1875–90)
Ch. réun.	Cour de Cassation, Chambres réunies
cif	cost, insurance, freight
CISG	United Nations Convention on the International Sale of Goods (Vienna, 1980)
Civ.	Cour de Cassation, Chambre civile
CLR	Commonwealth Law Reports (Australia)
Clunet	*Journal du droit international*, founded by CLUNET

Cmd., Cmnd.	Command Paper
Cod. Iur. Can.	Codex Iuris Canonici
Colum. J. Transnat'l L.	*Columbia Journal of Transnational Law* (from 1962)
Colum. L. Rev.	*Columbia Law Review*
Com.	Cour de Cassation, Chambre commerciale et financière
Comp. Int. LJS Afr.	*Comparative and International Law Journal of South Africa*
Comp. L. Yb.	*Comparative Law Yearbook* (from 1977)
Cornell L. Rev.	*Cornell Law Review* (from 1915, called *Cornell Law Quarterly* till 1967)
Crim.	Cour de Cassation, Chambre criminelle
Curr. Leg. Prob.	*Current Legal Problems* (from 1948)
D.	*Recueil Dalloz de doctrine, de jurisprudence et de législation* (1945–64); *Recueil Dalloz et Sirey de doctrine, de jurisprudence et de législation* (from 1965)
DA	Dalloz, *Recueil analytique de jurisprudence et de législation* (1941–44)
DC	Dalloz, *Recueil critique de jurisprudence et de législation* (1941–44)
DH	Dalloz, *Recueil hebdomadaire de jurisprudence* (1924–40)
DJZ	*Deutsche Juristenzeitung* (1896–1936)
DLR 2d	Dominion Law Reports, Second Series (Canada)
DNotZ	*Deutsche Notar-Zeitschrift*
DP	Dalloz, *Recueil périodique et critique de jurisprudence, de législation et de doctrine* (1825–1940)
DPCI	*Droit et pratique du commerce international* (from 1975)
DR	*Deutsches Recht*
Duke LJ	*Duke Law Journal*
ECE	Economic Commission for Europe
EEC	European Economic Community
Eng. Rep.	English Reports (1307–1865)
Ex. D.	Law Reports, Exchequer Division (1875–80)
F. (2d)	Federal Reporter (Second Series)
FamRZ	*Ehe und Familie im privaten und öffentlichen Recht* (from 1962); *Zeitschrift für das gesamte Familienrecht* (from 1954)
FGO	Ordinance of the Financial Court in Germany (Finanzgerichtsordnung)
fob	free on board
Foro it.	*Il Foro Italiano*
Foro pad.	*Il Foro padano*
F. Supp.	Federal Supplement
Gaz. Pal.	*Gazette du Palais*
Gaz. Trib.	*Gazette des Tribunaux*
Geo. Wash. L. Rev.	*George Washington Law Review* (from 1932)
GG	West German Basic Law (Grundgesetz)
Giust. civ.	*Giustizia civile*

GlU (NF)	Decisions of the Austrian Supreme Court (Oberster Gerichtshof), collection founded by GLASER and UNGER (new series from 1900)
GVG	Gerichtsverfassungsgesetz
Harv. L. Rev.	*Harvard Law Review*
HGB	West German Commercial Code (Handelsgesetzbuch)
HR	Dutch Supreme Court (Hoge Raad)
ICLQ	*The International and Comparative Law Quarterly*
Incoterms	International Commercial terms
Ind. LJ	*Indiana Law Journal* (from 1925)
Int. Enc. Comp. L.	*International Encyclopedia of Comparative Law*
Inter-Am. L. Rev.	*Inter-American Law Review*
Int. Leg. Mat.	International Legal Materials
Iowa L. Rev.	*Iowa Law Review*
JBl.	*Juristische Blätter*
JbOstR	*Jahrbuch für Ostrecht*
J. Bus. L.	*The Journal of Business Law*
J. Comp. Leg.	*Journal of Comparative Legislation and International Law*
JCP	*Juris-Classeur périodique, La Semaine juridique*
Jher.Jb.	*Jherings Jahrbücher für die Dogmatik des bürgerlichen Rechts*
J. Int. Jur. Komm.	*Journal der Internationalen Juristenkommission* (1957–68)
JL & Econ.	*Journal of Law and Economics* (from 1958)
J. Leg. Ed.	*Journal of Legal Education*
J. Leg. Stud.	*Journal of Legal Studies* (from 1972)
JR	*Juristische Rundschau*
J. Soc. Comp. Leg.	*Journées de la Société de législation comparée* (from 1979)
JSPTL	*Journal of the Society of Public Teachers of Law* (1924–38, from 1947), then, from 1981, *LS*
JT	*Journal des Tribunaux* (from 1881)
JurJb.	*Juristen-Jahrbuch*
Jur. Rev.	*Juridical Review* (from 1889)
JuS	*Juristische Schulung*
JW	*Juristische Wochenschrift*
JZ	*Juristenzeitung*
KB	Law Reports, King's Bench (1901–52)
KO	Konkursordnung
La. L. Rev.	*Louisiana Law Review*
L. and Soc. Rev.	*Law and Society Review*
L. Contemp. Probl.	*Law and Contemporary Problems*
LJ Ch.	Law Journal Reports, Chancery (1831–1949)
LM	LINDENMAIER, MÖHRING, *et al.*, Reference Work to the Decisions of the West German Supreme Court (Bundesgerichtshof)
LQ Rev.	*The Law Quarterly Review*
LR Ch. App.	Law Reports, Chancery Appeal Cases (1865–75)
LRCP	Law Reports, Common Pleas Cases (1865–75)

LR Ex.	Law Reports, Exchequer Cases (1865–75)
LRHL	Law Reports, English and Irish Appeals (1866–75)
LRPC	Law Reports, Privy Council Appeals (1865–75)
LRQB	Law Reports, Queen's Bench (1865–75)
LS	*Legal Studies* (from 1981, previously *JSPTL*)
LT	Law Times Reports (1859–1947)
LuftVG	West German Air Traffic Act (Luftverkehrsgesetz)
LZ	*Leipziger Zeitschrift*
McGill LJ	*McGill Law Journal* (from 1952)
Mass.	*Massimario*
MDR	*Monatsschrift für deutsches Recht*
Mich. L. Rev.	*Michigan Law Review*
Minn. L. Rev.	*Minnesota Law Review*
Mod. L. Rev.	*The Modern Law Review*
Mont.	Montagu, Reports of Cases in Bankrupty (1832)
Mot.	*Motive zu dem Entwurfe eines Bürgerlichen Gesetzbuches für das Deutsche Reich* (1896)
no.	number
NBW	Nieuw Burgerlijk Wetboek
NE (2d)	North Eastern Reporter (Second Series)
Ned. Jur.	*Nederlandse Jurisprudentie*
NJ	*Neue Justiz*
NJW	*Neue Juristische Wochenschrift*
NW (2d)	North Western Reporter (Second Series)
NWUL Rev.	*Northwestern University Law Review*
NY	Reports of Cases Decided in the Court of Appeals of the State of New York (1877–1921)
NYS (2d)	New York Supplement (Second Series)
NYL Forum	*New York Law Forum*
NYUL Rev.	*New York University Law Review*
NZULR	*New Zealand Universities Law Review*
ObTr.	Decisions of the Prussian Supreme Court (Obertribunal)
OER	*Osteuropa-Recht* (from 1955)
OGH	Austrian Supreme Court (Oberster Gerichtshof)
OGHZ	Decisions in civil matters of the Supreme Court for the British Zone of Germany
ÖJZ	*Österreichische Juristen-Zeitung*
OLGE	Decisions in civil matters of the Oberlandesgerichte in Germany
OR	Swiss Code of Obligations
Oxf. J. Leg. Stud.	*Oxford Journal of Legal Studies* (from 1981)
P.	Law Reports, Probate Division (from 1891)
P. (2d)	Pacific Reporter (Second Series)
Prot.	Protokolle der Kommission für die 2. Lesung des Entwurfs des BGB
QB	Law Reports, Queen's Bench (1891–1900, from 1952)
QBD	Law Reports, Queen's Bench Division (1875–90)

Qd.R.	Queensland Reports (from 1958)
RabelsZ	*Rabels Zeitschrift für ausländisches und internationales Privatrecht*
Rec. des Cours	Recueil des Cours (from 1923)
Req.	Cour de Cassation, Chambre de requêtes
Rev. Contemp. L.	*Review of Contemporary Law*
Rev. dr. int. dr. comp.	*Revue de droit international et de droit comparé*
Rev. hell. dr. int.	*Revue hellénique de droit international* (from 1948)
Rev. int. dr. comp.	*Revue internationale de droit comparé*
Rev. jur. Univ. Puerto Rico	*Revista jurídica de la Universidad de Puerto Rico* (from 1932)
Rev. Soc. L.	*Review of Socialist Law* (from 1975)
Rev. trim. dr. civ.	*Revue trimestrielle de droit civil*
RGZ	Decisions in civil matters of the German Imperial Court (Reichsgericht)
RheinZ	*Rheinische Zeitschrift für Zivil- und Prozeßrecht des In- und Auslandes*
Riv. dir. com.	*Rivista del diritto commerciale e del diritto generale delle obbligazioni*
Riv. it. sci. giur.	*Rivista italiana per le scienze giuridiche*
RIW	*Recht der internationalen Wirtschaft* (1954/55–1957 and from 1975)
ROHG	Decisions of the German Imperial Commercial Court (Reichsoberhandelsgericht)
ROW	*Recht in Ost und West*
RSFSR	Russian Socialist Federated Soviet Republic
RVO	German Imperial Insurance Ordinance (Reichsversicherungsordnung)
s.	section
S.	*Recueil Sirey* (1791–1954, 1957–64)
S. Afr. LJ	*The South African Law Journal*
SavZ/Germ.	*Zeitschrift der Savigny-Stiftung für Rechtsgeschichte, germanistische Abteilung* (from 1880)
SavZ/Rom.	*Zeitschrift der Savigny-Stiftung für Rechtsgeschichte, Romanistische Abteilung*
Scand. Stud. L.	*Scandinavian Studies in Law*
SchwzZBGR	*Schweizerische Zeitschrift für Beurkundungs- und Grundbuchrecht*
SE (2d)	South Eastern Reporter (Second Series)
SeuffA	*Seuffert's Archiv*
SJZ	*Schweizerische Juristen-Zeitung*
SLT	*Scots Law Times*
So.	Southern Reporter
Soc.	Cour de Cassation, Chambre sociale
Som.	Sommaire
Stan. L. Rev.	*Stanford Law Review*
StGB	West German Penal Code (Strafgesetzbuch)

StuR	*Staat und Recht* (from 1952)
StVG	West German Road Traffic Act (Strassenverkehrsgesetz)
Süddt. JZ	*Süddeutsche Juristenzeitung*
SW (2d)	South Western Reporter (Second Series)
Sydney L. Rev.	*The Sydney Law Review*
SZ	Decisions of the Austrian Supreme Court (Oberster Gerichtshof) in civil and judiciary matters
Tex. L. Rev.	*Texas Law Review*
TLR	Times Law Reports
Trib. civ.	Tribunal civil
Trib. com.	Tribunal de commerce
Trib. gr. inst.	Tribunal de grande instance
Trib. paix	Tribunal de paix
Tul. L. Rev.	*Tulane Law Review*
U. Chi. L. Rev.	*The University of Chicago Law Review*
UCC	Uniform Commercial Code
U. Ill. L. Forum	*University of Illinois Law Forum* (from 1949)
ULFIS	Uniform Law on the Formation of Contracts for the International Sale of Goods
ULIS	Uniform Law on the International Sale of Goods
UNCITRAL	United Nations Commission of International Trade Law
Unidroit	L'Unification du droit
U. Pa. L. Rev.	*University of Pennsylvania Law Review*
US	United States Supreme Court Reports
U. Tor. LJ	*University of Toronto Law Journal* (from 1935)
UWG	West German Law of Unfair Competition (Gesetz gegen den unlauteren Wettbewerb)
Va. L. Rev.	*Virginia Law Review*
Vand. L. Rev.	*Vanderbilt Law Review*
Verh. DJT	*Verhandlungen des Deutschen Juristentages*
VersR	*Versicherungsrecht*
VLR	Victorian Law Reports (1875–1956, Australia)
VRS	Verkehrsrechts-Sammlung
VVG	West German Law of the Insurance Contract (Versicherungsvertragsgesetz)
Wash. L. Rev.	*Washington Law Review*
WGO	*Die wichtigsten Gesetzgebungsakte in den Ländern Ost-, Südosteuropas und in den ostasiatischen Volksdemokratien* (1959–66), then *Monatshefte für osteuropäisches Recht*
Wis. L. Rev.	*Wisconsin Law Review* (from 1920)
WLR	Weekly Law Reports
WM	*Wertpapier-Mitteilungen*, Part IV
Yale LJ	*The Yale Law Journal*
ZaöRV	*Zeitschrift für ausländisches öffentliches Recht und Völkerrecht* (1929–44; from 1950)
ZBernJV	*Zeitschrift des Bernischen Juristenvereins*
ZBl.	*Zentralblatt für die juristische Praxis* (Austria)

ZfRV	(Austrian) *Zeitschrift für Rechtsvergleichung* (from 1960)
ZGB	Civil Code (Switzerland, East Germany)
ZgesHR	*Zeitschrift für das gesamte Handelsrecht und Wirtschaftsrecht* (1858–1944, from 1948)
ZgesStW	*Zeitschrift für die gesamte Staatswissenschaft*
ZPO	West German Code of Civil Procedure (Zivilprozessordnung)
ZSR	*Zeitschrift für schweizerisches Recht*
ZStW	*Zeitschrift für die gesamte Strafrechtswissenschaft*
ZvglRW	*Zeitschrift für vergleichende Rechtswissenschaft* (1878–1942, 1953 ff.)
ZVR	*Zeitschrift für Verkehrsrecht* (Austria)
ZZP	*Zeitschrift für Zivilprozeß*

Table of Cases

ANGLO-AMERICAN LEGAL FAMILY

AUSTRIA

FRANCE

GERMANY (EAST)

GERMANY (WEST)

Table of Statutes

AUSTRIA

GERMANY (EAST)

Zivilgesetzbuch

GERMANY (WEST)

PART I

PART I

A. GENERAL CONSIDERATIONS

I

The Concept of Comparative Law

ADAM, 'Ethnologische Rechtsforschung', in: Adam/Trimborn, *Lehrbuch der Völkerkunde* (3rd edn. 1958) 189.

BANAKAS, 'Some Thoughts on the Method of Comparative Law: The Concept of Law Revisited', *Rev. hell. dr. int.* 33 (1980) 155.

v. BENDA-BECKMANN, 'Einige Bemerkungen über die Beziehung zwischen Rechtssoziologie und Rechtsvergleichung', *ZvglRW* 78 (1979) 51.

——, 'Ethnologie und Rechtsvergleichung', *ARSP* (1981) 310.

CARBONNIER, 'L'Apport du droit comparé à la sociologie juridique', in: *Livre du centenaire de la Société de législation comparée* I (1969) 75.

CHEBANOV, 'Science du droit comparé en U.R.S.S.', *Rev. int. dr. comp.* 27 (1975) 121.

COING, 'Die Bedeutung der europäischen Rechtsgeschichte für die Rechtsvergleichung', *RabelsZ* 32 (1968) 1.

DÖLLE, 'Der Beitrag der Rechtsvergleichung zum deutschen Recht', in: *Hundert Jahre deutsches Rechtsleben, Festschrift zum 100jährigen Bestehen des Deutschen Juristentages 1860–1960* II (1960) 19.

DROBNIG/REHBINDER (eds.), *Rechtssoziologie und Rechtsvergleichung* (1977, with important contributions from Drobnig, Gessner, Heldrich, Rehbinder, Terré, Zweigert, and others).

GENZMER, 'Zum Verhältnis von Rechtsgeschichte und Rechtsvergleichung', *ARSP* 41 (1954/55) 326.

——, 'A Civil Lawyer's Critical Views on Comparative Legal History', 15 *Am. J. Comp. L.* 87 (1966).

HAILBRONNER, 'Ziele und Methoden völkerrechtlich relevanter Rechtsvergleichung', *ZaöRV* 36 (1976) 190.

LAMBERT, 'Conception générale et définition de la science du droit comparé', Procès-verbaux des séances et documents, Congrès international de droit comparé I (1905) 26, printed in: Zweigert/Puttfarken (eds.), *Rechtsvergleichung* (1978) 30.

MARTINY, 'Rechtsvergleichung und vergleichende Rechtssoziologie', *Zeitschrift für Rechtssoziologie* 1 (1980) 65.

NODA, 'Quelques Réflexions sur le fondement du droit comparé; Aspects nouveaux de la pensée juridique', in: *Recueil d'études en hommage à Marc Ancel* I (1975) 23.

POSPISIL, *The Ethnology of Law* (2nd edn., 1978).

POUND, 'Some Thoughts About Comparative Law', in: *Festschrift Ernst Rabel* I (1954) 7.

——, 'Comparative Law in Space and Time', 4 *Am. J. Comp. L.* 70 (1955).

RABEL, *Aufgabe und Notwendigkeit der Rechtsvergleichung* (1925), reprinted in: Rabel, *Gesammelte Aufsätze* III (ed. Leser, 1967) 1.

RHEINSTEIN, 'Legal Systems: Comparative Law and Legal Systems', in: *International Encyclopedia of the Social Sciences* IX (ed. Sills, 1968) 204.

——, *Einführung in die Rechtsvergleichung* (1974, rev. v. Borries).

SCHWARZ-LIEBERMANN V. WAHLENDORF, *Droit comparé, Théorie générale et principes* (1978).

SEIDL-HOHENVELDERN, 'Die Rolle der Rechtsvergleichung im Völkerrecht', in: *Völkerrecht und rechtliches Weltbild, Festschrift A. Verdross* (1960) 253.

STONE, 'The End to Be Served by Comparative Law', 25 *Tul. L. Rev.* 325 (1951).

TALLON, 'Comparative Law: Expanding Horizons', 10 *JSPTL* 265 (1968).

WENGER, 'Rechtsgeschichte und Rechtsvergleichung', in: *Mémoires de l'Académie internationale de droit comparé* III 1 (1953) 149.

YNTEMA, 'Roman Law as the Basis of Comparative Law', in *Law—A Century of Progress 1835–1935* II (1937) 346.

ZWEIGERT, 'Rechtsvergleichung und Rechtsfortbildung heute,' *Universitas* 1973, 27.

——/PUTTFARKEN (eds.), *Rechtsvergleichung* (1978).

I

BEFORE we try to discover the essence, function, and aims of comparative law, let us first say what 'comparative law' means. The words suggest an intellectual activity with law as its object and comparison as its process. Now comparisons can be made between different rules in a single legal system, as, for example, between different paragraphs of the German Civil Code. If this were all that was meant by comparative law, it would be hard to see how it differed from what lawyers normally do: lawyers constantly have to juxtapose and harmonize the rules of their own system, that is, compare them, before they can reach any practical decision or theoretical conclusion. Since this is characteristic of every national system of law, 'comparative law' must mean more than appears on the surface. The extra dimension is that of internationalism. Thus 'comparative law' is the comparison of the different legal systems of the world.

Comparative law as we know it started in Paris in 1900, the year of the World Exhibition. At this brilliant panorama of human achievement there were naturally innumerable congresses, and the great French scholars ÉDOUARD LAMBERT and RAYMOND SALEILLES took the opportunity to found an International Congress for Comparative Law. The science of comparative law, or at any rate its method, was greatly advanced by the occurrence of this Congress, and the views expressed at it have led to a wealth of productive research in this branch of legal study, young though it is.

The temper of the Congress was in tune with the times, whose increasing wealth and splendour had given everyone, scholars included, an imperturbable faith in progress. Sure of his existence, certain of its point and convinced of its success, man was trying to break out of his local confines and peaceably to master the world and all that was in it. Naturally enough, lawyers were affected by this spirit; merely to interpret and elaborate their own system no longer satisfied them. This outgoing spirit permeates all the Congress papers; the whole Congress was dominated by a disarming belief in progress. What LAMBERT and SALEILLES had in mind was nothing less than a common law of mankind (*droit commun de l'humanité*). A world law must be created—not today, perhaps not even tomorrow—but created it must be, and comparative law must create it. As LAMBERT put it (above p. 1, pp. 26 ff.), comparative law must resolve the accidental and divisive differences in the laws of peoples at similar stages of cultural and economic development, and reduce the number of divergencies in law, attributable not to the political, moral, or social qualities of the different nations but to historical accident or to temporary or contingent circumstances.

Comparative law has developed continuously since then, despite great changes in man's attitude towards existence. The belief in progress, so characteristic of 1900, has died. At best we believe that history comes in waves, the crest of a later wave being perhaps a little higher than its predecessor. World wars have weakened, if not destroyed, faith in world law. Yet despite a more sceptical way of looking at the world, the development and enrichment of comparative law has been steady. Comparative lawyers have come to know their field better, they have refined their methods and set their sights a little lower, but they remain convinced that comparative law is both useful and necessary. Scholars are more resistant to fashionable pessimism than people in other walks of life; they have no immediate aim, only the ultimate goal of discovering the truth. This is true also of research in comparative law; it has no immediate aim. But if one did want to adduce arguments of utility, comparative law must be at least as useful as it was, especially as technological developments since 1900 have made the world ever smaller and, to all appearances, national isolationism is on the wane. Furthermore, by the international exchanges which it requires, comparative law procures the gradual approximation of viewpoints, the abandonment of deadly complacency, and the relaxation of fixed dogma. It affords us a glimpse into the form and formation of legal institutions which develop in parallel, possibly in accordance with laws yet to be determined, and permits us to catch sight, through the differences in detail, of the grand similarities and so to deepen our belief in the existence of a unitary sense of justice.

Despite all this, comparative law still occupies a rather modest position in academic curricula (see further Ch. 2 IV below). Though LAMBERT's great claims in this respect, as developed in his report of 1900 (above p. 1, pp. 53 ff.) were much more realistic than his dream of a 'droit commun de l'humanité', they have not yet been realized anywhere in the world. He thought that it would be greatly to the good of society if pride of place in academic studies were accorded to comparative private law, the heartland of all comparative law. For if clear and consistent general principles of law were established, this would promote international trade and advance the general standard of living, and if lawyers were induced to look beyond their borders, international exchanges would increase. For a practising lawyer to be capable of this, he must have been exposed while still at university to comparative legislation and comparative law. A further reason for promoting comparative law in the academic curriculum is that its study renews and refreshes the study of national law, which suffers from confining itself to the interpretation of positive rules and neglecting broad principles in favour of tiny points of doctrine.

It may indeed be that the mere interpretation of positive rules of law in the way traditionally practised by lawyers does not deserve to be called a science at all, whether intellectual or social. Perhaps legal studies only become truly scientific when they rise above the actual rules of any national system, as happens in legal philosophy, legal history, the sociology of law, and comparative law.

Now it is precisely the broad principles which comparative law lets one see; it can help the economist by discovering the social preconditions of particular rules of law, and by the comparisons it makes across time it can assist the legal historian. Students today are often put off by textual disputes, arid logomachies, and logical demonstrations, which prevent their seeing the living problems which lurk behind these technical facades. For this reason LAMBERT claimed for comparative law a place in the curriculum equal to that of the home system: four lectures a week should be given in comparative law for each of three semesters. Everything he said is as valid today as when he said it in 1900, but though much has improved in many countries in the ensuing eighty years, the radical restucturing of the curriculum which he showed to be necessary has yet to take place.

II

Comparative lawyers compare the legal systems of different nations. This can be done on a large scale or on a smaller scale. To compare the spirit and style of different legal systems, the methods of thought and procedures they use, is sometimes called *macrocomparison*. Here, instead of concentrating on individual concrete problems and their solutions, research is done into methods of handling legal materials, procedures for resolving and deciding disputes, or the roles of those engaged in the law. For example, one can compare different techniques of legislation, styles of codification, and methods of statutory interpretation, and discuss the authority of precedents, the contribution made by academics to the development of law, and the diverse styles of judicial opinion. Here too one could study the different ways of resolving conflicts adopted by different legal systems, and ask how effective they actually are. Attention may be focused on the official state courts: how is the business of proving the facts and establishing the law divided between attorneys and judges? What role do lay judges have in civil or criminal proceedings? What special arrangements, if any, are made for small claims? But one should not confine one's study to the state courts and judges: one should take account of all actual methods of settling disputes. Studying the various *people* engaged in the life of the law, asking what they do, how, and why, is a very promising field of work for comparative lawyers. First of all one would look at the judges and the lawyers, the people, whatever they are called, who apply or advise on the law in any system. But it can also be profitable to compare other persons involved in the law, such as the lawyers in Ministries and Parliaments who work on forthcoming legislation, notaries, the experts who appear in court, the claims adjusters of insurance companies and, last but not least, those who teach law in universities.

Microcomparison, by contrast, has to do with specific legal institutions or problems, that is, with the rules used to solve actual problems or particular conflicts of interests. When is a manufacturer liable for the harm caused to a consumer by defective goods? What rules determine the allocation of loss in the case of traffic accidents? What factors are relevant for determining the custody of children in divorce cases? If an illegitimate child is disinherited by his father or mother, what rights does he have? The list of possible examples is endless.

The dividing line between macrocomparison and microcomparison is admittedly flexible. Indeed, one must often do both at the same time, for it is only by discovering how the relevant rules have been created and developed by the legislature or the courts and ascertaining the practical context in which they are applied that one can understand why a foreign legal system resolves a given problem the way it does and not otherwise.

Thus one cannot give a true picture of the American law regarding the strict liability of the manufacturer just by listing the elements of a successful claim at law. One must also say that the claim will be decided in a trial by jury and show what roles the judge, lawyers, and jury play in such proceedings and how this influences the substantive law, by noting, for example, that in such a claim the plaintiff's attorney normally stipulates for a fee of 30–50 per cent of the damages awarded and that the jury takes account of this fact when fixing the damages. Or take a patient's claim for damages against a doctor for malpractice. No study could be complete or accurate without saying how malpractice is proved in court and, in particular, whether the experts are appointed by the court, or are chosen by the parties themselves to battle it out in the courtroom, as happens in Common Law countries. In many respects, therefore, microcomparison only makes sense if one takes due account of the general institutional context in which the rules of the foreign systems under comparison are developed and applied.

III

In order to understand what comparative law really is, it is as well to distinguish it from related areas of legal science, that is, to show what comparative law is *not*.

Since comparative law necessarily has to deal with foreign law, it must be distinguished from those other branches of legal science which have to do mainly or occasionally with other legal systems. As has often been observed, the mere study of foreign law falls short of being comparative law. For example, in 1937 the League of Nations produced a study of The Status of Women in the World, consisting merely of reports from different countries on their own solution of the problem. There was no real comparison of the solutions presented, and so at most one could call it descriptive comparative law. One can speak of comparative law only if there are specific comparative reflections on the problem to which the work is devoted. Experience shows that this is best done if the author first lays out the essentials of the relevant foreign law, country by country, and then uses this material as a basis for critical comparison, ending up with conclusions about the proper policy for the law to adopt which may involve a reinterpretation of his own system.

The neighbouring areas of legal science which also deal with foreign law, and from which comparative law must be distinguished, are private international law, public international law, legal history, legal ethnology, and finally sociology of law.

1. *Comparative Law and Private International Law*

These two areas are, on the face of it, entirely distinct, but they interact. Private international law, or conflict of laws, is a part of the positive national law, while comparative law seems to present itself as a *science pure*. Private international law tells us which of several possible systems of law should be applied in a particular case which has foreign connections; it contains rules of competence which determine which specific national law is to be applied and which lead to its application. One could therefore say that private international law is basically more selective than comparative. Comparative law, on the other hand, deals with several legal orders at the same time, and does so without having any practical aim in view.

Yet comparative law is enormously valuable for private international law, indeed so indispensable for its development that the methods of private international law today are essentially those of comparative law.

The most striking example is the well-known theory of *qualification* or *characterization*, which tells us how to understand those concepts, such as marriage, contract, and tort, which figure as connecting factors in the national rules of private international law. On one view (qualification according to the *lex fori*) these concepts are to be given the same meaning as they have in the substantive national law; according to the theory of qualification developed by ERNST RABEL (see RABEL,'Das Problem der Qualifika-tion', *RabelsZ* 5 (1931) 241), they are to be understood in the light of comparative law, independently of the *lex fori*. Comparative law also has to be used in the *application of the foreign law* indicated by the conflict rules of the home system. Suppose that in a will which is governed by English law the widow is made 'life-tenant' or a third party is appointed 'trustee'. These terms must somehow be converted into the language of the legal system which is controlling the disposal of the estate. The only way of doing this is to compare the English institutions with the nearest thing in the legal system involved: the German lawyer would therefore consider *Vorerbschaft, Niessbrauch,* and *Testa-mentsvollstrecker.* Now in English law the estate does not vest directly in the 'heirs', but goes to a 'personal representative', that is, a person who must administer the estate on behalf of those entitled to it, and divide the estate between them after paying off its debts. In Germany, these English rules cause difficulties in drafting the certificate of entitlement (*Erbschein*) which persons with rights of succession may demand, and these difficulties can only be resolved by intensive researches of comparative law. 'For example, if a person dies intestate, leaving a widow and several adult children, the certificate must indicate that the moveables in the estate pass under English law to the administrator appointed by the English probate court, who must manage the property in trust (*zu treuen Händen*) for the beneficiaries and use the net proceeds of the estate, after payment of its debts, to provide the widow with the personal chattels and the sum of [£40,000] after which one half of the rest is divided between the children in equal portions, and the other half is administered in trust (*zu treuen Händen*) for the widow, the children being entitled to equal parts of it on her death' (see the instructive treatment of this question by GOTTHEINER, 'Zur Anwendung englischen Erbrechts auf Nachlässe in Deutschland', *RabelsZ* 21 (1956) 33 ff., 71). Comparative law is also essential for the proper treatment of the concept of *ordre public* in private international law. Sometimes a foreign rule which is indicated by the conflict rules of the forum is so shocking to the *ordre public* of the forum that it cannot be applied, but in order to discover whether this is so one must make a comparison between the foreign rule and the closest analogue in the home system. Finally, there is the question of *renvoi*, whether consistency of decision—the principal aim of private international law—is best advanced by applying or not applying the conflicts rule of a foreign system which remits the matter back to the forum. This also can only be solved by the comparative method, and it was ERNST RABEL'S comparative work on 'Conflict of Laws' which conclusively showed how absurd it was to carry on applying national tests in an area like conflicts law which is devoted to international intercourse (see especially vol. I (2nd edn., 1958), 3 ff., 103 f.).

2. *Comparative Law and Public International Law*

At first sight there is little in common between comparative law and *public international law*, for public international law, or the law of nations, is essentially a supranational and global system of law. Yet comparative law is essential to the understanding of 'the general principles of law recognized by civilized nations' which are laid down as being one of the sources of public international law by art. 38 (1) (c) of the Statute of the International Court of Justice—whether this means principles of law accepted by all nations without exception, which would include only a few trivial truisms, or rather the principles of law accepted by a large majority of nations. The recognition of such general principles is rendered more difficult by the basic differences of attitude between the capitalist countries of the West and the socialist countries of the East on the one hand, and between the developed and developing nations of North and South on the other. Now one of the aims of comparative law is to discover which solution of a problem is the best, and perhaps one could include as a 'general principle of law' the solution of a particular problem which emerges from a proper evaluation of the material under comparison as being the best. To do this would avoid reducing the valuable notion of 'general principles of law' to a mere minimum standard, and could gradually lead us to accept progressive solutions as being examples of such general principles.

The methods of comparative law can also be extremely useful in interpreting treaties, and in helping to understand some of the concepts and institutions of customary international law. The rule *pacta sunt servanda*, the idea behind the *clausula rebus sic stantibus*, and the theory of *abus de droit* in international law all have their roots in insitutions of municipal private law, and it is only through comparative law that they can be made to yield their full potential.

3. *Comparative Law, Legal History, and Legal Ethnology*

The relationship between comparative law and legal history is surprisingly complex. At first sight one is tempted to say that while comparative law studies legal systems coexistent in space, legal history studies systems consecutive in time. But there is more to it than that. For one thing, all legal history uses the comparative method: the legal historian cannot help bringing to the study of his chosen system, say Roman Law, the various preconceptions of his own modern system; thus he is bound to make comparisons, consciously if he is alert, unconsciously if he is not. Secondly, an expanded notion of comparative law would include comparative legal history, which proved especially fruitful when Roman legal scholars turned their attention to other systems of the ancient world, and 'extended their research over the whole field of law, public as well as private, ius gentium as well as ius civile, drawing on the different laws of Greece as well as the sense of justice common to them and taking into account the near Eastern systems in cuneiform . . . and the recently discovered laws of ancient societies in the Mediterranean basin . . .' (WENGER (above p. 2), 157). If one bears in mind that the founders of modern comparative law were nearly all great legal historians, that without a sense of history even modern comparatists cannot understand foreign solutions, that 'legal history actualises the past by spanning time' (H. MITTEIS), and that we have a more 'relative' sense of time and space than our predecessors, then the differences between legal history and comparative law nearly disappear, and amount quite simply to a practical division between those comparatists who look more to the past and those who look more to the present and the future. The legal historians of our time 'no longer believe that legal history unrolls independently, but see law and history as fully interfused and try to illuminate the extra-legal context and hidden stimuli of legal development. Legal history is therefore not simply self-serving, but contributes to a critical evaluation of the policy of law which is, after all, the principal aim of pure comparative law.' (GENZMER (above p. 1), 334.) The distinction between comparative law and legal history is therefore considerably reduced and it is only with such a qualification that one can accept the opposition between comparative legal history as 'vertical comparative law' and the comparison of modern systems as 'horizontal comparative law'.

The founders of comparative legal ethnology, J. J. BACHOFEN (*Das Mutterrecht* (1861)) and Sir HENRY MAINE, had an aim rather different from that of true comparatists, namely to produce a general world history of law as part of a general history of civilization. At its outset legal ethnology rested on a specific belief, stemming from the teachings of AUGUSTE COMTE, the historical dialectic of HEGEL, and BASTIAN's theories of elementary and folk ideas. This belief, now regarded as invalid, was that mankind, with its common psyche, follows the same path of development in everything regardless of location or race. This belief led scholars to focus on the so-called primitive systems of law, if systems they can be called, still to be found among backward peoples. From the legal practices of these peoples they drew conclusions about the condition many ages ago, at a period from which we have no legal muniments or even evidence of any kind, of the legal systems which are now highly developed. Foremost among such scholars were H. H. POST in his *Einleitung in das Studium der ethnologischen Jurisprudenz* (1886) and JOSEPH KOHLER in his *Zeitschrift für vergleichende Rechtswissenschaft*. The basic tenet of ethnological legal studies, namely that all peoples develop as it were in parallel from a common original condition, was controverted principally by the so-called theory of cultural groups (*Kulturkreislehre*) according to which every cultural development of any group anywhere was, as a historical event, unique. The adherents of this theory could not deny the surprising similarities between the legal institutions of different peoples at the same stage of development, but sought to explain them as being the result of adoption or migration. Certainly such events did take place, but they cannot explain all the instances of parallel development. The more modern view, represented by KOSCHAKER, is that the development of a legal system is the product of factors, some of which are typical and occur everywhere, and some of which are atypical. According to KOSCHAKER the typical factors are not natural and inevitable, like BASTIAN's elementary ideas, but historical: a group of people in a particular geographical social and economic situation develops in a particular way with regard to law as well as other things. Such a typical development may be influenced by atypical factors, such as race, special aptitudes, or historical accident. The principal aim of legal ethnology, therefore, must be to distinguish the typical factors from the atypical aberrancies, for otherwise no safe conclusions could be drawn for our original law from the legal practices of surviving primitive peoples.

Nowadays we see legal ethnology not so much as a constituent of a general history but more as a branch of ethnology and comparative law which concentrates on the legal aspects of surviving societies, unhappily called 'primitive' because they are not yet equipped with all the apparatus of civilization. Its discipline is historical only in seeking to discover 'the origins and early stages of law in relation to particular cultural phenomena' (ADAM (above p. 1), 192). But the few older societies hitherto untouched are being increasingly exposed to the modernizing influence of the expanding industrial revolution and being drawn into the community of mankind. Accordingly the task of modern legal ethnology is to study the changes suffered by societies already observed in adjusting to the intrusion of a higher civilization. Thus to a large extent legal ethnology has become a branch of modern comparative law, one of whose most pressing tasks it is to assist the legal systems of developing societies by giving them the benefits of its comparative researches. To this aim legal ethnology has its special contribution to make.

4. *Comparative Law and Sociology*

After the discussion in recent years of the relation between *sociology of law* and comparative law, it now seems to be generally agreed that the two disciplines not only have a great deal to learn from each other but also use much the same methods.

Sociology of law aims to discover the causal relationships between law and society. It seeks to discover patterns from which one can infer whether and under what circumstances law affects human behaviour and conversely how law is affected by social change, whether of a political, economic, psychological, or demographic nature. This is an area where it is very difficult to construct theories, but if one can support one's theory with comparative data from other nations and cultures, it will be much more persuasive.

Legal sociologists use a technique quite like the 'control group' of experimental natural scientists: if in a given sector of experience two systems have different rules and one can show that the relevant social facts in those countries are also different, this may point towards the hypothesis that the social facts and the rules are causally connected (see examples given below pp. 35 ff.). Likewise if one brings in the time dimension, one may be able to show that as the social development in different countries converges (or diverges) the rules in force there also converge (or diverge). If people behave the same way in similar situations despite a difference in the rules which purport to control their conduct, one may infer that the rules are ineffectual, and the same inference may be drawn when the rules are the same but people behave differently. On all this see

MARTINY (above p. 1): he shows how the sociology of law can use the discoveries of comparative law, while making it clear that the practice of international and intercultural legal sociology is a very difficult matter indeed.

If comparative sociology of law can make use of the experience and discoveries of comparative law, comparative lawyers undoubtedly have a great deal to learn from legal sociologists. This is important, first, for what one can call the *definition of the problem*. Comparative lawyers have long known that only rules which perform the same function and address the same real problem or conflict of interests can profitably be compared. They also know that they must cut themselves loose from their own doctrinal and juridical preconceptions and liberate themselves from their own cultural context in order to discover 'neutral' concepts with which to describe such problems or conflicts of interests (on this see further Ch. 3 II). Legal sociologists not only accept this but apply it with a rigour which the comparative lawyer finds stimulating, if also a bit worrying, for legal sociologists can sometimes show that concepts and features which the comparative lawyer regards as 'neutral' and therefore suitable for the definition of the problem are in fact nationally or culturally conditioned, or that they implicitly presuppose the existence of a particular social context which in reality exists in only one of the places under comparison and not in the other. Once the problem has been defined and it comes to the question of the *statement of the rules* which the systems under review use to resolve it, the situation is similar. Here too comparative lawyers agree that one must take account not only of legislative rules, judicial decisions, the 'law in the books', and also of general conditions of business, customs, and practices, but in fact of everything whatever which helps to mould human conduct in the situation under consideration (on this see below Chs. 2 and 3). Sociologists of law take this for granted, since they start out from the assumption that human behaviour is controlled by many factors other than law, but lawyers find it more difficult—and comparative lawyers are generally lawyers of some kind. They have to force themselves to be sufficiently receptive to the non-legal forces which control conduct, and here they have much to learn from the more open-minded sociologists of law. So also when the comparative lawyer comes to *explain his findings*, that is, to describe the causes of the legal similarities or differences which he has discovered. He knows, of course, that causal factors may exist anywhere throughout the fabric of social life, but often he will have to go to the sociology of law to learn just how far he must cast his net, so as to include, for example, the distribution of political power, the economic system, religious and ethical values, family structure, the basis of agriculture and the degree of industrialization, the organization of authorities and groups, and much else besides.

One must not forget that comparative law has several different goals. In its *theoretical–descriptive* form the principal aim is to say how and why certain legal systems are different or alike. In this respect it must, as we have shown, work on and profit from the theoretical models and empirical data produced by the sociology of law. But comparative law can also aim to provide advice on legal policy. In its *applied* version, comparative law suggests how a specific problem can most appropriately be solved under the given social and economic circumstances. In such cases the comparative lawyer often acts under considerable pressure: he may be pressed to say how the positive law should be altered on a particular point, how a perceived gap should be filled, or exactly what rules should be adopted in an international uniform law, and he may have to come up with detailed proposals in a very short time. In such circumstances he has to operate with assumptions which, plausible as they may be, would rightly be derided by the sociologist of law as simple working hypotheses. But this does not mean that they are necessarily false. Without in the least suggesting that the comparative lawyer can ignore the insights and discoveries of the legal sociologist, he often cannot avoid adopting, however tentatively and provisionally, theses which the sociologist of law would regard as unproven, but which are nevertheless cogent enough to carry weight in discussions or decisions about changing the law.

2

The Functions and Aims of
Comparative Law

AUBIN, 'Die rechtsvergleichende Interpretation autonom-internen Rechts in der deutschen Rechtsprechung', *RabelsZ* 34 (1970) 458.

BERNHARDT (ed.), *Das internationale Recht in der Juristenausbildung* (1981).

BLECKMANN, 'Die Rolle der Rechtsvergleichung in den Europäischen Gemeinschaften', *ZvglRW* 75 (1976) 106.

COING, Rechtsvergleichung als Grundlage von Gesetzgebung im 19. Jahrhundert', *Ius commune* VII (1978) 160.

DAIG, 'Zur Rechtsvergleichung und Methodenlehre im Europäischen Gemeinschaftsrecht', *Festschrift Zweigert* (1981) 395.

R. DAVID, 'La Place actuelle du droit comparé en France dans l'enseignement et la recherche', in: *Livre du centenaire de la Société de législation comparée* I (1970) 51.

——, 'The International Unification of Private Law', in: *International Encyclopedia of Comparative Law* II (1971) Ch. 5.

DÖLLE, 'Der Beitrag der Rechtsvergleichung zum deutschen Recht', in: *Hundert Jahre deutsches Rechtsleben, Festschrift zum 100jährigen Bestehen des deutschen Juristentages 1860–1960* II (1960) 19.

DROBNIG/DOPPFFEL, 'Die Nutzung der Rechtsvergleichung durch den deutschen Gesetzgeber', *RabelsZ* 46 (1982) 253.

DUTOIT, L'Importance du droit comparé dans l'enseignement juridique', in: *Recueil des travaux suisses présentés au IXe Congrès international de droit comparé* (1976) 21.

FERID, 'Die derzeitige Lage von Rechtsvergleichung und IPR in der Bundesrepublik Deutschland', *ZfRV* 22 (1981) 86.

HIRSCH, *Rezeption als sozialer Prozess* (1981).

JESCHECK, 'Die Bedeutung der Rechtsvergleichung für die Strafrechtsreform', *Festschrift Bockelmann* (1979) 133.

KAHN-FREUND, 'On Uses and Misuses of Comparative Law', 37 *Mod. L. Rev.* 1 (1974).

KÖTZ, 'Gemeineuropäisches Zivilrecht', *Festschrift Zweigert* (1981) 481.

KROPHOLLER, *Internationales Einheitsrecht, Allgemeine Lehren* (1975).

MARTINY, 'Autonome und einheitliche Auslegung im europäischen internationalen Zivilprozessrecht', *RabelsZ* 45 (1981) 427.

MARSCHALL V. BIEBERSTEIN, 'Überlegungen zum Gegenstand der Lehre des Privatrechts', *Festschrift Coing* II (1982) 341.

MARSH, 'Comparative Law and Law Reform', *RabelsZ* 41 (1977) 649.

NEUHAUS/KROPHOLLER, 'Rechtsvereinheitlichung—Rechtsverbesserung?' *RabelsZ* 45 (1981) 73.

NEUMAYER, 'Rechtsvergleichender Unterricht auf internationaler Grundlage', *RabelsZ* 32 (1968) 405.

——, 'Fremdes Recht aus Büchern, fremde Rechtswirklichkeit und die funktionelle Dimension in den Methoden der Rechtsvergleichung', *RabelsZ* 34 (1970) 411.

——, 'Rechtsvergleichung als Unterrichtsfach an deutschen Universitäten', *Festschrift Zweigert* (1981) 501.

PESCATORE, 'Le Recours dans la jurisprudence de la Cour de justice des Communautés Européennes à des normes déduites de la comparaison des droits des États membres', *Rev. int. dr. comp.* 32 (1980) 337.

POUND, 'The Place of Comparative Law in the American Law School Curriculum', 8 *Tul. L. Rev.* 161 (1934).

SCHLESINGER, 'The Role of the "Basic Course" in the Teaching of Foreign and Comparative Law', 19 *Am. J. Comp. L.* 616 (1971).

SCHMIDLIN/KNEUCKER, 'Der Beitrag der Rechtsvergleichung zum akademischen Unterricht', *ZfRV* 18 (1977) 241 and 251.

E. STEIN, 'Uses, Misuses—and Nonuses of Comparative Law', 72 *NWUL Rev.* 198 (1977).

TALLON, 'Les Perspectives de l'enseignement universitaire de droit comparé', *Festschrift Zajtay* (1982) 479.

UYTERHOVEN, *Richterliche Rechtsfindung und Rechtsvergleichung* (1959).

WATSON, 'Legal Transplants and Law Reform', 92 *LQ Rev.* 79 (1976).

ZWEIGERT, 'Rechtsvergleichung als universale Interpretationsmethode', *RabelsZ* 15 (1949/50) 5.

——/PUTTFARKEN, 'Die Bedeutung der Rechtsvergleichung in der Juristenausbildung der Bundesrepublik Deutschland', *ZvglRW* 75 (1974) 125.

I

IT is beyond dispute today that the scholarly pursuit of comparative law has several significant functions. This emerges from a very simple consideration, that no study deserves the name of a science if it limits itself to phenomena arising within its national boundaries. For a long time lawyers were content to be insular in this sense, and to some extent they are so still. But such a position is untenable, and comparative law offers the only way by which law can become international and consequently a science.

In the natural and medical sciences there is an international exchange of discoveries and opinions. This is so familiar a fact that it is easy to forget its significance. There is no such thing as German physics or Belgian chemistry or American medicine. All one can say is that the contributions of the various nations to the different departments of world knowledge have been outstanding, average, or modest. But the position in legal science is astonishingly different. So long as Roman law was the essential source of all law on the Continent of Europe, an international unity of law and legal science did exist, and a similar unity could be found in English-speaking countries, the unity of the Common Law, differing in substance from that on the Continent of Europe because Roman law had very little effect in England and North America. The basic unity of legal science in the Anglo-American world still exists, but on the European Continent it started to disintegrate in the eighteenth century with the appearance of the great national codes, based on the existing law, principally Roman in origin. The Code of Maximilian of Bavaria and the General Code of Prussia in the eighteenth century were followed by the French Civil Code (1804) and the German Civil Code (1896) and then by the great codes of the twentieth century, the Swiss codes, the new Italian Civil Code, and the new Greek Civil Code. After these national codifications lawyers contented themselves with the study of their national rules, and stopped looking over the border. At a time of growing nationalism, this legal narcissism led to pride in the national system. Germans thought German law was the ark of the covenant, and the French thought the same of French law: national pride became the hallmark of juristic thought. Comparative law has started to put an end to such narrowmindedness.

The primary aim of comparative law, as of all sciences, is knowledge. If one accepts that legal science includes not only the techniques of interpreting the texts, principles, rules, and standards of a national system, but also the discovery of models for preventing or resolving social conflicts, then it is clear that the method of comparative law can provide a much richer range of model solutions than a legal science devoted to a single nation, simply because the different systems of the world can offer a greater variety of solutions than could be thought up in a lifetime by even the most imaginative jurist who was corralled in his own system. Comparative law is an 'école de vérité' which extends and enriches the 'supply of solutions' (ZITELMANN) and offers the scholar of critical capacity the opportunity of finding the 'better solution' for his time and place.

Like the lively international exchange on legal topics to which it gives rise, comparative law has other functions which can only be mentioned here in the briefest way. It dissolves unconsidered national prejudices, and helps us to fathom the different societies and cultures of the world and to further international understanding; it is extremely useful for law reform in developing countries; and for the development of one's own system the critical attitude it engenders does more than local doctrinal disputes.

But four particular practical benefits of comparative law call for closer attention: comparative law as an aid to the legislator (II); comparative law as a tool of construction (III); comparative law as a component of the curriculum of the universities and law schools (IV); and comparative law as a contribution to the systematic unification of law (V).

II

Legislators all over the world have found that on many matters good laws cannot be produced without the assistance of comparative law, whether in the form of general studies or of reports specially prepared on the topic in question.

Ever since the second half of the nineteenth century legislation in *Germany* has been preceded by extensive comparative legal research. This was true when commercial law was unified, first in Prussia and then in the German Empire, and also, after the Empire had acquired the necessary legislative powers, of the unification of private law, law of civil procedure, law of bankruptcy, law of judicature (courts system), and criminal law. Account was taken not only of the different laws then in force in Germany, including the French law in force in the Rhineland, but also of Dutch, Swiss, and Austrian law (see COING and DÖLLE (above p. 13 and below)) As to the present, it can be said that no major legislation since the Second World War has been undertaken without more or less extensive research in comparative law. This is true not only of reforms in German criminal law (see JESCHECK (above p. 13)) and family law (see DROBNIG/DOPFFEL (above p. 13)), but also of numerous other laws, such as the law of commercial agents, company law, anti-trust law, the introduction of the dissenting opinion in the Federal Constitutional Court, the draft law of privacy (admittedly never enacted), the law for the compensation for victims of violent crime, the law regarding changes of sex, the law on legal advice for the indigent, and much more. Work in comparative law was also undertaken when the Federal Ministry of Justice was considering the reform of the law of obligations (see A. WOLF, *AcP* 182 (1982) 80, and the submissions of the Max Planck Institute for Foreign and International Private Law, 'Zur Neueren Entwicklung des Vertragsrecht in Europa', printed in: *Gutachten und Vorschläge zur Überarbeitung des Schuldrechts* I (ed. Federal Ministry of Justice, 1981) 1 ff.).

Comparative lawyers often propose that their own system should adopt, with regard to a particular problem, a solution which they have found to obtain abroad. Now one cannot resist such a proposal simply because it is foreign and *ipso facto* unacceptable. To those who object to the 'foreignness' of importations, RUDOLPH V. JHERING has given the conclusive answer:

'The reception of foreign legal institutions is not a matter of nationality, but of usefulness and need. No one bothers to fetch a thing from afar when he has one as good or better at home, but only a fool would refuse quinine just because it didn't grow in his back garden.' (*Geist des römischen Rechts*, Part I (9th edn., 1955) 8 f.)

Whenever it is proposed to adopt a foreign solution which is said to be superior, two questions must be asked: first, whether it has proved satisfactory in its country of origin, and secondly, whether it will work in the country where it is proposed to adopt it. It may well prove impossible to adopt, at any rate without modification, a solution tried and tested abroad because of differences in court procedures, the powers of the various authorities, the working of the economy, or the general social context into which it would have to fit.

The 'reception' of foreign law and the question whether and under what circumstances it can succeed has provoked an interesting controversy between KAHN-FREUND and WATSON (above p. 13). (See also STEIN and HIRSCH (above p. 14), all with further references.)—An example may indicate the difficulties involved. Many countries have realized that the individual who wishes to combat illegal conduct and obtain compensation often has very great difficulty in doing so within the framework of the existing legal remedies. This is true, for example, where although many people are affected by the illegal conduct, none of them is seriously enough hurt to warrant his bringing proceedings by himself. As a result, private litigation as a means of policing illegal conduct will be rare, and law-breakers may speculate that, by the simple device of committing numerous small wrongs, they may escape the arm of justice as long as they stay clear of criminal sanctions. Here there is a need to spur victims into suing, and thus acting as 'private Attorneys-General', by offering methods of 'aggregating' a lot of minor claims into a single lawsuit. The 'class action' is one of the ways in which this need has been met in the United States. Under certain conditions, where a large group of persons is affected, one of them may be allowed to sue not only for his own loss but also on behalf of everyone else similarly situated. A finding that the defendant is not liable becomes *res judicata*, binding also on those not involved in the trial, and if the claim succeeds, the damages awarded are divided among all the victims, including the plaintiff. It is true that the actual plaintiff has no very great interest in bringing such a class action, since at best he will only get compensation for his own harm, but his attorney has a major interest in winning, and thus in tracking down winnable cases, for his fee is then fixed by the court and constitutes a first charge on the damages awarded to the whole class of victims, including his client. This fee can reach astronomical levels if, as quite often happens, the class of victims numbers tens or hundreds of thousands, for the damages awarded may reach millions of dollars and the attorney may have spent much time and trouble on the preparation of the case. The attorney's time and trouble will certainly be wasted if the claim fails, but neither he nor his client has to pay the successful defendant's costs, since under the American rules even the winning party bears his own attorney's costs. The class action is undoubtedly a fascinating technique for making the private lawsuit an effective sanction, but whether it can be incorporated into German law, or any other law, is quite another question. In other countries there may be strong opposition, expressed in the rules on professional conduct, against the entrepreneurial role played by the plaintiff's lawyer in a class action, attorneys' fees may be determined by statute on the basis of the amount at stake in the litigation, the losing party may have to pay his successful opponent's attorneys' fees, and other devices may be available to stimulate private litigation as a means of redressing group wrongs through the courts. See KÖTZ, 'Public Interest Litigation, A Comparative Survey', in: *Access to Justice and the Welfare State* (ed. Cappelletti, 1981) 85.

III

Another practical use of comparative law lies in the interpretation of national rules of law. On this matter the standard textbooks say nothing, dealing only with the old question whether a law should be given the meaning attributed to it by the legislator at the time of enactment, or whether the statute, treated as leading a kind of independent life of its own, may not be interpreted in the light of changing social conditions. Our present question is whether the interpreter of national rules is able or entitled to invoke a superior foreign solution. It is clear that such foreign material cannot be used in order to bypass unequivocal national rules: the principle of respect for an unambiguous enactment must not be infringed in any legal system. But the question may be raised when the construction of a rule is doubtful, or where there is a lacuna in the system which the judge must fill. The purely logical techniques at our disposal are insufficient, and it is unconvincing to play with analogy or the *argumentum e contrario*. The rule applied all over the Continent which determines how a judge must find the law when all else fails is formulated in the Swiss Civil Code, art. 1 pars. 2 and 3, as follows:

'If no statutory provisions can be found, the judge must apply customary law, failing which he must decide according to the rule he would, were he a legislator, decide to adopt.—In so doing the judge must follow accepted doctrine and tradition.'

The principal thought underlying this provision is that gaps in the Swiss Civil Code are to be filled in the spirit of the national, that is, the Swiss, law. But will this do? If the judge is to decide in the way he would have decided had he been a legislator, must we not ask: how does a modern legislator reach his decisions? Now we have already seen that, to a great degree, the modern legislator takes his solutions from comparative law. Thus, thanks to the greater breadth of vision which we obtain from comparative law, we must include the comparative method among the criteria traditionally applied to the interpretation of national rules. There may still be questions about how far this can and should be done. For example, should one, in using the comparative law method of interpretation, consult only related systems like those of Switzerland and France, or also systems that are quite different in style, such as the Common Law or the law of socialist states? Can the judge choose whichever of the foreign solutions seems to him the best, or can he choose only a solution which is common to a number of other systems? May we, with the help of comparative law, reach an interpretation of our legal rules which is independent of, perhaps even at odds with, the conceptual structure of our own system? These questions, with the possible exception of the last one, should receive a bold rather than a timid answer (see further in ZWEIGERT (above p. 14)).

As may be seen from the law reports, comparative law has often helped the courts to clarify and amplify *German* law, though it is true that comparative law arguments are usually deployed in conjunction with normal methods of interpretation, and thus serve to confirm and support a result reached by a traditional route. One excellent example is the development by the Bundesgerichtshof of the principle that the victim of an invasion of the 'general right of personality' may claim damages at large (see vol. II, Ch. 20 II), a principle which the Bundesgerichtshof sought to defend against criticism by saying that

'In almost all the legal systems which, like ours, put a prime value on the individual, damages for pain and suffering are regarded as the proper private law sanction for invasions of the personality. The availability of such damages does not adversely affect the freedom of the press, which those systems also treat as of fundamental importance, so the objection that the award of such damages in cases of invasions of personality improperly invades or unduly imperils the constitutionally guaranteed freedom of the press is clearly without substance' (BGHZ 39, 124, 132). In another decision the Bundesgerichtshof held that the claim for such damages was limited to cases where the invasion of the right of personality had been particularly serious; the Court observed that such a limitation 'is also to be found in Swiss law, which is more concerned with legal protection of the personality than the BGB (see art. 49 I OR)' (BGHZ 35, 363, 369). Many further examples from German courts are analysed by AUBIN (above p. 13). The *Swiss* Bundesgericht accepts arguments from comparative law even more readily (leading examples are BGE 98 II 73 and 273. See also UYTERHOVEN (above p. 14), with further references). The *French* Cour de Cassation, on the other hand, seems utterly unreceptive to such arguments; this is to be explained by the very peculiar and characteristic style of its judgments, which pay no heed to the factual background of the law. (See below pp. 127 f.)

In general it must be said that comparative law has a much greater role to play in the application and development of law than the courts yet allow. The situation is rather better when *uniform laws* are being interpreted. Such laws normally result from international conventions, governmental co-operation, or supranational or international legislation, and since the underlying aim is to unify the law, their construction and development must be geared to this goal. This means that when a national judge is faced with a uniform law, he must not simply deploy his trusty old national rules of construction but modify them so as to arrive at an internationally acceptable result which promotes legal uniformity. This often calls for a *comparative law interpretation*: the judge must look to the foreign rules which formed the basis of the provision to be applied, he must take account of how courts and writers abroad interpret it, and he must make good any gaps in it with general principles of law which he has educed from the relevant national legal systems.

For details see KROPHOLLER (above p. 13) 258 ff., 278 ff., 298 ff.—This is undoubtedly a hard and demanding task, and it may be beyond the powers of national judges who have to apply uniform law only very seldom. The only sure way to avoid national divergences in the construction and development of a uniform law is to grant jurisdiction to an international court. For the member states of the Common Market the Court of Justice of the European Communities is the leading example: it has already used the method of comparative legal interpretation in a large number of decisions with great success. On this see BLECKMANN, DAIG, PESCATORE, and MARTINY (above pp. 13–14).

IV

1. Comparative law also has an important function in legal education. In legal education as in legal science generally it is too limiting smugly to study only one's national law, and for universities and law schools so to act at a time when world society is becoming increasingly mobile is appallingly unprogres-

sive. Comparative law offers the law student a whole new dimension; from it he can learn to respect the special legal cultures of other peoples, he will understand his own law better, he can develop the critical standards which might lead to its improvement, and he will learn how rules of law are conditioned by social facts and what different forms they can take. What he learns in this science, as in others, will prove useful in practice too. Here we need only mention how useful comparative law is in conflict of laws, for the interpretation of treaties, for those who are involved in international adjudication, arbitration, or administration, or concerned with the unification of law. The younger generation of lawyers, and probably their successors as well, will be faced with an unparalleled 'internationalization' of legal life. As the threat of war recedes, the relations between capitalist and socialist countries will become much closer and their ideological differences will probably diminish. Much the same is true of the relations between developed countries and the developing countries to the South, which are entitled to assistance with their legal development. Other long-term problems cast a particular responsibility on the lawyer: the improvement of the environment, the elimination of racial confrontations, and the extension of social justice. These problems cannot be solved by any one state in isolation; they call for full co-operation between all states and peoples. But it is the general educational value of comparative law which is most important: it counteracts positivism, dogmatism, and narrow nationalism, and thereby points to the universality of legal science and the transcendent values of law; by rising above mere technical specialization it leads to legal thinking at a higher and more general level, and it offers the mind thus induced to be critical a world-wide 'supply of solutions'.

2. Despite all this, and notwithstanding the considerable improvement as in the last few decades, the place occupied by comparative law in the university curriculum is still rather modest.

In *West Germany* the teaching of comparative law varies quite widely from university to university. For the moment almost all universities offer a general 'Introduction to Comparative Law' which, in addition to giving an overview of the legal systems of the world, covers the aims and methods of the discipline and its relationship with other specialties with an international legal flavour. Rather less common are lecture-courses on a particular legal system, such as French law, or a group of related legal systems, such as the Common Law or the socialist legal systems; even where such courses are on offer, it is noticeable that universities tend to specialize in, say, English law, or Soviet law, or French law. Even less common is the 'comparison of institutions' in which one tries to see what all the relevant legal systems, or several of them, do in a particular area of law, such as the law of succession or products liability. But if the teaching of comparative law is perhaps just acceptable, the picture is wretched indeed when one comes to the vital question of the place of comparative law in *examinations*. Comparative law has never been a compulsory examination subject, although relevant questions are occasionally set as a test of the candidate's 'general juridical culture'. A student will admittedly be examined in the subjects which fall within his chosen 'group of elective subjects', though not much weight may be given to it, but in many of the *Länder* comparative law and private international law figure in a heterogeneous group along with family law and the law of succession. BERNHARDT (*JZ* 1971, 581) complains of the 'provincialism of German legal training', and many others have done likewise. The diagnosis is still correct, and it is not much consolation that in other countries the position is no better. On the whole question see DAVID, DUTOIT, SCHMIDLIN/KNEUCKER, ZWEIGERT/PUTTFARKEN (above pp. 13–14), as well as the instructive materials and area reports given by BERNHARDT (op. cit.).

3. In order to see how the teaching of comparative law will and should develop, we must look at law teaching as a whole.

The critical feature of the academic teaching of law today is the constant increase in the bulk of the material to be learnt. Students in the past could learn to think like lawyers by concentrating on private law, but nowadays it is necessary to master not only criminal law, which has not increased so much in volume, but also the vast bulk of constitutional and administrative law, business law, labour law, and social security law. It is no longer possible to cram comparative law and legal sociology into a law course which already has to contain so much material.

Since there is a limit to the amount which students can absorb, it looks as if comparative law may be overtaken by the same fate as legal history and legal sociology, namely to be treated as a luxury subject in which the brightest students may indulge but which normal students cannot afford. This development is made more probable by the tendency to shorten the length of the law course so that students can graduate and start practising rather earlier.

But if comparative law, like legal history and sociology of law, were treated as an extra, suitable only for doctoral students and budding academics, the rest of legal education would be sadly impoverished: the law school would become a mere trade school, producing professionally competent technicians. The dangers of such a course should be obvious to Germans who consider the results of the different styles of law study in the last three generations. The generation of 1900 had lectures, seminars, and books which dealt with the topical problems—mainly questions of private law—by showing how they were solved by classical Roman law, by the pandectist law of the nineteenth century, and, to a lesser extent, by old German law, and then by comparing these solutions with those of the Civil Code. Thus legal instruction was comparative in the vertical, that is, the historical, sense, and the lawyers it produced were first-rate; of this the opinions of their leaders, the judges of the Imperial Court, are proof. After 1918 the historical approach declined, and students were indoctrinated with the rules and interpretation of positive German law, with an intensive analysis of judicial decisions. By focusing on the actual national law, they lost sight of the range of possible solutions to which nearly every legal problem is open: in consequence they became incapable of personal commitment to law as such, or of a critical approach to it. By and large this type of training produced lawyers who, though technically competent, lacked intellectual independence and that sound sense of values which was needed to oppose national socialism.

Today it is comparative law we must look to in order to discover all the types of solution developed by contemporary legal systems for any particular problem, and to acquire the means by which all these solutions, including our own, can be disinterestedly evaluated. Now since the bulk of material makes it impossible simply to cram comparative law into the syllabus, it follows that we must *integrate comparative law into the teaching of national law*. That means that the problem being studied must be set in the context of the solutions obtaining in the most significant legal systems; then one must make a critical appraisal in order to determine which solution is best suited here and now to the national society as it is. Such a method allows one not only to highlight the characteristics of the solution which is accepted in the positive law, but also at the same time to encourage the reforming spirit and to develop a sense of responsibility for improving the law.

It follows from this that a textbook of comparative law should not try to stuff the student full of further foreign legal data; it should rather lay out the different approaches to a problem, state the critical arguments which illuminate and enliven it, and then indicate which is the best solution here and now. This involves that 'national' textbooks should be rewritten in the light of comparative law, and that in the long run all teachers of law should master the comparative method so as to obtain the necessary information for themselves.

As early as 1934 ROSCOE POUND expressed, more precisely and tersely, the view here put forward:

'What is aimed at by such a course [sc. in comparative law] may be done more effectively by a group of teachers who are conscious of the possibilities of comparative law in their daily teaching and know how to realise those possibilities. Hence I suggest that the law teacher of the future should ground himself in comparative law and should bring out continually other modes of treatment of the questions he takes up from the standpont of our law, as shown by the civil law and the modern codes, just as he canvasses the modes of treatment in different English-speaking jurisdictions. I suggest that he continually seek to lead the student by concrete examples to appreciate that there is no one doctrine or rule or institution or conception for every case in every land in every time. In other words, I believe comparative law will best be taught, for the purposes of our professional instruction, in the course of teaching the law of the land, except as graduate students are able, after due training in the civil law, to go deeply into some of its particular problems' (above p. 14, p. 168). Such 'integrated' law teaching has been opposed by SCHLESINGER and NEUMAYER (*Festschrift Zweigert* 507 f.) and defended afresh by KÖTZ (*RabelsZ* 36 (1972) 570 ff.).

V

1. *Unification of Law—Concept and Function*

The final function of comparative law to be dealt with here is its significant role in the preparation of projects for the international unification of law. The political aim behind such unification is to reduce or eliminate, so far as desirable and possible, the discrepancies between the national legal systems by inducing them to adopt common principles of law. The method used in the past and still often practised today is to draw up a uniform law on the basis of work by experts in comparative law and to incorporate it in a multipartite treaty which obliges the signatories, as a matter of international law, to adopt and apply the uniform law as their municipal law. For states which are members of the European Communities, the harmonization of law by supranational means (Community guidelines and directives) is of ever-increasing significance.

Unification cannot be achieved by simply conjuring up an ideal law on any topic and hoping to have it adopted. One must first find what is common to the jurisdictions concerned and incorporate that in the uniform law. Where there are areas of difference, one must reconcile them either by adopting the best existing variant or by finding, through comparative methods, a new solution which is better and more easily applied than any of the existing ones. Preparatory studies in comparative law are absolutely essential here; without them one cannot discover the points of agreement or disagreement in the different legal systems of the world, let alone decide which of the actual or proposed solutions is the best. A model of such a preparatory study is ERNST RABEL, *Das Recht des Warenkaufs* I (1936: reprinted 1957); II (1958), which was of vital importance for the unification of international sales law.

Sometimes diverse rules within single states are unified; this may be called *internal unification of law*. This may happen when a central legislator creates a great codification, as in France after the Revolution, or in Germany after the founding of the Empire, or in confederations such as Switzerland, but we must also include the partial unifications which have been brought about in the United States through the introduction of 'uniform laws' which any state is free to adopt (for example, the Uniform Commercial Code—now in force in all the states except, in part, Louisiana).

The advantage of unified law is that it makes international legal business easier. In the area they cover, unified laws avoid the hazards of applying private international law and foreign substantive law. Unified law thus reduces the legal risks of international business, and thereby gives relief both to the businessman who plans the venture and to the judge who has to resolve the disputes to which it gives rise. Thus unified law promotes greater legal predictability and security. International treaties for the unification of law often try to obtain the accession of all the states in the world, but none has yet succeeded. All unification of law so far has been limited in its geographical area of application, by force of circumstance rather than by design. Sometimes, however, schemes for the unification of law are designed to apply only within a limited area (regional unification of law, for example, in Scandinavia or the Benelux countries; here one can include also the *rapprochement* or harmonization of laws envisaged by the Treaty of the European Economic Community).

Multilateral treaties are very difficult to achieve and rather clumsy in operation; furthermore, their results in the field of unification of law are not very satisfactory (see 3 below). Accordingly, one must think of alternative means of achieving the goal. One way would be to produce model laws, a method which has been used for the internal unification of law within the British Commonwealth and especially in the United States. This method is less heavy-handed since the adoption of such laws by the different countries is a matter of recommendation rather than of obligation.

Other methods have been proposed by RENÉ DAVID in his encyclopedia article: for example, the creation of a new and universal *ius commune*, applicable to international relationships to which national systems of law may be insufficiently adapted. As an example of this he cites the socialist countries which have replaced a competitive economy by a planned economy, and therefore no longer possess any internal commercial law which could be applied to international trade. Thus in 1963 Czechoslovakia produced an extensive Code of International Trade to be applied when an international transaction calls for the application of Czechoslovakian law, and East Germany followed suit in 1976.—DAVID also urges a more widespread and international use of the device of *Restatements of the Law*, as practised in the United States. Every several state in the United States has its own private and commercial law, and the legislative competence of the Congress in Washington is rather limited. Nevertheless the laws of the several states have a great deal in common, thanks to the Common Law tradition. This common law in each principal area of law is set out in a series of books, called *Restatements*, with additional volumes which give the deviations in each state (see below pp. 259 f.). DAVID proposes the extension of this system to the countries of Africa in the first instance, and thinks that something analogous might be done in Europe, possibly even for the whole world.

Welcome though any idea is which tends to the greater harmonization of laws, overall the most suitable method for the immediate future seems to be that of *model laws*, provided that they are carefully drafted on the foundations of comparative law.

Running parallel with uniform enacted laws there may arise a kind of universal contract law, since in certain spheres of activity (such as wholesale trade in primary commodities, banking, insurance, and transport) there are general conditions or customs of business which are the same or similar in many countries. Here one might instance the Conditions of Business of the London Corn Trade Association, the General Conditions for the Supply of

Plant and Machinery for Export, produced by the UN Economic Commission for Europe, and the so-called Incoterms (such as fob and cif clauses) and the Uniform Customs and Practices on Documentary Credits drawn up by the International Chamber of Commerce in Paris. Many observers think of these rules as forming a nascent, perhaps actual, *lex mercatoria* of a new and autonomous variety (on the whole question see KROPHOLLER (above p. 13) 119 ff.).

2. *Areas and Agencies*

Since the end of the nineteenth century the unification of law has produced its main results in private law, commercial law, trade and labour law, in copyright and industrial property law, and in the law of transport by rail, sea, and air, as well as in parts of procedural law, especially in connection with the recognition of foreign judgments and awards. Even where the substantive private law should not, or cannot, be unified, it may be possible to achieve a harmony of outcome by unifying the rules of conflicts of law, and thereby avoid differences attributable to the accident of the forum.

It is in private law in the widest sense that the world forces tending towards the integration of law are at their strongest.

The results already achieved by way of unification of law are too numerous to be listed here (compare ZWEIGERT/KROPHOLLER, *Quellen des Internationalen Einheitsrechts*, 3 vols. (1971 ff.)). The League of Nations and the United Nations Organization have done much for the law of negotiable instruments and of arbitration, the Rome Institute for the Unification of Private Law (founded in 1926) has worked on the law of sale of goods, the Hague Conferences have helped in private international law, and various international organizations have advanced the unification of the law of transport, copyright, and labour. In 1966 the United Nations Organization resolved to set up a Commission for International and Commercial Law (UNCITRAL) charged with promoting the harmonization and unification of international trade law. Its greatest achievement so far is the Convention on Contracts for the International Sale of Goods (CISG) concluded in Vienna in April 1980 (see SCHLECHTRIEM, *Uniform Sales Law* (1986); HONNOLD, *Uniform Law for International Sales Under the 1980 U.N. Convention* (1982)).

3. *Experience*

In the past, enthusiasts have planned to unify the law of the whole world; people now realize that only the specific needs of international legal business can justify the vast amount of energy which is required to carry through any project for the unification of law. These needs are most pressing in the fields of law mentioned above (less, for example, in land law, family law, and the law of inheritance), and even there only for particular topics or specific institutions.

Though the total quantity of unified law is still not very great, it is bound to increase as traffic between states intensifies.

It is striking that hitherto the law has been unified only in very specific areas and on particular topics. For example, Europe has treaties for the unification of the law of liability of hotel-keepers, the package holiday contract, and the liability of the owner of a motor vehicle. UNIDROIT, the Rome Institute for the Unification of Private Law, is working on treaties which would unify the law of warehousing, commercial agency, and leasing. Such a fragmentary approach to the unification of law may have been quite justified in times past, and will doubtless be unavoidable for some years yet, but we are beginning to realize that as a method of unifying law it raises considerable problems. One problem is that in this increasingly complicated patchwork the unified rules often overlap with each other and increasingly clash with the non-unified rules of national law. Again, it has been shown that one cannot unify the law on any problem without using general concepts of contract and tort. These basic concepts may well take the same verbal forms in different legal systems, so it is tempting to adopt them in uniform rules without more ado, but if one does so, one discovers later, when the national courts actually have to apply them, that beneath the same words lie very dissimilar concepts. In the long run, therefore, it is unsatisfactory to try to unify law in a manner which produces a congeries of bitty rules and neglects their common basis. Those engaged in unifying the law must strive to embrace the fundamentals of private law and to work out a set of general rules in contract and tort which command international consensus. This would help courts which are applying the actual rules of unified law to avoid the differences of interpretation we have mentioned and would prepare the ground for further instances of uniform law. On this see KÖTZ (above p. 13).

The preparation and adoption of uniform laws is beset with difficulties. Some of these have psychological causes, such as dislike of novelty or pride in the national law, others are technical (differences in legal concepts or presuppositions, which only intensive preparatory studies in comparative law can overcome) or political: national parliaments are reluctant to adopt in their entirety the agreed drafts of international conferences. These difficulties are lessened somewhat if the uniform law is made applicable only to international transactions. Then each state has two concurrent sets of rules in the same area: for example, in the sale of goods, municipal law would cover internal transactions while the uniform law would apply to sales which were international in the sense of affecting at least one other state.

When uniform laws are applied by national courts, there is always the risk that the uniformity of law apparently achieved in that area will be eroded by its being differently construed and applied in the different member states. This risk cannot be wholly excluded by even the most careful drafting of the uniform law. Just as in any country a Supreme Court of Cassation or Appeal is needed to procure that the law is uniformly applied, so in the long run an international court is necessary to ensure the uniform application of uniform laws. The uniform construction of the law of the European Economic

Community is guaranteed by the Court of the European Communities (arts. 164 ff., Treaty of Rome), and it is to be welcomed that the member states have also entrusted to this court the power to interpret legal concepts used in certain treaties made pursuant to art. 220, Treaty of Rome. But apart from a few minor exceptions, this is the only court so far with power to give a uniform construction to uniform law. Until an international court is set up, the best that can be done is to procure that the highest courts of the member nations at least know what their opposite numbers have decided. If a uniform law is being differently construed in the different member states, it is impermissible to have recourse to the rules of conflicts law in order to determine whether in a particular case it is the law as applied, for example, in France or as applied in Germany which is to control (*aliter* the French Court of Cassation in *Hocke*, Rev. crit. 53 (1964) 264, and the Federal German Supreme Court, IPRspr. 1962–1963 no. 44). If the substantive law has been unified, it is the substantive law which must control, and not the rules of conflicts law. In brief: *unification of substantive law excludes the application of private international law*. Until we have an international court for the construction of uniform laws, the highest municipal courts should adopt as their own whichever construction, proposed or actually adopted elsewhere, seems to them the best and proper one.

3

The Method of Comparative Law

ANCEL, *Utilité et méthodes de droit comparé* (1971).

CONSTANTINESCO, *Rechtsvergleichung* II: *Die rechtsvergleichende Methode* (1972).

DÖLLE, 'Rechtsdogmatik und Rechtsvergleichung', *RabelsZ* 34 (1970) 403.

DROBNIG, 'Methodenfragen der Rechtsvergleichung im Lichte der "International Encyclopedia of Comparative Law"', in: *Ius privatum gentium, Festschrift Max Rheinstein* I (1969) 221.

EÖRSI, *Comparative Civil (Private) Law* (1979).

ESSER, *Grundsatz und Norm in der richterlichen Fortbildung des Privatrechts* (2nd edn. 1964).

FIKENTSCHER, *Methoden des Rechts in vergleichender Darstellung*, 4 vols. (1975–7).

FRANKENBERG, 'Critical Comparisons: Re-Thinking Comparative Law', 26 *Harv. Int. LJ* 457 (1985).

JESCHECK, *Entwicklung, Aufgaben und Methoden der Strafrechtsvergleichung* (1955).

KAHN-FREUND, 'Comparative Law as an Academic Subject', 82 *LQ Rev.* 40 (1966).

LANGROD, 'Quelques réflexions méthodologiques sur la comparaison en science juridique', *Rev. int. dr. comp.* 9 (1957) 353.

LAWSON, 'Comparative Law as an Instrument of Legal Culture', in: LAWSON, *The Comparison (Selected Essays*, vol. II, 1977) 68.

——, 'Some Reflexions on Comparative Law', id. 58.

LOEBER, 'Rechtsvergleichung zwischen Ländern mit verschiedener Wirtschaftsordnung', *RabelsZ* 26 (1961) 201.

NEUMAYER, 'Ziele und Methoden der Rechtsvergleichung', in: *Recueil des travaux suisses présentés au Congrès international de droit comparé* 9 (1976) 45.

RABEL, *Aufgabe und Notwendigkeit der Rechtsvergleichung* (1925), reprinted in: Rabel, *Gesammelte Aufsätze* III (ed. Leser, 1967) 1.

——, 'Die Fachgebiete des Kaiser-Wilhelm-Instituts für ausländisches und internationales Privatrecht', in: *25 Jahre Kaiser Wilhelm-Gesellschaft zur Förderung der Wissenschaften* III (1937) 77, reprinted in: Rabel, *Gesammelte Aufsätze* III (ed. Leser, 1967) 180.

RHEINSTEIN, 'Comparative Law— Its Functions, Methods and Usages', 22 *Ark. L. Rev.* 415, printed in: RHEINSTEIN, *Gesammelte Schriften* I (1979) 251.

——, *Einführung in die Rechtsvergleichung* (1974) §2.

SANDROCK, *Über Sinn und Methode der zivilistischen Rechtsvergleichung* (1966).

SCHLESINGER, 'The Common Core of Legal Systems, An Emerging Subject of Comparative Study', in: *Twentieth Century Comparative and Conflicts Law, Legal Essays in Honor of Hessel E. Yntema* (1961) 65.

SCHMITTHOFF, 'Die künftigen Aufgaben der Rechtsvergleichung', *JZ* (1978) 495.

TUNC, 'La Possibilité de comparer le contrat dans des systèmes juridiques à structures économiques différentes', *RabelsZ* 27 (1962) 478.

ZACHER (ed.), *Methodische Probleme des Sozialrechtsvergleichs* (1977).

ZWEIGERT, 'Rechtsvergleichung, System und Dogmatik', *Festschrift Bötticher* (1969) 443.

——, 'Die kritische Wertung in der Rechtsvergleichung, *Festschrift Schmitthoff* (1973) 403.

——/PUTTFARKEN, 'Zur Vergleichbarkeit analoger Rechtsinstitute in verschiedenen Gesellschaftsordnungen', in: ZWEIGERT/PUTTFARKEN (eds.), *Rechtsvergleichung* (1978) 395.

I

ACCORDING to GUSTAV RADBRUCH, 'sciences which have to busy themselves with their own methodology are sick sciences' (*Einführung in die Rechtswissenschaft* (12th edn., 1969) 253). Though generally true, this is not a diagnosis which fits modern comparative law. For one thing, comparatists all over the world are perfectly unembarrassed about their methodology, and see themselves as being still at the experimental stage. For another, there has been very little systematic writing about the methods of comparative law. There are thus no signs of the disease in question. The same is true of comparative law as practised by legislators for a long time. Since the great codifications of Western Europe, national enactments and international regulations of all kinds have been preceded by critical and comparative surveys. This has been very successful and, because of its success, has given rise to no methodological worries. The same is true of modern comparative law as a critical method of legal *science*, as described and practised by RABEL, though the reasons for this are different: so recent a discipline could not be expected to have an established set of methodological principles. Even today the right method must largely be discovered by gradual trial and error. Experienced comparatists have learnt that a detailed method cannot be laid down in advance; all one can do is to take a method as a hypothesis and test its usefulness and practicability against the results of actually working with it. Earlier theories, some examples of which have been given in the previous chapter, committed the error of supposing that the basis, goals, and methods of comparative law could be determined a priori from a philosophy or scheme of law. Even today it is extremely doubtful whether one could draw up a logical and self-contained methodology of comparative law which had any claim to work perfectly. Most probably there will always remain in comparative law, as in legal science generally, let alone in the practical application of law, an area where only sound judgment, common sense, or even intuition can be of any help. For when it comes to evaluation, to determining which of the various solutions is the best, the only ultimate criterion is often the practical evidence and the immediate sense of appropriateness.

If there is a 'sick science' in RADBRUCH's sense today it is not comparative law but rather legal science as a whole. Though the hollowness of the traditional attitudes—unreflecting, self-assured, and doctrinaire—has increasingly been demonstrated, they are astonishingly vital. New and more realistic methods, especially those of empirical sociology, have been developed, but it is mere wishful thinking to suppose that they characterize our legal thought. One of these new methods is comparative law and it is preeminently adapted to putting legal science on a sure and realistic basis. Comparative law not only shows up the emptiness of legal dogmatism and systematics but, because it is forced to abandon national doctrines and come directly to grips with the demands of life for suitable rules, it develops a new and particular system, related to those demands in life and therefore functional and appropriate. Comparative law does not simply criticize what it finds, but can claim to show the way to a better mastery of the legal material, to deeper insights into it, and thus, in the end, to better law. It therefore makes good sense to pay quite close attention to the method of comparative law— not because comparative law is sick, but because legal science in general is sick, and comparative law can cure it.

We are concerned not only with a method of *thinking*—the principles whose application gives the right results— but also a method of *working*: How does one actually set about a task in comparative law? This at least the beginner can expect from an introductory work, to be told the lessons of experience so that he does not set to work without any guidance at all, and waste his time in unprofitable detours.

II

As in all intellectual activity, every investigation in comparative law begins with the posing of a question or the setting of a working hypothesis—in brief, an idea. Often it is the feeling of dissatisfaction with the solution in one's own system which drives one to inquire whether perhaps other legal systems may not have produced something better. Contrariwise, it may be the pure and disinterested investigation of foreign legal systems which sharpens one's criticism of one's own law and so produces the idea or working hypothesis. Thus JESCHECK (above p. 28, at pp. 36 f.), speaking of criminal law in particular, understandably observes that one's own view of what the law should be is material for a working hypothesis, and can act as a point of comparison (*tertium comparationis*). LANGROD (above p. 28, at pp. 363 f.) asks whether it is the material or the hypothesis which comes first. This is not quite the right question: the two may interact. Nor is he quite on point when he says (ibid.) that the hypothesis comes first, and that deductive reasoning plays the most important role. In fact the original idea is often not 'deductive'. As MAX WEBER said: 'The idea is normally bottomed on hard work.' For the comparatist the 'hard work' in question is the critical appreciation of his own law and the constant study of other people's.

The basic methodological principle of all comparative law is that of *functionality*. From this basic principle stem all the other rules which determine the choice of laws to compare, the scope of the undertaking, the creation of a system of comparative law, and so on. Incomparables cannot usefully be compared, and in law the only things which are comparable are those which fulfil the same function. This proposition may seem self-evident, but many of its applications, though familiar to the experienced comparatist, are not obvious to the beginner. The proposition rests on what every comparatist learns, namely that the legal system of every society faces essentially the same problems, and solves these problems by quite different means though very often with similar results. The question to which any comparative study is devoted must be posed in purely functional terms; the problem must be stated without any reference to the concepts of one's own legal system. Thus instead of asking, 'What formal requirements are there for sales contracts in foreign law?' it is better to ask, 'How does foreign law protect parties from surprise, or from being held to an agreement not seriously intended?' Instead of asking, 'How does foreign law regulate *Vorerbschaft* and *Nacherbschaft*?' one should try to find out how the foreign law sets about satisfying the wish of a testator to control his estate long after his death. To take another example: only in Germany does one meet with the concept of 'disappearance of enrichment' (*Wegfall der Bereicherung*, §818 par. 3 BGB), yet all systems must resolve the conflict which arises when a person who is bound to restore a thing received under an invalid contract no longer has the thing to restore. One must never allow one's vision to be clouded by the concepts of one's own national system; always in comparative law one must focus on the concrete problem.

The beginner often jumps to the conclusion that a foreign system has 'nothing to report' on a particular problem. The principle of functionality applies here. Even experienced comparatists sometimes look for the rule they want only in the particular place in the foreign system where their experience of their own system leads them to expect it: they are unconsciously looking at the problem with the eyes of their own system. If one's comparative researches seem to be leading to the conclusion that the foreign system has 'nothing to report' one must rethink the original question and purge it of all the dogmatic accretions of one's own system. The German legal system in particular is conceptually so highly developed that its practitioners think of it as being almost a product of natural law and have great difficulty in disentangling themselves from its concepts. It is only when one has roamed through the entire foreign legal system without avail, asking a local lawyer as a last resort, that one can safely conclude that it really does not have a solution to the problem. This hardly ever happens, but even if it does, that is no reason to terminate one's comparative study. To ask *why* a foreign system has not felt the need to produce a legal solution for a particular problem may lead to interesting conclusions about it, or about one's own law. Sometimes the solution in one's own system is quite superfluous, thought up in the interests of theoretical completeness by the academics who drafted the Code (compare the 'joke transaction' (*Scherzgeschäft*) of §118 BGB). Often a solution is provided by custom or social practice, and has never become specifically legal in form. The same is true if there is something about the structure of the foreign society which makes the adoption of a legal solution unnecessary. Again an inquiry into the source of so different a sense of justice may produce interesting conclusions. It may be, however, that no reason at all can be found for the absence of a legal rule: historical accident also plays some part in determining whether legal institutions arise or not.

This, then, is the negative aspect of the principle of functionality, that the comparatist must eradicate the preconceptions of his native legal system; the positive aspect tells us which areas of the foreign legal system to investigate in order to find the analogue to the solution which interests him.

The basic principle for the student of foreign legal systems is to avoid all limitations and restraints. This applies particularly to the question of 'sources of law'; the comparatist must treat as a source of law whatever moulds or affects the living law in his chosen system, whatever the lawyers there would treat as a source of law, and he must accord those sources the same relative weight and value as they do. He must attend, just as they do, to statutory and customary law, to case-law and legal writing, to standard-form contracts and general conditions of business, to trade usage and custom. This is quite essential for the comparative method. But it is not enough. To prepare us for his view of the full requirements of the comparative method, RABEL says: 'Our task is as hard as scientific ideals demand . . .' and then he proceeds:

'The student of the problems of law must encompass the law of the whole world, past and present, and everything that affects the law, such as geography, climate and race, developments and events shaping the course of a country's history—war, revolution, colonisation, subjugation—religion and ethics, the ambition and creativity of individuals, the needs of production and consumption, the interests of groups, parties and classes. Ideas of every kind have their effect, for it is not just feudalism, liberalism and socialism which produce different types of law; legal institutions once adopted may have logical consequences; and not least important is the striving for a political or legal ideal. Everything in the social, economic and legal fields interacts. The law of every developed people is in constant motion, and the whole kaleidoscopic picture is one which no one has ever clearly seen' (above p. 28, at pp. 3 ff.).

But one must be realistic. It is too much to say that one must systematically master all this knowledge and then keep it in mind before one is allowed to embark on any kind of comparative work. But RABEL's demands are justified if they are understood to mean that the comparatist must make every effort to learn and remember as much as he can about foreign civilizations, especially those whose law has engendered the great families of legal systems.

Writers often stress the number of traps, snares, and delusions which can hinder the student of comparative law or lead him quite astray. It is impossible to enumerate them all or wholly to avoid them, even by the device of enlisting multinational teams for comparative endeavours. The best advice one can give the novice is EICHENDORFF's: 'Hüte dich, sei wach und munter' (Watch out, be brave, and keep alert). Even so, the cleverest comparatists sometimes fall into error; when this happens the good custom among workers in the field is not to hound the forgivable miscreant with contumely from the profession, but kindly to put him right.

RABEL once said that in their explorations on foreign territory comparatists may come upon 'natives lying in wait with spears' (*RabelsZ* 16 (1951) 341); but let his wit not frighten us out of ours.

III

The comparatist who wants to find in a foreign system the rules which are functionally equivalent to those which interest him in his native law requires both imagination and discipline. Many instances could be given, some of which are treated *in extenso* in Volume II. Suppose that the question is how to enable persons incapable of acting for themselves (minors, lunatics, persons under interdict) to participate in legal affairs. For the European lawyer the notion of 'statutory representative' provides the ideal, if not the only imaginable answer. The idea is so self-evident that he thinks nothing of it: every child from the day he is born is provided with a person—the local youth authority if all else fails—who is comprehensively empowered by statute to represent him. Yet the Common Law has got by quite satisfactorily without any such legal institution. There the parents of a child are not automatically entitled or bound to represent him in legal affairs generally or in litigation in particular. When an infant is making a claim, he does so through a person appointed by the court for this purpose, called his 'next friend'. When an infant is being sued, the court similarly appoints a 'guardian *ad litem*'. Should a minor become entitled to an estate, the court in certain circumstances appoints an 'administrator *durante minore aetate*'. Furthermore a child may under certain circumstances be declared a 'ward of court', whereupon the court itself assumes powers of representation which in the normal case it later transfers to others. In the Common Law 'trustees' have the duties in relation to a child's property which on the Continent are performed by the statutory representative, for it has long been the rule in Anglo-American law to transfer property not to the child himself but to a trustee to manage on the child's behalf. This example shows that what the Continental lawyer sees as being a single problem and solves with a single institution is seen by the common lawyer as being a bundle of more specific problems which he solves with a plurality of legal institutions, most of them of ancient pedigree. (See further vol. II, Ch. 9 III.) One should be frank enough to say, however, that though the English system has a certain antiquarian charm about it, it is so extremely complex and difficult to understand that no one else would dream of adopting it.

But we must not too readily infer that it is only the Continental systems, with their tendency to abstraction and generalization, which develop the grand comprehensive concepts, while the Common Law, with its inductive and makeshift habits, produces low-level legal institutions specially adapted to solve particular concrete problems. Things may be the other way round. A counterexample demonstrates once again that even if the legal institutions in different systems are historically and conceptually quite different, they may still perform the same function in the same way. The counterexample is the Anglo-American *trust*. The trust stems from a brilliantly simple notion: interests in a piece of property are split between a 'trustee', who has powers of administration and disposition, and others, often successive in time, who have a defined right to part of the proceeds of the property. This unitary conception is used by common lawyers in family law, in the law of succession, in the law of charities and companies, and even in the law of unjust enrichment; the trust thus satisfies a great many needs well known to European lawyers who deal with them with the aid of a whole panoply of extremely heterogeneous legal institutions.

Many more examples could easily be given. One system may meet a need by the *rei vindicatio* or the *actio negatoria* while another satisfies it by a claim in tort; claims for support in one country may be replaced in another by public relief of poverty; claims for the division of property in one place may be paralleled by devices of inheritance law in another, or vice versa; and what one system does by general clauses (exploitation, for example) may be done in another by more specific rules with a limited sphere of operation (lesion). All these examples are instances of the replacement of one legal rule by another *legal* rule, albeit of a different conceptual stamp. But often the comparatist must go beyond the purely legal devices, for he finds that the function performed in his own system by a rule of law is performed in a foreign system not by a legal rule at all, but by an extralegal phenomenon. One can only discern this by investigating the facts behind the law. Thus there may be general conditions of business which have not found their way into the books, but which in practice supersede or bypass rules of law fixed by the legislature or the judiciary. There may also be unwritten rules of commercial practice, matters of implicit agreement, which inhibit a party from using a right which the legal system accords to him. It may even be the case that a particular social problem, regulated in one system by rules of law, is wholly unregulated somewhere else, being controlled by mechanisms which operate outside the legal system altogether. Of course such a situation must be investigated, and the results brought into the comparison, for where a problem is solved by extralegal means one cannot simply assert that the foreign *law* does not deal with the problem without giving a false and misleading picture even of that legal system.

An example of this is provided by the question, when are offers binding? In German law the offeror is bound by his offer, in the sense that he cannot effectively withdraw it, either during a period set by himself or during a reasonable period (§145 BGB). In the Common Law, barring legislative intervention, the offeror may withdraw his offer at any time until it has been accepted, even when he has said that it will remain open for a stated time. The *reality* in both systems is quite different from what one would infer from these legal rules. It is well known that German merchants often insert terms like 'freibleibend', 'ohne Obligo', and 'Lieferungsmöglichkeit vorbehalten', which often appear also in general conditions of business; such clauses not only prevent the offer from being binding, they may prevent its being an offer at all, and have the effect of turning it into an invitation to submit offers, an *invitatio offerendi*. Contrariwise, the Common Law has developed several devices which weaken the practical effect of the rule that offers are freely revocable. What is especially interesting for us is that there are extralegal inhibitions which limit capricious revocation: such a revocation is legally effective but it is regarded as unfair and therefore not done (see vol. II, Ch. 3 V).

Another example shows how the comparatist must sometimes look outside the law. All developed legal systems, one might think, must have legal rules which protect the purchaser of an interest in land from the harm which could result from any outstanding and unknown property rights of third parties. But the German system with its land register and its concept of 'public reliance' (*öffentlicher Glaube*) was and is nearly unique. It has been imitated recently by other countries, especially France, and even the Anglo-American systems have for some time been experimenting, though their register system operates successfully only in a few densely populated areas. But by and large England and the United States have stuck to the old 'conveyancing' system, whereby the purchaser's attorney has to search through the deeds provided by the vendor in order to see that there is an unbroken chain of title. This system is so tiresome and expensive that 'Title Insurance Companies' have sprung up in the United States. These are private insurance companies which guarantee the insured against any loss he may suffer should a third person's rights diminish the value of his property. Companies will enter such an insurance contract only when they have checked their own sources and have established that the risk of the emergence of any conflicting interest is slight. These companies often have a monopoly in their locality and they have often been in business since the turn of the century, so the evidence they possess is virtually complete. In fact the function performed by the German land register is performed in the United States by the files and books of Title Insurance Companies. For details of 'conveyancing' and 'Title Insurance Companies', see the comparative study of v. HOFFMANN, *Das Recht des Grundstückskaufs* (1982).

The examples we have given point to a conclusion which the comparatist so often reaches that one can almost speak of a basic rule of comparative law: different legal systems give the same or very similar solutions, even as to detail, to the same problems of life, despite the great differences in their historical development, conceptual structure, and style of operation. It is true that there are many areas of social life which are impressed by especially strong moral and ethical feelings, rooted in the particularities of the prevailing religion, in historical tradition, in cultural development, or in the character of the people. These factors differ so much from one people to another that one cannot expect the rules which govern such areas of life to be congruent. Should freedom of testation be curtailed in the interests of a decedent's widow and family? Should divorce be possible and, if so, under what conditions? Should it be possible to legitimate adulterine children? Should a married father be bound to support an adulterine child and, if so, under what circumstances? Different legal systems answer these questions quite differently, and the answers they give are sometimes maintained with such fervour that when courts have occasion, thanks to a rule of conflicts law, to apply the rule of a foreign country, they tend to ask whether that different rule is consistent with the *ordre public* of their own jurisdiction. So there are areas in comparative law where judgment must be suspended, where the student simply cannot say which solution is better. But if we leave aside the topics which are heavily impressed by moral views or values, mainly to be found in family law and in the law of succession, and concentrate on those parts of private law which are relatively 'unpolitical', we find that as a general rule developed nations answer the needs of legal business in the same on in a very similar way. Indeed it almost amounts to a '*praesumptio similitudinis*', a presumption that the practical results are similar. As a working rule this is very useful, and useful in two ways. At the outset of a comparative study it serves as a heuristic principle—it tells us where to look in the law and legal life of the foreign system in order to discover similarities and substitutes. And at the end of the study the same presumption acts as a means of checking our results: the comparatist can rest content if his researches through all the relevant material lead to the conclusion that the systems he has compared reach the same or similar practical results, but if he finds that there are great differences or indeed diametrically opposite results, he should be warned and go back to check again whether the terms in which he posed his original question were indeed purely functional, and whether he has spread the net of his researches quite wide enough.

It must be stressed again that this presumption does not apply in all areas of law. In those areas which are particularly marked by strong political or moral views and values it has no application, but in other areas of law which are more technical and morally more neutral one may assume as a useful working hypothesis that the practical results will be similar.

IV

One question poses particular problems for comparative law, especially for its methodology: can the legal systems of socialist countries be compared with others, and, if so, how? By 'socialist countries' we mean those which are ruled by a communist party and which regard themselves as socialist in accordance with their official version of Marxist–communist doctrine.

According to orthodox socialist legal philosophy, the function of law in a socialist society is entirely different from that in a capitalist society: bourgeois legal philosophy is said to see law only in a formal and legalistic light, to treat it as a given phenomenon existing independently of its social function, and therefore to be incapable of an objective view of its law as it really is, namely as an instrument of the mastery of one class in the class struggle. Socialist legal philosophy, on the other hand, perceives law in its social function, and therefore as it really is. For those who accept this point of view, an even-handed comparison of legal systems of the different types must be pointless, if not actually impossible. One view, previously the dominant view in the Soviet Union, was that the only proper function of comparative law was to demonstrate the superiority of socialist law. LOEBER (above p. 28) calls this 'contrastive comparative law', which is correct enough but far too mild: comparative law which denies that there is any meaningful basis for comparison is not comparative law at all. Fortunately there are many different opinions, especially in the other socialist countries. They emphasize that socialist law is different in kind, but do not wholly discount the capitalist theory of law, which they admit to be capable of perceiving its own social reality: this provides a basis for meaningful comparative law.

Western legal scholars are also divided in much the same way. BILINSKY, for example, an expert on Soviet law (*Das sowjetische Wirtschaftsrecht* (1968) 18), regards the comparison of socialist and capitalist law as fundamentally impossible and sterile, because the theoretical and, more important, practical differences in their economic and social structures are so great. On the other hand, an expert like LOEBER is confident that such comparisons can be significant and productive. LOEBER seems to have the right view. We should not be deterred by the orthodox Soviet doctrine on which BILINSKY relies heavily. It is the similarity of the factual needs answered by different legal systems which makes them comparable; only if these needs were entirely different in the Western and socialist systems would they defy comparison, and it does not seem that this is, or could be, the case.

In this area one must, of course, be particularly careful to inquire into the function of the legal institutions under comparison. Socialist and capitalist countries are clearly quite different in their economic structure, not only in theory but also in practice, and their legal systems reflect these differences. But it does not follow from this that the legal systems are wholly incomparable.

For one thing, there are whole areas where these differences are not so prominent. LOEBER draws an excellent distinction between those legal institutions which are system-conditioned and those which are not. Family law, for example, is not system-conditioned, and consequently comparative family law is perfectly possible, no more difficult, indeed, than the comparison of 'Western' legal systems. The same is true of such areas of private economic activity as may be permitted in a socialist legal system. So, too, with some qualifications, for criminal and procedural law, as well as for the law of external trade. Comparative researches are also possible in the law of copyright and the law of tort.

There remains, however, a hard core of 'system-conditioned' legal institutions. So far as private law is concerned, these include the contracts entered into by nationalized businesses in the planned state economy, the property of socialist organizations, and the law of inheritance; to this we must add the whole area of what we call 'public law', namely administrative and constitutional law, the law of state arbitration and jurisdiction over state economic organizations. If in such cases the factual circumstances covered by a legal institution are really so different that the legal needs are no longer the same or similar, then there will be no functionally comparable solutions (for details see ZWEIGERT/PUTTFARKEN (above p. 29)). But even here one should not too quickly defer to the suspicion that comparisons are impossible. A comparative analysis which carefully probed the reality behind the law might quite possibly disclose much more that was comparable or even identical than is asserted by ideologists on either side.

One thing is clear, and that is that *practical co-operation* between comparative lawyers from East and West is not in the least hindered or impeded by disputes over the comparability of their legal systems. In many international organizations such as UNCITRAL, the Commission for International Trade Law founded by the United Nations, or UNIDROIT, the Rome Institute for the Unification of Private Law, lawyers from the socialist countries have long been working, often in leading positions, with energy and expertise on the solution of practical problems, and the same is true of scholarly co-operation, for example, under the auspices of the *International Encyclopedia of Comparative Law* (see below p. 40) or in the many international congresses and symposia which deal with comparative law.

V

The question how the comparatist should set out and how far he should go in his search for material is intimately related to the meaning and purpose of comparative law, to its very methods of thought. That is why we have already dealt with it, concluding that he should go as deep as possible into his chosen systems. But there is an anterior question, namely which legal systems he should choose to compare in the first place. Here sober self-restraint is in order, not so much because it is hard to take account of everything as because experience shows that as soon as one tries to cover a wide range of legal systems the law of diminishing returns operates. There are good reasons for this. Mature legal systems are often adopted or extensively imitated by others; as long as these other so-called 'affiliated' legal systems maintain the style of the parent system, they usually do not possess to the same degree that blend of originality and balanced maturity in solving problems which characterizes the 'significant' legal system. While they are at this stage of development, the comparatist may ignore the affiliate and concentrate on the parent system. This proposition, however, is more of a working rule than a firm conclusion of comparative methodology, since in fact the matter is rather subtle and complex.

To show what delicacy is required, take the case of the scholar in private law who wants to include the Romanistic systems in his comparative study. In addition to France, the parent system, he must also consider Italy where, behind a façade prevailing in the early stages, one finds an impressive wealth of ideas on private law matters, attributable perhaps to a late flowering of legal history in the seed-bed of Roman law, further fertilized by the codification of 1942. The legal systems of Spain and Portugal, on the other hand, do not often call for or justify very intensive investigation.

Much the same can be said of the Anglo-Saxon legal systems. The eighteenth-century comparatist could safely have concentrated on the law of the British Isles and ignored North America. Today the situation is quite different, if not the other way round. Though England is unquestionably the parent system, the law of the United States, while staying in the family, has developed so distinctive a style—less antiquated in manner, and often substantially divergent—that a comparatist would fall into error if he drew only on English, to the exclusion of American, law.

It is difficult to speak generally of how the comparatist should limit his field of inquiry, since it all depends on the precise topic of his research. If he is comparing the style of different families of law, rather than particular institutions or solutions of particular problems, then he can generally limit himself to the parent systems of the great legal families. If, on the other hand, he is dealing with particular questions, the following rule of thumb may be suggested. Some problems of private law, especially in the law of transactions, obligations, and property, are 'classical'. For these it will normally be sufficient to study English and American law in the Anglo-Saxon family, French and Italian law in the Romanistic family, and, in the Germanic systems, Germany and Switzerland (though here perhaps the native lawyer stands too close to see properly). It is worth while to bring in the law of Denmark and Sweden of the Nordic systems, despite the language difficulties, because of their refreshing lack of dogma. For questions of a more specific nature, outside the heartlands of private law already mentioned, a different principle of selection applies, but even here it is rarely safe to ignore the parent systems. To give just a few examples: questions of anti-trust law will find more answers in the United States than in France; the limitation of liability of trading concerns is distinctively, though perhaps not best, treated in Liechtenstein; fairness of trial has received more attention in England than elsewhere. Finally there may be quite topical legal problems with which legislators and judges all over the world are currently grappling. Here the comparatist may often have to consider the solutions offered by quite small jurisdictions. Thus *France* and *Sweden* have enacted striking laws to deal with the problem of standard terms in contracts; the Canadian province of *Saskatchewan*, along with *Poland, Finland*, and *Sweden*, led the world in using social accident insurance as a model for dealing with the compensation of harm suffered in highway accidents, and *New Zealand* has extended this to the compensation of harm caused in *all* accidents (see vol. II, Ch. 19 VI); and in family law there is much to be learnt from the legislation of the *Scandinavian* countries. It is clear, therefore, that the rule proposed is simply a rule of thumb, and no substitute for the experience and flair which a comparatist urgently needs if he is to make a proper choice of legal systems to study.

DROBNIG (above p. 28) has doubted whether in principle the comparatist need study only the great 'parent' systems. He points out that these systems have no monopoly of legal inventiveness and that therefore the comparatist should invoke all the legal systems of the world which might make any contribution to the problem being studied. After such a world-wide investigation the comparatist should present, in the form it takes in a representative system, each of the different types of solution which are to be found. DROBNIG developed this view in the context of the *International Encyclopedia of Comparative Law*—an undertaking backed by enormous financial resources, in which hundreds of comparatists from all over the world participate. In the case of wholesale research like this (see ZWEIGERT, *RabelsZ* 31 (1967) 539), it is possible and justifiable to accede to DROBNIG's exacting demands, since provision was made for each of the participating scholars to visit libraries and question expert colleagues in almost every country, in order to obtain a complete picture of the world's legal systems. In such a situation there was no need to exclude a priori and without detailed investigation any legal system at all, even if it had no great legal experience and had not therefore been able to test by case-law and try by scholarly criticism the solutions adopted. But most comparative research is not done by international teams with world-wide coverage, and it might not be desirable if it were. Comparative law is still useful and necessary when undertaken by an individual, and the comparison of individual systems, as opposed to those of the whole world, is important, indeed indispensable. So although making a selection may be painful, it is unavoidable on practical grounds. If a selection must be made, a criterion of selection must be adopted, and for this purpose the rules of thumb outlined above—for they are no more than that—still seem to offer a useful point of departure.

VI

As one researches the chosen legal systems one makes comparisons the whole time, often quite unconsciously: comparison, indeed, stimulates the enterprise and determines the choice of materials. But as a creative activity going beyond the mere actual absorption of the data, the process of comparison proper starts only when the reports on the different legal systems have been completed. To present such reports before the comparison proper begins is an established method of research and a proven way of constructing works on comparative law. Separate reports should be offered for each legal system or family of legal systems, and they should be objective, that is, free from any critical evaluation, though containing all significant qualifications or modifications. Whoever reads or uses a work on comparative law must be made familiar with the basic material, or he will be in no position to make the necessary comparisons, but in any case it is useful to give jurists access to legal systems hitherto unfamiliar to them. Occasionally an unusual topic will demand a different method of treatment as did Esser's study 'Grundsatz und Norm in der richterlichen Fortbildung des Privatrechts'. Esser was studying the various ways in which judges develop the law. This basic problem, of which German lawyers at least were barely conscious, cannot be posed or answered in terms of statutory or dogmatic rules. It would have been impossible or futile to try to produce an objective report on this problem in the different countries, free from critical commentary, and so the material had to emerge from the comparison itself. Topics of this kind are, however, the exception; for all individual legal problems the researcher should first produce an objective statement of the law in each jurisdiction.

But merely to juxtapose without comment the law of the various jurisdictions is not comparative law; it is just a preliminary step. As Rabel put it: 'The inner relationship between the . . . legal systems is only discernible if in our comparative portrayal of their institutions we take the similarities and differences together' (*Fachgebiete* (above p. 28), at p. 186). This, the actual process of comparison, is the most difficult part of any work in comparative law, and the process is so much affected by the peculiarities of the particular problem and of its solutions in the different systems that it is impossible to lay down any firm rules about it. One can only tentatively state some basic generalities.

It goes without saying that a comparative analysis will bring out the differences between the actual solutions. It is, indeed, the feeling of surprise that such differences exist which first prompts us to undertake comparative researches. But one does not gain much by simply listing the similarities and differences one discovers: this is really just to repeat in a clearer form what is already contained in the reports on each jurisdiction. This may be sufficient where each of the jurisdictions gives a clear and easily comprehensible solution to the problem in question, but things are not often as easy as this, as our examples have shown. Furthermore, it is precisely the more taxing legal questions which justify comparative treatment. The process of comparison at this stage involves adopting a new point of view from which to consider all the different solutions. The objective report which sets out the law of a particular jurisdiction will give a comprehensive portrayal of its legal solution to a practical problem, but it does so 'on its own terms', with its particular statutory rules or decisions, its characteristic conceptual form, and in its systematic context: the significance of this has been brought out above. But when the process of comparison begins, each of the solutions must be freed from the context of its own system and, before evaluation can take place, set in the context of all the solutions from the other jurisdictions under investigation. This is one new point of view, the one required by the process of comparison itself. The other standpoint to be adopted by the comparatist is intimately connected with the first, indeed, a precondition of it, namely that of function. Earlier in this chapter it was shown how significant the principle of functionality is as a guide to one's investigations in the different legal systems. Now, in the process of comparison, we come to the aim of these investigations. Different legal systems can be compared only if they solve the same factual problem, that is, answer the same legal need. In other words, the institutions of different legal systems can be meaningfully compared only if they perform the same task, if they serve the same function. Function is the start-point and basis of all comparative law. It is the *tertium comparationis*, so long the subject of futile discussion among earlier comparatists. For the comparative process, this means that the solutions we find in the different jurisdictions must be cut loose from their conceptual context and stripped of their national doctrinal overtones so that they may be seen purely in the light of their function, as an attempt to satisfy a particular legal need. It means also that we must look to function in order to determine the proper ambit of the solution under comparison; for a solution may be unitary although in its own system parts or stages of it are regarded as separate and distinct, as, for example, 'rules of law' as opposed to matters of interpretation, or as case-law as opposed to merely factual phenomena of legal significance. Experience shows that it is unprofitable and misleading to compare parts of a solution only; only the principle of functionality can let us see a solution as a whole. In particular one must resist the temptation of comparing only the statutory rules or doctrinal principles to which the various systems themselves admit, for principles are often so heavily qualified by exceptions that it is sometimes hard for the observer to think of a case which would not be decided in the same way even in countries which have adopted fundamentally opposed principles. Sometimes what actually happens in practice can severely weaken the operation of an admitted principle. But it is impossible to make general statements about how to free a solution from its national conceptualism and to reduce it to its functional form, since so much depends on the particular problem being investigated. Sometimes an institution has to be discerpted into separate parts, as, for example, the trust: in its native systems it is regarded as a unitary institution, but for comparative purposes it must be separated out in accordance with the different legal needs it helps to satisfy. Contrariwise, one may have to go in for synthesis, as in the example of statutory representation: there several independent legal institutions must be treated as a single unit, because it is only their joint operation which provides the solution of the problem.

VII

The next step in the process of comparison is to build a system. For this one needs to develop a special syntax and vocabulary, which are also in fact necessary for comparative researches on particular topics. The system must be very flexible, and have concepts large enough to embrace the quite heterogeneous legal institutions which are functionally comparable. To give an example: all legal systems have somehow to distinguish those expressions of a person's will which have a binding effect from those which do not, but the legal techniques they use for this purpose are very different. One way is to insist on purely objective requirements (formality, typicality of object, quid pro quo), while at a more developed stage it may be left to the judge as a matter of pure interpretation. Thus a system of comparative law must have a category which includes 'form', 'causa' (in one of its protean meanings) and 'consideration', and which also suggests that it is concerned with distinguishing the legally binding expression of will from the merely social utterance: perhaps 'indicia of earnestness' would do.

To take another example. ESSER observes that the principle of enrichment is 'ubiquitous' (above p. 28, at p. 367). So it is, but it appears in various guises and serves very various functions. What in one system is seen as a claim for restitution appears in another as a claim in tort and in a third as a claim for rescission of contract. A system of comparative law must here find a higher concept related to the function common to all these claims, or several different higher concepts, one for each of the different functions of restitutionary claims and capable of including claims of a different cast but similar practical object: perhaps one might have 'restitution of payments gone wrong', 'restitution for appropriating the property of others', 'restitution for unjustifiably using another's thing', and so on (see v. CAEMMERER, 'Bereicherung und unerlaubte Handlung', *Festschrift Rabel* I (1954) 333). There are simpler examples: we should talk of 'breach of contract' rather than '*Unmöglichkeit*' [impossibility], 'liability for others' is a better expression than 'liability for assistants', 'liability for servants' or 'respondeat superior'; 'strict liability' is more comprehensive than '*Gefährdungshaftung*' or '*théorie du risque*', and so on.

A system of comparative law will thus seem to be rather a loose structure. The component concepts cast a wider net than those of national systems: this is because the functional approach of comparative law concentrates on the real live problem which often lurks unseen behind the concepts of the national systems. The system produced by comparative law is, however, functionally coherent: its concepts identify the demands that a particular slice of life poses for the law in all systems where the social and economic conditions are similar and provide a realistic context within which to compare and contrast the various solutions, however much they may differ technically or substantially. DROBNIG has shown that the wider the international coverage of a comparative work is, the more necessary, though the more problematical, the development of such structural concepts is (above p. 28, at pp. 228 ff.). The task is not, however, different in nature from that of the librarian who needs a supranational system of concepts if he is to arrange his foreign materials in factual categories rather than simply in national groupings.

It now becomes unmistakably clear that an international legal science is possible. After a period of national legal developments, producing academically and doctrinally sophisticated structures, each apparently peculiar and incomparable, private law can once again become, as it was in the era of natural law, a proper object for international research, without losing its claim to scientific exactitude and objectivity. To this recognition of the fact that law, and especially private law, may properly be studied outside national boundaries, comparative law has greatly contributed, though other legal disciplines also have long been pointing the way. The jurisprudence of interests, the *Freirechtsschule*, the sociology of law, legal realism—all these have played a part by criticizing purely national conceptualism, deprecating scholarship which is territorially limited, and emphasizing that legal science should study the actual problems of life rather than the conceptual constructs which seek to solve them. Law is 'social engineering' and legal science is a social science. Comparative lawyers recognize this: it is, indeed, the intellectual and methodological starting-point of their discipline. Comparative law is thus closely in tune with current trends in legal science when it asks what the function of legal institutions in different countries may be, rather than what their doctrinal structure is, and when it orders the solutions of the various systems upon a realistic basis by testing them for their responsiveness to the social needs they seek to fill. It adds the international dimension and generates a supply of material beyond the imagination of even the cleverest stay-at-home lawyer. The vision of a universal comparative legal science is already sketched in the preface to JHERING's *Geist des römischen Rechts*:

'. . . legal science has degenerated into the jurisprudence of states, limited like them by political boundaries—a discouraging and unseemly posture for a science! But it is up to legal science itself to cast away these chains and to rediscover for all time that quality of universality which it long enjoyed: this it will do in the different form of comparative law. It will have a distinct method, a wider vision, a riper judgment, a less constrained manner of treating its material: the apparent loss [of the formal community of Roman law] will in reality prove a great gain, by raising law to a higher level of scientific activity.' (JHERING, *Geist des römischen Rechts auf den verschiedenen Stufen seiner Entwicklung*, Part I (7th/8th edn., 1924) p. 15.)

JHERING's vision is on the point of becoming reality, and comparative law has greatly helped to bring this about. If law is seen functionally as a regulator of social facts, the legal problems of all countries are similar. Every legal system in the world is open to the same questions and subject to the same standards, even countries of different social structures or different stages of development. Our universal legal science must have a structure and all the conceptual apparatus for ordering, organizing, and transmitting its material; we have shown above what form these must take. These cannot be laid down a priori, but only achieved inductively through continuing experiments in comparative law. In doing this comparative law will itself begin to be truly international. Though great progress has been made, most German work in comparative law even today still starts from a particular question or legal institution in German law, proceeds to treat it comparatively, and ends, after evaluating the discoveries made, by drawing conclusions—proposals for reform, new interpretations—for German law alone. The same is doubtless true of comparative studies in other countries. This activity could be called national comparative law. What we must aim for is a truly international comparative law which could form the basis for a universal legal science. This new legal science could provide the scholar with new methods of thought, new systematic concepts, new methods of posing questions, new material discoveries, and new standards of criticism: his scientific scope would be increased to include the experience of all the legal science in the world, and he would be provided with the means to deal with them. Comparative law is primarily a heuristic method of legal science rather than a way of discovering positive law. Only if one forgets this can one deny the value of an international legal science founded on comparative law, as SANDROCK (above p. 28, at pp. 50, 58, 65, 68) has just done, at least implicitly, in Germany: he sees very little value, if any, in the comparatist's discovery of supranational legal types, legal concepts, or principles of solving legal problems, or indeed in the creation of a supranational system of law. But even for the modest purpose of facilitating understanding between jurists of different nationalities, and of avoiding the misunderstandings which come from the prejudices, constraints, and diverse vocabularies of the different systems, such legal types, concepts, principles, and systems are indispensable. The legal scholar has more to do than simply decide cases; law is a mechanism of social regulation which can and must be studied across national boundaries; such international study and co-operation, as in all other sciences, will extend and improve our knowledge. Only if one refuses to see this can one doubt the value of comparative law.

VIII

A necessary part of the comparatist's task is to make critical evaluation of what he has discovered by his comparisons. Often he will find that the different solutions are equally valid, or that, as RABEL said, 'a reasoned choice is hard to make' (*RabelsZ* 16 (1951) 357). Often he will find that one solution is clearly superior. Finally, he may be able to fashion a new solution, superior to all others, out of parts of the different national solutions. The comparatist must consider all this, and be explicit about it. It is true that RABEL wanted to distinguish such evaluation on policy grounds from comparative law properly so-called, as being a 'distinct activity . . . because, though neither task is free from subjectivity, the pure comparison of laws can in general claim for its conclusions and theoretical pronouncements a greater degree of general validity than can value-judgements and conclusions directed to practical matters like legislative policy . . .' ('Fachgebiete', above p. 28, at p. 186). Much could be said on the question whether the critical evaluation of law is a legitimate scientific activity; it raises the famous dispute over KELSEN's pure theory of law, and this is not the place to give a final answer. However, there is one important difference between the comparatist's criticism of law and the criticism made by the observer of a rule of municipal law: the comparatist's conclusions are not rendered superfluous by the word of the legislator, since his comparative and critical analysis takes him above the national systems, which merely provide him with his data. RABEL himself in the same breath speaks out against a division of labour as between comparison and criticism of law: 'Lawyers who are used to criticism and are animated by the desire to improve the law can hardly prevent themselves from seeing and commenting upon the better practical rule.'

In fact the comparatist is in the best position to follow his comparative researches with a critical evaluation. If he does not, no one else will do it, and if no one does it, comparative law will deserve BINDER's sour description of 'piling up blocks of stone that no one will build with'. The comparatist's standards of criticism are those used every day by all legal scholars, who consider which of various solutions is best adapted to its purpose and operates most justly, and give a reasoned conclusion. The comparatists must leave it to the philosopher of law to state what this implies, though he can help by producing a greater mass of relevant data than legal philosophy has hitherto been ready or able to use. To rebut the charge that evaluation is a subjective matter we must turn again to RABEL: 'If the picture presented by a scholar is coloured by his background or education, international collaboration will correct it' (*RabelsZ* 16 (1951) 359).

4

The History of Comparative Law

ANCEL, 'Les grandes Étapes de la recherche comparative au XXe siècle, in: *Studi in memoria di Andrea Torrente* (1968) 21.

——, 'Cent ans de droit comparé en France, in: *Livre du centenaire de la Société de legislation comparée* (1969) 3.

BROWN, 'A Century of Comparative Law in England: 1869–1969', 19 *Am. J. Comp. L.* 232 (1971).

CONSTANTINESCO, *Rechtsvergleichung* I (1971), Part 2.

——, 'Les Débuts du droit comparé en Allemagne', in: *Miscellanea W. J. Ganshof van der Meersch* II (1972) 737.

DAVID, *Droit civil comparé* (1950) 397–429.

DÖLLE, 'Der Beitrag der Rechtsvergleichung zum deutschen Recht', in: *Hundert Jahre deutsches Rechtsleben, Festschrift zum 100jährigen Bestehen des Deutschen Juristentages* II (1960) 19.

GORLA, 'Prolegomeni ad una storia de diritto comparato europeo', *Foro it.* 103 (1980) V 11.

HUG, 'The History of Comparative Law', 45 *Harv. L. Rev.* 1027 (1932).

JESCHECK, *Entwicklung, Aufgaben und Methoden der Strafrechtsvergleichung* (1955).

KADEN, 'Rechtsvergleichung', in: *Rechtsvergleichendes Handwörterbuch* VI (ed. Schlegelberger, 1938) 9.

v. MEHREN, 'An Academic Tradition for Comparative Law?', 19 *Am. J. Comp. L.* 624 (1971).

MOLINA PASQUEL, 'Veinticinco años de evolución del derecho comparado: 1940–1965', *Bol. Mex. der. comp.* NS 2 (1969) 57.

POLLOCK, 'The History of Comparative Jurisprudence', 5 *J. Soc. Comp. Leg.* (2nd ser.) 74 (1903).

POUND, 'Comparative Law in the Formation of American Common Law', in: *Acta academiae universalis iurisprudentiae comparativae* I (1928) 183.

——, 'The Revival of Comparative Law', 5 *Tul. L. Rev.* 1 (1930).

RABEL, *Aufgabe und Notwendigkeit der Rechtsvergleichung* (1925), reprinted in: Rabel, *Gesammelte Aufsätze* III (ed. Leser, 1967) 1.

——, 'Die Fachgebiete des Kaiser Wilhelm-Instituts für ausländisches und internationales Privatrecht', in: *25 Jahre Kaiser Wilhelm-Gesellschaft zur Förderung der Wissenschaften* III (1937) 77, reprinted in: Rabel, *Gesammelte Aufsätze* III (ed. Leser, 1967) 180.

RHEINSTEIN, *Einführung in die Rechtsvergleichung* (1974) §5.

SARFATTI, 'Les Premiers Pas du droit comparé', in: *Mélanges Maury* II (1960) 237.

STURM, 'Geschichte, Methode und Ziel der Rechtsvergleichung', *JR* (1975) 231.

ZAJTAY, 'Réflexions sur l'évolution du droit comparé', *Festschrift Zweigert* (1981) 595.

ZWEIGERT, 'Die Gestalt Joseph Storys', *ZgesStW* 105 (1949) 590.

——, 'Jherings Bedeutung für die Entwicklung der rechtsvergleichenden Methode', in: *Jherings Erbe, Göttinger Symposion zur 150. Wiederkehr des Geburtstags von Rudolph von Jhering* (1970) 240. Extended version in English: ZWEIGERT/SIEHR, 'Jhering's Influence on the Development of Comparative Legal Method', 19 *Am. J. Comp. L.* 215 (1971).

I

THE history of comparative law is really part of the history of ideas. While the history of law in general is concerned with the organic development in time of legal institutions, the history of comparative law is principally the history of the thoughts of individuals, and it is only recently that these thoughts have produced happenings in the outside world. Yet, as will be shown, this part of the history of ideas is intimately connected with the basic intellectual tendencies of their age.

It must be emphasized at the outset that true comparative law has as yet had a very short history. In earlier times there are only occasional unconnected occurrences, not yet forming part of a proper development of comparative law such as we witness today.

It is in *Greece*, owing to the characteristic interest of Greek thinkers in political structures, that we find the earliest comparative researches. In his *Laws*, PLATO makes a comparison of the laws of the Greek city-states; he not only describes them, but also tests them against the ideal constitution he constructs out of them. Prior to writing his *Politics*, ARISTOTLE also examined the constitutions of no less than 153 city-states, though only the portion devoted to Athens has come down to us. This work can be described as philosophical speculation on the basis of comparative law. The only trace of comparative private law is in a fragment of THEOPHRASTUS's 'On Laws': so far as we can tell, THEOPHRASTUS's approach is quite modern, for he tries to discover the general principles in the various Greek legal systems, and then, in another chapter, to set against these principles the deviant particular rules— the very method used more recently by OTTO VON GIERKE in his presentation of German private law, and most spectacularly by EUGEN HUBER in his portrayal of the private laws of the Swiss cantons.

The *Roman Empire* offers no examples of efforts in comparative law. The Roman jurists, like those of England in later times, were too convinced of the superiority of their legal and political system to pay much attention to foreign laws. CICERO described all non-Roman law as 'confused and quite absurd'. The occasional references to foreign rules of law are just historical footnotes or theoretical amusements. But an interesting work of comparative law comes from the post-classical era, say from the third or fourth century AD. This is the *Collatio legum Mosaicarum et Romanarum*, in which excerpts from the classical Roman jurists are set against the laws of Moses, presumably with the aim of furthering Christian belief by showing that Roman and biblical law were similar.

At the beginning of the *Middle Ages* legal skill was at a low ebb, and thereafter canon and Roman law acquired such authority that no other kind of law had any interest for scholars. Furthermore the warrior chiefs believed that the conqueror could impose his law on the peoples he conquered—a coarse idea inimical to comparative law. But if writings on comparative law are not to be found on the Continent, there are two works by FORTESCUE (died 1485) in England, *De Laudibus legum Angliae* and *The Governance of England*. In these we have comparison of English and French law; it is not, however, an objective analysis, but is obviously designed to demonstrate the superiority of English law.

In the *Age of Humanism*, when lawyers were interested in *elegantia juris*, there were more serious attempts at comparative legal analysis. Special mention should be made of STRUVE and STRYCK in the late seventeenth century, for their comparisons of Roman and German private law. The first representatives of the *Age of Enlightenment and Natural Law*, scholars like WOLF and NETTELBLADT, were very little likely to help comparative law on its way. For them, natural law was an intellectual construct to be produced by speculation a priori without reference to any empirically discovered material, though one is entitled to wonder whether behind their supposedly a priori system there does not lurk some 'concealed comparative law'. Yet two leading spirits of the age, BACON and LEIBNIZ, emphatically advanced the cause of comparative law without actually practising it. In his essay *De dignitate et augmentis scientiarum* (1623) BACON stated that the lawyer must free himself from the 'vincula' of his national system before he can estimate its true worth: the object of judgment (the national law) cannot be the standard of judgment. This perception, as valid now as ever, justifies all comparative researches. For his part, LEIBNIZ endorses comparative law from the standpoint of universal history: his plan for a 'Theatrum legale' involved a comparative portrayal of the laws of all peoples, places, and times. Nothing immediately came of these writings, but we find that subsequent natural lawyers such as GROTIUS, PUFENDORF, and MONTESQUIEU expressly used the method of comparative law to give empirical support to the teachings of natural law. The contribution of this age, therefore, is less the systematic practice of comparative law than the recognition of the theoretical value of its methods. Mention must also be made of SAVIGNY's predecessor at Göttingen, HUGO (died 1844), who aimed to produce an empirical natural law by making a comparison of all existing positive laws.

The *historical school of jurisprudence*, on the other hand, had a particularly repressive effect on the development of comparative law. At first sight this is not easy to understand, since comparative law might (though it also might not) have produced some support for their view that all law is a product of the *Volksgeist*. But SAVIGNY and his followers rejected the study of any but Roman and German law. This is comprehensible only because the historical school adopted a negative attitude towards all methods of thought which had any connection with natural law, with whose speculations comparative law, with its aim of seeking and finding better solutions, admittedly has a certain affinity.

II

Comparative law, as it is practised today, has two quite distinct roots: 'legislative comparative law', when foreign laws are invoked in the process of drafting new national laws, and 'scientific or theoretical comparative law', when the comparison of different legal systems is undertaken simply in order to improve our legal knowledge.

Legislative comparative law has the longer and more continuous history—though still not a very long one—and its methods raise fewer problems. In Germany it starts in the mid-nineteenth century. The older codes—the Prussian General Land Law of 1794 and the Austrian General Civil Code of 1811—are based more on natural law thinking than on extended comparative studies of foreign law. The same is true of the most influential code of the eighteenth century, the French Civil Code of 1804. This elegant practitioners' work, beautifully drafted, was produced in an astonishingly short time, with the principal aim—so far as it was comparative at all—of amalgamating the Roman *droit écrit* of Southern France with the principally Germanic *coutumes* of the North (compare below Ch. 6 II).

Legislative comparative law in Germany grew with the movement for the codification and unification of law within Germany. It started in that area of law where unification is most urgently called for—commercial law. The General German Negotiable Instruments Law of 1848 and the General German Commercial Code of 1861 were both based on comparative studies, not only of the laws of the different regions of Germany, which included in the Rhineland the French Commercial Code, but also of other European commercial codes, especially the Dutch Commercial Code (*Wetboek van Koophandel*) of 1838. Proof of this is to be found in the Prussian 'Entwurf eines Handelsgesetzbuches für die Preussischen Staaten nebst Motiven' (Berlin 1857) which laid the basis for the German Commercial Code of 1861 and the 'Protokolle der Kommission zur Beratung eines allgemeinen Deutschen Handelsgesetzbuches' (1857 ff.). The company law reforms contained in the Novellen of 1870 and 1884 were also based on extensive comparative researches which are preserved in the Parliamentary papers and contain a veritable treasure-house of material for the comparative history of European company law. All subsequent reforms of company law, up to the reforms of the law relating to corporate securities of the 1930s and the great reform of 1965, have also been based on wide-ranging comparative studies and affected at critical points by discussion of the foreign solutions.

But legislative comparative law was used elsewhere than in commercial law. Comparative studies preceded almost all the most important pieces of legislation, which this is not the place to list or itemize. Mention must, however, be made of the prolonged reforms of criminal law, for one of the early monuments of German comparative law is the fifteen volumes of the *Vergleichende Darstellung des deutschen und des ausländischen Strafrechts* (1905–09). To fulfil his duty to provide the legislator with proposals backed by comparative researches, the Imperial Minister of Justice obtained the participation of nearly all the reputable teachers of criminal law in Germany, and a work of scholarship was produced whose great significance has been recognized on all hands (compare JESCHECK (above p. 47) at 13 ff.). Then about twenty years later WOLFGANG MITTERMAIER, HEGLER, and KOHL-RAUSCH produced a draft General German Code of Criminal Law (*Entwurf eines Allgemeinen Deutschen Strafgesetzbuchs*) (1927). This used examples of foreign and comparative law to illuminate the most important problems of policy in criminal law, questions of international criminal law, and a few hotly debated practical issues. Extensive comparative researches also underlie the reforms of German criminal law now in process, after prolonged discussion, of being enacted.

One final instance of the successful use of legislative comparative law is that pinnacle of German private law scholarship, the German Civil Code, which unified the private law of Germany as from 1 January 1900. In the preparation of this Code, careful consideration was given to the solutions accepted in all the systems then in force in the various parts of Germany. These included the *Gemeines Recht*, the Prussian Law, and the French Civil Code which was in force in the Rhineland and also, in a modified form, in Baden. Furthermore, on nearly all the more important questions, the comparative research was extended to include Austrian and Swiss law. Now one might have expected that, in the theoretical and scientific task of expounding the Code, German legal scholars would have used this comparative method which had proved so useful in creating it. Instead of this, they encased the Code in a closed system of theoretical concepts, mostly taken from the *Gemeines Recht*, and for a long time shut their eyes to the empirical and functional methods of comparative law. Once the work of legislation was over, the new law put comparative law in the shade, and deprived it of continuing effect. Thus the Civil Code and other enactments of the period, though based on comparative legal research, had hardly any positive effect on the use of comparative law as a scientific method. But it is still, of course, the general practice for important legislative proposals to be preceded by intensive comparative studies.

III

Scholarly comparative law has had a very different development from legislative comparative law: while the latter has developed continuously, the history of the former is marked by hesitations and rejections followed by periods of exaggerated optimism.

1. It took comparative law a very long time to obtain recognition in Germany where lawyers had long been attacked for their parochialism. FEUERBACH was one of the first to reproach German legal scholars when he said in 1810 that 'all their scholarship was devoted exclusively to what was native or naturalised' (A. v. FEUERBACH, *Kleine Schriften vermischten Inhalts* (1833) 152, 162). It was FEUERBACH also who, in an essay entitled 'Idee und Notwendigkeit einer Universaljurisprudenz' (*Biographischer Nachlass* II (2nd edn., 1853) 378), published posthumously, put forward the idea of a universal legal science based on extensive comparative law, but it is true that he had very little experience as a comparatist. His charges were echoed a few decades later when JHERING lamented how legal science had degenerated into the law of political states—'a discouraging and unseemly posture for a science!' (see the full quotation above, p. 44). JHERING was no comparatist either, though there are a number of references to foreign laws scattered through his works, but had it not been for his successful struggle on behalf of a teleological approach to law in the context of real life comparative law could not have developed in the way it has. (For details, see ZWEIGERT, 'Jherings Bedeutung' (above p. 48) *passim*). RABEL himself in his first schedule of work had to remark on 'the striking introversion of our legal life' from which it took the Treaty of Versailles to shake the German jurists free (*Aufgabe* (above p. 47) at p. 17).

Neither the historical school of jurisprudence, with its equation—more dogmatic than historical—of the *Volksgeist* with Roman Law, nor the conceptual jurisprudence of the pandectists, nor yet the legal positivism of the turn of the century provided conditions in which comparative law could flourish: indeed, it had no recognized place in legal science. BIERLING may be taken as typical of the positivists: comparative law is 'of little or no use for learning the principles of law' (*Juristische Prinzipienlehre* I (1894) 33). Even when, in the early twentieth century, positivism yielded to the neo-Kantian search for 'just law', the attitude adopted towards comparative law remained ambiguous. STAMMLER unequivocally discountenanced comparative law as a means of discovering the just law: the comparison of laws which were factually conditioned could never lead to the perception of those unconditionally valid modes of thought which were needed for any scientific study of law (*Lehrbuch der Rechtsphilosophie* (1922) 11 f.). Even RADBRUCH, in an essay 'On Comparative Legal Method' (*Monatschrift für Kriminalpsychologie und Strafrechtsreform* 2 (1902/1906) 422), denied that comparative law had any significance for the underlying idea of law, though he powerfully defended its value for the legislator as 'a useful means of obtaining the widest possible view of actual law'. No amount of study of actual systems could teach us anything about just law, for the notion of just law is arrived at not empirically, but a priori (id., 423). In a later work he denied comparative law any place in the 'proper dogmatic and systematic' science of law, and classed it along with legal history and sociology of law as 'the social theory of law' (*Rechtsphilosophie* (4th edn. Wolf, 1950) 210).

It will be clear even from this brief sketch of the prevailing attitudes among German legal scholars how much opposition comparative law had to overcome in order to establish itself as a legal discipline. Its history may seem to show a steady development, but it was long regarded by most legal scholars all over the world as simply an esoteric game for a handful of outsiders. This attitude may be attributed to the fact that in their everyday activities lawyers have to deal mainly with the law of their own country, but it has been greatly reinforced during this period by the prejudices of positivism and of national legal cultures, and we cannot in good conscience say that this attitude has wholly disappeared. Even now comparative law is not yet regarded as an indispensable international component of a *culture juridique*.

2. Even if conscious antipathy to comparative law was not expressed so strongly and dogmatically elsewhere as it was in Germany, the picture was not very different; scholars were not much readier to busy themselves with other peoples' law; national prejudices were very widespread. In the same breath in which he attacked the introversion of German lawyers, RABEL felt bound to inveigh against the equally poor standing of comparative law in other countries (*Aufgabe* (above p. 47) at 12 ff.). It is against this background that we must see the successful development of comparative law.

3. There is an astonishing similarity in the way different countries in the early nineteenth century embarked on the purposive and systematic comparison of different legal systems, that is, modern comparative law. Its intellectual origins are also similar. The purposes are practical, namely reform and improvement of the law at home, rather than theoretical, philosophical, or speculative; but a part was played also by natural curiosity about other peoples' law and by the impartial feeling that perhaps those others had something to offer—a contrast with the haughty concentration of legal scholars on their own newly codified systems. ZACHARIÄ used quite characteristic language in the first issue of the world's first periodical devoted to comparative law—the *Kritische Zeitschrift für Rechtswissenschaft und Gesetzgebung des Auslandes* (no. 1 (1829) 25 f.):

'If, after this survey of the present extent of exchange between European peoples in literary matters, and of the previous situation with regard to law, we may conclude that legislative or jurisprudential developments in any European country will be of some interest in other European countries, the idea behind this periodical, namely to familiarize the German public with foreign laws and legal writings, requires no justification.'

In Germany special mention must be made of ZACHARIÄ's co-founder and co-editor, MITTERMAIER. He was professor at Heidelberg and the leader of a group of jurists, mainly from Southern Germany, who were interested in the practical uses of foreign and comparative law, probably, as HUG says (above p. 48, at p. 1056) under the stimulus of the recent introduction of the Code Napoléon in the Rhineland and in Baden. This did not limit the interests of the group, however, which extended to all modern legal systems, and it is especially noteworthy that this was the first time that European jurists demonstrated a deep understanding of the Common Law of England and the United States. The 28 volumes of the *Kritische Zeitschrift*, as WARNKÖNIG was to say (*KritZ* 28 (1856) 391), offer a nearly complete view of three decades of legislation and legal science abroad. It is true that the mere discovery and portrayal of foreign law is not comparative law, but the contributors almost always drew comparisons with their own legal systems.

MITTERMAIER was the first to practise comparative law by systematically juxtaposing, comparing, and evaluating the law of various systems, and he did it on the grand scale. It is true that his aim was primarily practical—the reform of criminal procedure in the *Gemeines Recht*—but that does not in the least diminish his achievement in producing a series of scientific works which withstand all criticism. MITTERMAIER's comparisons of particular areas of law or of legal institutions were both comprehensive and detailed. He did not stop at the statutory texts, but went into the reality of law as practised in the courts, and even into its factual, political, and social background, as the titles of his principal works on comparative law make clear. [. . .]

It was clearly MITTERMAIER's example which led FOELIX to found the *Revue étrangère de législation* in *France* in 1834. His avowed aim was to help French jurists improve their knowledge of foreign laws, as well as to promote the improvement of French law. This must have seemed a most unpromising undertaking at a time when French jurists regarded their Civil Code with an awe bordering on superstition, and after a few issues the journal, which kept changing its name, had to devote more and more space to purely French law. The portion devoted to foreign law, to which FOELIX as editor was restricted, kept shrinking, and in 1850 the *Revue* ceased to appear. Even so, FOELIX seems to have had more success in establishing comparative law as an independent discipline in France than MITTELMAIER and his group had in Germany, for the collapse of comparative law studies in France in the face of positivism was much less marked. A chair of comparative legal history was founded at the Collège de France in 1831, and after holding courses in comparative criminal law from 1838, the Faculty of Law at Paris founded a chair in that subject in 1846. Although FOELIX did not see the fulfilment of his wish to have courses given in comparative private law, it is fair to say that it was his initiative, and in particular his starting the *Revue*, which gave the first impetus to the development of comparative legal studies in France.

In England the Privy Council, as the highest court of the Empire, had to apply the law of several different foreign systems; this led to a need for 'a more ready access to the sources from whence an acquaintance might be derived with those systems of foreign jurisprudence' (BURGE, *Commentaries on Colonial and Foreign Laws* (1838) p. v). It was the aim of BURGE to satisfy this need with his *Commentaries on Colonial and Foreign Laws, generally, and in their conflict with each other, and with the Law of England* (1838). According to BURGE himself (id., vi) these included: the 'civil law' (as the English used to call Roman law); the law of Holland before the introduction of the French Civil Code; Spanish law; the *coutumes* of Paris and Normandy; the French law then in force; Scots law; English law; the local laws of the colonies in the West Indies and North America; the laws of the United States of America. BURGE's work had three aims: first, to give a comprehensive survey of the sources and rules of law in all the systems in force in the British Empire, secondly, to compare their family law, their law of persons, property, and succession, and thirdly, to show the principles of conflict of laws in the various topics. The book was highly regarded both on the Continent and in the United States as a basic work of comparative law (see HUG (above p. 47) at 1065), and in 1924 the exigent RABEL himself stated that though the work was designed for the use of the Privy Council, 'the range of material and quality of treatment make it useful as a substitute for a primer of comparative private law' (*Aufgabe* (above p. 47) at p. 12, no. 12).

A similarly practical aim, namely to satisfy the need of English tradesmen for information about the commercial law of other peoples, underlay the other notable first-fruit of English comparative law. This is LEONE LEVI's *Commercial Law of the World; or, the Mercantile Law of the United Kingdom, compared with the Codes and Laws of Commerce of the following Mercantile Countries* [58 are listed], *and the Institutes of Justinian* (1854). LEVI compared English commercial law with the trade laws of almost every country in the world. Each of his topical subdivisions begins with a short description of the relevant English law; then follows a statement of the foreign rules of law—concentrating on statutory texts and dealing rather superficially with judicial practice—and finally an 'analysis of the law' in which he indicates the similarities and differences between the various legal systems. It is worth noting that LEVI was so impressed by the success of the German General Ordinance on Bills of Exchange of 1848 that he put forward the idea of an international unified code of commercial law: this was to be achieved by international conferences, and his work was to be a basic document (see LEVI, id., vol. I, p. xv). Thus LEVI was the first to propose the international unification of a whole area of law on the basis of comprehensive comparative law.

The period 1800–50 saw an early flowering of comparative law in the United States of America as well. American law at this stage was far from being merely the child of English law, whose traditionalism ill suited the economic, social, and political conditions of a new land only just occupied and not yet developed. Furthermore the War of Independence and the later war of 1812 had left a distaste for England and everything English. It was therefore with full consciousness that, whenever new and more suitable rules had to be developed, the most famous and influential American jurists of this period reached for Roman and European law, especially for French doctrine. This was true of both JOSEPH STORY and JAMES KENT, of the former, perhaps, to an even more marked degree. Nor was this recourse to foreign legal sources just a matter of theory. The works of KENT and STORY had a great effect on the practice of the courts as well as on legal teaching; indeed KENT's *Commentaries* formed the essential basis of American law at this time. Furthermore, both writers were themselves judges and so, as never before to such an extent in any country in the Anglo-American legal family, we find a series of judicial decisions, many of them well known, which are openly and explicitly based on the Civil Law. (See, for details, POUND (above p. 47); POUND, 'The Influence of French Law in America', 3 *Ill. L. Rev.* 354 (1909)). This open interest in foreign law was not, as in other countries, the prerogative of a few scholars; it was part of the contemporary American legal scene. In 1829, the anonymous reviewer of two books on Roman law said that 'in the liberal course of professional studies general or comparative jurisprudence must be a constituent part' (2 *Am. Jurist* 60 (1829)). The syllabus and reading-list of the Harvard Law School contained a section on Civil Law which recommended JUSTINIAN'S *Institutes*, POTHIER's *Law of Obligations*, and DOMAT's *Loix civiles* among others (4 *Am. Jurist* 217, 220 (1830)). There was also at this time a great demand for a Chair of Civil Law at Harvard (see, in general, HUG (above p. 47), 1068 n. 176). This interest in Civil Law is attributable in great part to the natural law thinking of the American Independence movement; by the middle of the century it had greatly diminished, and by the time of the Civil War it had quite disappeared.

A similar, though less dramatic, decline in comparative law is observable in other countries, and we must agree with HUG (above p. 47, at pp. 1069 f.) that after the middle of the nineteenth century people lost almost all interest in comparative law as a method of discovering law and of putting the discoveries to practical use.

4. The idea of 'comparative law' remained alive, however, though it came gradually to refer to a pursuit which we have earlier (above pp. 9 f.) distinguished from modern comparative law, namely 'legal ethnology' or 'universal legal history'. This species of 'comparative legal science' as it was

known in Germany, became the practice of a veritable school, often influenced by significant trends of philosophical thought. In Germany the idea of development contained in HEGEL's philosophy of history, though not his dialectic, was the admitted source of the works of GANS (*Das Erbrecht in weltgeschichtlicher Entwicklung* I (1824), especially the Preface at p. xxxix), of UNGER (*Die Ehe in ihrer welthistorischen Entwicklung* (1850)), of POST (for example, *Bausteine für eine allgemeine Rechtswissenschaft auf vergleichend-ethnologischer Grundlage* I (1880)), of KOHLER (especially *Einleitung in die vergleichende Rechtswissenschaft* (1885)), and many others. In France LERMINIER's *Introduction générale à l'histoire du droit* (1829) was clearly influenced by GANS, and in Italy AMARI's *Critica di una scienza delle legislazione comparate* (1857) was written under the influence of VICO's philosophy (see in detail ROTONDI, above p. 47). The leading work of the English school is HENRY MAINE's *Ancient Law* (1861).

5. This school of (historical) comparative legal science played a great part in the revitalization of modern comparative law towards the end of the nineteenth century, marked by a sudden growth of institutions, such as learned societies, periodicals, and professorial chairs. This occurred first and most strongly in France. POLLOCK (above p. 47) points to 1869 as the year in which comparative law gained full recognition as a new branch of legal science. That year saw the founding of the 'Société de législation comparée' which, along with its periodical, now called the *Revue internationale de droit comparé*, is still in existence today. In 1876 an 'Office de législation étrangère et de droit international' was set up in the French Ministry of Justice. But it is its acceptance into the university curriculum which marks the final recognition of comparative law as a new scholarly discipline. The founding in Paris in 1846—in the first flowering of comparative law—of a Chair in comparative criminal law has already been mentioned. In 1892 a Chair of comparative maritime and commercial law was established, a Chair of comparative constitutional law in 1895, and finally, in 1902, a Chair of comparative private law, held by SALEILLES and LÉVY-ULLMANN among others (see DAVID (above p. 47) at 408 f.).

Almost nothing similar was happening in Germany at this time. The *Zeitschrift für vergleichende Rechtswissenschaft*, founded by BERNHÖFT and COHN in 1878, was primarily devoted to comparative legal history. Germany had to wait until the foundation of the Internationale Vereinigung für vergleichende Rechtswissenschaft und Volkswirtschaftslehre in 1894 in order to obtain a society analogous to the Société de législation comparée in France. The Vereinigung was the brainchild of FELIX MEYER, *Kammergerichtsrat* in Berlin, and although it had very considerable fame and success, full recognition of comparative law as a scholarly discipline was not achieved, as it was in France, by incorporation into the university syllabus before the Great War.

England at this time was also still heavily influenced by the historical school. Even in 1903 FREDERICK POLLOCK could still say, 'It makes no great difference whether we speak of historical jurisprudence or of comparative jurisprudence, or, as the Germans seem inclined to do, of the general history of law' (above p. 47, at p. 76). The early institutions in England must be considered in the light of this observation. HENRY MAINE became the first Professor of 'Historical and Comparative Jurisprudence' at Oxford in 1869, and in 1894 a Chair of 'History of Law and Comparative Law' was founded at University College in London, thanks to a bequest of £10,000 by the High Court judge SIR RICHARD QUAIN. But 1894 also saw the foundation of the 'Society of Comparative Legislation' on the French model, which gave modern comparative law a home in England. The Society has remained in existence up to the present day, as has its journal, now entitled the *International and Comparative Law Quarterly*.

It is a matter for speculation to what causes we should attribute this rebirth of interest in comparing the rules of foreign systems actually in force. No doubt the most important cause was the increase in economic and commercial contacts which called for a better knowledge of foreign rules or even of unified rules. The re-emergence of comparative law coincides with the first great efforts of international co-operation and unification of law, such as the treaties on copyright and trade-marks, the Universal Postal Union, and the first Hague Convention on Private Law. But the characteristic high-point of this stage of comparative law was the Paris Congress of Comparative Law of 1900. The aim set for comparative law by this Congress, so far as one can formulate it in view of the large number of contributors, was to discover the 'droit commun législatif' (SALEILLES) or the common 'stock of solutions' (ZITELMANN), and thus to bring the different systems of law closer together. The Paris Congress not only identified the aims of comparative law, as it then was; it also stamped its character with its optimistic and progressive pursuit of world unity, yet limited its scope, for its assumption that only similar things could be compared led to rather a narrow concentration on statutory law and on the legal systems of Continental Europe. MARC ANCEL's summing-up is quite accurate:

'At this stage in methodology, the principal aim and object of comparison is to create a rational science of law which could permit the formulation of norms appropriate to nineteenth century society in Continental Europe' ('Les Grandes Étapes' (above p. 47) at p. 26).

6. After the First World War the picture changes somewhat. German jurists were forced out of their 'remarkable introversion' (RABEL, *Aufgabe* (above p. 47) at 17) by Article X of the Treaty of Versailles which sought to regulate the pre-war legal relationships between nationals of combatant states. At first 'they naively supposed with their pre-war assumptions that German concepts

and methods would largely suffice to interpret and apply the Treaty of Versailles' (H. ISAY, quoted by RABEL, *Aufgabe* (above p. 47) at 19). But 'the Treaty was drafted in foreign languages, the German translation not being authentic, and it was the legal systems and perspectives of the victor nations, namely England and France, which provided the mode of drafting, the conceptual apparatus, the rules of interpretation, and the style. In such a situation there was no alternative but to investigate those systems . . .' (DÖLLE (above p. 47) at 20, citing references to works on the Treaty of Versailles). The comparative law thus required was admittedly a tool of advocacy designed to promote particular interests in litigation rather than objective scholarship, but the practical necessity of investigating so many cases produced results of value for science. It fell to RABEL, who himself had to interpret the Treaty as a member of the mixed Italian–German Court of Arbitration, to free comparative law from this merely ancillary role. He saw comparative law as an independent juristic discipline whose practical usefulness to those applying the Treaty of Versailles was, scientifically speaking, contingent and collateral, even if it produced interesting data. Indeed, when, in his first basic book, *Aufgabe und Notwendigkeit der Rechtsvergleichung* (1925), he states the arguments for comparative law, the Treaty of Versailles and the other consequences of the war are given only a passing mention (*Aufgabe* (above p. 47) at 18 ff.).

The fact that other countries also experienced it shows that this upsurge of interest in comparative law in Germany is not wholly attributable to the confrontation with other systems necessitated by the Treaty of Versailles. According to ANCEL ('Les Grandes Étapes' (above p. 47) at 26), the second phase of twentieth-century comparative law begins at the end of the First World War. In this phase the institutions are consolidated, individual research is devoted to concrete and realistic problems, and the limitation to Continental Europe is overcome. The foundation of the 'major' institutes for comparative law was not simply an advantage for technicians, but was of deep and substantial importance: the kind of work in comparative law which was just beginning urgently needed research institutes which united teams of experts and specialized libraries; the development of comparative law from that period up to the present day would have been impossible without them. Even during the War, in 1916, an Institute for Comparative Law was founded in the University of Munich, at RABEL's instigation, and several other German universities followed suit after the War was over. Then in 1926 the Kaiser-Wilhelm-Gesellschaft founded in Berlin the Kaiser-Wilhelm Institute of Foreign and International Private Law, under RABEL, at the same time as it founded the companion Institute for Public Law, Foreign and International, under VIKTOR BRUNS. The Institute very quickly became the centre of comparative legal studies in Germany and one of the most important research institutes in the world. It is now in Hamburg, under the name of the Max-Planck-Institut für ausländisches und internationales Privatrecht.

In France the Institut de droit comparé was founded in 1920 by ÉDOUARD LAMBERT in Lyons where special courses on comparative law had been held for a few years. This was followed in 1932 by the Institut de droit comparé of Paris University, founded by LÉVY-ULLMANN who was also its first director. At the international level, the Académie internationale de droit comparé emerged in 1924, and has since held periodic International Congresses of Comparative Law which have proved very useful. Nor must one underestimate the significance for comparative law of the founding in 1926, by the League of Nations at SCIALOJA's instigation, of the Institut international pour l'unification du droit privé (UNIDROIT) in Rome, although its aims are not purely comparative.

As these institutes made it possible to conduct more penetrating research, so the method of research altered. The accent shifted from the discussion of fundamental questions—what are the aims and uses of comparative law, and what is its place in legal science generally?—which had obsessed the Paris Congress of 1900 to individual studies of particular factual problems, so-called 'recherche concrète' (ANCEL, 'Les Grandes Étapes' (above p. 47) at 27). As RABEL said in 1924 (*Aufgabe* (above p. 47) at 22) 'the principal task for scholars is to work on the detailed questions with all the care and exactitude at our command'. Basic questions of principle were no longer in the forefront; RABEL could report as a fact in 1935 what he had proposed as a plan in 1924: people had realized that there was so much juristic material to be studied, so many insights to be won, that it would unduly limit comparative law to determine in advance what its goals should be or what place in the system it should adopt. 'In fact comparative law has as many different aims as legal science itself; it would be impossible to enumerate them, and we need not attempt it' (RABEL, 'Fachgebiete' (above p. 47) at 79).

As research became concrete its scope expanded. The Paris Congress sought to find its 'droit commun législatif' in the positive legislation of Continental Europe; it compared codes and texts. At the 'second stage' of comparative law in the twentieth century this limitation was definitively overcome: comparative law moved on to the comparison of the legal solutions whch 'are given to the same actual problems by the legal systems of different countries seen as a complete whole' (RABEL, 'Fachgebiete' (above p. 47) at 82). So far as method is concerned, this second stage is still with us: the method taught and practised today comes from the research which RABEL evolved and perfected.

There is a clear connection between the shift of focus from purely statutory law and the 'discovery' of the Common Law. RABEL and LAMBERT both recommended an intensive investigation of the Common Law when particular problems were being dealt with. The exclusive concentration of comparative law on the Romanistic and Germanic systems had already met with some opposition on the ground of the national and doctrinal constraints this imposed, but the extension to the Common Law was a step into the unknown. A handful of experts had some familiarity with a few special areas of law with an international flavour (for example, maritime law) but, apart from this, the Common Law was quite unknown to the jurists of Continental Europe. Admittedly work had started before the First World War on a project to produce a German commentary on English private law, undertaken by FELIX MEYER's Internationale Vereinigung für vergleichende Rechtswissenschaft, with financial support from the Berlin Chamber of Commerce and the Senates of Hamburg and Bremen, but the War had put an end to it. The gap between the Common Law and the Continental systems in history, structure, and method must have seemed unbridgeable; to cross it was a challenge to comparative law, but it was a challenge which let scholars see that if one poses one's questions properly, that is, in terms of function, and if one investigates a legal system in its entirety, such differences are really immaterial. At the turn of the century the axiom 'only comparables can be compared' was taken to mean that comparison was possible only between systems whose structures and concepts were comparable. This construction of the theoretical axiom was belied by the success of the practical 'Experiment' of RABEL's and LAMBERT's institutes, for in the 1920s and 1930s they produced a stream of first-rate works. The bridge between the Common Law and the Civil Law was admittedly built from both sides. American comparatists in particular looked more closely into the legal systems of Continental Europe, in part because Civil Law codes were still in force in Louisiana and Quebec (see below, pp. 119 ff.). It must be added that comparative law studies in the United States and in England were greatly benefited by the forced exile of German jurists after 1933.

Writers have sometimes exaggerated the significance for comparative law as a whole of the confrontation of Common Law and Civil Law, and have overestimated the difficulties of comparing systems which are conceptually so very different. Thus ASCARELLI said that the essential work of a comparatist lay in the dialogue between Civil Law and Common Law (cited by ANCEL, 'Les Grandes Étapes' (above p. 47) at 27; so also MOLINA PASQUEL (above p. 47) at 59), and DE SOLÁ CAÑIZARES advised the civilian who was embarking on comparative law to look first into related systems of law since it took an expert to venture into the difficulties of the Anglo-American systems. Such views are inconsistent even with the attitude of comparative lawyers between the wars. At any rate the principal German products of the period—the *Rechtsvergleichendes Handwörterbuch*, and *Das Recht des Warenkaufs*, the product of a team under RABEL's direction—are comprehensively international: the Common Law takes its proper place as one system among many. It is certainly true that it was the inclusion of the Common Law with Romanistic and

Continental European systems which broke the bounds set by the Paris Congress of 1900; after the necessary abandonment of the view that only systems with comparable systematic structures offered a basis for comparison, it was shown to be profitable and useful to compare systems which were entirely different, and that the true basis for comparison was *similarity of function and of social need*, the means of satisfying which may be conceptually very different. This provided comparative law with a methodologically sound starting-point and also, to a large extent, a tool for the investigation of extremely different legal systems, whether Common Law, oriental, or socialist. It was this wider viewpoint rather than the new ground immediately acquired which was the real gain from the concern with the Common Law. The intellectual and methodological basis was thus laid for the confrontation with socialist law, which took place in earnest only after the post-war annexation of the Eastern European countries.

Many causes have contributed to the modern form of comparative law— the extension of scope from European statutory law to areas not bounded by nationality, the adoption of a method which investigates a legal system in all its aspects but always with an eye to particular function, the establishment of special institutes, fully equipped with the personnel and plant needed for sustained work, and finally the representation of comparatists from all countries in the Association internationale des sciences juridiques. The methods of RABEL and his contemporaries at home and abroad have won through. The problems they identified and the programmes they established constitute the tasks of comparative law today.

B. THE LEGAL FAMILIES OF THE WORLD

5

The Style of Legal Families

ARMINJON/NOLDE/WOLFF, *Traité de droit comparé* I (1950) 42–53.
CONSTANTINESCO, 'Ideologie als determinierendes Element zur Bildung der Rechts-kreise', *ZfRV* 19 (1978) 161.
——, 'Über den Stil der "Stiltheorie" in der Rechtsvergleichung, *ZvglRW* 78 (1979) 154.
R. DAVID, *Traité élémentaire de droit civil comparé* (1950) 222–6.
——, *Les grands systèmes de droit contemporains* (8th edn., rev. Jauffret-Spinosi, 1982).
EÖRSI, *Comparative Civil (Private) Law* (1979).
A. ESMEIN, 'Le Droit comparé et l'enseignement du Droit', in: *Congrès international de droit comparé, Procès-verbaux des séances et documents* I (1905) 445.
LÉVY-ULLMANN, 'Observations générales sur les communications relatives au droit privé dans les pays étrangers', in: *Les Transformations du droit dans les principaux pays depuis cinquante ans* I (1922) 81.
MALMSTRÖM, 'The System of Legal Systems, Notes on a Problem of Classification in Comparable Law', *Scand. Stud. L.* 13 (1969) 127.
MARTINEZ-PAZ, *Introducción al estudio del derecho civil comparado* (1934, reprinted 1960) 149–60.
SAUSER-HALL, *Fonction et méthode du droit comparé* (1913).
SCHNITZER, *Vergleichende Rechtslehre* I (2nd edn., 1961) 133–42.
WIEACKER, *Privatrechtsgeschichte der Neuzeit* (2nd edn., 1967) 496–513.

I

THE theory of 'legal families' seeks to provide the answer to several distinct questions in comparative law. Can we divide the vast number of legal systems into just a few large groups (legal families)? How do we decide what these groups should be ? And, supposing we know what the groups should be, how do we decide whether a particular legal system belongs to one group rather than another? We make these groupings primarily for taxonomic purposes, so as to arrange the mass of legal systems in a comprehensible order. But there is another way in which this may make the comparatist's task easier. If one or

63

two legal systems prove representative of each of these large groups, then the comparatist can, under certain conditions, concentrate on those systems, at any rate at the present stage of comparative law.

Of the many attempts to devise such groupings, that of ARMINJON/NOLDE/ WOLFF is the most penetrating. ESMEIN had earlier divided the legal world into the Romanistic, Germanic, Anglo-Saxon, Slav, and Islamic families, but ARMINJON/NOLDE/WOLFF objected to this on the ground that the criterion of division was not evident. This objection is arguably unfair; ESMEIN's grouping was particularly good for his time, and he did state what principles of distinction he had in mind: 'For this purpose we must classify the laws of different countries, enacted or customary, by dividing them into a small number of families or groups, each of which constitutes an original system of law; and the teaching of comparative law, if it is to be scientific, must start with a survey of the historical sources, the general structure, and particular characteristics of each of these systems' (above p. 63 at p. 451). ARMINJON/ NOLDE/WOLFF also objected to LÉVY-ULLMANN's division into the Continental family, the family of English-speaking countries, and the Islamic family, though his main principle of distinction is made very clear, namely the differences in the sources of law recognized by the Continental and Anglo-American systems.

SAUSER-HALL in 1913 used *race* as the essential factor in his division, on the ground that 'it is only within an individual race that legal evolution can be traced' (above p. 63 at p. 102). Accordingly he distinguished the Indo-European, Semitic, and Mongolian legal families, as well as a family of uncivilized nations, and subdivided the Indo-European family into Hindu, Iranian, Celtic, Greco-Roman, Germanic, Anglo-Saxon, and Lithuanian–Slav subgroups. MARTINEZ-PAZ in 1934 adopted a genetic method of classification; he asked how far the development of each system had been affected by the *ius gentium*, by Roman law, by canon law, or by more recent democratic ideas. On this basis he arived at four groups, of which the 'grupo romano-canónico-democrático' united, rather to the reader's surprise, the systems of Latin America, Switzerland, and Russia (above p. 63 at pp. 154 f.). For a criticism of other proposed divisions, see ARMINJON/NOLDE/WOLFF (above p. 63) 43 ff.

ARMINJON/NOLDE/WOLFF themselves suggested that modern systems of law should be grouped in accordance with their *substance* 'paying due heed to orignality, derivation, and common elements', and without any reference to extrinsic factors such as geography or race. This produced an attractive division into seven legal families: the French, German, Scandinavian, English, Russian, Islamic, and Hindu (above p. 63 at pp. 47 f.).

RENÉ DAVID, whose treatise was published at about the same time, also criticized earlier writers for failing to produce convincing criteria of distinction, and himself concluded that only two such criteria were satisfactory: the criterion of *ideology* (the product of religion, philosophy, or political, economic, or social structure) and the criterion of legal technique: differences of legal technique being of secondary importance, the principal ground of distinction is philosophical basis or conception of justice. On this principle he distinguishes five legal families: Western systems, socialist systems, Islamic law, Hindu law, and Chinese law (Traité (above p. 63) at pp. 222 ff.). DAVID subsequently modified his position: he now has three legal families—the Romanistic–German family, the Common Law family, and the socialist family—along with a further loosely knit group of 'other systems', consisting of Jewish law, Hindu law, and the law of the Far East, along with a new group of African and Malagasy law (see *Les Grands Systèmes* (above p. 63) 19 ff.).

A few years ago MALMSTRÖM addressed the theory of legal families once more. His principal objection to the proposal of ARMINJON/NOLDE/WOLFF is that the legal systems which are European in origin have so many features common and exclusive to them that they should be classed in a Western (European–American) group; in this group MALMSTRÖM would put, in addition to the Romanistic and Germanic systems, the Latin American systems, the Nordic systems, and the Common Law systems. The socialist systems, the non-communist Asian systems, and the African systems would fall in another group (above p. 63 at pp. 145 ff.).

In a recent work, the first to offer a general theory of comparative law from the standpoint of Marxist legal theory, EÖRSI offers quite a different division (above p. 63). In his view the legal system in any country is determined by its relations of production, especially the ownership of the means of production and the consequent distribution of power in society. It follows that the world today knows two different 'law types': to the 'capitalist law type' belong the legal systems of countries where the means of production are privately owned, while the legal systems of countries where the means of production have been socialized and put in the hands of the working class belong to the 'socialist law type'. Within the 'capitalist law type' EÖRSI distinguishes four groups of European legal systems, depending on when and how the bourgeoisie succeeded in overcoming the relations of production typical of the phase of feudalism (pp. 109 f.). England and the Northern countries belong to the first group, for they reached 'an early compromise between the bourgeois and the feudal class'. The second group includes France, where the feudal powers were radically abolished at a stroke by the French Revolution, and the bourgeoisie took their place. In the German-speaking countries of central Europe, as well as in Hungary and other parts of Eastern and South-Eastern Europe, the bourgeoisie had a long struggle against feudalism and their victory was long delayed; these countries therefore constitute a fourth group. For criticism see KÖTZ, *RabelsZ* 46 (1982) 572.

II

ARMINJON/NOLDE/WOLFF's division of legal systems into seven families is the most convincing of the groupings so far put forward, especially in its rejection of external criteria: 'Any rational classification of modern legal systems must be based on a study of their substance' (above p. 63 at p. 47). The authors are, however, reticent about the standpoint to be adopted for such study. We are told that, as with languages in comparative linguistics, legal systems are to be put into families on the basis of similarities and relationship, but it is never made really clear which common qualities are the crucial ones. It is often obvious enough that one system is a parent system (like the Common Law of England), but we need more help with the difficult question whether a system is affiliated to one parent or to another, especially as legal systems have been known to adopt new parents.

Whenever one is concerned with the identification of legal families or the classification of a particular system, two matters in particular must be borne in mind.

1. The theory of legal families has so far proceeded as if the only law worth taking into account were what European lawyers call private law. This is partly because comparatists have hitherto concentrated on private law, and partly because it is only private lawyers, so far as one can see, who have been interested in the theory. ARMINJON/NOLDE/WOLFF alone make it clear that their division is based on, and therefore valid only for, private law (above p. 63 at p. 47). Such groupings, therefore, may be highly relative. For example, it is quite possible that a system is to be put in one family for private law purposes, and in another for purposes of constitutional law. Thus German private law unquestionably belongs in the German legal family, but one might well put German constitutional law in a group which included the United States and Italy and excluded England and France, depending on the weight one attributes to the presence or absence of judicial review of constitutionality as being the hallmark of a constitutional system. But even if one concentrates on private law, a similar difficulty may arise. Thus the Arabian countries unquestionably belong to Islamic law as far as family and inheritance law is concerned, just as India belongs to Hindu law, but the economic law of these countries (including commerical law and the law of contract and tort) is heavily impressed by the legal thinking of the colonial and mandatary powers—the Common Law in the case of India, French law in the case of most of the Arab states. So in the theory of legal families much depends on the area of law one has in mind.

2. Much also depends on the period of which one is speaking. Usually comparatists may largely ignore sudden legislative changes, since the meat of comparative law is not positive law but critical comparison. But the division of the world's legal systems into families, especially the attribution of a system to a particular family, is susceptible to alteration as a result of legislation or other events, and can therefore be only temporary. For example, contemporary developments in Japan make it seem increasingly advisable to consider taking modern Japanese law out of the oriental group and classifying it with those systems which have European origins. It is true that for a long time the many codes on the European model which were enacted in Japan had very little influence on the realities of legal life there, but now that it appears that

the traditional distaste for written rules of law and litigation is on the wane (see below pp. 366 ff.) it is increasingly doubtful whether Japanese law should be kept in the family of oriental systems. China presents a similar problem, save that it is the family of socialist systems with which it may now fall to be classed.

It is possible for a quite *new* legal family to emerge as time goes by, and we may at the moment be approaching the time when the systems of sub-Saharan Africa should be classed together as an *African legal family*. These African legal systems have long been an object of fascination to comparative lawyers, legal ethnologists, and legal sociologists, despite the appalling difficulties of doing research on them (see the instructive and comprehensive piece by BRYDE, 'Afrikanische Rechtssysteme', *JuS* 1982, 8). *Legal ethnologists* find Africa extremely important for research because in relation to family and land law and questions of dispute resolution the mass of Africans still live under indigenous customary law. The rules of such law vary enormously, partly because of the great differences in race, language, culture, and life-style between the various tribes and peoples on this vast continent, and partly because the existing 'traditional' law has been very variously influenced by Islamic law and the law of the ex-colonial powers. *Sociologists of law* love discussing African law, for it is a concrete instance of their central problem, namely the relationship between law and social change and, in special relation to African conditions, the question what contribution law, especially 'modern' law, has made and can or will make to the desired political, social, and economic 'development' in African countries, a question relevant to all developing countries (see, for example, TRUBEK/GALANTER, 'Scholars in Self-Estrangement: Some Reflections on the Crisis in Law and Development Studies in the United States', 1974 *Wis. L. Rev.* 1062; MERRYMAN, 'Comparative Law and Social Change: On the Origins, Style, Decline and Revival of the Law and Development Movement', 25 *Am. J. Comp. L.* 457 (1977); BRYDE, *The Politics and Sociology of African Legal Development* (1976); FUCHS, 'Recht und Entwicklungsländer', *ZvglRW* 80 (1981) 355). The African legal systems also provide a rich field of material for the study of the *reception of foreign law*, for all African legal systems are still influenced to a considerable extent by the laws of the earlier colonial powers, partly because European law has served as a model, especially in the area of the law of obligations, commercial law, criminal law, and administrative law, and partly because, by studying in Europe or at an African university founded on a European model, African lawyers have absorbed European legal traditions which have stayed with them in their subsequent careers as officials, judges, and lawyers. As a result there is still a deep divide between the previous French and Belgian colonies on the one hand, and those that were British on the other. This is why it is much easier for a lawyer from Ghana to understand a lawyer from Kenya, Uganda, or even from England, which are far away, than a lawyer from the Ivory Coast next door (see below pp. 237 ff.). Even so, the problems facing all African legal systems are basically similar, and with a little co-operation could be studied at a general level. Those for whom this is the main consideration may therefore speak of an African legal family, notwithstanding the differences we have mentioned (see in this sense M'BAYE, 'The African Conception of Law', II *Int. Enc. Comp. L.* Ch 1 (1975) 138).

It will be clear from these examples that one's division of the world into legal families and the inclusion of systems in a particular family is vulnerable to alteration by historical development and change. So in the theory of legal families much depends on the period of time of which one is speaking.

It follows that the comparative legal historian who practises 'vertical' comparative law will hit upon different legal families, depending on the period under review, from the comparatist who looks only to living systems of law. This distinction is one which SCHNITZER failed to observe in 1961 when he produced a classification based on the 'great cultural families'. He put primitive peoples into one legal family, and the ancient Mediterranean civilizations into another; he had a European–American legal family, 'arising from a mixture of the romanistic and Germanic cultures and impressed by Christian characteristics', a family of religious legal systems, and a legal family of the peoples of Africa and Asia (above p. 63 at pp. 138 ff.). Because of SCHNITZER's confusion of the methods of comparative legal history and comparative law his proposed scheme, which is defective in other respects as well, fails to serve the function of the theory of legal families, namely to assist us to comprehend and assimilate the great mass of detail.

III

The unsatisfactory feature of most previous attempts to distinguish the legal families and to attribute individual systems to them is that they are one-dimensional, that is, they seek to make everything turn on a *single* criterion. Even the most progressive of the schemes, that of ARMINJON/NOLDE/WOLFF, did not tell us what criterion to apply in 'studying the legal systems themselves'. RENÉ DAVID's first theory, that legal systems should be classed in accordance with their basic ideology in the widest sense, is also too one-dimensional; we cannot put such diverse systems as Continental law and the Common Law into the same box just because they share a sense of justice which differs from that of the socialist systems.

In our view the critical thing about legal systems is their *style*, for the styles of individual legal systems and groups of legal systems are each quite distinctive. The comparatist must strive to grasp these *legal styles*, and to use distinctive stylistic traits as a basis for putting legal systems into groups.

The concept of style which originated in the literary and fine arts has long been used in other fields. Style in the arts signifies the distinctive element of a work or its unity of form, but many other disciplines use this fertile concept to indicate a congeries of particular features which the most diverse objects of study may possess. In law we find the concept used in the Codex Iuris Canonici; canon 20 lays down that if there is no clear and express rule, the rule to be applied is to be found by analogy or inferred from the general principles of law consistent with canonical equity, from constant leading doctrine, and from the *style* and practice of the Roman Curia. Another social science, economics, uses the notion of the 'style of an economy' in one of its branches. ARTHUR SPIETHOFF defines it thus: the 'style of an economy' is the totality of features which flesh out a distinctive form of economic life; his subsequent discussion of methodological questions and of the 'determination of the characteristics of economic styles' is not relevant for us in view of the differences between the two disciplines. (See SPIETHOFF, 'Die Allgemeine Volkswirtschaftslehre als geschichtliche Theorie', in *Festgabe Sombart* (1933) 56, 75 ff.)

We must therefore ask which are the factors which contribute to the juristic style of whole groups of legal systems; for this purpose, experience, inadequate though it doubtless is, must be our guide. It is not every trivial difference between legal systems which can rank as an element in their style. Only 'important' or 'essential' differentiating qualities are hallmarks. As SPIETHOFF says: 'there can never be any final proof of what is "important" or "essential". How many styles a scholar identifies and how he identifies them are largely matters for his judgment. The aim, however, is quite clear: to see the differences in reality, past and present, contained in distinctive forms of economic life' (ibid., 57). One indication of the 'importance' of a feature in a legal system is if the comparatist from another system finds it very surprising. In consequence it is easier to discover the stylistically distinctive elements in a foreign system than in one's own. From this it follows that in the long run international co-operation will be needed to determine the different styles of law.

The following factors seem to us to be those which are crucial for the style of a legal system or legal family: (1) its historical background and development, (2) its predominant and characteristic mode of thought in legal matters, (3) especially distinctive institutions, (4) the kind of legal sources it acknowledges and the way it handles them, and (5) its ideology.

1. It is self-evident that *historical development* is one of the factors which determines the style of modern legal systems. The Common Law is perhaps the clearest example of this, but it is not so easy to group the systems of the European Continent. They stem from Roman and Germanic law, but should they all (with the admitted exception of Nordic law, which stands by itself) be put in one legal family, as DAVID and MALMSTRÖM do, or should there be a Germanic family (Germany, Austria, Switzerland, and a few affiliated systems) and a Romanistic family (France and all the systems which adopted the French Civil Code, along with Spain, Portugal, and South America)? ARMINJON/NOLDE/WOLFF seems to us to be right in opting for the latter alternative (above p. 63 at p. 50). Subsequent events may obliterate the stylistic significance of common origins, and here there are two subsequent events. First, the great movement of reception to which the French Civil Code gave rise and in which Germany, Austria, and Switzerland took no part.

Secondly, the development in German-speaking countries in the nineteenth century, under pandectist influence, of a formal legal technique with extremely clear-cut concepts which, far from forming the basis of a thorough codification in France, whose traditions look more to the political and forensic spheres, had hardly any effect there at all. If one puts into a single 'Romanistic–Germanic legal family' the Romanistic systems, the laws of Germany, Austria, and Switzerland, and even the Nordic systems, one may be misled into concentrating on the relatively abstract common features which distinguish them as a group from, say, the Common Law; one may too easily overlook the fact that in the concert of European law the three groups mentioned have each their own very distinctive voice. It is true, of course, that the Romanistic, Germanic, and Nordic systems each have a closer relationship with each other than with the Common Law; but given their recent development and the presence of the other stylistically distinctive features to be mentioned shortly, clarity requires us to put them into different legal families. The independent historical development of the Common Law makes it necessary to classify it separately, and the same is true of Islamic and Hindu law. Western law was received into Russia, but Russian law must be separately classified because of recent events, and so must the non-communist systems of the Far East by reason of their distinctive mode of thinking.

2. Another hallmark of a legal system or family is a *distinctive mode of legal thinking*. Thus the Germanic and Romanistic families are marked by a tendency to use abstract legal norms, to have a well-articulated system containing well-defined areas of law, and to think up and to think in juristic constructions. When one looks at the very different situation in the Anglo-Saxon legal family one realizes just how distinctive these stylistic elements are.

The tradition of the English Common Law has been one of gradual development from decision to decision; historically speaking, it is case-law, not enacted law. On the Continent the development since the reception of Roman law has been quite different, from the interpretation of JUSTINIAN's Corpus Iuris to the codification, nation by nation, of abstract rules. So Common Law comes from the court, Continental law from the study; the great jurists of England were judges, on the Continent professors. On the Continent lawyers, faced with a problem, even a new and unforeseen one, ask what solution the rule provides; in England and the United States they predict how the judge would deal with the problem, given existing decisions. These differences in style run through the whole legal system. On the Continent lawyers think abstractly, in terms of institutions; in England concretely, in terms of cases, the relationship of the parties, 'rights and duties'. On the Continent, the system is conceived as being complete and free from gaps, in England lawyers feel their way gradually from case to case. On the Continent lawyers delight in systematics, in England they are sceptical of every generalization. On the Continent lawyers operate with ideas, which often, dangerously enough, take on a life of their own; in England they think in pictures; and so one could continue.

These differences in style correspond with the differences in the Continental and English mentalities, attributable to different historical developments, especially those of an intellectual order. If we may generalize, the European is given to making plans, to regulating things in advance, and therefore, in terms of law, to drawing up rules and systematizing them. He approaches life with fixed ideas, and operates deductively. The Englishman improvises, never making a decision until he has to. As MAITLAND said, he is an empiricist. Only experience counts for him; theorizing has little appeal; and so he is not given to abstract rules of law. Convinced, perhaps from living by the sea, that life will controvert the best-laid plans, the Englishman is content with case-law as opposed to enactments. But recently the attitudes of Common Law and Continental law have been drawing closer. On the Continent statute law is losing something of its primacy; lawyers no longer see decision-making as a merely technical and automatic process, but accept that the comprehensive principles laid down by statutes call for broad interpretation, and have begun to treat the *jurisprudence constante* of the courts as an independent source of law. At the same time the need for large-scale planning and ordering of social affairs has forced Anglo-American law into using abstract norms, though its methods of interpretation still show many of the stylistic differences we have mentioned (see further below Ch. 20).

Another characteristic element in the style of Continental legal systems is their *antiformalism*, their opposition to needless formality in the law. In private law this shows itself in consensualism, that is, the rule that agreement creates contractual obligations, no matter how it is expressed.

Consensualism is to be found at an advanced stage of every legal culture. In the early stages we meet its opposite, formalism, the requirement of strict forms for the few recognized types of transaction. Consequently and subsequently there arises the 'factitious transaction' where the intended transaction, not being recognized by the law, is forced into the form of one that is so recognized, or the fictive lawsuit, brought collusively by the parties to a transaction in order to avoid the inconveniences of formalism. At the final stage of development we find a struggle on behalf of the 'victims of form', those who failed to achieve what they sought only because they omitted, perhaps through ignorance, the requisite form.

The formalism present in all primitive systems is also to be found in developed Anglo-American law, in the Statute of Frauds. In Europe the tendency to antiformalism is strong, especially in Germany, Switzerland, and Scandinavia, less so in France, which in this respect is untypical because of the age of its Civil Code. At a late stage in legal culture critical lawyers realize that factitious transactions and fictive lawsuits are simply evasive devices, and since they no longer believe in the importance of forms in law, they approach them in a liberal spirit: the doors to freedom of type and form are opened.

There is another stylistic element in legal thinking which is found in several legal families, indeed in all Western law. It is what RUDOLPH V. JHERING called the 'struggle for law'. The principle is that though the goal of law is peace, one must struggle to achieve it. In other words, it is the duty of a person, owed both to himself and to the idea of law itself, to fight for his rights. Our Western laws of procedure are bottomed on this view. JHERING thought it was invariable and many people today regard it as a truism, but the comparatist who turns his eyes to the Far East finds that this is not so of the legal systems th're, as they were at any rate until recently.

In those systems law is a secondary and subordinate means of achieving social order, and it is used only as a last resort. The harmony of society is seen as reflecting the general harmony of the world as evidenced in nature and the cosmos. The arid logic and external compulsion inherent in law make it a very rudimentary means of achieving order, though no doubt it is suitable for uncivilized peoples. Among civilized peoples, principles of behaviour should be obeyed voluntarily, and then they will prove effective in the community life of family, clan, and village; they come not from the law, but from a mass of unwritten rules of behaviour harmoniously integrated by tradition. These rules are not directed to procuring that everyone obtains his due, but to preserving social harmony. In consequence is is no solution to a dispute to have a winner and a loser; instead the claimant must take great care to let his opponent 'save face'. Thus in the Far East law does not lead to a judicial decision in favour of one party, but to a peaceable settlement or amicable composition (see further below p. 409). There is much of the wisdom of the Orient here, and there are some echoes of it in the West. Thus a bad settlement, we say, is better than a good lawsuit, and a legal adviser may pride himself on never having had to go to court. Despite this, there is still this critical difference in style, that in the West man naturally fights for his rights and seeks a clear decision, treating a compromise as a thing perhaps to be settled for, and in the East the face-saving compromise is the ideal and a firm decision only a necessary evil.

In this area the assistance of legal sociology is especially needed by comparative law. Our example of the Far Eastern systems shows that statutes and codes, which in Japan were technically and substantially comparable with those of Europe, may be quite peripheral features of a legal system, surprisingly remote from the real forces which mould legal life. The student of other legal systems will have to ask himself similar questions. Thus the information we have about the operation of the legal systems of Latin America suggests that there also written law is not very significant in practice, and that as a means of resolving social conflicts formal proceedings before an independent state judge have nothing like the importance they do in Europe or North America. (See, for example, GESSNER, *Recht und Konflikt, Eine soziologische Untersuchung privatrechtlicher Konflikte in Mexico* (1976).) Much work remains to be done: comparative sociological research in law has only just started.

3. *Certain legal institutions* are so remarkable that they lend a distinctive

style to a legal system. In Common Law systems one could instance agency, consideration (vol. II, Ch. 6 II), estoppel, the absence in principle of remedies *in specie* (vol. II, Ch. 12 IV), the trust, the amazing casuistry of tort law (vol. II, Ch. 17 III), many peculiarities of property law with its various degrees of property and the division between real and personal property, the relativity of legal personality, the vesting of a decedent's estate in an executor, and many oddities in the law of evidence. In the Romanistic family there are institutions such as *cause* (vol. II, Ch. 6 III), abuse of right, the direct action, the oblique action, the *actio de in rem verso* (vol. II, Ch. 14 III), the extent of strict liability in tort (vol. II, Ch. 19 III), and *negotiorum gestio*, common to the Continental systems but so foreign to the Common Law. In the Germanic family one can perhaps mention the *clausulae generales* which open the door to judge-made law, the concept of the legal act (vol. II, Ch. 1 I), the theory of the abstract real contract, liability based on *culpa in contrahendo*, the doctrine of the collapse of the foundations of a transaction (vol. II, Ch. 14 II) the entrenched position of the institution of unjustified enrichment (vol. II, Ch. 15 II), and the land register. The institutions which give the socialist systems their distinctive style would include the different kinds of ownership (below Ch. 26), the peculiarities of contract in a planned economy (below Ch. 27), the equal treatment of legitimate and illegitimate children, and many others.

4. The style of legal systems is obviously also marked by the choice of *sources of law* which they recognize and by the methods of interpreting and handling them in connection with the court machinery and rules of procedure. Since LÉVY-ULLMANN many introductions to comparative law, books and articles have been devoted to these topics, especially and repeatedly to the supposed opposition between statutory and case-law systems, with all the refinements of the doctrine of precedent and the niceties of statutory construction (see below Ch. 20). No one can deny that differences exist on this matter, but they have generally been exaggerated. For comparative law as a whole and for the theory of legal families in particular, the question of sources of law is of minor importance. The legal institutions which we have mentioned as giving legal systems their characteristic stamp are much more significant, and deserve much closer attention.

5. Finally, the *ideology* of a legal system, in the sense of political or economic doctrines or religious belief, may have a distinctive effect on its style. This is manifest in the case of the religious legal systems and of the socialist systems. The legal ideologies of the Anglo-Saxon, Germanic, Romanistic, and Nordic families are essentially similar, and it is because of other elements in their styles that they must be distinguished, but the communist theory of law is so extremely different that we must put into a special legal family the Soviet Union, the People's Republic of China, Mongolia, Vietnam, North Korea, and the socialist states of Europe.

IV

These are the stylistic factors which enable us to identify the families of legal systems and to attribute individual systems to them, but the weight to be given to each of these factors varies according to the circumstances. As was said above, ideology is an effective ground for distinguishing the religious and socialist systems, but does not help us to separate the legal families of the West. There it is history, mode of thought and distinctive institutions which distinguish the legal families. Sources of law are a distinguishing feature of Islamic and Hindu law and also help us to divide the Anglo-Saxon from the Continental legal families, but we cannot use them as a basis for distinguishing between the Germanic, Nordic, and Romanistic families.

There are some 'hybrid' systems of law which it is not easy to put in the right family—Greece, for example (below Ch. 12 IV), Louisiana in the United States (below Ch. 8 VII), the Province of Quebec in Canada (below Ch. 8 VII), Scotland (below Ch. 16 VI), South Africa (below Ch. 18 VI), Israel (below Ch. 18 VII), the Philippines, Puerto Rico, the People's Republic of China, and some others. With them the question must be which family they are closest to in style. This calls for delicacy. Often one finds that some areas of law in a system bear the marks of one 'parent', others of another. In such a case an exclusive attribution to one or other is impossible, except with regard to particular areas of law such as family law or inheritance law or commercial law. Sometimes a legal system is in the process of moving towards a particular legal family; in such a case it is often extremely doubtful at which point of time the change of family is complete, and it may not be possible to fix upon an exact moment. In any case, as the example of 'hybrid' systems shows, any division of the legal world into families or groups is a rough and ready device. It can be quite useful for the novice, by putting the confusing variety of legal systems into some kind of loose order, but the experienced comparatist will have developed a 'nose' for the distinctive style of national legal systems and will either not use the device of legal families at all, or will use it with all the circumspection called for by any attempt to force into a schematic order social phenomena as highly complex as living legal systems.

One must therefore keep calm when new proposals for divisions of legal systems are aired and the view here proposed is subjected to criticisms based on quite different assumptions. As we have said, experts may differ on what features and criteria are 'essential' when one is dividing legal systems into families, and different classifications may well be called for if new concepts are developed by comparative work in sociology of law, ethnology of law, or political science. Furthermore the aptness of the criteria one adopts depends on the aim one has in mind. As this 'Introduction' is designed for teaching purposes, it seemed right to treat the Romanistic, Germanic, and Nordic systems as separate legal families in order to emphasize the different timbres they bring to the concert of law in Europe. Those with other aims may make other divisions. We quite agree with DAVID, who concluded his treatment of the controversies of classification by saying: 'Much ink has been spilt on the subject, but to little purpose. "Legal families" do not exist like human families: the idea is used purely for explanatory purposes, to indicate the extent of difference and similarity in the various legal systems. It follows that all classifications have their utility: it all depends on the point of view adopted by the writer in question and the aspects of the matter which interest him most.' (*Les Grands Systèmes*, 22.)

It was not the aim of this excursus to offer a new grouping of legal systems but rather to use the concept of style in the context of law to elucidate better than has hitherto been done the criteria which should be employed in grouping the legal systems together and deciding which group a particular system belongs to. The grouping to which we are led and which will serve as our basis for the introduction to the great legal systems of the world is only slightly different from that of ARMINJON/NOLDE/WOLFF: (1) Romanistic family; (2) Germanic family; (3) Nordic family; (4) Common Law family; (5) socialist family; (6) Far Eastern systems; (7) Islamic systems; and (8) Hindu law.

I. THE ROMANISTIC LEGAL FAMILY

6

The History of French Law

ARMINJON/NOLDE/WOLFF, *Traité de droit comparé* I (1950) 120 ff.

BRISSAUD, *Manuel d'histoire du droit privé* (1935).

DAWSON, 'The Codification of the French Customs', 38 *Mich. L. Rev.* 765 (1940).

——, *The Oracles of the Law* (1968).

A. ESMEIN, *Précis élémentaire de l'histoire du droit français de 1789 à 1814* (1908).

——, *Cours élémentaire d'histoire du droit français* (15th edn., 1925).

FENET, *Recueil complet de travaux préparatoires du Code civil* (1836).

HEINSHEIMER, *Die Zivilgesetze der Gegenwart* I (1932): *Frankreich, Code civil,* Introduction V ff.

HEYMANN, 'Romanische Rechtsordnungen', in: *Handwörterbuch der Rechtswissenschaft* V (1928) 151.

KOSCHAKER, *Europa und das römische Recht* (2nd edn., 1953).

LE CODE CIVIL, LIVRE DU CENTENAIRE, 2 vols. (1904), with essays by SOREL, ESMEIN, VIGIÉ, SALEILLES and others.

MITTEIS, 'Die germanischen Grundlagen des französischen Rechtes', *SavZ/Germ.* 63 (1943) 137.

OLIVIER MARTIN, *La Coutume de Paris—Trait d'union entre le droit romain et les législations modernes* (1925).

RABEL, 'Private Laws of Western Civilization—The French Civil Code', 10 *La. L. Rev.* 107 (1950).

SAVATIER, *L'art de faire les lois—Bonaparte et le Code civil* (1927).

WILHELM, 'Gesetzgebung und Kodifikation in Frankreich im 17. und 18. Jahrhundert', *Ius commune* I (1967) 241.

——, 'Portalis und Savigny', in: *Aspekte europäischer Rechtsgeschichte, Festgabe für Coing* (1982) 445.

I

THE Code civil of 1804 is not only the heart of private law in France but also the great model for the codes of private law of the whole Romanistic legal family. The Code was generated by the spirit of the French Revolution which sought to eradicate the feudal institutions of the past and to implant in their place the natural law values of property, freedom of contract, family, and family inheritance. The revolutionary events of the years after 1789 were very important for the Code, but there is more to it than that. For all the impetus of revolution, the Code carefully absorbs the results of a long historical development, and most of it is a felicitous blend of traditional legal institutions from the *droit écrit* of the South, influenced by Roman law, and the *droit coutumier* of the North, influenced by the Germanic–Frankish customary law. Though in many respects the Code civil makes a revolutionary take-off, it bears throughout the marks of its heritage of the pre-revolutionary law, the *ancien droit*. Accordingly we shall first trace the development of French law up to the Revolution, so far as this is necessary in order to understand the achievement of those who drafted the Code civil. Then we shall deal briefly with the *droit intermédiaire* of the revolutionary period and with the legislative history of the Code, before turning to the Code itself.

II

The Romans established their law in Gaul as they did in all the provinces they conquered, but when the Western Roman Empire collapsed in 476, Roman law did not lose its validity in the Germanic states which succeeded it; it survived, especially in the kingdoms of the Visigoths and the Burgundians, as the law for the subject peoples of non-German origin. In 506 Alaric II, King of the Visigoths, passed a statute—the Breviarium Alaricianum or Lex Romana Wisigothorum—containing a résumé of and commentary on the Codex Theodosianus and some other Roman sources; this contributed to the survival of some knowledge of Roman law in the southern part of France despite the great migrations of the fifth and sixth centuries. In the North of France, on the other hand, the incursion of the Franks and the founding of the Frankish state did largely oust Roman law, since the Franks brought with them their own developed customary laws of Germanic origin, and later crystallized them in several statutes of which the most important is the Lex Salica. The renaissance of Roman law studies in North Italy in the eleventh and twelfth centuries was immediately taken up in the South of France; the study of the Corpus Iuris was well established in the Universities of Montpellier and Toulouse in the twelfth century. Acquaintance with Roman law gradually filtered north-wards, without of course displacing the traditional customary laws of the Franks. Thus the territory of France became divided for legal purposes into the area of *droit écrit* in the South influenced by Roman law, and the area of *droit coutumier* in the North, based on Germanic customs (*coutumes*). The dividing line ran parallel with the Loire from the mouth of the Gironde to the Lake of Geneva, so that the northern three-fifths of France as it is today were controlled by the *droit coutumier*, the southern two-fifths by the *droit écrit*.

One must not overestimate the sharpness of the division between the *droit écrit* and the *droit coutumier*. In the South, for example in the urban regions of Bordeaux and Toulouse, there were written *coutumes* influenced by Roman law but containing strong Germanic elements. Nor was Roman law entirely rejected by the *droit coutumier* in the North. Some parts of the law, for example contract law, were inadequately regulated by the *coutumes* and therefore lawyers readily had recourse to the better developed and more refined Roman law; and the view was accepted in the North that Roman law as *ratio scripta* could be called upon to supplement and explain the *coutumes* when they gave no answer to particular questions. But it must be noticed that, unlike the later situation in Germany when Roman law was received, Roman law was not regarded as authoritative or valuable on the ground that it was the law of the Roman Empire. On the contrary, the French Kings were especially interested in protecting their sovereignty against the Empire and the Emperor, and the royalist lawyers emphasized that if Roman law was accepted in France, this was not because it had been laid down by Rome, but on the ground that it had been accepted by custom or by reason of its inherent quality: *non ratione imperii sed imperio rationis*. Thus in France, unlike Germany later, there was never any serious discussion of a complete reception of Roman law into France; it was effective only in so far as this was the local custom, as in the South, or, as in the North, on the grounds of its inherent merit.

In the tenth and eleventh centuries, as the Carolingians gave way to the Capetians, Frankish law broke up into many different systems, according to the territories, some extremely small, won by princes and prelates (compare MITTEIS, above p. 76, at pp. 152 ff.). A number of law-books were written in the thirteenth century, mainly by famous practitioners, recording the custom of a particular region. Among the most important are the *Livre de Jostice et de Plet* which portrayed the *Coutume* of Orleans, strongly impressed by Roman and canon law, the *Coutumes de Beauvaisis* by PHILIPPE DE BEAUMANOIR, and the great collection of Norman customary law (*Grand Coutumier de la Normandie*) which to this day provides the basis for the private law of the Channel Islands. It remained true, however, that the customary laws of Northern France depended principally on oral tradition; the judge who did not know the appropriate rule of the relevant *coutume* had to discover it by means of an 'enquête par turbe', in which a number of local inhabitants had to say what they remembered the substance of the *coutume* to be. The proliferation of *coutumes* and the difficulty of discovering their content naturally gave rise to great legal uncertainty. This called the French King on to the scene in the fifteenth century. By the Ordonnance of Montils-les-Tours of 1454, Charles VII ordained that the customs of the various territories should be written down and that those which were already recorded should be drafted anew, with the co-operation of a royal commission of experts. The task of recording the *coutumes* took longer than expected. Charles VII's instruction had to be repeated several times by his successors, and they also had to overcome the opposition of some of the territories, especially

Normandy (see the detailed description in DAWSON, above p. 76). But the intervention of the King greatly strengthened the power of the traditional customary laws to withstand Roman law. As the French historian of law OLIVIER MARTIN wrote, 'That France was saved from the massive reception of Roman law which took place in Germany is clearly attributable to the King's success in having the customs recorded in the sixteenth century' (above p. 76, p. 13). It is also clear that the recording of the *coutumes* was necessary for the gradual development of a common customary law of France (*droit coutumier commun*), and finally for the amalgamation of *droit coutumier* and *droit écrit*, without which the Code civil of 1804 could never have unified the law in France.

By the end of the eighteenth century all the important customs of more than purely local significance had been recorded in accordance with the royal mandate. Yet on the eve of the French Revolution, on one estimate, there were no fewer than 60 customary laws of extensive significance (*coutumes générales*), some of which were interrelated, and as many as 300 *coutumes* of limited territorial application (*coutumes locales*).

The juxtaposition of different *coutumes* led to legal problems whenever a case had connections with more than one region, as where a Breton drew up his will in Paris, where the *coutume* laid down different rules regarding testamentary capacity or form. Thus in the sixteenth century French lawyers were especially active in the area of law which today we call private international law; the names of DUMOULIN (1500–66) and, even more, D'ARGENTRÉ (1519–90) stand out; see the fundamental work of GAMILL-SCHEG, *Der Einfluss Dumoulins auf die Entwicklung des Kollisionsrechts* (1955).

While the writing down of the more important *coutumes* could reduce the uncertainty of the law, it could not diminish the substantial differences between them, much less the great legal division between the *pays du droit écrit* and the *pays du droit coutumier*. As the French Kings consolidated their power, the multiplicity of legal systems became more and more unsatisfactory, and the creation of a unitary private law common to the whole of France was increasingly felt to be necessary.

The assimilation of the particular customary laws was considerably promoted by the *Coutume de Paris*. It became increasingly important after its publication in 1510. This was mainly attributable to the influential decisions of the Parlement de Paris, whose very wide jurisdiction included almost the whole of the area of *droit coutumier* with the exception of Brittany and Normandy. Its judges therefore had to apply a very broad range of different *coutumes*, and, as one would expect, when they had to solve disputed questions or fill gaps in the law, they tended to develop unitary rules. Consistently enough, the new and extended edition of the *Coutume de Paris* in 1580 contained a digest (*abrégé*) of the decisions of the Parlement on *questions générales*. Gradually it came to be accepted that the *Coutume de Paris* could be applied everywhere, even in preference to Roman law, so as to supplement any gaps in the regional laws.

A series of important jurists played a most conspicuous role in the gradual development of a common private law for the whole of France. They were not professors, but practitioners, attorneys, legal advisers, royal administrators, and judges. Of these, DUMOULIN is pre-eminent. He was the first to state the view that there was such a thing as a common law of France; it consisted of the totality of the ideas of law which found expression in the different *coutumes*. His works, especially his famous and influential' commentary on the First Book of the *Coutume de Paris*, were mainly directed to discovering these general legal principles; to this end he constantly made critical comparisons of the different *coutumes*, and applied the principle that 'deficiente consuetudine ... non est recurrendum ad ius Romanum, sed ad vicinas et generales et promiscuas consuetudines Galliae' (see GAMILLSCHEG (above p. 76) at 88 ff.). COQUILLE (1523–1603) wrote a commentary on the *Coutume* of the County of Nevers, and an *Institution au droit français*, both of which expressly used the methods of comparative law in the interest of harmonizing and assimilating the various customs—the very task which comparative law still has to perform today, with the difference that it is no longer the customs of localities but the legal systems of nations which have to be assimilated and harmonized.

DUMOULIN, COQUILLE, and other like-minded authors of the sixteenth century could not by themselves have had such a determinative effect on the development of a common customary law had there not been, especially in Paris, a well-regarded and powerful body of professional lawyers pledged to achieve the same goals. As KOSCHAKER has emphasized, the careful and moderate aceptance of Roman law in France, like its rejection in England, of which we shall shortly be speaking, is attributable to the fact that in both countries there developed early a well-organized and therefore powerful group of practising lawyers, allied with the King, interested in the centralization of justice in the royal courts, and devoted to the national law.

By the fourteenth century professional judges, trained in the law and of bourgeois background, had replaced the clergymen, barons, and noble courtiers in the Court of Paris; before long they were appointed by the King, not just for particular cases or particular sessions, but for an indeterminate period ('à tant qu'il nous plaira') and were normally chosen from the group of practising lawyers and legal advisers on the proposal of the Parlement. We may find it very shocking today that in the fifteenth and sixteenth centuries the King allowed judicial positions to be sold and inherited, but it contributed to the consolidation of the legal profession in France.

'The fact that he could sell his office made the judge in practice irremovable, and the fact that the office could be inherited led to the development of a large number of families with a strong juristic tradition. ... In consequence there arose a sort of hereditary nobility of lawyers, une noblesse de robe, of families proud of their status, with education and style of living to match, which prevented the bureaucratisation of the judiciary which occurred in Germany. . . . It was men like these, in practice as lawyers with the Parlement of Paris, whether as judges or as attorneys or as legal authors, who created the common private law of France. This law was largely the old law of France, partly because the coutume de Paris, though not strictly speaking common law, was much more important than the other customs, but it did not lose its connection with Roman law, from which it took some mature concepts and also some substantive rules of law. Just as in England it was the jurists who rejected the reception of Roman law, so here it was the jurists who, if they did not reject the reception, at least tempered its influence and so were able to maintain a large part of the national law' (KOSCHAKER (above p. 76) 169, 223).

In the seventeenth and eighteenth centuries we find the first jurists whose works provided the draftsmen of the Code with material and model. First there is BOURJON, a Parisian lawyer expert in the Custom of his native city; his influential work had the significant title *Le Droit commun de la France et la coutume de Paris réduit en principes* (1720). DOMAT (1625–96) was less a practitioner than a philosopher like his influential friend PASCAL; he was a great systematizer and his work *Les Loix civiles dans leur ordre naturel* (1689), in which he put into an order suggested by the new ideas of natural law the rules of Roman law adapted to the needs of the time, greatly contributed to the scientific basis of the Code civil. The jurist with the greatest influence on the draftsmen of the Code civil was POTHIER (1699–1772). He was not a great organizer of a vast mass of material nor a very original thinker; indeed, according to the historian A. DUMAS, 'he sometimes did no more than repeat in good French what DUMOULIN had already said in bad Latin'. Yet POTHIER knew both Roman and customary law inside out, though he took from them both rather eclectically, and his numerous small writings on the law of obligations, sale, hire, gift, and so on are characterized by great elegance of style, extreme lucidity, and conceptual accuracy.

Royal ordinances also had a certain effect on the eventual unification of French law. Until the sixteenth century these ordinances dealt with questions of feudalism, procedural law, and court organization. Only later did they regulate areas of substantive private law as well. The Ordonnance de Moulins (1566) dealt with a subject close to procedure. It laid down that oral testimony should be inadmissible in lawsuits worth more than 100 pounds. This formalistic rule is preserved in the Code civil (art. 1341; see vol. II, pp. 49 ff.) though of course the monetary limit has been altered. From the seventeenth century we have the Ordonnance du Commerce (1673) and the Code de la Marine (1681) which contained special rules for commercial law and maritime law, and thereby laid the basis for that division between private law in the narrow sense and commercial law which the Romanistic and Germanic legal families (except Switzerland and Italy) still recognize by having different codes, much to the surprise of Anglo-American lawyers. Louis XIV's Chancellor DAGUESSEAU was responsible for three ordinances of particular importance; one concerned the law of gift (1731), the second

the law of wills (1735), with the remarkable feature of laying down different rules for
the *pays du droit écrit* and the *pays du droit coutumier*, and the third the law of
fideicommissa (1747). The Civil Code incorporated significant parts of the first two
ordinances, but there was not much scope for the third since the *fideicommissum* was
regarded by the Code civil as an institution of a feudal system which had been rendered
obsolete. On the whole matter see WILHELM, 'Gesetzgebung und Kodifikation' (above
p. 76).

Despite all these efforts France on the eve of the Revolution was still very
far indeed from having a unified private law. The chasm between *droit écrit*
and *droit coutumier* was as wide as ever. It is true that all the important
coutumes of more than local significance had been codified, but this only made
it easier to see the differences between them. VOLTAIRE's mockery was
justified:

'Is it not an absurd and terrible thing that what is true in one village is false in
another? What kind of barbarism is it that citizens must live under different
laws? . . . When you travel in this kingdom you change legal systems as often as you
change horses' (*Œuvres de Voltaire* VII (1838) Dialogues p. 5).

The idea of a 'droit coutumier commun' or, as people were coming to say
more often, a 'droit français' had been clearly formulated for a century and a
half. It had become the leading theme of French jurisprudence and this had
laid the intellectual basis for the great work of unification of law in theory and
practice. But before this idea of a unified French private law could become
reality, two things were needed: first the powerful political impetus of the
French Revolution, secondly the authority and decisiveness of NAPOLEON.

III

The 'droit intermédiaire', the law of the revolutionary period between the first
session of the Assemblée Constituante of 1789 and the coming to power of
NAPOLEON BONAPARTE in 1799, altered the traditional social order with
almost unparalleled speed and thoroughness. All the institutions of the *ancien
régime* were rooted out in very short order—the absolute monarchy, the
interlocking powers of King, nobility, clergy, and judiciary (*noblesse de robe*),
the old territorial division of the country into provinces, the feudal regime of
land, the courts system, and the tax system. In its place was put the vision of
the Enlightened Society, as sketched by DIDEROT, VOLTAIRE, and ROUSSEAU:
according to this, man is a rational and responsible creature who acquires at
birth an inalienable right to freedom of conscience, belief, and economic
activity. No longer does man have to deal with the intermediary status groups
of the *ancien régime*, but only with the state itself, which is bound through its
legislation to free its citizens from the traditional authority of feudal, church,
family, guild, and status groups, and to equip all its citizens with equal rights.

In pursuit of these aims the hectic legislation of the early years of the Revolution was sometimes too radically individualistic in the area of private law, and many of the extreme positions it adopted had to be abandoned by the more composed draftsmen of the Code civil. In 1791, decrees of the Assemblée Constituante abolished without compensation all feudal servitudes and cancelled all the privileges of primogeniture along with all the other differences based on age and sex which existed in the laws of succession. Estates both moveable and immoveable were to be divided completely and equally between the descendants or other heirs in intestacy: 'All heirs of equal degree succeed in equal parts to the property which vests in them by law.' This still left the possibility that the decedent might by *will* seek to prefer some persons over others, or to attempt to bind the inheritance for a long period of time. This possibility the Revolution also did away with; fideicommissary substitutions, which performed the same function as the *Nacherbfolge* of German law, were forbidden, and they even went so far, in the interests of dividing up landed property, as to abolish freedom of testation and donation. The National Convention in 1793 decreed that 'the power of disposing of one's goods whether on death, or inter vivos, or by contractual donation in direct line, is abolished: in consequence all descendants will have an equal part of the property of ascendants'. The testator with children could dispose by will of only one-tenth of his estate, the testator with collaterals of only one-sixth, and this only in favour of third parties unrelated to him, for otherwise the 'sainte égalité' of relatives entitled to succeed would have been infringed.

The changes in family law were equally far-reaching. *Patria potestas*, which in the *pays du droit écrit* had allowed the father to exercise some paternal power even over adults, was abolished as being inconsistent with the rights of man. Restraints on marriage laid down by canon law were severely curtailed, and the requirements of marriage, particularly the requirement of parental consent, reduced to a minimum. Marriage itself was regarded as a civil contract (*contrat civil*), with the consequence, amazing for its time, that either spouse could announce a wish to terminate the contract and then obtain a divorce; it was sufficient to assert that there was 'incompatibility of temperament or character' between the spouses. The justification for this principle was made clear: 'individual freedom entails the freedom to divorce, since it would be lost if the engagement of marriage were irrevocable'. Only civil marriages were lawful, and the central register of civil status was introduced. Illegitimate children recognized by their parents were equated with legitimate children, save that 'adulterine' children, that is, children at the time of whose conception either parent was married to a third party, could not have more than one-third of the inheritance of a legitimate child.

One of the most important aims of the Revolution from the very beginning was to unify the private law. The Assemblée Constituante itself had decreed: 'A code of civil law common to the whole kingdom will be drawn up.' In 1793

CAMBACÉRÈS tendered a first draft which was immediately rejected on the ground of being too comprehensive and complicated, although it had only 697 articles: what was wanted were 'simpler and more philosophical conceptions' (see FENET (above p. 76) I, p. XLVIII). The next year CAMBACÉRÈS offered a second draft with only 297 articles, but this time the National Convention found it too sparse and terse. The indefatigable CAMBACÉRÈS produced a third draft in 1796 and laid it before the Council of Five Hundred, the Directorate's legislative organ, but its protracted consideration of the draft was rudely interrupted by NAPOLEON's taking power at the end of 1799.

Things now began to move more briskly. Under the constitution introduced by NAPOLEON the executive power and the power of initiating legislation was vested in three Consuls; NAPOLEON was the First Consul, and the two others had only advisory roles. Draft legislation was to be prepared by the Conseil d'État on the proposal of the Consuls, and was then to be referred by the Consuls to the Tribunat, who could adopt or reject the draft, but not alter it. Then the draft had to be laid before the Corps Législatif, which was just a caricature of a Parliament, since it also had no power to discuss the draft, but only to hear the views of the representatives of the government and the Tribunat and then to adopt it as a law or to reject it. After this constitution was adopted, NAPOLEON devoted himself with energy and circumspection to the creation of a Code civil. He appointed a Commission of only four persons to draft it; these were no revolutionary hotspurs, but experienced practitioners. The representatives of the *droit coutumier* were TRONCHET, President of the Court of Cassation, and BIGOT DE PRÉAMENEU; both had previously been advocates at the Parliament of Paris; the representatives of the *droit écrit* were PORTALIS, a high administrative official and a brilliant speaker and writer, and MALEVILLE, judge of the Court of Cassation. In the astonishingly short period of four months this Commission produced a draft. It was shown to the Court of Cassation and the Courts of Appeal and then, along with their views on it, laid before the Conseil d'État for discussion under the chairmanship of a Consul, normally NAPOLEON himself. There the decision was taken to divide the Code into large sections and to submit these sections separately to the legislative process. But the very first section met with opposition in the Tribunat. Some of its members were very suspicious of the abolition of the Directorate and the rise to power of the young General NAPOLEON. One of these was BENJAMIN CONSTANT, who expressed strong opposition to the First Consul in the salon of his close friend MADAME DE STAËL, and was later to gain fame for the polemics he wrote in exile. Suspicion and envy rather than reasons of substance led the Tribunat to reject the first portions of the Code, and the Corps Législatif to follow suit. NAPOLEON's reaction must have surprised them. He withdrew the whole legislative project, saying that the calmness and unanimity required for so important a project had not yet been achieved. He then purged the Tribunat of all the members hostile to him, including CONSTANT, and procured that in future the Tribunat should be asked unofficially what position it would take before the draft law was laid before it and the Corps Législatif. After the lapse of only a year, NAPOLEON set the legislative process in motion again, and in 1803 and 1804 thirty-six separate statutes were passed without opposition; they were finally consolidated by the law of 31 March 1804 and brought into force under the title of 'Code civil des Français'.

What part did NAPOLEON himself take in the creation of the Code civil? As we have seen, his energy and determination were needed to force the Code through the legislative process, but we are now interested in his influence on its form and substance. NAPOLEON, as chairman, took a very lively part in no less than 57 of the 102 meetings at which the Conseil d'État considered the text of the drafting committee. Of course, NAPOLEON had no legal training; he was a soldier, and indeed was heavily preoccupied at the time in question by military adventures against the English. He was absent when some important matters, such as, for example, the law of obligations and the law of matrimonial property, were being discussed by the Conseil d'État, and he took very little part in purely legal debates. Yet his contribution to the formation of the Code civil was quite substantial. Then a man of 34 and head of state, NAPOLEON had, according to all contemporary evidence, a most powerful and fascinating personality. At the meetings of the Conseil d'État he constantly focused attention on the realities of life rather than the technicalities of law; he immediately saw the practical relevance of abstract rules; he put an abrupt end to any hair-splitting discussions, and by clear and simple questions kept bringing the discussion back to the practical and concrete; above all, he insisted on a style of drafting which was transparently clear and comprehensible to a non-lawyer like himself. It has been said that the Code civil owes the clarity and comprehensibility of its language to the fact that its draftsman had constantly to ask himself whether the words he had chosen would withstand the criticisms of a highly intelligent layman like NAPOLEON, unfamiliar with the jargon of the law. THIBEAUDEAU, who took part in the discussions as a member of the Conseil d'État, is probably not exaggerating in the following passage from his memoirs where he describes NAPOLEON's participation:

'He started, maintained and guided [the discussion], and when it flagged he revived it. . . . He spoke quite simply and naturally, without affectation, but with the freedom and tone one finds in a conversation whose natural flow depends on the subject-matter, the diversity of opinions and the stage of the discussion. At this no member of the Council was better than he; in his capacity to go straight to the heart of a question, in the appropriateness of his ideas and the strength of his arguments he was as good as any: in originality of expression and apt turn of phrase he was often the best.' (Quoted in SOREL, *Livre du Centenaire* I, pp. xxv f.)

NAPOLEON left many marks on the actual substance of the Code, too. His support for the idea of a strong patriarchally organized family was constant and eloquent; here his central idea was, in SAVATIER's words (above p. 76, at p. 25), 'A strong family in an omnipotent state with a Napoleon at the top'. His strong support for divorce by mutual consent and for adoption may be explained on personal grounds. At the time NAPOLEON planned to found a dynasty, having obtained by referendum in 1802 the consulship for life as well as the right to nominate his successor, and since he knew that his marriage to JOSEPHINE BEAUHARNAIS would remain childless, remarriage and adoption seemed to be ways to procure a family and thus a successor. NAPOLEON himself was very proud of his part in creating the Code civil, as is shown by his famous observation, made years later in exile on St. Helena: 'It is not in winning 40 battles that my real glory lies, for all those victories will be eclipsed by Waterloo. But my Code civil will not be forgotten, it will live forever.'

7

The Spirit and Essential Features
of the Code Civil

In addition to the literature cited above p. 76:
AUDIT, 'Recent Revisions of the French Civil Code', 38 *La. L. Rev.* 747 (1978).
BOEHMER, 'Der Einfluß des Code Civil auf die Rechtsentwicklung in Deutschland',
    AcP 151 (1950/1951) 289.
——, 'Grundlagen des französischen Privatrechts im 20. Jahrhundert, *RabelsZ* 18
    (1953) 480.
DAVID, *English Law and French Law* (1980).
——, *French Law, Its Structure, Sources and Methodology* (1972).
FERID, *Das französische Zivilrecht*, vol. I (1971) Chs. 1 and 2.
FIKENTSCHER, *Methoden des Rechts in vergleichender Darstellung*, vol. I (1975) Ch. 6.
FRIEDRICH, 'The Ideological and Philosophical Background', in: *The Code Napoleon
    and the Common Law World* (ed. B. Schwartz, 1956) 1.
GÉNY, *Méthode d'interprétation et sources en droit privé positif*, 2 vols. (2nd edn., 1954).
KAHN-FREUND/LÉVY/RUDDEN, *A Source-Book on French Law* (1973).
LAWSON, 'The Approach to French Law', 34 *Ind. LJ* 531 (1959).
——, Réflexions d'un juriste anglais sur le cent-cinquantenaire du Code civil, *Rev. int.
    dr. comp.* 6 (1954) 665.
MURDOCK, 'Le Code civil vu par un Américain', *Rev. int. dr. comp.* 6 (1954) 678.
PORTALIS, *Discours, rapports et travaux inédits sur le Code civil* (ed. F. Portalis, 1844).
RIPERT, *Le Régime démocratique et le droit civil moderne* (2nd edn., 1948).
SAVATIER, Les *Métamorphoses économiques et sociales du droit privé d'aujourd'hui*, 3
    vols. (3rd edn., 1959–64).
——, 'Destin du Code civil français', *Rev. int. dr. comp.* 6 (1954) 637.
THIEME, *Das Naturrecht und die europäische Privatrechtsgeschichte* (1947).
TUNC, 'The Grand Outlines of the Code', in: *The Code Napoleon and the Common Law
    World* (ed. B. Schwartz, 1956) 19.
——, 'Methodology of the Civil Law in France', 50 *Tul. L. Rev.* 459 (1976).
WIEACKER, *Das Sozialmodell der klassischen Privatrechtsgesetzbücher* (1953).
——, *Privatrechtsgeschichte der Neuzeit* (2nd edn., 1967) 322 ff.

I

OTHER great codes came into force in Central and Western Europe at the end
of the eighteenth and the beginning of the nineteenth centuries, but beyond
doubt the French Code civil is intellectually the most significant and
historically the most fertile. Like the General Land Law for the Prussian

87

States (1794) and the General Civil Code of Austria (1811), the Code civil is founded on the creed of the Enlightenment and the law of reason that social life can be put into a rational order if only the rules of law are restructured according to a comprehensive plan. The means by which these codes sought to achieve this goal and the historical situations in which they tried to do so were very different. Despite the recurrent influence of the spirit of the Enlightenment, the Prussian Land Law remains essentially rooted in the class structure of Frederick's state: its paternalistic authoritarianism did not leave the subject much room for play, and judges and scholars were inhibited from creative development by its rigid specificity of detail. The Austrian General Civil Code, in contrast, is much more strongly pervaded with the idealism and rationalism of the Enlightenment, and differs from the Prussian Land Law in being brief, general, lucid, and easily comprehended: but it was in advance of social reality, for in the early nineteenth century Austria under METTERNICH was the great champion, at home and abroad, of the restoration of absolute monarchy, and those were not propitious conditions for a powerful development of the liberal ideas of the Code. In France the situation was different; the Prussian and Austrian codes were decreed by an enlightened despot; in France it was the *bourgeoisie* which by revolutionary means had brought down the socially obsolete institutions of the *ancien régime*, had founded the new state on the principle of the equality of citizens, and had then, *out of this very situation*, created a code which vindicated the demands of the Revolution for liberty and equality. Only in France was the Code the product of a revolutionary movement, only in France was there complete congruence between social reality and the idea of society on which the Code was based.

Of course one must distinguish ideology and reality. Contemporaries saw the Code civil as a product of revolution, but closer investigation shows that it rests also on a large number of traditional legal institutions tenaciously conserved. Certainly the Code does not discard the great achievements of the revolution—the principle of equal division of estates, the complete secularization of marriage, the total abolition of feudal servitudes, and the prohibition of fideicommissary substitutions, to take a few examples. But the Code did abandon or qualify many rules of the *droit intermédiaire* which seemed to have gone too far. Thus divorce is retained, but the ground of mutual consent is severely restricted by many complex rules of procedure. The freedom to dispose of one's property on death or in life had been largely abolished in the aim of parcelling out landed estates; it was reintroduced by the Code, though only up to the 'quotité disponible', that is, to a much lesser degree than in the German or Anglo-American legal systems.

To the *droit intermédiaire*, it was inconsistent with the rights of man that an adult's freedom to marry be dependent on his parents' consent. The conflict between the individual's interest in free self-determination and the social interest in maintaining patriarchally organized family groups was resolved by the Code in favour of the latter: a man under the age of 25 and a woman under the age of 21 could not marry at all without the permission of their parents or, if the parents were dead, their grandparents. At 25, a man could marry without his parents' consent but only if he had sought their consent three times by issuing at monthly intervals a 'respectful request' (*sommation respectueuse*) served by a *huissier*. For a man of 30, a single sommation was sufficient. A similar step, which some would see as retrogressive, was taken in matrimonial law in relation to the equality of husband and wife. To begin with, the revolutionary principle of the equality of citizens had been quite simply applied between spouses; thus CAMBACÉRÈS in his First Draft had proposed that 'the rights of spouses in the administration of their property are equal. Every legal act which sells, binds, burdens or pledges the property of either spouse requires the consent of both.' (FENET (above p. 76) I. 20.) But in his Third Draft CAMBACÉRÈS abandoned this position and, as the Code civil was later to do, gave the right to administer the property to the husband alone: it was true that all social relationships should be controlled by the principle of equality, but in the matrimonial sphere the precedence of the husband was part of the 'natural order' and to deny it would lead to 'quarrels which would destroy the pleasures of domestic life'. (FENET (above p. 76) I. 156.) It was much the same in the law of divorce. The Code civil did not hesitate to lay down that the husband could demand a divorce simply by proving his wife's adultery, whereas the wife could seek divorce on the ground of the husband's adultery only 'when he has kept his mistress in the matrimonial home'. PORTALIS seemed to regard this rule as self-evident: 'The infidelity of a wife bespeaks greater vice and has more dangerous consequences than that of a husband.'

In the difficult problem of making an accommodation between the *droit coutumier* and the *droit écrit*, the draftsmen of the Code civil showed a sure and skilful touch. Their main aim here was to produce a reasonable and balanced compromise. In his *Discours Préliminaire* PORTALIS wrote:

'We have made a compromise, if such an expression may be used, between the droit écrit and the customs, whenever we have been able to reconcile their provisions or to modify each in the light of the other, without infringing the unity of the system or causing widespread dissatisfaction.' (FENET (above p. 76) I. 481.)

The *droit écrit*, which was nearly pure Roman Law, provided almost the whole of contract law, the draftsmen having relied extensively on the classical treatment by POTHIER, as well as the law of neighbours, the law of wills, and the system of dowry as a contractual property regime. The *coutumes*, especially the Custom of Paris, won through principally in family law and in the law of inheritance, with their strong emphasis on the unity of the family and on the domestic power of husband and parents, in the forced heirship of relatives, in the statutory property regime of community of moveables, in the so-called 'recognition' of illegitimate children (see below Ch. 10), and in the administration of wills. Acquisitive prescription in good faith (see art. 2279 Code civil) is also in line with Germanic legal thinking; but the principle of publicity in German land law is found in the Code civil only in the shadow form of a system of transcription and inscription. By and large one must accept the paradoxical conclusion that the French Code civil, the leading code of the Romanistic family, contains more Germanic legal ideas than the German Civil Code a century later which, owing to the influence of the Historical School of Law and the pandectists, belongs much more to the Roman tradition.

It is often asked how much the Code civil was influenced by *natural law* thinking. As a matter of intellectual history it is clear that the Code as a whole would never have existed but for the idea of codification which comes from natural law. Furthermore the Code civil is based on the tenet of natural law that there are autonomous principles of nature, quite independent of religious belief, from which one can infer a system of legal rules which, if given intelligible form according to a plan, can act as the basis for an orderly, reasonable, and moral life in society. The early versions of the Code civil, more strongly and directly influenced by the Revolution, are largely dominated by this idea; but its hold diminished as work on the Code progressed.

On this matter see THIEME (above p. 87) 25 ff., 38 ff.; HEINSHEIMER (above p. 76) at 7; WIEACKER, *Privatrechtsgeschichte der Neuzeit* (2nd edn., 1967) 322 ff.—The Draft of the Commission originally contained an introductory section, clearly taken from DOMAT's introduction to his *Loix civiles*. Art. 1 was as follows: 'There is a universal and unchanging law which is the source of all positive laws: it is none other than natural reason, which governs all mankind.' Elsewhere the judge who finds the applicable statute unclear is instructed to decide as a 'ministre d'équité'; by 'équité' is understood 'the return to natural law, or to practices accepted in the absence of positive law' (FENET (above p. 76 II. 3, 7). The Conseil d'État deleted almost the whole of this introductory section on the practitioners' argument that *omnis definitio in iure periculosa*: 'Laws are acts of will. Definition, teaching and scholarship are the matter of science. The matter of legislation is command and disposition properly so-called' (PORTALIS (above p. 87) at p. 100).—The weakening of the influence of natural law thinking can also be seen in the changing attitude to the value of traditional legal institutions: CAMBACÉRÈS believed that nothing but obstacles to thorough legal reform could be found 'in our institutions, our customs and our habits' (FENET (above p. 76) I. 140)—This antihistorical attitude, quite typical of the reformist zeal of natural lawyers, was not shared at all by the Drafting Committee: 'It is useful to maintain everything which it is not necessary to destroy: laws should respect social practices unless they are vicious. We too often act as if at every moment the human race came to a complete stop and made a fresh start, without any kind of communication between one generation and the next. . . . We have recently been too fond of change and reform; where institutions and laws are concerned, if centuries of ignorance have made for abuse, centuries of enlightened philosophy have too often made for excess.' (FENET (above p. 76) I. 481 f.)

Thus although the idea and conception of the Code civil are the product of the natural law of the eighteenth-century Enlightenment, the value of historical continuity was increasingly recognized as it took practical shape. The Code seemed to many contemporaries to be a 'reaction against the Revolution', but succeeding generations who have seen its extraordinary influence have acclaimed it on the ground of its 'spirit of moderation and wisdom'.

II

The draftsmen of all the natural law codes were much exercised by the question of the proper position of the judge in relation to statute. Doctrinaire adherents of the principle of separation of powers often held the exaggerated view that the judge should have no power at all to develop the law and that statutes should be so detailed that the judge could apply them quite mechanically.

Thus in the decree which introduced the Land Law of Prussia, FRIEDRICH WILHELM II expressly forbade the judges 'to indulge in any arbitrary deviation, however slight, from the clear and express terms of the laws, whether on the ground of some allegedly logical reasoning or under the pretext of an interpretation based on the supposed aim and purpose of the statute'; otherwise 'Our very great displeasure and severe sanctions will be incurred'; in cases of doubt the judges were to submit the problem to the statutory commission. The Land Law with its 17,000-odd paragraphs often amuses us today by the detail into which it descends, but its intention was to give the judge a precise answer to every question and thus to render interpretation, so far as possible, wholly unnecessary.

Here also the draftsmen of the Code civil adopted a more sensible course. It is true that during the period of the *droit intermédiaire* the principle of division of powers was still taken very seriously; thus in 1790 a statute ordained that the courts 'must apply to the Corps législatif whenever they believe it necessary either to interpret a law or to make a new one'. The Tribunal de Cassation—later the Cour de Cassation—was set up about the same time to quash judicial decisions which by these standards had misconstrued the written law. The new system, based on the teaching of MONTESQUIEU, had no place for the sort of judicial development of law which had occurred in the Parlements under the *ancien régime*. Of course the principle that the courts must submit questions of interpretation to the Corps Législatif for a decision was never really taken seriously. The drafting committee were emphatic in their opposition to any such proceeding: the function of the legislator was to set up *general* rules; interference with the resolution of questions of interpretation affecting the affairs of private individuals would be time-consuming and undignified, the quality of legislation would suffer and lawsuits would be prolonged. Consequently art. 4 Code civil provides without any qualification that if a judge refuses to make a decision 'on the ground that the law is silent or obscure or inadequate' he may be held responsible.

The Code civil also avoids the danger of being too detailed. The draftsmen clearly realized that even the most ingenious legislator could not foresee and determine all the possible problems which might arise and that therefore room must be left for judicial decisions to make the law applicable to unforeseen individual cases and suited to the changing circumstances of society. PORTALIS's observations on this matter are among the most impressive in his *Discours Préliminaire*: they show clearly that the dichotomy between statute-law of the Continental variety and the case-law of the Common Law is by no means so fundamental as theorists of the sources of law keep trying to tell us:

'The task of legislation is to determine the general maxims of law, taking a large view of the matter. It must establish principles rich in implications rather than descend into the details of every question which might possibly arise. The application of the law belongs to the magistrate and the lawyer, steeped in the general spirit of the legislation. . . . There is a legislative skill as well as a judicial skill, and the two are quite distinct. The skill of the legislator is to discover the principles in each area which most conduce to the common weal; the skill of the judge is to put these principles into action, and to extend them to particular circumstances by wise and reasoned application. . . . To the courts may be left those unusual and extraordinary cases which no reasonable legislation could deal with, the varied and contested trivia with which the legislator had no time to deal, and all those matters which it would be futile to try to foresee, and which could not be safely defined even if one did cursorily foresee them. We shall leave some gaps, and they will be filled in due course by experience. National codes are created in time; indeed, people do not really create them at all.' (FENET (above p. 76) I. 470, 475 f.)

The best-known example of the compressed legislative style of the Code civil is found in arts. 1382–6. These five laconic paragraphs cover the entire French law of delict, a subject-matter to which the General Civil Code of Austria, otherwise so terse, having only half as many paragraphs as the Code civil, devotes about 40, and the German Civil Code 31. These rules of the Code civil, now 160 years old, are still in force, almost unaltered despite all the economic and technological changes which have taken place, and it is therefore no surprise to find that today they are barely recognizable under a heavy gloss of case-law to which new layers are added every year. Perhaps the draftsmen of the Code civil went too far in compression here (see vol. II, Ch. 17 IV); yet in 1804, when the Industrial Revolution had hardly started, the social problem of compensating the victims of accidents had nothing like the importance it has today.

The way the Code civil is drafted gives the courts room for interpretation, for its terms are often inexact, incomplete, or ambiguous, far from having the terminological exactitude which the German Civil Code inherited from the pandectists. Thus according to art. 778 of the Code civil, an inheritance may be accepted either 'dans un acte authentique ou privé' or by means of an 'acte qui suppose nécessairement son intention d'accepter': here in the same sentence the word 'acte' is used in the sense of 'deed' and in the sense of 'action', a lapse of which the fathers of the German Code would certainly not have been guilty. In arts. 544 ff. Code civil, the notion of 'propriété' is used in the sense of ownership of things (moveable or immoveable), while in the Title of the Third Book ("des différentes manières dont on acquiert la propriété') it is used in the sense of wealth of all types. According to art. 1147 Code civil, a person has to pay damages for breach of contract, unless he proves that a 'cause étrangère qui ne peut lui être imputée' was the reason for non-performance; according to art. 1148 the duty to make compensation ceases in the event of 'force majeure' or 'cas fortuit'. The relationship between 'cause étrangère', 'force majeure', and 'cas fortuit' is never made clear. The list of technical inaccuracies of this kind could easily be prolonged.

On the other hand, the Code civil is a masterpiece from the point of view of style and language. It has often been praised for its clear and memorable phrases, and for the absence of cross-references and jargon, all of which has significantly contributed to the popularity of the Code in France. STENDHAL is said to have read part of the Code every day in order to refine his feeling for the language ('pour prendre le ton'), and PAUL VALÉRY described the Code civil as 'the greatest book of French literature' (cited by THIEME (above p. 87) at 38 f.). The dry and dogmatic language of the *German* Code is very unattractive in comparison. For example, compare art. 212 Code civil with §1353 BGB. The French provision is concrete: 'Spouses owe each other the duty of fidelity, succour and companionship'. The German text offers the rather pale technical term of 'matrimonial community'. Art. 312 Code civil is almost an epigram: 'The child conceived in marriage takes the husband for its father'; in §1591 BGB the legislator goes straight into the technical details of the requirements for legitimacy. The idea *pacta sunt servanda* is given in art. 1134 Code civil a striking and almost moving formula: 'Agreements made according to law have the force of law for the parties to them'. §241 BGB on the other hand instructs us, somewhat didactically, that 'by reason of the creditor–debtor relationship . . . the creditor is entitled to demand performance from the debtor'—a textbook formulation which admittedly makes it perfectly clear, to the lawyer at any rate, what meanings are going to be attributed in the succeeding paragraphs to the ideas of 'creditor–debtor relationship' and 'performance'. Yet the elegant sheen of the wording in the Code civil is often paid for by a lack of substance, as closer investigation shows. WINDSCHEID made the criticism 'that the famed precision of its expressions is quite often only superficial, not that true inner precision which comes from complete clarity of thought' (*Zur Lehre des Code Napoleon von der Ungültigkeit der Rechtsgeschäfte* (1847) V). An example can immediately be given: the famous formula 'en fait de meubles la possession vaut titre' (art. 2279). This provision could hardly be bettered for dramatic tautness, but one must realize that it gives only the shadowiest indication of the underlying thought: it was left to the courts of France to resolve the following questions: Under what conditions is possession a ground of defence to a *rei vindicatio*? What is meant by 'possession'? Is good faith required? If so, what constitutes good faith, and at what moment of time must it be established? §932 BGB may lack the urbanity of art. 2279 of the Code civil, but it certainly contains more precise information.

The subject-matter of the Code civil is set out as follows. A brief introductory title contains only six articles, all that remains of the much fuller *Livre préliminaire* originally planned. The *First Book* is entitled 'Des Personnes' (arts. 7–515). It opens with provisions concerning the enjoyment of civil rights; these rights, according to art. 8, attach to every Frenchman. Rules about the acquisition and loss of French nationality followed, well demonstrating the national character of the Code, but in 1927 these rules were greatly expanded and promulgated in the form of a special statute. The following few articles about the legal status of foreigners have formed the basis on which the French courts have created an impressive structure of private international law and procedure, and of law relating to foreigners. The next section contains an extensive treatment of the register of civil status; this is a matter which a German lawyer could hardly imagine as forming part of his Civil Code but it seemed especially important to the draftsmen of the Code for whom the secularization of family relationships was one of the achievements of the Revolution. The following sections deal with domicile, disappearance, marriage, divorce, legitimacy and illegitimacy of children, adoption, paternal (not parental) power, and guardianship. *Book Two* ('Des biens et des différentes modifications de la propriété'; arts. 516–710) starts with general provisions about things, distinguishing moveables and immoveables and dealing with components and accessories. The ownership of things, their fruits and profits, is then covered, followed by rules about usufruct and the rights of use and habitation, as well as servitudes. The acquisition of ownership by means of contract is not dealt with here, because French law adheres to the principle that a contractual act automatically operates as a conveyance of ownership (gift, sale, exchange: see arts. 938, 1138, 1583); thus there is no separate conveyance contract or delivery, actual or constructive, to be regulated by the law of property (contrast §§873, 925, 929 ff. BGB).

All the rest of the Code civil—twice as many articles as in the first two books together—falls in *Book Three*, under the title 'Des différentes manières dont on acquiert la propriété' (arts. 711–2281). First there are the rules of succession, which is seen as a special form of the *acquisition of ownership*, like gift, with which it is closely associated. There follows a section on the general law of contract, with articles concerning capacity, construction, joint debtors, contractual penalties, set-off, formal requirements, and rules of evidence; next there is a section on 'obligations formed without agreement', consisting of eleven provisions on the law of unjustified enrichment ('quasi-contracts'; see vol. II, Ch. 15 III); and then the five articles on the law of delict. Next comes matrimonial property law, and then the special contracts— sale, exchange, lease, the contract of services and of service (employment being treated, on the Roman model, as a 'contrat de louage'), then partnership, loan, deposit, agency, suretyship, and compromise. Book Three ends with security rights (pledge, hypothec, and lien) and prescription.

The structure of the Code civil is plainly unsatisfactory. Matrimonial property law would be much better placed next to the law of husband and wife in the First Book, and the law of succession, instead of being placed with the property law in Book Three, might have been better grouped with family law or put in a separate book of its own. To say that a claim for compensation based on tort is a special 'mode of acquiring ownership' seems to miss the point. PLANIOL is justified in saying that Book Three is a rag-bag of heterogeneous matters:

'It is not very logical to put all these various topics in a single book' (*Traité élémentaire de droit civil* I (5th edn., 1950) 33). It is true that PLANIOL does not regard the absence of scientific order in the Code civil as very serious: 'A scientific order, although very suitable in a lecture-course or a textbook, is neither necessary nor even useful in a code. Teaching requires a special method because it is a kind of initiation. Codes are made for people who have completed their studies, practitioners who are familiar with the law. In consequence, it is enough that the topics be set out in a clear and convenient manner' (id., 36).

III

The original Code civil was the law-book of the third estate, the bourgeoisie which in the French Revolution had worsted the feudal groups dominant in the *ancien régime* and subsequently, in the Restoration after the fall of NAPOLEON, had consolidated its position with growing self-confidence and political influence. The ideal man in the mind of the draftsmen is therefore not the little man, the artisan or the day-labourer, but the man of property, the responsible man of judgment and reason, knowledgeable about affairs and familiar with the law, and it is this ideal which gives the Code its particular flavour. In this view, the existence of the bourgeoisie depended on guaranteed personal freedom, especially the freedom to engage in economic activities, and on property, especially landed property. Freedom of contract is therefore the principle which dominates the law of obligations in the Code civil, restricted as little as possible by mandatory rules of law, called in France 'lois d'ordre public' (see art. 6). Consonant with this view of the citizen's responsibility is the conclusion evinced by the general formula of art. 1382 Code civil, that if a person causes harm by behaviour which is reprehensibly careless ('faute') he must pay for it; this accommodated both the freedom of activity and the individual's desire for responsibility which *stricter* forms of liability might have narrowed and constrained. The great problem of how to regulate the position of the dependent worker was not recognized by the legislator, but unlike the draftsmen of the German Civil Code of 1896, he is not really to be blamed for this, since in 1804 industrial mass production had hardly started. The rules of family law in the Code civil reflect the patriarchal family typical of the successful bourgeoisie of the early nineteenth century; the husband and father is head of the family, and it is he alone who has paternal power over the children, including the power, by refusing his permission, to prevent the marriage of his son until 25 and his daughter until 21. As for the relationship of the spouses, the original art. 213 Code civil speaks for itself: 'The husband must protect the wife, the wife obey her husband.' The wife was supposed to be running the household and educating the children, and to be unexperienced in business affairs; without her husband's permission therefore she could neither enter contracts nor conclude dispositions, even when the spouses had chosen by antenuptial contract to retain their separate property. Interference by the state in the closed family circle was regarded as intolerable; the supervision of guardians and juveniles now performed by officials was given to a 'conseil de famille', including more distant relatives such as uncles, aunts, cousins, and in-laws, who were then part of the family in a way which is not usual today. The great protection afforded to the family circle is a leading characteristic of French family law, and its concern to preserve the family property has had an effect on the law of succession as well. There are severe restrictions on the freedom to dispose on one's assets by gift or will as one chooses: even today in France a person can dispose only of a *part* of his property—the so-called 'quotité disponible'; as to the rest, called the 'réserve', members of the family have more than just a right to monetary payment of their statutory part, they are actually forced heirs.

When one considers what economic and social changes have occurred since the time of NAPOLEON, and how differently the family is now regarded, one may well ask how the Code civil can have remained in force in France until this day. How can a Code which came into force 180 years ago have withstood the tremendous political, economic, and social storms which have raged over France in the nineteenth and twentieth centuries?

In many areas, especially in family and inheritance law, it is the *legislator* who has kept the Code in line with changing social reality by altering its text. *Patria potestas* has been gradually eroded, the business capacity of the married woman admitted, her position on the death of her husband improved, and the right of illegitimate children to be maintained or recognized by the father accepted. In the law of contract also, wherever it was clear that the free play of contractual autonomy led to consequences which seemed unaccept-able to new social value-judgments, the legislator has expanded or modified the rules of the Code civil, mainly by special statutes. Thus in the contracts of lease, carriage, employment, and insurance so many mandatory provisions are imposed by law that almost nothing is left of the unrestrained freedom to conclude and determine the content of contracts which so appealed to the draftsmen of the Code civil.

But the *courts* (jurisprudence) as well as the legislator have played a leading part in adjusting the rules of the Code civil to modern requirements; they have continually been construing these rules so as to develop, extend, or limit them and have brought new legal ideas into play as well as developing old ones. The task of the courts in this has been made easier because, as we have already seen, the principles of the Code civil are often unclear and deliberately designed to require completion, the concepts used are frequently indefinite and ambiguous, many individual rules are incomplete, and the systematic interplay of different provisions is often faulty. It is easy to give examples of the creative legal activity of the French courts. For instance, out of the rule of art. 1384 of the Code civil they have developed a law of *accident compensation* which is much better adapted to the special dangers of the modern world with its advanced technology than the system of compensation which the draftsmen of the Code had in mind (see vol. II, Ch. 19 III). In labour law the courts, strongly supported by the legislature, have developed rules for the social protection of workmen and employees which go far beyond the inadequate provisions of arts. 1780 f., and indeed this whole important area of law now really falls outside the Code civil and, as in Germany, is widely regarded as being an independent area of law. The courts developed the doctrine of abuse of rights which has proved useful in limiting the right of the owner of property to deal with it exactly as he chooses (see art. 544 Code civil), the right to dismiss an employee, the right to strike, the right to take steps in legal procedure and other rights, for if the exercise of a right seems to a court to constitute an abuse of right (*abus d'un droit*), an injunction may be issued or liability in damages imposed (see vol. II, Ch. 17 IV). Art. 1121 Code civil permits some contracts for the benefit of third parties and invalidates others, all in rather obscure language; here the courts developed rules relating to the *insurance contract*, which the legislature took over into the statute of 1930. The courts also developed a general claim based on *unjustified enrichment*, which had received an extremely patchy treatment in arts. 1376 ff. Code civil in relation to the payment of a thing not due (see vol. II, Ch. 15 III). There was no statutory regulation at all of the 'astreinte', a legal device for enforcing judicial orders for performance, and this the courts themselves developed. The practice of the courts has also played a significant part in family and inheritance law. Thus, to give a few examples, the courts have so qualified the strict prohibition of successive heirship in art. 896 Code civil than one can now create successive entitlements to an inheritance simply by having one's will skilfully drafted. Many years before the enactment of the basic reform statutes, the courts had accepted claims for maintenance by an illegitimate child, although this was hard to reconcile with the original meaning of art. 340 Code civil, according to which *any* 'recherche de la paternité' was excluded.

'Thus quite large areas of French private law have ceased to be *droit écrit* and have become common law, almost without our noticing it. The famous and striking opposition between the sources of law recognized by Anglo-Saxon and French law respectively has been very materially reduced.' (RIPERT (above p. 87) II. 15, no. 9.) There have frequently been lively disputes in France on the question whether or not judicial decisions are strictly speaking a source of law. The dominant view is still that they are not; but great scholars like PLANIOL, JOSSERAND, LAMBERT, and HÉBRAUD have accepted that they are. Fortunately people are becoming tired of this question, for it is now clear that one's answer depends entirely on one's definition of 'source of law'. If the test of a rule is its validity in social reality and its viability in fact, then there can really be no doubt at all that the rules which have been created by the courts and confirmed by repeated decision have all the qualities of rules of law.

As the Code aged, *legal writing* (doctrine) became increasingly significant in the development of French private law. In the years immediately following the enactment of the Code legal writing went through an unfruitful and positivistic stage, merely expounding the text of the Code, grammatically and logically, and ignoring judicial decision entirely (*école de l'exégèse*). The picture changed, however, towards the end of the nineteenth century. Under the influence of GÉNY and SALEILLES, scholars realized that the school of exegesis was not giving any help to judges in the task of applying the Code civil to changed circumstances; GÉNY's new school, called the 'école de la libre recherche scientifique', allowed the judge a greater freedom with the text of the Code and encouraged him to construe the Code not simply logically and systematically, but in the light of the requirements of society as it developed, the actual usages and practices in the relevant areas of commerce, and also the results of the researches of sociologists and comparative lawyers.

In this dispute between the schools the multi-volume treatises of French private law, of which the three most important and comprehensive are those of BAUDRY/LACANTINERIE, BEUDANT, and PLANIOL/RIPERT, took an intermediate position. These treatises all have their own refined systematic structure, often quite different from the statutory structure of the Code civil, but, thanks to the practical and sober good sense of French jurists, never lose themselves in exalted subtleties of doctrine. They all deal carefully with judicial decisions, which are sometimes criticized quite severely, though never with that dogmatic tone of dismissal occasionally to be found in German textbooks. In language and style these treatises are often of splendid eloquence and perfect lucidity, even if one sometimes has the feeling that the text could be compressed somewhat without any loss of substance. This is less true of the more recent textbooks, of which those of COLIN/CAPITANT, CARBONNIER, MARTY/RAYNAUD, and MAZEAUD call for especial mention. Often enough the development of French law has been spurred on not by textbooks or articles, but by case-notes; those by THALLER and LABBÉ, the best-known 'arrêtistes' of the nineteenth century, are especially important for the basis of modern French private and commercial law.

With the help of legislation, judicial decision, and legal writing, the Code civil has been able to adapt itself to modern developments; this can be seen from the fact that though there have frequently been demands for a thorough overhaul of the Code, all attempts have so far proved abortive. In the centenary year of the Code civil, 1904, a committee was set up to reform it, consisting of 100 persons, many of whom were not lawyers; their labours soon ground to a halt. Another committee charged with the reform of the Code civil was set up in 1945, in the first flush of post-war feeling; it had only 12 members, under the chairmanship of JULLIOT DE LA MORANDIÈRE, Professor of the Paris Faculty of Law. In 1954 this committee produced the draft of an Introductory Book and of Book One, on the law of persons and the family, and in 1961 it produced a draft of Book Two, on the law of inheritance and gift, but neither of these drafts led to actual legislation. Recently the work of the committee of reform has come to a complete stop, and instead the French legislator has undertaken partial reforms of the Code civil, of which the most important concern matrimonial property law, the law of adoption, the legal position of illegitimate children, and the rules of incapacity.

Although the proposals for total reform led to nothing, the discussion and documents of the committee of reform (Travaux de la commission de réforme du Code civil (1974 ff.)) are full of interest to those concerned with questions of comparative law and unification of law. On this, see JULLIOT DE LA MORANDIÈRE, 'The Reform of the French Civil Code', 97 *U. Pa. L. Rev.* 1 (1948); HOUIN, 'Les travaux de la commission de réforme du Code civil', *Rev. trim. dr. civ.* 49 (1951) 34; PASCAL, 'A Report on the French Civil Code Revision Project', 25 *Tul. L. Rev.* 205 (1951); ANCEL, 'The Revision of the French Civil Code', 25 *Tul. L. Rev.* 435 (1951). The recent reforms in family law and the way they have been incorporated in the Code civil are described by AUDIT (above p. 87).

8

The Reception of the Code Civil

AMOS, 'The Code Napoleon and the Modern World', 10 *J. Comp. Leg.* 222 (1928).
ARMINJON/NOLDE/WOLFF, *Traité de droit comparé* I (1950) 136 ff.
BARHAM, 'A Renaissance of the Civilian Tradition in Louisiana', 33 *La. L. Rev.* 357 (1973).
——, 'Methodology of the Civil Law in Louisiana', 50 *Tul. L. Rev.* 474 (1976).
BATIZA, 'Origins of Modern Codification of the Civil Law: The French Experience and Its Implications for Louisiana Law', 56 *Tul. L. Rev.* 477 (1982).
BAUDOUIN, 'The Impact of the Common Law on the Civilian Systems of Louisiana and Quebec', in: Dainow (ed.), *The Role of Judicial Decisions and Doctrine in Civil Law and Mixed Jurisdictions* (1974) 1.
BLAGOJEVIĆ, 'L'influence du Code civil sur l'élaboration du Code civil serbe', *Rev. int. dr. comp.* 6 (1954) 733.
BOEHMER, 'Der Einfluß des Code civil auf die Rechtsentwicklung in Deutschland, *AcP* 151 (1950/1951) 289.
BRIERLEY, 'Quebec's Civil Law Codification', 14 *McGill LJ* 521 (1968).
CAPPELLETTI/MERRYMAN/PERILLO, *The Italian Legal System, An Introduction* (1967).
CASTÁN VÁZQUEZ, 'El sistema del derecho privado iberoamericano', *Estudios de derecho* 28 (1969) 5.
CHABANNE, 'Napoléon, son code et les Allemands', *Études Lambert* (1975) 397.
CHABAS, 'Réflexions sur l'évolution du droit sénégalais', in: *Études juridiques offertes à Julliot de la Morandière* (1964) 127.
DAINOW, 'Le Droit civil de la Louisiane', *Rev. int. dr. comp.* 6 (1954) 19.
EICHLER, 'Privatrecht in Lateinamerika', in: *Aus Österreichs Rechtsleben in Geschichte und Gegenwart, Festschrift Hellbling* (1981) 481.
FOKKEMA/CHORUS/HONDIUS/LISSER (eds.), *Introduction to Dutch Law for Foreign Lawyers* (1978).
HEINSHEIMER, *Die Zivilgesetze der Gegenwart* I (1932): *Frankreich, Code civil,* Introduction XVI ff.
HEYMANN, 'Romanische Rechtsordnungen', in: *Handwörterbuch der Rechtswissenschaft* V (1928) 163 ff.
HOOD, 'The History and Development of the Louisiana Civil Code', 33 *Tul. L. Rev.* 7 (1958).
ISHIMOTO, 'L'Influence du Code civil français sur le droit civil japonais', *Rev. int. dr. comp.* 6 (1954) 744.
KOSCHAKER, *Europa und das römische Recht* (2nd edn., 1953).
LE CODE CIVIL, LIVRE DU CENTENAIRE II (1904), with articles on the effects of the Code civil in Germany, Belgium, Canada, Egypt, Italy, the Netherlands, Romania, and Switzerland.

LIMPENS, 'Territorial Expansion of the Code', in: *The Code Napoleon and the Common Law World* (ed. B. Schwartz, 1956) 92.

LUTHER, *Einführung in das italienische Recht* (1968).

MOUSSERON, 'La réception au Proche-Orient du droit français des obligations', *Rev. int. dr. comp.* 20 (1968) 37.

NEUMAYER, 'Deutsche und französische Zivilrechtswissenschaft—Besinnliches zu einem Nachbarschafts- und Partnerschaftsverhältnis unter Verwandten', in: *Ius privatum gentium, Festschrift Max Rheinstein* I (1969) 165.

NODA, 'La réception du droit français au Japon', *Rev. int. dr. comp.* 15 (1963) 543.

ORTUN, 'L'Unification du droit civil espagnol', *Rev. int. dr. comp.* 18 (1966) 413.

PIRET, Le Code Napoléon en Belgique', *Rev. int. dr. comp.* 6 (1954) 753.

v. RAUCHHAUPT, 'Vergleich und Angleichbarkeit der Rechte Süd- und Mittelamerikas', *RabelsZ* 20 (1955) 121.

SALACUSE, *An Introduction to Law in French-Speaking Africa* I: *Africa South of the Sahara* (1969).

SCHNITZER, *Vergleichende Rechtslehre* I (2nd edn., 1961) 200 ff.

SOLUS, 'Die französischen Besitzungen und Kolonien', in: *Rechtsvergleichendes Handwörterbuch* I (ed. Schlegelberger, 1929) 535.

TRAVAUX DE LA SEMAINE INTERNATIONALE DE DROIT 1950 (1954), with essays on the effects of the Code civil in Europe, America, and the Near East.

TUCKER, 'The Code and the Common Law in Louisiana', in: *The Code Napoleon and the Common Law World* (ed. B. Schwartz, 1956) 346.

TYAN, 'Les Rapports entre droit musulman et droit européen occidental, en matière de droit civil', *ZvglRW* 65 (1963) 18.

VALLADAO, *Le Droit latino-américain* (1954).

WENGLER, 'Der Entwurf für ein neues portugiesisches Zivilgesetzbuch', *AcP* 167 (1967) 64.

YIANNOPOULOS, 'Louisiana Civil Law: A Lost Cause?', 54 *Tul. L. Rev.* 830 (1980).

ZAJTAY, 'Les Destinées du Code civil', *Rev. int. dr. comp.* 6 (1954) 792.

——, 'La Réception des droits étrangers et le droit comparé', *Rev. int. dr. comp.* 9 (1957) 686.

I

IN order to understand the extraordinary influence of the Code civil in the nineteenth and twentieth centuries, it is useful to recall the very favourable circumstances attending its birth. On the one hand, the Code was still inspired by the enlightened enthusiasm of the French Revolution, appealing to all the forces of progress; it was the first codification in the world to loosen all the bonds of feudalism and shed the shackles of the past, and it implemented those demands of the Revolution which were most to influence the future: it gave equality to all citizens, it secularized family law, it emancipated landed property, it granted freedom to engage in economic activities, and it protected the family. On the other hand, when the Code was drafted the fanaticism of the Revolution had cooled off considerably, and in the relatively stable political situation under NAPOLEON people could have second thoughts without seeming reactionary. Thus the draftsmen of the Code could make good use of the principles of law which had been slowly developed by the courts of the *ancien régime* and which had been carefully elaborated and refined by the writers of the seventeenth and eighteenth centuries. In this way, a happy compromise was struck between the powerful appeal of revolutionary ideas and the solid craftsmanship of traditional legal institutions.

Furthermore, NAPOLEON's part in the Code civil seemed to the world to lend it some of his charisma, and its language was forceful and thrilling, free from heavy logic and detailed digression. The Code civil answered the needs and interests of the nineteenth-century bourgeoisie but still offered great scope for variant progressive interpretation, since many of its outline principles called for amplification and it had many technical faults, omissions, and imprecisions, all of which were creatively used by French judges and writers to great effect as the Code grew older. This may help to explain why the Code civil spread not only to the Latin peoples of Europe, but also to Eastern Europe, the Near East, to Central and South America, and even to some parts of North America, and why it had a prolonged influence on the development of law in other European countries, especially Germany.

One must not suppose, however, that the Code civil was received in these countries as the result of a careful evaluation of its merits, in the way that a customer in a shop might choose the goods which best suited him. PAUL KOSCHAKER has shown that the reception of foreign law is not so much a 'question of quality' as a 'question of power': 'reception occurs when the law being received is in a position of power, at least intellectually and culturally, as being the law of a country which still enjoys political power or did so until so recently that its strength and culture are still clearly remembered' (above p. 100, p. 138). KOSCHAKER used this idea primarily to explain the reception of Roman law in Central Europe, which in his view was attributable not to any qualitative superiority of Roman law, but to the fact that as the law of the Imperium Romanum, and consequently the law of the Holy Roman Empire of the Germans, its authority and claim to validity could rest on the idea of Roman civilization. But KOSCHAKER has also applied his idea to the reception of the Code civil: it had such a wide influence 'because it was the Code of the French Empire, whose military prowess, backed by a brilliantly integrated civilization, made such a deep impression on people not only during its brief life but many years after it was over' (above p. 100, p. 136). This is certainly right, especially if we remember that the reception is attributable not only to the political power of the *French Empire*, or to the spiritual influence of *French civilization*, but also in a great measure to the merits of the *Code civil* itself; for in the nineteenth century the Code enjoyed intellectual authority and an almost supernatural appeal as the Code of the Great Revolution, which had abolished the *ancien régime* and produced for the first time legal unity and equality for the citizens of a centrally organized national state. Nor must one forget that the spread of the Code civil throughout the world was greatly helped by its admirable language and the easy flexibility of its expression, in brief, by its very *quality*.

II

Between 1804 and 1812 the Code civil came into force in many regions as the result of French military expansion eastwards under the revolutionary regimes and later under NAPOLEON; they were later to win or win back their sovereignty, but their private law retained the impress of the ideas of the French Code. We shall look first at Belgium, Luxembourg, and the Netherlands.

(*a*) The territory we now know as *Belgium* was ruled by Austria from 1713 until its cession to France by the Peace of Campo Formio of 1797. The territory was incorporated into France, and the Code civil came into force there automatically in 1804, and remained in force despite the fall of NAPOLEON and the unification of Holland and Belgium by the Congress of Vienna under WILLIAM I of Orange. When Belgium became independent in the revolution of 1830, its new Constitution contained a provision that the French codes, the Code civil and the Code de Commerce of 1807, should be fundamentally revised 'dans le plus court délai possible'. So far as the Code civil is concerned, this provision has remained unimplemented to the present day. Instead, the Belgian legislature has, as time went by, passed a large number of special laws in order to modernize the Code civil; often the legislature has followed in the wake of new French legislation, but frequently enough it has gone its own way and on occasion has anticipated reforms in France—for example, in the field of mortgage the unsatisfactory rules of the Code civil were replaced in Belgium in 1851, four years earlier than in France. Although the Belgian courts apply nearly the same statutory text as the French courts, they have sometimes reached divergent results (much the same thing happens in the European sphere where different national courts apply the identical texts of unified laws, such as the law of negotiable instruments, and reach divergent interpretations which cannot be resolved until the foundation of a European court with jurisdiction to watch over the unity of law). In general, however, legal thought and judicial decision in Belgium are very close to those in France:

'Despite the important independent work of Belgian courts and scholars, it is obvious that they have never made a systematic break with their counterparts in France. For us . . . Dalloz, the Revue trimestrielle, Colin et Capitant, Planiol et Ripert are used almost as frequently as our own periodicals and treatises' (DE HERVEN, *Travaux* (above p. 101) 610).—The same is true, *mutatis mutandis*, for Luxembourg, which came to France in 1795 also from the Habsburgs; the Code civil remained in force during the Union of the Crown with the Netherlands and on its independence in 1890. Indeed, the version of the Code civil which is in force in Luxembourg today is closer to the original text than are the current versions in France and Belgium. On this, see BERNECKER, *RabelsZ* 27 (1962/1963) 263.

(*b*) For a time after the outbreak of war between the French revolutionary government and the coalition of the Kings of Europe, the *Netherlands* maintained an uneasy neutrality, but as the French were militarily successful came more and more under their sway. In 1806 NAPOLEON forced the Dutch to accept his brother LOUIS as King, and saw to it that in 1809 a version of the Code civil was enacted with marginal adaptations to Dutch legal practices. After the abdication of LOUIS in 1810, NAPOLEON brusquely annexed the territory of the Netherlands, as a mere 'alluvium from French rivers', and brought the Code civil in its original form into effect. The Code civil remained in force after the liberation of the country and the creation of a kingdom of the Netherlands which included the territory of Belgium; work immediately started on the preparation of a new code, though it would have been difficult to harmonize the Dutch law and the Code civil which was fully accepted in the Belgian territory. This project came to an end with the separation of Belgium in 1830, but a new commission was appointed and a few years later produced a draft which came into force in 1838 under the name 'Burgerlijk Wetboek' (BW).

The Burgerlijk Wetboek is not a brand new project, but derives mainly from the Code civil, most of its provisions being word-for-word translations of the French equivalent. This is rather surprising since in the seventeenth and eighteenth centuries Holland had developed a great independent legal culture, a blend of the old Dutch customary law and the Roman law in which their universities excelled, which the Dutch then introduced into their overseas colonies and which still forms the law today of South Africa and Ceylon, heavily influenced though it has been by the Common Law (see below Ch. 18 VI). But in the Netherlands itself the Code civil won out, though the order of topics in the Burgerlijk Wetboek is different, and there are also differences of substance on certain points, especially in the law of matrimonial property.

A new Civil Code is about to be introduced in the Netherlands. Like the Codes of Switzerland and Italy, it abandons the obsolete division between private and commercial law, and deals with both within the same covers. Work on the Code began in 1947 when an eminent scholar from Leiden, Professor MEIJERS, was entrusted by royal decree with the task of preparing the text. In essence MEIJERS worked alone. It is true that he continually took the advice of the relevant men of affairs and practising lawyers, and consulted with a governmental committee; he also submitted 49 questions on the most disputed points to the Chamber of Deputies of the Dutch Parliament, whose answers were not to bind the future course of legislation. But in essence the first four books of the draft Code are the work of a single man. MEIJERS died in 1954, and the work passed to a committee of three, who have relied much more than MEIJERS on a permanent staff of assistants.

The Code is divided into nine books. *Book One* deals with the law of persons and family law, and came into force in 1970, though the section on the law of divorce has already had to be brought up to date. *Book Two*, in force since 1976, deals with all the law relating to legal persons, including company law, the law of incorporated bodies, and foundations. *Book Three* deals with 'the ius rerum in general'. Here, in addition to rules on agency and trust (*bewind*), are to be found provisions on juristic acts, their nullity on the ground of immorality or illegality, and their voidability on the ground of duress, deceit, or 'abusive exploitation of the circumstances'. To some extent therefore the new Burgerlijk Wetboek follows the German BGB in 'factoring out' the general rules regarding juristic acts as part of the *ius rerum*. *Book Four*, on the law of succession, strengthens the rights of the surviving spouse, and *Book Five* deals with the law of property so far as it has not been covered in Book Three. Obligations in general form the substance of *Book Six*. Contract rules relate to breach, assignment, assumption of debts, adoption of contracts, and contracts for the benefit of third parties. In the law of tort, there is a considerable extension of strict liability independent of fault. There is also a very modern-looking section on money debts, with rules on non-cash transactions, on the place and time of payment, and on debts in foreign currencies. Finally there are some general rules on contracts, especially standard form contracts (on this see vol. II, Ch. 1 III). *Book Seven* deals with the individual types of contract, such as sales contracts (instalment sales being fully included), contracts for the transfer of the use of property, and 'contracts for services to others', including the contract of employment and collective bargains. *Book Eight* includes the whole of the law of carriage in a very modern form. *Book Nine* was to have contained the law of patents, trade marks, and copyrights, but the European Community is on the verge of unifying the law of patents and the Benelux Treaty on the harmonization of trade mark law is already in force, so it looks as if the plans for Book Nine will be abandoned, as it would be very difficult to incorporate these provisions in the new Burgerlijk Wetboek. This shows how unification of law at the international level, and even proposed unification, may limit the national legislator's freedom of action. Books Three to Six and important parts of Book Seven are so far through the legislative process that one can expect them to come into force before 1990; but the drafts have already had a considerable 'pre-echo' effect, since courts tend to look at them while applying the existing law. Can the new Burgerlijk Wetboek be regarded as still in the French tradition? The answer is very doubtful. It is certainly based on extensive comparative research, as the accompanying materials show; perhaps it has discovered a style of its own, based on the *ius commune* of Continental Europe. See MEIJERS, 'La Réforme du Code civil néerlandais', *Bull. Soc. lég. comp.* 71 (1948) 199; SNIJDERS, 'Vers un nouveau Code civil néerlandais', *Rev. dr. int. dr. comp.* 56 (1979) 223; HARTKAMP, 'Vers un nouveau Code civil néerlandais', *Rev. int. dr. comp.* 34 (1982) 319.

III

In large parts of Germany and Switzerland also the Code civil had a prolonged influence.

(a) In *Germany*, the Code civil automatically came into force in 1804 in those territories West of the Rhine which had already passed to France by the Treaty of Lunéville so as to form part of French territory. In addition, after the creation of the Rheinbund and especially after Napoleon's successful Prussian campaign of 1806–07, the Code civil crossed the Rhine and penetrated far to the east: it came into force in the Kingdom of Westphalia, in the Grand Duchies of Baden and Frankfurt, in Danzig, and even in Hamburg and Bremen, as parts of the 'Hanseatic Departments'. It was also to be introduced in the other principalities of the Rheinbund. This development came to an end with the War of Liberation, but the Code civil kept its hold in all the territories west of the Rhine and in a few other parts of the Rhenish province of Prussia. In the Grand Duchy of Baden it remained in force in a translation called the 'Badisches Landrecht', which contained a number of judicious additions by Brauer to fit it to German circumstances.

One result of the fact that the Code civil was in force in the Rhineland and in Baden for almost a century until the enactment of the BGB and was applied by the courts there, with appeal, after 1879, to the Imperial Court (Second (Rhenish) Civil Chamber), was that great German scholars applied to French law the methods which German legal science had developed in the nineteenth century, and produced work which had a strong effect in France itself. The *Handbuch des französischen Civilrechts* (1808) by Zachariä von Lingenthal has pride of place here. This was the first methodical and systematic treatment of French private law anywhere which broke away from the unsatisfactory structure of the Code civil. It was soon translated into French by Aubry and Rau, professors at Strasbourg, and as edition followed edition the work developed in independence and strength; the latest is the seventh edition, produced by Esmein and Ponsard. Earlier editions contributed much to the overthrow of the École de l'Exégèse in France, and the work had a steady influence on the courts; even today it is regarded by French writers as the most significant textbook of private law of the nineteenth century. The names of Crome, Kohler, Heinsheimer, and Saleilles are particularly associated with the manifold cross-fertilizations between German and French legal scholarship; on this, see Boehmer, above p. 101, Neumayer, above p. 101, and Andreas B. Schwartz, 'Einflüsse deutscher Zivilistik im Auslande', in: *Symbolae friburgenses in honorem Ottonis Lenel* (1935) 425, 435 ff.

(b) In *Switzerland*, the Code civil applied in the Canton of Geneva and in the Bernese Jura as from 1804, for both of these territories belonged to the French Republic. Both territories joined the confederation in 1815 after the fall of Napoleon, but the Code remained in force. During the nineteenth century, the Swiss cantons produced their own codes; throughout western Switzerland, in the Cantons of Vaud (1819), Fribourg (1834/1850), Ticino (1837), Valais

(1855), and Neuchâtel (1854/1855), the French Code served as the model; it was often only in family and inheritance law that local legal customs survived. In 1912 these cantonal laws were replaced by the Swiss Civil Code in which, as we shall see (below Ch. 14), French legal institutions still play a part, though not so significant a one as native and German elements.

IV

Although the enactment of the BGB and the ZGB greatly diminished the influence of French law in Germany and Switzerland, the legal systems of *Italy, Spain*, and *Portugal* must still be reckoned as belonging to the Romanistic legal family.

(*a*) In *Italy*, as elsewhere, the Code civil entered in the train of NAPOLEON's armies. Sicily and Sardinia escaped French occupation thanks to the help of the English fleet, but in the rest of Italy the Code civil came into force, if only for a short time. In the enthusiasm of liberation from the dominance of NAPOLEON, the Code was repealed almost everywhere in 1814, but it soon became clear that the traditional law of canon and Roman origins was inadequate for the needs of the time, and so the individual Italian territories gradually produced new civil codes all of which were based on the Code civil; it was only in the territories ruled by Austria, especially Lombardy and the Veneto, that the Austrian ABGB of 1811 controlled. Although there were many different civil codes in Italy their common reliance on the Code civil formed a basis for a unified private law, and it was not long after the Kingdom of Italy was called into being in 1861 by the great national movement for unification called the 'Risorgimento' that the enactment of the Codice civile of 1865 unified the law of Italy. This Code was substantially based on the French codification, but differed from it, for example, by having an introductory portion 'disposizioni preliminari', in which for the first time private international law, at the instance of the great Italian lawyer and statesman MANCINI, was accorded detailed regulation.

It is not surprising that the Italian lawyers of the nineteenth century looked exclusively to France. The works at their disposal consisted almost exclusively of translations of French authors of the École de l'Exégèse, with several Italian translations of the work of AUBRY and RAU. But a change was felt towards the end of the nineteenth century, as Italian legal scholars came more and more under the influence of the historical and dogmatic methods of the *German* school of pandectists. There was an enormous upsurge of research into legal history, especially Roman legal history, but in private law also Italian authors seized on and developed ideas from German legal scholarship, as SCIALOJA did in his famous work on *Negozi giuridici* (1893). Even today as one goes through the incredibly copious Italian legal literature, one finds late echoes of German pandectist methods—in particular a tendency to think in purely theoretical and unrealistic terms and a striking absence of any critical evaluation of judicial decisions (on this, see the apt observations of CAPPELLETTI/MERRYMAN/PERILLO (above p. 100, at pp. 170 ff.)). Only recently has a change gradually set in, thanks to the beneficial influence of comparative law.

In the social changes which followed the First World War, a plan for a complete reform of civil and commercial law was mooted. A reform commission set up in 1923 reported in 1930–6 with the drafts of four books of a new Codice civile; the first three dealt with the law of persons and family, the law of succession, and the law of property. Book Four, which dealt with the law of obligations and contracts, was a faithful translation of a draft produced in 1928 by a joint commission of French and Italian representatives under the chairmanship of SCIALOJA and LARNAUDE with the aim of unifying the law of obligations in France and Italy.

In 1939 however a decision was suddenly taken to expand the Civil Code substantially: it was to deal not only with private law in the traditional sense, but with all the possible personal and professional relationships of the citizen. One particular consequence of this was a demand to include commercial law. The existing draft of Book Four was withdrawn, and in its place a new Book Four was produced which in addition to sale, lease, and services dealt with the more sophisticated transactions of modern economic life, such as carriage, agency, forwarding, insurance, and bank credits. There was also a new Book Five, entitled 'Del lavoro', which dealt not only with the law of collective and individual labour, but also with the law of partnerships and companies, with the names of firms and trade marks, patents, unfair competition, and the law of monopolies. The concluding Book Six deals with the protection of rights; in the tradition of the Code civil it contains rules relating to evidence, hypothec and pledge, enforcement of judgments, and prescription. The Codice civile came into force on 21 April 1942, and contains 2969 articles.

Apart from including nearly the whole of commercial and economic law (on this, see ROTONDI, 'Entstehung und Niedergang des autonomen Handelsrechts in Italien', *AcP* 167 (1967) 29), the Codice civile makes no radical break with the French tradition: 'the main lines of the Code Napoleon can still be found today in the Italian civil code which, indeed, is not easily understood without some familiarity with the great French work . . .' (BERRI, *Travaux* (above p. 101) 631). The Codice shows its modernity, however, by dealing with many fact situations unknown at the time of the older codifications in France and even Germany. Thus, for example, arts. 1341 f. of the Codice civile contain provisions relating to *general conditions of business*, and transactions formed by signing sets of *standard terms* or printed *contractual forms* ('moduli o formulari'). The *assumption of contracts* is dealt with in arts. 1406 ff. The rules relating to *contracts for the benefit of third parties* stem from French judicial decisions based on art. 1121 Code civil, with some contribution from §§328 ff. BGB (compare arts. 141 ff.). The Codice accepts the French principle relating to breach of contract that an unperformed contract can be rescinded only on judicial complaint made by the innocent party; he is, however, afforded the possibility of making a written demand for performance within a set period, on the expiry of which the contract is rescinded by force of statute (art. 1454). The Codice civile did not adopt all the abstract conceptual refinements of the German BGB and in particular not the General Part. The notion of 'legal act' was also found uncongenial; instead arts. 1321 ff. deal with 'contracts in general' by saying that their rules are also to be applied, if possible, to 'unilateral *inter vivos* acts affecting property or obligations' (art. 1324). As in France, the law of unjustified enrichment distinguishes between the payment of a thing not due (arts. 2033 ff.) and the 'general claim for enrichment' (arts. 2041 f.) which was developed by the French courts without statutory basis. In the law of delict the Codice is also generally in line with French judicial decision, but there is the noteworthy limitation that damages for pain and suffering can be awarded only when the harmful behaviour is also criminal (art. 2059 Codice civile, 185 Codice penale).

If the basic principles of the law of obligations are clearly similar in the Italian and French codes, there are fundamental differences in the area of matrimonial law. In post-revolutionary *France* the principle of separation of church and state has been strictly observed, while in *Italy* the so-called Lateran Treaty of 11 Feb. 1929 brought the state and the Catholic church into very close association: according to art. 1 of the Treaty the Catholic religion is 'la sola religione dello stato'. The old Codice civile of 1865 regarded marriage as a secular affair in the tradition of the Enlightenment, and therefore accepted the principle that marriage must be entered into before the civil authorities. But by art. 34 of the Concordat the Italian state 'accords private law effects to the sacrament of marriage regulated by canon law'. It follows from this that marriage may be concluded not only before state officials but also before Catholic priests; in the latter case the state official is bound forthwith to enter the marriage in the state register, whereupon the same effects follow, as from the date of the ceremony, as attach to a marriage made before the state officials. About nineteen out of every twenty marriages made in Italy today take this 'canonical' form, also called the 'concordat form' (LUTHER (above p. 101) 77). In addition to the official and the canon forms of marriage, the Codice civile offers a third form for non-Catholic citizens: if the general preconditions set out in arts. 84 ff are satisfied, they may be married before the minister of any religious community recognized by the state; such a marriage must also be entered in the state register.

The Codice civile used not to recognize the possibility of divorce at all. Under art. 151 Codice civile a court could grant a request for separation from a spouse who was in gross breach of his matrimonial obligations, by desertion, maltreatment, or threatening or insulting behaviour, but the bond of matrimony remained intact and neither of the separated spouses could remarry. After many years of bitter public disputes, a law was brought into force in December 1970 which makes civil law divorce possible. Efforts were made to topple this law by means of a referendum and recourse to the Italian Constitutional Court, but they were fruitless.

The law of divorce in Italy today is based essentially on the principle of the breakdown of the marriage. The court will decree a divorce when the affective harmony and communal life of the spouses can no longer be maintained or restored. This is presumed by law after five years of separation. Such separation must be based on an agreement of the spouses confirmed by the court or, in the absence of such an agreement, on a separation order by the court if life together is found to be intolerable. Divorce may also be granted, on the basis that the marriage is deemed to have broken down, if the defendant spouse has tried to kill or maltreat the plaintiff or their children, or if he has been sentenced to fifteen or more years of imprisonment, or convicted of an immoral crime; so, too, if the defendant is a foreigner who has already obtained a divorce decree abroad.

(*b*) The most striking thing about the development of the law in *Spain* is the continuing vitality of the *fueros*, or laws particular to different localities, which developed in the course of the Middle Ages in individual provinces, counties and boroughs. *Las Siete Partidas*, a thirteenth-century law-book heavily influenced by Roman sources, also had particular importance, for in Castile it obtained the force of statute, and in other parts of the country it gradually obtained subsidiary force, after the local *fueros*. Thus until the nineteenth century the law of the Spanish kingdom was the so-called 'fuero system': the 'compilaciones' of royal laws and ordinances had force everywhere, then there were the *fueros* or local customary laws, and finally *Las Siete Partidas*. In the nineteenth century there was a plan to create a unified Spanish private law, stimulated by the impressiveness of the French Code, but the resistance of the several provinces was too great. Only the most urgent reforms, of land law and the law of mortgage, could be carried through by special statutes. Commercial law was codified in 1829, after the French model, and was greatly modernized in 1885, but the Código civil had to wait until 1889. This code, which is still in force, relies heavily on the Code civil, especially in the area of the law of obligations, where most of the provisions are a simple translation of the French text. In family and inheritance law, on the other hand, the Código contains many institutions indigenous to Spain, especially those from prior Castilian law. For Roman Catholics, canon law directly controls the forms of marriage as well as the conditions of nullity and voidability.

But even the Código civil has not produced complete legal unity in Spain. Only the rules of matrimonial law and the general provisions in the introductory section concerning the effect of statutes and of private international law are valid throughout the country. The other parts of the Código civil have only subsidiary force in those regions which previously had the *fuero* system (see art. 12). These regions cover about a quarter of the Spanish territory and include parts of Northern Spain which are extremely important economically and culturally, and where there is a continuing or renewed movement for autonomy, for example Catalonia (with Barcelona), the

Basque provinces of Álava, Vizcaya, and Navarra (wih Bilbao and Pamplona), and Galicia (including Corunna). The fueral laws of these regions are often contained in materials of very varied historical provenance and an attempt is being made to codify them: the fueral law of Aragón was collected in 1925 and brought into force as an appendix to the Código civil; it is only recently that the fueral laws of most of the other regions have been identified and enacted in statutes. These fueral laws are being codified not only in the interest of legal certainty, but also so as to provide a basis for the future creation of a private law common to the whole of Spain. This aim is also being advanced by the Supreme Court of Spain, which applies common legal ideas when the applicable fueral law is uncertain or inadequate; in doing this the Court may rely on art. 6 Código civil, which instructs the judge, in the absence of statutory provisions, to apply the local customs and then 'los principios generales del derecho'. On this matter see HIERNEIS, *Das besondere Erbrecht der sogenannten Foralrechtsgebiete Spaniens* (1966).

(c) In *Portugal* the law has been fairly well unified since the fifteenth century, consisting of the ordinances of King ALFONSO V, as edited and expanded by his successors, especially PHILIP III in 1603; the room left for the operation of local customs and canon law was relatively slight. The modern codification movement started in Portugal at the beginning of the nineteenth century, but came to nothing by reason of the stressful political conflict between the liberals and the restorationists. Commercial law, because of its wider implications, was codified in 1833 on the basis of the private work of FERREIRA BORGES, who relied on French law; this was replaced in 1888 by a sleeker and more modern version which took account of the Commercial Codes of Italy and Spain which had followed on the Code de Commerce. Professor SEABRA of the University of Coimbra was entrusted with the preparation of a Civil Code, and his draft came into effect in 1867, after the approval of King and Parliament, as the Código Civil. This code is significantly different in style and structure from the French Code, and it is immediately apparent that it was drafted by an academic. The language is highly didactic, and full of very abstract definitions; the structure is extremely forced, for example, in the organization of the very large Second Part of the Code, which deals with the acquisition of rights. The First Book deals with those rights which can be acquired by the activity or will of the creditor *without the co-operation* of others (including, for example, prescription and copyright); a Second Book deals with those rights whose acquisition needs the participation of others (for example, contractual rights, mortgage and matrimonial property); finally the Third Book deals with those rights which arise solely from the acts of others or by force of statute (for example, the law of succession and *negotiorum gestio*). So far as the content is concerned, the Código civil of 1867 generally reflects French legal institutions, but defers to the Portuguese tradition particularly in family and inheritance law.

A new Código Civil came into force in Portugal on 1 June 1967. Formally speaking, this Code marks a great advance on the old Code of 1867. It is also remarkable for the intelligent attention it pays to foreign legislation—especially German, Swiss, and Italian—to the point where one may wonder whether Portuguese private law ought still to be included in the Romanistic legal family. At the same time, when one compares it with the modern Italian and the forthcoming Dutch codifications, it seems a rather retrogressive and conservative product. On the one hand, labour law and commercial law have been rigorously excluded, and it deals only with what remains of 'classical' private law; on the other hand, much to the surprise of the German comparatist, it adopts the pandectist divisions of the BGB and much of its conceptual apparatus. Family and inheritance law disclose conservative features characteristic of Mediterranean Europe.

Apart from its inclusion of private international law, the 'General Part' of the Código Civil deals with essentially the same materials as the BGB: first, the law of natural persons (with admirably far-reaching protection of the individual's personality against invasions of his privacy and publication of his picture or private letters) and of juristic persons (corporations and foundations), followed by the law of property, under the influence of §§90 ff. BGB, and finally the rules relating to acts in law (*factos juridicos*), using the concepts of 'negocio juridico' with which the German reader is quite familiar, and 'declaração negocial'; it contains rules on error, deceit, duress, form, agency, conditions, legality and immorality, usury, and so on; in the case of usury, the code in art. 283 offers the exploited party the interesting possibility of demanding that the other party *modify* the contract 'segundo juizos de equidade'. The section on the exercise and protection of rights follows the romanistic tradition in including the law of proof. Book Two of the Código Civil, the law of obligations, is divided into two parts; the first part deals with creditor–debtor relationships 'in general', and the second deals with the special types of contract. The first section follows the Italian Codice civile in many points (for example, in the rules of assumption of contracts and the collapse of the foundation of a transaction) and deals also with the law of delict and, according to the German pattern, *negotiorum gestio* and the law of unjustified enrichment. It is noteworthy that all security rights such as suretyship, the transfer of securities, pledge, mortgage, rights of priority, and also the oblique action of a creditor, are dealt with in the general law of obligations. Book Three contains the law of property (possession, ownership, and real rights), while Books Four and Five, as in the German BGB, deal with family law and the law of succession. It is worth noting in relation to matrimonial law that since 1940, when a concordat between church and state was agreed after SALAZAR had brought them closer together once more, canonical marriage is again recognized alongside civil marriage, which had been the only recognized form of marriage after the republican revolution of 1910. Until 1975 divorce was only possible if the marriage had been made in civil form; by deciding on the form of marriage, therefore, the parties could determine whether or not it could be ended by divorce. Since 1975 divorce is possible whatever form of marriage has been chosen.

V

In the nineteenth century France was one of the greatest colonial powers in the world, with particular spheres of influence in the Near East, in Africa, in Indochina, and in Oceania. Almost all these territories are now fully independent, but in all of them, though to varying degrees, the French legal tradition is still influential. This will be illustrated very briefly for the Near East, the states of the Maghreb, and francophone Africa.

(*a*) Halfway through last century, nearly the whole of the Near East was under the control of the Turks, though that control was shortly to collapse. In this vast area private law was codified only in part. The Ottoman rulers had introduced a Code of Commerce (1850), an Ordinance regulating procedure in commercial cases (1861), and a few other special statutes relating to commercial law, all based on French models. But Islamic law controlled the heartland of private law; there was a rather incomplete and casuistic code called the Majalla, promulgated between 1869 and 1876, which covered the law of property and obligations (see also below p. 379), but family and inheritance law were not codified, the special courts for the different religious communities each using relevant sources.

In the 1870s Egypt became largely independent, as to both home and foreign affairs, within the Ottoman Empire. It had become strategically very important after the completion of the Suez Canal and was heavily in debt, so it was the great European powers, especially the principal creditors, England and France, who had most influence in the country rather than the Egyptians themselves. In 1876 Egypt signed a treaty with the European countries which treated the so-called 'Mixed Tribunals'. The judges in these tribunals were mostly European and had competence, by and large, for all civil and commercial suits in which either party was a foreigner. They applied the so-called 'Codes Mixtes', which, agreeably to the European powers, were principally French in origin, being indeed no more than hastily compiled epitomes of the Code civil (apart from the law of family and inheritance), the Code de Commerce, and other French codes. The so-called Mixed Tribunals had no jurisdiction in suits concerning family and inheritance law; if foreigners were involved, special consular courts had jurisdiction, while if Egyptians were involved the relevant courts of the different religious communities stepped in. Native courts were set up in 1883 for litigation between Egyptians concerning property and obligations, and 'Codes Mixtes', with a few concessions to the relevant Islamic law, were brought into force for them also. There thus arose in Egypt a sharp division between cases involving family relations or inheritance, for which there were *religious* courts applying *religious* law, mainly Islamic, and disputes on economic matters, for which there were *state* courts applying law principally of *French* origin. A similar situation obtains in most of the states of the Near East even today; it follows that, even if the religious courts have been largely abolished, the legal system of these countries should be classed with the Islamic legal systems as regards family or inheritance law (see below Ch. 29), and with the Romanistic legal family as regards the law of economic relations.

A few years after the First World War, Egypt became an independent kingdom but had to concede extensive privileges to England in relation to the Canal Zone and other installations. Not until 1937 could Egypt arrange by treaty that the jurisdiction of the consular courts should pass to the 'Mixed Tribunals' which would cease to operate after a transitional period of twelve years. It was determined at the same time to proceed with the preparation of a new Egyptian Civil Code.

This Civil Code came into force in 1949, and rests largely on the work of the Egyptian legal scholar AS-SANHŪRĪ. Although AS-SANHŪRĪ and the Egyptian legislator emphasized that Islamic law was considered throughout in the preparation of the Code, the Code appears on closer investigation to be principally orientated towards *French* law, and to contain only a few rules of Islamic origin, such as those relating to gift and pre-emption. The code draws on the French–Italian draft Code of Obligations of 1928 (see above p. 108), the Italian Civil Code of 1942, and also on many legal ideas developed by the French courts. Thus, for example, we find in codified form the French doctrine of liability in damages for abuse of rights (see vol. II, Ch. 15 III); here too we find the doctrine of the collapse of the basis of a transaction, not accepted by France but adopted by the Codice civile (see vol. II, Ch. 14 III). The Egyptian Civil Code did not adopt the obsolete rules of the Code Civil concerning the avoidance of a contract on the ground of material disproportion between performance and counterperformance (see vol. II, Ch. 5 V); instead it adopts a rule similar to that in §138.2 BGB which it has been proposed to enact in France. On this, see MOUSSERON (above p. 101) 74 ff., and MAURY, *Travaux* (above p. 101) 840 ff., who concludes his study of the Egyptian Code as follows: 'It is always clear that the Civil Code of Egypt is closely related to the Code civil of France and, even more so, to French private law as a whole; taking everything into acount, they are members of the same family; but the more recent code does not simply follow or imitate its predecessor; the Egyptian legislator thought afresh and made corrections and additions; the work he produced is in many respects original' (above p. 101, p. 842). The Egyptian Civil Code is silent on family and inheritance law: on these matters religious law still applies. Nevertheless the special jurisdictions of the religious courts in Egypt were abolished in 1955; a code of family and inheritance law has been being prepared for many years, there being as yet just a few special statutes.

After the collapse of the Ottoman Empire, *Syria* and the *Lebanon* were put under French mandate in 1922 by the League of Nations. Turkey itself replaced its traditional private law by the Swiss Code in 1926 (see below Ch. 14 III), but in Syria and the Lebanon Islamic law remained in force. In economic matters the Majalla was gradually replaced by modern codes. Thus in 1932 the Lebanon enacted a Code des Obligations et des Contrats, drafted by French lawyers, led by Professor JOSSERAND. The Lebanese Code of Procedure of

1933 and Code of Commerce of 1942 are also largely based on French law. In Syria French influence was relatively slight, but a series of codes came into force there after the Second World War closely following the Egyptian texts and thus indirectly influenced by the Romanistic legal tradition. This is especially true of the Civil Code which they borrowed from Egypt in 1949.

The same is true of the Civil Codes of *Libya* and *Iraq*, though it must be noted that Islamic law is more prominent in the Civil Code of Iraq than in the Egyptian Civil Code (on this see KÜPPERS, Das Irakische ZGB', *ZvglRW* 62 (1960) 181, 63 (1961) 1 and JWAIDEH, 'The New Civil Code of Iraq', 22 *Geo. Wash. L. Rev.* 176 (1953)). By and large the law of property and obligations is much the same throughout the states of the Arab League today now that civil codes based on the Egyptian model are in force in Syria (1949), Iraq (1951), Libya (1953), Qatar (1971), Somalia (1973), North Yemen (1976), Kuwait (1980), as well as in Algeria (1975).

(b) In *Algeria, Tunisia*, and *Morocco*, the states of the Maghreb, the main political influence since the beginning of the nineteenth century has been French. In consequence their law of obligations and commercial law has been virtually identical with the French equivalent. Thus in Algeria the Code civil and the Code de commerce were introduced *in toto* in 1834, while Tunisia and Morocco acquired a Code des obligations et des contrats in 1906 and 1913 respectively, which was a version of the relevant sections of the Code civil adapted to local circumstances. All these colonial statutes remained in force when French domination came to an end except in so far as they were inconsistent with independence. The reforms of recent years such as the new Tunisian Commercial Law of 1959 and Export Trade Law of 1962 leave French influence as unmistakable as ever. This is true even of Algeria which, like Somalia in 1973, responded to the pan-Arab movement by enacting a new Code civil in 1975, based largely on the Egyptian Civil Code which itself reflects French legal traditions.

Where family and inheritance law are concerned the picture is quite different. Litigation between resident French citizens was heard by special courts applying the Code civil, while disputes between natives were resolved by the religious courts applying Islamic, Christian, or Jewish law. However, natives of Algeria and later Morocco and Tunisia had the right to opt for the French civil regime, and thus to have their will or marriage regulated by the provisions of the Code civil. This possibility of opting for French law was abolished when independence was fully achieved, and today the family and inheritance law applicable to all Muslim citizens of these countries is Islamic law, which was codified in Tunisia in 1956 and in Morocco in 1958.

(c) The most extensive French colonies, all of which have now obtained national independence, were in sub-Saharan Africa. There are still many economic and cultural links between the new African states and France, but French attempts to forge a closer legal liaison, like the Commonwealth, by means of the 'Union française' and later the 'Communauté française' have not been a lasting success.

One of the great units of the French empire was French West Africa; despite efforts to maintain its unity as a state, since 1960 this territory has broken into no less than eight independent states: *Senegal, Mauretania, Mali, Niger, Guinée, Upper Volta, Ivory Coast*, and *Dahomey*. Much the same is true of French Equatorial Africa which in 1960 produced *Gabon, Congo (Brazzaville), Chad*, and the *Central African Republic*. We must add *Togo* and *Cameroon*, previously German but administered by France after the First World War, and also *Madagascar* which was under French control from 1885 until independence in 1960. If one takes into account the previous Belgian colonies— *Ruanda* and *Burundi* (which were earlier part of German East Africa) as well as the *Congo*—it will be clear how significant a part of Africa is French-speaking and influenced by French and Belgian legal ideas.

The French introduced their codes, especially the Code civil and the Code de commerce, sometimes with modifications in the light of particular circumstances, into all their colonial territories shortly after taking possession of them. Any alterations made in these laws at home were regularly followed in the colonies. It is true that the French laws did not apply to everyone. They applied to all French citizens who had left France to reside in the colonies, their offspring (who were French citizens by blood), and naturalized citizens, but in principle no one else was subject to the French statutes, especially not the natives of African origin. It is true that these people obtained French citizenship by art. 80 of the French Constitution of 27 Oct. 1946, but they remained 'citoyens français de statut local', subject not to the rules of the Code civil but to the rules of African customary law, or, should they be Muslims, the rules of Islamic law. This division of substantive law was reflected in a division of jurisdictions. The French had their own courts system, closely allied to that of France and even divided between private law courts and administrative courts, from which there might be a final appeal to the Court of Cassation or the Conseil d'État in Paris; the natives had their own native courts, staffed by tribal dignitaries, Islamic judges (cadis), French colonial officials, and, in the upper courts, some French career judges.

French colonial policy always sought in the long run to assimilate the native populations. English policy was different: true to the principle of 'Indirect Rule' (see below p. 238), English colonial administrators relied as much as possible on existing native rulers, kept the local courts decentralized, and left mature native law almost intact. The French, on the other hand, inspired by the egalitarian ideals of the Great Revolution and a belief in the superiority of 'civilisation française', constantly strove to lead the native population step by step to the higher level of metropolitan culture. In consequence French colonial legislation always offered the African population the possibility of opting for French law. Thus in all the colonies Africans could conclude individual legal acts, such as marriage or a will, under French law, or submit a particular dispute to French law, whether by agreement or implicitly by calling on a French court for adjudication. Furthermore it was made relatively easier for natives in the colonies to become naturalized French citizens, and in this way opt for French private law. But all these attempts to procure a legal assimilation were unsuccessful, except in Senegal, the most developed of the colonies; French law never really displaced the personal law of the African populations, whether African customary law or Islamic law.

On obtaining independence the new African states undertook a fundamental reconstruction of their law. In particular they abolished the system of divided courts; all courts now apply French law, which still, in principle, regulates constitutional, administrative, commercial, labour, and social law, as well as the African customary law and Islamic law which control family and inheritance. New codes are in process of preparation everywhere, using French legal terminology and French techniques of codification. Thus in 1964 Senegal enacted a Code des obligations, a thoroughly modern and original version of the rules of contract and delict of the Code civil. The codification of family and inheritance law has also been undertaken, but here there are very great practical difficulties, stemming principally from the differences between the African customary laws and Islamic law.

VI

After long and bloody struggles in the early nineteenth century *South* and *Central America* wrested their independence from the colonial power of Spain. The newly founded states of Latin America needed national and unifying civil codes; the only available model was the French Code civil. Spanish law was out of the question as being the law of the previous colonial power; in any case it was neither codified nor uniform even in Spain where local customary laws survived. In contrast, the French Code civil was a product of the Great Revolution, rooted in a world of ideas on which the Latin Americans had frequently drawn to justify their own struggles for independence. In its compactness and terseness of phrase the Code civil was far ahead of any other model, and furthermore it was so full of traditional concepts and ideas, especially from Roman law, that its reception represented no breach with the legal institutions familiar to the Spanish and Portuguese settlers. The civil codes of the Latin American states are consequently heavily influenced by the Code civil, though to different degrees. It is true that French influence has declined in the twentieth century, rather more in commercial than in private law, since legislators have increasingly drawn on other sources, especially Italian, German, and Swiss law, and even, in some cases, the Common Law, as by introducing the Anglo-American trust. Even so, there can be no doubt today that as regards private law the states of Central and South America belong to the Romanistic legal family.

Within the systems of Latin America, we can first distinguish a group whose codes are especially close to the Code civil, as being more or less translations of it: in this group fall the codes of Haiti (1825), Bolivia (1830), and the Dominican Republic (1845/1884). A second and more significant group is headed by the Civil Code of Chile (1855), which despite its reliance on French law is, along with the Civil Code of Argentina, the most independent and original product of Latin American legislation.

The draftsman chosen by the government of Chile was the Venezuelan ANDRÉS BELLO. He spent twenty years on the task, drawing on the Roman legal tradition as well as on French sources, and paying particular attention to *Las Siete Partidas* and to SAVIGNY's thinking. But the Code also contains ideas which in view of its date—before the middle of last century—are remarkably novel and original. This Code was the first to devote a special title in Book One on the Law of Persons to *juristic* persons, it is generous in its recognition of contracts for the benefit of third parties, and contains detailed rules on fiduciary ownership, which the Code civil did not recognize. In its structure it is superior to the Code civil, and in its language it is equally clear and forceful. The Code was later adopted by Ecuador (1860) and Colombia (1873) as well as by several of the Central American states; it also had a great influence on other Latin American legal systems, especially on the Civil Codes of Venezuela (1862) and Uruguay (1868). On the Civil Code of Chile see ARNOLD, *JZ* 1956, 773, and on the importance of ANDRÉS BELLO, see SAMTLEBEN, *RabelsZ* 46 (1982) 421.

The Argentinian Civil Code of 1869 is the work of DALMACIO VÉLEZ SARSFIELD, professor at the University of Córdoba in Argentina; he was also largely responsible for the Commercial Code of Argentina which had come into force in 1859. The Code civil was his principal model, but he also relied on French and other legal writers, as is shown by his frequent footnotes, which are still reproduced in modern editions of the Code; for example, he took several provisions directly from the textbook of AUBRY and RAU, and his private international law mainly from teachings of SAVIGNY and STORY. But VÉLEZ SARSFIELD also used the Civil Code of Chile, statutes of Spain, the preparatory materials for the Brazilian Code, and other sources, in a brilliantly eclectic manner. The Code he produced was later introduced, almost word for word, in Paraguay (1876).

Brazil had no civil code until 1916, though there were numerous drafts, especially from TEIXEIRA DE FREITAS and BEVILAQUA. In addition to the Code civil it was able to draw on the Portuguese and Italian codes, as well as those of Germany and Switzerland. The structure of the Code, especially its 'General Part', is largely traceable to German influence.

VII

In *North America* there are two areas where the French legal tradition is still vital: *Louisiana* and *Quebec*. The survival of Romanistic law in these two territories is of the greatest interest to comparative lawyers, for Louisiana and Quebec are both members of federal states otherwise entirely dominated by the Common Law; at a time of constantly increasing interfusion on an economic and cultural plane it is clear that the Common Law must exercise a strong influence on these 'islands' of the Romanistic legal tradition, to the point, indeed, that the question has been raised whether in these regions the traditional Civil Law can for long resist its effects. Not only are important areas of private law in Louisiana and Quebec covered by statutes of federal force throughout the United States or Canada which are drafted in the language and spirit of the Common Law, but there are also covert influences of Anglo-American legal thought since, for example, many lawyers in Louisiana are educated in law schools orientated towards the Common Law, and the Supreme Court of Canada, which as a final court of appeal also applies the law of Quebec, is mainly staffed by judges who feel more at home in the Common Law. In Louisiana the consciousness of linguistic and cultural separateness is less marked than it is in Quebec, and the danger, if danger it be, of gradual erosion of the characteristic differences in its style of legal thinking must be taken seriously, though it is sought to resist it by insisting on the particular methods of 'civilian' legal thought. Louisiana and Quebec offer the comparatist a rare chance to observe, as it actually occurs, the interaction of different styles of law, and it is therefore natural that both places should have flourishing and world-famous centres of comparative legal studies.

On the precarious situation of the 'outposts' of 'civilian' jurisprudence in the legal territories of the Common Law, which include Scotland and South Africa as well as Louisiana and Quebec (below Ch. 16 VI, Ch. 18 VI), see SMITH, 'The Preservation of the Civilian Tradition in "Mixed Jurisdictions" ', in: *Civil Law in the Modern World* (ed. Yiannopoulos, 1965) 3.

(a) *Louisiana*, named after LOUIS XIV, became a French colony at the end of the seventeenth century; at that time it included the whole of the Mississippi valley and marched in the north with the Canadian possessions of the French king. French law obtained, primarily the royal ordinances, followed by the Coutume de Paris. In consequence of her difficulties with England, the other great colonial power in North America, France ceded to Spain in 1762 the city of New Orleans and all of Louisiana west of the Mississippi. The Spanish governors immediately introduced the law of Spain, though they did not succeed in obliterating the French law of the settlers. In 1800, under the threat of NAPOLEON's new military power, Spain had to cede Louisiana back to France; NAPOLEON's attention was fixed on the European scene, so in 1803 he sold this immense territory at a bargain price to the United States, which administered the southern part, the Louisiana of today, as a federal 'Territory of Orleans'; in 1812 it was admitted to the Union as an independent state.

A few years after its accession to the United States, Louisiana's House of Representatives commissioned the drawing up of a Civil Code, which was to codify the law in force—that is, the Spanish law. Nevertheless the draftsmen of the Code turned mainly to *French* law, not only because it was familiar and had proved satisfactory during the period of Spanish rule, but principally because any lawyer then entrusted with the task of producing a code was bound to be drawn first and foremost to the model of the Code civil which had just come into force. It is disputed whether the draftsmen had at their disposal the final version of the Code civil, or only the draft produced by NAPOLEON's commission, or even just the final draft of CAMBACÉRÈS. In any case the Code which came into force in 1808, apart from some infiltrations from Spanish sources, especially from *Las Siete Partidas*, is firmly based on French law, and the new edition and expansion of the Code in 1825 and 1870 did not alter that situation to any great extent.

In many important areas of law the connection between the law of Louisiana and the law of its neighbouring states is extremely close. This is true not only in areas which are governed by federal laws in the United States, such as bankruptcy, patent, and trade mark law, but also in areas where the individual states have legislative power, as in the law of bills and notes, the law of securities and banking, insurance and company law, for here Louisiana has followed the style and content of the legislation in neighbouring states, and it may well be that the *construction* of these statutes by its courts is in line with the practice of American law in general. Louisiana has finally, after many years of hesitation, adopted most, though not all, of the Uniform Commercial Code, that great work of unification of law in the United States (see below p. 260). Strong influences of the Common Law are to be found even outside trade and economic law. Thus, for example, the legal institution of the trust, a typical creation of the Common Law, has been taken over in modified form by a special statute in Louisiana. So far as the law of delict is concerned, though the rules in the Civil Code are an almost literal translation of the articles of the Code civil (see arts. 2315 ff. Civil Code of Louisiana), the courts have surreptitiously brought in the ideas and forms of action of Anglo-American negligence law, to such an extent 'that one can say today with little fear of contradiction that the Code Napoleon is wholly devoid of effect in Louisiana in the area of quasi-delict' (HUBERT, *Travaux* (above p. 101) 778, 782; by 'quasi-delict' is meant the careless infliction of harm, see vol. II, Ch. 17 IV). In the law of contract also the concealed influence of Anglo-American legal ideas is very considerable, since Louisiana provides a very narrow base for the development of an independent civil legal doctrine, and contact with modern French legal science is made very difficult by the language barrier. It is true that recently parts of the Civil Law textbooks of AUBRY and RAU and of PLANIOL have been translated into English and that the universities of the state lay great store by the scientific practice of Civil Law, but only the future will show what effect this will have on the law in action. Today Louisiana belongs neither entirely to the Civil Law nor yet to the Common Law; it is in an intermediate position and seems to be a 'système juridique sui generis' (DAINOW (above p. 101) 32).

(*b*) The territory which is now the Canadian province of *Quebec* was originally part of the huge French colony of 'New France', which stretched from the mouth of the St. Lawrence far into the Middle West of what is now the United States. Here too French domination came to an end with their defeat in the war with England: by the Peace of Paris France had to cede its Canadian possessions to England. The English accorded the French Canadians full religious freedom by the Quebec Act, 1774, and recognized French law, especially the Coutume de Paris, as the basic private law of the province. We shall not dwell on the disputes between the French and English populations of Canada which have lasted with fluctuating intensity until the present day, save to say that the legal separateness of the Province of Quebec, whose population amounts to nearly one-third of that of the whole of Canada, has never been lost.

The basis for the separate legal position enjoyed by Quebec in the federal state of Canada, the rest of which is dominated by the Common Law, is the 'Code civil de la Province de Québec' of 1866. The Code came into existence because in the middle of the nineteenth century the law in force had become unmanageable, consisting as it did of the Coutume de Paris, the French royal ordinances which came into force before 1763, the subsequent provincial statutes, and the decisions of the courts of Quebec. Parliament instructed the draftsmen not to draw up a substantially new code, but simply to put the existing law in an orderly form; the French Code civil was to be taken as a model, but commercial law was to be included.

The Civil Code so produced is very strongly influenced by the Code civil but it is by no means a mere copy. The Common Law has made its influence felt on many points, and in some others, especially the law of succession, French law was not followed, on the ground that its rules seemed unsuitable for the particular circumstances in Quebec. The most striking feature in the Civil Code is the inclusion of commercial law, in deviation from the French tradition. To achieve this, the draftsmen added to the first three books of the Code, which are modelled on those of the Code civil, a fourth book, entitled 'Lois commerciales', which included the law of bills, notes, and cheques, subsequently regulated by federal statute, and also insurance and maritime law, both of which were strongly influenced by the Common Law. Throughout the Code one finds many individual provisions in which special rules are laid down if the transaction in question constitutes an 'affaire de commerce' or an 'opération commerciale'. The role played by federal commercial law in Quebec is large and will probably grow.

Work on a new Civil Code has been going on in Quebec since the early 1960s. The Code civil of 1866 was thought obsolete in structure and content and to need modification in the light of modern conditions. Another aim was doubtless to assert Quebec's cultural and legal independence by producing a code in the Civil Law tradition. A complete draft of the Civil Code with supporting materials was issued in 1978. Book Two, which deals with family law, came into force in 1981, except for rules on divorce, for which the Federal Parliament has legislative competence under the present Canadian Constitution. See the Report on the Quebec Civil Code, 2 vols. (ed. Civil Code Revision Office, 1978), and on it CRÉPEAU, 'La Réforme du Code civil du Québec', *Rev. int. dr. comp.* 31 (1979) 269.

Civil Law has a better chance of maintaining itself against the emanations of the Common Law in Quebec than in Louisiana. For in Quebec the French tradition exists outside the legal system as a decisive factor in the whole cultural life of French Canadians. Furthermore the Province of Quebec, with its large population and significant economic power, has a much larger influence in the federation of Canada than Louisiana has in the United States. It is also important that in the legal life of Quebec the French language is still more current than English. Of course French Canadian lawyers complain that French legal language has been ruined by the adoption of Anglicisms, and that judges of Anglo-Canadian background often surreptitiously introduce legal ideas of the Common Law by using English expressions. Nevertheless most of the important books on the private law of Quebec which are used in the universities and in practice are written in French, and access to recent French legal literature is certainly much easier in Quebec than in Louisiana. In any case the legal systems of Louisiana and Quebec offer the comparatist fascinating models of a symbiosis of Civil Law and Common Law, and show that a political unit may comprise states of different legal traditions, even when those legal traditions are as different as those of Rome and Westminster.

9

Courts and Lawyers in France and Italy

BELLET, 'Grandeur et servitudes de la Cour de Cassation', *Rev. int. dr. comp.* 32 (1980) 293.

——, 'France: La Cour de Cassation', *Rev. int. dr. comp.* 30 (1978) 193.

BORÉ, *La Cassation en matière civile* (1980).

BRETON, 'L'Arrêt de la Cour de cassation', *Ann. Université des Sciences Sociales de Toulouse* 23 (1975) 5.

CAPPELLETTI, 'Der italienische Zivilprozeß, Ein rechtsvergleichender Überblick', *RabelsZ* 30 (1966) 254.

——, MERRYMAN/PERILLO, *The Italian Legal System* (1967).

——, PERILLO, *Civil Procedure in Italy* (1965).

CORVES, 'Zur Praxis der Kassation in Frankreich', *DRiZ* (1966) 139.

R. DAVID, *Le Droit français* I: *Les Données fondamentales du droit français* (1960).

DAVID/DE VRIES, *The French Legal System* (1958).

HAMELIN/DAMIEN, *Les Règles de la nouvelle profession d'avocat* (3rd edn., 1977).

HERZOG, *Civil Procedure in France* (1967).

——, HERZOG, 'The Reform of the Legal Profession and of Legal Aid in France', 22 *ICLQ* 462 (1973).

LEMAIRE, *Les Règles de la profession d'avocat et les usages du barreau de Paris* (3rd edn., 1975).

LINDON, 'La motivation des arrêts de la Cour de cassation', *JCP* 1975.I. 2681.

LUTHER, 'Studium und Richterlaufbahn in Italien', *JZ* 1956, 84.

MIMIN, *Le style des jugements* (4th edn., 1978).

OLIVIER, 'The Future of the Legal Profession in France', 53 *Aust. LJ* 502 (1979).

PÉDAMON, Anwaltsberuf im Wandel (no. 111 of *Arbeiten zur Rechtsvergleichung*, 1982) 37.

RIEG, 'Die Reform einiger rechtsberatender Berufe in Frankreich', *JZ* 1972, 581.

SCHILL, 'Die Stellung des Richters in Frankreich', *Eine rechtshistorische Darstellung unter Einbeziehung der Gerichtsverfassung* (1961).

SGROI, 'La cour de cassation d'Italie', *Rev. int. dr comp.* 30 (1978) 393.

STURM, 'Juristenausbildung in Frankreich und Italien', *JZ* 1969, 241.

TOUFFAIT/TUNC, 'Pour une motivation plus explicite des décisions de justice, notamment de celles de la Cour de cassation', *Rev. trim. dr. civ.* 72 (1974) 487.

ZWEIGERT, 'Der Jurist in Frankreich und Deutschland, Versuch einer vergleichenden Typologie', in: *Festschrift Hans G. Ficker* (1967) 498.

I

JUST as the French Code civil has served as a model for the private law of many countries of the Romanistic legal family, so has the French *system of courts.* We shall concentrate here on the *Court of Cassation*, the highest French court in civil and criminal matters, which deserves special attention, since it differs in characteristic respects from the comparable supreme courts of the Anglo-American and German legal families.

The Court of Cassation was created by the legislation of the French Revolution. Under its original title 'Tribunal de Cassation', its first function was to assist the legislature rather than to act as a court: its task was to see that the courts did not deviate from the text of the laws and so encroach on the powers of the legislature. In those days even the *construction* of a statute ranked as a 'deviation' from its text, as did the judicial completion of an incomplete law. This was because the provincial courts of the *ancien régime*— the 'Parlements'—had often used the device of construction to evade or restrict the reforming laws of the king. Furthermore it seemed to conflict with the principle of separation of powers for the judges to be empowered to construe statutes; so courts were allowed to refer doubtful questions of construction to the legislature—the 'référé facultatif'. The fact that the Tribunal de Cassation was originally outside the courts system proper had two consequences: first, it could only quash ('casser') the decisions of the courts, not substitute its own decision on the merits; secondly, the courts were not bound by the decisions of the Tribunal de Cassation, but could decide the matter on remand exactly as they had done the first time; if this second decision was questioned, the Tribunal de Cassation was bound to lay the question in dispute before the legislature for final solution—the 'référé obligatoire'.

The revolutionary distrust of judicial legal development in all its forms evaporated fairly quickly; the courts never used the 'référé facultatif', and the text of the Civil Code itself recognizes the need for judicial interpretation (see above Ch. 7 II), so the Tribunal de Cassation, which NAPOLEON renamed the 'Cour de Cassation', itself gradually took over the task of construing the statute and of quashing the judgments of lower courts which had misconstrued it. The principle still remains, however, that the Court of Cassation cannot itself render a decision on the merits, but can only quash the decision under attack and remit the matter for rehearing to another court of the same level. Even today that court is not bound to follow the view of the Court of Cassation: if it refuses to do so and this second judgment is brought to the Court of Cassation, the combined chambers of the court of Cassation decide the matter. If the second decision is quashed, the matter is remitted to a third court, which is then bound to follow the view of the law laid down by the Court of Cassation.

In *Italy* this rather cumbrous procedure is simplified. There also the Corte di Cassazione may only quash the decision under attack, but the court to which the matter is remanded is thereupon bound to follow the view of the law laid down by the Court of Cassation; see art. 384, par. 1 Codice di procedura civile.

It should be noticed that in principle every decision of a French court is liable to attack before the Court of Cassation, provided that other remedies are unavailable or have been exhausted. Thus decisions which are unappealable, because of their low monetary value, for example, may be taken to the Court of Cassation which may therefore have to review the decision of a *tribunal d'instance*. If the preconditions are satisfied the Cour de Cassation is *obliged* to render a decision: it has no power to select cases of special significance. In consequence the Court is grossly overworked, delivering about 15,000 decisions on applications for review every year.

In *Italy* the right to have judicial decisions reviewed by the Court of Cassation is laid down in the *Constitution* of 1948: see art. 111. It is true that the Codice di procedura civile of 1942 denies review to judgments of *juges de paix* which are not subject to appeal (art. 360), but art. 111 of the Constitution, as construed by the courts, permits review by the Court of Cassation even in these cases; see Cass. 9 Feb. 1962, n. 271, Giust. Civ. Rep. 1962, s.v. 'Cassazione civile' n. 163.

In principle the Court of Cassation only answers *questions of law*; *questions of fact* are left to the 'uncontrolled judgement of the judges of fact' (*appréciation souveraine des juges de fait*). Of course the distinction between questions of law and questions of fact is notoriously difficult, so the Court of Cassation can very often determine the extent of its activities. The principal factor it considers is whether any decision it makes will be of general significance and so help to maintain uniformity in the courts. Contrariwise, the Court of Cassation adopts a position of restraint when it appears that a legal development is still in full flood; in such a case it often leaves the issue unresolved, saying that it is (ostensibly) a question of fact on which the trial judge has the final say.

For the French Court of Cassation, foreign law is in principle a question of fact; it therefore refuses to quash a judgment on the ground that foreign law has been wrongly applied, but it reserves the right to intervene in a case where the court below has wholly failed to apply foreign law as required by a rule of French conflicts law, or where a very gross error has been made in applying foreign law, or where it is a question of general significance (compare ZAJTAY, *Zur Stellung des ausländischen Rechts im französischen internationalen Privatrecht* (1963)).—The construction of *contracts* is also in principle a matter for the trial courts, but the Court of Cassation may intervene when general conditions of business or standard form contracts are being construed, or when the trial judge has 'denatured' the contract by his construction, or has attributed to it a meaning inconsistent with the words of a 'clause claire et précise'.—Art. 360 par. 5 Codice di procedura civile puts the Italian Court of Cassation in a similar position to indulge in covert appreciation of questions of fact.

The French Court of Cassation has six chambers. Three chambers deal with litigation arising out of the general private law, a fourth deals with trade and economic law, the fifth with labour and social security matters, and the sixth with criminal law. Each civil chamber has fifteen judges, and the criminal chamber seventeen, so that in the Court of Cassation as a whole there are about 90 judges, in addition to about 25 'conseillers référendaires', junior judges who do preparatory work on the cases for decision and take part in the consideration of the decision, though without voting on it. A quorum of seven judges is required in the civil and criminal chambers. With such a large number of judges there is a risk that different benches may adopt different methods of judging cases, so when there may be contradictory decisions or when there is a 'question de principe' to solve the President of the Court or the individual chambers can remit a decision to a 'Chambre Mixte'. The 'Chambre Mixte' is made up of judges from the chambers concerned in the matter in question, each chamber sending its President, it senior judge, and two other judges. Judges chosen in this way from *all* the chambers constitute the 'Assemblée Plénière' (formerly the Chambres Réunies). Apart from ceremonial occasions, the Assemblée Plénière meets only when a decision is up for review a second time, because of the refusal of the lower court to which the matter was remanded after being quashed on the first occasion to adopt the view of the law enunciated by the Court of Cassation. The Court of Cassation also has a special team of state attorneys, led by the Procureur Général, who co-operate not only in criminal matters, but in all civil matters as well; the French view is that at the level of the Court of Cassation the public, whom the state attorney represents, has an interest in the maintenance of law even in *civil* matters. In lower courts the participation of a state attorney in civil suits is necessary only in questions involving status and guardianship, though there is a right of intervention in all cases.

The content, structure, and phraseology of the decisions of the Court of Cassation, and to a lesser extent those of lower courts, are extremely characteristic of the particular style of French legal thought. From the external point of view every decision of a French court consists of a single sentence, which in the case of the Court of Cassation reads either 'The court . . . dismisses [the demand for cassation]' or 'The Court . . . quashes [the judgment under attack] and remits the matter to the Court of . . . '. All the reasons for the judgment are to be found betweeen the subject and predicate of this sentence, in the form of a string of subordinate clauses, all beginning with the formula 'attendu que . . .' ('whereas . . .'). There is no particular section devoted to the facts of the case or the history of the litigation; indeed, the facts are referred to only so far as may be necessary to clarify the particular grounds on which cassation is urged ('moyens'), the reasoning of the lower court or the particular view of the Court of Cassation, and even then the reference may be very allusive. Furthermore, especially in the Court of Cassation, every effort is made to make the text of the judgment as dense and compact as possible. Subsidiary considerations are eschewed; and when the decision must be quashed on one ground, other grounds are not even considered. Asides, divagations, and efflorescences are never to be found in the Court of Cassation, and hardly ever below; nor are there references to the background of the case, legal history, legal policy, or comparative law. In a widely used guide to the style of judgments MIMIN wrote:

'Extrajuridical arguments which do not assist in the solution of a case are among those which lend a merely sophistical appearance to a decision. To invoke considerations of economics, sociology or diplomacy is to confuse different types of arguments and to conceal the correctness of sound reasoning' (above p. 123, pp. 255 f).

Judgments of the Court of Cassation never contain references to previous decisions made by itself or any other court, or even references to legal writing; such references occasionally appear in the judgments of lower courts, but MIMIN regards them as objectionable even there (above p. 123, pp. 273 ff.). In consequence, decisions of the Court of Cassation are very rarely longer than 4–5 pages of typescript, and are often no more than a few lines long. They are generally marked by polished elegance, formal clarity, and stylistic refinement; often, however, they seem to be frozen in a pedantic ritual of empty formalism, inappropriate to the uniqueness of the concrete facts of life behind the case, which indeed can often only be guessed at. It is difficult to believe that these decisions are the work of judges of flesh and blood who ever indulged in the luxury of doubt; it seems to be required by the 'majesté de la loi' that a judgment should appear in perfect purity as the act of an anonymous body.

The style of judgments in the Cour de Cassation has been criticized by French writers as well as by foreigners (see DAWSON, *The Oracles of the Law* (1968) 375, 410 f.; KÖTZ, *Über den Stil höchstrichterlichen Entscheidungen* (1973)). TOUFFAIT/TUNC (above p. 123) have shown that because the judgments generally give only the decision and not the real reasons behind it, no dialogue between the Cour de Cassation and the legal public is possible and they make clear with a wealth of examples how trying it is for a French lawyer to have to venture a view on the possible scope of a terse and cryptic judgment without any expectation that the court will ever respond to what he says. They therefore propose that the Procrustean method of giving decisions in the form of 'attendus' be abandoned and that the judges should be required 'to give their reasoning, with an explanation why they decided in the way they did, and without concealing any of the relevant considerations'. Needless to say, these proposals have had no effect so far; indeed, they have been roundly dismissed (see BRETON (above p. 123)).

Since the reforms of 1958 the French courts system below the level of the Court of Cassation is of the two-tier model familiar elsewhere in Continental Europe. Civil matters are decided at first instance by a single judge in the *tribunaux d'instance*, of which there are 456 in the whole of France, an average of 5 for each of the 90 departments. They can hear cases whose monetary value does not exceed 10,000 NF; their decision in litigation involving less than 3,500 NF is unappealable, though recourse to cassation is always possible. All other civil suits go first of all to one of the 175 *tribunaux de grande instance*, where three judges sit. Commercial cases, whatever their value, are first heard by *tribunaux de commerce* set up by governmental decree as required in the centres of commerce. At the moment there are about 230 of them. Three judges also sit on a *tribunal de commerce*, but instead of being career judges they are indirectly elected by the tradesmen of the jurisdictional area. Many of them, of course, have a basic knowledge of law, since in France legal education is nothing like as specialized as it is in Germany, and many educated laymen know some law. Labour disputes go first of all to the *conseil de prud'hommes*, which are also staffed by honorary lay judges. A bench is normally constituted by equal numbers of employers and workmen, but in the event of disagreement a judge with a casting vote is called from the *tribunal d'instance*. Special first instance tribunals exist for litigation arising out of tenancies, social security, and eminent domain.

Although, as we have seen, there are several special tribunals at first instance, alongside the general civil courts, on appeal the principle of unified jurisdiction is observed; since the reforms of 1958 all appeals go to the *cours d'appel*, no matter whether the judgment in question was rendered by a *tribunal d'instance*, a *tribunal de grande instance*, or one of the special tribunals; the only exception is for some social security cases. If the sum in issue is less than 3,500 NF, no appeal is possible, even in commercial or labour disputes. As there are only 31 courts of appeal this makes justice in France very centralized. Most of them serve two to four departments, though the court of appeal of Bastia hears appeals only from the department of Corsica. The Court of Appeal of Paris is especially important, for its catchment area includes nearly a fifth of the whole population of France; it has nearly 170 judges whose prestige, position, and pay are greater than those of the judges in the provinces. Courts of Appeal sit in chambers with three judges, which may specialize in particular areas of law, especially in the larger courts.

II

Judges in France, like those in Italy and Germany, are *career judges*; they opt for a judicial career early in life, they are appointed by the state after passing the necessary examinations, and they are generally promoted to more important positions in higher courts on the basis of their performance and years of service. Here is RENÉ DAVID's picture of the career of the judge and the state attorney, both of whom in France are called 'magistrats':

'In France it is often family tradition or personal inclination which attracts people to the career of magistrat. In addition, it also appeals to some people who are not very ambitious, who prefer the security of a modest but assured salary to the risks of competition or the uncertainties of a life in business. A person who chooses to be a magistrat can count on a quiet life whose early years at any rate will be spent in a provincial town, and this life will not be troubled by undue responsibility: a judge in

France sits alone only in very small cases, private or public; matters of any importance come before a tribunal with several members, whose decisions, in accordance with a principle of French law, are anonymous' (above p. 123, pp. 49 f.)

In France lawyers of different branches follow different systems of training. Certainly future advocates, notaries, judges, and state attorneys must all follow the same four-year law course in a university, which leads to the 'licence en droit' once the university examination is passed. But then the paths diverge. The future 'magistrat' has to pass a further, rather difficult examination conducted by the state, success in which gives him the right to attend the 'École Nationale de la Magistrature' in Bordeaux. This school was founded in 1958 on the model of the famous 'École Nationale d'Administration', and it admits about 200 young lawyers a year. They are sworn in as 'auditeurs de justice' and are paid by the state during their two-year period of training. They spend time at different courts and state attorney's offices, and receive intensive instruction to develop their specialist legal knowledge, including disciplines like forensic medicine, criminology, and business accounting. This period of training culminates in a further examination, and then the successful candidates, usually not more than 27 years old, take up posts as judges and state attorneys; the range of choice available to them depends on their performance in the final examination.

French judges are guaranteed complete independence: they cannot be removed or even promoted against their will. The promotion of judges depends principally on the decision of a central committee on promotion, which contains prominent judges as well as officials of the Ministry of Justice and has before it the annual reports submitted by Presidents of Courts on the performance of the judges set under them. When judges are to be named to the Court of Cassation the Conseil supérieur de la Magistrature plays an important part; this is a committee of eminent judges whose members are chosen by the President of the Republic from a list prepared by the superior courts. This procedure more or less ensures that the political views of judges play no part in their promotion; if, on the other hand, men of a very independent cast of mind are not very likely to be promoted, this is not a fault of the French system in particular, but one which exists whenever the bridge between 'inferior' and 'superior' judges has to be crossed on the basis of a superior's evaluation of an inferior's performance in office.

In contrast to the judge in the Anglo-American legal system, the judge in France can hardly ever make a name for himself during his professional career. Only on trivial cases in the lowest courts does he sit alone; if he is one of a bench of judges, he is not permitted to deliver a dissenting opinion, and even if he writes the decision of the court the rigorous style of judgments in France requires him to repress all his personal characteristics. Yet this obviously reflects the internal attitude of French judges: the fact that in France today (unlike Italy) there is no judicial review of the constitutionality of a statute is attributed by RENÉ DAVID to the unwillingness of French judges to take on this responsibility. One also begins to understand why they cling so stubbornly to the myth that statute is the only source of law: there is no doubt at all that in large areas of French private law the rules are a pure fabrication of the judges, often with only the most tenuous connection with the text of the Code civil, but a French judge would be extremely unhappy to admit that he is at all creative in his legal activity:

'Judges in France do not like to put themselves forward as creating rules of law. In practice, of course, they have to do so; it is not, and could not be, the function of a judge mechanically to apply well-known and predetermined rules. But judges in France make every effort to give the impression that this is how it is: in their decisions they keep claiming to be applying a statute; only rarely, if ever, do they put forward unwritten general principles or maxims of equity which might suggest to observers that judges were being creative or subjective' (DAVID, above p. 123, p. 50). In fact judges all over the world like to be seen as 'applying' the law rather than as forming it, even interstitially, in a creative manner. MAX WEBER concluded that 'the very judges who, objectively speaking, are the most "creative" have felt themselves to be just the mouthpiece of legal rules, as merely interpreting and applying them, latent though they may be, rather than as creating them.' (*Wirtschaft und Gesellschaft* II (4th edn., 1956) 512).

III

Until recently the business of advising and representing parties in legal affairs, which has long been done in Germany by the unified profession of the *Rechtsanwalt*, was in France divided between the *avocat* and the *avoué*. The two professions have now been fused into the 'nouvelle profession d'avocat' by a reform law of 31 Dec. 1971, but it is still worth taking a brief look at the old system, for the division still applies in appellate matters and it is necessary for an understanding of the present rules regarding the profession.

The old-style *avocat* appeared in court and delivered oral argument on behalf of the party he was representing; the *avoué* dealt with all the rest of the case, the documentary part, taking the necessary steps preliminary to trial, drafting the statement of claim, reply, and any other documents, preparing the written pleadings, collecting the judgment, lodging the appeal, seeing to the executory process, and so on. As they said in France, the *avocat*'s business was 'la plaidoirie'; the *avoué*'s business was 'la procédure, l'écriture et la postulation'. Each branch of the profession had the exclusive right to perform its tasks: neither could do those of the other.

Unlike the *avocat*, the *avoué* was not a member of an independent profession; like the notary, he was an 'officier ministériel', in many respects like a civil servant. For example, the *avoué* had to make his services available to any person who sought them, and his fees were calculated according to an official tariff. But the best evidence of the official nature of the *avoué*'s profession was the fact that only a limited number of *avoués* were admitted by the various courts: no one could be made an *avoué* by the Minister of Justice unless he was 'presented' by a retiring *avoué* or his heir; in other words, an applicant had to obtain the place of an *avoué* by purchase or otherwise, and the purchase price of such a place might be very high indeed, especially in the big cities.

This strict division of practising lawyers into two professionally and functionally separate groups survived until recently because in the French view there was a fundamental difference between taking the steps required to bring a case to court—that being basically a technical matter—and presenting orally in court the facts of the case and the issues of law it raised—this being a task calling for special eloquence, a grasp of principle, a wide education, and a certain detachment and distance from the procedural details. The *avoué*, it was thought, should be a practical man, knowledgeable and familiar with the technical details of procedure, while the *avocat* should take a lofty view of the facts of the case, present it rhetorically, and rise above the banal formalities by elaborating the legal issues and relating them to great legal principles. Accordingly the *avoué* acted at the instance of the client and in his name, under a contract, and for a fee, while the *avocat*, acting in his own name, came spontaneously into court to protect the party's right, not, according to the earlier view, for a contractual fee, but receiving an honorarium prompted by gratitude and recognition. Only in 1957 did a statute give the *avocat* a general right to sue for his fees; previously this had been regarded as unprofessional.

In recent years there was increasing criticism of this functional distinction between 'postulation' and 'plaidoirie'. Litigants could not see why they should have to retain two professionals in even a simple case: having two advisers prolonged the affair and also made it more costly, because the two were in large part doing the same work. Furthermore, there were often difficulties in drawing the boundary between their activities because no sensible distinction can be made between collecting and writing up the facts on the one hand and working out their legal significance and arguing it in court on the other. Sometimes, especially in the big cities, all the *avoué* did was to have documents drafted by the *avocat* typed out under his letterhead, sign them, and hand them in to the court. Even before the reforms of 1971 the theoretical distinction between the two professions of *avocat* and *avoué* was not quite reflected in practice. Representation before the Court of Cassation and the Conseil d'État, the highest administrative court in France, was in the hands of a special group of lawyers who performed the functions of the *avoué* as well. In the *tribunaux d'instance*, rent tribunals, and labour courts all the litigation could be conducted by either an *avoué* or an *avocat*, and in the commercial courts by the so-called *agréé* as well. Another factor favouring the fusion of the professions was the satisfactory experience with a unified profession in

Alsace and Lorraine where the situation was left as it had been under German rule, without any harmful consequences.

A final reason for unifying the legal profession was that this would make the French system more like those of other European countries and so facilitate for lawyers the freedom of establishment which is sought within the European Community. In Great Britain the legal profession is still divided between barristers and solicitors (see below Ch. 17 III) but elsewhere in Europe it is different. Apart from Belgium no country has seen fit to adopt the French practice, and even in Belgium it has been abandoned. The legal profession in the Netherlands and Luxembourg has been unified for many years. Italy admittedly makes a distinction between the *procuratore* and the *avvocato*, the dividing line being theoretically the same as in France until recently, with the *procuratore* taking the purely technical and procedural steps while the *avvocato*, regarded as the successor of the *juris consultus* of ancient Rome, makes the purely legal submissions. In practice, however, the distinction is virtually irrelevant, since any *procuratore* may become an *avvocato* without any trouble: a university graduate with the degree of 'dottore in giurisprudenza' is admitted as *procuratore* after a year in practice and a further examination; after six years in practice he can forthwith be admitted as *avvocato*, and after nine further years as *avvocato* before the Corte di Cassazione.

Now that the reforms are in force, it is only before the appellate courts that the prior division of legal labour in France still obtains. In other courts all procedural steps are taken by the 'nouvel avocat'. Indeed it is only in the *tribunal de grande instance* and the higher courts that an attorney is required at all, for in other courts the parties may be represented by other persons. But in one respect the old distinction between *avocat* and *avoué* is retained in the *tribunal de grande instance*: although the *nouvel avocat* may plead before any *tribunal de grande instance* in France, he is like the *avoué* before him in being unable to take the purely procedural steps in a lawsuit except in the court in whose area he has his chambers. Thus a person who wants a Paris attorney to represent him in litigation in Bordeaux has to retain an attorney with chambers in Bordeaux as well, so that he may do what was previously done by the *avoué*. It is different in the *tribunaux d'instance* and the commercial and labour courts, where the 'nouvel avocat' may conduct the entire lawsuit irrespective of geographical considerations. The *nouvel avocat* may not appear before the Cour de Cassation or the Conseil d'État, where the representation of litigants is still entrusted to a special group of lawyers, who, like the former *avoués*, are *officiers ministériels* rather than independent professionals. So far as remuneration goes, the old distinction between 'postulation' and 'plaidoirie' has been maintained. For purely procedural steps the 'nouvel avocat' receives payment in accordance with a fixed tariff just like the former *avoué*, but he can negotiate the honorarium for advice and pleading with his client just like the former *avocat*, without reference to any tariff.

The professional life of the attorney has been reformed in other major respects. Traditionally the French lawyer was a sole practitioner, a generalist able to deal with business of all kinds. Nowadays, however, thanks to economic and social developments in France as elsewhere, a client can only get proper advice from someone with specialist knowledge and expertise, which no attorney can possess in all areas of law at the same time. Furthermore, a modern attorney's office requires staff and equipment such as no sole practitioner could afford. There was thus an increasing need for new forms of co-operation between attorneys. A Law of 1954 allowed attorneys to form partnerships—this had previously been regarded as unprofessional—and a whole range of other forms of professional co-operation have been authorized by the reforms of 1971 and the subsequent decrees. Various forms of office-sharing are possible, as well as legal partnerships of the kind known in Germany, and one can even incorporate a company of attorneys (*société civile professionnelle*). Such a company has independent legal personality, its own firm name, and its own capital, but the personal liability of the attorneys who are members of it remains unlimited. All these forms of professional co-operation have been widely welcomed in France, especially in Paris (see PÉDAMON (above p. 123)).

The training of attorneys is in the hands of the venerable 'ordres d'avocats' or 'barreaux'. Wherever there is a Court of Appeal or a *tribunal de grande instance* there is a local Bar. They are quite independent, have their own disciplinary jurisdiction, and keep a close eye on the maintenance of professional standards of conduct. In order to be admitted as an 'avocat stagiaire' one must not only have completed his university studies and obtained a 'maîtrise en droit' but also have passed the examination for the 'certificat d'aptitude à la profession d'avocat' for which he can prepare while still at university by following courses jointly organized by the Faculty and the Bar. As an *avocat stagiaire* he spends three to five years working in the office of an attorney, during which time he may appear in court by himself, whether for a legal aid client or on the instructions of his supervising attorney, and takes part in the training sessions of a 'centre de formation professionnelle'. These are geared to practice, and emphasize the development of forensic rhetoric and the acquisition of professional skills. There is no examination at the end of this training period. On being inscribed in the list of members of the Bar he acquires the right to appear as *avocat* in any court in France except the Cour de Cassation and the Conseil d'État.

IV

One may often throw some light on the characteristic style of a legal system by asking which *type of lawyer* it regards as representative. France and Germany are alike in not having developed the type of the wise judge which other people find so remarkable in the Anglo-American systems. But France and Germany differ, if we are right, in that in France the representative type of lawyer is the *avocat*, the lawyer who pleads before the courts, while the ideal German lawyer is the learned Doctor Iuris, the trained scholar who is to be found in all legal careers, especially among professors, but among judges and barristers as well.

In France the lawyer most often in the public eye is the *avocat* with his brilliant oratory and his special prestige. Although the traditional view that the *avocat* has no monetary contractual relationship with his client is virtually without significance today, the social prestige of the *avocat* still rests on the belief that when he appears in court he comes not so much as the agent of a particular party as in the exercise of a kind of public office. There are historical reasons for the high reputation of the *avocat*, for he is the representative of the self-confident French bourgeoisie which emerged triumphant from the Revolution of 1789. From that Revolution, like the July Revolution of 1830, the French lawyer learnt that one has to fight for the rights of the individual not in the study, but in the forum, on the floor of Parliament, and in the halls of justice. This explains the public standing of the French *avocat* and his importance in French politics. For a long time one could justly say that the Parliament of France consisted half of mayors and half of advocates. Thus the revolutionary spirit of the French bourgeoisie has lived on in the advocate for two hundred years. It is true that like the French bourgeoisie, these advocates are by our standards today rather conservative, but theirs is a conservatism rooted in the belief that one should act with energy and commitment for the protection of freedom once won, for the maintenance of rights which have been earned, of 'droits acquis'. The German lawyer, on the other hand, is typical of a bourgeoisie which is the product of revolutions which failed to succeed or failed to occur. While the impression of the French Revolution and the War of Liberation was fresh the German lawyer was still ready enough to leap on the barricades—consider the dispute between Thibaut and Savigny—but after 1848 he withdrew from public life like the rest of the bourgeois intelligentsia. At the time, towards the beginning of the nineteenth century, when the lawyers in France were constructing the noble edifice of administrative law—especially through the jurisprudence of the Conseil d'État—to protect the freedoms of the citizens against high-handed intervention by the state, the German lawyer was turning to the meditative cultivation of private law, supposed to be 'unpolitical'. At the turn of the century in Germany lawyers who had theretofore abstained from public life and politics and had shut themselves up in the ivory tower of legal learning began to co-operate with the established powers; but this was the very time in France when the conscience of the nation was shocked by the Dreyfus affair. It is significant that ÉMILE ZOLA's famous article in *L'Aurore* of 13 Jan. 1898 started with the words: 'J'accuse . . . ' and continued in the style of a prosecutor's speech in court; this is a further indication of how the methods of thought and speech characteristic of the *avocat* are consciously used in France in the interests of maintaining the standards of law and morality in the public life of the nation.

One can also see marked differences when one asks which *legal virtues* are regarded as specially important in Germany and France. The ideal qualities of a German lawyer are expressed by ideas such as thoroughness, exactitude, learnedness, a strong tendency to tolerate academic disputes, the ability to construct concepts of law with which to master the variety of legal life. The French lawyer, especially the *avocat*, but also the judge, aims at clarity and brevity of expression, eloquence, style, effect, and form. This form is not something purely external, but structural in legal thought itself: 'La forme donne l'être à la chose.' French lawyers have no time for pedantry, for the 'querelles d'Allemand', for the urge to be right in trivia irrelevant to the solution of actual problems. The German lawyer, on the other hand, willingly dons the cloak of learning and is eager to widen his knowledge. This is immediately obvious when one compares the style of judgments of German and French courts. The superior German court gives reasons which are wide-ranging and loaded with citations like a textbook, while the French Court of Cassation goes in for lapidary 'whereas'-clauses. But the same conclusion follows from the characteristics of the legal language in the two countries. STENDHAL may, according to tradition, have read the Code civil frequently in order to improve his style, but one could hardly advise a German novelist to attend to the Prussian General Land Law or the BGB. Indeed, one has the impression that in France there is very little room for a special legal language and that the French legal writer is the equal of the great masters of the French novel in writing in a manner which is clear and unpretentious and often brilliantly elegant. Germany, on the other hand, has developed a specialist legal language in which obscurity too often rates as profundity and which, even when it is not pure jargon, still makes it more difficult for the intelligent citizen to know what is going on in the law than is really desirable for public faith in its activities.

This also helps to explain why in France, unlike Germany, legal studies are part of a *general education*, why the Frenchman regards a basic legal knowledge—as RENÉ DAVID writes (above p. 123, p. 46)—as an 'élément presque normal de la culture générale'. Many young people at French universities study law without having any intention of taking up a legal career: laws is not just the object of a special training but an area in which one can learn to think clearly, to express oneself lucidly, and to practise oratorical skills. The other side of the coin is that the teaching of law in France is often a matter of rarefied principle, of not being occupied with the practical question of finding the right legal solution for the problems of social reality. But to study law in this general, unpractical, and rather 'literary' manner is a way of furthering the education of young people who are not going to be lawyers. Therefore among educated Frenchmen one often meets with a certain familiarity with basic legal ideas. It may or may not be true, as one says, that the French peasant keeps a copy of the Code civil next to his Bible. But it does seem as if SOREL was right to say: 'There is, so far as I know, no other country where the private law has entered so deeply into the customs of the country, and forms so intimate a part of its intellectual, emotional and literary life' (*Livre du Centenaire du Code Civil* I (1904) p. xxxv).

10

The Legal Position of Illegitimate Children—A Distinctive Feature of the Style of the Romanistic Legal Family

COLOMBET/FOYER/HUET-WEILLER/LABRUSSE-RIOU, *La filiation légitime et naturelle* (1973).

HOLLEAUX, *De la filiation en droit allemand, suisse et français, Essai de droit comparé* (1966).

MADLENER, *Das französische Unehelichenrecht* (1969).

——, 'Das französische Familienrecht nach dem Gesetz vom 3.1.1972'. *FamRZ* 1972, 336.

MASSIP/MORIN/AUBERT, *La Réforme de la filiation* (3rd edn., 1979).

SAVATIER, *La Recherche de la paternité* (1927).

SCHMIDT-HIDDING, *Die Stellung des unehelichen Kindes in den romanischen Rechtsordnungen Europas, das sogenannte Anerkennungssystem und seine Abschwächungen* (1967).

FOR text, please see first edition, I. 123–32.

II. THE GERMANIC LEGAL FAMILY

11

The History of German Law

BOEHMER, *Grundlagen der bürgerlichen Rechtsordnung,* Book 2, Part. 1 *Dogmenge-schichtliche Grundlagen des bürgerlichen Rechts* (1951).
COING, *Epochen der Rechtsgeschichte in Deutschland* (1967).
KOSCHAKER, *Europa und das römische Recht* (2nd edn., 1953).
HANS SCHLOSSER, *Grundzüge der neueren Privatrechtsgeschichte* (4th edn., 1982).
THIEME, *Das Naturrecht und die europäische Privatrechtsgeschichte* (1947).
WESENBERG, *Neuere deutsche Privatrechtsgeschichte im Rahmen der europäischen Rechtsentwicklung* (2nd edn., rev. Wesener, 1969).
WIEACKER, *Privatrechtsgeschichte der Neuzeit* (2nd edn., 1967).

NOT everyone would agree that among the legal systems of Continental Europe, leaving aside Eastern Europe, a distinction should be drawn between a *Romanistic* and a *German* legal family. It is certainly true that the Romanistic and German legal families are much more closely related to each other than either of them is to the Common Law, but in our view this consideration does not by itself justify us in ignoring the important differences of style to be found in the Continental European systems. We have mentioned some of the differences already in Ch. 9, when we were comparing Germany and France, the representative systems of the German and Romanistic legal families, with regard to the style of their statutory language, the form of their judgments, and the type of jurist they see as characteristic. But the point and purpose of distinguishing these two legal families becomes much clearer if we also take historical development into account. It is for this reason that we shall say something about the history of German private law. What follows is in no way intended as an integral sketch of German legal history; for this purpose the reader should rely on authors of repute and consult, for example, the basic works of WIEACKER, WESENBERG, and KOSCHAKER. In line with the aim of this book, we shall here try briefly to tell the *foreign* reader in what characteristic points German legal history has diverged from that of the French–Romanistic systems and the English system. Since a different historical development may have a decisive influence on the modern character of a legal system, such a historical sketch can surely help us to understand the particular style which distinguishes the German from the Romanistic legal families today, and both of them from the systems based on the Common Law.

II

During the Middle Ages the whole of Europe came into contact with ancient civilization; the influence of Roman law as a part of ancient civilization was therefore felt throughout medieval Europe, England included. Certainly Roman law had a different impact at different times in different countries. When Germany came in contact with Roman law it was relatively late—not before the middle of the fifteenth century to any great extent, but its effects, which we call the 'reception of Roman law', were much greater in Germany than in France and enormously greater than in England. This contact meant not only a widespread acceptance of legal institutions and concepts of Roman law but also a much more extensive scientific systematization of legal thought than occurred elsewhere.

The reasons which gave the reception in Germany this particular character are to be found in the political situation in Germany after the Hohenstaufens. Central imperial power was weakened and the power of the territorial rulers and boroughs was correspondingly increasing. Though this decentralization of power had many consequences for German history, we cannot here inquire whether it was attributable to the Emperors' having overextended themselves in Italy to the neglect of the inner Empire, or because the defects in the German feudal system, as compared with France and England, made it incapable of producing a tight centralization of power. In any case it is certain that the reduction of imperial power in favour of the principalities was very conducive to the reception of Roman law, since because of it there was no common German private law, no common German courts system, and no common German fraternity of lawyers which could, as the examples of France and England show, have opposed and delayed the introduction of Roman law.

In the Germany of the Middle Ages there were no central political and judicial organs to lay the foundations of common German private law by pruning, rationalizing, and elaborating the traditional and very diverse laws of the various peoples and cities. In particular there were no strong central courts endowed with royal authority nor any group of royalist lawyers to make the effort to produce a unified private law for the Empire, a German common law. England had the royal courts in London, attended by an organized corporation of lawyers with great political influence; Paris was not only the seat of the French King and the royal organs and offices, but also the seat of the most important court in the land, so it was also the residence of the best judges, lawyers, and legal writers, who were eager to increase the King's influence since his interests coincided with their own; but in Germany the imperial power grew weaker and weaker while the power of the territorial rulers grew. The German King had no fixed abode and did his business on the move; there were no central administrative bodies, no staff of royal officials, no effective royal jurisdiction. It is true that there was the Reichshofgericht, which as the highest court of the Empire could in theory call up from the lower courts any case which had not been finally decided, and which acted as a court of appeal for all the regular courts of the Empire. But its influence was not very great since it was not wholly independent of the Emperor, its judges did not have tenure, and it did not even stay in the same place. Furthermore, the landed rulers had enough political power to exact privileges *de non evocando* and *de non appellando* which gravely reduced the jurisdiction of the Reichshofgericht. The Reichskammergericht with career judges and a fixed abode (originally in Frankfurt) was set up in 1495; but for the development of a common German private law 1495 was too late (see KOSCHAKER (above p. 138) 212 ff.).

The weakness of imperial power in Germany, the absence of a strong system of imperial justice, and the non-existence of an influential class of imperial jurists made it easier for the reception of Roman law to make its way in Germany, but this does not explain why Roman law came into Germany in the first place, why its entry was so triumphant, and why the local laws, variegated though they might be, seemed to be so unsatisfactory. The fact is that the legal methods developed by Germanic law became increasingly unsuited to the needs of the time. In the accepted view, the judge made his decisions on the basis of traditional legal knowledge, practical wisdom, experience, and practicality, and from an intuitive perception of what best answered the objective and concrete facts of the case. But such an irrational method of finding law, unreasoningly based on tradition, seemed increasingly incongruous as the social and economic circumstances of the later Middle Ages became more complex, variegated, and developed. There was thus a legal vacuum and Roman law flowed in, not because its rules were substantially better or juster than those of the traditional German law but because it offered a whole range of concepts and methods of thinking which enabled lawyers to grasp difficult factual problems, to place them in a rational framework, to see their implications, and to make them the object of reasoned argument. Had the indigenous law been collected, ordered, and rationalized by an organized group of judges and jurists, the categories of Roman law could have been used, as the French experience shows, to enrich it and make it suitable to the altered circumstances of the times, but in Germany the necessary social and political conditions just did not exist; the traditional law was still in a 'pre-scientific' stage, diverse and disorderly, so that instead of being harmoniously integrated into the local legal culture under the supervision of an organized class of lawyers, Roman legal ideas and institutions were adopted wholesale in many parts of the country and for many areas of law. A further factor was that

Roman law was not just another foreign law, but was the law of the *imperium romanum*, which could claim authority on the ground that the Holy Roman Empire of the Germans, as its name suggests, was the successor of the Roman Empire, and that the German Kaiser saw himself as the heir of the Roman Caesar (see the extensive development in KOSCHAKER (above p. 138) 70 ff., 113 ff.).

Jurists trained in Roman law were first employed in ecclesiastical institutions, the principalities, and the boroughs, but by the end of the fifteenth century they had increasingly taken the practice of law from the untrained practitioners and had themselves moved into judicial positions. At first, these jurists all obtained their legal education in the famous Law Faculties of North Italy, but later the German universities began to give regular courses in Roman law, at the instance of rulers eager to maintain their cadre of lawyers. In the course of the sixteenth and seventeenth centuries these lawyers, in their roles as law teachers in universities, as clerks to courts and cities, as writers of legal opinions, as legal advisers of rulers and boroughs, as draftsmen of the legal documents of principalities and towns, created the 'usus modernus pandectarum' out of the Roman law which had been received and the indigenous legal ideas which continued in force everywhere. Admittedly no unified German common private law was developed: the political impotence of the Empire and the manifold particularism of small and tiny principalities and cities made this impossible. While France under an energetic monarchy and a growing centralization could set about creating a 'droit français commun', in Germany it was only in a few large jurisdictions that any synthesis of the Roman and native laws was achieved, for example Saxony (CARPZOV, 1595–1666), the Baltic States (MEVIUS, 1609–70), and Württemberg (LAUTERBACH, 1618–78).

III

A decisive change occurred in the intellectual climate of Europe in the seventeenth century: that powerful march of mind called '*The Enlightenment*' sought to free the individual from his medieval shackles by subjecting the traditional authorities in religion, politics, law, and culture to rational criticism, and to make it possible for him to create a new view of the world on the basis of reason. The effects of this intellectual movement on the law were immense. It gave the lawyer a standpoint from which he could see his way through the *usus modernus pandectarum* with its variety of historically conditioned detail, purge it of obsolete legal institutions, and put it in a new systematic order. One particular product of the Enlightenment is the idea of *codification*, the idea that the diverse and unmanageable traditional law could be replaced by comprehensive legislation, consciously planned in a rational and transparent order. These new intellectual movements had quite different effects in different parts of Europe. *English* law was the least influenced, since it had been so stamped by historical experience and contemporary empiricism that it was very unreceptive to the ideal of a theoretical and unhistorical law of reason, such as was to be developed on the Continent. It is true that the codification of English law on a rational basis found a redoubtable champion in JEREMY BENTHAM (1748–1832), but the conceptual methods of legal thinking of the Enlightenment and the law of reason could never make headway against the sober, practised, and traditionalistic conservatism of the English lawyers, especially of the tightly organized class of judges and attorneys in the Inns of Court. In *France* it was different: here DOMAT and POTHIER had reviewed the traditional legal materials from the standpoint of the law of reason and had presented them in systematic form in influential books, with the result that in many areas of law the future draftsmen of the Code civil found fully fashioned rules ready for them to adopt. More important, however, and crucial for the French experience, was the fact that in France the ideas of the Enlightenment and the law of reason took the form of *direct political action* and led to the Revolution of 1789, to the overthrow of the *ancien régime*, to the constitution of a unitary state resting on the ideal of the equality of all citizens, and finally to the creation of a Civil Code, not *laid down* by an enlightened despot but, leaving aside the midwifery of NAPOLEON, *forced through* by a triumphant third estate.

In *Germany* it was different again: here the law of reason gradually broke loose from its roots in general philosophy and became a system of principles of private law to be taught and learnt. The great systematizers were PUFENDORF, THOMASIUS, and CHRISTIAN WOLF; by rigorous logical–mathematical deduction they inferred rules of increasing particularity from the most general principles of the law of reason and made the law appear as an artful and articulated system, orderly and comprehensible. A rational and abstract method of thought gradually came to predominate in the universities, often more concerned with the refinement of learned definitions and the construction of consistent systems than to keep in touch with social reality, of whose value the *usus modernus pandectarum*, for all that it was difficult, opaque, and obsolete, had had a greater sense. It was in this period that 'the German professor, with all his good and bad points, theoretical, unworldly and doctrinaire, entered the German faculties of law and . . . stamped them with the characteristics they have basically retained to this day' (KOSCHAKER (above p. 138) 249).

The ethereal intellectual constructions of the professors of the law of reason had no direct influence on German legal practice, but the German princes and their high officials, brought up in the spirit of the Enlightenment, found these new ideas very appealing; they became the intellectual stimulus for the many movements for reform in the eighteenth century which sought to humanize the practice of law in the German principalities and to free their legislation from the grip of Roman authorities. These attempts were not, as in France, the product of a passion for freedom and a tempestuous demand for reform by a large class of citizens, but came from the altruistic paternalism of enlightened authorities eager to perform their duty. The first of the codes of this period was the Codex Maximilianeus Bavaricus Civilis of 1756, written by the Bavarian Chancellor v. KREITTMAYR—a code which essentially contains the Bavarian variants of the *usus modernus pandectarum* but nevertheless clearly shows the contemporary legislator's belief in reason, for it solves long-contested questions in a reasonable manner and it is drafted in clear and pointed German. But, apart from the General Civil Code of Austria of which we shall speak in Ch. 13, the most important of the great codifications of the Age of Reason is the *General Land Law for the Prussian States*, which prevailed in the old Prussian territories of Germany from 1794 until the BGB came into force.

The first steps towards this Code took place early in the eighteenth century, but work on the project only began in earnest on the initiative of FREDERICK II, who in this venture was very much the pupil of the French *philosophes*. His men v. CARMER and SUAREZ impressed it with the spirit of the law of reason and the atmosphere of FREDERICK's special brand of enlightened absolutism. Its structure reflects the system of PUFENDORF who saw man as having a 'double nature', as an individual on the one hand, and on the other as a part of larger groups in society; thus the first part deals with the rules relating to the individual's property, and the second part with the individual's legal position in the various communities of which he was a part; here the Land Law deals with the legal position of the individual as member of a family, as member of a household (including the domestic staff), as member of associations or companies, as member of one of the various classes (burghers, farmers, nobility), and finally as a citizen of the state. The contrast with the radical egalitarianism of the Code civil will be immediately apparent, for the Land Law remains rooted in the class structure of FREDERICK's Prussia; this Code was not designed to alter society but to portray it faithfully, completely, and objectively so that everyone could be told in comprehensible if condescending language just where he stood in the state complex. There is no suggestion in the Code that the citizen in society should ever be free from the tutelage of the state or given the opportunity to create his own social world in a responsible manner: 'the real driving force [in the General Land Law] is the claim of an omnipotent administration to look into and regulate permanently and completely every detail of the life of its subjects' (KUNKEL, *SavZ/Rom.* 71 (1954) 534).

Given this passion for completeness and comprehensiveness and the enlightened wish to make the Code comprehensible, popular, and educational, the legislator had to abandon juristic and conceptual consistency and to adopt a style of language which was discursive and pedagogic; with so many individual rules the Code has about 17,000 paragraphs, and though practical and realistic in substance, and in style often quite striking and objective, the Code as a whole is extremely hard going, almost impossible for either professor or practitioner to master: KUNKEL (above p. 138) described it as a 'monstrous anti-intellectual undertaking', not only because of its mass of special cases but also because it kept the judges and the subjects of law in leading strings. We have already said that judges were threatened with punishment if they went in for any 'independent' construction and development of the statute, and that if they were in any doubt about the meaning of a provision they were to call on the Law Commission or the Minister of Justice (see above Ch. 7 II); it was consistent, then, to lay down in §6 of the Introduction that in judicial decisions thenceforth 'the opinions of legal writers or previous decisions of the courts will be ignored . . .'. The consequence was that the Land Law never attracted independent judicial or scholarly elaboration; must less was it capable of acting as a model for the unification of private law within Germany.

IV

As the eighteenth century gave way to the nineteenth and the codes of Prussia and Austria came into force, the star of the law of reason was already sinking. KANT's critique of perception had put paid to the optimistic hypothesis that human reason could discover generally valid ethical postulates. The law of reason had also forfeited its enlightening spirit of reform by compounding with the enlightened absolutism of Central Europe, often in statutory form; to the ambitious bourgeoisie of the nineteenth century it came to seem more and more the tool of territorial authoritarianism, a device for regulating the citizen's existence without allowing him any room for play. Rationalism was ousted by the new intellectual movements which now started. HERDER had made people see that cultural manifestations like poetry and language are not produced by abstract reason but evolve historically, as he thought, from the people who keep them in a process of constant change. The Romantic movement uncovered the elemental irrational powers in human life and dealt in concepts like 'people', 'development', 'soul', 'feeling', and 'sensibility'. At such a time it is not surprising that the optimistic rationalism of the Enlightenment should seem a dull placebo.

It was in this intellectual situation that the German *Historical School of Law* arose with FRIEDRICH CARL V. SAVIGNY, one of the great figures of German law, as its unquestioned head (1779–1861). In contrast to the Enlightenment view that the legal order is a deliberately planned and purposive creation of an official legislator guided by reason, SAVIGNY and the Historical School of Law saw law as a historically determined product of civilization, having its roots deep in the spirit of the people and maturing there in long processes. Like language, poetry, and religion, law is the product not of the formative reason of a particular legislator, but an organic growth, rather like a plant, of the 'inner secret powers' of the 'spirit of the people' working through history. For the adherents of the Historical School of Law all true law is customary law, developed, handed down, and captured in usage and manners; the law-bearers are the people and, as the people's representatives, the lawyers.

This root idea of the Historical School of Law emerged very clearly in the famous confrontation in 1814 between SAVIGNY and THIBAUT, a professor at Heidelberg, on the desirability of a unified German civil code. In the wave of patriotism which swept Germany after the Wars of Liberation THIBAUT had written a piece entitled 'Über die Nothwendigkeit eines allgemeinen bürgerlichen Rechts für Deutschland' in which he proposed to replace the intolerable diversity of the German territorial laws by a general German civil code, on the pattern of the Code civil, and thus to lay the basis for the political unification of Germany. At the time this proposal had no chance of bearing fruit, since the fall of NAPOLEON was followed immediately in Central Europe by the Restoration, and the dynasticism of the various German rulers rendered democratic integration of the whole of Germany and so the unification of German law very unlikely. But SAVIGNY's opposition, added to these unpropitious political circumstances, finally killed THIBAUT's proposals. In a polemical piece entitled 'Vom Beruf unsrer Zeit für Gesetzgebung und Rechtswissenschaft' SAVIGNY maintained that the time was not yet ripe for the production of a unified German civil code. He did not accept the Code civil and the Austrian Code as precedents; as a conservative, traditionalistic, and class-conscious aristocrat he found their egalitarian tendency and antihistorical rationalism quite repellent, and he criticized their faults of structure and substance very sharply, if somewhat superficially. SAVIGNY's basic view was that legislation, being inorganic and unscientific, was not the right way to create a common German law and would do violence to the traditions it opposed; what was needed in his view was a thorough absorption and cultivation of the legal material which was to hand, as it had grown through time, a task he would entrust to an 'organically progressive legal science which would be common to the whole nation'.

Since for SAVIGNY all law was the product of history, he and his followers concentrated on the historical development of law. In this, SAVIGNY realized that the *Germanic* sources of law had played a great part, and consequently he insisted on the study of *this* aspect of legal historical development and thereby greatly stimulated the study of Germanic law in Germany. But he and his followers turned exclusively to *Roman* law, not in the form it had taken in the Middle Ages or in the *usus modernus pandectarum* but in the form of *ancient* Roman law as it appeared in the Corpus Iuris. It was rather inconsistent of them to give this preference to Roman law in its original form since in the programme of the Historical School of Law *all* the forces which had had effects on German legal history must be equally entitled to attention. The real reason was that SAVIGNY accepted the educational principles of contemporary humanism and adopted the aesthetic ideas of classicism, just as WINCKELMANN had done for the plastic arts and GOETHE for poetry; for him, therefore, the highest educational value resided in a return to the purity and truth of ancient law. This idealization of Roman law led SAVIGNY and, to an even greater extent, his followers to the thoroughly unhistorical view that the legal forms and institutions created by the Romans belonged to a higher and purer conceptual world and possessed a sort of eternal validity. They did not recognize or did not admit the fact that even in Roman times law was simply a means to the end of a rational ordering of communal life and thus must be seen as dependent on the changing social, economic, and cultural conditions of Roman society. Instead they thought that the Corpus Iuris placed at their disposal a store of legal institutions of eternal validity which could be put to direct use as valid law, if only they were set in the right order. Accordingly SAVIGNY and his followers, from PUCHTA to WINDSCHEID, addressed themselves to schematizing, ordering, and integrating the concepts of Roman law; so it was that the Historical School of Law produced the *Pandectist School* whose only aim was the dogmatic and systematic study of Roman material. Their method of treatment was once again marked by that exaggerated dogmatism which we noted in the period of the law of reason, save that it was directed to rules of Roman law rather than particular postulates supposedly grounded in reason. For them the legal system was a closed order of institutions, ideas, and principles developed from Roman law: one only had to apply logical or 'scientific' methods in order to reach the solution of any legal problem. In this way the application of law became a merely 'technical' process, a sort of mathematics obeying only the 'logical necessity' of abstract concepts and having nothing to do with practical reason, with social value-judgments, or with ethical, religious, economic, or policy considerations. No matter how urgently commerce might demand that a claim should be assignable without the co-operation of the debtor, that a debt should be capable of being taken over by a third party, or that a contract should be enforceable by a third party, if such a legal construction could not be arrived at with the devices present in the legal system, then it was 'logically impossible' and the devil might take the hindmost. A method of legal thinking which put 'conceptual calculus' before the careful observation of social reality could only arise in a legal culture which was dominated by remote and theorizing professors and which lacked an organized and powerful class of practising lawyers such as had contributed in France to the development of a unified code whose merits were everywhere recognized, or such as had helped to maintain in England the traditional stock of juristic techniques. But in Germany at the time there was neither a unified private law nor a centralized judiciary, there was no class of practising lawyers bound together by professional solidarity, and the integration of legal life on the *political* and *practical* levels was delayed by the unbroken influence of powerful territorial rulers until late in the nineteenth century. In such a situation the Pandectist School could at least claim for itself that by producing a method of studying law which was common to the whole of Germany it had brought about integration at the *theoretical* level. The pandectists created a set of clear and clearly distinguished concepts which contributed much to the technical sophistication of the BGB, and which had a considerable effect abroad as well, because of the Roman legal materials on which it was grounded. But they did not bother to seek out the real forces in legal life, and they did not ask what ethical, practical, or social justification for their principles there might be; consequently much of what they wrote is hairsplitting pedantry and legal spillikins. This has admittedly been recognized for some time, yet these methods of conceptual jurisprudence are still at work behind the scenes in Germany. As is especially evident to comparative lawyers, trained by their ecumenical experience to be sceptical of the dogmatisms of particular nations, the situation today is that while no one has a good word to say for conceptual jurisprudence lawyers in Germany are still a very long way from adopting in their everyday activity a method of solving problems which is related to their factual content.

V

The first moves towards the codification of unified German private law occurred about the middle of the nineteenth century. The pacemakers were the internationally significant topics of commercial law and the law of negotiable instruments. The law of negotiable instruments was unified in 1848 by the Wechselordnung, and commercial law by the General German Commercial Code of 1861; both enactments were gradually adopted word for word by all the states of the Deutscher Bund. Work also began with the unification of general private law. In 1865 a draft of the law of obligations (Dresdner Entwurf) was produced by a team of famous professors and judges; this pure pandectist production was later to serve as a model for the law of obligations in the BGB. After BISMARCK's efforts had led to the creation of the Empire in 1871, the first priorities were unification of the courts system, civil procedure, and bankruptcy; the ensuing 'Reichsjustizgesetze' which came into force in 1879 are still law in West Germany today, though they have been altered in many particulars. Under the Imperial Constitution central legislative competence in private law was limited to the law of obligations, commerce, and negotiable instruments, but in 1873 on the proposal of the National Liberal members LASKER and MIQUEL this was extended to the whole of private law; this was the signal for work to start on the codification of German private law, work which was to last for more than twenty years.

In 1874 a *First Commission* was appointed and charged with producing a draft. It had eleven members, including six judges, three officials from the Ministry, and two professors (though no practising lawyer); the leading figures were probably GOTTLIEB PLANCK, a prominent judge also famous as a liberal politician, and BERNHARD WINDSCHEID, the most outstanding pandectist professor of his day. The Commission did its work in seclusion, without any contact with representatives of commerce or other social groups, and thirteen years later, in 1887, published a First Draft with supporting 'Motive'. A storm of criticism broke out. In addition to a host of suggestions for improvements on points of detail, there were attacks of principle. There was general objection to its unduly scholastic structure, largely attributable to the abstract conceptualism of the Pandectist School, as well as to the legal jargon in which it was drafted, accurate and precise at the cost of clarity and comprehensibility, and finally to its unduly complicated system of cross-referencing. The criticism of OTTO V. GIERKE made a great impression; in a very spirited attack he took exception to the Draft for bypassing many legal traditions of Germanic origin which were still vital among the German people, and for ousting the traditional ethical obligations and relationships of trust in family and society in favour of an extreme and impersonal individualism. The objections of ANTON MENGER, a Viennese academic socialist, were even more pointed, though not much notice was taken at the time; his book on *Das bürgerliche Recht und die besitzlosen Volksklassen* (1891) showed how the principle of freedom of contract could lead to the suppression of the socially weaker classes because the socially stronger could dictate the terms of contracts, and how the institutions of private property and succession guaranteed to the propertied classes, who alone benefited from them, the perpetuation of their power of controlling the means of production. These criticisms had no great practical effect. It is true that the *Second Commission* which was called into being in 1890 included a few laymen (one bank director, one chief forester, a professor of national economy, and no less than three of the landed gentry!), and that their labours were more public than those of the First Commission. But the alterations made by the Second Commission, necessary and insufficient though they were, were mainly to the *language* of the draft; in substance they added only a few 'drops of socialist oil' to the soulless individualism of the First Draft. The Second Draft with its 'Protokolle' was published in 1895, passed through the legislative process with a few relatively insubstantial alterations, and was adopted in the summer of 1896 by the Reichstag, only the Social Democrats voting against. At the Emperor's personal request, the date of entry into force was set for 1 Jan. 1900; the new century was to have a brilliant start.

12

The German Civil Code

BOEHMER, *Einführung in das bürgerliche Recht* (2nd edn., 1965) 65 ff.
COING, 'Erfahrungen mit einer bürgerlich-rechtlichen Kodifikation in Deutschland', *Zvgl RW* 81 (1982) 1.
DIEDERICHSEN, 'Die Industriegesellschaft als Herausforderung an das bürgerliche Recht', *NJW* 1975, 1801.
DÖLLE, *Vom Stil der Rechtssprache* (1949).
——, 'Das Bürgerliche Gesetzbuch in der Gegenwart', in: *Fünfzigjahrfeier des deutschen Bürgerlichen Gesetzbuches* (ed. Nipperdey, 1950) 14 ff.
ESSER, 'Gesetzesrationalität im Kodifikationszeitalter und heute', in: Vogel, *100 Jahre oberste deutsche Justizbehörde, Vom Reichsjustizamt zum Bundesministerium der Justiz* (1977) 13.
R. GMÜR, *Das schweizerische Zivilgesetzbuch verglichen mit dem deutschen Bürgerlichen Gesetzbuch* (1965).
HEDEMANN, 'Fünfzig Jahre Bürgerliches Gesetzbuch', *JR* 1950, 1.
ISELE, 'Ein halbes Jahrhundert deutsches Bürgerliches Gesetzbuch', *AcP* 150 (1949) 1.
LAUFS, 'Beständigkeit und Wandel—80 Jahre deutsches BGB', *JuS* 1981, 853.
RABEL, 'Zum 25. Geburtstag des Bürgerlichen Gesetzbuchs', *DJZ* 26 (1921) 515, reprinted in: Rabel, *Gesammelte Aufsätze* I (ed. Leser, 1965) 389.
——, 'The German and the Swiss Civil Codes', 10 *La. L. Rev.* 265 (1950).
F. SCHMIDT, 'The German Abstract Approach to Law, Comments on the System of the Bürgerliches Gesetzbuch', 1965 *Scand. Stud. L.* 131.
ANDREAS B. SCHWARZ, *Das schweizerische Zivilgesetzbuch in der ausländischen Rechtsentwicklung* (1950).
——, 'Einflüsse deutscher Zivilistik im Auslande', in: *Symbolae friburgenses in honorem Ottonis Lenel* (1935) 425 ff.
WIEACKER, *Privatrechtsgeschichte der Neuzeit* (2nd edn., 1967) 468 ff.

I

CODES of private law are stamped by the particular historical situation in which they are produced. Many codes consolidate the results of a recent reconstruction of society; their advantage is that the idea of man and the model of society which inspired them may be expected to remain valid for a considerable period. Other codes, by contrast, are created at a time of relative social and political stability; their spirit is often retrospective and reflective, seeking to maintain a situation favourable to the establishment. The German BGB is one of these rather conservative codes: RADBRUCH said that it is more 'the cadence of the nineteenth than the upbeat to the twentieth century', and

ZITELMANN observed (*DJZ* 1900, 3) that 'rather than boldly anticipating the future it prudently sums up the past'. The Code does indeed accurately reflect the society of BISMARCK's Empire. The chief role in the state at that time was played by a liberal *grande bourgeoisie* which had produced the imperial German nationstate by co-operating with the conservative powers of authoritarian Prussia. It was the day of a marked liberalism in economics, of the belief that the general good would spontaneously ensue from the interplay of economic forces provided that the state did not interfere. In the 1870s and 1880s, admittedly, some movements towards social justice, paternalistic though they were, led to the enactment of provisions to protect workmen and to the impressive statutory construction of a social insurance system. But in private law these progressive tendencies made no headway; private lawyers were so concerned with positivistic exegesis that they either did not see or deliberately blinded themselves to the great social challenges of the time which any onlooker with insight could easily see. For example, the draftsmen of the BGB seem to have taken no notice of the great social change which was occurring in Germany in the final decades of the nineteenth century; commerce and industry were becoming much more important economically than farming, and urban populations were expanding rapidly, especially with industrial workers. Yet for the BGB the typical citizen is not the small artisan or the factory worker but rather the moneyed entrepreneur, the landed proprietor, and the official, people who can be expected to have business experience and sound judgment, capable of succeeding in a bourgeois society with freedom of contract, freedom of establishment, and freedom of competition, and able to take steps to protect themselves from harm.

II

In language, method, structure, and concepts the BGB is the child of the deep, exact, and abstract learning of the German Pandectist School with all the advantages and disadvantages which that entails. Not for the BGB the simple common sense of the Austrian General Civil Code, the clear and popular style of the Swiss Code, or the sprung diction of the Code civil, instinct with the ideal of equality and freedom among citizens. The BGB is not addressed to the citizen at all, but rather to the professional lawyer; it deliberately eschews easy comprehensibility and waives all claims to educate its reader; instead of dealing with particular cases in a clear and concrete manner it adopts throughout an abstract conceptual language which the layman, and often enough the foreign lawyer as well, finds largely incomprehensible, but which the trained expert, after many years of familiarity, cannot help admiring for its precision and rigour of thought. The concepts used by the draftsmen— 'Verfügung', 'Vollmacht', 'Einwilligung', 'unverzüglich', 'in gutem Glauben', and many others—are always used in exactly the same sense. Sentence construction indicates where burden of proof lies, and repetitions are avoided by means of cross-references to amplifying sections. But the BGB has none of the elegance and rich compactness of the Code civil, none of its epigrammatical pith and suppressed passion; instead, in deference to accuracy, clarity, and completeness it often goes in for a prim Chancery style, complex syntax, and rather Gothic cumbrousness, even where it would have been easy enough to hit upon more lively and clearer words. The BGB, then, is no work of literature, but 'the legal calculating machine par excellence' (A. B. SCHWARZ, *Das schweiz. ZGB* (above p. 149) 8), 'legal filigree work of extraordinary precision' (ISELE (above p. 149) 6), 'perhaps the code of private law with the most precise and logical legal language of all time' (GMÜR (above p. 149) 28). In France, Austria, and Switzerland ordinary citizens may have a feeling of warm affection, of closeness to their Code; in Germany not even the lawyer does; instead, the undeniable technical merits of the BGB exact a cool, even grudging, admiration.

Following the divisions arrived at the Pandectist School, the BGB has five books, each devoted to a different subject matter. Two of these areas deal with questions related at the factual level: *Family Law* (Book IV) and the *Law of Succession* (Book V). The *Law of Property* (Book III) and the *Law of Obligations* (Book II) concern 'iura in rem' and 'iura in personam' respectively, a conceptual division derived from Roman law. Thus the *law of property* deals with 'real rights' which a person enjoys *in respect of a particular thing* and can assert against *all the world*, such as ownership, mortgage, usufruct, and pledge. In the *law of obligations*, on the other hand, we are concerned with 'personal' rights, which give one person a claim against another *particular person* on the basis of contract, unjustified enrichment, or tort. This division makes for clarity of thought but it has the consequence that rules governing a single transaction may be placed in widely separated parts of the Code, while provisions closer together may concern quite distinct factual problems. For example, it is obvious to the Anglo-American lawyer for the 'law of sale' should deal not only with the question whether and when the purchaser can demand delivery of the goods he has agreed to buy, but also with the question whether and when the ownership in those goods passes to him. In contrast, the BGB deals with the first of these questions in the law of obligations (§§433 ff.) and with the second a long way away in the law of property (§§929 ff.). The Anglo-American follows the view that all aspects of a unitary transaction should be dealt with in the same place in the system, while the German lawyer recognises that since ownership in things may pass not only by a reason of a sale but also by *gift* or *exchange*, it conduces to the orderly and rational disposition of the law to give unitary treatment to the passing of ownership as a whole.

Contrariwise, a common lawyer cannot see much affinity between the law of sale and the law of tort; even in the lecture-room he treats them as quite independent areas of law. For the BGB, a common characteristic of sale and tort is that they both afford one person a right 'to claim something' from another, so that both matters are dealt with in the law of obligations and still form part of the same course of instruction.

These four books on Obligations, Property, Family Law, and Succession are preceded by a book with the title 'General Part' (*Allgemeiner Teil*)—a legacy of the Pandectist School whose value to the BGB has been gravely doubted. The General Part does not contain general rules about the exercise of rights in society (see art. 2 ZGB) or basic principles of the construction of statutes, customary law, the powers of the judge, or burden of proof (see art. 1 ZGB, 1 ff. Codice civile), which would have been perfectly sensible and indeed desirable. Instead, the General Part sets out to expound certain basic institutions common to the whole of private law which the lawyer meets with in the law of obligations as well as the law of property, family law, and the law of succession. As GUSTAV BOEHMER said, these matters are 'factored out'. It was thought that this would make for greater logical compactness and internal economy in the Code and would avoid tiresome repetitions. The legal institutions which appear in the General Part were not invented by the draftsmen of the BGB; they were taken over from the learned pandectists of the nineteenth century who distilled them from particular cases by means of a long and wearisome process of increasing generalization. Here are to be found general provisions concerning 'natural persons' (capacity, majority, interdiction, domicile) and 'legal persons', ending with a detailed regulation of the law of juristic entities and foundations, not really suitable for a 'General' Part, followed by some definitions appertaining to the law of property, and finally general rules about 'legal acts' and prescription. Much of this material is in the General Part only because of an exaggerated passion for abstraction: the provisions on 'natural persons' (§§1 ff.) and on 'things' (§§90 ff.) could simply have been included in family law and property law respectively. The idea of 'legal act' is also far too abstract a notion (see vol. II, Ch. 1 I). For the German scholar, 'legal act' includes not only the normal type of contract such as sale or lease and also the so-called 'real contract', namely that special agreement needed in German law to transfer a real right or create a real right over another's property (see Ch. 15 of the first edition), but it also includes the contract of family law, such as the contract of adoption or the agreement made by bride and bridegroom before the registrar at the marriage ceremony, and even includes the making of a will, the giving of notice to terminate or to rescind a contract, as well as, for example, the resolution to increase a company's capital made by a formal meeting of its shareholders. Although legal declarations of such diverse sources and significance fall within the concept of 'legal act', the BGB enacts rules about voidabilty on the grounds of error, deceit, or duress, about agency, conditions, and so on, which it solemnly asserts to be applicable to *all* legal acts of whatever type. This extreme position has proved an inexhaustible source of controversy about the range of application of these general rules. In fact it was only the normal contracts which the draftsmen of §§116 ff. BGB had in mind, and so the provisions we have mentioned apply only to *this* type of legal act; it would therefore be preferable to have the rules on voidability on the ground of error, deceit, and duress, rules about agency and so on, contained in the *law of contract* and to direct the judge to apply these rules, if really applicable, to other kinds of legal declarations, deeds or relationships as well (as in art. 7 ZGB, 1324 Codice civile, §876 ABGB). Of course it makes no difference for the practical operation of law where in the Code the concept of domicile is defined, where agency is regulated, or where one finds the rules which determine when a contract may be rescinded for fraud: the judge or lawyer who knows his way around the Code will find the applicable paragraphs (and also, through the commentaries, the relevant judicial decisions) regardless of the internal 'correctness' of their location in the system. But the abstract conceptual calculus of the General Part may still mislead the novice, and sometimes the practising lawyer as well, by suggesting that the correct solution of a living problem depends more on being able to classify it correctly than on seeing and understanding all its factual aspects.

For German discussions of the merits and demerits of the General Part, see WIEACKER (above p. 149) 486 ff.; A. B. SCHWARZ, *Das schweiz. ZGB* (above p. 149) 25 ff.; BOEHMER (above p. 149) 68 ff.; KOSCHAKER, *Europa und das römische Recht* (2nd edn., 1953) 279 ff.; all these contain further references. For the criticisms of a Swedish lawyer, see FOLKE SCHMIDT (above p. 149).

More than anything else, the general theories elaborated by the German pandectists and the General Part of the BGB which rests on their achievements have exercised a particular fascination on foreigners. We have already seen the effect of these doctrines on *Italian* law (see above Ch. 8 IV) and will shortly see their importance for *Austrian* and *Swiss* law. In *France* also the General Part has had a strong influence, principally through the mediation of RAYMOND SALEILLES, a pioneer of comparative law; his two influential works on the general law of obligations in the BGB and on the theory of the declaration of will induced the authors of French textbooks on private law to break away from the structure of the Code civil and present 'general theories' such as we find in equivalent German books. In England the teaching of the pandectists had very little effect. This is hardly surprising since England had always denied admission to Roman institutions and methods of thought: English lawyers, if only to secure their professional monopoly by keeping the law obscure, blocked any attempts to rationalize the concepts and structure of their law. German teaching did have a great influence on a few professors of law, especially JOHN AUSTIN (1790–1859), the acknowledged founder of 'jurisprudence', the legal discipline known in Germany as 'Allgemeine

Rechtslehre'. After profound study of the Civil Law and its theoretical foundations he declared that an English jurist who can get to the Continent to study law 'escape[s] from the empire of chaos and darkness to a world that seems by comparison the region of order and light' (*Lectures on Jurisprudence* (5th edn., 1885) 58). Other famous Anglo-American jurists such as HOLLAND, SALMOND, ANSON, POLLOCK, and MAITLAND were also familiar with German pandectist teaching and used their knowledge of those methods in their textbooks on 'jurisprudence' and the 'law of contract'. MAITLAND's observation when the BGB came into force shows that these English lawyers recognized the intellectual merits of German pandectism; he said that it was 'the best code that the world has yet seen'; 'never, I should think, has so much first-rate brain power been put into an act of legislation'.

On the influences of German private legal scholarship abroad, see ANDREAS B. SCHWARZ, 'Einflüsse deutscher Zivilistik im Auslande' (above p. 149) 471, from which the citations from MAITLAND are taken.—The Civil Codes of *Brazil* and *Portugal* have followed the BGB in having a General Part, though with many deviations (see above p. 112); the same is true of the *Greek* and *Japanese* Codes (see below Ch. 12 IV, Ch. 28 II), and the new Civil Code of the *Netherlands* also follows the German model to a limited extent (see above Ch. 8 II). During the work on the reform of the Code civil in France which started after the Second World War but has since been abandoned there was much discussion of the question whether the new code should have a 'Livre préliminaire' containing at least the rules concerning the 'acte juridique'; see *Travaux de la Commission de réforme du Code civil* (1945/1946) 97 ff. and (1946/1947) 229 ff.; also *Travaux de l'Association Henri Capitant* I (1945) 73 ff. The outcome was an agreement to have a 'livre préliminaire' containing only the rules of conflicts of law in time and space; the doctrine of legal acts was to be contained in a special Book IV ('des actes et des faits juridiques'), to follow the first three books on Persons, Succession, and Property. See JULLIOT DE LA MORANDIÈRE in: *Avant-projet du Code civil* (ed. Ministère de la Justice, 1955) 25 ff.—The General Part was *not* adopted in *Switzerland* or *Italy*.—On the whole question see IONESCU, 'Le Problème de la partie introductive du Code civil', *Rev. int. dr. comp.* 19 (1967) 579.

III

Given that the BGB is impregnated with the legal values of bourgeois liberalism and is thus, to use an expression of RADBRUCH, 'more cadence of the nineteenth century than the upbeat of the twentieth', how has it been able, without fundamental revision, to survive the political, economic, and social crises and catastrophes of recent German history, including the period of total perversion of law under Hitler? Here we can make only a few observations about the development of the law of contract and delict, and of family law.

The *law of contract* in the BGB is unequivocally dominated by the bourgeois idea that contracting parties are formally free and equal. This idea expresses itself in the legal principles of freedom of contract and the duty to respect contracts: on the one hand, everyone—servant as well as master, consumer as well as manufacturer—is entitled to decide, freely and on his own responsibility, what contracts to enter and on what terms; on the other hand, contracts so formed must be adhered to in all cases, precisely because they arose from the free decision of reasonable contracting parties of sound judgment. Only a few marginal rules seek to protect those for whom the freedom of contract is nugatory, as being economically inferior to the other contracting party or dependent on him in some other way: thus contracts are void under §138 BGB if they are *contra bonos mores* or if one party has exploited the plight, inexperience, or lack of judgment of the other. In addition, contractual penalties may be modified by the court if they are unduly high (§343 BGB). Yet the tenant receives virtually no special protection, and the section on the contract of employment contains only a few rules requiring the 'person entitled to the services' to see to the safety of the place of work and to provide sick-pay within limits.

These few 'drops of oil' have proved to be quite inadequate. As the bourgeois state of the nineteenth century gave way to the social democracy of our own time, legislator and judge alike have had to qualify and limit the liberal principles of the law of contract wherever they gave one party power to threaten those basic conditions of decent life which the social state of today must guarantee to its citizens. Where, as often happened, the interlocking rules of the BGB afforded no sufficient basis on which the legal power of the individual might be modified in the interests of social morality, development had to take the form of creating important areas of law *outside* the Code. This happened in the law of competition and monopolies, in the law of housing, landlord and tenant, and agricultural holdings, but most of all in the law of employment. The draftsmen of the BGB simply did not see the great problem of how to regulate the situation of dependent labourers; indeed they adopted an anti-labour, almost a police-state position, since they deliberately gave trade unions the legal form of the 'corporation without legal personality' with the quite unsatisfactory consequence that trade unions could not even sue in their own name. (But see now BGHZ 42, 210; 50, 325.) Here the *legislator* stepped in and produced a fundamental change by means of provisions concerning security of employment, worker participation, minimum rates of pay, and so on, but the *courts* also without much statutory basis imposed on the employee a general duty of fidelity and on the employer a general duty of care for the safety and welfare of his employees and a duty to treat them equally, principles which are used today to solve the very great variety of concrete problems which may arise out of the contract of employment. Thus developed the great mass of *labour law*, largely independent of the provisions of the BGB which were inadequate, incomplete, and old-fashioned even in 1900.

But this tendency to emphasize the mutuality of social responsibility has led to extremely significant legal developments even in the area of private contractual law. This 'moralization' of contractual relations was made possible by the famous 'general clause' of §242 BGB, which is still much relied on today. That clause simply says in quite general terms that everyone must perform his contract in the manner required by good faith (*Treu und Glauben*) in view of the general practice in commerce, yet the courts, left more or less in the lurch by the draftsmen, have had to rely on it in order to solve the extremely important economic and social problems which arose after the First World War with the collapse of the economy, inflation, and revaluation, and after the Second World War from the loss of East Germany and the change of currency. The rigorous individualism of the original contract law of the BGB has been qualified by means of devices developed by the courts, with names such as 'clausula rebus sic stantibus', 'collapse of the basis of the transaction' (see vol. II, Ch. 14), 'improper exercise of rights', 'venire contra factum proprium' and 'Verwirkung' (forfeiture of right, especially by laches). The courts long used §242 BGB in order to control the content of General Conditions of Business: standard terms excluding or limiting one party's liability were invalidated as inconsistent with good faith if 'they are inequitable on a balancing of the interests of those who typically enter such transactions' (BGH NJW 1963, 99, 100; for the actual position today see vol. II, Ch. I III 1). Thus the general clause of §242 BGB has proved a splendid device for adapting the law of contract to the changed social and moral attitudes of society. HEDEMANN has called this 'the flight into the general clauses' and though the development was inevitable, it is true that it runs the risk of producing judicial decisions which are undirected, exuberant, and variable. Legal writers here have an important and responsible task, to put some order into the variety of cases so that they may be surveyed, learnt, and mastered, to reveal and criticize the value-judgments of the courts, and so to produce some degree of certainty in the law even where the general clauses and legal institutions they engender are being applied.

The *tort* law of the BGB still rests on the principle of liability for fault. So far as compensation for *accidents* is concerned, this principle has been greatly weakened both by statute and by judicial decision. There are special statutes for important types of accidents which grant the victim compensation for his loss without his having to prove any fault in the defendant. These cover industrial accidents, railway accidents, traffic accidents, aircraft accidents, and accidents in electricity, gas, and nuclear power stations, as well as many others. But the general principle of liability for fault has also been altered in response to the growing need to protect large sections of the community from the distress and impoverishment which an accident may cause: here the courts have greatly improved the victim's position in many ways—by vastly extending the duty of care, by treating the mere facts as evidence of fault, or even by openly reversing the burden of proof and sabotaging §831 BGB (see vol. II, Ch. 18 II)—to such a degree indeed that it is not easy in practice to distinguish between liability for fault and strict liability. This development was made very much easier because *insurance*, now much more widely used by the public and often required by law, provides a device for spreading individual losses among the community at large and so diminishes the chance that a defendant held liable in damages will be personally ruined. Apart from the case of accidents, the principle of fault still applies in full force to compensation for material and immaterial harms. The courts have gradually extended protection against intentional and negligent invasions to some interests which the draftsmen of the BGB did not see fit to protect: here one may mention interests of personality and the so-called 'right in an established and active trade or business' (see the full treatment in vol. II, Ch. 7 II, Ch. 20 II).

In *family law* also the BGB originally bore the marks of the conservative and patriarchal age of the bourgeoisie. It was for the husband to make decisions during the marriage and it was the husband who exercised parental power. The rules of matrimonial property were devised on the basis of the prevailing practice among the classes of officers and officials that the spouses brought to the marriage an interest-bearing capital sum which was to be administered by the husband. The rules of divorce and illegitimacy were influenced by Christian morality. Accordingly, the BGB used to permit divorce only when the breakdown of the marriage was attributable to the fault or insanity of the defendant spouse. In comparison with legitimate children illegitimate children were deliberately disfavoured, for fear that extramarital adventures, which the law discountenanced, might otherwise be legalized and that immorality and undesirable concubinage might be encouraged. An illegitimate child was treated in law as unrelated to his father; instead he was fobbed off with a claim for maintenance whose amount depended on his *mother*'s social position and which came to an end when he was 16.

Most of the work of bringing family law into line with altered social and economic circumstances has been done by the legislature, through the only really deep incisions which have been made in the text of the Code. The work of reform after the Second World War received a striking impetus from the Basic Law which provides that men and women should have equal rights and that all rules of private law inconsistent with this principle should cease to have effect on 31 March 1953 (see art. 3 par. 2, 117 GG). The legislature, however, allowed this date to go by without taking any action, so there was a lacuna in the law which had to be filled by the courts. Four years elapsed before the Law of Equal Rights of Man and Woman came into force in 1957; it made important alterations in private law, some of which had been anticipated by judicial decision. Thus in *matrimonial property* law the statutory régime is to be one of separate property, with the modification that acquisitions by the spouses during the marriage are to be divided between them; on *divorce* the proceeds are to be divided equally between the spouses, while if the marriage is dissolved by *death*, the surviving spouse's statutory right of succession is proportionately increased (the so-called property regime of 'community of acquisition'). The draftsmen of the Law of Equal Rights decided to maintain the husband's priority in regard to the exercise of *parental power* (called *parental care* since 1979) and especially the right to be the *statutory representative* of his children, only to be told by the Federal Constitutional Court that such a provision was void as being inconsistent with Art. 3 GG (BVerfG NJW 1959, 1483). The legal position of *illegitimate children* has been decisively improved by a law which came into force in 1970, also pursuant to express constitutional mandate (see art. 6 par. 5 GG). The preconditions and consequences of *divorce* are now determined by a Law of 1976. This Law abandons the principle of fault and adopts the principle of breakdown of the marriage, for it declares that a marriage may be dissolved 'when it has collapsed' (§1565 BGB). The fault of the parties is in general equally irrelevant for the *consequences* of divorce, especially with regard to the validity and extent of a claim for maintenance. An important innovation deals with the adjustment of pension rights and rights to other benefits (*Versorgung*): if during the marriage one spouse has acquired greater rights of this sort than the other, the latter is to receive one half of the difference. This is done by creating new entitlements in the disadvantaged party (and proportionally diminishing those of the partner) carrying an independent personal claim against the body liable to provide the benefit or pension in the future. Furthermore, the law of adoption was reconstructed by an enactment in 1976, and the law of parental care by a Law of 1979. Indeed, there is hardly a paragraph in family law that is recognizably the same as in 1900.

Despite this, the structure of the BGB, taken by and large, looks very much the same as it did eighty years ago, for all the intervening changes in economic and social conditions since then. In part this is explained by the fact that areas of law which were developing very rapidly have assumed an independent existence outside the BGB but many areas of law, especially family law, have been greatly altered and modernized by intervening *legisation*. Still, the maintenance of the general structure of the BGB is really the work of the *courts*, whose performance in fitting the original text of the code to modern demands and keeping it socially vital has been as significant as it has often been misunderstood. In the result, whole parts of the BGB, just as of the Code civil, are covered by a heavy gloss of judicial decision, often to the point where a mere reading of the text will not disclose the law as it actually is. But while in France it was the gaps and technical imperfections of the Code civil which gave the judges their opportunity to develop the law, the courts in Germany have relied above all on the general clauses of §§138, 157, 242, and 826 BGB. These general clauses have operated as a kind of safety valve, without which the rigid and precise terms of the BGB might have exploded under the pressure of social change.

But now we must ask whether this increasing divergence between the rules in the Code and the rules of the actual law is still acceptable. Certain types of contract and heads of liability which are vital for the citizen receive no mention at all in the BGB; contracts of other types are hived off in special laws which can fall outside the purview of commentators and scholars; in many areas judge-made law has become so predominant that the foundation of codal texts could be withdrawn without any risk of having the edifice collapse. This is why the Ministry of Justice is considering redrafting the law of obligations in the BGB with a view to bringing it back into touch with modern legal practice. On this see the *Reports and Proposals for the Remoulding of the Law of Obligations* (2 vols., ed. Federal Ministry of Justice, 1981), and the comments of WOLF and DIEDERICHSEN, *AcP* 182 (1982) 80 and 101.

IV

In the course of the nineteenth century the Historical School of Law and the Pandectist School exerted an influence which reached far beyond the boundaries of Germany and gave new life to legal theory in many European countries, especially Italy, France, and Austria, but even England as well. Thus when the BGB came into force in 1900 it could count on lively interest abroad because it expressly sought to give legislative form to the pandectist achievements in method and concept. The Code, indeed, was much admired on all sides, more perhaps abroad than in Germany at the time, but it really only influenced legal *theory* and legal *doctrine*; there was very little *practical* reception of the BGB, at any rate very much less than of the Code civil a century earlier. One reason for this was that its sophisticated structure and abstract conceptualist language was seen abroad as a typical product of German scholarship which, despite its technical merits, was not likely to take root very easily in alien legal soil, but the critical fact was that the more developed states of the world outside the Common Law family had already equipped themselves with civil codes during the nineteenth century and there was therefore no widespread need to import foreign models.

Even so, in the years following its enactment, the BGB had a great influence in quite widespread regions of the world, though political changes since then have diminished or extinguished it. One such area of influence in the early days was *Eastern and Southern Europe*. Thus, for example, the civil codes which came into force in the 1920s in the different republics of the *Soviet Union* were very like the BGB in structure and sometimes also in content (see FREUND, 'Russland', in: *Rechtsvergleichendes Hand-wörterbuch* I (ed. Schlegelberger, 1929) 200 ff.). *Hungary* repealed the Austrian General Civil Code in 1861 after gaining a certain degree of independence in the Austro-Hungarian Empire; the courts then relied increasingly on German law, in addition to old Hungarian customary law and principles of Austrian law; German law also provided a series of statutes on commercial law and civil procedure. Several drafts for a Hungarian Civil Code were based on German law, and though they never actually became law, the courts treated them rather as if they had (see HEYMANN, *Das ungarische Privatrecht und der Rechtsausgleich mit Ungarn* (1917); Eörsi, 'Richterrecht und Gesetzesrecht in Ungarn', *RabelsZ* 30 (1966) 117). *Czechoslovakia* and *Yugoslavia* came into existence in 1918; the principal influence was originally Austrian law, but subsequent legislation and drafts of private law statutes paid considerable attention to German law (see Korkisch, 'Das Privatrecht Ost-Mitteleuropas in rechtsverglei-chender Sicht', *RabelsZ* 23 (1958) 201). *Romania*, in contrast, then belonged to the Romanistic legal family (see Constantinescu, *Travaux de la Semaine internationale de droit 1950* (1954) 664). Almost all the countries we have mentioned adopted new civil codes after the Second World War. Some of the legal institutions they adopted or retained are German and their structure is partly based on the BGB, but the political changes were such that on grounds of their ideology they will be considered in the section on the socialist legal family (below Chs. 23 ff.).—In the *Far East* the BGB used to have considerable influence. Between 1924 and 1935 the Kingdom of *Siam* introduced a Civil Code which, apart from family law and the law of succession, derived principally from German law. The same is true of *China* (see Arminjon/ Nolde/Wolff, *Traité de droit comparé* II (1950) 427 ff. with further references). About the turn of the century *Japan* adopted much of the German BGB, but was exposed to strong *Anglo-American* legal influence after the Second World War (see below Ch. 28).

The Pandectist School and the BGB had a particular influence on the Civil Code of *Greece*. Plans for a Greek civil code go back to the War of Liberation of 1821–27 in which the Greek people won their independence from Turkish domination. For a long time it remained doubtful what the model for such a code should be. Since the Greek Liberation Movement was essentially based on the ideas which led to the French Revolution, many voices were raised in favour of a reception of the Code civil but others wanted to codify the law of Roman Byzantium which, primarily in the form of a private collection of statutes of Harmenopoulos from 1345, had been the law of Greece during the nearly four centuries of Turkish domination. This was the view which won through in the course of the nineteenth century. During this period Greek lawyers increasingly ignored the alterations and additions which Byzantine Emperors had made to the Corpus Iuris of Justinian and concentrated instead on the Roman law of the Corpus Iuris as elaborated by the German pandectists. Contact with Germany was established in 1835 when the Wittelsbachs came to the Greek throne in the person of Prince Otto, for he brought with him a group of legal advisers, including v. Maurer, a professor from Munich, whose contribution to procedural and penal legislation constituted a valuable form of 'legal aid to developing countries'. As a result of these contacts with Germany, the second half of the nineteenth century saw *German* professors teaching pandectist law at Athens University and writing textbooks alongside *Greek* professors trained in Germany; this meant that the Roman law familiar to the Greeks by reason of their history came in practice to take the form it had received at the hands of the pandectists. After many abortive attempts, preparatory work on a Civil Code for Greece entered a decisive phase in 1930, by which time all were agreed to look first to the *German* Code as being in closest contact with Roman law. The Greek Civil code was promulgated in 1940 but involvement in the Second World War and German occupation of the country delayed its entry into force until 23 February 1946.

In its structure the Greek Civil Code reflects the BGB. The General Part precedes books on the Law of Obligations, the Law of Property, Family Law, and the Law of Succession. In content also the Greek Civil Code relies predominantly on the German Code, but it always takes account of subsequent German legal practice which filled gaps in the BGB or developed its rules. At the same time there are many echoes of Swiss law, and to a lesser extent rules have also been taken from the French Code civil and the Italian Code. In linguistic and conceptual style the Code steers a middle course between the German and the Swiss Codes, avoiding the sophisticated interfusion and the abstract conceptualist language of the BGB without aiming for the simple and popular tone characteristic of the Swiss Code.

The *General Part* of the Greek Civil Code deals by and large with the same subject-matters as Book One of the BGB, adding only private international law. As is only reasonable, the general provisions relating to 'things' are taken out of the General Part and placed at the head of the Book on the Law of Property. For the rest, the Greek Code largely follows the provisions of the German Code; where it deviates, it is mainly more progressive. Thus it gives protection against invasions of personality (art. 57), a derivation from the Swiss law, and it restricts the conditions laid down by the BGB for rescission on the grounds of error (arts. 140–6). Art. 281 of the Greek Code shows how far it has freed itself from the individualism of the German Code; it provides that the exercise of a right is impermissible 'if it manifestly exceeds the limits laid down by good faith or good social practice or by the social or economic purpose for which the right was granted'. This provision, whose final part stems from the Civil Code of the Russian Soviet Republic of 1922, is described by Greek scholars as a 'royal paragraph', and it plays in judicial decisions today a role similar to that played in Germany by the general clause of §242 BGB. It should be noticed also that the Greek Civil Code adopts the German doctrine of liability for *culpa in contrahendo*: art. 198 lays down that 'a person who reprehensibly causes harm to another during negotiations prior to a contract . . . [is] bound to make compensation even if the contract does not eventuate'.

About three-quarters of all the provisions in the *law of obligations* come from the BGB, with improvements in their verbal form. Here too the Greek legislator has often codified rules which were first developed in Germany by the courts; thus there are rules for the collapse of the basis of the transaction (art. 386). In keeping with the openness of the statute on social matters, the law of employment is regulated in detail and contains, for example, provisions about inventions made by workmen, the availability of set-off against salary or wages, and the duty of the employer to pay for overtime and to grant holidays. The law of delict in the Code is a remarkable example of mixture of systems. On the one hand there is a general clause similar to art. 1382 Code civil and art. 41 par. 1 OR which lays down that everyone is bound to make compensation who 'reprehensibly causes harm to another in a manner contrary to law' (art. 914); on the other hand, the principle of special cases, as in §§824–6 BGB, is also respected. The German law has had less influence on the *law of property, family law*, and the *law of succession*. So far as *property law* is concerned, this is largely attributable to the fact that there is no cadastral register of land in Greece, and so in lieu of the German land register the Greek Code had to adopt the Romanistic system of transcription and inscription. The particular flavour of Greek *family law* results from the tradition of the Greek Orthodox church.

Taking all things together, it seems to us indubitable that the Greek Civil Code, in view of its historical origins, structure, and content, must be reckoned as belonging to the German legal family. But two things must be borne in mind. The first is that the Greek Code is very far from being a servile copy of the BGB; on the contrary, its draftsmen, setting to work with critical care, recognized and avoided the stylistic defects of the BGB, its exaggerated conceptualism, and its obsolete social values. Secondly, the Greek Civil Code is not the result of a 'reception' of a 'foreign' law. Reliance on German law was entirely natural, because the BGB rested on the same principles of Roman law as the established and traditional Greek law which it was the function of the legislator to codify.

On the origins and content of the Greek Civil Code, see MACRIS, 'Die Grundgedanken für die Ausarbeitung des Entwurfs eines griechischen Zivilgesetzbuchs', *RabelsZ* 9 (1935) 586; GOGOS, 'Das griechische Bürgerliche Gesetzbuch vom 15.3.1940', *AcP* 149 (1944) 78; ZEPOS, 'The New Greek Civil Code of 1946', 28 *J. Comp. Leg.* 56 (1946); ZEPOS, 'Der Einfluss des schweizerischen Privatrechts auf das griechishe Zivilgesetzbuch', *SJZ* 1960, 358; MARIDAKIS, 'La Tradition européenne et le Code civil hellénique', in: *L'Europa e il diritto romano, Studi in memoria di Paolo Koschaker* II (1954) 157; PLAGIANAKOS, *Die Entstehung des griechischen Zivilgesetzbuches* (1963); SONTIS, 'Das griechische Zivilgesetzbuch im Rahmen der Privatrechtsgeschichte der Neuzeit', *SavZ/Rom.* 78 (1961) 355.

13

The General Civil Code of Austria

EBERT, Gesetzgebung und Rechtswissenschaft, Ein Beitrag zur Zeit des späten Naturrechts in Österreich', *SavZ/Germ.* 85 (1968) 104.

ARMIN EHRENZWEIG, *System des österreichischen allgemeinen Privatrechts* I 1 (2nd edn., 1951) 17 ff.

——/GSCHNITZER, *Kommentar zum Allgemeinen Bürgerlichen Gesetzbuch* I, 1 (2nd edn., 1964).

VON HARRASOWSKY, *Der Codex Theresianus und seine Umarbeitungen* I (1883).

KLANG,'Der Oberste Gerichtshof und die Entwicklund des bürgerlichen Rechts', in: *Festschrift zur Hundertjahrfeier des österreichischen Obersten Gerichtshofes* (1950) 80.

——/GSCHNITZER, *Kommentar zum Allgemeinen bürgerlichen Gesetzbuch* I, 1 (2nd edn., 1964).

FRANZ KLEIN, 'Die Lebenskraft des Allgemeinen Bürgerlichen Gesetzbuches', in: *Festschrift zur Jahrhundertfeier des Allgemeinen Bürgerlichen Gesetzbuches* I (1911) 1.

KLEIN-BRUCKSCHWAIGER, '150 Jahre österreichisches ABGB', *JZ* 1963, 739.

KORKISCH, 'Die Entstehung des österreichischen Allgemeinen Bürgerlichen Gesetzbuches', *RabelsZ* 18 (1953) 263.

VON MAYR, 'Das Bürgerliche Gesetzbuch als Rechtsquelle, Einst und jetzt, in: *Festschrift zur Jahrhundertfeier des Allgemeinen Bürgerlichen Gesetzbuches* I (1911) 379.

OGRIS, *Der Entwicklungsgang der österreichischen Privatrechtswissenschaft im 19. Jahrhundert* (1968).

PFAFF/HOFMANN, *Excurse über österreichisches allgemeines bürgerliches Recht* I (2nd edn., 1878).

VON SCHEY, *Das österreichische Allgemeine Bürgerliche Gesetzbuch, Vortrag aus Anlaß der Jahrhundertfeier* (1911).

STEINWENTER, 'Der Einfluß des römischen Rechts auf die Kodifikation des bürgerlichen Rechts in Österreich', in: *L'Europa e il diritto romano, Studi in memoria di Paolo Koschaker* I (1954) 403.

UNGER, *System des österreichischen allgemeinen Privatrechts* I (5th edn., 1892).

WEISS, 'Hundertvierzig Jahre Allgemeines Bürgerliches Gesetzbuch', *JBl.* 1951, 249.

WELLSPACHER, 'Das Naturrecht und das ABGB', in: *Festschrift zur Jahrhundertfeier des Allgemeinen Bürgerlichen Gesetzbuches* I (1911) 173.

VON ZEILLER, *Commentar über das Allgemeine Bürgerliche Gesetzbuch für die gesammten deutschen Erbländer der oesterreichischen Monarchie* I–VI (1811–13).

I

THE third of the great codes which came into force in Europe at the end of the eighteenth and the beginning of the nineteenth century is the Austrian *General Civil Code* of 1811. Like the Prussian Land Law and the Code civil, this Code is founded on the ideal of codification characteristic of the Age of Enlightenment, on the belief, later so fiercely contested by SAVIGNY, that comprehensive legislation, deliberately planned, rationally and lucidly constructed, and backed by the authority of the state, should replace the unwieldy and old-fashioned traditional law, often cumbrous and uneven. Among these three great codes of natural law the Austrian Code has its own flavour and distinctive characteristics.

Preparatory work on the code started in the middle of the eighteenth century when the Empress MARIA THERESIA was embarking on the fundamental administrative reforms which were to turn the Austrian hereditary territory into a state in the modern sense. One of the great obstacles was the variety and complexity of the laws in the various parts of the royal Austrian territory, so in 1753 the Empress charged a Commission with the task of preparing a code; her instruction was

'that in drafting the code the Commission should limit itself to *private law*, leaving the present law in force so far as may be, and bringing the various laws of the provinces into agreement so far as conditions permit, using the *Gemeines Recht* and its best exponents as well as the laws of other countries and always referring back to the common law of reason whenever correction or completion is called for' (cited by ZEILLER (above p. 163) I. 7 f.).

The Empress's instructions make it clear that the Code which was envisaged was, unlike the Prussian Land Law, to be limited to *general* private law, leaving aside not only the particular laws of special groups or classes of persons but also the whole of public law as well as any other 'political' law. The bodies of law which were to be incorporated in the Code were also specified: the laws of the various territories, the Roman *Gemeines Recht* (in the form of the *Usus modernus pandectarum*), and finally the 'common law of reason'.

In 1766 the Commission produced a draft, called the *Codex Theresianus*. It was immediately considered in the Austrian Imperial Council but the reception was predominantly critical: the draft was far too comprehensive, it was too like a textbook, and it was incomprehensible without a knowledge of Roman law, in which it was too firmly rooted. The Empress agreed with the view of her Council and called for a reworking of the Code on the basis of the following principles:

'1. Statute and textbook should not be confused; definitions and divisions and such other matters as smack more of the lecture-room than the legislative chamber should be left out of the Code. 2. Everything should be stated as briefly as possible, consistently with clarity . . . Unusual cases should either be omitted or brought under general principles. 3. Ambiguity and vagueness must be carefully avoided. But even in respect of clarity moderation must be observed; clarity must not be used as a pretext for introducing unnecessary repetitions nor for explaining cases where a reasonable man would have no doubts. 4. The Code should not be tied to Roman law but should be founded throughout on natural equity . . .' (cited by v. HARRASOWSKY (above p. 163) 11 f.).

FREDERICK II is said to have made a similar criticism of the size of the draft of the Prussian Land Law when it was put before him: 'But it is very big; laws must be short and to the point.' In Austria, however, the draftsmen paid heed to such criticisms. They first attacked the law of persons and reduced it from 1,500 paragraphs to a bare 300; this was brought into force in 1787 under the Emperor JOSEPH II as the *Josephinisches Gesetzbuch*. Reworking of the other parts of the Codex Theresianus started under LEOPOLD II: in 1790 he appointed a new Commission under the chairmanship of MARTINI, an eminent exponent of the law of nature at Vienna University and head of the Imperial Ministry of Justice. In 1796 MARTINI produced a 'Draft of a General Civil Code' (*Entwurf eines Allgemeinen Bürgerlichen Gesetzbuches*) which broke free from the Codex Theresianus and from Roman law, and for the first time gave weight to the doctrines and postulates of the law of reason. This draft was put before the administration of the Austrian territory for their views, and in 1801 was referred to a new Commission for final polishing, along with the reservations ('Monita') which had been entered. The leading spirit of the Commission was FRANZ v. ZEILLER, who ranks along with MARTINI as the real creator of the Austrian code. ZEILLER was also an adherent of natural law which he had learnt from MARTINI at Vienna University and taught there after him but, perhaps under the influence of KANT's theory of knowledge, he had broken away from the dry and doctrinal formalism of the law of reason; he sought to make a compromise between the claims of natural reason and the empirical realities of Austrian life. ZEILLER formulated the supporting considerations which accompanied the final version of the draft of the Commission, submitted to the Emperor FRANZ I in 1808:

'Laws rest on the general and unchanging principles of reason and justice . . . This is why the civil codes of civilized nations agree in most of their provisions and why the states of Europe have been able to use old Roman law as a principal source of rules for deciding disputes. At the same time every state needs its indigenous and peculiar statutes suited to its own particular circumstances . . . The climate, resources, commerce, traditional forms of intercourse, and the candid or devious character of the inhabitants, all these have a definite effect on the rules concerning the legal form and various types of legal transaction, wills, contracts, securities, and the right to compensation for harm' (quoted by PFAFF/HOFMANN (above p. 163) 62 f.).

As a convinced supporter of the philosophy of the Enlightenment, ZEILLER took the ultimate source of all law to be reason, but his sound practical sense led him to keep out of the Code those dogmas of the law of reason which were unduly theoretical and remote from life. Thus the law of reason afforded the draftsmen a firm standpoint amid the unmanageable and largely obsolete chaos of the old *Gemeines Recht* and it also influenced the structure and phrasing of the Code, giving it at many points its unmistakable natural law flavour (see §§7 and 12 ABGB). On the other hand the Code is quite free from exaggerated and unrealistic dogmatism and it retains many institutions of the *Gemeines Recht* and provincial laws which seemed to the draftsmen to be reasonable and appropriate. Thus, rather like the Code civil, the Austrian Code of 1811 strikes a happy balance between the critical rationality demanded by the times and a sound sense of the value of tradition.

II

The General Civil Code was founded on enlightened principles—equality of citizens, freedom of private legal relationships from state control, freedom of economic activity—but this was in striking contrast with the actual social conditions in Austria in 1811 when the Code came into force. Thus although §16 ABGB laid down that 'every human being is entitled to be treated as a person by reason of his intrinsic rights, made manifest by reason', the peasantry in large parts of the Austrian kingdom at the time was in a state of feudal dependence barely distinguishable from serfdom; indeed §1146 ABGB laid down that the 'rights and obligations . . . between the owners of land and the local peasantry are to be found in the constitution of the relevant province and in political provisions'. So while the Code is based on the aim of easing legal commerce between citizens, it makes no attempt to curtail the numerous rights and privileges of feudal classes, which were controlled by 'political' provisions relating to 'hunting, forests, commerce, the servant classes, or the relationship between landed proprietors and the local peasantry'. §7 ABGB is forward-looking in giving the judges freedom, under certain conditions, to fill gaps in the law by calling upon 'principles and natural law', but in the decades after the Code came force the Imperial administration kept issuing petty decrees dealing with the most insignificant legal questions, almost as if Austria had had the 'reference to the statutory commission' of Prussian law or the 'référé' of the *droit intermédiaire* of France. In spirit the General Code was far ahead of actual social conditions in the authoritarian and absolutist Austrian state, and FRANZ KLEIN is right to say that the Austrian code was really 'an anachronism' at the date of its enactment (above p. 163 p. 17).

A turning-point came in 1848, the year of revolutions. The only specifically legal change was the abolition of the status of rural subservience but the new ideas of the liberty of the press, freedom of occupation, and the right to participate in politics and matters of state spread gradually from the bourgeoisie throughout society. In the period of restoration after 1848 there were admittedly many retrogressive steps. Thus imperial legislation pursuant to the Concordat of 1855 subjected to canon law the marriage of Catholics which had been regulated in the ABGB, gave jurisdiction in matrimonial matters to ecclesiastical courts, and put almost all education under the supervision of the church. The Concordat was replaced only twelve years later after the constitutional reforms of 1867 had brought a liberal majority into the Austrian Reichstag; recognition was accorded only to civil marriage, matrimonial litigation was returned to the secular courts, and the supervision of schools was taken away from the church. In the 1870s and 1880s as rural conditions gradually changed, as industry caught on, as the country was opened up to commerce, and as the economic institutions of capitalism came to the fore, the ABGB with its libertarian and individualist outlook came increasingly to be congruent with social and economic reality in Austrian life (see KLEIN (above p. 163) 16 ff.).

The decisions of the Austrian courts show a similar development. Just as in Prussia after 1794 and in France after 1804, the enactment of the Code was followed by a period of pure exposition, the judges hewing to the letter of the statute with neither wish nor taste for the historical or comparative varieties of legal study. Here too the situation did not change until after 1848. Then Austria came into contact once again with German scholarship, which in the juristic field meant contact with the Historical School of Law and with the Pandectist School which grew out of it. The leader of this pro-German school of thought was JOSEF UNGER, professor at Vienna University since 1855. In his writings he sharply attacked the 'literalism' of the exegetical school, their 'reasoning on the surface of the law', their 'logical petit-point'. One can almost hear the voice of SAVIGNY in UNGER's statement that in lieu of the exegetical method one must adopt "the historical–philosophical method, which consists in learning to understand the peculiar phenomena of the present by means of a deep and loving study of the past'. UNGER said 'that the only hope for law in Austria is to be found in the School of Historical Law founded by SAVIGNY and PUCHTA . . .'; he was therefore emphatic in urging his colleagues to 'water the fallow fields of Austrian legal study with the abundant stream of German scholarship' (UNGER (above p. 163) pp. iii–v, 640 f., 647; see also OGRIS (above p. 163) 11 ff.).

UNGER's own work greatly helped to forge the links between Austrian law and German pandectist doctrines. Although his *System des österreichischen allgemeinen Privatrechts* (1856 ff.) was never finished, it absorbed all the scholarship of German pandectist literature and dealt lovingly and in detail with the General Part of private law without which, as he said (above p. 163, p. 641), the lawyer is at sea in the law 'like a pilot without a compass'. UNGER and his followers had to erect the structures of pandectist theory on a statutory text based on natural law, a task which clearly presented grave difficulties (see examples in OGRIS, above p. 163, pp. 16 ff.). UNGER had very little time for the 'principles of natural law' occasionally referred to in the ABGB. In §7, where the judge is directed to use these principles as a standard of construction, UNGER saw 'no more than the satisfaction of a purely theoretical bias of the draftsmen'. He found that §§16 and 17, where a human being is described as the titulary of intrinsic natural rights which entitle him to legal personality, were 'wholly otiose paragraphs without any practical significance' (above p. 163, p. 71). Since the time of UNGER, Austrian and German legal scholars have worked closely and fruitfully together; his *System* had an effect on Austrian legal writing comparable to that of ZACHARIÄ's Handbook on the French (see above pp. 106 f.); since then, unlike the Code on which they are grounded, textbooks of private law in Austria all include a generous 'General Part' containing general theories, as developed by the German pandectists, on the sources of law, persons, property, and legal acts.

III

In its formal and technical construction the ABGB is much clearer, more comprehensible, and more 'modern' than the Prussian Land Law, much criticized by ZEILLER for its 'artificial structure which even the most indefatigable legal expert can barely master' (quoted in PFAFF/HOFMANN (above p. 163) 48). Instead of the streamlined phrasing of the French Code civil the ABGB has many explanatory and theoretical provisions of a rather fatherly tone, and though these are strictly unnecessary they somehow make the Code clearer and easier to understand. (On this compare v. MAYR (above p. 163) 385 ff.). §14 ABGB specifies the parts into which the Code is divided, a matter which was already clear from the Table of Contents. Countless provisions kindly inform the reader that a particular question is dealt with elsewhere (see, for example, §§450, 603). The Code contains many purely explanatory or instructive definitions without juristic content. Thus §44 ABGB explains the marriage contract by saying that thereby 'two persons of different sexes [declare] their will in legal form to live together in indissoluble community, to have children, to educate them, and to give each other mutual support'. The Code is often drafted with a wealth of specific detail; while it seldom reaches the tiresome prolixity of the Prussian Land Law (but see the nearly laughable casuistry of §§487–503, 556–683), it is very far from the glacial phraseology of the *German* Code 85 years later. Compare, for example, the provision in §45 ABGB on the law relating to premarital engagements: 'Regardless of the circumstances in which it is made or the conditions to which it is subject, the contract of affiancement or preliminary promise of marriage creates no legal obligation either to proceed to the marriage itself or to do what was promised in the event of withdrawal.' §1297 BGB, in contrast, reads:

'No claim for the fulfilment of a promise to marry will lie. The promise of a penalty in the event of failure to marry is null.'

With only 1,502 paragraphs the ABGB is strikingly shorter than the Code civil or the BGB. The draftsmen were able to achieve this brevity only by leaving significant gaps which have caused considerable difficulties for the Austrian courts. Thus the personal rights and duties of spouses are dealt with in four paragraphs of extreme generality (§§89–92 ABGB); there are no regulations at all to cover *real burdens* or the *brokerage contract*; and the original rules on the contract of employment and the contract of services were jejune in the extreme.

In view of the gaps in the Code as well as the many defects which had come to light in comparison with the German Code, the Austrian government accepted UNGER'S proposal to set up a 'Commission to Revise the ABGB'. This Commission and its successors worked for ten years and it was not until 1914–16 that three *Teilnovellen* were enacted, of which the third in particular made considerable alterations in the text of the Code. About 180 provisions in the ABGB were redrafted, completed, or repealed; these emendations, all based on the model of the German BGB, affected nearly all the areas of law dealt with in the ABGB, especially the general law of contract, tenancy, and lease, and contract of employment and services. The Teilnovellen excited considerable criticism, but in EHRENZWEIG's judgment they have proved generally satisfactory: 'Laws get better year by year as the magic wand of practice makes their defects disappear' (above p. 163, p. 35).

The structure of the ABGB is much like the system of the Institutes of GAIUS: there is a short introduction followed by three sections devoted to the Law of Persons, the Law of Property and 'Provisions Common to the Law of Persons and the Law of Property'.

The Introduction includes general provisions about entry into force, area of application, retroactive effect, and statutory construction. We have already mentioned §7 ABGB, a remarkable provision, very progressive in comparison with the Prussian Land Law, which instructs the judge how to act when faced with a gap in the law: when a case cannot be decided on the basis of the words or the natural meaning of a statute, the judge must look to the solutions laid down by the statute for comparable cases and to the reasons underlying other allied statutes: if the matter is still in doubt, it must be decided by the judge 'by applying the principles of natural law to the particular facts of the case, carefully sifted and maturely evaluated'. In practice this provision has not been used very much, because the judges preferred to make law behind a smokescreen of traditional techniques of construction rather than be openly creative (see KLANG (above p. 163) 84 ff.).

The *First Part* of the ABGB 'On the Rights of Persons' contains in its first principal division a great variety of rules concerning the 'Rights attaching to personal qualities or relationships'. Here there are rules about legal capacity, the protection of mental defectives, the position of the 'moral person', and finally some rules relating to foreigners and private international law, which was the subject of a totally new Law of 1978. The second principal division deals with *matrimonial law*. This was fundamentally altered by several reform laws of the 1970s, and now reflects the principle of equality of treatment in art. 7 of the Austrian Constitution. The same applies to the Law of Children and Guardianship in the third and fourth principal divisions.

The *Second Part* is devoted to the Law of Property and is by far the longest in the ABGB. Its first section deals with *Real Rights in Things*—possession, ownership, pledge, servitudes, and, astonishingly enough, the law of succession, regarded as the right to succeed to a decedent's estate or part of it (see §§308, 532)—and the second section deals with *Personal Rights in Property*, 'by dint of which one person is bound to perform something for another' (§§307, 859); it is at this point we find the whole of the law of contract and delict.

First we have the *general* rules of contract law: they deal with offer and acceptance, capacity, and invalidity of contacts on the ground of error, deceit, or duress—rules which strike us today as rather progressive (see vol. II, Ch. 8 II)—followed by rules relating to illegality and immorality and formal requirements. All these provisions are found in Germany in the General Part of the BGB where they are laid down as applicable not only to contracts but generally to all 'legal acts'. In the ABGB, on the other hand, §876—which was brought into the Code by the Third Teilnovelle— provides that the rules on error, deceit, and duress are to be applied 'to other expressions of will requiring communication'.—The general rules on breach of contract (§§918–21 ABGB) likewise stem from the Third Teilnovelle and indirectly from the BGB.—It is worth noting that in §§922 ff. ABGB responsibility for defects in property supplied for a consideration is dealt with in a *unitary* manner, whereas the BGB makes distinctions depending on whether the defective property is delivered pursuant to sale, lease, or hire.—It is interesting to note that some basic rules which give protection against general conditions of business which are 'unusual in content' or which 'grossly disadvantage' one of the parties have been incorporated into the ABGB (see §§864 *a*, 879 III), whereas in Germany the matter—one of the most important questions of contract law—is not mentioned in the BGB itself but is dealt with in ancillary legislation.

These general provisions are followed by rules for the *special types of contract*: here we find the treatment of, for example, gift, deposit, loan of both kinds, sale, and also marriage settlements between spouses. Of historical interest is the section on 'Powers of Attorney and Other Forms of Agency'. The legislator does not make the distinction between the power to act for another and the underlying contract which confers that power—the distinction was 'discovered' by LABAND in Germany only seventy years later—and treats the two as a unitary transaction, the 'Contract creating a power of agency' (*Bevollmächtigungsvertrag*) (§1002 ABGB). The general rules relating to lease, for both types of which (*Miete*, *Pacht*) the Code uses an old-fashioned expression (*Bestandsvertrag*), have been largely replaced or greatly restricted by the numerous special statutes provoked by the housing shortage. Much the same is true of the provisions relating to the contract of employment, thoroughly overhauled though they were in the Third Teilnovelle: they are almost completely overshadowed by the mass of modern statutes on industrial matters.

The *tort law* of the ABGB clearly shows the influence of natural law thinking; deliberately rejecting the multiplicity of Roman forms of action in delict, §1295 adopts a general clause, valid for liability in contract and delict alike: 'everyone who has suffered harm is entitled to claim compensation from the person who was at fault in causing it'. The Third Teilnovelle rather unnecessarily added a subsection to §1295 in reliance on §826 BGB which imposes liability in damages on the person who 'deliberately causes harm in a manner which offends the general moral sense'.

The ABGB recognises no cases of liability *without* fault. Even where the harm is caused by an animal or by the collapse of a building or structure, or by the fall of parts of it, the custodian of the animal or the possessor of the building can avoid liability if he proves that he had taken all necessary precautions (see §§1319 f.). In the rules relating to *vicarious liability* the Third Teilnovelle reintroduced the distinction between contractual and tortious liability: if the contractor uses the assistance of another person in the performance of a *contractual* obligation, he is liable to his contractor for the faults of that person without more ado (§1313a ABGB), but a person against whom a *delictal* claim is brought, though liable without proof of *culpa in eligendo*, is liable only if his assistant, in the eyes of the court, was 'incompetent' (*untüchtig*) (§1315 ABGB).—Modern developments in the area of accident law have taken place outside the ABGB, just as in Germany they have taken place outside the BGB; if a person is accidentally injured at work, on the highway, or by means of a train or airplane, his claim is controlled by special statutes which do not require any fault on the part of the defendant. There is one point, however, on which the Austrian courts have been more courageous than their German neighbours: they have recognized that even in the absence of a special statute liability may be strict when the harm has been caused by the 'dangerous activity' of the defendent entrepreneur; it is for the judge to decide when an activity is 'dangerous' (see vol. II, Ch. 19 II).

The *Third Part* of the ABGB deals with 'Regulations common to the law of persons and the law of property'. In addition to extinctive and acquisitive prescription, we here find *suretyship* and the *pledge contract* under the title 'Reinforcement of Rights', and under the title 'Alteration of Rights' a special treatment of *assignment* and the *taking over of a debt*. In the section on 'Termination of Rights' are the rules concerning the various ways of extinguishing a debt, for example, *set-off*, *release*, and *payment*; it is in an appendix to the provisions on payment that we find the rules on unjustified enrichment, under the rubric 'Payment of a Thing Not Due'. In comparison with the orderly structure of the *German* BGB this may seem very capricious, but erroneous though the location of this legal institution may be, no one has shown that it has in the least affected its *functional operation*. By and large the brevity and theoretical inadequacies of the ABGB have made it possible to adopt a flexible construction: 'It has been possible to exploit its poverty and turn its need into a virtue' (GSCHNITZER, JBl 1957, 371).

IV

The ABGB has not had anything like the effect abroad of the Code civil. This is not so much because Austria after 1811 did not conquer any lands on which to confer its Code as NAPOLEON did in Holland, Italy, and Germany. More important for the lack of external effect is the fact that the ABGB was the Code of a restoration-minded monarchy in thrall to the powers of the past during the decades under METTERNICH and soon to be faced with the constant danger of that inner collapse which threatens polyethnic states. The Code civil, on the other hand, was the law-book of a powerful unitary state, born of a successful revolution and politically outward-looking throughout the nineteenth century. Furthermore, no famous statesman and charismatic leader like NAPOLEON stood over the cradle of the ABGB, only the enlightened officials of an absolute and authoritarian state. In consequence it is not surprising that the ABGB has relatively little effect on the outside world. Yet as the nineteenth century proceeded, the Code had an effect in many of the non-German speaking parts of the Austro-Hungarian Empire: in Hungary it was in force for only a few years, but it was accepted in Croatia and Slavonia and in Bosnia and Hercegovina, as well as, somewhat abbreviated, in the adjacent territories of Serbia and Montenegro. The ABGB was in force in Lombardy and the Veneto until the Risorgimento. Even after the break-up of the Austro-Hungarian monarchy in 1918 the ABGB maintained a tenacious hold in the parts of Poland, Yugoslavia, and Czechoslovakia which had theretofore been Austrian, for it was only after the Second World War that it was replaced there by the new civil codes of the socialist states.

Although since 1719 *Liechtenstein* had been an Imperial Principate and consequently not part of the Austro-Hungarian Kingdom, it received large parts of Austrian law including the ABGB. After the First World War Liechtenstein separated from Austria and turned to Switzerland, since when its legislation has largely followed the Swiss model, the only parts of the ABGB left with practical effect being those relating to succession, marriage, and children. See, in detail, GSCHNITZER, *Gedächtnisschrift Ludwig Marxer* (1963) 19.

14

The Swiss Civil Code

DESCHENAUX, 'Der Einleitungstitel [des schweizerischen Zivilgesetzbuchs]', in: *Schweizerisches Privatrecht* II: *Einleitung und Personenrecht* (ed. Gutzwiller, 1967) 1.

EGGER, 'Einleitung und Personenrecht,' in: *Zürcher Kommentar zum Schweizerischen Zivilgesetzbuch* I (2nd edn., 1930).

——, 'Das schweizerische Zivil- und Handelsrecht,' in: Egger, *Ausgewählte Schriften und Abhandlungen* I (ed. Hug, 1957) 145.

ELSENER, 'Geschichtliche Grundlegung, Rechtsschulen und kantonale Kodifikationen bis zum Schweizerischen Zivilgesetzbuch', in: *Schweizerisches Privatrecht* I: *Geschichte und Geltungsbereich* (ed. Gutzwiller, 1969) 1.

GAUYE, 'Eugen Huber und das deutsche Bürgerliche Gesetzbuch' [with a hitherto unpublished essay by Eugen Huber of 1910 entitled "Das Verhältnis des schweizerischen Zivilgesetzbuches zum deutschen Bürgerlichen Gesetzbuche"], *ZSR* 80 (1961) 63.

RUDOLF GMÜR, *Das schweizerische Zivilgesetzbuch verglichen mit dem deutschen Bürgerlichen Gesetzbuch* (1965).

GUTZWILLER, Der Standort des schweizerischen Rechts, *ZSR* 80 (1961) 243.

HIRSCH, 'Die Einflüsse und Wirkungen ausländischen Rechts auf das heutige türkische Recht', *ZgesHR* 116 (1954) 201.

HIRSCH, *Rezeption als sozialer Prozess, Erläutert am Beispiel der Türkei* (1981).

EUGEN HUBER, *Schweizerisches Civilgesetzbuch, Erläuterungen zum Vorentwurf* (1902).

KOHLER, 'Eugen Huber und das schweizer Zivilgesetzbuch', *RheinZ* 5 (1913) 1.

LIVER, 'Das schweizerische Zivilgesetzbuch, Kodifikation und Rechtswissenschaft', *ZSR* 80 (1961) 193.

——, 'Einleitung', in: *[Berner] Kommentar zum schweizerischen Zivilrecht* I (1966).

——/MERZ, 'Das schweizerische Zivilgesetzbuch, Entstehung und Bewährung', *ZSR* 81 (1962) 9, 30.

MERZ, 'Fünfzig Jahre schweizerisches Zivilgesetzbuch', *JZ* 1962, 585.

——, 'Die Quellen des schweizerischen Obligationenrechts von 1881, Ein Beispiel interner Rechtsvereinheitlichung', *Festschrift Zweigert* (1981) 667.

——, 'Das schweizerische Obligationenrecht von 1881, Übernommenes und Eigenständiges', in: *Hundert Jahre schweizerisches Obligationenrecht* (Peter/Stark/Tercier ed., 1982) 3.

VON OVERBECK, 'Some Observations on the Role of the Judge under the Swiss Civil Code', 37 *La. L. Rev.* 681 (1977).

PRITSCH, 'Die Rezeption des Schweizerischen Zivilrechtes in der Türkei', *SJZ* 23 (1926/27) 273.

——, 'Das Schweizerische Zivilgesetzbuch in der Türkei', *ZvglRW* 59 (1957) 123.

RABEL, 'Bürgerliches Gesetzbuch und schweizerisches Zivilgesetzbuch', *DJZ* 15 (1910) 26, reprinted in Rabel, *Gesammelte Aufsätze* III (ed. Leser, 1967) 144.

——, 'Streifgänge im schweizerischen Zivilgesetzbuch', *RheinZ* 2 (1910) 308, 4 (1912) 135, reprinted in Rabel, *Gesammelte Aufsätze* I (ed. Leser, 1965) 179, 210.

——, 'Einige bemerkenswerte Neuheiten im schweizerischen Zivilgesetzbuch', *GZ* 62 (1911) 161, reprinted in Rabel, *Gesammelte Aufsätze* I (ed. Leser, 1965) 268.

—— 'The German and the Swiss Civil Codes.' 10 *La. L. Rev.* 265 (1950).

SAUSER-HALL, 'La réception des droits européens en Turquie', in: *Recueil de travaux publié par la Faculté de Droit de l'Université de Genève* (1938) 323.

ANDREAS B. SCHWARZ, *Das schweizerische Zivilgesetzbuch in der ausländischen Rechtsentwicklung* (1950).

SIEHR, 'Die Zeitschrift für schweizerisches Recht und das schweizerische Privatrecht in der deutschen Rechtspraxis', *ZSR* 100 (1981) 51.

SIMONIUS, 'Zur Erinnerung an die Entstehung des Zivilgesetzbuchs', *ZSR* 76 (1957) 293.

STARR/POOL, 'The Impact of a Legal Revolution in Rural Turkey', 8 *L. and Soc. Rev.* 534 (1974).

TUOR, *Das schweizerische Zivilgesetzbuch* (8th edn., rev. Schnyder, ed. Jäggi, 1968).

VELIDEDEOGLU, 'Erfahrungen mit dem schweizerischen Zivilgesetzbuch in der Türkei', *ZSR* 81 (1962) 51.

YUNG, 'Le Code civil suisse et nous,' *ZSR* 80 (1961) 323.

I

UNLIKE the Holy Roman Empire, the German-speaking part of Switzerland did not experience a comprehensive reception of Roman law. It is true that in many areas, such as Basle and Schaffhausen, Roman law had a certain validity and that the Swiss were ready enough to take over individual institutions of Roman law in order to make good the gaps in indigenous legal practices, but the self-determination and independence of the community of the confederacy was such that there was never any question of the reception of Roman law as a whole. After defending their independence against the German Emperor almost continually throughout the fifteenth century, the Swiss felt themselves to be no part of the Empire and so never tasted the quality of Roman law as *imperial* law. Furthermore, in Switzerland, unlike the German Territories, there were no princely administrations and no staffs of educated lawyers with an interest in the extension of Roman law. Thus until the end of the eighteenth century the law in the compact territory of the confederation of German-speaking Switzerland was a popular law based on indigenous legal practices and applied by elected lay judges (see LIVER, *Berner Kommentar* (above p. 173) nn. 14 ff.; ELSENER (above p. 173) 26 ff.).

After the French Revolution the Enlightenment idea of codification also took root in Switzerland. The territory of the confederacy was occupied by the French army in 1798 and with French aid a unitary state of Switzerland, the 'Eine und Unteilbare Helvetische Republik', was set up, but it lasted only a very short time. Meanwhile a decision to create a unified private law was immediately taken. When NAPOLEON fell, Switzerland quickly reverted to being a loose union of relatively independent cantons but the Enlightenment idea of collecting the private law into a code remained, though now at the level of the canton, and led to the adoption by almost all cantons of their own civil codes in the course of the nineteenth century.

In the west and south of Switzerland, cantons such as Geneva, Vaud, Valais, and Ticino (see above p. 106) had long been close to legal developments in France and it was natural that their codes should be substantially founded on the Code civil. The first of the German-speaking cantons to adopt a code was Berne in 1826/1831, which gave a lead to a second group of cantons. The Bernese Code, founded on old Bernese law, took its structure and much else from the Austrian ABGB which seemed to the conservative cantonal government at that time of restoration to be a more acceptable model than the Code civil. The cantons of Lucerne, Solothurn, and Aargau followed the Bernese model. The important private law code of the canton of Zurich (1853/1855) led the third group. It was the first code to contain reflections of the new German theories of the Historical School of Law and the Pandectist School, which KELLER, professor at the Political Institute in Zurich and pupil of SAVIGNY, had made known. The creator of the Code was BLUNTSCHLI who, like KELLER, had absorbed the teachings of the pandectists by prolonged study in Germany; at the same time he had an intimate knowledge of the private law of Zurich and thus was particularly well suited for the work of codification. This Code had a much greater effect than any other cantonal code on the Civil Code of Switzerland; it maintains strong links with the native legal traditions which it incorporates with remarkable originality into the system of the *Gemeines Recht* and in addition it is drafted in an especially clear and popular style. The codes of many cantons in Northern and Eastern Switzerland followed the Zurich model.

Throughout the second half of the nineteenth century the need for unification of law in Switzerland gradually made itself felt. Commerce was increasingly crossing cantonal borders, and with the growing movement of population inside Switzerland citizens were often adopting as their domicile a canton other than the one where they were born. In consequence intercantonal conflict of laws became disproportionately significant: 'A legal system is bound to suffer when preliminary questions regarding the area of validity of laws and rules regarding their application bulk much larger than substantive law' (EGGER, *Zürcher Kommentar* (above p. 173) General Introduction, n. 19). A lively discussion now took place on the constitutional question whether the federal legislature should be given competence to legislate on mattters of private law. The old arguments from the dispute between SAVIGNY and THIBAUT were heard once again but the principal fear expressed was that any extension of federal competence might lead to a sad levelling of the vital variety of cantonal laws. The constitutional reforms of 1874 gave the federal legislature competence in some areas of private law, especially for the law of obligations and commercial law; this made it possible for a unified Swiss law of obligations to come into force in 1881, based primarily on the General German Commercial Code of 1861 and the 'Dresdner Entwurf' of 1865 (see above Ch. II IV). It now fell to the Schweizerische Juristenverein to take a decisive initiative on the question of general codification: in 1884 it resolved that a comprehensive and comparative portrayal of the private law of all the Swiss cantons should be made so as to clear the path for the unification of law. Professor EUGEN HUBER, who was then teaching in Basle, was prevailed upon to accept this task and thus came on the scene the man whose splendid talents were largely responsible for giving Switzerland its Civil Code.

Within a few years HUBER had written his 'System und Geschichte des schweizerischen Privatrechts' (1886/1893), a work whose first three volumes took stock of the existing legal systems in the cantons and whose fourth volume contained a history of Swiss law. Even before the last volume appeared RUCHONNET, who as head of the department of police and justice in the confederacy performed the the functions of a Swiss Minister of Justice, had charged HUBER with the preparation of a draft code. The Swiss Civil Code is thus really the work of a single man. The first version of HUBER's draft was already complete when, in 1898, an alteration of the Constitution of the confederacy gave the federal legislature competence for the whole of private law. In 1900 the draft was laid before the public for discussion, considered by a commission of experts, and finally brought before the Swiss parliament. From the very beginning right through to the successful outcome, HUBER was closely involved in all stages of legislation; not only did he draft the Code but he also piloted it with great deftness through all the procedures of Parliament, of which he was himself to become a member. His experience as a journalist, for after his doctoral dissertation he became for a while the Chief Editor of the *Neue Zürcher Zeitung*, also helped him to win public support for the Code by means of newspaper articles and public lectures.

Biographical studies of EUGEN HUBER are numerous; in particular see MAX RÜMELIN, *Eugen Huber* (1923); GUHL, 'Eugen Huber', in: *Schweizer Juristen der letzten hundert Jahre* (1945) 323; EGGER, 'Eugen Huber und das schweizerische Zivilgesetzbuch', in: Egger, *Ausgewählte Schriften und Abhandlungen* I (ed. Hug, 1975) 105.

The Civil Code was adopted by the Swiss Parliament on 10 December 1907. According to the Swiss Constitution any federal statute is subject to referendum if 30,000 citizens or eight cantons so demand, but no referendum was called for. The interval before the coming into force of the Code on 1 January 1912 was used to amplify the code of obligations of 1881 and to fit it to the Civil Code. Time was too short to do more than update the general provisions of the law of obligations (including the general law of contract and the law of delict and unjust enrichment) and the law of the special types of contract. This revised part of the law of obligations came into force at the same time as the Civil Code. It is in the form of a special federal statute with separately numbered articles but it is clear from the title of the law that the Law of Obligations is substantially the fifth part of the Civil Code of which the first four parts deal with the law of persons, family law, the law of succession, and the law of property. The rest of the law of obligations, dealing with the whole of the law of associations (including the law of companies and partnerships) as well as, *inter alia*, the law of business associations and negotiable instruments, was not revised until 1936 when it was attached to the law of obligations. In 1971 the section dealing with the contract of service (*Dienstvertrag*) was recodified under the more modern heading of contract of employment (*Arbeitsvertrag*) (arts. 319–62 OR).

It follows from this that Switzerland has no special commercial code. In principle the same rules apply to commercial and civil transactions, as they did in the Zurich code of private law. Nevertheless there are some special provisions which apply only to *commercial* transactions: thus, for example, by arts. 191, 205 OR, in the case of a contract of sale, buyer and seller may calculate their damages *in abstracto* only if the transaction is one 'in line of commerce'.

It should be noted that in Switzerland the rules enacted since the Second World War in order to protect the weaker contracting party have not been sidetracked into special laws, as has happened in most of the European systems, but have been incorporated into the OR. So, too, with labour law, including the law of industrial relations, to be found since 1971 in arts. 319–62 OR; sales contracts involving payment by instalments have been integrated into the sales law of the OR (arts. 226a–228), and consumer credit law, under active review for some time, will also be included in the OR.

II

With the coming into force of the Swiss Civil Code the concert of European private law codes was enriched with a powerful new voice representing the particular style of Swiss legal thinking. Most lawyers abroad admired the Code and many expressed themselves in ecstatic tones; in Germany, indeed, voices were raised in favour of the immediate repeal of the BGB and its replacement by the Swiss Civil Code. In fact, the admirers of the ZGB necessarily included all those who found the language and technique of the German code too complex, its structure too sophisticated, and its conceptualism too extreme. In Switzerland all these defects had been avoided. The new Code was drafted in a popular and clear *language*, had an easily comprehended, relatively open *structure*, and instead of the 'abstract casuistry' which the BGB carried even into detail, made its statutory rules *deliberately incomplete* so that often it only sketched in an area within which the judge had to operate, using the standards of what was appropriate and reasonable and equitable.

So far as the *linguistic style* of the code is concerned, the primary aim of EUGEN HUBER was to produce a code which was readable and easily understood:

'the code must speak in popular ideas. The man of reason who has thought about his times and their needs should have the feeling, as he reads it, that the statute speaks to him from the heart . . . The injunctions of the legislator must therefore, so far as the material permits, be comprehensible to everyone, or at least to those who are involved in the activities regulated by the statute. Its provisions must mean something to educated laymen, even if they will always mean more to the specialist' (HUBER (above p. 173) 2,12).

The code therefore avoids technical jargon and internal cross-references. Nor does it try surreptitiously to allocate the burden of proof by peculiarities of sentence construction. Instead we find clear and striking expressions and terms: the husband 'fixes where the spouses will live, and must provide for the proper maintenance of wife and child' (art. 160.2); the wife 'stands by the husband in word and deed' (art. 161.2); land may be burdened by a servitude 'for a person's special use, such as for target practice or for passage on foot or by vehicle' (art. 781); 'marriage emancipates' (art. 14.2); 'everyone has capacity . . . ' (art. 1.1), and so on. Simple sentences are always preferred to complex sentences, even if juristic elegance is sometimes lost; short codal articles are preferred to long ones; German words are preferred to foreign ones picturesque expressions are preferred to blander words, even at the expense of precision (see, in general, HUBER (above p. 173) 14 ff.).

The *structure* of the ZGB, with its five sections on the law of persons, family law, law of succession, law of property, and law of obligations, by and large reflects the divisions developed by the pandectists (HUBER (above p. 173) 20 ff.). There are historical reasons for the location of the law of obligations at the end, but it can also be justified on the principle that the law of persons and the law of the family should precede the law of economic intercourse, and on the aesthetic ground that the relatively short sections on the law of property and the law of inheritance could not well be placed after the law of obligations which, with the inclusion of the whole of commercial law and the law of companies, extends to more than 1,100 articles. But there is another and more important respect in which the ZGB abandons the system of the pandectists: it has no General Part. One explanation is that the codes of the cantons never had a General Part and no unfortunate consequences had ensued; again, the old law of obligations of 1881 had general rules about *contracts* so that any attempt to make general rules about *legal acts* would have involved a crucial alteration of the law of obligations which was generally satisfactory. But most of all, the good practical sense of the Swiss led them to realise that these general rules are applied principally in the *law of obligations* and that it is essentially doctrinaire to insist that rules for the *whole* Code be contained in a separate General Part (*Botschaft des Bundesrates zum schweizerischen ZGB* (1904) 9). Thus the general rules on persons and things which appear at the outset of the German Code are placed in the Swiss Civil Code in the context in which they have their practical application, that is, in the law of persons and property; instead of having general rules on legal acts, art. 7 ZGB contains a provision according to which 'the general provisions of the law of obligations regarding the creation, performance and termination of contracts . . . are applicable to other relationships of private law'. RABEL was one of the most severe critics of this rule. In 1912 he predicted that it would lead to grave practical difficulties since the writers and the courts—especially the lay judges of Switzerland—would not be equal to the task posed by art. 7 ZGB: apart from these practical advantages, there was an aesthetic need to 'put the roof on the structure of legal principles' by having a General Part; otherwise the rest of the code would lie about 'like disordered heaps of rubble' (*RheinZ* 4 (1912) 14 f.). RABEL's prediction does not seem to have been fulfilled. At any rate after half a century of experience with the Code neither the practising lawyers nor the scholars in Switzerland have found the absence of a General Part to be a serious defect: 'It may be said with assurance that the fears that the courts might not be adequate to the task of sensibly applying the provisions of the Code of Obligations by analogy to other relationships have shown themselves to be unfounded' (FRIEDRICH, in: *Berner Kommentar zum ZGB* I 1 (1962) art. 7, n. 28; see also GMÜR (above p. 173, 53).

Another characteristic of the Swiss ZGB is the *deliberate incompleteness* of its statutory rules. The draftsmen of the BGB felt bound to make the Code complete, and therefore qualified their abstract principles with exceptions and limitations which are often carried down with scrupulous care to the last detail; the ZGB, on the other hand, is content to give merely an outline of the legal institution in question which it is then for the judge to fill in on the basis of the way he sees the particular case in front to him: 'At the point where the greatest difficulties begin, the BGB settles down to the task with particular satisfaction and the ZGB gives up completely (RABEL, *RheinZ* 2 (1910) 320). In consequence the length at which topics are treated in the two codes varies greatly. Thus to the question of future interests under a will the ZGB devotes 5 articles, the BGB 47. Contracts for the benefit of third parties get two articles in the OR, eight in the BGB. For adoption there are 18 Swiss articles as against 32 articles in the BGB, in matrimonial property law 74 as against 144, in the law of succession 192 as against 464; in total the ZGB (including the first two parts of the Code of Obligations, which correspond to law of obligations in the BGB) disposes in roughly 1,600 articles of the material which occupies 2,385 articles, normally longer, in the BGB.

Another characteristic of the ZGB is that it makes very extensive use of general clauses which the judge must particularize by constructing rules, maxims, and standards, by differentiating distinct types of cases and by specifying the relevant viewpoints. The BGB, on the other hand, in its concern for certainty in the law and predictability of judicial decision, makes much more use of precisely determined sets of facts so as to reduce judicial discretion to the minmum. Of course many general clauses are common to the two codes. Art. 2 ZGB reads: 'Everyone . . . in exercising his rights and in performing his duties [must] act in good faith' (*nach Treu und Glauben*); and the BGB in §§157, 242 has similar provisions which perform the same function although their more modest location in the Code makes their moral significance less striking. But often the ZGB is content with a general clause or a concept of rather vague reference where the BGB prefers exactitude and precision, even if it is often, as time has shown, much more ungenerous and rigid. It is easy to give examples.

According to art. 28 par. 1 ZGB, 49 OR, a person who has been injured by another 'in his personal circumstances' (in seinen persönlichen Verhältnissen) may seek an injunction and, if the other has been at fault, damages. Since it was deliberately left to the judge in Switzerland to decide what were injuries to 'one's personal circumstances', the Swiss courts were in a position to afford legal protection to outraged honour and invaded privacy. The draftsmen of the BGB, on the other hand, with equal deliberation, refused to include 'honour' or 'personality' in the list of protected rights in §823 par. 1 BGB, doubtless because they were extremely difficult to define. It took the Bundesgerichtshof to bring about a change here with its cases on the 'right to personality'. These cases also raise the question of damages for *immaterial harm*: here too the courts in Germany had to break loose from the unduly narrow rule of §253 BGB; now damages for pain and suffering (Schmerzensgeld) are allowed in Germany, as they are by art. 49 OR, where the injury to personality is especially severe (see vol. II, Ch. 20 II).—To take another example: if a person has caused damage by a tort, in Switzerland it is the task of the judge according to art. 43 par. 1 OR to determine in what form and in what amount compensation must take place; here the judge must 'take account of the circumstances as well as the seriousness of the fault'. If the tortfeasor caused the harm unintentionally and without gross negligence, the judge can reduce the amount of damages if the payment of *full* compensation would reduce the tortfeasor to a state of want (*Notlage*) (art. 44 par. 2 OR). By art. 99 par. 3 OR these rules also apply where liability is based on *breach of contract*; here the judge has further room for manoeuvre since the extent of liability is to be determined 'according to the special nature of the transaction' and in particular is to be moderated 'if the transaction was one which offered no advantage for the debtor'. German law, on the other hand, is committed in these cases to the 'all-or-nothing' principle, whereby the defendant either has to pay full compensation or none at all. For a long time there have been suggestions that the law should be changed so as effectively to introduce into Germany the more flexible Swiss system (compare LANGE, WILBURG, and HAUSS in *Verh. DJT* 43 (1960)).—Or take art. 45 par. 3 OR. By this provision a tortfeasor who has killed a person is bound to compensate all those who by the death have lost 'the person who supported them' (Versorger). §844 par. 2 BGB is differently drafted: a person can claim damages for wrongful death only if the decedent 'was actually or potentially bound by law to support him'. No doubt this rule is clearer; but a girl whose fiancé or a child whose stepfather is killed can have no claim in Germany since the stepfather is never 'bound by law to support' the child and the fiancé becomes bound to support the girl only on marriage. The Swiss Bundesgericht came to a different conclusion in BGE 66 II 219, 72 II 165. Of course it may on occasion be difficult to determine whether the affiancement was seriously intended or whether the stepfather was in fact supporting the child; this difficulty Swiss law is prepared to accept but German law, more concerned with certainty in the law, is not.—It is consistent, therefore, that the Swiss law of delict should start with a general clause (see art. 41 OR) while the BGB specifies the several combinations of factual circumstances which give rise to a remedy. In the view of the draftsmen of the BGB, a general clause would not have answered 'the dominant conception among German people regarding the position of the judge'; therefore it seemed better 'that the statute should provide the judge with a certain objective standard on which to base his decision' (Protokolle II p. 571). As things have turned out, the rigid system of the BGB has long since been exploded by the courts and to all intents and purposes replaced by a general clause (see the basic article of v. CAEMMERER in: *Hundert Jahre deutsches Rechtsleben, Festschrift zum 100jährigen Bestehen des Deutschen Juristentages* II (1960) 49).

The deliberate reliance of the Swiss Civil Code on judicial amplification can be explained in large part by the peculiar nature of Swiss legal practice even today. As we have said, Switzerland never really had a reception of Roman law and this meant in particular that the legal system never got into the hands of 'learned' jurists and was not turned into an esoteric science as happened in the German Empire. Law has always had an open and popular quality in the exposed community life of the Swiss cantons and the citizen who goes to law does not expect the judge to justify his decision by linking it in a completely logical manner with some leading principle. It is the personal qualities of the judge which lend authority to his judgment; he is not *appointed* by a higher authority on the ground of his specialist knowledge but normally *elected* as a leading citizen by the inhabitants of the immediate area. This tradition is still vital in Switzerland today. Below the Bundesgericht it is the law of the cantons which determines the courts structure and the law of civil procedure; even today judges of first instance in some cantons are laymen with the assistance of a specialist 'clerk of court' (*Gerichtsschreiber*) especially for the drafting of the decision. It is natural in these circumstances that the Civil Code should use more open rules, that it should on many points be deliberately incomplete, and be drafted in an easily comprehensible style; an unduly specialist or 'learned' code might well have provoked a referendum.

It must also be borne in mind that the Civil Code had the difficult task of creating legal unity in a federal state whose member cantons had always been especially proud of their independence and which had almost all equipped themselves with their own codes towards the end of the previous century. The Civil Code therefore had to leave room for cantonal rules at many points, for example, where the topic was intimately connected with the locality (as in neighbour law) or with the authorities of the canton (for example, in the law of guardianship). Some questions are openly left to local usage or 'the form normal in the locality' (see, for example, art. 642, 644 ZGB). On one matter it was impossible to reconcile the rules of the French-speaking cantons and the cantons in Central and Eastern Switzerland, namely the question whether siblings of a decedent should be automatically entitled to part of his estate and if so, to what part; here, in art. 472, the ZGB left the matter to cantonal law. Often also the ZGB permits the choice of several local versions of a particular legal institution: security in land may be created in any one of three ways (*Schuldbrief, Gült, Grundpfandverschreibung*). Doubtless the especial problems of unifying Swiss law led the legislator to avoid too detailed a regulation of individual questions and instead to leave a certain room for play to the discretion of the judges. Had he not done so, the susceptibilities of the cantons might have been aroused and the risk of a referendum increased.

In view of what has been said, it will be clear why the Swiss Civil Code, in its famous art. 1, openly admits the gaps in the law, entrusts the judge with the task of filling these gaps and gives him standards with which to proceed to the task. In art. 1 par. 2 and 3 we read:

'If no relevant provision can be found in a statute, the judge must decide in accordance with the customary law and, in its absence, in accordance with the rule which he would, were he the legislator, adopt. In so doing he must pay attention to accepted doctrine and tradition.'

There is really nothing fundamentally new in this provision, because ever since the decline of conceptualist positivism everyone has recognized that a legal order will still have gaps, even after all the possibilities of reasonable interpretation and analogy have been exhausted, and that they have to be filled by creative judicial activity. But the ZGB has won admiration and applause for putting this idea in such a fine verbal form and in a place where it cannot be overlooked. 'This is probably the first time that a modern legislator has given official recognition in a great formula to the fact that the judge is his indispensable auxiliary' (GÉNY, *Méthode d'interprétation et sources en droit privé positif* II (2nd edn., 1954) 328). Note, however, that art. 1 ZGB does not allow the judge to fill the gap in the law on the basis merely of his subjective feeling of what would be just in the particular case before him. He is bound to decide the particular case on the basis of a general *rule* and in order to find this rule he must pay attention to 'accepted doctrine and tradition'. HUBER has well dealt with the objection that this makes the judge too free and independent:

'[The judge] will certainly be freer than he is today when he is expected to be able to find everything in the statute, using if necessary the most suspicious artifices of interpretation, but he will perform his function in a much worthier manner if such artifices are not expected of him. He will have to recognize that the law as enacted has its gaps which cannot be filled by construction. Once he has recognized this, he will give his judgment not on the basis that the statute has no gaps but on the ground that the legal system as a whole has none; he will state the rule of law which he would, as legislator, choose as being congruent with the other rules in the system.' (HUBER (above p. 173) 37.)

In conclusion, then, we see that the characteristic traits of the ZGB are largely attributable to the particular circumstances in Switzerland and the traditions of its legal life. This is a fact one must always bear in mind when comparing the ZGB and the BGB. In particular one must not apply to these codes criteria which their draftsmen did not see as relevant in the historical, political, and social circumstances attending their work. All the German lawyers at the end of the nineteenth century had passed through the School of the Pandectists and so were equipped to deal with a technically splendid code that promised legal certainty; to such persons legislation like the Swiss code which leaves the solution of important questions entirely to the judges would have seemed a return to the 'pre-scientific' stage. Contrariwise, the practice of law in the cantons of Switzerland was far too localized and personal and the Swiss judges were too little specialist for the adoption of a code like the BGB with its demanding, difficult, and pedantic techniques, its precise, disciplined, and artificial language. But perhaps we may make one prediction; the day may not be too far distant when the project of a *European Civil Code* will be undertaken; if so, the style of legislation to be aimed at will be that of the ZGB and not of the BGB. This is not because *popularity* is an ideal for which such a code should aim; such an ideal may make sense in the intimate confines of Switzerland but to suppose that it is apt for modern life all over Europe seems to be sheer romanticism. The open texture of the Swiss model with its style of draftsmanship which calls for judicial amplification seems preferable on two other grounds: first because the legal unification of Europe would be impossible unless judges were left with a defined area of play, and secondly because we have come to understand and approve of the procedure by which a judge can gradually develop the scope of legislative provisions which have been openly drafted, and we no longer see in this, as the draftsmen of the BGB with their positivistic outlook did, any great risk for the certainty of law.

EUGEN HUBER himself, when the draft of the ZGB was being debated in the Swiss Parliament, expressed the hope that after its unification Swiss law would 'as international law develops, gain respect of a quite different order from that which could be expected of cantonal laws, a law which, if it should ever come to the creation of a *European Code*, might have a not insignificant influence of the outcome' (quoted by EGGER, in: 'Vom Krieg und vom Frieden', *Festschrift für Max Huber* (1944) 44). On the same theme see also A. B. SCHWARZ (above, p. 174) 55 ff., RUDOLF GMÜR (above p. 173) 195 ff., and especially HANS MERZ (above p. 173) 589.

III

The Swiss ZGB won great admiration abroad because of its intrinsic merits. Almost every legislator in countries whose private law is codified has learnt something from the Swiss experience which he has used in drafting a new civil code—as in Italy and Greece—or in reforming existing laws. But there has been only one *total reception* of the Swiss ZGB, namely in *Turkey*. After KEMAL ATATÜRK created the Republic of Turkey in 1922 the Swiss Code, including the Code of Obligations, was brought into force almost word for word as the new Turkish Civil Code of 1926.

It is not entirely clear precisely why the Turkish legislature opted for the Swiss ZGB. HIRSCH, who spent many years in Turkey as Professor of Law and legal adviser to the Turkish government, attributes it to the 'chance' that the then Minister of Justice had studied law in Switzerland and had been convinced by his teachers there that the Swiss laws were the best and most modern in the world: 'If the Minister of Justice had studied in Germany, [he would] have recommended the adoption of the German BGB with equal enthusiasm . . . , perhaps not the most modern of Codes, but . . . much better suited to Turkish jurists who have a long tradition of purely scholarly legal education than the Swiss laws with their numerous gaps which call for a free and unliteral method of interpretation' (above p. 173, p. 206). But in the view of SAUSER-HALL the decision of the Turkish legislature was based also on the formal merits of the Swiss ZGB, especially its brevity, lucidity and comprehensibility, as well as on the fact that it would be much easier to translate the French version of the ZGB and use commentaries in French because French is much more commonly understood in Turkey than German (above p. 174, 345 f.).

This instance of reception is especially interesting because it is so remarkable. In order to effect a radical modernisation of Turkish life, the legislator, at a stroke, abolished the Islamic legal practices which had been valid for centuries, having hardly been affected at all by the reform legislation of the last Sultans of the Ottoman Empire; in their place was introduced a code which was adapted to the needs of a society entirely different in its social, religious and economic structure. Nowhere else in the world can one so well study how in the reception of a foreign law there is a mutual interaction between the interpretation of the foreign text and the actual traditions and usages of the country which adopted it, with the consequent gradual development of a new law of an independent nature.

The adoption of Swiss family law has led to very grave difficulties, which have not yet been overcome. Under the old law, for instance, a marriage was validly constituted if the future spouses or their parents made the relevant contractual declaration in front of witnesses; it was normal, though not necessary to the validity of the marriage, for an Islamic priest to be involved in the ceremony. The new code of 1926 recognized only civil marriages, but the Turks in the country and small towns held fast to their old usages, the more so since the new form of marriage was not dissolved by repudiation; the result was that the number of children who were illegitimate by statute but legitimate in the eyes of the people became so large that a series of special statutes had to be passed so as to legitimate them. On this and kindred problems arising from the reception of Swiss law in Turkey, see the essays of HIRSCH, PRITSCH, STARR/POOL and VELIDEDEOGLU (above pp. 173–74), as well as the various contributions to Annal. Fac. Istanb. 5 (1956).

15

The Doctrine of the Abstract Real Contract—A Distinctive Feature of the Style of the Germanic Legal Family

BRANDT, *Eigentumserwerb und Austauschgeschäft* (1940).

BYDLINSKI, 'Die rechtsgeschäftlichen Voraussetzungen der Eigentumsübertragung nach österreichischem Recht' in: *Festschrift Larenz (1973) 1027.*

V. CAEMMERER, 'Rechtsvergleichung und Reform der Fahrnisübereignung,' *RabelsZ* 12 (1938/1939) 675.

DUTOIT, 'La Cession de créance: Acte causal ou abstrait? Le Code suisse des obligations dans la perspective du droit comparé', in Peter/Stark/Tercier (eds.), *Hundert Jahre schweizerisches Obligationenrecht* (1982) 453.

FELGENTRAEGER, *Friedrich Carl v. Savignys Einfluß auf die Übereignungslehre* (1927).

FRIEDRICH, 'Übereignung', in: *Rechtsvergleichendes Handwörterbuch* VI (ed. Schlegelberger, 1938) 606.

HAEHL, 'Dingliche oder obligatorische Wirkung der Vertragsaufhebung bei Irrtum, Rücktritt und Wandlung?' *ÖJZ* 1977, 533.

HOYER, 'Stilbildende Elemente der deutschsprachigen Rechtskreises, Eine rechtsvergleichende Skizze', in: *Liber amicorum Adolf F. Schnitzer* (1979) 341.

KAGEN, 'Zum Problem der Fahrnisübereignung im schweizerischen Recht,' in: *Fetschrift für Hedemann* (1938) 245.

KEGEL, 'Verpflichtung und Verfügung, Sollen Verfügungen abstrakt oder kausal sein?', *Festschrift für F.A. Mann* (1977) 57.

LARENZ, *Lehrbuch des Schuldrechts* II (12th edn., 1981) 10 ff.

LUIG, 'Zession und Abstraktionsprinzip', in: *Wissenschaft und Kodifikation des Privatrechts im 19. Jahrhundert* (ed. Coing and Wilhelm) II (1977) 112.

NEUNER, 'Abstrakte und kausale Übereignung beweglicher Sachen', *RheinZ* 14 (1926) 9.

RAPPAPORT, 'Über die Bedeutung des Titels für die Gültigkeit der Eigentumsübergabe nach dem allgemeinen Bürgerlichen Gesetzbuch', in: *Festschrift zur Jahrhundertfeier des Allgemeinen Bürgerlichen Gesetzbuches* II (1911) 399.

RANIERI, 'Die Lehre von der abstrakten Übereignung in der deutschen Zivilrechtswissenschaft des 19. Jahrhunderts', in: *Wissenschaft und Kodifikation des Privatrechts im 19. Jahrhundert* (ed. Coing and Wilhelm) II (1977) 90.

WILHELM, 'Bergriff und Theorie der Verfügung', in *Wissenschaft und Kodifikation des Privatrechts im 19. Jahrhundert* (ed. Coing and Wilhem) II (1977) 213.

FOR text, please see first edition, I. 178–89.

III. THE ANGLO-AMERICAN LEGAL FAMILY

16

The Development of the English Common Law

BAKER, 'The Future of Equity', 93 *Law Q. Rev.* 529 (1977)

BRUNNER, *Geschichte der englischen Rechtsquellen im Grundriß* (1909).

R. DAVID, *Introduction à l'étude du droit privé de l'Angleterre* (1948).

——, *English Law and French Law* (1980).

EMSLIE, 'The Law of Scotland, Its Interest for the Comparative Lawyer', 1982 *Curr. Leg. Prob.* 25.

FIKENTSCHER, *Methoden des Rechts in vergleichender Darstellung* II (1977).

HANBURY, *English Courts of Law* (5th edn., rev. Yardley, 1979).

HEYMANN, 'Überblick über das englische Privatreht', in: *Enzyklopädie der Rechtswissenschaft* II (2nd edn. Holtzendorff and Kohler, 1914) 281.

HOLDSWORTH, *A History of English Law*, 16 vols. (1903 ff.).

——, *Some Makers of English Law* (1938).

JENKS, A. *Short History of English Law* (6th edn., 1949).

KEETON, *English Law, The Judicial Contribution* (1974).

KIRALFY, *The English Legal System* (6th edn., 1978).

——, 'English Law' in: *An Introduction to Legal Systems* (ed. Derrett, 1968) 157.

MAITLAND, *Equity* (2nd edn., rev. Brunyate, 1936).

——, *The Forms of Action at Common Law* (1936).

MANCHESTER, *Modern Legal History of England and Wales 1750–1950* (1980).

MILSON, *Historical Foundations of the Common Law* (1969).

PETER, *Actio und Writ, Eine vergleichende Darstellung römischer und englischer Rechtsbehelfe* (1957).

——, 'Englisches Recht', in: *Handwörterbuch zur deutschen Rechtsgeschichte* I (ed. Erler and E. Kaufmann, 1967) 922.

——, *Römisches Recht und englisches Recht* (1969).

PLUCKNETT, *A Concise History of the Common Law* (5th edn., 1956).

POLLOCK/MAITLAND, *The History of English Law Before the Time of Edward I*, 2 vols. (1898, reprinted 1952).

POTTER, *Historical Introduction to English Law and Its Institutions* (4th edn., rev. Kiralfy, 1958).

SCHMITTHOFF, 'Die englische Equity', *Festschrift von Caemmerer* (1978) 1049.

ANDREAS B. SCHWARZ, 'Das englische Recht und seine Quellen', in: *Die Zivilgesetze der Gegenwart* (founded by Heinsheimer) II 1 (1931) 1.

——, 'Equity', in: *Die Zivilgesetze der Gegenwart* (founded by Heinsheimer) II 1 (1931)

101, reprinted in: Schwarz, *Rechtsgeschichte und Gegenwart, Gesammelte Schriften zur Neueren Privatrechtsgeschichte und Rechtsvergleichung* (ed. Thieme und Wieacker, 1960) 206.

T. B. SMITH, *British Justice: The Scottish Contribution* (1961).

——, *Scotland, The Development of Its Laws and Constitution* (1962).

——, *Studies Critical and Comparative* (1962).

STEIN, 'The Influence of Roman Law on the Law of Scotland', 1963 *Jur. Rev.* 205.

——, *Roman Law and English Jurisprudence Yesterday and Today* (1969).

——, 'Logic and Experience in Roman and Common Law', 59 *Boston UL Rev.* 433 (1979).

WALKER, 'Some Characteristics of Scots Law', 18 *Mod. L. Rev.* 321 (1955).

WILLOCK, 'The Scottish Legal Heritage Revisited', in: Grant (ed.), *Independence and Devolution, The Legal Implications for Scotland* (1976) 1.

I

To the lawyer from the Continent of Europe English law has always been something rich and strange. At every step he comes across legal institutions, procedures, and traditions which have no counterpart in the Continental legal world with which he is familar. Contrariwise, he scans the English legal scene in vain for much that seemed to him to be an absolute necessity in any functioning system, such as a civil code, a commercial code, a code of civil procedure, and an integrated structure of legal concepts rationally ordered. He finds that legal technique, instead of being directed primarily to interpreting statutory texts or analysing concrete problems so as to 'fit them into the system' conceptually, is principally interested in precedents and types of case; it is devoted to the careful and realistic discussion of live problems and readier to deal in concrete and historical terms than think systematically or in the abstract.

More than any other legal system now in force, English law demands a study of its historical origins. Of course modern Continental systems too can only be fully understood in the light of their history; the well-known dictum of HOLMES: 'The life of the law has not been logic: it has been experience' (*The Common Law* (1881) 1) is true of other systems though it was coined for the Anglo-American one. Yet some legal systems are more consciously tied to their past than others, more attached to traditional forms of legal thinking despite social and economic change, and none more than England. In fact no country has clung as firmly as England to its own style of law throughout the centuries or been so free from major convulsions in its legal life. Many areas in Germany accepted Roman law in its entirety and Roman law had an essential influence on the principles of the law in France, although traditional law was not entirely ousted, but the influence of Roman law on the Common Law of England has never been more than peripheral. Nor was England affected in practice by the idea of *codification*, the idea, born of the law of nature and the

Enlightenment, that the disorderly and patchy historical growth of law could be pruned and planed into a generally comprehensible form as a result of deliberate and planned legislation based on a rational system. And, finally, England never had an explosive *political upheaval* such as occurred in France in 1789, where one of the principal effects of the Revolution was to overturn the legal system of the *ancien régime* and replace it by a radically new system which, for all that it kept the old institutions, as we have seen, nevertheless represented a decisive new start; such a thing has never happened to English law.

In view of this, we must start our brief introduction to Anglo-American law with a sketch of the principal threads of English legal history. This will help to explain why England never experienced a reception of Roman law or a movement for codification and consequently why English law has had that unbroken development which so fascinates the Continental observer, and the legal historian above all. But even if the reader has no interest in the past, he will find it useful to take this trip into legal history; without it he would have difficulty in understanding the special style, the technical expressions, and the conceptual divisions of the Common Law as it is today.

II

English legal history begins in 1066 when the Normans under WILLIAM I dealt a crushing defeat to the Anglo-Saxons in the Battle of Hastings and thereby made possible the gradual domination of nearly the whole of the British Isles in the following years. It is true that in the previous centuries England had had its own legal practices, some of which were in written form, when it was a loosely organized state under the Anglo-Saxon kings, especially ALFRED THE GREAT (871–900). WILLIAM I did not abrogate these traditional laws or make any sudden change in English law in 1066, but the subsequent effect of the Norman kings and their officials on the administration of law was so profound that we can confidently ignore any earlier influences.

One of the great achievements of WILLIAM I and his successors was the construction of a tight, integrated, and rather simply organized *feudal system*, with the King as the supreme feudal overlord. WILLIAM regarded himself as the lawful heir to the Anglo-Saxon throne and treated his opponents as rebels; he therefore took all their land and divided it in fee among some 1,500 of his most important followers; as a condition of holding the land granted to them or letting others hold it from them as inferiors they had to take an oath of fealty and perform specified services or pay sums of money. Thus the view that all title to land was traceable directly or indirectly to the Crown was accepted in England very early, and ever since the thirteenth century the expression 'fee' ('feodum' or 'feudum'), which on the Continent was mainly restricted to military knight-service, has been used in England to describe *any* heritable right to hold land. Even modern English land law rests on the supposition, which is admittedly insignificant in practice, that all land in England is in the ownership of the Crown and that the citizen cannot have more than a limited right to use a particular plot of land (see the extensive treatment in MEGARRY/ WADE, *The Law of Real Property* (5th edn., 1984) 12 ff., and HEYMANN (above p. 187) 311 ff.).

WILLIAM I and his successors saw to it that the land of their magnates was geographically dispersed; great feudal estates were allowed only on the marches of the country, where they served to protect the borders against the hostile Scots and Welsh without presenting any real threat to the central power. The barons of England therefore never obtained the position of power achieved by the possessors of the great crown fiefs in France and Germany, whose political influence often greatly exceeded that of the central authority of King or Kaiser, to whom they submitted in France only in the fourteenth century and in medieval Germany not at all.

Given the strict construction of the feudal pyramid and the consequent centralization of power in the King, the Normans, with the talent for organization which they had demonstrated in founding other states elsewhere, were able to develop an effective central royal authority. The tax system was put on a new basis by WILLIAM I himself who had all property holdings inscribed in the Domesday Book in 1086. The taxes paid by feudal inferiors were thoroughly checked by the Curia Regis, a council consisting of the King and his advisers; gradually, under HENRY I (1110–35) there developed out of the Curia Regis a supreme Treasury—the Exchequer (Scaccarium Regis)— which was not simply an investigative body but gradually took on the character of a court as it decided all legal questions connected with taxes.

Fiscal reasons also underlay the increasing intervention by the central royal administration in civil and criminal law (see HOLDSWORTH (above p. 187) II. 173 f.). The most important taxpayers were the biggest landowners. The Curia Regis therefore had an interest in private legal disputes over large estates, especially when their holders were 'tenants in chief' whose right to the land depended directly on the King. If the taxes were regularly to come in there must be peace in the land. Thus the King took exclusive jurisdiction over all serious crimes; the fines and confiscations proved a significant new source of income. In this way royal justice developed in the twelfth and thirteenth centuries from a special jurisdiction for affairs of state into a general jurisdiction of wide coverage; in consequence there gradually developed out of the Curia Regis three permanent central courts, staffed by professional judges, capable of acting in the absence of the King, and fixed at Westminster; their jurisdiction was established by 1300 and lasted unaltered into the seventeenth century.

In addition to the Court of Exchequer, these were the Court of Common Pleas, with jurisdiction over normal lawsuits between private individuals and power to supervise and review the traditional lower courts, which had been run since 1066 by royal officials called sheriffs, and the Court of King's Bench which dealt mainly with matters of particular political importance. In addition, the King sent 'travelling justices' (*justiciarii itinerantes*) into the provinces with increasing frequency from the twelfth century onwards, where they replaced the sheriffs and held court in the name of the King—an institution which still exists in England today.

Thus started a development in England which in the following centuries led to the centralization of justice and to the unification of English law. The jurisdictions of local borough and feudal courts diminished in importance, not only because of the prestige and authority of the royal judges but also because the *procedure* of the royal courts was more modern and progressive, as were the *forms of action* made available by the royal administration (see immediately below pp. 192 ff.). At the same time the local rules of law which had come down from the Anglo-Saxon times gradually lost their importance; they were never formally abrogated but they gradually faded into insignificance beside the law applied by the royal judges. Thus England very early enjoyed a unified law, called for this reason the 'common law', whereas the 'droit commun français' did not develop in France until the sixteenth century, or the '*Gemeines Recht*' in Germany until the nineteenth century and even then only in the theory of the pandectists. Thus there never existed in England one of the essential motor powers behind the idea of codification, which even on the Continent rested on the practical need to unify the law as well as on the philosophy of the Enlightenment and the thinking of natural lawyers.

Litigation in the middle ages was founded on 'writs'. In those days a writ (Latin: *breve*) was a letter from a superior, ecclesiastical or secular, containing a message to the addressee, normally a request or an instruction. In law, 'writ' meant a command of the King directed to the relevant official, judge, or magistrate, containing a brief indication of a matter under dispute and instructing the addressee to call the defendant into his court and to resolve the dispute in the presence of the parties. Such writs were issued in the name of the King by the highest royal officials—the Capitalis Justiciarius, later the Chancellor—on payment of a fee by the plaintiff, without hearing the defendant. Since many of the complaints in respect of which the plaintiff sought a writ were substantially similar, the text of the individual writs very soon became standardized with only the name and address of the parties having to be filled in, and they became known to practitioners by short titles ('forms of action'). Towards the end of the twelfth century the Chancellor was issuing about 75 established types of writ, a number which grew considerably in the thirteenth and fourteenth centuries. They were collected together in semi-official collections, the 'Registers of Writs', which had a wide circulation among practising lawyers.

In the early days most writs were designed to implement claims arising out of feudal law. Thus, for example, the *writ of right* enabled a vassal to demand that the defendant refrain from interfering with his right to possess and use a plot of land. By the *writ of customs and services* the feudal superior could come before the royal courts to demand that the vassal perform his services, and the latter could use the *writ of replevin* to make good his claim that the superior release the chattels on which he had distrained in order to exact the feudal services (see the extensive treatment by PETER, *Actio und Writ* (above p. 187) 21 ff., 105 ff.). Two royal judicial officials, GLANVILL (died 1190) and BRACTON (died 1268), wrote books which show how 'procedural thinking' dominated English law at the time. These books, the oldest works recognized as a source of law by English legal writers ('books of authority'), present the law in force in the form of a list of the writs current in practice, with comments and, in the case of BRACTON, notes on decisions of the royal courts.

The plaintiff embarking on litigation had to give very careful consideration to the question which writ suited the substance of his complaint and would best help him to pursue it. It was important to make the correct choice, since the complaint would be dismissed if the wrong writ were chosen, and it was difficult, because each set of facts had its own writ and the distinction between the different set of facts became increasingly complex as the number of writs increased. In addition, each writ had its own special rules of procedure. This allowed the Chancellor and the judges to attach more up-to-date methods of proof to particular writs and thus to make royal justice more attractive to the public. In certain types of complaint the royal officials were able to abandon the methods of proof by ordeal (as by battle) and by oath, which gradually came to seem antiquated, and to replace them by using a 'jury' of twelve sworn men to find the facts.

But the Chancellor was never free to invent new writs simply because he thought this would help the proper and orderly development of the law. The royal judges would sometimes treat new writs to which they were unaccustomed as void, and the barons were constantly irritated because the uncontrolled issuance of writs amounted to legislation in which they had no part. An attempt was made to curb the powers of the Chancellor and his office in the Statute of Westminster II in 1285. The statute allowed the Chancellor or his officials to issue a new writ if the facts were 'in consimili casu' with a situation for which a writ already existed, but in cases of dispute or doubt the matter should be submitted to the next session of Parliament.

On this basis the Common Law had a remarkably continuous period of growth from the fourteenth to the seventeenth century; many forms of action gradually died away and were forgotten, but others had offshoots which became independent in the course of time and led in their turn to new developments. We cannot go into this process in greater detail here but we must give at least a brief indication of the striking history of the writ of trespass (for a lengthy treatment, see MAITLAND, *Forms of Action* (above p. 187) 53 ff., 65 ff.). Originally a writ of trespass could be issued only where a person had caused bodily injury to another or had interfered with his possession of tangible property forcibly or by breach of the peace—*vi et armis contra pacem domini regis*. But soon cases appeared in which there was no direct physical attack or where the harm to the plaintiff was only an indirect result of a particular act or omission on the part of the defendant. From about 1350, ostensibly relying on the formula in the Statute of Westminster, 'in consimili casu', the Chancellor allowed an 'action of trespass sur le case' or 'action on the case' which not only developed in time into the different sets of fact which now afford a remedy in the law of *tort* (see vol. II, Ch. 17 III) but also became the basis of the subsequent law of *contract*. In a famous case in 1348 the claim was that the defendant ferryman had overloaded his ship and caused it to founder, thereby causing the loss of the plaintiff's horse which had been entrusted to him for carriage. At that time there was no general claim for damages based on breach of contract. Certainly some claims of a contractual nature could be brought under the writs of *covenant* and *debt*, but *covenant* could not be used here since there was no document under seal and *debt* applied only to claims for a sum fixed in advance, such as a claim for the amount of a loan or agreed rent. Nor could a claim be based on *trespass*, for the loss of the horse was not directly attributable to any act of the ferryman. In this case the Chancellor allowed an 'action on the case', basing himself on the fact that the ferryman in performing a public service undertook ('assumpsit') the duty to bring his customer's property unharmed to the other bank. Thus gradually 'assumpsit' became a special variant of the 'action on the case', available at first only where a person had misperformed in some public calling, such as ferryman, farrier, or physician, but later extended to other cases of misperformance, and not long afterwards to cases of nonperformance of contractual promises. The various counts in *quasi-contract*, by means of which the Common Law deals with claims based on unjustified enrichment, are also offshoots of the 'action on the case' (see vol. II, Ch. 15 IV).

It will already have struck the careful reader of the last few pages that the development of the Common Law in the Middle Ages is very similar to the development of *Roman law* in many points. Rome, like England, gave judicial protection to rights only if the plaintiff could obtain a particular document of claim (formula, writ) from a non-judicial official (Praetor, Chancellor). In both systems the number of such documents of claim was normally limited, they were collected together in registers (*Edictum perpetuum*, Register of Writs), and they increased in number as new claims were developed in course of time (*actiones utiles*, writs 'in consimili casu'). The very similar ways in which litigation was initiated led legal practitioners in Rome and England to think not so much in terms of rights as in terms of types of action, and to interest themselves more in the concrete *facts* which fell within the various actions or writs rather than in elaborating the substantive law into a *system* based on some rational method. Thus Roman law and medieval Common Law were both dominated by 'procedural thinking'; in both systems the rules of *substantive law* emerged later, 'secreted in the interstices of procedural law' (MAINE, *Early Law and Custom* (1889) 389). In many other respects also the historical development of the two legal systems ran parallel, despite the intervening millennium. POLLOCK and MAITLAND were right to say that at the very time when the Glossators and Commentators of Western Europe were trying 'to adopt as their own the ultimate results of Roman legal history, England was unconsciously reproducing that history' (above p. 187, II. 558).

Compare the detailed studies of PETER, above p. 187, especially *Actio und Writ*, which successfully combine research in legal history and comparative law.—If we remember the unconscious parallelism of legal development in Rome and England we will find it easier to understand the really astonishing fact that in point of legal techniques the English lawyers have much more in common with the Roman lawyers than do the nineteenth century pandectists who expressly followed the Roman tradition: 'It may be a paradox, but it seems to be the truth that there is more affinity between the Roman jurist and the common lawyer than there is between the Roman jurist and his modern civilian successor. Both the common lawyer and the Roman jurist avoid generalisations and, so far as possible, definitions. Their method is intensely casuistic. They proceed from case to case, being more anxious to establish a good working set of rules, even at the risk of some logical incoherence which may, sooner or later, create a difficulty, than to set up anything like a logical system. That is not the method of the Pandectist. For him the law is a set of rules to be deduced from a group of primary principles, the statement of which constitutes the 'Allgemeiner Teil' of his structure. It is true that he has to make concessions to popular needs and that the superstructure is not quite so securely based on these fundamental principles as might have been expected. But the point of interest is that his method is not that of the Roman or of the common lawyer. (BUCKLAND/MCNAIR, *Roman Law and Common Law* (2nd edn., 1952) p. xiv).

III

Towards the end of the fourteenth century the legal creativity of the royal courts gradually began to wane. It became clear that the procedure of these courts was in many respects too crude and formalistic and that the applicable law was too rigid and incomplete; suits were being lost because of technical errors, because witnesses had been bribed, because of tricks of procedure, or because of the opponent's political influence. Thus as early as the fourteenth century parties who had lost a lawsuit in the King's courts on one of these grounds or who could not obtain an appropriate writ petitioned the King for an order compelling his adversary to do as morality and good conscience, if not the strict rules of the Common Law, required. The King used to transmit such petitions to his highest administrative official, the Chancellor. The Chancellor had an intimate knowledge of the Common Law and its remedies since it was he who issued the writs, and as the 'keeper of the King's conscience' and a prominent churchman he was best fitted to judge whether in the particular case the petitioner ought to receive the favour he sought 'for the love of God and in the way of charity'. In time these petitions were addressed directly to the Chancellor and the decisions he made developed into a complex of special rules of law which are still referred to in England, as they have been ever since the fifteenth century, as '*equity*'.

The Chancellor's special procedure for dealing with these petitions was fundamentally different from that of the royal courts. Unless the substance of the petitioner's claim was obviously hopeless, the Chancellor called the person named in the petition to a hearing which took place before himself rather than before a royal court. The defendant was called by a special writ carrying the threat of a steep penalty—*sub poena centum librarum*—and therefore called a 'writ of subpoena'. Since the purpose of the hearing before the Chancellor was to discover whether, as the petitioner complained, the defendant had behaved in a way which was contrary to morals and good conscience, the formal rules of proof used in the royal courts did not apply: the petitioner's opponent had to make a sworn statement to the Chancellor about the whole affair and give answers under oath to his questions. The Chancellor decided all matters of fact and law by himself without a jury, and the decision he eventually reached was executed by a process involving heavy penalties.

Throughout the fifteenth century the Chancellor decided more or less as he thought fit; decisions were consequently much coloured by the individual preferences of the churchman then in office. But after 1529 when the first secular Lord Chancellor, THOMAS MORE, was appointed, equity jurisdiction began to follow the model of the Common Law and developed rules and doctrines, originally in a very fluid and uncertain form, to which the Chancellor had recourse when similar fact-situations arose. Regular publication of the Chancellor's decisions began towards the end of the sixteenth century and before long he felt almost as bound by precedent as the judges of the Common Law courts. His activity came to be seen as being more and more *judicial*, and his office became the separate Court of Chancery; at the outset the Chancellor was the sole judge, but from 1730 onwards he was helped by his immediate subordinate, the Master of the Rolls. In the eighteenth century it was beyond doubt that 'equity', the rules of law applied by the Court of Chancery, was as much fixed by decisions and as much formed into technical legal rules as the rules of the Common Law.

It will be clear by now that the expression 'Common Law' has several meanings. Often 'Common Law' denotes the totality of the law of the Anglo-American legal family, as opposed to 'Civil Law' which denotes the law of the Continental legal systems and their followers, heavily influenced by law from Roman sources. In a *narrower sense* 'Common Law' refers only to that part of the law which was created by the King's courts in England, as opposed to 'statute law', on the one hand, which comprises the enactments of Parliament, and the rules and practice of 'equity' on the other. By 'equity' is meant not a group of maxims of fairness, but a part of substantive law distinguished from the rest by the fact that it was developed by the decisions of a particular court, the Court of Chancery.

In practice the most important group of rules developed by equity are the rules of 'trusts' (earlier called 'uses'). As early as the twelfth and thirteenth centuries it had become normal for a vassal who wanted to avoid the feudal burdens attaching to land to transfer to a 'trustee' the land he held of his superior; to the outside world the 'trustee' would appear to own the land, but he was bound to let the settlor have possession and profits during his lifetime and then, either on his death or when his heirs reached manhood, to deal with the property in a prescribed way in favour of another ('cestui que trust' or 'beneficiary'). If a trustee refused to deal with the property in the way he had undertaken, performance of the trust could not be enforced by complaining to the royal courts, because there was no writ to vindicate such claims and the procedure of the Common Law courts was then too rigid and formalistic to permit the trust agreement to be fully established. Here the Chancellor came to the assistance of the settlor and the beneficiaries; he saw the trustee's behaviour in breach of the trust agreement as being contrary to morality, as an offence against 'good conscience', and held that while the property in question doubtless belonged to the trustee 'at law', that is, in accordance with the rules of the Common Law, nevertheless he was obliged 'in equity' to deal with the property in the way he had promised by the trust agreement. In his decisions the Chancellor gradually refined this principle into very detailed rules; after the feudal system had disappeared they were utilized in the most varied areas of law, with the result that the trust can now be described as an institution typical of the style of Anglo-American law.

Equity also developed a number of *remedies* which greatly supplemented the rather crude system of pleas in the Common Law. Thus the old common Law with its archaic formalism clung to the view that a person could not protect himself *in advance* against the illegal behaviour of another, but had to wait until the harm had already been caused and then bring a claim for damages. This was unacceptable to the Chancellor with his more sensitive conscience. Under certain circumstances he would grant an '*injunction*' to prevent a future legal wrong which would be unconscionable. The Chancellor had eventually to decide many ancillary questions: under what conditions might an 'injunction' be issued, given the various cases which might occur? Could the injunction be used to prevent a threatened *breach of contract*? Could it be used as a temporary device pending the final judicial determination of a disputed question? and so on. In making such decisions, the Chancellor never operated *deductively* by developing a general principle recognized as sound, but *inductively* by dealing with each concrete problem as is came before him.

While the rules of Equity and Common Law were applied in different courts, as they were in England until 1873, the Chancellor was sometimes ready to issue an 'injunction' to prevent a party from instituting or continuing a lawsuit before the Common Law courts, or from executing a judgment he had obtained there. In the seventeenth century this practice led to a violent confrontation between Lord Chancellor ELLESMERE and Chief Justice COKE: COKE was of the view that the Chancellor had no right to sit in judgement over the Common Law courts by brusquely forbidding the continuation of active lawsuits or forbidding the execution of judgments lawfully obtained. ELLESMERE calmly answered that 'when a judgment [of the Common Law Courts] is obtained by oppression, wrong and a hard conscience, the Chancellor will frustrate and set it aside, not for any error or defect in the judgment, but for the hard conscience of the party'; *Earl of Oxford's Case* (1615) 1 W. & T. 615, 21 Eng. Rep. 485, 487. The dispute was submitted to King JAMES I, who decided it in favour of his Chancellor. Since that time it has been clear that in cases of conflict the rules of equity should prevail, but no other open confrontation between equity and Common Law has arisen.

'Specific performance' is another legal remedy which developed in equity jurisprudence. The remedies offered by the Common Law to victims of breach of contract were insufficient because, having developed out of the writ of trespass, they only sounded in damages. Cases were therefore brought before the Chancellor, and if he felt that it was unfair to restrict the innocent party to a claim for damages, he would allow, under conditions which gradually became fixed and clear, a claim for *performance of the contract in specie*.

On this, see the detailed treatment in vol. II, Ch. 12 IV.—Another of the Chancellor's inventions is the '*equitable doctrine of part performance*': if parties have concluded a contract for the sale of landed property which is invalid for want of form, the purchaser who in reliance on the contract 'has materially changed his position' may demand 'specific performance' from the Chancellor although 'at law' the contract is void. See vol. II, Ch. 12 IV.—Here is a further example: like Roman law, the Common Law long held to the view that claims could not be transferred and that the transferee of a claim could enforce it only with the agreement of the transferor. Here also the Chancellor's intervention was helpful: claims which he himself had developed by his decisions, such as the claim of a beneficiary under a trust, he held to be assignable without more ado, but he could not simply decree the transferability of claims which were enforceable 'at law', such as a claim for damages in tort, for that would have been an open alteration of the Common Law. Instead, he could issue a judgment ordering the assignor to agree to the assignee's enforcing the claim; the assignee, equipped with this judgment, was then in a position to sue the debtor, admittedly in the Common Law court which had jurisdiction (see vol. II, Ch. 10 IV). A survey of the important rules and doctrines of Equity, including those mentioned here, may be found in SCHWARZ, 'Equity' (above p. 187, pp. 122 ff.) and WEIR, 'The Common Law System', II *Int. Enc. Comp. L.* Ch. 2 (1974) 77; see also, apart from treatises devoted to the law of trusts, MAITLAND, *Equity* (above p. 187); HANBURY, *Modern Equity* (11th edn., Maudsley and Martin, 1981); SNELL's *Principles of Equity* (28th edn., Baker and Langan, 1982).

These examples will have made it clear that the rules of Equity did not openly contradict those of the Common Law and did not seek to oust or replace them. Instead, equity added marginalia, glosses, and supplements to the Common Law; they are often extremely important and sometimes go so far, to speak frankly, as effectively to neutralize the Common Law rules. To the outward eye, however, the Chancellor always professed reverence for the

Common Law, and announced that his decisions simply created *supplementary* rules. Thus it is possible, though it is not easy, to imagine English law without *equity*, but it is impossible to conceive of English law without the *Common Law* in the narrow sense. MAITLAND wrote on this:

'We ought to think of the relation between common law and equity not as that between two conflicting systems, but as that between code and supplement, that between text and gloss. And we should further remember this, that equity was not a self-sufficient system—it was hardly a system at all—but rather a collection of additional rules. Common law was, we may say, a complete system—if the equitable jurisdiction of the Chancery had been destroyed there would still have been law for every case, somewhat rude law it may be, and law imperfectly adapted to the needs of our time, but still law for every case. On the other hand, if the common law had been abolished, equity must have disappeared also, for at every point it presupposed a great body of common law' (*Equity* (above p. 187) 153).

IV

The nature of English law and the course of its development were fundamentally affected by the fact that very early in its history there arose a class of *jurists* who organized themselves in a kind of guild and so exercised very great political influence. Because the King's entourage and the royal courts which gradually emerged from it were all located in London in the early Middle Ages they attracted a large number of persons skilled in law; these were mainly churchmen to begin with, but later included laymen as the knowledge of law spread outside the church. Then, as today, a distinction was drawn between attorneys (*attornati*), experienced men of business who advised the parties on the law, and pleaders (*advocati*), who specialized in the oral presentation of cases before the courts. Around the beginning of the fourteenth century these legal practitioners organized themselves in several independent guilds (Inns of Court) of which four still exist today: Lincoln's Inn, Gray's Inn, Inner Temple, and Middle Temple. These lawyers' guilds were controlled by 'benchers', a group of successful senior practitioners with power to co-opt new members. They represented the guild in its external affairs, strove to prevent 'unfair competiton' by lesser breeds who knew the law, kept careful watch over the maintenance of professional etiquette, and possessed extensive disciplinary powers. Whereas on the Continent legal education has always been the province of *universities* and consequently rather theoretical and remote from practice, in England it was the monopoly of the Inns of Court throughout the whole Middle Ages and until the nineteenth century. It is obvious that in these circumstances legal education would tend to be primarily practical and empirical, more the development of a professional skill than a scholarly science. The acolyte learnt his law by taking part in court proceedings, by appearing in moots (hypothetical lawsuits) in which the benchers acted as judges, by attending regular lectures delivered by practitioners of experience, and above all by constant association with his seniors, who advanced their own education by daily discussions of practical problems. At the end of this training there was the solemn 'call to the Bar', conducted by the benchers of each Inn, as it still is today, in the four Inns already mentioned; the state had and has no part in it at all. But these guilds of lawyers were interested not only in teaching their young members law but also in forming their character, giving them a general education, and creating professional solidarity. For this purpose lawyers and aspirants lived cheek by jowl in the buildings of the guild, took their meals together, attended divine service together, made common use of the library which each Inn possessed, and joined in making music and organizing solemn feasts and dramatic entertainments. SHAKESPEARE's *As You Like It* is said to have had its world première in the Hall of the Middle Temple in 1601.

As early as the time of HENRY III (1216–72) there had been a tendency to choose the judges of the royal courts from the ranks of lawyers; from the beginning of the fourteenth century this became a fixed practice which is still adhered to today although not required by statute. Indeed, the judges in the early days were chosen from a particularly small élite of lawyers, the 'serjeants-at-law' (*servientes ad legem*). Only the most competent and well-regarded lawyers were promoted to the rank of serjeant by the Chancellor on the nomination of the judges in the Court of Common Pleas. On nomination they left their own Inn of Court and joined the *Serjeants Inn* where they stayed even if later appointed to the judiciary. The relations between the judges and this élite group of lawyers were therefore particularly close and friendly, for not only did they meet in court but they also had frequent social intercourse as members of the same Inn where they could talk shop. A serjeant was publicly referred to as 'brother' by the judges and could, by taking part in any lawsuit as 'amicus curiae', lend assistance to his 'brother' on the bench.

In the sixteenth century the opposition between barristers, who appeared in court, and attorneys, the other legal advisers, became more marked. Until that time members of both professions had lived together in the same Inns. Now the barristers began to claim that they appeared in court not as the representative of either party but pursuant to the *nobile officium* of independent counsel; they consequently declined to involve themselves with the ministerial tasks attaching to the institution of lawsuits, they regarded direct contact with the client, unless introduced by an attorney, as undesirable, and they treated it as unprofessional to make a formal legal claim for the payment of fees. Towards the end of the sixteenth century the attorneys, who were in direct contact with the parties and who were concerned with the preparation of lawsuits, especially the collection of evidence and procedural steps, were excluded from membership of the Inns of Court. Solidarity among those who remained, barristers specializing in oral presentation of cases and in giving legal opinions, became consequently even closer.

The attorneys were concerned with procedural steps before the Common Law courts; the same functions were performed before the Court of Chancery by the newer profession of *solicitors*. In 1739 the 'Society of Gentlemen Practisers in the Courts of Law and Equity' was founded to include both attorneys and solicitors. This was the predecessor of the 'Law Society' which is today the professional body of business lawyers, now given the common denomination of 'solicitors' (see below Ch. 17 III).

MAX WEBER has pointed out how great an influence on the style of law in a society is exercised by the professional training, activity, organization, and interests of its most prestigious lawyers, whom WEBER calls 'lawyers of rank' (*Rechtshonoratioren*). This idea is especially illuminating when applied to the English legal scene. The character of English law has unquestionably been deeply marked by the fact that the leading lawyers have never been professors or officials but always legal practitioners, that they lived, judges and barristers alike, in the closest social and professional contact at the central seat of the major courts, that they were strictly organized in powerful professional bodies, and that the Inns of Court not only saw to the recruitment of new lawyers and admitted them to the profession but also had a monopoly of their legal education. This has never been better described than by MAX WEBER who, after a sketch of the training programme in the Inns of Court in the Middle Ages, wrote:

Legal teaching of this kind naturally led to a rather formalistic treatment of law, dominated by precedent and analogy ... Legal practitioners did not aim ... to produce reasoned structures but rather lists of contracts and actions which would be useful in practice because they suited the typical and recurrent particular needs of litigants. This produced what in civilian countries is called 'cautelary jurisprudence' ... No system of rational law, nor even a rational systematization of law, can emerge from the forces inherent in cautelary jurisprudence. Such ideas as it produced were linked to fact situations which were formal in the sense of being concrete, recognizable, current, and quotidian, and the principle of distinction between them turned on external factors; if these ideas needed extending, this was done by the methods already indicated. They were not general concepts, which are formed by means of abstraction from the particular and by the logical processes of generalization and subsumption, and then applied syllogistically in the form of norms. When legal practice and teaching are purely empirical, legal thinking always moves from the particular to the particular and never tries to rise from the particular case to the general principles from which the decision in the particular case can then be deduced. Instead, it is trapped in words which it applies, construes, and stretches in all directions as the need of the moment dictates; should this prove inadequate, it has recourse to 'analogies' or technical fictions. Nevertheless, if the lists of contracts and actions required by the practical needs of litigants are sufficiently elastic, it is possible for the positive law to retain an extremely archaic character and remain formally unaltered despite great changes in the economic sphere ... But no rational legal education or legal theory can develop from such a situation. For when legal practitioners, and barristers in particular, are in control of legal education and have a guild-like monopoly of admission to legal practice, economic factors, namely an interest in fees, become very important and help to stabilize the positive law; this ensures that it will continue to be applied in a purely empirical manner and that its rationalization by legislation or scholarship will be obstructed. Any assault on traditional legal procedure threatens the material interests of the practitioners, for it is they who control the relation of the lists of contracts and actions to the formal norms on the one hand and to the needs of litigants on the other.' MAX WEBER, *Wirtschaft und Gesellschaft* (4th edn., 1956) 457 f.; see also the apt observations of KOSCHAKER, *Europa und das römische Recht* (2nd edn., 1953) 170 ff.

This sociological view of the professional background of English legal life helps us to understand why England never had a comprehensive reception of *Roman law*. Of course, from its earliest days the Common Law had manifold contacts with Civil Law. Thus in the middle of the twelfth century, a time when Roman law was hardly known at all in Germany, it was being taught in Oxford or Canterbury by Magister VACARIUS from Bologna. Roman-canon law was applied by the ecclesiastical courts which obtained jurisdiction over matrimonial affairs and succession to moveables under the first Norman kings. BRACTON himself as a churchman was familiar with Roman law, but he used its concepts and methods of thought only so far as was necessary to put some articulation and order into the indigenous English legal material. Finally, one can find some influences of Roman law in the equity practice of the Chancellor, himself a churchman until the sixteenth century, for he used canon law as a model for the *inquisitorial procedure* which he introduced in his court.

In mercantile and maritime law Roman influences were rather stronger. Trade in the Middle Ages was mainly in the hands of commercial men of different nationalities who travelled from country to country and from fair to fair and had special 'international' legal customs which were strongly coloured by Roman law. The normal procedure of the Common Law courts was ill adapted to dealing with the legal transactions of commercial men; instead, special courts grew up at the most important fairs and places of trade, and they applied an 'international' *lex mercatoria* rather than the Common Law. Much the same was true for maritime law; special courts of shipping arose in the major ports and the King later set up several courts of Admiralty which mainly applied Civil Law. Until the nineteenth century these special commercial courts had to fight for their jurisdiction with the Common Law courts, a struggle which terminated in favour of the Common Law courts. One result of this was that the 'law merchant' has long since ceased to be a separate body of law and has been completely incorporated into the Common Law, especially through the decisions of the famous judge LORD MANSFIELD (see p. 203). Nevertheless, the influence of Roman law in the areas of mercantile and maritime law was relatively strong and can be detected even today: 'This branch of English Law has undoubtedly drunk deep out of the well of old Roman Law, as well as the living waters of mercantile custom' (POTTER (above p. 187) 204).

At only one period in English legal history did the Common Law face the threat of being entirely ousted or at least pushed into the wings by Roman law: this was the period of the Tudors and Stuarts in the sixteenth and seventeenth centuries, the time of the great conflict between Parliament and the English kings who wanted an absolute monarchy. In this dispute Roman law had a great appeal for the royalists for it alone could support the political claim that whatever pleased the king had the force of law. Common Law was somewhat weakened at this time because, beside the courts which had existed time out of mind, a series of new royal courts and quasi-judicial bodies were created, especially the 'Star Chamber', a superior court which dealt with crimes of political significance; these courts were set up directly to implement the royal will and used a procedure based on the Roman-canon model. The lawyers who worked in these courts as judges and advocates, like those in the Courts of Admiralty, had been educated in Civil Law at the English universities, and had formed a special guild in Doctor's Commons since 1511. The intellectual climate of the period was also quite favourable for the reception of Roman law. Churchmen and educated laymen, though admittedly not practising lawyers, had such a passion for the ideas of the Renaissance and humanism that they often complained of the 'barbaric' and formalistic nature of the Common Law and were in favour of adopting the Civil Law which seemed to them to be clearer and more comprehensible (see the extensive treatment in HOLDSWORTH (above p. 187) IV. 217 ff.).

Despite all this, England never did have a comprehensive reception of Roman law. We have already seen one reason—the closed organization, the professional solidarity, and the political influence which the class of English lawyers, who were devoted to the maintenance of the Common Law on grounds of principle and profit alike, had built up over three centuries. But it is equally important that these lawyers consciously threw all their weight behind Parliament, the eventual victor in the political battles of the time. The Common Law became a mighty weapon in the hands of the Parliamentary party in the struggle against the absolutist prerogatives of the King, for in its long history it had developed a certain tenacity, its very cumbrous and formalistic technique serving to make it less vulnerable to direct attack from above. Ever since then, Englishmen have thought of the Common Law as being the essential *guarantee of freedom*, serving to protect the citizen against the arbitrary inroads of absolute authority, a function which on the Continent is performed by the *Constitution*.

The leader of the movement against absolute monarchy was one of the most famous of English lawyers, EDWARD COKE (1552–1634). As Chief Justice of the Court of Common Pleas and later of the Court of King's Bench, COKE was the most famous lawyer of his day and a passionate admirer of the Common Law. We have already seen how he fought for the precedence of Common Law over equity, and how he was false-footed in this question only by the fiat of the King. Shortly after this dispute COKE fell into disfavour with the King and was dismissed from judicial office. He then devoted himself to leading the Parliamentary opposition in the struggle against the royalists. He was also a splendid writer whose best-known book is a commentary on a work on land law by LITTLETON, published in 1481. 'Coke upon Littleton', a 'book of authority', greatly helped to preserve in the English land law of today many concepts and ideas which can be traced through COKE's book right back to the early Middle Ages.

After bitter struggles in the course of the seventeenth century the absolutist claims of the Stuarts were defeated and brought under firm Parliamentary control; thereupon all threats to the survival of the Common Law as the 'supreme law of the land' disappeared and a long period of internal peace began ('Age of Settlement'). In this period the English Bar produced a whole series of eminent judges, under whom Common Law and equity developed peacefully, adapting themselves to the needs of a country where industry and trade, internal and external, increasingly vied in importance with agriculture. Here we can only mention LORD MANSFIELD (1705–93) who was Chief Justice of the Court of King's Bench for more than thirty years, an expert in Civil Law, and the founder of English commercial law.

All the great English lawyers hitherto, from GLANVILL and BRACTON to COKE and MANSFIELD, were practitioners and almost always important judges, but in the eighteenth century we first find in WILLIAM BLACKSTONE (1723–80) a lawyer who, after a merely moderate career as a barrister, became Professor in Oxford and—one might almost say, nevertheless—had a lasting influence on English law. BLACKSTONE's fame rests on his *Commentaries on the Laws of England*, a four-volume systematic portrayal, based on his lectures of the whole of English law, not only private law and the law of procedure but also constitutional law and criminal law. On its first appearance, the *Commentaries* had an amazing success, and since then it has been reproduced in countless editions not only in England but also in other Common Law countries The book was praised for the pleasant clarity of its style, the sure accuracy of its legal propositions, and its intelligent concentration on what was vital and central. The *Commentaries* certainly do not reach that level of systematical and theoretical mastery of the legal material which was being achieved on the Continent at the time, but BLACKSTONE did not have a centuries-old tradition of university-taught doctrine on which to build. BLACKSTONE's significance lies in his being the first to order and control the *rudis indigestaque moles* of amorphous English case-law which the occasional irruption of statute rendered even more confused, and to present it in a clear and comprehensible manner and in a form which from the literary and didactic point of view was extremely successful; he made English law seem comprehensible to the educated layman as well as to the professional lawyer.

For an evaluation of BLACKSTONE, see ANDREAS B. SCHWARZ, *Das englische Recht* (above p. 187) 67 f.; ANDREAS B. SCHWARZ, 'Der Einfluss der Professoren auf die Rechtsentwicklung im Laufe der Jahrhunderte', printed in: SCHWARZ, *Rechts-*

geschichte und Gegenwart (1960) 181, 193; HOLDSWORTH, *Some Makers* (above p. 187)
238 ff.; THIEME, *Das Naturrecht und die europäische Privatrechtsgeschichte* (1947) 32 ff.

V

After the defeat of NAPOLEON England's external position was one of the
unprecedented strength but internally the nineteenth century started with a
period of serious political and social crisis. The centre of economic activity
had moved to trade and industry and workers had increasingly migrated to the
cities, but both Houses of Parliament were still composed of extremely
conservative aristocrats, bishops, and landed gentry. The Continent of
Europe, impoverished by NAPOLEON's wars, offered a very poor market
outlet for English industry, so that the number of unemployed grew
alarmingly and wages dropped. The landed proprietors nevertheless introduced tariffs on corn which prevented the import of cheap grain and thus
increased the misery of the people. As starvation, strikes, and Luddism
spread, the forces of progress in England began to realise that political and
social reforms were inevitable if a revolution was to be avoided. The electoral
legislation of 1831/2, over the opposition of the House of Lords, gave the
middle classes a share of political power for the first time; this meant that
important reforms could be carried through in other areas as well. The poor
law was fundamentally reconstructed, the employment of children was
limited, and the great change was made from protective tariffs to free trade;
finally, through legislative intervention, the legal scene was given the
modernization it badly needed.

The intellectual voice of the age, often called the 'Age of Reform' in
England, was JEREMY BENTHAM (1748–1832), a social reformer and lawyer. He
was the leader of the Utilitarian School which scrutinized the traditional
institutions of society in order to determine whether they were appropriate
and useful to the central aim of any social order, namely 'the greatest good of
the greatest number'. Such a school, unhistorical in its method and concerned
only with considerations of expediency, was bound to find a perfect butt in the
traditional institutions of the Common Law. Indeed, for BENTHAM, the rules
of Common Law, often based on historical accident rather than rational
design, were simply obstacles in the way of major social reform, and the same
was true of the traditionalism of the conservative practitioners typified by the
English barrister whom BENTHAM savagely criticized. His particular wrath
was reserved for BLACKSTONE whose classical and conservative presentation
of the results of history BENTHAM rightly found to be wholly uncritical. Thus
BENTHAM became a passionate propagandist for thorough reform of English
legal life, a reform he thought could be achieved only by comprehensive
codification.

BENTHAM's views had an enormous influence on English law in the nineteenth century but his call for complete codification of the Common Law found little response. Given their practical sense and their collective interests, English lawyers could not tolerate the thought of replacing the Common Law with a code worked out at a table on the basis of a particular social philosophy. But credit must be given to the reformist proposals of BENTHAM and his school for the many special enactments, especially in the latter half of the nineteenth century, which altered the courts structure and the law of civil procedure in England and, to a lesser degree, the substantive law.

At the time, indeed, the English law of procedure presented a picture which any uncommitted observer must have found in many respects grotesque. There was a baroque profusion of courts whose jurisdictions sometimes overlapped and sometimes differed in a manner so complex as to be comprehensible only to adepts. There were special rules of procedure for every court, indeed for every form of action brought before a particular court, often with technical peculiarities which had long since lost all meaning. The courts of Common Law and the Courts of Equity controlled separate parts of the substantive law with the result that the victim of a simple occurrence who wanted both an injunction and damages had the bother of going to two different courts. Attempts were made to overcome these inconveniences step by step by a series of special statutes until finally the courage was summoned up for a great reform of the courts structure and the law of procedure, by the enactment of the Judicature Act, 1873; it came into force in 1875 and still constitutes the basis of the present situation in England.

The main thrust of the reform was to transform the *courts system*. The numerous independent courts were brought within a single *Supreme Court of Judicature*, consisting of the High Court of Justice and the Court of Appeal. The High Court contains several divisions of which each specializes in types of litigation which were formerly within the exclusive jurisdiction of an independent court or courts. Claims which previously had to be *rejected* because the court had no jurisdiction can now be simply *transferred* to the relevant division within the same court. To begin with, the three divisions of Queen's Bench Division, Exchequer Division, and Common Pleas Division reflected the business of the prior independent courts of those names, but since 1881 these three divisions have been amalgamated in the *Queen's Bench Division*. Legal matters which were previously heard by the Court of Chancery were now transferred to the *Chancery Division*. Finally, questions of the validity of wills and marriages, and questions of admiralty law, for which there had previously been three separate courts, were referred to a single division, namely the *Probate, Divorce, and Admiralty Division*. These areas of law, familiarly referred to as 'wills, wives, and wrecks', seem rather heterogeneous, but the explanation is that the rules of succession, matrimonial law, and admiralty law which this division was to apply were all rather strongly coloured by Roman law. Sitting over the High Court with its three divisions is the *Court of Appeal*, an amalgamation of the several different courts which before the reform operated independently as courts of appeal. A third instance, not forming part of the Court of Judicature, was provided by a statute of 1876, in the special Judicial Committee of the House of Lords; it is composed of the Lord Chancellor and other judges raised to life peerages for this purpose.

The second important effect of the reform was to *consolidate* the areas of Common Law (in the narrow sense) and equity. This means that all divisions of the High Court as well as the Court of Appeal must apply all the rules and principles of English law, regardless of whether they were developed 'at law' or 'in equity'. Previously, for example, the Court of the Queen's Bench could not give effect to a defence which was recognized only 'in equity'; the litigant had to go to the Court of Chancery so that in a *second* suit the plaintiff in the *first* suit might be enjoined from continuing it. Today, the Queen's Bench Division *itself* can and must test the 'equitable defence' and, if it is established, reject the plaintiff's claim. The conflict between 'law' and 'equity', which is theoretically possible, is resolved by Judicature Act, s. 25(11), which lays down that the rules of equity shall prevail. Now one must not conclude from the 'fusion' of these two bodies of law that the difference between them has become without meaning. Within the High Court the division of business is such that even today the matters which must be determined by the rules of equity, however diverse they may be, are dealt with by the Chancery Division. This means that there are some barristers who specialise in 'chancery work' and it is from these specialists that the judges of the Chancery Division are chosen. Thus despite the 'fusion' of the bodies of 'law' and 'equity', the distinction is still vital today in the mind of the English lawyer, and the division is maintained in legal education and in legal writing, the two areas still being covered in different lecture courses and different books.

The final achievement of the reform of 1873 was to abolish the technical procedural consequences of the *writ-system*. In BLACKSTONE's time the plaintiff still had to announce at the outset of the litigation which of the 70–80 different forms of action his demand was based on. His choice was final and it conclusively determined which precedents could be invoked to decide the case, how the defendant was to be summoned, how evidence was to be adduced, and how the judgment should be executed. It often happened in such a system that the plaintiff in a difficult case chose the wrong form of action and thus lost his claim on purely technical grounds. The Judicature Act, by abolishing the 'forms of action', put the finishing touch to a development carried forward by a series of special statutes from 1832 to 1860. Today all trials in the High Court are started by the same 'writ of summons', that is, a formal demand in which the plaintiff describes the basis and substance of his claim in untechnical language; he no longer has to specify a particular type of claim. At the same time the Judicature Act went far to unify the rules of procedure. It is true that many details of procedure still depend on whether the plaintiff is seeking a divorce, probate of a will, or a judgment in damages, but these differences are now seen to be variations in what is in principle a unitary form of procedure before the High Court rather than fundamentally different types of process depending on the particular 'form of action'. This is not to say that the Judicature Act has in any way weeded out the traditional 'procedural type of legal thinking'. Modern presentations of the law of contact, tort, unjustified enrichment, and property still often divide up the material in terms of the traditional forms of action so that the 'forms of action', while they may have lost their procedural significance, have maintained their function as a method of ordering ánd developing the substantive law: 'The forms of action we have buried, but they still rule us from their graves' (MAITLAND, *Forms of Action* (above p. 187) 2).

Substantive law also was more altered by legislation in the nineteenth century than theretofore. It is true that in all periods of English legal history, including the earliest, there had been statutes affecting private law, but such statutes did not aim at any complete or comprehensive regulation of a particular area of law; they were generally simply *ad hoc* enactments, designed to change individual rules developed by the case-law whose practical effects seemed to the King and his advisers, and subsequently to Parliament, to be inconvenient. BENTHAM and his school would have accorded a much more important role to legislation, since they believed that legislation was the only way to achieve legal certainty and to bring the law into a simpler and generally comprehensible form. On this last point BENTHAM's demands coincided with the interests of English commerce, and so towards the end of the nineteenth century several comprehensive laws were enacted which covered specific areas of commercial law: the Bills of Exchange Act, 1882, the Partnership Act, 1890, the Sale of Goods Act, 1893, and the Marine Insurance Act, 1906. But these statutes did not deliberately represent any legal breakthrough: they were simply 'codifying statutes', that is, orderly presentations of existing rules which had been developed by the courts of Common Law. It follows that if there is any doubt about the purpose of a provision, it is permissible to go back to judicial decisions rendered *before* the statutes came into force. Apart from commercial law, such statutes as regulate important areas of private law are almost all products of the twentieth century. As yet there is no comprehensive codification of family law or the law of succession or the law of contract or the law of tort. For this purpose England still prefers special statutes which deal with particular questions, such as the law of matrimonial property, intestate succession, adoption, illegitimacy, administration of estates, or credit transactions, and even these statutes can be understood only against the background of the unwritten Common Law, for they use the concepts and categories and invariably presuppose the rights and doctrines which have been developed by the courts.

The Law of Property Act, 1925, is a very good example of this. This statute constituted a fundamental reform and simplification of English land law among other matters, but at every stage it uses the traditional basic concepts of the Common Law which in this area are especially old-fashioned. The foreign lawyer will therefore find this statute a perfectly closed book until he masters the basic concepts of English land law; the statute itself does nothing to explain them.

In the area of modern social legislation the English practitioner is overwhelmed by new enactments just as much as his German and French colleagues. For some time now, just as on the Continent, the English legal practitioner has barely been able to wade through the proliferating comprehensive enactments regarding housing, the protection of tenants, industrial law, social security, traffic and insurance law, the law of unfair competition and monopolies, and many other matters.

It follows from all this that the dichotomy, once so familiar, between the Common Law as a creation of the judiciary and the Civil Law as a creation of the legislature has lost much of the plausibility it enjoyed even at the beginning of this century. It is beyond dispute that the English courts have lost their leading role as creators of law to Parliament and to ministers with power to issue statutory instruments, especially in modern social law, while on the Continent the courts base themselves on the actual words of the ageing codes only in the most technical sense and the legislator in enacting *new* provisions is perfectly willing to adopt general formulae which throw the burden of legal creativity on to the courts. Today the old question whether statute or judicial decision is the primary source of law gives us very little help towards understanding the basic difference between Common Law and Civil Law. The more important question, in our view, is whether in deciding individual cases judges on the Continent and in England use *methods of finding and applying law* which are different in character. To this matter we shall shortly return.

VI

If our survey of English legal history has given the impression that the Common Law of England covers the whole of the British Isles, this false impression should be allayed. Great Britain is not legally unified at all; Scotland, in particular, with which we shall now briefly deal, has a legal system quite different from the Common Law.

But the *Channel Islands*, including Jersey and Guernsey, have their own legal system, too, as fairly independent dominions of the British Crown. At the time when England was conquered by the Normans, these islands were part of the Duchy of Normandy, a fact which leads Channel Islanders to joke that England is their oldest colony; this explains why the law of these islands still rests today on Norman customary law as contained in the Grand Coutumier de la Normandie (see above p. 78) and in later collections.

Until the beginning of the eighteenth century Scotland and England were independent kingdoms on British soil. Their relations had their ups and downs. In 1292 EDWARD I, King of England, defeated the Scots and brought the whole island under the control of the English Crown, but only a few years later the Scots conducted a great war of liberation and won their independence back again. These events taught the Scots that the only way to fend off their powerful neighbour to the South was to make an alliance with some power hostile to England: that power was France. For more than 200 years the Auld Alliance with France was the corner-stone of Scottish policy in opposing English aggression. Thanks to this alliance Scotland was opened to cultural influence from Continental Europe and for centuries Scots law developed in close contact with European legal scholarship. In the fourteenth and fifteenth centuries Scots lawyers went to the Universities of Orleans, Avignon, and Louvain for their education and to Leyden, Utrecht, and Groningen after Scotland turned to Calvinism. Thus Scotland had a true reception of Roman law; at the same time, in contrast to the Common Law which developed in insular self-sufficiency, Scots law acquired a cosmopolitan and 'international' character, with a very distinctive combination of indigenous customary law (especially the feudal land law), Scots statutes, Roman law, and the teachings of natural law. *The Institutions of the Law of Scotland* (1681) by LORD STAIR, statesman and judge, is a work designed on the Romanistic model and still a classical portrayal of Scots law.

From the beginning of the seventeenth century the same monarch wore the crowns of Scotland and England, and in 1707 the two countries combined from the point of view of constitutional and international law also. Both Parliaments ratified a treaty by which both Scotland and England ceased to exist as independent states and which instead created the 'United Kingdom of Great Britain'. Thereafter it has been a solecism, albeit a very common one, to refer to the 'English' Parliament, the 'English' Constitution, or the 'English' Crown.

The Treaty of 1707 laid down that the traditional courts system of Scotland should remain unimpaired; it further provided

that the Laws which concern public Right, Policy and Civil Government may be made the same throughout the whole United Kingdom; but that no alteration be made in Laws which concern private Right, except for evident utility of the subjects within Scotland.

The union of the two kingdoms thus left Scots law essentially as it was. It is true that towards the end of the eighteenth century the contacts with European legal scholarship were broken: traffic with the Continent became impossible in the Napoleonic Wars and when peace returned to Europe the position had been decisively changed, for the Code civil had been introduced in France and Holland and was monopolizing attention everywhere.

In the period starting with the nineteenth century Scots law came very strongly under the influence of English Common Law. Enactments of the British Parliament, both numerous and important, in the areas of private law, commercial law, economic law, administrative law, and social law apply in England and Scotland identically or alike. Decisions of the House of Lords have introduced into Scots law many unwritten rules of the Common Law. Until 1876 there were no Scots lawyers in the House of Lords in its judicial capacity and even today they constitute a minority of the judges who hear appeals from Scottish decisions, so it has quite often happened, as Scots lawyers never tire of saying, that the purity of Scots law has been sullied by the introduction of English legal ideas. English influence also comes from the fact that even where rules of Scots law should really be applied Scots lawyers and judges often have recourse to English decisions and textbooks, which are naturally more numerous. Scotland has also adopted the English doctrine of the binding force of precedent, though with some limitations. But the Scottish courts also pay great attention to the so-called 'institutional writers'; these are a dozen or so Scots writers, especially STAIR, MACKENZIE, ERSKINE, and BELL, who between 1680 and 1820 wrote basic works on Scots law and enjoy in Scotland a reputation analogous to that formerly enjoyed on the Continent by DOMAT, POTHIER, or GROTIUS.

Despite these overt or covert effects of English Common Law, Scots law has so far managed to maintain its independence in the heartland of private law, not least because that independence has been powerfully asserted since the Second World War by brilliant scholars in the Scottish Law Faculties such as T. B. SMITH and WALKER (above p. 188).

See, however, the criticisms of WILLOCK (above p. 188).—The law of contract, for example, as on the Continent, rests on the principle that every agreement intended to be contractually binding by the parties, according to the judge's finding, is valid and actionable; Scots law does not have the additional requirement of consideration (see vol. II, Ch. 5 II). Scotland, unlike England, accepts contracts for the benefit of third parties; the claim for specific implement of a contract is in principle *always* admissible, not just exceptionally as in England (see vol. II, Ch. 12 IV). Since the time of the 'institutional writers', Scotland has accepted the view that all claims for the return of an indebitum rest on a unitary basis, while English Common Law still operates with a heterogeneous group of actions of 'quasi-contract' (see vol. II, Ch. 15 IV). In Scotland almost the whole of the law of delict is covered by general liability for culpa (which developed from the *actio legis Aquiliae*) and the *actio iniuriarum*; here, in contrast to English law with its great profusion of separate torts (see vol. II, Ch. 17 III), the law of Scotland operates with only a few high-level principles and concepts, thereby demonstrating that inner economy which 'civilian' legal thought regards as a virtue.

It is an open question whether Scots law will be able in the long run to resist the influence of Common Law and whether in the future the area within which it can develop its own solutions may not become more and more restricted.

One must realize that Scots law is not reinforced by codification, as the law of Louisiana is, nor by using a separate language, like the law of Quebec; nor is Scotland in the position of South Africa (see below Ch. 18 VI) of being its own legislator, for Scotland must often trim its legal sails to the winds blowing from Westminster. However this may be, it is clear that Scots law deserves particular attention from comparative lawyers as a special instance of the symbiosis of the English and Continental legal traditions; this may be of some assistance to those who embark on the great project of the future, namely to procure a gradual approximation of Civil Law and Common Law.

17

Courts and Lawyers in England

ABEL, 'The Decline of Professionalism', 49 *Mod. L. Rev.* 1 (1986).
ABEL-SMITH/STEVENS, *In Search of Justice—Society and the Legal System* (1968).
BENSON REPORT, The Royal Commission on Legal Services (Chairman: Sir Henry Benson) Cmnd. 6748 (1979).
BUNGE, *Das englische Zivilprozessrecht, Eine systematische Darstellung mit einer Auswahlbibliographie* (1974).
EVERSHED, 'The Judicial Process in Twentieth Century England', 61 *Colum. L. Rev.* 761 (1961).
GOLDSCHMIDT, *English Law from the Foreign Standpoint* (1937).
GRIFFITHS, *The Politics of the Judiciary* (1976).
HAZELL (ed.), *The Bar on Trial* (1978).
JACKSON, *The Machinery of Justice in England* (7th edn., 1977).
JOLOWICZ, 'Les Décisions de la Chambre des Lords', *Rev. int. dr. comp.* 31 (1979) 521.
KIRALFY, *The English Legal System* (1984).
MANN, 'Fusion of the Legal Professions?', 93 *Law Q. Rev.* 367 (1977).
MEGARRY, *Lawyer and Litigant in England* (1962).
MILTON, *The English Magistracy* (1967).
RADCLIFFE/CROSS, *The English Legal System* (6th edn., 1977).
REID, 'The Judge as Lawmaker', 12 *JSPTL* 22 (1972).
SCARMAN, 'The English Judge', 30 *Mod. L Rev* 1 (1967).
SHETREET, *Judges on Trial, A Study of the Appointment and Accountability of the English Judiciary* (1976).
STEVENS, *Law and Politics, The House of Lords as a Judicial Body 1800–1976* (1978).
WILSON, *Cases and Materials on the English Legal System* (1973).
ZANDER, *Lawyers and the Public Interest, A Study in Restrictive Practices* (1968).
——, *Cases and Materials on the English Legal System* (1973).
——, *Legal Services for the Community* (1978).
——, 'Promoting Change in the Legal System,' 42 *Mod. L. Rev.* 489 (1979).
——, 'The English Legal Profession,' in: *Anwaltsberuf im Wandel* (Arbeiten zur Rechtsvergleichung no. 111, 1982) 59.

I

LAWYERS from other countries have long been fascinated by the institutions of English legal life and by the men who run them. This fascination has not always conduced to objectivity of judgment about English justice. The European who addresses himself to this theme often has in his mind's eye the romantic picture of a judge, robed in scarlet and heavily bewigged, holding

court in a splendidly panelled hall and making law with wise authority from fat volumes of reports. People are especially surprised to be told that an industrial state like England with nearly 50 million inhabitants can get by with only a few dozen judges. One sometimes hears the view that this tiny number of judges is explained by the fact that lawyers' fees and court fees are so exorbitant in England that law is only open to plutocrats, or the view that Bench and Bar conspire to preserve a legal system which has lots of old world charm but is seriously in need of reform, or the view that young English lawyers are trained exclusively in offices, on the theory that a university education in law is not only unnecessary but actually harmful. There may or may not be a grain of truth in these views but they certainly give a one-sided and false impression of English justice; in the following section we shall try to present a picture, necessarily only in outline, which is rather nearer the truth.

II

The English citizen who is involved in civil litigation normally comes into contact not with the High Court in London, much less the Court of Appeal or the House of Lords, but with the Magistrates' Courts or the County Courts which are spread throughout the land.

1. *Magistrates' courts* are staffed by 'Justices of the Peace', magistrates without any legal training, three of whom constitute a bench under a chairman chosen by themselves. Only in the larger towns are there professional paid 'stipendiary magistrates' who have legal training and who sit alone. Justices of the Peace, of whom at the moment there are about 19,000 in England, divided between about 1,000 courts, are nominally appointed by the Queen but really chosen by the Lord Chancellor from lists provided by local commissions. The choice is normally made from people who have shown some interest in public affairs by being active in local government, trades unions, professional organizations, chambers of commerce, or in some other way; but party political considerations also play some part in the selection of magistrates. To be a Justice of the Peace is not a full-time job and many of them are retired; it is an honorary position which attracts only a small payment for expenses. But the social prestige attaching to the position is considerable: persons of rank in provincial towns and even tycoons see it as an honour to be a Justice of the Peace and to be able to put the initials JP after their names.

The jurisdiction of Magistrates' Courts is mainly in *criminal law*, where they deal with all minor offences, especially the vast number of traffic offences. Their procedure is summary, without a jury, and is very swift, especially since the defendant in trivial cases often pleads guilty and no evidence need be called.

For more serious crimes where a jury is called for, there is a special court, the Crown

Court. Depending on the gravity of the charge, cases in the Crown court are tried either before a full-time judge or before a 'Recorder', an experienced barrister or solicitor in professional practice who is commissioned to serve as judge from time to time. The Crown Court may also contain up to four Justices of the Peace.

So far as *private law* is concerned, the jurisdiction of Magistrates' Courts is principally in matters of family law: they hear claims for maintenance between spouses and between parents and children, legitimate or illegitimate, issue separation orders, apply the laws about the care of children, agree to adoptions, supervise guardians, and have extensive competence in matters concerning the protection of children.

Although for some time Justices of the Peace have been required on nomination to follow courses which introduce them to the most important legal questions likely to arise, it is nevertheless necessary to have a skilled lawyer constantly at their side to advise them. In the Magistrates' courts this function is performed by the so-called 'clerk to the justices', a solicitor whose task it is, part-time or, in the larger towns, full-time, to supervise the administration of the court, to see to the procedure in court, and above all to advise the Justices when problems arise during a sitting. For this purpose the clerk may, should the justices so wish, take part in the deliberations prior to judgment.

2. *County Courts* were introduced in England by statute 'only' in 1846. The aim was to provide within easy reach of the parties courts which could determine private law disputes involving relatively low sums at rather small cost.

There are over 400 County Courts in England, so situated in the country that everyone is within easy distance of one. The courts are manned by a single judge, of whom there are at present about 125. Thus most of the judges attend regularly in several different County Courts in turn, which together form a single jurisdiction. But in many of the larger cities the jurisdiction consists of only one court so that the judge always sits in the same place. The cases for which County Courts are competent are almost exclusively private law matter, mainly claims arising from tort or breach of contract for sums of not more than £2,000, though larger claims may be heard with the defendant's consent. County Courts may now hear equitable claims involving property amounting to as much as £10,000. Divorce cases are reserved to the High Court, unless they are undefended. Some County Courts have been given jurisdiction for disputes arising from bankruptcy and admiralty law, and here the jurisdictional limit is higher. Furthermore, modern social legislation has reserved for the County Courts a whole series of very important matters, notably those arising from housing law and legislation protecting tenants. The practical importance of the County Courts is shown by the fact that about 85 per cent of all civil actions are first heard in these courts: 'If we consider that from a social point of view the importance of a court is the number of *persons*

whose affairs it deals with, there can be no doubt that County Courts are the most important civil courts in the country. (JACKSON (above p. 212) 33).

The judges in the County Courts are circuit judges, chosen from the ranks of the barristers and appointed by the Queen on the proposal of the Lord Chancellor. Each County Court also has a Registrar, a solicitor who may or may not have a private practice of his own, depending on local circumstances, and who may serve several courts if they are not very busy. The Registrar controls the administrative staff of the County Court, but he also performs judicial functions: he conducts the procedure prior to the oral trial, he issues judgments by default or confession, and may himself decide claims involving less than £200 or larger claims if the parties agree.

Parties in the provinces who want a dispute resolved in the High Court do not necessarily have to go to London, for since the earliest days of English legal history High Court judges have been travelling into the provinces in order to decide civil and criminal matters on the spot. The practice continues to this day, save that civil matters are heard only if the judge has free time after hearing the criminal cases in the Crown Court. London is by far the most important economic centre in the country and the great majority of barristers practise there, so many more civil matters are dealt with in London than the relative population would justify.

3. When people abroad or even in England speak of English justice, they think in the first place of the *High Court of Justice* in London. As we have seen, this court consisted of three divisions: the Queen's Bench Division, the Chancery Division, and the Probate, Admiralty and Divorce Division. The statute of 1970 transformed the last of these divisions into the 'Family Division'; at the same time succession disputes were transferred to the Chancery Division and admiralty cases to the Queen's Bench Division, indeed to a special Admiralty Court there. The number of High Court judges has risen from only 25 in 1925 to 75 at the present time, and it will probably increase still more. Each judge is attached to one of the three divisions mentioned. Today there are 47 judges in the Queen's Bench Division, presided over by the Lord Chief Justice; there are 12 in the Chancery Division under the Vice Chancellor, and a further 16 in the Family Division under the President. Except for appeals for judgments of lower courts and for some proceedings of an adminstrative nature, all cases in the High Court are decided by single judge.

The division of business in the High court gives to the judges of the Queen's Bench Division the cases which before 1873 fell within the jurisdiction of the old Common Law courts. The most frequent cases in practice involve claims for damages for breach of contract or tort, normally in the context of traffic or industrial accidents. There is no jurisdictional limit but if the case involves only a small sum of money the judge has discretion to refer it to the County Court; if he retains and deals with the case in the High Court, and the case is not one which has some importance apart from its value in financial terms, he can decree that the successful plaintiff should recover from the defendant only the relatively low costs that he would have obtained had the case been brought in the County Court.

The judges of the Chancery Division operate only in London so now all cases with a strong equity content, such as administration of the estates of decedents, bankrupts, or incompetents, or questions of the law of trusts, or the liquidation of companies, or the law of mortgage, are heard in the Chancery Division in London, unless the property in dispute is worth less than £10,000, when the County Court has concurrent jurisdiction.—Much the same is true with cases previously falling within the jurisdiction of the Probate, Divorce, and Admiralty Division. Probate and admiralty cases go to the High Court if they are important and to the County Courts if they are not. All matrimonial cases were heard in London until 1920, when some Assize Courts were given jurisdiction in divorce cases, first for specified and later for all types of case. Because of the steady increase in divorce suits, the expedient was adopted in 1946 of equipping County Court judges with the robe, wig and jurisdiction of a High Court judge and commissioning them to hear divorce suits in specified provincial towns. Since 1968 most County Courts themselves have jurisdiction for undefended divorces but all 'defended' divorces must still be heard even today in London or by judges from London. An obvious solution would be to give County Courts jurisdiction over all divorces but the well-organized opposition of the barristers has prevented this: barristers have an exclusive right of audience before High Court judges and were chary of the competition of solicitors who have a right of audience in County Courts.

A number of important judicial tasks in the High Court are performed by the many 'masters' and 'registrars', who are chosen from barristers or solicitors with a certain professional experience. They perform many varied tasks (see DIAMOND, 76 *LQ Rev.* 504 (1960)) of which the main one is to work closely with parties and their legal advisers in the preliminary steps of procedure so that when the matter comes before the judge, it can be decided without delay in a single oral hearing. The master also decides, with appeal to a judge, whether the trial should be referred to a County Court or should be heard in London or on circuit, what security, if any should be given, and questions regarding expert opinions and methods of proof. Furthermore, on proper motion of the parties, he sees to it that before the oral trial begins the parties provide their opponent with full information about the facts they propose to prove and the relevant documents in their possession. The master also tries to get the parties to agree as many facts as possible so as to reduce the amount that must be proved and thereby lighten the task of the judge. Because the trial is so carefully prepared and because the parties must fully disclose what positions they propose to adopt, many suits are terminated by compromise, admission or withdrawal of claim before the oral trial ever starts.

4. The *Court of Appeal* hears appeals from judgments of the High Court, and, with some limitations, appeals from the County Courts as well. In theory

the Lord Chancellor presides but in practice his role is performed by another judge, called the 'Master of the Rolls'—a title borne since the seventeenth century by the Chancellor's senior subordinate in Chancery. In addition to the Master of the Rolls the Court of Appeal consists of 22 'Lord Justices of Appeal', who sit in divisions of three or occasionally two. The Court of Appeal reviews every point of law on which the judgment below was based but often feels itself bound by trial judge's findings of fact, even if they have legal consequences. Thus the Court of Appeal does not hear again the evidence presented at the trial and new evidence is admitted only within very strict limits.

5. The *House of Lords* is the highest court, not only for England, but also for Scotland (except for criminal cases) and Northern Ireland, which in other respects have their own system of courts. Decisions are made by a special judicial committee which contains, apart from the present Lord Chancellor and predecessors who have demitted office on a change of government, ten judges who bear the title 'Lord of Appeal in Ordinary', called 'Law Lords' for short. The committee is normally composed of five judges and hears appeals from judgments of the Court of Appeal provided that, in view of the importance of the case, leave to appeal has been granted either by the Court of Appeal or by the House of Lords itself.

Brief mention must finally be made of the *Judicial Committee of the Privy Council*. The Privy Council is an advisory body which developed out of the old Curia Regis and the task of its judicial committee is to give the Queen advice, which is invariably followed, on petition made to her as the fount of justice by parties who have unsuccessfully exhausted the legal procedures in the national courts of Commonwealth countries. Appeal to the Privy Council has been abolished by many important members of the Commonwealth: Canada, India, Pakistan, and, in 1982, Australia have all declared that the decisions of their own highest courts are final. But even today it is not uncommon for the Privy Council to hear cases from countries as diverse as New Zealand, Sri Lanka, Sierra Leone, and Malaysia, an impressive indication of the world-wide spread of the Common Law tradition.

6. High Court judges are nominated by the Queen on the proposal of the Lord Chancellor who selects them from among barristers with at least ten years practical experience; on appointment they receive the accolade of a knighthood. As a member of the government, the Lord Chancellor is a politician who has often spent many years in the House of Commons but it must be said that for the last fifty years at least political considerations have played next to no part in the nomination of judges. In the narrow and familiar circle of barristers a *communis opinio* readily determines which of their number are fit for judicial office and a Lord Chancellor would quickly incur public reproach or, worse still, public ridicule if he proposed for a judgeship a barrister who was politically committed but professionally incapable. Once appointed, judges are wholly independent. Under the formula of the Act of

Settlement 1701, which is still in force today, a judge holds his office only 'during good behaviour subject to a power of removal by His Majesty on an address presented to His Majesty by both Houses of Parliament', but no English judge has ever been removed from office since that date and no one in England is quite sure how exactly one would set about it (see JACKSON, above p. 212, pp. 461 f.). Even desire for promotion, which can temper the independence of professional judges on the Continent, plays no great role in England. High Court judges have already reached a peak position and for many of them a further move up to the Court of Appeal or the House of Lords would be unattractive as the business there is rather different and there is very little financial incentive. A Lord Justice of Appeal earns only a little more than a High Court judge (£68,400 as against £62,100), while a Law Lord earns only a little more than that (£71,400).

The fact that judges are chosen from the closed circle of eminent and successful barristers ensures that the higher courts are manned by judges who are extremely competent and very experienced in practice, able to command the respect of the whole legal profession. But in the view of many people, this restricted principle of choice has the disadvantage that the English judges tend to be of an extremely conservative temperament: a person who has enjoyed a brilliant professional career will hardly be disposed to criticize and reform the very circumstances which made it possible. This tendency to stability may also be reinforced by the fact that a judge is never appointed before he is 40, and usually not until he is past 50, and that until recently there was no age for retirement; this was first introduced in 1959, with some resistance from the judges, and was fixed at 75. To be more specific, the charge has occasionally been made that the marked individualism of English judges led them, especially until the Second World War, to adopt a perverse attitude to modern social legislation and give an unduly restrictive construction to many of their provisions contrary to the clearly discernible will of Parliament (see JACKSON (above p. 212) 472 ff., and ABEL-SMITH/STEVENS (above p. 212) 166 ff.).

Parliament itself has reacted to this. According to many writers, it was in a deliberate attempt to render modern statutes on social security, tax, agricultural holdings, and landlord and tenant 'judge-proof' that Parliament referred disputes in these areas not to the ordinary courts but to special 'tribunals', of which there are now an enormous number; their procedure is relatively simple and cheap, they are often staffed by laymen, and they are often closely linked with relevant government departments. The number of appeals to the High Court in these areas is small and diminishing. This very fact helps us to understand how England gets by with so relatively small a number of judges, especially when one considers that West Germany, for instance, has three levels of separate courts for administrative and social matters.

Whatever one may think of the conservatism of the English judges, it seems clear that England has never been readier for reform or more energetically critical of the existing system than today. Some radicals have demanded the 'nationalization' of all professional lawyers, much as doctors were nationalized in the National Health Service, and would leave no part of the courts system untouched. In present circumstances these proposals may seem unrealistic but it must be granted that an increasing number of leading and influential jurists see it as necessary to undertake drastic reforms of substantive law, and especially of the law of procedure and and the system of courts. Thus in 1963, before becoming Lord Chancellor, LORD GARDINER, in association with MARTIN, produced a book with the striking title *Law Reform NOW*, containing wide-ranging proposals for the modernization of English law. One proposal envisaged the creation of a special permanent Commission for the reform of the law. This proposal has already been realized: since 1965 England and Scotland have each had a five-man 'Law Commission' which has the help of a well-equipped staff in its demanding task

'to take and keep under review all the law . . . with a view to its systematic development and reform, including in particular the codification of such law, the elimination of anomalies, the repeal of obsolete and unnecessary enactments, the reduction of the number of separate enactments and generally the simplification and modernisation of the law' (Law Commissions Act 1965 s. 3). Many of the Law Commission's proposals have resulted in legislation which has modernized and improved English law on important topics. The Law Commission's programme of work originally contained a plan to codify the whole law of contract. This project has been abandoned. The advantages and disadvantages of the codification of English law are discussed in many recent articles of great interest to anyone from a Civil Law jurisdiction: see, for example, SCARMAN, *A Code of English Law?* (1966); HAHLO, 'Here lies the Common Law: Rest in Peace', 30 *Mod. L. Rev.* 241 (1967): DIAMOND, 'Codification of the Law of Contract, 31 *Mod. L. Rev.* 361 (1968); DONALD, 'Codification in Common Law Systems', 47 *Austr. LJ* 160 (1973); KERR, 'Law and Reform in Changing Times', 96 *LQ Rev.* 515 (1980); NORTH, 'Problems of Codification in a Common Law Country,' *RabelsZ* 46 (1982) 94; ANTON, 'Obstacles to Codification', 1982 *Jur. Rev.* 15.

In recent years various aspects of the English legal system have repeatedly come under investigation by Committee and criticism by writers. It may be that London's importance as a legal centre will diminish as the limits on the financial jurisdiction of the County Courts are raised and more criminal cases are heard by the Crown Courts. Noteworthy, too, are the English experiments with novel forms of 'informal' resolution of minor disputes in private law. In non-litigious matters advice to the relatively deprived has been provided not only by solicitors but also, most successfully, by 'Citizens Advice Bureaux'. Such fascination as the English system of justice still exercises on the Continental observer depends now not so much on the admittedly astonishing position of the English judge as on the interesting question how in the years to come England will manage to effect a compromise between its tendency to cling tenaciously to traditional legal institutions and the need which exists in all modern societies to provide effective justice for every citizen.

III

Professional lawyers in England are divided into *solicitors* and *barristers*. This distinction, which has cropped up several times in the preceding pages, is a further peculiar characteristic of English legal life which must now be briefly considered.

1. The typical English *solicitor* is an independent lawyer who gives legal advice to a client on personal and business affairs. In practice on his own or in partnership with other solicitors, he carries through transactions involving land, drafts contracts and wills, undertakes the administration of estates, and advises his client on tax, commercial, insurance, and company law matters. Solicitors alone are empowered to take the necessary steps prior to trial. They may also act in the name of their client in the procedure which precedes the oral hearing before the judge. In the trial itself they have a right of audience only in the Magistrates' Courts and the County Courts, but not in the High Court or most Crown Courts, much less in higher courts (see *Abse* v. *Smith*, [1986] 1 All ER 350 (CA)). Most solicitors' offices are in the provinces and naturally are not so much concerned in the preparation, initiation, or conduct of trials as with transactions concerning land. Registers of land exist in most areas of the country, but they are not as sophisticated as in Germany. If the title is not registered, the title of a vendor or mortgagor must be investigated carefully by any purchaser or mortgagee. Even if it is registered, most people who are buying and selling houses wish their interests to be protected from the contractual stage to the completion of the transaction. This business, called 'conveyancing', falls mainly to solicitors (who had, indeed, a legal monopoly of it until very recently), and the fees for the conveyancing of houses constitute about 30% of the profession's total income.

In 1986 the total number of solicitors authorized to practice was about 46,000. Of these about half were either sole practitioners or profit-sharing partners; the remainder were either salaried partners or assistant solicitors in larger firms or were in employment in local government or in commerce and industry. There were about 7,500 full-time solicitors' offices, about one-third of them having only one solicitor, nearly a half having two to four partners, and less than a fifth having five or more. A few very large firms of solicitors in the City of London have forty or fifty partners or even more.

The professional organization of solicitors is the *Law Society*, of which as many as 85 per cent of all practising solicitors are members. There is no legal requirement for a solicitor to be a member but the Law Society has statutory power to lay down rules, with the agreement of the Lord Chancellor and other leading judges, regarding the training and admission of solicitors. The Law Society also finances the Solicitors' Complaints Bureau which can bring disciplinary proceedings before the Solicitors' Disciplinary Tribunal, an independent judicial body. Solicitors' fees in private matters are normally a matter for agreement between solicitor and client. The courts, however, retain the power to review a solicitor's charges in any case involving court proceedings, and in other cases the Law Society will do so if a client complains.

2. *Barristers* specialize in advocacy before the higher courts, essentially the preparation of written documents and the oral presentation before the court. Here barristers have a monopoly which rests not on the provisions of any statute but on a long-estabished practice of the judges according to which a party who does not appear *personally* can have no legal adviser in court other than a barrister. Barristers also give oral legal advice or written opinions and draft complicated wills, land contracts, or trust deeds; indeed, some barristers do nothing else. In these areas there is a certain competition between barristers and large firms of solicitors, but it is quite normal for a solicitor in a case of particular difficulty to seek the opinion of a barrister, many of whom specialize in particular topics and therefore have an extremely detailed knowledge of the relevant judicial precedents. One very striking fact is that the etiquette of the Bar forbids any direct contact with the client. Thus a person who wishes to institute a suit in the High Court or to obtain a barrister's opinion must always do so through a solicitor. If a conference becomes necessary between the barrister and the client who is thus brought into contact with him, the barrister is bound by professional etiquette to hold his conference in the presence of the solicitor and in his own chambers, so far as possible. The choice of barrister normally falls to the solicitor since only a few litigants have any preferences, so it follows that a barrister's success depends very much on his links with the large firms of solicitors.

Even today barristers are not entitled to form partnerships. Instead, barristers occupy 'sets of chambers' in loose groups of about twelve to fifteen, often specializing in particular areas of law. In London all these chambers are situated in the Inns of Court, in buildings possessed for centuries and steeped in tradition, not far from the High Court. The chief of staff in these sets of chambers is the *clerk*. The clerk makes the contact between solicitors and the barristers in his chambers, fixes appointments, gives information about the individual barrister's programme of work, and agrees with the solicitor on the fee payable to the barrister by the client. The amount of these fees is not fixed by statute but depends on the difficulty and importance of the case as well as the reputation and standing of the barrister in question. Since the clerk receives a fixed percentage of the fees paid to the barristers in his chambers, he is naturally interested in fixing the fee as high as possible, without losing the business to another set of chambers. Until recently it was regarded as unprofessional for barristers and solicitors to have *direct* transactions regarding fees without the clerk as intermediary, and this is still extremely unusual; even today a barrister cannot sue for his fees.

The method of fixing fees and the prohibition of partnership make it difficult for young barristers to make a living at the outset of their career, but the more they succeed in obtaining a certain reputation and in maintaining good contacts with firms of solicitors, the more sought-after they become and the higher the fees they can, through their clerk, prescribe. For barristers who are greatly in demand the burden of work can be very heavy, since advocacy can only be performed in person and the barrister is in principle obliged to accept every brief which is offered provided that the stipulated fee is paid. At a certain moment in a very successful career barristers will face the question whether they should not lighten their work-load by petitioning the Lord Chancellor to submit their name to the Queen for nomination as *Queen's Counsel* (abbreviated QC). Queen's Counsel form the élite of the Bar from whom High Court and Circuit judges are normally chosen. They stand in high regard in court and in the Inns, and are entitled to wear a robe of silk. For this reason, when a person has recently been promoted to the rank of Queen's Counsel, one says that 'he has taken silk'. Queen's Counsel can demand particularly high fees and normally appear in court in company with a 'junior' barrister, for whom of course the party must pay an additional fee; in consequence of this great expense, Queen's Counsel are briefed only for important and interesting suits. No barrister may *claim* to be appointed Queen's Counsel; whether the Lord Chancellor accepts such a petition and proposes nomination to the Queen depends on whether the petitioner has, in practice at the Bar for at least ten years, achieved the requisite degree of success in his profession and renown among his peers. About one in ten of the 5,500-odd active barristers in 1986 were Queen's Counsel, and of these over 90 per cent had chambers in London.

The professional organizations for barristers are the four *Inns of Court*, all of equal standing, known as 'The Honourable Society of Lincoln's Inn', 'of the Inner Temple', 'of the Middle Temple' and 'of Gray's Inn'. The business of these four Inns is conducted by the so-called 'benchers', not elected by the members of their Inn but co-opted for life by the other benchers. Most of them are now practising barristers, mainly Queen's Counsel, but some are judges, for judges remain members of their Inn even after appointment.

In addition to running the business of their Inn of Court and administering its property, benchers admit students, who must become members of an Inn before their training, and call them to the Bar once they have completed it. Other institutions are of general importance for barristers. The most important of these is the *General Council of the Bar*. As the governing body of the Bar, it lays down and implements general policy with regard to all matters affecting the Bar. Its 93 members include at least 51 practising barristers (39 elected at large and 12 by the Circuits), as well as 12 members appointed by the Benchers of the Inns. The *Council of the Inns of Court* formulates consistent policies for the Inns and liaises with the *Council of Legal Education*, which organizes the training of future barristers under the general direction of the Bar Council. In matters of discipline, charges are preferred by the *Professional*

Conduct Committee of the Bar Council before a *Disciplinary Tribunal* chaired by a judge, which acts in the name and on behalf of the Inns Council.

For details on the profession of the barrister and his position in the whole context of English legal life, reference may be made to the works of MEGARRY and ABEL-SMITH/ STEVENS (above p. 212). The former is written from the point of view of a successful Queen's Counsel and gives a clear and flowing account of the activities of English barristers and judges; it conveys the impression that everything is really all for the best in the state of justice in England, and that drastic reforms are unnecessary if not actually harmful. ABEL-SMITH/STEVENS, on the other hand, have done some empirical sociological research and raise the question whether the practice of law in England today is responsive to the demand of a modern society that it should be a 'social service'. The authors give a distinctly negative answer to this question and they do so with details which will give the foreign lawyer pause for thought, especially if he is unduly in love with English law. ZANDER (*Lawyers and the Public Interest*, above p. 212). He sees the principal aim of the monopolies and professional duties of English barristers and solicitors, whether fixed by statute or tradition, as being to limit free competition in the production and distribution of legal services. The crucial question is whether these restrictive practices are justified as being in the public interest; the author thinks that by and large they are not. See also the critical analysis in HAZELL (above p. 212). Copious data are to be found in the BENSON REPORT (above p. 212) on which see also ZANDER, 1980 *Curr. Leg. Prob.* 33.

3. The *training of lawyers* in England also has many features which will surprise the observer from abroad. The training is directed to the profession of *lawyer*, rather than of *judge* as in Germany and, in part, in France (see above Ch. 9 II). This is only natural because there is no such thing as a 'judicial career' in England: one only becomes a judge after many years of successful practice as a barrister. Again, the bifurcation of the legal profession means that there are different methods of training and examination for solicitors and barristers. As one would expect from the historical development of the legal professions in England, these methods of training and examination are the responsibility of the respective professional organizations, the Law Society and the Bar Councils, not of the state or the universities. Of course it is possible to study law in almost all of the British universities and to emerge, normally after three years, as a Bachelor of Laws (Bachelor of Arts in Oxford and Cambridge), and it is true that most of those admitted as barristers and solicitors possess a university degree. But it is nowhere laid down that a degree is required, and there is certainly no requirement that the degree be one in law. Nor is a degree in law sufficient to qualify one as a professional lawyer: it simply exempts the graduate from some of the professional examinations.

Of those who inscribed with the Law Society as student solicitors in 1986, over 75% had a university degree in law, about 15 percent a degree in some other discipline, and nearly 9 per cent no degree at all. Whereas a few years ago the newly admitted barristers included 13 per cent with no degree, the Inns of Court have now decided that only graduates may be admitted as 'bar students', though their degree need not be in law.

If the budding *solicitor* has studied law at university he must follow a nine-month course at the College of Law, the law school run by the Law Society, or at a specified polytechnic in the provinces or London. Practical subjects such as conveyancing, estate management, revenue, commercial and company law, and the law of succession are obligatory. In addition to passing the final examinations the young lawyer must spend two years as an apprentice or 'articled clerk' doing his 'articles' in a solicitor's office. He is then admitted as a solicitor, but must still serve for three years as an assistant solicitor before he can practise on his own or as a partner in a firm of solicitors: in this way the public can be protected from lawyers of undue youth and inexperience.

The training of *barristers* is roughly similar. If, as is now normal, he has a university degree in law the 'bar student' must be inscribed in an Inn of Court and follow a one-year course held in the Inns of Court School of Law. After the final examinations he 'devils' as a 'pupil' in one or more sets of chambers for a year, during the second half of which he may act on his own account.

The bar student must also keep a specified number of 'dining tems'. 'Dining terms', of which there are four per year, are periods of about three weeks during which bar students may take an evening meal in the Dining Hall of their Inn. One 'keeps a dining term' by dining at least three times during it, and one must keep eight terms in this manner, that is, have dined on twenty-four occasions, before one may be admitted as a barrister. The explanation of this institution is that in the old days the communal dinner was an occasion for contact between barristers and youngsters, for conversations on legal matters and for moots. In our times this practice has largely lost its point, especially in view of the large numbers of students: 'Today it is difficult to find any student who can see any value or utility in the ritual of dining in hall. The food, it is said, is poor or scanty or both, and the conversation does no more than pass the time; but the Inn requires it, and so one must go through the pointless ceremony' (MEGARRY (above p. 212) p. 114; see also the criticisms contained in the BENSON REPORT (above p. 212) 641 ff.

After passing his exams the candidate is 'called to the Bar' in a formal ceremony, and thereby becomes a barrister.

4. Whether the division of the legal profession into two branches should be maintained is the subject of recurrent and lively debate in England. *In favour* of the split, it is said that to have barristers who specialize in advocacy is a great advantage for the parties and for the court: for the *parties* because the barrister is more detached from the case, can see it with fresh eyes, and has special experience in pleading, gained by constant practice; for the *court* because co-operation with lawyers can be made easier, more trusting, and free from friction if judges have to deal with only a small circle of experienced

specialists. *Against* the division of the legal professions one often hears the objection that it greatly increases the expense and duration of legal proceedings, since the same case is being worked on by two lawyers one after the other, and sometimes both together. One thing is sure, that the division between barristers and solicitors gives both groups a strong economic interest in 'the maintenance of the status quo', a fact which, as the dispute over the divorce jurisdiction of County Courts shows, may serve to prevent or delay a reform of the courts system which would be in the public interest. It is clear that it makes sense to have specialized competences within the legal profession, as, for example, for conveyancing or for the conduct of cases in court. What is in issue is only whether the kind and extent of such specialization should be fixed by compulsory rules as in England, or whether it should not be left, as on the continent and in the United States, to the free play of the forces of the market (see JACKSON (above p. 212) 448 ff., ABEL-SMITH/ STEVENS (above p. 212). 304 ff), with a reply by F.A. MANN (above p. 212).

The Royal Commission on Legal Services a few years ago considered in great detail the advantages and disadvantages of the 'fusion' of the two branches of the legal profession; at the end of the day they opted unanimously for the maintenance of the present system. See BENSON REPORT (above p. 212) 187 ff. The question has, however, been recently reopened, with the solicitors pressing for rights of audience before the superior courts. The Commission also found that the numerous other restrictive practices characteristic of the solicitors' and barristers' professions were in general compatible with the public interest.

18

The Spread of the Common Law
Throughout the World

ALLOTT (ed.), *The Future of African Law* (1960).
——, *New Essays in African Law* (1970).
——, *Judicial and Legal Systems in Africa* (2nd edn., 1970).
BAKER, *The Legal Systems of Israel* (1968).
BENTWICH, 'The Migration of the Common Law: Israel', 76 *LQ Rev.* 64 (1960).
BOSE, 'The Migration of the Common Law: India', 76 *LQ Rev.* 59 (1960).
COTRAN, 'The Place and Future of Customary Law in East Africa', in: *East African Law Today* (ed. British Institute of International and Comparative Law, 1966) 72.
DANIELS, *The Common Law in West Africa* (1964).
DANNENBRING, 'Heutiges römisch-holländisches Recht', Vom Privatrecht der Republik Südafrika', *ZfRV* 6 (1965) 56.
DERRETT, 'The Role of Roman Law and Continental Laws in India', *RabelsZ* 24 (1959) 657.
——, 'Justice, Equity and Good Conscience', in: *Changing Law in Developing Countries* (ed. Anderson, 1963) 114.
DHAVAN, 'Borrowed Ideas: On the Impact of American Scholarship on Indian Law', 33 *Am. J. Comp. L.* 505 (1985).
ELIAS, *British Colonial Law, A Comparative Study of the Interaction between English and Local Laws in British Dependencies* (1962).
FRIEDMANN, *The Effect of Foreign Law on the Law of Israel* (1975).
GALL, *The Canadian Legal System* (1977).
GLEDHILL, *Pakistan, The Development of Its Laws and Constitution* (2nd edn., 1967).
——, *The Republic of India, The Development of Its Law and Constitution* (2nd edn., 1964).
GUTTMANN, 'The Reception of the Common Law in the Sudan', 6 *ICLQ* 401 (1957).
HAHLO/KAHN, *The Union of South Africa, The Development of Its Laws and Constitution* (1960).
——, *The South African Legal System and Its Background* (1968).
HOSTEN, 'The Permanence of Roman Law Concepts in South African Law', 2 *Comp. Int. LJS Afr.* 192 (1969).
HOSTEN etc., *Introduction to South African Law and Legal Theory* (1980).
JAIN, *Outlines of Indian Legal History* (4th edn., 1981).
JENNINGS/TAMBIAH, *The Dominion of Ceylon, The Development of Its Laws and Constitution* (1952).
KASER, 'Das römische Recht in Südafrika', *SavZ/Rom.* 81 (1964) 1.
LASKIN, *The British Tradition in Canadian Law* (1969).

LATHAM, 'The Migration of the Common Law: Australia', 76 *LQ Rev.* 54 (1960).

MCWHINNEY (ed.), *Canadian Jurisprudence, The Civil Law and Common Law in Canada* (1959).

VON MEHREN, 'Law and Legal Education in India: Some Observations', 78 *Harv. L. Rev.* 1180 (1965).

MORAN, 'The Migration of the Common Law: The Republic of Ireland', 76 *LQ Rev.* 69 (1960).

NICHOLLS, 'The Migration of the Common Law: Canada', 76 *LQ Rev.* 74 (1960).

PATON (ed.), *The Commonwealth of Australia, The Development of Its Laws and Constitutions* (1952).

RAJANAYAGAM, 'The Reception and Restriction of English Commercial Law in Ceylon', 18 *ICLQ* 378 (1969).

READ, 'The Judicial Process in Common Law Canada', 37 *Can. Bar Rev.* 265 (1959).

SANDERS, 'The Characteristic Features of Southern African Law', 14 *Comp. Int. LJS Afr.* 328 (1981).

SAWER, *The Australian and the Law* (1968).

SCHREINER, *The Contribution of English Law to South African Law; and the Rule of Law in South Africa* (1967).

SETALVAD, *The Common Law in India* (1960).

——, *The Role of English Law in India* (1966).

ZELTNER, 'Das Vertragsrecht des Staates Israel', *RabelsZ* 39 (1975) 56.

——, 'Einführung in das israelische Privatrecht', in: *Beiträge zum deutschen und israelischen Privatrecht* (Neue Kölner rechtswissenschaftliche Abhandlungen no. 81, 1977) 9.

ZIMMERMANN, *Das römisch–holländische Recht in Südafrika* (1983).

I

NEARLY a third of all the people alive today live in regions where the law has been more or less strongly marked by the Common Law. This is the legacy of the fact that Great Britain was once the greatest colonial power in the world. By centuries of tenacious effort the Britons succeeded in establishing themselves on every continent and gradually brought vast overseas territories under the control of the British Crown; they created and maintained an enormous colonial empire, by peaceful colonization, through the establishment and furtherance of trade links, and by military exploits against indigenous rulers or competing European colonial powers, especially France. In the train of this colonial expansion English settlers, merchants, and administrators took the Common Law to North America, India, Australia, New Zealand, and to large parts of Africa and South-east Asia. Almost all the overseas possessions of the British Crown are now independent. As early as 1776 the United States declared its independence and broke away from the British state. Canada, Australia, New Zealand, India, Pakistan, the Republic of South Africa, and a large number of important states in East and West

Africa, including Ghana, Nigeria, Kenya, Uganda, and Tanzania, are all now completely independent in internal and external affairs, although most of them remain within the Commonwealth and thus have close political and economic links with the United Kingdom. Nevertheless the whole law of these countries—not just the substantive law, but also the law of procedure, the courts system, the structure of legal professions, the whole style of legal thought and debate— is still strongly influenced by the legal ideas, institutions, and methods of the Common Law.

From the historical standpoint one can distinguish two groups of British colonies. One group comprises those territories which at the time of their first settlement were either unoccupied or occupied only by natives at a very early stage of civilization and not yet politically organized; in these colonies, called 'settled colonies', such as Australia, New Zealand, and North America, the Common Law of the incomers applied automatically, except in so far as particular social, economic, geographical, or climatic circumstances might render any of its rules inappropriate. The second group of colonies comprised lands already controlled by native princes or other European colonial powers which came under British control by conquest or cession ('conquered' or 'ceded colonies'): here it was a firm principle of English colonial policy to leave intact the law already in force in these territories, and often the existing courts system as well. Thus when they took over the French possessions in North America, the English recognized, in the Quebec Act, 1774, that the French-Canadians should retain their private law, then based on the Coutume de Paris (see above Ch. 8 VII b). By the same principle of English colonial policy, the Roman–Dutch law which had been introduced by the Dutch in the middle of the seventeenth century into their territories in Southern Africa was left in force there when those territories were incorporated into the British colonial empire (see the full development below Ch. 18 VI). The English followed this principle even when the law they found in the new territories was not, like French or Roman–Dutch law, a variant of the Civil Law: in India and in the colonies of Africa the British administration did not try to replace the Islamic, Hindu, or unwritten African customary law then in force with the rules of the Common Law. After incorporation into the British Empire, these territories retained the family law, marriage law, and law of succession of the native populations. Of course if the local law had no appropriate rules or the rules they had were undesirable in the eyes of the English the colonial legislature filled the gaps by following the model of the Common Law. Hence many areas of law which are not codified or are only partially codified in Great Britain even today are regulated in the colonies by comprehensive statutes; one instance is the law of contract.

In the following pages we shall attempt to show how the Common Law spread throughout the world by taking a few chosen countries as examples.

II

Dutch sailors had set foot in *Australia* several times in the course of the seventeenth century, but their descriptions of the country made it seem so inhospitable that for more than a hundred years no one made any attempt at settlement. Only after JAMES COOK landed on the East Coast of Australia in 1770 and took the country in the name of the British Crown did England embark on a process of settlement, for which at first they used transported convicts as labourers. The law in force was the English Common Law, and a statute of the British Parliament in 1828 laid down that the law of the existing Australian colonies should be the Common Law with the addition of such English statutes as were in force in England on 25 July 1828. In the first half of the nineteenth century all the Australian colonies, starting with New South Wales, were gradually given the right to elect a local legislature. Soon after gold was discovered and the economy started to prosper the transportation of convicts ceased to be necessary, for tens of thousands of settlers, mainly of English, Scottish, and Irish descent, flooded into the land; between 1830 and 1860 the population grew from 70,000 to 1,100,000. Towards the end of the century it became necessary to federate the several Australian colonies. There were considerable difficulties but finally a draft Constitution was agreed, adopted by referendum in the several colonies, and brought into force by the British Parliament as the Commonwealth of Australia Constitution Act, 1900. Under the Constitution Australia is a federal state with six members (New South Wales, Victoria, Queensland, Tasmania, South Australia, and West Australia), each of which has its own constitution, its own government, and its own Parliament. The federal legislature has competence only in the areas specified by the Constitution, such as external relations, defence, currency and coins, customs, as well as insurance and banking, negotiable instruments and bankruptcy, the protection of trade, and matrimonial law. All the rest of private and commercial law, as well as criminal law, is reserved to the competence of the several states. In consequence, although Australia has only 14 million inhabitants, it contains six different legal systems, one of which, that of Tasmania, applies to a bare 400,000 inhabitants. To these one must add the territories which are federally administered, where federal law applies. But when one looks more closely, one finds that in the principal areas of private law, commercial law, and procedural law all these legal systems are nearly identical, or at least very similar. This is because throughout Australia the law has come from the English Common Law without any serious deviation either in judicial decisions or legislation. It is true that the courts of Australia are not bound by English precedents, but English decisions, especially those of the Court of Appeal and House of Lords, are treated with great respect and normally followed, even if this means that Australian courts have to abandon a previous decision of their own. Thus DIXON J., in a judgment of the highest court in Australia, said:

'I think that if this Court is convinced that a particular view of the law has been taken in England from which there is unlikely to be any departure, wisdom is on the side of the Court's applying that view to Australian conditions, notwithstanding that the Court has already decided the question in the opposite sense . . . Where a general proposition is involved the Court should be careful to avoid introducing into Australian law a principle inconsistent with that which has been accepted in England. The common law is administered in many jurisdictions, and unless each of them guards against needless divergences of decision its uniform development is imperilled.' *Waghorn* v. *Waghorn* (1941–2) 65 CLR 289, 297.

In their legislation also, the member states have often limited themselves to adopting English models or relying heavily on them. Thus all states except New South Wales adopted the English court reforms of 1873; they have also adopted, word for word, numerous statutes on commercial matters, such as the English Sale of Goods Act, 1893. Their general law of contract and land law are very similar. Yet on occasion Australia has developed original solutions of its own: thus in *family law* there is the modern Family Law Act of 1975 (see FINLAY, *Family Law in Australia* (2nd edn., 1979)), and in *land law* a land registration system, not unlike the German one, was introduced in the middle of the nineteenth century, at the instance of TORRENS, who was not a lawyer, and over the bitter opposition of those who were; it now operates with great success in the whole of Australia and is beginning to attract adherents in other countries of the Anglo-American legal family.

With regard to the system of courts, one must distinguish between the courts of the several states and the Commonwealth courts. The *states* have lower courts rather like the English Magistrates' Courts and County Courts to deal with minor disputes. The highest court of each state, the Supreme Court, acts both as a court of appeal and as a court of first instance in important civil and criminal matters. Hearings are normally before a single judge, from whom an appeal lies to a bench of three judges in the same court. The *Commonwealth* courts, apart from those in the commonwealth territories, do not act as full courts of first instance but as superior courts; by far the most important is the *High Court of Australia*. It hears appeals from the judgments of the Supreme Courts of the several states, whether federal law or state law is involved. Furthermore the High Court also deals with constitutional disputes, such as suits between the Commonwealth and a state or between states, and cases where a Commonwealth statute is alleged to be void as being outside the legislative competence of the Commonwealth. On the other hand, the High Court has no power to strike down a statute on the ground that it infringes a constitutionally protected right of the citizen: unlike the American Constitution, the Australian Constitution contains no catalogue of 'basic rights'.

By no means all the states in Australia have adopted the English distinction between barristers and solicitors, though the most densely populated states have done so, namely New South Wales, Queensland, and Victoria. In the other three states every lawyer is admitted as both barrister and solicitor though it is possible, and in the larger cities even normal, for a lawyer to specialize as a barrister or as a solicitor in the course of his professional career.

All in all, one can conclude that Australian law and English law are still very similar in their method and procedure, in their basic legal ideas, in the way their law is applied, and in their techniques of drafting and construing statutes. Even where differences exist, English and Australian lawyers have no difficulty at all in understanding each other. It seems that of all the great countries outside Europe which belong to the Anglo-American legal family, Australia is the one whose law is still closest to that of England.

III

Canada, like Australia, is a federal state composed of previous British colonies but, unlike Australia, much of it was not originally settled by colonists from England, Scotland, and Ireland; the region of the St. Lawrence River was already heavily settled by French citizens when it was ceded to Britain along with all the other French possessions in North America by the Treaty of Paris in 1763. At first there was a distinct preponderance of French in the population of the Canadian colonies but during the American War of Independence many thousands of loyalists left what is now the United States and moved North of the Great Lakes, and the Anglo-Saxon population of 'Upper Canada' gradually approximated to the French settlement in 'Lower Canada'. In 1791 an Act was passed by the British Parliament which divided Canada into two parts, one predominantly French and one predominantly English, both under the sovereignty of the British Crown but each having its own Parliament and its own government. There then ensued in both parts repeated movements for independence and much unrest and revolt, so in 1840 the British Colonial Office tried another system under which both regions were united and each was given an equal number of seats in the common Parliament. This system also proved unstable by reason of the constant rivalry between the two almost equal populations, and a lasting solution was only reached with a plan to found a federation containing not only Upper Canada and Lower Canada but also the other colonial regions subject to the British Crown in North America. In 1867, Parliament in London enacted the *British North America Act* on the basis of proposals originating in Canada. This statute created the federal state 'Dominion of Canada' of which originally there were four member provinces: Quebec, Ontario, New Brunswick, and Nova Scotia. Two years later with the agreement of the British Parliament Canada paid £300,000 and obtained all the sovereign rights which the

Hudson's Bay Company had enjoyed since 1670 over the huge area of the North West Territories, on the basis of an English royal patent. In 1871 British Columbia joined the Canadian union, and independent provinces were carved out of the North West Territories and admitted to the federation—Manitoba in 1870 and Saskatchewan and Alberta in 1905. Finally, in 1949, Newfoundland became a province of Canada; since that date the entire North American continent has been divided between the United States and Canada.

The relationship between the federation and the member provinces under the new Canadian Constitution (Canada Act 1982, replacing the British North America Act 1867) is much like that in the United States and in Australia, legislative competence in private law being left in principle to the member provinces. The law in the different provinces may thus differ quite markedly, and of course there is a deep chasm between the Province of Quebec, an outpost of 'civilian' jurisprudence, and the other provinces of Canada where the Common Law had applied since they were first settled (see above Ch. 8 VII b). But even in commercial law or in the modern areas of economic law Canada is far from being legally unified. In part this is attributable to the fact that the Privy Council, which heard appeals from Canadian judgments until 1949, tended to give an extremely narrow construction to the constitutional provisions regulating the legislative competence of the federal Parliament, very much narrower than the Supreme Court of the United States has done in relation to the 'commerce clause' of the American Constitution (see below Ch. 19 III). Efforts have been made to achieve a degree of legal unity by preparing model laws for particular areas of law and recommending their adoption to the various provinces, but so far this has had much less success in Canada than in the United States where, for example, the Uniform Commercial Code has been adopted by all the states with the exception of Louisiana, which has adopted most of it.

The system of courts in Canada is much like that in Australia: in addition to the provincial courts with a Court of Appeal at the head of each, there are federal courts—the Federal Court which has jurisdiction essentially over acts of the federal administration, and above all the *Supreme Court of Canada* whose principal task is to hear appeals from the highest provincial courts.

The law in Canada, apart from Quebec, was quite unequivocally modelled on law in England until recently. Canadian courts regarded decisions of the House of Lords and the Privy Council as binding and treated decisions of other English courts as having 'persuasive authority'. English methods of legal education prevailed; law teachers in Canada usually had a degree in law from an English university. But since the end of the Second World War and especially since the abolition of appeals to the Privy Council in 1949, though its effect was primarily psychological, there seems to have been an increasing independence in Canadian legal thought; instead of being guided solely by the methods and institutions of English law, more attention is being paid to promptings from the United States.

IV

In the sixteenth and seventeenth centuries *India* was a country with a large population and a high level of cultural development which had long been ruled by powerful Grand Moguls of the Islamic faith. There was thus no question of the Portuguese and Dutch, or later the French and English, being able to colonize the country on their arrival in India. Their aim was rather to forge as strong trade links as possible while fully respecting the sovereignty of the native princes. This explains why it was not the governments of the European colonial powers which had dealings with India but special trading companies acting under royal patent, of which the most famous and successful was the English 'East India Company' which came into being in 1600 with the blessing of ELIZABETH I. In 1612 the Grand Mogul of India allowed this company to establish its first settlement in Surat, north of Bombay, and in the following decades it set itself up in many other places on the east and west coasts and gradually ousted the competition of other European colonial powers. In the eighteenth century the Grand Mogul's empire gradually fell to pieces and the country was rent by frequent wars; the English occasionally had to resort to arms in self-defence and British influence was maintained by winning over the local Indian potentates by persuasion, bribery, or threats, or by making deft use of their disputes. So alongside the original desire of the English to engage in profitable trade with the Indians there gradually developed a stronger interest in open political control of the country and finally in the extension of the British colonial empire. We cannot here give the details of this development, but at the beginning of the twentieth century the whole of the Indian subcontinent, including Burma, was under English control. About 60 per cent of this immense land mass was British territory directly administered by British officials; the rest comprised a very large number of native states whose princes had recognized the sovereignty of the British crown and who administered their states under the eye of the British.

Under the original patent issued to it, the East India Company was given power to make regulations for the administration of its overseas settlements and their senior officials could punish on the spot those who broke these rules or committed criminal acts. This naturally applied only to Englishmen in the Company's service, but in the course of time as the number of Company outposts increased and trade prospered, numerous Indians entered the service of the Company and centres of administrative activity and trade developed. Of these, the so-called 'Presidency towns', the ports of Madras, Bombay, and Calcutta, were especially important. In 1726 an ordinance of the British Crown gave these three towns special royal courts—the 'Mayor's Courts'—to resolve disputes between parties in those towns, whether English or Indian, and to give judgment 'according to justice and right'; 'justice and right' meant the English Common Law with the addition of such English statutes as were in force in 1726, in so far as these rules were not inapplicable because of local conditions. It soon became apparent that the Common Law was inappropriate to disputes between Indians on family or succession matters and towards the end of the eighteenth century the Mayor's Courts in the three cities mentioned were abolished and replace by Supreme Courts, staffed by professional English judges; these courts were mainly to apply the Common Law, but Islamic or Hindu law was to control in litigation between Muhammadans or Hindus concerning family or succession law. Judges were to supplement their familiarity with these legal systems by obtaining information from named experts in the two religions.

In the course of time very large territories came under the administration of the East India Company as a result of treaties with Indian princes and the occasional military exploit. Here the situation was much the same. The provincial courts, introduced by the English towards the end of the eighteenth century and staffed by English administrators, were instructed to apply Islamic or Hindu law depending on the faith of the parties whenever the case involved 'inheritance, marriage, caste and other religious usages and institutions'. In all other matters without religious connotations and in every case where the parties were neither Muhammadan nor Hindu the court was instructed to decide 'according to justice, equity and good conscience'.

Under these circumstances the Common Law, apart from family and succession law, naturally became the 'common law' of India in the course of the nineteenth century. In the 'Presidency towns' this followed from the fact that the courts were bound to apply the Common Law, except in religious cases. It is true that in the provinces the principle of decision was to be 'justice, equity and good conscience' but even there the administrative officials were soon replaced as judges by barristers trained in England who tended to suppose, conveniently enough, that 'justice, equity and good conscience' meant simply the rules of the Common Law with which they were familiar, so far as they were appropriate to Indian conditions. As the Privy Council, the final court of appeal from Indian courts after 1833, once observed in a judgment:

'the matter must be decided by equity and good conscience, generally interpreted to mean the rules of English law if found applicable to Indian society and circumstances' (*Waghela Rajsanji* v. *Shekh Masludin* [1887] LR 14 IA 89, 96; see the further decisions mentioned by JAIN (above p. 226) 576 ff.).

Other judges took the wider view that one could only find out what 'justice, equity and good conscience' implied in particular cases by making a critical comparative survey of the developed legal systems of the world; in many judgments one finds well-educated and open-minded judges taking the Civil Law, especially Roman law, into account in addition to the Common Law (see the extensive treatment by DERRETT (above p. 226) I). But by and large it may certainly be said that the whole of the Common Law, except family law and the law of succession, established itself in India and took up residence there, though often in a very modified form.

Admittedly the law at that time was in an extremely confused, even chaotic condition. In addition to English statutes prior to 1726, of which it was often not clear whether they should be treated as received into India, there were English statutes subsequent to that date so far as they professed to apply in India, and finally there were regulations from the provincial governments in Bombay, Madras, and Calcutta which often differed since they were produced quite independently. Furthermore the courts in the 'Presidency towns' applied the Common Law to a greater extent than the provincial courts to whom the formula 'justice, equity and good conscience' offered considerable room for play. In this situation the unification and codification of Indian law struck many people as a matter of urgency; there was agreement and support in England, where many Members of Parliament were swayed by the ideas of BENTHAM. A British statute in 1833 therefore provided that a 'Law Commission in India' be set up; it was to collect together the rules of positive law in India, to put them into some order, and then codify them in a manageable way. The first President of this Commission was MACAULAY, the famous English historian, essayist, and politician. In a very short time he succeeded in producing a draft of an Indian Penal Code; it was mainly based on English criminal law, itself largely uncodified, but it also paid some attention to European models, especially the French Code pénal. These efforts at reform had no practical consequences before 1857, the year of the great mutiny in northern India, in consequence of which the British Crown itself took over responsibility for the administration of India from the East India Company. In 1859 a Code of Civil Procedure, in 1860 the Criminal Code drafted by MACAULAY, and in 1861 an Ordinance relating to Criminal Procedure were enacted. Further statutes followed in quick succession.

The Indian Succession Act came into force in 1865. It unified the law of succession for all Indians, such as Christians and Jews, who were not subject to either Islamic or Hindu law. Though this statute too was based on the Common Law, it deliberately abandoned many archaic formalities of English succession law.—The Indian Contract Act of 1872 is especially interesting. It codified rules from the sanctum of classical judge-made law in England, such as the rules concerning the formation of contracts by offer and acceptance (see vol. II, p. 29 ff.), consideration (see vol. II, p. 62 ff.), mistake, deceit, duress and misrepresentation (see vol. II, pp. 88 ff.), illegality and immorality, breach of contract, unjust enrichment (under the unhelpful heading 'Of certain relations resembling those created by contract'), as well as suretyship and agency (see vol. II, p. 99 ff.). The portions of the Indian Contract Act concerning sale of goods and partnership were later replaced by the Sale of Goods Act, 1930, and the Partnership Act, 1932, both of which are nearly congruent with the English prototypes. Other statutes in this area are the Specific Relief Act, 1877, the Transfer of Property Act,

1882, and the Indian Trusts Act, 1882. All these statutes are still in force today both in India and Pakistan, though they have been redrafted or much modified.

The striking fact about political development in India in the twentieth century is the long drawn out process by which the Indian people obtained the right to legislate for and administer their country from an unwilling and unyielding British government, first internally in the provinces and then centrally for external affairs as well. It became clear that the Muslims and the Hindus would prefer not to live together in a single Indian state after independence, and so when the British Parliament granted complete independence by means of the India Independence Act, 1947, *two* new states immediately came into being: India and Pakistan. The Indian princes, more than 500 of them, who had theretofore lived under the sovereignty of the British Crown also obtained full freedom; they were entitled to attach themselves to either of the two states as they wished, and in the following years all of them did so.

The Constitution of India came into force in 1950. Constitutionally India is a federal state with 15 member states, including Kashmir, and a number of federal territories. The central Parliament is given exclusive jurisdiction in some areas, such as large industry and big business, external trade, banking and insurance, company law, and the law of negotiable instruments. The member states have exclusive jurisdiction in matters of local importance such as local administration, police, and land management. Private law, criminal law, and procedural law fall within the concurrent legislative competence of the federation and the member states. Important areas of Hindu family and succession law, about 85 per cent of the total population of India today being Hindu, have since been unified by federal statutes; as all the statutes from the colonial period which were in force on the day of independence have in principle remained in force, the private law of India today is mainly codified law.

Unlike the Constitutions of Australia and Canada, the Constitution of India contains a list of basic rights; any statute which infringes these basic rights can be held void by the High Courts, the highest courts of the member states, or by the *Supreme Court of India*, the highest court in the land. The Supreme Court is not only a constitutional court, however; it also decides appeals against judgments of the High Courts in cases involving more than a certain value, or if leave has been given in a matter of important principle by the High Court or the Supreme Court itself.

Court procedure in civil and criminal matters basically follows the Common Law. Thus the binding force of precedent, the position of the judge, free to deliver concurring or dissenting judgments, the importance of procedure in legal remedies, the role of lawyers in matters of procedure, and much else remind us clearly of the Common Law model. Given the diversity of language, race, religion, and civilization among the people of India, with the grave risks this presents for its political unity, the relative homogeneity of the legal system throughout India, resting as it does on the Common Law, must rank as one of the most important contributions of the departed colonial masters to the integration of the country.

V

The Common Law also had a great influence on the legal systems of those states which formed part of the British empire in Africa. In West Africa these countries are *Sierra Leone, Gambia, Nigeria,* and *Ghana; Liberia,* founded in 1821 as a settlement for emancipated slaves from the United States and an independent republic since 1847, has a legal system which bears the marks more of American than of English Common Law. In East Africa the countries which belonged to the British zone of influence were principally *Kenya* and *Uganda,* and, since 1920, Tanganyika; Tanganyika had previously been German East Africa, and united with Zanzibar to form the *Republic of Tanzania* in 1964.

In 1814 the *Seychelles,* an archipelago in the Indian Ocean about 950 miles off the coast of Africa, was ceded by France to Britain and incorporated into the British Empire. The French Code civil and Code de Commerce which were in force at that time remained in force, but numerous English ordinances were introduced during the next 150 years. The results were inconvenient until the enactment in 1976, the year of independence, of a Code civil thoroughly reworked and modernized by the comparatist CHLOROS. This is an interesting 'experiment in Franco-British codification'. See CHLOROS, The Projected Reform of the Civil law of the Seychelles: An Experiment in Franco-British Codification', 48 *Tul. L. Rev.* 815 (1974); CHLOROS, *Codification in a Mixed Jurisdiction, the Civil and Commercial Law of Seychelles* (1977).

The student of legal development in these countries of East and West Africa will see that the reception of the Common Law took a similar form everywhere: it was provided, either by order in council issued by the monarch or by ordinance of the colonial legislature, that the law of the colony in question should be

'the common law, the doctrines of equity and the statutes of general application which were in force in England on the 24th day of July, 1874'—to take the rule in the Gold Coast, now Ghana. The formulas by which the reception was made in Sierra Leone in 1862, in Kenya in 1897, in Uganda in 1902, and in Tanganyika in 1920 were very similar. These formulas raised numerous questions in practice. For example, it might be a matter of doubt whether an English statute was designed for a specifically 'English' problem or whether the law was a statute 'of general application' so as to have validity in the colonies also. The judges enjoyed a certain room for play as a result of the widespread proviso which laid down that English law was to be applied by the colonial courts 'so far only as local circumstances permit and subject to such qualifications as local circumstances may render necessary'. Again, it might be a question of doubt whether or in what cases colonial judges should regard decisions of English courts subsequent to the date of reception as being binding precedents, as having 'persuasive authority', or as being simply negligible. On this, see ALLOTT, *Systems* (above p. 226) 9 ff.

The special legislation of the British colonies and their independent successors are also based on British models.

Thus the English Sale of Goods Act, 1893, applies in all four states of West Africa, some of which enacted it before and some after independence, often with alterations; the Sales Act, 1962 of Ghana is particularly interesting as an attempt to modernize the English law of sales (see MERTENS, 'Das Kaufgesetz Ghanas von 1962', *RabelsZ* 27 (1962/1963) 519). The courts of these countries had previously applied the English Sale of Goods Act on one of two grounds: either it was a 'statute of general application' which automatically became law in the colony because it was in force in England at the time of the reception of the Common Law in that colony, or it was simply a codification of judge-made law and therefore in substance 'common law' (in the narrow sense) and applicable as such in the colonies by reason of the general formula of reception. East Africa generally followed the Indian legislation and consequently adopted the Indian Contract Act, 1872, and later, still following the Indian example, the English Sales of Goods Act as well. The Indian Contract Act has since been repealed in the East African states; Kenya and Uganda adopted English contract law by general reference in 1960, and in 1961 Tanganyika replaced it by a new Contract Act which admittedly greatly resembles that of India. The numerous statutes which these African states have passed since independence in order to regulate the economy and its administration are also patterned in form and substance on English enactments.

All this might lead one to the conclusion that in the areas of Africa which were previously under British rule most legal relations today are governed by the rules of English Common Law. This conclusion would be wholly erroneous. The fact is that to much the largest part of the African population the Common Law is of almost no practical significance; the legal relations of Africans, in contract and land matters as well as family and succession matters, are principally governed by the rules of customary African law, and in many regions also by the rules of Islamic law. This is a consequence of the principle of English colonial policy which we have already mentioned, namely that the population of a region which had been annexed or ceded or conquered should generally retain its existing law and that the administration of the territory should so far as possible be left in the hands of the traditional executive and judicial bodies (the principle of 'Indirect Rule'). This principle had two particular consequences for the African parts of the British Empire: unwritten African customary laws, which often varied from tribe to tribe, remained in force for the native population, as did the Islamic law prevalent in many regions, provided that in the view of the colonial masters they were not 'repugnant to natural justice and morality'. Secondly, the existing African courts, where the tribal chief or other notables applied the customary law, were basically left unaffected; the colonial administrators were only interested in seeing that certain elementary principles of procedure, mainly in criminal cases, were adhered to, and that there was a possibility of appeal to higher courts, eventually to a final court staffed by English judges. In this way the imported English law, the African customary laws, and, where applicable, Islamic law coexisted in the African territories of the British Empire.

Obviously enough, this quite often gave rise to doubts whether English law or customary law should be applied in a particular case. Thus, for example, it might be a question whether the English law of succession should apply when an African died in a city where he had lived for a long time in the European style with his close family. Should African customary law apply to a contract between Africans concluded in writing in the English language? Which law of divorce was to apply when the marriage was valid by African customary law because the bride's father had entered the contract and paid the price, and also by English law as being in the *statutory* form, which Africans could always use, of celebration before state officials, with or without a church ceremony? The rules by which one decides which of the competing legal systems is to be applied are usually called 'interpersonal private law', on the analogy of 'international private law'.

During the colonial period the English showed very little interest in African customary laws; in the main they regarded them simply as an object for anthropological study, perhaps secretly expecting that in the long run they would die out and be gradually replaced by English law. Today the attitude has changed, and it seems that the African states are eager to maintain all the indigenous institutions and values which their peoples have in common. Thus many of them have started on the task, normally with the help of English specialists, of recording the various customary laws and making an orderly 'Restatement' of them; many states regard such a 'Restatement' simply as a means of finding one's way about, while others want to give it statutory force and thus replace unwritten law by written law. At the same time these countries must try so far as possible to approximate the different customary laws which are in force in their territory or even to unify them, though such a task will be horribly difficult wherever there is a great diversity of race, language, and life-styles among the tribes and peoples which constitute a state. In any case the dual system of courts from the colonial period, some applying only customary law and others applying the Common Law, has been abolished everywhere and decisions in the lower courts are being given more and more not by tribal elders and other such people but by professional African judges who have often been educated at the newly founded universities in Africa, most of which still have English and American lawyers on their staffs. The great task in the future for these African states will be to unify their internal legal system, so far as possible, and to codify their law, using the legal terminology and statutory techniques of the Common Law and incorporating the basic values and institutions of African customary law, especially in the field of family and inheritance law. At the same time the legislators should try to keep in mind the goal of unifying the commercial law of Africa as a whole, and for this purpose they should do their best to avoid closing off their national law or giving its development any special twist.

VI

African customary law co-exists with rules of law of European origin in the *Republic of South Africa* as well. More than four-fifths of the population of about 33 million are black; pursuant to the governmental policy of apartheid, they live in specially designated territories which have considerable powers of self-administration or in separate living regions in the cities, where their disputes are normally heard by special 'native courts' which apply customary Bantu law. Here, however, we shall concentrate on the law of the dominant *white* population; it merits the particular attention of comparatist, first because Roman law has shown a greater vitality in South Africa than anywhere else in the world by surviving to the present day, and secondly because in the course of its history this Roman law has interacted quite remarkably with English Common Law.

It is really a historical accident that Roman law still survives in South Africa. In 1652, on the orders of the Dutch East India Company, the Dutchman JAN VAN RIEBEECK established a settlement at the Cape of Good Hope; its principal purpose was to provide water and victuals for Dutch ships which were making the long journey to the Dutch East Indies. Very soon this victualling station developed into a flourishing colony which increased its population by attracting Dutch, French, and German settlers and enlarged its land area by gradually extending its borders to east and north. The law of the Cape Colony was the law of the metropolis, specifically the law of the Province of Holland, the most influential province of the Republic of the Netherlands and the seat of the Dutch East India Company at the time. The law then in force in the Province of Holland was Roman law. It had been received into Holland in the form given to it by the Glossators and Commentators, and in the seventeenth and eighteenth centuries Dutch legal scholars, after historical research, had adapted it to the practical needs of the time with an admixture of a good deal of old Dutch customary law; of these we may mention HUGO GROTIUS (1583–1645), ARNOLDUS VINNIUS (1588–1657), JOHANNES VOET (1647–1713), CORNELIS VAN BYNKERSHOEK (1673–1743), and DIONYSIUS VAN DER KEESSEL (1738–1816). In 1795, during the Napoleonic Wars, the English seized the Cape in order to secure their sea links with India and finally took it into possession in 1806 as a British colony; the 'Roman–Dutch law' which then obtained in the Cape Colony remained in force. In the Dutch homeland, however, Roman–Dutch law was abolished by the decree of NAPOLEON and replaced in 1809 by the Code civil; the Burgerlijk Wetboek of 1838 which was based on it was later introduced into the Dutch East Indies. Thus Roman–Dutch law survived only in those areas which had come under British rule and had left the Dutch Empire before it adopted a Civil Code on the French model. The only countries of which this is true apart from South Africa are *Sri Lanka*, previously *Ceylon* (since 1799) and parts of *Guyana* (since 1803).

But Roman–Dutch law has not been able to hold on as well in Sri Lanka as in South Africa, mainly because Dutch and Afrikaans are no longer spoken in Sri Lanka and so there is no longer access to the Dutch or even the Roman sources. English Common Law clearly dominates in Sri Lanka, especially in the law of contract and in commercial law; on this, see JENNINGS/TAMBIAH (above p. 226) and RAJANAYAGAM (above p. 227). In British Guiana the tenure of Roman–Dutch law was precarious from the very beginning and in 1916 it was replaced by the English Common Law (see DALTON, 'The Passing of Roman–Dutch Law in British Guiana,' 36 *S. Afr. LJ 4* (1919)).

The influence of English Common Law made itself felt in the Cape Colony as soon as it was incorporated into the British Empire. The first interest of the British was to organize and modernize the constitution, administration, and courts system of the new colony. The law of evidence and procedure in both civil and criminal matters were immediately reconstructed on the pattern of the Common Law, and English was introduced as the sole language of the courts. Since very close economic connections developed between South Africa and Great Britain, and Roman–Dutch law had no rules suited to modern commercial practice, it was only natural that many English statutes were adopted almost word for word in South Africa in the fields of negotiable instruments, bankruptcy, maritime law, insurance, and partnership law. But English law also seeped into South Africa surreptitiously. Whenever Roman–Dutch law seemed to be unclear, inadequate, or obsolete, the courts had a tendency to rely on English case-law with which the lawyers and judges, most of whom had been trained in London, were certainly more familiar than with the old texts of GROTIUS and VOET. The strength of the influence of English legal ideas can be partially explained by the fact that in the second half of the nineteenth century Great Britain stood at the peak of its political and economic power in the world. Furthermore at the time there was very little independent legal scholarship in South Africa to keep Roman–Dutch traditions alive. Nor must it be overlooked that in the course of the nineteenth century many thousands of Boers, disenchanted with the English for abolishing slavery and afraid that their life-style would be anglicized, quit the Cape Colony and trekked to the North where they founded three independent Boer republics, Natal, the Orange Free State, and Transvaal. In the course of time all three of these republics were incorporated into the British Empire, the Orange Free State and Transvaal only after the English won the Boer War in 1902. Shortly after the end of the Boer War the white population of the colonies in Southern Africa came to realize that on economic grounds at least they must become more closely linked. In 1910 the Cape Colony and the three previous Boer republics joined together to form the 'Union of South Africa', whose constitution was laid down by the British Parliament in the South Africa Act, 1909.

Some parts of Southern Africa remained for the time being under British administration and did not join the Union. Today they are independent (*Lesotho, Botswana, Swaziland, Zimbabwe*). In all these states Roman–Dutch law of the South African stamp applies, at least to the white population. But Britain had other territories lying further to the north, which are independent today under the names of *Zambia* and *Malawi*; apart from the African customary law their law is basically English Common Law.

After the creation of the Union of South Africa in 1910 the progressive anglicization of the law came to a stop. Several factors contributed to this, such as the sense of political independence from Britain, the recognition of English and Afrikaans as equal languages, and the blossoming of South African universities which not only took over the training of native jurists but also worked on the sources of Roman–Dutch law and made it accessible to the public. Since then the courts of South Africa have clearly been paying great attention to the texts of the old Dutch writers and to the rules which have developed from them; they evaluate them with care and adapt them to modern circumstances. The Common Law still dominates in constitutional and administrative law, and in commercial and procedural law; and the traditions of English law are still strong in the courts structure, the position of the judge, the doctrine of binding precedent, and the activities of the legal professions. On the other hand, Common Law has had negligible influence in family and succession law and in the law of property, all of which are unequivocally dominated by Roman methods of thinking. Thus, for example, South Africa has held to a unitary concept of ownership, sharply distinguished from limited real rights and from possession in a way quite foreign to the Common Law. A clear distinction is also made between the *contract* which involves the passing of property and the *conveyance transaction*, which is effective only if in addition to delivery or constructive delivery there is the necessary consent of the parties. South African judges and lawyers make constant use in appropriate cases of such legal figures as *occupatio, accessio, specificatio, traditio* and *constitutum possessorium*. Nor has South Africa received the Anglo-American legal institution of the trust, although the courts have succeeded in producing most of the desired legal effects by using Roman concepts: thus *fidei commissum* performs the function of the testamentary trust, the *stipulatio alteri* performs that of the trust declared *inter vivos* and the *donatio ad pias causas* performs the functions of a charitable trust for the public benefit.

On this see the extensive treatment by HAHLO, 'The Trust in South African Law', 78

S. Afr. LJ 195 (1961).—Common Law influences are rather stronger in the general law of contract and in the law of tort. Thus the South African courts have taken over the 'mail-box' theory and the concept of innocent misrepresentation (see vol. II, Ch. 3 II, Ch. 8 IV); towards the end of the nineteenth century there was an intensive flirtation with the doctrine of consideration, which was subsequently and conclusively jilted. The foundations of the law of tort today are certainly the *actio legis Aquiliae* and the *actio iniuriarum* but there are clear echoes of English law in the doctrine of causation and contributory negligence; vicarious liability and the action of defamation, indeed, are pure Common Law. But by and large even in the law of contract and tort the basic conceptual structure of the Roman law has been maintained and in the solution of particular questions citations from the texts of the Digest and the old Dutch writers are fruitfully and unselfconsciously made. See, by way of example, *Essa* v. *Divaris*, 1947 (1) SA 753 (AD), where the court was faced with the question whether the strict liability of the *stabularius* for the loss of a horse he had lodged, as laid down in the Praetor's Edict (D. 4.9.1 pr.), could be applied to the proprietor of a parking lot for the loss of a truck which had been parked there. Here and in other cases the continental reader is surprised, not so much that the problem is raised in the terms of Roman categories of thought, for this is often true today in Germany and France as well, as by the fact that in the decisions of the South African courts the development of the law, from the classical Roman jurists through JUSTINIAN and the Gloss and VOET and VINNIUS up to modern times, stands out as being so continuous. European lawyers today are not generally so conscious of the continuity of legal development because the civil codes give the impression of having interrupted it, even if this is not the case.

No simple answer can be given to the question whether the law of South Africa should be put in the Anglo-American legal family or whether it should be classed with those legal systems which have developed on the basis of Roman law. The latter view will be adopted by those who think the critical factor is the nature of the basic concepts and structures of the legal order in question; in South Africa, these are unquestionably Roman, at any rate if one concentrates on the uncodified law. But those who pay more attention to the techniques of applying the law in the courts today will have a different opinion; the way the trial is conducted, the methods of proof, the treatment of precedents, as well as the courts structure and the activities and position of judges and lawyers are all clearly based on English models; and the same is true of the law in very important areas such as trade and partnership law, which is codified. Thus South African law appears as a 'hybrid' law in which, as it seems to us, the elements of Roman–Dutch and English law are so intermixed that it cannot without distortion be put in one or other pigeon-hole:

'Like a jewel in a brooch, the Roman–Dutch law in South Africa today glitters in a setting that was made in England. Even if it were true (which it is not) that the whole of South African private law and criminal law had remained pure Roman–Dutch law, the South African legal system as a whole would still be a hybrid one, in which civil- and common-law elements jostle each other' (HAHLO/KAHN, *The South African Legal System* (above p. 226, 585 f.).

VII

It is no easier to decide to which legal family the law of *Israel* should be allocated. This is principally because the present law in Israel comes from different historical strata: some from the Ottoman period, some from legislation influenced by the Common Law during the British Mandate (1922–48), and some from enactments of the Israeli legislature since 1948, as further developed by the courts.

After Great Britain received Palestine from the League of Nations as a Mandated Territory in 1922, the British Palestine Order in Council of 10 August 1922 came into force. This provided in art. 46 that the courts were to apply the Ottoman law in force on 1 November 1914 and subsequent Ottoman laws, plus rules brought into force by the mandatary authority. In line with normal British colonial administration (see above Ch. 18 IV) it was further provided that where no legislative rule was applicable the courts were to decide "according to the substance of the common law, and the doctrines of equity', always 'subject to such qualifications as local circumstances render necessary'.

Even the Ottoman law in force in Palestine in 1922 had very various origins. The law of property was laid down in the Majalla (a collection of rules of Islamic law of the Hanafi brand (see pp. 377 f.), made between 1869 and 1876 by the Turkish administration); in the area of family and succession law, uncodified Islamic law applied, while enactments lifted verbatim by the Turkish sultans from French sources controlled much of commercial law. The law in Palestine was extensively Anglicized during the British Mandate, though it lasted barely thirty years. This was done in part by replacing the Ottoman laws of French provenance by provisions of English origin, in part by introducing laws already in force in Great Britain, for example as regards bills of exchange, partnership, companies, and intangible property. In tort and criminal law, for instance, statutes were introduced which reproduced the rules of English case-law in the form of paragraphs, case-law being easier to export to the colonies in this form. The Anglicization of the law was facilitated because the courts applied the Common Law not only where there was no positive law on the particular issue (or indeed in the whole area, such as restitution or conflicts of law), but also where existing provisions were unclear and required interpretation, a not uncommon occurrence with the Ottoman laws.

After the foundation of the State of Israel on 14 May 1948 one of the first acts of the legislature was to enact the Law and Administration Ordinance of 1948, §11 of which provided that the law in force at the time should remain in force except in so far as it was altered or repealed by ordinances of the new legislature. Much alteration and repeal has taken place. But one must distinguish: the Common-Law-based ordinances from the time of the Mandate are still very much in force, so that commercial and company law remain largely English, notwithstanding that since 1972 decisions of English courts construing these enactments are only of persuasive authority and no longer binding. By contrast, the rules of Ottoman origin are much less significant, since the Majalla has been largely ousted by numerous statutes enacted by the Israeli legislature since 1965 to reform parts of the law of obligations and property. Many of these enactments touch the law of contract (see ZELTNER, *RabelsZ* 39 (1975) 56), agency and assignment, and contracts of sale and gift, as well as the law of real property and succession. These laws, which will eventually be brought together in a civil code, are Continental in *Form*, laying down only essential principles, often using indefinite terms whose specification is left to the courts, sometimes deploying general clauses, and consciously avoiding the baroque detail characteristic of English lawmaking (see below Ch. 20 III). As to *content*, the Israeli legislature has learnt much from comparative law, using, in addition to the Common Law, the law of Continental European systems and the Uniform Sales Law of The Hague. It inheres in the comparative law background of these statutes—and indeed it is expressly provided in some of them—that their terms should be construed, any lacuna filled, and their application developed 'autonomously' and 'self-referentially' rather than by recourse to English law. There is no doubt that the influence of the Common Law on the *content* of Israeli positive private law is on the wane, but it remains true that the style and methods of legal development are in the traditions of the Common Law:

'Israeli case-law remains typical of that in countries following the common law tradition. The manner of discussion, the mode of reasoning and the general approach are all characteristic of the common law systems. This is also true of the attitude of judges, jurists and attorneys to precedent, to the role of the courts and to their contribution to the development of law' (FRIEDMANN (above p. 226) 22).

19

The Law of the United States of America

ABRAHAM, *The Judicial Process* (4th edn., 1980).

COING, 'Neue Strömungen in der nordamerikanischen Rechtsphilosophie,' *ARSP* 38 (1949) 536.

FARNSWORTH, *An Introduction to the Legal System of the United States* (1963).

FIKENTSCHER, *Methoden des Rechts* II (1975).

FRIEDMAN, *A History of American Law* (1973).

FULDA, *Einführung in das Recht der USA* (1966).

GILMORE, *The Ages of American Law* (1977).

GOWER/PRICE, 'The Profession and Practice of the Law in England and America,' 20 *Mod. L. Rev.* 317 (1957).

GRISWOLD, *Law and Lawyers in the United States, The Common Law Under Stress* (1964).

HAY, *An Introduction to United States Law* (1976).

HONNOLD (ed.), *The Life of the Law, Readings on the Growth of Legal Institutions* (1964).

HURST, *The Growth of American Law* (1950).

JESCHECK, *Bedingungen und Methoden des Rechtsunterrichts in den Vereinigten Staaten* (1970).

KAHN-FREUND, 'English Law and American Law—Some Comparative Reflections,' in: *Essays in Jurisprudence in Honor of Roscoe Pound* (1962) 362.

KARLEN, *Appellate Courts in the United States and England* (1963).

——, *Judicial Administration—The American Experience* (1970).

KIMBALL, *Historical Introduction to the Legal System, Cases and Materials* (1961).

MERRYMAN, 'Judicial Responsibility in the United States', *RabelsZ* 41 (1977) 332.

PARKER, *Das Privatrecht der Vereinigten Staaten von Amerika* (1960).

POUND, *The Formative Era of American Law* (1938).

——, 'The Development of American Law and Its Deviation from English Law,' 67 *LQ Rev.* 49 (1951).

RABEL, 'Deutsches und amerikanisches Recht,' *RabelsZ* 16 (1951) 340.

RHEINSTEIN, 'Die Rechtshonoratioren und ihr Einfluß auf Charakter und Funktion der Rechtsordnungen,' *RabelsZ* 34 (1970) 1.

RUESCHEMEYER, *Juristen in Deutschland und in den U.S.A., Eine vergleichende Untersuchung von Anwaltschaft und Gesellschaft* (1976).

RUMBLE, *American Legal Realism* (1968).

SCHLESINGER, *Die Rolle des Supreme Court im Privat- und Prozeßrecht der Vereinigten Staaten* (1965).

SHARTEL, *Our Legal System and How It Operates* (1951).

STEIN, 'The Attraction of the Civil Law in Post-Revolutionary America,' 52 *Va. L. Rev.* 403 (1966).

WEISS, *Die Theorie der richterlichen Entscheidungstätigkeit in den Vereinigten Staaten von Amerika* (1971).

WENGLER, 'Die Anpassung des englischen Rechts durch die Judikatur in den Vereinigten Staaten,' in: *Festschrift Rabel* I (1954) 39.

YNTEMA, 'American Legal Realism in Retrospect,' 14 *Vand. L. Rev.* 317 (1960).

I

THE United States of America occupies an especially important place in the Common Law family, and thus calls for a more detailed treatment even in an introductory work such as this. This is not only because the United States is one of the mightiest countries in the world in terms of political influence and economic and military power, but mainly because in the two hundred years since the Declaration of Independence its law has gone through a quite distinctive development and has in many ways left its English model far behind. Unlike England, the United States has a written Constitution which gives the country a federal structure and contains a list of basic rights which may not be infringed by the legislature, the judiciary, or the executive. But other factors, the particular political ideals of the Founding Fathers, the diversity of the population in terms of race, religion and culture, the vast extent of its territory, and above all the astonishing vigour of its social and economic development, all these have helped American law to devise methods and solutions which make its study much more interesting and challenging for the Continental observer than English law, which is often too absorbed in cherishing its traditions.

Settlement of the North American continent began in the first half of the seventeenth century. Small colonies were set up first in Virginia and later elsewhere on the East Coast; they had little contact with each other and their links even with England were rather loose. In the early days when the main task facing the settlers was to secure their own survival against the elements and the Red Indians, there was hardly any need for courts and lawyers. Furthermore many of the colonies such as Massachusetts and Pennsylvania had a religious regime in which any disputes which arose were settled by ministers with the Bible rather than by lawyers with the Common Law. At the beginning of the eighteenth century this picture began to change; there was an increase in trade between the colonies and abroad, especially with England, and theocracy lost its hold in the various settlements. A class of lawyers gradually arose, many of whom had received their training in the Inns of Court in London, often before emigration. Gradually, too, law-books from England became widespread, especially BLACKSTONE's *Commentaries on the*

Laws of England, almost as many copies of which were sold in the relatively unpopulated colonies of America as in England. The Reaction to English imperialism in the mid-eighteenth century gave rise to the movement for American independence; on both sides the principal spokesmen were lawyers, and there were no less than 25 lawyers among the 56 signatories of the Declaration of Independence of 1776. Throughout the war with England until its end in 1781 the representatives of the newly independent American states strove for closer political links with each other, but it was not until 1787 that the Constitutional Convention of Philadelphia, where again more than half of the participants were lawyers, was able to thrash out a Federal Constitution which came into force in 1789 for its 13 member states and which is still, with the addition of a few amendments, in force today. The continuity of the Constitution is amazing; the United States has spread across the whole North American continent, it has developed from a prairie on the edge of civilization into the greatest industrial nation in the world, and it has survived a Civil War and two World Wars, yet still the Constitution has remained virtually unchanged.

Even before independence the American settlers were agreed that in principle the English Common Law, along with statutes already enacted in England, should be the law of the several colonies, apart from any statutes which had been passed specially for them. But it was also recognized that the English Common Law should not be applied to the extent that it was unsuited to local conditions in the colonies.

These principles enabled the American courts to modify the English Common Law in many respects, even in the colonial period but especially in the course of the nineteenth century. Thus, to take an example, the rule in England was that the occupier of land was responsible for the harm which his cattle had caused on the land of a neighbour, regardless of any fault on his part; such a rule might work satisfactorily in a heavily populated land in which one may expect farmers to fence in their beasts so as to prevent harm to their neighbours. But in America, with huge areas almost devoid of people and fit only to be used as pasturage, it was different. Here the principle evolved that it was not for the farmer to fence in his beasts but rather for the occupier of buildings, woods, or agricultural land to protect his property by fencing the beasts out. The rules of the English Common Law regarding the use of water were also unsuited for the dry areas of the American West, where water is extremely scarce and must therefore be available not just to the riparian but also to other landowners for irrigation. The English rules of mining law were also inappropriate: quite different rules for the delimitation of mineral rights were naturally called for in a 'gold-rush' situation when tens of thousands of prospectors simultaneously rushed into unoccupied areas in search of the precious metal. These and other examples from American legal history decisively demonstrate how much the content of law is determined by the climatic, geographical, economic, and social conditions obtaining at the time, and how they change together. On the way the American courts applied English law, see WENGLER (above p. 247) and KIMBALL (above p. 246) 205 ff., 267 ff., which contains very remarkable documentary sources.

The rules of English Common Law were also much altered by *legislation* in the various states. Many of the American settlers had left their European homes precisely because they were politically, spiritually, or economically oppressed by the rulers there, so the political ideals of an extremely egalitarian and radically democratic society dominated the Houses of Representatives of the American states at the beginning of the nineteenth century and found their strongest expression during the presidency of ANDREW JACKSON (1829–37). Accordingly, the several states passed a great number of statutes which purged land law, family law, and law of succession of its feudal English elements, and also simplified court procedure, abolished professional monopolies, protected needy debtors, especially small manual labourers, against recourse by creditors, and rendered criminal law rather more humane. The actual practice of law was also affected by this development. The view that one could not be a lawyer or a judge without special training or special knowledge struck many people as smacking of medieval privilege, and many of the states enacted provisions whereby every citizen, without more, could practise as a lawyer, unless he were actually in trouble with the criminal law. Provisions of this kind survived in Massachusetts until 1935 and in Indiana until 1933. ROSCOE POUND has described this as a 'deprofessionalisation' of the practice of law; one consequence is that the behaviour of lawyers in court and their standards of professional conduct still strike the foreign observer as being in many respects distinctly informal. In those days it also seemed undemocratic that judges should be nominated by the executive and left in office for long terms or even for life. Consequently almost all states enacted laws providing that judges should be elected by the House of Representatives or directly by the people and that they should stand for re-election after relatively short periods in office. Even today in a clear majority of American states judges are chosen directly by the people in public elections in which candidates mostly appear quite openly on the 'Democratic' or 'Republican' ticket and have their electoral campaigns supported by the relevant party organization. The judges in the rest of the states and the judges in the federal courts are nominated by the executive (the Governor in the states, and the President for federal office), though the agreement of the legislature is often called for. Even in these cases the choice of judge does not simply depend on their professional qualifications, but is affected to an astonishing degree by considerations of party loyalty, of patronage, and of political bargaining. This is clearly true for the judges of the lower state courts but even the federal judges nominated by the President are normally members of his party.

For a detailed treatment, see KAYSER, *Die Auswahl der Richter in der englischen und amerikanischen Rechtspraxis* (1969); ABRAHAM (above p. 246) 26 ff. and the authors excerpted in HONNOLD (above p. 246) 195 ff.—For many years the Bar Associations, the professional organizations of lawyers in America, have been trying with some success to procure that professional competence plays a larger part in the selection of judges. In consequence of their efforts many states have abolished popular election for judicial office and have adopted a system whereby the Governor chooses a judge for each vacant seat from a list of three qualified candidates proposed by an independent committee; the judge who is nominated in this way must put himself up for popular election when his period in office expires, but as no candidate is opposed to him he can normally count on confirmation. The Bar Associations also try to influence the choice of judges by the chief executive. Names of candidates being considered for federal judgeships are normally submitted to a special committee of the American Bar Association, and it is very rare for a President to nominate a candidate whom this committee, after close investigation, has found unsuitable, for in such a case there would be unfavourable publicity.

Another great question of legal policy in the nineteenth century was whether the Common Law in its American form should be comprehensively codified. In 1811 JEREMY BENTHAM wrote a letter to President MADISON, in which he persuasively laid out the advantages of such a step and offered to undertake the task of preparing a code himself. He received a polite but firm refusal. Nevertheless the ideas of BENTHAM and his school were so influential, the example of the French Code so impressive, and the discontent over the unmanageable condition of the Common Law so widespread that the idea of codification took root, first of all in Massachusetts and then in New York, where it found a splendid protagonist in DAVID DUDLEY FIELD, a New York lawyer; from there the idea of codification spread to the other states of the Union and provoked serious discussion everywhere, rather reminiscent of the dispute between THIBAUT and SAVIGNY taking place in Germany about the same time (see p. 145). First of all, FIELD drafted a Code of Civil Procedure whose principal feature was the abolition of the traditional distinction between actions 'at law' and 'in equity', a reform which greatly simplified court procedure in civil matters. New York adopted this code in 1848, and in the following years it became the model for similar codes of procedure in many other states. But with the Civil Code, in which he also had the principal hand, FIELD had less success. The movement for codification had already lost much of its impetus in 1865 when he published his draft. The recent diffusion of the commentaries and treatises of KENT and STORY had helped American law to seem more manageable and orderly but, even more important, the idea of codification ran into strong opposition from the legal profession, which had become organized on the East Coast in the mid-nineteenth century and had become a very influential part of the bourgeois establishment; lawyers had very little interest in seeing their familiar techniques of legal research rendered valueless by means of a code such as FIELD proposed. But the situation was different in many states of the American *West* where the simpler social circumstances of the 'frontier society' still obtained; here belief in the value of a code whose rational structure made it comprehensible to a simple layman greatly outweighed the interest of lawyers in maintaining received legal traditions. Towards the end of the century the 'Field Code' came into force in North Dakota, South Dakota, Idaho, Montana, and California, and it is still in force in those states today, though with many alterations; one must, however, recognize that its practical significance as a source of law is quite different from what a civil lawyer would expect of a civil code in his own country (see below Ch. 20 III).

In the course of the nineteenth century there was increasing tension between the industrialized and commercial North, with its concern for protective tariffs, and the planter aristocracy of the agrarian South. This tension came to breaking point over the question of slavery. In a notorious decision of 1857, *Dred Scott* v. *Sandford* (19 How. 393), the Supreme Court decided that a negro slave could not be a citizen of the United States even if he had lived for a time in a state where slavery was not accepted. This decision provoked enormous anger in the North; after ABRAHAM LINCOLN was elected President in 1860 as the candidate of the Republic party which had been founded only a few years previously, the Southern states seceded from the Union and civil war became inevitable. The victory of the North saved the unity of the federation, reinforced federal power, especially by developing the emergency powers of the President, and made the abolition of slavery possible.

II

After the end of the Civil War headlong economic expansion took place in the United States. Enormous progress was made in a few decades: the American West was opened by the construction of railroads, new industries were built up, and the mineral resources of the country were exploited. This called for legal creativity in the fields of company law, the law of insurance and carriage, and in credit, banking, and stock exchange law. These legal creations naturally reflected the prevalent ideas of the time concerning the proper way to order the economy and society as they had been set down, for example, in the works of the English philosopher HERBERT SPENCER, especially in his book *Social Statics* (1850): in this view the only way to ensure the progress of civilization and the maximization of the general good was to give entrepreneurs the greatest possible scope for their freedom of activity, their enterprise, and their individualism. Governmental intervention in the economic process in the interests of protecting the weak was seen as wrong; sacrifices had to be borne by the individual in the name of progress and economic growth. It was not only the substance of the law but also the manner of its presentation and application which answered the needs of the entrepreneurs: financiers, industrialists, and investors were interested in the predictability and stability of judicial decision, and so a situation arose towards the end of the century similar to that in Germany at the height of conceptual jurisprudence when the economic and social policies were very similar: the law took more fixed forms and the judges saw their primary task as being to put the existing stock of rules in dogmatic order; they had a tendency to draw legal consequences from the place in the system where the applicable legal rule had previously been put; this allowed the judges to enjoy the illusion that they could thus insulate themselves from the political and social conflicts of the time and serve as the mere ministers of a timeless sense of justice.

The powerful upsurge of economic activity after the Civil War and the opening up of new and complex areas of law led to major changes in the way American lawyers were trained. Theretofore it had been normal for youngsters to obtain the necessary skills either in the English Inns of Court or by apprenticing themselves to an American lawyer so as to learn trial procedure and the drawing up of deeds, to acquire the tricks of their master's trade and perhaps even to read a little in the *Commentaries* of BLACKSTONE or KENT. Already by the end of the eighteenth century there were some universities where professors were charged with delivering lectures on law. That the study of law should be regarded as a practical preparation for the legal profession and not, as at the English universities, a means of furthering a general education was a view which was accepted under the influence of STORY, a professor at the Harvard Law School from 1829 and a judge of the Supreme Court as well (see KEGEL, *RabelsZ* 43 (1979) 609). The level of legal education, which normally lasted no longer than a year, was admittedly fairly low. Students were admitted to study law without any preparation and normally there were no examinations at all. But a fundamental change set in after 1870. The pacemakers of this development were the Law School of Harvard University and its Dean LANGDELL. Thanks to his efforts the Faculty was greatly increased, the length of the period of instruction was extended to three years, a strict control of performance was established by examinations, and gradually a college education was demanded as a precondition to admission to the Law School. LANGDELL also invented the so-called 'case method', a style of teaching which is still prevalent in American legal education today, though with many variations. The basic idea of this method is that the rules of law should be presented to the student in the context of actual decided cases and should be explained, set in relation to other rules, and subjected to critical discussion only in the context of such cases. The American Bar Association, which had a professional interest in the improvement of legal education, helped to procure the adoption of the demanding Harvard model by the law schools of other universities. The habit of learning practical legal skills in an attorney's office as an apprentice gradually died away and in the United States now, unlike England (see above Ch. 17 III 3) law schools have an unchallenged monopoly of legal education.

As the law schools began to flourish, a group of lawyers came on the scene who were to be of great significance for American law in the course of the twentieth century: these were the *professors*. Their influence is connected with a fundamental alteration in legal methods of thinking, coinciding with a change in the view of American society about its ethical and social obligations. This change is best seen in the gradual weakening of the extreme individualistic ideas of the 'social Darwinism' of the period of expansion, and in the growing tendency of the state from the beginning of the twentieth century to subject economic life to supervision and control and deliberately to limit the freedom of activity of the entrepreneur whenever it might cause unacceptable hardship to individual citizens. Even before the turn of the century Congress had moved to repress really gross abuses of contractual freedom; for example, it subjected railroad companies to state supervision and created for this purpose the Interstate Commerce Commission in 1887, the first of the great federal authorities which supervise economic affairs. The Sherman Act of 1890 and the Clayton Act of 1914, with the construction given to them by the courts, afford the federal authorities very extensive powers to repress agreements and practices which are in restraint of trade. Electricity, water, and gas utilities, the news industry, broadcasting, road transport, shipping, and air traffic, all of which are still conducted in the United States, unlike Europe, by private undertakers, were all gradually subjected to state control which soon moved from merely restraining abuses to taking positive action to procure that consumers should receive a proper service at a reasonable price. Numerous statutes were also enacted to protect workmen: federal or state legislation brought in social accident insurance, fixed minimum wages, limited child labour, and set maximum daily hours of work. In this the United States was reproducing a situation which had been brought about in Germany many decades earlier by the social legislation of Bismarck's Empire, patriarchal and paternalistic in tone.

These measures of economic and social policy met with determined opposition from the entrepreneurs of America, in which they could often count on the support of the judges until the 1930s. Thus in 1905 the Supreme Court struck down as unconstitutional a New York statute which forbade the employment of bakers for more than ten hours per day and sixty hours per week: according to the majority such a statute deprived the workers as well as the entrepreneurs of the freedom to conclude contracts of employment 'without due process of law', that is, in breach of the Fourteenth Amendment. But Justice HOLMES delivered a passionate dissenting opinion, whose high-point was the lapidary observation 'The Fourteenth Amendment does not enact Mr. Herbert Spencer's Social Statics' (see *Lochner* v. *State of New York*, 198 US 45 (1905)). As late as 1918 the Supreme Court struck down a federal statute which under certain conditions prohibited the transport of goods whose production involved the employment of children under 14 years of age (see *Hammer* v. *Dagenhart*, 247 US 251 (1918)). Indeed the first of the New Deal legislation with which President ROOSEVELT aimed to bring the country out of the great economic crisis of the 1930s was frustrated by a bare majority of the Supreme Court on constitutional grounds. Here, however, the Court went too far. With ROOSEVELT's enormous electoral majority in the autumn of

1936 it became clear that the greater part of the people approved of his legislative plans and he put before Congress the drafts of a statute which would have given him the power to nominate an additional judge to the Supreme Court whenever one of the existing judges, nominated for life, reached the age of 70 without retiring; no less than six of the nine judges were over that age at the time. The President vigorously defended his 'court-packing plan' in public: 'We have reached the point as a nation where we must take action to save the Constitution from the court and the court from itself' (*New York Times*, 10 March 1937, p. 1). Whether Congress would at the end of the day have approved the plan is uncertain; the question never had to be answered, as one of the judges altered his position and thus converted the minority into the majority— an event not unfairly described by the witticism 'A switch in time saved nine'.

As one can imagine, the analytical and conceptual methods current at the beginning of the century gradually came to seem very implausible in the face of the development of a reformist economic and social policy relying increasingly on purposive legislative intervention such as we have outlined; a contributory factor may well have been the general acceptance in the United States between 1910 and 1930 of the pragmatic philosophy of WILLIAM JAMES and JOHN DEWEY which opposed all kinds of formalistic, deductive and abstract reasoning; even lawyers must have felt its impact. As early as his publication in 1881 of 'The Common Law' HOLMES in a famous passage attacked the view that the Common Law was an eternally valid manifestation of higher reason hovering over the troubled waters of the present, which could be concretized for the individual case by an act of perception on the part of an intellectually detached judge operating on logical and deductive principles:

'The life of the law has not been logic: it has been experience. The felt necessities of the time, the prevalent moral and political theories, intuitions of public policy, avowed or unconscious, even the prejudices which judges share with their fellow-men, have had a good deal more to do than the syllogism in determining the rules by which men should be governed' (id., 1).

In many other places as well, including many of his judgments in court, HOLMES brilliantly critized traditional modes of thought. But ROSCOE POUND, who ranks in America as the founder of 'sociological jurisprudence' was the first to turn these criticisms into a complete new programme. POUND and his school saw a legal system as being a phenomenon which intimately interacts with the prevalent political, economic, and social circumstances in a given society and which constantly alters with them in a living process of development. They are not interested in the abstract content of 'black letter rules' nor in the logical and analytical connections which may exist between them in a particular system. What they want to discover about legal rules is what concrete effects in social reality they aim to produce as soon as they become 'law in action' by the behaviour of judges or administrative authorities. Thus for POUND law is in the first place a means for the ordering of social interests, and the judge in balancing out these interests should be a 'social engineer' who can only perform his task properly if he has an accurate knowledge of the actual circumstances on which his decision will have an effect. POUND also insisted that teachers of law should have this knowledge:

'The modern teacher of law should be a student of sociology, economics and politics as well. He should know not only what the courts decide and the principles by which they decide, but quite as much the circumstances and conditions, social and economic, to which these principles are to be applied . . . [and] the state of popular thought and feeling which makes the environment in which the principles must operate in practice. Legal monks who pass their lives in an atmosphere of pure law, from which every worldly and human element is excluded, cannot shape practical principles to be applied to a restless world of flesh and blood. The most logical and skillfully reasoned rules may defeat the end of the law in their practical administration because not adapted to the environment in which they are to be enforced' (POUND, 'The Need for a Sociological Jurisprudence,' 19 *Green Bag* 611–12 (1907), cited by RUMBLE (above p. 246) 13).

The theories of sociological jurisprudence were further developed in the 1930s by a group of American lawyers representing the school of 'legal realism' and carried by them, in the view of many, to extremes. The best-known members of this group were KARL N. LLEWELLYN and JEROME N. FRANK, who are much more sceptical than POUND in their view of the value of abstractly formulated rules of law as descriptions or predictions of the actual behaviour of judges. For them law cannot be learnt from the 'paper rules' of textbooks but only from keen observation of 'judicial behaviour', that is, *what the courts actually do*. In this they adopt the standpoint of HOLMES, who said in a phrase which has become proverbial, that by law he understood 'the prophecies of what the courts will do in fact, and nothing more pretentious' ('The Path of the Law,' 10 *Harv. L. Rev.* 457, 460 f. (1897)). So LLEWELLYN: he describes judges, judicial officials and lawyers as 'officials of the law' and then defines as follows: 'What these officers do about disputes is, to my mind, the law itself' (*The Bramble Bush* (1951) 12). Pursuant to this idea, the 'realists' see their principal task as being the discovery and analysis of the factors which lead the 'law official', especially the judge, to decide the concrete case in the way he does and not otherwise. They started from the conviction that the traditional doctrines of law were relatively insignificant for the actual decision on the merits in many cases and simply offered a means whereby the judge could *ex post facto* 'rationalize' a decision which he had arrived at by another path. Even the principle of the binding force of precedents seemed to the 'realists' to be very far indeed from guaranteeing that certainty of law and predictability of future decisions claimed for it by orthodoxy: for, as LLEWELLYN tried to show, the judge had at his disposal dozens of techniques by which he could cull exactly what he wanted out of previous decisions. What really determined the disposal of a case—and that was that legal scholarship and research should look to—was rather the particular social and economic context of the particular case, a matter wholly ignored by the traditional rules of law which are generally far too widely framed. Another determinant is the judge's personal predilections and antipathies, as well as his moral values and his political beliefs; a further critical factor is the degree to which the judge at first instance got the facts of the case wrong or failed to understand them.

Many of the ideas developed by 'sociological jurisprudence' and 'legal realism' obviously underlie the 'École de la libre recherche scientifique' in France (see above p. 98) and the 'Freirechtsschule' in Germany, as well as the frequent demands that we should investigate the facts behind the law and have greater co-operation between the sciences of law and sociology. But in Germany and France these ideas did not have the enormous response in all areas of legal life which the ideas of POUND and the realists had in the United States: 'the attitude towards legal problems, characterised as realistic jurisprudence . . . has dominated legal thinking in the United States during the past generation, even to the point of becoming commonplace' (YNTEMA (above p. 247) 325). For example, in the area of *legal education*, a glance at a recent American casebook shows that law courses nowadays cover much more than court decisions and the rules of law formulated in them; they also cover economic facts, medical, psychiatric, and criminological information, the usages of business life, and the standard forms of contract. Consistently enough, the faculties of the large law schools today often include political scientists, doctors, and sociologists who co-operate closely with the lawyers in both teaching and research. Even in the practice of the courts there are many alterations which can be traced back to this new way of thinking. Thus already in 1907, in the case of *Muller* v. *Oregon*, 208 US 412 (1908). LOUIS BRANDEIS put before the Supreme Court, of which he was later to become a famous judge, a brief containing a wide range of factual data and comparative legal material germane to the question of law in dispute; the 'Brandeis brief' caused a sensation at the time but it has since become a fixed concept in America and has established itself in constititutional disputes and also in other matters. Then there are many judges in the United States whose judgments demonstrate the influence of 'sociological jurisprudence' by displaying a scepticism about doctrine, a sense of reality, and an open weighing of the social interests at stake. And finally *legal writing* shows how firmly established in the United States these new ideas are. For while in Germany, with few exceptions, these questions are discussed only at the level of principle and philosophy in a rudimentary manner, in the United States for some decades past writers have addressed themselves to the much more difficult task of testing the value of sociological research methods by applying them to practical problems of law.

Rules of law have thus been analysed in the light of sociology and political science. Recently they have also been analysed in terms of *economics*. POSNER's *Economic*

Analysis of Law (2nd edn., 1977) is the leading work. Its hypothesis is that in order to maximize the general welfare the limited resources available in any society should be made available to those individuals who can use them to best advantage. This is normally achieved through exchange transactions whereby a person gives up certain assets, such as property or services, in order to obtain from his partner other assets which have a greater value for him than those he gives up. Under certain conditions the situation produced by such operations is 'efficient', since all scarce resources have been channelled by market operations to the place where their use is of the greatest value, and the general good cannot be increased by any further exchange operations. This hypothesis can be used to test legal rules in order to see whether they contribute to an 'efficient' distribution of scarce resources or, to put the point in another way, whether they promote a situation in which the acts of individuals directed to their own private gain also conduce to the advantage of society. To take an example from the law of tort, one can show that the courts habitually classify conduct as 'negligent' and therefore impose liability if the steps which the person causing the harm could have taken to avoid it would have cost less than the expense due to the occurrence of the damage. Or in contract law one could say that whether or not the courts should hold an exculpatory clause invalid as being 'contrary to good faith', 'unconscionable', or 'unfair' should depend on whether or not it places the relevant risk on the party who can more cheaply avoid it or, in the case of a risk which it is impossible or uneconomic to avoid, insure against it. This 'economic analysis' is applied to all aspects of law by professorial votaries in the leading laws schools in the United States, and there are special periodicals for its practitioners and critics. Of course there are limits to the utility of this approach but there is no doubt that it can help one to recognize the conflicts of aim which lurk in problems of legal policy, to determine the necessary priorities, and to discuss them rationally after a sober evaluation of means and ends, cost, and utility.

III

The United States has been said to possess 'perhaps the most complicated legal structure that has ever been devised and made effective in man's effort to govern himself' (GRISWOLD (above p. 246) 3). The point of this observation becomes clear when one sees the problems which have arisen in the United States from the complexities of the concurrence of federal and state law, and from the fact that both the United States and the several states possess fully equipped courts systems.

Under the Constitution the United States Congress has legislative competence only in specified areas: apart from currency and coin, the levying of taxes and excises, foreign affairs, and defence, the most important are citizenship, the protection of trade and copyright, bankruptcy, maritime law, and finally the control of commerce with foreign nations and among the several states. It can be seen from this that the whole of private law and the rest of commercial law fall within the competence of the 50 individual states. Given these facts, one must ask whether one can really talk of 'American law' in the way one talks of German or English law and, if so, with what qualifications.

Regarding the division of legislative power between the United States and the member states, the Supreme Court has always been able to construe the Constitution in such a way that the development of a large and economically integrated internal market in the United States has not been seriously inhibited by legal differences. Art. I §8 of the Constitution provides that the United States has power, in addition to the powers expressly attributed to it, to enact laws 'necessary and proper' for carrying these powers into execution. As early as 1819 the Supreme Court under Chief Justice MARSHALL, himself an outstanding judicial statesman, used this clause to construct the doctrine of implied powers which gives the United States very generous room for play in its legislative activities; *McCulloch* v *Maryland*, 4 Wheat. 316 (1819). But the principal device for extending the federal powers and thereby restricting those of the states has been the 'commerce clause', that provision of the Constitution which gives the United States power to pass laws to regulate commerce among the several states. The way the scope of this clause has been gradually extended to suit the needs of an expanding economy is one of the most fascinating chapters in the development of American constitutional law. Even today the United States has no power to pass laws regulating economic matters in 'intrastate commerce', that is, matters which occur within the boundaries of one state only, but by the decision in which the Supreme Court endorsed the New Deal legislation this principle was so emptied of content that it no longer really limits the power of the United States to pass such laws if it has any reasonable interest in doing so.

But in the central areas of private law the competence of the several states is as large as ever. This means not only that the legislatures of each of the 50 states can pass their own statutes in the area of family and succession law, contract and tort, land law, partnership, insurance, and negotiable instruments law, but also that the judges in these areas are free to develop the law of their state in different directions, as in fact they often do. Thus the United States can be seen as a gigantic laboratory for legal policy in which any state can move forward in any direction by legislation or judicial decision and thus gain experience and reach views which enrich the debates on legal policy and may serve as an encouraging or horrifying example to other states.

Of course the egoism of individual states sometimes leads them on fairly obvious grounds to marked deviations—the extensive divorce practice of Nevada and the generous company law of Delaware are well-known examples—but there are also institutions which help the cause of legal unification or help to emphasize the similarities which already exist. Here we must mention the American *law schools*. Of course every law school is located in one state or another and law schools are largely financed by the resources of their home state unless they form part of a private university. Nevertheless most law schools would not think of training their students only in the law of New York or the law of Michigan, for example; instead, these law schools teach their students, who themselves come from all over the country, a *common American law* which admittedly does not exist as positive law anywhere. Classes and casebooks by no means ignore the interesting results which particular states may have arrived at, but they are looked at as being merely local variations of a theme which in principle is unitary and they are approached with the critical detachment of a person who knows that there are always other rules somewhere which have different formulations but reach the same results. So in the training of American lawyers the critical methods of comparative law play an important part from the very beginning; at the same time the young lawyer comes to think of American law as something which is basically unitary, though this will be counteracted by the state chauvinism which he will later meet in his professional career.

Another indication of the unitary basis of American private law, despite all the local variants, is the success with which it has for some time been being compiled in the so-called 'Restatements'. Since the increasing flood of precedents was making the law cumbrous and unmanageable it seemed sensible to record it in a clearly ordered and systematically constructed 'Restatement'; this task was entrusted to the 'American Law Institute', founded in 1923 by the American Bar Association in conjunction with judges and law teachers. The following procedure was adopted. A leading scholar is selected as 'Reporter' for each legal topic; his task is to absorb all the existing case-law, to extract general rules, and, in association with a group of advisers including experienced lawyers, judges, and professors, to formulate a text which needs the endorsement of certain committees of the American Law Institute before it is published as a 'Restatement'. The task of the reporter is to lay down the law in its *present positive form* and not to improve or modernize it. Nevertheless in cases where the rules of the various states are inconsistent they may choose the solution which seems to them to be the more progressive, even if it obtains only in a minority of states. By this means Restatements have been produced for all important areas of American private law except family law and the law of succession—for example, the general law of contract, tort, trusts, conflicts of law—and many of them have already appeared in a second edition. Restatements are rather like the Civil Law codes in their systematic structure of abstractly formulated rules, and in many cases the Continental jurist can use them as a means of easy access to the rules of American private law in the first instance. Warning should be given, however, not to use them too uncritically, for the only way to be sure whether a particular rule is in force in a particular state is by consulting the judicial decisions of that state. If the problem in question has not yet been decided or clearly decided in that state, an American judge will often have recourse to the Restatement, but will normally accord it only fractionally more weight than he would to a leading textbook, and that, in a Common Law country, is not very much.

As early as the end of the nineteenth century it was recognized in the United States that it would be very desirable to have particular topics regulated by identical statutes in all the states. On the prompting of the American Bar Association, all states eventually agreed to send three to five representatives to a national body, the *National Conference of Commissioners on Uniform State Laws*, which was given the task of drafting Uniform Acts for those areas where intra-American unification seemed especially desirable, and to propose them to the legislatures of the several states for enactment with the minimum possible amendment. This Conference met for the first time in 1892 and has since worked on many dozens of such Uniform Laws, most of them dealing with very specific and narrow questions, but sometimes also covering whole areas of law, such as the law of bills and notes. Many of the Uniform Acts so produced have been adopted by all the states, while others have had only sporadic success, but by and large the efforts of the Conference have substantially promoted legal unification in the American states, especially in the area of commercial law where the need for unitary rules is outstandingly clear.

So far, the *Uniform Commercial Code* is the most significant and successful undertaking of the Conference, in association with the American Law Institute. In 1940 the Conference determined on a fundamental revision of the existing Uniform Laws on commercial matters, of which, for example, the statute on negotiable instruments had been adopted by all states and the law of sales by most; they were then to be brought together in a Commercial Code. The work was put in charge of LLEWELLYN who left his mark on the construction, scope and methods of the Code. In 1952 a first draft was submitted for comment to hundreds of merchants, commercial agents, bankers, carriers, and warehousemen. Note was taken of their criticisms and in 1956 a final version appeared which has subsequently been adopted in all the states of the Union. Louisiana has not adopted it in its entirety, and many states found it necessary to make verbal alterations, but they do not amount to much. Thus essentially the same rules apply today in all of the United States to sale, transactions involving negotiable instruments, cheques, warehouse receipts, bills of lading, certificates of deposit, and so on, as well as to the collection of commercial paper and the very important area of credit and security, with the exception of mortgage. See MALCOLM, 'The Uniform Commercial Code in the United States,' 12 *ICLQ* 226 (1963).

Enough has been said to make it clear that there is often a confusing hodgepodge of federal law and state law. As a rule of thumb one can say that the law relating to the control of the economy is federal law, although the states often have concurrent laws or even act in place of the United States, as in the control of the insurance industry. Important areas of commercial law, especially the sale of goods and connected credit and security arrangements, are regulated by state law, but with substantially the same content in consequence of the introduction of the Uniform Commercial Code. Other areas of commercial law, such as company law (except for the federal supervision of the stock exchange and share dealings) and the law of insurance, are covered by the laws of the various states which still show marked divergencies, while the law of bankruptcy, the protection of industrial property, and maritime law fall within the exclusive competence of the United States by reason of the Constitution. In the general law of contract, in tort and land law, and in family and succession law the legal systems of the several states control; they are in general agreement in basic concepts, methods, and solutions, but often show so marked a variation on individual points that it is of the greatest importance to know which state law applies to a case which has connections with several states. Here the rules of conflicts of law, mainly unwritten, apply, being themselves part of state law and therefore capable of variation from state to state, subject to minimum standards inferred from the Constitution (see SCHLESINGER (above p. 246) 6 ff.).

The situation in the United States is rendered even more complicated by the fact that there are complete courts systems not only in each of the several states but also in the United States. So far as the *federal courts* are concerned, by art. III § 1 of the Constitution, the judicial power of the federation is vested in the Supreme Court and 'such inferior Courts as the Congress may from time to time ordain and establish'. In 1789, in one of the very first Acts passed by it, Congress exercised the power to create lower federal courts by establishing *District Courts* as federal courts of first instance and, as courts of appeal, courts which were later called *Courts of Appeals*. There are close to 100 District Courts in the United States, many states having only one while other states with large populations may be divided into two or four districts each of which has a District Court; furthermore many districts have more than one judge, so that in total there are about 550 'District Judges' who normally sit alone. For appeals from judgments of the District Courts there are 12 Courts of Appeals: the catchment area or 'circuit' of 11 of them includes several states each, and there is one for the District of Columbia Circuit. There are about 168 judges in these Courts of Appeals who sit in benches of three. Finally, at the head of the federal courts stands the Supreme Court in Washington with nine judges.

In order to keep the Supreme Court's workload within limits, an Act of 1925 gave the judges discretion to decide which cases were important enough to justify an appeal being heard by the highest court of the land. According to the normal practice, the Supreme Court will 'grant *certiorari*' and proceed to a decision on the merits if, after a summary consideration of the case, at least four judges are in favour of so doing. If not, no reasons are given for refusal, though very occasionally one of the justices will briefly say why he would have chosen to hear the case. It does not follow from the grant of *certiorari* that there will be oral argument. The Court may decide the matter on the basis of the briefs which have been submitted; such a decision 'per curiam' is normally unanimous and contains either no reasons at all or only very brief reasons for confirming or quashing the judgment in question. In a specific group of cases the parties are entitled to a decision on the merits, for example, where the highest court of a state has held a state statute constitutional, despite attack, or a federal statute unconstitutional, or where a federal court has held a federal statute unconstitutional in a case to which the United States is a party. In these cases there must be a decision on the merits but not necessarily oral proceedings, as the Supreme Court may give a summary judgment upholding the decision in question if it is of the view that the case raises no real question of principle in federal law. In 1985–86 the Supreme Court gave decisions on the merits in only 273 of the 4,374 cases which were laid before it and only 161 of these had fully reasoned judgments.

The courts systems of the different states are so diverse that one can hardly make any general statements. In rural areas trivial matters both civil and criminal are dealt with by part-time judges of the peace; they hardly ever have any legal training and the procedure they employ is a very simplified one. In the large cities the lowest courts are often the so-called 'Municipal Courts', staffed by qualified judges, which as 'Traffic Courts' concentrate on highway offences or as 'Small Claim Courts' deal with civil matters of small importance. Civil and criminal matters which are more serious first go to courts which always have a single judge, in many states called 'County Courts', in others 'District Courts', and in New York even the 'Supreme Court'; their procedure is formal and may involve a jury in specified cases. Appeals against judgements of these courts often go straight to the highest court of the state; only about 15 states with large populations have an intermediate court of appeal, thus providing three levels of court.

By far the largest number of civil suits in the United Sates is decided by state courts. Federal courts have jurisdiction only under specified conditions, most of which are laid down in the Constitution, for example, cases in which the United States is a party and cases where the complaint is based on a provision of federal law ('federal question jurisdiction'). The fear that the courts of a state might not afford complete justice to a party domiciled in another state explains the existence of federal jurisdiction in another class of case: the Constitution provides that the federal courts shall be competent if the parties are citizens of, that is, are domiciled in, different states ('diversity of citizenship jurisdiction'), but a federal statute imposes a further requirement, that the matter in issue must exceed $10,000 in value. A legal person counts as a citizen of the state of its incorporation, and if it has its chief place of business in some other state it counts as a citizen of that state also.

It follows from the rules of jurisdiction in 'diversity of citizenship' cases that, to take an example, a federal court sitting in California can decide a suit brought by a Texan for damages in tort against a Californian defendant. The question immediately arises whether the federal court should apply Californian or Texan tort law or whether it may not have to apply federal tort law instead. For nearly a century after the Supreme

Court decision in *Swift* v. *Tyson*, 16 Pet. 1 (1842) it was established that in areas of judge-made law such as tort, the federal courts should apply not the case-law of any particular state but rules of federal law which were to be independently developed. This decision was based on the hope that in this way the decisions of the federal courts might gradually build up a 'federal common law' which might be taken over by the courts of the several states and thus form a point around which unified American law might crystallize. This hope has not borne fruit. The courts of the states were far from following decisions of the federal courts and often enough hit upon deviant rules. This gave litigants an incentive to try all kinds of devices to bring the case before the federal rather than the state courts or vice versa, depending on whether federal or state common law offered them the more favourable rule. These unfortunate effects induced the Supreme Court in *Erie Railroad Co.* v. *Tompkins*, 304 US 64 (1938) to abandon its previous holding and decide that, except in cases controlled by a federal statute, federal courts should in principle apply the written or unwritten law of the state in which it sat. This applies also to questions of conflicts of law; thus in the example with which we started this paragraph, the federal court must answer the question whether Californian or Texan tort law is to be applied in accordance with the conflict rules of California, the state in which it sits, and not by federal rules.

20

Law-Finding and Procedure in Common Law and Civil Law

AMOS, 'The Interpretation of Statutes', 5 *Camb. LJ* 163 (1933–5).

BRIDGE, 'National Legal Tradition and Community Law: Legislative Drafting and Judicial Interpretation in England and the European Community', *J. Common Market Studies* 1981, 351.

CAPPELLETTI, 'The Doctrine of Stare Decisis and the Civil Law: A Fundamental Difference—Or No Difference at All?', *Festschrift Zweigert* (1981) 381.

CARDOZO, *The Nature of the Judicial Process* (1921).

COOPER, 'The Common Law and the Civil Law—A Scot's View', 63 *Harv. L. Rev.* 468 (1950).

CROSS, *Precedent in English Law* (3rd edn., 1977).

——, *Statutory Interpretation* (1976).

——, 'Stare Decisis in Contemporary England', 82 *LQ Rev.* 203 (1966)

——, 'The Ratio Decidendi and a Plurality of Speeches in the House of Lords', 93 *LQ Rev.* 378 (1977).

DAINOW (ed.), *The Role of Judicial Decisions and Doctrine in Civil Law and in Mixed Jurisdictions* (1974).

DAWSON, *The Oracles of the Law* (1968).

DICKERSON, *The Interpretation and Application of Statutes* (1975).

ESSER, *Grundsatz und Norm in der richterlichen Fortbildung des Privatrechts* (2nd edn., 1964).

FIKENTSCHER, *Methoden des Rechts* IV (1977) 269.

——, 'Die Theorie der Fallnorm als Grundlage von Kodex- und Fallrecht (code law and case law)', *ZfRV* 1980, 161.

FRANKEL, *Partisan Justice* (1978).

FRANKFURTER, 'Some Reflections on the Reading of Statutes', 47 *Colum. L. Rev.* 527 (1947).

FRIEDMANN, 'A Re-Examination of the Relations Between English, American and Continental Jurisprudence', 20 *Can. Bar Rev.* 175 (1942).

GOODHART, 'Precedent in English and Continental Law', 50 *LQ Rev.* 40 (1934).

HERMAN, 'Quot iudices tot sententiae: A Study of the English Reaction to Continental Interpretive Techniques', 1981 *JSPTL* 165.

KÖTZ, *Über den Stil höchstrichterlicher Entscheidungen* (1973).

——, 'Zur Funktionsteilung zwischen Richter und Anwalt im deutschen und englischen Zivilprozess', *Festschrift Zajtay* (1982) 277.

LAWSON, 'The Art of Drafting Statutes', *Festschrift Zweigert* (1981) 879.

LLEWELLYN, *The Bramble Bush* (1930).

MARSH, *Interpretation in a National and International Context* (1974).

v. MEHREN, 'The Significance for Procedural Practice and Theory of the Concentrated Trial: Comparative Remarks', *Festschrift Coing* (1982) 361.

MUNDAY, 'The Common Lawyer's Philosophy of Legislation', *Rechtstheorie* 14 (1983) 191.

POUND, 'What Is The Common Law?', in: *The Future of the Common Law* (1937) 3.

——, *The Spirit of the Common Law* (1921).

——, 'Common Law and Legislation', 21 *Harv. L. Rev.* 383 (1908).

RABEL, 'Civil Law and Common Law', 10 *La. L. Rev.* 431 (1949), reprinted in: Rabel, *Gesammelte Aufsätze* III (ed. Leser, 1967) 312.

RADBRUCH, *Der Geist des englischen Rechts* (1947).

RADIN, 'A Short Way with Statutes', 56 *Harv. L. Rev.* 388 (1942).

RHEINSTEIN, 'The Common Law and the Civil Law: An Elementary Comparison', *Rev. jur. Univ. Puerto Rico* 22 (1952/1953) 90.

RUDDEN, 'Courts and Codes in England, France and Soviet Russia', 48 *Tul. L. Rev.* 1010 (1974).

SAUVEPLANNE, *Codified and Judge Made Law, The Role of Courts and Legislators in Civil and Common Law Systems* (1982).

SCHMITTHOFF, 'Der Zivilprozess als Schlüssel zum englischen Rechtsdenken', *JZ* 1972, 38.

——, 'Systemdenken und Fallrecht in der Entwicklung des englischen Privatrechts', *JZ* 1967, 1.

——, 'Non stamus decisis', *Festschrift Coing* (1982) 469.

SCHWARZ-LIEBERMANN v. WAHLENDORF, *Introduction à l'esprit et à l'histoire du droit anglais* (1977).

STEVENS, *Law and Politics, The House of Lords as a Judicial Body* (1978).

WIEACKER, 'Gesetzresrecht und richterliche Kunstregel, Zu Essers Buch "Grundsatz und Norm"', *JZ* 1957, 701.

ZANDER, *The Law-Making Process* (1980).

I

BEFORE embarking on a comparison of the different methods of law-finding characteristic of Common Law and Civil Law jurisdictions respectively, it is as well to remind ourselves of the great differences in political, social, and intellectual history in England and on the Continent, for they affected the whole of legal life, including the way that sources of law were dealt with. As we have seen, the Kings of England had succeeded by the early Middle Ages in concentrating the practice of law in just a few courts in London; this made it possible for a Common Law effective throughout the country to evolve from native sources. A well-organized guild of influential layers grew up around these central courts, with independence enough to select, train, and admit new members to practice and even to procure that only their own members should be appointed to the judiciary. Things were quite different in Germany, whose history in the Middle Ages is the story of the progressive enfeeblement of the Empire; this delayed the growth of central courts and administrative agencies, and prevented the rise of a 'class of Imperial jurists', which made it difficult for the indigenous law to put up much opposition to the advance of Roman law (see above Ch. 11 II). Roman law as it appeared on the scene was 'scholars' law'—professors had rediscovered it in the universities of Northern Italy, professors had refined and developed it with the methods of scholasticism and humanism, and only professors taught it—one had to go to university to learn it. Thus the law in Germany after the Reception had a rather *academic and theoretical* quality, not the *forensic and pragmatic* character it had acquired in England; it was controlled by *university teachers* rather than by *legal practitioners* and it was to be found in *textbooks* rather than in *law reports*. Here also we find the origins of the habit which still survives in Germany of treating the practice of law as a function of the state bureaucracy and the judiciary as a part of the civil service. The civilian jurists who established themselves in Germany during the Reception were mainly employed on the administrative staffs of the many territorial rulers where their dependent position as the princes' official advisers made it impossible for them to combine in guilds or professional bodies and achieve the power which an independent social group can acquire. Although in the course of the eighteenth century the practice of law became detached from the general internal government of the state, it nevertheless kept its administrative flavour, the more so as procedure of the roman–canonical cast—written, secret, and authoritarian—was replacing the old method of resolving disputes by means of lay judges and jurors. In France, too, after the Revolution had destroyed the 'noblesse de robe' of the *ancien régime*, the judges of the restored Empire, like the judges of Prussia and Austria, saw themselves as 'servants of the state', anonymous members of a Ministry of Justice which appointed, promoted, remunerated, decorated, and pensioned them off, operating a code conceived as comprehensive and conclusive, and following an extreme doctrine of the separation of powers which sought to restrict to the minimum the judges' scope for creativity and which claimed that the disputes of real life could be resolved by mere acts of subsumption.

Given that the development of political ideas and institutions in Western Europe was quite different from that in England and that in consequence the standing of the judge, the role of the advocate, the methods of legal education, and the forms of procedure all differed widely, it will come as no surprise that the techniques of discovering and applying the law, indeed the typical methods of legal thought as a whole, have developed very differently. ROSCOE POUND described this difference as follows:

'Behind the characteristic doctrines and ideas and technique of the common-law lawyer there is a significant frame of mind. It is a frame of mind which habitually looks at things in the concrete, not in the abstract; which puts its faith in experience rather than in abstractions. It is a frame of mind which prefers to go forward cautiously on the basis of experience from this case or that case to the next case, as justice in each case seems to require, instead of seeking to refer everything back to supposed universals. It is a frame of mind which is not ambitious to deduce the decision for the case in hand from a proposition formulated universally . . . It is the frame of mind behind the sure-footed Anglo-Saxon habit of dealing with things as they arise instead of anticipating them by abstract universal formulas' (*What is the Common Law?* (above p. 264) 18 f.).—LORD COOPER (above p. 264, p. 470 f.), an eminent Scottish judge familiar with both the Common Law and the Civil Law, expressed himself similarly: 'A civilian system differs from a common law system much as rationalism differs from empiricism or deduction from induction. The civilian naturally reasons from principles to instances, the common lawyer from instances to principles. The civilian puts his faith in syllogisms, the common lawyer in precedents; the first silently asking himself as each new problem arises, "What should we do this time?" and the second asking aloud in the same situation, "What did we do last time?" . . . The instinct of a civilian is to systematise. The working rule of the common lawyer is *solvitur ambulando*.

But here it is as well to issue a word of warning. Undoubtedly there are differences in the style of legal thinking in the countries of the Common Law on the one hand and on the Continent of Europe on the other, but it would certainly be wrong to make out that there was an unbridgeable opposition between the former's method of inductive problem-solving and the latter's method of systematic conceptualism. Such an antithesis would emphasize the dominant trends and tendencies in the Common Law and Civil Law but, in its absolute form, it would be an increasingly inaccurate and incomplete reflection of what can actually be seen happening in these two great legal families today when lawyers set about the task of discovering the law.

II

According to a view expressed in England in 1934 by GOODHART, the critical difference between Continental and English methods of legal thinking lies in the doctrine of the *binding force of precedent* (*stare decisis*) (above p. 264, p. 42). At first sight this view seems plausible even today. The doctrine lays down that every English court is bound by all decisions handed down by courts superior to it in the hierarchy; and, until quite recently, the doctrine laid down that the superior courts, namely the Court of Appeal and the House of Lords, were bound to treat their *own* previous decisions as absolutely binding. A previous decision is 'binding' in the sense that it must be followed whether it forms part of a series of similar decisions or whether it stands quite alone, whether it was handed down the previous year or a century ago, and even if the rule it lays down now seems inappropriate because of altered social circumstances or for some other reason. It had always been recognized in England that courts which were faced with the task of discovering the law should take note of previous decisions and follow them whenever this seemed proper on the facts of the case. Indeed, given the absence of any comprehensive legislative regulation this was the only reasonable thing to do unless every individual case was to be decided *de novo* in a form of cadi-justice. But it was only in the late nineteenth century that the doctrine took the rigorous form we have sketched above—decisions binding even if the result seems repellent to the judge, superior courts bound by their own decisions; it was a product not of legislation but of judicial decision; the courts forged their own fetters.

Of course English judges have devised various ways and means which enable them to 'distinguish a precedent', that is, to avoid following a previous decision which is unsatisfactory. A previous decision is binding only where the basic reason underlying the decision, the so-called 'ratio decidendi', covers the instant dispute. But in many cases it is extremely doubtful what the 'ratio decidendi' of the previous decision is, and what is merely 'obiter dictum'. Take the case where a mother suffers a nervous shock as a result of witnessing a traffic accident in which her child is killed, and a court grants her claim for damages against the careless driver. The *ratio decidendi* of this decision will certainly cover a subsequent case in which, all the other facts being the same, a *father* witnesses the death of his child, but it is not clear that the *ratio decidendi* of the first decision would require the driver to be held liable in a later case where the child was only injured or merely endangered instead of being killed, or where the plaintiff was not a relative of the child. Before the judge can resolve these questions he must scrutinize the precedent keenly, he must examine the arguments presented by the advocates before him, but above all he must carefully sift any related decisions handed down before or after the precedent in question: this intellectual process follows certain rules of the judicial art but it is open at every step to the influence of conscious or unconscious *value-judgments*.

The discovery of the *ratio decidendi* can be particularly difficult when the previous judge based his decision on two concurrent and equal lines of reasoning or when the precedent comes from a superior court whose judges, unanimously or by a majority, agreed on the result but differed as to the method of reaching it. Again, can a decision of a court be ignored if it is inconsistent with another decision of the same court? Can it be ignored as given *per incuriam* if it overlooked a legislative provision or if a particular legal point was not put forward by the advocates or raised by the court? English law has developed a whole series of sophisticated doctrines in reponse to these and similar questions. On this see the writings of CROSS (above p. 264). CROSS concludes that the technique of 'distinguishing a precedent' is now so lax that one must ask 'whether the spectacle of an English judge labouring under the brutal fetters of a rigid doctrine of precedent is not something which, if it exists at all, exists only in the minds of academic lawyers' (82 *LQ Rev.* 203, 214 (1966)).

The attitude of *American* courts in this matter is more flexible still. Legal publishers in the United States issue hundreds of volumes of judicial decisions every year without making any critical selection of them and the mass of material is so enormous that it is virtually impossible to expect that *all* relevant precedents be taken into account. But, more than this, the political, social, and economic development of the United States has been so dramatic and the consequent alterations in the substance of the legal order so swift that the superior courts could never have adopted the view that they were absolutely bound by their *own* previous decisions. It was clear that the *Supreme Court*, dealing with constitutional matters, had to be free to depart from a previous decision ('to overrule a precedent') since otherwise the only way to overcome its obsolete decisions would have been by amending the *text* of the Constitution, an extremely complex and slow procedure requiring the ratification of three-quarters of the component states. But in the *states* as well the highest courts have shown an increasing readiness in the last few decades to ask whether the rules laid down in the case-law, even those which have repeatedly been confirmed in a series of decisions, are still in touch with the needs and interests of the times.

Such an investigation often leads to the conclusion that the old rules are no longer apt; an 'overruling decision' is rendered and a fundamental change in the case-law takes place; this can be inferred from the way courts and writers keep discussing the question what protection, if any, should be given to persons who entered into transactions in reliance on the 'old' judicial decisions. Many American courts adopt the practice of 'prospective overruling': in the judgment in which the 'new' rule is laid down for the first time they state that it is to be effective only in the future (see KNITTEL, *Zum Problem der Rückwirkung bei einer Änderung der Rechtsprechung, Eine Untersuchung zum deutschen und US-amerikanischen Recht* (1965)).

Even in England it seems that the doctrine of binding precedent is not accepted as wholeheartedly as it was some years ago. Indeed, the most objectionable part of the doctrine, the rule that the House of Lords was strictly bound by its own previous decisions, was abandoned in 1966. This did not, as one might have expected, occur by Act of Parliament or in the course of a judicial decision; instead the Lord Chancellor simply made a declaration ('Practice Statement') in open court in the name of all the Law Lords. It read as follows:

Their Lordships regard the use of precedent as an indispensable foundation upon which to decide what is the law and its application to individual cases. It provides at least some degree of certainty upon which individuals can rely in the conduct of their affairs as well as a basis for orderly development of legal rules.

Their Lordships nevertheless recognise that too rigid adherence to precedent may lead to injustice in a particular case and also unduly restrict the proper development of the law. They propose, therefore, to modify their present practice and, while treating former decisions of this House as normally binding, to depart from a previous decision when it appears right to do so.

In this connection they will bear in mind the danger of disturbing retrospectively the basis on which contracts, settlements of property and fiscal arrangements have been entered into and also the special need for certainty as to the criminal law.

This announcement is not intended to affect the use of precedent elsewhere than in this House.' ([1966] 1 WLR 1234.)

By taking this step, which is primarily of psychological significance, the House of Lords has abandoned only one of the extreme outposts of the doctrine but it is probable that it will gradually lead to further restrictions on the doctrine, for in the present day it is, in its rigorous form, 'an antiquated English peculiarity', as RABEL put it (*RabelsZ* 16 (1951) 340, 344). If the view that 'too rigid adherence to precedent may ... unduly restrict the proper development of the law' is taken seriously, it must follow that in future the *Court of Appeal* should also free itself from the binding force of its own previous judgements and that all courts should be readier to depart from *older* decisions.

The question whether the Court of Appeal also should not cease to be bound by its own previous decisions was raised recently in *Gallie* v. *Lee*, [1969] 1 All ER 1062. LORD DENNING was of the view that the Court of Appeal should follow the example of the House of Lords: the principle of binding precedent was 'a self-imposed limitation; and we who imposed it can also remove it. The House of Lords have done it. So why should not we do likewise? We should be just as free, no more and no less, to depart from a prior precedent of our own, as in like case is the House of Lords or a judge of first instance. It is very, very rare that we will go against a previous decision of our own, but if it is clearly shown to be erroneous, we should be able to put it right' (at p. 1072). RUSSELL, LJ was of the contrary opinion: the *House of Lords* was justified in abandoning the doctrine of precedent, since otherwise a rule of law which had become obsolete could only be overturned by the *legislature*, and Parliament was too busy with urgent new legislation to make this a real possibility. But judgments of the *Court of Appeal* could be appealed from and under these circumstances the interest in legal certainty justified adherence to the doctrine that the Court of Appeal was bound by its own previous decisions. 'An abandonment of the principle that this court follows its own decisions on the law would, I think, lead to greater uncertainty and tend to produce more litigation' [1969] 1, All ER 1076). In subsequent decisions, however, LORD DENNING stuck steadfastly to his guns (for example, *Davis* v. *Johnson* [1979] AC 264, 281–3 (CA)) though without finding any support in the House of Lords; see, for example, LORD DIPLOCK (ibid. at 323–8). The arguments on either side of this question are interestingly marshalled by RICKETT, 'Precedent in the Court of Appeal', 43 *Mod. L. Rev.* 136, 147 ff. (1980).

A quick look round the Continent shows that, apart from the doctrine of courts being bound by their own decisions, matters are not very different there. It is true that there is never any legal rule which compels a judge to follow the decisions of a higher court, but the reality is different. In practice a judgment of the Court of Cassation or of the Bundesgerichtshof in Germany today can count on being followed by lower courts just as much as a judgment of an appeal court in England or in the United States. This is true not only when the judgment of the superior court follows a line of similar decisions; in practice even an isolated decision of the Bundesgerichtshof in Germany enjoys the greatest respect, and it is very rare and not at all typical for a judge openly to deviate from such a decision. In France the situation is much the same:

See, for example, DAVID/DE VRIES, *The French Legal System* (1958) 113 ff.: 'Despite the absence of a formal doctrine of stare decisis, there is a strong tendency on the part of the French courts, like those of other countries, to follow precedents, especially those of the higher courts . . . The Cour de Cassation can, of course, always overrule its own prior decisions. But it is equally certain that it will not do so without weighty reasons . . . The attitude of the lower courts toward decisions of the Cour de Cassation is in substance quite similar to that of the lower courts in common law jurisdictions towards decisions of superior courts. Even a single precedent established by the Cour de Cassation will usually be followed, though it cannot be cited as the only basis for the decision. Certain factors may, however, induce the lower courts to seek reasons for deciding contrary to a prior decision of the Cour de Cassation. One such factor may be the expectation that an old decision of the Cour de Cassation would not be followed by that court in the light of new conditions.' See also ANCEL, 'French Case Law', 16 *J. Comp. Leg.* 1 (1934), and DAVID, *Le Droit français* I (1960) 160 ff.

Accordingly it is hardly an exaggeration to say that the doctrine of *stare decisis* in the Common Law and the practice of Continental courts generally lead to the same results: 'The practical differences . . . are microscopic' (RABEL in *RabelsZ* 16 (1951) 340, 345, criticized by CAPPELLETTI (above p. 264)). In fact, when a judge can find in one or more decisions of a supreme court a rule which seems to him relevant for the decision in the case before him, he will follow those decisions and the rules they contain as much in Germany as in England or France. Of course in order to be able to *follow* a rule, the judge must first have extracted it from the case-law; and in the *method of extracting such rule* there are still very considerable differences between the Common Law and the Civil Law.

The Common Law judge's technique of approaching the case-law and extracting its rules and principles is the product of a mature and workmanlike tradition of 'reasoning from case to case'. The Anglo-American judge starts his process of decision with the individual precedents which counsel for the parties before him have adduced as being most in point. In these precedents he recognizes certain 'rules', that is, solutions of particular concrete living problems. He observes how these 'rules' have been limited, extended, and refined by other 'precedents' and then, constantly keeping the practical problems in the forefront of his mind, gradually draws out of them high-level 'principles' and 'standards' which he uses to make a tentative resolution of the case before him; his solution he then tests for its appropriateness against the background of similar cases and finally arrives at the decision itself (on this, see the basic work of ESSER (above p. 264) 183 ff. and *passim*, which contains a wealth of jurisprudential and comparative insights). All these steps take place in open discourse: arguments for and against are presented in speeches and rebuttals between actual or imaginary opponents. *Ambulando solvitur.*

The Anglo-American civil trial provides the ideal forum for raising problems in this discursive manner. Throughout its history it has been strongly marked by the requirements of *trial by jury*, although today it is only in the United States that the jury has any practical importance in private law. The proceedings take place in a single session, spread over several days if necessary, and all the facts, as well as questions of law, are orally presented there and then by the litigants and discussed in an open and argumentative manner, with the judge taking part. For more detail, see below Ch. 20 V.

This inductive way of thinking, based on the particular factual problem of the case, and the intensive treatment of precedents associated with it are not to be found in Continental law, at any rate not to anything like the same extent. This is because Continental judges, in Italy and France rather more than in Germany, are still imbued with the old positivistic idea that deciding a case involves nothing more than 'applying' a particular given rule of law to the facts in issue by means of an act of categorization; indeed, they often entertain the further supposition that ideally the rules of law to be 'applied' are statutory texts and that, by contrast, rules and principles judicially developed can only be officially recognized if they have 'hardened into customary law' by somehow attracting a 'communal endorsement of their validity evidenced by practice'. This old-fashioned doctrine of legal sources is obviously at odds with what we can see actually happening on the Continent when judges set about discovering the law today, but the style of the judgments of the highest courts of France, Italy, and even Germany shows how stubbornly these ideas remain alive.

A striking piece of evidence for this is the grudging manner in which the facts of a case are treated in Continental judgments. We have already mentioned that the French Court of Cassation often does no more than make cryptic allusions to them (see above Ch. 9 I). The courts in Germany are required to include 'a compressed version of the facts and the history of the suit' (§313.1 no. 3 ZPO), but when the judgment is printed in periodicals or law reports there is a characteristic tendency to curtail or even to omit it—a proceeding which the common lawyer would find unthinkable. Again, the French Court of Cassation does not even quote its *own* previous decisions, much less say why it follows one decision rather than another. Of course the judges of the Court of Cassation do in fact go through the case-law with great care, but they like to give outsiders the impression that the judgment springs from the text of the statute at a wave of the magic wand of subsumption (see the excellent treatment of this in DAWSON (above p. 264) 400 ff.). Above all, judgments of supreme courts on the Continent still sometimes reflect the traditions of the authoritarian state of a hundred years ago: judgments should primarily be impersonal acts of state which parade the majesty of the law in front of citizens in awe of authority; therefore they must not let it emerge that judges reach their decisions through a hesitant and doubtful balancing of the pros and cons of concrete solutions of the problem thrown up by the 'case', rather than by sheer intellect and cold logic. (See further KÖTZ (above p. 264).)

Another indication of how underdeveloped the art of 'reasoning from case to case' remains is the uncritical use made of the 'headnotes' (*Leitsätze*) which precede published judgments all over the Continent. These headnotes present a very brief and abstract version of the essential legal proposition basic to the court decision but they omit the underlying facts or only hint at them and never give the reasoning on which the decision was founded. Common Law countries also have these 'headnotes' but they serve the judge only as a preliminary indication of the probable content of the decision which follows and never as a substitute for its investigation in detail. On the Continent, on the other hand, these headnotes, prised loose from their roots in the facts, are often treated as independent polished formulas and used in legal practice much as if they were statutory rules. In Italy, indeed, this occurrence is facilitated by the fact that most decisions of the Court of Cassation are published only in the form of headnotes (*massime*); it thus becomes practically impossible to go back to the facts of the case and discover the real scope of the headnote. In reality the principles contained in these headnotes should be treated only as working hypotheses which must be subjected to critical scrutiny in the light of later cases and the altering needs of life, for they may have to be extended or limited or refined; courts on the Continent no doubt often do this subconsciously, but they far too rarely let outsiders know, and thus be in a position to check, that they are doing so.

III

In the matter of *statutory construction* also one can observe characteristic differences between the methods of Common Law and Civil Law; they stem from the very different part played in the development of English law by statutes enacted by Parliament from that played by legislation on the Continent. Until the nineteenth century the English, again rather like the Romans, regarded legislative activity as necessary only in order to counteract some specific social or economic mischief. With their practical empiricism and habit of going step by step from case to case the English would have regarded it as dangerous and unnatural to prescribe the outcome of comparable cases in advance by making general regulations to cover the whole area of life; 'we will cross the bridge when we come to it'. Thus English statutes were originally sporadic *ad hoc* enactments which as legal sources had much less force than the unwritten Common Law which had been developed by the judges through the centuries and which covered all areas of the law equally. The judges saw statutes as being evil, a necessary evil, no doubt, which disturbed the lovely harmony of the Common Law and they devised rules of statutory construction which, as POLLOCK observed, obviously stemmed from the conviction that 'Parliament generally changes the law for the worse, and that the business of the judge is to keep the mischief of its interference within the narrowest possible bounds' (*Essays on Jurisprudence and Ethics* (1882) 85). More specifically, the idea arose that every statute which deviated from the unwritten Common Law must be of an exceptional nature and therefore must be narrowly construed and applied only to the precise situations which were unquestionably covered by its terms; if the statute so construed did not cover the case in issue, then the case fell to be decided according to the general rules of the Common Law. In the Civil Law it is different: there the judges seek to avoid the obscurities and gaps in a statute by going back to the purpose of the *statute itself*; in so doing they see themselves as being in a real partnership with the legislature; they do not think that all legislative incursions into the field of private law should be met with vigilant scepticism, if not outright resentment.

It is not unknown for English judges of a conservative temperament to use the principles of construction we have mentioned in order to limit or circumvent provisions of modern social legislation which they find uncongenial. Their argument is that such provisions adversely affect the freedom of contract protected by the Common Law, and that therefore they must be restrictively interpreted (see JACKSON, *The Machinery of Justice* (7th edn., 1977) 472 f.).

It is consistent with the low value they attach to statute as a source of law that Common Law judges very rarely use statutory provisions as a starting-point for judicial creativity. Here again matters are different on the Continent: in order to solve doubtful questions the Civil Law judge refers first of all to available statutory rules. He asks whether there may not underlie these rules a principle of resolving the conflicting interests which might be applied to the problem in issue, and whether they may not offer an analogy or an argument *e contrario*. Indeed, one might, with only a little exaggeration, say that in the Civil Law *statutory rules* constitute the materials of argument in decision-making much as *precedents* do in the Common Law.

See POUND, 67 *LQ Rev.* 50 (1951): 'The common-law lawyer thinks of a body of law as characteristically customary or traditional. He is at his best in developing a decision from a body of decided cases, thinking of a statute as only fixing a rule for defined situations of act but not as something to be reasoned from by analogy . . . On the other hand, the Continental lawyer thinks of a body of law as characteristically legislative. He is at his best in developing and applying legislative texts, reasoning from them by analogy . . .' This accounts for the fact that even in Common Law jurisdictions where a comprehensive code with thousands of paragraphs has been brought into force, the legislator's original aim of doing away with much of the unwritten Common Law has been frustrated. California offers an example. The judges have not been prepared to treat the Civil Code as a unity independent of the Common Law or to make it a new starting-point for legal development. Admittedly the Civil Code must be followed where its provisions deviate from judicial rules of law, but in other cases the Common Law is developed by the traditional method of 'reasoning from case to case'; if the ensuing solution can be supported by some provision of the Civil Code, so much the better. But once such a provision has been construed in a judicial decision, that *decision* rather than the legislative text becomes the start-point for further argument. One can therefore say that the Civil Code in California has lost most of its independence as a source of law in the surrounding mass of Common Law.

The adoption by English judges of these restrictive techniques of construction helps to explain the peculiarities of the *drafting* of English statutes. Continental observers are struck by the pedantic and prolix detail in which statutes deal with the simplest matters, obviously so as to make it more difficult for the judges to get round them: where a Continental legislator would be satisfied with a single comprehensive notion, the English legislator, simply in order to bind the judges, will use *five* specific terms, without adding anything to the meaning. In POLLOCK's view, the art of legislation towards the end of the eighteenth century was 'to pile up as many words as possible, significant and insignificant, on the chance that in their multitude the intention of the enactment might find safety' (*A First Book of Jurisprudence* (6th edn., 1929) 359); it must be said, with all respect, that one can quite often find traces of this attitude even in modern legislation. There is one common practice which the Continental observer finds amazing: the terms used in a statute are collected together in a kind of lexicon near the beginning and defined in what is often a rather pedagogic manner; this technique AMOS once described as 'the device of making a statute contain its own miniature dictionary' (above p. 264, p. 170). Indeed, the English Interpretation Act, 1899 consists *exclusively* of such verbal explanations. There, for example, we find the following proposition solemnly announced: 'In this Act and in every Act passed after the year one thousand eight hundred and fifty ... unless the contrary intention appears,—(a) words importing the masculine gender shall include females; and (b) words in the singular shall include the plural, and words in the plural shall include the singular.' The technique of statutory construction in a country has to be in a parlous condition to require trivial aids of this sort.

The pedantry and pettiness of legislative language is attributable not only to the desire to leave judges the least possible scope for construction, but also to a certain formalism of legal thought, significant traces of which are still to be found in England today. Contracts and wills as well as statutes may still be drafted in a style of language which strikes the Continental jurist as positively medieval. In Germany a contract of lease will simply say: 'The lessor leases to the lessee the following dwelling ...', but in England or America a contract of lease might well read something like this: 'The Landlord has let and by these presents does grant, demise and let unto the Tenant and the said Tenant has agreed to hire and take, and does hereby hire and take as Tenant the following space in the apartment building ...' (cited in WILLISTON, *Contracts* VII

(2nd edn., 1938) 6111). Many comparable examples are to be found in books of forms and precedents in England and in the United States. Of course all this serves the professional interests of the lawyers who must be quite content to have simple affairs made to appear occult with the help of technical jargon, so that the layman needs a professional to help him master them.

There is no space here to portray the dense web of rules and principles engendered by statutory construction in England; there are enough of them to fill big books in England, and they 'strike the Continental jurist as very anachronistic' (ESSER (above p. 264) 131). For example, there is the so-called 'golden rule', which makes it permissible to depart from the clear meaning of a statute if otherwise the result would be absurd or impractical. This is contradicted by the so-called 'literal rule': according to the literal rule one must follow the very words of the statute at all costs, provided that any clear meaning emerges from them: 'If the words of an Act are clear, you must follow them, even though they lead to a manifest absurdity. The Court has nothing to do with the question whether the legislature has committed an absurdity' (LORD ESHER in *R.* v. *The Judge of the City of London Court*, [1892] 1 QB 273, 290). The so-called 'mischief rule' comes from a decision of 1584 (*Heydon's Case*, 3 Co. Rep. 7a, 76 Eng. Rep. 637); according to this rule the judge must construe the statute so as to promote its underlying aim, namely the avoidance of a particular mischief which the general Common Law did not deal with. But another rule makes it difficult to find out what the aim of the legislator was because it forbids the judge in his construction of a statute to refer to statements made in Parliament or on Parliamentary committees during the discussion or enactment of the statute. The standard justification for this rule is that such statements are notoriously unreliable, incomplete, or biassed. In many cases this may be true, but one could surely leave it to the judge to decide what weight to attribute to such statements in any particular case; it is not at all clear why he should *invariably* be prevented from taking them into account (for details see MARSH, above p. 264, pp. 56 ff.). Finally, when we learn that it is still a serious question in England whether the judge in construing a statute may refer to its punctuation, titles, or sectional headings, our surprise turns to amazement.

It is true that in the past few years Englishmen have begun to realize how very important it is to free the judges from the shackles of these technical rules of construction, to allow them more freedom in their approach to statutes, and to make them into *partners* rather than *opponents* of the legislature whose work they are attempting to construe.

LORD DENNING speaks for those who favour such a style of statutory construction. Not only should the judge, in his view, be able to consider all the preliminary legislative materials (see *Davis* v. *Johnson* [1979] AC 264, 276 f.; *contra*, House of Lords, id. 329, 337) but he should also be able to promote the goal envisaged by the legislature by openly filling in any gaps in the statute and resolving any ambiguities: 'We do not sit here to pull the language of Parliament and of Ministers to pieces and make nonsense of it. That is an easy thing to do, and it is a thing to which lawyers are too often prone. We sit here to find out the intention of Parliament and of Ministers and carry it out, and we do this better by filling in the gaps and making sense of the enactment than by opening it up to destructive analysis' (*Magor & St. Mellons RDC* v. *Newport Corp.* [1950] 2 All ER 1226, 1236). This earned LORD DENNING a sharp rebuff in the House of Lords. According to LORD SIMONDS it is improper to fill in a gap in line with the apparent purpose of the enactment: 'It appears to me to be a naked usurpation of the legislative function under the thin disguise of interpretation. And it is the less justifiable when it is guesswork with what material the legislature would, if it had discovered the gap, have filled it in' (*Magor & St. Mellons RDC* v. *Newport Corp.* [1952] AC 189, 191). LORD DENNING nevertheless adhered to his opinion, most cogently in cases where a rule of European Community law fell to be construed: 'It would be absurd that the courts of England should interpret it differently from the courts of France, or Holland, or Germany . . . We must, therefore, put on one side our traditional rules of interpretation. We have for years tended to stick too closely to the letter—to the literal interpretation of the words. We ought, in interpreting this convention, to adopt the European method. . . . They adopt a method which they call in English by strange words—at any rate they were strange to me—the "schematic and teleological" method of interpretation. It is not really so alarming as it sounds. All it means is that the judges do not go by the literal meaning of the words or by the grammatical structure of the sentence. They go by the design or the purpose which lies behind it. . . . They then interpret the legislation so as to produce the desired effect. This means that they fill in gaps, quite unashamedly, without hesitation. They ask simply: what is the sensible way of dealing with this situation so as to give effect to the presumed purpose of the legislation? They lay down the law accordingly. . . . In interpreting the Treaty of Rome (which is part of our law) we must certainly adopt the new approach. Just as in Rome, you should do as Rome does. So in the European Community, you should do as the European Court does.' (*Buchanan & Co.* v. *Babco Forwarding & Shipping Ltd.* [1977] QB 208, 213–14; see also *HP Bulmer Ltd.* v. *J. Bollinger S.A.* [1974] 1 Ch. 401, 425.)

The Law Commissions of England and Scotland have taken a significant, though circumspect, step in the direction indicated by LORD DENNING. In a Report issued in 1969 it set out and evaluated the rules of statutory construction and proposed, *inter alia*, that a statute be passed which allowed the judges to refer to *travaux préliminaires* when they were construing a statute. It was also to be one of the principles of statutory interpretation that

'a construction which would promote the general legislative purpose underlying the provision in question is to be preferred to a construction which would not'—a thing self-evident to continental jurists. (See Law Commission, The Interpretation of Statutes [1969] Law Com. no. 21.)—As one can learn from the work of RADIN, above p. 265, and FRANKFURTER, above p. 264, the courts in the *United States* have long since adopted a less constrained and more flexible attitude towards statutes. LLEWELLYN has shown that the canons of construction to be found in the older cases can be paired off in such a way that one rule contradicts the other; it is thus always possible to find a suitable rule of interpretation to justify a decision arrived at for quite *other* considerations. (See LLEWELLYN, *The Common Law Tradition—Deciding Appeals* (1960) 521 ff.) In view of this, the Uniform Commercial Code lays down in §1–102 that the only purpose of construing the statute is 'to promote its underlying purposes and policies'. On this the Official Commentary says: 'The text of each section should be read in the light of the purpose and policy of the rule or principle in question, as also of the Act as a whole, and the application of the language should be construed narrowly or broadly, as the case may be, in conformity with the purposes and policies involved.' See MENTSCHIKOFF, 'The Uniform Commercial Code', *RabelsZ* 30 (1966) 403, 409 ff.

IV

The student making a comparison of the methods of legal thinking in the Common Law and the Civil Law must be constantly on his guard against one-sided views, for they are only too easily adopted by the superficial observer in this area. One can still find Anglo-American lawyers who think that in Civil Law countries the principal role of the judge is mechanically to apply statutory rules so closely interwoven that there is no room left for any vital development of the law by the judge. We have already shown in several passages how erroneous this view is. In the first place, there are large areas of law where, for various reasons, statute offers either no rules at all or only general clauses or outline provisions; here, then, is scope for judicial law-making. But more generally one can say that as the civil and commercial codes on the Continent grow older they lose their power and potential and that as the legislator is increasingly overtaxed by the need to make specific regulations for the novel problems of life which arise, case-law must increasingly leap into the breach; statute is thus losing the position of pre-eminence it once held and, as RABEL once said, 'is now no more than an expression of a global conviction' ('Die Fachgebiete des Kaiser Wilhelm-Instituts', in: Rabel, *Gesammelte Aufsätze* III (ed. Leser, 1967) 180, 201). It is true that many lawyers are not yet fully conscious of this basic change and that the processes of law, especially court decisions, still cling to traditional styles and forms. In substance, however, it is really undeniable that in Civil Law countries judges are playing a large and constantly growing part in the development of law.

As the development of uncodified law on the Continent falls increasingly to the judges, it becomes all the more important for the Civil Law to take cognisance of the techniques and methods by which judge-made law may reconcile the demand for legal certainty with the need to have rules appropriate for the changing circumstances of life. Here the accumulated experience of the Common Law should be of the greatest interest to the Continental lawyer. Anglo-American lawyers have a much more careful and precise way of delving into the distinctive facts of a case, of distinguishing these from apparently similar cases, and of delicately drawing out general rules and principles, as abstract as may be necessary but as concrete as is possible, while keeping close to the problem in hand and to its factual setting; furthermore they discuss these matters more frankly and openly than Continental lawyers who often still feel drawn to a forced 'categorization' of the facts of the case, even a rather crude and simplistic one, in order to bring the case as quickly as possible within the ambit of the closest 'leading principle' (*Leitsatz*).

If one suggests that the inductive and casuistic technique of the Common Law may be of help for the development of judge-made law on the Continent one may be charged with underrating the orderliness and rationality which come from systematic thinking and with exposing the consumer of law to a chaos of special cases. In our view this idea, though frequently expressed, is just as erroneous as the notion that the Civil Law is simply a well-organized system of exact and calculable legal concepts. The case-technique of the Anglo-American legal systems is 'not decisional pointillism, but rather the fragmentary indication of constant real principles' (ESSER (above p. 264) 284). In other words, even the Common Law technique requires the judge to look for the *general rule* behind the actual decisions in the relevant precedents, for that is the only way he can tell whether this or that decision really controls the case before him. These general rules and principles, which Common Law judges have drawn out of the mass of case material by an inductive and comparative method, give the case-law a considerable degree of inner systematic order and hence of community and predictability. It is certainly true that in a system of pure judge-made law the intrinsic forces which make for order may on occasion prove inadequate and it is undeniable that there are some areas in the Common Law where in the view of English and American specialists the case-law has reached such a state of complexity and obscurity that the intervention of the legislature is urgently required to put it in order. But observant common lawyers are increasingly aware of this danger. In American law especially there have long been attempts in various areas of the law to make a wholesale and systematic revision and reordering of the legal material. The Restatements (see above pp. 259 f.) are a good example; but the important legislative achievements of recent years, such as the Uniform Commercial Code, would have been impossible without a great deal of preliminary systematization and processing of the solutions contained in the case-law. A similar development appears to be in train in England. Here we may cite *The Law of Restitution* (3rd edn., 1987) by GOFF and JONES, who make a manful attempt to put some order into the baroque complexity of English remedies for unjustified enrichment by bringing them under a few general principles (see MARTINEK, *RabelsZ* 47 (1983) 284). But the best evidence in England of the growing need for systematization and rationalization of the law is the establishment of the Law Commission, which is expressly given the task 'to take and keep under review all the law . . . with a view to its systematic development and reform, including in particular the codification of such law'. It is true that codification of the heartland of English private law, such as the law of contract, still seems to be a very distant prospect, but it has been much discussed in the literature in England recently, and much of the discussion has centred on Civil Law codes (see the references above p. 219). Certainly contact with Continental law, especially through the European Community, has contributed to the criticism now being levelled at the traditional techniques of statutory construction in England (see above pp. 275 f.), and DALE concludes his exhaustive comparative study of techniques of codification and styles of legislation by saying that in this area the English have much to learn from the Civil Law (above p. 264).

To sum up: on the Continent the days of absolute pre-eminence of statutory law are past; contrariwise, in the Common Law there is an increasing tendency to use legislation in order to unify, rationalize, and simplify the law. On the Continent, law is increasingly being developed by the judges and consequently there is more room for an inductive method and style related to the actual problems; contrariwise, the Common Law is seeing the need to bring the rules developed by the judges into a systematic order, so as to make them easier to understand and master. There are therefore grounds for believing that although the Common Law and the Civil Law started off from opposite positions, they are gradually moving closer together even in their legal methods and techniques.

V

Comparative lawyers tend to asume that in all developed legal systems in the world similar needs are met in ways that are similar, if not precisely the same. The assumption is hard to maintain when one turns to *procedural law* and compares the preparation and progress of a simple civil suit in the Common Law and the Civil Law, the way the facts are presented to the court, especially the way witnesses and experts are selected and examined, and the way the different tasks and functions are allocated to the court, the parties, and the lawyers in the different phases of the proceedings. Here the Common Law and the Civil Law have developed quite differently.

One decisive fact explains many of the peculiarities of Anglo-American procedure: it is that the procedure results from the *jury trial*. Jury trials admittedly occur only in criminal cases in England today, and then only when the crime is serious and the accused has pleaded 'not guilty', but even so, civil litigation in England is still instinct with the traditions of the jury trial. For example, all trials, civil as well as criminal, take the form of a single continuous oral hearing, lasting many hours or even days, if necessary. Since one cannot keep recalling the members of a jury, the oral hearing once started must continue without interruption. This compression of the Anglo-American trial into a single oral hearing gives rise to a whole series of further consequences, from the totality of which the Common Law trial has gained its unmistakable characteristics. (On this see also VON MEHREN (above p. 265).)

The first consequence is that enormous importance attaches to the *preparation* of the trial by the attorneys. This is not so in the Civil Law, where the division of the trial into several hearings separated by intervals means that if one party makes any surprising assertions or arguments the other party has until the next session to produce further evidence or facts in rebuttal, so that gradually, as the proceedings are resumed and with energetic assistance from the judge, the essential matters of fact get defined, what is in dispute is winnowed out from what is not, and the basis for decision is achieved step by step. But in an Anglo-American trial there is only a single hearing, so before it ever begins each party must not only have thought out his own arguments and evidence, but must also know his opponent's, because if unexpected evidence emerges one cannot simply propose an adjournment. This has two consequences: every attorney (in England, solicitor) must interview 'his' witnesses before the trial and ascertain exactly what they will say, conduct which would strike the German attorney as verging on the unprofessional in view of the risk of improper influence. Secondly, each party has the right under Anglo-American procedural law to make the other party disclose information and produce documents relevant to the forthcoming trial.

We cannot go into the details of 'discovery' here, a procedure so potent as to be capable of abuse, especially in the United States: 'a powerful litigant in a complex case may impose costly, even crushing, burdens, by demands for files, pretrial testimony of witnesses and other forms of discovery . . . A litigant may contrive to dump truckloads of unassorted files on the party demanding discovery, hoping, often not in vain, that the searcher will be so exhausted that the damaging items will be overlooked or never reached' (FRANKEL (above p. 264) 18).

When the Anglo-American trial starts, the attorneys will be carefully prepared for it, but the judge will have only the vaguest idea of what the issues and testimony may be. He is supposed to rely on the attorneys to present all the necessary facts and law by word of mouth. *How* the presentation is effected is a matter for the attorneys: they alone decide which witnesses to call, how many, and in what order; it is the attorneys also who question the witnesses, each witness after examination by 'his' side being 'handed over' for cross-examination to the other side.

The same is true of *experts*. In a medical malpractice suit, for example—or proceedings involving a question of foreign law—each party produces its own expert in court, and such experts are subject, just like any other witnesses, to examination and cross-examination by the attorneys for the two sides. This spectacle of formalized duelling between experts, with the attorneys displaying their *ad hoc* knowledge in an intrepid if amateur manner, is quite a thrill for the Continental observer, but he may be tempted to ask whether it would not be cheaper, simpler, and quicker for the *court* itself to appoint a single reputable expert whose independence and neutrality would be guaranteed by the fact that his loyalty was due to the court rather than to either of the parties.

When witnesses and experts are being questioned, the judge just listens attentively. If he speaks, it will be to rule, at the request of a party or on his own motion, on the admissibility of a question put to a witness or party, or to ensure adherence to the rules of the game in some other respect. The judge may indeed question the witness himself, but self-restraint is the rule here, as in the story of the English judge who, conscious of his tendency to ask too many questions, placed a little notice on the bench telling himself to 'Shut up!'. LORD GREENE's advice to his fellow-judges not to involve themselves in questioning witnesses is often quoted: he added that a judge who does so 'descends into the arena and is liable to have his vision clouded by the dust of the conflict' (*Yuill* v. *Yuill* [1945] P. 15, 20). A common saying is that 'The judge who opens his mouth closes his mind'. In this connection *Jones* v. *National Coal Board* [1957] 2 QB 55 is well worth reading: there the Court of Apeal remanded a case for a new trial on the sole ground that the judge at first instance had asked too many questions and made it impossible for the parties to present the evidence in the way they thought best.

The role of the Anglo-American judge may be relatively passive because knowing nothing of the case at the outset, he must learn about it as it proceeds, but the reason for giving the leading role to the parties and their lawyers has to do with certain deeply held views about the best way to get at the truth, or something akin to it, in the course of a court hearing. It is thought best to let the parties battle it out, each presenting and defending a consciously one-sided view of his own case, with the judge standing passively by, essentially seeing simply that the rules of the game are observed. '. . . truth is best discovered by powerful statements on both sides of the question', said a famous Lord Chancellor, LORD ELDON, 150 years ago (*Ex parte Lloyd*, Mont. 70, 72 n. (1822)). And a statement of LORD DENNING positively reeks of the battlefield: 'In litigation as in war. If one side makes a mistake, the other can take advantage of it. No holds are barred' (*Burmah Oil Co.* v. *Bank of England* [1979] 1 WLR 473, 484). The 'adversary procedure' which common lawyers see as the ruling principle of procedural law manifests itself in this determined if regulated confrontation between the parties to the lawsuit.

In Germany and neighbouring countries in Continental Europe procedural law is rather based on the idea that it will be easier to get at the truth if the *judge* is given a stronger role: he should be entitled, indeed bound, to question, inform, encourage, and advise the parties, lawyers, and witnesses so as to get a true and complete picture from them, as free as possible from inconsistency and ambiguity, and to counteract any mistakes due to lack of care or skill on the part of the suitors or their attorneys. It is true that the German judge cannot of his own motion call a witness simply because his evidence might cast light on the matter; it is also true that in normal civil litigation the *Verhandlungsmaxime* applies, the principle that the judge may take account only of what has been led in evidence. Even so, writers from the Common Law do not hesitate to describe the German civil trial, as compared with the Anglo-American trial, as 'inquisitorial', and the German judge as a 'paterfamilias—also endowed, to be sure, with some of the characteristics of a bureaucrat; . . . he is constantly descending to the level of the litigants as an examiner, patient or hectoring, as counselor and advisor, as insistent promoter of settlements. Withal he has not entirely lost his character as a civil servant, though of a special type, . . . in a government department' (KAPLAN, VON MEHREN, SCHAEFER, 'Phases of German Civil Procedure', 71 *Harv. L. Rev.* 1193, 1443, 1472 (1958)).

In the *United States* 'adversary procedure' is practised with particular rigour. This is largely because civil suits are still tried there by a jury in the first instance, at any rate if it is a Common Law claim as opposed to one in Equity (see above Ch. 16 III). In practice this means that almost all damages claims, such as arise from traffic accidents, are tried before a jury.

Many matters fall to the jury for decision, many more than to the lay judges occasionally used in civil and criminal cases on the Continent. For example, at the end of a hearing of, say, a claim for damages arising out of a traffic accident, the jury, in the absence of the judge, decides what *facts* have been proved. During the trial the judge will have instructed the jury on the applicable *rules of law*, but the actual application of those rules is for the jury alone. They thus decide whether on the facts as found the defendant acted 'negligently', whether the plaintiff was guilty of any 'contributory negligence', and what damages he should receive by way of compensation for pain and suffering and material harm. The right to trial by jury is constitutionally guaranteed by the Seventh Amendment, so that abolition is hardly imaginable. Indeed, there are even constitutional objections to any reduction of the number of jurymen from the traditional twelve or any qualification, in favour of a majority verdict, of the historic requirement of unanimity.

The attorney's knowledge that at the end of the day the crucial questions in the case will be decided by a group of laymen will obviously affect his tactics at the trial. First of all, he must see that the jury is composed of the 'right' persons. By law each attorney may object to a certain number of proposed jurors without giving any reason, and to an unlimited number if reason is given. In big criminal cases this 'voir–dire' examination, or selection of the jury, can last several days; hundreds of proposed jurors may be questioned by the attorneys only to be dismissed. Once a jury is impanelled, the attorney will strive to present the facts in as striking and dramatic a manner—and as favourably to his client—as possible. He will use every trick of forensic rhetoric. The questions he puts to his witnesses will often have been studiously rehearsed. Of course the attorney on the other side will be striving with equal vigour to frustrate these efforts. He will try to impugn the witnesses' credibility by putting tricky questions (for which they will have been prepared).

There is a complex set of rules, called the 'law of evidence', which determines what evidence may be given by witnesses and what questions they may be asked in examination and cross-examination. There is no counterpart for this in the Civil Law, where evidence is heard by professional judges who, in a civil suit, should get to hear *everything*; after all, they are experienced, even hardened, enough to make a 'free evaluation of the evidence' and separate the grain from the chaff. In a jury trial, by contrast, a 'law of evidence' is necessary to prevent laymen being led up the garden path by 'hearsay evidence', suggestive 'leading questions', and other tricks. It will be obvious that 'adversary procedure' encourages attorneys to go to the very limits of what is morally and professionally acceptable, perhaps sometimes even to overstep them, by 'preparing' their witnesses rather intensively for examination and cross-examination, and by dressing up as unalloyed truth what the attorney well knows to be a pack of lies. Scruples are easily allayed by the consideration that the other side can do likewise. Nor is the problem rendered any less acute by the prevalence of the contingent fee in the United States, for then victory or defeat in the courtroom may mean riches or ruin for the plaintiff's attorney.

If the principle of adversary procedure is sacrosanct in American writing, there has been much discussion of the question when abuse begins and how it should be met. FRANKEL mounts a spirited attack against the 'excesses, distortions and perversions' of adversary procedure, against 'the tricks, stratagems, dodges and ruses that wily advocates everywhere have learned and employed in one form or another, to win unfairly, take unfair advantage, and achieve what detached observers would condemn, and have always condemned as unjust results' (FRANKEL, above p. 264) reviewed by KÖTZ in 48 *U. Chi. L. Rev.* 478 (1981)); a contrary position is adopted by FREEDMAN, *Lawyers' Ethics in an Adversary System* (1975); and the authors exchange views in 123 *U. Pa. L. Rev.* 1031 and 1060 (1975).

21

The Trust—A Distinctive Feature of the Style of the Anglo-American Legal Family

BOLGÁR, 'Why No Trusts in the Civil Law?', 2 *Am. J. Comp. L.* 204 (1953).

FRATCHER, 'Trust', *International Encyclopedia of Comparative Law*, vol. VI, Ch. 11 (1973).

GUBLER, 'Besteht in der Schweiz ein Bedürfnis nach Einführung des Instituts der angelsächsischen Treuhand (trust)?', *ZSR* 73 (1954) 215a.

KEETON, *Social Change in the Law of Trusts* (1959).

——, *The Law of Trusts* (9th edn. 1968).

KÖTZ, *Trust und Treuhand, Eine rechtsvergleichende Darstellung des anglo-amerikanischen trust und funktionsverwandter Institute des deutschen Rechts* (1963).

LEPAULLE, *Traité théorique et pratique des trusts* (1932).

MAITLAND, *Equity, A Course of Lectures* (2nd edn., Brunyate, 1936). 23 ff.

MAYDA, '"Trusts" and "Living Law" in Europe', 103 *U. Pa. L. Rev.* 1041 (1955).

NUSSBAUM, 'Soziologische und rechtsvergleichende Aspekte des "trust"', *AcP* 151 (1950) 193.

REYMOND, 'Le Trust et le droit suisse', *ZSR* 73 (1954) 119a.

ROTH, *Der Trust in seinem Entwicklungsgang vom Feoffee to Uses zur amerikanischen Trust Company* (1928).

SCHNEIDER, 'The Reception of the Trust in Louisiana', 57 *Tul. L. Rev.* 89 (1982).

SCOTT, 'Fifty Years of Trusts', 50 *Harv. L. Rev.* 60 (1936).

——, 'Trusts in the United States', 31 *J. Comp. Leg.* 11 (1949).

——, *The Law of Trusts*, 6 vols. (3rd edn., 1967).

SIEBERT, *Das rechtsgeschäftliche Treuhandverhältnis, Ein dogmatischer und rechtsvergleichender Beitrag zum allgemeinen Treuhandproblem* (1936).

UNIKEN VENEMA, *Trustrecht en bewind* (1954).

WEISER, *Trusts on the Continent of Europe* (1936).

DE WULF, *The Trust and Corresponding Institutions in the Civil Law* (1965).

FOR text, please see first edition, I. 275–84.

IV. THE NORDIC LEGAL FAMILY

22

Scandinavian Law, Past and Present

CHYDENIUS, 'The Swedish Lawbook of 1734: An Early German Codification', 20 *LQ Rev.* 377 (1904).

DANISH AND NORWEGIAN LAW, *A General Survey* (ed. Danish Committee of Comparative Law, 1963).

EEK, Évolution et structure du droit scandinave', *Rev. hell. dr. int.* 14 (1961) 33.

EINFÜHRUNG IN DAS SCHWEDISCHE RECHTSLEBEN, *Vorlesungen gehalten an der Juristischen Fakultät Lund* (1950).

VON EYBEN, 'Inter-Nordic Legislative Cooperation', *Scand. Stud. L.* 6 (1962) 63.

THE FINNISH LEGAL SYSTEM (ed. Uotila, 1966).

FISCHLER/VOGEL, *Schwedisches Handels- und Wirtschaftsrecht mit Verfahrensrecht* (3rd edn., 1978).

GAMELTOFT-HANSEN/GOMARD/PHILIP (eds.), *Danish Law, A General Survey* (1982).

GINSBURG/BRUZELIUS, *Civil Procedure in Sweden* (1965).

GOMARD, 'Civil Law, Common Law and Scandinavian Law', *Scand. Stud. L.* 5 (1961) 27.

HELLNER, 'Unification of Law in Scandinavia', 16 *Am. J. Comp. L.* 88 (1968).

——, 'Rechtsvereinheitlichung im skandinavischen Rechtskreis', in: *Methoden der Rechtsvereinheitlichung* (Arbeiten zur Rechtsvergleichung vol. 69, 1974) 27.

JÄGERSKIÖLD, 'Roman Influence on Swedish Case Law in the 17th Century', *Scand. Stud. L.* 11 (1967) 175.

JØRGENSEN, 'Grundzüge der Entwicklung der skandinavischen Rechtswissenschaft', *JZ* 1970, 529.

——, 'Les Traits principaux de l'évolution des sources du droit danois', *Rev. int. dr. comp.* 23 (1971) 65.

KORKISCH, *Einführung in das Privatrecht der nordischen Länder* I (1977).

MATTEUCCI, 'The Scandinavian Legislative Cooperation as a Model for European Cooperation', in: *Liber Amicorum of Congratulations to Algot Bagge* (1956) 136.

MUNCH-PETERSEN, 'Main Features of Scandinavian Law', 43 *LQ Rev.* 366 (1927).

ORFIELD, *The Growth of Scandinavian Law* (1953).

REHFELDT, 'Rezeption in Schweden', *SavZ/Germ.* 82 (1965) 316; 85 (1968) 248.

SCHLEGELBERGER/VON SETH/WREDE/DIX, *Das Zivilrecht der nordischen Länder*, Part I: *Finnland und Schweden* (1933 ff.).

SCHMIDT/STRÖMHOLM, *Legal Values in Modern Sweden* (1964).

STRÖMHOLM (ed.), *An Introduction to Swedish Law* (1981).

——, 'La Philosophie du droit scandinave', *Rev. int. dr. comp.* 32 (1980) 5.

SUNDBERG, 'Civil Law, Common Law and the Scandinavians', *Scand. Stud. L.* 13 (1969) 179.

VINDING KRUSE, *A Nordic Draft Code for Denmark, Finland, Iceland, Norway and Sweden* (1963).—Literature in English, French, and German dealing with the law of the Nordic countries may be found in GINSBURG, *A Selective Survey of English Language Studies on Scandinavian Law* (1970); FRYKHOLM in *Scand. Stud. L.* 5 (1961) 155, 18 (1974) 238 (Swedish law); SØNDERGAARD in *Scand. Stud. L.* 7 (1963) (Danish Law); HAUKAAS in *Scand. Stud. L.* 10 (1966) 239 (Norwegian law) and REINIKAINEN, *English, French and German Literature on Finnish Law in 1860–1956* (Helsinki 1957). Information on Scandinavian legal literature may be found in JUUL/MALMSTRÖM/SØNDERGAARD, *Scandinavian Legal Bibliography* (1961).

I

WRITERS on comparative law often make the implicit assumption that the legal systems of the Western world belong either to the Common Law or to the Civil Law. The difficulties inherent in such an assumption are shown by asking how this scheme accommodates the legal systems of Northern Europe— Denmark, Finland, Iceland, Norway, and Sweden. It is clear that these Nordic laws cannot be allocated to the Common Law, for the only legal systems which belong to the Common Law are those which are historically traceable to medieval English law, and the history of the Nordic systems has been quite independent of English law. Furthermore, Nordic law has few, if any, of the 'stylistic' hallmarks of the Common Law, such as the typical methods of finding law, the strong emphasis on judicial decisions in important areas of private law, and the standing and career of the Anglo-American judge. More difficult is the question whether the Nordic laws can be attached to the Civil Law, that great family of legal systems such as those of Continental Europe which have been more or less imbued with Roman law and which traditionally rely on statutes or indeed comprehensive codes as the primary means of ordering their legal material. There is no denying that Roman law has played a smaller role in the legal development of the Nordic countries than in Germany, and the Nordic states have as yet no codes like the civil codes of France or Germany. Nevertheless we are of the opinion, as will be seen from what follows, that it would be right to attribute the Nordic laws to the Civil Law, even although, by reason of their close interrelationship and their common 'stylistic' hallmarks, they must undoubtedly be admitted to form a special legal family, alongside the Romanistic and German legal families.

The expressions 'Nordic' and 'Scandinavian' will here be treated as synonymous, despite the fact that neither Denmark nor Iceland forms part of Scandinavia in the geographical sense.

II

The close interrelationship of the Nordic legal systems is explained by the fact that the political and cultural ties between the Scandinavian countries have always been very close. It is true that the complete unification of the three Nordic kingdoms of Denmark, Norway and Sweden was only temporary, in the time of the Union of Kalmar (1397–1523), but the links between Sweden and Finland on the one hand, and between Denmark, Norway, and Iceland on the other, proved much more durable and lasted for centuries. In the twelfth and thirteenth centuries Finland was conquered by Sweden and then formed part of the Swedish Empire until 1809 when Sweden was forced, as a result of an unsuccessful war against Russia, to cede Finland to the Tsars. Even so, Finland had considerable autonomy within the Russian state as an independent Grand Duchy and the Tsarist administration interfered very little with its legal system. Thus when Finland broke loose from Russia after the October Revolution and declared its independence in 1918, its legal unity with Sweden had not been greatly impaired. In *Western* Scandinavia, Denmark, Norway, and Iceland stayed under the central control of the Danish royal family for more than four centuries from the end of the fourteenth century so that Danish law was essentially in force in Norway and Iceland as well. In 1814 Denmark had to cede the territory of Norway to Sweden, but the Norwegians were able to secure a considerable degree of independence within the Swedish Empire and in 1905 peacefully obtained complete autonomy. Finally, Iceland became an independent state in 1918, though it remained under the Danish monarch until the end of the Second World War.

Historically speaking, all the Nordic laws were based on old Germanic law, though there were certain local variations in the different parts of Scandinavia. In the twelfth century these rules began to be written down in a large number of local laws and then city laws. With the increasing centralization of power the law began to be collected and unified. In the fourteenth century Sweden was able to replace the particular laws of counties and towns with a *Land Law* effective throughout the lowlands and a *City Law* valid in all towns of the Empire. By the seventeenth and eighteenth centuries progress was such that in Denmark as well as in Sweden comprehensive codes could be produced. The preparatory work was carefully done and they unified the entire private law, criminal law, and procedural law in both countries. In *Denmark* the *Danske Lov* of King CHRISTIAN V came into force in 1683; in Norwegian territory it came into force under the title *Norske Lov* in 1687. It is divided into six books; the first deals with the practice of law, the second with the church, the third with the secular classes, trade, and matrimonial law, the fourth with maritime law, the fifth with the rest of property law and the law of succession, and the final sixth book with criminal law. The Swedish code of 1734 (*Sveriges rikes lag*) is divided in a more sophisticated way. It has nine parts, of which the first five cover most of private law: these sections deal with matrimonial law, succession law, land law, building law, and the law of obligations and contract. The Swedish law-book has only 1,300 paragraphs; like the Danish law, it is drafted in a simple, clear, and homely style and prefers a wealth of casuistic detailed rules to the theoretical generalization and pedagogic conceptualism that was being currently practised on the continent by the system-builders of natural law.

This is by no means to say that Swedish and Danish law has developed in complete isolation from the law of Continental Europe. Indeed, in the seventeenth century, Sweden was in close contact with legal scholarship on the Continent. This was a consequence of the fact that at the time of the Thirty Years War Sweden had become a great power with an important role in European politics and considerable territorial interests in the Baltic regions, territories in which the *usus modernus pandectarum* was flourishing both in legal practice and in the universities. These political and intellectual relations with central and Eastern Europe allowed continental legal thinking to make its way into Sweden. In particular, young Swedish noblemen who sought a career in the administration or in legal practice in the Swedish Empire used to obtain their legal training in the *Gemeines Recht* at the universities of Protestant Germany, and as time went by, at the universities of Uppsala and Lund as well. GUSTAVUS ADOLPHUS founded new supreme courts as part of his administrative reforms—both the Svea hofrätt in Stockholm, founded in 1614, and the Göta hofrätt in Göteborg, founded in 1634, still exist today— and it was natural that these courts, in marked contrast to England, should be staffed by learned career judges who were also familiar with Roman law. We can thus see how Roman ideas and rules came to play an important part in the supreme courts of Sweden in the seventeenth century, as JÄGERSKIÖLD (above p. 286) has shown, especially in the area of contract law, the law of real and personal security, and the law of partnerships and bankruptcy, areas where the law books of the fourteenth century was most deficient. But remarkably enough the influence of Roman law on the code of 1734 is not at all prominent, even in the part devoted to contract and commercial law. This is probably connected with the fact that under CHARLES XII Sweden had lost its position as a great European power in consequence of an unfortunate foreign policy and a series of military defeats, and suddenly found itself nearly forced out of the European continent. In consequence there was a reversion to nationalism and the draftsmen of the code of 1734 thought it advisable to link it closely in construction, style, diction, and casuistry with the traditions of the old Swedish city and land laws (see REHFELDT, above p. 286). Nevertheless the contact with Roman law was so powerful that the links with legal thought in Continental Europe were never broken and have always been much closer than in England.

Neither the Danish–Norwegian law of 1683/1687 nor the Swedish law of

1734 has been formally repealed, but of course most of their rules have been rendered obsolete by changes in circumstances or have been replaced by new statutory law.

Nevertheless many questions of some practical importance are still solved by reference to certain provisions of these codes. Thus in its section on contract and commercial law the Swedish code contains a provision regarding the good faith acquisition of ownership which is still valid today (see HESSLER, 'Der gutgläubige Erwerb in der neueren schwedischen Rechtsentwicklung und dem nordischen Gesetzentwurf', *RabelsZ* 32 (1968) 284). A rule of the Danske lov and Norske lov still regulates vicarious liability in Denmark and Norway: the owner of an enterprise is liable regardless of his personal fault for harm caused to a third party by one of his subordinates or employees. As one can imagine, these old statutory texts, now over two centuries old, today merely indicate the general direction in which the jurisprudence of Denmark and Norway was to develop (see GOMARD (above p. 286) 35). Here we can see, more clearly than in the case of the relatively recent codes of France and Germany, how as a code grows its power diminishes, for it becomes so overlaid with an ever-increasing encrustation of case-law that it gradually loses its independent validity.

The disturbances of the Age of Napoleon brought about great changes in the political conditions and intellectual climate of Scandinavia as elsewhere. The connections which had existed for centuries between Sweden and Finland and between Denmark and Norway were broken. The national and liberal ideas of the French Revolution found ready acceptance in Scandinavia and helped, on the one hand, to strengthen the Scandinavians' sense of cultural and linguistic separateness and, on the other hand, to vanquish what remained of absolutist government and to increase citizen participation in affairs of state. The success of the Napoleonic codification evoked proposals in Sweden that the old code of 1734 should be fundamentally reformed, and indeed in 1811 the Swedish Parliament set up a commission charged with the preparation of a new code. The draft which was produced in 1826 was heavily influenced by the French Code civil, and its family and succession law in particular departed from old Swedish law with its underlying model of patriarchally organized kin-groups. For example, under the old law unmarried women had no legal capacity, whatever their age, and they could not marry without the consent of their father or other representative of their kin-group; under the new Code women, like men, gained capacity on reaching a certain age, husband and wife were given equal rights in matrimonial property, sons and daughters were granted the same statutory right of inheritance, and many old-fashioned differences between city-dwellers and countrymen in questions of matrimonial property and succession were abolished. This draft could not be brought into force as a whole because of conservative opposition but many of its ideas were implemented in separate reforming laws. This is the way in which, starting in the middle of the nineteenth century, Denmark and Sweden have modernized their old codes, especially in family and succession law, where they brought about the legal emancipation of women usually well in advance of countries on the Continent.

Stimulated by a sense of their common historical and cultural heritage, as well as by an increase in mutual trade and the improvement of traffic, the Nordic states started to co-operate closely in the field of legislation in the last third of the nineteenth century. This was facilitated by the fact that the Scandinavian languages, except Finnish, are very closely related, so that Scandinavian lawyers can speak their own language and still understand each other quite well. In 1872 a congress of Scandinavian jurists, convened in Copenhagen with the express purpose of advancing legal unification in Scandinavia, resolved that the first and most important goal was to unify the Nordic law of negotiable instruments. This challenge was taken up by the Ministers of Justice in Sweden, Denmark, and Norway, and they carried through the preliminary work with such speed that in 1880 the unified law of negotiable instruments came into force simultaneously in all three countries. In the following years attention was still concentrated on the unification of commercial law, and before the end of the nineteenth century nearly identical laws had come into force on trade marks, commercial registers, firms, and the law of cheques. The maritime law of Scandinavia was also put on a unified statutory basis in 1891/3.

It gradually appeared that the legislation emerging from this co-operation among the Nordic states was better in *quality* as well. Since Sweden even today has only 8 million inhabitants and Denmark, Norway, and Finland between 4 and 5 million each, the experience of each country is relatively limited; only on the basis of their consolidated experience is it possible to draft good statutes. Bolder plans for unification appeared around the turn of the century. In 1899 the Danish Professor LARSEN proposed that in addition to commercial law the whole of the rest of private law should be unified, with a Scandinavian Civil Code as the eventual goal. The governments of the Nordic states were in general agreement with this proposal but the ambitious project of producing a civil code was shelved in favour of unifying specific areas of the law of property and obligations. The first fruit of these efforts was a draft statute on the sale of moveables, which came into force in Sweden in 1905, in Denmark in 1906, in Norway in 1907 and in Iceland in 1922.

In preparing the Scandinavian Sales Act the draftsmen took account of the English Sale of Goods Act, 1893 and the German BGB but they also paid much more attention than usual to the viewpoints of the commercial interests involved. This had two results: first, the Sales Act is 'a simple system of simple and clearly formulated concepts' (RABEL, *Das Recht des Warenkaufs* I (1936) 311), and secondly it answers the strict demands of mercantile practice and the need to get contracts over and done with simply and swiftly. Thus, according to the statute, a vendor is in delay if he has failed to deliver the goods to the purchaser or to the carrier at the proper time; no notice is needed to put him in delay, nor indeed need he be *responsible* for the delay in delivery. If the vendor is in delay and the delay is 'material', the purchaser, instead of demanding performance, is entitled to repudiate the contract without allowing any further time for performance; such a repudiation of the contract does not have the consequence provided by §326 BGB, that the contract is avoided *ab initio*, with the result that the purchaser has no basis for claiming damages. §24 of the Scandinavian Sales Act gives the same result as German law, but is much better formulated: the vendor of generic goods who has failed to deliver is freed from liability in damages if, and only if, the performance of the contract was rendered impossible by reason of a circumstance 'which the vendor was not bound to envisage at the time of the contract, such as the destruction of the entire class of goods or such portion of it as was to form the object of the contract, the outbreak of war, the imposition of import restrictions or similar events'. It may be added that if the goods delivered are *defective*, the Scandinavian Sales Act holds the vendor of generic goods liable for damages even in the absence of fault. All these rules are substantially incorporated in the Uniform Sales Act (see below vol. II, ch. 13 VI).

Another important product of Nordic co-operation is the 'Law of contracts and other legal transactions in the law of property and obligations', to give it its Swedish name, which came into force in Sweden, Denmark, and Norway between 1915 and 1918 and in Finland in 1929. This Act, which has about 40 sections, does not purport to deal with all the questions covered by the BGB in its chapter 'Acts in Law' in the 'General part'; it confines itself to a few problems of proven practical importance, with rules concerning the *conclusion of contracts, agency*, and the *invalidity of legal acts*. It is very clear that the draftsmen kept an eye on the general private law doctrines of the German Pandectist School as well as the texts of the German and Swiss codes, but thanks to those twin virtues of Scandinavian jurists, namely reasonableness and realism, the Act shows no signs of that exaggerated passion for putting general rules 'right out front' which we find in the BGB (see above Ch. 12 II). This is already evident from the fact that the statute very sensibly purports to apply only to those legal acts which occur in the law of property and obligations, excluding family law and the law of succession; nor does the statute include any rules concerning the legal invalidity of legal acts on the ground of *minority*; those rules seemed to be functionally associated with the law of children, so they were kept for a special law dealing with the legal position of minors in all its aspects. The Contracts Law also has its own way of solving many practical problems, particularly by giving strong protection to good faith in business matters.

Thus a party who concludes a contract under the influence of mistake may in principle resile from the contract only if the other party knew or should have known of the error and therefore has no right to have his reliance on the validity of the contract protected. Offers to contract are binding, so that the offeree may count on his acceptance bringing a contract into being, provided it is communicated to the offeror within the period for which the offeror can reasonably be expected to wait. In its section on agency the Contracts Law has detailed provisions to protect those who contract in good faith with an agent whose powers have been limited or even terminated by a principal who has not made his intention sufficiently clear. This strong emphasis on the protection of commerce may be explained by the fact that in Scandinavia, as in England, commercial law has never been seen as a 'special law' for businessmen, but has always been incorporated into the general private law with a few special rules for the transactions of private citizens not in commerce. This can also be seen in §36 of the Contracts Law, a new version of which was produced in Denmark and Sweden in 1975–6. Under this provision a court may invalidate or modify a term of a contract if, given the subject-matter of the transaction and the attendant or supervening circumstances, it can be held to be 'unfair'. This applies in principle to commercial and non-commercial transactions alike, although there is an express reference to the relevance of the need to protect the consumer or other weak contracting party, and it applies to all 'unfair' terms, whether they are standard terms or individually negotiated.

In addition to the Sales Act and the Contracts Law there are several other statutes in the law of property and obligations which have come into force in Scandinavia in a unified form; one can instance the laws concerning Commission Agents. Trade Representatives, and Commercial Travellers, the Law on Instalment Sales, the Law on Insurance Contracts, and the Law on Bonds. All these laws were preceded by careful research in comparative law, scanning English as well as Continental, especially German, law for rules suited to Scandinavian conditions. Because their construction, diction, and style are almost identical with those of Continental legislation, and their basic legal concepts in harmony, the German or French lawyer finds it very much easier to cope with Scandinavian enactments than with the statutes of Anglo-American law.

With the enactments we have mentioned the Scandinavian countries have developed a substantially unified law of contract; where there are no applicable statutory provisions the device of *analogy* is very widely used by courts and writers alike. Thus in Sweden the provisions of the Sales Act regarding the delivery of defective goods have been applied by analogy to the contract of services which is not covered by the law of 1734. In the same way when judges have to decide a case involving the assignment of choses in action or the right of recourse between joint debtors, they ask whether perhaps the provisions of the Law on bonds may not be applied analogically. Again, there is no general clause in any Swedish statute which requires good faith in the performance of contracts, though specific rules to this effect can be found in the Law of Instalment Sales (1915), Law on Insurance Contracts (1927), and in the Law of Bonds (1936); in 1948 the Supreme Court of Sweden announced that contractual terms which offended against the principle of good faith were to be regarded as void in *all* contracts, even where there was no special statutory mandate. The list of such examples could easily be extended.

Scandinavian countries, with Sweden in the forefront, have been especially innovative in the field of *consumer protection*, and their ideas have often served as models elsewhere. In addition to the general clause in §36 of the Contracts Law, which has already been mentioned, Sweden has enacted special statutes which fix the terms of certain types of contract entered into by consumers. Contracts of sale are an instance: the *Consumer Sales Law* of 1973 grants inalienable rights to the consumer who buys goods for private use from a supplier, especially where the goods are defective or not delivered on time. Since 1979 all forms of credit provided to consumers fall under the *Consumer Credit Law*; where the credit is for the purchase of goods—the most important case in practice—the regulation is very detailed, and in some circumstances the consumer who has a defence against the supplier of the goods may use it against the supplier of the credit. Finally in 1981 the *Consumer Insurance Law* came into force; it gives very extensive rights to private citizens who take out property insurance against fire, accident, burglary, and other misfortunes, but not life insurance or sickness insurance. The Swedes have long realized that consumer protection can never be adequate so long as the individual consumer has to go to court to vindicate his rights in a particular case, so since 1970 they have had an Office of Consumer Protection, headed by a 'Consumer-Ombudsman'. Among its extensive powers since 1971 is the right to take a firm to a special 'Market Court' and seek an injunction against continued use of General Conditions of Business if the objectionable terms are 'unfair to the ultimate consumer with regard to the price and other circumstances'. The details may be found in BERNITZ, 'Schwedishes Verbraucherschutzrecht', *RabelsZ* 40 (1976) 593. Most other Scandinavian countries have enacted similar provisions. See also vol. II, Ch. 1 III.

In the field of *family law* there has also been productive co-operation between the Nordic states, although here the variations from nation to nation are rather more marked than in the law of obligations. The law of marriage, the law of children, and the law of adoption are similar in principle throughout Scandinavia, and often in their details as well. It must be noticed that many questions on which reform was proposed in Continental Europe only after the Second World War were raised or even solved in Scandinavian law much earlier: one may mention the equality of husband and wife, the abandonment of the principle of fault in divorce law, the equal treatment of legitimate and illegitimate children, and the improvement in the position of the surviving spouse in succession law.

III

This survey shows how successful the Nordic countries have been in their efforts over the last hundred years to bring their legal systems closer together; indeed, the Scandinavian achievement has been put forwards as a model for co-operation in Europe as a whole (see MATTEUCCI, above p. 286). On the other hand, further progress may have become more difficult as it appears that the reformist zeal has become less pronounced in some Scandinavian countries than in others (see HELLNER, above p. 286). Also it must be remembered that the conditions for achieving the present degree of legal harmony, if not unity, were particularly propitious in the Scandinavian countries. Their historical development was very similar, their cultural links were very close, their languages were very alike, there were no serious political differences, their population and economic power was approximately equivalent, and they were all perched on the edge of Europe; all these circumstances made co-operation in good faith much easier, co-operation which for some time has extended beyond the joint preparation of draft statutes to questions of economic, social, transport and cultural policy, especially, since 1952, under the auspices of the Nordic Council. But the principal explanation for the success of this co-operation in legal matters is the fact that the law in these Nordic countries, starting from a common basis of Germanic legal ideas, has developed historically on parallel lines. Thus Roman law reached the Scandinavian countries from the South only in the seventeenth century, at a time when the traditional legal institutions had long been stabilized in provincial and city laws and were being applied in a well-constructed courts system. The influence of Roman law was therefore confined to these areas in which the rules of the medieval codes were particularly deficient: in essence contract law, the law of credit and securities, partnership and bankruptcy law. Thus the reception of Roman law in the Nordic countries took a very weak form and the links between Scandinavia and Continental legal science, although much closer than they were in England, did not lead to so extensive a 'scientification' of legal doctrine and practice as did the reception of Roman law in Germany. Furthermore, the Age of Enlightenment's idea of codification lost some of its allure in Scandinavia, as so many continental ideas seem to do when they enter the cooler climate of the North. In order to modernize their old codes the Scandinavians in the nineteenth century relied principally on a number of individual statutes indistinguishable in style and construction from similar products on the Continent. The more advanced idea of codifying the whole of private law in a comprehensive manner has not worked out in any of the Scandinavian countries; the last step in this direction, the proposal of the Danish scholar VINDING KRUSE in 1948 to draw up a draft Nordic Civil Code, has recently come to a halt. This is in line with the attitude of Nordic legal science. It has always paid attention to events on the continent and in the nineteenth century it unquestionably got its legal wares from the pandectists' shop. But the tendency to undue conceptualism and the construction of large-scale integrated theoretical systems has never really been followed in the North, thanks to the realism of the Scandinavian lawyers and their sound sense of what is useful and necessary in practice. Thus while the Scandinavian legal systems have participated in the legal development of Continental Europe they have also maintained their local characteristics, and this justifies us in allocating them to a special 'Nordic' legal group within the Civil Law.

V. THE SOCIALIST LEGAL FAMILY

23

Distinctive Features of the Style of the Socialist Legal Family

BUTLER, *Soviet Law* (2nd edn., 1988).

FELDBRUGGE/VAN DEN BERG/SIMONS (ed.), *Encyclopedia of Soviet Law* (2nd edn., 1985).

GEILKE, *Einführung in das Recht der Sowjetunion* (2nd edn., 1983).

IOFFE, *Soviet Civil Law* (1988).

——, *Development of Civil Law Thinking in the USSR* (1989).

IOFFE/MAGGS, *The Soviet Legal System, A Legal Analysis* (1987).

——/——, *Soviet Law in Theory and Practice* (1983).

IZDEBSKI, 'Economic Reforms in Socialist Countries', 37 *Am. J. Comp. L.* 703 (1989).

LAPTEV, 'Socialist Enterprises', 17 *Int. Enc. Comp. L.* Ch. 16 (1978).

MARKOVITS, 'Pursuing One's Rights under Socialism', 38 *Stan. L. Rev.* 689 (1986).

QUIGLEY, 'Socialist Law and the Civil Law Tradition', 37 *Am. J. Comp. L.* 781 (1989).

REICH, *Marxistische Rechtstheorie* (1973).

——/REICHELT (ed.), *Einführung in das sozialistische Recht* (2nd edn., 1975).

I

TEN years ago it was a truth universally acknowledged that there was such a thing as a socialist legal family, its members being those countries where a communist party had engrossed political power and sought to make society march to the drum of Marxist–Leninist philosophy. Up to 1945 this had occurred only in the Soviet Union and Outer Mongolia, which adopted Soviet law as its model after being helped to independence in the 1920s, but a whole socialist legal family became possible at the end of the Second World War when the Red Army thrust deep into Central Europe. Communist parties were installed in Romania, Bulgaria and Albania, in Poland, Hungary and Czechoslovakia, in eastern Germany and Yugoslavia.

Opposition was reduced to deathly silence, and the political, social, and economic scene was quickly reconstructed to match that of the Soviet Union or at least reflect the tenets of Marxism-Leninism. A similar development took place in the People's Republic of China, founded when Mao Tse-Tung's troops had cleared the mainland of the Japanese and the Nationalist Chinese, and in Africa the leaders of some newly-independent countries invoked Marxism-Leninism to support their claim to sole political power and justify their policies.

Today, however, the very existence of a socialist legal family is seriously in question. Communist power structures have collapsed throughout central and eastern Europe, more or less quietly and at breathtaking speed. East Germany has been incorporated in the Federal Republic. Pluralist democracy and a market economy are firmly established in Poland, Czechoslovakia and Hungary, and in Romania and Bulgaria the process is under way. Estonia, Latvia and Lithuania have regained their independence. In Yugoslavia the state structure has broken down, and Slovenia and Croatia are about to acquire full independence. Even the Soviet Union has experienced changes unimaginable a few years ago. The political system was reformed under Gorbachev in the name of *Glasnost* and *Perestroika*: the provision of the Constitution which granted sole power to the Communist party has been repealed, and free elections have been held for some members of the Supreme Soviet, which can influence the government of the Union, despite the considerable increase in the executive powers of the President. The economy, however, has so far seen no radical reform: land and the other means of production are still vested exclusively in the state and state-supervised organizations, and all major economic decisions are still subject to state planning and comprehensive regulation. But *Glasnost* and *Perestroika* have had a further effect: the various peoples of the Soviet Union now openly assert their cultural, linguistic, and religious identities, reject the tutelage of the central powers in Moscow, and have gained autonomy in political and economic as well as cultural affairs.

It is too soon to say that the 'socialist legal family' is dead and buried. No one can predict possible political and economic developments in the Soviet Union. In China the government has reasserted its Marxist–Leninist stance after mowing down the student movement in 1989, and Communist parties elsewhere—in Cuba, some African countries and even, it seems, Serbia—are reluctant to give up their monopoly of power or permit the development of a free political and economic order. Even in countries where the changes seem irreversible the traces of more than forty years of complete subjection to political ideology will take a long time to erase. It therefore seems right to offer a brief survey of the basic tenets of Marxist–

Leninist ideology, the role it ascribes to law and the implications this has had for the practice of law and the economy in countries of the socialist legal family, as well as for their concepts of property.

II

The Marxist theory of law is founded on the doctrines of *dialectical and historical materialism*. These doctrines—if we may simplify slightly—proceed from the philosophical axiom that the sole reality in the world is material, discoverable only in objectively perceptible and discernible relationships and circumstances. Anything spiritual, ideal, or conceptual, on the other hand, is merely a reflection of the particular material reality on which it is dependent and by which its content is determined. Marxism applies this fundamental thesis of materialism to the social life of man: a social order is not based on ideas about the proper way to order social life which men may entertain as a result of their religion, metaphysics, or conception of justice; the real basis of any social order is material, namely the economic and social conditions of life in the society in question.

The Marxist doctrine of *foundation and superstructure* is a logical consequence of this view: according to this theory, the basis of any social order is its economic foundation, characterized by the particular structure of the current *relations of production*. The relations of production are in their turn determined by the manner in which the forces and factors of production (manpower, land, raw materials, mineral wealth, machines) are organized and exploited by those classes of society which control them. On this foundation arises the *superstructure*, comprising people's views and ideas on religion, morals, philosophy, and art and that whole stock of political and legal rules and institutions which we comprehensively call the state and the law. State and law are thus not independent at all and in particular they do not derive from any given, eternal, and unchangeable idea of law and justice. They are rather parts of the superstructure which simply reflect the economic foundation and the relations of production, especially by serving as the tools which the ruling class uses to maintain its existing position of power in society and the economy.

This Marxist model of society obtains inner dynamism from the further proposition that the economic foundation *alters* through history, not in any straightforward manner but by dialectical leaps and bounds. As new forces of production, such as the steam engine, arise, develop, and spread, the contradiction with existing relations of production which are based on other productive forces, such as those of a feudal agrarian society, increases and leads eventually to a revolutionary change in the relations of production, which then in turn produces a similar alteration in the superstructure. Thus for Marxist doctrine there is a law of historical development: society starts in a condition where no legal system is needed because all property is owned in common, and it develops through the slave-owning society of ancient times through medieval feudalism and then capitalism to socialism; after socialism there will once again be a classless society in which all economic contradictions are resolved and all 'exploitation of man by man' ended; the state and legal order will then die away, for they will have no function left. For Marxists this development is not a Utopian dream, but an inevitable, scientifically established necessity.

As to the role to be played by law in the intermediate period between the acquisition of power by the Communist Party and the arrival of the classless society Marxist legal philosophers differed, but the day was won by the view that law remained an essential means of assuring, stabilizing and moulding social conditions. Of course the direction and stimulus which the law must give to society during this period must be carefully tailored to the stage which that society had reached on its predestined route to communism. To do this was the prerogative and task of the Communist Party, which alone had insight into the progress of social development and ultimately, as the keeper of the Holy Grail of Marxist–Leninist ideology, must determine the content of the law.

Thus law for the Marxist is wholly dependent on its political function.

Marxism rejects the view that law may aim at the realization of other independent values, be they established by a god-given law of nature, by an idea of justice, or by the particular legal tenets of a given culture; in particular Marxism opposes the view that the law may set limits to political action by guaranteeing to the individual citizen certain spheres of freedom immune from control by the state, even if such control seemed justified by the needs and demands of politics and society.

This is not in the least to say that in Western legal systems law is 'policy-free'. On the contrary, even in Western countries every legal rule is set in a context of more or less explicit policy, without which it would be almost impossible to understand how the rule originated or how it is applied in practice. Indeed, many statutes deliberately seek to advance some economic or social policy in reconstructing social life. But the implementation of such policy goals is not the only or exclusive aim of the legal order. Law always has the additional function of *setting limits* to politics, by recognizing autonomous zones of freedom for the citizen which cannot simply be taken over in the interests of society as a whole. This may be seen in the constitutional guarantees of civil rights, in the many rules of criminal procedure which protect personal freedom, and in the institution of judicatures, especially constitutional courts, which are independent of the executive. In brief, this idea finds expression in all the institutions which in

Western legal systems are often comprehensively included in the 'Rule of Law', whose purpose it is to protect the zones of freedom of the citizen from invasion by the authorities. It is true that the boundaries of these reserved areas have been significantly eroded by developments in the past few decades. Wherever the exercise of rights might constitute the exercise of social power, increasingly narrow limits have been set by modern economic and social legislation. The question where precisely the boundary should be drawn between the areas of liberty of the individual and society's need for an equitable division of property, for the protection of the economically inferior, and for the guarantee of a humane and worthwhile life for all citizens is a problem which in Western countries has given rise to incessant dispute between the interests and values of widely varying philosophies, religions, modes of life, and attitudes to society. It is entirely different in countries where the doctrines of Marxism–Leninism obtain. There it is a matter for pride that these antagonisms within society have been overcome. Indeed, those who are possessed of a doctrine which makes precise predictions about the way in which human history will develop until it reaches a condition of perfect social justice and who accord to this doctrine the irrefutability of a law of nature are not likely to permit disputes within society about the direction which should be taken or to tolerate the freedom which is necessary for such a discussion. In such circumstances it makes no sense to attribute to law the function of limiting politics. For if society is set on a path which demonstrably leads to the greatest human happiness, anyone who in the name of law sought to oppose such a policy must be an enemy of society. On the contrary, law is exclusively the instrument or tool of politics, determined by the doctrines of Marxism–Leninism as interpreted by the Communist Party.

III

Anyone who wants to understand the actual role played by law in socialist states must first grasp the concept of 'socialist legality'. As has already been said, Marxism–Leninism teaches that the development of social life follows certain objective and ineluctable laws of nature susceptible of scientific demonstration, according to which human society moves from capitalism to socialism and from socialism to communism. In charge of this development is the Communist Party, whose leaders alone have the necessary training and education to enable them to evaluate the position reached by society and thus to organize and advance the developing process in accordance with the natural laws and to ordain the rules of positive law appropriate to the current stage of social development. Since the practice of law is tied to the principle of 'socialist legality', all those involved in applying the law must always act in harmony with the objective legality of social development as interpreted by the Communist Party at the time.

Thus in socialist legal systems statements to the effect that judges are 'independent and subject only to the law' mean something rather different from superficially similar guarantees of judicial independence in Western countries. All that is meant is that in deciding a particular case a judge is to be protected from direct intervention by the local party and the union organs. Throughout his entire career, however, the judge is bound to serve the political objectives set up by the Communist Party, and he remains permanently subject to party control, supervision and accountability. Under such circumstances the judiciary clearly cannot have the status of a 'third power'; indeed the very doctrine of separation of powers, conceived as a weapon born of the eighteenth-century struggle between the bourgeoisie and the absolutist nobility, would be quite out of place in a system from which class antagonisms have been banished. Judges in socialist systems are accordingly appointed and dismissed on political grounds. They are nominated by the party, trade unions and other organizations loyal to the party, and they are appointed for the duration of their legislative mandate by representatives of the people, to whom they are answerable and to whom they must report. They are subject to dismissal at any time for breach of duty.

An important stylistic feature of law in socialist states is the degree to which it has *educational functions*. According to Marxist–Leninist doctrine, one of the tasks of politics—and therefore also of law—is to alter the consciousness of individuals, to purge them of traces of bourgeois morality, and to coach them in socialist thought and behaviour. In Western democracies it is otherwise: Western law is designed in principle to provide an orderly setting in which people can live peaceably together; pledged to the idea that men living in freedom should develop themselves—it stops short of regulating their morals and attitudes.

The principal educational task of socialist law is the reform of persons charged with an offence. Consistently with continental tradition, though perhaps surprising to the lawyer from the Anglo-American system, what is involved is not simply judgement of the *act* but also judgement of the *actor*; of its own motion the court investigates the personal history of the accused, his family background, the circumstances of his life, his previous record, and much more, all of which plays a large part in the determination of the sentence. But the procedural systems of socialist states go much further than this, for they contain a whole range of provisions and institutions designed to extend involvement in the proceedings to groups of people not directly implicated, and thus exert an educational effect on a wider public. In criminal matters, for example, the 'collective' to which the accused belongs—his workmates or neighbours—may, with the permission of the judge, send a representative to the proceedings; such a representative is accorded considerable procedural rights, and may either side with the state attorney as 'social prosecutor' or, more commonly, appear with the accused as 'social defender', depending on whether, after discussing the matter between themselves, the collective regards the accused's conduct as grave or venial. Indeed the court can suspend the sentence and put the accused on probation, handing him over to the collective for re-education and improvement, and if, when the collective reports back to the court, the accused has betrayed the trust reposed in him, the court can cancel the suspension of the sentence. Members of the collective to which the accused belongs may be delegated to attend the criminal proceedings, and in appropriate cases the judge can even transfer the whole hearing to the factory or apartment block to which the accused or the parties belong or which is affected by the conduct in question.

Another typical feature of socialist law is its readiness to transfer some of the legal functions of the state to purely social units. In agricultural co-operatives, offices, hospitals and schools, residential areas and village communities one finds so-called 'social courts', composed of lay judges elected by the members of the collective on the proposal of the party or the union. Their jurisdiction includes cases of indiscipline at work, shirking of family responsibilities (especially failure to maintain), housing disputes and other minor private law controversies. Their procedure, free from the constraints of the Code of Civil Procedure, is extremely informal. Proceedings normally take place in the presence of the collective, which can make its views known by direct intervention. Such courts are designed not only to relieve the state organs of the minor disputes of daily life but also to educate the people by involving them personally in conflict resolution.

A striking feature of the state courts is their willingness to sidestep the general rules of jurisdiction whenever the seriousness, interest or difficulty of a case suggests that it be heard in a higher court or a court elsewhere. The 'inquisitorial principle' applies throughout, so that even in civil matters, given a general interest in having the whole truth revealed, the courts, untrammelled by the manner in which the parties present their case, can ex officio order evidence of facts not asserted by the parties. The state attorney is accordingly entitled to take part in civil as well as criminal proceedings and, like the presidents of the higher courts, is even empowered, whenever necessary in the light of higher principles, that is, in the interests of the uniform implementation of political goals, to enter a 'protest' against, or have quashed, verdicts and even final judgments.

This brief survey will have shown how the typical institutions of the socialist law of judicature and procedure reflect Marxist–Leninist insistence on the political function of law. The forms and guarantees found in court structures and procedural law in Western countries—the 'independence' of the judge from the exigencies of day-to-day politics, the inalienable right of the citizen to his 'statutory judge', the 'binding force' of judicial decisions, the principle of the 'day in court'—cannot, in a state which makes a total claim to lead and mould society, enjoy an independent value proof against all political considerations. On the contrary, a state which embraces a demonstrable doctrine of salvation must naturally prefer the implementation of *substantive political correctness* to the guarantee of *formal areas of freedom* such as underlie the rules of procedure in Western countries.

IV

Property and ownership, both in theory and in the actual forms they take, are quite different in countries of the socialist legal family from those in capitalist countries. This is a direct consequence of the teachings of Marxism. In capitalist societies, by definition, the means of production may be privately owned, and the owner thereby empowered to exploit other individuals, groups, or classes. In socialist society, by contrast, according to Marxist theory, class antagonisms and the exploitation of man by man are avoided by socializing the means of production, putting them into social or socialist ownership, where they are at the disposition of the whole people organized as a state, or of collective economic groups recognized by the state.

In order to implement these basic principles, socialist legal systems have created quite novel legal categories. They have three distinct types of property: *state property, property of co-operative organizations* (which together constitute 'socialist property') and finally *personal property*. State property is the highest and most important form of ownership. Co-operative property is vested in farming co-operatives (*kolkhozes*) and other communal units of production such as trade unions and other mass organizations. Individual citizens may have personal property. Different kinds of owner can own different kinds of thing: the most important productive assets belong exclusively to the state, and only the least important kinds of thing to the individual citizen. Indeed a citizen can own only things which are intended to satisfy his material and cultural needs, such as earned income and savings, household furniture and goods and a private car, though he may also have the right to use a plot of land with a small dwelling or holiday home on it. Land aside, state enterprises—sometimes rather euphemistically called 'people's enterprises'—form the most significant item under state ownership: they dominate industry and commerce, including the service industries, and even in agriculture state farms may play an important role, especially in the Soviet Union (*Sovchozes*). Although a state enterprise is a part of the state and an organ of it, it has, as a legal person, limited capacity to enter such legal relations with other state or co-operative organizations or individual citizens as may be required by the tasks imposed on it. The enterprise does not, however, own the property asigned to it to work with. Ownership remains vested in the state, and the enterprise obtains a mere 'right to operative management'.

This right is seen as an offshoot of ownership, by dint of which state enterprises may use the state property conferred on them and dispose of it within the limits laid down by law and consistent with the tasks imposed on them by the state economic plan. Thus a state enterprise's powers of disposition over the property it 'administers in operation' are narrowly determined by the tasks laid down in the plan and the purpose served by the property in the production process. As a matter of legal technique this is done by creating separate funds (*Fonds*) with different legal regimes. Thus if an enterprise wishes to dispose of an item of property, it makes a great difference whether it belongs to the 'basic fund' (e.g., a machine), the 'stock fund' (e.g. raw materials or half-finished goods) or the 'circulation fund', consisting of finished goods. Any disposition at variance with the current plan or purpose is *ultra vires* and void as a matter of private law.

This principle that property is bound by its purpose in the plan applies not only to state enterprises but also to co-operative productive enterprises. Thus while a farming co-operative or *kolkhoz* has legal personality and owns the business installations, machines, vehicles, livestock, and the agricultural products thereby engendered, it cannot deal with this property just as it likes. In respect of 'its' property the *kolkhoz* has only such powers as are consistent with the role it must play in the national production plan. The *kolkhoz* cannot by itself dispose of objects in the basic fund; it may not, for example, lease out an orchard or sell a harvester in order to pay for deliveries of fertilizer or satisfy the wage-claims of the participating farmers. The powers of the *kolkhoz* over its agricultural products are subject to special regulation: products may be sold to the state in quantities and at the prices fixed by the plan; only the surplus may be 'freely' disposed of.

To abolish private ownership of productive assets and suppress all private enterprise, business competition and individual incentives is to switch off the market mechanism which in capitalist economies regulates the relations between the component members of the economy. In socialist countries its function is taken over by the *plan*, which not only determines the long-term development of the economy but also, sometimes in great detail, specifies the total productive output, regulates the circulation of goods and services, and fixes the prices to be charged for them.

In practice the 'plan' consists of a great number of extremely different plans. *Perspective plans* are long-term plans which cover many years and are of special importance for the large-scale direction of the economy. They state what goals are to be achieved in the most important sectors of the economy, what essential research tasks must be solved, and what procedures to alter the structure of the economy must be carried out within the period of the plan. A perspective plan lays down the basic priorities for future economic development, in accordance with policy decisions taken by government and party. It contains, for example, the decisions about whether existing resources should be devoted primarily to the development of agriculture or industry, to light or heavy industry, to the production of investment goods or consumer goods or armaments, or whether they should be concentrated on particular technical projects (for example, space travel, development projects, and so on).

In socialist economies perspective plans are rendered more specific by annual plans, which spell out for a single economic year the detailed implications of the long-term plan's global aims as they affect each area of the economy and type of production. At this point individual businesses and enterprises may indicate their experience and wishes. Yearly plans are normally drawn up by a 'State Planning Commission' under one of the highest governmental organs and, after government approval, are enacted in the form of law. They are then broken down into a number of individual plans to deal with such matters as the production required of the individual units of the economy, the allocation of materials, the transport required of transport undertakings, deliveries in and out, the provision of credit, and insurance cover for the businesses. Individual businesses learn what the plan requires of them only when the relevant planning authority intimates particular 'target figures'. These state what *quantity* of goods or services the business must produce, what *value* they must have or what *quality*. The target figures often require the business to achieve a certain productivity as well, such as a minimum rate of interest on the capital property allocated to it, or on the currency attributed to it, or a specified increase in profit. On the basis of these 'target figures' every undertaking finally produces an *undertaking plan* for the approval of superior authority; this fixes the details of how the general requirements imposed on the business are to be satisfied.

Dealings between individual state enterprises are not directly determined by the plans, but rather by so-called 'planning acts' based on the plans.

Planning acts are administrative acts by means of which the competent authorities issue specific instructions to the individual businesses—by directing them to deliver a specified quantity of goods to a named consignee or to collect them from a named supplier, to carry out a specified piece of building work for another, to afford credit up to a certain amount or to accept it, to carry specified goods for a specified distance to a particular consignee, and so on. Planning acts give rise to a relationship of administrative law between the addressee and the authority which issues them and to a duty of private law between the various addressees, namely a duty to conclude a contract containing the details of the exchange required in outline by the planning acts. If a processing factory A is instructed by planning act to obtain 1,000 tons of corrugated iron from an ironworks B and the ironworks B is instructed by a mirror-image planning act to deliver the same quantity to A, A and B must regulate by contract those points not already specified in the two planning acts. For example, they must agree what qualities, strength, and shape the iron should have, in what instalments and to what destinations it should be sent in the course of the planning year, and how it should be packed. There is more freedom to contract about products whose circulation is *not* determined by planning acts. These are goods which are not so important economically, which are not in short supply or which are produced in smaller businesses in the locality. Thus, for example, a state trading organization can decide by itself what groceries or other goods, not subject to planning acts, it will stock; in many cases, indeed, it may choose from which of several local suppliers it will take a particular product. Even here suppliers and trading organizations are subject to the plan in so far as they must achieve a certain quantity of production or throughput of goods, but the precise manner of achieving these planned goals—with what types of goods, with what articles within particular classes of goods, in what sort of quantity, and from what contractors—is largely left open to the individual businesses if the goods are not subject to planning acts.

It is important to realize that even before the radical changes of recent times there were great variations between different countries in the system given here in outline. Thus the range of goods subject to planning acts varied from country to country, and within each country from year to year, for every socialist state must face the problem of reconciling central planning, which is politically obligatory, with a system of material incentives which is economically desirable. In Hungary, notably, economic reforms in the 1980s restricted the role of state planning to strategic matters and left it to individual enterprises to solve their own problems. Nowadays Central and Eastern Europe realizes that one cannot mix fire and water, and that if one wants democracy and material well-being, one must have a market economy, even if the price to be paid in the transition from one form of economy to the other is social disruption and crisis which may strain the polity to the limit. Only in the Soviet Union does the government still seem to nurse the belief that lesser reforms will suffice and that state ownership of the means of production and central planning can in essence be retained.

24

The Development of the Socialist Legal Family

In addition to the works cited in the Bibliography to Ch. 23 above:

ARLT/STILLER, *Entwicklung der sozialistischen Rechtsordnung in der DDR* (1973).

BARRY etc. (eds), *Soviet Institutions and the Administration of Law* (1979).

——/GINSBURG/MAGGS (eds.), *The Citizen and the State in Contemporary Soviet Law* (1977).

BERMAN, *Justice in the U.S.S.R., An Interpretation of Soviet Law* (1963) 187 ff.

——, 'The Dilemma of Soviet Law Reform', 76 *Harv. L. Rev.* 929 (1963).

BRUNNER, *Einführung in das Recht der DDR* (2nd edn., 1979).

BUTLER, 'Sources of Soviet Law', 1975 *Curr. Leg. Prob.* 223.

——, *Soviet Law* (1983).

DEKKERS, *Introduction au droit de l'Union soviétique et des Républiques populaires* (2nd edn., 1971).

EMINESCU/POPESCU, *Les Codes civils des pays socialistes, Etude comparative* (1980).

EÖRSI and others, *Das ungarische Zivilgesetzbuch in fünf Studien* (1963).

FELDBRUGGE (ed.), *Encyclopedia of Soviet Law*, 2 vols. (1973).

FOSTER, 'Codification in Post-Mao China', 30 *Am. J. Comp. L.* 395 (1982).

FREUND, *Das Zivilrecht Sowjetrußlands* (1924).

GEILKE, *Einführung in das Sowjetrecht* (1966).

——, 'Die Sowjetisierung von Staat und Recht in den europäischen Volksdemokratien', *WGO* 5 (1963) 10.

——, *Einführung in das Recht des Polnischen Volksrepublik* (1971).

——/ JESSEL, *Einführung in das Recht der Bulgarischen Volksrepublik* (1975).

GSOVSKI/GRZYBOWSKI, *Government, Law and Courts in the Soviet Union and Eastern Europe*, 2 vols. (1959).

HAZARD, 'The Soviet Legal Pattern Spreads Abroad', 1964 *U. Ill. L. Forum* 277.

——, 'Unity and Diversity in Socialist Law', 30 *L. Contemp. Probl.* 270 (1965).

——, 'Marxist Models for West African Law', in: *Ius privatum gentium, Festschrift Max Rheinstein* I (1969) 285.

——, *Communists and Their Law, A Search for the Common Core of the Legal Systems of the Marxian Socialist States* (1969).

——/BUTLER/MAGGS, *The Soviet Legal System, Contemporary Documentation and Historical Commentary* (3rd edn., 1977).

IOFFE, 'Soviet Law and Roman Law', 62 *Boston UL Rev.* 761 (1982).

——/MAGGS, *Soviet Law in Theory and Practice* (1983).

——/TOLSTOI, 'The New Civil Code of the R.S.F.S.R., A Soviet View', 15 *ICLQ* 1090 (1966).

JOHNSON, *An Introduction to the Soviet Legal System* (1969).

KIRALFY, 'The New Civil Code of the R.S.F.S.R., A Western View', 15 *ICLQ* 1116 (1966).

KLIBANSKI, *Handbuch des gesamten russischen Zivilrechts*, 2 vols. (1911/1917).

KNAPP, 'Codification du droit civil dans les pays socialistes', *Rev. int. dr. comp.* 31 (1979) 733.

KORKISCH, *Fragen des ostmitteleuropäischen Rechts* (1979).

LOEBER, 'Die Rechtsstruktur des Ostblocks', *OER* 6 (1960) 196.

LÜBCHEN/POSCH, 'Die Herausbildung des sozialistischen Zivilrechts', *NJ* 1979, 239.

MAKAROV, 'Das Privat- und Wirtschaftsrecht der Sowjet-Union', *RabelsZ* 13 (1940/1941) 754.

MEDER, *Das Sowjetrecht, Grundzüge der Entwicklung 1917–1970* (1971).

MÜNZEL, *Das Recht der Volksrepublik China* (1982).

PETEV, *Sozialistisches Zivilrecht* (1975).

POSDNJAKOW, *Das Zivilrecht der asiatischen Länder der Volksdemokratie* (1959).

ROGGEMANN, 'Entwicklung und allgemeine Grundlagen des sowjetischen Zivilrechts', *JbOstr* 12 (1971) 149.

ROZMARYN and others, *Introduction à l'étude du droit polonais* (1967).

SCHROEDER, 'Gesellschaftsgerichte und Administrativjustiz im vorrevolutionären Russland', *OER* 8 (1962) 292.

——, 'Das neue Bürgerliche Gesetzbuch der Russischen Sowjetrepublik', *ROW* 9 (1965) 1, 49.

SCHULTZ, *Russische Rechtsgeschichte von den Anfängen bis zur Gegenwart einschließlich des Rechts der Sowjetunion* (1951).

TSCHCHIKVADZE/ZIVS, 'Structure and Divisions of the Law: The System of Socialist Law', *International Encyclopedia of Comparative Law*, vol. II, Ch. 2 (1974) 115.

ZWEIGERT, 'Stilelemente des sozialistischen Rechtskreises', in: *Zbornik radova* 4 (1966) 541.

25

The Administration of Law in the Socialist States

ADLER/ALICH, 'Zur Rolle der Anwaltschaft in der DDR nach dem Gesetz über die Kollegien der Rechtsanwälte vom 17.12.1980', *ROW* 1982, 71.

BARRY/BERMAN, 'The Soviet Legal Profession', 82 *Harv. L. Rev.* 1 (1968).

BILINSKY, 'Das neue Gesicht der sowjetischen Rechtsanwaltschaft', *ROW* 12 (1968) 239.

——, 'Die "gesellschaftliche Rechtspflege" in der Sowjetunion', *ROW* 4 (1960) 89.

BREITBARTH, 'Kollegien der Rechtsanwälte: dem Sozialismus gemässe Form rechtsanwaltlicher Tätigkeit', *NJ* 1981.

BRUHN, 'Die Rechtsanwaltschaft in der DDR', *NJW* 1981, 1189.

BUTLER, 'Comradely Courts in Eastern Europe', 1972 *Curr. Leg. Prob.* 200.

CAMERON, *The Soviet Lawyer and his System* 1 (1978).

ČCHIKVADZE (ed.), *The Soviet State and Law* (1969).

COLLIGNON, *Les Juristes en Union Soviétique* (1977).

ESER, *Gesellschaftsgerichte in der Strafrechtspflege* (1970).

FEIFER, *Justice in Moscow* (1964), also in German translation, *Justiz in Moskau* (1965).

FRIEDMAN/ZILE, 'Soviet Legal Profession: Recent Developments in Law and Practice', 1964 *Wis L. Rev.* 32.

GIDDINGS, 'Social Legal Consultation', 1 *Rev. Soc. L.* 261 (1975).

HAYDEN, 'Who Wants Informal Courts?, Paradoxical Evidence from a Yugoslav Attempt to Create Workers' Courts for Labor Cases,' 1985 *Am. Bank Fed. Res. J.* 293.

HAZARD, *Settling Disputes in Soviet Society, The Formative Years of Legal Institutions* (1960).

KUCHEROV, *The Organs of Soviet Administration of Justice, Their History and Operation* (1970).

KURCZEWSKI/FRIESKE, 'The Social Conciliatory Commissions in Poland', in: *Access to Justice*, vol. II (Cappelletti/Weisner (eds.) 1978) 153.

LAMMICH, 'Merkmale des sozialistischen Gerichtsverfassungsrechts', *ROW* 1978, 251.

——, 'Das Problem der richterlichen Unabhängigkeit im sozialistischen Gerichtsverfassungsrecht', *JZ* 1979, 93.

MALONE, 'The Soviet Bar', 46 *Cornell LQ* 258 (1961).

MARKOVITS, 'Law or Order, Constitutionalism and Legality in Eastern Europe', 34 *Stan. L. Rev.* 513 (1982).

——, 'Pursuing One's Rights Under Socialism', 38 *Stan. L. Rev.* 689 (1986).

MEDER, *Das Sowjetrecht* (1971).

O'CONNOR, 'Soviet Procedures in Civil Decisions: A Changing Balance Between Public and Civil Systems of Public Order', 1964 *U. Ill. L. Forum* 51.

PETEV, *Sozialistisches Zivilrecht* (1975).

RACZ, 'Le Contrôle de l'administration par la Prokuratura dans la République populaire de l'Hongrie', *Rev. int. dr. comp.* 31 (1980) 771.

RÉVÉSZ, *Justiz im Ostblock, Richter und Strafrecht* (1967).

ROGGEMANN, 'Das sowjetische Zivilverfahrensrecht', *OER* 12 (1966) 229, 13 (1967). 1.

SCHMIDT, *Die sowjetischen Gesellschaftsgerichte* (1969).

——, 'Wesen und Entwicklung der Konflikt- und Schiedskommissionen in der DDR (1952–1969)', *JbOstR* 10 (1969) II, 57.

SMITH, *The Soviet Procuracy and the Supervision of Administration* (1978).

——, 'The Impact of Socialism on Soviet Legal Institutions and Procedures', 23 *Colum. J. Transnat'l L.* 315 (1985).

ULč, *The Judge in a Communist State, A View from Within* (1972).

WÜNSCHE, 'Rolle und Funktion der juristischen Berufe [in der DDR]', in: Nationales Kommitee für Rechtswissenschaft der DDR (ed.), *Berichte zum XI. Internationalen Kongress für Rechtsvergleichung Caracas 1982* (1982) 62.

WOLFF, 'Aufgaben und Stellung des Rechtsanwalts im entwickelten gesellschaftlichen System des Sozialismus', *NJ* 1969, 615.

26

Ownership in the Socialist Legal Family

BILINSKY, 'Persönliches Eigentum im Lichte der neuen Verfassung der UdSSR', *ROW* 1980, 104.
BUTLER, 'Marxian Concepts of Ownership in Soviet Law', 23 *Colum. J. Transnat'l L.* 281 (1985).
DROBNIG, 'Eigentum und Vertrag im sozialistischen Recht', *Jahrbuch für Sozialwissenschaft* 2 (1951) 157.
HASTRICH, 'Das persönliche Eigentum der Sowjetbürger in der Übergangszeit zum Kommunismus', *OER* 9 (1963) 26.
HAZARD, 'Whither Communist-Led Society? An Approach Through Property Law', 39 *Ind. LJ* 732 (1964).
IONASCO, 'Les Types et les formes de propriété en droit socialiste,' *Rev. int. dr. comp.* 21 (1969) 499.
JAKOBS, *Eigentumsbegriff und Eigentumssystem des sowjetischen Rechts* (1965).
——, 'Das Eigentum als Rechtsinstitut im deutschen und sowjetischen Recht', *RabelsZ* 29 (1965) 694.
LAPTEV, 'Rechtiche Stellung der sozialistischen Staatsbetriebe in der UdSSR', *ZgesHR* 134 (1970) 1.
LUCAS, 'Das Wohnhauseigentum in der UdSSR', *JbOstR* 3 (1962) I, 205.
LUKIĆ, 'Notions de la propriété dans l'Europe socialiste et dans les États capitalistes', *RabelsZ* 26 (1961) 238.
MERRYMAN, 'Toward a Comparative Study of the Sale of Land', in: *Ius privatum gentium, Festschrift Max Rheinstein* II (1969) 737.
PFAFF, *Das sozialistische Eigentum in der Sowjetunion* (1965).
PFUHL, 'Begriff und Stellung des Eigentums in der Sowjetunion', in: *Das Eigentum im Ostblock* (ed. Institut für Ostrecht, München, 1958) 25.
L. RAISER, 'Das Eigentum als Rechtsbegriff in den Rechten West- und Osteuropas', *RabelsZ* 26 (1961) 230.
SARKÖZY, *Die Theorie des gesellschaftlichen Eigentumsrechts im Verlauf der sozialistischen Wirtschaftsreformen* (1980).
THOMSON, 'Das persönliche Eigentum im Recht der UdSSR', in: *Das Eigentum im Ostblock* (ed. Institut für Ostrecht, Munich, 1958) 51.
WIEDEMANN, *Das sozialistische Eigentum in Mitteldeutschland* (1964).

27

Contract in the Socialist
Planned Economy

ABOVA, 'Plan und Vertrag in der sozialistischen Wirtschaft der UdSSR', in: *Deutsches und sowjetisches Wirtschaftsrecht* (ed. Max-Planck-Institut für ausländisches und internationales Privatrecht, 1981) 37.

BILINSKY, *Das sowjetische Wirtschaftsrecht* (1968).

BRATUS/LUNZ, *Fragen des Wirtschaftsvertrages* (1956).

BRUNNER/KALMAN, *Vertragsrecht und Vertragsfreiheit in der Volksrepublik Ungarn* (1971).

CHALFINA, *Wesen und Bedeutung des Vertrags im sowjetschen sozialistischen Zivilrecht* (1958).

DROBNIG, 'Der Vertrag in einer plangelenkten Staatswirtschaft, Zum Vertragsgesetz der DDR vom 11. 12. 1957,' *JZ* 1960, 233.

EÖRSI/IOFFE/SUCH, 'Contract in the Socialist Economy,' VII *Int. Enc. Comp. L.* Ch. 5 (1981).

GROSSFELD, 'Money Sanctions for Breach of Contract in a Communist Economy,' 72 *Yale LJ* 1326 (1963).

HEMMERLING and others, *Grundfragen des Vertragssystems* (1958).

KNAPP, 'Verträge im tschechoslowakischen Recht, Ein Beitrag zur Rechtsvergleichung zwischen Ländern mit verschiedener Gesellschaftsordnung,' *RabelsZ* 27 (1962/1963) 495.

LAPTEV, 'Socialist Enterprises,' XVII *Int. Enc. Comp. L.* Ch. 16 (1978).

——, 'Rechtsstellung der Betriebe und Vereinigungen in der UdSSR', in: *Deutsches und sowjetisches Wirtschaftsrecht* (ed. Max-Planck-Institut für ausländisches und internationales Privatrecht, 1981) 7.

LOEBER, 'Plan and Contract Performance in Soviet Law', 1964 *U. Ill. L. Forum* 128.

——, *Der hoheitlich gestaltete Vertrag, Eine rechtsvergleichende Untersuchung über den Planvertrag im Sowjetrecht und den 'diktierten Vertrag' im Recht der Bundesrepublik Deutschland* (1969).

PLEYER, 'Der Wirtschaftsvertrag in der DDR, Entwicklung, Gegenwartsprobleme, Reform', *AcP* 181 (1981) 459.

RADWANSKI, 'Grundfragen des Vertragsrechts in den sozialistischen Staaten,' *JBl.* 1979, 70.

RAISER, 'Das Vertragsgesetz der DDR vom 25.2.1965,' *JZ* 1967, 338.

SUCH, *Der Liefevertrag* (1967).

TUNC, 'La Possibilité de comparer le contrat dans des systèmes juridiques à structures économiques différentes,' *RabelsZ* 27 (1962/1963) 478.

ZILE, 'Law and the Distribution of Consumer Goods in the Soviet Union,' 1964 *U. Ill. L. Forum* 212.

VI. OTHER LEGAL FAMILIES

28

The Far Eastern Legal Family

BEER/TOMATSU, 'A Guide to the Study of Japanese Law,' 23 *Am. J. Comp. L.* 284 (1975).

BLAKEMORE, 'Post-War Developments in Japanese Law', 1947 *Wis. L. Rev.* 632.

BODDE/MORRIS, *Law in Imperial China* (1967).

BÜNGER, *Zivil- und Handelsgesetzbuch sowie Wechsel- und Scheckgesetz von China* (1934).

CH'Ü, *Law and Society in Traditional China* (1961).

COHEN, 'Chinese Mediation on the Eve of Modernization', 54 *Calif. L. Rev.* 1201 (1966).

——/EDWARDS/CHEN, *Essays on China's Legal Tradition* (1980).

DAVID, 'Deux conceptions de l'ordre social', in: *Ius privatum gentium, Festschrift Max Rheinstein* I (1969) 53.

EUBEL etc., *Das japanische Rechtssystem, Ein Grundriss mit Hinweisen und Materialien zum Studium des japanischen Rechts* (1979).

HAN PAO MA, 'Legal System of the Republic of China', *RabelsZ* 37 (1973) 101.

HENDERSON, *Conciliation and Japanese Law, Tokugawa and Modern*, 2 vols. (1964).

ISHII, *Japanese Legislation in the Meiji Era* (1959).

ISHIMOTO, 'L'influence du Code civil français sur le droit civil japonais', *Rev. int. dr. comp.* 6 (1954), 744.

JIANPAN, 'Building New China's Legal System', 22 *Colum. J. Transnat'l L.* 1 (1983).

KIM/LAWSON, 'The Law of the Subtle Mind: The Traditional Japanese Conception of Law', 28 *ICLQ* 491 (1978).

KITAGAWA, 'Das Methodenproblem in der Dogmatik des japanischen bürgerlichen Rechts', *AcP* 166 (1966) 330.

——, *Rezeption und Fortbildung des europäischen Zivilrechts in Japan* (1970).

MCALEAVY, 'Chinese Law', in: An Introduction to Legal Systems (ed. Derrett, 1968) 105.

MACNEIL, 'Contract in China: Law, Practice, and Dispute Resolution', 38 *Stan. L. Rev.* 303 (1986).

VON MEHREN (ed.), *Law in Japan, The Legal Order in a Changing Society* (1963).

MÜNZEL, *Das Recht der Volksrepublik China* (1982).

MURAKAMI, *Einführung in die Grundlagen des japanischen Rechts* (1974).

NODA, 'The Far Eastern Conception of Law', II *Int. Enc. Comp. L.* Ch. 1 (1975).

——, *Introduction to Japanese Law* (1976).

OPPLER, *Legal Reform in Occupied Japan, A Participant Looks Back* (1976).
RÖHL, *Fremde Einflüsse im modernen japanischen Recht* (1959).
ROKUMOTO, 'Juristen und zivilrechtliche Streitigkeiten in Japan, Die Problematik der Verkehrsunfälle', *Recht in Japan 3* (1980) 47.
——, 'Tschotei (Schlichtung), Eine japanische Alternative zum Recht: Verfahren, Praxis und Funktionen', *Jb. f. Rechtssoziologie* 6 (1980) 390.
RUETE, *Der Einfluß des abendländischen Rechtes auf die Rechtsgestaltung in Japan und China* (1940).
VON SENGER, 'Über das Normbewusstsein der Japaner', *ZfRvgl* 1981, 265.
——, 'Grundlagen und Eigenart des Rechts der Volksrepublik China', *SJZ* 1981, 1.
STEVENS, 'Modern Japanese Law as an Instrument of Comparison', 19 *Am. J. Comp. L.* 665 (1971).
WANG, *Les Sources du droit japonais* (1978).

I

A LEGAL system is allocated to a family or circle of legal systems on the basis of its distinctive features. One of these may be the importance it attaches to law as a means of ordering social life. This is the point on which the legal systems of the Far East differ fundamentally from the legal families dealt with so far. All Western systems, whether they belong to the Civil Law, the Common Law, or the socialist legal family, agree that the important questions of social life should primarily be regulated by *rules of objective law* rather than simply by conventions or habits or mores. These rules of law assure to individual citizens certain claims, a certain status, and certain entitlements; statute and judicial decision specify in general terms the conditions under which all persons are to have particular *rights*, such as the right to performance of a contract or to compensation for harm, or the right to obtain a divorce or payment of maintenance money. If a person's rights are infringed or questioned by others, he is not only *entitled* to assert and vindicate them but, as RUDOLF VON JHERING said in his book *The Struggle for Law*, may actually be *bound* to do so; the mechanism used for this purpose is court proceedings, in which a judge provided by the state resolves the dispute on the basis of objective law by issuing a conclusive and binding judgment. A glance at the legal systems of the Far East shows that this is not the only possible method: in some societies disputes are resolved by techniques other than suits at law. It is true that even in the Western world there are many conflicts which are not usually or easily resolved with finality by judicial decision—there are examples in international law and in labour law, and even in areas where court proceedings are available and effective one can discern a tendency to avoid the publicity of a duel before state courts and to resolve the dispute in a friendly manner by compromise or settlement instead. This may help to maintain a sense of trust which commercial men or the parties to a contract of service or licence may hold more important for their future relations than the establishment of their legal rights. We know far too little about the extent and operation of these informal mechanisms of resolution in the Western world, but in the Far Eastern legal family they are enormously more important, to a degree which constantly surprises the Western observer. It is this very fact which makes the study of Far Eastern law so interesting, for it clearly demonstrates the temporary and local nature of attitudes which in the Western world we too easily take to be axiomatic.

In this section we shall first make a brief survey of the development in *China*, where the doctrines of CONFUCIUS very quickly led to a tradition of scepticism about general rules of law and all forms of court enforcement. This Chinese tradition still has a certain effect on the law in the People's Republic of China today, though it is certainly diminishing. It had a great influence in Korea and Indo-China, and is of great importance even today for the Chinese inhabitants of Hong Kong, Indonesia, and Malaysia. Then we must pay special attention to *Japanese* law. It is true that Japan, thanks to its physical insularity, was never ruled by the Chinese Emperors, but from the sixth and seventh centuries Chinese culture had such a powerful influence in Japan that Japanese law was greatly affected. The modern law of Japan is of particular interest to comparative lawyers for another reason: the tradition of solving conflicts outside the courts is still vital but it coexists with modern codes and codes of procedure, originally modelled on German and French law and now, since the end of the Second World War, on American law as well.

II

In the Chinese view, social relations are part of the natural order. This view is to be found in the doctrines of Confucianism, and it helps us to understand why in the Far East they set so little store by law and the resolution of conflicts by courts. CONFUCIUS lived from 551 to 479 BC; his importance lies not so much in the originality of his thought, which reflects the philosophical and ethical tenets of his time, as in the way he developed and refined these in discussions with his pupils which were later recorded, and especially in the way in which his admirable personal life embodied the ideals he propounded. In the following centuries his teachings were further developed, especially by the philosopher TUNG CHUNG-SHU (176–104 BC) who incorporated elements of popular beliefs into Confucianism and produced a doctrine of cosmic harmony. It is this form of Confucianism which constituted the ideology of the Chinese empire until the revolution of 1911. It starts from the proposition that man and God, Heaven and earth, all things living and inert are organic parts of a harmoniously ordered and integrated universe. The most important goal of man must therefore be to keep his thoughts, feelings, and actions in perfect accordance with cosmic harmony; in particular men must so conduct themselves as not to disturb the natural balance of their existing relations. The rules of 'proper' behaviour were called 'li' and their content characteristically depended on the social status of the person to whom they applied, his status in his family, in his clan, in the neighbourhood, in the official hierarchy, and in the state. For Confucianism, the different positions which an individual might occupy by reason of his age, sex, career, family position, employment status, and social prestige were all part of the prescribed natural order and had to be respected if one was not to disturb the balanced harmony of the world. Thus the 'li' or appropriate behaviour was carefully determined for each situation differently, according as it involved relations between superior and inferior, between older and younger, nobleman and citizen, between relatives, friends, or strangers, between father and son, older and younger brother, or husband and wife (on this see in detail CH'Ü (above p. 315) p. 226 ff.). The ideal man in the Confucian view is the person conscious of the natural order of the world who recognizes the necessity and purpose of these rules of behaviour, follows them spontaneously, and thus modestly and quietly represses his own interests in order to maintain that harmony.

It will be clear that Confucianism could have no great regard for rules of law or their enforcement by courts. Since all law tends to schematize and typify the relations of life in a simple and orderly way, it is in no position to take account of all the various imponderables inherent in the social position of the parties. Much less could Confucianism approve of establishing legal rights through court procedures. According to the ethics of Confucianism a citizen who thought that someone else had neglected the rules of 'li' in his behaviour towards him does better to seek an equitable resolution by peaceful discussion than to accentuate the existing discord by insisting on his rights or calling in a judge. The wise and virtuous man wins a gold star in the eyes of the community and of God by exercising a degree of forbearance in a conflict and by accepting the injustice he has suffered. Anyone who disturbed social tranquillity by calling in a state court and trying to put a fellow-citizen publicly in the wrong was regarded as a disruptive, boorish, and uncultivated person who lacked the cardinal virtues of modesty and readiness to compromise.

For a long time after his death in 479 BC it seemed that the doctrines of CONFUCIUS must sink in the welter of political events. For two centuries the country was incessantly riven by armed conflict between rival territorial princes and the circumstances were such that the Confucian view of law could hardly thrive. Instead, the school of the so-called 'Legists' won the upper hand; they harried the Confucians badly, and adopted the opposite stance on all important questions. CONFUCIUS and his school believed that man was intrinsically good and could be brought by education and the example of his rulers to see the need for virtuous conduct, whereas the 'Legists' held that man was basically selfish, concerned only to advance his personal interests, and therefore had to be strictly disciplined by state legislation. While CONFUCIUS taught that the differences of status in a hierarchically ordered society should be seen as an expression of the higher harmony of the world and must therefore be scrupulously observed, the 'Legists' believed that all men were equal before the law and that the proper social behaviour which could not be induced by philosophical teaching should be inculcated through severe penal sanctions imposed by every form of state coercion regardless of the person involved. Finally in 221 BC the Ts'IN dynasty emerged victorious from the wars, and China for the first time in its history found itself under unified rule; it seemed that the ideas of the 'Legists' must also be victorious, for the Ts'IN Emperors, who set up a strong centralized administration, passed draconian laws, and imposed fearful burdens on the population, also pursued the followers of CONFUCIUS and burnt their writings. But the hated Ts'IN regime lasted only a short time: fighting broke out again and in 206 BC the imperial power passed to the HAN dynasty which ruled the country for more than four centuries. Under the HAN Emperors Confucianism became the ideology of the state; its teachings were propagated throughout the land by travelling disciples and Confucianism was recognized as the spiritual and philosophical basis of the Chinese state for the next two thousand years. Readings of the classics of Confucianism played a very important role in school education and a thorough knowledge of the writings of CONFUCIUS and his pupils was called for in the state examinations which every candidate for the mandarinate and for advancement within it had to pass. Furthermore, in the course of time, the imperial magistrates, highly educated and literate men who were sent into the provinces to perform administrative duties, spread the doctrines of Confucianism throughout the entire country.

One must not infer from the triumph of Confucianism that China abandoned the use of written law or that as a result of following the unwritten rules of 'li' social life was perfectly free from disruption. Confucian thinkers had to admit that under existing conditions state laws were needed for regulating human conduct, although they had much less value and merit than the 'li'. Even before the imperial unification of China there were codes, and under the Ts'IN and HAN dynasties there was an unbroken succession of them; the older codes are lost save for chapter headings or fragments, and the earliest code which has survived complete is a code of the T'ANG dynasty from about the seventh century AD. It is worth noticing that these codes deal almost exclusively with questions of criminal and administrative law, though often in a sophisticated manner; questions of family and succession law are mentioned only in connection with criminal law or administrative law, for example for taxation purposes, and the codes pay hardly any overt attention to the law of commerce and commodities. This reflects the Confucian doctrine which sees legislation as a necessary evil, only to be invoked where the state must impose a criminal sanction because the cosmic order has been very seriously disturbed, or where the organization of the state administration is in issue.

Even in the criminal law one finds the unmistakable influence of Confucianism; it finds expression, for example, in the careful gradation of the penalties for homicide and assault, not only in relation to the intention of the criminal and the external circumstances of the crime, but also in relation to the social position of the criminal and his victim. Thus the severity of the sentence depended very much on whether, for example, a father had injured his son, a husband his wife, or a master his slave, and equally it made a great difference if a wife had been maltreated by her husband or vice versa; if an older brother struck a younger, no penalty was imposed at all, but if a younger brother struck his elder, he might receive thirty months of hard labour and ninety strokes of the bamboo (for details, see BODDE/MORRIS (above p. 315) 29 f.).

Given that the great bulk of the legislation in ancient China appertained to criminal and administrative law and that the practice of law was mainly the practice of *criminal law*, how were conflicts of 'private law' decided? Here, in deference to the teachings of Confucianism, there developed a wide variety of forms of conflict-resolution outside the courts. For difficulties within the family the head of the family acted as conciliator, or else more remote relatives or even outsiders who were so respected because of their extreme age or high standing in the region or on other grounds that there was no 'loss of face' to either side in accepting the compromise they proposed. The standards applied by these conciliators in seeking a compromise came from the rules of behaviour of the 'li', the practices obtaining in the area, and also their own experience and knowledge of the world. If the first proposal for compromise was not accepted by the parties, discussions continued until finally the conciliator, whose prestige enabled him to bring considerable social and moral pressure to bear, succeeded in obtaining agreement. Similar procedures applied where the parties were not related to each other but belonged to the same kin-group or lived in the same village or were members of the same mercantile guild: here the oldest of the kin-group, the local mayor, other persons of the local élite, or the seniors of the guild were invited to act as conciliators. It was always open to the parties in these cases to take their way to the state courts which were held by imperial officials in the chief city of the province or region, but it was normal for parties to try the local conciliation procedures first, as indeed they had to if they were to avoid social censure; anyone who rejected a compromise proposed by a respected conciliator and brought the case before the officials would have to bear in mind that his behaviour would be castigated by the tight community of which he was a part. Furthermore, the procedures of the state courts were extremely prolonged and expensive, and the imperial magistrates had a reputation for being preoccupied, corrupt, and lazy (on this see COHEN, above p. 315).

Thus one can see that only a very small proportion of 'private law' disputes ever came before the state courts in imperial China. This was perfectly acceptable to the Chinese emperors and their governments, for it meant that most of these disputes were 'self-regulating' within the local communities on the basis of the traditional rules of behaviour which were dependent on status, that individuals stayed rooted in their narrow social context, and that the state administration was largely relieved of the duties of judicature and legislation in the field of Civil Law. Not until the end of the nineteenth century was there a gradual change. From about 1850 China had to enter many 'unequal treaties' with England, France, Germany, Russia, and Japan; these opened up Chinese ports and trading centres, granted extraterritoriality and a degree of separate jurisdiction to foreign nationals, and involved the cession or 'lease' of territories on the edge of the Chinese Empire. In 1899 indeed, the great powers, apparently in preparation for a grand annexation of the whole of China, entered a treaty which divided up the territory among them into 'spheres of interest'. The last MANCHU Emperors had to recognize that thorough internal reforms were needed if China was to be able to withstand competition from the European powers and avoid becoming the plaything of imperialist ambition. But this realization came too late. The Chinese Empire was powerless aboard, there were riots against foreigners, there were power struggles between reformists and conservatives, and the foreign debt was growing; this led to the abdication of the MANCHU dynasty in 1911, whereupon a Constitution was hastily drawn up and the Chinese state became a republic. The republican government of the following years was admittedly only a shadow government, since most of the country was in the power of mutually hostile generals and party leaders, and there was no time to think of the central reforms which were urgently needed. A degree of stability was first achieved in 1926/1928 when the Kuomintang party and their army under CHIANG KAI SHEK, schooled on the Russian pattern, succeeded in freeing China and bringing peace to the country for a few years. This period was used to codify the whole of private law; following the example of Japan and taking advantage of the Japanese experience, the codes were principally based on German and Swiss law (on this see BÜNGER and RUETE, above p. 315). In the 1930s the country was thrown into armed unrest once again. Japan annexed Manchuria in 1931 and attacked Central China four years later; at the same time there were communist uprisings throughout the country. The communist soldiers were forced to make the famous 'Long March' back to Northern China, but then the Soviet Union started to support the Chinese communists and sought to free China from the Japanese. With this Soviet help it only took a few years for the Chinese revolutionaries under MAO TSE-TUNG to clear the troops of the National Government from mainland China. When the People's Republic of China was established in 1949, one of the first acts of the new government was to abrogate all the legislation of the Kuomintang period as being 'reactionary' and 'Western in spirit'. But apart from the Marriage Law of 1950, there was nothing new to put in its place. Many starts were made in the liberal period of the 1950s but only recently, since the end of the 'Great

Proletarian Cultural Revolution' in 1976, has the work of codification been vigorously embarked upon. A Criminal Code came into force on 1 Jan. 1980, and work is far advanced on a Civil Code for China.

III

Like Korea and Indo-China, *Japan* came under the influence of the highly developed Chinese civilization at an early stage. Chinese writing came to Japan in about the fifth century AD and Buddhism in the following century. In the seventh and eighth centuries the rulers of Japan were great admirers of Chinese intellect; they were familiar with Chinese literature and art, they adopted Buddhism, and they reorganized their state on the Chinese pattern by instituting a hierarchy of salaried officials and making their own position one of individual omnipotence, rather like that of the Chinese Emperors. The earliest of the Japanese statutes which have come down to us are also very like those of the Chinese T'ANG dynasty.

The Mikados were not able to maintain their unlimited governmental power against the powerful territorial rulers for long. From about the twelfth century they were emperors only in name; the Mikado was hidden away from the people in his palace and real power was exercised in his name by the Crown Field Marshal of the day, the Shogun. As the powerful families in the country waged constant war in an attempt to win the shogunate for themselves and to make it hereditary, Japan experienced hardly any extended period of internal peace until the late sixteenth century. The situation became stabilized only under the Shogunate of the TOKUGAWA family (1603–1867). At that time the country had a strongly feudal and stratified social structure: at the bottom of the social pecking-order were the craftsmen and the tradesmen, above them the farmers, who paid heavy taxes to lease their land from the feudal leaders, and above them, predominantly from the Samurai class, were the priests, doctors, and scholars, along with officials and soldiers of the princes; the Shogun was the feudal superior of all. The social philosophy best adapted to this stratified society was Confuciansim, which was dominant in the TOKUGAWA period in a variant suited to Japanese conditions. Although a comprehensive courts system developed in the course of time, disputes of 'private law' were mainly resolved, just as in China, by conciliation procedures in the relevant social groups (on this see in detail HENDERSON (above p. 315) vol. I).

It was the policy of the TOKUGAWA Shoguns to cut their Empire off as completely as possible from the outside world: no Japanese person might leave the land nor any stranger come to it. This did not apply to the Chinese, with whom trade relations continued, and the Dutch had permission, under extreme security precautions, to enter specified harbours for the purpose of trade. But gradually an interest in Western learning manifested itself. In the early eighteenth century there was a relaxation of the ban on the import of Western books, and Western technology played some part in the early development of industrialization, notably in iron production and ship-building. But the corresponding Western interest in trade with Japan grew very much more rapidly, and in the nineteenth century was so great that the isolation desired by the Shoguns could not be maintained for long. In 1853 the Americans gave dramatic expression to their wish for trade links by sending a fleet of warships to cruise off the Japanese coast, and this induced the Shogun to enter 'unequal treaties', first with the United States and then with England, Russia, and the Netherlands. These treaties gave foreigners the right to settle in specified cities, to indulge in trade, and to have consular representation. These policies of the Shogun evoked passionate opposition in Japan, based as much on xenophobia as on a growing desire to get rid of the Shogunate. The Emperor emerged from his retreat and placed himself at the head of the opposition; only a few years later the position of the Shogun was so weakened that in 1867 he had to withdraw and place full governmental power in the hands of the Emperor. The Emperor's advisers had meanwhile seen that the country needed to enter into close links with foreign nations and to learn from their superior technical and scientific knowledge. Even the conservative leaders soon accepted this view, and within a few decades the old feudal state had been changed into an absolute monarchy, admittedly retaining its patriarchal social structure. The army and the administration were moder-nized on the European model, the technology of the West was adopted, and finally, in 1889, a new Constitution was introduced, modelled on that of Prussia, which made Japan into a constitutional monarchy. All powers of decision remained with the Emperor, however; only the wealthiest citizens, about 2 per cent of the population, could vote in elections to the Lower House and only persons who were noble by birth or by imperial accolade could sit in the Upper House.

In the 'unequal treaties' Japan had had to agree that consular courts rather than the Japanese courts should have jurisdiction over foreign nationals in both private and criminal matters. In order to rid themselves of this discrimination, the Japanese were eager from the very beginning to alter their law on the European model. For this purpose they called Professor BOISSONADE from Paris and gave him the task of drafting a criminal code and a code of criminal procedure. After BOISSONADE had completed his task and seen his drafts, strongly orientated to French law, come into force in 1880, he turned to the preparation of a civil code. Concurrently Professor ROESLER, a German, was charged with drafting a commercial code. BOISSONADE's draft was largely based on the Code civil, save that family and succession law were drafted by a Japanese committee. Along with ROESLER's draft of a commercial code it was placed before the Japanese Parliament in 1890 and was due to come into force in 1893, but there was lively opposition to both drafts in

Parliament. Many members objected that the draft civil code was too biased in favour of French law and should have been drawn on a broader comparative basis; others thought that the time for such codification was not yet ripe and that in any case much more attention should have been paid to traditional Japanese legal institutions. The 'codification dispute' gradually broadened into a general conflict between conservatives and progressives and the end of the affair was a successful proposal to shelve both drafts. The preparation of the civil code was now given to a commission consisting of three Japanese professors. The draft produced by this committee in 1896/8 showed sporadic influences of French law and the Common Law here and there, but followed the two drafts of the German BGB in important points of structure and content. It was only in family law and the law of succession that the draftsmen adopted any number of Japanese institutions, notably the so-called 'family system'.

On this, see PLAGE, 'Der Hausverband im modernen japanischen Zivilrecht', *ZvglRW* 43 (1927) 13; TANIGUCHI, 'Über das heutige japanische Familiensystem', *RabelsZ* 10 (1936) 477.—It is hard to say why the pendulum finally swung so markedly in favour of German law during the preparation of the Japanese Civil Code. One important factor was certainly the fact that at the time the BGB rated as the most mature product of the Continental art of legislation; another was that several technical defects had already become apparent in the Code civil. Nor did the Japanese find the heavy learning and conceptualism of the German Code at all uncongenial; rather the reverse. As time was to show, Japanese legal scholars were much drawn to systematic theorizing, and the German code went far to answer this tendency. Perhaps an additional factor was that the BGB was a product of the German Empire, whose political stance must have seemed thoroughly appealing to the extremely conservative leaders of Japan at the time.

In 1898 the Japanese Civil Code came into force and in the following year the Commercial Code; both were squarely based on their German counterpart. The organization of the courts and procedure in civil matters were also regulated by statutes on the German pattern; indeed, large parts of the Japanese Code of Civil Procedure of 1890 are simply literal translations of the German one. It is therefore no surprise that thereafter the principal stimulus for Japanese scholarship in private law came from Germany; it has been said that towards the end of the First World War this influence was so great 'that one could find in Japanese law a true reflection of German legal scholarship' (KITAGAWA, *AcP* 166 (1966) 330).

After the Second World War the Common Law, especially North American law, had the strongest influence on Japanese law. American legal ideas underlie the new Japanese Constitution of 1946, which considerably strengthened the judiciary and contained a list of basic rights directly binding on the courts. Criminal procedure was reformed on the American model in 1948, and even the Code of Civil Procedure was altered on some points so as to curtail the judge's power to control the proceedings and to leave more room for the initiative of the parties and their counsel. The constitutional requirement of equal treatment of man and wife necessitated a fundamental reconstruction of the family and succession law in the Civil Code and the old Japanese 'family system' had to be abandoned. In order to democratize the economy, the American occupying force insisted on the enactment of a strong 'antimonopoly law', and a new company law was enacted as well as laws on the supervision of the stock market and the issuance of shares, all based on American models. Japanese legal scholars also adopted new methods as a result of contact with Anglo-American legal thought: there is now much less of the purely dogmatic approach of the pre-war period; instead, one finds Japanese legal scholars producing many more studies of the interaction of law and society and the practical operation of individual legal institutions.

Basic information on the development and present state of Japanese law can be found in *Law in Japan, The Legal Order in a Changing Society* (ed. von Mehren, 1963), a co-operative work in which Japanese authors with American advisers report on the modern constitutional, criminal, family, and economic law. In addition see KITA-GAWA, *Rezeption und Fortbildung des europäischen Zivilrechts in Japan* (1970), which gives a picture of Japanese legal history from the time of the MEIJI until the present day.

IV

This historical sketch of Japanese law must have caused many readers to ask themselves whether the numerous statutes imported into Japanese law between 1890 and 1900 really struck root, whether they became 'living law' and were implemented in practice in the same way as in their European countries of origin. Of course, Japanese society at the end of the MEIJI period was very different from the acquisitive bourgeois society of the end of the nineteenth century for which the codes were suited. In Western Europe it was the heyday of liberalism, of the idea that the responsible individual should be in a position to determine his own fate independently of traditional social and religious authority. So, too, in the economic sphere liberalism saw individual initiative and enterprise as the motors of progress and called on the legal order to afford the individual entrepreneur the requisite room for manoeuvre by guaranteeing freedom of contract and the freedom to deal with his property more or less as he chose. Such individualism was quite foreign to Japanese society. It is true that the modernization of the state administration was precipitate, the adoption of technical knowledge and skills from abroad swift, and the reception of foreign legal institutions massive, but all this did nothing to loosen the social bonds which tradition imposed on the individual by reason of his place in the family, kin-group, and village community, on the artisan and tradesman by his membership of the guild, or on the farmer by his relationship with the landowner. It is true that within a few decades thriving industries had grown up in Japan, but they did not owe their existence to the activity and risk-taking of individual competitive entrepreneurs. On the contrary, these industries were founded by the imperial administration in order to speed up economic development and were then transferred to the feudal lords of yesteryear, rather as compensation for the loss of political influence. Industrialization changed very little in the social structure of the country to begin with: capitalist privilege took the place of feudal privilege and the patriarchal *tai-kun* was replaced by the patriarchal tycoon.

Given these circumstances it is clear that until well into the twentieth century these imported statutes had very little practical effect on Japanese legal life. Even then very few citizens made use of the legal rights that the new laws put at their disposal because in all sections of society, but especially among the farmers, the distaste for bringing one's disputes into the open before state courts was still so strong, rooted as it was in the Confucian tradition. The traditional forms of peaceful conciliation and arbitration continued to predominate and the very fact that the written law and the procedures of the state courts were so largely unused may have contributed to the extreme devotion with which Japanese legal scholars until the Second World War followed the unrewarding art of dealing in pandectist conceptualism.

One might think that at the present day the traditional tendency to resolve disputes without resort to the courts must be beginning to weaken. Indeed there is some evidence for this. At the same time, the Western observer is surprised to find how tenaciously the Japanese cling to their old practices despite all the changes in the circumstances of life. Disputes between members of a family are still predominantly resolved by internal procedures, without invoking the courts. For example, before a marriage the families of the fiancés normally commission a middleman to help with all the questions connected with the wedding, to serve as best man, and especially to intervene as arbitrator and reconciliator in any difficulties which may subsequently arise between the spouses or between them and their families. For a divorce in Japan there is no need to go to court except in the rare cases where the parties cannot agree on it. If they do agree, the divorce is effective as soon as the parties have communicated their agreement to the registry office. As to the *consequences* of a divorce—the distribution of the property, maintenance, the custody of children—agreement is reached through the offices of the middlemen we have mentioned and of relatives and friends of the spouses; attorneys hardly ever figure. Disputes between neighbours or the parties to a lease are settled so far as possible by amicable arrangement. In the case of a traffic accident, the victims or their dependants, rather than go to court, often make their claims good with the help of experienced third parties, perhaps a retired policeman, or the personnel officer in the victim's firm, or a trade union official, or a respected businessman with relevant experience (see ROKUMOTO, above p. 316). Even where difficulties arise in the performance of contracts, the courts are regarded as the last resort. This is because in deciding the case the judge cannot take account of the many imponderables which give any contract its unique flavour, such as the importance, size, age, and reputation of the business involved, the length and nature of their mutual trade relations, the actual economic situation of the parties to the contract, and much else. Instead of this the judge must always apply abstract, impersonal, and schematic rules of law and usually he will have to give an all-or-nothing decision which will do right to one party at the price of doing wrong to the other. In the view of Japanese businessmen this is a crude, even a rude way of proceeding. It is much better to negotiate a compromise, for even if the compromise may not reflect the true legal position at least it does not disturb the harmony of the mutual relationship and it spares the parties the pain of winning a total victory or suffering a total defeat.

Even if it is not possible to reach agreement by negotiation or through conciliation by third party, polarized procedure before the state judge may still be avoided. Japanese law offers the parties a special statutorily regulated arbitral procedure. On the request of a party the court may set up an arbitral committee containing two or more laymen under a judge whose chairmanship is largely nominal. This arbitral committee issues invitations to all the parties to the dispute, listens to what they have to say and tries to move them towards a friendly agreement. If this fails, a complaint can still be raised by regular procedure; and, apart from a few matters in family law, there is no need to try the arbitral procedure at all before making a claim in court. In practice, however, arbitral proceedings are very important and the regular courts themselves often adjourn a legal dispute and refer the matter to the arbitral committee.

HENDERSON has established some statistics for 1959: over 40% of all the disputes which came before the Japanese courts were terminated by settlement before the arbitral committee, and over 20 per cent by settlement before the court; in a further 14 per cent of all cases the parties reported to the court that the dispute was over, doubtless usually as a result of a compromise reached outside the court, and in only 26 per cent of the cases was there a court decision on the merits. See the detailed picture, with interesting statistical material in HENDERSON (above p. 315) p. 919 ff. and KAWASHIMA, 'Dispute Resolution in Contemporary Japan', in: VON MEHREN, *Law in Japan* (above p. 315) 41 ff.; see also KITAGAWA, *Rezeption* (above p. 315) p. 154 ff. ROKUMOTO (above p. 316) has more up-to-date statistics and provides us with criticism of the arbitrarial process.

But it would be wrong to overemphasize the Japanese preference for resolving disputes uncontentiously. Many people familiar with Japan believe it to be a myth that the Japanese are reluctant to litigate. They do not deny that there is much less resort to the courts in Japan than in West Germany or other industrialized countries of the West, but they say that this is due not so much to the conditioning effect of Confucianism as to the somewhat duller explanation that the court system in Japan has long been under strain, that there are fewer judges and lawyers than elsewhere, and that a case may take many years to come to trial; that is why arbitration or other forms of dispute resolution are preferred to the courts. They also point out that some recent lawsuits in Japan, particularly in the area of environmental law and products liability, have involved thousands of plaintiffs, massive publicity, and a degree of passion and animus rarely found elsewhere. Full details are given by HALEY, 'The Myth of the Reluctant Litigant', *J. of Japanese Studies* 4 (1978) 359.

29

Islamic Law

AFCHAR, 'The Muslim Conception of Law', II *Int. Enc. Comp. L.* Ch. 1 (1975).
ANDERSON, *Law Reform in the Muslim World* (1976).
BADR, 'Islamic Law: Its Relation to other Legal Systems', 26 *Am. J. Comp. L.* 187 (1978).
CHARLES, *Le Droit musulman* (4th edn., 1972).
CHEHATA, *Études de droit musulman* (1971).
COULSON, 'Islamic Law', *An Introduction to Legal Systems* (ed. Derrett, 1968) 54.
——, *A History of Islamic Law* (1964).
——, *Conflicts and Tensions in Islamic Jurisprudence* (1969).
FYZEE, *Outlines of Muhammadan Law* (4th edition 1974).
HILL, 'Comparative and Historical Study of Modern Middle Eastern Law', 26 *Am. J. Comp. L.* 279 (1978).
KHOJA, *Elements of Islamic Jurisprudence* (1977).
LIEBESNY, *The Law of the Near and Middle East, Readings, Cases and Materials* (1975).
LINANT DE BELLEFONDS, *Traité de droit musulman comparé*, 3 vols. (1965–73).
RAMADAN, *Das islamische Recht, Theorie und Praxis* (1980).
SCHACHT, *The Legacy of Islam* (2nd edn., 1974).
——, *The Origins of Muhammadan Jurisprudence* (1950).
——, *An Introduction to Islamic Law* (1964).
WIEDENSOHLER, 'Grundbegriffe des islamischen Rechts', *RabelsZ* 35 (1971) 632.

I

THE Shariah, as Islamic law is called in Arabic, is the complex of divinely revealed rules which the faithful Muslim must observe if he seeks to perform the duties of religion. The crucial difference between Islamic and Western law is immediately apparent from this description. The unique ground of validity of Islamic law is that it is the manifested will of the Almighty: it does not depend on the authority of any earthly law-giver. The consequences of this difference are manifold.

One of these consequences is that Islamic law is in principle *immutable*, for it is the law revealed by God. Western legal systems generally recognize that the content of law alters as it is adapted to changing needs by the legislator, the judges, and all other social forces which have a part in the creation of law, but Islam starts from the proposition that all existing law comes from ALLAH who at a certain moment in history revealed it to man through his prophet MUHAMMAD. Thus Islamic legal theory cannot accept the historical approach of studying law as a function of the changing conditions of life in a particular society. On the contrary, the law of ALLAH was given to man once and for all: society must adapt itself to the law rather than generate laws of its own as a response to the constantly changing stimulus of the problems of life. Admittedly Islamic legal theory recognizes that the divine revelation did not start out in a comprehensible and orderly form and that it needed many centuries of work by Islamic jurists to extract the full content of the recognized sources of law and fit it for practical use. But according to the orthodox Islamic view these efforts were directed not to the creation of a *new* law but to the discovery, understanding, and formulation of a law which *already exists*.

Since Islamic law reflects the will of ALLAH rather than the will of a human lawmaker, it covers *all* areas of life and not simply those which are of interest to state or society. Thus Islamic law regulates the prayers a Muslim must make, the periods of fasting he must observe, the alms he must distribute, and the pilgrimages he must undertake. The observance of these precepts may not be enforced, but even so the shariah claims to be a comprehensive ethic or doctrine of duties (*fiqh*) which controls the entire earthly existence of Muslims and shows them the way in which they must perform their religious duties in order to earn the promised reward of bliss in a better world.

With its fundamental claim to regulate the totality of human behaviour, Islamic law is followed by as many as 500 million human beings, nearly a sixth of the entire population of the world. Although Islam is the most recent of the three monotheistic world religions, its propagation was immensely wide. MUHAMMAD died in 632, and barely a century later, when the Caliphs of the Ummayyad dynasty were in power, Islam had spread in the train of the Arabian hordes across the whole northern coast of Africa and deep into Spain; in the East it crossed Persia and reached the Indus. In the fifteenth century a second wave of conquest led by the Sultans of the Ottoman dynasty overthrew the Byzantine Empire, conquered Constantinople (1453) and established the dominance of Islam in South-Eastern Europe; Yugoslavia, Albania, and Bulgaria still have significant Muslim minorities. In *Asia*, too, Islam had great success; indeed after the Second World War the Muslims succeeded in establishing Pakistan as a state of their own; in the Republic of India about 10 per cent of the inhabitants, some 50 million people, are adherents of Islam. The non-Chinese population of Malaysia and Indonesia is predominantly Muslim. In *Africa* missionaries and tradesmen won the Nile Valley, the Sudan of today, for Islam, and it spread from there along the trade-routes of the Sahara to the West, so that not only Northern Nigeria but also most of the states in what was previously French West Africa (see above Ch. 8 V c) have populations which are mainly Muslim. On the East Coast of Africa as well Islam is fairly widespread; Somalia is almost entirely Islamic and Tanzania and Kenya have strong Islamic minorities.

II

The highest and most important source of Islamic law is the Koran, a collection, made a few years after his death, of the utterances of the prophet MUHAMMAD which are considered to be based on divine revelation. Only a few of the statements in the Koran constitute rules of law capable of direct application. It consists mainly of precepts of proper ethical behaviour too generally phrased to have the precision and point of legal rules. For example, the Koran prescribes that a Muslim must take pity on the weak and helpless, that in his business dealings he must act in good faith, that he must not bribe judges, and that he must abstain from usury and gambling, but it does not specify what legal consequences, if any, attach to a disregard of these commandments. Furthermore most of the rules of behaviour contained in the Koran concern the rituals of prayer, fasting, and pilgrimage; even where it deals with legal problems in the narrower sense, such as those of family law, it does not offer an integrated system of rules but simply gives the solution of a few individual problems with which MUHAMMAD was concerned as a judge and prophet of the law. In this role MUHAMMED always started from the customary law prevalent among the Arab peoples; he altered or added to it only where it seemed to him inadequate or unsatisfactory, or where it ran counter to his political goal of replacing the old Arab tribalism with a community of men bound together by belief in ALLAH.

For instance, MUHAMMAD found a rule in customary Arab law that only the male relatives of a decedent might succeed him; rather than replace this rule with another rule, he modified it by recognizing that the daughters, widows, and sisters of the deceased had certain rights of succession as well as his male relatives. This represented a move away from the traditional patriarchal organization of the tribe based on the blood group towards a new model of society in which the *family* formed the basic unit in a community bound together by belief in ALLAH. In another respect also MUHAMMAD improved the legal position of the wife. He softened the old rule that a husband could at any time unilaterally repudiate his wife without any restriction by holding that the husband could repudiate his wife only if he took equitable account of her needs and always made suitable provision for her maintenance thereafter. Whether this commandment is to be seen as a general ethical guide or as a legal duty with definite legal consequences is not a question to which the Koran offers any answer.

After the death of MUHAMMAD (632) the political leadership, which carried with it the position of supreme judge, passed to the Caliphs (literally 'representatives') of whom the first four were his disciples. In giving judgment, they and the judges they appointed mainly applied the existing customary law, having regard to any instructions the Koran might give. The greater part of the law remained 'indifferent to religion' and 'if this situation had continued there might have developed a law only sporadically influenced by the doctrines of religious duties but mainly based on practice, useful in practice, and applied in practice' (BERGSTRÄSSER, above p. 329, p. 12). The political rulers then became secularized and this provoked a reaction, especially among those who regarded themselves as guardians of the religious tradition. It was this reaction which finally brought all law into the field of the Islamic religion. After the death of the fourth Caliph, ALI, the son-in-law of MUHAMMAD, the great family of the UMMAYYADS from Mecca came to power; in the tradition of the old Arab princely leaders they saw themselves mainly as politicians and statesmen and used their seat of government in Damascus as a base from which to direct the world-wide operations of the Arabian armies.

One group of Muslims believes that the title of Imam is hereditary in the family of ALI and that only his successors can accede to the Imamate or leadership of the Islamic religious community. They therefore regard the first three Caliphs and the Ummayyads in particular as usurpers. This group is called the *Shi'a*, which means 'the party' (ALI's party). It is now split into several factions with different views about the line of ALI's succession. Their religious and legal practices differ in many respects from those of other Muslims, called the *Sunni*. About 8% of all Muslims today are Shi'a, most of whom live in Iran and in the Southern Republics of the Soviet Union, especially Turkestan, Kazakhstan, and Uzbekistan.

The Ummayyads were soon criticized for the secular style of their government. The critics were based in Medina where a group of pious scholars maintained that life in all its aspects must be subservient to the claims of religion and that all human behaviour must therefore be tested by the standard of the Islamic doctrine of duty. In examining the law in all areas to see whether it was consistent with the ethical mandates of MUHAMMAD, they had to discover what legal consequences flowed from the rules of the Koran; this was not easy since they were basically only general ethical and religious guidelines for the human behaviour which would be pleasing to the Almighty. It soon became clear that the Koran by itself would not do, so its shortcomings in this respect were made good from the sayings and doings which tradition attributed to the prophet himself or to his immediate disciples. There is no doubt that the Sunna, as this tradition is called, is very largely unhistorical and that it was invented by Islamic scholars more or less in good faith in order to lend support to their views. Islamic scholars today see the Sunna as being 'documents not of the time to which they claim to belong, but of the successive stages of doctrinal development during the first centuries of Islam' (SCHACHT, *Origins* (above p. 329) p. 4). However this may be, Islamic theory still holds the Sunna to be the second great source of law, after the Koran.

The *Abbasides* who took over the Caliphate in 750 gave strong support to the efforts of the pious legal scholars. They gave religious law greater influence in the state, recognized the authority of the leading legal scholars, and called many of them to high judicial office. Meanwhile several centres for the study of the divine revelation had grown up and were flourishing in the great Arab

Empire. In addition to Medina there was the city of Kufa in Iraq where a group of important legal scholars gradually formed a school of consistent legal doctrine. The legal school of Kufa is called the *Hanafi* shool, after ABU HANIFA, one of its earliest and most respected members, while the school of Medina is called the *Maliki* school, after the scholar MALIK. In the course of time serious disagreements arose between these schools of law. Individual scholars were originally allowed to make up their own mind on matters not foreclosed by the Koran and the Sunna, but the members of the different schools, which were geographically far apart, were influenced in their views by the style of life, the stage of development, and the legal practices of the surrounding population, so it was only natural that the schools should reach different views—a fact which was redeemed in Islam by reference to a saying attributed to MUHAMMAD: 'Differences of opinion in my community are a sign of the goodness of ALLAH'. Towards the end of the ninth century there arose two further law shools which are still vital: *Shafi'i*, so called after the famous scholar AS-SAFI'I, of whom we shall have to speak in a moment, and the *Hanbali* school, named after its founder IBN-HANBAL.

In the course of time these four schools of law established themselves in definite parts of the Islamic world: the Maliki in North, West and Central Africa, the Hanafi in the Near and Middle East and the Indus Valley, the Shafi'i in East Africa, Malaysia and Indonesia, and the Hanbali in Saudi Arabia. Each school of law recognized the legitimacy of the others; although the holy law is in principle unitary, the different versions are seen as divinely ordained.

Nevertheless the manifold differences of doctrine between individual scholars and schools led to some concern lest Islamic law disintegrate in a plethora of private opinions. In order to counter this risk AS-SAFI'I, a famous scholar who died in 820, produced a doctrine of the four 'roots' of Islamic law, which was to provide jurists with a fixed and common method of finding law. The first 'root' of Islamic law is naturally the *Koran*. The second 'root' is the *Sunna*, the sum total of the inspired practice of the prophet, so important for interpreting and clarifying the rules of the Koran. The third 'root' is the *igma*, the consensus reached by the entire Islamic community, laymen as well as lawyers, on any question of the doctrine of the duties of the faithful. The fourth and last 'root' is analogy (*qiyas*), that is, the application to new and similar cases of rules established by the Koran, the Sunna, or *igma*. Subsequent doctrine made only one change in this scheme, a change in the idea of *igma* which greatly increased its practical significance: a proposition was to be regarded as a rule of law if at any time the living *legal scholars* of all or even one of the schools of law agreed on it—a principle which perhaps has some historical connection with the Roman idea of *communis opinio prudentium*. It will be obvious that this classical system of the four 'roots' of Islamic law comprises very different things, namely two *sources*—the Koran and the

Sunna—*a method*—the use of analogy—and a *judgement*—that of *igma*; and it will be equally clear that among these roots the agreed judgment of scholars has the critical role, for it alone can finally decide, with or without the use of analogy, what valid rule of law can be taken from the Koran or the Sunna.

III

After the classical doctrine of the 'roots' of Islamic law had been embraced by all the schools of law, the legal creativity of Islamic jurists gradually began to dry up. Whereas the earlier practice had been to resolve doubtful questions in a relatively free manner while still adhering to the spirit of the Koran and the Sunna, this was now regarded as improper, and as more and more open questions were answered by the agreement of scholars, the solutions became part of the divine law and closed to critical investigation. From about the ninth century the view prevailed that it was not open to jurists to adopt an independent opinion founded directly on the Koran or Sunna; jurists were to confine themselves to the explanation and interpretation of books of law regarded as authoritative in the individual law schools. Thus Islamic legal scholarship gradually became quite rigid and dry, a fact which may have contributed to the subsequent development of certain areas of law outside the shariah and the religious courts.

It was still implicitly recognized that the Caliph, as head of government, was entitled to refer disputes in *constitutional* and *administrative* law to special judges with an indication of the rules they were to apply; *administrative crimes* and *disputes over land* were also reserved for special courts since for political reasons the law had to be effective in these areas and the traditional courts had methods of proof by witnesses and oaths which were extremely cumbrous. Thus despite its theoretical claim to control the *totality* of human life, the practical significance of the shariah was really limited to the area of *private law*.—The doctrinal immutability of religious law and the actual immobility of legal scholarship led the courts to accept a large number of *acts of evasion*. For example, loans at interest were rendered impermissible by the prohibition of usury in the Koran, so the device of the '*double sale*' was used instead: the borrower 'sold' some object or other to the lender, which the lender immediately 'sold back' to the borrower at a 'price' inflated by the agreed amount of interest and payable only after the period of the loan was up. Such 'legal tricks' (*hiyal*) made it possible for the courts to do what was required by the exigencies of practice while adhering to the doctrine in the rules of the shariah. (For more detail, see COULSON, *History* (above p. 329) 138 ff.; SCHACHT, *Introduction* (above p. 329) 78 ff.)

Until the beginning of the nineteenth century the social condition of the peoples of the Islamic world developed very slowly and the shariah remained quite appropriate to their needs despite its doctrinal rigidity. But from 1850 onwards it faced a decisive challenge. As the Ottoman Empire went into gradual decline there was an increase in the political influence of the great

European powers in the Near East, and the leaders of the Islamic world came to see, after contact with the outside world, that administration and law must be completely modernized if any stand were to be made against the political and economic competition of the European powers. Naturally, any proposals for reform in the state conflicted with the traditional Islamic doctrine that the holy law prescribed for it was immutable and immune to legislative intervention.

The reform legislation of the Ottoman rulers between 1840 and 1876 (see above Ch. 8 V a) was nevertheless carried through without very great resistance from conservative circles. The adoption of the Code de commerce and the French maritime law concerned areas in which conflict with traditional Islamic law could rarely arise. Then the Code of Commercial Procedure gave jurisdiction over disputes relating to property and obligations to a special secular court. This, too, was unobjectionable, since by Islamic tradition the state was entitled to prescribe the external conditions of life for the community of the faithful; this was the extent of its entitlement, but it included making regulations in constitutional and administrative law and also for the organization of the courts and their procedure. The Turkish rulers went a step further in passing the *Majalla* (1869–76), an enactment of about 1850 articles which attempted to consolidate the Islamic law of property and obligations according to the Hanafi school. This step was as necessary as it was novel: *necessary* because the secular courts which had just obtained jurisdiction over disputes concerning property and obligations could hardly study the medieval law books, and *novel* in that here for the first time the rules of the shariah were produced in the form of paragraphs in the European style and brought into force with the authority of the state (see TEDESCHI, 'Le Centenaire de la Mejelle', *Rev. int. dr. comp.* 21 (1969) 125). None of these reforms yet involved any state interference with the heartland of the shariah, that is, the law of family and the law of succession.

In regions which were directly controlled by the colonial powers the development was different. There too it was always recognized that the rules of the shariah should be applied in disputes between Muslims. But in *British India*, for example, cases were decided by judges who were British by birth or education and in the last resort by the judges of the Privy Council in London, so in the course of time Islamic law absorbed much of the Common Law, to a degree which makes it possible even to speak of 'Anglo-Muhammadan Law'. This is because wherever the judges found the rules of the shariah to be deficient, obscure, obsolete or inconsistent with 'justice, equity and good conscience', they had recourse, often quite unconsciously, to the principles and concepts of the Common Law with which they were more familiar. It is also because of British traditions that 'Anglo-Muhammadan Law' is treated as *case-law* in India and Pakistan today and accepts the principle of binding precedent. Furthermore, a whole series of statutes which substantially codify the Common Law of property and obligations were brought into forcing starting in 1872 (see above Ch. 18 IV) so that

'Anglo-Muhammadan Law' retains its significance today only for family law and the law of succession.—In *French Algeria* the religious courts kept their jurisdiction in matters of family and succession law but even there the influence of appeal courts staffed by French judges gradually modified the pure Islamic law of the Maliki school until it became a 'droit musulman algérien'. The situation was much the same in Morocco and Tunisia (on the whole question see COULSON, *History* (above p. 329) 163 ff.; SCHACHT, *Introduction* (above p. 329) 94 ff.).

As the world entered the twentieth century, government reforms began to reach even family law and the law of succession. In 1917, under one of the last Sultans, the Ottoman Law of Family Rights was enacted in which, instead of accepting all the rules of the Hanafi school which had authority in the Ottoman Empire, the legislator quite openly adopted some more progressive rules from the Hanbali and Maliki schools. Egypt and the Sudan, then an Anglo-Egyptian condominium, followed suit with similar statutes in the 1920s and 1930s, and after the Second World War laws regulating family and succession matters were enacted or proposed in nearly all Arab states. Jordan passed such a law in 1951, Syria in 1953, Tunisia in 1956, Morocco in 1958, and Iraq in 1959, and elsewhere drafting is in hand. These laws have several reforms in view: they seek to lay down conditions for the exercise of the husband's right to repudiate his wife unilaterally, to give *wives* a certain right to divorce their husband, to put limits to the way parents and guardians could arrange for the marriage of minors, and to diminish or abolish the practice of polygamy. None of the countries we have mentioned has found that these reforms required the abandonment of the shariah as the basis of family law and its replacement by something entirely new. Only Turkey found it necessary to take so drastic a step: the Swiss Civil Code which was introduced in 1926 made a radical break with traditional Islamic practices in family and succession law, and has had great difficulty in winning gradual recognition among the population at large (see above Ch. 15 III).

The decision in other Islamic countries to hold fast to the shariah as the basis of family law has also had its difficulties. For orthodox Muslims Islamic law, being based on divine revelation, was in principle unalterable and could not be substantially changed by the state legislature just because some reform might be thought necessary. In order to justify the new statutory solutions in the eyes of the public and especially the faithful, it had to be shown that each of the changes was in harmony with the principles of the shariah. One transparent device was to change the substantive law by means of adopting a *procedural* rule which was within the competence of the legislator. To begin with, for example, Egypt did not explicitly forbid the marriage of minors which the Koran permitted; it was simply enacted that courts could render decisions in matrimonial affairs only if the marriage was registered, and that a marriage could only be registered if the parties to it had reached a certain age. Another principle was of more importance in practice: this was that where the views of the Islamic law schools differed the legislator had the right to prescribe by formal law which view should be applied by the judges. Even in the Majalla the legislator did not always choose the *dominant* view within the Hanafi school, but sometimes preferred the view of a *minority*. The Ottoman Law of Family Rights of 1917 went a step further, for it sometimes adopted the view dominant in other law schools. Gradually it came to suffice as justification for a statutory rule if it could be based on a view ever expressed by any author in the whole of Islamic legal history. Sometimes a provision even took its major premiss from one author, its minor premiss from another, and the conclusion from a third. A modern view which is still greatly controverted goes the full extent of saying that a jurist may reach his own conclusion in the light of contemporary requirements without regard to the classical authors of the different schools if the conclusion can be based on the Koran and the Sunna.

An example may make this clearer: the Koran says that a man may take up to four wives, but that he should be able to maintain them all in a suitable manner. The dominant view in all four schools of law was always that the Koran was simply making a moral appeal to the conscience of the husband. In Syria the legislator in 1953 read the Koran differently, to the effect that the ability to look after two wives was a *precondition* of a second marriage. Syrian law accordingly lays down that a judge may refuse the necessary permission for a second marriage if the husband is in no position to make suitable provision for both wives. The legislator in Tunisia was bolder still. A verse of the Koran says that a husband must treat his several wives with complete impartiality: this was held to mean that marriage with a second wife cannot take place unless this impartiality on the part of the husband can be guaranteed in advance. But, said the reformers, complete impartiality is practically unattainable, things being what they are; therefore the Tunisian statute of 1956 simply and tersely lays down: 'Polygamy is forbidden.'—Further examples may be found in COULSON, *History* (above p. 329) 182 ff.

Recent developments in the Arab states have weakened the sharp division between commercial law and the law of obligations which have been codified mainly on the French model (see above p. 114) and the uncodified Islamic law applicable to the family and successions. Family and succession law are increasingly being codified now and many European legal ideas, dressed up with an Islamic pedigree, are being introduced, especially in the law of marriage. The time when European rules of contract, tort and commercial law were copied word for word is over: the Iraqi Civil Code of 1953 made valiant efforts to apply Islamic legal ideas in this area as well. The tendency for the difference between property and family law to break down is best seen in the fact that most of the Arab states are trying to abolish the dualism of secular and religious courts and to replace it with a unitary system of courts in which judges, salaried and educated by the state, will apply codified law to property and family disputes alike. Egypt consolidated the secular and religious courts

in 1955; Tunisia took the step in 1957 and other Arab states are preparing to
follow suit.

It would be an error to suppose that Islamic countries are tending towards a
complete 'Westernization' of their law. No country in the Islamic world today
is minded to emulate the radical solution adopted by Turkey. On the other
hand, the consequences that flow from the shariah as a divinely revealed law
are now difficult to accept. The classical scholars of Islamic law succeeded in
turning the Islamic doctrine of religious duties into a comprehensive system of
legal rules covering almost all aspects of human life. Although these legal rules
were created by the Islamic legal scholars and perfectly reflected their time, the
fact that they were all traced back to divine authority, even if by complex and
devious ways, supported the claim that they were all immutable, that they
required no endorsement by the state, and that they could not be abrogated by
earthly powers. In truth the legal scholars of the classical period were
themselves legislators and the most powerful legislators in the country; once
they had achieved a consensus among themselves they had an authority which
European legal scholarship never possessed even in its proudest days. This is
no longer acceptable for the Islamic states of today are nationalistic,
authoritarian, and committed to the progressive improvement of the common
good. This does not mean that they must abandon the idea of a law which rests
in the last analysis on the basis of religion, but it does mean that a new
compromise must be found between the basic and categorical demands of the
Islamic region and the need in a changing world for law which is capable of
change.

30

Hindu Law

DERRETT, 'Hindu Law: The Dharmasastra and the Anglo-Hindu Law—Scope for Further Comparative Study', *ZvglRW* 58 (1956) 199.
——, *Introduction to Modern Hindu Law* (1963).
——, 'Hindu Law', in: *An Introduction to Legal Systems* (ed. Derrett, 1968) 80.
——, *Religion, Law and the State in India* (1968).
——/IYER, 'The Hindu Conception of Law', II *Int. Enc. Comp. L.* Ch. 1 (1975) 107.
——/SONTHEIMER/SMITH, *Beiträge zum indischen Rechtsdenken* (1979).
JOLLY, *Recht und Sitte [der Hindus]* (1896); translated into English, *Hindu Law and Custom* (1928).
KANE, *History of Dharmaśāstra*, 5 vols. (1930–62).
——, *Hindu Customs and Modern Law* (1950).
LINGAT, *Les sources du droit dans le système traditional de l'Inde* (1967).
MAYNE, *Hindu Law and Usage* (11th edn., rev. Chandrasekhara Aiyar, 1951, reprinted 1953).
MULLA, *Principles of Hindu Law* (14th edn., rev. Desai, 1974).
PARAS DIVAN, *Modern Hindu Law, Codified and Uncodified* (2nd edn., 1974).
SARKAR, *Epochs in Hindu Legal History* (1958).
SEN-GUPTA, *Evolution of Ancient Indian Law* (1953).
SONTHEIMER, 'Recent Developments in Hindu Law', 13 *ICLQ* 32 (Supp. 1964).

HINDU law today applies to about 450 million Hindus. The vast majority, about 400 million, live in the Republic of India where they compose about 80% of the total population; most of the others live in minorities in Pakistan, Burma, Singapore, and Malaysia, and in countries on the East Coast of Africa, principally Tanzania, Uganda, and Kenya. It will be seen from this that the applicability of Hindu law does not depend on a person's being a national of a particular state or a domiciliary of a particular region: Hindu law applies regardless of nationality or domicile to all persons who are *Hindus*, that is, who accept the complex mass of religious, philosophical, and social ideas compendiously referred to as Hinduism. For practical purposes one may say that Hindu law applies to all people racially derived from the population of India except adherents of the Islamic, Christian, Jewish, or Parsee religions.

Unlike other religions Hinduism does not require its members to accept particular religious doctrines about God, the soul, the creation, redemption, and so on. It is open to every Hindu to believe in one god or another, in many or none; furthermore, Hinduism embraces a great variety of cults and rituals.

Though it lacks a clearly defined theological doctrine. Hinduism does offer certain basic convictions of a religious or philosophical order which are accepted one way or another by the majority of Hindus.

In the course of time several religious creeds have developed out of this common fund of convictions, such as Buddhism or the religions of the Jains and the Sikhs; these may be regarded either as independent religions or as sects of Hinduism, but modern Indian legislation makes the rules of Hindu law apply to Buddhists and Sikhs and other devotees of these creeds.

Among the fundamental tenets of Hinduism the most important are the doctrines of the migration of souls and of *Kharma*. According to this, all the deeds, good and bad, which an individual commits on earth form the germ of his next existence, whose quality is determined by the moral balance, plus or minus, of the life just passed. If a person suffers greatly in his present life or finds himself very low in society, he is atoning for sins committed by his soul in earlier embodiments, while a person who devotes himself to the holy life and behaves with striking virtue and piety may entertain the hope that he may be born again under more propitious circumstances, perhaps as a member of a higher caste, or that his soul may even be released from the eternal circle of death and rebirth and become part of the divine nature as a higher spritual being. This doctrine is the basis, indeed the justification, for the caste structure of Hindu society which is intrinsic to Hinduism as a religious, philosophical, and social system. A caste is a group of persons, normally in specific occupations or groups of occupations, who subscribe to a corpus of rules which regulate their behaviour towards each other and, more important, towards members of other castes. There are several thousand castes and sub-castes in the Hindu population, traditionally divided into four large groups; the *Brahmins* (originally the priests), the *Kshatriyas* (warriors), the *Vaishyas* (tradesmen), and the *Sudras* (servants and artisans). There is no way of moving from one caste to another; in particular, one cannot move upwards by dint of professional success, wealth, or political power. The castes stand in a hierarchical order, sustained by the idea that each caste has a certain 'purity' which must not be sullied by contact with certain objects, much less by contact with members of lower castes. There are therefore many rules which prohibit marriage, sexual relations, and eating with members of lower castes of lesser purity, or even being in their vicinity.

These rules of behaviour were not just mere conventions, for their infraction often had specific legal consequences recognized by the courts. Thus the Indian Courts had an intricate set of rules to determine under what circumstances a 'mixed marriage' of members of different castes was valid and what the legal position of children of such 'mixed marriages' might be, until the Hindu Marriages Validity Act, 1949 provided that 'no marriage between Hindus shall be deemed to be invalid or ever to have been invalid by reason only of the fact that the parties thereto belonged to different religions, caste, sub-castes or sects'.

In pursuance of a mandate contained in the Indian Constitution, legislation in India has now abrogated all the rules which attached a legal consequence to membership of a caste, but many Hindus still conduct themselves in accordance with the traditional rules of behaviour. It is still very rare for Hindus of different castes to marry, especially when the bride belongs to a higher caste than her groom; nor is it very common, at least among the members of the higher castes, for a widow to remarry, although in 1856 the old rule of Hindu law which rendered such a marriage invalid and the children it produced illegitimate was abolished by statute. Certainly there are signs that in many areas of life the influence of the old traditions is weakening. The whole caste system is caught up today in the process of fundamental change in a country with a modern political structure, promoted by general and equal suffrage, the gradually increasing mobility of occupation among Indians, the influence of the mass media, and the growing contact with Western culture.

II

It is often said that the Hindu legal system is the oldest in the world, but this requires some qualification. It is true that the *Veda*, that congeries of Indian religious songs, prayers, hymns, and sayings produced at various times during the second millennium BC or even earlier, contains the earliest texts in which, with some difficulty, rules for human conduct may be descried, but although the Hindus regard the Veda as a divine revelation and as the source of their religion and law, its practical influence on the spiritual life of the Hindu population has been very slight for many centuries; it cannot be said that the Veda has had much impact on the development of Hindu law, especially as it contains very little material with a specific legal content.

The oldest writings in Hindu literature any part of which can be described as 'law-books' are the *smritis*, a Sanskrit word denoting the 'remembered' wisdom of the old priests and scholars. It is extremely difficult to date them as the precise chronological ordering of particular historical events does not accord with the Hindu belief in a world process with neither beginning nor end. Consequently one must rely on conjectures that the *smritis* were produced between 800 BC and 200 AD. The oldest of them consist of aphorisms about the magic and religious rituals that should attend the important events of life. While they reflect the religious practices in early Indian history, they contain almost no rules of juristic content. Next came the so-called *dharmasutras*. These are the first law-books which lay down in detail how members of the different castes should conduct themselves towards the gods, the king, the priests, their forebears, their relatives, their neighbours, and animals, but these rules—'dharma' in Sanskrit—make no clear distinction between the mandates of religion, morals, custom, and law. The development of law took a further step forward with the *dharmasastras*: these are comprehensive collections of the rules of *dharma* in metrical form, ascribed to famous scholars. The best-known of these works in the *Manusmitri*, a collection from the second century BC, attributed to the legendary *Manu*. Here for the first time we find a relatively clear and orderly presentation of rules which today might form part of private and criminal law. The orthodox view is that all *smritis* rest on the writings of the holy Veda and it is assumed that the compilers of the *smritis* knew many texts of the holy Veda which have since disappeared. In fact, however, the *smritis* are based on the religious practices and social customs followed by the Hindus of the time. The reason why the *smritis* differ so much from each other is that, contrary to the view of orthodox doctrine, they were written at different times by writers who attempted to account for customs which had recently arisen.

In the following period, from about 200 BC until the arrival of the British, the most important legal works were collections, extracts and commentaries which made no claim to originality but simply sought to expound the *smritis* and adapt them to practical use. Many writers sifted through the old texts, extracted the passages which seemed most topical, and presented them in a comprehensible manner. In this way the *smritis* were 'modernized' and much obsolete material gradually disappeared. Other authors wrote commentaries on the *smritis* or on subject-matters treated in them, such as the law of succession or the law of adoption. Although the *smritis* were treated as binding, since the official doctrine was that they stemmed from the Veda, the commentators had considerable scope for interpretation of the texts which were often many centuries old, ambiguous, incomplete, and inconsistent. There was a special theory and complex art of interpretation but even so the end result naturally tended to be affected by the customs and practices prevalent in the circle surrounding the authors. In view of the great variety of geographical, climatic, and racial conditions in India it is not surprising that some writers had only a local following and so, rather as happened in Islamic legal scholarship, schools of law gradually emerged in the eleventh and twelth centuries, the Dayabaga school in Bengal and the Mitakshara school, with several offshoots, in the rest of India. Furthermore Hindu law has always recognized that customs long followed in a particular region or by a particular caste, clan or family, are to be regarded as a source of law. Such customs, if known to the court or proved before it, are taken into account in interpreting the rules laid down in the *smritis* and the commentaries and are even allowed to take precedence over them.

III

The classical Hindu law of the period before British colonization rested neither on formal laws laid down by secular rulers nor yet on court decisions; essentially it rested on the works of private scholars, on the *smritis* and the commentaries and collections associated with them. Formally linked to the divine revelation of the Veda, in substance these works were comprehensive and systematic portrayals of the customary law obtaining among Hindus, though doubtless the holy Indian lawyer–priests played a large part in determining which customs deserved legal recognition. This classical Hindu law—called '*dharmasastra*' in Sanskrit, that is, the doctrine of proper behaviour— changed a great deal during the period of British rule. In the area of *property and obligations law* the traditional rules were very soon replaced by the Common Law (see above pp. 234 ff.), but things were different in the area of *family law and the law of succession*: here the principle was that 'all suits regarding inheritance, marriage, caste and other usages or institutions' were to be determined in accordance with the rules of Hindu Law. Admittedly this was not an easy principle for the British judges to apply. At the outset very few works out of the enormous legal literature had been translated from Sanskrit into English, and the judges must often have been very puzzled by them since they did not really know anything of the conditions of life among the Hindus or of their oral legal traditions. At first pandits, that is, natives learned in the *dharmasastra,* were attached to the courts, and the British judges could seek information from them on particular questions. This institution was aban-doned in 1864; by then the judges had acquired some experience in dealing with Hindu law, the number of law-books in translation had increased, and, above all, there was a considerable case-law. The judges used prior decisions not only as a starting-point for argument but as binding authorities in accordance with the principle of 'stare decisis'. Although this was perfectly typical of the way English judges made law it was very far from the traditions of Hindu law which did not regard judicial decisions as binding at all; the judges not only could but should decide each case anew in relation to the relevant rules of law.

In content also, Hindu law during the period of British rule diverged considerably from the rules of *dharmasatra*. This was not so much the result of legislation, for the British used statutes only to abolish a few provisions of Hindu law which they found particularly repellent, such as the prohibition of a widow's remarriage and the rule that a Hindu forfeited all his property and rights of succession if he abandoned his religion or was excluded from his caste. It was *judicial decision* which had a much greater practical effect in modifying law, indeed, one could even say in corrupting it. The judges had at their disposition only a small part of the classical legal literature in English translation. This meant that they relied exclusively on such works, to the neglect of more recent or reliable writings. Furthermore the judges naturally found or thought they found many gaps or ambiguities in the traditional texts. Here they exercised a free judicial discretion, often with reference to 'justice, equity, and good conscience', and developed rules which, consciously or unconsciously, were influenced by the viewpoints of the Common Law or rested on 'general principles of law' which the judges found by making a comparative survey of the legal systems of the world. Thus classical Hindu jurisprudence was gradually ousted by 'Anglo-Hindu Law', as it was called; it soon stopped having direct recourse to traditional legal literature and was practised as pure case-law by the Indian courts.

During the struggle for independence a plan was mooted for complete codification of Hindu law, and soon after the achievement of independence in 1947 the Indian Government laid before Parliament the draft of a 'Hindu Code' which was to give a unified and statutory form to the whole of family law and the law of succession. The draft was strongly opposed by the archconservatives for whom any code was anathema and also by those who were unprepared to give up the special customary laws of their locality. Stormy debates in parliament and elsewhere forced the Indian government to withdraw the project. It then decided to produce separate drafts of the most important parts of Hindu law. This method succeeded. The first statute to come into force was the Hindu Marriage Act of 1955 which unified the marriage law of the Hindus and adapted it to modern thinking.

According to the traditional doctrine of the *dharmasastra*, marriage is a sacrament which inaugurates an unbreakable community between the spouses. Orthodox Hindus therefore regarded divorce as impermissible, though in many regions of India and among the lower castes custom often allowed it. Although the termination of marriage was prohibited in principle, the husband might take a second wife under certain circumstances, as when the first wife had neglected her matrimonial obligations; polygamy, however, was never much practised among the Hindus. For Hindus, marriage was primarily an affair for the *families* involved and so it was commonly arranged by the parents of the spouses, as it still often is today; according to the rules of the *dharmasastra*, the express assent of the spouses themselves was not required nor was there any minimum age for marriage. Hindu law also has a remarkable number of obstacles to marriage. We have already mentioned that marriage between members of different castes was ruled out but in addition there were detailed provisions which forbade marriage even between very distantly related parties; indeed it could be enough that the family names of the parties were similar. During the past 150 years these traditional rules have been much modified by court decision and by legislation. Admittedly the legal system does not forbid voluntary adherence to these rules and it is to be supposed that people still follow them today, especially in rural India. In this respect the Hindu Marriage Act may be in advance of social reality in curtailing the number of prohibited degrees and in abolishing the ban on marriage between members of different castes. The statute also permits divorce and forbids polygamy.

Three further statutes came into force in 1956, the Hindu Minority and Guardianship Act, the Hindu Succession Act, and the Hindu Adoptions and Maintenance Act; in consequence most of Hindu law is now codified. Indian judges and lawyers now go first to the provisions of the new statutes and to the judicial decisions which construe them. Only in the relatively unimportant areas for which there is no statutory regulation does Anglo-Hindu Law have any role to play in India. Outside India the work of codification has gone much less far and 'Anglo-Hindu Law' applies as it did before; but even there practising lawyers today look mainly to the judgments of the courts and only very rarely to the classical legal literature of the *dharmasastra*.

PART II

PART II

A. CONTRACT

I. THE FORMATION OF CONTRACTS

31

Juristic Act, Contract, and General Conditions of Business

ATIYAH, *The Rise and Fall of Freedom of Contract* (1979).

BERLIOZ, *Le Contrat d'adhésion* (2nd edn., 1976).

——, 'The Protection of the Consumer in French Law', 1985 *J. Bus. L.* 342.

BORRIE/DIAMOND, *The Consumer, Society and the Law* (4th edn., 1981).

BYDLINSKI, 'Die Grundlagen des Vertragsrechts im Meinungsstreit', *Basler jur. Mitt.* 1982, 1.

——, 'Die Kontrolle allgemeiner Geschäftsbedingunen nach dem österreichischen Konsumentenschutzgesetz', *Festschrift Meier-Hayoz* (1982) 65.

CALAIS-AULOY, *Droit de la consommation* (1980).

CARBONNIER, *Théorie des obligations* (1963).

CORNU, 'L'Évolution du droit des contrats en France', in: *Journées de la Société de législation comparée* 1979, 447.

DEUTCH, *Unfair Contracts, The Doctrine of Unconscionability* (1977).

FRIEDMANN, *Law in a Changing Society* (1959) 90 ff.

GORLA, 'The Theory of Object of Contract in Civil Law', 28 *Tul. L. Rev.* 442 (1954).

HAHLO, 'Unfair Contract Terms in Civil Law Systems', 70 *S. Afr. LJ* 70 (1981).

V. HIPPEL, *Verbraucherschutz* (2nd edn., 1979).

HERSBERGEN, 'Unconscionability: The Approach of the Louisiana Civil Code', 43 *La. L. Rev.* 1315 (1983).

HONDIUS, *Standaardvoorwaarden* (1978).

——, 'Unfair Contract Terms: New Control Systems', 26 *Am. J. Comp. L.* 525 (1978).

JACOBS, 'The Battle of the Forms: Standard Form Contracts in Comparative Perspective', 34 *ICLQ* 297 (1985).

KESSLER, 'Contracts of Adhesion, Some Thoughts About Freedom of Contract', 43 *Colum. L. Rev.* 629 (1943).

——, 'Freiheit und Zwang im nordamerikanischen Vertragsrecht', *Festschrift für Martin Wolff* (1952) 67.

KRAMER, *Die 'Krise' des liberalen Vertragsdenkens* (1974).

——, 'Vertragsrecht im Umbau', *ÖJZ* 1980, 233.

KREJCI/SCHILCHER/STEINIGER, *Konsumentenschutzgesetz, ABGB und Verfahrensrecht* (1978).

KREJCI (ed.), *Handbuch zum Konsumentenschutzgesetz* (1981).

LE CONTRÔLE DES CLAUSES ABUSIVES DANS L'INTÉRÊT DU CONSOMMATEUR DANS LES PAYS DE LA C. E. E., *Rev. int. dr. comp.* 34 (1982) 505–1113 with contributions by BOURGOIGNIE/DOMONT-NAERT, GOMARD, DE LAMBERTERIE/WALLAERT, VOULGARIS, PHILLIPS, BESSONE, HOFFMANN, STEENHOFF, RIEG, SALVAT/TALLON.

LETOWSKA, 'Die Problematik der allgemeinen Geschäftsbedingunen in der sozialistischen Rechtslehre', *JbfOstr* 17 (1976) 25.

LLEWELLYN, 'What Price Contract?, An Essay in Perspective', 40 *Yale LJ* 704 (1931).

VON MEHREN, 'A General View of Contract', VII *Int. Enc. Comp. L.* (Contracts in General) Ch. 1 pp. 64 ff.

MINOR, 'Consumer Protection in French Law', 33 *ICLQ* 108 (1984).

POUND, 'Promise or Bargain?', 33 *Tul. L. Rev.* 455 (1959).

PRAUSNITZ, *The Standardization of Commercial Contracts in English and Continental Law* (1937).

L. RAISER, 'Vertragsfunktion und Vertragsfreiheit', *Hundert Jahre deutsches Rechtsleben, Festschrift zum 100jährigen Bestehen des Deutschen Juristentages* I (1960) 101.

——, *Das Recht der Allgemeinen Geschäftsbedingungen* (1935).

RAKOFF, 'Contracts of Adhesion, An Essay in Reconstruction', 96 *Harv. L. Rev.* 1173 (1983).

REICH/MICKLITZ, *Verbraucherschutzrecht in der Bundesrepublik Deutschland* (1980).

RICHTERLICHE KONTROLLE VON ALLGEMEINEN GESCHÄFTSBEDINGUNGEN, *Arbeiten zur Rechtsvergleichung* no. 41 (1968) with contributions from HAUSS, NEUMAYER, WILSON, MARTIN, MERZ, LANDO, L. RAISER, and YADIN.

F. SCHMIDT, 'The German Abstract Approach to Law', 9 *Scand. Stud. L.* 133 (1965).

SINAY-CYTERMANN, 'La Commission des clauses abusives et le droit commun des obligations', *Rev. trim. dr. civ.* 84 (1985) 471.

TITZE, 'Rechtsgeschäft', V *Rechtsvergleichendes Handwörterbuch* (ed. Schlegelberger) (1936) 789.

VÉKÁS, 'Konsumentenschutz und das ungarische Zivilrecht', *ZfRV* 24 (1983) 17.

WILSON, 'Freedom of Contract and Adhesion Contracts', 14 *ICLQ* 172 (1965).

I

LAWYERS on the Continent, particularly in Germany, are familiar with the notion of *juristic act* (*Rechtsgeschäft*). This is one subcategory of the concept of *legal act* in the wider sense (*Rechtshandlung*), signifying any act of a legal person which has effects in private law; other subcategories in the sophisticated German system are *acts in fact* (*Realakte*), such as finding an old thing or making a new one, and *unlawful acts*. Now the critical difference between juristic acts and other legal acts is that the latter have their legal effect regardless of the actor's intention, while in the former the effect ensues precisely because the actor so intended: 'The law makes itself the instrument of his intention' (POLLOCK, *Jurisprudence* (6th edn., 1929) 145). It is because of a person's *declaration of intention (Willenserklärung)* that his juristic act has its legal effect, the declaration of intention being composed of the intention to do the act and the conduct which evinces that intention. As compared with declaration of intention, the notion of juristic act is the more comprehensive: all juristic acts necessarily contain a declaration of intention, but they may include other components as well. To give an instance, in German law the transfer of a moveable is a *juristic act* composed of the *declarations of intention* of both parties (*Einigung*—agreement) and the *act in fact* of delivery (§929 BGB).

All legal systems worth the name must recognize juristic acts as events which actually occur in life and so require some kind of regulation, but they can do this without grasping the concept of juristic act in its pure form. Thus many legal systems have rules, statutory or judicial, which regulate only the commonest type of juristic act, namely the contract, and take no account of the juristic act as a basic structure.

1. *German legal family.*—The expression 'Rechtsgeschäft' (juristic act) is quite recent. Roman law had no concept at all like it. Canons 103 and 104 of the Codex Iuris Canonici admittedly deal with the 'actus' and the effect that error, duress, and deceit may have on it, but 'actus' here means any act with legal significance, 'Rechtshandlung' in the wider sense. In Roman law itself, 'negotium' could mean either any piece of business (as in 'negotiorum gestio'), which is broader than the concept of juristic act, or just contract, which is narrower. The importance of the declaration of intention as the fundamental component of the juristic act escaped the Roman lawyers. The natural lawyers of the age of enlightenment used the concepts of 'actus juridicus' and 'declaratio voluntatis' which may be traced back to NETTELBLADT. Thus one can find a doctrine of the declaration of intention in the Prussian General Land Law, a natural law code, though it did not use the word *Rechtsgeschäft* whch was brought into German legal language by HUGO at the beginning of the nineteenth century. The juristic act became a leading topic in the General Parts of books on the *Gemeines Recht* (the Roman-based law applied in Germany before 1900) and remained so in the BGB and in modern doctrine, though the main question today is how the theory of the juristic act can accommodate modern phenomena like general conditions of business and those purely factual acts which have obligatory effects analogous to those of contracts.

The doctrine of the juristic act developed by the scholars of the *Gemeines Recht* has made many converts throughout the world. While the Saxon Civil code of 1865 had only a few provisions on the juristic act (§§88 ff.), it is in the BGB that the institution is dealt with most extensively. This part of the German Civil Code is still reckoned to be unsurpassed in its happy blend of clarity and compressed conceptualism but, like the BGB as a whole, it is more admired abroad than by scholars at home. French legal theory was enriched by SALEILLES's writings on the German doctrine of the juristic act and the Englishman MAITLAND is reported to have said: 'Never, I should think, has so much first-rate brain power been put into an act of legislation.'

See SALEILLES, *De la déclaration de volonté, Contribution à l'étude de l'acte juridique dans le Code civil allemand* (1929), and also ANDREAS B. SCHWARZ, 'Einflüsse deutscher Zivilistik im Auslande', *Symbolae friburgenses in honorem Ottonis Lenel* (1935) 425, reprinted in SCHWARZ, *Rechtsgeschichte und Gegenwart* (*Gesammelte Schriften*, 1960) 43. See also Ch. 12.

The BGB, being more abstract than other codes, deals with the formation of contract under the doctrine of the juristic act. In the systematic textbooks of the *Gemeines Recht*, contract always appeared at the head of the law of obligations, because the obligatory contract is the commonest form of agreement in the broader sense, but according to the theory of the BGB contract is a basic act of importance in the law of property, family law, and the law of succession as well. Accordingly, many rules of contract law, including those dealing with the formation of contract, are believed to form part of the doctrine of the juristic act and are therefore laid down in the General Part of the Code rather than in the Part dealing with obligations. Of the other Germanic codes, the *Austrian* ABGB has no doctrine of the juristic act (§§859 ff.), and even the *Swiss* Civil Code and Law of Obligations reject the sharp systematization of the BGB, to which they are in many respects superior, and place the essentials of the doctrine of the juristic act at the outset of the law of obligations under the heading 'The Formation [of Obligations] by Contract'. Such a deviation from a logically sound structure produced by doctrinal theory may well be justified in the interests of rendering a code more comprehensible. In fact, the theory of the juristic act in Switzerland is very like the German theory, owing mainly to the writings of ANDREAS V. TUHR on the General part of German private law and the Swiss Law of Obligations. The *Greek* Civil Code, despite all its modern qualities, clearly follows the German model in arts. 127 ff.

2. *The Romanistic Legal Family.*—The *French* Code civil—to take the parent system first—shows little sign of a doctrine of the juristic act; under POTHIER's influence the rules relating to it are unsystematically strewn about Book Three. Nevertheless French scholars in private law have maintained SALEILLES's interest in the German doctrine of the juristic act. Like the Code civil, French textbooks on private law have no General Part, but they do discuss 'principes généraux' before they proceed to the positive law, and the chapter on 'actes juridiques' includes the most important parts of the general doctrine of the juristic act.

In Italy SCIALOJA (*Negozi giuridici* (3rd edn., 1933)) and several others demonstrated the merits of the doctrine of the juristic act as developed in the *Gemeines Recht*, but in the new Codice civile of 1942 the rules relating to juristic acts were still placed in the law of contract: provisions regarding form, illegality and immorality, agency, construction, error, deceit, duress, and so on are therefore to be found in arts. 1321 ff. under the heading 'Contracts in General'. Nevertheless, art. 1324 povides that in principle all these rules should also be applied to 'unilateral acts inter vivos of economic significance' (*atti unilaterali tra vivi aventi contenuto patrimoniale*). The *Brazilian* Civil Code of 1916 generally follows the BGB, and its General Part contains nearly eighty articles on the doctrine of the juristic act (arts. 81–158).

3. *Common Law.*—Its case-law tradition has made the Anglo-Saxon legal family sceptical of theories and very resistant to the temptation to indulge in extreme abstraction. In consequence one hardly finds any theoretical treatment of juristic acts in general in the Common Law, though there are discussions of its most important embodiment, namely contract.

In books on jurisprudence, however, English and American authors are given to adopting Continental concepts. Thus SALMOND deals with juristic acts and distinguishes between those 'vestitive acts' which are 'voluntary' and those which are 'involuntary'; the *Realakte* of German doctrine he calls 'acts of the law', while *Rechtsgeshäfte* are called 'acts of the party' or 'acts in the law' (see *Jurisprudence* (10th edn., 1947) 345 ff.). So also when HOLLAND speaks of 'juristic act' he is referring to the *Rechtsgeschäft* of German doctrine (see *Jurisprudence* (13th edn., 1924) 117 ff.).

4. As a contribution to scholarship, the doctrine of the juristic act is less valuable than has been thought. There is only one element common to all the transactions brought under the concept of juristic act, and that is the 'declaration'. But the concept of juristic act is overstrained if it is made to cover those declarations which are linked with real acts (like the transfer of moveables in German law) as well as synallagmatic contracts, conveyances, acts affecting family status, unilateral declarations with constitutive effects, and much else besides. Furthermore, while the doctrine is of some use for systematic purposes, it is of no help in the most important task of law, which is to establish goals and ideals for the solution of social conflicts. Thoughtful criticisms of the doctrine have recently come from CARBONNIER and FOLKE SCHMIDT, and one must agree with them in large part. CARBONNIER emphasizes that contract law provides almost all the subject matter for the doctrine of the juristic act, 'tandis que les actes juridiques non contractuels sont tellement différents entre eux que leurs règles propres ne se prêtent pas à la généralisation' (above p. 347, p. 77). According to FOLKE SCHMIDT, the BGG is unduly conceptual except in family law and the law of succession, where it is more functional: 'The foreign student of German law will perhaps first ask whether all these distinctions between different levels of abstraction are truly necessary. Would it not be possible to arrange the material and describe the

relevant rules without resort to such a great number of specific concepts? Is it necessary to distinguish between juristic act (Rechtsgeschäft), declaration of intention (Willenserklärung) and contract (Vertrag) with the offer (Antrag) as a component of the contract? The Anglo-Amerian legal systems have a less intricate terminology; their palette has only two colours, the contact and the promise' (above p. 348, p. 148). For a functional method like comparative law, a concept such as 'juristic act' is not, in our view, a useful tool.

II

1. 'Juristic act', then, is an artificial concept of the *Gemeines Recht* which, whatever its expository and systematical value, is not very useful as a perceptual tool for the social ordering of private law. *'Contract'*, on the other hand, immediately strikes the observer as a natural institution of the law, an original device without which the law could not exist. To the extent that the world cannot survive without economic exchange contracts such as barter and sale this is and always has been quite true, but once German jurists with their passion for abstraction set to work on the concept of contract and extended it from the mutual credit transactions of the law of obligations to other phenomena such as conveyances and transfers, the events of family law such as affiancement and marriage, treating as a contract every 'agreement' which has any legal consequences whatever, the concept becomes etiolated, a thin and functionless form. Definitions such as SAVIGNY's, 'Contract is the union of two or more people in an agreed declaration of intention directed to altering their legal relations', miss the point much as if, for example, one were to say that the essence of marriage lay in the exchange of the words 'I will' before the registrar. The moment of agreement has some importance in the genesis of contracts, though even this is true only in those situations where consensus is the appropriate means of creating contracts, namely where scope is left for 'self-created' order between individuals in society: quite different methods of creation can be imagined and some, such as majority vote or decision of representatives, actually exist in situations where order is produced collectively rather than by individuals. To say that in these situations consensus is created by offer and acceptance seems to be pointless.

But if, instead of concentrating on the ways in which contracts may arise, one focuses on the functions they perform, one finds that the only contract with any real function is the contract of the law of obligations: conveyances or the contracts of family or succession law have very little left to do once they have come into being by agreement, for they only serve as the gateway to a new status such as ownership, marital status, marriage, and succession, whose contents are not 'self-created' or determined by what the contract says but are rather fixed in advance by the laws laid down for such institutions. This explains why in some systems the notion of 'contract' covers only the contract of the law of obligations; this is especially true of the Common Law, but French law also recognizes a distinction between 'contrat' and 'convention'.

The essence and function of the obligational contract has received much more thoughtful attention in the Common Law and in the Scandinavian systems (on which see JØRGENSEN, *Vertrag und Recht* (1968) 34 ff., 40) than in other legal families. For the Common Law the essence of contract lies not in the simple fact of agreement but in the 'promise' expressed by the parties in the contract. Thus the American Restatement (Second) of Contracts (1981) has the following definition in §1: 'A contract is a promise or a set of promises for the breach of which the law gives a remedy, or the performance of which the law in some way recognises as a duty.' ROSCOE POUND found in the Common Law seven theories which attempt to explain why contractual promises are enforceable: (1) a will-theory, that the legal order is implementing the promisor's intention to be bound; (2) a theory that genuine intentions must carry some external guarantee; (3) the theory that breach of promise is delictal in character; (4) the theory that promises are binding only if some counterprestation is provided (compare below Ch. 36); (5) the theory of the sanctity of promises: promises are enforced because they are intrinsically sacrosanct; (6) the theory that reliance on promises must have some legal backing; (7) the theory that promises are enforceable only if they are part of a 'bargain'. POUND himself clearly inclines to the sixth of these theories and rejects the 'moribund requirement of consideration'. Whatever the value of these different theories may be, one certainly comes closer to the essence and function of contract if one sees its legal enforceability as based on 'promise' rather than on 'agreement', as is the view in Continental systems.

Common lawyers used to discuss whether the true function of the law of contract is to satisfy the promisee's legitimate expectations of performance or to give him a guarantee against loss. This is not really an important question. The discussion simply reflects the peculiarity that in the Common Law the normal sanction against a party in breach is money damages, 'specific performance' being granted only exceptionally 'in equity' (see below Ch. 42).

Another point, however, is of real importance. If we survey the whole range of mutual promissory transactions, we find that two types predominate in number and importance: contracts to provide goods and contracts to provide services. In the form of sales contracts, employment contracts, and services contracts, they generate and accompany the economically vital transactions. Seen from the standpoint of economic and social policy, the individual contract is the basic economic–social act reflected in law. Thus, as LUDWIG RAISER saw, the function of the law of contract (as opposed to the formal legal mechanisms of 'formation') is 'contractual justice'. Contractual justice rather than contractual freedom is the material function and principle of contract law throughout the world today.

2. Some codes have tried to identify the component elements of a contract,

as opposed to the stages of formation by offer and acceptance. The French Code civil lists them in art. 1108 as *consentement, capacité, objet certain*, and *cause licite*, much as the new Italian Codice civile lists *accordo, causa, oggetto*, and *forma* in art. 1325.

On looking outside the Continental codes the comparatist discovers that only agreement and capacity are universal requirements. It is otiose to require an 'object', since people do not contract if there is nothing to contract about.

If 'object' is used to mean more than this, systems which require it, as the French Code civil does, are not only terminologically confusing, they are including under the notion of 'object of the contract' matters which are very disparate and diverse. Thus the following topics have been brought under the category of 'object of the contract': *res extra commercium*, forbidden performance, initial impossibility, legal impossibility, future goods, rights in a future succession, and others, and the brutal consequence of this is that the contract runs the risk of being nullified if the requirement of 'object' in art. 1108 of the Code civil is unsatisfied. In fact, reference to the rule that contracts must have an object is of no use at all in solving cases which raise the questions of these types, as is admirably shown by GORLA (above p. 347).

The other requirement is 'causa', a peculiarity of Continental codes and other attempts at systematization, and one of very doubtful value. The concept is unknown in England and the United States, where an informal contract is enforceable as an obligation only if it is a non-gratuitous promise backed by 'consideration', that is, performance or a promise of performance from the other party (see below Ch. 36). Apart from agreement and capacity then, the elements of contract as specified by the codes mentioned are difficult to grasp and not very rewarding.

3. For a long time, and during nineteenth-century liberalism in particular, the crux of the law of contract was to realize *private autonomy* and *freedom of contract*. The notion of private autonomy still has some validity today, in the sense that the expressed will of the parties serves as the impetus to the formation of contract and as the justification for its legal enforcement. One may, however, question the underlying assumption that if the parties have come to an agreement, that is enough and no investigation of the economic and social circumstances in which they did so is called for. One must note, furthermore, that in many legal systems this doctrine of private autonomy has led to consequenecs which are not commercially satisfactory, especially in cases involving error, since the ready granting of recission for error unjustifiably transfers the risk of error from the person who made the mistake to the person who relied on him. Nevertheless, if we leave aside the process of formation of a contract, private autonomy still represents a legitimate principle for giving contracts a legal basis and legal sanctions, within the limits of public order.

Private autonomy is often confused with freedom of contract, which is much more problematical. Can we really say that freedom of contract is, subject to exceptions, still a principle of contract law, or should we not admit that the principle has so far lost its validity that it is only in exceptional cases that it applies at all?

Freedom of contract has always had many meanings, even if we confine ourselves to obligational contracts. Given that the limits of public order are not overstepped—'limits which have moved ever closer to the centre with the development of ethical consciousness' (O. v. GIERKE, *Die soziale Aufgabe des Privatrechts* (reprinted 1943) 23)—freedom of contract means the freedom to select and enter contracts of any imaginable type, the freedom to decide whether to contract or not, and the freedom of each contractor to fix the terms of his own promise, subject to the agreement of the other party. The freedom to choose what type of contract to adopt is just a variation of the freedom to choose what the content and consequences of one's contract are to be, so in asking whether freedom of contract is still a vital principle today we can confine ourselves to the question whether parties still have a free choice *whether* to conclude a contract and *how*, or on what terms. Indeed, the 'whether' and 'how' of contracting often, perhaps even usually, coalesce into just one single question, since whether a person will contract at all commonly depends on the terms open to him.

Exponents of the principle of freedom of contrast urged that no rules of law, statutory or judge-made, should constrain its exercise. This was purely legalistic. What they did not realize was that this freedom was obstructed by social or economic facts. Indeed, the freedom to contract is best seen in the 'freedom to hire and fire'.

We now realize that true freedom of contract cannot exist unless the parties to the contract are economically and socially equal.

Judge PITNEY made this point brilliantly in *Coppage* v. *Kansas*, 236 US 1, 17 (1915): 'It is impossible to uphold the freedom of contract and the right of private property without at the same time recognising as legitimate those inequalities of fortune that are the necessary result of the exercise of those rights. . . . Indeed, a little reflection will show that whenever the right of private property and the right of free contract co-exist, each party, when contracting, is inevitably more or less influenced by the question whether he has much property or little or none: for the contract is made to the very end that each may gain something he needs or desires more urgently than that which he proposes to give in exchange.'

Thus true freedom of contract could only operate in a Utopia, in a society in which businesses were independent, economically equal, and fully automated, with neither labour nor management. If the parties are not socially and economically equal, only the stronger party is free to determine whether and how to form a contract. Since such a society of equals does not exist anywhere, even in socialist countries, and probably never will, since it is a dream, freedom of contract in its pure form is itself a chimera, a fantasy, and not in any way a reality. In the vast majority of the contracts which are concluded in modern society there is no freedom of contract, for the suppliers have fixed the conditions which the consumer can do nothing to alter. Freedom of contract exists only in contracts between large undertakings over atypical objects, and possibly in the area of labour law in the wage-scale contracts produced by modern collective bargaining. Legal scholars must give up the habit of proclaiming that freedom of contract is a *principle* and then listing the exceptions to it. The main task today is to discover criteria and procedures for the development of *contractual justice*, which the absence of freedom of contract makes it all the more necessary to promote.

The achievement of such contractual justice is no easy matter, and much further thought will have to be given to its answer. It may be necessary to consider protective procedures to redress inequalities which have become intolerable and produce new collective forms of contractual freedom; this is the present posture of modern collective labour law. But we are still a long way from a satisfactory solution of the contractual injustice which is often wrought by general conditions of business. It is true that in the last twenty years many countries have enacted legislation empowering their courts, and occasionally even administrative bodies, to scrutinize the fairness of contract terms under given circumstances (see below). It remains to be seen how effective these provisions will prove.

It is occasionally said that the development of private law from 'status' to 'contract' (HENRY MAINE) has shown signs in the last few years of going into reverse: instead of being formed by 'contract' freely reached, the legal relations between individuals are becoming more and more fixed as 'status'-relations. The truth is that contract, seen as a social institution, is being readjusted, so as to make it more just. The phenomena which are seen as examples of retrogression into 'status' are in fact instances of the degeneration of contract. Its regeneration is possible and has already started. It falls to us to advance it.

III

Standard terms in contracts, or *general conditions of business (Allgemeine Geschäftsbedingungen—AGB)*, are a byproduct of the industrial revolution of the nineteenth century. Just as the production of goods and services was standardized, so were the terms on which such goods and services were supplied. To standardize terms of contract in this way helps to rationalize big business: standard terms make it unnecessary to negotiate the provisions of each transaction separately, they may be fuller, clearer, and more suitable than the terms which would otherwise be implied by law, and finally they facilitate the conduct of transactions and the calculation of their effect. But rationalization of business is rarely the sole aim when standard terms are used. Firms also use them in order to shift to the other party as many as possible of the risks involved in the transaction. Typical clauses may exclude the firm's liability for non-performance or misperformance, or permit it to raise the price or supply substitute goods; conversely, they may prevent the *customer* from setting off debts due to him, withdrawing from the deal, or cancelling the contract, or they may impose penalties or liquidated damages in the event of delay on his part. If the proposed standard terms seem too one-sided, the customer can in theory go elsewhere, but the standard terms of other possible contractors will often prove to be just the same or very little better. Experience shows that whereas there may be competition so far as the price and quality of goods or services are concerned, competition hardly ever exists with regard to the terms on which they are supplied. Freedom of contract suggests that ideally the customer can dicker with the supplier in the hope of bettering the standard terms proposed, but the reality is different. Sometimes it is evident from the outset that negotiations will be futile because the firm is so big and rich that it need not budge. Often the customer lacks the necessary business experience or acumen. But even if the supplier were ready, and the customer were able, to dicker over the terms, such bargainng would often be unprofitable for the customer, for the time and effort needed to read the small print and formulate and discuss counterproposals would be out of all proportion to the likelihood that any of the risks put on him by the standard terms would actually arise.

Everyone has now come to realize that the law must protect the customer against standard terms of business which unfairly affect his rights and liabilities. The idea is not entirely new. It has long been recognized that in certain types of transaction one of the parties is normally much weaker than the other and therefore has to be protected: instalment sales, residential leases, contracts of employment, and insurance contracts are instances. Thus all legal systems have laws which more or less fix the terms of certain types of contract, by laying down mandatory provisions which oust deviant terms adverse to the customer, whether they are standard terms or *ad hoc* agreements. The German Instalment Sales Act, enacted as early as 1894, is such a law, and modern examples are the Swedish laws on Consumer Sales (1974), Consumer Credit Transactions (1977), and certain Consumer Insurance Contracts (1979). But only in the last twenty years have lawyers fully realized that protection against standard terms of business is a *general* problem which in principle affects all contracts, and it is mainly in the last decade that the various European countries have responded to the problem by passing legislation. The methods adopted vary tremendously.

1. *German Legal Family*. For a long time the only protection against unfair conditions of business in the Federal Republic of Germany, apart from the special statutes already mentioned, was afforded by the courts. They first

asked whether the standard terms in question had ever become part of the contract at all. This might be a matter of doubt where the terms of business were in print so small as to be barely legible, or where they were only brought to the customer's attention by an obscure reference on the back of a hat-check or by a notice displayed in the foyer of a bank. Here the judges were fairly tolerant. The Reichsgericht took the view that to contract on standard terms was hardly to make a 'genuine' contractual agreement at all, but rather, as the Court said in DR 1941, 1210, 'to submit to a legal regime already in existence'; and 'when a person voluntarily enters a legal regime it is hardly relevant what detailed knowledge of its contents he possessed'. Though the Bundes-gerichtshof has not spoken in such terms, it has not hesitated to treat standard terms of business as incorporated when they are in common use and a customer who was properly alert would have known of their existence and applicability (see, for example, BGHZ 32, 216, 219). The Bundesgerichtshof has, however, held that terms cannot be regarded as validly incorporated into a contract unless they are such that 'the customer could fairly and justly suppose that they might be included' (BGHZ 17, 1, 3): the agreement of the customer does not extend to 'unexpected' or 'unusual' clauses. But the best-tried method, used by the courts in countless cases, is that of *strict construction*. They first hold that the terms in dispute are unclear or ambiguous—and what document is not, when keenly scrutinized by a lawyer?—and then they resolve the uncertainties in favour of the customer, by invoking the rule that in case of doubt any restriction of liability is to be construed narrowly, or the rule that ambiguous clauses are to be construed *contra proferentem*, that is, against the party putting them forward.

But the real reason for the judges' going in for 'strict construction' or holding that 'surprise' clauses were not really agreed to was that they disapproved of the substance of the clause in question: they were exercising a 'covert' or 'camouflaged' control of the terms of the contract. But it is only when the courts' control becomes 'open' that the real question in these cases, namely, whether the term is acceptable in substance or not, can be properly addressed. The German courts have taken this step. At the outset the Reichsgericht would only do it where a firm was using a monopoly position to impose terms on the customer, that is, where 'firms with a virtual monopoly of an essential trade exploit the general need for their services in order to gain for themselves advantageous terms incompatble with law and in restraint of trade'. (RGZ 103, 82, 83). But economic superiority is not the only case where freedom of contract is abused by the imposition of standard terms of business: it also occurs where the draftsman 'deploys the intellectual superiority of the legal virtuoso' and trades on the customer's indifference and inexperience, as LUDWIG RAISER pointed out in 1935 in his pathbreaking book, *The Law of Standard Terms of Business* (*Das Recht der AGB*) (at p. 284). Judgments after the Second World War took up this idea, and since the middle 1950s the

Bundesgerichtshof has practised 'open control' of standard terms on a wide front. The courts quickly developed guidelines for testing the fairness of such terms, distinguishing different types of clause and different types of case. The judgments may invoke §242, the general clause of the BGB, but the invocation is mere ritual, since that paragraph simply says that contracts are to be performed in accordance with 'good faith' and therefore contains no concepts 'capable of subsumption'. What we have here is judge-made law of the purest kind, and in creating it the German courts have done a remarkable and praiseworthy job without parallel elsewhere.

In the 1970s it was generally agreed that the time had come for the legislature to act. Lawyers wanted a firm statutory basis for court decisions of such importance and increasing detail, and politicians were keen to have something to show in the way of consumer protection. A draft bill was rapidly produced. There was no doubt that it was a measure for consumer protection, for it subjected standard terms of business to control only when a non-merchant was party to the contract. This was severely criticized, especially on the cogent ground that almost all the transactions which had come before the Bundesgerichtshof had been transactions between merchants. The bill was therefore redrafted and came into force on 1 April 1977 as the Act for the Control of the Law of General Conditions of Business (AGBG). Contrary to the wish of those who felt that the matter should be dealt with in the BGB, the Act was passed as a separate statute outside the Code.

Many sections of the Act simply enact principles already laid down by the courts. These include the 'ambiguity rule' (§5), that is, the principle of 'customer-friendly' construction of ambiguous terms *contra proferentem*, the principle that an *ad hoc* agreement takes precedence over standard terms in case of conflict (§4), and the rule that 'surprise' clauses do not become part of the contract at all if they are so 'unusual that the other party could not be expected to suppose that they would be there' (§3). Nor is there anything new in §6, which says that when a standard term is invalid, the rest of the contract remains in force, the invalidated clause being replaced by the terms implied by the BGB or other legislation. The general clause in §9 gave the draftsman a good deal of trouble. Though it is longer than §242 BGB, all it does is add a few resonant but empty tropes. It says that standard terms are invalid when they 'unfairly' disadvantage the customer by modifying 'essential' rights or duties which arise from the 'nature of the contract' in such a manner 'as to imperil the achievement of the contractual purpose'.

Resort to the general clause of §9 is unnecessary if the standard terms in issue are of the kind specified in the compendious 'catalogue of terms' in §§10 and 11. Here the legislature, still guided by the valuable experience of the courts, could clarify and generalize some of the judge-made rules and include in the 'blacklist' some clauses which had not yet come before the courts.

We cannot here go through all the terms specified in §§10 and 11. The main thing the comparatist will want to know is the coverage of the Act as regards parties and subject-matter. As to the *subject-matter*, the law applies only to 'standard terms' as defined in §1, that is, 'contract terms which have been drafted beforehand for use in a number of transactions and which one party (the user) puts to the other when the contract is being formed'. It is a solution which has advantages and disadvantages. One of the disadvantages is that the dividing line between standard terms and *ad hoc* agreements can often be debatable. Take the case, for example, that the parties leave it to a notary to draw up the contract and he takes from a book of precedents an exculpatory clause which unfairly restricts the rights of one of the parties. In one such case the Bundesgerichtshof has held that the clause was a standard term (BGHZ 74, 210), a view which is hard to reconcile with the actual wording of §1, though it doubtless advances the AGBG's aim of protecting the consumer. Another disadvantage is that the law does not bite where the parties have 'negotiated' *ad hoc* agreements, although here too standard terms may be accepted because of an 'imbalance' in negotiating power and their substance may be very unfair. The *advantage* of the Act as drafted is that in most cases it is quite clear whether the Act applies or not, without having to go into the very difficult question whether one of the parties was greatly superior to the other in business acumen, legal experience, and bargaining power. To this extent the Act promotes legal certainty.

As to the *parties* covered, the Act applies whenever general terms of business have been used, even if both parties are merchants. Thus it is clear that the Act is not exclusively concerned with consumer protection. It is true that by §24 of the Act transactions between merchants are exempted from certain other provisions of the Act, including §§10 and 11, with their automatic invalidation of standard terms of the specified types, but the general clause of §9 remains applicable, and, in general, when merchants use a clause which falls within one of the prohibited categories of §§10 and 11, the courts have not hesitated to invoke §9 in order to hold it invalid.

Austria has adopted a quite distinctive solution. For a long time the only relevant provision was §879 ABGB, which rendered void any contract prohibited by law or in conflict with good morals, but a new 'general clause' has now been added (§879 par. 3), according to which collateral agreements contained in general conditions of business or contractual forms are also void if in view of all the circumstances of the case they are 'grossly' disadvantageous to one of the parties. Also inserted in the ABGB is a further provision that clauses in standard terms are not incorporated in a contract if their content is 'unusual', that is, where the party prejudiced by them 'could not, in all the circumstances of the case, especially in view of the ostensible nature of the document, reasonably expect them' (§864A). It was unnecessary to add an 'ambiguity' rule because this rule of construction, applicable to *all* contracts, was already present in §915 ABGB.

The two provisions we have mentioned seek to protect *all* those disadvantaged by standard terms which are substantially unfair or unusual. They apply even where the party prejudiced is a firm with experience in mercantile and legal affairs, though it may not be so easy to find that such a firm was 'grossly' prejudiced by, or surprised by, the 'unusualness' of the terms in issue. But special protection for consumers is provided by the new Consumer Protection Act, effective 1 July 1978, many of whose rules apply only to contracts between 'entrepreneurs' and 'consumers'. Under the definition in §1, an 'entrepreneur' is a person who is engaged in an independent economic activity and a 'consumer' is a person who is not. If a contract is made with a consumer by an entrepreneur in the course of the latter's business, any provisions of the contract which fall foul of the numerous rules which the statute lays down in order to protect the consumer are void. The statute invalidates exclusion clauses of all kinds, excessive penalties, and restrictions on the consumer's rights of recission, cancellation, and so on. In Austria, unlike Germany, even contractual terms 'specifically negotiated' with the consumer are also invalidated, but some clauses, listed in §6 par. 2 and regarded by the legislature as less objectionable, are invalidated only if they are contained in standard terms.

The concept of 'consumer transaction' may be adequate in the normal case to separate the sheep that need protection from the goats that do not, but as the Austrian legislature was well aware, some 'entrepreneurs' are much less powerful and experienced than the person with whom they are doing business and, conversely, some 'consumers' do not in the least need the protection of a Consumer Protection Act. According to the explanation accompanying the Act, the judge may protect the 'weaker' entrepreneur by treating the transaction as a consumer transaction although it falls outside the statutory definition, and may also treat a particular transaction as not being a 'consumer transaction' where the 'consumer' clearly does not need the statutory protection. This is all very well, but then why use the notion of 'consumer transaction' at all, especially as the general clause of §879 par. 2 ABGB applies in any case?

Switzerland is one of the few European countries with no statutory control of unfair conditions of business. The protection afforded by the courts, such as it is, is based on the common law, and is almost always 'covert' or 'camouflaged'. Thus there is a rule about 'unusual' clauses, that general conditions of business which the person disadvantaged had no reason to expect are not binding. For example, the Bundesgericht has held a clause to be 'unusual' if in the case of a person unfamiliar with business it provides for jurisdiction elsewhere than at his domicile; such a clause escapes invalidity only if it is contained in 'an explicit declaration clearly separated from the other provisions of the contract, unequivocal in content and clearly expressive of the intention to found jurisdiction elsewhere' (BGE 91 I 11, 14). The 'ambiguity rule' also does yeoman service. Yet the courts which could exercise genuine control over the actual terms of contracts by reference to the standards of good morals or public order or undue restraint of freedom are very reluctant to do so (compare art. 19 f. OR, 27 par. 2 ZGB; and see, for example, BGE 51 II 281 and 67 II 128).

In dealing with exclusion clauses the courts are on firmer ground: such clauses are always ineffectual against liability for intentional or grossly negligent fault (art. 100 par. 1 OR). This rule applies to all exclusion clauses, not just those contained in standard terms of business. With regard to control of standard terms, legal writers have urged the courts to be stricter (see, for example, BUCHER, *Schweizerisches Obligationenrecht* (1979) 130 ff. with references), but only a few people seem to think that the legislature should intervene.

2. *Romanistic legal family.*—The courts in *France* have no statutory mandate to police standard terms of business. They occasionally help by invoking the ambiguity rule, and they have sometimes refused to enforce standard terms of business so drafted as to be incomprehensible or illegible. Furthermore French courts invalidate exemption clauses under certain circumstances. No such clause, for example, can be invoked by a contractor guilty of intentional fault or gross negligence (*dol ou faute lourde équivalente au dol*), and since the rules of tort law are regarded in France as being *d'ordre public*, any attempt to exclude liability arising under arts. 1382 ff. Code civil is void. One principle of great practical importance has been established by the courts, namely that a commercial seller is to be treated as if he were aware of any defects in the goods he sells. Art. 1643 Code civil then makes it impossible to invoke a contractual exemption clause, so such a clause, whether in standard terms or a specific agreement, is void unless the buyer himself knew of the defect or is himself a merchant who deals in goods of that kind and therefore does not need protection (see Civ. 30 Oct. 1978, and Com. 6 Nov. 1978, JCP 1979. II. 19178, note GHESTIN). Furthermore, exemption clauses in contracts for the carriage of goods are invalidated by art. 103 Code de Commerce.

The rules we have so far mentioned are not specifically directed towards consumer protection since they apply to exemption clauses whether they are contained in standard terms of business or result from individual negotiations. Consumer protection is, however, the aim of many recent enactments which fix the terms of certain transactions entered into by consumers in such detail as to leave no room for deviant standard terms. Notable among such contracts are residential leases, consumer credit arrangements (the rules depending on whether the credit is for goods or land), correspondence courses, 'doorstep agreements' (distinguishing sales from credit arrangements), and purchases of dwellings or buildings already built or to be built. The details can be found in DE LAMBERTERIE/WALLAERT in *Le Contrôle des clauses abusives* (above p. 348) 701 ff.

The French legislature has also taken action against unfair contract terms (clauses abusives) regardless of the type of contract. It is action of a very distinctive kind. The Law of 10 January 1978 (no. 78-23) empowers the government to issue decrees prohibiting specified clauses in contracts between professionals and consumers in so far as they give the professional an unfair advantage and seem to have been imposed by him on the consumer 'by an abuse of economic power' (art. 35). The Law sets up a 'Commission des clauses abusives', whose 15 members include judges, civil servants, experts, and representatives of producers and consumers. The 'Commission' makes proposals for decrees to the government and may also give advice about suppressing or modifying certain 'clauses abusives'; such recommendations, however, are binding neither on the supplier nor on the courts.

This Act, it should be observed, does not of itself empower the courts to nullify unfair terms of business. The original draft of the measure did in fact grant the courts such power, but the proposal was withdrawn after opposition in Parliament. The courts can therefore invalidate as 'clauses abusives' only the clauses specified in a decree issued under the Act. Only one such decree has been issued so far (no. 78-464 of 24 March 1978). It strikes at clauses which purport to incorporate terms not contained in the document signed by the consumer, clauses which remove or restrict the purchaser's right to have defective goods repaired or replaced, and clauses which entitle the supplier to provide substitute goods or services. For the details see DE LAMBERTERIE/WALLAERT (above p. 348, p. 684), and CALAIS-AULOY (above p. 347, pp. 321 ff.). CALAIS-AULOY, himself a member of the 'Commission', would like to see the judges' powers strengthened, and regrets that the recommendations and proposals of the 'Commission' are ignored by suppliers and unimplemented by the government.

The special interest of the law in *Italy* is that the problem of standard terms of business has been specifically addressed by the Codice civile ever since it came into force in 1942 (arts. 1341 f., 1370). But progress has destroyed the advantage of modernity enjoyed by the Codice civile as compared with other European civil codes: the rules which seemed modern in 1942 are no longer adequate, largely because they permit only 'covert' and 'camouflaged' rather than 'open' control of standard terms. In art. 1370 we find the familiar rule of construction that in cases of doubt (so the article provides) clauses in standard terms of business or form contracts are to be construed in favour of the party on whom they are imposed. Art. 1342 provides that where there is a conflict between words added by the parties and the preformulated text, the former take precedence. The incorporation of standard terms into the contract is dealt within art. 1341. According to para. 1 of this article it is sufficient if the customer knew of the conditions of business at the time the contract was concluded, or should, as a normally careful person, have known of them. The requirements of para. 2 are somewhat stricter: here there is a list of 'dangerous' clauses which are valid only if they are 'specifically approved in writing' by the consumer. Included here are clauses which limit the liability of the supplier, clauses which entitle him to withdraw from the contract or to withhold further performance, clauses which limit the time within which the customer must assert his rights, clauses which limit his freedom to contract with others (for example, subsales at fixed prices), clauses which provide for a tacit prolongation or renewal of the contract, jurisdiction clauses, and arbitration clauses.

The practical application of art. 1341 par. 2 has caused a lot of problems, not so much on the question whether a clause is 'dangerous', for here the courts have interpreted the catalogue extensively and have applied art. 1341 para. 2 to clauses not specified but similar in effect, but rather because it can be very difficult to decide when a clause has been 'specifically approved in writing' by the customer. For example, suppose that a customer is handed a complete set of the standard terms of business for signature on the dotted line: must the 'dangerous' clauses be reproduced verbatim just above the dotted line, perhaps even in bold or larger print, or is it enough if they are referred to by number only? (See Cass. 29 May 1973, no. 1610, Foro pad. 1973 I 177; Cass. 5 Nov. 1974, no. 3355, Temi 1977, 151, and BESSONI in *Le Contrôle des clauses abusives* (above p. 348, pp. 827 ff.).) This is simply to make the solution depend on the typographical skills of the draftsman, for surely no customer will be deterred from signing a clause, or spurred on to press for its modification, just because it is printed in bold type? But rules like those of art. 1341 par. 2 are actually worse than useless, for they may lead us to believe that clauses signed by the customer have been really agreed to by him and that therefore they should not be subject to much, if any, control of their *content*. Indeed 'open' control of the terms of standard form contracts is not practised by the Italian courts. Writers have suggested that with a little goodwill the judges might justify a more stalwart control of standard term of business by reference to arts. 1175 and 1375, whch are comparable with §242 BGB, but these proposals have fallen on stony ground. Other writers have concluded that the time is ripe for intervention by the legislature.

3. *Common Law. English* law is sometimes said to be in thrall to the dogma of freedom of contract. Certainly some dicta of English judges are as uncompromising as one could wish:

'. . . if there is one thing which more than another public policy requires it is that men of full age and competent understanding shall have the utmost liberty of contracting, and that their contracts when entered into freely and voluntarily shall be held sacred' (*Printing and Numerical Registering Co.* v. *Sampson*, (1875) LR 19 Eq. 462, 465, per Sir George JESSEL).

But even in the nineteenth century unfair contract terms were quite often invalidated. For example, in the so-called 'ticket cases' the courts repeatedly refused to uphold exemption clauses which had not been brought to the attention of the passenger in the proper manner, whether because they were printed on the back of the rail ticket or merely figured in the 'Conditions of Carriage' available for consultation in the railway station. Again, a person who hires a deck-chair on the beach cannot be expected to suppose that on the back of the ticket he receives is a clause which takes away his right to damages for personal injury caused by the deck-chair's collapse (*Chapelton* v. *Barry*

UDC [1940] 1 KB 532). And the 'ambiguity' rule has long been a favourite tool of the English courts for drawing the teeth of unfair conditions of business.

The history of the matter has been narrated by LORD DENNING in his inimitable style (*George Mitchell* v. *Finney Lock Seeds*, [1983] QB 284, 296–7):

'None of you nowadays will remember the trouble we had—when I was called to the Bar—with exemption clauses. They were printed in small print on the back of tickets and order forms and invoices. They were contained in catalogues or timetables. They were held to be binding on any person who took them without objection. No one ever did object. He never read them or knew what was in them. No matter how unreasonable they were, he was bound. All this was done in the name of 'freedom of contract'. But the freedom was all on the side of the big concern which had the use of the printing press. No freedom for the little man who took the ticket or order form or invoice. The big concern said, "Take it or leave it." The little man had no option but to take it. The big concern could and did exempt itself from liability in its own interest without regard to the little man. It got away with it time after time. When the courts said to the big concern, "You must put it in clear words", the big concern had no hesitation in doing so. It knew well that the little man would never read the exemption clauses or understand them. . . . Faced with this abuse of power—by the strong against the weak—by the use of the small print of the conditions—the judges did what they could to put a curb upon it. They still had before them the idol, "freedom of contract". They still knelt down and worshipped it, but they concealed under their cloaks a secret weapon. They used it to stab the idol in the back. This weapon was called "the true construction of the contract". They used it with great skill and ingenuity. They used it so as to depart from the natural meaning of the words of the exemption clause and to put upon them a strained and unnatural construction. . . . In short, whenever the wide words—in their natural meaning—would give rise to an unreasonable result, the judges either rejected them as repugnant to the main purpose of the contract, or else cut them down to size in order to produce a reasonable result.'

Only after the Second World War does one find any move towards 'open' control of contract terms. Of particular interest here is the judge-made rule that an exemption clause was no defence to a claim based on a 'fundamental breach of contract'. The justification for this was that if a breach of contract was 'fundamental', the contract as a whole was to be regarded as at an end, with the result that the exemption clause also disappeared. Of course there were problems in distinguishing a 'fundamental' from a 'normal' breach of contract, and it was never quite clear whether the rule was simply a 'rule of construction', whereby in a case of doubt an exemption clause was to be construed as not covering a fundamental breach, or rather a 'rule of law' which invalidated an exemption clause *ipso iure* whenever there was a fundamental breach.

Leading cases include *Karsales (Harrow) Ltd.* v. *Wallis*, [1956] 1 WLR 936; *Suisse Atlantique Société d'Armement Maritime SA* v. *NV Rotterdamsche Kolen Centrale*, [1967] 1 AC 361; *Harbutts 'Plasticine' Ltd.* v. *Wayne Tank & Pump Co.*, [1970] 1 QB 447.

In 1980, however, in the important case of *Photo Production* v. *Securicor Transport*, [1980] AC 827, the House of Lords closed the door on the doctrine of 'fundamental breach of contract'.

The plaintiff's factory was totally destroyed by a fire which was started by a nightwatchman employed by the defendant security firm and which got out of control because of the inflammable material lying around. When the plaintiff claimed damages, the security firm rested its defence on a clause in the contract providing that 'under no circumstances' should it be liable for harm caused by its employees. The exemption was not to apply to harm which could have been avoided by the exercise of proper care on the part of the defendant itself, but it was agreed that the firm was not to blame as it had exercised proper care with regard to the employee in question. Nevertheless the Court of Appeal gave judgment for the plaintiff on the ground that to start a fire in an inflammable building was a 'fundamental breach' of the contract of a security firm, and that therefore the exemption clause was inapplicable. The House of Lords, however, reversed. The doctrine of 'fundamental breach' must be abandoned, and the agreement of the parties was to control, including the exemption clause which in the instant case, on its proper construction, covered the situation. In his speech LORD WILBERFORCE recognized that while the doctrine of fundamental breach had helped the courts to get round unfair exemption clauses, its application in practice had been problematical. In the meantime Parliament had enacted the Unfair Contract Terms Act 1977. This Act made it possible to nullify unfair exemption clauses, especially when they were deployed against consumers: 'After this Act, in commercial matters generally, when the parties are not of unequal bargaining power, and when the risks are normally borne by insurance, not only is the case for judicial intervention undemonstrated, but there is everything to be said, and this seems to have been Parliament's intention, for leaving the parties free to apportion the risks as they think fit and for respecting their decisions' (ibid. p. 843).

Indeed, Parliament in Britain has addressed the problem of unfair conditions of business in a whole series of statutes, such as the Consumer Credit Act 1974, which regulates credit arrangements with consumers, and, most important of all, the Unfair Contract Terms Act 1977, with its wide powers of control over clauses which purport to exclude or limit liability.

This very complex enactment is hard enough for the English lawyer, let alone the foreigner, to understand. 'It is certainly not a masterpiece of the draftsman's art' (CHESHIRE/FIFOOT p. 172). Now in England no one objects to the judges' using vague and indeterminate concepts and particularizing them as cases come up. But this applies only when those concepts are Common Law concepts created by the judges themselves. When it comes to legislation, the draftsman seems determined to leave the judges no room for play at all, and uses endless statutory definitions and other devices in his unsparing efforts to render his terms of art pedantically precise. (On this, see p. 275.) Despite its name the Act does not deal with all 'unfair contract terms', but only with those which seek to exclude or limit liability. In principle the Act applies only to 'business liability', that is, a liability which arises from some business or governmental activity, or from the possession of premises used for commercial or governmental purposes. Many provisions of the Act apply with full force only when the buyer contracted 'as a consumer', for example ss. 5–7, relating to the exclusion of the manufacturer's or seller's liability for physical or legal defects in goods. The Act is concerned mainly with contractual liability, but s. 2 applies to claims for damages in tort as well: liability in damages for *personal injury or death due to negligence* cannot be excluded or limited by any contractual clause or unilateral notice. An exemption clause which the defendant can establish to be 'reasonable' (s. 2(2), 11 (5)) may be valid in the case of *property damage* negligently caused. The test of 'reasonableness' is used in other provisions of the Act as well, in particular where the exemption clause is in a contract not made with a consumer. An exclusion of liability is 'reasonable' when it can be said that 'the term shall have been a fair and reasonable one to be included having regard to the circumstances which were, or ought reasonably to have been, known to or in the contemplation of the parties when the contract was made' (s. 11(1)). The circumstances which the judge is to take into account in determining the 'reasonableness' of an exemption are listed in 'Guidelines' in a Schedule to the Act.

The law in the *United States* is so complex that only a few basic points can be made here. Courts there, as elsewhere, will under certain circumstances deny that standard terms were incorporated in the contract, construe them *contra proferentem*, or disregard them if they conflict with a specific agreement (on this see §§203, 206, 211 Restatement of Contracts (Second), with extensive case-references). In addition, many enactments, mostly quite recent, lay down terms for certain kinds of contract typically entered into by consumers, such as sale, credit bargains, and so on. The courts do, however, have a general power of control in the principle that contractual clauses are void if they are contrary to public policy. On this basis the courts strike down clauses whereby 'common carriers' that is, carriers which offer their services to the public at large, try to immunize themselves from liability for faulty conduct, and they adopt a similar approach towards 'public utilities' such as telephone companies, radio and television stations, and health-care institutions, which in the United States are often privately run. Recently courts have held 'that a banking business is a public business, and like the common carrier, the banking institution is not allowed to exculpate itself from its own negligence' (CORBIN §1472 [Suppl. 1982]).

But the most important source of judicial control of contract terms is now to be found in §2–302 of the Uniform Commercial Code. This section permits the judge to invalidate a sales contract or individual terms in it if the contract or its terms are 'unconscionable'. This provision applies whether or not the terms in issue are standard ones, and whether or not the parties to the contract are both merchants: a sales contract made with a private individual is covered. The concept 'unconscionable' is nowhere defined. It is thus a general clause every bit as vague as §242 BGB. Being rather unfamiliar to American lawyers, it led to a flood of publications.

One particularly influential article was LEFF, 'Unconscionability in the Code, The Emperor's New Clause', 115 *U. Pa. L. Rev.* 485 (1967); see also EPSTEIN, 'Unconscionability: a Critical Reappraisal', 18 *JL & Econ.* 293 (1975); KORNHAUSER, 'Unconscionability and Standard Forms', 64 *Calif. L. Rev.* 1151 (1976); HILLMAN, 'Debunking Some Myths about Unconscionability: A New Framework for U.C.C. §2-302', 67 *Cornell L. Rev.* 1 (1981). The court decisions applying §2-302 UCC are well laid out in ANDERSON, *Uniform Commercial Code* (3rd edn., 1982).

The courts have taken to this provision with enthusiasm, using it in preference to the traditional Common Law methods of avoiding contracts— undue influence, duress, and misrepresentation (see below pp. 447–58); indeed the Comments to §2-302 suggest that its principal purpose was to replace the familiar techniques of 'concealed' control of terms. The section has been applied in hundreds of decisions; so popular is it, indeed, that although strictly speaking it applies only to contracts of sale, it is commonly applied to other types of contract which fall within the Uniform Commercial Code, and even to other contracts, on the basis that it is 'merely declaratory of a general pre-existing principle' and therefore applicable throughout the whole law of contract. That is the conclusion reached by the Restatement of Contracts (Second) (1981), for §208 says:

'If a contract or term thereof is unconscionable at the time the contract is made, a court may refuse to enforce the contract, or may enforce the remainder of the contract without the unconscionable term, or may so limit the application of any unconscionable term as to avoid any unconscionable result.'

4. This comparative survey shows that in their efforts to ensure contractual justice all legal systems have increasingly restricted the freedom of the parties to fix the terms of their contracts. It also shows what very different methods and combinations of methods have been adopted. Those who believe that injustice is particularly apt to occur when the terms of the contract are fixed by one party in his general conditions of business tend to check terms for fairness only where they are contained in such general conditions of business. This is the origin of those techniques of indirect control of standard terms whch are so widespread, such as construing ambiguous standard terms in a 'customer-friendly' manner, that is, *contra proferentem*, or imposing special requirements for their incorporation in the contract (express reference, sufficiency of notice, special written declaration by the customer, and so on). The greater protection against unfairness afforded by the legislator in Germany focuses specifically on standard terms: only standard terms are subject to the 'open' control provided by the Act of 1977, 'individual agreements', however unfair, remaining entirely unaffected.

The same viewpoint underlies some parts of the English Unfair Contract Terms Act: according to s. 3, a party who enters a contract 'on the other's written standard terms of business' is not bound by contract terms which 'unreasonably' limit or exclude that other's liability for breach of contract.

Another approach is to identify specific types of term and invalidate them regardless of their form. One example of this is the common rule that no clause can exempt a person from liability for intentional or grossly negligent conduct (for example see art. 100 par. 1 OR; art. 1229 par. 1 Codice civile, and the decisions of the courts in France). Again, §2-302 UCC renders contract terms invalid if they are 'unconscionable', regardless of whether these terms are standard or not, though in fact they usually are.

The general clause in §36 of the Swedish Contracts Act of 1976 is interesting in this connection. It empowers the judge to modify or invalidate a contract term if and to the extent that it appears to him to be 'unfair', and it applies whether or not the term is a standard one, and regardless of the status of the party prejudiced, whether consumer, farmer, artisan, or entrepreneur. On the other hand, the 'unfairness' of a contract term is to be tested in the light of all the existing and subsequent circumstances, so that the question whether the party prejudiced was in a position of relative weakness either as a consumer or for other reasons receives particular attention, as §36 makes clear. Thus while §36, unlike §9 of the German Act, is not confined to standard terms of business, its main purpose was surely to afford protection against such terms. A general clause in similar terms is to be found in §12 of the *Danish* Contracts Act.

Finally, the lawmaker may be concerned with *consumer protection*. Thus the Unfair Contract Terms Act makes the validity of certain exemption clauses turn on whether or not the party prejudiced 'deals as consumer'. To a large extent the Austrian Law of 1977 is also, as its name suggests, a 'consumer protection Act', and the same is true of the French Law of 1978 (no. 78-23) which strikes at 'clauses abusives', defined as one-sided and excessively advantageous clauses inserted by an entrepreneur into agreements with 'non-professionnels ou consommateurs'.

As to methods, the lawmaker also has a choice: he can issue a 'general clause' or he may list terms which are particularly unfair in a 'catalogue of prohibited clauses'. Again he can either fix the terms of specified types of contract, such as sales or credit bargains, or he may alternatively or additionally lay down *general* rules prohibiting specified clauses regardless of the type of contract in which they feature.

In countries whose private law is contained in a compendious code a further question arises: should these new provisions be built in to the civil code or should they be contained in separate laws? The question has both technical and ideological aspects. As to legal technique, inclusion in the civil code has the advantage of forcing the legislator to put in only what is essential and permanent, and to express his aims tersely in concepts with a well-established meaning. As against this it is said that the old-fashioned structure of the codes sometimes makes it hard to incorporate the new material, and that in any case a civil code is no place for the administrative, penal, and procedural provisions which the legislature may regard as essential for dealing with the problem. But much of the discussion has concentrated on the ideological aspects of the question. Some people swear by the 'unity of private law' and insist that the code which ensures such unity should duly absorb new developments and so be saved from social obsolescence. Others dismiss the 'unity of private law' as a nineteenth-century myth and want 'consumer law' to be laid out in separate statutes so as to emphasize the novelty and independence of this very dynamic area of private law with its main aim of advancing social policies and interests.

5. When a particular unfair term in a contract is invalidated, whether by statute or by judge-made law, the party whom it would otherwise prejudice is thereby enabled to sue his contractor or defend a claim brought by him. This is important, of course, but more is needed if we are to put an end to the abuse of unfair contract terms, and unfair standard terms in particular. After all, resort to the courts is often not a sensible or practicable step for the party in question to take, because in addition to the deterrent effect of the risk and trouble, the costs involved in a trial may be very much greater than any harm he would suffer by simply accepting the unfair contract term without a struggle. In addition, very little effect attaches to a court ruling *inter partes* that a clause is invalid: it does not reach other firms which use the same clause, and the very same firm can continue to use it in dealings with *other* customers in the hope that they will not resist it.

For these reasons many countries now offer, in addition to litigation between the individual parties to a contract, special 'abstract' proceedings for determining the validity of standard terms. Here, too, there is a wide variety of solutions.

Germany and *Austria* use the *Verbandsklage* or group action, which has proved useful in other areas of law. Specified groups, such as consumer associations, are given standing to seek an injunction in the ordinary courts to prevent the defendant from continuing to use standard terms void by law. Should an injunction issue, not only must the defendant desist from using those terms in future dealings with its customers, but he is also barred from invoking such clauses in contracts already formed and still on foot (BGH NJW 1981, 1511). Other firms which use similar terms are admittedly not bound by the judgment, but the judgments are reported in a public register and are generally published in the specialist press, so such firms know that they face the risk of an injunction (and costs as well).

The *Scandinavian countries* have adopted original and far-reaching solutions. Sweden led the field with an Act in 1971 which provides that an entrepreneur can be enjoined from continuing to use unfair contract terms in contracts with consumers. Such proceedings are brought not in the ordinary courts but in the 'market court', a special body with a general jurisdiction for matters of competition and consumer protection. Proceedings may be instituted only by the 'Consumer Ombudsman', head of a public body empowered to protect consumers not only against unfair conditions of business but also against misleading competition, dangerous products, and so on.

In practice it is rather rare for the Consumer Ombudsman to invoke the market court. He spends most of his time in negotiations with groups of producers, trying to secure that the terms of business they recommend are substantially fair. The Ombudsman can back up his suggestions by the threat of going to the market court, but that is a last resort and even where he does not prevail in the first round of talks, it may be sensible for him to come back to the issue after a while in the light of further experience and only if he then fails to get the contract terms modified, to seise the market court of the matter. Experience with this device has so far been very favourable in Sweden, whereas the Danes are apparently rather disappointed with their own very similar solution. On this see HONDIUS, 26 *Am. J. Comp. L.* 534 ff. (1978), and in general on the Swedish law, BERNITZ, 17 *Scand. Stud. L.* 13 (1973); 20 *Scand. Stud. L.* 13 (1976); 40 *RabelsZ* 593 (1976); and HELLNER and BERNITZ in *An Introduction to Swedish Law* (ed. STRÖMHOLM, 1981) 201–56 (with extensive references to the literature).

Great Britain also has a special authority, the Office of Fair Trading, set up by the Fair Trading Act 1973, which, *inter alia*, supervises the market behaviour of firms with regard to practices

'which may adversely affect the interests (whether they are economic interests or interests with respect to health, safety or other matters) of consumers' (s. 2)). The campaign against unfair terms of business is only one of the authority's functions. For example, it can invite the government to issue regulations to prohibit or require certain standard terms of business, and it can seek an injunction in court against a firm which is using standard terms contrary to law, be it criminal or private law.

One of the great successes of the Office of Fair Trading in recent years has been to get major groups of tradesmen to draw up voluntary codes of practice to be followed by those supplying certain goods and services to consumers (for example, automobiles, furniture, package holidays). These codes of practice admittedly apply only to the members of the association in question, some of whom may even prefer to leave the association and draw up their own terms of business, but even so, the utility of the code of practice is unquestioned (on this see BORRIE, 1978 *J. Bus. L.* 317; 1980 *J. Bus. L.* 315).

32

Contractual Capacity

BRUCKEN et al., 'Mental Illness and Contracts', 57 Mich. L. Rev. 102 (1959).
HETTESHEIMER, 'Die Fähigkeit Minderjähriger zu selbständigem, rechtgeschäftlichem Handeln, Eine rechtsvergleichende Darstellung', Dissertation Tübingen (1956).
GRAF LAMBSDORFF, 'Minderjährigkeit', V Rechtsvergleichendes Handwörterbuch (ed. Schlegelberger) (1936) 335.
HARTWIG, 'Infants' Contracts in English Law: With Commonwealth and European Comparisons', 15 ICLQ 780 (1966).
LAROCHE, 'La Condition juridique des malades mentaux', Gaz. Pal. 1968. Doctr. 12.
MONTANIER, 'Les Actes de la vie courante en matière d'incapacités', JCP 1982 D. 3076.
RAISON, Le Statut des mineurs et des majeurs protégés (3rd edn., 1979).
TREITEL, 'The Infants' Relief Act, 1874', 73 LQ Rev. 194 (1957).

I

ONLY if people have reached a certain minimum level of understanding and ability and are regarded by the law as having 'contractual capacity' can they bind themselves by contract. All legal systems have rules which deny contractual capacity to minors, lunatics, and incompetents under certain conditions. The function of these rules is basically protective: those whose mental powers are undeveloped or underdeveloped should be prevented from doing themselves an injury by their legal declarations and contracts. Obviously there must be exceptions, for to invalidate all his transactions would be an ill office to the minor one was seeking to protect, since then no one would be be ready to make a contract with him even if it were essential to his well-being or very advantageous for his estate.

The protective aim which underlies all rules relating to contractual capacity is valued so highly that it takes precedence over the needs of business. A person who deals with a minor is never safe simply because he believed the minor to have capacity, even if his belief that the minor was of age was perfectly reasonable. But all legal systems concur in answering the needs of commerce on one point: once a certain age has been reached, people are vested with contractual capacity regardless of their individual ability to look after their own affairs in a sensible way; it is on the question at what age this occurs that systems differ somewhat.

It used to be the rule that one reached the age of majority on one's twenty-first birthday; only the socialist countries set the age of majority at 18. But in the 1970s most of the countries of Continental Europe reduced the age of majority to 18, though in

Austria it is 19 (§21 ABGB) and in Switzerland 20 (art. 14 ZGB). Eighteen is also the age of majority in England and in almost all the states in the United States, but in Japan it is 20, and in Argentina, Brazil, and Chile 21.

While all countries fix a point at which complete contractual capacity begins, only Germany and Austria have a fixed age, namely seven, before which children have no contractual capacity at all. In other systems this depends on the circumstances of the individual case; they ask whether the child's capacity for judgment and comprehension is such as to enable him to understand the significance of what he was saying; if not, his declaration has no legal force.

It is mainly in the intervening period that problems arise, when the child is capable of understanding the consequences of his act but has not yet reached the age of majority. On this point all legal systems distinguish between contracts which juveniles can validly conclude on their own and other contracts which may be void *ab initio* or voidable or subject to reduction in favour of the minor.

Lunatics and incompetents raise much the same problem. People who have been interdicted on the ground of mental illness are incapable of contracting altogether, but the case of incompetents and drunkards is more delicate since it is impossible simply to annul or to uphold all their contractual declarations.

II

To go by the words of the Code civil, *French* law starts from the principle that minors' contracts are valid, since only where the law expressly invalidates a minor's obligation (as in art. 1123 Code civil) must his statutory representative contract in his place. In fact the courts start from the opposite principle that a minor's transactions are invalid, unless there is a special reason for holding otherwise.

Under the Code civil itself an adolescent may enter many of the transactions of family law without the consent of his statutory representative (marriage, marriage contracts, recognition of illegitimate children: for the details see MAZEAUD, *Leçons de droit civil* I(3) (6th edn., 1976) nos. 1251 ff.); in addition, the courts uphold 'actes conservatoires', measures taken by a minor which are necessary to ward off a danger to his property and which do not entail too great a financial burden.

Thus, for example, a minor may register a mortgage for the purpose of maintaining priority, he may put a debtor in default, he may interrupt prescription, and, to take a textbook example, he may make a contract with a builder to secure his house from collapse, provided that the price is low compared to the value of the building.

All other transactions by a minor are in principle invalid. To establish this invalidity, a court action is required (*action en rescision*), but it is not enough simply to prove that the complainant was a minor at the time the contract was concluded (as in Italian law, art. 1425 Codice civile). In addition the minor must prove that the transaction would cause him an economic disadvantage (*lésion*). This extremely important limitation used to be reflected in the maxim 'Minor non restituitur tamquam minor sed tamquam laesus', and nowadays it is based on arts. 1305 ff. Code civil. The practical effect is that a minor's transactions are binding unless they are disadvantageous. Where performance and counterperformance are objectively disproportionate such a disadvantage obviously exists, and it also exists where the estate of the minor is such that it would be unreasonable to proceed with the transaction even if what he has promised is reasonable in relation to what he is to receive. Under art. 1306 Code civil, however, a minor's transaction is not rendered disadvantageous by the mere fact that an accident ('un événement casuel et imprévu') has robbed him of the benefit he was to have received. If the transaction is to the minor's benefit, the other party is bound as well: see art. 1125 Code civil.

If the contract is one which the minor's statutory representative could only conclude on his behalf by observing special forms (such as the agreement of the family council or the approval of the authorities responsible for wards) it will be absolutely void, regardless of lesion, if concluded by the minor himself. This means that some quite important transactions, such as sales of landed property, cannot be concluded by a minor even if the terms are greatly to his advantage. Contrariwise, the transactions of daily life which juveniles normally enter are generally effective as they are seldom to his disadvantage.

In 1970 this idea of the courts was adopted by the Code civil. Under arts. 389–3 and 450 a minor's statutory representatives need not be involved in cases 'dans lesquels la loi ou l'usage autorise le mineur à agir lui-même'. Admittedly this applies only to transactions of daily life which pose no serious risk for the minor. Thus while a minor may *rent* a motor-car on fair terms by himself (Civ. 4 Nov. 1970, Bull. civ. 1970. I. 241), the intervention of his statutory representative is required if he wishes to *buy* one, even with funds at his free disposal (Civ. 9 May 1972, Bull. civ. 1972. I. 110).

A minor who attemps to rescind an unfavourable contract may be met with an *exceptio doli* if his contractor can prove that in negotiating the contract the minor used fraudulent manœuvres. A mere representation that he was of full age is not, however, enough (see also art. 1426 Codice civile), for if the rule were otherwise the adult could always protect himself against an action of rescission by asking the minor his age. The real reason for allowing the defence of fraud is that it constitutes a tort and the best way to make the minor liable is to hold him to his contract.

The picture is only complete if we ask what happens when a minor applies to rescind a contract which has been performed on both sides, especially when a minor who has consumed what he received demands the return of what he gave. This problem is dealt with in detail in Ch. 46 IV 3 below.

Mention must finally be made of *emancipation*, a striking institution of the law of minority in Romanistic systems, which only superficially resembles the emancipation of Roman law (compare arts. 476 ff. Code civil, arts. 390 ff. Codice civile).

Under the new French law of 14 December 1964, emancipation arises either from a formal declaration by the person with parental power over a minor at least 18 years old or by force of law when the minor marries. Its effect is to extinguish parental power and to clothe the minor with full contractual capacity. The emancipated minor may also enter into trading contracts if his statutory representative has given the special authorization required by art. 2 Code de Commerce (art. 487 Code civil).

The protection of *adults* suffering from some incapacity was reformed by the law of 3 January 1968. The previous device of taking away the capacity from the adult by judicial order (interdiction) and of charging a 'conseil judiciaire' with the task of acting on the person's behalf has been replaced by three new types of protection: protection by the court (*sauvegarde de justice*), tutorship (*tutelle*) and curatorship (*curatelle*). In the first of these cases the person's contractual capacity is in principle unrestricted, but lesionary transactions may be rescinded by the court or given only a limited effect. If a person needs constant representation in all the doings of daily life, a wardship may be set up on application or ex officio. The ward is basically incapable of contracting, but judicial decree may grant him the power to enter certain types of transaction on his own or with the support of his tutor. For a person who is capable of acting by himself but who needs protection or supervision, curatorship may be set up, even against his will. The person under care can enter quotidian transactions by himself but needs the consent of his curator for other matters (on this see LAROCHE, above p. 372).

III

Unlike Continental legal systems, the *Common Law* has no all-purpose legal representative (see below Ch. 39 III); equally, it does not have a general concept of the minor's incapacity to contract. Casuistical as always, it has been concerned to identify the types of case where a minor's contract must be invalidated for his own protection.

This is apparent in the doctrine of 'necessaries', the most interesting feature of the Anglo-American law of minority. For centuries the courts have held that despite his minority a juvenile must pay a reasonable price for 'necessaries' supplied to him. This is not a contractual liability but a liability in 'quasi-contract' which arises only when the minor receives the 'necessaries' delivered. In consequence it is not the agreed price but a reasonable sum which he must pay for the 'necessaries', though the reasonable price is usually the same as the normal commercial price.

According to the definition in the *English* Sale of Goods Act, 1979, s. 3, 'necessaries' are

'goods suitable to the condition in life of the minor . . . and to his actual requirements at the time of the sale and delivery'.

Thus food and clothes and medicines are classified as 'necessaries', whether they are for the minor himself or for his family. Also included are medical and similar services, education, and the hire of a car. The question ultimately turns on whether the judge in the individual case accepts that the minor really needed the objects in question and that the expenditure was reasonable in view of his income and style of life.

The *English* courts seem to have a more generous conception of 'necessaries' than the courts of the *United States*. For example, two diamond rings bought by a minister's son as engagement gifts were treated as 'necessaries' although they cost £80: *Elkington & Co.* v. *Amery*, [1936] 2 All ER 86. See also *Nash* v. *Inman,* [1908] 2 KB 1.—A great number of *American* decisions deal with the question whether *motor cars* are necessaries. Here again it is a question of fact: if the minor bought the car to drive to work in, and the distance involved and the absence of other means of transport made the purchase reasonable, he is bound to pay the normal trade price: see *Crocket Motor Co.* v. *Thomson*, 117 Ark. 495, 6 SW 2d 834 (1930); *Robertson* v. *King*, 225 Ark. 276, 280 SW 2d 402 (1955); *Braham & Co.* v. *Zittel*, 232 App. Div. 406, 250 NYS 44 (1931).—Contracts of employment, apprenticeship, and education are binding if they are shown to be advantageous and useful to the minor: see *Roberts* v. *Gray*, [1913] 1 KB 520; *Doyle* v. *White City Stadium, Ltd.*, [1935] 1 KB 110. See also *Chaplin* v. *Leslie Frewin (Publishers) Ltd.*, [1966] Ch. 71 (Charlie Chaplin's 19-year old son had, for a fee, licensed a publishing house to publish his autobiography, written with the aid of a ghost-writer and sharply critical of his parents: was the contract binding?)—Yet there is no general rule that *all* economically advantageous contracts are binding on the minor. Thus contracts in a minor's trade or business may be avoided even if they are advantageous. For *England* see *Cowern* v. *Nield*, [1912] 2 KB 419; *Mercantile Union Guarantee Corp.* v. *Ball*, [1937] 2 KB 498; in the *United States* more subtle distinctions are drawn; the cases are cited in WILLISTON §242 no. 15.

All other contracts, including contracts for the purchase of objects which cannot be classed as 'necessaries', are voidable. The *English* Infants' Relief Act, 1874, actually makes such contracts 'absolutely void', but it is agreed that this does not deprive them of all legal effect. On the contrary, the other party, if capable of contracting, is wholly bound by the contract although not suable for specific performance. A minor who wants to avoid a contract need not bring an action for this purpose: all he need do is simply inform the other party or rely on his infancy as a defence to any claim.

In English law, a minor who has bought and paid for goods other than 'necessaries' can only claim back the price he paid if there was a 'total failure of consideration', that is, if he obtained no part whatever of what he was promised. If he has used the objects in question at all he cannot claim his money back: *Valentini* v. *Canali*, (1889) 24 QBD 166; *Pearce* v. *Brain*, [1929] 2 KB 310; compare TREITEL, 73 *LQ Rev.* 202 ff. (1957) and ATIYAH, 74 *LQ Rev.* 101 ff. (1958). The notion underlying this rule is that it is inequitable to allow the minor to claim back what he has given if he cannot return what he has received. In the two cases just cited, the minor attempted to avoid the contract after using furniture and a motor car respectively for several months. The cases on this point are much more numerous in the *United States*, but not unanimous. In most jurisdictions the minor may claim back what he paid even if he has consumed or destroyed the goods he received. If the goods are still in his possession, though diminished in value by reason of his use, he may claim back the price if he returns the goods, and need not make any allowance for the diminution in their value. There is a contrary view, however, and it seems to be gaining ground. See WILLISTON §278 for further references, and below Ch. 46 IV 3.

In Common Law a minor is in principle liable for the harm he causes by his torts, but this principle is applied with great caution, especially in the *English* courts, when the tort was committed in connection with a contract. The minor's immunity for breach of contract should not be subverted by making him liable in tort: only where the tort is independent of contract should a minor be liable.

On occasion this leads to very fine distinctions: if a minor hires a horse and injures it while riding it he is not liable, but he will have to pay damages if he injures the horse while jumping it after being told that the horse is not for jumping: *Burnard* v. *Haggis*, 143 Eng. Rep. 360 (1863).—A fraudulent representation of majority cannot ground a claim in tort. The leading case is *Leslie* v. *Sheill*, [1914] 3 KB 607, where a minor obtained a loan of £400 after representing that he was of age. The lender's claim for his money back was rejected even in terms of tort law, although the rules of equity would have allowed him a restitutionary claim if the money borrowed by the infant had still been ascertainable in his hands: compare *Stocks* v. *Wilson*, [1913] 2 KB 235; and ATIYAH, 22 *Mod. L. Rev.* 273, 280 ff. (1959). This rule will be considered later (below Ch. 16 IV) along with the doctrine of disappearance of enrichment (*Wegfall der Bereicherung*) in Continental law.—The American courts are more inclined to allow a claim in tort when the minor has been fraudulent; see WILLISTON §§245 f. for further references.

Not long ago the English Law Commission proposed reforms in the law relating to infants (Law Com. no. 134). It had examined, but finally rejected, a radical suggestion which would have solved all the existing uncertainties at a stroke, namely that contracts of those under 16 would *never* be enforceable and those of persons over 16 would *always* be. Fears were expressed that such a rule would give inadequate protection to young persons of 16 and 17, so the Law Commission stood by the principle of 'qualified enforceability' despite the intrinsic difficulty of distinguishing contracts which are to be enforceable from those which are not. Nor could they bring themselves to propose a comprehensive 'Code for Minors' Contracts': the considerable effort of codifying even a part of the law of contract might be wasted, since Parliament might not adopt it (ibid. no. 3.4). The Commission therefore proposed only some minor amendments where the existing law was particularly unsatisfactory.

English law makes a distinction between contracts made by lunatics and those made by incompetents: if the mental affliction has been judicially ascertained, the contracts of the 'lunatic so found' are void; a 'lunatic not so found' can rescind his contracts on proof that at the time of contracting he was incapable of discernment and that the other party knew it. On the other hand, a person mentally ill is always liable to pay a reasonable sum for 'necessaries' delivered to him. In the *United States* most jurisdictions allow a person mentally ill to avoid the contract only if he is still in a position to return what he received from the other party. An exception is made if the other party knew or should have known of the affliction of his contractor or if, by reason of a judicial determination of the mental illness, the contract is void rather than voidable. Considerable differences exist between the several states on this point.

IV

In the *German* legal family a distinction is drawn between incapables and persons with limited capacity. Declarations of intention made by incapables are entirely without legal effect. Those who have limited capacity, that is, children of 7 and over in Germany and Austria and children in Switzerland who are 'capable of judgment', can indeed make declarations of will, but their contracts are 'provisionally invalid' (*schwebend unwirksam*) in the sense that the ratification of their legal representative is required to validate them. If no such ratification occurs the 'provisional invalidity' of the contract turns into permanent invalidity, equivalent to nullity.

If the parties to such an invalid contract have already performed their parts each is bound to return what he received, in accordance with the general principles of unjustified enrichment (see also art. 280, 411 ZGB). A minor who has received the price and spent it can defend himself on the ground that his enrichment has disappeared, on the basis of §818 par. 3 BGB (see below Ch. 16 IV 3b). §819 BGB does not stand in his way even if he knew that his minority made the contract invalid (RG JW 1917, 461; §1433 ABGB contains the same idea), but if he used the money for necessary purposes and thereby saved expenditure of his own funds he is bound to pay to the extent of his savings.

While the validity of the contract remains in doubt the other party can free himself from the contract provided he did not know of the minority (for the details see §109 BGB). In Swiss law, on the other hand, he remains bound by the contract unless he has allowed the legal representative a reasonable time to make his decision (art. 280, 410 ZGB).

In certain exceptional cases a minor is bound by a contract formed by his declaration of intention just like a person with unlimited capacity. This is so in German law when the contract 'procures only a legal advantage' to the minor (§107 BGB, and see also art. 19 ZGB, §865 ABGB), but the mere fact that its execution would have a beneficial effect on the minor's estate does not render a contract advantageous in this sense: the contract must not impose even the slightest obligation on the minor, however favourable the balance of advantage to him might be.

Since none of the contracts of the law of obligations, with the exception of promises of gifts to the minor, are legally advantageous in the sense of §107 BGB, this provision applies in practice only to conveyance contracts, though this has led to extremely fine distinctions; see STÜRNER, *AcP* 173 (1973) 402.—The views of *Swiss* writers are to much the same effect: see BUCHER, *Berner Kommentar zum schweizerischen Privaterecht* II 1 (3rd edn., 1976) Art. 19 n. 155 ff.

The *German* BGB has a 'pocket money paragraph' which provides that a minor's contract is valid if he can perform his part of it with means provided specially or generally by his legal representative or by some third party with the representative's consent. The principal instances which fall within this provision are cases where parents have given their minor child an allowance or the means of supporting himself away from home at school or college.

Austria has had a similar rule since 1973: if a minor enters a contract such as 'is normally entered by minors of his age and relates to a triviality of daily life', the contract is binding under §151 par. 3 ABGB as soon as the contractual duties affecting the minor are performed.

Under §§112, 113 BGB the minor may be given partial capacity to conclude employment contracts and contracts in the course of a business conducted by him; see also arts. 280, 412 ZGB, §§152, 246 ABGB.

The laws of *Germany*, *Switzerland*, and *Austria* are in general agreement in their treatment of the mentally ill. 'Lunatics, madmen, and fools' (§21 ABGB) or, as art. 16 ZGB puts it, persons who 'in consequence of mental illness, mental weakness, drunkenness, or similar circumstances lack the capacity to behave in a reasonable manner' are entirely without contractual capacity. Persons under interdict are also legally incapable but a person under interdiction who is still 'capable of judgment' and a person whose interdiction is 'limited' or based on grounds other than mental illness (see art. 19 ZGB, §114 BGB) is treated so far as business capacity is concerned in the same way as a minor with limited contractual capacity.

V

The three systems under review all start from the fundamental proposition that a minor, acting by himself, cannot bind himself by contract, but they differ considerably in the exceptions they make to this principle.

In the *Romanistic* systems a minor remains bound by his contracts until he brings a claim for rescission: in *French* law he must then prove that the execution of the contract would be disadvantageous to him, except in the cases—the most important transactions—where in addition to the agreement of his legal representative the ratification of the family council or the wardship authorities is required and lacking. In practice, therefore, minors are bound by all less important transactions, provided that they are economically advantageous.

In contrast, the *German* legal family hardly admits any exceptions to the principles that the contractual declarations of minors require ratification. The pocket money paragraph is not a true exception, for if the parents give the child an allowance they normally agree that he may conclude the contracts which such an allowance permits.

In comparison, the rules of *Swiss* and *Austrian* law seem very satisfactory in allowing the minor who lives away from home to have free disposition of his earned income and consequently granting him the capacity to bind himself to this extent. Since more and more juveniles are living independently on their earnings today it seems artificial to validate their contracts only on the fiction of parental ratification.

A minor is generally not bound by his contract in the *Common Law* either, but if he has had 'necessaries' supplied to him he must pay the going price. This Common Law rule has an affinity with the *French* rule, for much the same factors are taken into account by French judges asking whether the execution of a contract would involve a 'lésion' for the minor and by English judges asking whether the objects involved were 'necessaries'. Thus in both legal systems a minor can by his own acts bind himself contractually or at least 'quasi-contractually', given that in the particular circumstances of the case such an obligation is in reasonable relation to his interests.

The German legal family, however, takes no account of the minor's interests when testing the validity of his contracts. If the legal representative does not ratify the contract, it is invalid even if the obligations it contains for the minor are perfectly trivial and if the judge concludes that in all the circumstances the execution of the contract would be reasonable and proper for the minor. True though it is that this conduces to clarity and legal certainty, it not only restricts the independence of the juvenile more than his protection justifies but it also prejudices legal dealings by fobbing the contractor off with an enrichment claim where it would be only right and proper in the circumstances to make the minor contractually liable.

Only German law allows the other party to resile from a contract which the minor's legal representative has not ratified (§109 BGB). In both the Romanistic and Common Law systems the adult contractor is bound and even in Swiss law he can be freed only if the legal representative has remained silent during the period set for his decision. It is not at all clear why a person should be freed from a contract just because his declarations were made to a minor. He may, of course, want to be assured of the fate of the contract as soon as possible but it would be enough to allow him to set a reasonably short period for ratification, failing which the contract would finally become void as to both parties.

33

Offer and Acceptance

AUBERT, *Notion et rôle de l'offre et de l'acceptation dans la formation du contrat* (1970).

BRAUCHER, 'Offer and Acceptance in the Second Restatement', 74 *Yale LJ* 302 (1964).

v. CAEMMERER, 'Die Ergebnisse der Haager Kaufrechtskonferenz hinsichtlich der Vereinheitlichung des Rechts des Abschlusses von Kaufverträgen', *RabelsZ* 29 (1965) 101.

COHEN, *Des contrats par correspondance en droit français, en droit anglais et en droit anglo-américain* (1921).

DILGER, 'Das Zustandekommen von Kaufverträgen im Außenhandel nach internationalem Einheitsrecht und nationalem Sonderrecht', *RabelsZ* 45 (1981) 169.

FARNSWORTH, 'Formation of International Sales Contracts: Three Attempts at Unification', 110 *U. Pa. L. Rev.* 305 (1961–2).

GOLDSTAJN, 'Formation of Contract', in: *Unification of the Law Governing International Sales of Goods* (ed. Honnold 1966) 41.

KAHN, 'Some Mysteries of Offer and Acceptance', 72 *S. Afr. LJ* 246 (1955).

KEYES, 'Consideration Reconsidered: The Problem of the Withdrawn Bid', 10 *Stan. L. Rev.* 441 (1958).

LAGERGREN, 'Formation of Contract', in: *Unification of the Law Governing International Sales of Goods* (ed. Honnold 1966) 55.

LITVINOFF, 'Offer and Acceptance in Louisiana Law: A Comparative Analysis', 28 *La. L. Rev.* 1, 153 (1969).

MACNEIL, 'Time of Acceptance: Too Many Problems for a Single Rule', 112 *U. Pa. L. Rev.* 947 (1964).

NUSSBAUM, 'Comparative Aspects of the Anglo-American Offer-and-Acceptance Doctrine', 36 *Colum. L. Rev.* 920 (1936).

RABEL, *Recht des Warenkaufs* I (1936) 69–93.

RODIÈRE (ed.), *La Formation du contrat* (1976).

SCHLESINGER *et al.*, *Formation of Contracts, A Study of the Common Core of Legal Systems*, 2 vols. (1968).

F. SCHMIDT, 'The International Contract Law in the Context of Some of its Sources', 14 *Am. J. Comp. L.* 1 (1965).

R. SCHMIDT, 'Der Abschluß des Vertrages nach dem italienischen Zivilgesetzbuch von 1942', *Festschrift Nipperdey* I (1965) 701.

WINFIELD, 'Some Aspects of Offer and Acceptance', 55 *LQ. Rev.* 499 (1939).

I

A CONTRACT is formed when parties express their agreement in congruent declarations, a prior offer and a subsequent acceptance.

Contracts are quite different from unilateral legal acts. It is often said that while a unilateral legal act is the declaration of a single person's intention a contract needs the declarations of two persons, but there is more to the phenomenon of contract than that. If it were only a matter of the number of persons who declared their intention, one might think of a contract as comprising two unilateral legal acts, namely offer and acceptance. This would be an error. Far from being acts with independent legal consequences, offer and acceptance are declarations of will which must be reciprocal in order to generate a contract in law. The German BGB clearly takes the view that a contract is something over and above a pair of unilateral legal acts, for while the unilateral legal act of a minor is held to be invalid (§111) the validity of a contract he has entered into is left in suspense (§108).

A contract therefore emerges not out of two unilateral legal acts but out of the agreement produced by two binding declarations of intention. Offer and acceptance can therefore be defined as declarations of intention which are not unilateral legal acts.

Given this, what problems arise in the formation of contracts?

The formation of contract depends on the agreement of the parties expressed in the offer and acceptance. No difficulty arises when the contract is concluded between persons who are in the same place or who, though separated, are in immediate communication, by telephone or otherwise. In such a case it is the invariable rule that the offer lapses if the offeree does not accept it on the spot.

It is when a contract is to be concluded at a distance, *inter absentes*, by the exchange of letters or other embodiments of the parties' declarations, that the problems arise. Since the two declarations must be given in succession, the offer has to remain in force for some period of time, since otherwise, the two declarations being necessarily successive, it cannot be united with the acceptor's expression of will so as to form a contract. The question therefore is what legal effects attach to the offer as an individual declaration of will directed towards the making of a contract. This is the well-known problem of the binding force of offers.

Here the comparative lawyer meets with a remarkable legal doctrine, the so-called Löfte-theory of the Scandinavian countries. Whereas in most legal systems a true obligation arises only after the contract is formed, obligations under the Löfte-theory arise not from the agreement of the parties but from the duty undertaken by each party in his contractual declaration. Thus a vendor's duty to deliver the goods stems from the declaration he made, and it is because of the purchaser's declaration that he owes the price. This difference is admittedly of more theoretical than practical importance, for in the most important type of contract, the commutative contract such as the contract of sale, the unilateral duty of one party is suspensively conditioned on the other party's assumption of the corresponding duty. Nevertheless the Löfte-theory makes it clear that the offeror is bound by his offer; what is more, provided that the declaration of the acceptor is in line with the offeror's expectations, the principal obligation of the offeror dates back to the time when the offer arrived, even if it was accepted some time later.

Of the three solutions in the legal systems of the world to the problem of the binding nature of offers, the offeror is least bound in the Anglo-Saxon legal family and most strongly bound in the German systems, the Romanistic legal family adopting an intermediate position.

There exists a two-volume work which contains a comprehensive comparative treatment of all the problems connected with 'offer and acceptance'. This is *Formation of Contracts*, produced by a team of nine comparatists from all over the world under the leadership of SCHLESINGER. The general topic of 'offer and acceptance' is broken down into more than twenty complexes of problems, for each of which the contributors have produced national reports; these are then worked into general reports which show the areas of agreement and divergence. For an extensive description of this interesting method of comparative research see SCHLESINGER, 'The Common Core of Legal Systems—An Emerging Subject of Comparative Study', in: *Twentieth Century Comparative and Conflicts Law—Legal Essays in Honor of Hessel E. Yntema* (1961) 65.

II

In Anglo-American law an offer empowers its addressee to accept it and so conclude a contract; it remains capable of acceptance from the time it arrives until it lapses through the expiry of a period fixed by the offeror or determined in accordance with the circumstances. Until the offer has been accepted, however, the offeror remains free to withdraw it at any time and even if he has declared his readiness to be bound to his offer for a stated period he is legally free quite capriciously to withdraw it before that period elapses.

The reason why the Common Law will impose no obligation on the offeror is to be found in the doctrine of consideration, that is, the principle of Anglo-American contract law whereby a promise, unless contained in a document 'under seal', generates a binding obligation only if the promisee has rendered or promised a counterperformance (see below Ch. 36). Offers are normally made without any counterperformance by the addressee and they are hardly ever clothed in solemn form, so normally the offeror is not bound by his offer.

The basic rule of the Common Law can cause hardship to an offeree who has not paid the offeror not to withdraw his offer (option contract) for he may have entered engagements or incurred expenditure in reliance on the continuation of the offer which the offeror now revokes. In such cases American courts tend to hold that the offer may not be withdrawn, notwithstanding the doctrine of consideration. If a general contractor bases a tender on the price quoted by a subcontractor and his tender is accepted, the subcontractor is not entitled forthwith to withdraw his offer and so throw out all the general contractor's calculations. Where the subcontractor knew and intended that the main contractor would rely on his offer in calculating his bid the courts, with varying reasonings, hold that the offer may not be withdrawn: see *Northwestern Engineering Co.* v. *Ellermann*, 69 SD 397, 10 NW 2d 879 (1943); *Drennan* v. *Star Paving Co.*, 51 Cal. 2d 409, 333 P. 2d 757 (1958); and also 59 Colum. L. Rev. 355 (1959); but see also *James Baird Co.* v. *Gimbel Bros., Inc.*, 64 F. 2d 344 (2d Cir. 1933), noted in 20 Va. L. Rev. 214 (1933). This development in the courts has been followed by Restatement (Second) of Contracts (1981) where §87 par. 2 lays down that an offer is to be regarded as irrevocable if, as the offeror should reasonably have expected, it induces action or forbearance of a substantial character on the part of the offeree. In such a case, however, the offer is to be regarded as binding only 'to the extent necessary to avoid injustice'. The need to attribute some binding effect to offers is especially strongly felt in commerce. The Uniform Commercial Code, now in force in all American states except Louisiana, where most of it is enacted, lays down that if written offers to buy and sell commercially are stated to be binding, they may not be withdrawn during the prescribed period or, if no period is prescribed, for a reasonable period not exceeding three months (§2-205); this is the general rule in New York; see NY Personal Property Law s. 33(5), and 43 Colum. L. Rev. 487 (1943).—In England the Law Revision Committee proposed in 1937 (Cmd. 5449) than 'an agreement to keep an offer open for a definite period of time or until the occurrence of some specified event shall not be unenforceable by reason of the absence of consideration' but no action has yet been taken. The whole subject is covered in SCHLESINGER/MACNEIL (above p. 381) 747 ff., 1393 ff.

In the absence of any statutory regulation the basic principle still applies that offers may be freely withdrawn at any time until they have been accepted by the offeree. But the hardship of this rule is somewhat modified by the special rule of the Common Law regarding the time when acceptance makes the contract binding. This rule goes back to the famous leading case of *Adams* v. *Lindsell*, (1818) 1 B. & Ald. 681, 106 Eng. Rep. 250, the source of the 'mailbox' theory. According to this rule it is not when the acceptance reaches the offeror that the contract is formed but at the earlier time when the offeree despatches it, that is, puts it in the mailbox or otherwise entrusts it to the Post Office. The 'mailbox' theory was originally based on the view that the offeror implicitly authorized the Post Office to act as his agent for the receipt of acceptances, so that the contract was formed on posting just as if the declaration of acceptance has been handed to the offeror in person. This construction is now seen to be unrealistic and unpersuasive. The real reason for the rule was the need to minimize the period during which the offeror could withdraw his offer; to put it another way, the offeree had to be relieved of the risk of the offer's being withdrawn as from the moment when he posted his acceptance rather than the later moment when it arrived.

Foreign observers may find it hard to reconcile the 'mailbox' theory with the consensual nature of contract. Even in the Common Law all other declarations (offers, withdrawal of offers, the giving of notice, and so on) must reach the addressee before they are effective, yet a *contract* can come into existence without the offeror's knowledge. A valid contract arises even if the acceptance is lost in the post, though of course the offeree must be able to prove that he really did post his acceptance.

The 'mailbox' theory is also difficult to reconcile with the fact that postal rules everywhere allow a letter to be withdrawn even in transit. This fact induced the American Court of Claims to abandon the 'mailbox' theory; see *Dick* v. *United States*, 82 F. Supp. 326 (Ct. Cl. 1949); *Rhode Island Tool Co.* v. *United States*, 128 F. Supp. 417 (Ct. Cl. 1955). Writers generally oppose it as well. See 34 *Cornell LQ* 632 (1949); 62 *Harv. L. Rev.* 1231 (1949); 59 *Yale LJ* 374 (1950); 54 *Mich. L. Rev.* 557 (1956). The traditional rule is however retained in Restatement (Second) of Contracts (1981) §63: 'An acceptance made in a manner and by a medium invited by an offer is operative . . . as soon as put out of the offeree's possession, without regard to whether it ever reaches the offeror.'

III

In the *Romanistic* legal systems the binding force of offers is rather stronger. In France, after many fluctuations, the principle whereby any offer can be withdrawn until it has been accepted by the offeree has been greatly modified by the courts. If the offeror has set a given period for acceptance the offer can be withdrawn before this period has expired but the withdrawal renders the offeror liable in damages (Civ. 10 May 1968, Bull. civ. 1968. III. 162). As the courts do not require that any particular period be expressed the same is usually true of offers which contain no set period for acceptance: it is sufficient if it appears from the circumstances of the individual case or from normal trade usage that the offer was to be open for acceptance for a 'délai raisonnable'. What period for acceptance, if any, is to be regarded as implicitly agreed is decided as a matter of fact by the trial court in the light of the particular circumstances of the case (Civ. 10 May 1972, Bull. civ. 1972. III. 214). If an offer is revoked before this period elapses, the offeree, while unable to form the contract *stricto sensu* by purporting to accept, can nevertheless claim compensation for the loss which the premature revocation causes him.

Where the owner of a plot of land made an offer to sell it to an interested party and agreed that the premises might be viewed on a particular day, there was an implicit agreement that the offer would remain open until the day of viewing, and the previous withdrawal of the offer rendered the owner liable in damages; instead of money damages, there may be 'réparation en nature', which in such a case takes the form of requiring the offeror to perform the terms of the offer (see Civ. 17 Dec. 1958, D. 1959, 33; Civ. 10 May 1968, Bull. civ. 1968. III. 162).

There is some dispute about the legal basis for the offeror's liability in damages. Many writers (for example, MAZEAUD/TUNC I nos. 116 ff. and RIPERT/BOULANGER II no. 329) see the offeror as being liable in tort under art. 1382 Code civil: while there may be a right to withdraw an offer its withdrawal may in certain circumstances constitute an abuse of right for which the offeror is liable (see below pp. 660 ff.). On another widely held view, the offeror offers not only to enter the principal transaction but also a preliminary contract which binds him to keep the principal offer open for a certain time. This preliminary contract, being purely advantageous for the offeree, is concluded by tacit acceptance. If the offeror then withdraws the offer to enter the principal transaction, he is liable in damages for breach of the preliminary contract. (So, for example, PLANIOL/RIPERT VI no. 131; MAZEAUD II no. 365.)

This was the theory used by the Court of Appeal at Colmar in a case where a subcontractor who had based his offer on an error of calculation had withdrawn it after the offeree had used it as the basis for a successful tender. The court held that an offer was binding 'dès lors qu'il résulte d'un accord exprès ou tacite, mais indiscutable, qu'elle a été formulée pour être maintenue pendant un délai déterminé', but found that in the case before it no such agreement was proved: when the offeror made his offer he did not know that the offeree was intending to use it as a basis for making a tender (Colmar, 4 Feb. 1936, DH 1936, 187).

This construction is obviously very forced: it is a sheer fiction to say that the parties have made a special preliminary contract to the effect that the offer should remain open. There is a third theory, that the offer is an example of a unilateral binding declaration of will (maintained earlier by COLIN/CAPITANT, *Cours élémentaire de droit civil français* II (4th edn., 1924) 270 ff.) but the doctrinal objection to this theory is that there is no such institution as 'engagement unilatéral' in French law.

It is difficult to tell from the cases what amount of damages, if any, may be ordered against an offeror who has withdrawn his offer. This is attributable in part to these theoretical differences but in part also to the fact that when it comes to determining the quantum of damages French judges have a very considerable room for discretion, not subject to the control of the Cour de Cassation. Decisions based on art. 1382 Code civil normally allow the disappointed offeree only the equivalent of the expenses he incurred in reliance on the offer's remaining open (see Bordeaux, 17 Jan. 1870, S. 1870. 2. 219); yet the offeror can also be required by way of damages to put the offeree in the position he would have enjoyed had the contract come to fruition (compare PLANIOL/RIPERT VI no. 132, and, in great detail, SCHLESINGER/BONNASSIES (above p. 381) 769 ff.).

The Commission charged with the reform of the French Code civil proposed a rule whereby offers stated to be open for a certain period could not be withdrawn until that period elapsed unless the withdrawal reached the offeree before the offer; the same was to apply when a period during which the offer was to remain open could be inferred from the circumstances (art. 11 of the avant-projet of 'Sources and Formation of Obligations'). Art. 2 of the Franco-Italian Draft Law of Obligations, never enacted, was to the same effect.

The new Italian Codice civile proceeds on this modern path in arts. 1328 f. An offer cannot be withdrawn before the expiry of any specified period. If no period is specified in the offer it can be withdrawn until acceptance, but if the offeree has relied on the offer in good faith he has a claim for damages for the loss he suffered in preparing to perform.

Just as in the Common Law, the problem in the Romanistic systems can only be seen as a whole if one asks at what moment acceptance concludes the contract.

On the various doctrinal views see, for example, PLANIOL/RIPERT VI nos. 158 ff.—Of course this moment determines when an offer ceases to be revocable but it is important in practice for other reasons too: since the purchaser of specific goods becomes owner of them at the moment when the contract is concluded, he bears the risk of their accidental loss from that time (see art. 1138, 1583 Code civil); and the place where the contract is concluded may determine which court has territorial jurisdiction over any disputes which arise (see art. 420 Code de procédure civile).

The French Cour de Cassation has constantly held that the time of effective acceptance depends on the circumstances of the individual case, especially on the intention of the parties, and is therefore not a proper question for the highest court. This attitude of the Cour de Cassation is quite incomprehensible to lawyers from countries where this matter is regulated by statute. It is not very helpful to be told to interpret the will of the parties since frequently one has to determine whether the parties ever reached any agreement at all. Nevertheless the French trial courts seem to reach equitable results with the power afforded to them by the Cour de Cassation.

According to art. 1326, 1335 Codice civile a contract comes into being as soon as the offeror knows of the acceptance; such knowledge is presumed as soon as the declaration of acceptance arrives at the offeror's normal address unless he can prove that his ignorance is not attributable to negligence.

IV

In Germany the offeror is bound by his offer, in the sense that he cannot withdraw it, for the period of time he specifies or, if he specifies no period, for a reasonable time. As the wording of the BGB makes clear, the offeror is not simply under a duty not to withdraw the offer but actually has no power to do so; instead of giving rise to liability in damages, therefore, an attempted withdrawal simply has no legal effect at all. This rule has been taken over in essence by the Brazilian and Greek civil codes; it also applies in Switzerland (art. 3, 5 OR).

The offeror can prevent his offer's having binding force by using express phrases designed to have that effect ('freibleibend', 'ohne Obligo'). Normally a declaration so qualified is not an offer in the legal sense but simply an invitation to make offers: the declaration of the other party becomes the offer which in its turn requires acceptance, but in fact the German courts tend to hold that the necessary acceptance has been given if the original uncommitted proposer remains silent; good faith in the circumstances would require him to reject the offer expressly and his failure to do so counts as assent.

The BGB has no special rule for the question when *acceptance* is effective; quite rightly it sees this as simply an instance of a general problem which calls for comprehensive regulation since it affects all communicable declarations. The real problem is to divide the risks of transit fairly between the person sending the declaration and the person he sends it to. In §130 the BGB strikes a middle course between the rival theories of the old *Gemeines Recht*, traces of which may still be seen in French law. Every declaration of will, including the acceptance of an offer to contract, is effective as soon as it 'arrives', that is, as soon as it comes into the sphere of influence of the addressee. This effects a sound apportionment of the risks of transit. The person who sends off a declaration chooses the medium and route of communication and consequently must bear the attendant risks, but the risks incident to the addressee's own zone of influence must be borne by the addressee himself: if a bird-lover, to take an old school example, chooses not to empty the letter-box in his garden for fear of affrighting the tomtits within, the declaration is treated as having arrived.

V

This comparative survey has shown that the three different systems attach different legal consequences to the issuance of an offer. In the Common Law an offer has no binding force at all and is not even a ground for liability in damages. In the Romanistic legal systems the premature withdrawal of an offer leads to liability in damages, always in the case of offers with fixed periods, usually for offers without such periods attached. In German law every offer is irrevocable; a purported withdrawal has no legal effect whatever unless the offeror has excluded the binding effect of his proposal.

The critic is forced to conclude that on this point the German system is best. It is true that in practice the differences between the German system and the Common Law are slighter than might at first glance appear. Even in German law an offer may be withdrawn until before it reaches the offeree, and in the Common Law an offer becomes irrevocable once the offeree has put his acceptance in the hands of the carrier. This means that in the Common Law the offeree bears the risk of revocation only for the extra period between the arrival of the offer and the despatch of the acceptance, the period during which he is considering whether to accept or not; unless the offer is stated to be open for a certain time this period is normally very short. Even so, the German system is superior. Experience shows that its results are practical and equitable; the offeree can act with assurance in the knowledge that his acceptance will bring about a contract. It also makes sense to put the risk of any changes in supplies and prices on the offeror: it is he who takes the initiative, it is he who invokes the offeree's reliance, and so it must be for him to exclude or limit the binding nature of his offer, failing which it is only fair to hold him bound.

The apostle of unification of the law on this problem would find it difficult to convert the Anglo-American lawyers. Although it may seem odd to the Continental jurist that an offeror cannot bind himself even if he wants to do so unless he goes to the unusual trouble of entering a remunerated option contract, the doctrine of consideration which is deeply rooted in their contract law is strongly opposed to the binding force of offers. Nevertheless there is a clear trend in state legislation in the United States towards making offers binding and there are also extralegal factors which limit the capricious withdrawal of offers: withdrawal may be legally permissible but it is recognized to be unfair and commercial men consequently avoid it.

The critical comparatist who approves of the German solution to the problem of the binding nature of offers will also approve of the rule of the BGB that a declaration of intention *inter absentes* becomes effective when it arrives with the addressee. The 'mailbox' theory leads to unsatisfactory results because it means that a contract is concluded even if the acceptance is lost in the post or is withdrawn by a telegram which the offeror receives earlier than the letter. But the principal objection to the 'mailbox' theory is that it is inconsistent with all the postal regulations which allow those who send letters to recall them until they reach the addressee. The older Continental theory which required the addressee to have knowledge of the declaration hinged on an internal event, something which a legal order should try to avoid because of difficulties of proof. German law makes the question turn on *arrival*, that is, the entry of the declaration into the addressee's zone of influence. This is not a special rule for the acceptance of contractual offers but applies to all declarations of will which need to be communicated; it not only allocates the risk of transmission as between sender and addressee in a fair manner but also makes the outcome turn on an ascertainable and provable event.

VI

The variety of these solutions might lead one to think that any attempt at international unification of the law in this area was doomed to fail. The Uniform Law on the Formation of Contracts for the International Sale of Goods (ULFIS) proves otherwise. This law, in force in West Germany since 1974, unifies the rules which determine the formation of international sales contracts. Admittedly ULFIS did not adopt the clear solution of making an offer generally binding; indeed, it starts from the principle that offers may be withdrawn. However, such important exceptions are made to this principle in art. 5 pars. 2 and 3 that in practice it comes very close indeed to the German solution of §145 BGB. Thus an offer is irrevocable if it specifies a period for acceptance or if it states that it is binding or not subject to withdrawal. Furthermore an offer can be held to be binding in all the circumstances of the case, on the basis of previous negotiations, the practices of the parties, or trade usage, and withdrawal is inadmissible if it 'is not made in good faith or in conformity with fair dealing'. (On the whole subject see in detail v. CAEMMERER (above p. 381, pp. 119 ff.).)

In the cases where an offer may be withdrawn at all the withdrawal must, according to art. 5 par. 4 of the Treaty, reach the offeree before the offeree has sent off his acceptance. In allowing the recipient of a revocable offer the chance of curtailing the period of vulnerability by prompt despatch of an acceptance, the Conference took an idea from the 'mailbox' theory but it did not follow the 'mailbox' theory's rule that the mere posting of the acceptance concludes the contract: posting the acceptance puts an end to the offer's revocability but it does not conclude the contract. For the problem of the moment when contractual declarations become effective the Conference adopted the German rule: under arts. 5, 6, 8, 10, and 12, a contractual declaration, whether it be an offer, an acceptance, or the withdrawal of either of these, becomes effective at the time it arrives with the addressee, for which purpose arrival at the address of the person for whom it is destined is sufficient.

The same basic idea underlies the Convention on Contracts for the International Sale of Goods (CISG), concluded in Vienna in 1980 under the auspices of the United Nations but not yet in force. After stating the principle that an offer is revocable until the offeree has despatched his declaration of acceptance (art. 16), the Convention provides that an offer may be rendered irrevocable if the offer so provides or if there are special circumstances, such as its containing a period for acceptance. In addition, an offer is irrevocable if the offeree reasonably supposed it to be irrevocable and has taken action on the basis of that supposition.

On the whole it is a matter for regret that ULIS and CISG did not adopt the clear German solution throughout. The practical differences are very slight but the solution of starting from the old-fashioned principle that offers can be withdrawn and then rendering it meaningless by a series of exceptions made for very complex drafting. However, one can hardly complain too much of lack of legal elegance when in fact a considerable degree of legal unity has been achieved with regard to the conclusion of international sales contracts.

34

Formal Requirements

BROOKE, *Treatise on the Office and Practice of a Notary in England* (8th edn., rev. Cranstoun, 1925).

BROWN, 'The Office of the Notary in France', 2 *ICLQ* 60 (1953).

COMMENT, 'The Statute of Frauds and the Business Community: A Re-Appraisal in Light of Prevailing Practices', 66 *Yale LJ* 1038 (1957).

EBEL, *Recht und Form, Vom Stilwandel im deutschen Recht* (1975).

FRIDMAN, 'The Necessity for Writing in Contracts within the Statute of Frauds', 35 *U. Tor. LJ* 43 (1985).

FULLER, 'Consideration and Form', 41 *Colum. L. Rev.* 799 (1941).

HÄSEMEYER, *Die gesetzliche Form der Rechtsgeschäfte* (1971).

——, 'Die Bedeutung der Form im Privatrecht', *JuS* 1980, 1.

K. HELDRICH, 'Die Form des Vertrags', *AcP* 147 (1941) 89.

V. HOFFMANN, *Das Recht des Grundstückskaufs, Eine rechtsvergleichende Untersuchung* (1982) §5.

JHERING, *Geist des römischen Rechts auf den verschiedenen Stufen seiner Entwicklung*, Pt. II(2) (4th edn., 1883) §§43 ff.

KÖBL, 'Die Bedeutung der Form im heutigen Recht', *DNotZ* 1983, 207.

LLEWELLYN, 'What Price Contract?—An Essay in Perspective', 40 *Yale LJ* 704, 746 ff. (1931–2).

LORENZ, 'Das Problem der Aufrechterhaltung formnichtiger Schuldverträge', *AcP* 156 (1957) 381.

——, 'Rechtsfolgen formnichtiger Schuldverträge', *JuS* 1966, 429.

MANN, 'Die Urkunde ausländischer, insbesondere englischer Notare und der deutsche Rechtsverkehr', *NJW* 1955, 1177.

VON MEHREN, 'The French Civil Code and Contract: A Comparative Analysis of Formation and Form', 15 *La. L. Rev.* 687, 693 ff. (1955).

MEURISSE, 'Le Déclin de la preuve par écrit', *Gaz. Pal.* 1951. 2. Doctrine 50.

PERROT, Juris-Classeur civil, Artt. 1315–69 Code civil.

RABEL, 'The Statute of Frauds and Comparative Legal History', 63 *LQ Rev.* 174 (1947).

SCHLESINGER, The Notary and the Formal Contract in Civil Law, Report of the [New York] Law Revision Commission (1941), Study Relating to the Seal and to the Enforcement of Certain Written Contracts, p. 59.

STERNBERG *et al.*, 'Formvorschriften', *III Rechtsvergleichendes Handwörterbuch* (ed. Schlegelberger) (1931) 454.

STEVENS, 'Ethics and the Statute of Frauds', 37 *Cornell LQ* 355 (1951–2).

WEHRENS, 'Das Notariatswesen in Frankreich', *DNotZ* 1964, 7.

I

In all modern legal systems there are some transactions which have to be in a special form if they are to receive legal recognition. Such formal requirements are, however, always exceptions to a general *principle of informality*. In many legal systems this principle is made explicit, as in art. 11 OR, which lays down that the validity of contracts depends on a particular form 'only if' the law so specifies (see also §883 ABGB). The German Civil Code, on the other hand, brief and abstract as usual rather than clear and popular, leaves it to be inferred from §125 that legal transactions are generally valid regardless of form.

The principle of informality has not always been recognized. In ancient Roman law, as in other early legal systems, legal obligations could *only* be engendered by observing special forms. The requirement of form was not a means of advancing legal goals such as certainty of proof; the form was the actual reason for the desired legal result; it was 'effective form' rather than 'protective form', to use an expression of DULCKEIT (*Festschrift Fritz Schultz* I (1951) 161). Accordingly, ancient forms combined ritual solemnity and obviousness of import; in ancient Rome spoken formulas with prescribed words had occasionally to be accompanied by stipulated gestures, such as the grasping by the purchaser in mancipatio of the person or thing sold. As Roman law developed, legal transactions which required no form became increasingly important, especially the consensual and real contracts, until in the sophisticated transactional law of the classical period they constituted the rule. At this stage formality was required for protective purposes; practically the only known form in the post-classical period was a written record of the transaction which is still the typical formal requirement today, though it has many variants, from simple writing to a document officially attested.

It is not difficult to identify the *functions* served by rules which specify formal requirements: basically they are to facilitate proof or to confirm seriousness of intention.

The former seems to be historically the older. The very title of the English Statute of Frauds, 1677—parts of it are still in force in England and most of the states of North America adopted it *in toto*—suggests why it introduced formal requirements for certain types of transaction: it was to prevent judges being misled by perjury or other fraudulent manœuvres into holding that the parties had made a certain contract, or 'for the prevention of many fraudulent practices which are commonly endeavoured to be upheld by perjury and subornation of perjury', to quote the Preamble. The same is true of the even older French rule in art. 54 of the Ordonnance de Moulins, 1566, which prohibited oral evidence in respect of disputed contracts involving more than a hundred pounds. Today we see that formal requirements may have evidentiary functions even where the parties have no improper motives, for the required form facilitates proof not only of the *conclusion* of the transaction but also of its *content*, whether the document is simply presumed to be accurate and complete or whether proof of a divergent oral agreement is excluded (see below Ch. 37 V). We can tell that the provisions we have mentioned were originally designed to strengthen the proof of the agreement because failure to observe the requisite form leads not to the substantive invalidity of the legal transaction but only to *procedural* sanctions; a contract defective in form is 'unenforceable' in Anglo-American legal systems and 'unproveable' by means of witnesses in France (art. 1341 Code civil; 'il n'est reçu aucune preuve par témoins').

The private international lawyer must not be misled by the fact that in many foreign systems a failure to observe the specified forms has only procedural sanctions. It is certainly an unwritten principle of the conflict of laws that the judge applies his own procedural law and never that of a foreign system, but it does not follow that a German judge must treat a contract to which French law applies as valid on the sole ground that the sanctions attached to the defect in form by French law, namely the exclusion of proof by witnesses, are procedural. Although it is dressed up in procedural terms, the French rule performs the substantive legal function of a formal requirement. Accordingly, the German judge should treat the contract as invalid on the ground of want of form. The Bundesgerichtshof has decided otherwise and has been criticized for it by GAMILLSCHEG (*JZ* 1955, 702).

Rules which impose formal requirements are often concerned with *seriousness of intention*; in prescribing the conditions which the transaction must satisfy if it is to be enforced as being presumptively serious, the aim is to give persons unfamiliar with business an opportunity for thoughtful consideration and so protect them from surprise. It is true that it takes only a few seconds to draft even a contract of guarantee so that the requirement of writing does not necessarily entail a period of delay sufficient to permit reappraisal, but to insist on writing does suggest, especially to laymen, that one is leaving the area of merely social engagements and has to face the question whether one wants to enter a genuine business obligation or not.

A formal requirement is clearly directed to assuring seriousness of intention if it lays down that the transaction must be attested by an independent official with legal training such as the notary in Germany, who is bound

'to ascertain the will of the parties, explain the content of the transaction, instruct the parties about the legal consequences of the transaction, and record their statements clearly and unequivocally. In so doing he should take care that errors and doubts are avoided and that inexperienced and unknowledgeable parties are not disadvantaged' (§17 Beurkundungsgesetz).

Officials of this type exist in almost all Continental legal systems. It is true that their exact legal position differs considerably in different countries, indeed sometimes within a single country. In many countries notaries belong to an independent profession, in others they are officials, and in socialist countries they form the changing personnel of a permanent state authority under the control of the Minister of Justice (see STERNBERG (above p. 391) and SCHLESINGER (above p. 391)).

In the Anglo-American legal family, on the other hand, there is no official comparable with the notary who is entrusted with the recording of legal transactions; in consequence the Common Law never insists on anything like the 'notarial document' (§ 128 BGB), the 'notarial act' (for example §551 ABGB), or the 'acte authentique' (art. 1312 Code civil). It is true that in England there is a respected profession of 'Public Notary', to which applicants of at least seven years professional experience may be admitted by the Court of Faculties under the supervision of the Archbishop of Canterbury (for details see BROOKE (above p. 391). p. 31 ff., MANN (above p. 391) p. 1178), but the typical task of the Public Notary is to draw up documents for use abroad by parties who need them under foreign law. The *American* 'Notary Public' has nothing in common with the Continental notary except the name. They are normally persons with little or no legal training who are empowered under the laws of the individual states to record sworn statements, to certify signatures and so on.

In private international law cases the question often arises whether the German requirement that a legal transaction be inscribed or a signature attested by a notary is satisfied if these acts are done by a foreign 'Notary'. What must be decided in each case is whether the foreign official is the equivalent of the home product, given the purpose underlying the German rule. Certainly if the rule is designed to ensure that the parties should have the advice of a legal expert before concluding the transaction, the participation of an American Notary Public, for example, would be quite inadequate (see DÖLLE, *RabelsZ* 27 (1962/1963) 201, 238 ff.; NEUHAUS, *Grundbegriffe des Internationalen Privatrechts* (2nd edn., 1976) 351, and BGHZ 80, 76).

II

The civil codes of the Romanistic legal family follow the French Code civil and make a basic distinction between cases where certain formalities must be observed as a precondition of the *validity* of the legal transaction and other cases in which an informal transaction, though valid, cannot be *proved* in court or can be proved only by limited means of proof. In practice the distinction between invalidity and unproveability is not very great; if a transaction is *invalid* for want of form it must be treated by the court on its own motion as non-existent, while a transaction which is valid but simply *unproveable* may possibly be recognized by the party liable.

There are very few cases in French law where the observance of a formality is a precondition of validity and in those cases the requisite formality is always the notarial act. This class of case includes the promise of a gift (art. 931 Code civil, art. 782 Codice civile) and the marriage contract (art. 1394 Code civil, arts. 162 f. Codice civile). Holographic wills apart, simple writing is never a formal requirement in the strict sense. The provision of art. 2044 par. 2 Code civil that an agreement to compromise a dispute must be in writing has been construed by the courts as rendering the proof of an oral compromise more difficult, not as rendering it invalid.

The Italian Civil Code of 1942 is more exacting than the French Code civil, for it requires a whole list of contracts to be in writing and specifies that the contract is void if this form is not observed ('sotto pena di nullità', art. 1350). Included in this list are contracts appertaining to the transfer of land and to the creation, alteration, or transfer of real rights.

Although in France one may sell land, undertake guarantees, and create servitudes quite validly without observing any form, parties in fact normally do these things in writing or by notarial document because of the practical difficulty of enforcing purely oral contracts. The difficulty arises from art. 1341 Code civil which prescribes that all transactions of more than 5,000 f. in value (50 f. until 1980) must take the form of private writing ('acte sous seing privé') or notarial document ('acte notarié'), and sanctions the non-observance of these forms by excluding the testimony of witnesses (so also art. 2721 Codice civile, where the limit of value is 5,000 lire).

The same rule is laid down by art. 1985 Code civil for powers of agency: if the value of the transaction to be concluded by the agent exceeds 5,000 f. the principal may prove the agency only by documents and not by witnesses. The Codice civile has a different rule: the power of agency must be in the form required for the contract which the agent is to conclude (art. 1392 Codice civile; the rule of §167 par. 2 BGB is different).

In principle, then, apart from everyday transactions, the conclusion of a contract must be proved by a notarial or private document. By notarial document, as has already been explained, is meant a document in which the transaction in question has been recorded, with the observance of the specified formalities, by a proper notary. It is rather more difficult to say what constitutes a private document (*acte sous seing privé, scrittura privata*). In French, unlike German, law, if the contract is commutative there must be as many originals of the contractual document as there are parties (see art. 1325 Code civil). On the other hand, difficult though this is to reconcile with art. 1325 Code civil, a letter from a purchaser accepting an oral offer of sale constitutes an *acte sous seing privé* (see Req. 6 Feb. 1928, DH 1928, 133). A document recording a unilateral undertaking to pay a sum of money or do something else, such as to take over a guarantee, will only serve as a valid *acte sous seing privé* if either it has been written out and signed in the hand of the obligor or it is signed and contains at least a handwritten acceptance ('approuvé' or 'bon pour') specifying in words the amount of the debt undertaken (art. 1326 Code civil). These convoluted provisions have been dropped from the Italian Codice civile.

If an agreement is recorded in writing as required, there may be difficulties in giving evidence of any preliminary, contemporary, or subsequent oral variation of the contract (see below Ch. 37 V). If the required written form is not observed, witnesses cannot give evidence at all. This principle is, however, subject to far-reaching exceptions.

The evidence of witnesses is not excluded when the oral agreement is a commercial transaction. Art. 109 Code de commerce admittedly says only that the conclusion of commercial *sales* may be proved by witnesses but it is agreed on all hands that this text is simply a particular instance of the general principle that any evidence is admissible to prove the conclusion of commercial transactions. Commercial men must often act very speedily and it would be inept to force them to do their business in writing by rendering oral agreements difficult to enforce. It is worth noting that in the case of transactions which are commercial on one side only—where, for example, the sale is a commercial transaction only for the purchaser and not for the vendor—there is no relaxation of the means of proof if this would adversely affect the party for whom the transaction has a private character.

The most important limitation on art. 1341 Code civil is that the testimony of witnesses is admitted whenever the party wishing to introduce it can offer a 'commencement de preuve par écrit', that is, can start off his evidence with a written document. By this is meant a document emanating from the opponent which constitutes good evidence that the oral contract really was concluded between the parties (art. 1347 Code civil, art. 2724 par. 1 Codice civile). Accordingly, if there is a document signed by the opponent which for some formal reason does not satisfy the requirements of a valid *acte sous seing privé*, the testimony of witnesses may be admitted for it will normally constitute a 'commencement de preuve'. Thus a creditor claiming the repayment of a loan may call witnesses to prove the oral loan if he can put in evidence a letter from the defendant thanking him for 'the favour performed': if in all the circumstances of the case this document makes it probable that the loan was made, the plaintiff is allowed, art. 1341 notwithstanding, to use any means of proof, including proof by witnesses, to establish the fact to the satisfaction of the judge.

The notion of 'commencement de preuve' has been so widely construed by the courts that in practice the rule of art. 1341 has lost a great deal of its force. A written document in the narrow sense may not even be required: some courts have been satisfied with oral statements recorded on tape (Dijon 29 June 1955, JCP 1955. II. 8856). Under art. 336 Code de procédure civile, a court may find a 'commencement de preuve' if a party properly summoned fails to appear or give satisfactory answers and his conduct suggests that the contract was indeed orally concluded. Courts occasionally reach the same result by pointing to the dispositive nature of art. 1341 and then treating the conduct of a party as a silent estoppel: thus a party who has actively participated in the examination of witnesses called by his opponent can no longer claim the exclusion of oral proof under art. 1341 (Soc. 24 March 1965, JCP 1965. II. 14415). This principle was adopted by the Code civil in 1975. Art. 1347 par. 3 now provides that the judge can infer a 'commencement de preuve' from statements made by a party in court, from the silence of a party in court, or from the failure of a party to appear at the oral proceedings.

Finally, a plaintiff who has no contractual document may still call witnesses if he can show that on factual or moral grounds it was impossible for him to procure such a document (see art. 1348 Code civil). For example, in transactions between spouses, fiancés, siblings, or between parents and children, it is not exactly tactful to insist on the safeguard of a note of hand; the courts recognize the social dilemma in such cases by abandoning the requirement of written proof (for example, see Req. 2 Feb. 1920, DP 1921. 1. 40; Req. 27 June 1938, Gaz. Pal. 1938. 2. 586).

It will be seen that in practice very little survives of the impressive principle contained in art. 1341 Code civil. A judge who has heard the parties and finds the plaintiff's assertion that a contract was orally concluded prima facie credible will always discover means of allowing him to prove the matter by witnesses. This is true without qualification for commercial transactions but in other cases a judge can use documents written by the defendant or even the defendant's actual behaviour to reach the conclusion that the transaction in question was 'probable'. In the absence of such 'commencement de preuve' the court can still say that it was 'moralement impossible' for the plaintiff to obtain a proper document. But while it may be true that a well-grounded claim very seldom fails by reason of the evidentiary restriction of art. 1341 Code civil, it remains the case that this text acts as a strong inducement in non-commercial affairs to have one's transactions written down, for it is always difficult to say in advance *whether* the court will, on one ground or another, let in proof by witnesses notwithstanding art. 1341, and people try to avoid this uncertainty so far as possible.

III

In the Romanistic legal family, as we have seen, provisions which lay down formal requirements are principally directed to questions of proof. Failure to observe the requisite form does not invalidate the transaction but just makes it harder to prove since the evidence of witnesses, regarded with disfavour because of its notorious unreliability, may be excluded. But proof by witnesses is let in if the interest in enforcing promises is backed up by even a sketchy document or other facts which suggest that the promise was really made.

In the *German* legal family matters are quite different. Certainly their provisions as to the form of transactions have some evidentiary functions but in contrast to French law, this is subsidiary. This is shown by the fact that in Germany, Austria, and Switzerland the presumption that a written contractual agreement is accurate and complete may be rebutted even by the testimony of witnesses, but it is shown most clearly by the fact that in the German legal family want of form invariably makes a transaction invalid, even if it can be proved beyond a shadow of doubt that the promise was actually made or that the contracting parties actually made the agreement in question. The only explanation for attaching such a strong sanction to want of form is that the legislator was also concerned with the seriousness of the parties' intention.

Only against the background of this fundamentally different point of view do the many peculiarities of the legal rules in the German legal family become comprehensible. Thus Germany and Switzerland put in the General Part the rule that a legal transaction not in the form legally prescribed is in principle void or invalid (§125 BGB, art. 11 OR). The precise formal requirements are to be found here and there throughout the civil codes wherever the legislator specifies in relation to each type of transaction whether simple writing is sufficient or whether notarial attestation is required, whether the declaration of one contractor or of both must be in the proper form, whether formal invalidity may be cured by subsequent performance, and so on. Such *ad hoc* rules are needed in the German legal family because the need for protection from surprise varies from one kind of transaction to another. Problems of proof, on the other hand, are common to all transactions, so the Romanistic legal systems can develop general clauses like art. 1341 Code civil.

Confining ourselves to the law of obligations, we can quickly indicate the kinds of transaction which require particular forms. Although *sales contracts* are valid regardless of form and regardless of the value of the object sold, Germany and Switzerland make an exception for sales of land (§313 BGB, art. 216 OR). In Austria, by contrast, an oral contract for the sale of land is binding; a notarial document must indeed be drawn up in order to register the transfer of ownership in the land register (§432 ABGB), but the oral contract entitles the purchaser to demand the vendor's co-operation in drawing up this document, that being part of his duties. The same is true in Austrian law for hire-purchase or conditional sales transactions (see §24 Consumer Protection Act). In Switzerland and West Germany, on the other hand, such transactions are void unless they are in writing (art. 226a OR; §1a Abzahlungsgesetz).

Switzerland alone requires *assignments* of claims to be in writing (art. 165 OR). In Germany this is required only if the claim being assigned is secured by a mortgage; this is for reasons connected with the Land Register (§1154 BGB).

Contrariwise, all systems see the need for protection against surprise in *suretyship*. Thus they all require writing for the validity of a guarantee, though it is only the guarantor's promise which must be in writing since he is the only one who needs protection. In Switzerland the matter is regulated in detail by a special law of 1941: the document of guarantee must specify an upper limit in figures, written in the hand of the guarantor if he is an individual guaranteeing the claim of a private creditor, and the guarantee must be officially recorded if the limit of liability exceeds 2,000 Swiss francs (see art. 493 OR).

In German and Austrian law an *oral* guarantee is valid if it constitutes a commercial transaction from the guarantor's point of view (§350 HGB). This recalls the rule of French law that the requirements of form are generally relaxed for commercial transactions, but while the normal explanation in France is that commercial intercourse must not be hindered by undue formalities (see PERROT (above p. 391), arts. 134 ff.Fasc. D, no. 4), the German provision is based on the realization that a commercial man entering commercial transactions requires no protection from surprise.

In Germany and Austria *promises of gifts* require to be notarized, as do promises of gifts of land in Switzerland, where other gifts are valid if in writing (art. 243 OR).

IV

In *Anglo-American* law a promise unsupported by consideration (see below Ch. 36) is binding only if it is contained in the form of a document 'under seal'. Thus one requirement of form springs directly from the doctrine of consideration; the nullity of an informal gratuitous promise leads the promisor to use a 'deed', as a sealed document is called. A promise under seal is valid without any acceptance or even knowledge by the promisee (*Macedo* v. *Stroud* [1922] 2 AC 330).

Another kind of formalism is often the *indirect* effect of the doctrine of consideration. As will be explained below in Ch. 36 II, the validity of a promise does not depend in any way on the *equivalence* or *adequacy* of the consideration provided for it. Thus if a person wants to make a binding offer to sell a valuable property to another any time during the next ten years, he can create a fully effective option by asking the prospective purchaser to pay or promise one dollar as consideration. In such a case it is clear that the optionee's promise to pay the dollar is purely formal.

There may have been a time when the sealing of a document was a solemn act but today it is a mere formality involving little more than writing. The only other thing required is to affix to the document a little label which may be had in any stationer's shop or to write the letters 'LS' (*loco sigilli*) or the word 'seal' on it. Then the promisor must do some act or other to show his intention of uttering this sealed document in favour of the promisee. This is normally done by handing over the document, but the courts have relaxed even this requirement very considerably (see, for example, *Xenos* v. *Wickham*, (1867) LR 2 HL 296).

Most of the states of the United States have abolished the formality of documents under seal by legislation. This normally provides that a promise without consideration is ineffective even if it is contained in a deed. (On this, see the details in CORBIN §254.)

There are very few other cases in Anglo-American law where the observance of a particular form is a precondition of validity. The normal result of failing to observe the forms legally required is to render the transaction not invalid but rather 'unenforceable', that is, incapable of forming the basis of a claim in court. The most important of these formal requirements are to be found in the Statute of Frauds, 1677, already mentioned, which requires 'a note or memorandum of the agreement in writing and signed by the party to be charged therewith' in the following cases:

1. The promise of an executor or administrator of a decedent's estate to be personally liable for the debts of the decedent;
2. A promise to answer for the debt of another;
3. A promise in relation to a forthcoming marriage;
4. A contract for the transfer of landed property or real rights therein;
5. A contract to be performed a year or more after the formation of the contract;
6. Contracts of sale where the price exceeds £10, unless the purchaser has accepted the goods or part of them, or has himself performed, by giving an earnest or paying part of the price.

In the three centuries since its enactment English lawyers and judges, both in court and extrajudicially, have criticized the Statute of Frauds as a very unhappy piece of legislation. It aimed to prevent fraudulent plaintiffs from bringing claims on non-existent contracts but its terms gave equally unscrupulous defendants the opportunity of avoiding obligations which they had in fact assumed, though only by word of mouth. Always uneasy at legislative interventions in private law, the English judges have done their best to restrict the area of application of the Statute of Frauds, helped in their tortuous construction by the remarkable opacity of the statutory text. The result was that by the end of the nineteenth century the original words of the statute had virtually disappeared under a thick patina of case-law; student and practitioner alike faced, in the words of CHESHIRE/FIFOOT, 'a wilderness of cases through which it is possible only to indicate the hazardous and inconsequent paths trodden by the unwilling feet of litigants' (*The Law of Contract* (6th edn., 1964) 167 f.).

In England repeated efforts to abolish the Statute of Frauds were successful only in 1954: most of it was repealed by the Law Reform (Enforcement of Contracts) Act, 1954, only promises of guarantee (above no. 2) and contracts relating to land (above no. 4, now s. 40 of the Law of Property Act, 1925), remaining subject to the formal requirements.

In the United States, on the other hand, the provisions of the Statute of Frauds are still very much in force, since nearly all the states of the Union speedily enacted it, with variations in the precise wording and in the figure fixed for sales contracts (see above no. 6). American courts therefore still have the task of applying this antique enactment. CORBIN's outstanding textbook on the law of contract in the United States devotes one whole volume out of six, with more than 800 pages and a mass of cases, to expounding all the detailed application of the Statute of Frauds. Like other American writers, CORBIN would welcome the repeal or restriction of the statute in the more than fifty jurisdictions but he sees no chance of this happening: 'its repeal would deprive attorneys at law of one of their cherished defences' (CORBIN §275 (1964 supplement)).

Before the recent introduction of the Uniform Commercial Code the question whether to maintain the requirement of writing for sales contracts (above no. 6) was debated at length. In the result the old rule was adhered to, as LLEWELLYN desired (40 *Yale LJ* 704, 747 (1931)): according to §2-201 UCC, contracts for the sale of goods costing $500 or more are 'enforceable' only if the conclusion of the contract is evidenced by a written document, signed at least by the party whom it is sought to make liable. Various arguments have been adduced to show why it is reasonable for the United States to maintain a formal requirement for sales contracts which has been abolished in modern English legislation: it is said that claims based on doubtful oral promises are more likely to be brought in the United States than in England for the American plaintiff, unlike his English counterpart, runs no risk of paying the attorney's costs of a successful defendant, and also that in the United States contract suits are quite often tried before a jury, which is more liable to be taken in by a party's manœuvres if he is not required to produce a document (BRAUCHER, 40 *Cornell LQ* 696, 705 (1955)). These arguments are pretty unconvincing.

V

Every rule which requires contracts to be in a particular form has some legislative purpose behind it: it may be to exclude the testimony of witnesses on the ground that it is undesirable or to make a sharp demarcation between the finalized transaction and the preliminary negotiations or to give a party the opportunity for reflection or the benefit of legal advice. But once a provision requiring a certain form is enacted, it breaks away from its underlying purpose and falls to be applied even in cases where the aims of the legislator are already fully satisfied in other ways. Under the 'blinkered' provision of §766 BGB an admitted oral promise of guarantee is void even if there is no problem of proof and even if the guarantor would not have considered the matter more anxiously had it been reduced to writing. Thus provisions regarding form often cut more deeply than is required to implement the underlying policy grounds, and to apply them rigidly may lead to results so offensive to feelings of justice that legal systems must face the question whether in some circumstances they should not be ignored. For the comparative lawyer this raises the following questions: does this problem actually arise in all legal systems? What conceptual devices are used to solve them? What different solutions are reached?

The *German* lawyer is well aware of the problem for there are a great many court decisions on it. Most of these cases involve a contract for the sale of land which is not notarized and so infringes §313 BGB. The purchaser may be demanding possession from the vendor *despite* the want of form, or the vendor may be claiming to repossess from the purchaser *because of* the want of form. The courts' approach has been to ask whether in all the circumstances of the case the claim or defence is consistent with the basic principle of good faith (*Treu und Glauben*) (§242 BGB). Until very recently it was unanimously agreed that it was contrary to good faith for the vendor to reclaim possession if he had deliberately or negligently induced the purchaser to think that no particular form was needed; such circumstances also deprived the vendor of his defence to the purchaser's claim for performance (RGZ 107, 357; BGH NJW 1954, 425; BGHZ 12, 286, 304). Recently, however, the Bundesgerichtshof has abandoned even this hard-won position, which had at least the merit of clarity.

The plaintiff was a communal housing authority which had erected a number of terraced houses on its own land. Towards the end of 1957 they agreed in writing with the married defendants that the latter should purchase one of these houses for about DM 32,000. A 'definitive contract', it was agreed, should be drawn up later. This was never done. Differences of opinion arose between the parties and led to the present suit, wherein the plaintiff demanded that the defendants give up possession of the house after nearly four years' occupation. The Bundesgerichtshof expressly found that the want of form was due to the fault of the plaintiff. According to a long series of precedents, this finding alone was sufficient to justify the dismissal of the claim, but the Bundesgerichtshof produced a new formula: one could not refuse to apply §313 BGB simply because there would be a 'hard result' for the party affected; 'the result must be actually intolerable'. In the case in question it would certainly be 'hard' for the defendants to have to give up the house they had lived in for many years, but it was not 'actually intolerable' since the fault of the plaintiff afforded them a claim for damages based on *culpa in contrahendo* (NJW 1965, 812; see the critical notes of MARSCHALL V. BIEBERSTEIN, *NJW* 1965, 1014, and LORENZ, *JuS* 1966, 429). See also BGH 21 Apr. 1972, NJW 1972, 1189, where the plaintiff, who had purchased a house without the necessary formality, was nevertheless allowed to demand a formal conveyance, because he was already advanced in years, the house was to be his retirement home, and there was reason to fear that if he were remitted to a claim for damages, he might die before it succeeded.

The basic question with regard to the enforcement of contracts for the sale of land which are void for want of form is whether in the particular case the policy underlying the formal requirement makes it necessary to hold the informal promise invalid. This is not the case when a contractor deceitfully or negligently leads his trusting partner to believe that the written contract is valid and then, *veniens contra factum proprium*, seeks to turn the formal invalidity to his own advantage; that is to sever the rule from its rationale and use it as camouflage for a breach of contract. Again, the formal rule must give way if the parties have performed a contract in whole or in part in the innocent belief that it was valid and one of the parties has so conducted himself that to hold the contract invalid would constitute a grave breach of the principle that justifiable reliance should be protected (in this sense see also LORENZ, *AcP* 156 (1957) 381, 413). It is for the courts to decide when this stage has been reached, by progressively identifying proper types of case; very little help is provided by ritualistic formulae which distinguish between the case which is simply 'hard' and the case which is 'actually intolerable'.

Much may be learnt with regard to this problem from the *Anglo-American* method of developing the law by careful and constant attention to precedent (see LORENZ, *AcP* 156 (1957) 381, 410 ff.). Although the Statute of Frauds made oral contracts for the sale of land 'unenforceable', the Courts of Equity soon developed the doctrine of part performance, whereby the vendor may be forced to perform an oral contract of sale if the purchaser has acted in such a way that a detached observer would regard his actions as constituting partial performance of the contract.

In adopting the formal requirements of the Statute of Frauds in relation to contracts for the sale of land, the Law of Property Act 1925 also recognized the doctrine of part performance (s. 40). This was not done in the Continental manner of attempting to codify these judicial rules but by simply enacting: 'This section . . . does not affect the law relating to part performance.'

The doctrine requires that the 'plaintiff, by acting on the promise of the other party, must have changed his position for the worse, so as to render it unfair that the other should be be bound by the contract' (ANSON/GUEST, *English Law of Contract* (22nd edn. 1964) 79).

The following decisions are instructive: United States: *Townsend* v. *Vanderwerker*, 160 US 171 (1895); *Sears* v. *Redick*, 211 F. 856 (8th Cir. 1914); *Hoffmann* v. *F. H. Duehay*, 65 F. 2d 839 (DC 1933); *McGrory* v. *McCormick*, 400 Ill. 203, 79 NE 2d 485 (1948). Restatement (Second) of Contracts (1981) §129 sums up the American case-law as follows: 'A contract for the transfer of an interest in land may be specifically enforced notwithstanding failure to comply with the Statute of Frauds if it is established that the party seeking enforcement, in reasonable reliance on the contract and on the continuing assent of the party against whom enforcement is sought, has so changed his position that injustice can be avoided only by specific enforcement.' (See also §139.)—Among the English decisions see *Wakeham* v. *MacKenzie*, [1968] 2 All ER 783; *Steadman* v. *Steadman*, [1976] AC 530.

Payment of the purchase price does not by itself constitute part performance, since it can be returned without the purchaser's suffering any further
loss, but decisions in the United States are divided on the question what other
acts on the part of the purchaser are sufficient to constitute part performance.
In most states the mere fact of taking possession of the land with the
acquiescence of the vendor is not regarded as sufficient. The decision has been
otherwise when the taking of possession was accompanied by the payment of
the price or if the purchaser's possession lasted for a considerable time, or if, in
reliance on the validity of the contract, he had made substantial expenditures
on the property, or if on other grounds it would be grossly unfair to the
purchaser to undo the effects of the performance on either side. (See the full
treatment in CORBIN, §§420 ff.)

English writers are not entirely agreed on the exact basis of the doctrine of part
performance. Most interesting is the view of POLLOCK that the doctrine can be traced to
the principle of estoppel: 'A man cannot be allowed to set up the legal invalidity of an
agreement on the faith of which he has induced or allowed the other party to alter his
position' (*Principles of Contract* (12th edn., 1946) 514); see also LORENZ, above p. 391
pp. 41 f.). American courts are also given to treating the plaintiff's part performance of
the contract as a circumstance which renders the defendant 'estopped' from insisting
on the want of form (CORBIN §422 A (1964 Supplement) with further references).

In *French* law the problem of upholding contracts which are void for want
of form does not seem to arise at all, even though the well-developed concept
of *abus de droit* provides an apt and ready tool with which to solve the
problem. Finding 'nothing to report' in France analogous in function to the
doctrine of part performance or the German doctrine of the irrelevance of
want of form, the comparative lawyer investigates further and finds out why.
In Germany, and often in countries of the Anglo-American legal family as
well, the question whether a party can rely on the absence of a statutory form
arises in cases where the parties admit that there was a contractual agreement
between them, though not in the form required by statute. Cases of this kind
present no problems whatever for French judges. As we have seen, the formal
requirements of art. 1341 Code civil are related to questions of proof; if a fact
is admitted it does not need to be proved and so there is no room for the
application of art. 1341. Thus once a party admits that the agreement on
which he is being sued did in fact take place he cannot rely on the absence of
writing, and the question never arises whether if he did seek so to rely this
would be an abuse of right or contrary to good faith. Even where a party does
deny the conclusion of an oral agreement the judge can make a liberal
application of the doctrine of *commencement de preuve* and help his opponent
to prove the matter by witnesses. As has been shown, the doctrine, by relying
on intrinsic factors, answers the requirements of good faith, so there is no need
to have recourse to the general prohibition of abuse of rights in order to solve
the cases we are concerned with.

VI

This survey suggests that while no legal system can entirely dispense with formal requirements the trend is towards informality, at any rate in the area of classical private law. One indication of this is the unanimity in favour of informality when the law of international sales contracts was being unified (see art. 15, Uniform Law of Sales and the observations of Riese, *RabelsZ* 29 (1965) 1, 26 ff., as well as art. 3 of the Uniform Law on the Formation of Contracts and the comments of v. Caemmerer, *RabelsZ* 29 (1965) 101, 114 ff.). The same tendency can also be seen in the repeal of the Statute of Frauds in England in 1954, which left contracts of guarantee and contracts for the sale of land as the only transactions requiring writing. France has gone particularly far in dispensing with formal requirements: commercial transactions never require any particular form and in other areas the doctrine of *commencement de preuve* has been so extended by the courts that a plausible claim hardly ever fails merely because there is no written evidence. Meurisse has used the phrase 'déclin de la preuve par écrit' (above p. 391) and other French writers have even proposed the repeal of art. 1341 Code civil (see Perrot (above p. 391) arts. 1341 ff., Fasc. A no. 25). Only in the systems of the German legal family is there no comparable development, those being the systems where the formal requirements are primarily designed to protect inexperienced persons from surprise rather than just restrict the methods of proof.

The declining importance of these formal provisions in France and England is easier to understand if we remember that art. 1341 Code civil is designed to restrict the undesirable testimony of witnesses and that the Statute of Frauds was primarily directed to preventing perjury and false witness. When courts were bound by strict procedural rules, especially rules of evidence, and could not, in countries of the Anglo-American legal family, reverse jury verdicts even if they were obviously wrong, such provisions may have made sense. Today, however, nearly everyone accepts that all evidence should be admitted for what it is worth, and courts are much better able to guard against the misdoings of witnesses and parties; there is therefore no longer the same need to provide indirect protection by insisting on formal requirements.

This makes it all the more surprising that in the United States the rules of the Statute of Frauds are still in force and that even the Uniform Commercial Code, so modern in other respects, requires contracts for the sale of goods to be in writing if the price exceeds a certain amount. It is no justification to say that in the United States the risk of false claims is particularly great (compare above p. 401) or that, as in 1677, it is a real danger that a plaintiff may drum up a whole troupe of corrupt witnesses to persuade a jury that a contract was concluded. Llewellyn emphasizes that in modern commerce all transactions tend to be put in writing but even this is no argument for making writing mandatory, unless one is prepared to infer a rule from a practice. In 1936, even before the Statute of Frauds was repealed in England, RABEL observed that a merchant there would be thought dishonourable and would imperil his commercial reputation if he defended an otherwise meritorious claim by relying on the absence of writing (*Recht des Warenkaufs* I (1936) 112; so also RABEL, 63 *LQ Rev.* 174, 187 (1947): 'honest parties to a suit resort to the Statute of Frauds only as an auxiliary defence against an unjust action'). CORBIN's conclusion points in the same direction:

'Very many cases are found in which the Court has seemed to apply the statute with vigor and approval, but in which its review of the evidence shows that the decision might well have been the same had there been no statute to apply' (§275).

If this is true, the main effect of abolishing the formal requirements for sales contracts would be to force courts to disclose the true reasons for their decisions. It would also dissipate the fog of those technical doctrines which have evolved over the centuries to counteract the excessive requirements of form, an oddity of American law which the modern comparative lawyer would like to see abolished in the interests of the global harmonization of sales law.

Even the more modern practice of imposing formal requirements so as to protect parties from surprise and draw their attention to dangers should be approached with a certain caution. People are literate today and there is no place in the modern law of contracts for the heavy Prussian paternalism evident in the excessive formal requirements of the General Land Law. It must be granted that the German BGB observes a praiseworthy restraint in this matter. Whether the formal requirement of §313 BGB can be justified by the consideration that landed property normally forms the most important item in the vendor's wealth is open to doubt, for it gives immoveable property a special status not justified by modern conditions, but it is any case unavoidable to require some degree of formality for transactions in land since otherwise there would be no clear basis for making entries in the Land Register. That formalities be required for guarantees is sound—significantly enough, they were first introduced in the Reichstag (see MUGDAN, *Materialien zum BGB* II (1899) 1295)—because even quite literate people may not see all the dangers inherent in becoming a guarantor. Even so, lawmakers must constantly bear in mind that every provision requiring a certain form exacts a high price: not only does it inhibit commercial intercourse and set traps for the unwary but it brings the legal system into disrepute, for it is only when the courts apply formal requirements and disregard the equities of the particular case in the interests of abstract order that the layman normally becomes conscious of them.

35

Illegality and Immorality

ABRAHAM, 'Die Doktrin der Public Policy', *AcP* 150 (1949) 385.

BONNECASE, 'La Notion juridique de bonnes mœurs; sa portée en droit civil français', *Études à la mémoire de Henri Capitant* (1939) 91.

CELLINI/WERTZ, 'Unconscionable Contract Provisions: A History of Unenforceability from Roman Law to the UCC', 42 *Tul. L. Rev.* 193 (1967).

COING, 'Allgemeine Rechtsgrundsätze in der Rechtsprechung des Reichsgerichts zum Begriff der guten Sitten', *NJW* 1948, 213.

DWYER, 'Immoral Contracts', 93 *LQ Rev.* 384 (1977).

GORDLEY, 'Equality in Exchange', 69 *Calif. L. Rev.* 1587 (1981).

v. HOFFMAN, *Das Recht des Grundstückskaufs, Eine rechtsvergleichende Untersuchung* (1982) §6.

JULLIOT DE LA MORANDIÈRE, 'L'Ordre public en droit privé interne', *Études à la mémoire de Henri Capitant* (1939) 381.

D. LLOYD, *Public Policy, A Comparative Study in English and French Law* (1953).

MALAURIE, *L'Ordre public et le contrat, Étude de Droit civil comparé: France, Angleterre, U.R.S.S.* (1953).

MAYER-MALY, 'Renaissance der laesio enormis?', *Festschrift Larenz zum 80. Geburtstag* (1983) 395.

v. MEHREN, 'The French Doctrine of lésion in the Sale of Immovable Property', 49 *Tul. L. Rev.* 321 (1974).

K. SIMITIS, *Gute Sitten und ordre public* (1960).

SZLADITS, 'Illegality of Prohibited Contracts, Comparative Aspects', in: *Twentieth Century Comparative and Conflicts Law—Legal Essays in Honor of Hessel E. Yntema* (1961) 221.

THOMMEN, *Beitrag zur Lehre vom Begriff der guten Sitten im schweizerischen Privatrecht* (1954).

WINFIELD, 'Public Policy and the English Common Law', 42 *Harv. L. Rev.* 376 (1928).

I

DESPITE the prevalence in the Western world of the principle of freedom of contract, every legal system must reserve the right to declare a contract void if it is legally or morally offensive, 'contraire aux bonnes mœurs ou à l'ordre public' or contrary to 'public policy'. The rules which determine whether a contract is void on these grounds are all very much the same, whether they are the product of legislation or judicial decision. In all systems the principal task falls to the judge, who has to test the circumstances of the individual case in

407

order to discover whether the contracting parties have gone beyond the
bounds of the permissible. In doing so, the courts strive to reduce the vague
concept of ethical behaviour or public policy to meaningful principles by
carving out discrete sets of case and formulating concrete criteria of
distinction, and so to minimize the irrational element necessarily contained in
general clauses.

One difficulty is that ideas of what is unethical alter in the course of time:
behaviour which seemed offensive yesterday can be found morally acceptable
today, and vice versa.

The unbroken legal development of the Common Law makes such a change
of attitude particularly clear and it comes as no surprise to find that the
English judges are very conscious of the changing content of legal values: 'The
determination of what is contrary to the so-called "policy of the law"
necessarily varies from time to time. Many transactions are upheld now by our
courts which a former generation would have avoided as contrary to the
supposed policy of the law. The rule remains, but its application varies with
the principles which for the time being guide public opinion.' (*Evanturel* v.
Evanturel, (1874) LR 6 PC 1, 29).—For example, claims arising from betting
transactions were perfectly enforceable until the nineteenth century, even if
the object of the bet, to modern sensibilities, was highly immoral. In 1771, in
the case of *March* v. *Pigot*, (1771) 5 Burr. 2802, 98 Eng. Rep. 471, the parties
had 'run their fathers each against the other', that is, had bet on whose father
would die first, and the transaction was held valid. Gaming transactions were
first rendered void by the Gaming Act, 1845.—In the area of sexual morals the
change is especially striking. Conduct which would have been regarded as
utterly repulsive twenty years ago may be tolerated, if not eagerly endorsed, by
the law nowadays. In the Australian decision of *Andrews* v. *Parker*, [1973] Qd.
R. 93, 104, Stable J. said this:

'Surely, what is immoral must be judged by the current standards of morality of the
community. What was apparently regarded with pious horror when the cases were
decided would, I observe, today hardly draw a raised eyebrow or a gentle "tut-tut" . . .
George Bernard Shaw's Eliza Doolittle (*circa* 1912) thought the suggestion that she
have a bath in private with her clothes off was indecent, so she hung a towel over the
bathroom mirror. One wonders what she would have thought and said to a suggestion
that she wear in public one of today's minuscule and socially accepted bikinis, held
miraculously in place apparently with the aid of providence, and, possibly, glue.'

In all the systems of the world illegality and immorality are seen as facts
which invalidate *contracts*. For this reason both Anglo-American law and the
Romanistic systems deal with the question in the law of contract. Only in
Germany is it treated as a factor which nullifies other legal acts as well as
contracts. Swiss and Italian law reach the same practical result, since they
apply the rule of nullity in contract law by analogy 'auf andere zivilrechtliche

Verhältnisse' (art. 7 ZGB) and 'per gli atti unilaterali tra vivi aventi contenuto patrimoniale' (art. 1324 Codice civile); in fact this is done even in systems where the concept of legal act is unknown, as in the Common Law.

When we speak here of the nullity of contracts on the ground of illegality or immorality, we mean that such contracts give rise to no claim for performance or damages. It is a quite different question whether a party to such a contract may have to give back what he received under it. For the comparatist this latter problem falls to be categorized not as a question of contract law, where it often appears in Common Law writings, but as an instance of the great class of restitutionary problems arising when something has been transferred or done without legal ground. For this reason the problem of reclaiming what was transferred under an illegal or immoral contract will be dealt with at a later stage (see below Ch. 46 III).

The question what makes a contract immoral or illegal is one which receives different answers in the various systems. The emphasis differs since ethics differ from country to country and traditional value-judgments still play a significant role; this can be seen if one looks at the cases relating to contracts which facilitate divorce or contracts to maintain concubines or agreements to divide up the estate of persons still in life. This is not the place to make a comparative study of all the cases on the question, so we will deal with three matters only. First we shall mention the rules in the codes of Civil Law jurisdictions; then we shall look at the Common Law to see the most important types of case involving illegality and immorality; finally we shall deal comparatively with one or two special instances.

II

In all the great European codes this problem is covered by general clauses which refer to other prohibitory rules or to the concept of good morals.

In Italy and France the invalidity of contracts on the ground of illegality or immorality is dealt with in connection with the doctrine of 'causa' or 'cause'. Thus art. 1131 of the French Code civil says that an obligation 'sur une cause illicite' is void, and this is defined in art. 1133:

'La cause est illicite quand elle est prohibée par la loi, quand elle est contraire aux bonnes mœurs ou à l'ordre public.'—Art. 1343 of the Italian Codice civile is almost identical: 'la causa è illecita quando è contraria a norme imperative, a l'ordine pubblico o al buon costume.'

To deal with this matter in relation to 'cause', which in French law is simply the generalized motive behind a promise (see below Ch. 36 III) is clearly unsatisfactory. The situation is further confused by the fact that in French law a contract can also be held invalid if its *objet* is unpermitted ('objet illicite': see in the same sense art. 1346 Codice civile). If a person promises to commit a crime for a reward, then—according to PLANIOL/RIPERT VI no. 276—the obligation is invalid since the *objet* of the contract, the promised act, is forbidden. The object of the other party's obligation, namely to pay the reward, is by contrast, intrinsically 'neutral' but the promise is equaly invalid because the *cause* underlying it, here understood as the purpose of the promise, is forbidden.

Distinctions such as these are quite artificial. There is really no reason to say any more than that a contract is void if the content of a contract and the attendant circumstances, including the motives of the parties, show that its whole character offends against the proper standards.

This is clearly formulated in the German BGB in §138 par. 1; it makes offensiveness to good morals the ground of invalidity and makes no particular reference to the object of the contract or its legal basis.

§134 BGB adds that a legal act is void if it contravenes a statutory prohibition, but since this only applies if the prohibitory rule does not provide otherwise (see also art. 174 of the Greek Civil Code) the judge has to inquire whether or not the intention behind the prohibitory statute was to invalidate the contract as a matter of private law.

Thus in RGZ 60, 273, 276 the Reichsgericht held that a transaction concluded on a Sunday was not invalid on the ground that §41a of the Trade Ordinance then in force made sales on a Sunday punishable. In many of the states of the United States, on the other hand, there are 'Sunday laws' which render transactions concluded on a Sunday invalid unless they are 'works of necessity or charity'.—The Cour de Cassation in France has held that transactions entered into by a warehouse-man on his own account were not invalid although forbidden by a police ordinance (Req. 25 Jan. 1909, S.1910. I. 77). More recently courts have been much occupied with the question whether prohibitions in European economic law have any effect on contracts in private law which offend against their provisions. The Bundesgerichtshof has upheld a contract which contravened the rule against discrimination in the Treaty establishing the European Coal and Steel Community (BGHZ 30, 74) and a contract which offended against the prohibition of monopolies in the same treaty has been upheld by the Cour de Cassation (Clunet 88 (1961)120).—There are a large number of comparable cases. They disclose that all legal systems call for a functional construction of the prohibitory statute involved. One particular point to check is whether the sanctions imposed by the statute itself, such as monetary fines, are adequate to achieve the purpose behind it. It is also important to ask whether the other party's interest in having the contract upheld is worth protecting.

III

To discover what contracts are illegal or immoral in Anglo-American law one must resort to the cases. One quickly discovers that there are certain groups of situations which the courts regularly deal with in terms of illegality, but when it comes to categorizing these various groups of case in some systematic order almost every English writer seems to have his own method, whilst American textbooks normally just make a list of them.

POLLOCK/WINFIELD (p. 260) distinguish between 'illegal' contracts, 'immoral' contracts and contracts which offend 'against public policy'. In the first group they put contracts to commit a crime or defraud third parties, marriages between persons too closely related, gaming and betting contracts, and many others.

A contract is immoral, according to POLLOCK/WINFIELD, if a reasonable man would find it scandalous for a court to uphold it. Basically this is the same test as the German courts express in the phrase 'feeling of decency of the just and fair-minded man', the English formula being more forceful and objective, the German one more domestic.

It is in this connection that the Common Law normally deals with agreements which may adversely affect matrimonial life or induce disregard of matrimonial duties. Here English law has treated as invalid the promise by one spouse to pay maintenance to the other in return for her consent to a divorce (*Brodie* v. *Brodie*, [1917] P. 271). So also a promise to marry is invalid if it is made by a person already married, as this might provide an incentive for the promisor to dispose of his spouse one way or the other (*Spiers* v. *Hunt*, [1908] 1 KB 720); the Reichsgericht reached the same conclusion in RGZ 170, 72.—On the other hand, a person who has already obtained a decree of divorce from his spouse may validly promise to marry another and be liable in damages for breach, even if at the time of the promise the decree of divorce was not yet finalized (*Fender* v. *St. John-Mildmay*, [1938] AC 1; see especially the interesting judgment of LORD ATKIN which contains an anthology of the most striking expressions of English judges on the problem of public policy).

The group of contracts which offend against public policy includes a whole string of very diverse types of case. The following may be of particular interest for the Continental lawyer.

Contracts are void if they aim to effect an improper 'restraint of trade'. As well as the case where a person promises not to compete with another in a particular trade, this covers the whole field of contractual limitations on competition by cartel and price restrictions—an area of law where the United States is especially rich in practical instances and theoretical distinctions.

'Bargains harmful to the administration of justice' are also void, including agreements whereby a person is paid not to institute a prosecution. On the other hand, it is not necessarily illegal in the United States for a litigant to promise to pay a witness to give evidence. This is connected with the fact that in the American law of procedure it is up to the parties themselves to procure witnesses to attend in court, since the court itself does not summon them. Only a witness who is resident within the jurisdiction of the court which is seised of the case can be required to pay a penalty (subpoena) if he fails to appear; in such a case promises to pay for evidence are void, since they contain a risk of influencing the evidence given. On the other hand, it is perfectly valid to promise a witness who lives outside the jurisdiction a sum of money for his appearance in court, though not for giving particular evidence or conditionally on the outcome of the trial

Arbitration agreements used also to be included in the group of contracts regarded as being harmful to the administration of justice and therefore to public policy (see POLLOCK/WINFIELD p. 310 f.). The Common Law has always been very suspicious of arbitration clauses because of their tendency to take the decision of legal disputes away from the courts which are so venerated in the Anglo-American legal family. An agreement to submit all future disputes to arbitration is invariably void but an arbitration clause may be valid if it covers only specified disputes sufficiently described. Such a clause does not prevent the party's going to court but simply means that his doing so amounts to a breach of contract which gives rise to a claim for damages, supposing any damage can be proved. In England (unlike Germany—see §274 par. 2 no. 3 Code of Civil Procedure) a party cannot demand the dismissal of a claim which has been brought in breach of a domestic arbitration agreement: the judge has a discretion to stay the court proceedings (s. 4(1) Arbitration Act 1950). No such discretion exists if either party or the agreed forum is foreign (s. 1 Arbitration Act 1975).

IV

The same conduct is sometimes regarded differently in different countries by reason of differing ethics. Some cases relating to attorney's fees provide a good example.

The general view in *Germany* is that while an agreement to pay an unduly high fee to an attorney may be a breach of the attorney's professional ethics, it is not of itself void as being offensive to good morals. Such an agreement will only be void if there are other circumstances in the case such as the elements of exploitation specified in §138 par. 2 BGB or taking unfair advantage of the client by steps which come close to extortion (compare RGZ 83, 109).

But the Reichsgericht has taken a much sterner view where the payment of the fee is made conditional on success. It once had to deal with a case in which the attorney had demanded a special honorarium over and above the statutory fee amounting to 5% of the sum recovered in the trial plus 10% of the excess over $10,000 (the so-called *pactum de quota litis*). The Reichsgericht held that such a percentage fee was morally offensive. The lawyer, as 'an organ of the law', must serve the law, not just the interests of his client; his objectivity in this regard would be imperilled if he 'confused his own interest in a fair remuneration for his efforts with the interests of his client by making the former dependent on success in the trial' (RGZ 115, 141). Since that decision the German courts have always held that fees conditional on success and fees calculated as a percentage of the sums recovered by suit are immoral and void under §138 BGB.

For examples, see RGZ 142, 70; BGHZ 39, 142; 51, 290. But if a conditional fee contract is made with an American attorney and is governed by *American* law, the attorney can claim the payment in Germany: this is not an offence against German *ordre public* barred by art. 30 of the Introductory Law of the BGB (see BGHZ 22, 162).—Outside Germany also the *pactum de quota litis* is regarded askance, as in Austria (see §875 par. 2 no. 2 ABGB, and JAHODA, ÖJZ 1954, 605), Switzerland (see BGE 41 II 474; Cass. Zurich, BlZüRspr. 54 (1955) no. 83), France (see LEMAIRE, *Les Régles et les usages du barreau de Paris* (3rd edn., 1975) 471 ff.), and Italy (see art. 2233 par. 3 Codice civile). Contingent fees are also banned in England, though not without dissent (YOUNGWOOD, 28 *Mod. L. Rev.* 330 (1965); WHITE, 41 *Mod. L. Rev.* 286 (1978)).

A wholly different view is taken in the *United States* where it is perfectly normal for attorneys to stipulate for contingent fees expressed in the form of a percentage of the proceeds of suit. Such an agreement is only regarded as immoral if the attorney undertakes to pay the costs of the trial himself or promises to indemnify the client for the costs of an unsuccessful suit, the reason being that an attorney has no business to incite a client to sue for the attorney's own benefit (see CORBIN §1424).

These different ways of viewing the same matter are of interest to the comparative lawyer. The German notion that the attorney is to rise above the interests of the parties and to protect the objective law is quite different from the American view. Of course attorneys must act lawfully in the United States as well, but their principal task is to use all legal means to obtain the maximum recovery for their clients. The underlying consideration is that if both attorneys deliberately present the case as 'one-sidedly' as possible the judge will be best placed to reach the correct solution. This is probably a more realistic way of looking at the matter than the German view that the attorney, just like the judge, should act as a detached protector of the law and treat the interests of the parties as subsidiary.

This is reflected in legal education in the two systems; in American law schools the law student is trained to argue doubtful cases as imaginatively and effectively as possible, whereas in the law faculties of European universities the student is ideally prepared to decide a case as a judge would decide it.

Thus behind the difference in the case-law lies a difference in the view of the professional obligations of the attorney. The American view seems to us to be preferable because it is more realistic. Nor is there any danger in it: the untrammelled advocacy of the attorney for one party is balanced out by that of the other party's counsellor, and so a good judge is enabled to see the case from all sides. That the German concept of the attorney as the dispassionate protector of the law can lead to unfortunate consequences could be seen during the Hitler era when defence counsel used to address the People's Court in much the same tones as the state prosecutor, in the belief, consistent with the teaching of the National Socialist regime, that this was the best way to serve the 'public good'.

V

It is worth taking a moment to consider whether the validity of a contract may depend on there being a reasonable relationship between what the parties respectively undertake.

The historical development on this question is instructive even for the comparative lawyer of today. In classical Roman law the parties to a contract of sale were entirely free to fix the price, and neither party could resile on the ground that there was a gross disproportion between the price promised and the true value of the object of sale. Under JUSTINIAN, however, if the true value of the object was more than twice the price (*laesio enormis*), the vendor was entitled to demand the object back from the purchaser on condition of returning the price, though the purchaser could retain the object on paying the difference between price and value.

This doctrine was elaborated in the Middle Ages—especially under Thomistic influence—into the theory of the just price, the 'iustum pretium', that in any kind of contract the mutual promises had to be equivalent in value. This doctrine survived for a long time, for even POTHIER was ready to apply it to all commutative contracts. But at the very time he was writing, a contrary movement was afoot in France which exempted a whole string of contracts from the doctrine of *laesio enormis*, including the contract for the sale of goods.

The result of this development in *France* may be seen in art. 1118 Code civil. Only certain types of contract can be rescinded by an adult on the ground of 'lesion': these are contracts for the division of a decedent's estate and contracts for the sale of land. If under a contract for the division of an estate a joint heir obtains less than three-quarters of his entitlement under the law of succession, he can rescind the contract without proving any error or deceit (art. 887 Code civil, compare also art. 783 Code civil). The vendor (but not the purchaser) of land has the same right under arts. 1674 ff., if the price he has agreed to accept is less than seven-twelfths of the true value of the land, and this right is not lost by express waiver or by a purported gift of the shortfall to the purchaser.

Under *Austrian* law both parties to *any* contact, including contracts for the sale of goods, are entitled to rescind the contract if the performance of one party is worth more than twice the other's (Verkürzung über die Hälfte, §934 AGBG), unless the transaction was a commercial one on the side of the party seeking rescission (§351a Austrian Commercial Code), or he had stated in the contract that 'the object is being transferred at an unusual price in consideration of love and affection' (§935 ABGB). In addition, Austrian law contains a general provision that contracts may be invalid if they are legally or morally offensive (§879 ABGB).

In *Italy*, too, the Codice civile of 1942 maintains the possibility of rescinding a contract on the grounds of a quantitative disproportion between performance and counterperformance. Under art. 1448 a contract may be set aside for 'lesione' if the disadvantaged partly received less than half the value of his performance under a contract which exploited the difficulties of his situation.

In *Germany* the doctrine of lesion formed part of the *Gemeines Recht* until the end of the nineteenth century but the draftsmen of the BGB declined to adopt it because they found it inconsistent with the principle of freedom of contract. Under the positive law, a 'striking' disproportion makes a contract invalid under §138 par. 2 BGB if the beneficiary has exploited the distress, inexperience, lack of judgment, or pliancy of the party prejudiced; additional factors may render a transaction immoral and therefore void under §138 par. 1 BGB.

Laesio enormis came to life again, though not for long, in a notorious decision of the Oberlandesgericht Stuttgart (NJW 1979, 2409). The question for decision was when a contract for the repayment of a loan by instalments was to be regarded as immoral. The position of the BGH had been that a contract which did not fall within the special case of §138 par. 2 was to be regarded as immoral only if, in addition to there being an obvious misrelation between performance and counterperformance, the lender had consciously exploited the borrower's relative poverty or had at least wantonly closed his mind to the fact that the borrower was only entering the transaction because of it. The view of the Stuttgart court was that resort to these subjective criteria was unnecessary under §138 par. 1 if the disproportion between performance and counterperformance was not just 'obvious' but 'particularly gross'. The disproportion would always be 'particularly gross' if the agreed interest was more than twice the market rate. To show that this was not an arbitrary point at which to draw the line the Stuttgart court invoked §934 ABGB, which allows the disadvantaged party to claim rescission of the contract in a case of 'overreaching beyond the moiety'. The Bundesgerichtshof refused to accept this line of thought (BGHZ 80, 153). There are indeed good reasons against making the validity of a contract depend on the precise ratio of the values of performance and counterperformance, but it was wrong for the court to say that it was 'an error . . . for the court below to rely on rules from a foreign jurisdiction', for provided that a rule in a foreign jurisdiction is functionally comparable, it is always proper to use it as an argument, though whether the argument is compelling or not is another question.

The Common Law of *England* and the *United States* has no doctrine analogous to *laesio enormis*. It is true, as will be shown below (see Ch. 36), that a contract will only be valid if each party made his promise in return for the promise of the other party (consideration), but there is no need for the counterperformance to stand in any reasonable relation of value to the performance promised. On the other hand the relationship of performance to counterperformance is very important when the question is whether the contract is void for 'unconscionability' under §2—302 of the UCC (see above p. 367) or duress or fraud (see below Ch. 38 VI). The greater the disproportion between performance and counterperformance, the more likely it is that the contract will be held invalid. According to GORDLEY, indeed, the courts regard the objective imbalance between performance and counterperformance as *decisive* and where such imbalance exists will treat a contract as invalid even if the disadvantaged party was neither in actual difficulty nor misled by the other party (above p. 407, pp. 1645 ff.).

After careful consideration one is forced to condemn the doctrine of lesion, traces of which may still be found in Austrian law and in the law of the Romanistic systems. In systems of private law based on the freedom of contract it is for the parties themselves to determine the relationship of performance and counterperformance, though in times of economic stress exceptional laws may be passed relating to maximum prices or price freezes. Another exception is presented by cases where there was no freedom of contract at all, performance and counterperformance being disproportionate because a state of difficulty or distress has been exploited or a position of monopoly or superior economic power abused. Since the power of the parties to fix the relation of performance and counterperformance is a product of freedom of contract, the only ground on which the courts can be invited to interfere with it is that in the particular case no such freedom existed at all.

36

Indicia of Seriousness

ATIYAH, *Consideration in Contracts: A Fundamental Restatement* (1971).

BECKER, *Gegenopfer und Opferverwehrung* (1958).

BOYER, 'Promissory Estoppel: Principles from Precedents', 50 *Mich. L. Rev.* 639, 873 (1952).

——,'Promissory Estoppel: Requirements and Limitations of the Doctrine', 98 *U. Pa. L. Rev.* 459 (1950).

CAPITANT, *De la cause des obligations* (3rd edn., 1927).

CHLOROS, 'The Doctrine of Consideration and the Reform of the Law of Contract', 17 *ICLQ* 137 (1968).

DAVID, 'Cause et Consideration', *Mélanges Maury* II (1960) 111.

DAWSON, *Gifts and Promises, Continental and American Law Compared* (1980).

DENNING, 'Recent Developments in the Doctrine of Consideration', 15 *Mod. L. Rev.* 1 (1952).

FRIDMAN, 'Promissory Estoppel', 35 *Can. Bar Rev.* 279 (1957).

FULLER, 'Consideration and Form', 41 *Colum. L. Rev.* 799 (1941).

GILMORE, *The Death of Contract* (1974).

GORLA, *Il Contratto*, Vol. I (1954) 327 ff.

HAMSON, 'The Reform of Consideration', 54 *LQ Rev.* 233 (1938).

HENDERSON,' Promissory Estoppel and Traditional Contract Doctrine', 78 *Yale LJ* 343 (1969).

E. v. HIPPEL, *Die Kontrolle der Vertragsfreiheit nach anglo-amerikanischem Recht* (1963).

KESSLER, 'Einige Betrachtungen zur Lehre von der consideration', *Festschrift Rabel* I (1954) 251.

——, 'Der Schutz des Vertrauens bei Vertragsverhandlungen in der neueren amerikanischen Rechtsprechung', *Festschrift v. Caemmerer* (1978) 873.

KÖNDGEN, *Selbstbindung ohne Vertrag* (1981) 65 ff.

KÜHNE, 'Der Vertrauensgedanke im Schuldvertragsrecht', *RabelsZ* 36 (1972) 275.

LLEWELLYN, 'Common Law Reform of Consideration', 41 *Colum. L. Rev.* 863 (1941).

LOCHER, 'Causa' in II *Rechtsvergleichendes Handwörterbuch* (ed. Schlegelberger) (1929) 614.

LORENZ, 'Entgeltliche und unentgeltliche Geschäfte, Eine vergleichende Betrachtung des deutschen und des ango-amerikanischen Rechts', *Festschrift für Max Rheinstein* II (1969) 547.

LORENZEN, 'Causa and Consideration in the Law of Contracts', 28 *Yale LJ* 621 (1919).

MARKESINIS, 'Cause and Consideration: A Study in Parallel', 1978 *Camb. LJ* 53.

——, 'La Notion de consideration dans la common law', *Rev. int. dr. comp.* 35 (1983) 735.

MASON, 'The Utility of Consideration—A Comparative View', 41 *Colum. L. Rev.* 825 (1941).

NEWMAN, 'The Doctrine of Cause or Consideration in the Civil Law', 30 *Can. Bar Rev.* 662 (1952).

PATERSON, 'An Apology for Consideration', 58 *Colum. L. Rev.* 929 (1958).

RHEINSTEIN, *Die Struktur des vertraglichen Schuldverhältnisses im anglo-amerikanischen Recht* (1932) 55 ff.

SEAVEY, 'Reliance on Gratuitous Promises', 64 *Harv. L. Rev.* 913 (1951).

SHATTUCK, 'Gratuitous Promises—A New Writ?', 35 *Mich. L. Rev.* 908 (1937).

SHATWELL, 'The Doctrine of Consideration in the Modern Law', 1 *Sydney L. Rev.* 289 (1955).

SUTTON, *Consideration Reconsidered, Studies on the Doctrine of Consideration of the Law of Contract* (1974).

VON MEHREN, 'Civil-Law Analogues to Consideration: An Exercise in Comparative Analysis', 72 *Harv. L. Rev.* 1009 (1959).

WRIGHT, 'Ought the Doctrine of Consideration to be Abolished from the Common Law?' 49 *Harv. L. Rev.* 1225 (1936).

I

ALL legal systems must decide whether to treat every bilateral agreement as a contract or whether to require something extra in order to make a transaction enforceable. Lawyers in the German legal family make a distinction between promises which give rise to a legal obligation and mere acts of kindness and other purely social engagements of no interest to the law: every first-year law student learns that invitations to dance at a ball, invitations to a party, and so on give rise to no claims at law.

Throughout the world it is regarded as normal for binding promises to be given for payment or some counterpart in kind. Gifts and gratuitous promises, on the other hand, are regarded as something abnormal and the law always treats them in a special way, though the ways differ.

The French Code civil has special provisions about gift in arts. 894, 931 and 932. These rules are not very clearly drafted, but their effect is that an informal gift, the so-called manual gift, is valid if it is immediately executed but that a promise of a gift requires to be notarized (Req. 28 Oct. 1935, DP 1936. 1. 29).

Both of these principles were later formulated with clarity in the codes of the German legal family, in §§516 and 518 BGB in Germany, and in art. 242 and 243 OR in Switzerland, the only difference being that in Germany promises of gifts have to be notarized while in Switzerland writing suffices. The new Italian Codice civile is more severe: in principle it requires the notarial form for every gift and promise of gift; an exception is made for manual gifts of moderate value, for which 'tradizione' or delivery f the thing itself suffices (arts. 782, 783 Codice civile), as it does in Germany for *all* manual gifts.

Thus all the great codes have special rules for gratuitous transactions and insist on a special formality as evidence of the intention to enter legal relations. The Common Law and the Romanistic systems go further and lay down general requirements to distinguish those promises which are legally significant from those which are not, to distinguish serious from unserious promises and thus to determine which promises are actionable and which are not.

II

In the Common Law of England and the United States of America a promise is treated as serious only if it is made against a 'consideration', that is, some counterpart from the promisee. Since a promise with no such counterpart is not actionable, the presence of consideration is an actual precondition of validity for all contracts in Anglo-American law, unless they are 'under seal', that is, contained in a sealed document.

In the United States the sealing of a document is now an empty formality: all that is required is to affix to the document a paper label which may be procured in any drugstore and it is even sufficient if the letters 'LS' (*loco sigilli*), printed or written, appear at the bottom of the text. More than half the states of the Union, including New York and California, have enacted that a contract without consideration is not rendered valid by 'sealing', while others have provided that the effect of a 'seal' or even of mere writing is to raise a rebuttable presumption that consideration was given.

The idea of consideration as it has developed in England and the United States is extremely complex and subtle. This makes it all the more difficult to define. One classic definition was given by the Exchequer Division of the English High Court in 1875:

'A valuable consideration in the sense of the law may consist either in some right, interest, profit or benefit accruing to one party, or some forbearance, detriment, loss or responsibility given, suffered or undertaken by the other' (*Currie* v. *Misa*, (1875) LR 10 Ex. 153). See also the definition of LORD BLACKBURN in *Bolton* v. *Madden*, (1873) LR 9 QB 55.

More recent definitions emphasize that the promisor must have intended to induce the promisee to give the requested counterpart: the relation between the parties must be of the *do-ut-des* type. Thus Restatement (Second) of Contracts (1981) §71 has the following definition:

(1) 'To constitute consideration, a performance or a return promise must be bargained for.' (2) 'A performance or return promise is bargained for if it is sought by the promisor in exchange for his promise and is given by the promisee in exchange for that promise.'

To give some substance to these definitions one must go to the cases. A good introduction is provided by the famous English decision *Stilk* v. *Myrick* in 1809 (2 Camp. 317, 170 Eng. Rep. 1168):

A shipowner hired a crew in London for a voyage to Petersburg under contracts of employment which obliged the sailors to perform their services to the best of their strength notwithstanding the dangers of the journey. Some of the sailors jumped ship in Kronstadt and no replacements could be found for them, so in order to keep the remaining members of the crew in good spirits the captain promised to pay them extra if they did the work of the runaways. The men agreed and on their return asked for the additional pay they had been promised. The shipowner refused to pay and the sailors brought an action. The court dismissed the claim on the ground that the captain's promise was invalid and not actionable since the sailors, as promisees, had given him no consideration for it: they were already obliged by the original contract to take on any extra duties which might arise during the voyage, including the work of those who had jumped ship.

One will see from this holding that the doctrine of consideration makes for difficulties when claims are brought on contracts which have been varied since their conclusion. Take the case that a builder agrees to dig foundations for $1,000 and then, when he starts digging, unexpectedly happens upon rock. If the site-owner thereupon promises $1,500 for the job, his promise of the extra amount is not enforceable since the builder, being already bound to make the excavation, has not given any consideration for the extra $500. This result cannot be justified by saying that otherwise a contractor would be tempted to do the work sloppily or threaten not to do it at all so as to exact a higher price; such extreme cases can always be dealt with under the general rules of defects of consent.

See the American cases *King* v. *Duluth, Missabe and Northern Ry. Co.*, 61 Minn. 482, 63 NW 1105 (1895); *Western Lithograph Co.* v. *Vanomar Producers*, 185 Cal. 366, 197 P. 103 (1929); *Linz* v. *Schuck*, 106 Md. 220, 67 A. 286 (1907); *Lange* v. *United States* 120 F. 2d 886 (4th Cir. 1941).—These implications of the doctrine of consideration do not answer the requirements of modern commerce in goods and services; accordingly, the Uniform Commercial Code provides, in §2–209, that 'an agreement modifying a contract . . . needs no consideration to be binding'. It is true that this provision applies only to contracts of sale, but at least it means that a subsequent agreement to vary the price, the date of delivery, the place of delivery, and so on is effective without any counterpart from the person who benefits from the variation. But even outside the law of sales, the courts uphold subsequent modifications of a contract not yet wholly executed, even if there is no consideration for them. See Restatement (Second) of Contracts (1981) §89 and the cases there cited.

The doctrine of consideration also gives rise to difficulties regarding the release of debtors. If a creditor states that he will accept the immediate payment of $800 in full settlement of a debt of $1,000 and waive the rest, this release is invalid for want of consideration since the debtor has done nothing extra for it.

Such was the decision of the House of Lords in *Foakes* v. *Beer*, (1884) 9 App. Cas. 605; CHESHIRE/FIFOOT (p. 81) describe it as 'hardly satisfactory', which is about as far as English academics will go in England in criticizing decisions of the Upper House. Although most decisions in the United States take the same line, half a dozen states have abolished the rule by legislation, two supreme courts have held the rule inapplicable in terms, and in many other states its area of application is being narrowed by the development of special doctrines. On this see the detailed treatment in CORBIN §175.

A further consequence of the doctrine of consideration is that services rendered by the promisee prior to the promise do not constitute consideration: 'past consideration is no consideration'. This is shown, for example, by *Brawn v. Lyford*, 103 Me. 362, 69 A. 544 (1907):

A vendor sold a house and assigned to the purchaser his rights under a current fire insurance policy. After the contract of sale had been performed by both parties and the property had vested in the purchaser, both parties remembered that the policy had to be put into the purchaser's name. The vendor agreed to send the policy to the insurance agent for this to be done but he forgot, and failed to tell the purchaser. Shortly afterwards the house burned down.—The Continental lawyer would allow the purchaser's claim for damages, basing it either on the vendor's duty to perform collateral duties in the contract or on an agency agreement, but the American court dismissed the claim: the vendor's promise to send off the policy for transfer into the purchaser's name was a gratuitous promise without any consideration since it had been made after the contract of sale had been concluded and performed.—In *Siegel* v. *Spear*, 234 NY 479, 138 NE 414 (1923), however, the court was able to come to the opposite result.

Many judges have tried, and none more strenuously than LORD MANSFIELD, to make 'past consideration' into 'good consideration', at any rate when the past services of the promisee made it a matter of moral duty for the promisor to reward them and his promise was intended to confirm this moral duty. Nevertheless the efforts to establish this exception have not been generally successful. Indeed, if the doctrine of consideration is accepted as sound, it is perfectly logical to repulse LORD MANSFIELD's efforts, for MANSFIELD's doctrine of 'moral consideration' would wholly have destroyed the institution of consideration which is so typical of English law: since *every* promise engenders a moral duty to perform it the equation of consideration with moral duty must logically have driven the requirement of consideration out of the common law of contracts.

An extreme case in the United States shows how harshly the rule as to past consideration can operate unless perceptive judges are prepared to get round its technicalities: A saved B's life but in doing so was himself so severely injured that he was crippled for life. In gratitude, B promised A to pay him the sum of $30 per month, but when B died his heirs refused to continue the payments. Technically, B's promise to pay should be invalid since the act of rescue was already over and done with when the promise was made and therefore could not constitute good consideration. Even so, the court gave judgment for the plaintiff and rightly, however strained its reasoning.

(*Webb* v. *McGowin* 27 Ala. App. 82, 168 So. 196 (1935). (But see *Harrington* v. *Taylor*, 225 NC 690, 36 SE 2d 227 (1945), where in a similar case the court said: 'However much the defendant should be impelled by common gratitude to alleviate the plaintiff's misfortune, a humanitarian act of this kind, voluntarily performed, is not such consideration as would entitle her to recover at law.' Restatement (Second) of Contracts (1981) now takes a different view: §86 provides that promises in recognition of a benefit previously received are binding, though only 'to the extent necessary to prevent injustice'.

The shifts to which courts may be put in order to reach a reasonable result despite the doctrine of consideration may be seen in the decision of the English Court of Appeal in 1956:

Mr Byham had lived in unmarried bliss with Mrs Ward for several years and a daughter was born to them. They agreed that the daughter should stay with the mother and Mr Byham promised to pay her £1 per week so that the child 'be well looked after and happy'. Mrs Ward subsequently married another man and Mr Byham stopped paying. On being sued, he argued that his promise to pay was invalid for want of consideration since by English law it is the mother of an illegitimate child who is obliged by statute to maintain it. This argument was rejected by LORD DENNING on the ground—admittedly at variance with the general view—that the performance of one's statutory duty is 'sufficient consideration', and by the other two judges on the ground that the mother had promised not merely to maintain the child but to look after it well and to make it happy! (*Ward* v. *Byham*, [1956] 2 All ER 318.)

To the adequacy of consideration, on the other hand, the courts pay no attention. Freedom of contract is maintained alongside the doctrine of consideration but naturally there are limits. If someone promised to give $600 for one cent, the cent would not be good consideration since it could not possibly be intended as a proper counterpart; but provided that the counterpart was seriously intended as such, the validity of a contract is not impaired by even a very gross difference in the value of what is given on the two sides.

There is a remarkably interesting doctrine in American law which is used to avoid the unfair results of the doctrine of consideration in certain types of case: this is the doctrine of 'promissory estoppel'.

The primary stimulus for the development of this doctrine came from the so-called 'subscription cases', concerned with citizens' subscriptions to communal, charitable, or religious purposes. Contributions promised to a parish for the building of a church could be withheld even if the parish had relied on them and proceeded with the work; the parish could not sue for the promised contribution since there was no consideration for it and it was naturally hardly ever under seal.

See *Y.M.C.A.* v. *Estill*, 140 Ga. 291, 78 SE 1075 (1913); *Furman University* v. *Waller*, 124 SC 68, 117 SE 356 (1923); *Allegheny College* v. *National Chautauqua County Bank of Jamestown*, 246 NY 369, 159 NE 173 (1927) (famous opinion of Judge CARDOZO).

The same problem arises in a whole series of cases in which a person has spent his own money in reliance on a promise unenforceable for want of consideration. The case of *Devecmon* v. *Shaw*, 69 Md. 199, 14 A. 464 (1888) offers a textbook example:

An uncle promised to finance his nephew's studies for a year if he spent the year in Paris and immersed himself in European culture. The nephew, who had means of his own, went to Paris in reliance on this promise and studied there for a year; after his return he sought to have his expenses paid by his uncle.

Undoubtedly there is here an informal promise without consideration and it should therefore be unenforceable, but the American courts have developed a doctrine which appears in the following form in Restatement (Second) of Contracts (1981) §90(1):

'A promise which the promisor should reasonably expect to induce action or forbearance on the part of the promisee or a third person and which does induce such action or forbearance is binding [even in the absence of consideration] if injustice can be avoided only by enforcement of the promise. The remedy granted for breach may be limited as justice requires.'

This means that the promisor may be bound even by a gratuitous and informal promise if the promisee 'has changed his position' materially and definitively in reliance upon it and such reliance might have been foreseen by the promisor. This is a very reasonable qualification of the doctrine of consideration in favour of giving protection to detrimental reliance.

The principle laid down in Restatement (Second) of Contracts (1981) §90 was first used by the courts where the promised performance was gratuitous, but more recently they have extended the principle much further, to cases in which one of the parties to negotiations for a bilateral contract arouses expectations on which the other predictably relies: if the envisaged contract does not eventuate, the disappointed party can claim damages for his wasted expenditure and even, under certain circumstances, the benefit of the bargain. Here the German lawyer would use the doctrine of *culpa in contrahendo*. Leading cases in the United States include *Chrysler Corp.* v. *Quimby*, 51 Del. 254, 144 A. 2d 123(1958); *Hoffman* v. *Red Owl Stores Inc.*, 26 Wis. 2d 63, 133 NW 2d 267 (1965). The matter is dealt with in detail by KESSLER, *Festschrift von Caemmerer*; KÖNDGEN amd KÜHNE (above p. 417). The notion of promissory estoppel also underlies some *English* decisions, especially *Central London Property Trust* v. *High Trees House*, [1947] KB 130. But in contrast with the United States a person who relies on a promise for which there is no consideration obtains only a defence against a claim by the promisor and cannot sue for performance of the promise or for damages for non-performance; on this see *Combe* v. *Combe*, [1951] 2 KB 215 (CA) and CHESHIRE/FIFOOT pp. 83 ff.

III

In the Romanistic systems the same function, namely, to distinguish between promissory transactions which are binding and those which are not, is performed by the doctrine of *cause* or *causa*.

Cause in France is admittedly something of a conceptual hippogriff. According to art. 1131 Code civil, promissory contracts are valid only if they have a cause. The concept of 'cause' has altered much during the history of French law but today it means something like the typical reason for which people make the sort of promise in question. If the proper construction of a transaction shows that the promisor wished to make a *gift* out of his estate for the benefit of the recipient, art. 931 Code civil requires the promise to be notarized. Here is an example before the French Court of Cassation.

In order to give 'une preuve de l'amitié que nous lui portons', Baron de Kaerbout had promised in writing to make an annuity to a family retainer. After the Baron's death his heirs refused to continue the payments. The Court held that because the employee had faithfully fulfilled a position of responsibility in the management of the estate the promise had 'une cause suffisante dans les services que Justine Moufflard avait rendus au baron de Kaerbout'. In consequence it was not a gift (Civ. 3 Feb. 1846, DP 1846. 1. 59). Similar cases are Req. 14 Apr. 1863, DP 1863.1. 402; Civ. 19 July 1894, DP 1895. 1. 125; Aix 30 Jan. 1882, DP 1883. 2. 245. In all these cases a person was held bound by an informal promise to pay money or convey land because although he had received no 'true' return he was seeking some intangible advantage such as the prestige which comes from ostentatious generosity. See also Req. 23 March 1870, DP 1870. 1. 327; Caen, 22 March 1911, S. 1911. 2. 271. Everything depends on the circumstances of the individual case, and here the Cour de Cassation accepts the findings of fact in the trial courts; this is clearly stressed in Req. 7 Jan. 1862, DP 1862. 1. 188 and Civ. 23 May 1876, DP 1876. 1. 254.

The calls of honour and decency have very frequently been held to be 'cause suffisante' by the courts. A man's written promise, not in notarial form, to support his mother-in-law was held binding although under art. 206 Code civil he was under no legal obligation to maintain her, his wife having died childless. (Trib. civ. Béziers 26 Nov. 1945, Gaz. Pal. 1946. 1. 115). So too was the promise of a father to maintain the mother of an illegitimate child not recognized by him (Civ. 27 May 1862, DP 1862. 1. 208; Civ. 15 Jan. 1873, DP 1873. 1. 180). Finally we may cite an interesting decision of the Court of Cassation in 1923.

After the outbreak of the First World War a certain M. Bailly promised the City of Nancy to give 100,000 francs to set up a fund to support the families of combatants. The city did so and then claimed the promised sum from M. Bailly which he refused to pay. The Court of Appeal of Nancy decided that the promise of a subscription gave rise not only to an 'engagement d'honneur' but to a legal duty; this took it out of the law of gift and away from the formal requirement of art. 931 Code civil. It was a 'contrat innomé', admittedly gratuitous *vis-à-vis* the families who were to benefit, but a 'contrat commutatif' *vis-à-vis* the organizers of the fund, their counterpart consisting of the services they performed in raising revenue and in administering and distributing the fund (17 March 1920, DP 1920. 2. 65). The Court of Cassation upheld this decision (Civ. 5 Feb. 1923, DP 1923. 1. 20).

In essence, therefore, cause is simply a generalized reasonable motive for making a contractual promise and the French writers who oppose the doctrine are doubtless correct in maintaining that the whole concept now lacks content. Indeed, the rule expressed in the French Code civil that a contract without a lawful cause is void means no more than that a contract is invalid and unenforceable if, on a reading of its whole content, it is contrary to law or morals. WALTER G. BECKER, who makes a comparison of cause and consideration in his monograph on the English law of consideration (above p. 417, p. 237), is certainly correct in saying that in French law today cause is simply 'the content of a contract as a whole'.

IV

Let us now try to compare and evaluate the rules relating to the so-called indicia of seriousness, taking the German legal family into account as well.

The idea underlying the doctrine of consideration is certainly sound: it is a fact that most serious promises actually made in the world are made in relation to some counterperformance. It is therefore perfectly consistent to say that promises without consideration are unenforceable unless the promise is given in a particular form, as it might be 'under seal'.

One thing, however, is certain: even where there is no counterpart there may well be a serious intention to be bound. By taking counterperformance as the sole indication of seriousness, then, the Common Law renders it impossible to do justice in all cases. This is particularly evident where the doctrine of consideration prevents offers (see above Ch. 33 II) or modifications of an existing contract from being binding. It is clear from the case of the runaway sailors that one may perfectly reasonably promise a bonus to persons already employed so as to spur them to greater exertions. By outlawing this on the ground that the employees are already bound to do any extra work which may become necessary, the consideration doctrine makes it radically impossible for contractors to make reasonable variations in their arrangements. Then in the case of the fire insurance policy, where the promise was unquestionably serious, the Continental lawyer would say that a promise by the vendor to procure that insurance cover is transferred into the name of the purchaser was part of the sales transaction and perfectly enforceable as such. To deny that this additional promise is binding is to fail to recognize that a contract may give rise to collateral duties as well; as HEINRICH SIBER has very pertinently observed, a contractual relationship is an organism which produces a whole range of duties before, during and after the conclusion of the contract, all arising directly from it and all forming part of it. The only obstacle to the obviously just solution of these cases is the doctrine of consideration which, though right in its basic idea, is wrong in making the enforceability of promises turn exclusively on the existence of a counterpromise instead of construing what the parties said and evaluating the particular circumstances of the case in order to discover more generally whether there was a serious intention to be bound. This point was made by one of the most eminent English critics of the doctrine of consideration, LORD WRIGHT:

'I cannot resist the conclusion that the [consideration] doctrine is a mere incumbrance. A scientific or logical theory of contract would in my opinion take as the test of contractual intention the answer to the overriding question whether there was a deliberate and serious intention, free from illegality, immorality, mistake, fraud or duress, to make a binding contract. That must be in each case a question of fact' (49 *Harv. L. Rev.* 1225, 1251 (1936)). This is indeed the attitude of Scottish law which does not accept the doctrine of consideration. (See NORMAND, 'Consideration in the Law of Scotland,' 55 *LQ Rev.* 358 (1939).)

In France and the other countries of the Romanistic legal family it is 'cause' which serves the criterion for separating transactions which are legally binding from those which are not. The resulting view that a serious promise must be based on some comprehensible social–economic purpose recognized by the mores of the time is already more liberal and flexible than the doctrine of consideration.

The German legal family does not refer to the *causa* of a contract in this connection. It is true that in bilateral contracts the *causa* for one promise is the expectation of counterperformance, but this observation is simply a relic from the old books on the *Gemeines Recht*. It is an inherent feature of bilateral contracts that each promise is in fact given in relation to the other; the concept of *causa* is quite unnecessary as a criterion for the seriousness of a promise. This was made clear by the American scholar LORENZEN in his now classic essay on 'Causa and Consideration in the Law of Contracts':

'As regards bilateral and real contracts obviously no special element is requisite in addition to what the nature of the particular class of contracts demands. It goes without saying that if the legal duty of one party to a bilateral contract does not arise the other party is not bound either. Calling the duty of one party the *causa* of the duty of the other adds nothing to what is implied from the nature of the contract' (above p. 417, pp. 625 f.).

In Swiss and German law the only gifts which require a special form are promises to transfer property. Other gratuitous promises, such as the promise to do or not to do something (*Auftrag*), or the promise to give an interest-free loan or a contract in favour of third parties are valid even if informal. The Italian comparatist GORLA (above p. 417, pp. 84 ff., 322 ff., 475 ff.) finds it illogical that these gratuitous promises should be exempt from the requirements of form and explains it on the historical ground that an obligation to donate property used to seem much more serious than an obligation to render gratuitious services; today, however, work is paid for and a much higher percentage of all economic activities take the form of services than of transfers of property. This may well be true, but it is not a sufficient reason for imposing formal requirements on gratuitous promises to perform services or on contracts for third parties. GORLA advocates the reception of the doctrine of consideration into Continental law (above p. 417, pp. 467 ff.) but it can hardly be desirable to import a doctrine which is so powerfully and cogently criticized in its country of origin.

In the German legal family, then, *causa* plays virtually no part in the law of contracts. It is an important concept when property has been transferred, for it is used to answer the question whether a person is entitled to keep an object he has received. It is in the category of unjustified enrichment that *causa* is at home for lawyers of the German legal family. A person who has received a thing without a *causa* must give it up. Thus *causa* is the right to hold on to something which one has received, a *titulus retinendi*, and a thing is obtained with *causa* and its retention justified by it if the thing was transferred pursuant to a valid contract, pursuant to a liability, or as a gift—gift being interesting since it creates a *titulus retinendi* although there was no preceding obligation: retention is also justified according to §814 BGB if at the time of the transfer the transferor knew that he was not obliged to make it.

The doctrine of *causa*, then, does not provide the criterion of distinction between serious promises and those which are not binding in German and Swiss law; a quite different method, namely the *construction* of the trans- action, is used. Whereas the doctrines of consideration and cause look to fixed indicia, the German legal family permits a free inquiry whether the promise was intended to be legally binding or whether it fell outside the legal sphere as being a mere social courtesy or act of friendship. This method of abandoning specific indicia of seriousness and leaving the matter in the hands of a qualified judge is certainly the best way of dealing with the problem.

It is true that the German rule on promissory gifts is not quite in tune with the needs of the times (§518 BGB), for this cautionary provision takes account of the donor's interests only and pays no heed either to the purpose of the gift or to the interest of the promisee, who may well have altered his position for the worse in justifiable reliance on the promise. We have mentioned the case of the uncle who promised to finance his nephew's studies; the German judge would have to dismiss the student's claim because the promise was not in notarial form, whatever result a balancing of the interests of the parties might produce. Again, German law has to resort to tortured reasoning in order to deal with the person who goes back on his written promise to contribute to a charitable fund. A decision of the Reichsgericht of 1905 comes to mind (RGZ 62, 389).

In 1900 a cremation society solicited contributions towards the building of a crematorium at an estimated cost of 50,000 marks. S. stated orally and in writing that he was prepared to contribute 50,000 marks and the society embarked on the work of construction. After two payments of 10,000 marks each, the contributor refused to pay any more and subsequently died. The society brought a claim against his heirs and the claim succeeded before the Oberlandesgericht of Stuttgart which based its decision on the following grounds. It was an essential element of gifts and promises of gifts that the donee be enriched by the gift executed or envisaged, but that was not the case here since the society was only to be a trustee, the crematorium being built on public land. This reasoning was endorsed by the Reichsgericht: 'These reasons contain no error of law. In denying that the contract between S. and the plaintiff was a promise of gift the court below asked to what type of contract it belonged; the answer is that the traditional division of transfers of property into those which are *obligandi, credendi,* or *donandi causa* is not exhaustive but simply indicates the commonest and most important purposes for which transfers are made. A causal, as opposed to an abstract, transaction which is not donative may perfectly well impose no duty to make any counterperformance or restitution; the aim may be different, as it is in the case where the recipient is to undertake an act for charitable, communal, or altruistic purposes.'

The disposition of this case is admirable but the reasoning is obviously very strained.

Swiss law is greatly superior on this point, for only writing is required to make a gratuitous promise valid and some attention is paid to the *purpose* of the gift. A promise pursuant to a moral duty is not regarded as a gift at all and is therefore valid even if not in writing (art. 239 par. 3 OR). This admirable provision leaves it to the judge to decide, on the basis of construction, whether in the particular case the promise was made in pursuance of a moral duty or not.

The decisions of the Swiss Bundersgericht on this matter are fairly flexible. A striking example is BGE 53 II 198, where the Bundesgericht held a person liable on an oral promise to maintain and educate a minor waif, made on the erroneous assumption that he was morally obliged to do so (compare also BGE 44 II 6 and BGE 45 II 298). According to the commentary on the law of obligations by OSER/SCHÖNENBERGER, 'gifts for charitable or public purposes on the occasion of public disasters' also fall in the category of performance of a moral duty (*Das Obligationenrecht* (1936) art. 239 note II 2 a). Though no Swiss decision on this point has been found, it is clear that the 'subscription cases' which cause difficulty in English and American law could properly be solved in Switzerland by reference to art. 239 par. 3 OR.

Not all cases can be solved by concentrating on the purpose behind the gift. The excellent idea of promissory estoppel in the American cases may be useful in enforcing informal gratuitous promises where the promisee, as the promisor might well have foreseen, has altered his position to his detriment in justifiable reliance. This is a good idea well worth adopting, and the German courts could adopt it without waiting for legislation. When an enactment is as old as the German BGB it should be extended beyond its literal meaning by bold and progressive interpretation in the light of comparative law.

37

The Construction of Contracts

CHAFEE, 'The Disorderly Conduct of Words', 41 *Colum. L. Rev.* 381 (1941).
FARNSWORTH, '"Meaning" in the Law of Contracts', 76 *Yale LJ* 939 (1967).
HOLMES, 'The Theory of Legal Interpretation', 12 *Harv. L. Rev.* 417 (1899).
HUG, 'Betrachtungen zum Gerichtsgebrauch über Abschluß und Auslegung der Verträge', *SchwzZBGR* 36 (1955) 1.
LARENZ, *Die Methode der Auslegung des Rechtsgeschäfts* (1930, repr. 1966).
LÜDERITZ, *Auslegung von Rechtsgeschäften, Vergleichende Untersuchung anglo-amerikanischen und deutschen Rechts* (1966).
MARTY, 'Rôle du juge dans l'interprétation des contrats', *Travaux de l'Association Henri Capitant* V (1950) 84.
MEIER-HAYOZ, *Das Vertrauensprinzip beim Vertragsschluß* (1948).
MORRIS, 'Palm-Tree Justice in the Court of Appeal', 82 *LQ Rev.* 196 (1966).
OFTINGER, 'Einige grundsätzliche Betrachtungen über die Auslegung der Verkehrsgeschäfte', *ZSR* 58 (1939) 178.
PATTERSON, 'The Interpretation and Construction of Contracts', 64 *Colum. L. Rev.* 833 (1964).
POUND, 'The Role of Will in Law', 68 *Harv. L. Rev.* 1 (1954).
RIEG, *Le Rôle de la volonté dans l'acte juridique en droit civil français et allemand* (1961).
SIMONIUS, 'Über die Bedeutung des Vertrauensprinzips in der Vertragslehre', *Basler Festgabe zum Schweizerischen Juristentag* (1942) 235.
SWEET, 'Contract Making and Parol Evidence: Diagnosis and Treatment of a Sick Rule', 53 *Cornell LQ* 1036 (1968).
TITZE, 'Rechtsgeschäft' in V *Rechtsvergleichendes Handwörterbuch* (ed. Schlegelberger) (1936) 841.
WILLIAMS, 'Language and the Law', 61 *LQ Rev.* 71, 179, 293, 384 (1945); 62 *LQ Rev.* 387 (1946).
YOUNG, 'Equivocation in the Making of Agreements', 64 *Colum. L. Rev.* 619 (1964).
YUNG, 'L'Interprétation supplétive des contrats', *ZBernJV* 97 (1961) 41.

I

LIKE the other gestures and symbols which men use to mark their entry into legal relationships words, whether written or spoken, can never fully express what was intended. Furthermore, the parties making a contract may well not have turned their minds to certain matters which later prove to be relevant. Judges are therefore constantly faced with the task of deciding the rights of parties who have expressed themselves unclearly or incompletely. This process of determining the meaning of ambiguous or incomplete expressions is called 'construction'.

Construction is called for when it is known what the parties said, wrote, or otherwise expressed, but not obvious what they meant by it. Construction may start from either of two opposed premisses, neither of which is found in the pure form in practice today. On one view, it is the *intention* of the promisor which counts; this is justified by the principle of private autonomy which treats the free will of legal persons as the source and measure of legal consequences: 'Intention *per se* is really the only important and effective thing, which needs a sign by which we can recognize it only because it is an internal and invisible phenomenon' (SAVIGNY, *System des heutigen römischen Rechts* III (1840) 258).

On the other view, priority is given to the external phenomenon of *expression* on the ground that the legal order is concerned with protecting commercial intercourse: the internal will of the promisor is treated as significant only in so far as it coincides with the normal objective meaning that a reasonable man would attribute to its expression.

Roman law shows the shift in methods of construction from one of these extremes to the other. To interpret external expression strictly and literally is historically the older method. To give an example, a will in classical Roman law was invalid if the testator, in instituting his slave as heir, forgot to emancipate him. Institution of heir and emancipation of slave were seen as being quite distinct transactions and the older lawyers would have thought it improper to say that since it was common knowledge that only free persons could own property, a person who was instituting a slave must, in a case of doubt, have meant to emancipate him (Inst. 1, 6, 2; 2, 14 pr.): 'cum in verbis nulla ambiguitas est non debet admitti voluntatis quaestio' (D. 32, 25, 1). It was only JUSTINIAN who laid down in one of his constitutions (C. 6, 27, 5) that in such a case the instituted slave must be deemed to have been emancipated as well 'cum non est verisimile eum quem heredem sibi elegit, si praetermisit libertatis dationem, servum eum manere voluisse, et neminen sibi heredem fore'. Thus the development ends with a strong emphasis on the *voluntas* as against the *verba*, not only in the law of wills but also in the law of contracts: 'in conventionibus contrahentium voluntatem potius quam verba spectari placuit' (D. 50, 16, 219). The post-classical developments are fully treated in KASER, *Das römische Privatrecht* II (1959) §201, I, II.

II

The draftsmen of the European codes had widely differing views of the value of prescribing rules of construction. The *Romanistic* civil codes in particular contain a great many canons of construction (see arts. 1156 ff. Code civil, 1362 ff. Codice civile), all of very dubious merit. It is not really for the legislator to instruct the judge in what is practically reasonable or to control his application of the law by technical rules which are virtually empty of content. In any case, a judge who is construing a contract must pay such close attention to the special circumstances of the case before him that it can only make for error if he is constrained by rules enacted generally and in the abstract. It can safely be left to judges and scholars to develop proper rules of construction.

A glance at the rules of construction laid down in the French Code civil confirms this view. According to art. 1156, one should seek out the common intention of the parties rather than adhere to the meaning of their words; in case of doubt, a contract should be construed so as to have validity (art. 1157) and where one expression is ambiguous it should be given the meaning 'qui convient le plus à la matière du contrat' (art. 1158). Again, it is the contract as a whole rather than its individual provisions which indicates which indicates the right construction (art. 1161); general words should be limited to the particular contractual objects intended though, on the other hand, where only *one* situation has been mentioned one must ask whether others are not included (arts. 1163 f.). In cases of doubt, one should construe the contract against the creditor and in favour of the debtor (art. 1162) and sales contracts should be construed against the vendor (art. 1602 par. 2).

Some of these rules are simply banal, others are rules of thumb of doubtful value. The provision of art. 1162 (*in dubio pro debitore*) is clearly based on the popular fallacy that the creditor is rich and the debtor is poor, though it suffers from the further disadvantage that it may not always be clear which of the parties is the creditor and which is the debtor in regard to a particular term in the contract.

This is illustrated by a case decided by the Court of Appeal of Douai (10 Nov. 1898, DP 1900. 2. 47) which held that the captain of a vessel had no right to require the consignees to take delivery of the cargo at night, although according to the contract of carriage the unloading was to be effected 'as soon as possible and immediately after permission to unload has been granted by the customs authorities'. The Court saw this term as having been included in favour of the captain and owner of the ship and based its decision against the shipowner, *inter alia*, on the ground that the clause 'doit être interprétée contre celui qui stipule et en faveur de celui qui a contracté l'obligation'. It is just as likely, however, that the term was included in the contract in the interests of the *consignee* who might well have had a considerable interest in the quickest possible delivery, especially at a time of falling prices.

The Court of Cassation has held that in art. 1162 the legislator was merely giving advice and that the decisions of lower courts are not to be quashed for not following it (Civ. 10/11 May 1948, Gaz. Pal. 1948. 2. 41).

The justification adduced by PLANIOL/RIPERT VI no. 373 for the rule of art. 1602 par. 2 (*in dubio pro emptore*) is that the vendor knows the goods better than the purchaser and normally also drafts the conditions of the contract. This is not very convincing. Quite apart from the fact that art. 1602 is not limited to terms concerning the qualities of the goods, goods today are not usually handcrafted but industrially mass-produced and distributed through a whole series of middlemen, with the result that vendor and purchaser are often equally ignorant about the goods.

Nor is art. 1157, which says that the aim of interpretation is to uphold the contract, beyond criticism. Such a provision may be relevant to the construction of wills since it can be assumed that to invalidate the will and bring on an intestacy is the worst of all solutions since that is certainly contrary to the testator's intentions, but in the construction of contractual promises there may be much more important considerations such as the principle that contractual declarations must be construed in the sense in which they would be understood by their addressee.

If it comes to a conflict between objective and subjective construction, French theorists still incline to the latter even today. Just as art. 1156 Code civil insists that the judge seek out 'la commune intention des parties contractantes', so the writers stress the importance of ascertaining their real intention. If it is impossible to descry any common intention of the parites—to which many writers add 'la volonté virtuelle ou présumée'—then one must have recourse to the statutory rules of construction in the Code civil:

'Telle est la doctrine française moderne de l'interprétation des actes juridiques: rechercher avant toute chose la volonté des auteurs d'un acte, et si cette recherche ne donne pas de résultats, appliquer les règles objectives d'interprétation formulées par le code civil' (RIEG (above p. 429) p. 367).

Most court decisions also refer to the end-product of construction as the 'commune intention des parties', but a closer study of the more recent decisions suggests that this reference is no more than a verbal obeisance to the doctrine of intention which has in fact been largely abandoned.

On the retirement of a director, Camille Blanc, a company undertook to pay him a pension and after his death to continue paying half of it to 'Mme. Camille Blanc'. Mme. Blanc died first and the widower remarried. After his death the second Mme. Blanc demanded the continuation of the pension payments but her claim was rejected because the Court of Appeal found that 'dans l'intention des parties' only the first wife was to be entitled (Req. 31 Oct. 1934, DH 1934. 602). In the circumstances of the case this construction may be quite correct, but it is sheer fantasy to suppose that at the time the contract was concluded the parties had even considered the possibility of the aged pensioner's remarriage, let alone formed any common intention about it.

The lower courts' tendencies to very subjective constructions are limited by a doctrine of 'clauses claires et précises', developed by the Court of Cassation. According to this doctrine the court can only inquire into the probable or supposed intention of the parties if on an objective construction the words of the contract contain ambiguities or contradictions. A well-known decision of 1942 shows how far the Court of Cassation is prepared to go in limiting freedom of interpretation in the lower courts by insisting on a construction directed to the actual words of the contract itself.

A purchaser had agreed to buy a certain quantity of cod on the terms that the vendor should be entitled to reduce this quantity if he was so empowered by the Cod-Dealers' Association. The Association did so decide and the vendor delivered only 50% of the quantity originally agreed. The purchaser claimed damages and the Court of Appeal of Bordeaux allowed the claim. The Court of Cassation quashed this decision and remanded it to another Court of Appeal because in its view the clear text of the contract left no doubt about the vendor's right to reduce the quantity to be delivered. This second court also gave judgment for the plaintiff, apparently because in reaching their agreement the parties had implicitly assumed that the Association would permit a reduction of quantity only if the catch diminished and not, as was the case, because of a sharp increase in demand. This decision also was quashed: the term of the contract was so unambiguous that there was no room for any further inquiry into the parties' intentions. In his note on the case, LEREBOURS-PIGEONNIÈRE, one of the judges involved in the case, was quite specific: 'Si la clause litigieuse est claire, il n'y a pas lieu de rechercher l'intention commune des parties pour en déterminer la portée' (Civ. 14 Dec. 1942, D. 1944, 112; see also Civ. 23 April 1945, D. 1945, 261, noted LEREBOURS-PIGEONNIÈRE).

III

When we turn to the *German* legal family, we find that despite all the efforts to harmonize the provisions of the BGB there still remains a clear conflict between the doctrine of intention and the expression theory. On the one hand, §133 BGB, just like art. 1156 Code civil and art. 1362 Codice civile, says that the aim of construction is 'to discern the real intention'. This must mean that the crucial thing is the actual historical will of the parties. This is supported by the fact that the section on 'Ascertainment of Intention' in the Motives for the BGB rejects as 'unacceptable' the perfectly reasonable view that 'in contracts what matters is not what real intention lay behind what one contractor said but what the other contractor must in the circumstances have understood him to mean' (Motive I p. 155). On the other hand, §157 BGB applies a strongly objective standard and requires that construction be 'in accordance with good faith with reference to normal commercial usage'. It is true that §157 BGB falls in the section of the Code limited to contracts, while §133 BGB applies only to declarations of intention, but this does nothing to resolve the contradiction since from the point of view of method there is no difference between the construction of a contract and the construction of a declaration of intention.

One can still find traces of the confusion caused by this contradiction. ENNECCERUS/ NIPPERDEY state that the judge must 'treat the actual intention as conclusive if it is at all ascertainable in the expression' (*Allgemeiner Teil des Bürgerlichen Rechts* II (15th edn., 1960) §205. I 2). Only a few pages later, we read that declarations of will which call for acceptance must be given the meaning which their addressee attributed or should have attributed to them in the prevailing circumstances. Even this is qualified again by a subsequent statement that when one is construing declarations of intention calling for acceptance it would be quite wrong to 'totally disregard' §133 BGB which treats subjective intention as conclusive (ibid., §205 I 5, and note 17).

Despite these occasional variations in emphasis, lawyers in Germany are unanimous that if the addressee's justifiable reliance on the objective meaning of the declaration deserves protection there is no room for §133 BGB with its stress on subjective intention of the parties. This is especially true in cases where it becomes clear at the stage of *performance* that a common text agreed on at the time of the *conclusion* of the contract was understood in different ways or contained no term to cover a particular question. It is obvious that in such cases there is no point in seeking the 'true intention' of the parties. A formula often adopted in such cases is that the judge should determine the 'hypothetical intention of the parties', that is, should inquire how the parties would have regulated the disputed matter if some third party had indicated the gap or uncertainty in the contract. This cannot be accepted. The suggestion that the judge should somehow retrospectively discern, by means of psychological clues, what terms the parties would probably have agreed on cannot be right. Besides, if one took this doctrine seriously, the judge would always align himself with the economically stronger party since it would naturally be the terms in his favour which would have been adopted. Finally, when one is deciding what rights were conferred on the parties by the contract under construction one cannot take into account circumstances and occurrences *subsequent* to the conclusion of the contract, for this also can lead to great unfairness.

In RGZ 92, 318 (320), the Reichsgericht hit upon a good formula: 'When gaps in a contract have to be filled, it is not a question of completing the contractual intentions of the parties but only of completing the contract; the judge must use the principle of commercial good faith and the guidelines of the intention expressed in the contract for the relationship envisaged in order to fashion the rules which are to apply in the situation which has unforeseeably arisen.'

When all is said and done, the purpose of construing ambiguous or incomplete contracts is to achieve an objectively fair and functional solution appropriate to the facts of the concrete case. In particular, the judge must ask whether one of the parties should have not realized that the other might reasonably attribute a special meaning to the term of the contract in question. If so, the meaning honestly attributed to the declaration must be treated as conclusive and the subjective intention of the person making the declaration must be ignored. The intention theory may have been sound enough in times gone by when individual contracts were amicably made between neighbourly farmers and merchants who knew all the personal circumstances, but in the present day of impersonal mass transactions only the expression theory can provide the right solution.

IV

This view finds the clearest support in the *Common Law*. The conflict between the theories of intention and expression has attracted much less thought and writing there than on the Continent. POTHIER and SAVIGNY may have had some influence on English jurists in the nineteenth century and even today one happens upon statements that the essence of contract is a 'meeting of the minds' or 'consensus ad idem', but the courts have always clung to the position that the construction of a legal transaction is geared to the external phenomenon of expression rather than the subjective intention of the parties. As CHESHIRE/FIFOOT put it at p. 22:

'Agreement, however, is not a mental state but an act and, as an act, is a matter of inference from conduct. The parties are to be judged, not by what is in their minds, but by what they have said or written or done. While such must be, in some degree, the standpoint of every legal system, the common law . . . lays peculiar emphasis upon external appearance . . . The function of an English judge is not to seek and satisfy some elusive mental element but to ensure, as far as practical experience permits, that the reasonable expectations of honest men are not disappointed.'

An observation of the famous American Judge LEARNED HAND goes even further:

'It is quite true that we commonly speak of a contract as a question of intent, and for most purposes it is a convenient paraphrase, accurate enough, but, strictly speaking, untrue. It makes not the least difference whether a promisor actually intends that meaning which the law will impose upon his words. The whole House of Bishops might satisfy us that he had intended something else and it would make not a particle of difference in his obligation . . . Indeed if both parties severally declared that their meaning had been other than the natural meaning, and each declaration was similar, it would be irrelevant' (*Eustis Mining Co.* v. *Beer, Sondheimer & Co.*, 239 F. 976, 984 (SDNY 1917).—See also O. W. HOLMES, 10 *Harv. L. Rev.* 457, 464 (1897)).

This basic attitude of the Common Law explains why the courts in England and the United States, when required to construe a contract, spend as long as possible on its actual words and only advert to the attendant circumstances if there is no other way of arriving at a solution. If an unequivocal clause in the contract fits the circumstances under dispute the court will often apply that clause even if there is good reason to suppose that the parties probably did not intend the point at issue to fall under the clause, clear as it is. This is even done in the construction of wills where the idea that the reliance of a good faith addressee should be protected has hardly any force at all. This can be shown by two English decisions which would almost certainly have been decided the other way on the Continent.

In *Re Gale*, [1941] 1 Ch. 209, the testator left a house to trustees with the direction that his wife was to occupy it free of rent 'during her widowhood'. After the testator's death it was found that he had never been married to the beneficiary, though they had lived together for 26 years and had produced four children. The court held the disposition void, since the beneficiary was not married and therefore could not be a 'widow' as the will required: 'The testator intended to benefit the lady by his will, but he has used language which, in my judgment, unfortunately, cannot have that effect.' ([1941] 1 Ch. 209, 218, criticized by WILLIAMS, 61 *LQ Rev.* 393 (1945).)

A similar rigid legalism appears in the House of Lords decision, *National Society* v. *Scottish National Society*, [1915] AC 207.

In his will a Scotsman left a legacy of £500 to the 'National Society for the Prevention of Cruelty to Children'. There was a society of that name in London and it claimed the legacy, but it was opposed by the 'Scottish National Society for the Prevention of Cruelty to Children'. On proof that the estate was located in Scotland, that the legacy in question appeared in the will amidst other dispositions in favour of Scottish charities, and that the testator had had his attention drawn to the Scottish Society two years before he drew up the will, both Scottish courts gave the legacy to the Scottish Society. However, in view of the unequivocal words of the will, the House of Lords, with expressions of regret, found it impossible to do otherwise than to accord the money to the London Society. LORD DUNEDIN said: 'My Lords . . . I cannot help having the moral feeling that this money is going probably to the society to which, if we could have asked him, the testator would not have sent it.' ([1915] AC 207, 214.) See also *Re Rowland*, [1963] 1 Ch. 1.

One must not be too quick to dismiss these decisions as obviously unjust. It must be borne in mind that in Common Law jurisdictions, unlike the Continent, wills are almost invariably drawn up by lawyers and there is therefore no need to tolerate lapses and imprecisions in expression which would be excusable in a layman. Moreover, such a rule excludes undesirable testimony as to the way the testator's mind was going. Finally, such a method of construction has a certain educative effect: on the one hand, it holds the person responsible for drafting the will to the most extreme precision in his choice of words and, on the other hand, it increases the certainty of the law by making it possible to predict the result of judicial construction with some assurance.

In both these cases the document was in itself clear and unequivocal. But the reluctance of the Common Law to refer to the mind of the draftsman when construing a document can also be seen in cases where the language used is so imprecise that no construction is possible without reference to outside facts; in such a case the Anglo-American courts do not ask what the actual intention of the party was and whether it is 'at all ascertainable' in the document but refer instead to all the circumstances surrounding the making of the declaration. If in the light of these circumstances the other party would attribute a particular meaning to what was said and if the speaker should, had he been alert, have realized this, the latter cannot rely on the fact that the intention underlying the declaration was quite different.

On this see CORBIN §537 and the decisions cited there, especially *Right Printing Co.* v. *Stevens*, 107 Vt. 359, 179 A. 209 (1935) where the following was said: 'It is a general rule of construction of contracts that the language and acts of a party to a contract are to receive such a contruction as at the time he supposed the other party would give them, or such a construction as the other party was fairly justified in giving to them.'

V

An allied problem concerning written agreements is how far to admit evidence of collateral oral agreements, prior or contemporaneous, which alter or extend the import of the contract as written.

The Common Law solves this problem in a manner consistent with its objective approach to construction: 'If there be a contract which has been reduced to writing', said LORD DENMAN in *Goss* v. *Lord Nugent*, (1833) 5 B. & Ad. 58, 110 Eng. Rep. 713, 'verbal evidence is not allowed to be given of what passed between the parties, either before the written instrument was made, or during the time that it was in a state of preparation, so as to add to or subtract from, or in any manner to vary or qualify the written contract.'

American law is to the same effect: see CORBIN §573 and Restatement of the Law of Contracts §§237 ff. The whole matter is covered in LÜDERITZ (above p. 429) 111 ff.

This very important rule is really only a consequence of the theory of expression, the only theory appropriate today; both parties to a written document are entitled to act on the basis that should a dispute occur the courts will treat the text of the written contract as complete and exhaustive; it also promotes legal simplicity and certainty by inducing parties to include in the contract, should they write it down at all, *all* the terms to which they want to be bound.

This 'parol evidence rule' is not applied if it is shown that a valid contract never came into being at all, whether from want of consideration or by reason of fraudulent misrepresentation, substantial error, or an offence against public policy. Witnesses may only be admitted to testify to the circumstances attending the formation of the contract if the written document requires construction because the words are ambiguous, a finding which Anglo-American courts are often very reluctant to make.

For example, see *Great Western Railway* v. *Bristol Corp.*, (1918) 87 LJ Ch. 414.— Some American decisions have gone very far in holding that a clause in a contract is unambiguous so that the testimony of witnesses is excluded. In *Le Witt* v. *Park Ecclesiastical Society*, 103 Conn. 285, 130 A. 387 (1925) the vendor of land undertook to transfer it free of third party rights. The land was actually burdened by a right of way in favour of a third party and the purchaser demanded the return of his deposit. The vendor had a whole string of witnesses ready to prove that at the time the contract was concluded the purchaser was aware of the right of way and that the parties had agreed that this should not constitute a 'third party right' for the purposes of the contract. Both lower courts held that the evidence of these witnesses was inadmissible since the clear meaning of the contract could not be got round by 'parol evidence'. To the same effect see *Inman* v. *American Cereal Co.*, 113 Iowa 71, 110 NW 287 (1907); CORBIN §535 and SWEET (above p. 429) are critical.

The comparable rule in Continental jurisdictions is much weaker. It is true that art. 1341 of the Code civil in *France* states that the evidence of witnesses is inadmissible to show that there was an oral agreement before, during or after the conclusion of a contract in writing or notarial form (to the same effect see art. 2722 Codice civile), but this rule is severely limited in practice. It is inapplicable when the written contract constitutes a commercial transaction nor does it apply if the party can bring a 'commencement de preuve par écrit', that is, can produce documents emanating from the other party which establish with some probability that the oral agreement actually took place (see above pp. 396 ff.). Moreover, the courts will always hear evidence to the effect that a party was deceived into concluding the written contract or that the parties intended the document to be a sham, in whole in in part. Finally, the evidence of witnesses is held to be admissible whenever the contract clause in question is obscure or ambiguous (Civ. 3 March 1969, D. 1969, 477).

The probative force of written agreements is even weaker in *Germany*. The drawing up of a written document containing legal declarations merely gives rise to a presumption that it is accurate and complete. Informal collateral agreements are valid if they can be proved by the party asserting them.

Thus the difference between the Continental legal systems and the Common Law lies in the force of the rule: while Continental systems make it a mere presumption with the result that the person asserting an oral collateral agreement is entitled to prove it, the rule in the Common Law has the more rigorous effect of a fiction, and proof to the contrary is in principle inadmissible.

By contrast, all systems seem to deal with the problem of *falsa demonstratio* in the same way. When parties contracted to buy and sell a cargo of 'Haakjöringsköd' (sharksmeat) under the common misapprehension that the term meant whalemeat, the contract was effective in the sense in which they intended it (RGZ 99, 147). A clause in a charterparty which incorporated an American statute was effective although the clause erroneously referred to the charterparty as a bill of lading (*Adamastos Shipping Co. Ltd.* v. *Anglo-Saxon Petroleum Co. Ltd.*, [1957] 2 QB 233, 248 f.; [1959] AC 133, 154). In these cases the words are given the meaning intended by the speaker and understood by the addressee, but this is not because of the intention theory. In cases of *falsa demonstratio* the intention of the parties is only given priority over the normal meaning of the expressions they used because there is no reliance by the addressee which falls to be protected: the reasonable interests of both parties are best answered by construing their expressions in accordance with what they meant rather than with what they said.

Where the parties attribute divergent meanings to ambiguous expressions, it is always held that no valid contract arises though such cases are not always put in a special category.

In the Common Law the problem is dealt with under the heading 'Rule in *Raffles* v. *Wichelhaus*' ((1864) 2 H. & C. 906, 159 Eng. Rep. 375). This case involved a contract for the sale of a floating cargo of cotton wool 'ex Peerless from Bombay'. It transpired that two ships by that name had left Bombay and that the parties in contracting had different ships in mind. The court held that the contract was void.—For the modern state of the doctrine see the very full article by YOUNG, 64 *Colum. L. Rev.* 619 (1964).

In most legal systems, and even in German law, the problem raised by expressions which are hopelessly ambiguous when objectively construed is dealt with in the law of contracts. In truth the problem occurs throughout the law of legal acts; ambiguous notices of termination and ambiguous notices of rescission are also invalid. And it is simply a consequence of the rule relating to *falsa demonstratio* that an ambiguous offer may well lead to a contract if it is accepted by an addressee who understands it in the sense intended by the offeror.

38

Mistake, Deceit, and Duress

AMORTH, *Errore e inadempimento nel contratto* (1967).

ATIYAH/BENNION, 'Mistake in the Construction of Contracts', 24 *Mod. L. Rev.* 421 (1961).

DAWSON, 'Economic Duress, An Essay in Perspective', 45 *Mich. L. Rev.* 253 (1947).

DREXELIUS, *Irrtum und Risiko, Rechtsvergleichende Untersuchungen und Reformvorschläge zum Recht der Irrtumsanfechtung* (1964).

FROEB, 'Der Irrtum beim Vertragsabschluß im amerikanischen Recht', Diss. Bonn (1962).

GHESTIN, *La Notion d'erreur dans le droit positif actuel* (2nd edn., 1971).

GOODHART, 'Mistake As To Identity in the Law of Contract', 57 *LQ Rev.* 228 (1941).

Gow, 'Mistake and Error', 1 *ICLQ* 472 (1952).

HALL, 'New Developments in Mistake of Identity', 1961 *Camb. LJ* 86.

HENRICH, 'Unbewußte Irreführung', *AcP* 162 (1963) 88.

HOFF, 'Error in the Formation of Contracts in Louisiana, A Comparative Analysis', 53 *Tul. L. Rev.* 329 (1979).

KEMPERMANN, *Unlautere Ausnutzung von Vertrauensverhältnissen im englischen, französischen und deutschen Recht* (1975).

LAWSON, 'Error in substantia', 52 *LQ Rev.* 79 (1936).

LITVINOFF, ' "Error" in the Civil Law', in: *Essays on the Civil Law of Obligations* (ed. Dainow, 1969) 222.

MAX-PLANCK-INSTITUT FÜR AUSLÄNDISCHES UND INTERNATIONALES PRIVATRECHT, *Die materielle Gültigkeit von Kaufverträgen, Ein rechtsvergleichender Bericht*, 2 vols. (1968).

MEIER-HAYOZ, *Das Vertrauensprinzip beim Vertragsschluß* (1948).

MOKRI, *Les Conditions de l'invalidité des actes juridiques pour cause de dol en droit français et en droit suisse* (1956).

NEWMAN, 'Relief for Mistake in Contracting', 54 *Cornell LQ* 232 (1969).

PALMER, *Mistake and Unjust Enrichment* (1962).

RODIÈRE (ed.), *Les Vices du consentement dans le contrat* (1977).

ROLLIN, 'Irrtum und Reurecht', Diss. Hamburg (1964).

SCHMIDLIN, 'Das Vertrauensprinzip und die Irrtumslehre im deutschen und schweizerischen Recht', *ZSR* 89 (1970) 225.

v. SCHWIND, 'Der Irrtum im Verkehrsrecht des ABGB und BGB, Eine rechtsvergleichend-rechtspolitische Betrachtung', *Jher. Jb.* 89 (1941) 119.

SMITH, 'Error in the Scottish Law of Contract', 71 *LQ Rev.* 507 (1955).

SLADE, 'The Myth of Mistake in the English Law of Contract', 70 *LQ Rev.* 385 (1954).

STOLJAR, *Mistake and Misrepresentation* (1968).

TITZE, 'Rechtsgeschäft', in V *Rechtsvergleichendes Handwörterbuch* (ed. Schlegelberger, 1936) 789.

——, 'Vom sogenannten Motivirrtum', *Festschrift Ernst Heymann* (1940) 72.

TYLOR, 'General Theory of Mistake in the Formation of Contract', 11 *Mod. L. Rev.* 257 (1948).

WADE, 'Consensus, Mistake and Impossibility in Contract', 7 *Camb. LJ* 361 (1939–41).

WINTTERLIN, *Die Haftung für fahrlässige Irreführung im englischen Delikts- und Vertragsrecht unter vergleichender Berücksichtigung des deutschen und nordamerikanischen Rechts* (1968).

ZWEIGERT *et al.*, 'Der Entwurf eines einheitlichen Gesetzes über die materielle Gültigkeit internationaler Kaufverträge über bewegliche Sachen', *RabelsZ* 32 (1968) 201, 342.

I

NOT every error entitles a promisor to evade the consequences of his promise. On this all legal systems are agreed. Equally there is no doubt that in exceptional circumstances a promisor who has made a mistake may be able to shift its consequences to the other party, even at the cost of frustrating the other party's reliance on the validity of the promise. Where the dividing line is to be drawn between errors of which the law will take account and those which it will disregard is a question as old as it is controverted.

The problem is a difficult one, and there are many plausible points of view one might adopt when faced with a case of mistake. Suppose that a person has a Chinese vase which he thinks is simply a middling example of standard native ware; he sells it at a low price, delivers it to the purchaser, and then discovers that it was a priceless specimen of the Ming Dynasty. Can the vendor rescind the contract and demand the return of the vase just because he was mistaken as to its value? Does it make any difference if the vendor himself was an expert who could have found out the true value of the vase, but failed to do so, either recklessly or carelessly? What if the purchaser was aware of the true value of the vase and concealed the fact, and what if he could have discovered it? What if the parties to the contract were both experienced orientalists? Is it relevant that the purchaser, in the supposition that his purchase is valid, might meanwhile have contracted to resell the vase, or that he may already have delivered it at his own expense? Suppose that the purchaser, acting in the best of good faith, had assured the vendor that it was only an average sort of vase, and the vendor concluded the contract in the belief that this was true? If the purchaser is ready to pay the difference in value may the vendor still demand the return of the vase?

One cannot solve these difficult cases by simple reference to grand concepts such as the doctrine of intention and the expression theory, the principle of private autonomy and the protection of commerce. We shall try to discover the proper tests and standards by using the established method of comparative law, by ascertaining the legal situation in countries with distinctive rules relating to mistake, and then trying to come to a critical and comparative conclusion.

II

The fundamental distinction in the German legal family is made in §119 BGB: a mistake in the transaction is relevant while a mistake of motive is not. The distinction between these two categories of mistake turns on rather subtle psychological considerations: it is a material error in the transaction when the promisor has formed his intention quite correctly but has made a mistake in expressing it, and it is an error of motive when the intention itself, being based on an error, is incorrectly formed.

For example, if a person intended to buy ten bottles of soda water for a birthday party and orders a hundred bottles by mistake, he may rescind the contract, but if a person orders ten bottles of soda water because he mistakenly thinks that his guests are teetotallers, he has no right to recind. As we shall see, however, the distinction is not always so easy to draw: if a testator, in instituting his 'statutory heirs', has in mind those who would be statutory heirs under a statute which has been repealed this is a mistake in the transaction under §119 par. 1 BGB (RGZ 70, 391, 394); the same is true if a guarantor mistakenly believes that the creditor's claim is a secured one (RGZ 75, 271). So also, according to STAUDINGER/COING, *Bürgerliches Gesetzbuch* (11th edn., 11 1957) §119 note 14, it is a mistake in the transaction if a person buys a specified forest in the belief that it contains 100,000 trees whereas in reality it only has 85,000. If so, the purchaser may rescind without any inquiry into the question whether the contract, reasonably construed, might not put the risk of any inaccuracy in the estimate of quantity on him rather than on the vendor.

It is true that the question whether the error is one in the transaction or one of motive is not of great practical importance in Germany. This is because under §119 par. 2 BGB one may also rescind for errors of motive, provided they concern qualities of the person or the thing 'which are normally regarded as essential'. More specific meaning has been given to this general clause by the decided cases.

In the case of the Chinese vase, the Reichsgericht allowed the vendor to rescind on the ground of mistake as to an essential quality (RGZ 124, 115). So too an error over the development potential of a plot of land may be raised (RGZ 61, 86), as may an error as to the creditworthiness of the other party to a credit transaction (RGZ 66, 385). Even an adoption, which in German law is treated as a contract subject to the approval of the court, can be rescinded on the ground of error on a material quality if it transpires that at the time of the adoption the child had latent vices ineradicable by education (RGZ 147, 310; 152, 228).—But the concept of essential qualities includes 'only those factual and legal qualities of things which specifically characterize them, not factors which only have an indirect effect on their value' (BGHZ 16, 54, 57). Thus it is not an essential quality of a piece of land that it does not belong to the vendor (BGHZ 34, 41), nor that it is worth less than the purchaser supposed when he bought it (RG HRR 1932 no. 224, invariable holding).

What is remarkable about this rule is that it wholly ignores the question whether the promisor was at fault in being mistaken and whether the mistake was ascertainable to the other party or caused by him, even quite innocently.

The *Austrian* Civil Code offers a most original, attractive and satisfactory solution. A 'mistake in the reasons for contracting' being in principle irrelevant (§901 sent. 2 ABGB), a mistake is significant, as in the German BGB, only if it is one 'which concerns the principal object or an essential attribute of it to which the intention was principally and expressly directed' (§871 ABGB); but even if he makes a mistake of this kind the mistaken party cannot rescind his promise unless in addition he proves one of three facts: that the other party *caused* the mistake, that the mistake must have been *obvious* to the other party in all the circumstances, or finally that the mistake was *notified* to the other party in good time.

According to the cases, a mistake may be *caused* though it was induced neither deliberately nor negligently; any behaviour which causes the mistake is sufficient. Even silence can 'cause' a mistake in the sense of §871 ABGB if one party should have informed the other that the assumptions he would normally make about certain facts related to the transaction were erroneous.

Thus the Oberste Gerichtshof granted recission in a case in which the purchaser of a house erroneously believed that it was of massive construction. The court concluded that in the light of the attendant circumstances the vendor should have drawn the purchaser's attention to the fact that the house was not substantially built. Thus the vendor 'caused' the mistake and rescission was in order (OGH 20 April 1955, SZ XXVIII 103).

Rescission may also be granted for a mistake concerning 'the principal object' if it is shown that the other party *knew* of the error or *would have known* if he had exercised normal and proper care. Failing this, the mistaken party may show that he *notified* the error 'in good time', that is, brought it to the attention of the other party before the other party had acted in reliance on the mistaken promise, as by incurring expenses in performing the contract (compare OGH 31 Oct. 1951, SZ XXIV 288).

Thus a vendor in error concerning the qualities of the thing, even an 'essential' quality in the sense of §871 ABGB, loses his right to rescind as soon as the purchaser resells the object or lets it out on hire, or takes possession of the house which he bought, or rearranges his business around the purchased machinery. This rule applies unless the vendor can show that the purchaser caused his mistake or should have known of it.

Compare KLANG/GSCHNITZER, *Kommentar zum ABGB* (2nd edn., 1953) §871 note 3.—In OGH 3 March 1932, SZ XIV 40, a creditor who had received part payment erroneously declared that he had received payment in full. The court allowed him to rescind this declaration, even although in the circumstances of the case the mistake might well not have been known to the debtor, since 'according to the law a mistaken party is not bound to his mistaken declaration when its addressee, though entitled under the doctrine of reliance to treat it as accurate, has been informed of the error before he took any action or made any arrangements in reliance on the declaration'.

While German law gives the promisee a claim for the harm he suffered in reliance on the promise now rescinded (§122 BGB), Austrian law does not. There is a good reason for this. In Austrian law the limitations on rescission for error are such that there is no need for a claim of this sort: in the few cases where rescission is permitted, either the promisee has suffered no reliance damage worth mentioning or he deserves no protection because he himself was responsible for causing the error or not knowing of it.

Swiss law also makes the fundamental distinction between an error of motive and an error in the transaction; art. 23 OR declares that only an essential error may be taken into account, and art. 24 par. 2 OR states that an error in motive is not essential. At first sight the concept of 'essentiality' appears to be more specific than in German law since four types of essential error are listed, including errors concerning the nature of the transaction and error concerning the identity of the other party or the object of the contract. These types of error remind us of the *error in negotio, error in persona*, and *error in objecto* known to the Roman-based *Gemeines Recht* in force before the Continental codes became effective. An error is also essential if it concerns the quantity to be provided under the contract (art. 24 par. 1 no. 3 OR).

An example of such an error may be found in BGE 105 II 23: a ring was displayed in a jeweller's window, priced at 1,380 S. fr. A customer paid this sum for the ring and took delivery of it. On a showing that the price had been affixed by mistake and that the intended price had been 13,800 S. fr., the jeweller was allowed to rescind the sale under art. 24. par. 1 no. 3 OR, subject to paying damages under art. 26 OR because the error was due to his own negligence.

Finally an error is essential if it concerns a particular feature of the contract 'which the mistaken party, in accordance with good faith and normal commercial practice, regarded as a necessary foundation for the contract' (art. 24. par. 1 no. 4 OR).

Only the last of these errors, the so-called 'fundamental error' (*Grundlagen-irrtum*), is important in practice, being treated as an error of motive which is exceptionally to be taken into account. The broad terms of the Code leave the courts a free hand to determine when an error is fundamental, in line with the general habit of Swiss law to leave the decision of difficult questions to the discretion of the judges.

Surprisingly enough, Swiss law does not draw a clear distinction between cases of unilateral mistake and the cases which are treated in Germany under the heading of 'failure of the basis of the transaction' (*Wegfall der Geschäftsgrundlage*); cases of both types are dealt with under art. 24 par. 1 no. 4 OR. For an error to be fundamental it is generally agreed that a subjective and an objective element must concur: the mistaken party must have regarded the fact misconceived as the necessary basis for the transaction and it must have been one which businessmen would normally regard as a *sine qua non* of contracting (BGE 53 II 153; 56 II 426). In making this objective evaluation the courts have occasionally considered which of the parties should bear the risk of misconception in the circumstances of the case and also whether the promisee could have known of the mistake.

See BGE 55 II 189; 79 II 272; GUHL, *Das schweizerische Obligationenrecht* (7th edn., 1980) 123 ff.; BUCHER, *Schweizerisches Obligationenrecht, Allgemeiner Teil* (1979) Ch. 13.

Although the damages payable by a person who seeks rescission of a contract for mistake may, if the judge thinks it equitable, exceed the reliance interest, no damages are payable at all unless it was his own fault he made the mistake (art. 26 OR). Unlike §122 BGB, this rule follows out the logic of *culpa in contrahendo*, but it is perhaps not beyond criticism in view of the risks to which a party is exposed by another's mistake even when it is not due to his negligence.

III

When we turn to the Romanistic legal family and consider *French* law, we find that the rules in the Code civil offer the judges even less in the way of firm standards for the solution of mistake cases than German, Austrian, or Swiss law: what the Code civil says is that an error can be taken into account only if it affects the substance of the thing contracted about—'la substance même de la chose'—and that an error concerning the other party to the contract is not to be taken into account unless the identity of the other party was a principal ground for contracting (art. 1110 Code civil).

On the basis of these rather sketchy rules, the courts and writers have reached the following position. An error may only be taken into account if it was a principal motive in concluding the contract (*motif principal ou déterminant*) and concerned basic qualities of the object of the contract (*qualités substantielles*).

A mistake constitutes the determining motive if the mistaken party would never have concluded the contract but for the mistake; it is not sufficient if he would have concluded the contract on different terms. Thus if a person undertakes a guarantee in the erroneous belief that the creditor's claim is secured and that the securities will pass to him should he pay, he cannot rescind the guarantee on the ground of this error if it appears at the trial that he had other reasons for undertaking the guarantee (Req. 16 March 1898, DP 1898. 1. 301). Naturally a person cannot point to a detail which is objectively trivial and claim that his error on that matter was the principal inducement for entering the contract. Thus while it is a relevant error to think that the picture one is buying is by Rubens, when it is not (Paris 22 Feb. 1950, D. 1950, 269), it is not a relevant error to suppose that a picture, correctly attributed to Delacroix, had hung in the painter's bedroom, even if the purchaser alleges he was induced to buy it because he thought it had. (Trib. civ. Seine 8 Dec. 1950, D. 1951, 50; similarly, Trib. paix Nantes, 23 Jan. 1947, D. 1947, 220, and Civ. 26 Jan. 1972, D. 1972, 517.)

It is a further requisite that the error be as to a 'qualité substantielle'. The courts have not done much to render this general clause more specific, and nearly every author puts the cases in a different order. An error of motive is generally said to be immaterial except in very special cases.

If a person assigns a debt in the mistaken belief that the real rights which secured it have expired, he cannot rescind the assignment even if the supposed extinction of the securities is referred to in the document of assignment (Civ. 26 May 1891, DP 1891. 1. 352; see also GHESTIN (above p. 440) 64 ff.). But it is different when in a contract for the sale of property the rental income is said to be 466 f. per *month* and turns out to be 466 f. per *quarter* (Trib. gr. inst. Fontainebleau, 9 Dec. 1970, D. 1972. 89, noted by GHESTIN; see also LOUSSOUARN, *Rev. trim. dr. civ.* 70 (1972) 386 ff.).—Trial courts sometimes go badly off the rails in the other direction, as happened when a Paris court, in a holding characterized by chivalry rather than law, allowed a lady to reclaim the price of a theatre ticket she had just bought on the ground that she did not realize that her husband had already bought a ticket for the same performance (Trib. com. Seine 2 April 1943, Gaz. Pal. 1943. 2. 81).—If the transaction is gratuitous, the courts are much more ready to take errors of motive into account: thus an heir who disclaimed his rights of succession in the expectation that the estate would devolve on a particular third party whom he wanted to benefit was allowed to rescind his disclaimer when he found that this did not occur (Civ. 15 June 1960, JCP 1961. II. 12274; see also Civ. 24 May 1948, D. 1948, 517 and 12 Jan. 1953, D. 1953, 234, and also COLIN/CAPITANT, *Traité de droit civil* II (1959) no. 658).

It is also agreed—although the Code civil says nothing whatever about it— that an error can be taken into account only if it is *excusable*. Cases in which a party has signed a written contract without reading it properly are often placed under this heading, although really they are not cases of mistake at all (see Trib. civ. Vitré 23 Dec. 1949, JCP 1950. II. 5271). The principal instance of an inexcusable and therefore irrelevant mistake occurs when the mistaken party had the means of acquainting himself with the true state of facts before entering the contract. A person who makes an excavation pursuant to contract and quite unexpectedly hits rock cannot rescind if he had had the opportunity of investigating the ground beforehand (Paris 30 June 1866, DP 1874. 2. 182). A lessee of hunting rights who finds much less game than he expected cannot rescind the contract if a walk through the land would have disclosed the state of the game (Amiens 30 Nov. 1954, D. 1955, 420). A person who takes out an insurance policy without realizing that he already has cover for that risk cannot rescind the contract if his affairs were in evident disarray and he was a person with 'une certaine expérience des assurances' (Civ. 29 June 1959, Bull. civ. 1959. I. 267).

The rules of the new *Italian* Codice civile (arts. 1427–33) are very forward-looking, having been influenced by Austrian and Swiss law as well as by the decisions of the French courts.

They quite rightly abandon the notion of error in motive, and take account of mistakes only if they are essential, under art. 1429, and if the other party could have been aware of them. A mistake is essential if it concerns the nature or object of a contract; it is also essential if it concerns the identity or qualities of the contractual object or of the other party to the contract, provided that these were factors determinative of entering the contract, either objectively or in the circumstances of the case. An error of law is also essential if it was the only or principal reason for entering the contract.

In addition it must always be shown that the error would have been noticed by the other party had he exercised reasonable and proper care. If a picture bought as a real Picasso turns out to be a forgery, the purchaser can only rescind if the vendor could have known that it was a forgery; this requirement was held satisfied in a case where the vendor himself was a painter (App. Milano 5 June 1951, Foro pad. 1951. I. 874).

IV

The doctrine of mistake in the law of *England* and the *United States of America* is rather complex.

The first striking feature about the Common Law is that, unlike Continental systems, it makes a separate category of those cases where the mistake is caused by an inaccurate statement or misrepresentation by the other party. If the other party made the mis-statement with the deliberate intention of misleading or deceiving, this is a fraudulent misrepresentation which entitles the mistaken party to rescind the contract and claim damages, but even if the other party was in perfect good faith, that is, it was an innocent misrepresentation, the mistaken party may still rescind if he acts quickly enough. Previously, this was his *only* right and he could *not* claim damages, but the English law on this point has been changed by the Misrepresentation Act, 1967. Under s. 2(1) of the Act the mistaken party, while adhering to the contract, can claim damages even if the defendant had no intention of misleading him, unless the defendant can prove that at the time of conclusion of the contract he believed that what he said was true and that he had reasonable grounds for so believing. The mistaken party in the case of an innocent misrepresentation retains his previous right to rescind the contract but here also the Misrepresentation Act makes a significant change: under s. 2(2) the court may hold the mistaken party to the contract and grant him damages instead if it is of opinion that

'it would be equitable to do so, having regard to the nature of the misrepresentation and the loss that would be caused by it if the contract were upheld, as well as to the loss that rescission would cause to the other party'. Thus in effect one may now rescind a contract for innocent misrepresentation only if in all the circumstances this is fair: on the whole matter see ATIYAH/TREITEL, 30 *Mod. L. Rev.* 369 (1967), FAIREST, [1967] *Camb. LJ* 239, and v. METZLER, *AWD* 1968, 252.

It is not always clear precisely what constitutes a misrepresentation. In general a misrepresentation is a false statement made before or at the time of the conclusion of the contract which caused the misrepresentee to enter the contract or contributed to his doing so. A statement as to the law or as to matters lying in the future is not taken into account, and the same is true of mere statements of opinion and of commercial puffs which no one in business could reasonably take seriously.

There may be difficult borderline cases. For example, the inaccurate statement by an auctioneer of agricultural land that it was 'very fertile and capable of development' was held to be 'a mere flourishing description by an auctioneer' (*Dimmock* v. *Hallett*, (1866) LR 2 Ch. App. 21) while the statement of a vendor of land that it was let to 'a most desirable tenant' gave rise to rescission when it was shown that at the time of the contract the tenant was already several months in arrears with the rent (*Smith* v. *Land and House Property Corp.*, (1884) 28 Ch. D. 7).—Even if a misrepresentation is such as to entitle the misrepresentee to rescind, the misrepresentee must nevertheless stand by the contract if he allows an unreasonably long time to elapse before attempting to rescind on the ground of his error (compare *Leaf* v. *International Galleries*, [1950] 2 KB 86), or if the contract has been conclusively affirmed in some other way. Claims to rescind on the ground of innocent misrepresentation used also to be barred if the false statement, often an inaccurate description of the qualities of goods sold, had been *incorporated* in the contract or if the ensuing contract had been executed by either party. These artificial limitations have also been done away with by the Misrepresentation Act (see s. 1).

By 'mistake' the Common Law means only such errors as are *not* caused by mis-statements. In this area the doctrine of error in *English* law is particularly complex because the Common Law courts and the Equity Courts treated cases of mistake differently and these divergent views still coexist in judicial decision and legal writing. It was a Common Law rule that contracts are 'void ab initio' if at the time the contract was concluded the object of the contract had ceased to exist.

This was extended from cases where the object sold had ceased to exist before the contract was concluded or where it already belonged to the purchaser to cover the case in which two persons entered a separation and maintenance agreement on the erroneous assumption that they were married (*Galloway* v. *Galloway*, (1914) 30 TLR 531), and the case where neither party to a transfer of the right to receive the proceeds of a life insurance policy knew that the *cestui que vie* was already dead (*Scott* v. *Coulson*, |1903| 2 CH. 249); see also PALMER (above p. 440) 33 ff.—In the case of a mere 'unilateral mistake', that is, a mistake made by only one party, the contract stands; this is so, according to the leading case of *Smith* v. *Hughes*, (1871) LR 6 QB 597, even if the other party knew of it. On this see LORD ATKIN in *Bell* v. *Lever Bros. Ltd.*, [1932] AC 161, 224.

The Courts of Equity were rather readier than the Courts of Law to take account of mistakes; where the Common Law offered no remedy, equity could undo a contract on the ground of mistake (recission) or order 'rectification' or 'reformation' of contracts which had been inaccurately recorded in writing. More recently there has been a tendency to extend the devices which were developed 'in equity', as may be seen in the landmark decision of LORD DENNING in *Solle* v. *Butcher*, [1950] 1 KB 671, 693, where he makes the general statement that

'a contract is also liable in equity to be set aside if the parties were under a common misapprehension either as to facts or as to their relative and respective rights, provided that the misapprehension was fundamental and that the party seeking to set it aside was not himself at fault'.—See also *Grist* v. *Bailey*, [1967] Ch. 352. It remains true, however, that it is only in the rarest cases that even the Courts of Equity will rescind a contract on the ground of a mere unilateral mistake not caused by the other party.

American law has an equally strong tendency to limit the cases where contracts may be avoided for error, but it does not make all the fine and sometimes strained distinctions of English law. This may be because the principle of *stare decisis* is rather less strong in the United States than in England, so that unhappy precedents have a less marked effect on subsequent developments, and because the much larger number of decisions on mistake in the United States makes it proportionally less likely that a subtle technicality will survive.

So far as can be seen, American courts which have to decide cases involving mistake are ready to entertain all the considerations which can reasonably be adduced in this context. The veniality of the error of the mistaken party, whether the other party should have realized it, the extent to which the other party has acted or acted reasonably in reliance on the mistaken party's promise, the possibility of resuming the status quo ante—all these circumstances play a part in proportion to their importance in cases of the type before the court.

Unfortunately there is no room here to go through the cases and show how the American courts actually take account of these various considerations, so we can only give a few instances. In *Grant Marble Co.* v. *Abbot*, 142 Wis. 279, 124 NW 264 (1910), the plaintiff had contracted to put marble floors in a building with six storeys, but his tender was calculated on the erroneous basis that the building had only five. After the work had been carried out, the plaintiff claimed a reasonable supplement, but his claim failed since the court held that the contract was binding notwithstanding the mistake: 'Such mistake cannot be charged to defendant, but must rest upon the party whose negligence caused it. All the facts were within reach of plaintiff and he had but to open his eyes and see them. His own architect who had full knowledge of the facts was within call and could have been consulted upon the subject if plaintiff had desired.'—See also *Leonard* v. *Howard*, 67 Ore. 203, 135 P. 549 (1913) and *Steinmeyer* v. *Schroeppel*, 226 Ill. 9, 80 NE 564 (1907).—The decision is different if the offeree purports to accept an offer which he knows to have been made in error: in such a case even a negligent offeror is not bound by the contract; see *State of Connecticut* v. *McGraw & Co.*, 41 F. Supp. 369 (D. Conn. 1941).—The courts are especially ready to bar rescission for error if the promisee has already, in reliance on the validity of the contract, undergone a 'change of position' which makes it difficult or impossible to reinstate the status quo ante; on this see the cases cited in CORBIN §606. A partial explanation of this may lie in the fact that American law does not yet impose a general duty on the mistaken party to compensate the other party for his reliance damage (see PALMER (above p. 440) 58 ff.) and that therefore a court would rather leave the *mistaken party* to suffer the consequences of his error than shift the loss to the other party by giving effect to the mistake.—The rules which American courts apply when rescission is sought on the ground of mistake or misrepresentation may conveniently be approached through Restatement (Second) of Contracts (1981) §151 ff.

V

We can now turn to an analysis and evaluation of the various rules relating to mistake.

The commonest distinction drawn in Continental legal systems is the distinction between error in motive, which is not taken into account, and error in the transaction, which is. Errors of motive are irrelevant because they relate to what the promisor had in mind before making his promise; error in the transaction is significant because the declaration of intention does not reflect the intention correctly formed.

Whether or not the distinction between error in motive and error in transaction is psychologically meaningful, it is very doubtful whether it is legally useful. If a person misreads an offer to sell a thing for 500 DM as an offer to sell for 300 DM, and accepts it in this sense, this is held to be an error in the transaction. If a person receives a telegram saying 'I offer my racehorse Rhi' and accepts this offer on the false supposition that the horse is the well-known Derby-winner of that name, this is an irrelevant error of motive, since it was only a mistake as to what was meant which induced him to accept. If I quote too low a price because I have done my sums wrong, this is an error of motive which must not be taken into account; if my sums are right but I mis-state the price when I make the offer, this is an error of transaction.

No reasonable layman would accept these distinctions for a moment. From the point of view of justice mistakes of both categories may be equally important. Moreover, when one considers the matter more closely, every error in transaction involves an error in motive as well, and many pure errors of motive are so important that they have to be treated as errors in transaction in order to permit the mistaken party to rescind. If a person buys a silver bread-basket for a wedding, unaware that the engagement has been broken off, a reasonable observer would say that there was obviously no real congruence between intention and promise. In countries where this distinction obtains, most jurists make a distinction between motives which coexist with the contractual promise (relevant error) and motives which have already ceased to exist at the time the contract was formed (irrelevant error of motive). From the psychological point of view, this distinction is unsound, since antecedent motives do not simply die off but survive and accompany the making of promise. The distinction between the decision to contract and the act of contracting, widespread though it is, is fundamentally factitious, and the distinction between error of content and error of motive is not juridically sound or useful.

If we reject this method of distinguishing material and immaterial mistakes, what do we put in its place? One could make the following suggestion. The question raised by cases of mistake is which party should reasonably and fairly bear the risk of an error. Should the promisee be held to his promise despite his error, or should the other party, though not in error, suffer the risk of rescission? Now it is not at all obvious why cases of error in contract law should be decided differently from the way fate decides the consequences of error in life itself, and in life itself the mistakes one makes are borne by oneself. If one accepts this natural principle and treats contract as a feature of the impersonal mass commerce of today rather than as a very individuated phenomenon, it will be seen that the risks of making a mistake must rest with the party who makes it; one will then discard as socially inappropriate those remnants of the doctrine of intention which lurk in Continental rules relating to mistake. If risks are properly allocated in this way, rescission for error will always be very exceptional. This has been much more clearly appreciated in the Common Law and in Austrian law than in most Continental legal systems.

Thus it would be right to bar rescission if the other party was prepared, once the error was discovered, to perform the contract in the sense intended by the mistaken party (on this, see in detail ROLLIN (above p. 440)). Statutory rules to this effect are to be found in art. 25 par. 2 OR in Switzerland, in art. 1432 of the Italian Codice civile, and in the civil codes of Greece, Turkey, and Egypt; it is an idea which the Austrian courts have adopted without statutory authority.

Our comparative and criticial analysis of the problems of mistake gives support to the view put forward by HEINRICH TITZE (above, p. 441), though it met with no response at the time: an error accompanying the making of a contractual promise is in principle irrelevant. This should be obvious when the mistake relates to the value of the goods being sold, or their saleability or other matters such that decent businessmen would say that one party should not have to suffer because the other party got the facts wrong. But even in other cases where the error is *essential* in the sense indicated, rescission should only be allowed if there are other special reasons for not protecting the other party's reliance on the validity of the contract. Such reasons exist (1) if at the time of the contract the other party *knew or should have known* of the error being made; in such cases avoidance is allowed in Italian, Austrian, and Scandinavian law (see arts. 1428, 1432 Codice civile, §871 ABGB, art. 32 par. 1 Scandinavian Contract Law); (2) if the other party, even in the best of good faith, *caused* the mistake; here Austrian law allows the contract to be avoided (§871 ABGB) and the Common Law grants rescission for innocent misrepresentation; (3) if a *gratuitous* transaction is entered under a mistake; here the other party cannot oppose rescission since he has no claim that his reliance be protected. In all these cases, however, rescission should be barred if the other party is ready forthwith to perform the contract in the sense in which the mistaken party intended it.

It is to be hoped that one day, as part of a *unified* law concerning the substantial validity of contracts, we shall have international rules on the avoidance of contracts for error. One would start with rules which are important for international sales. The International Institute for the Unification of Private Law in Rome (UNIDROIT) is striving to extend the 'Uniform Sales Law' which covers the substantive law of sales, though only of 'international' sales (see below Ch. 43 V), by a series of other treaties, so-called 'satellite treaties', which are to unify the important marginal areas of law which are relevant to the law of sales. In particular, work has for many years been being done on a uniform law on the substantive validity of international sales contracts, which aims, *inter alia*, to unify the rules for avoidance on the grounds of error, deceit, and duress. For this purpose the Max Planck Institute for Foreign and International Private Law drew up a very comprehensive comparative report (see the references cited above p. 440); it has also, in pursuance of a commission from the International Institute for the Unification of Private Law, produced a draft uniform law for discussion (see ZWEIGERT *et al.*, *RabelsZ* 32 (1968) 201, 342), which contains a thorough comparative and critical discussion of the problems under consideration here. In the meantime the UNIDROIT draft of such a uniform law (see 17 Int. Leg. Mat. 282 (1978)) has been submitted to the UN Commission on International Trade Law (UNCITRAL).

VI

All legal systems see the connection between being mistaken and *being deceived*, the difference being that in cases of mistake the stress is laid on the misconception of the mistaken party while in cases of deceit the stress is laid on another's misbehaviour. That the dividing line between the two need not be sharply drawn is shown by the way the Common Law treats innocent misrepresentation as an instance of mistake caused by the other party.

The phrases used in the Continental codes to describe the concept of deceit differ somewhat. In the German legal family one speaks of 'deceitful' or 'deliberate' misleading, or, as in §870 ABGB, of causing a mistake by 'fraud', whereas in the Romanistic systems the phrases refer to the acts by which the deceit is effected.

Thus art. 1116 Code civil speaks of 'manœuvres', art. 1439 Codice civile of 'raggiri', the Burgerlijk Wetboek of 'kunstgrepen' (art. 1364), and the Spanish Código civil of 'maquinaciones insidiosas' (art. 1269).

In fact nothing turns on this distinction: all systems recognize that a simple lie may be enough to render a contract voidable, depending on the circumstances.

It is also common ground that in the case of deceit there is no room for the complex distinctions between material and immaterial errors, errors in transactions and errors in motive: art. 28 par. 1 OR in Switzerland expressly states that if a mistake is caused by deceit it need not be essential, and under art. 39 of the previous Polish Law of Obligations the party deceived might avoid the consequences of his promise 'without regard to the question whether the error was a reason for contracting or affected the content of the contract or whether it was a material one or not'. The reason for this is obvious: a swindler should not be favoured just because the error he deceitfully induces is one which his less practised contractor may regard as immaterial or collateral.

Court decisions to like effect may be found in Austria (OGH 3 Feb. 1932, SZ XIV 18), in Germany (RGZ 81, 13, 16), in the Netherlands (HR 27 Jan. 1950. Ned. Jur. 1950 no. 559), and in the United States: *New York Life Insurance Co.* v. *McLaughlin*, 112 Vt. 402, 26 A. 2d 108 (1942), and *De Joseph* v. *Zambelli*, 392 Pa. 24, 139 A. 2d 644 (1958).

In the Romanistic legal family the French Code civil maintains an old doctrinal distinction: a contract may be avoided only for *dolus causam dans contractui*, that is, when the party deceived would not have decided to enter the contract but for the deceit, and not for *dolus incidens in contractum*, where the contract would have been concluded, albeit on different terms, even if no deceit had been practiced; in such a case the party deceived can simply claim damages, usually in the form of a reduction of the price.

See Civ. 15 Feb. 1898, DP 1898. 1. 192; Conseil d'Etat 14 Dec. 1923, DH 1924, 52.— This view finds support in the wording of art. 1116 Code civil (and also art. 1440 Codice civile, and art. 1270 par. 2 of the Spanish Civil Code): deceit constitutes a ground for rescission 'lorsque les manœuvres pratiquées par l'une des parties sont telles qu'il est évident que, sans ces manœuvres, l'autre partie n'aurait pas contracté'.—The courts in

Switzerland have gone both ways on this question, see BGE 40 II 114, 64 II 142, 81 II 213.

There is no doubt that this is a most unfortunate distinction. It makes it necessary for the judge to go in for a retrospective and hypothetical psychological reconstruction of what the parties would have agreed had the deceptive manœuvres never occurred.

In Anglo-American law deceit is called 'fraudulent misrepresentation' or simply 'fraud'. For this it must be shown that the representor made statements of fact (and not simply standard commercial puffs) in the knowledge, at the least, that they might well be false.

According to the leading case of *Derry* v. *Peek* (1889) 14 App. Cas. 337, 374: 'Fraud is proved when it is shown that a false representation has been made knowingly without belief in its truth, or recklessly, careless whether it be true or false.' The Restatement of the Law of Contracts defines fraud as 'misrepresentation known to be such'. There is an exhaustive treatment of the matter in the Report of the Max-Planck-Institut (above p. 440) 11 f.

Courts everywhere are agreed on what constitutes deceit, though there are often slight variations, as in the question when mere silence regarding a relevant fact may amount to deceit so as to entitle the other party to avoid the contract.

In view of the German courts, failure to state a fact constitutes deceit only if there was a duty to declare it, and it depends on the circumstances of the individual case whether there was such a duty or not. For example, it is recognized that in negotiating a sales contract parties cannot expect to be told of the general market conditions relevant to the price; on the other hand, it has repeatedly been decided that good faith requires the disclosure of such circumstances concerning the object of the sale as are evidently material to the decision whether to enter the contract or not.

Thus the Reichsgericht granted rescission of a contract when the vendor had stated that the motor being sold was more than three years old, when in fact it was over twelve years old and the vendor in the circumstances knew that the purchaser would never have bought the motor had he known its true age (RGZ 62, 149).—It was also held deceitful for a banker to sell shares in a mining company at the normal daily price when he already knew that the mine had been flooded (see RGZ 111, 235).—In the opinion of the Bundesgerichtshof the vendor of a well-maintained car is bound to volunteer the fact that the car has been involved in a collision: if he fails to do so the purchaser may avoid the contract on the ground of deceit (BGH NJW 1982, 1386).—The Court of Cassation in France has stated the following principle: 'Le dol peut être constitué par le silence d'une partie dissimulant à son cocontractant un fait qui, s'il avait été connu de lui, l'aurait empêché de contracter.' (Req. 23 May 1933, DP 1933. 1. 142; but see also Civ. 30 May 1927, DH 1927, 416.)—Art. 6. 5. 2. 11 of the Draft Civil Code of the Netherlands (The Meijers Draft) lays down that a contract may be avoided 'si une partie avait compris que l'autre partie se trouvait dans l'erreur et que, sans cette erreur, cette autre partie n'aurait pas conclu le contrat'. On the whole matter see the Report of the Max-Planck-Institut (above p. 440) 105 ff.

If a person fails to put express questions to the other party and draws erroneous conclusions from his silence on these matters, the Common Law seems readier to hold him to his contract.

The problem is one which has exercised jurists throughout the ages. CICERO put the case that at a time when a famine in Rhodes had caused a sharp increase in prices a merchant arrived there from Alexandria with a cargo of corn. Must he let the Rhodians know that a lot of other merchants, whose ships he had passed on the way, were also coming to Rhodes with corn? CICERO thought the merchant must disclose what he knew (*De officiis*, 3. 50 and 57), but GROTIUS held otherwise: the Rhodians' mistake had nothing to do with any quality of the goods themselves, and the merchant had not told any actual lie, but had only acted '*licita sollertia*', that is, with permissible craftiness. (*De iure belli ac pacis libri tres* (1625) II 12. 9. 2.) Likewise Chief Justice MARSHALL in *Laidlaw* v. *Organ*, 4 US 72 (1817): during the war of 1812–14 between England and the United States the price of tobacco in New Orleans fell drastically because of the British blockade. One morning the plaintiff learnt that a treaty of peace had been signed in Ghent and immediately proceeded to buy a great quantity of tobacco from the defendants who suspected no such thing; as one would expect, the price of tobacco forthwith rose, by some 50%. The contract was upheld.—A similar decision in England is *Smith* v. *Hughes*, (1871) LR 6 QB 597, where the vendor knew that the purchaser was labouring under a misconception regarding the quality of the goods he was buying, but did nothing to correct the error. The court held that the purchaser was bound by the contract: 'the question is not what a man of scrupulous morality or nice honour would do under such circumstances . . . Whatever may be the case in a court of morals there is no legal obligation on the vendor to inform the buyer that he is under a mistake, not induced by the act of the vendor' (ibid. p. 603, 607). LORD WRIGHT has observed of this judgment that 'the maxim that a vendor may passively take advantage of the self-deception of the buyer is calculated to encourage people to say that law is a mean and sordid business' (59 LQ Rev. 122, 127 (1943)). It may be, in view of recent developments, which PALMER describes as the 'gradual whittling away of the maxim caveat emptor' (above p. 94, p. 83), that these precedents will not always be followed either in England or in the United States; see LORD DENNING in *Solle* v. *Butcher*, [1950] 1 KB 671, 692 f.—This very interesting question has not yet been properly investigated on a comparative basis.

Another difficult problem arises when the deceit is practised not by the promisee himself but by some third party. In such circumstances German law permits rescission only if the promisee was himself aware or should have been aware of the deception or if the deception was practised by a person whose behaviour in all fairness is attributable to him; in such circumstances the promisee's reliance deserves no protection.

Thus if deceit is practised by a representative of the promisee or by any other person whom he allowed to assist him in the conclusion of the contract the contract may be rescinded although the promisee himself had no knowledge or means of knowledge of the deception (BGHZ 20, 39; BGH NJW 1962, 2195).—The same principles apply in Austria (§875 sent. 2 ABGB), in Switzerland (art. 28 par. 2 OR), and also in the Anglo-American legal systems: see Restatement (Second) of Contracts (1981) §164(2), and *Lloyd* v. *Grace, Smith & Co.*, [1912] AC 716.

The French courts seem to insist that for fraud to be a ground of rescission it must be the fraud of the other party to the contract: 'Le dol ne peut entraîner la nullité que s'il émane du cocontractant': Civ. 26 Jan. 1977, Bull. civ. 1977. I. 40; (see also Civ. 27 June 1973, D. 1973. 733, noted by MALAURIE). In both cases a suit by a creditor against a surety met the defence that the surety had been fraudulently deceived by a third party, namely the principal debtor. In neither case was the surety allowed to rescind. German law would be more generous here: the surety would be able to rescind not only if the creditor knew or should have known of the deception but also if the principal debtor could be seen as the creditor's 'negotiating agent', manifestly acting in the interest and at the instance of the creditor in procuring the suretyship. See BGH NJW 1962, 2195 and WM 1966, 92; see also Civ. 7 July 1960, Bull. civ. 1960. I. 305.

VII

In all Continental legal systems the third 'defect of will', after mistake and deceit, is '*duress*'. Duress does not include physical compulsion, when, legally speaking, there is no declaration of will at all; duress is concerned only with psychical pressures.

Continental systems draw a sharp distinction between duress and the abuse of a necessitous condition. No such distinction is known to Anglo-American law. This is because the Common Law, in the narrower sense, treated as 'duress' only those cases in which a person made a promise under threats of physical violence or imprisonment. The concept of 'undue influence', gradually developed by the Courts of Equity, is used for the cases which are dealt with under the concept of duress in the Continental Civil Codes. Comparatists who enter this area must therefore investigate the doctrine of 'undue influence' as well. Although the term is principally used in cases of abuse of positions of particular trust, such as exist between parent and child, guardian and ward, lawyer and client, doctor and patient, and confessor and penitent, cases of unfair exploitation of a person's difficulty, which are dealt with in German law as exploitation (*Wucher*) under §138 par. 2 BGB, are also dealt with in Anglo-American law as instances of 'undue influence'.

As in the case of deceit, all the great legal systems are in general agreement about the objective and subjective requirements for duress.

On this see the report of the Max-Planck-Institut (above p. 440) 123 ff.—Of course one must not be taken in by the fact that some legal systems seem to emphasize aspects of the problem which others apparently ignore. For example, the German lawyer can cite a great number of cases for the proposition that while it is duress to threaten an evil which it lies in the power of the threatener to bring about, it is not duress merely to point to an imminent or actual misfortune; the reason for this is probably that quite early on a Supreme Court decision emphasized this aspect of the matter and that subsequent judges, hypnotized by the precedent, have tended to see the cases before them in this light. The same principle unquestionably applies in the Common Law although it is not always made express there.

A contractor can rescind a contract on the ground of 'duress' if he entered it under the influence of an unlawful threat of physical violence or some other evil, but it is a question whether a case of 'duress' exists when one party, to the knowledge of the other, was in such an economic crisis that he had really no option but to enter the contract as he did. Can such a person claim rescission of the contract for 'economic duress'? In the *United States* some decisions hold that he may (on this see DAWSON (above p. 440), and Restatement (Second) of Contracts (1981) §176 propounds rules to similar effect). The American courts can usually help here by holding the contract 'unconscionable'. (See above Ch. 31 III.) In *England* the House of Lords has indicated a general acceptance of the American position, but has stressed the importance of finding that the claimant's will must have been coerced and vitiated so that his entering the contract was not really a voluntary act (*Pao On* v. *Lau Yiu Long*, [1980] AC 614, 635–6). (For a critical view of this, see ATIYAH, 98 *LQ Rev.* 197 (1980).) LORD DENNING had previously made a famous attempt at synthesis:

' . . . English law gives relief to one who, without independent advice, enters into a contract upon terms which are very unfair or transfers property for a consideration which is grossly inadequate, when his bargaining power is grievously impaired by reason of his own needs or desires, or by his own ignorance or infirmity, coupled with undue influences or pressures brought to bear on him by or for the benefit of the other.' (*Lloyds Bank* v. *Bundy*, [1975] QB 326, 339.) The House of Lords has disapproved this venture (*National Westminster Bank* v. *Morgan*, [1985] AC 686, where LORD SCARMAN said, at p. 708, 'I question whether there is any need in the modern law to erect a general principle of relief against inequality of bargaining power.') Yet in *Universe Tankships* v. *Int'l. Transp. Workers Fed'n*, [1983] 1 AC 366, 384, LORD DIPLOCK had said of economic duress that its rationale 'is that [the party's] apparent consent was induced by pressure exercised on him by [the] other party which the law does not regard as legitimate, with the consequence that the consent is treated in law as revocable unless approbated either expressly or by implication after the illegitimate pressure has ceased to operate on his mind. It is a rationale similar to that which underlies the avoidability of contracts entered into and the recovery of money exacted under colour of office, or under undue influence or in consequence of threats of physical duress.' See also *North Ocean Shipping Co.* v. *Hyundai Constr. Co.* (*The Atlantic Baron*), [1979] QB 705.

The problem of duress applied by a third party is of interest here too, and, at the expense of many other equally attractive questions, we shall investigate it in slightly greater detail.

The view underlying the German BGB is that a person threatened has a greater claim to be freed from his contract than a person deceived, and the result is that the party threatened can rescind even against a contractor who was in good faith.

This view is shared by the Romanistic legal family: see art. 1111 Code civil, art. 1434 Codice civile, art. 1268 Código civil, art. 1359 Burgerlijk Wetboek.

In Austria and in the Common Law, on the other hand, deceit and duress are treated alike on this point: the party threatened can rescind the contract only if the other party was aware of the threat.

Under §875 ABGB it is sufficient if the other party 'must obviously have known' of the threat; the same is true in the United States: see Restatement (Second) of Contracts (1981) §175(2); in England, apparently, actual knowledge is required; see *Kesarmal* v. *Valliappa*, [1954] 1 WLR 380, 386; *Talbot* v. *von Boris*, [1911] 1 KB 854.

A further variation is found in Scandinavian law, where if a person is subjected to a particularly serious threat of dire evil capable of immediate production, he may rescind even against a contractor in good faith, whereas in cases of less grievous pressure rescission is available only if the contractor is in bad faith, as under the Anglo-American rule: see art. 28 f. of the Scandinavian Law of Contract.

The solution of Swiss law is particular original and progressive. A person who has entered a contract as a result of threats by a third party may rescind the contract even if his contractor was in good faith, but if equity so requires he must compensate his contractor for his reliance damage (art. 29 par. 2 OR). It is this solution which the Max-Planck-Institut has proposed for the Uniform Law on the Substantive Validity of International Sales Contracts (on this, see ZWEIGERT *et al.* (above p. 441) p. 241 f.).

39

Representation

AMES, 'Undisclosed Principal—Rights and Liabilities', 18 *Yale LJ* 443 (1909).

BASEDOW, 'Das Vertretungsrecht im Spiegel konkurrierender Harmonisierungsentwürfe', *RabelsZ* 45 (1981) 196.

CAPELLE, Das Außenverhältnis bei der Vertretung fremder Interessen nach skandinavischem Recht', *Festschrift Leo Raape* (1948) 325.

CONARD, 'What's Wrong with Agency?', 1 *J. Leg. Ed.* 540 (1948–9).

DORIS, 'Die unmittelbare Stellvertretung des BGB im Lichte funktions- und strukturähnlicher Rechtsgebilde anderer Rechtsordnungen', *Festschrift Larenz* (1983) 161.

FERSON, *Principles of Agency* (1954).

FRIDMAN, *The Law of Agency* (4th edn., 1976).

GOODHART/HAMSON, 'Undisclosed Principals in Contract', 4 *Camb. LJ* 320 (1932).

HIJMANS, 'La Représentation dans les actes juridiques', *Travaux de l'Association Henri Capitant* IV (1949) 121.

HAMEL, *Le Contrat de commission* (1949).

LÉVY-ULLMANN, 'La Contribution essentielle du droit anglais à la théorie générale de la représentation', *Acta Academiae Universalis iurisprudentiae comparativae* I (1928) 341.

MECHEM, *Outlines of the Law of Agency* (4th edn., 1952).

MONTROSE, 'The Basis of the Power of an Agent in Cases of Actual and Apparent Authority', 16 *Can. Bar Rev.* 757 (1938).

MÜLLER-FREIENFELS, *Die Vertretung beim Rechtsgeschäft* (1955).

——, *Stellvertretungsregelungen in Einheit und Vielfalt, Rechtsvergleichende Studien zur Stellvertretung* (1982; including reprints of most of the following articles).

——, 'Die "Anomalie" der verdeckten Stellvertretung (undisclosed agency) des englischen Rechts', *RabelsZ* 17 (1952) 578, 18 (1953) 12.

——, 'The Undisclosed Principal', 16 *Mod. L. Rev.* 299 (1953).

——, 'Comparative Aspects of Undisclosed Agency', 18 *Mod. L. Rev.* 33 (1955).

——, 'Law of Agency', 6 *Am. J. Comp. L.* 165 (1955).

——, 'Legal Relations in the Law of Agency: Power of Agency and Commercial Certainty', 13 *Am. J. Comp. L.* 193, 341 (1964).

——, 'The Law of Agency', in: *Civil Law in the Modern World* (ed. Yiannopoulos, 1965).

MÜNCH, 'Auftrag', in II *Rechtsvergleichendes Handwörterbuch* (ed. Schlegelberger) (1929) 277.

POPESCO-RAMNICEANO, *Représentation dans les actes juridiques en droit comparé* (1927).

POWELL, *The Law of Agency* (2nd edn., 1961).

REYNOLDS, 'Agency: Theory and Practice', 94 *LQ Rev.* 224 (1978).

ROUAST, 'La Représentation dans les actes juridiques', *Travaux de l'Association Henri Capitant* IV (1949) 110.

SCHMITTHOFF, 'Agency in International Trade', *Rec. des Cours* 129 (1970–1) 107.

SEAVEY, *Studies in Agency* (1949).

SELL, *Agency* (1975).

DE THEUX, *Le Droit de la représentation commerciale, Étude comparative et critique du statut des représentants salariés et des agents commerciaux*, 2 vols. (1975/77).

WAHL, *Vertragsansprüche Dritter im französischen Recht* (1935).

WÜRDINGER, *Die Geschichte der Stellvertretung (agency) in England* (1933).

I

THE device of representation is an unavoidable necessity in any developed system which depends on the division of labour for the production and distribution of goods and services. The manufacturer delegates the purchase of raw materials to an agent, the heirs entrust the sale of the estate to an auctioneer, and the wholesaler sells his goods through trade representatives or commission agents. For any number of reasons these people, instead of acting themselves, as they may be unable or unwilling to do, use the assistance of persons who transact with third parties 'for them', 'on their account', 'as agents', or 'in their interest'. The function of these auxiliaries is the same everywhere: they make it possible for people to participate in commercial transactions. We shall use the word 'representation' to denote what they do, and eschew for the moment the technical terms which have been employed.

For many Anglo-American lawyers even this would be too narrow a circumscription of our topic. According to a widespread view in the Common Law, 'agency' includes not only the cases where a person transacts on behalf of another but also the cases where a master is held liable in tort for the acts of his employee or servant (see below Ch. 48). In consequence the American Restatement of Agency is forced to define an agent in rather an empty manner in §12, to the effect that he is in a position 'to alter the legal relations between the principal and third persons'. The comments make it clear that such an alteration of legal relations occurs when the agent's misconduct exposes his principal to tort liability towards a third party. In the American textbooks and in most English textbooks as well the problem of responsibility for others is dealt with not only in the law of torts but also in the law of agency.

This American view is traceable to the influence of HOLMES who attempted to make of agency an independent area of law which included all the instances in the law of contract, the law of torts, and the law of companies where he could discern the notion 'qui facit per alium facit per se'. In this way the 'doctrine of respondeat superior' which describes the tort liability of the master for the damage caused by his servants entered the law of agency. On this see CONARD (above p. 459).

Nevertheless, for the purposes of comparative law, it seems best to maintain the distinction between the situations where a principal is held to declarations, especially contracts, made on his behalf and where he is made liable for the harmful conduct of his staff. It is true that the brocard 'qui facit per alium facit per se' covers both cases, since the end result of both is that the superior is made liable for the behaviour of an assistant, and it may therefore be didactically sound to present both grounds of liability under a single heading. Nevertheless the two cases of liability rest on fundamentally different bases: in the one case it is the fact that the principal has *authorized* his assistant to enter legal transactions with third parties which makes him responsible, in the other case it is the fact that he has charged persons under his control with an *activity* which has proved harmful to third parties in an unforeseen manner.

This point is taken by Common Law writers but no consequences are drawn from it and they continue to link agency and vicarious liability. FERSON, for example, writes: 'The two basic relations are strange bedfellows. The liability of a master under the doctrine of respondeat superior and the subjection of a principal to the power of his agents are utterly different . . . There is a wide difference between contracts and torts, and there is a corresponding difference between the liability of an employer as such and the subjection of a principal to the power of his agent' (above p. 459, p. 12). To the same effect, see MECHEM (above p. 459) 4 f., FRIDMAN (above p. 459) 21, 197 ff.; SEAVEY (the Editor of the Restatement) dissents (above p. 460) 72: 'That there may be different reasons of policy in the two cases is clear, but it does not follow that a master is liable upon one ground and a principal upon another.'

II

The theory of VON JHERING and LABAND that not only is there a conceptual distinction between the grant of authority and the legal relationship which gives rise to it but that they have quite different legal consequences is one of the best-known achievements of German legal scholarship in the later nineteenth century. Their idea was adopted in the German BGB and then made a triumphal procession around the world. In fact no subsequent civil code has failed to make the distinction in one form or another between agency as a contract and agency as an authority.

Full details are to be found in MÜLLER-FREIENFELS, *Die Vertretung beim Rechtsgeschäft* (1955) 2 f.

The Austrian ABGB, on the other hand, treats them both together as 'contracts of authorization' in §1002; this falls in the 22nd Chapter entitled 'Of Authorization and Other Methods of Conducting Transactions', which makes no distinction between the internal and external aspects of the relationship, as is shown by §1017 which describes a contractual limitation of the representative's power as a 'secret authorization'.

Nor does the French Code civil contain any general treatment of representation. After a whole series of other contracts it finally deals with 'mandat', defined in art. 1984 as 'un acte par lequel une personne donne à une autre le pouvoir de faire quelque chose pour le mandant et en son nom'. Despite the absence of any statutory basis, however, French lawyers today use the concept of 'représentation' both in relation to the 'acte juridique' and in the general law of contracts.

The Committee set up to reform the Code civil posed the following question: 'Faut-il construire une théorie générale de la représentation commune à tous les actes juridiques ou au contraire se contenter de renvoyer cette matière au livre des contrats?' The first alternative was accepted, and in 1948 the draft of a section 'De la représentation' was proposed for inclusion in the chapter 'De la formation des actes juridiques' (Travaux de la Commission (1947/1948) 34, 399 ff.). See also the earlier draft of the Franco-Italian Law of Obligations of 1927, arts. 30 ff.

A different picture is presented once again by Anglo-American law where it is generally recognized that there is a Janus-quality about agency: it can be seen on the one hand as a contract engendering rights and duties, and on the other hand as the transfer of an authority.

Thus SALMOND/WILLIAMS, *On Contracts* (2nd edn., 1945) 393 say: 'We are here concerned with agency not in its aspect as a relationship or contract between principal and agent imposing and conferring rights and obligations between the parties, but in its aspect as a grant by the principal to his agent of authority to represent him in the exercise of his power of making contracts with third persons.' For England, see also DOWRICK, 17 *Mod. L. Rev.* 24 ff. (1954); FRIDMAN (above p. 459) 9 f.; POWELL (above p. 459) 296; for the United States, see SEAVEY (above p. 460) 69 f.; FEARSON (above p. 459) 216 f.; MECHEM (above p. 459) 11. The Restatement observes that 'It is not essential to the existence of authority that there be a contract between the principal and agent or that the agent promise or otherwise undertake to act as agent' (note (*a*) to §26).

This insight is not, however, put to any systematic use. It is mainly used to explain that in situations of peril an 'agency by necessity' may arise without any underlying contract or that where no consideration is provided there may still be a grant of authority although there cannot be a contract properly speaking.

This is another instance of the special style of legal thought in the Anglo-Saxon legal family: on the Continent the tendency to abstraction has led to the gradual induction from all the various fact-situations describable as 'acting for others' of a general concept of 'representation', juristically very refined but smelling rather of the lamp; the Common Law, on the other hand, with its pragmatic and dimensional way of seeing things, never loses sight of the integrated quality of the principal–agent relationship and is always concerned to see the law of agency as 'knitting together the whole subject of the employment of one man by another, whether for one job or life, and whether on commission or on payroll'.

See CONARD (above p. 459) 548. Sometimes the absence of a basic concept well anchored in theory has perceptible consequences: thus CONARD (above p. 459) reports that in the United States recently the law of agency has been threatened with discerption among neighbouring areas of law—torts, contracts, labour law, business transactions, and partnerships (on this see also MECHEM, 2 *J. Leg. Ed.* 203 (1949/1950)).

III

The comparative lawyer often discovers that an institution which he takes for granted in his own legal system almost as if it were part of the natural order of things is really no more than a contingent product of historical and sociological conditions which, much to his surprise and edification, is unknown in other systems and unregretted at that. Thus one might reasonably believe that comprehensive statutory representation was the ideal, if not the only imaginable, way of allowing incapable persons such as minors, persons under interdict, and the mentally unsound to take part in legal matters. Nevertheless, it transpires that the Common Law gets by quite nicely without having any such legal institution.

For the full details see MÜLLER-FREIENFELS, *Die Vertretung beim Rechtsgeschäft* (1955) 166 f.—It is probable that the Common Law has no comprehensive statutory representation because it did not have the concept of *patria potestas*. The care of incompetents in early German legal history lay with the family and it was only as urban civilization developed that any need was felt for a rationally organized and publicly supervised welfare system, which in the absence of autochthonous legal institutions was best answered by adopting the tutela of Roman law.

In English and American law the parents as such are not automatically the general representatives of minors in legal matters, nor are they either entitled or bound to appear on their behalf in court. In England, certainly, both parents are equally 'guardians', unless otherwise provided (Guardianship Act 1973, s. 1); the guardian is the person to accept the rents of landed property and manage the moveable property of the child. More important in practice are a whole series of other persons who represent the child in different matters and look after his various interests. For example, the practice in Anglo-American law, if a child receives property *inter vivos* or *mortis causa*, is to create a 'family settlement' or 'testamentary trust' so that the legal title in the property goes to a trustee until the beneficiary is of full age, the child being 'equitable owner' for the meanwhile and only entitled to call for the proceeds of the property if this accords with the directions of the donor or testator. When property is thus held 'in trust' for the minor—since 1925 this has been a statutory requirement in England for land (see the Law of Property Act, 1925 s. 1 (6)) and it is the general practice everywhere for moveables of value—the trustee's powers of management and disposition are exclusive of all other persons; these powers may be vested in the *parents* but, if so, this is only because they have been expressly appointed trustees by the donor or testator or, in particular cases, by the court.

Nor does the Common Law treat parents as general representatives of minors when it comes to the making of contracts. The Common Law does not make the validity of minors' contracts depend on the consent of parents or anyone else. Minors' contracts are valid if they are contracts for 'necessaries' or beneficial contracts of employment, apprenticeship, or education (see above Ch. 32 III); parental approval is not required. All other contracts may be avoided by the minor under certain circumstances whether ratified by parents or not.

Even in the law of procedure the Common Law has no 'statutory representation'. Suits by the minor are brought through a person appointed by the court, called a 'next friend', and suits against him are brought against a 'guardian ad litem' similarly appointed. The court usually appoints the father but it is by no means bound to do so. The court can also declare a minor to be a ward of court, with the result that the court itself acts as representative; if the ward owns property, the court normally appoints trustees to manage it.

IV

At the outset of this chapter we said, with a deliberate lack of specificity, that representation takes place whenever one party acting at the instance of a second party serves as a go-between in legal transactions with third parties and thus enables the second party to take part in legal affairs without personally appearing on the scene. This description will not quite do for German law, for German law makes a basic distinction depending on whether the transaction with the third party is conducted in the middleman's own name or in the name of his principal. Only when the third party knows, either from the middleman or from the circumstances, that the transaction is a transaction of another does the middleman's activity have any direct effects on the person of his principal, and it is only in such cases that German law speaks of 'representation'. If the middleman transacts in his *own* name, he alone acquires rights and duties under the contract even if, just as in a case of 'true' representation, he was acting on the principal's business and account without having any personal interest in the transaction at all.

This basic dichotomy in the law of representation appears, at least in a weak form, in all Continental legal systems. The definition of mandate in art. 1984 Code civil suggests otherwise, since it states that the mandatary must act 'pour le mandant et en son nom', but it is recognized that even where the mandatary acts in his own name, as might a commission agent, there may still be a contract of mandate in the sense of the Code civil. Such a mandate, however, according to the writers, is a 'mandat sans représentation' and the principal is not directly affected. For this to happen 'représentation' is required and, just as in German law, the transaction must be conducted in the name of the principal. The Italian Codice civile also, in art. 1388, requires that the representative's activity be 'in nome e nell'interesse del rappresentato'; if the middleman acts in his own name, he alone acquires rights and duties even, according to art. 1705, when the third party knew that the middleman was acting on behalf of a principal.

Such a distinction is unknown to the Common Law: if an agent acting within the scope of his authority concludes a contract with a third party on his principal's account, the principal acquires rights and duties under this contract even if the middleman acted as an 'undisclosed agent', that is, made the transaction in his own name and did not reveal the fact that he was acting for a principal.

Although eminent English and American jurists have thought of this rule as an anomaly of the Common Law, it is regarded by Continental lawyers as a forward-looking doctrine which could serve as a landmark for legal development.

Full references are given in MÜLLER-FREIENFELS, *RabelsZ* 17 (1952) 578 ff.—Much ingenuity has been devoted to the question of the true basis of this 'anomalous' doctrine of the Common Law. AMES saw the principal as being the beneficiary of a trust relationship between agent and third party. For GOODHART and HAMSON the principal takes over the contract concluded by the agent. LÉVY-ULLMANN's theory, based on Common Law writings, would make representation a mere aspect of the contract between representative and third party. FRIDMAN simply proposes 'to treat the whole idea of the undisclosed principal as an anomaly introduced into and accepted by the common law for reasons of convenience'. In Germany MÜLLER-FREIENFELS has investigated these problems comprehensively and intensively (*RabelsZ* 17 (1952) 578, 18 (1953) 12). He concludes that it is because the Common Law focuses on the persons between whom the exchange is to take place, as it does in cases of consideration, that the undisclosed principal directly acquires rights and liabilities; here these persons are the principal and the third party, the agent being simply a middleman for effecting the exchange. This is criticized by POWELL (above p. 459) p. 153.

The Continental lawyer will immediately ask how well the doctrine of 'undisclosed agency' serves the practical interests of principal and third party. Two problems call for special attention and will be investigated in some detail here: what protection is given to the third party who, having concluded a contract, as he thought, with the other party to the negotiations, finds himself sued for performance by a principal hitherto undisclosed? And again: how is the reverse case to be justified, that the third party contractor can demand performance not only from the middleman who contracted in his own name but also from his principal, although at the time the contract was made the contractor had no suspicion of his existence?

V

On the first question the Common Law has worked out a whole series of rules which take much of the bite out of the principle that the undisclosed principal may sue. According to MECHEM, these rules may be stated in the formula that 'The undisclosed principal may not enforce the contract where the effect is to prejudice the third party.' In other words, the principal's right to sue must not be allowed to put the third party in a worse position than he would have been in if the contract were between him and the agent only.

In *Greer* v. *Downs Supply Co.*, [1927] 2 KB 28, the defendant made a purchase from an agent only because he had a time-barred claim against the agent which he hoped to be able to set off against the price: the undisclosed principal, on whose account the agent had contracted, was not allowed to sue. The plaintiff in *Said* v. *Butt*, [1920] 3 KB 497 was minded to attend the première of a play but the management of the theatre was ill-disposed towards him and would have refused to sell him a ticket, so he had the ticket purchased by a friend. This did him no good, since the defendant, the manager of the theatre, refused to allow the plaintiff to his seat. The plaintiff sued on the ground that he was entitled as undisclosed principal to demand admission on the basis of the contract concluded by his agent. His claim was dismissed. The result can be summed up as follows: if, on a proper analysis of the situation, the third party has a justifiable interest in rendering performance only to the contractual party he knows, the undisclosed principal may not sue. As instances of cases in which the third party was found to have no such interest, and was therefore held liable to perform directly to the prinicpal, one may cite *Kelly Asphalt Block Co.* v. *Barber Asphalt Paving Co.*, 211 NY 68, 105 NE 88 (1914); *Dyster* v. *Randall & Sons*, [1926] Ch. 932.

If a person contracts with another not knowing that the latter has a principal, he may raise against the principal who subsequently appears all the defences he could have raised against a claim by the agent. Thus the third party can defend on the ground that he has already performed to the agent, believing him to be the other party to the contract, and he can set off against the principal's claim any claim which he had against the agent at the time the contract was formed.

See *Browning* v. *Provincial Ins. Co. of Canada*, (1873) LR 5 PC 263; *Montagu* v. *Forwood*, [1893] 2 QB 350; *Cooke* v. *Eshelby*, (1887) 12 App. Cas. 271; FRIDMAN (above p. 459) 168 ff. The same is true in the United States: see Restatement of the Law of Agency §§306 f.

It will be seen that in the Common Law the practical effect of allowing the undisclosed principal to sue is generally consistent with the principle of publicity in the protection of commerce which is always used on the Continent to justify the distinction between 'real' and merely indirect representation. One might compare the balancing of interests which occurs in the German law of assignment of choses in action: the way the BGB protects the debtor who may have a new creditor thrust on him without his consent is very like the way the Common Law protects the third party who finds himself sued by a principal of whose existence he was unaware. Thus, for example, just as the undisclosed principal's claim may be excluded by reason of the special nature of the contractual relations between agent and third party, so in German law §399 BGB would operate to prevent the assignment; and just as the undisclosed principal may run into the defence of set-off or other matters arising from the third party's relations with the agent, so may the assignee under §406 and §407 BGB. This shows that there is no necessary connection between the publicity principle of the Civil Law and the distinction between direct and indirect representation which is inferred from it. Indeed, the Common Law proves that one can make a fair accommodation between the undisclosed principal's interest in suing on a contract concluded on his account and the third party's right to rely on the identity of his apparent contractor, just as the interests of assignee and debtor are reconciled in Germany.

It must also be pointed out that, notwithstanding the publicity principle, Continental legal systems have ways of allowing the person indirectly represented to intervene in a contract concluded on his behalf by a middleman. In the Romanistic legal family, the *action directe* and other devices may make it possible for the mandator to sue his mandatary's contractor.

Thus according to art. 1994 par. 2 Code civil, the mandator has a direct suit against the third party to whom the mandatary has delegated the execution of the mandate. For example, see Req. 28 Oct,. 1924, DH 1924, 683; Paris 17 Oct. 1934, Gaz. Pal. 1934. 2. 781 (the customer of a bank may bring a direct action against another bank to which his own had entrusted the execution of the mandate); Rouen, 2 Feb. 1950, Gaz. Pal. 1950. 1. 345 (the depositor of goods can sue the warehouseman chosen by the mandatary); Civ. 1 Dec. 1896, Gaz. Pal. 1897. 1. 10 (direct suit by consignor against carrier, passing over the freight forwarder). On this see BAILLY in: *Le Contrat de commission* (ed. Hamel, 1949) 274 f. and on the *action directe* in general WAHL (above p. 460) 67 ff.—The position of Italian law is even more clearly stated in art. 1705 par. 2 Codice civile 'Il mandante, sostituendosi al mandatario, può esercitare i diritti di credito derivanti dall'esecuzione del mandato'; on this see GIORDANO, *Riv. dir. com.* 51 (1953) 93.—The same is true of Swiss law (art. 399 par. 2 OR).

German law is much less ready to allow a person to intervene in a contract indirectly concluded on his behalf. MÜLLER-FREIENFELS (*RabelsZ* 18 (1953) 36) attributes this to the fact that in Germany the distinction between mandate and representation is drawn so sharply that any interaction between the internal relationship of mandator and mandatary and the external relationship of mandatary to third party would be regarded as a sin against LABAND's theory. Of course, the courts may often reach a just result by finding that even although the name of the party represented was not actually mentioned in the negotiations, the case is one of true representation, given that in all the circumstances of the case the transaction was intended to be a third party transaction.

If a transaction is one 'for whom it may concern', its obligatory effects may, according to the writers, enure to the principal, provided that the third party was indifferent to the identity of his contractor and so needs no protection under the publicity principle. Switzerland even has a special provision that in the absence of any reference to agency the undisclosed principal may directly acquire contractual rights and duties 'if under the circumstances the other contractor must have inferred that there was an agency, or if he was unconcerned as to the identity of his contractor' (art. 32 par. 2 OR). In Germany it may be possible to use §328 BGB so as to give the undisclosed principal a direct claim against the third party if the circumstances were such as to show that the agent, though transacting in his own name, was intending to create rights not only for himself but also for his principal; for example, see OLG Hamburg, MDR 1948, 52.

Other texts, such as §392 par. 2 HGB, art. 401 OR and art. 547 par. 2 Code de commerce, also call for mention here. To a certain extent these provisions accord to the principal special rights in relation to the agent's transaction, for they allow him to prime the agent's general or judgment creditors in respect of any claims against the third party vested in the agent as a result of the execution of the agency.

In Scandinavia the principal of a commission agent is even given a direct claim against the third party if the agent is in breach of his obligations under the agency: see art. 57 par. 2 of the Swedish Law on Commission Agency of 18 April 1914 (also in force in Denmark and Norway) and, on it, CAPELLE (above p. 459) 330 ff.

VI

Although the Continental and Common Law systems set out from very different positions regarding the ability of the undisclosed prinicpal or person indirectly represented to intervene in the transaction of his middleman, the practical results they arrive at are really very similar, as we have seen. The picture alters, however, when we turn to the rights of the third party against the principal who remains in the background.

In the Common Law the third party may sue the principal once he has discovered his identity, unless he stated at the moment of concluding the contract that he would look only to the agent, whatever might happen. Apart from such exceptional cases, the only dispute is whether the third party who knows the principal's identity loses his claim against the principal by suing the agent, and especially by suing him to judgment, or whether, on the other hand, the undisclosed principal and the agent remain jointly and severally liable.

The first of these views is generally accepted in England and the United States: see the decisions cited in the textbooks and Restatement §210.—The opposite view has, however, been held in the United States (see MECHEM (above p. 459) 105 f.; SEAVEY,

Proceedings of the American Law Institute 7 (1929) 256 f.; and many Pennsylvania decisions such as *Joseph Melnick Bldg. & Loan Ass.* v. *Melnick*, 361 Pa. 328, 64 A. 2d 773 (1949)).

The position adopted by the German legal family is quite different. If one concludes a contract with a person who transacts in his own name, only that person may be treated as the contracting party even if it was known that the transaction was being undertaken for someone else.

For this reason the third party is well advised to attach or garnish the middleman's claim to be indemnified by his prinicpal under §670 BGB, and if necessary to sue for its transfer. But the third party obtains no privileged right by doing so. If the middleman goes bankrupt or another creditor attaches the indemnity claim before him, the third party ranks along with the other creditors.

This is the position in the Romanistic and Nordic legal families as well. In France it is the almost unanimous view of scholars and courts that the third party has no direct claim against the principal.

See WAHL, *Précis de droit commercial* (1922) 464; LYON-CAEN/RENAULT, *Traité de droit commercial* III (5th edn., 1923) 474; RIPERT and ROBLOT, *Traité élémentaire de droit commercial* II (9th edn., 1981) no. 2658; the contrary view is held only by STARCK, *Le Contrat de commission* (ed. Hamel, 1949) 167. However, the Court of Cassation has decided not only that art. 1994 par. 2 Code civil gives the principal a direct action against the third party to whom the agent entrusted the execution of the business, but also that the third party has a direct action against the principal (Civ. 27 Dec. 1960, DH 1961, 491, with a critical note by BIGOT). This was a case where an attorney had instructed a *huissier* to investigate the condition of a rented dwelling. The *huissier* brought a direct action for payment of his expenses against the attorney's principal and the Court of Cassation allowed the claim; unfortunately the judgment is extremely terse and leaves the background facts wholly in the dark.—Art. 1705 par. 2 sent. 2 of the Italian Codice civile is quite explicit: 'I terzi non hanno alcun rapporto col mandante.'—This is also the posture of Scandinavian law, see CAPELLE (above p. 459) 326.

Lawyers in Common Law countries normally explain their minority position by saying that because the principal sets the agent into legal motion by authorizing him to conclude the transaction he should, as against outsiders, be held responsible for the consequences of the agent's activity.

Thus FERSON (above p. 459) 249 writes: 'It is well settled that an undisclosed principal is bound by the acts of his agent acting within his authority . . . It seems rational that the undisclosed principal should be held. He has consented to the agent's power; he has manifested that consent to the agent. Why should there be any doubt or hesitation about holding the principal?' MÜLLER-FREIENFELS (*RabelsZ* 18 (1953) 53) also justifies making the third party into the principal's creditor on the ground, *inter alia*, that 'by giving his authority to the middleman the principal is to a certain extent an "indirect actor" who causes the "loss" to the third party contractor'.

Common lawyers may be persuaded that this makes it right to give the third party an action against the principal, but in our view an evaluation of the interests involved shows that this Anglo-Saxon attitude should not be imitated. Continental legal systems have adopted a sounder position by putting the risk of the middleman's insolvency on the third party and denying the third party any direct claim against the principal; this is in line with the reasonable view that if a person is wrong about the credit-worthiness of the person he deals with he must bear this risk himself. Why, in the case of an agency for purchase, should the third party vendor, at the expense of the principal or his creditors, be able to derive any advantage from the fact, possibly unknown at the time, that his purchaser was buying the goods not for himself but for someone else? Of course it is true that the principal has given the middleman his authority to conclude transactions but it does not follow, as the Common Law supposes, that he is prepared to incur liability towards all third parties with whom the middleman may contract. In any case, the third party in such cases is usually a vendor of goods who may take the usual security precautions of reserving his property rights and of taking an assignment from the middleman of the latter's indemnity claim against his principal.

40

Assignment

ARNDT, *Zessionsrecht, Beiträge zum Recht der Forderungsabtretung im internationalen Verkehr* (1932).

BAILEY, Assignment of Debts in England From the Twelfth to the Twentieth Century', 47 *LQ Rev.* 516 (1931); 48 *LQ Rev.* 248, 547 (1932).

FONTAINE, 'La Transmission des obligations "de lege ferenda" ', in: *La transmission des obligations (IXes Journées d'études juridiques Jean Dabin*, 1980) 611.

GHESTIN, 'La Transmission des obligations en droit français positif', in: *La Transmission des obligations (IXes Journées d'études juridiques Jean Dabin*, 1980) 3.

HUWILER, *Der Begriff der Zession in der Gesetzgebung seit dem Vernunftrecht* (1975).

JÄGGI, 'Zur "Rechtsnatur" der Zession', *SJZ* 67 (1971) 68.

KLEIN, 'Die Abtretung von Forderungen nach englischem Recht', *WM* 1978, 390.

KOESSLER, 'Assignment of Accounts Receivable', 33 *Calif. L. Rev.* 40 (1945).

LUIG, *Zur Geschichte der Zessionslehre* (1966).

——, 'Zession und Abstraktionsprinzip', in: *Wissenschaft und Kodifikation des Privatrechts im 19. Jahrhundert.* (ed. Coing and Wilhelm) II (1977) 112.

MALCOLM, 'Accounts Receivable Financing Under the Uniform Commercial Code', *RabelsZ* 30 (1966) 434.

MAIER, 'Zur Geschichte der Zession', *Festschrift Rabel* II (1954) 205.

MARSHALL, *The Assignment of Choses in Action* (1950).

MOECKE, *Kausale Zession und gutgläubiger Forderungserwerb* (1962).

MUMMENHOFF, 'Vertragliches Abtretungsverbot und Sicherungszession im deutschen, österreichischen und US-amerikanischen Recht', *JZ* 1979, 425.

NEUMAYER, 'La Transmission des obligations en droit comparé', in: *La Transmission des obligations* (IXes Journées d'études juridiques Jean Dabin, 1980) 193.

SCHUMANN, *Die Forderungsabtretung im deutschen, französischen und englischen Recht* (1924).

——, 'Abtretung' in II *Rechtsvergleichendes Handwörterbuch* (ed. Schlegelberger) (1929) 34.

I

IN societies whose economy calls for a sophisticated system of circulating currency and credit it seems axiomatic that one should be able to transfer that form of intangible property which consists of the right to claim something from someone else. In the modern world such claims are mobile items of wealth, one of the many possible forms which 'capital' may take as a factor in production in economic life, much like goods or land, and it is therefore essential to ensure that, like other items of wealth, they should be easily transferable. In all modern legal systems there are legal forms by which this may be effected, though they differ in many respects.

But the transferability of debts and other claims was achieved only at the end of a long historical development. Like the old English Common Law, Roman law started from the position that personal rights could not be transferred at all. Along with the principle that third parties can acquire no rights by contract, this was based on the view that a claim is something highly personal which cannot be severed at will from the particular legal relationship between creditor and debtor which gave rise to it. Nevertheless in the course of time both Roman law and Common Law adopted devices which made it possible to some extent to satisfy the growing economic need to make claims transferable without the co-operation of the debtor. Thus in Roman law the creditor might authorize the 'assignee' to act as cognitor or procurator *in rem suam* in a suit against the debtor, to bring the claim in his own name and to retain any proceeds of suit. This solution had its drawbacks: the creditor could withdraw his authority before the suit was started, he could bring the claim himself, for he always remained its owner, and he could accept payment of the debt and so release the debtor. The assignee could seek to guard against these hazards by having the assignor promise by *stipulatio* that he would do nothing to frustrate the assignment. In Imperial times the purchaser of a decedent's estate was given an *actio utilis* against the debtor; this was subsequently extended to the purchaser of an individual claim and finally, under JUSTINIAN, to every assignee. The assignor retained a right of suit such as was given to the assignee, though under JUSTINIAN it was admitted that payment to the assignor by the debtor would not release the debtor if the assignee had intimated the assignment to him. On the whole matter see KASER, *Das römische Privatrecht* I (1955) 545 ff.

The Common Law had the institution of 'power of attorney' which performed a function rather similar to that of '*procurare in rem suam*': here the creditor gave the 'assignee' authority to use the creditor's name to collect on the claim—called a 'chose in action' to this day—and retain the proceeds. This device also fell short of a proper assignment of a chose in action, since the creditor could at any time withdraw his authority to sue on his behalf and it normally terminated on his death. Until the end of the sixteenth century the English courts were reluctant to give any further protection to the assignee for fear that undesirable persons would take assignments of claims simply in order to bring them to court.

See WINFIELD, 35 *LQ Rev.* 143 (1919).—In the natural law codes, too, a certain odour of fraud seems to stick to assignment. For instance, they generally provide that the assignment of a disputed claim is void if the assignee is a court official, lawyer, or notary in the area of the court which would or could decide a dispute over the claim; see ALR §385 I 11, art. 1597 Code civil, and, to the same effect, art. 1261 Codice civile.— Another example is the remarkable rule of arts. 1699 ff. Code civil, modelled on the *lex*

Anastasiana: If a disputed claim is transferred for a consideration, the debtor can acquit himself by giving the assignee what he paid for the debt rather than the amount of the debt itself. This rule also rests on the view that trading in disputed claims should be discouraged on the ground of the public good. Today we reject such *general* prohibitory or protective provisions, and rightly so; instead we check the particular circumstances of doubtful cases and declare an assignment void as being against public policy if it was made in pursuit of a forbidden aim; for Switzerland, see BGE 58 II 162; for Germany RGZ 81, 175 and BGH MDR 1959, 999; for the United States: *Ellis* v. *Frawley*, 165 Wis. 381, 161 NW 364 (1917) and further cases cited in WILLISTON §417.

In the early seventeenth century the Equity Courts of England started to come to the aid of the assignee. The way in which they did so was typical of equity jurisprudence: they did not dispute the Common Law rule that claims were not transferable, but in practice they emptied it of content by allowing the assignee to bring a bill 'in equity' so that they could require the assignor to lend his name for the necessary action 'at law' against the debtor. This procedure was very cumbrous since it involved two trials, but it was only necessary where the right which had been assigned was a '*legal* chose in action' which had to be sued for 'at law' before the King's judges. If the claim was an '*equitable* chose in action' or claim recognized or enforced in equity, such as the claim of a beneficiary under a trust or of a legatee under a will, then the equity judges allowed the assignee to bring the claim directly in his own name.

The transfer of claims was also recognized by the *Gemeines Recht* in Germany. WINDSCHEID himself, in his *Textbook of the Pandects* in 1865, accepted that singular succession to claims 'is established as valid by customary law today' (§329 note 9). 'It is another question' admittedly 'what theoretical construction can be given to the rule established by customary law, that is, how it can be explained by established concepts.' On this point, indeed, every conceivable theory was expressed. Many authors were of the view that according to the Roman sources claims were conceptually non-transferable and that the assignee acquired at best a personal right to exercise someone else's obligation. WINDSCHEID wanted to give the assignee a claim of his own, with the qualification that the claim remained concurrently vested in the assignor until the debtor learnt of the assignment by a communication from the assignee which he called a 'denunciation' (ibid. §331). The opinion of BÄHR was that the contract of assignment made the assignee the sole creditor but that the debtor had a defence if he had paid the debt to the assignor in ignorance of the assignment (*JherJb.* 1 (1857) 351, 41 ff., in accordance with the Prussian General Land Law in §§376 ff. I 11. (For the full story of the development in the *Gemeines Recht* see LUIG, *Zur Geschichte der Zessionslehre* (1966).)

II

The last of these views is the one adopted into the *German* legal family by the

BGB. On the conclusion of the contract of assignment the assignee takes the place of the previous creditor without any need that the debtor be informed, much less that he agree (§398 BGB). This is also the standpoint of *Austrian* and *Swiss* law (§§1392 ff. ABGB, arts. 164 ff. OR).

The *Greek* Civil Code of 1940, which so often follows the German BGB, adopts a different position. Art. 455 certainly makes the claim pass to the assignee by means of the contract of assignment without any requirement that the debtor agree, but this applies only as between assignor and assignee. As against the *debtor* and other *third parties* the assignee becomes entitled to the claim only when either he or the assignor has informed the debtor of the assignment (art. 460 Greek Civil Code). As will shortly be shown, this is also the solution of the Romanistic legal family.—The *Turkish* Civil Code, on the other hand, adopts the rule of Swiss law (art. 162).—The courts in *Austria* have special rules for assignments by way of *security*, differing from the general rules of assignment. Like the creation of a pledge (§§451f. ABGB), an assignment by way of security requires 'titulus' and 'modus': there must therefore be not only a valid written contract of assignment but also an externally perceptible public act, either the express agreement of the third party debtor or some special entry in the books of the assignor. On this see the leading opinions of the Austrian Supreme Court in 15 Jan. 1929, SZ XI 15, and also OGH 21 Feb. 1973, JBl. 1974, 90, note BYDLINSKI.

The debtor who has a new creditor thrust upon him without his consent requires some protection. The rule therefore is that the debtor who pays the assignor is discharged, provided that he did not know of the assignment. This is the result in all the Germanic legal systems, though the formula they use vary somewhat—'knows' of the assignment (§407 BGB), 'the transferee has been made known to him' (§1396 ABGB), or that he is not 'in good faith' in rendering performance 'to the previous creditor' (art. 167 OR). If the debtor has *any* knowledge of the assignment, whether he received it from the assignor, from the assignee, or in any other way, performance to the assignor does not release him. This is also true of other legal arrangements, such as release, stay, and set-off, which the debtor may make with the assignor in the supposition that he is still the creditor (§§407 BGB; BGE 56 II 363; KLANG/WOLFF, *Kommentar zum ABGB*, vol. VI (2nd edn., 1951) addendum to §1395).

The debtor *may* thus treat payment to the assignor as extinguishing his liability to the assignee, but he *need* not do so: he may treat the payment to the assignor as the payment of an *indebitum* and demand it back as an unjustified enrichment. This has been recognized by the courts in Germany (RGZ 83, 188; BGH LM §407 no. 3), but Austrian writers take a different view (KLANG/WOLFF (ibid.) addendum to §1395; SWOBODA, *JBl.* 60 (1935) 283). This is probably wrong, since the purpose of §§407 BGB, 1395 ABGB, is to give the debtor an *additional* protection by allowing him to treat his performance as discharging the claim which has been assigned; he should remain entitled to the *condictio* under the general provisions.

A special feature of the legal systems under consideration is the way they treat the assignment of a claim as 'abstract', that is, as a disposition independent of the contractual agreement underlying it. A claim may be transferred pursuant to a sale or a gift, in lieu of something else which was *in obligatione*, or as a security, and the systems of the German legal family make a sharp distinction between the assignment itself and the sale or gift or whatever other obligational relationship may exist between the assignor and assignee. Not only are the two transactions distinguished, they are actually independent in law, the principle being that defects in the underlying transaction do not affect the assignment, which constitutes the performance of the transaction; thus a claim which has been transferred pursuant to a contract of sale or agreement to give security remains vested in the purchaser or the secured creditor even if the contract of sale is later rescinded for error or justifiably repudiated or if the secured claim has already been paid off.

It is clear from art. 165 OR that the *Swiss* law of assignment accepts this distinction between the obligational transaction and the performance transaction; it says that an assignment requires writing for its validity but that 'the obligation to conclude a contract of assignment may be concluded without any particular form'. Arts. 171 ff. OR specify when the assignor warrants the existence and collectibility of the claim being assigned and distinguish according to whether the assignment is 'for value' or 'gratuitous'. This is not quite logical. Strictly speaking, the assignment as such cannot be either for value or not for value, since it merely concerns property rights; only by looking at the underlying transaction can one tell whether the assignee is bound to pay for the assignment or whether it was to be a gift. No doubt the lay reader would expect to be told about the guaranteeing of claims during the discussion of their transfer, and this may justify the Swiss method of presentation, but the German legislator deals with the question in connection with the underlying transactions in pursuance of which the assignment is made: in sale (§§437 f. BGB), in gift (§523 BGB), in transfer of claim in lieu of other performance (§365 BGB). Since it was first developed in the *Gemeines Recht* (see LUIG (above p. 471) 74 ff., 125 ff.), the principle of 'abstraction' (namely, the idea that the obligational transaction and the performance transaction are to be distinguished—see Ch. 15) is unknown to the *Austrian* ABGB of 1811. Austrian doctrine is divided: see, for example, KLANG/WOLFF (above p. 471) §1392 addendum II, with further references.

The practical importance of the principle of abstraction in the law of assignments should not be exaggerated. If it appears from the circumstances of the individual case that the parties intended the basic transaction and the assignment to form a single transaction, the invalidity of part of the composite act may involve the nullity of the whole transaction (compare §139 BGB). The same result occurs if it can be inferred that the parties intended the assignment to be conditional on the underlying transaction's being and staying valid.—Indeed, the principle of abstraction, with its artificial separation of basic transaction and assignment, may not be worth retaining in this area of the law. In Switzerland the doctrine has excited a great deal of criticism; see

BUCHER, *Schweizerisches Obligationenrecht, Allgemeiner Teil* (1979) 501 ff.; MOECKE (above p. 471) and JÄGGI (above p. 471). The Bundesgericht which has endorsed the principle of abstraction (BGE 67 II 123), has also expressed the view that there should be 'a renewed investigation of this basic question of the law of assignments' (BGE 84 II 355).

The central problem in the law of assignments is how to protect the debtor. It has already been observed that if the debtor is unaware of the assignment he will be discharged by payment to the assignor. The same idea applies if the creditor has made several successive assignments of the same claim. In such a case all Germanic systems apply the principle of priority and hold that only the first assignee acquires title. Since after the first assignment the claim no longer forms part of the property of the assignor, a subsequent assignee could only obtain title if protection were given to his honest but erroneous belief that the assignor was still a creditor. None of the legal systems here under investigation does this, nor does a subsequent assignee improve his position by being the first to inform the debtor that he has become the 'creditor'.

If an assignee is in good faith, the debtor may be barred from raising certain defences to his action. Thus if he has given the assignor a written acknowledgement of the debt and the creditor made use of this document in making the assignment, the debtor cannot raise as against the assignee the fact that the assignor had agreed that the claim should not be transferable, or that the claim was a mere sham (§405 BGB, art. 18 par. 2, 164 par. 2 OR). The same is true if a creditor makes a written assignment of a debt on an understanding with the assignee that this should merely be a simulated transaction; if the assignee then assigns the claim to a third party in good faith along with the document, the claim passes to that third party at the expense of the original creditor (RGZ 90, 273, BGE 23 I 818).—Once again Austria has an exceptional rule for assignments for security purposes: if the same claim is assigned to several assignees for security purposes, it is acquired by the assignee who first completes the required act of publicity, usually obtaining the acknowledgement of the original debtor.

The question which of several assignees becomes owner of the claim must be distinguished from the question which of them can discharge the debtor by receiving performance from him. Once again it is a matter of the debtor's knowledge of the assignment. If he pays an assignee who, having already transferred the claim, is no longer the true creditor, the debtor is discharged if at the time of payment he was unaware of the prior assignment.

This is laid down in §408 BGB and art. 167 OR. The ABGB does not advert to the question, and there is a dispute among the writers. KRAINZ/EHRENZWEIG, *System des öst. allg. Privatrechts* (5th edn., 1915) §330 II, adopt the standpoint of German and Swiss law, contrary to KLANG/WOLFF (above p. 471)§1396 addendum II.—If payment to the subsequent assignee discharges the debtor, the subsequent assignee should not be able to retain the payment as against the first assignee. German and probably Swiss law therefore allow the first assignee to bring a direct claim based on unjust enrichment against the subsequent assignee (see §816 par. 2 BGB); here again KLANG/WOLFF (above p. 471) take a different view, unlike EHRENZWEIG (below p. 583).

If the problem of protecting the debtor arises when he has transactions with a *supposed* creditor, it can also arise when there is no doubt about the assignee's entitlement, but the question is what defences the debtor can raise against his claim for payment. Since the assignment takes place without the consent of the debtor, the invariable principle is that it must not curtail the defences he can raise against the assignee. If the debtor had a good defence against the assignor on any ground, be it that the claim never arose or has ceased to exist, been stayed, or become time-barred, he may use it against the assignee (§404 BGB, art. 169 OR, §1396 ABGB). For this purpose it is immaterial that the facts giving rise to the defence took place only after the debtor had knowledge of the assignment, provided that the emergence of such a defence was inherent in the obligation before the assignment.

Thus if a contractor assigns the fee for his services and the assignee claims it from the employer, the latter may defend on the ground that the contractor was in breach of contract and had thereby caused him harm; this defence is open even if the breach occurs only after the assignment had been made and notified to the employer (RGZ 83, 279; BGH NJW 1958, 1915; Obergericht Zürich, BlZüRspr. 41 (1942) no. 65).

The same is true for set-off; the debtor may set off against the assignee any claim he had against the assignor at the time he learnt of the assignment. A counterclaim which falls due only after the assignment is notified can only be set off by the debtor if the claim assigned falls due even later (§406 BGB, art. 169 OR). Finally, the debtor can oppose a suit by the assignee by showing that the assignment was invalid and that the plaintiff has consequently no title to sue. For example, he can point to the fact that the assignor lacked capacity at the time of the assignment or that the assignment is void as a simulated transaction under §117 BGB, art. 20 OR. But the principle of 'abstraction' takes effect here: the defence is good only if the assignment as such is invalid; objections based on the nullity of the *underlying transaction* are no more use to the debtor than the argument that although the assignee became entitled to the claim, the underlying transaction contained an agreement not to sue or not to sue yet.

See for example RGZ 102, 385; BGE 50 II 392; OGH 22 Dec. 1931. SZ XIII 271 and 4 Jan. 1934, SZ XVI 3.

III

The *French* Code civil deals with the assignment of debts in the law of *sales*, since the eighteenth-century jurists always saw the assignor as selling the claim assigned and the assignee as buying it (arts. 1689 ff.). Assignment is therefore not an 'abstract' transaction independent of the underlying agreement. The *Italian* Codice civile of 1942 deals with assignment in the chapter headed 'Delle obligazioni in generale' (arts. 1260 ff.), where it also covers the question when the assignor guarantees the existence of the claim and the solvency of the debtor.

In the Romanistic legal systems also, an assignment transfers the debt to the assignee without any co-operation on the part of the debtor. This is explicitly stated in art. 1260 Codice civile; it has to be inferred from art. 1689 Code civil which, using the language of the law of sales, states that under an assignment 'delivery' of the claim from assignor to assignee is effected by a transfer of the document evidencing the claim. Of course the French courts recognize that a claim may be transferred even without the delivery of any relevant document, provided that the parties contractually agree thereon (Paris 12 July 1911, DP 1913. 2. 189).

This applies, however, only as between the parties to the assignment: 'entre le cédant et le cessionnaire' (art. 1689 Code civil). As against *third parties* the assignment is treated as complete only when the assignor or assignee has informed the debtor of the assignment by making the appropriate communication through the agency of a *huissier* ('signification'), or when the debtor has 'acknowledged' the assignment by judicial or notarial document ('acceptation')—(see art. 1690 Code civil, 1264 f. Codice civile). It follows that by itself the agreement to assign procures a merely relative transfer of the claim, that is, only as between assignor and assignee; this view is shared by almost all writers in France and Italy.

As ARNDT (above p. 471) p. 74 ff. has shown, no practical consequences are drawn from the proposition that the contract of assignment transfers the claim as between assignor and assignee. He therefore holds that the transfer is never complete unless there has been either 'signification' or 'acceptation' in accordance with art. 1690 Code civil.

Art. 1690 Code civil has several very important consequences. Unless the debtor has been informed of the assignment in the manner prescribed, or has 'acknowledged' the assignment by public document, he may discharge himself by paying the assignor, since it is the assignor who remains the creditor of the claim which has been assigned (see art. 1691 Code civil). Not only *may* the debtor pay the assignor, he *must* do so. If there has been neither 'signification' nor 'acceptation', he cannot defend on the ground that he knows in some other way that the claim being sued on has already been assigned (Civ. 20 June 1938, Gaz. Pal. 1938. 2. 435; Civ. 27 Nov. 1944, Gaz. Pal. 1945. 1. 13).

The courts have, however, qualified these rules in several respects. The assignee's statement of claim against the debtor may amount to a 'signification' provided it makes clear that the plaintiff is suing as assignee (Civ. 17 Feb. 1937, DH 1937, 221). Again, the courts do not always require that the 'acknowledgement' of art. 1690 par. 2 Code civil be contained in a public document. A private written document may suffice, or even an implicit declaration of acceptance; the result is that the assignee rates as creditor and can demand payment from the debtor (Civ. 6 Feb. 1878, DP 1878. 1. 275; Req. 27 Dec. 1933, DP 1934. 1. 13; Req. 22 Dec. 1937, DH 1938, 83). In certain cases the assignee may even sue a debtor who has paid the assignor before 'signification' or 'acceptation': if at the time of payment the debtor had actual knowledge of the assignment and his behaviour constituted a fraudulent conspiracy with the assignor to the detriment of the assignee, his payment will not discharge him (Req. 17 Feb. 1874, DP 1874. 1. 281; Paris 11 Oct. 1912, Gaz. Pal. 1913. 1. 501). On occasion the courts show a tendency to infer fraud on the part of the debtor from the mere fact of payment with knowledge of the assignment.

See Civ. 10 Jan. 1905, S. 1905. 1. 328. The trend appears to be against allowing the debtor to discharge himself by making payment to the assignor if he has even a 'connaissance de fait' of the assignment (on this see PLANIOL/RIPERT VII no. 1122). If this position were achieved, the practical result in French law would be much the same as in the German legal family, where payment to the assignor does not discharge a debtor who knows of the assignment (for example, see §407 BGB). This step has already been taken by the *Italian* legislator: according to art. 1264 Codice civile payment made by a debtor before 'notificazione' does not release him if the assignee can prove that the debtor had knowledge of the assignment. The actual legal position in France on this question is so unclear that writers advise debtors when sued by the assignor to bring in the assignee as a third party so as to avoid the risk of having to pay twice.

In a suit by the assignee the debtor may use any defence which he had acquired against the assignor up till the time of 'signification' or 'acceptation' (Req. 5 Nov. 1889, DP 1890. 1. 379). For set-off this is made explicit in art. 1295 par. 2 Code civil (as in art. 1248 par. 2 Codice civile), which permits the debtor to set off against the assignee's claim any counterclaims which are available against the assignor at the time of 'signification' (see Paris 23 March 1939, Gaz. Pal. 1939. 1. 768). If the debtor has given an 'acceptation', however, he can only set off counterclaims if there was an express reservation to that effect in the declaration of acknowledgement (art. 1295 par. 1 Code civil, 1248 par. 1 Codice civile).

If the assignment to the plaintiff of the lessor's right to receive the rent of a dwelling has been 'acknowledged' by the defendant lessee in accordance with art. 1690 par. 2, and the defendant can show that the dwelling was unfit for habitation at the appointed time, the claim will be diminished by the amount the defendant had to pay for the work required to put it in order. This is not because of set-off, which would not be permitted because the 'acceptation' was unqualified, but because the claim assigned was liable to this reduction *ab initio*, and such a defence is good against the assignee even if the debtor's acknowledgement of the assignment was without reservation (Req. 4 Feb. 1889, DP 1890. 1. 121; see also BGH NJW 1958, 1915, which deals with the same problem in relation to the assignment of a fee for services).

As we have seen, assignment is treated, in relation to third parties, as vesting the claim in the assignee only when the requirements of art. 1690 Code civil are satisfied. 'Third parties' for this purpose include not only the debtor but any creditor of the assignor as well, and also any other party to whom the assignor makes a subsequent assignment of the claim. If follows that the assignor's creditors may attach a debt even if it has already been assigned, provided that the assignment has not been notified to the debtor or that he has not 'acknowledged' it in the form required by art. 1690 Code civil. By like reasoning the debt, though assigned, still falls in the estate of a bankrupt assignor provided that the bankruptcy proceedings are opened before 'signification' or 'acceptation'; in line with this, the courts have held that notification is ineffective once bankruptcy proceedings have been opened against the estate of the assignor (Req. 6 Feb. 1934, DP 1936. 1. 39). If the creditor makes successive assignments of the same debt to two different assignees, the debt is acquired not by the one to whom it was first *assigned*, but by the one who first *notifies* the debtor (see Civ. 29 Aug. 1849, DP 1849. 1. 273; this is explicit in art. 1265 Codice civile).

These rules have also had to be modified by the courts. Applied strictly, art. 1690 Code civil leads to astonishing results where a party who knows of the assignment tries to take advantage of its invalidity on the ground that formal 'signification' or 'acceptation' have not taken place. For example, is it right that one of the assignor's creditors should be able to rely on the absence of notification when at the time of attaching the debt he knows that his debtor had long since assigned the debt to a third party? The courts have not yet evolved a clear rule on this point. The original standpoint of the Court of Cassation was that mere knowledge of the assignment was not sufficient to deprive the attaching creditor of his rights and that actual fraud must be shown (Civ. 24 Dec. 1894, DP 1895. 1. 206), but in another case it was held sufficient that there be a 'connaissance spéciale et personnelle' (Civ. 7 July 1897, DP 1898. 1. 483). A similar problem arises when the assignor has made successive assignments of the same debt. What should the decision be if the second assignee was the first to notify the debtor but knew of the first assignment at the time he did so? The lower courts have on several occasions decided in favour of the first assignee, without requiring proof of any particular fraud on the part of the second assignee (Trib. com. Seine 4 April 1892, Gaz. Pal. 1892. 1. 665; Trib. civ. Seine 5 Jan. 1905, Gaz. Trib. 1905. 2. 473 and 1 Dec. 1903, Gaz. Trib. 1904. 2. 317).

Businessmen obviously have a considerable interest in having a simple procedure for the assignment of debts such that the assignee becomes owner of the debt not only against the assignor but also against the debtor and his creditors, and can make it good in bankruptcy proceedings. For example, a merchant can hardly obtain money for, or raise money on, the debts his customers still owe him if he cannot transfer them effectively as against the whole world without having to make a formal intimation to each of his customers. The relevant provisions of the Code civil, especially art. 1690, are not really practical. In practice, therefore, other legal devices have been sought and found. One method relies on the fact that the transfer of debts incorporated in a negotiable instrument, such as a bill of exchange, requires no formality: unlike the position in German law, if a creditor draws a bill on his debtor and endorses it over to a third party the underlying claim ('provision') is also transferred even if the debtor has not accepted the bill and even if the requirements of art. 1690 have not been observed (see GHESTIN(above p. 471); MEZGER, *RIW* (1981) 213, 214). Furthermore, the Code civil itself contains a legal institution ('subrogation personnelle') which can be used to sidestep art. 1690: if a debt is paid off by a third party rather than by the debtor himself, the third party acquires the creditor's claim if the creditor so agrees (art. 1249, 1250 no. 1, Code civil). This is the method used in France today in the factoring business, for example: if a businessman who wishes to realize the debts owed to him by his customers declares to the factoring bank that he accepts payment by the bank as being payment by the debtor and agrees that the debts vested in him should now vest in the bank, 'subrogation' transfers the debts to the bank without the cumbrous formalities of art. 1690 (see GHESTIN (above p. 471) 36 ff., and the full details in MESTRE, *La Subrogation personnelle* (1979) 57 ff., 229 ff.). Finally the French legislature intervened. The Law to Facilitate Business Credit of 2 January 1981 enables a businessman to use the debts owed to him as security for credit afforded by a bank by listing the debts in a 'bordereau' or annexure following the statutory formalities. The delivery of this 'bordereau' to the bank constitutes an assignment of the debts listed in it.

It will be seen that lawyers, courts, and legislature in France have developed many different ways of effecting assignment of debts which get round the obsolete rules contained in the Code civil. Thought is now being given to reforming the rules themselves. The suggestion in the Benelux countries is that an assignment made by the assignor in writing should be valid *erga omnes* if either he or the assignee has given notice of it to the debtor. FONTAINE (above p. 471, pp. 622 ff.) would go a step further and abandon all formal requirements. He cogently points out that the debtor can be fully protected even when there are no formalities at all, and that no practical problems have arisen in 'subrogation personnelle', an existing method of transferring debts without notifying the debtor.

IV

Until 1873 *English* law adhered to the position that suits on 'legal choses in action', such as claims for the repayment of a loan, or for the price of goods or for damages for breach of contract, must be brought by the assignor or at any rate in his name, and not by the assignee. If the assignor was unwilling to lend his name in an action at law against the debtor, the assignee could require him to do so by a prior process 'in equity'. Procedurally speaking, the Judicature Act 1873 which amalgamated the independent jurisdictions of Common Law and Chancery as well as the rules developed by them brought about an important simplification in the law of assignment: although it was still necessary for the assignor to be involved in the suit against the debtor of a 'legal chose in action', the assignee could henceforth bring him into the principal action, since the court which was seised of the matter was bound to apply not only the '*legal*' rules relevant to the suit against the *debtor*, but also the '*equitable*' principles which controlled the suit against the *assignor*.

But the Judicature Act 1873 made another very important change in the law of assignment as well. By s. 25(6) (now s. 136 Law of Property Act 1925) the owner of a 'legal chose in action' was empowered to transfer his rights to an assignee in such a way that the latter could exercise those rights against the debtor without any further co-operation on the part of the assignor. If the assignor makes the assignment in writing and signs it, such a 'statutory assignment' is effective *erga omnes* once the debtor has been informed of it in writing. If the requirements of an effective 'statutory assignment' are not satisfied, whether because the debtor has not been informed or because the assignment is purely oral, one must always check whether the transaction may not still be a valid 'equitable assignment' in accordance with the traditional rules of equity. An assignment may be valid 'in equity' although it is perfectly informal and has not been intimated to the debtor. One must still ask whether the claim assigned would have been, before 1873, a claim 'at law' or 'in equity', however, for even today the equitable assignee of a legal chose in action will fail in his suit against the debtor if the assignor is not made a party to the suit, either as plaintiff or as defendant.

See *Performing Rights Society* v. *London Theatre of Varieties, Ltd.*, [1924] AC 1: the plaintiff, a society for the vindication of the rights of authors, claimed an injunction and damages against the defendant theatre for infringing a copyright of which the plaintiff had become owner by assignment. The House of Lords found that although there was no 'statutory assignment' since the special requirements of the Copyright Act had not been met, the transfer was nevertheless valid as an 'equitable assignment'. Even so, the plaintiff's claim failed: the copyright, being a '*legal* chose in action' could only be established in court if the plaintiff's assignor was also a party to the proceedings. After expounding these rules, VISCOUNT FINLAY said: 'We must decide according to law, however much we may regret that success in the action should depend upon a mere technicality which has no relation to the merits of the case' ([1924] AC 1, 19).

In the *United States* the requirements of modern commerce have ousted these vestiges of medieval assignment law. Founding on legislation which liberalized the law of procedure and abolished the technical distinctions between 'law' and 'equity', American courts today accept that an assignment may be valid although it is informal and although the debtor has not been notified, and allow the assignee as 'the real party in interest' to bring suit against the debtor in his own name without any participation by the assignor (see WILLISTON §430, CORBIN §856).

Since the creditor may change without the debtor's knowledge (except in the case of the English 'statutory assignment'), the debtor must be protected if he relies on the assignor's continuing to be his creditor. This protection is afforded both in England and in the United States by the rule that the debtor may use as against the assignee all the defences which at the time he learnt of the assignment he could have opposed to the assignor. In practice the courts in Common Law countries reach the same results as German courts applying §§404, 406, 407 BGB.

For instance, if a person who has performed contractual services assigns the right to the fee and then breaks the contract, the assignee may be met by a defence based upon the breach of contract. See *Newfoundland* v. *Newfoundland Railway Co.*, (1888) 13 App. Cas. 199, 213, with which it is not easy to reconcile the later case of *Stoddart* v. *Union Trust Ltd.*, [1912] 1 KB 181 (noted by LUMLEY in 28 *LQ Rev.* 184 (1912)). A large number of American decisions are cited in WILLISTON §433. See also GILMORE, 74 *Yale LJ* 217 (1964) and Restatement (Second) of Contracts (1981) §336.

Two typical situations show that the validity of an assignment does not depend on the debtor's having been notified of it: one is the case where the assignor's creditor attempts to garnish or attach a debt already assigned, and the other is the case where the assignor makes successive assignments of the same debt.

In the first of these cases the Common Law holds that the creditor's attempts to garnish or attach a debt already assigned has no effect; it makes no difference whether the debtor knew of the assignment or whether the creditor honestly believed that the debt was still owed to his debtor.

See *Holt* v. *Heatherfield Trust Ltd.*, [1942] 2 KB 1.—The decision is the same in the United States: *Smith* v. *Harris*, 127 Cal. App. 2d 311, 273 P. 2d 835 (1954); *Seamon* v. *Federated Films Inc.*, 142 NY 2d 324 (City Ct. 1955); *Oklahoma Oxygen Co.* v. *Citizens State Bank*, 274 P. 2d 372 (Okla. 1954). In Louisiana the rule is different, for the terms of the Louisiana Civil Code (arts. 2642 f.) approximate closely to those of the French Code civil (see *Gordon* v. *Vallee*, 119 F. 2d 118 (5th Cir. 1941)). See also Restatement (Second) of Contracts (1981) §341.

The position adopted by the Common Law in regard to successive assignments is not so uniform. *English* law gives precedence to whichever good faith assignee first gave notice of the assignment to the debtor (rule in *Dearle* v. *Hall*, (1828) 3 Russ. 1, 38 Eng. Rep. 475). Most American states follow a different 'American' rule to the effect that priority is determined by the order of the assignments, with the consequence that a subsequent assignee who has received payment from the debtor must give it up to the first assignee.

This rule has been applied, for example, in the courts of New York: *Superior Brassiere Co.* v. *Zimetbaum*, 214 App. Div. 525, 212 NYS 473 (1925); *State Factors Corp.* v. *Sales Factors Corp.*, 257 App. Div. 101, 12 NYS 2d 12 (1939).

But the 'American' rule has been much modified in most of the states. An assignee for value without knowledge of a prior assignment may retain what he has been paid by the debtor, and if he has obtained judgment against the debtor or has made an agreement with him which amounts to a novation of the debt, he can even claim priority over the first assignee.

Massachusetts in particular adopts this position, which has been accepted by the Restatement (Second) of Contracts (1981) in §342. On this very disputed question, see KOESSLER (above p. 471) with extensive references to articles and cases. The decision of the Supreme Court of the United States in *Salem Trust Co.* v. *Manufacturers Finance Co.*, 264 US 182 (1924) is of particular interest: it unequivocally rejects the 'English' rule of *Dearle* v. *Hall* and endorses the 'American' rule, though without indicating any preference for the 'New York' rule or the 'Massachusetts' rule.

In the early 1940s the problem of the priority between successive asssignees suddenly became very important in the United States in relation to bulk assignments of claims for the price of goods delivered, 'accounts receivable financing' being a very common method of securing bank advances in that country. In several decisions the federal courts, applying a section of the Federal Bankruptcy Act, held that a trustee in bankruptcy could disregard an assignment by the party now bankrupt if at the time of the assignment there was any possibility at all under applicable state law that a subsequent assignee in good faith could obtain priority.

See *Corn Exchange National Bank & Trust Co.* v. *Klauder*, 318 US 434 (1943); *In re Vardaman Shoe Co.*, 52 F. Supp. 562 (ED Miss. 1943); *In re Rosen*, 157 F. 2d 997 (3d Cir. 1946).

Now the assignee could be primed by a subsequent assignee not only in the states which accepted the 'English' rule of *Dearle* v. *Hall* but also in states whose courts accepted the Restatement's variant of the 'American' rule. The practical effect of this construction of the Bankruptcy Act was thus to deprive bulk assignments of their usefulness as a device for securing credit. Individual states attempted to prevent this by enacting legislation which preserved the priority of the first assignee even if a later assignee gave notice to or received payment from the debtor first, a result which in many states was made conditional on the entry of the first assignment in a public register. There was much discussion whether to alter the law so as to make public registration a precondition of the validity of a bulk assignment by a party who subsequently went bankrupt. The Uniform Commercial Code resolved the question in favour of registration, just as England had done in the Bankruptcy Act, 1914, s. 43, so that there is now a uniform solution to the problem of the priority of multiple assignees, at any rate in the case of bulk assignments of claims for the price of goods delivered.

On this series of events and the law under the Uniform Commercial Code, see RIESENFELD, 'Kollisionen zwischen der dinglichen Sicherung von Lieferantenkredit und Bankkredit [im amerikanischen Recht], printed in a publication of the same name by the Gesellschaft für Rechtsvergleichung (no. 23, Arbeiten zur Rechtsvergleichung (1964) 41 ff.) and MALCOLM, 'Accounts Receivable Financing under the Uniform Commercial Code', *RabelsZ* 30 (1966) 434; see also 'Priority Problems in Receivables Financing: The German Experience and the UCC Compared', 11 *Boston Coll. Ind. & Com. L. Rev.* 355 (1970).

V

As the legal historian and the comparative lawyer both discover, the law of assignment is dominated by the conflict between two interests. One of these is the interest of commerce in increasing the circulation of credit: money claims, like other items of wealth, should be capable of being transferred by mere agreement between assignor and assignee so that the transfer is effective against all third parties without any further requirement, especially without any need for any form of co-operation or agreement on the part of the debtor. Opposed to this is the interest of the *debtor* in not having his legal position adversely affected by the transfer of the claim against him: this not only means that he should be able to use against the assignee any defences he had against the assignor, but it also suggests that no change of creditor should take place without his agreement or at any rate his knowledge. Our survey of the rules of different legal systems shows that the German legal family and the Common Law have preferred the commercial interest while the Romanistic laws still incline to the protection of the debtor.

The Romanistic legal systems appear to assume that payment made by the debtor can only discharge his liability if it is made to the person who actually owns the debt in question under the substantive law. Since it is necessary in order to protect the debtor that he be discharged if he pays in ignorance of the assignment, it follows that the substantive law cannot admit to a change of creditor until the debtor has knowledge of the assignment. In order to avoid the difficulties of proving such knowledge the Romanistic civil codes go one step further and lay down that the assignment must be notified to the debtor in a particular manner, namely by having the statement of the assignment delivered to him by an officer of the court.

Yet it is plain that legislators and judges can perfectly well decide that the debtor is discharged by paying the person he takes to be his creditor even if that person is no longer the actual creditor by substantive law. The German legal family and the Common Law show that it is possible to protect the debtor even if one allows a change of creditor without his participation.

It has also become manifest that the provisions of the French Code civil lead to unnecessary difficulties in practice. These do not arise so much when the assignee brings a claim against the debtor, for here, as has been seen, the debtor is bound to pay even if the formalities of art. 1690 Code civil have not been satisfied prior to suit. But suppose the *assignor* raises a claim after making the assignment but before there has been any notification: must the debtor then pay the assignor? Here the debtor who has learnt by some other means that the assignment has taken place is faced with a difficulty, for if he pays the assignor with knowledge of the assignment he may later be charged with a fraudulent manœuvre at the expense of the assignee. It is hardly a satisfactory answer that he should make good the defects in the substantive law by making the assignee a party to the suit. Another unsatisfactory aspect of French law is that if there has been no notification to the debtor it allows the assignor's creditor to attach the debt as still forming part of the creditor's patrimony. The purpose of notification, after all, is to protect the debtor, not the assignor's creditors. It is true that the French courts have occasionally restricted this rule by holding such an attachment invalid if the creditor knew of the assignment at the time, but this still makes the extent of the creditor's estate available to his creditors depend on the opinions formed by the latter, which is rather remarkable.

The better principle is the one accepted in the German legal family and in the Common Law, that a debt is transferred directly by the contract of assignment between assignor and assignee. This does not adversely affect the debtor. It is true that the 'statutory assignment' of English law does not transfer the debt to the assignee until the debtor has received a written intimation of it, but this requirement is not too important in practice, since transfers which are ineffective as a 'statutory assignment' for want of notification may still be held valid as an 'equitable assignment'. In the United States, moreover, the validity of an assignment never depends on notification.

Although they start from common ground, the German legal systems and most of the Common Law systems differ in their view of the legal position of the second assignee, that is, the second person to whom the assignor has assigned the same debt. While the unanimous view in the German legal family is that the second assignee obtains nothing, English law gives him precedence if he is a good faith assignee for value and gave notice to the debtor before the first assignee (rule in *Dearle* v. *Hall*).

The practical result of this solution accords with that of the Romanistic systems, though a difference must be noted. Under *Dearle* v. *Hall* the first assignee becomes owner of the debt, but loses it to the second assignee if the latter is the first to notify the debtor. In France and Italy the debt assigned remains in the estate of the assignor until one of the assignees notifies the debtor.

English writers have maintained that the rule in *Dearle* v. *Hall* is justified by the principle of protecting the debtor (see especially POLLOCK/WINFIELD, pp. 176 f.), but this overlooks the point that the question payment to whom discharges the debtor has nothing to do with the question which of the assignees owns the debt as a matter of substantive law. Writers in England and France also say that this rule discourages fraudulent practices by the assignor. A person negotiating for the assignment of a debt can always ask the debtor if he has received notification from any other assignee; if not, the inquirer can be sure that he will own the debt if he informs the debtor immediately after the assignment.

Thus COLIN/CAPITANT treat the real purpose of art. 1690 Code civil as being to guarantee 'publicité de la cession' (*Traite de droit civil* II (1959) no. 1648 f.). The same argument has been mustered in favour of the rule in *Dearle* v. *Hall*, although in *Ward* v. *Duncombe*, [1893] AC 369, 393 f. LORD MACNAGHTEN did not think much of it.

It may well be that the rule in *Dearle* v. *Hall* diminishes the risk that an assignee will be deluded into believing that his assignor still owns the debt, though it is worth noting that a debtor is by no means bound to inform a stranger about prior assignments. However this may be, any advantages proceeding from the rule in *Dearle* v. *Hall* and the corresponding rules in France are brought at the price of a severe restriction on all assignments, especially assignments for security, in which the parties have a reasonable interest in not informing the debtor of the transfer of the debt. If it appears to the legislature that certain kinds of assignment for security purposes, especially bulk assignments of claims for the price of goods delivered, are hazardous to commerce and credit, then special provisions requiring publicity, of the sort to be found in the Uniform Commercial Code and the English Bankruptcy Act, may always be enacted. A rule which requires *every* assignee to notify the debtor on pain of losing his claim goes rather too far.

41

Contracts for the Benefit of
Third Parties

BRESCH, 'Contracts for the Benefit of Third Parties', 12 *ICLQ* 318 (1963).

BROCKMANN, 'Der Vertrag zugunsten Dritter im französischen Recht mit rechtsvergleichenden Hinweisen zum deutschen Recht' (Diss. Bonn, 1981).

v. CAEMMERER, 'Wandlungen des Deliktsrechts', *Hundert Jahre deutsches Rechtsleben, Festschrift zum 100jährigen Bestehen des Deutschen Juristentages* II (1960) 49, 59 ff.

CORBIN, 'Contracts for the Benefit of Third Persons', 46 *LQ Rev.* 12 (1930).

DOLD, *Stipulations for a Third Party* (1948).

DOWRICK, 'A Jus Quaesitum Tertio by Way of Contract in English Law', 19 *Mod. L. Rev.* 374 (1956).

HAITAMI, *La Stipulation pour autrui en droit anglais et en droit anglo-américain* (1925).

KÄSER, 'Der Vertrag zugunsten Dritter im englischen Recht', *RabelsZ* 21 (1956) 418.

KESSLER, 'Die soziale Funktion des Vertrages zugunsten Dritter im nordamerikanischen Recht', *Festschrift E. Wahl* (1973) 81.

LORENZ, 'Die Einbeziehung Dritter in vertragliche Schuldverhältnisse—Grenzen zwischen vertraglicher und deliktischer Haftung', *JZ* 1960, 108.

MILLNER, 'Jus quaesitum tertio: Comparison and Synthesis', 16 *ICLQ* 446 (1967).

PACCHIONI, *I Contratti a favore di terzi* (Milan, n.d.).

SIMPSON, 'Promises Without Consideration', 15 *ICLQ* 835, 848 ff. (1966).

WESENBERG, *Verträge zugunsten Dritter* (1949).

WILLIAMS, 'Contracts for the Benefit of Third Parties', 7 *Mod. L. Rev.* 123 (1944).

I

THE normal intention of persons who enter a commutative contract, such as a contract of sale, is that the rights and obligations engendered by the contract should attach to themselves alone. The same is true even if the parties provide that each of them may discharge his liability under the contract by rendering performance to someone else: if the purchaser, at the vendor's request, is to pay the price to the vendor's bank rather than to the vendor himself, or if the vendor is to deliver the goods to the purchaser's order rather than to him personally, each of them in rendering performance to a third party is performing an obligation which he owes only to his contractor and not to the third party. Quite different is the situation where the parties contract in such a manner that the third party, not himself involved in the formation of the contract, is to be entitled not only to receive the promised performance but actually to demand it in his own name: this brings us into the realm of contracts for the benefit of third parties.

It is by no means obvious that a contract should be able to create such rights in those who are not parties to it. A look at legal systems past and present shows that the concept of contracts for the benefit of third parties has been far from receiving invariable acceptance. No legal system has been able to ignore the fact that there is a great practical need to recognize contractual benefits conferred on strangers, but it is one thing to admit that occasionally the third party may be entitled to sue, and quite another to recognize the contract for the benefit of third parties as a basic institution of legal thought. The main obstacle to this is a rather dimensional and unabstract way of looking at the problem, of seeing a contract as a bond binding the parties, as a 'vinculum juris', for this makes it difficult to understand how a third party who is a stranger to the contract can take under it in the way suggested. It is not only lawyers who go in for this dimensional manner of approaching things, it is a general method by which *homo sapiens* attempts to impose order on the variety of surrounding phenomena. It is extremely useful in law since it enables one to discern and transmit different types of situation, but such typology has its own dangers, since the striking pictures it develops may prove delusive in time. The picture of a contract as a necessarily bilateral 'vinculum juris' is one of these and it has led the Common Law to the dogma of 'privity of contract'.

Classical Roman lawyers granted no independent right to a third party who was a stranger to a contract: 'alteri stipulari nemo potest' (ULPIAN, D. 45, 1, 38, 17). In the post-classical law of the Empire a few exceptions were admitted, and JUSTINIAN's men increased their number. One case was where a person made a gift on the terms that the donee was to do something for a third party: in such a case the third party was given an *actio utilis* against the donee. Another instance of the recognition of contracts for the benefit of third parties lies in dispositions from one member of a family to another member or to a trustee with the direction that the transferee, possibly on the death of the transferor, transmit the property to third parties, normally descendants in need of support (on this, see WESENBERG (above p. 488) 29 ff.).

By and large the natural law codes adhered to these principles. It is true that the General Prussian Land Law laid down in §74 I 5 that 'a contract may have as its object the benefit of a third party'; but it added that 'the third party [obtains] a right from such a contract, in the formation of which he was involved neither directly nor indirectly, only if he accedes to the contract with the agreement of the principal parties' (§75). Making the third party's right depend on a formal declaration of adhesion proved unsatisfactory in practice, as emerges clearly from a passage in the famous lecture on 'The Worthlessness of Jurisprudence as a Science' [*Die Werthlosigkeit der Jurisprudenz als*

Wissenschaft] delivered in 1848 by the Prussian philosopher and state attorney
v. KIRCHMANN. Dealing with the farm surrender contract, used by an ageing
farmer to dispose of the property on the condition that the transferee pay part
of the price directly to his siblings, he says:

'People familiar with this institution had no doubt that, unless the father said
otherwise, the siblings had an independent claim to the funds destined for them, even if
they had not adhered to the contract. But the Land Law unfortunately overlooked this
institution and its only applicable provisions were the general terms of I 5 §75 . . . When
these provisions were applied to the institution in question, intolerable hardships
occurred. From the very outset attempts of every kind have been made to prevent §75
having this destructive effect on the institution. Fictions, conversions, anticipated
successions, and other artificial constructs of this sort were all tried out . . .' (v.
KIRCHMANN (id. 3rd edn., 1948) 21 f.).

In fact the Prussian courts contrived to give the siblings an independent
right of suit notwithstanding the unsatisfactory terms of the Land Law: they
simply held that the transferee's promise to pay his siblings must be deemed to
have been accepted by the father as 'their representative'.

The plenary decision to this effect, made by the Prussian Obertribunal on 25 Aug.
1846, is very instructive (ObTr. 14, 68). The reasoning is so tortured that v.
KIRCHMANN took it as further evidence for his view that most of legal science consisted
of ignominious rehabilitation of moribund legislation—'so repellent a business that it
is surprising so many are ready to take to it'.

Be this as it may, it is beyond question that when the legal scholars of the
Gemeines Recht rethought the problem of the contract for the benefit of third
parties, they performed a valuable service for they produced the conceptual
clarity needed for the mature solutions of the German BGB. Even the
pandectists sometimes heeded the exigencies of practice. Only a few of them,
such as BRINZ (*Pandektenrecht* IV (1892) 389 f.), thought that a contract for
the benefit of third parties was a 'logical impossibility', a view which, when
expressed by lawyers, inevitably discloses the untenability of the proposition it
is adduced to support. Most of the law professors of the period saw that the
new life insurance contracts or annuity contracts or the farm surrender
contracts already mentioned could not be dealt with by Roman law alone.
They therefore proposed a wide variety of theories, all using existing
institutions, to justify giving the third party an independent claim. The device
used by the Prussian Obertribunal is just one example. It was also suggested
that the third party's right of suit could be based on fictional assignment, and
that the third party could bring his claim as the agent of the promisee, but the
view which finally won through was that the contractual will of the parties was
powerful enough by itself to engender the third party's right to claim. This was
the view of WINDSCHEID in particular, and he was led to this conclusion by the
fact that 'in Germany . . . theory and practice have always gone beyond [the

Roman principles]. This is a fact which cannot be ignored and which gives good evidence of the tendency of modern legal consciousness' (*Lehrbuch des Pandektenrechts* II (1865) §316, pp. 189 f.). It was through WINDSCHEID that the proper view of the matter entered the BGB.

II

The German BGB starts off with the proposition that one may by contract so bargain for performance to a third party that 'the third party directly acquires the right to demand performance' (§328 par. 1). The statement that the third party acquires the right 'directly' means that in order to acquire the right in his own name the third party need not make any declaration of adhesion or acceptance, or participate in any way; indeed he need not even know of the conclusion of the contract. It also follows that the right to claim to receive performance vests only in the third party; it never vests in the promisee, even for a 'legal second', although he may acquire the right to claim that performance be rendered to the third party. The third party need not, however, accept the right; he may decline it by making a declaration to this effect *vis-à-vis* the promisor (§333 BGB).

In answering the question under what circumstances a contract for the benefit of third parties is to be found, the BGB followed WINDSCHEID; if the contract contains no express provision the judge is to make an inference 'from the circumstances, especially the purpose of the contract'. The BGB facilitates the judges' task somewhat by drawing up presumptions for particular cases: in case of doubt, if the payments under life assurance contracts and annuity contracts are to be made to a third party, they are to be treated as contracts for the benefit of that third party. The same is true for farm surrender contracts and other gratuitous dispositions with provisions in favour of third parties (§330 BGB). By contrast, arrangements to pay a contractor's creditor are *not*, where any doubt arises, to be treated as contracts for the benefit of the third party: the presumption here is that the creditor, not being a party to the contract, cannot claim payment from the debtor's contractor as well as from the debtor himself (§329 BGB).

§331 deserves particular attention: if the parties have agreed that the promisor is to render performance to the third party only after the death of the promisee, the third party, in case of doubt, acquires his right only at the time of the promisee's death. In practice this means that the promisee can rescind or alter the benefit to the third party at any time during his life. There is a special rule on this in the law relating to the insurance contract [*Versicherungs-vertragsgesetz*] (§§166 ff.), but more important is the general recognition in §331 BGB of the validity of contracts for the benefit of third parties which mature on the death of the promisee. Accordingly, a person who wants a particular person to have an item of property after his death may achieve his aim by making a contract whereby his contractor promises to transfer the object to the destinatee after the promisee's death. In practice, of course, this amounts to a disposition *mortis causa*, but the formal requirements regarding wills or contracts of succession can be disregarded because, as is laid down, the third party obtains his right to performance 'directly', that is, he does not acquire it through the estate of the deceased.

The Reichsgericht always held that if a 'testator' made an informal agreement with his bank or savings bank that after his death the latter should transfer all or part of his funds to a third party, the third party obtained a claim to payment of these funds on the death of the testator and did so outside the succession (RGZ 88, 137; 106, 1). This was much criticized by writers who pointed to §2301 BGB (see, for instance, HECK, *Grundriss des Schuldrechts* (1929) §§50, 4; 95, 2; KIPP/COING, *Erbrecht* (13th edn., 1980, §81 IV)), but even so, the Bundesgerichtshof has repeatedly endorsed this line of cases (BGH NJW 1975, 382 and NJW 1976, 749) and extended them to cover contracts whereby a person deposited shares or bonds with a bank on the terms that on his death a third party should be entitled to claim the papers from the bank (BGHZ 41, 95).

A contract for the benefit of third parties has also been found in cases other than the very important ones mentioned in §§329–31 BGB.

If the lessor of a private clinic provides in the lease that a named specialist should have the right to reserve beds in it, the contract may be construed under §328 BGB so as to give the specialist an independent contractual right against the lessee (BGHZ 3, 385).—The circumstances under which a person opens an account in a bank or savings bank, especially the name chosen for the account, may show that a third party should also have an immediate right to draw on the funds in the account (BGHZ 21, 148).— The dowry promised by the bride's father to his future son-in-law can be construed as a contract in favour of the daughter (RGZ 67, 204).—If a collective agreement between a trade union and an employers' federation contains a promise not to strike and the promise is broken, an individual employer may be able to claim damages in respect of the harm suffered by *himself*, since the contract made by the employers' federation is to this extent a contract in favour of the individual employers who are its members (BAG NJW 1957, 647).

This is not, however, the right place to deal with the many cases in which the German courts use the contract for the benefit of third parties in order to impose a contractual duty to pay damages on a person who causes harm by breach of the general duty of care required in the circumstances although in fact there are no contractual relations between him and the victim of such breach.

An example is the well-known case decided by the Reichsgericht in 1930. A tenant contracted with a repair firm for the repair of a gas water-heater which was in the dwelling, and owing to fault on the part of the gas-fitter, the heater exploded and caused injuries to the cleaning woman employed by the tenant (RGZ 127, 218).—See also BGH NJW 1965, 1757: A cookery club hired a room from the defendant in which to hold its foundation celebrations, during which a member of the club slipped and hurt herself on the floor (see also RGZ 160, 153).

The courts held that the victims had *contractual* claims for damages against the repair firm and the landlord of the room respectively. Originally the courts based this result directly on §328 BGB. In the light of objections raised by LARENZ (*Schuldrecht* I (7th edn., 1964) 126 ff.) the Bundesgerichtshof now bases the contractual claim for damages on the consideration that

'third parties are to be brought within the protective ambit of a contract if the duty of care and protection arising from the contract should be owed, in good faith and in accordance with the purpose of the contract, not only to the contracting party but also to certain other persons' (BGHZ NJW 1965, 1757). The Bundesgerichtshof has gone a step further in BGHZ 66, 51: a child who slipped on the floor of a self-service store while accompanying her mother on a shopping expedition was held entitled to claim damages from the occupier on a *contractual* basis. It was immaterial whether or not the mother had already bought the groceries: if she had, the child was protected under the contract of sale; if not, she was protected under the business contact arising between the parties when the customer entered the shop.

The sole purpose of these decisions is to put the accident victim in a better position than if his only claim for damages were based on delict. Under German law, with regard to prescription, burden of proof, and especially liability (see Ch. 48 below), a victim is in a much better position to claim damages if he can claim in *contract* for the harm he has suffered. Not the slightest blame attaches to the German courts for using the contract for the benefit of third parties in order to get round the misconceived legal policy contained in §831 BGB; nor is there anything wrong with what they have done as a matter of positive law. Nevertheless it must be seen that these are cases where the harmful consequences of *accidents* are attributed to the person responsible, not because he is guilty of any breach of specifically *contractual* duties but because he has committed a breach of general duties of care imposed by the law of *delict*. The position of German law may be excused by the necessity caused by the unfortunate policy of §831 BGB, but the comparative lawyer has to classify problems according to the true significance of their actual facts. These cases must therefore be put in the law of tort, as is done everywhere else in the world. In doing so, the comparatist must realize that it may be necessary to study a person's contractual relations with third parties in order to discover *to whom* he owes his delictual duties of care not to cause harm; this is well put with references to foreign systems by LORENZ (above p. 488; see also the extensive treatment by v. CAEMMERER (above p. 488)).

Austria and *Switzerland* also recognize contracts for the benefit of third parties. Originally the ABGB, like all other natural law codes, took a contrary position, for §811 laid down that no one could accept a promise for another, and contracts for the benefit of third parties remained inadmissible until the adoption of the Third Teilnovelle to the ABGB in 1916. This amendment followed the German BGB by declaring that the entitlement of the beneficiary 'is to be judged from the agreement and the nature and the purpose of the contract'. The presumptions of §§329–31 BGB were replaced by a rather empty formula that in cases of doubt the beneficiary acquires an independent right 'if performance will principally be to his benefit'. The same presumption applies to farm surrender contracts as in Germany. The *Swiss* rule in art. 112 OR is even terser. The third party may himself demand performance of the contract 'if this accords with the intention of the contractors or if it is in line with practice'.

III

The thesis that a contract is a *vinculum juris* which creates rights and duties only for and against the parties to it is expressly stated in the *French* Code civil. Immediately afterwards, however, the legislator qualifies this by saying that the principle does not apply to contracts for the benefit of third parties. Art. 1165 Code civil provides:

'Les conventions n'ont d'effet qu'entre les parties contractantes; elles ne nuisent point au tiers, et elles ne lui profitent que dans le cas prévu par l'article 1121.'

It is only under very strict conditions that art. 1121 declares a 'stipulation au profit d'un tiers' to be admissible; this shows that while French lawyers at the end of the eighteenth century were ready to abandon the Roman principle that 'alteri stipulari nemo potest', they were still very far from accepting the modern principle that contracts for the benefit of third parties should be allowed generally. Under art. 1121 the 'stipulation au profit d'un tiers' is only valid if the person who promises to render performance to the third party simultaneously promises something to the other contractor as well, or if the contracting party makes the promisor some gift in connection with the transaction. If these requirements were taken seriously, it would mean that in order for an uncle to make a binding promise to a father to render some performance to his son, either the uncle must promise something to the father as well or receive something from the father as a gift, on condition of the performance to the son. Nowadays, however, it is established that a contract for the benefit of third parties may be perfectly valid even if these requirements are not satisfied. The performance which the promisee must make to the promisor under art. 1121 need no longer be a gift: any economic transfer will suffice, and the alternative requirement of the Code, that the promisee must at the time of the contract always stipulate for something for himself, has been understood by the courts as being satisfied if any 'profit moral' accrues to him as a result of the transaction. In the case of insurance such a 'profit moral' exists in the certainty of the insured that the insured sum will be paid to the third party on the occurrence of the insured event (Civ. 16 Jan. 1888, DP 1888, 1. 77).

These decisions have been adopted in the *Italian* Codice civile, whose art. 1411 states that a 'stipulazione a favore di un terzo' is valid if the promisee has an interest in the third party's being benefited. The Italian courts were prompt to state that it is sufficient if the interest is 'di natura morale' (Cass. 24 Oct. 1956, no. 3869, Giust. civ., Mass. 1956, 1318).

In practice, therefore, the limitative requirements imposed by the Code in 1804 for contracts for the benefit of third parties have been effectively struck out by the French courts: 'l'un des exemples les plus souvent cités de l'œuvre créatrice des tribunaux' (MAZEAUD II no. 787).

With regard to the theoretical explanation of the 'stipulation pour autrui' even the modern French textbooks follow the old doctrines to the effect that the beneficiary is a fictive assignee of the promisee's right, or that the beneficiary ratifies the unauthorized agency (*negotiorum gestio*) of the promisee in undertaking the matter on his behalf. All these theories are now of merely historical interest; it is no longer necessary to refer to other institutions of law since it is simply admitted that it is a practical necessity that the beneficiary acquire a direct claim in his own name. French law differs from German law, however, on the question whether the third party's right may be rescinded by subsequent act. Whereas in Germany this depends on the intention of the parties (see §§328 par. 2, 331 BGB), in France it depends on whether the third party has 'accepted' the right accorded to him: if he has done so the promisee can no longer rescind the disposition in his favour (see art. 1121 sent. 2 Code civil and art. 1411 par. 2 Codice civile). This is also the position of Swiss law (art. 112 par. 3 OR).

Contracts for the benefit of third parties are of practical importance today in much the same areas as in Germany. *Annuities* are specially provided for in art. 1973 Code civil, which expressly grants a right to the beneficiary, as does art. 1875 Codice civile. Life assurance contracts, now specially covered by the French Law of Insurance of 13 July 1930 (arts. 54 ff.), had to be dealt with prior to its enactment simply as contracts for the benefit of third parties under art. 1121 Code civil; indeed the application of that article to life assurance contracts was the acid test which purified that article of its Roman dross. The French courts are also ready to recognize other arrangements as contracts for the benefit of third parties if the promisee wants to procure that a third party receive one or more payments from the promisor. Although such a disposition is normally gratuitous as between the promisee and the beneficiary, it is generally agreed that the formal requirements for donations, such as art. 931 Code civil, do not apply.

This is laid down by art. 1973 par. 2 for annuity contracts in particular, but it is also admitted generally: one of the reasons given will be familiar to German lawyers, that under a *stipulation pour autrui* the third party's rights flow not from a conveyance of property by the promisee but from the conclusion of the contract (see MAZEAUD II no. 776 and Montpellier 22 Dec. 1932, Gaz. Pal. 1933, 421).

These contracts for the benefit of third parties are typically cases where the promisee wants to secure the support of dependants by giving them contractual claims against the promisor, but the institution is used by the French courts in many other cases as well.

For example, the purchaser of a business conducted on leased premises may acquire a contractual right to have the lease extended if the lessor had agreed with the tenant that the lease would be extended if the business were sold (Civ. 30 May 1962, Bull. civ. 1962. I. 247).—The contract between the owner of a house and a concierge may be seen as a contract for the benefit of the tenants, so that the tenants acquire their own contractual claims against the concierge if he fails to fulfil the duties he assumed in the contract (Trib. civ. Seine 4 March 1944, DA 1944 J. 84).—If the Centre National de transfusion sanguine, pursuant to a contract with a hospital to provide a blood donor if required by a patient, provides a syphilitic donor and the patient becomes worse, the patient has a contractual claim for damages against the Centre National de transfusion sanguine since the hospital's contract is for the benefit of the patient in accordance with art. 1121 Code civil (Civ. 17 Dec. 1954, Gaz. Pal. 1955. I. 54).

The Romanistic legal families have another institution, very similar in its practical effects to the contract for the benefit of third parties but entirely different from the point of view of juristic construction. This is the so-called 'action directe' ('azione diretta'). In a few specified cases the French Code civil gives a person an independent right of suit if he has a special interest in the performance of a contract concluded between two other parties. Thus art. 1994 par. 2 Code civil provides that a principal has a direct claim against the third party to whom his agent has delegated the performance of the authorized task (so art. 1705 par. 2 Codice civile; see also above Ch. 39 V). Art. 1753 Code civil further provides that if a tenant is in arrears with the rent the landlord can proceed directly against the subtenant (so art. 1595 Codice civile). The building subcontractor may bring a direct claim against the site-owner if the main contractor still owes him money and still has claims against the site-owner for his services (art. 1798 Code civil; to the same effect art. 1676 Codice civile). But the most important instance of the *action directe* in practice occurs in the law of insurance: if a tortfeasor is covered in respect of an accident by a policy of liability insurance, the victim can sue the insurer direct (art. 53 of the French Law of Insurance of 13 July 1930; *contra*, art. 1917 Codice civile and Cass. 4 Dec. 1952, no. 3121, Foro it. Mass. 1952, 719).

What these cases have in common with the *stipulation pour autrui* is that a third party who takes no part in the formation of the contract may 'force' himself as creditor on the contractual debtor and demand that performance be rendered to himself. But while under a *stipulation pour autrui* the third party's right to claim is inferred, often with the help of construction, from the will of the *parties*, in the case of the *action directe* it is the *legislator* who decides on the basis of an abstract balancing of the interests involved that the third party should have a right to intervene, regardless of whether this is in accordance with the will of the parties or not.

IV

English law has not yet been able to bring itself to adopt the contract for the benefit of third parties as a legal institution of general application. All the textbooks start their discussion of the matter with the observation of VISCOUNT HALDANE in a decision of the House of Lords:

'My Lords, in the law of England certain principles are fundamental. One is that only a person who is a party to a contract can sue on it. Our law knows nothing of a ius quaesitum tertio arising by way of contract. Such a right may be conferred by way of property, as, for example, under a trust, but it cannot be conferred on a stranger to a contract as a right to enforce the contract in personam' (*Dunlop* v. *Selfridge*, [1915] AC 847, 853).

It is true that there are a few decisions from the middle of the eighteenth century in which English courts enforced contracts for the benefit of third parties, but there are also decisions in the same period which go the other way (on this see 70 *LQ Rev.* 467 (1954)). But it was the leading case of *Tweddle* v. *Atkinson*, (1861) 1 B. & S. 393, 4 LT 468 which finally set England on the path of principled refusal to accept contracts for the benefit of third parties.

Mr Tweddle and Miss Guy were married rather young, and in order to contribute to the young couple's living expenses both fathers entered a written contract in which each bound himself to pay a named sum of money to Mr Tweddle. They further agreed 'that the said William Tweddle has full power to sue the said parties in any court of law or equity for the aforesaid sums hereby promised and specified'. The bride's father, Mr Guy, died without paying, so Mr Tweddle raised a claim against his executor, Atkinson. The claim was dismissed: the court could not bring itself to accept that the plaintiff, a third party and a stranger to the contract, had any right to sue on it.

Courts and writers in England seek to justify this rule by reference to two basic principles of the English law of contract: the doctrine of consideration and the doctrine of 'privity of contract'.

In the doctrine of 'privity of contract' we meet once again the old idea of contract as a basically bilateral *vinculum juris*. All that 'privity of contract' really means is that a contract can generate rights and obligations only for and against the parties to it. This is a very reasonable principle so far as it means that a contract may not impose burdens on third parties, since in principle no one should be lumbered with contractual obligations unless he agrees to them, but it is far from clear to the comparative lawyer why contracts in favour of third parties should offend against the doctrine of privity, especially as English law, as will be shown in a moment, has itself abandoned this principle in a whole series of cases.

The doctrine of consideration states that promises are only legally enforceable if they are given in return for some counterprestation from the promisee, that is a 'consideration'. It is the promisee who must give the consideration: 'Consideration must move from the promisee'. This is a proposition which, as RHEINSTEIN had already shown (*Die Struktur des vertraglichen Schuldverhältnisses im anglo-amerikanischen Recht* (1932) 58 f., 111 f.), by no means entails the inadmissibility of contracts for the benefit of third parties. English authors who deny this fail to see that it is not the third party who is the promisee but always the other contracting party, and that it is the latter who gives consideration in return for the promise to him of performance to the third party. It must be admitted that the English writers often formulate the doctrine of consideration to the effect that the consideration must be provided by the person who seeks to enforce the contract: 'Only a person who has given consideration may enforce a contract'. This formulation does make it impossible to give legal recognition to a contract for the benefit of a third party, but one must still ask whether this is a necessary consequence of the function performed in the Common Law by the consideration doctrine. So far as we can see, the function of this doctrine is to distinguish serious binding promises from those which are not binding, by putting the question whether the promise was given with a view to a counterprestation (see above Ch. 36). If a person has made a promise in return for consideration provided by the other contractor, the seriousness of his intention to contract is established, and it should not be reckoned any weaker simply because the agreement provides that what was promised should be capable of being demanded not only by the other contracting party but by the beneficiary as well.

Although the theoretical justification for the refusal to accept the 'ius quaesitum tertio' is unconvincing, the fact remains that in general England still denies the validity of contracts for the benefit of third parties. We must wait and see whether it will take the stiff broom of the legislator to sweep away those old doctrines or whether the courts will be able to abandon them on their own. English lawyers have often exposed the present rules to cogent criticism (see in particular DOWRICK (above p. 142)), and LORD DUNEDIN in his dissenting judgment in *Dunlop* v. *Selfridge* ([1915] AC 847, 855) accurately observed that the effect of refusing to accept contracts for the benefit of third parties was

'to make it possible for a person to snap his fingers at a bargain deliberately made, a bargain not itself unfair, and which the person seeking to enforce it has a legitimate interest to enforce'.

The problem of recognizing contracts for the benefit of third parties was ventilated at length in several courts quite recently. This was in the case of *Beswick* v. *Beswick*. A Lancashire coal merchant more than 70 years old made a written contract with his nephew: the merchant was to transfer his whole coal business to the nephew, and in return the nephew was to pay £6 per week to the coal merchant while he lived and, after his death, £5 per week to his widow. After the old man died, the nephew refused to make the agreed payments to his widow, and the widow sued him both in her quality as administratrix of the estate of her deceased husband and in her own right. Her claim was rejected at first instance ([1965] 3 All ER 858), but the Court of Appeal allowed her appeal ([1966] 3 All ER 1), holding that the plaintiff was entitled to claim *in her own right*. LORD DENNING, one of the most reformist and progressive of English judges, supported this conclusion by saying that the Common Law had always allowed third parties who were strangers to contracts to demand performance of them and that *Tweddle* v. *Atkinson* and other precedents could be 'distinguished'; furthermore, in company with DANCKWERTS, LJ, he was of the view that this result could also be based on s. 56 of the Law of Property Act 1925.

According to the text of this somewhat obscure provision 'a person may take . . . the benefit of any . . . agreement over or respecting land or other property, although he may not be named as a party to the conveyance or other instrument'. It was admittedly an extremely bold assertion that this provision, ready to hand but noticed by no one, had introduced the contract for the benefit of third parties into English law; see the criticism in CHESHIRE/FIFOOT 411 ff.

The case finally went to the House of Lords, who held that the plaintiff had no claim *in her own right*: contrary to what LORD DENNING had said below, such a claim could not be based on the rules of Common Law, nor yet on s. 56 of the Law of Property Act, properly construed. Nevertheless the claim was allowed, because in her capacity as administratrix of her husband's estate she could exercise the claim to specific performance which formed part of that estate.

(See *Beswick* v. *Beswick*, [1968] AC 58, and the comments of TREITEL, 30 *Mod. L. Rev.* 687 (1967).) Since it was more or less a coincidence that the plaintiff was also administratrix, this should not have been determinative for the decision in the case: if someone else had been executor or administrator and had refused to insist on the nephew's performing his promise, the widow would have gone away empty-handed, which is absurd.

Now the only reason English law has been able to reject the 'ius quaesitum tertio' for so long is because whenever the practical need has been greatest it has found other methods of allowing third parties to sue on contracts (see the details in KÄSER (above p. 488)). For example, s. 11 of the Married Women's Property Act 1882 provides that if a person insures his life in favour of his spouse or children the beneficiary is to be regarded as the beneficiary of a trust, and therefore entitled to claim on the death of the insured. So also in motor insurance the 'permitted driver', though not a party to the insurance contract, may demand an indemnity from the insurer: *Williams* v. *Baltic Ins. Co.*, [1924] 2 KB 282, accepted the fiction that the insured becomes trustee of the claims under the insurance policy for the 'permitted driver', a solution which the legislator has since adopted in s. 148(4) of the Road Traffic Act 1972.

Apart from these instances where the *legislature* has given the third party a right to claim, English law holds in reserve other legal institutions which may under certain circumstances be used to give the desired result. The trust must be mentioned first of all. In essence, a trust arises when a person transfers an item of property to a trustee so that the latter may manage it in favour of third persons according to the instructions of the transferor. Cases like the German farm surrender contracts can thus be solved in the Common Law by saying that the transferee of the farm holds the farm as trustee and is obliged 'in equity' to make certain contributions from the farm to his relatives as beneficiaries of the trust. But in English law the trust has been used as a substitute for the contract for the benefit of third parties much more extensively than this, for a trust may exist not only in things but also in claims: if A has concluded a contract with B, A's claim under the contract may be asserted by C if the court accepts that the claim vested in A is held by him as trustee for C.

One of the first cases to use this trust construction was *Tomlinson* v. *Gill* (1756) Ambler 330, 27 Eng. Rep. 221. The defendant had promised a widow that if she would consent to his being called as executor of the will he would pay off the debts of her deceased husband. The question was whether one of the deceased's creditors could bring a direct claim against the defendant. The German judge would ask whether by the agreement between the widow and the defendant the latter simply promised the widow to pay off her debts ('Erfüllungsübernahme', see §329 BGB) or whether the agreement was meant by the parties to confer on the creditors a right to demand performance from the defendant and thus to constitute a genuine contract for the benefit of a third party. The English judge asked whether in the circumstances of the case it would be right to conclude that it was only as trustee for the creditors that the widow held her claim to have the debts paid off. It was so held, and the creditor's claim was allowed. On this see KÄSER (above p. 488) and CORBIN (above p. 488).

In the last few decades the courts of England have shown themselves much less ready to use the trust as a substitute for the contract for the benefit of third parties. The reason for this may perhaps be that the trust is really an institution of property law and that if every contractual right were treated without more as the object of a fictive trust in favour of beneficiaries not party to the contract, the principle of privity of contract might by unduly weakened. (On this see WILLIAMS (above p. 488) 130 ff. and CHESHIRE/FIFOOT 408 ff.)

The state courts of the *United States* have long since accepted contracts for the benefit of third parties. Indeed in many states this legal institution has been endorsed by the legislature. In California, for example, §1559 of the Civil Code provides:

'A contract, made expressly for the benefit of the third person, may be enforced by him at any time before the parties thereto rescind it.' On this see LANGMAID, 27 *Calif. L. Rev.* 497 (1939).

The American courts distinguish according to whether the transaction represents a gratuitous disposition or the payment of a debt. An instance of the first would be when a person takes out a life assurance policy and names his wife as the beneficiary: here the wife obtains a claim to payment of the insured sum without having given anything to her husband in exchange, so in American terminology she ranks as a 'donee beneficiary'. One speaks of 'creditor beneficiaries' on the other hand when a person wishes to pay off a debt and instead of paying the creditor himself he procures another person to promise him that he will make the necessary performance to the creditor. This distinction is of no significance for the critical question whether in a particular case a third party actually obtains an independent right to claim as an 'intended beneficiary', or whether he is simply an 'incidental beneficiary'. The almost unanimous view is that the answer depends on whether at the time of concluding the contract the parties intended the third party to have an independent right. If the agreement leaves the matter open, then just as in Germany it depends on the circumstances of the case, the purpose of the contract, and the intention of the promisee as known to the promisor.

For the details, see Restatement (Second) of Contracts (1981) §§302 ff., CORBIN §776, WILLISTON §357, KESSLER (above p. 488), and the decisions there cited.—These rules apply even where the statute provides, as it does in California, that the contract must be concluded 'expressly' in favour of the third party; see LANGMAID (above p. 488) 510 f.

In the United States parties often also use the legal institution of the trust in order to set up legal relationships which on the Continent would be classified as contracts for the benefit of third parties.

The German lawyer will be particularly interested in the cases where a person makes an agreement with his bank that the funds standing to his account will be held by him on trust for a named third party so that he will be able to administer the account until his death and that after his death any funds left in the account shall be paid out to the third party beneficiary. The leading case in this area is the decision of the New York Court of Appeals in *Matter of Totten*, 179 NY 112, 71 NE 748 (1904), which gave the name of 'Totten trusts' to devices of this kind. The American courts are perfectly aware that this is a way of getting round the formal requirements for testamentary dispositions, but the device is so practicable and so useful in commerce that the objections are bypassed (see SCOTT, *On Trusts* I (2nd edn., 1956) §58).

V

Comparative lawyers sometimes say that its highly developed art of applying judicial decisions makes it easy for the Common Law to adapt itself quickly to changes in economic and social circumstances by modifying its legal principles and standards. This is contrasted with the way law develops on the Continent, where it is said to have a tendency to limp some way behind the changing world, being mainly the product of the legislator, and to be prevented from looking reality squarely in the face because its legal scholars have an undue predilection for abstract conceptualism and generalization. There may be a grain of truth in these observations, but the example of contracts for the benefit of third parties shows that they could well be stood on their heads.

It was in France that the courts, faced with the intractable text of art. 1121 Code civil, set themselves energetically to the task of remoulding the law and developed rules which helped them to control the new phenomenon of 'life assurance'. And it has been seen that the mature manner in which the German BGB deals with the contract for the benefit of third parties is very largely attributable to the conceptual clarity with which the scholarship of the *Gemeines Recht* illuminated this institution.

Contrariwise, it is astonishing how stubbornly English law still clings to the view that a 'ius quaestium tertio' is in principle inadmissible. The manner in which many writers and judges in England seek to deduce this principle from the doctrines of 'privity' and 'consideration', notwithstanding the practical needs which it ignores, would do credit to many a Continental theoretician of the purest water. One of the recognized rules of good judicial behaviour in England is that abstract principles should not be laid down in a case if they go further than the concrete facts of the case demand. Yet this principle did not deter VISCOUNT HALDANE in *Dunlop* v. *Selfridge* ([1915] AC 847) from laying down as an inevitable truth, without even a reference to precedent, the general proposition that 'Only a person who is a party to a contract can sue on it'. In consequence a simple case like *Beswick* v. *Beswick*, which any first-year student on the Continent could solve correctly and with ease, had to pass through three courts in England, causing lucubrations of the most complex variety on the way.

42

Claims to Performance and Their Enforcement

BORÉ, 'La Liquidation de l'astreinte comminatoire', D. 1966 *Chron.* 159.

DAWSON, 'Specific Performance in France and Germany', 57 *Mich. L. Rev.* 495 (1959).

FRÉJAVILLE, 'L'Astreinte', D. 1949 *Chron.* 1.

——, 'La Valeur pratique de l'astreinte', JCP 1951. I. 910.

FRY, *A Treatise on the Specific Performance of Contracts* (6th edn., 1921).

R. GOLDSCHMIDT, 'Las astreintes, las sanciones por contempt of court y otros medios para conseguir el cumplimiento de las obligaciones de hacer y de no hacer', *Scritti giuridici in onore della Cedam* I (1953) 61.

GROSSFELD, *Die Privatstrafe* (1961) 22 ff.

——, 'Money Sanctions for Breach of Contract in a Communist Economy', 72 *Yale LJ* 1326 (1963).

HÉBRAUD, 'L'Exécution des jugements civils', *Rev. int. dr. comp.* 9 (1957) 170.

HUSTON, *The Enforcement of Decrees in Equity* (1915).

JACKSON, 'Specific Performance of Contracts in Louisiana', 24 *Tul. L. Rev.* 401 (1950).

JEANDIDIER, 'L'Exécution forcée des obligations contractuelles' *Rev. trim. civ.* 74 (1976) 700.

KAYSER, 'L'Astreinte judiciaire et la responsabilité civile', *Rev. trim. civ.* 51 (1953) 209.

KRASSA, 'Interaction of Common Law and Latin Law: Enforcement of Specific Performance in Louisiana and Quebec', 21 *Can. Bar Rev.* 337 (1943).

POMEROY, *A Treatise on the Specific Performance of Contracts* (1926).

RABEL, *Das Recht des Warenkaufs*, vol. I (1936) 269 ff., 375 ff.

RASSAT, 'L'Astreinte définitive', JCP 1967 D. 2069.

RAYNAUD, 'La Distinction de l'astreinte et des dommages-intérêts dans la jurisprudence française récente', *Mélanges Secrétan* (1964) 249.

RHEINSTEIN, *Die Struktur des vertraglichen Schuldverhältnisses im anglo-amerikanischen Recht* (1932) 138 ff.

SAVATIER, 'L'exécution des condamnations au payement d'une astreinte', D. 1951. *Chron.* 37.

SCHOBERT, 'Die Realerfüllung, insbesondere nach anglo-amerikanischem Recht', (Diss. Berne, 1952).

SZLADITS, 'The Concept of Specific Performance in Civil Law', 4 *Am. J. Comp. L.* 208 (1955).

TREITEL, 'Specific Performance in the Sale of Goods', 1966 *J. Bus. L.* 211.

——, 'Remedies for Breach of Contract', VII *Int Enc. Comp. L.* Ch. 16 (1976) 6 ff.

TUNC, 'Le Renouveau de l'astreinte en droit français', *Festschrift Riese* (1964) 397.

I

A PERSON who enters a contract expects the other party to do as he promised. He may be disappointed. The goods may not be delivered, the purchased premises may not be vacated, the tenant may stay on after the end of the lease, the singer may not give the covenanted recital, or the ex-employee may set himself up in competition contrary to his promise. The question then arises what forms of relief the legal system will offer the innocent contractor who has been deceived in his expectation that the contract will be performed. One point is agreed in all modern legal systems: the creditor must not simply proceed to help himself and snatch the goods from the vendor, thrust the tenant into the street, or use similar private and forcible methods to compel the other contracting party to perform his promise. The innocent party must go to court and establish the claims which accrue to him on non-performance of the contract before he takes any further steps against the debtor, and those steps too must proceed under the supervision of the state.

The contractor who has suffered a loss because he has not got what he was promised may be content with monetary compensation. This will normally be the case if something as good as what was promised can be procured elsewhere, even at a higher price, for the innocent party will be content to sue the defaulter for damages for the extra he has to pay. But what is to be done when it is difficult or even impossible to calculate the harm, or when no calculation one can do will reflect any special interest the creditor may have in having the contract performed? If a man buys a picture which has a 'sentimental value' for him, inestimable in money, perhaps because it is a portrait of a noted ancestor, is he only to claim damages if the picture is not delivered or can he ask a court to order the auctioneer to deliver the picture to him? Under what circumstances—and this is our first question—may a court, at the instance of the plaintiff, order the defendant to perform his contract *in natura*, that is, order the auctioneer to deliver the picture, the tenant to vacate the dwelling, the singer to give the concert as promised, and the employee to cease from competition?

Even if the court grants the creditor's claim for performance, he still does not have what he really wants, for many debtors do not satisfy a claim even if it has been established in court, either because they cannot do so or think they cannot, or because they do not want to. Here the state helps the creditor by set procedures for using its coercive powers to satisfy his claim against the debtor's will, unless the debtor's co-operation is required, when it will influence his will with forceful sanctions, threatened or applied.

We shall devote no further attention to the execution of money claims such as judgments for the price of goods. This is done in all countries by having state execution officials seize and sell the property of the debtor and then hand the proceeds of the sale to the creditor. Legal systems naturally have different procedures depending on the type of property which is to be seized: a creditor who wishes to execute on the moveables of the debtor of a money claim in England must ask the court for a writ of 'fieri facias' and hand it to the 'sheriff' as the execution officer, while in Germany and France the court execution official ('huissier') proceeds to seizure ('saisie-exécution') as soon as the creditor has obtained a judgment containing a clause of execution or 'formule exécutoire'.

For the details of the procedure in France see art. 583 ff. Code de procédure civile, in England Orders 45 ff. Rules of the Supreme Court, and for Germany, where the rules are extremely detailed, §§704 ff., 803 ff. Code of Civil Procedure, as well as the provisions of the Law of Forced Auction Sales (*Zwangsversteigerungsgesetz*).—It may be mentioned here that the non-payment of a judgment debt in modern legal systems hardly ever leads to 'personal execution' against the debtor in the form of imprisonment. In France the 'contrainte per corps' was abolished for private claims by the law of 22 July 1867; so also in England, where, however, s. 5 of the Debtors Act 1869, leaves the judge power to imprison a debtor for up to six weeks if he malevolently refuses to pay: in Germany a rule which is hardly ever invoked permits the imprisonment of a debtor after seizure has proved fruitless if he unjustifiably refuses to draw up a complete inventory of his assets and guarantee its accuracy under oath: see §§807, 899 ff. Code of Civil Procedure.

Two questions therefore remain for discussion. Under what circumstances may a contractor ask a court to issue judgment ordering the other party to perform the contract? How is such a judgment, not being simply a money judgment, actually executed?

II

In *German* law and in related systems it is axiomatic that a creditor has the right to bring a claim for performance of a contract and to obtain a judgment ordering the debtor to fulfil it. For this purpose it is immaterial whether the debtor's obligation is to deliver goods pursuant to a sale, to vacate a dwelling house, or to produce a work of art. The view that it is of the very essence of an obligation that it be actionable in this sense is so fundamental that it is not expressly stated in any legislative text, but the words of §241 of the Civil Code, that the creditor is entitled, on the grounds of the creditor–debtor relationship, 'to demand performance from the debtor', imply that actual performance may be demanded before a court and that a judgment ordering performance in kind may be issued by it.

A judgment ordering the debtor to perform his contract in kind can be issued only if performance by the debtor is still *possible*. As the Reichsgericht once said, it would be 'nonsensical to order a person to perform when it has been established that performance is objectively impossible' (RGZ 107, 15, 17). Accordingly a judgment for performance cannot be issued if, for instance, a picture has been destroyed after sale, or if a ship has been requisitioned while under charter, or if, just before the première, an opera-singer is rendered so hoarse by a bad cold that for the duration she cannot sing; in such cases the creditor can bring only a claim for damages.

This can admittedly lead to unfair results when goods are in very short supply. Suppose that a person hands a gold wrist-watch to a jeweller for repair and that the watch is stolen from the jeweller because he failed to look after it properly. A claim for money damages is not of much use in a situation such as existed shortly after the Second World War when money was virtually valueless and watches could not be bought at all but only obtained in exchange for other goods of value. The courts were able to assist here by invoking the view contained in §249 BGB, that the principal obligation of a person bound to make compensation is to 'bring about the situation which would have existed were it not for the occurrence of the circumstance which rendered him liable to make compensation'. This basic principle of 'restitution in kind' (*Naturalrestitution*), which is not of great significance in normal times, was then brought into play in cases where the defendant was responsible for his inability to hand over a specific chattel intact or at all; he was ordered to make compensation, not by the payment of money, which was then almost worthless, but by transferring to the plaintiff a different chattel of approximately the same value, either one out of his own stock or one which he had obtained in exchange for goods of his own. Thus in the case given above, the defendant jeweller was ordered to deliver a watch of equal value (AG Hamburg Süddt. JZ 1946, 180; compare also OLG Hamm MDR 1947, 100; LG Oldenburg Süddt. JZ 1946, 179). Decisions of this type ceased when the economic situation returned to normal.

When the contract fixes a time for performance and the debtor has allowed the time to elpase, another type of impossibility may arise. If the performance is such that, in itself or in the context of the contract, it can take place only within the fixed period—for example, the delivery of a wedding-cake or the participation of a singer in a Christmas concert—then, when the due date has gone by, the performance has become *impossible* and no judgment for performance can be given. But suppose a parcel of goods is to be delivered by the vendor in late October; delay does not necessarily render delivery futile, and so in November or December the purchaser can insist on a judgment for performance. In such a case the vendor may of course be in some doubt whether he is still bound to deliver or whether he must just be ready to pay damages. Doubts of this kind are undesirable, especially in commercial matters, as §376 Commercial Code shows: this provision lays down that if in a contract of sale a specific date or fixed period is set for performance and not adhered to, the innocent party can, under certain conditions, demand damages or else withdraw from the contract; if despite the delay, he wants to insist on performance in kind, he must so notify the other party as soon as the contractual date has passed; if he does not do so, his claim for performance will fail. The same result flows from §326 BGB on the expiry of the extra time allowed to dilatory contractor (compare below Ch. 43 II 2).

It is clear from the Civil Code and the Code of Civil Procedure that their draftsmen believed that a disappointed contractor who decided to sue would always choose to claim performance. This is not what happens in practice, but their belief explains the fact that several texts concern themselves in loving detail with the creditor who, having brought a claim for performance, then finds that this is not the right step and that a claim for damages makes better sense. Thus, according to §268 Code of Civil Procedure, it is not a change of claim (*Klagänderung*) of which the defendant can complain as being an unfair surprise or procedural trick if a plaintiff in the course of a suit abandons his claim for performance in kind and prosecutes his claim for damages instead. A plaintiff who has actually obtained a judgment for performance may, instead of executing it, wish to proceed immediately to a judgment for damages; this case also has been foreseen and carefully regulated. By §283 Civil Code the creditor who has obtained judgment for performance can fix a time within which performance from the debtor must be forthcoming. On the expiry of this period the plaintiff can forthwith institute a claim for damages, against which the only admissible defence is that performance has been rendered impossible by circumstances not entailing the defendant's responsibility and arising after the judgment for performance was handed down (see RGZ 107, 15, 19). These well-intentioned provisions are rarely used today. They stem from the legislator's belief that the creditor who did not know or could not prove that performance by the debtor was impossible would always bring a claim for performance. Today commercial men resolve this uncertainty differently: they grant the debtor an additional period for performance in accordance with §326 Civil Code and, if this period elapses without result, they forthwith institute a claim for damages (see below Ch. 43 II 2).

Claims for performance may not be very frequent in practice, since creditors bring them only when their interest in performance cannot easily be reckoned in money, but it remains the theory that, in a case where performance is still possible and the creditor so elects, the courts are bound to deliver judgment ordering the debtor to perform. Such a judgment is, however, only of use if the legal system provides the means to make it effective. Accordingly one must turn to the question whether and how such a judgment can be enforced.

The way in which the question is dealt with in German law is quite characteristic. The Code of Civil Procedure carefully distinguishes all the various types of claim which might underlie a judgment for performance, and provides quite distinct forms of execution for each of them. Thus §§883–6 of the Code deal with the execution of judgments on claims for the delivery of property. The method provided—the only method—is for the bailiff (*Gerichtsvollzieher*) to take the chattel from the debtor or to require him to leave the premises, with the help of the police, if necessary, and then to hand over the chattel or premises to the creditor. If the claim on which the creditor has obtained judgment is that the debtor should take some positive action other than handing over property, a distinction is made. If the act in question is one which could be equally well performed by someone else, that is, it need not be performed by the debtor personally but is, as the Code of Civil Procedure puts it, *vertretbar*, then the method of execution—the only method—is for the creditor, on the authority of the court granted at his request, to have the act performed by a third party at the expense of the debtor (*Ersatzvornahme*, §887 Code of Civil Procedure).

As examples of acts which are *vertretbar*, or capable of substitute performance, one may cite manual tasks which call for no especial talent and can therefore be carried out by third parties—the execution of building operations (LG Hagen JR 1948, 314), the installation of a lift in an apartment block (KG JW 1927, 1945), the printing of a manuscript (OLG Munich MDR 1955, 682). The making of an extract from the books of a business or the production of its accounts may also be 'vertretbar' if an expert could do it after inspecting the debtor's records (OLG Hamburg MDR 1955, 43).

If the act to which the creditor lays claim is one which can be performed only by the debtor himself, it is said to be *unvertretbar*. In such a case the method of execution provided by the Code of Civil Procedure (§888) is to threaten the unwilling debtor with a fine or imprisonment. Should the debtor still not perform, he may be imprisoned for up to six months in all; fines, unlimited in amount, are collected like judgment debts, and go to the Treasury.

These means of execution are available only when the act in question 'depends exclusively on the will of the debtor', in the words of §888 Code of Civil Procedure. They are therefore not available if, for the performance of the required act, the debtor needs the co-operation of others over whose behaviour he has no direct influence such as is enjoyed by an employer over his staff or by a parent over his children. For example, suppose that a lessee has obtained a judgment which requires the lessor to maintain peace and quiet in a house occupied by third parties; such peace and quiet cannot be ensured by the good intentions of the lessor alone, but requires that of the residents as well; in such a case the minatory sanctions of §888 Code of Civil Procedure cannot be deployed against the lessor (OLG Munich ZZP 1929, 361). Nor can they be used against a debtor whose obligation is to do something which calls for special artistic or scientific talent, for here also the performance of the act does not depend exclusively on the debtor's will. However good his intentions may be, a composer cannot compose his sonata nor a law professor write his commentary without the right inspiration, mood, energy, and other preconditions of great spiritual creativity (see OLG Frankfurt OLGE 29, 251). Finally the Code of Civil Procedure lists in §888 several more specific cases where these methods of penal pressure are unavailable. Thus one may not execute a judgment obtained by one spouse requiring the other to reconstitute the conditions of married life, and one may not execute a judgment which orders the defendant to perform services under a contract of employment. The employer may certainly obtain a judgment which imposes on the employee the duty to perform his obligations under the contract of service (so, in terms, RGZ 72, 393, 394), but this judgment cannot be enforced, because the employee must at all times remain free to decide how to dispose of his labour, even if this involves a breach of contract: in such a case the employer must content himself with a claim for damages.

There is a special regulation for the case where the positive act required of the debtor by the judgment is a declaration of intention or consent (*Willenserklärung*); the effect of §894 Code of Civil Procedure is that as soon as the judgment is final the declaration is deemed to have been made.

If, instead of requiring the debtor to take positive action, the judgment orders him to *abstain* from action or to *permit* someone else to take action, §890 Code of Civil Procedure applies: should the debtor act in breach of such a duty, the court may, on the application of the creditor, imprison him or fine him, the fine going once again to the Treasury. The debtor must have notice that such sanctions are to be invoked: this notice is normally contained in the original judgment.

III

In the *Romanistic* systems also the claim for performance of a contract is generally recognized. Art 1184 par. 2 of the French Code civil provides that a party to a synallagmatic contract who has not received what he was promised is entitled to demand resolution of the contract and damages or 'to require the other to perform the agreement in so far as that is still possible' (see Civ. 6 Jan. 1932, DH 1932, 114; see also art. 1453 Codice civile). Sales contracts are covered by a special provision of the Code civil: according to art. 1610, instead of seeking resolution of the contract for non-delivery, the purchaser may demand that the vendor put him in possession of the goods. In the same way the creditor may obtain a judgment requiring the debtor to perform the promised services (Civ. 20 Jan. 1913, S. 1913. 1. 386), to provide business particulars (Civ. 7 Nov. 1923, D. 1926. 1. 171), to vacate a dwelling (Paris 28 April 1948, JCP 1948. II. 4333), or to name an arbitrator (Paris 1 March 1951, DH 1951, 1. 315).

There is, however, another provision of the French Code civil which seems in terms to prohibit any judgment which obliges a debtor to act or refrain from acting in a particular way. This is art. 1142 Code civil: 'toute obligation de faire ou de ne pas faire se résout en dommages et intérêts, en cas d'inexécution de la part du débiteur'. ('The obligation to do or not to do something gives rise, on non-performance, to liability in damages.')

The underlying idea is that, man being a free and responsible being, he should not be coerced by the state into behaving in a particular way. This is a most praiseworthy idea but it is far too vague, and its formulation in art. 1142 Code civil, as experience has shown, is much too sweeping. In consequence, the vendor's obligation to deliver the goods is treated as an 'obligation de donner' and not as an 'obligation de faire' (see art. 1101 Code civil), so that the purchaser, who becomes owner of the goods at the time of the contract, if they are specific, and at the time of ascertainment, usually, if they are purchased by description (see art. 1138 Code civil), can make good his claim to delivery, once it is reduced to judgment, by having the *huissier* seize the goods *manu militari* from the vendor and transfer them to him ('saise-revendication' under art. 826 Code de procédure civile). The basic principle is further restricted by arts. 1143 and 1144. Under art. 1144 a court may empower the creditor to have a third party do the act promised by the debtor and charge the debtor with the cost. Of course this is done only where the personal participation of the debtor is not required, that is, in cases where the act in question is impersonal or, as §887 of the German Code of Civil Procedure has it, 'vertretbar'. But although the 'surrogate performance' of art. 1144 Code civil looks like what German jurists would call an act of forced execution, in fact it is rather different. Forced execution in Germany only begins after the trial is over and the consequent judgment falls to be implemented, but the French courts use art. 1144 during the trial itself, either to authorize the creditor to procure the performance of the act or to grant the creditor's claim for payment of the expense of the substitute performance, as costs rather than as damages.

The courts have occasionally used this article where a disappointed purchaser has bought goods in a covering transaction: the person who has bought generic goods and not received them can buy similar goods from another source and then charge the vendor at fault with the excess costs as 'surrogate performance' under art. 1144 Code civil; by trade usage this does not require the usual judicial authorization in advance. Such a covering transaction would never be seen as an act of execution in the proper sense by German lawyers, but simply as an act which crystallizes the amount of harm suffered by the purchaser.

Art. 1143 Code civil also anticipates the execution of judgments already rendered by permitting the court to threaten a defaulting debtor with special sanctions during the trial. If the debtor is bound to refrain from certain behaviour, art. 1143 empowers the creditor to demand the removal or avoidance of anything made or done by the debtor in breach of this duty (for example, see Civ. 17 Dec. 1963, Gaz. Pal. 1964. 1. 158). In order to 'execute' this claim for avoidance, according to art. 1143, the creditor may himself, under judicial authorization, remove anything constructed by the debtor in breach of his duty, such as a building put up in contravention of a servitude, and charge the debtor with the expense of so doing.

We may sum up by saying that French law generally admits the issuance of judgments for performance in kind but enforces them in a very grudging manner. Leaving aside the execution of claims for payment, only judgments for the delivery of specified goods are covered by special rules of execution: these the *huissier* may seize directly. If the judgment concerns other acts or abstentions neither the Code civil nor the Code de procédure civile prescribes any specific means of execution, although if the promised act is impersonal the creditor can ask at the trial for power under arts. 1143 f. Code civil to do or have someone else do what the debtor shoud have done and to charge him for it.

This legislative coverage of compulsory execution of judgments in specie is obviously quite inadequate. In an attempt to fill the gaps, the French courts have, since the beginning of the nineteenth century, developed a special coercive technique called the 'astreinte'. On issuing a judgment requiring a debtor to perform *in natura* a court may order that for every day he remains in default the debtor must pay a specified sum of money to the plaintiff as 'astreinte'. The courts have two forms of *astreinte* at their discretionary disposal. The 'astreinte provisoire' (or 'astreinte comminatoire') is so called because when the court later comes to finalize the amount of *astreinte* payable by the debtor it is not bound by its prior decision and may order the payment of a lesser sum than was threatened. But there is also the 'astreinte définitive', where the original judicial order is final, especially with regard to the amount to be paid per day, week, or month; later proceedings do the simple arithmetic of multiplying the sum fixed in the judgment by the number of units of time during which the debtor has remained in default contrary to the terms of the judgment. The threatened *astreinte* expires at the end of the period fixed in the judgment, but if the debtor has still not performed, the creditor can ask the court to apply a new *astreinte* for a further period.

See, for example, Riom 10 Dec. 1956, S. 1957, 112, where the creditor had obtained a judgment carrying an *astreinte* and ordering the defendant to execute certain building operations. The judgment remained unsatisfied and the creditor sought both to 'liquidate' or quantify the amount of *astreinte* to be paid by the debtor, and also to have a new *astreinte* imposed for a further period of three months. The court accepted the plaintiff's claim, held the debtor liable to pay an *astreinte* of 900,000 francs and ordered him 'to proceed with the execution of the works specified in the order of 31 May 1954 within a new period of three months starting from the date of this judgment, on pain of an astreinte of 10,000 francs per day of default . . . '

It must not be supposed that an *astreinte* is available only where the statutory methods of execution are inapplicable or impractical. An *astreinte* may be issued to promote the delivery of a specified motor vehicle (Com. 12 Dec. 1966, Bull. civ. 1966. III. 424) or the conveyance and delivery of landed property (Req. 18 Nov. 1907, S. 1913. 1. 386), although in such cases direct execution through the *huissier* is perfectly possible. Judgments ordering a tenant to vacate a dwelling may be executed by having the *huissier* expel the tenant by force, with the assistance of other state organs if necessary, but the courts regularly apply the *astreinte* in such judgments for possession because in the post-war years when homelessness was a serious risk the state authorities used to refuse to assist in executing such judgments. The courts therefore resorted to coercion by means of the *astreinte* so as to induce the tenant to agree to quit. This device the leglislator also defused by enacting in a law of 21 July 1949 that judgments for possession against tenants could carry only *astreintes provisoires* which could be finalized only after the tenant had vacated the premises and must never amount to more than the loss actually sustained by the owner.

Nor do the courts hesitate to impose *astreintes* in cases where the creditor might have used the method of 'surrogate performance' offered by art. 1144 Code civil, as where a neighbour was ordered to remove a boundary wall (Civ. 7 April 1965, Bull. civ. 1965. I. 192) or a vendor to dismantle faulty machinery he had delivered (Civ. 20 Jan. 1913, S. 1913. 1. 386). The Court of Cassation has recently held that an *astreinte* may even be attached to a money judgment, at least if the creditor has no other effective means of enforcing his claim for payment. This was the situation in Com. 17 April 1956, JCP 1956. 9330 (noted VELLIEUX). The city of Marseilles had failed to honour a judgment rendered against it in respect of compensation for expropriation; the civil judge threatened it with an *astreinte* if it persisted further in delay and was upheld by the Court of Cassation.

Such cases will not often arise, since the *saisie-exécution* of arts. 583 ff. Code de procédure civile provides the normal means of executing money judgments. Nor will a vendor often be required under pain of *astreinte* to deliver generic goods, since the purchaser can normally cover himself in the market and so has no interest in performance by the vendor personally (but see Req. 21 Dec. 1920, DP 1921. 1. 62). But the situation may be different in wartime when goods are in short supply; then the purchaser might well seek performance by the vendor *in natura*, and the latter could be ordered to deliver on pain of *astreinte* if he did not (for example, see Trib. com. Seine 16 Dec. 1919, DP 1920. 2. 34; Besançon 4 Dec. 1946, Gaz, Pal. 1947. 1. 20).

The *astreinte* really comes into its own when there is no statutory means for executing judgments, for example, where the debtor has been ordered to do something other than pay money or deliver things, such as issue a certificate of employment (Soc. 29 June 1966, Bull. civ. 1966. IV. 534), or move his business

(Com. 6 Oct. 1966, Bull. civ. 1966. III. 424). The *astreinte* is also used where the plaintiff wants to prevent the defendant from doing something, the difference here being that the amount of the *astreinte* depends on how often the debtor contravened his duty to desist rather than on how long he remained in breach. Thus when a soft drink manufacturer was enjoined from using bottles so like those of the plaintiff as to constitute unfair competition, the *astreinte* was in the form that the defendant should pay 10 francs 'par infraction constatée' (Com. 31 March 1965, Bull. civ. 1965. III. 219).

Superficially it might seem that the *astreinte* is like the money penalties which may be imposed *in terrorem* under §§888 and 890 of the German Code of Civil Procedure in judgments which order the debtor to cease and desist or to co-operate in doing the requisite act. There is an important distinction, however, since the *astreintes* go into the pocket of the creditor while the monetary penalties go to the state treasury.

This significant difference becomes comprehensible if we remember that in France it was the courts which invented the *astreinte* and had to do it *extra legem*, 'en marge des textes', for they realized that in view of the inadequacy of the statutory methods of execution the only way of ensuring that judgments were satisfied was by threatening defaulting debtors with monetary penalties. Even if the idea that such payments might be made to the *state* had occurred to the French courts, they could hardly have acted on it in the absence of any statutory basis. It was much simpler to see the *astreinte* as a special form of threatening and granting *compensatory damages*, and so link it to a well-known institution of private law. This indeed was the basic point of departure for the French courts. Since the *astreinte* was a *threat* designed to induce the debtor to co-operate, it was seen that the amount he was threatened with having to pay should not be limited to the harm suffered by the creditor but should depend on the probable recalcitrance of the debtor and his capacity to perform. But when it came to quantification or 'liquidation' of the *astreinte*, the judge was to fix it solely in relation to the amount of economic harm provably suffered by the creditor through the failure to perform or delay in performing. In the nineteenth century the debtor in these cases was always threatened with the payment of 'dommages et intérêts': the word 'astreinte' entered legal language rather later.

But if at the end of the day the *astreinte* turns into an award of damages it loses all its coercive character. As French writers have often said, there is little point in a judge's threatening a debtor with a draconian *astreinte* in the event of non-performance if it is clear that he will never have to pay more than simple compensation. After many years of indecision in the courts, there are now many cases where the Court of Cassation has held that the *astreinte* has nothing to do with compensation and should normally be related in amount to the degree of the debtor's fault in not performing and to his economic circumstances. This clearly gives the institution a penal character: no longer is it a special form of damages award, but the open threat of a real private punishment.

The leading decision, noted by HOLLEAUX, is Civ. 20 Oct. 1959, D. 1959, 537. The defendant electricity company, sued by a neighbour, had been ordered 'sous astreinte' to execute certain building operations on its land. The defendant failed to do the work, and the plaintiff had the *astreinte* 'liquidated'; at the same time he asked for a new *astreinte*, and the court granted it, for a period of three months. This too failed to have any effect and again the plaintiff obtained a liquidation and yet another *astreinte*, limited as before to three months, of 10,000 francs per day. Yet again nothing happened. Only when the court fixed the amount of the *astreinte* at 900,000 francs (90 days at 10,000 francs per day) was the defendant stirred to action. He argued that on liquidation an *astreinte* must be limited to the amount of harm actually suffered. The court of appeal rejected this argument and upheld the judgment (Riom 10 Dec. 1956, S. 1957, 112), as did the Court of Cassation, which said that the *astreinte provisoire* is 'une mesure de contrainte entièrement distincte des dommages-intérêts . . . un moyen de vaincre la résistance opposée à l'exécution d'une condamnation'. It is not intended as compensation for the harm the creditor may have suffered as a result of the delay in performance but should normally be quantified 'en fonction de la gravité de la faute du débiteur récalcitrant et de ses facultés'. To the same effect see Civ. 20 Jan. 1960, JCP 1960. II. 11483; Civ. 12 July 1960, Bull. civ. 1960. I. 319; Civ. 17 March 1965, Bull. civ. 1965. I. 143.

Although the *astreinte* is an entrenched institution of French court practice, it has constantly been criticized in legal writings, and these criticisms gain in force as its coercive and penal character is increasingly admitted by the courts. Indeed, it is not at all clear why the creditor, in addition to receiving compensation for the harm he has suffered, should also obtain the amount of the *astreinte provisoire* which is designed to overcome the debtor's reluctance to honour the judgment, especially if the *astreinte* is fixed in relation to the culpability of the debtor's behaviour and to the extent of his financial resources. The hybrid nature of the *astreinte* seems to cause a certain malaise in France: when a bill to put the *astreinte* on a proper statutory footing was being discussed in 1971, it was seriously proposed—though the proposal was not adopted—that the sum payable by the debtor should go half to the state and half to the creditor. The Law of 5 July 1972 provides that the *astreinte* goes in full to the creditor, and also makes clear that the purpose of the *astreinte* is to put pressure on the debtor rather than to compensate the creditor.

Art. 5 of the statute empowers the courts, even of their own motion, to impose an *astreinte* 'pour assurer l'exécution de leurs décisions'. Art. 6 makes it crystal clear that the *astreinte* 'est indépendante des dommages-intérêts'. For a detailed explanation of the statute see CHABAS, D. 1972. *Chron.* 271.—It is to be noted that in recent years other European legal systems have imported the *astreinte*: for *Belgium*, see art. 1385 bis, Code judiciaire, and GLANSDORFF, *JT* 95 (1980) 312; DHOORE, *JT* 96 (1981) 529; MOREAU-MARGREVE, *Ann. Fac. Liège* 47 (1982) 11, and DAVID-CONSTANT, *Études Alex*

Weill (1983) 185; for the *Netherlands*, see arts. 611a ff. Civil Procedure Ordinance, soon to be arts. 3.11.5 ff. new Civil Code; for *Portugal*, see art. 829-A Código civil, with the peculiarity that the sum is divided in equal parts between the state and the creditor; for *Yugoslavia* see art. 294 Law of Obligations, and STUDIN, *Jugoslav Law* 1982, p. 3.

IV

In both German and French law, as we have seen, a contractor is in principle entitled to demand that his contract be performed in specie. The standpoint of the *Common Law* is quite different: if a contractor does not do as he promised, the innocent party's only right, in general, is to bring a claim for breach of contract, a claim which is historically derived from the tort remedy of trespass and which always leads to monetary compensation or damages. The idea that the conclusion of the contract engenders an enforceable duty to perform it is a notion foreign to the Common Law; instead, it starts from the proposition expressed by O. W. HOLMES (*The Common Law* (1881) 301) that 'the only universal consequence of a legally binding promise is that the law makes the promisor pay damages if the promised act does not come to pass'.

In saying that the Common Law does not render judgments obliging the debtor to perform his promise, we are referring only to the Common Law in the narrow sense, that is, to the rules of law historically developed by the royal courts. But in addition the equity of the Chancellor and later of the Court of Chancery gradually produced rules which in very hard cases mollified the rigid principle that claims for performance were inadmissible. Under these rules a plaintiff could exceptionally claim 'specific performance' if he could persuade the Equity Court that the remedies available to him 'at law', especially the action for damages for breach of contract, were inadequate. In both England and the United States today the distinction between the jurisdictions of the courts of law and of equity has largely been abolished and all courts now apply concurrently the rules developed 'at law' and 'in equity', but the idea still remains that the claim for specific performance is exceptional. Even today it is constantly emphasized that the grant of a decree of specific performance remains 'in the complete discretion' of the judge, although this discretion, as a result of much court practice, has long been exercised in accordance with fixed rules, subject to the principle of *stare decisis* as much as other areas of Anglo-American Law.

The most important requirement which a person must satisfy if he seeks a decree of specific performance is that the normal sanction of damages is 'inadequate' and that he has an interest in the performance of the contract which cannot well be translated into money terms. Where the contract is to transfer land or real rights, the creditor's interest in the land in question cannot be adequately estimated in money if there is no identical or similar plot of land in existence or for sale. The situation would of course be different if the sale were of a terraced house or a standard plot of land in a new develpment area. Even so the claim for performance is *always* granted in such cases, even if on the facts a claim for damages would be quite adequate. Sales of other property are treated differently. With regard to sales of securities, a distinction is made: the claim for damages is perfectly adequate as a remedy for the purchaser of treasury bonds, but if the sale concerns shares which are not to be bought in the stock-market or privately, a claim for specific performance is granted. The sale of *goods* is covered by legislation. English courts may apply s. 52 of the Sale of Goods Act 1979 at the instance of the purchaser of 'specific or ascertained goods' and issue judgment 'that the contract shall be performed specifically'. It is in the court's direction whether to issue such a judgment or not. In the United States §2-716(1) of the Uniform Commercial Code prescribes generally that specific performance may be decreed 'where the goods are unique or in other proper circumstances', and a claim for performance is normally granted if the sale is of specific goods which are very rare or extremely valuable or of a special sentimental value to the purchaser, such as an heirloom, a triptych, a Renaissance mirror, a valuable snuff-box, or a horse already familiar to the purchaser. In sales of generic goods, on the other hand, a claim for damages is normally adequate since the purchaser can fairly easily cover himself by buying from elsewhere. The courts have sometimes granted specific performance even of sales of generic goods, especially in the United States where they are rather sceptical of the old doctrine that the claim for specific performance is exceptional. This is true, for example, of the 'requirement contract', whereby a supplier binds himself to supply a customer with raw materials or other goods as his needs arise. Here the courts decree specific performance against the supplier even if the materials could, at a pinch, be procured from elsewhere, provided that the supply would be uncertain or unreliable or would make for grave difficulties in the customer's business.

According to the official commentary to §2-716 UCC, cases of this sort present 'the typical commercial specific performance situation', but the courts in England are very hesitant in this area and have been criticized for it by TREITEL (above p. 504) 225 ff. For the American cases, see, for example, *Curtice Brothers' Co.* v. *Catts*, 72 NJ Eq. 831, 66 A. 935 (1907); *Elk Refining Co.* v. *Falling Rock Coal Co.*, 92 W. Va. 479, 115 SE 431 (1922); *Griffin* v. *Oklahoma Natural Gas Corp.*, 37 F. 2d 545, (10 cir. 1930); *Eastern Rolling Mill Co.* v. *Michlovitz*, 157 Md. 51, 145 A. 378 (1929). Even in England a recent decision points in this direction. In *Sky Petroleum* v. *VIP Petroleum*, [1974] 1 WLR 576 the defendant had a long-term contract to supply large quantities of petrol for the plaintiff's petrol stations. A tremendous increase in the price of oil made the defendant reluctant to perform the contract, and he ceased delivering for no sufficient reason. The plaintiff sought an injunction to prevent the defendant from withholding supplies of petrol. GOULDING J. stated that this was really a claim for specific performance since the plaintiff wanted the defendant to do something, namely to resume the contractual deliveries, rather than to desist from doing something. Although normally the non-delivery of generic goods gives rise to a claim for damages only, the judge here issued the order sought because petrol was so exceptionally scarce that the plaintiff had no other source of supply.

The inadequacy of a claim for damages is not the only relevant factor when a decree of specific performance is sought. The courts often ask whether the *execution* of a judgment for performance would involve great inconvenience. It is an argument *against* the granting of a decree of specific performance that the court might find it very difficult or time-consuming to ascertain whether it had been obeyed or that such ascertainment, in the case of long-term contracts, might be long delayed. Thus during the trial itself the court has an eye to the possibilities of prompt enforcement of the judgment, and for the same reason a claim for specific performance is denied if the debtor's obligation under the contract is so imprecise that it would be difficult to execute any judgment on the ground of 'vagueness' or 'uncertainty'.

The leading case in England is *Ryan* v. *Mutual Tontine Westminster Chambers Association*, [1893] 1 Ch. 116. In a lease to the plaintiff tenant the defendant landlord had undertaken to engage a porter to live in the basement of the dwelling and do specified tasks for the plaintiff. The plaintiff sought judgment against the defendant ordering him to perform his obligation *in natura*. The court rejected the claim on the ground that specific performance could not be decreed as the proper execution of such a long-term contract required 'constant superintendence by the Court'.—Difficulties in enforcement also provide the reason for denying specific performance of contracts for the construction of houses or the carrying out of large building operations, but the courts make exceptions where a claim for damages would not answer the plaintiff's interests, where the building operations have been sufficiently specified by plans or drawings, and, where finally, at any rate in England, the defendant is in possession of the land where the building is to take place: see *Wolverhampton Corp.* v. *Emmons*, [1901] 1 KB 515; *Carpenters' Estates Ltd* v. *Davies*, [1940] Ch. 160.—Here, too, American courts grant specific performance more readily: see, for example, *Fleischer* v. *James Drug Stores*, 1 NJ 138, 62 A. 2d 383 (1948); *Gregson-Robinson Stores Inc.* v. *Iris Construction Corp.*, 8 NYS 2d 133, 168 NE 2d 377 (1960); *Roberts* v. *Brewer*, 371 SW 2d 424 (Tex. 1963).—*City Stores Co.* v. *Ammermann*, 266 F. Supp. 766 (DDC. 1967) is an excellent example of the care with which American courts weigh the plaintiff's interest in obtaining an order for specific performance as against the difficulties which a court would face in determining whether or not the defendant had conformed to the order granted. See also Restatement (Second) of Contracts (1981) §366 and LINZER, 81 *Colum. L. Rev.* 111 (1981).

Specific performance will not be granted if the contract calls for personal services from the defendant. One reason given for this is that otherwise the defendant would be forced into a kind of involuntary servitude; another and more realistic reason is that services performed under such coercion would probably be of doubtful quality, and a third, not very convincing, reason is that it would be extremely difficult for the court to determine whether the services so performed were in accordance with the contract. In consequence, a singer cannot be ordered by judgment to give the concerts she had contracted to give. The court can however help the plaintiff in such a case by issuing a judgment forbidding the singer to appear for any of the plaintiff's competitors during the period of the contract. Such a judgment is called an 'injunction' and can only be rendered if two conditions are satisfied: first, it must clearly appear from the contract that the defendant is bound not to work for the contractor's competitors; secondly, the injunction must not debar the defendant from all activity whatsoever, since otherwise he would be indirectly forced, unemployment not being a real alternative, to perform the contract for the plaintiff.

On this see *Lumley* v. *Wagner*, (1852) 1 De GM & G. 604, 64 Eng. Rep. 1209; *Whitwood Chemical Co.* v. *Hardman*, [1891] 2 Ch. 416; *Mortimer* v. *Beckett*, [1920] 1 Ch. 571; *Warner Bros.* v. *Nelson*, [1937] 1 KB 209. For the American cases, see CORBIN §§1204 ff.

If judgment has been issued against the defendant ordering him to do or not to do a particular act, apart from the payment of money, and the defendant fails to obey the order for performance or acts in breach of the injunction the court has a whole series of different ways of enforcing the judgment. Like most of the law of procedure the relevant rules are to be found in the Rules of the Supreme Court rather than in a comprehensive code of procedure, the Rules of the Supreme Court being laid down pursuant to a legislative mandate in s. 99 of the Supreme Court of Judicature (Consolidation) Act, 1925 by a special committee, called the 'Rule Committee', composed of the Lord Chancellor, senior judges, and lawyers.

Since time immemorial, English judges have reserved the right, though it is nowhere written down, to treat many kinds of behaviour as 'contempt of court'; they treat the non-performance of a judgment as a 'contempt' and imprison or fine the debtor for it. This power is recognized and regulated by the Rules of the Supreme Court (see Orders 45 and 52), but what strikes the German observer is that there are no specific rules to limit the extent and kind of punishment which may be imposed or the ways in which the execution of the decision to punish ('order of committal') is started or stopped. In all these questions the judges have a very extensive discretion. Instead of fining or confining the debtor, the court may issue a 'writ of sequestration': the sheriff then confiscates the entire moveable and immoveable property of the debtor 'until the defendant shall clear his contempt'. If the debtor has been ordered to hand over a moveable, the judge can issue a 'writ of delivery' which instructs the sheriff to take the thing from the debtor and deliver it to the creditor. The same function is performed by the 'writ of possession' if the debtor has to deliver up landed property. A judge may also, if this seems practicable to him, empower the creditor or a third party to do or procure to be done the act required of the debtor and to charge the debtor for the expense of so doing. It lies in the proper discretion of the judge to decide which of these various possibilities of enforcement to adopt in a particular case.

On the whole matter see Order 45 of the Rules of the Supreme Court. American rules are to much the same effect; see for example, Rule 70 of the Federal Rules of Civil Procedure: if a judgment ordering the debtor to convey land, to give particulars, or to 'perform any other specific act' remains unperformed, the court may order performance by a sutstitute, it may confiscate the debtor's property in an effort to cure his recalcitrance, it may punish him for 'contempt of court', it may issue a 'vesting order' to transfer the property if that is the debtor's duty, or it may issue the relevant 'writ' to the sheriff and empower him to seize from the debtor the thing which is required. The provision does not specify which method is to be adopted in which cases, this obviously being left to the judge's view of the requirements of the individual case.

V

It is plain enough that the legal systems under consideration give very different answers to the questions posed at the beginning of this section. On the Continent a plaintiff is in principle always entitled to a judgment requiring the defendant to perform his contract, while in the Common Law this is allowed only exceptionally. Once such a judgment is issued every legal system has its own special techniques for enforcing it; again these differ quite considerably.

While it is true that a claim for performance is the normal sanction in German and French law and that specific performance is regarded as exceptional in the Common Law, closer scrutiny reveals that the actual contrast is not quite so sharp. In Germany, on the one hand, where the claim to performance is regarded as the primary legal remedy, it does not in practice have anything like the significance originally attached to it, since whenever the failure to receive the promised performance can be made good by the payment of money commercial men prefer to claim damages rather than risk wasting time and money on a claim for performance whose execution may not produce satisfactory results. On the other hand, the traditional Common Law view, explicable only on historical grounds, that specific performance is an exceptional remedy is apparently losing some of its force. This is certainly true in the United States: according to CORBIN there is no doubt 'that the American courts have become progressively more liberal in the granting of this effective remedy and have become less astute in enforcing the requirement that the remedy in damages shall be inadequate' (§1139). And the purpose of §2-716 UCC, according to the official commentary, is to encourage a more generous use of this legal institution in the courts. England is naturally more attached to the old ideas, but even there TREITEL has asked whether it would not be proper to allow the purchaser to claim specific performance in sales contracts generally and to refuse him this remedy only where the defendant vendor has some justifiable interest in resisting it (above p. 504, pp. 215 f.).

In recent years a great debate has taken place in American periodicals on the question whether the judge-made rules regarding the grant of specific performance as opposed to damages are 'efficient' in the economic sense (see Ch. 19 II). The discussion was started by POSNER. In his *Economic Analysis of Law* (2nd edn., 1977) 89 f., he takes the case of a seller who has promised to deliver a specific thing to a buyer for 100. If a third party now offers the seller 200 for the same thing and the buyer in the case of nondelivery would suffer harm of only 150, it is 'efficient' for the seller to break this promise, to pay the buyer 150 and to deliver the thing to the third party for 200, for then the thing ends up in the hands of the person for whom it has the greatest value. It is because the buyer cannot obtain an order for specific performance in such a case that the seller is able to deliver the thing to the third party; the rule is therefore 'efficient'. The ensuing discussion gives an idea of the leading—or, as many would say, misleading—principles of the 'economic analysis of law'. See KRONMAN, 45 *U. Chi. L. Rev.* 351 (1978); SCHWARZ, 89 *Yale LJ* 271 (1979); LINZER, 81 *Colum. L. Rev.* 111 (1981); MURIS, 1982 *Duke* LJ 1053.

The difference in the theoretical bases of the Continental laws and of the Common Law on the point under investigation remains fundamental, to such an extent that, as RABEL predicted long ago (see *RabelsZ* 9 (1935) 1, 69 ff. and 5 *U. Chi. L. Rev.* 543, 549 f. (1938)), attempts to unify the law of international sales on this point have had only a very modest success. Art. 16 of the Uniform Law of Sales allows a court to decline either to order a vendor to deliver the goods or to enforce a judgment ordering him to do so if that is what the court would do if it were applying the *lex fori* to a wholly *domestic* contract. The same rule is now to be found in art. 28 of the (UNCITRAL) Vienna Convention on Contracts for the International Sale of Goods of 1980. In practice this means that an *English* judge, faced with an international sales contract, can dismiss the buyer's claim for performance although a *French* court seised of the same matter would have granted it. There is no doubt that, however unavoidable it may have been, this provision represents a foreign body in a Uniform Law of Sales. A uniform solution analogous to that of the Common Law, was, however, reached by refusing to allow the purchaser to claim performance if he could have entered a covering transaction and it would have been good commercial practice to do so (art. 25; on this see RABEL, *Recht des Warenkaufs* I (1936) 375 ff.).

One can accept such a restriction on the claim to performance without at all endorsing the very much more hesitant attitude of the Common Law to this legal institution as a whole. The view that a claim for performance has an 'exceptional character' is not at all persuasive, although it is perfectly comprehensible from the historical point of view and it admittedly reflects the statistical fact that in practice claims for damages are common and claims for performance are not. This does not, however, justify the way in which the Common Law makes it more difficult for a plaintiff to obtain performance of a contract than to obtain damages for breach of the same contract.

Not all the reasons adduced to support the restrictions on the grant of specific performance are convincing. It is certainly very reasonable to say that a claim for performance is unnecessary where damages would satisfy the plaintiff's interests, but it is not at all clear why it should be for the *court* to decide what the plaintiff's interests are. The very fact that he is seeking judgment for performance shows that the plaintiff thinks damages inadequate, and the fact that the court thinks differently can hardly by itself justify the rejection of his claim. In saying this we are following more progressive American writers, such as DAWSON, who has described the rule in question as an 'unnecessary and irksome restriction on specific performance' (above p. 503, p. 532).

The Common Law rule that a judgment for performance will not issue if its execution would present the court with difficult problems is more comprehensible. Anglo-American judges seem to avoid issuing such judgments as far as possible, and often support their refusal with the argument that the court would find it impossible or difficult to determine whether the debtor's purported performance of the judgment was consonant with the contract. This is not a convincing reason since the question whether performance conforms with the contract is constantly raised in claims for damages and it is no more difficult to answer when it arises in proceedings for enforcement. Perhaps the explanation of this judicial distate for intervening in execution proceedings is to be found in the fact that the Common Law rules in this area are still in a state of disorder, unlike the comparable rules of German law. It is true that the Common Law has all the means of coercion at its disposal, including seizure of property by the sheriff, substitute performance by the creditor, and punishment of the debtor by imprisonment and fines, but whereas the German Code of Civil Procedure sets out a clear system which distinguishes the various types of claim and lays down particular coercive techniques for each type of claim, the underlying idea being that the debtor should only be exposed to the sanctions of fine and imprisonment where satisfaction cannot be had by other less forcible means, the various coercive devices of the Common Law are not put in any rank or order at all, and one cannot find even the fairly obvious idea that punishment for 'contempt of court' should only be imposed under judgments for delivery if an attempt to execute the judgment by seizing the property has been unavailing. Indeed, the idea that judgments for contempt should be the last resort is quite unknown, and it may be that the supposition, which closer inspection shows to be groundless, that every judgment for performance may immediatley lead to the drastic sanctions of fine or imprisonment if the debtor fails to obey it constitutes a further ground for the very circumspect hesitancy with which judges approach claims for specific performance in the Common Law.

On the whole matter see the extremely thoughtful comparative treatment by

DAWSON (above p. 503). He severely criticizes the various doctrines which the Common Law has developed in order to limit the claim for performance and finds it a particular disadvantage that the Anglo-American judge enjoys so great a discretion in the enforcement proceedings: 'Not only the initial decision whether or not to grant specific performance, and on what terms, but the choice and the severity of the sanctions imposed are all remitted to the judge's discretion. Particularly after studying the provisions of the German law one is struck with our own failure to analyze and organize our system of sanctions. Instead of a carefully adjusted scale in which each mode of enforcement is assigned to its special task, we have almost no rules at all to regulate the choice or severity of sanctions' (above p. 503, p. 533).

As we have seen, Continental legal systems, unlike the Common Law, start from the position that if a contractor seeks a judgment for specific performance the court may always grant it. So far as the *enforcement* of such a judgment is concerned, French law with the *astreinte* takes a path different from both German law and the Common Law. The *astreinte* is perfectly comprehensible, indeed inevitable, if one remembers the historical and systematic development of French law and bears in mind that the provision made by the legislator in arts. 1143–4 Code civil for the enforcement of judgments requiring an act or an abstention is highly unsatisfactory. But from the independent position of a comparative lawyer the *astreinte* appears to be an institution of rather dubious value. The fact that the amount of the *astreinte* always goes into the pocket of the creditor has made it sometimes appear in the guise of damages and sometimes wear the dress of a private penalty, but for most of the history of French law it has occupied a rather uncertain and shadowy zone between the two. The closer the *astreinte* comes to a damages claim, the less practical value it has as a means of coercion; the more it takes on the colouring of a private penalty—and this is the direction in which the pendulum has swung in recent years, leading to the Law of 5 July 1972—the more insistent becomes the question why the creditor of a defaulting debtor in such cases should be able to claim not only compensation but an extra profit as well. It may be right from the standpoint of French law to accept that this unjustified enrichment of the creditor is a lesser evil than having no effective means of enforcing judgments at all (as TUNC says, above, p. 504, p. 404), but the comparatist will prefer a solution according to which fines are imposed only where enforcement is impossible without them, as in Germany, and the proceeds of such fines go to the treasury, as they do in the Common Law as well.

43

Breach of Contract

BARTELS/MOTOMURA, 'Haftungsprinzip, Haftungsbefreiung und Vertragsbeendigung beim internationalen Kauf', *RabelsZ* 43 (1979) 649.

A. BLOMEYER 'Schuldverhältnis—Nichterfüllung, Synallagmatischer Vertrag' in VI *Rechtsvergleichendes Handwörterbuch* (ed. Schlegelberger) (1938) 312–49.

BORRICAND, 'La Clause résolutoire expresse dans les contrats', *Rev. trim. dr. civ.* 55 (1957) 433.

V. CAEMMERER, 'Das deutsche Schuldrecht und die Rechtsvergleichung', *NJW* 1956, 569.

——, 'Probleme des Haager einheitlichen Kaufrechts', *AcP* 178 (1978) 121.

——, 'Die wesentliche Vertragsverletzung im internationalen Einheitlichen Kaufrecht', *Festschrift Coing* II (1982) 33.

——, 'Vertragspflichten und Vertragsgültigkeit im internationalen Einheitlichen Kaufrecht', *Festschrift Beitzke* (1979) 35.

CONSTANTINESCO, *Inexécution et faute contractuelle en droit comparé* (1960).

DAWSON, 'Judicial Revision of Frustrated Contracts: The United States', 64 *BUL Rev.* 1 (1984).

DEVLIN, 'The Treatment of Breach of Contract', 1966 *Camb. LJ* 192.

ESMEIN, 'L'Obligation et la responsabilité contractuelles', *Le droit privé français au milieu du XXe siècle, Études offertes à Georges Ripert*, vol. II (1950) 101.

FARNSWORTH, 'Legal Remedies for Breach of Contract', 70 *Colum. L. Rev.* 1145 (1970).

HUBER, 'Zur Dogmatik der Vertragsverletzungen nach Einheitlichem Kaufrecht und deutschem Schuldrecht', *Festschrift v. Caemmerer* (1978) 837.

——, 'Empfiehlt sich die Einführung eines Leistungsstörungsrechts nach dem Vorbild des Einheitlichen Kaufgesetzes?', in: *Gutachten und Vorschläge zur Überarbeitung des Schuldrechts* (ed. Bundesministerium der Justiz, 1981) 647.

JØRGENSEN, 'Die skandinavische Lehre der Vertragsverletzung', *Festschrift Larenz* (1973) 549.

KEGEL/RUPP/ZWEIGERT, *Die Enwirkung des Krieges auf Verträge in der Rechtsprechung Deutschlands, Frankreichs und der Vereinigten Staaten von Amerika* (1941).

LANDFERMANN, *Die Auflösung des Vertrages nach richterlichem Ermessen als Rechtsfolge der Nichterfüllung im französischen Recht* (1968).

LAWSON, 'Fault and Contract, A Few Comparisons', 49 *Tul. L. Rev.* 295 (1975), reprinted in: *The Comparison* (Selected Essays, vol. II, 1977) 347.

RABEL, *Die Unmöglichkeit der Leistung, Festschrift für Bekker* (1907) 171; reprinted in: RABEL, *Gesammelte Aufsätze*, vol. I (1965) 1.

——, 'Über Unmöglichkeit der Leistung und heutige Praxis', *RheinZ* 3 (1911) 467; reprinted in: RABEL, *Gesammelte Aufsätze*, vol. I (1965) 56.

——, 'Zur Lehre von der Unmöglichkeit der Leistung nach österreichischem Recht', *Festschrift zur Jahrhundertfeier des ABGB*, vol. II (1911) 821; reprinted in: RABEL, *Gesammelte Aufsätze*, vol. I (1965) 79.

——, *Das Recht des Warenkaufs*, vol. I (1936, reprinted 1957), vol. II (1958).

——, Zustandekommen und Nichterfüllung schuldrechtlicher Verträge im allgemeinen', *Deutsche Landesreferate zum internationalen Kongreß für Rechtsvergleichung im Haag* (1932) 28 ff.; reprinted in: RABEL, *Gesammelte Aufsätze*, vol. III (1967) 119 ff.

——, 'Zu den allgemeinen Bestimmungen über Nichterfüllung gegenseitiger Verträge', *Festschrift für Dolenc u.a.* (Ljubljana, 1937) 703; reprinted in: RABEL, *Gesammelte Aufsätze*, vol. III (1967) 38 ff.

REU, *Die Unmöglichkeit der Leistung im anglo-amerikanischen Recht* (1935).

RHEINSTEIN, *Die Struktur des vertraglichen Schuldverhältnisses im anglo-amerikanischen Recht* (1932).

RODIÈRE, 'Une notion menacée: La faute ordinaire dans les contrats', *Rev. trim. dr. civ.* (1954) 201.

SIMONÉTOS, *Das Recht der Leistungsstörungen nach dem Entwurf eines griechischen Zivilgesetzbuchs und nach dem Entwurf der Akademie für Deutsches Recht* (1938).

STAEHELIN, *Die Vertragsverletzung im englischen und schweizerischen Privatrecht* (1954).

HEINRICH STOLL, *Die Lehre von den Leistungsstörungen* (1936).

SZLADITS, 'Discharge of Contract by Breach in Civil Law', 2 *Am. J. Comp. L.* 334 (1953).

TITZE, *Die Unmöglichkeit der Leistung nach deutschem bürgerlichem Recht* (1900).

TREITEL, 'Remedies for Breach of Contract', VII *Int. Enc. Comp. L., Contracts in General* (1976) ch. 16.

TUNC, 'Force majeure et absence de faute en matière contractuelle', *Rev. trim. dr. civ.* 43 (1945).

WEITNAUER, 'Vertragsaufhebung und Schadensersatz nach dem Einheitlichen Kaufgesetz und nach geltendem deutschen Recht', *Rechtsvergleichung und Rechtsvereinheitlichung, Festschrift zum 50jährigen Bestehen des Instituts für ausländisches und internationales Privat- und Wirtschaftsrecht der Universität Heidelberg* (1967) 71.

ZWEIGERT, 'Aspects of the German Law of Sale: Some Comparative Aspects of the Law Relating to Sale of Goods', 13 *ICLQ* (Suppl. 1, 1964).

I

IF a vendor refuses to deliver the goods or if the owner of a dwelling declines to allow the tenant to enter on the day fixed in the lease, the buyer or tenant may want to go to court and establish a claim for performance of the contract. The question when he can do this has been dealt with in the previous chapter. But quite other questions may arise. If the goods have been destroyed or the dwelling burnt down, the only questions left for the buyer or tenant are whether this has brought the contract to an end, whether they can reclaim any advance payments they have made and whether they can sue for damages. The same questions also arise if the goods or dwelling are still intact, but the vendor or landlord are late in performing or prove that unforeseen events have made it very difficult or unduly onerous for them to perform. These questions arise also when the purchaser or tenant have been put in possession but the goods are unfit for the purpose envisaged or the house is uninhabitable because the roof leaks or the heating does not work. Finally, even if the actual contract has been performed to the letter, the vendor or landlord may be in breach of other duties which have to be performed if the transaction is to fulfil the purpose for which it was concluded. In such cases it often makes no sense to ask whether the buyer or the tenant still has a claim to performance *in natura* since it is of no practical interest. What the buyer and the tenant in such cases will normally want to know is whether they are still bound by the contract, if and how they may resile from it, and whether they may obtain damages.

The common factor in these situations is the disturbance of the smooth exchange of performances agreed on in the contract owing to the fact that one of the parties, for some reason, has failed to perform the contract altogether or fully or at the right time or place or in some other respect. We shall treat all these cases under the heading of 'breach of contract', including every case in which the performance in fact rendered falls short in some way of what was promised in the contract. In exceptional cases the contracting party will not be responsible for this shortfall, and one might object that one can hardly speak of a 'breach' of contract in such cases. Nevertheless the term 'breach of contract' is preferable to 'non-performance', since it is more flexible, it is used with this meaning in most legal systems, and it perfectly covers the normal case in which the debtor is responsible for the non-performance.

II

The *German* BGB has no unitary concept of breach of contact. Instead it is concerned with two reasons for non-performance and distinguishes between them: *impossibility* of performance and *delay*.

1. *Impossibility*

Under the impression that it was Roman, the BGB adopted the doctrine of impossibility developed in the *Gemeines Recht* by MOMMSEN and WINDSCHEID: a contract is invariably void if at the time the contract was formed the promised performance was objectively incapable of being rendered by anyone ('impossibilium nulla obligatio', §306 BGB; see also art. 20 OR and §878 ABGB). The Code seeks to modify this result by making the contractor who knew or should have known of the initial impossibility pay compensation to the innocent party for any harm he suffers in reliance on the validity of the contract (§307 BGB). An exception is made to the principle of §306 BGB in the case of the sale of a right: if the right does not exist, the sale contract obviously cannot be performed by anyone, but despite §306 BGB it is held valid and the vendor is liable to the purchaser for the loss of his bargain (§437 BGB).

It is now generally agreed that the policy behind the absolute rule of §306 BGB is unsound and that it should be restrictively interpreted (see ZWEIGERT, *Süddt. JZ* 1949, 415).

If an architect promises a house-owner that the house can be reconstructed under his supervision for a certain price, the contract can be construed as meaning that the architect is to pay from his own pocket any excess over the price. Proof that no one in the world could achieve the reconstruction for the stipulated price does not make the contract void under §306 BGB (see RG SeuffA 75 no. 9).—Where a contract, properly construed, puts the risk that performance may be impossible on one of the contracting parties, the courts use the notion of 'undertaking a guarantee' (*Garantieübernahme*), hold the contract valid, and impose full liability for non-performance. The Oberlandesgericht in Hamburg had to decide a case involving a contract for the sale of 1,000 boxes of new potatoes from the Canary Islands 'aboard S.S. *Thekla Bohlen* afloat'. When the vessel arrived in Hamburg it was found that only 106 boxes had been loaded, but the court held that the vendor must pay damages for non-performance. It was certainly true that as the contract was for the whole of an identified cargo this was a sale of specific goods and that the delivery of the specified parcel of goods was impossible, since at the time of the contract not all those goods were on board. Nevertheless the vendor was liable 'because in the sale of a cargo described as "afloat" merchants take the contractual declaration of the vendor to be a warranty or the undertaking of a guarantee that the cargo has been loaded on the named vessel'. (SeuffA 65 no. 160.)

Although the idea of undertaking a guarantee enables the courts to avoid the inequitable consequences of §306 BGB, the regrettable enactment of this rule of initial impossibility has made it necessary to draw a lot of artificial distinctions. Thus as a matter of positive law 'initial impossibility' ('anfängliche Unmöglichkeit') under §306 must be distinguished from 'initial inability' ('anfängliches Unvermögen') where the promisor cannot do what was promised, but someone else could. In 'initial inability' cases most writers and the courts hold that the debtor is always liable even if not at fault. It is said that every person who enters a contract guarantees his ability to perform it, and if this ability does not then exist, for whatever reason, he must nevertheless pay the other party the benefit of the bargain. But is it not perhaps too much to apply this doctrine to *all* cases of initial inability? The real question here, as in cases of initial impossibility, is which of the contracting parties should, in the view of reasonable businessmen, bear the risk of the debtor's inability to perform. As it happens, the dominant view almost always reaches the right result, but this is only because the obstacles which prevent a party from performing are usually attributable to him, so that it is normally correct on the facts to assume that the debtor guaranteed his ability to perform.

One clear case for inclusion here is where a vendor does not own the goods at the time of the sale and is therefore in no position to transfer them to the purchaser (BGH NJW 1960, 720; WM 1972, 656). It is not quite such a clear case if the goods have just been stolen from the vendor without his knowledge before the contract is formed. The Reichsgericht treated this as a case of initial impossibility and declared the contract of sale void under §306 BGB (RGZ 105, 349). This view should be abandoned, not because performance is not 'objectively impossible' (since in theory the vendor and the thief might co-operate and transfer both ownership and possession to the purchaser) but because §306 BGB is a legislative lapse which should be narrowly construed and certainly not applied where the specific goods which have been sold are still in existence. We can treat this as a case of initial inability without having to make the vendor liable for the benefit of the bargain. The sale by a private citizen to a musician of a valuable violin which has just been stolen without the parties' knowledge may fall to be decided differently from a sale by an importer of a cargo of coffee supposedly lying in a warehouse at Santos at the time of the contract but actually removed by thieves. In the latter case tradesmen would hold the *seller* responsible, regardless of fault, if the goods are not in the place specified by the contract, but it would be inequitable to give the purchaser a claim for the loss of his bargain in the case of the violin.

Events which render performance impossible are divided by the BGB into those which are 'initial', existing at the time of the formation of the contract, and those which are 'subsequent' and arise only later. In cases of subsequent impossibility, unlike those of initial impossibility, the question is not whether performance was objectively or just subjectively impossible; the important question is who is to blame for the obstacle to performance. If it is the debtor, he is liable to pay damages (§§280, 325 BGB); if it is the creditor who must answer for the obstacle to performance, the debtor is freed and may even be able to demand what was promised to him (§§275, 324 BGB); if neither party is responsible for the obstacle to performance, both are freed (§§275, 323 BGB, art. 119 OR). In all these cases the general rule, inferred from the principle 'pacta sunt servanda', is that the debtor who fails to perform is liable unless he proves that he was not answerable for the obstacle to performance (§282 BGB).

Each party must answer for obstacles to performance which occur because of a lack of proper care on their part or on the part of those who were helping them to perform (§§276, 278 BGB, arts. 99 and 101 OR). For example, if a picture is destroyed on being despatched by one of the gallery's employees, the purchaser may claim damages for non-performance unless the gallery proves that there was no negligence either on its own part or on the part of its assistants. If this proof is forthcoming, both parties are released; the gallery cannot claim the price and the purchaser cannot claim damages, though it is open to the purchaser to hold the gallery to the contract and claim from it any 'surrogate benefit' ('stellvertretendes commodum') such as the proceeds of an insurance policy received by the gallery in lieu of the picture (§281 BGB and BGE 43 II 234).

Instances of an impossibility for which neither party is answerable occur when a house is destroyed during the tenancy by a fire for which neither of the parties is to blame (RG JW 1905, 718), or if a bye-law prohibits dancing during the lease of a place of entertainment (RGZ 89, 203), or if an architect cannot execute the contractual works because of prohibitory building regulations (BGH LM §275 no. 7). In the last two cases one must take account of the possibility that the prohibition of dancing and building may be lifted, and ask whether in all the circumstances the parties can be expected to defer the contract until such time as that happens.

An important qualification of the general rule that a debtor is answerable only for those obstacles to performance which are attributable to his fault is contained in §279 BGB. If the contract is for things of a kind rather than for a particular thing, the vendor who cannot deliver is responsible for his inability to deliver even if he and his assistants are entirely blameless. Thus if the vendor of a quantity of cocoa of specified quality is unable to deliver on the due date because of business difficulties or a strike or because his own suppliers have failed to deliver in time, he is liable in damages for non-performance even if he is clearly not to blame for any of these obstacles. In order to exclude this strict liability, parties often include war clauses and strike clauses, or a 'subject to availability' clause ('richtige und rechtzeitige Selbstbelieferung vorbehalten'). In the absence of any such clause, a vendor is only freed from his duty to perform if the entire genus to which the object of the sale appertained has been destroyed.

It is possible, however, for the vendor to be released despite the continued existence of goods of the specified type if delivery is prevented by an embargo imposed by some foreign state (RGZ 93, 182) or by a directive that all such goods must go to a state-controlled distribution centre (RGZ 95, 20) or by requisition (RGZ 88, 287). On the other hand, a merchant who at the beginning of 1914 sold malt for delivery at the end of December 1914 or January 1915 was still held liable in damages when he could not deliver because the malt producers stopped supplies by reason of price controls introduced by the government on 19 December 1914. He should have realized that the authorities might interfere with the malt trade in this manner. 'A person who sells goods of any type in the uncertain circumstances of wartime should already have them in his possession or at his disposition so that he may use them at any time in satisfaction of his obligation. Unless he knows that thoroughly reliable suppliers have such goods and are in a position to deliver them, he relies on supplies from third parties at his own risk, and cannot defend on the ground that performance was rendered impossible by events for which he was not responsible' (RGZ 93, 17).

In practical terms, then, §279 BGB reflects the opinion of merchants that anyone who undertakes to deliver goods of a certain type or goods which he is to procure by purchase gives a guarantee of his ability to supply such goods when the time for delivery arrives.

Whether a contract is or is not for generic goods is a question of the construction of the contract. If a dairy agrees to supply a hotel with a set quantity of milk every day and the dairy's own production is adversely affected by some disturbance of its business it must procure the agreed quantity on the open market and deliver it to the hotel. On the other hand, if a farmer agrees to supply a dairy with a certain quantity of milk every day he would be partially released from his obligation if a murrain decimated his herd: it can be inferred from the nature of the transaction that the farmer only bound himself to deliver such milk as was produced on his farm ('beschränkte Gattungsschuld', see RGZ 91, 312 and BGE 57 II 110).

After the appalling inflation which followed the First World War the German courts developed a doctrine that even under §279 BGB a debtor might exceptionally be released from an obligation which it was not wholly impossible to perform if as the result of an unforeseeable collapse of the currency, a change of legislation, or a political upheaval performance would involve quite exceptional hardships which went beyond the call of duty ('überobligationsmässig'). These cases will be considered in the next chapter (Ch. 14) on the discharge of contracts by reason of subsequent events.

While the German BGB adopted MOMMSEN's doctrine of impossibility—thereby 'entering sine beneficio inventarii into the joyless inheritance of pandectist scholasticism', to use TITZE's phrase—the *Austrian* ABGB was spared most of the effects of the dogma 'impossibilium nulla obligatio'. The Austrian provisions on impossibility of performance are thus much more amenable to reasonable construction than those of German law. We cannot go into the details of Austrian law here but despite the intervening adoption of the Teilnovellen to the ABGB the observations of RABEL are still apt (*Gesammelte Aufsätze* I 79 ff., and III 138 ff.).

2. Delay

If the promise is capable of performance but has not been performed within the time allowed by the contract, the question arises whether the creditor can demand compensation for the damage the delay has caused him and whether he can withdraw from the contract and refuse to accept late performance.

In Germany a claim for damages for lateness in performance can only be brought if the debtor is in 'default' ('Verzug'). In order to put the debtor in default after performance has fallen due the creditor must make a protest ('Mahnung'); this starts the default running unless the debtor can prove that the lateness of performance is attributable to a circumstance for which, under rules already stated, he is not responsible (§§284 ff. BGB). In Switzerland too a protest is required to put the debtor in default, but the debtor need not be to blame and will be liable for interest even if he is not; he is not liable for other damages, however, if he can show that he is free from fault (arts. 102 ff. OR; the same is true in Austria, see OGH 29 Dec. 1954, SZ XXVII 334).

If the contract fixes a date for performance, directly or indirectly, a protest is not necessary to put the debtor in default ('dies interpellat pro homine': §284 par. 2 BGB, art. 102 par. 2 OR); the same rule is applied by the courts if it appears on a proper construction of the contract that the time for performance is of vital importance (see BGH NJW 1959, 933).

Although putting the debtor in default gives the creditor a claim for damages for delay, it does not in principle free him from the duty to accept performance, late though it is. The creditor can only withdraw from the contract or claim damages for non-performance if he fixes a period during which the defaulting debtor must complete performance and states that he will refuse to accept after the expiry of that period (§326 BGB, §918 ABGB, art. 107 OR). Such a period may be fixed at the same time as making the protest (RGZ 93, 180), and if the period fixed is too short, a reasonable period will be substituted (RGZ 106, 90; OGH 5 Dec. 1951, SZ XXIV 332). No such period need be fixed if the delay has robbed eventual performance of any interest the creditor had in it, as might be the case with late delivery of seasonal articles (§326 par. 2 BGB, art. 108 no. 2 OR). Neither protest nor a fixed period is required if it would serve no purpose in view of the construction of the contract or the nature of the transaction, as in the case of import sales with fixed dates for loading and delivery (RGZ 71, 308; BGH MDR 1955, 343). Finally, neither protest nor a fixed period is called for in the case of a 'Fixgeschäft', where a definite period for performance is specified and the judge can infer from the terms of the contract or the surrounding circumstances that the parties intended the transaction to 'stand or fall' depending on whether the time fixed for performance was observed or not (RGZ 108, 58). If the 'Fixgeschäft' is a commercial transaction for either party and the time for performance has gone by, the innocent party may resile forthwith or, if the other party is responsible for the delay, claim damages, but he will only have a claim for performance if he expressly demands it after the time for performance has elapsed (§376 HGB; see also art. 108 no. 3, 190 OR, and applying them, BGE 54 II 31).

It is important to note that a creditor enjoys these rights under §326 BGB only if the debtor is in default in performing a major or principal obligation ('Hauptpflicht'). Whether an obligation is such a major obligation or a minor or collateral one depends once again on the construction of the contract. In sales contracts the obligation of the vendor to deliver the goods is a principal obligation, but if the purchaser is in default in accepting the goods tendered, the vendor can only claim damages for delay: the vendor cannot withdraw from the contract after setting a time for acceptance in accordance with §326 BGB and claim damages for non-performance, unless it is a case where he has a pressing interest in prompt acceptance, as in the sale of the materials of a house being demolished or in the sale of bulky goods occupying needed space in the vendor's warehouse. Even if he has delivered the goods the vendor may still be under a principal obligation to provide the accompanying document: for example, the purchaser of a motor vehicle can exercise his rights under

§326 BGB if the vendor has failed to deliver the motor licence along with the car (BGH NJW 1953, 1347; the same result was reached with different terminology in *Bentworth Finance, Ltd.* v. *Lubert*, [1968] 1 QB 680).

If the debtor unequivocally evinces his intention not to perform the contract, the innocent party may immediately exercise his rights under §326 BGB even before performance has fallen due and need not make a protest or fix any period for performance (RGZ 67, 317; BGH NJW 1976, 326; art. 108 no. 1 OR). Most writers agree with the courts in explaining this by saying that the refusal to perform is a 'positive breach of contract' (*positive Forderungsverletzung*) which can give rise, as we shall see, to a claim for damages without any protest or fixing of a period for performance. As RABEL indicates (*Recht des Warenkaufs* I 382 ff.), these cases are better explained on the view that this is not a case of faulty breach of contract at all, but rather that the debtor is bound by his declaration that he will not perform and cannot complain if the other party 'takes him at his word'. On this see LESER, 'Die Erfüllungsverweigerung', *Festschrift für Max Rheinstein* II (1969) 643, with further references.

3. *Positive Breach of Contract ('Positive Forderungsverletzung')*

Under both the German BGB and the Swiss Code of Obligations, a judge who is faced with a breach of contract must put it in one of two legal categories: either it is a case of *impossibility* of performance—(the Code of Obligations speaks of 'Ausbleiben der Erfüllung')—or it is a case of *delay*. It has to be said that this dichotomy is misconceived. A debtor is of course bound to perform and he is bound to perform at the right time, but that is not the end of the matter. He may in addition have further obligations arising from the contract, failure to perform which cannot be categorized either as 'impossibility of performance' or as 'delay'; in such cases the courts have for long been holding that he is liable on the ground of 'positive breach of contract', unfortunate though the name is. If, contrary to his promise, a vendor supplies a third party with similar goods, or if a site-owner fails to give the necessary details to the building contractor, the innocent party can claim compensation for the harm caused by this breach of duty; furthermore, he can insist on performance, and if the breach of contract imperils the whole purpose of the transaction in such a way that in all the circumstances of the case the innocent party cannot be expected to continue with the contract and to perform his own obligations under it, then he is entitled, without setting any fixed period for performance, to claim damages for non-performance of the whole contract or to withdraw from the contract, as under §§325, 326 BGB.

For example, if a charterer is slow in loading the ship which the shipowner puts at his disposal in a foreign port and gives other grounds for supposing that he cannot perform the charterparty as he should, the shipowner may be entitled forthwith to abandon the contract and sail away, and claim damages for non-performance of the charter (BGHZ 11, 80).—As has already been stated, the courts hold likewise in cases of anticipatory refusal to perform (RGZ 149, 403).

The courts also use the notion of 'positive breach of contract' in cases where a reprehensible breach of contractual duties of care has caused personal injury or property damage to the other party. For example, if a guest trips and falls on the stairway of a hotel or a passenger is injured while riding in a taxi, a claim for damages for 'positive breach of contract' arises against the hotelier or the taxi-firm. So, too, where harm is caused by faulty medical treatment or where, owing to the hairdresser's negligence, a customer's hair is singed under the hair-drier (RGZ 148, 148; see also BGHZ 8, 239 and 27, 236).

There is some doubt whether it is the victim in these cases who must prove that the harm was caused by the unlawful and faulty conduct of the other contracting party or whether it is the latter who must discharge the burden of proving that he used all the precautions called for in the situation. The courts ask which of the parties is responsible in the light of the contract for the area of danger in which the accident arose. This is normally the defendant, since these accidents usually occur after the victim has entered the defendant's area of responsibility by patronizing the hotel or entering the taxi or submitting to the operation. On this see HANS STOLL, 'Die Beweislastverteilung bei positiven Vertragsverletzungen', *Festschrift für Fritz von Hippel* (1967) 517.

The delivery of defective goods does not constitute a case of non-performance of a contract for the sale of specific goods. Most writers in Germany hold that the delivery of the defective goods constitutes performance of the contract and that the purchaser can only exercise the claims based on the guarantee, specially regulated in §§459 ff. BGB, in respect of which the vendor's liability is strict. The general provisions regarding impossibility and delay are not applicable if specific goods are defective on delivery, but the rules of 'positive breach of contract' may be (see BGH NJW 1965, 533). If generic goods prove to be defective when delivered, the purchaser has a choice: he may exercise the claim arising from guarantee if he chooses, but instead he may assert that the delivery of the defective goods was not a performance of the contract, call for delivery of sound goods, and, in proper circumstances, exercise his rights under §326 BGB. Different considerations yet again apply if the vendor has been unable to provide the purchaser with unencumbered title to the goods (§§434, 440, 480 BGB): under the BGB this is a case of non-performance of the contract, to which the general provisions fall to be applied.

III

Unlike the Germanic civil codes, those of the *Romanistic* family do have a unitary conception of 'non-performance' of bilateral contracts. If one party to a bilateral contract fails to perform his duties under it, the other is entitled to have the contract rescinded by court judgment (art. 1184 Code civil, 1453 Codice civile). In the French Code civil this rule is dressed up in old-fashioned concepts, to the effect that every bilateral contract is concluded under the implicit resolutory condition of the proper performance of the reciprocal duties, but in essence it simply means that non-performance gives the other party the right to have the contract rescinded, for which purpose he must bring a claim. (This is made clear in art. 1453 Codice civile.) Thus each party has a choice between bringing a claim for performance (dealt with in Ch. 42 above) and bringing an action to rescind the contract, which may be combined with a claim for damages. Once a claim for performance has been raised, the plaintiff may switch to a claim for rescission and damages, but not vice versa.

This rule may be found in art. 1453 par. 2 Codice civile. In France it is different: until a final judgment of rescission has been rendered, a claim for performance may be brought, even if the value of the performance has risen in the meantime; see Civ. 6 Jan. 1932, DH 1932, 114.

In a claim for rescission it must be shown that the defendant has failed to perform his contractual obligations (see art. 1184: 'ne satisfera point à son engagement'). This includes not only total non-performance because of impossibility, but also late or incomplete performance as well as breach of ancillary or collateral duties under the contract. In each case the judge decides in his discretion whether in view of the purpose of the contract the breach is serious enough to justify immediate rescission. In so doing he takes account of all the circumstances of the case, including whether and how much the defendant is to blame for the non-performance, how much harm the plaintiff has already suffered as a result of the non-performance, and whether it would be fair to hold him to the contract and restrict him to a claim for damages.

See Req. 24 Jan. 1939, Gaz. Pal. 1939. 1. 586; Req. 13 Feb. 1934, Gaz. Pal. 1934. 1. 782, and the details in LANDFERMANN (above p. 523) 35 ff., 53 ff.—The Italian Codice civile puts the same point in a different way in art. 1455 in saying that a contract is not to be rescinded 'if the non-performance by one party is immaterial in view of the interests of the other'.

This balancing act is especially necessary in cases where the contract has been performed only in part or not at the right time. If part performance is of no advantage to the plaintiff, the judge will consider rescinding the contract as a whole; otherwise he can hold the parties to the contract so far as it has been performed; as for the rest he will in a suitable case rescind the contract and give the plaintiff a claim for damages (see Req. 21 Dec. 1927, DH 1928, 82; Req. 21 June 1935, Gaz. Pal. 1935. 2. 35).

French law also allows the judge to set a period in which the defendant must render the promised performance ('délai de grâce': art. 1184 par. 3 Code civil), and if he does so, he normally issues a simultaneous order that the contract be rescinded if the period of grace expires without performance (Req. 16 May 1933, Gaz. Pal. 1933. 2. 422). If performance was due on a specified date which had already passed when the claim for rescission was brought, no such period of grace can be allowed (Civ. 18 Oct. 1927, S. 1928. 1. 22).

On this see LANDFERMANN (above p. 523) 52 f.—Under the Italian Codice civile it is the innocent party rather than the judge who can fix a reasonable period for performance by the other party and declare that the contract will determine forthwith if this period elapses without performance. In such a case there is no need for a court judgment which is usually a prerequisite for rescission (see art. 1454 Codice civile).

Should the defendant make a late tender of performance during the trial, the judge must determine whether to rescind the contract even so. Once again it is a matter of all the circumstances of the case, whether the court sees the debtor's original refusal to perform as simply an attempt to delay performance or whether the plaintiff has a justifiable interest in rejecting the late performance, possibly because the market situation has altered.

See Civ. 17 March 1954, Gaz. Pal. 1954. 2. 88; Civ. 30. Nov. 1949, Gaz. Pal. 1950. 1. 38. The decision of the Court of Cassation of 27 Nov. 1950 (Gaz. Pal. 1951. 1. 132) gives a good indication of the extent of judicial discretion in this area. The plaintiff had transferred some land to the defendant in return for the defendant's promise to clothe, feed, and care for her for the rest of her life. Irreconcilable differences arose between the parties, the defendant refused to do as promised, and the plaintiff sought rescission. Both lower courts, refusing to rescind the contract, issued a judgment of Solomon to the effect that the defendant must pay the plaintiff an annuity to the value of the promised services, so that there would be no need for personal contact between the parties. The Court of Cassation upheld this decision on the ground that the differences between the parties made it impossible for them to perform *in natura* and that the trial judge was justified in exercising his 'pouvoir souverain d'appréciation des circonstances de fait' so as to award the plaintiff a 'rente viagère compensatrice'. The courts here were really reconstructing the contract rather than rescinding it as requested, even if the terms used by the Court of Cassation suggest that it was awarding 'damages' in the form of the annuity. For further decisions of judicial 'reconstruction' of contracts after breach, see LANDFERMANN (above p. 523) 60 ff.

Judicial rescission of a contract is in principle only possible if the plaintiff has made a protest to the defendant. Such a protest must be in writing and delivered through a *huissier*. Ths rule has, however, lost almost all its importance in practice since the Court of Cassation decided that the institution of a claim for rescission may itself be seen as constituting a protest (Civ. 19 Oct. 1931, DH 1931, 537).

A rule that only courts may rescind contracts must obviously make for practical difficulties in commerce, for if it really meant that the innocent party remained fully bound by his contractual obligations until a final judgment of rescission the result would be that the vendor of goods could not resell them nor the purchaser buy in from elsewhere. The French courts have avoided this intolerable result by holding that it is not a breach of contract for the innocent party before going to court to declare the contract over by reason of the other party's non-performance, to refuse to perform his own part, and to enter covering transactions (see Paris 18 April 1912, S. 1915. 2. 66; Req. 4 Jan. 1927,

S. 1927. 1. 188); this is subject to the proviso that a court would have ordered immediate rescission of the contract had it been seised of the matter, an assumption which a contractor who frees himself from a contract makes at his own risk.

The rule that only courts may rescind contracts is also weakened by the fact that unequivocal agreements to discharge the contract in certain events are effective; on this see BORRICAND (above p. 523) and LANDFERMANN (above p. 523) 73 ff.). Businessmen usually include such a clause and lawyers always do. It is often called a 'pacte commissoire', and its advantages are that the parties can specify exactly the circumstances which are to entitle the innocent party to declare the contract over; in this way one may avoid the uncertainty inherent in judicial rescission that one cannot predict whether the judge may not treat a particular breach of contract as relatively trivial and so refuse to grant rescission or grant it only after a period of grace. The parties can also agree that a contract shall only be rescinded if the innocent party makes a protest to the other or sets a period for performance, and if performance at the right time is particularly important the parties may agree that when that time has gone by the contract should be rescinded by simple declaration to that effect.

The Italian legislator has realized that judicial rescission of contracts is not very practical, and has provided that parties to a contract may agree that it be determinable by simple declaration without going to court (art. 1456). Another case of extrajudicial termination of contracts under the Codice civile arises when a contracting party has in writing set a reasonable further period for performance and this period has expired (art. 1454). Finally, if a party has promised to perform by a particular date and the observance of this limit is 'essential' for the other party in all the circumstances of the case, the expiry of that period automatically determines the contract, unless within three days the interested party informs the party in default that he insists upon performance (art. 1457).

The innocent party will often be more interested in claiming *damages* than in procuring the *rescission* of a contract which has not been performed in time. Here a distinction must be made. If performance of the contract still seems possible, the innocent party can seek to hold his opponent to the contract and bring a claim for performance as well as for damages for the harm caused by the delay ('dommages-intérêts moratoires'). But if the other party cannot or will not perform, one looks to a claim for damages for non-performance of the contract ('dommages-intérêts compensatoires') which normally goes hand in hand with a claim for rescission. The Code civil itself permits this cumulation of a claim for rescission and a claim for damages, for art. 1184 par. 2 provides that the creditor has the right either to demand performance of the contract or 'd'en demander la résolution avec dommages et intérêts'. The draftsmen of the German BGB ruled out such a combination of rescission and damages on the ground that one could not claim damages at the very time one was seeking to undo the contract which was its basis, and §326 BGB therefore requires the creditor to choose which of these two rights to exercise. This causes endless difficulties. French lawyers are quite aware of the formal objections to cumulating claims for resolution and damages but do not give them much weight since the practical advantages of allowing such cumulation are so great. (On this see LANDFERMANN (above p. 523) 65 ff., 91 ff.)

In principle no claim for damages, whether for delay or for non-performance, can be brought until the debtor has been put in default by a formal protest (art. 1146 Code civil, 1219 Codice civile), but as has already been stated, the courts hold that a protest is unnecessary if the terms of the contract make the consequences of delay ensue without any protest, as in the case where a particular time for performance is agreed (see Req. 16 Feb. 1921, DP 1922. 1. 102; Civ. 18 Oct. 1927, S. 1928. 1. 22) or there is a clause 'livrable de suite' (Req. 21 June 1933, DH 1933, 412). The same is true if protest would be a mere formality, as in the case where the debtor has already refused to perform (so Req. 4 Jan. 1927, S. 1927. 1. 188 and, in terms, art. 1219 no. 2 Codice civile), or is in no position to perform.

A claim for damages will only succeed if the circumstance which prevented the performance of the contract is 'imputable' to the debtor. This is expressed in art. 1147 of the French Code civil in the form that a debtor in default is freed from liability in damages only if 'l'inexécution provient d'une cause étrangère qui ne peut lui être imputée' (so also art. 1218 Codice civile); art. 1148 says the same thing in different words, by providing that an obstacle to performance serves as a defence only if it occurs 'par suite d'une force majeure ou d'un cas fortuit'. 'Force majeure' and 'cas fortuit' are synonymous, and since the courts and writers agree that they can be invoked only if the debtor is free from fault, 'absence de faute' and 'force majeure' mean very much the same thing in this connection (on this see TUNC (above p. 523)). The same principle also underlies the rule of art. 1302 Code civil that a person who is bound to deliver specific goods is freed from his obligation if the goods are destroyed without his fault ('sans la faute du débiteur'). The inference is drawn that the vendor of goods by description is only freed if they had already been properly ascertained at the time they were accidentally destroyed.

There is no space here to go into the details of the question of 'transfer of risk': if a debtor is freed from his obligation to perform by some obstacle for which he is not responsible, can he nevertheless claim what was promised to him? We can simply point to the several distinctions which are drawn in this matter in the law of sales. In most of the Romanistic legal systems the risk passes to the buyer along with ownership at the time of the formation of the contract if the goods are specific, and at the time they are ascertained if the goods are generic (art. 1138 Code civil, 1465 Codice civile; but this rule is also found in art. 185 par. 1 OR). In German, Austrian, and Scandinavian law, on the other hand, as well as under the Uniform Law of Sales, the risk passes only on delivery of the goods (§§446 BGB, 1049, 1051 ABGB, art. 17 Scandinavian Law of

Sales, art. 97 Uniform Law of Sales). On the whole matter see the magisterial work of RABEL, *Recht des Warenkaufs* II (1958) 291 ff.

The critical question therefore is in what cases the courts are ready to treat an obstacle to performance as 'force majeure' or 'cas fortuit' and so to free the debtor from his obligation to pay damages. The writers say that an obstacle to performance only serves as a defence if it is an 'obstacle imprévisible et irrésistible' which renders it 'absolument impossible' for the debtor to perform (see PLANIOL/RIPERT VII no. 838). Although the courts tend to stress one of these criteria at the expense of the others, it is certain that an obstacle to performance will not serve as a defence if the debtor had even the slightest chance of avoiding it and neglected to avail himself of it. Even the very great difficulties in procuring, transporting, or delivering goods which occur in wartime do not free the vendor.

In one case a vendor who had sold 4,000 cwts. of oats from his 1914 crop had his whole crop requisitioned by the military authorities, but he had to pay damages all the same when it emerged that he had carelessly passed up an opportunity to get the goods in transit to the purchaser before the requisition (Civ. 6 May 1922, DP 1922. 1. 130; see also Req. 25 Jan. 1922, DP 1922. 1. 71).—In another case ten tons of potatoes had been sold and were requisitioned at the railway station when they were being loaded and this was held to be 'force majeure' (Civ. 19 June 1923, DP 1923. 1. 94).—The purchaser of a parcel of rice failed to open a credit making the price available to the vendor in Saigon as promised, because he did not obtain the necessary authority under the French exchange regulations which were already in force at the time of the contract; he was held liable in damages (Req. 4 Jan. 1927, S. 1927. 1. 188).—In cases where a strike prevents the production, transport, or delivery of goods, the courts are readier to find that the strike constitutes a defence the more general and unforeseeable it is proved to have been (see Civ. 2 March 1915, D. 1920. 1. 108; Civ. 20 April 1948, Gaz. Pal. 1948. 1. 285). Many other decisions are cited in PLANIOL/RIPERT VII nos. 838 ff. and in KEGEL/RUPP/ZWEIGERT (above p. 523) 223 ff.

The rules which determine whether an obstacle to performance may constitute a defence do not apply to contracts which could never be performed at all. Here, like the German legal family, the Romanistic legal systems make a concession to the doctrine 'impossibilium nulla obligatio', and render such contracts void (art. 1346, 1418 par. 2 Codice civile). The French Code civil expressly covers the case of specific goods which are already destroyed at the time of the sale: such a contract is void (art. 1601), regardless of whether in the circumstances of the case the promisor was to bear the risk that he might not be able to perform. The Romanistic legal systems seek to qualify the harshness of this result by granting the creditor a claim for damages based on delict or *culpa in contrahendo* if the debtor knew or should have known that what he promised was impossible (see Req. 11 Feb. 1878, S. 1879. 1. 196; art. 1338 Codice civile), and the quantum of damages is not limited to the extent of the plaintiff's reliance, as it is under §307 BGB.

Claims for damages based on the *mis*performance of contractual duties are of very great importance in Romanistic systems. These include contractual claims for compensation brought by a patient, guest, or traveller for the harm caused to them by bad medical treatment, the defective furnishings of a restaurant, or the fault of the carrier's employees. In this area the French courts have developed an interesting doctrine which distingushes the contractual 'obligation de résultat' from the 'obligation de moyens'. If the obligation is of the former type, the contractor is bound to ensure a specified *result* and his failure to do so makes him liable in damages unless he can prove that it was attributable to a cause not imputable to himself ('cause étrangère'), either a 'cas fortuit' or the fault of the victim himself ('faute de la victime') or the fault of a third party ('faute d'un tiers'). Examples of such *obligations de résultat*, which are also called 'obligations déterminées', are the duty of the vendor to deliver the goods at the right time and at the specified place (see the full details in MAZEAUD III no. 948), the duty of a carrier to carry the goods to the specified destination (art. 1784 Code civil), the duty of a person letting a thing on hire to provide it at the proper time and in the proper condition, and the obligation of a building contractor to do the promised work (see NAST, DC 1941. J. 54). But in the interests of improving the legal position of victims the courts have gone further than this and have imposed such an *obligation de résultat* in other cases: thus the carrier of persons is bound by such an *obligation de résultat* to deliver the traveller to his destination unharmed (Civ. 10 May 1921, DP 1923. 1. 209), and the proprietor of a merry-go-round must so manage the installation that his clients can go round and come away unimpaired in health (Req. 13 May 1947, D. 1947, 348; Civ. 1 July 1964, Gaz. Pal. 1964. 2. 316).

If the contractor's duty is only an 'obligation de moyens', on the other hand, it is for the victim to prove that his injury is attributable to faulty behaviour on the part of his contractor. The doctor, for example, owes only an *obligation de moyens*: he is not bound to produce a specific result (making the patient well) but simply has to use the requisite care and skill in the choice and application of his methods of treatment (Civ. 27 June 1939, DC 1941. J. 53); in consequence the patient must adduce proof of the doctor's breach of duty.

If a movie-goer falls on the stairway of the cinema, the occupier is only liable for the injury if the victim proves that he did not take proper security precautions: 'l'entrepreneur de spectacles s'oblige seulement à observer dans l'organisation et le fonctionnement de son exploitation les mesures de prudence et de diligence qu'exige la sécurité du spectateur [*obligation de moyens*] et n'assume pas l'obligation [*de résultat*] de rendre celui sain et sauf à la sortie de son établissement' (Civ. 17 March 1947, D. 1947, 269). For more cases on the borderland between *obligations de moyens* and *obligations de résultat*, see SCHAEFFER, *RabelsZ* 28 (1964) 676 ff.; on the theoretical aspects of the distinction, see TUNC, JCP 1945. I. 449 and ESMEIN (above p. 523) 108 ff.

The vendor satisfies his obligations under the contract of *sale* by delivering the goods to the purchaser at the right time and in the right place; if the goods have defects or even if the purchaser does not obtain unencumbered ownership the purchaser cannot claim that the contract has not been performed (it is otherwise in the case of delivery of defective goods sold by type, see RABEL, *Rechts des Warenkaufs* II (1958) 121 ff.). The purchaser must rely on the special guarantees laid down in the Code, a guarantee that the goods are free from defect and a guarantee against eviction by better title in a third party, both of which the vendor may restrict in the contract.

The French courts have, however, had no real difficulty in granting the purchaser extensive claims for damages when defective goods have been delivered. Art. 1645 Code civil certainly provides that a vendor is liable in damages only if he knew of the defect and that otherwise his liability is limited to returning the purchase price and paying the 'frais occasionnés par la vente' (art. 1646), but in the interests of protecting the consumer the courts have construed these provisions very generously. They regularly hold that a seller who is in the business of selling goods of the kind in question is to be treated as if he knew of the defects in the goods. The effect of this is that he is liable in damages, even if in the contract of sale he had sought to exculpate himself from such liability. On this see H. C. FICKER, *Die Schadenersatzpflicht des Verkäufers und seiner Vormänner bei Sachmängeln in der französischen Rechtsprechung* (1962), and RADOUANT, 'Les Dommages-intérêts dus par le vendeur dans la garantie des vices cachés de la chose en droit français', *Mélanges Secrétan* (1964) 241. Recent cases include Civ. 30 Oct. 1978 and Com. 6 Nov. 1978, JCP 1979. II. 19178, noted by GHESTIN.

IV

The *Anglo-American* systems look at contracts in a quite different way from the Continental systems; this has a very profound effect on the rules relating to difficulties which arise in the execution of contracts.

In the German and Romanistic legal families a contractor is thought of as a person who promises to behave in a certain way; generally he binds himself to do a particular thing or not to do it, and if necessary he can be forced by court action to conform to his promise. This being the principle, the Continental legal systems naturally sanction breaches of contract only if the debtor can be blamed for non-performance; only if in the circumstances of the case the debtor could be expected to behave as promised, that is, when he can be blamed for behaving otherwise than agreed in the contract, does non-performance of a contract involve his legal liability. In sales, however, the point of the contract is not that the vendor should *try* to see that the goods have the right qualities but that he should actually *ensure* their freedom from defect, so in dealing with sales contracts Continental systems have to use the special concept of *guarantee*, and make a sharp systematic distinction between the provisions concerning the guarantee of title and quality in things and the general provisions relating to the non-performance of contracts.

In the Common Law the position is rather the reverse. As the result of a long historical development, portrayed in RHEINSTEIN's *Die Struktur des vertraglichen Schuldverhältnisses im anglo-amerikanischen Recht*, the Common Law treats all contracts as *guarantees* leading to a claim for damages for 'breach of contract' if the guaranteed result is not produced by the debtor. This basic principle explains a great many of the numerous differences between the systems which strike anyone making a comparative study of Continental and Common Law. First, Anglo-American law has no need to separate and systematize the various causes of non-performance of a contract as German law does with its careful distinction between impossibility, delay, and positive breach of contract: it does not much matter in the Common Law whether the debtor has wholly failed to perform as promised or has performed too late or has performed unsatisfactorily in one way or another, since if the promised result has not been procured, the guarantee undertaken has not been observed and a 'breach of contract' has occurred. Furthermore, claims for damages do not depend on whether any blame for the breach attaches to the debtor or his employees. Admittedly the Common Law sometimes releases a debtor from liability when he has been prevented from performing, but this is not because he and his staff are free from blame regarding the non-performance of the contract, but rather on the ground that on a proper view of the contract he is not responsible for performance in *all* circumstances and that his guarantee does *not* cover certain obstacles to performance (on this see further below pp. 566 ff.). Finally, the Common Law does not have to have any special way of dealing with defects in goods, work, or premises since for Anglo-American lawyers the breach of guarantees in contracts of sale, services, and lease are just like all other breaches of contract which themselves arise from broken guarantees: 'Claims in respect of defects are actually the paradigm of contractual liability in the Common Law as a whole' (RHEINSTEIN (above p. 524), 155). This fusion of guarantee and general liability for breach of contract explains why the vendor of defective goods is strictly liable for the harm caused to the purchaser by the defect.

Whenever one party to a contract fails to perform the duties it imposes on him, the innocent party has a claim for damages for 'breach of contract'; under certain circumstances, namely when the term of the contract which has been broken is 'essential', the innocent party may in addition regard his own contractual obligations as over and refuse further performance or reclaim whatever he has transferred. In answering the question whether a contractual provision is 'essential' in this sense or not, English courts normally use the concepts 'warranty' and 'condition' which are of extremely variable meaning (see on this STOLJAR, 69 *LQ Rev.* 485 (1953) and RHEINSTEIN (above p. 524) 192 ff.). Every contractual term, express or implied, is in law a 'warranty' (express or implied). If such a term is broken, the innocent party is entitled to claim damages for breach of contract, but must continue to perform his own side of the bargain. The innocent party may only resile from the contract if the term which his opponent has broken is also a 'condition', that is, if it is especially important for the performance of the contract.

Continental lawyers find the use of the word 'condition' in this context very peculiar. 'Condition' for them signifies a future uncertain event whose occurrence or non-occurrence may trigger or suppress certain legal consequences. The word is used in this sense in the Common Law also, as in the phrases 'conditions precedent' and 'conditions subsequent', but in addition the concept of 'condition' is used in the law of contract to do what is done on the Continent by the concept of synallagma: if one party to a contract is bound to perform first or if the performance of the two parties is to take place simultaneously, common lawyers say that the duty of one contractor to perform is subject to the 'condition' that the other contracting party has already performed or is ready and willing to perform at the agreed time. Finally, English lawyers use the word 'condition' to denote an essential term of a contract whose non-performance gives the innocent party the right both to refuse to perform his own obligations and to claim damages for non-performance of the whole contract. On this and the other constructs used by English law to explain withdrawal from a contract on the ground of non-performance, see the full details in RHEINSTEIN (above p. 524) 192 ff.

The Common Law view that the only terms of a contract which are 'conditions' are those which are vital for the execution of the contract is very like the position in Germany where the exercise of the rights granted by §326 BGB depends on whether the party in delay is in breach of a 'principal duty' ('Hauptpflicht') or, in the case of positive breach of contract, 'has so imperilled the purpose of the contract that the innocent party cannot be expected to continue with it' (above p. 530). Similar phrases may be found in the English cases; for example, it has been said that a 'condition' exists if 'the particular stipulation goes to the root of the matter, so that a failure to perform it would render the performance of the rest of the contract by [one party] a thing different in substance from what the [other party] has stipulated for'.

See *Bettini* v. *Gye* (1876) 1 QBD 183. This distinction goes back to a judgment of that eminent judge LORD MANSFIELD in 1779: in *Boone* v. *Eyre* (1779) 1 H. Bl. 283, 126 Eng. Rep. 160 he decided that the purchaser of a plantation was not entitled to withdraw from the contract on the ground that the vendor was unable to provide good title to the concomitant slaves. There is an interesting application of this principle in the case of *Hongkong Fir Shipping Co. Ltd.* v. *Kawasaki Kisen Kaisha Ltd.* [1962] 2 QB 26. The vessel provided for the defendants at the start of a two-year time charter was unseaworthy in that the engine-room was understaffed and the staff were not trained to cope with the aged engines. On a journey from Liverpool to Osaka the ship was out of commission for five weeks because of engine failure, and after the vessel had been held up in Osaka for a further fifteen weeks the defendants threw up the charter and demanded damages, although there was no reason to believe that the ship would not be seaworthy after the repairs were finished. The shipowner argued that this withdrawal was unjustified and therefore a 'breach of contract' and claimed damages for the loss of the charter: this amounted to no less than £158,729 because freight rates had fallen greatly during the charter period and the ship could only find a substitute charter on much less favourable terms. In extended judgments the Court of Appeal held that the plaintiff had certainly broken its obligation to provide a seaworthy vessel (and thereby made itself liable to pay damages to the defendant) but that in the circumstances of the case this breach was not serious enough to justify the defendant in withdrawing from the contract. The obligation to provide a seaworthy ship was thus held not to be a 'condition' and the shipowner's claim was granted, subject to a counter-claim for damages by the charterer. On this decision, see LORD DEVLIN (above p. 523).

Lawyers in England now realise that 'warranty' and 'condition' are concepts too formalistic to solve the real problem of distinguishing between essential and inessential terms of a contract. In the United States, Restatement (Second) of Contracts (1981) dispenses with these concepts on this question and grants a claim for damages for 'total breach' if the party is entitled to refuse performance of his outstanding obligations by reason of the other party's breach. This will be the case if the other party's breach constitutes a 'material failure' of performance (§§243, 237). §241 lists the circumstances which are significant in deciding whether a failure of performance is 'material' or not: whether the innocent party has received, or can still receive, essentially what was promised, whether in such circumstances damages would be an adequate remedy, and whether and to what extent the behaviour of the party in breach is consistent with 'standards of good faith and fair dealing'.

So far we have been concerned mainly with *part* performance and *mis*performance, but of course cases where the party has *wholly* failed to perform or has not performed in time are of great importance as well, for example, where goods have not been delivered under a contract of sale, where the promised work has not been done, or where the premises have not been handed over to the tenant. The Common Law makes no distinction between 'impossibility' and 'delay'; the time fixed for performance is a term of the contract like any other and its breach gives the innocent party a claim for damages and, if the temporal provision is 'essential' to the contract, the right to resile as well. Whether the provision as to time of performance is 'essential' in this sense—English lawyers use the phrase 'of the essence of the contract'— is determined according to the circumstances of the case. The old Common Law rule was that any time for performance expressly fixed in the contract was *always* 'essential', but the Courts of Equity developed a milder rule which allowed the judge to decide whether the date was really of such importance to the parties, and this rule has now been generalized by s. 41 of the Law of Property Act, 1925. The courts usually hold time to be of the essence in commercial contracts, especially contracts for the sale of goods, because it would be intolerable in a time of fluctuating prices if the parties were left in uncertainty about whether they were bound to accept a late tender or free to proceed forthwith with a covering transaction.

Examples of English cases are *Lock* v. *Bell*, [1931] 1 Ch. 35; *Harold Wood Brick Co.* v. *Ferris*, [1935] 2 KB 198. The same rule is laid down for the United States in Restatement (Second) of Contracts (1981) §242.

If no 'essential' time for performance is specified in the contract, the debtor must perform 'within a reasonable time'. Even here the creditor, unlike his opposite number in Germany, need not make any protest to the debtor or fix a further period for performance before withdrawing from the contract, but it is nevertheless good commercial practice to do so unless the contract contains an 'essential' time for performance. Thus GUTTERIDGE reports that 'A reputable merchant who has bought goods without specifying a time for delivery does not rush off to his solicitor with instructions for the issue of a writ if he considers that there has been unjustifiable delay. He sits down and writes a stiff letter demanding delivery by a certain date and does not embark on litigation until this demand has been ignored by the seller.' (14 *Brit. YB Int. L.* 75, 87 (1933).)

The courts approve of this practice. A party to a contract which contains no 'essential' time for performance is entitled to fix a period within which the other party must perform. If the court finds this period reasonable, its final date is treated as being 'of the essence of the contract' with the consequence that the creditor can thereafter treat the unperformed contract as discharged, and in suitable cases claim damages.

See *Stickney* v. *Keeble*, [1915] AC 386; *Rickards (Charles) Ltd.* v. *Oppenhaim*, [1950] 1 KB 616; see also the American decisions *O'Brien* v. *Bradulov*, 80 NE 2d 685 (Ohio 1948); *Sliter* v. *Creek View Cheese Factory*, 173 Wis. 137, 179 NW 745 (1920), and WILLISTON §852.

Cases of 'anticipatory breach' of contract are accorded special treatment in the Common Law. In principle a party can only sue for non-performance of contractual promises when the time for the performance of those promises as fixed in the contract has elapsed. But even before then, if the party clearly shows, by express declaration or deliberate behaviour, that he is not minded to perform the contract, the other party can hold him to such behaviour, treat it as a 'breach of contract', consider the contract discharged, and claim damages for non-performance. The innocent party is not bound to do this, however; he may stand by the contract, wait for the time for performance, and then claim his damages.

If a young man promises his fiancée to marry her when his father dies and he breaks the engagement without any good cause she may forthwith bring a claim for damages and need not wait for his father to die. See *Frost* v. *Knight* (1872) LR 7 Ex. 111. An innocent party may, however, have an interest in holding the other party to the contract despite his refusal to perform, as in *White & Carter (Councils) Ltd.* v. *McGregor*, [1962] AC 413. If he does so, however, the innocent party bears the risk that the contract may in the meantime be avoided on some other ground, such as an exculpatory event which prevents performance. If the girl in *Frost* v. *Knight* had decided to delay bringing her claim for damages until the death of her fiancé's father, as she might have done in order to claim higher damages in view of her increased age and diminished marriageability, she would have been exposed to the risk of her fiancé's predeceasing his father and of thereby losing her claim altogether. A case decided under this rule is *Avery* v. *Bowden* (1855) 5 E. & B. 714, 119 Eng. Rep. 647. The charterer of a ship refused to load it, but the shipowner nevertheless kept the ship at the charterer's disposal. During this period the Crimean War broke out, with the result that the charter voyage could not have been performed even if the charterer had been ready to proceed with it. This event was at the shipowner's risk, and his claim for payment of the agreed hire was dismissed.

In the Common Law a contractor's liability in damages is not affected by the reason for his failure to perform his promise properly. In particular, in contrast with Continental law, it is irrelevant whether he was to blame for the non-performance or not: '. . . it does not matter whether the failure to fulfil a contract by the seller is because he is indifferent or wilfully negligent or just unfortunate. It does not matter what the reason is. What matters is the fact of performance. Has he performed it or not?' (*Nicolene Ltd.* v. *Simmonds*, [1952] 2 Lloyd's Rep. 419, 425, *per* SELLERS J.; *aff'd* [1953] 1 QB 543 (CA)). Since a contractor's liability in damages is based on breach of the guarantee he has given, the question when he is released from liability by external events must depend on the extent of his guarantee. This was the position from which the English courts started and they were originally extremely strict in holding the debtor to the promise he had actually made, though they allowed him to make express exceptions in the contract. Thus in the leading case of *Paradine* v. *Jane* (1647) Aleyn 26, 82 Eng. Rep. 897, a lessee tried to meet a claim for outstanding rent with the defence that during the period of the lease he had been forcibly extruded from the premises by the troops of a foreign prince. The defence was unsuccessful: 'When the party by his own contract creates a duty or charge upon himself, he is bound to make it good, notwithstanding any accident by inevitable necessity, because he might have provided against it by his contract.'

During the course of the nineteenth century the English judges invented some exceptions to qualify this principle that promises contractually given were absolutely binding. One exception covers cases where the German lawyer would speak of 'initial impossibility'. An important decision in this area is *Couturier* v. *Hastie* (1856) 5 HLC 673, 10 Eng. Rep. 1065. The parties agreed to buy and sell a cargo of corn on a named vessel, not knowing that it had already been disposed of by the captain, acting as agent of necessity, because it was spoilt. The vendor's claim for the price was dismissed since the court held that the contract was based on the parties' assumption that the goods were still in existence at the time they were sold. Subsequent English decisions have treated analogous cases as instances of error and have held that a contract based on a 'common mistake' of the parties is not binding (see above p. 448). These decisions and the similar rule in art. 1601 of the French Code civil led to the adoption in the English Sale of Goods Act of the following rule

'Where there is a contract for the sale of specific goods and the goods without the knowledge of the seller have perished at the time when the contract was made, the contract is void' (s. 6). On the historical development of this rule in English law see RHEINSTEIN (above p. 524) 183 ff. The same rule is to be found in §2-613 UCC. Even so, the courts of England the United States are always careful to check whether on a proper construction of the contract one party may not have taken the risk of the possiblity of performance. See the American decisions cited in CORBIN §§1362 ff. and the Australian case of *McRae* v. *Commonwealth Disposals Commission*, (1950) 84 CLR 337.

A contractor may also be relieved from his guarantee liability in certain circumstances where obstacles to performance arise *subsequently* to the contract. The courts so hold if the performance of the contract presupposes the continued existence of a specific thing which is accidentally destroyed before the time for performance arrives. These are cases where the German lawyer would speak of 'subsequent factual impossibility' ('nachträgliche (tatsächliche) Unmöglichkeit').

The leading case is *Taylor* v. *Caldwell* (1863) 3 B. & S. 826, 122 Eng. Rep. 309. The plaintiff hired the defendant's music hall for the promotion of concerts on four future dates. Before the first of these occasions the hall was accidentally destroyed by fire, and the plaintiff claimed damages for the loss he had suffered by reason of the non-occurrence of the concerts. The claim failed, not because the owner of the hall was unable to perform the contract by reason of an event for which he was not responsible—as would have been the basis for the decision in Germany under §275 BGB—but because the contract of hire was construed to contain an 'implied condition' that 'the parties shall be excused in case . . . performance becomes impossible from the perishing of the thing without default of the contractor'.—In *Howell* v. *Coupland* (1874) LR 9 QB 462 this rule was applied to a contract of sale. The defendant sold 200 tons of potatoes to be grown on a specified field, but blight reduced his potato crop to 80 tons. The purchaser's claim for damages for the non-delivery of 120 tons was rejected. This rule has also been adopted by the Sale of Goods Act: 'Where there is an agreement to sell specific goods and subsequently the goods, without any fault on the part of the seller or buyer, perish before the risk passes to the buyer, the agreement is avoided' (s. 7).

Finally, a contractor may be discharged if subsequent events in fact or law render performance of the contract impossible for the duration. For example, a contract whereby an English factory was bound to deliver machinery to a Polish purchaser in Danzig was discharged when, subsequently to the contract, war broke out between Germany on the one hand and Poland and England on the other, and the territory of Poland was occupied by German troops (*Fibrosa* v. *Fairbairn*, [1943] AC 32). The same is true if a chartered ship is requisitioned by the government for an indeterminate period, if the execution of specified building works is forbidden by administrative act, or if a sales contract is prohibited by a statute regulating trading with the enemy or is rendered incapable of performance because of rationing regulations.

See *Bank Line Ltd.* v. *Arthur Capel & Co.*, [1919] AC 435; *Metropolitan Water Board* v. *Dick, Kerr & Co.*, [1918] AC 119; *Distington Hematite Iron Co.* v. *Possehl & Co.*, [1916] 1 KB 811; *Peerless Casualty Co.* v. *Weymouth Gardens Inc.*, 215 F. 2d 362 (1st Cir. 1954); *Texas Co.* v. *Hogarth Shipping Co.*, 256 US 619 (1921).

There is a further class of case where performance is still possible but is rendered materially more difficult or actually futile by reason of unforeseen events such as a fall in the currency, a strike, or the closure of a sea route or a frontier. These cases will be dealt with in the next chapter (Ch. 44).

V

One's first impression on looking at all this material might be that the underlying doctrines are so fundamentally different that it makes no sense to compare the solutions.

Now it is certainly true that in the problems under investigation the theoretical starting-points are widely divergent and that every legal system uses technical expressions recognized nowhere else. Tell a Continental lawyer that in the Common Law every contractual duty is treated as a guarantee and he will think he is entering another legal world altogether. Contrariwise, it is hard for an Englishman to credit that the delivery of a specific thing which is useless for its intended purpose amounts to complete performance of the vendor's contractual duty to deliver and does not constitute a breach of contract at all. The German attempt to categorize the various types of non-performance of contracts and to draw sharp distinctions between 'impossibility', 'delay', and 'positive breach of contract' has not been greatly esteemed elsewhere, and neither Germanic nor Anglo-American lawyers have much time for the idea in the French Code civil that it takes a judicial decree to release parties from their contractual obligations.

Despite all this, attentive readers will repeatedly have noticed that the practical results in the legal systems under investigation are much more often in agreement than one would expect in view of their theoretical starting-points. Thus while it is true that in principle the Common Law sees a guarantee in every term of a contract, the vendor of specific goods is not liable in damages if they are accidentally destroyed without his fault before the risk passes. So also while in the Germanic and Romanistic legal families a debtor is in principle responsible only for those obstacles to performance for which he is to blame, he is still liable regardless of fault if he has promised to deliver generic goods and is unable to do so. Despite the theoretical differences, then, the actual problems are solved in much the same way, since each legal system makes concessions to its original position.

To take another example: all legal systems must face the question whether the innocent party can only claim compensation for the harm caused by breach while himself remaining bound, or whether in addition he may free himself from the bargain, refuse further performance, and bring his claim for damages for non-performance. In German law the creditor can exercise his rights under §326 BGB only if the debtor is in delay regarding a 'principle obligation' ('Hauptpflicht') (see above pp. 530 ff.); if the debtor is in breach of a 'collateral' obligation the creditor may only regard himself as discharged from the contract and claim damages for non-performance if the conduct of the debtor constitutes a 'positive breach of contract' whch so imperils the purpose of the contract that it would be unfair to hold the creditor to it. In French law it is much the same, for the judge is bound to use his discretion to discover whether the 'gravité' of the breach is such that the contract should be rescinded. The same idea underlies the English distinction between 'condition' and 'warranty': the innocent party may only treat himself as discharged from his obligations and claim damages for non-performance if the other party has broken a term which is 'essential' and thus constitutes a 'condition'. If the other party is in breach of some other, inessential term ('warranty'), the innocent party can still claim damages, but must continue to perform his obligations under the contract. Thus one can see that the substantial criterion applied to similar actual problems is much the same despite the differences in the technical modalities.

This being so, it should not surprise us that these questions have proved quite amenable to legal unification. In April 1964 the Hague Conference for the Unification of the Law of Sales adopted the Uniform Law on the International Sale of Goods (ULIS) and the Uniform Law on the Formation of Contracts for the International Sale of Goods (ULFIS). These conventions unify the law of 'international sales contracts' as between the states that ratify them. So far the number of ratifications is rather lower than expected, but the two Laws of Sales are nevertheless in force in six countries of the Common Market, namely Belgium, Great Britain, Italy, Luxembourg, the Netherlands, and West Germany. Thus a German court which has to deal with a dispute arising from an 'international' sales contract between parties domiciled in any two of those six states will apply the Uniform Laws directly rather than the rules of whichever legal system is indicated by German private international law. But a sales contract is 'international' only if a further requirement is satisfied, namely that the goods sold are to cross a frontier, or, failing that, that the offer and acceptance forming the contract did so (see art. 1 ULIS). Thus if a sales contract is formed and performed within a single state, the Uniform Laws do not apply unless the parties decide to declare it applicable, as art. 4 of ULIS permits them to do.

For the antecedent history of these Conventions see LESER, in 'Introduction' to Ernst RABEL, *Gesammelte Aufsätze*, vol. III (1967) 26 with further references. ULIS and ULFIS were ratified by West Germany in enactments of 17 July 1973 (BGBl I 856, 858). Many commentaries on them have been published, such as DÖLLE (ed.), *Kommentar zum Einheitlichen Kaufrecht* (1976); MERTENS/REHBINDER, *Internationales Kaufrecht* (1975).—In view of the fact that the developing countries and the socialist countries did not participate in the negotiations leading to the Hague Conventions and that the United States did so only at the end, it was not to be expected that a world-wide unification of the law of international sales would result. So in 1966 the United Nations Committee on International Trade Law (UNCITRAL) took up the question of the unification of sales law, and as they were able to build upon the work of the Hague Conference, the business could be completed relatively swiftly. In 1980 sixty-two states attended a conference convened in Vienna by the United Nations and produced a Convention on Contracts for the International Sale of Goods which is essentially a shorter and terser version of the Hague Sales Laws (now in a single text). On this see SCHLECHTRIEM, *Uniform Sales Law* (1986) and HONNOLD, *Uniform Law for International Sales Under the 1980 United Nations Convention* (1982).

ULIS is of particular interest to us here because it contains a complete treatment of breach of contract based on intensive comparative legal studies and succeeds in 'resolving in a higher unity the peculiarities still remaining in national laws from times past, and does so without any loss and with very great gain' (RABEL in *RabelsZ* 9 (1935) 6). For this reason we shall enrich our critical evaluation of the various laws on this matter by noting the standpoint adopted by ULIS.

VI

The German BGB was flawed at birth by its unfortunate division of breaches of contract into impossibility, objective and subjective, and delay. So incomplete was this coverage that the courts had to adopt the institution of 'positive breach of contract' as a residual category for the types of breach of contract not covered. The subtle distinctions in the BGB are also inappropriate to the subject matter. No one denies that special rules are needed for the case of 'delay' since it poses a problem which does not arise in cases where performance is impossible, namely of determining how late a performance the creditor, who admittedly will have a claim for damages, must nevertheless accept. But although such special provisions are required, it is unnecessary to create a theoretically independent type of breach of contract called 'delay'. It is equally unsatisfactory that the 'doctrine of impossibility' should have led German law to produce an independent category of contracts envisaging a performance which is 'objectively impossible' which §306 BGB renders void, thereby making it necessary to distinguish initial impossibility, itself subdivided into objective impossibility and subjective inability, from subsequent impossibility. The liability of a debtor who has failed to perform his contract cannot sensibly depend on whether his inabilty to perform existed at the time of the contract or occurred only later, or whether, though he himself could not perform at the time of the contract, there was someone else somewhere who could. In all these cases the critical question must be the same: is the fact which prevented, delayed, or otherwise perverted the execution of the contract one of those which, given the purpose of the transaction and the views of relevant businessmen, fall within the debtor's area of risk? If this is accepted, the way is open for a unitary concept of breach of contract, matched by an equally unitary concept of the defence arising from obstacles to performance.

In their present state the Continental legal systems are very far from accepting the general definition of 'exculpatory obstacle to performance' just given. The German and Romanistic legal families release a contractor from his duty to perform if he can prove that he was not to blame for the obstacle to performance. The Common Law, on the other hand, starts from the idea, qualified in many respects, as we have seen, that the debtor guarantees the result promised in the contract and instead of inquiring whether the debtor was at fault regarding the obstacle to performance it asks whether, on a proper construction of the contract, the obstacle falls within the guarantee. Once again we must emphasize that in spite of the theoretical differences the same or similar results emerge in practice. Thus we have seen that in cases of 'initial impossibility' the German courts are ready, if this is necessary in order to get round the inconveniences of §306 BGB, to find that a contractor who has promised an 'impossible' result has actually guaranteed it. Indeed, in cases of 'initial inability', the debtor is always regarded as guaranteeing his ability to perform. So far as subsequent obstacles to performance are concerned, the most important case is the delivery of generic goods, and both on the Continent and in the Common Law the view of commerce is that in entering the contract the debtor undertakes that whatever happens he will be in a position to produce the promised goods at the right time. Finally, if the vendor of specific goods later finds it impossible to deliver, the Common Law, both in its sales legislation and in the decisions following *Taylor* v. *Caldwell*, holds that the accidental destruction of the thing is not normally covered by the guarantee of performance. Where different theories lead to much the same results, the comparative lawyer must choose the most appropriate one. Here it seems to us that the Common Law should be preferred. In the modern world exchange transactions are very largely standardized and they must be quickly and painlessly executed: it is truer to the reality of 'contract' as a social phenomenon if we normally treat the parties not as simply promising to do their best to produce the envisaged result but as actually guaranteeing it. It is also the better legal policy.

This is the standpoint adopted by ULIS. Under arts. 18 and 19 the vendor is obliged to deliver and to pass title in goods which conform to the contract, along with the accompanying documents, these obligations being specified in greater detail in arts. 20 ff., 33 ff., 50, and 54. If the vendor delivers goods which are disconform to the contract (regardless of whether they lack a feature stipulated in the contract, a quality which was guaranteed, or a characteristic necessary for normal use, whether, indeed, they are the wrong goods altogether), if he delivers too much or too little, too early or too late, or in the wrong place, or if his performance is defective in some other respect, this is a breach of contract which entitles the purchaser to demand performance or to withdraw from the contract or, in the case where the goods are defective, to claim an abatement of the price; in addition he can always claim damages.

It will be obvious that the conditions under which the purchaser can exercise the rights just mentioned depend on the type of breach of contract. For example, if defective goods are delivered, the purchaser can claim damages or a reduction of the price only if he has given notice of the defect promptly after discovering it (arts. 38–40) If the seller is in default regarding the time or place of delivery, the buyer may bring a claim for performance only if it is not normal or practicable to buy similar goods elsewhere (art. 25). Again, when the vendor is in breach of other duties not specified in ULIS, the buyer can claim damages for the loss thereby occasioned to him, but only if the breach is 'fundamental' may he withdraw from the contract (art. 55); according to the definition in art. 10 a breach is 'fundamental' if a reasonable person similarly situated would have refrained from entering the contract had he foreseen the breach and its consequences.

Underlying all these special rules in ULIS is the idea that non-performance or defective performance always constitutes a breach of contract for which the vendor is responsible. It makes no difference whether the facts which prevented performance occurred before or after the contract was concluded, or whether they affected everyone in the world or only the vendor. Nor does it matter whether the non-performance or defective performance is attributable to any fault on the part of the vendor. There is only one provision in ULIS which releases the vendor, and in proper cases the purchaser, from his liability for breach of contract. This is art. 74, which provides that a party is released from liability if he proves that the non-performance is attributable to circumstances which he was not bound, in view of the purpose of the parties in concluding the contract, to take into account, to avoid, or to overcome; the intentions of the parties, if not expressed in any way, are assumed to be those which would be entertained by reasonable persons similarly situated. The aim of this provision is to create a unitary criterion for solving the question whether or not a contracting party is liable for initial or subsequent obstacles to performance; the criterion relates to the allocation of risks actually or presumptively, on a construction of the contract, intended by the parties. ULIS thereby adopts the criterion which all legal systems, whether openly or not, recognize as crucial and which explains the general similarity of the results of decided cases (on this see in detail RABEL, *Recht des Warenkaufs* I (1936) 346 ff.; v. CAEMMERER, *AcP* 178 (1978) 141 ff.; DÖLLE/STOLL, *Kommentar zum Einheitlichen Kaufrecht* (1976) Art. 74).

It will be seen that ULIS treats warranties of title and quality as part of the general system of breach of contract rather than as an independent institution: the delivery of goods which are physically or legally defective is a breach of contract just as much as a delivery which is faulty in point of time or place or in some other respect. So far as legal defects are concerned or physical defects in generic goods, this comes as no surprise to German lawyers, but it is a reasonable way of dealing with physical defects in specific goods as well. While it may seem perfectly accurate to say that the vendor has done all that he promised to do when he has delivered the specified goods, even if they are in a defective condition, the fact remains that all legal systems in the world hold him liable, and this is ultimately because commercial men know that the goods must be delivered in a proper condition.

Once liability for defective goods is thus removed from its traditional place among the aedilician remedies, it becomes possible to incorporate the *actio redhibitoria* into the general law relating to the right to resile, and so to resolve some of its great technical complexities, witnessed by German theories as to the legal nature of *Wandlung* (cancellation). Here ULIS utilizes ideas traditionally found only in the law relating to breach of contract; in particular, the distinction between 'material' and 'immaterial' breaches of contract now has a role to play when the vendor's liability is based on defects in the goods.

If the vendor delivers goods which are 'disconform to contract' (art. 33), this may or may not be a 'fundamental' breach. If it is, the purchaser has a short time after giving notice of the defect within which to declare the contract avoided, provided that failure to deliver proper goods on time would also have constituted a 'fundamental' breach (art. 43). If late delivery would only be an 'immaterial' breach and if the shortcomings of the goods are also 'immaterial', the purchaser must be prepared to accept satisfactory goods unless this would cause him inconvenience or considerable expense. But even in this case the purchaser does not have to wait for ever: he can fix a reasonable time for proper delivery and declare the contract at an end if it is not observed (art. 44). According to art. 45, these rules are equally applicable when the goods themselves are satisfactory in point of quality but have been delivered in the wrong quantity, whether the difference is material or not. On this see RIESE, *RabelsZ* 29 (1965) 57 f.

So fully is liability for defects incorporated into the law of breach in ULIS that a purchaser who receives defective goods is not only entitled, as he is in systems in the Roman tradition, to reject them or demand an abatement of the price, but, as in the Common Law, he also has a claim for damages even if the vendor is not at fault. This is the most significant difference between ULIS and the law in most Continental countries and it was the subject of lively discussion at the last Hague Conference.

On this see RABEL, *Recht des Warenkaufs* II (1958) 267 ff.; RABEL, *RabelsZ* 17 (1952) 222 f.; RIESE, *RabelsZ* 22 (1957) 60 ff.; RIESE, *RabelsZ* 29 (1965) 53 ff., 78 ff.

This is not the place to record the detailed considerations which led to the adoption in ULIS of the Common Law view on this matter, but it is worth noticing that even the German courts have contrived to hold the vendor of defective goods liable in damages even though he was not at fault, on the ground that he had given an 'assurance' or a 'guarantee' that the goods had certain qualities or did not have certain defects (compare §465 BGB).

To take an example, the Oberlandesgericht in Cologne has held that by trade usage the vendor of heating oil 'implicitly' assures the consumer that the heating oil does not contain an abnormal quantity of water (VersR 1964, 541). Again, if a producer of polyester fibre advertises by name ('Trevira') a fabric which is woven by third parties to his specifications and under his supervision, any contract of sale in which the goods are designated as 'Trevira' is taken to contain an 'assurance' that the specifications have been observed; if the material has defects attributable to non-observance of the specifications, the vendor is liable in damages even if he is not its producer and was himself under no obligation to follow the specifications or to test them (BGHZ 48, 118; see also BGHZ 59, 158).

On the other hand, it must be borne in mind that art. 74 extends to cases of defective goods; in consequence the vendor of defective goods may escape liability in damages if he can prove that the allocation of risks contained in the contract did not require him to take account of, to avoid, or to overcome the defect which has appeared in the goods. This should be of assistance to many *commercial* vendors: if at the time of the contract a purchaser knows or ought to know that the vendor is a middleman who is not himself in possession of the goods and who cannot for other reasons be expected to inspect the goods, whether because this is not the usual practice or because he has insufficient technical knowlege, it is quite possible that the sales contract should be so construed that the risk of the goods being disconform to the contract does not fall on the vendor so far as liability in damages is concerned. Here one could make a further distinction between mere economic harm suffered by the purchaser through the non-performance of the contract and physical injury to person or property which he suffers as a consumer of the defective thing. Furthermore the vendor is permitted to limit his liability for damages by an appropriately agreed clause.

The question 'whether the law on breach of contract should be reformed on the pattern of the Uniform Sales Law' was the subject of a report commissioned from Professor HUBER by the West German Ministry of Justice. HUBER (above p. 523) convincingly demonstrates that it should be so reformed, and drafted a big bill patterned on the unitary notion of 'non-performance' in ULIS. The innocent party to a bilateral contract would have the right to resile whenever the non-performance constituted a 'material breach of contract'; this would normally be the case where there was delay beyond the period for performance set by the innocent party. Damages would always be claimable for non-performance unless its cause was one which the debtor was not, according to the terms of the contract, bound to anticipate, avoid, or overcome. The innocent party to a bilateral contract could claim damages as well as withdraw from the contract, if justified.

44

The Effect of Supervening Events

AUBREY, 'Frustration of International Contracts of Sale in English and Comparative Law', 12 *ICLQ* 1165 (1963).

BAMBINO, 'Eccessiva onerosità della prestazione e superamento dell'alea normale del contratto', *Riv. dir. com.* 58 (1960) 416.

BERMAN, 'Excuse for Nonperformance in the Light of Contract Practices in International Trade', 63 *Colum. L. Rev.* 1413 (1963).

CHAPMAN, 'Contracts—Frustration of Purpose', 59 *Mich. L. Rev.* 98 (1960).

COHN, 'Frustration of Contract in German Law', 28 *J. Comp. Leg.* 15 (1946).

CORBIN, 'Frustration of Contract in the United States of America', 29 *J. Comp. Leg.* 1 (1947).

DAVID, 'Frustration of Contract in French Law', 28 *J. Comp. Leg.* 11 (1946).

DAWSON, 'Effects of Inflation on Private Contracts, Germany 1914–1924', 33 *Mich. L. Rev.* 171 (1934).

——, 'Judicial Revision of Frustrated Contracts', 1982 *Jur. Rev.* 86.

DESCHENAUX, 'La Révision des contrats par le juge', *ZSR* 61 (1942) 509 a.

DRACHSLER, 'Frustration of Contract: Comparative Law Aspects of Remedies in Cases of Supervening Illegality', 3 *NYL Forum* 50 (1957).

FARNSWORTH, 'Disputes over Omission in Contracts', 68 *Colum. L. Rev.* 860 (1968).

GOTTSCHALK, *Impossibility of Performance in Contract* (1938).

GOW, 'Some Observations on Frustration', 3 *ICLQ* 291 (1954).

HAY, 'Frustration and its Solution in German Law', 10 *Am. J. Comp. L.* 345 (1961).

——, 'Zum Wegfall der Geschäftsgrundlage im anglo-amerikanischen Recht', *AcP* 164 (1964) 231.

IGARASHI/RIEKE, 'Impossibility and Frustration in Sales Contracts', 42 *Wash. L. Rev.* 445 (1967) (Japanese law).

KEGEL, 'Empfiehlt es sich, den Einfluß grundlegender Veränderungen des Wirtschaftslebens auf Verträge gesetzlich zu regeln? [with comparative reports on different systems]; *Verhandlungen des 40. Deutschen Juristentages*, vol. I (1953) 135.

——, /RUPP/ZWEIGERT, *Die Einwirkung des Krieges auf Verträge in der Rechtsprechung Deutschlands, Frankreichs, Englands und der Vereinigten Staaten von Amerika* (1941).

LARENZ, *Geschäftsgrundlage und Vertragserfüllung* (3rd edn., 1963) [with comparative reports on different systems].

LEE, 'Frustration of Contract in the Union of South Africa', 28 *J. Comp. Leg.* 5 (1946).

LESGUILLONS, 'Frustration, Force majeure, Imprévision, Wegfall der Geschäftsgrundlage', *DPCI* 1979, 507.

LITVINOFF, 'Force Majeure, Failure of Cause, and Théorie de l'imprévision: Louisiana Law and Beyond', 46 *La. L. Rev.* 1 (1985).

McElroy/Williams, 'The Coronation Cases', 4 *Mod. L. Rev.* 241 (1941); 5 *Mod. L. Rev.* 1 (1942).

McNair, *Legal Effects of War* (3rd edn., 1948) 133 ff.

Meijers, 'La Force obligatoire des contrats et ses modifications dans les droits modernes', *Unidroit* 2 (1951) 99.

Merz, 'Die Revision der Verträge durch den Richter', *ZSR* 61 (1942) 393 *a*.

Mignault, 'The Frustration of Contracts, A Study in Comparative Law', 21 *Can. Bar Rev.* 32 (1943).

Popescu, *Essai d'une théorie de l'imprévision en droit français et comparé* (1937).

Posner/Rosenfield, 'Impossibility and Related Doctrines in Contract Law: An Economic Analysis', 1977 *J. Leg. Stud.* 83.

Reu, *Die Unmöglichkeit der Leistung im anglo-amerikanischen Recht* (1935).

Rheinstein, *Die Struktur des vertraglichen Schuldverhältnisses im anglo-amerikanischen Recht* (1932) 160 ff.

Rodhe, 'Adjustment of Contracts on Account of Changed Conditions', *Scand. Stud. L.* 3 (1959) 153.

Savatier, 'La théorie de l'imprévision dans les contrats', *Études de droit contemporain* II (1959) 1.

Schmitthoff, *Frustration of International Contracts of Sale in English and Comparative Law: Report of the Proceedings of the International Association of Legal Science* (Helsinki, 1961) 127.

Schmitz, 'Clausula rebus sic stantibus' in II *Rechtsvergleichendes Handwörterbuch* (ed. Schlegelberger) (1929) 634.

Smit, 'Frustration of Contract: A Comparative Attempt at Consolidation', 58 *Colum. L. Rev.* 287 (1958).

Smith, 'Impossibility of Performance as an Excuse in French Law', 45 *Yale LJ* 452 (1936).

Trakman, 'Frustrated Contracts and Legal Fictions', 46 *Mod. L. Rev.* 39 (1983).

Travaux de la Semaine Internationale de Droit, *La Révision des contrats par le juge* (1937) [with a general report by Niboyet, and separate reports on England, France, Germany, Hungary, Italy, Japan, Yugoslavia, Lebanon/Syria, Norway, Poland, Romania, Switzerland, and Turkey].

Wallach, 'The Excuse Defense in the Law of Contracts, Judical Frustration of the U. C. C. Attempt to Liberalize the Law of Commercial Impracticability', 55 *Notre Dame L.* 203 (1979).

Zepos, 'Frustration of Contract in Comparative Law and in the New Greek Civil Code of 1946', 11 *Mod. L. Rev.* 36 (1948).

I

A PERSON who fails to perform his contract properly is generally liable for breach of contract. If, however, he is prevented from performing by circumstances whose occurrence, according to the intention of the parties, is not at his risk, then an exception is made. In the previous chapter we tried to show that *impossibility* of a factual or legal nature may often act as an 'exculpatory obstacle to performance'. Cases of such impossibility arise if the specific object or supply of goods contracted for are destroyed without any fault on the part of the vendor or if the factory which was to produce the goods is accidentally burnt down or if a ship under short-term charter is requisitioned for a long time for naval purposes; since the actual destruction of goods, the burning of the factory, and the requisitioning of the ship are circumstances which are not, according to the general view of businessmen, at the risk of the debtor, the debtor is not liable to the creditor for non-performance of the contract. But suppose that the unforeseen change of circumstances does not exactly render it *impossible* for the debtor to perform the contract but makes it so much more difficult or so vastly more expensive that the two sides of the contract are now quite out of proportion. What is to be done in such cases of 'distortion of parity'? And what is to be done in cases of 'frustration of purpose', when one party under the contract is to pay a sum of money and can easily do so but finds that the other party's performance has now been rendered valueless for him by subsequent events?

The distinction here drawn between circumstances which render the performance of the contract *impossible*, those which render it much *more difficult* and those which *frustrate the purpose* of the transaction, is made only so as to help classify and clarify the cases by separating them into different types. In fact, all these cases are closely interconnected, as may be seen from the following example.

Suppose that a manufacture of fertilizer makes a long-term contract to produce a special fertilizer for tobacco plants and deliver it to a dealer for export to places overseas where tobacco is grown. If the fertilizer factory is then nationalized or if the manufacture of fertilizer is forbidden or if a government decree requires all fertilizers to be delivered to a state export organisation, we have a case of *impossibility*. It would be an instance of *distortion of parity* if after the conclusion of the contract enormous import duties were imposed on the import of the raw materials required for the manufacture of the fertilizer; finally, *frustration of purpose* would occur if the importation of fertilizer was forbidden in the consumer country: it remains possible for the manufacturer to produce the fertilizer and for the dealer to accept and pay for it but it is now impossible to achieve the only purpose for which, as the manufacturer knew, the dealer entered the contract, namely to deliver the fertilizer to the consumer country. We are not concerned at the moment with the question whether or how far the nationalization of the factory, the increase of import duties, or the prohibition of importation into the consumer country may release the parties from their duties to deliver or accept the fertilizer, but it is important to realize that the critical question may be put in the same form *in all three cases*: given the express contract they have made and the typical intention of parties to such contracts, which of the parties has accepted the risk that such circumstances might arise? If it is the *manufacturer* who has accepted the risk that his factory may be nationalized or that production costs may soar, then, if either event occurs, he must still deliver the fertilizer or compensate the dealer for the damage which failure to deliver causes. If the dealer has accepted the risk that the goods may not be imported into the consumer country, then he must either take the fertilizer and tender the price or pay damages for non-acceptance. If *both* parties bear the risk of the circumstances in question, the manufacturer is released from his duty to deliver and the dealer from his obligation to accept; both lose the chance of making any profit from the execution of the contract.

II

The question whether a person may be released from his contractual obligations by supervening events has been familiar to Continental jurists for centuries. It appeared in the *clausula rebus sic stantibus*, a doctrine which, as its name suggests, made the validity of a contract depend on the continuance of the circumstances obtaining at the time of its formation. This doctrine may be traced through the Middle Ages from the Glossators right up to GROTIUS and PUFENDORF; it was accepted in the Codex Maximilianeus bavaricus civilis of 1756 and then in the Prussian General Land Law of 1794 (on the historical development, see KEGEL (above p. 554) 135 ff., and LARENZ (above p. 554) 11 ff. with further references).

The Prussian General Land Law starts out with the proposition that in general one may not refuse to perform a contract 'on the ground of altered circumstances' (§377 I 5) but proceeds to add:

'If, however, an unforeseen change of circumstances makes it impossible to achieve the aim of both parties as expressed in the contract or inferable from the nature of the transaction, then each of them may resile from the unperformed contract' (§378 I 5). 'If the alteration of circumstances frustrates the express or obvious purpose of one party alone, that party may withdraw from the contract on condition, if the alteration is a personal matter, of fully indemnifying the other party' (§380 I 5).—There is a comparable rule in the Austrian ABGB but it is restricted to preliminary contracts, which remain binding only 'if . . . the circumstances have not so changed in the meanwhile as to frustrate the purpose expressed in the contract or inferable from the circumstances' (§936).

The scholars of the *Gemeines Recht* rejected the doctrine of the *clausula rebus sic stantibus*. Its vagueness was thought to be unconducive to legal certainty, and the fact that it had been welcomed by the natural law codes gave the adherents of the Historical School of Law an additional reason for rejecting it. Not until the middle of the nineteenth century did WINDSCHEID's 'doctrine of the contractual assumption' (*Lehre von der Voraussetzung*) make it possible once more to give proper effect to supervening events. According to WINDSCHEID, parties make contracts on the assumption 'that the intended legal consequence should only occur under certain circumstances'. Although the effects of the contract are to be dependent on the 'assumed' state of affairs, the parties' promises are not, strictly speaking, conditional, and the contract remains valid even if the assumption is falsified, but since this is not in accordance with the 'real' intention of the contractors, the contract, though valid and effective from the formal point of view, ceases to have any substantial justification. If the assumption is falsified, therefore, the contracting party may demand the rescission of the contract. In practical terms it is very much as if the contract had been concluded under a *condition* that the 'state of affairs' remain the same, so WINDSCHEID was able to call the assumption an 'inchoate condition' (*unentwickelte Bedingung*) lying midway between a mere motive and a true condition (*Lehrbuch des Pandektenrechts* (1865) §§97 ff.).

Like a few of WINDSCHEID's other ideas, the doctrine of the 'assumption' failed to gain entry into the BGB. It was severely criticized by LENEL (AcP 74 (1889) 213) who quite rightly pointed out that the 'assumption' was a kind of intermediate thing between a unilateral motive and a condition mutually agreed, and that commerce would be imperilled if it were recognized. The Commission which revised the draft BGB agreed with him and stated 'that this doctrine endangers the security of commerce'; there was also a risk 'that it might obscure the distinction between condition and motive and induce lawyers to give mistaken weight to the effect of a motive not incoporated in the contract' (Protokolle II 690 f.). Accordingly, neither the German BGB nor the Swiss codes have any general provision concerning the effect of change of circumstances in contract law.

The Swiss Code of Obligations does, however, have an isolated rule. The person who contracts to render services must do the work for the agreed price even if it proves more arduous or expensive than was foreseen. If, however, extraordinary circumstances which could not be foreseen or which were outside the assumptions made by both parties make it impossible to do the work or make it disproportionately difficult, the judge has a discretion to raise the price or rescind the contract (art. 373 part. 2 OR; see also art. 1793 Code civil).

After war broke out in 1914 the German courts were increasingly often faced with cases of supervening events, and since the legislator had left them in the lurch they had to work out equitable solutions on their own. At first they hewed to the words of the BGB and declared performance 'impossible' in the sense of §275 BGB even when it was only a case of so-called 'economic impossibility'. Two groups of decisions may be discerned (on this see KEGEL/ RUPP/ZWEIGERT (above p. 554) 51 f., 71 ff.). In one series of decisions the Reichsgericht saw economic impossibility in the fact that if performance was rendered after the removal of the obstacle, the delay caused by war, revolution, or transport problems, it would be *entirely different* in substance from what was originally promised in the contract.

This view was applied to contracts for the delivery of foreign raw materials which the war made it impossible or very difficult to import. In such cases the Reichsgericht released the vendor from the contract if 'delivery after the end of a prolonged war would take place in economic conditions entirely different from those prevailing in peacetime when the contracts were originally entered into' (RGZ 94, 68, 69 f.; see also RGZ 88, 71; 90, 102 and RG JW 1919, 717).

In another line of cases the Reichsgericht used to release the vendor for reasons of 'economic impossibility' if in the circumstances of the case to make him produce the goods was 'too much to ask' (*unzumutbar*).

'The chance event must not simply make it more difficult to produce the object contracted for, as by rendering it much harder to procure or more expensive to buy, but must involve such extraordinary difficulties that commercial men would say it was impossible' (RGZ 57, 116, 118 f.). Thus the vendor of salmon was freed from his obligation since the war had destroyed the German market in such foreign wares, even although the vendor had 'sporadically and exceptionally found ways and means' of obtaining some supplies previously (RG JW 1919, 499).—If goods which had been sold were requisitioned because of the war, the vendor was freed if the procurement of alternative supplies was not simply difficult and expensive but thoroughly uncertain and, if possible at all, not at a marketable price (RG WarnRspr. 1917 no. 161). On the other hand, in the case of bulk sales of generic goods with a speculative element the Reichsgericht clung stoutly to the view that the vendor remained bound by the contract notwithstanding considerable price increases, even of more than 100%, provided that there was still a market in the goods (RGZ 88, 172; 92, 322; 95, 41): 'even such an extraordinary rise in prices does not release the vendor provided that the goods are still being bought and sold in the market and are available in sufficient quantity for the performance of the contract. What the situation would be if just a few parcels of goods could be obtained only by a fantastic offer or from a single supplier need not now be decided' (RGZ 88, 172, 177).

This established rule that a vendor cannot be released by a mere increase in prices was nevertheless qualified by the Reichsgericht in several cases. If because of inflationary price increases performance of the contract on the terms originally agreed would involve the ruin of the vendor's business and bring about his immediate bankruptcy, then he may exceptionally have the 'defence of ruination' (*Einrede der Existenzvernichtung*).

See RGZ 100, 134; 101, 79.—Similar considerations can be found in the so-called 'reservoir case' decided by the Swiss Bundesgericht (BGE 45 II 386). By contract made in 1827 and renewed in 1863 the owner of a plot of land was bound to keep a reservoir on his land in good order and repair in return for a fixed 'water rate'. In 1910, as a result of changed economic conditions the cost of maintenance so greatly exceeded the water rate that the owner of land, actually a charitable institution, was faced in the long run with certain ruin. The Bundesgericht released the owner from the contract: this was permissible in an exceptional case if 'extraordinary circumstances which could not reasonably have been foreseen had the effect of rendering the debtor's obligation so onerous that to insist on it would involve his economic ruin'. But see also BGE 59 II 372, where the emphasis was laid not so much on the question of economic ruin, which unduly favours parties without resources, as on the question whether the debtor's obligations had been rendered so 'greatly, strikingly and disproportionately' more severe that the other party would be exploiting the debtor's embarrassment if he insisted on the contract. This line has been followed by the Bundesgericht in many other decisions (see BGE 62 II 45, 67 I 300, 68 II 173, criticized by MERZ, *Berner Kommentar* I (1962) art. 2 ZGB notes 230 ff.).—In NJW 1959, 2203 the German Bundesgerichtshof was faced with a case strikingly similar to the 'reservoir case'. A contract made in 1898 gave the plaintiffs the right to mine potash on the defendant's land for an unlimited period of time on payment of an annual sum of 1,200 marks as an 'interim payment' until the right was exercised. In 1959, the year of the decision, the 'interim payment' had only one-third of its purchasing power in 1898. Nevertheless the Bundesgerichtshof held the parties to the contract: not every alteration in the relative value of performance and counterperformance justified a departure from the principle of adherence to contracts; 'on the contrary, there must be such a fundamental and crucial change in the relevant circumstances that continued adherence to the original contract would lead to an intolerable result quite incompatible with one's sense of justice'. This requirement was not fulfilled in the present case. Any other view would, according to the Bundesgerichtshof, lead to 'the general implication of an index clause into all long-term contracts' (to the same effect BGH NJW 1966, 105 and 1976, 142). The Bundesgerichtshof has exceptionally permitted the revaluation of a money claim devalued by inflation where the money was to cover the creditor's *living costs*: the employer was required to negotiate a modification of the payments due under an old-age pension if the cost of living had risen by more than 40% since the last review (BAG BB 1973, 522; and BGHZ 61, 31). The Law of 19 December 1974 for the Improvement of Old Age Pensions now enacts this principle of judge-made law (see §16, applied in BAG NJW 1976, 1861 and NJW 1977, 2370).

German legal writers soon set themselves to producing a general theory to serve as a basis for the courts' decisions on the problem of altered circumstances. The most important of these attempts was OERTMANN's doctrine of the 'basis of the transaction' (*Geschäftsgrundlage*). Like WIND-SCHEID's theory, it starts from the proposition that a contract may lapse as a result of altered circumstances if the expectations, assumptions, or supposi-tions entertained by the parties at the time of the contract are frustrated by subsequent events. OERTMANN's theory can also be described as 'psychologi-cal' in as much as it turns on the actual state of mind of the parties at the time they concluded the contract, but he differs from WINDSCHEID in one respect: it is not enough that the assumption belied by the future course of events was privately entertained by the party now trying to resile from the contract; the assumption must either be shared by both parties or, if entertained by one party only, at least manifested by him at the conclusion of the contract and acquiesced in by the other party. An 'assumption' which satisfies these requirements OERTMANN calls the 'basis of the transaction' (*Geschäfts-grundlage*).

It will obvious that OERTMANN's doctrine is inapplicable in precisely the most important cases, where the subsequent alteration of circumstances *could* not reasonably be foreseen by the parties at the time of the contract; the parties in such a case naturally regard the continuance of the existing circumstances as self-evident and therefore do not consciously form, much less express, any assumptions about the future course of events. Nevertheless the Reichsgericht continually used the theory of the 'basis of the transaction', and the expressions they used may still be found today in the decisions of the Bundesgerichtshof. One should not pay too much heed to this, however, for cases where performance has unexpectedly been rendered much more difficult depend very much on their own particular facts, especially on the type of contract involved, which may suggest how the risk that these circumstances might occur is to be allocated between the parties. The only use of general theories like OERTMANN's is to give the courts phrases in which to dress up the really material considerations.

This is evident in the very first decision in which the Reichsgericht used the doctrine of the basis of the transaction. Property was sold which did not yet belong to the vendor but which he hoped to obtain from the then owner, a company in process of liquidation. The purchase price was in line with the market value at the time of the contract. The liquidation of the company was, however, very prolonged, and meanwhile the price of land increased many times over owing to the depreciation of the currency. In view of this the vendor asserted that he was no longer bound by the contract. The Reichsgericht agreed in principle, holding that the parties had assumed that the relationship between performance and counterperformance existing at the time of the contract would remain constant, and that this was the 'basis of the transaction' in OERTMANN's sense. But the defendant vendor could not simply resile from the contract; instead, the judge must 'adjust the price in view of the existing devaluation so as to avoid the rescission of the contract' and give the plaintiff the opportunity of buying the land at the higher price. Only if the plaintiff did not so agree could the defendant resile from the contract (RGZ 103, 328). As may be seen from the reasons given by the court, the critical factor in this decision was that it was a sale of specific property without any speculative element. In refusing to put on the vendor all of the loss resulting from a fundamental alteration in the currency, the Reichsgericht was making a 'demarcation of areas of risk on the basis of policy considerations' (KEGEL/RUPP/ZWEIGERT (above p. 554) 151); it is sheer fiction for the Reichsgericht to say that at the time of the contract the parties 'assumed' the continuance of the parity of performance and counterperformance and thus made it the 'basis of the transaction'.

This decision already contains the seeds of the Reichsgericht's famous line of cases on revalorization. After 1923 the Reichsgericht relied on §242 BGB to make the owner of mortgaged property pay the mortgagee a supplementary sum over and above the nominal value of the mortgage so as to alleviate the very marked devaluation of paper money in Germany (RGZ 107, 78). In 1925 the legislator adopted this solution and laid down in the Law of Revalorization (*Aufwertungsgesetz*) that the owner could only extinguish a mortgage on his property by paying a sum amounting to 25% of the value of the mortgage in gold marks, and that if the owner had already extinguished the mortgage by making payment in worthless paper money, the creditor could under certain conditions demand the reinstatement of the mortgage in the land register. This statutory resuscitation of the mortgage was very hard on the person who had sold his land 'free of mortgage' for he became liable to pay it off 'a second time', and in gold marks at that, so in another famous decision the Reichsgericht gave the vendor a 'contribution claim' against the purchaser who had to pay a subvention towards the expense of paying off the mortgage, in an amount depending on the circumstances of the case; if the purchaser refused, the vendor could rescind the contract of sale (RGZ 112, 329; see also RGZ 119, 133). The doctrine of the collapse of the basis of the transaction figures once more in the judgment, but still as a purely ornamental feature. A like decision was made in a case where the parties had fixed the purchase price in sterling on the assumption that the English pound would remain on the gold standard. When England unexpectedly abandoned the gold standard, the disadvantaged vendor was allowed to claim an increment towards the loss attributable to the devaluation (RGZ 141, 212; compare also RGZ 145, 51).

After the Second World War the courts were faced with unprecedented problems. Millions of people had to abandon their homes and their entire mode of life, domestic and business premises were very largely demolished and dismantled, and in the East expropriation added its toll. Such a catastrophe was bound to present the courts with the problem of the effect of altered circumstances on contracts.

The courts got very little help from the legislature. A law of 26 March 1952 (*Vertragshilfegesetz*) allowed the debtor under contracts antedating the day of currency reform, 21 June 1948, to seek a court judgment deferring or reducing his liability if he made a declaration of his assets; the judge was bound to grant the request 'if and in so far as due and complete performance by the debtor appears excessive on a just balance of the interests and situations of both parties'.

There were very many other cases. The courts continued to employ the doctrine of the collapse of the basis of the transaction, but stressed that in the last resort the critical thing was 'applying the standard of good faith to the circumstances of the individual case. The defence applies only . . . if and in so far as the result flowing from strict adherence to the contract would be intolerable for the debtor in view of the new situation' (OGHZ 1, 62; see also BGHZ 2, 188 and BGH LM §284 BGB no. 2). To this it has justly been objected that whether or not it would be 'intolerable' for the person disadvantaged to be kept to the contract is not the only consideration (see LARENZ (above p. 554) 117 ff.); what is essentially in issue is the division of risks typical of the type of contract in question, a question which the courts' approach tends to obscure.

We shall mention only one of these cases, the well-known 'pneumatic drill case', decided by the Bundesgerichtshof (MDR 1953, 282). The plaintiff had agreed to produce and deliver to the defendant a number of pneumatic drills of a particular model. The model was already obsolete, and the plaintiff knew that the defendant intended to send them to East Germany, that being the only place where pneumatic drills of this design could be used. After the contract had been concluded the side-effects of the Berlin Blockade made delivery of pneumatic drills to East Germany impossible. The Bundesgerichtshof quite rightly started out by saying that in contracts of sales and services the purchaser or employer must bear the risk of not being able to use the goods as originally intended, but it went on to say that 'although the blockade was in operation at the time the contract was concluded both parties shared the assumption that the delivery of pneumatic drills to East Germany would remain possible for the foreseeable future'. Thus the use which the plaintiff had in mind was 'admittedly not part of the contract, but the basis of the contract'. The defendant was therefore released from his obligation to accept and pay for the pneumatic drills, but as the contract had to be *adapted* to the new situation in the light of the demands of good faith he must pay one-quarter of the total agreed sum. This would go some way to compensate the plaintiff for its expenditures in beginning to carry out the contract.— This decision must be emphatically repudiated. A purchaser who buys goods on his own account in the hope of gaining from a resale must bear the risk of such a resale becoming impossible. This risk typically rests on him, and if he wants the vendor to share it he must so stipulate in the contract, and will doubtless find that the enhanced risk will cause the vendor to increase his price. The Swiss Bundesgericht was therefore right to decide a similar case the other way. At the end of 1939, a Swiss arms producer contracted with the French government to deliver certain weapons for the French army. He needed some special parts to fulfil the contract so on 4 June 1940 he placed an order for them with the plaintiff. Both parties knew what they were for and what the current French military situation was, but when armistice occurred between Germany and France sooner than was expected, the arms manufacturer repudiated the contract. The plaintiff claimed damages for the ensuing loss and obtained judgment from the Bundesgericht (BGE 69 II 139).

III

It has already been noted in the chapter on breach of contract (above p. 536) that the French courts are extremely chary of the defence that supervening events have rendered performance much more difficult, and treat an obstacle to performance as releasing a party only if it is an unforeseeable event, not attributable to the debtor, which renders it quite impossible to perform the contract for the duration. Transport problems, import and export restrictions, strikes, confiscations, and such matters free the debtor only if in the circumstances of the individual case they render performance impossible as a matter of fact.

After the First World War the inflexibility of the courts induced French legal scholars to make all manner of attempts to render a change of circumstances legally relevant one way or another, under the comprehensive heading of 'imprévision'. Some writers sought to expand the concept of 'force majeure' so as to include mere difficulties of performance, or to reduce the liability of a person unable to perform by using art. 1150 Code civil, which makes damages payable only for *foreseeable* harm. Others pointed out that according to art. 1134 par. 3 contracts are to be performed in good faith ('de bonne foi'), while yet others tried to use the probable intention of the parties (see art. 1156 Code civil) as a ground for adapting a contract to the altered circumstances (see WAHL, note to Civ. 4 Aug. 1915, S. 1916/1917. 1. 17). On occasion the old theory of the *clausula rebus sic stantibus* was trundled out and proclaimed to be an unwritten principle of law. Lower courts in France occasionally followed these ventures, but in the cases which came to it the Court of Cassation held rigidly to its previous view. Only the Conseil d'État, the highest adminstrative court in France, adopted new and more flexible doctrines.

It was in a series of decisions around the middle of the nineteenth century that the views of the Court of Cassation were crystallized. The cases involved the practice of taking cover against the lottery of conscription with an insurer who promised to find a substitute if the insured were called up. On 13 April 1843 a law suddenly raised the number of conscripts from 80,000 to 140,000, and the insurance companies, arguing that this near doubling of the contingent had falsified the underlying calculations, claimed to be released from their contracts. Some of the lower courts adhered to the old principle that a contract was unaffected by difficulties and unforeseen events if its performance still remained possible and also pointed to the aleatory nature of such insurance contracts (Orléans 24 May 1854, DP 1854. 2. 132; upheld by Civ. 9 Jan. 1856, DP 1856. 1. 41). In other courts, however, there was a reaction against the rigid decisions of the Court of Cassation: it was said that the 'base essentielle' of the contract had been completely altered in an unforeseeable manner, some decisions relying on the probable will of the parties, others simply declaring that the increase in the number of conscripts constituted an instance of *force majeure* (see the decisions in DP 1854, 2. 128 ff.). Decisions which rescinded the contract of insurance were quashed by the Court of Cassation which tersely observed that this was not a case of absolute impossibility of performance (Civ. 9 Jan. 1856, DP 1856. 1. 35).

A further attempt to introduce the idea of altered circumstances into French law was made by the Court of Appeal in Aix in a judgment of 31 Dec. 1873, apparently the last such attempt before the World War. The facts were very similar to those of the Swiss 'reservoir case' (above p. 559).

In a contract dating from the sixteenth century one party had agreed for a certain sum to irrigate an orchard by means of a canal which was to be built. The agreed sum was now ridiculously small and went no way toward covering the maintenance cost of the canal. The trial court and the Court of Appeal at Aix handed down decisions referring only to 'équité' and raised the sum to a reasonable figure. The Court of Cassation quashed these decisions (Civ. 6 March 1876, D. P. 1876. 1. 197, where the lower court decisions may also be found), and once again encapsulated its views in the formula 'that, however equitable their decision might seem, tribunals must never use lapse of time or other circumstances in order to modify the agreements of parties and substitute new clauses for those which were freely accepted by the parties themselves'.

The Conseil d'État, by contrast, proved readier to adapt contracts to altered circumstances. Contracts for public works came first, then concessions of vital and essential undertakings, and contracts for the provision of public utilities such as gas, water, and electricity. The reason for such decisions is the public interest in the continuance of contracts which are essential to the orderly conduct of public life. This is made clearest in the decision of the Conseil d'État of 30 March 1916 (DP. 1916. 3. 25):

By contract dated 8 March 1904 the City of Bordeaux granted a company a concession for the provision of gas and electricity within the city limits for a period of thirty years. The price of gas consumed for public lighting was fixed at 8 centimes per cubic metre. After the outbreak of war the price of coal rose from roughly 28 francs to 114 francs, and the company sought to have the price of gas adapted to the altered circumstances. As no amicable settlement could be reached the parties went to the administrative courts. At first instance the company's claim was rejected but the Conseil d'État granted it. The Conseil d'État observed that coal was a necessary raw material for the production of gas and that it had risen enormously in price since the outbreak of war because the coal-producing areas of central Europe were in enemy hands and ocean transport had become extremely difficult. This had subverted the whole economic basis of the contract. The public interest in an assured and continuous supply of gas, as well as the particular circumstances of the case, called for a solution which could not be achieved simply by applying the words of the contract. If the parties were unable to reach an amicable settlement on this basis, the court must grant the utility company a claim for contribution from the consumer so as to cover some part of the loss which would otherwise be caused by the continuance of the contract (see also Conseil d'État 9 Dec. 1932, S. 1933. 3. 39, and 15 July 1949, S. 1950. 3. 61).

The civil courts were quite unmoved by such decisions of the Conseil d'État. Apart from a few lower court decisions the view has remained intact that even catastrophic effects on contracts only justify rescission if the very strict conditions of 'force majeure' are satisfied. This is the position in France to this day.

The following cases may be consulted: Civ. 6 June 1921, D. 1921, 1. 73: Civ. 17 Nov. 1925, S. 1926. 1. 37; Civ. 15 Nov. 1933, Gaz Pal. 1934. 1. 68; Com. 18 Jan. 1950, D. 1950, 227.

This being the attitude of the civil courts in France, the legislator had to intervene after both World Wars. This very fact shows that it is wrong of the French courts to treat contracts in the private and the public sphere differently in this respect: the legislator's intervention shows that even in private law it may be against the public interest, properly understood, to require that debtors always perform their contracts according to their terms, notwithstanding a fundamental alteration in economic conditions. After the First World War a law of 21 Jan. 1918 named after Deputy FAILLIOT gave courts the power to rescind pre-war contracts for the delivery of goods and, if the case required, to grant damages

'if performance by the contractor would cause hardship or loss greatly in excess of what could reasonably be expected at the time of the contract'. A law of 22 April 1949 made similar provision for contracts concluded before the Second World War. In addition, there was comprehensive legislation for the modification of long-term leases affected by the war. Judges were even empowered under certain conditions to defer or diminish the price in sales contracts between commercial enterprises (on this see KEGEL (above p. 554) 166 ff.).

French businessmen have reacted in their own way to the restrictive attitude of the French courts. They incorporate war- or currency-clauses in long-term contracts so as to effect an express allocation of risks, or have recourse to arbitral tribunals which they absolve from strict adherence to law and empower to adapt the contract to the changed circumstances in the light of what is fair and reasonable (see DAVID (above p. 554) 13 f.).

Other Romanistic jurisdictions, with the exception of Belgium, have declined to follow the French example. (See KEGEL (above p. 554) 170 ff.). *Italy* calls for special mention here. The effect of subsequent changes of circumstances on contracts is covered by arts. 1467 ff. of the Codice civile of 1942. A contract which is to be performed after a long delay or in deferred or periodic instalments may be rescinded by the court on the application of a party for whom the performance of the contract would be excessively onerous ('eccessivamente onerosa') as a result of extraordinary and unforeseeable events. There are two limitations to this general principle. First, the contract will not be rescinded if the subsequent difficulty falls within the normal risks of the contract ('nell'alea normale del contratto'); secondly, the other party can resist rescission of the contract by offering to alter its terms in an equitable manner.

IV

The *English* doctrine of the effect of altered circumstances on contracts—the 'doctrine of frustration of contracts'—has two distinct historical sources. One of them has already been noted in the previous chapter, the rule in *Taylor* v. *Caldwell* (see above p. 545). This decision laid down the principle that a party was freed from his contractual obligation (and consequently from liability for damages for breach of contract) if performance of the contract required the continued existence of a particular chattel and this chattel was accidentally destroyed before the time fixed for performance. This principle was subsequently extended in several ways. It was applied in a case where a pianist was disabled through illness from appearing at a concert as promised (*Robinson* v. *Davison*, (1874) LR 9 QB 462), the analogy with *Taylor* v. *Caldwell* lying in the fact that by falling ill the pianist had lost a quality whose continuance until the moment of her appearance was essential to the contract. See also *Nickoll* v. *Ashton*, [1901] 2 KB 126: the vendor of a cargo of Egyptian cottonseed was to load it in Alexandria in January 1900 on SS *Orlando*, but the *Orlando* grounded in the Baltic the previous month. A majority of the judges used *Taylor* v. *Caldwell* to support their view that the contract contained an 'implied condition' to the effect that the vendor was to be freed if 'performance becomes impossible by reason of the particular specified thing—that is, the steamship "Orlando"—ceasing to exist as a cargo-carrying ship without the defendants' default'. The other judge made a more convincing analysis of the case and asked whether it was not unfair to put the risk of the timeous arrival of the *Orlando* on the purchaser alone: after all, it was the *vendor* who, with knowledge of its location, had nominated the ship and chartered it for the carriage of the goods he had sold.

Finally, the rule in *Taylor* v. *Caldwell* was applied in the famous 'coronation cases'.

In *Krell* v. *Henry*, [1903] 2 KB 740, the plaintiff had a house on the route of King Edward VII's coronation procession and he hired it to the defendant for the day. The coronation procession was cancelled, and the hirer refused to pay the hire. The owner's claim was rejected: the rule in *Taylor* v. *Caldwell* was applicable not only 'where the performance of the contract becomes impossible by the cessation of the existence of the thing which is the subject-matter of the contract, but also in cases where the event which renders the contract incapable of performance is the cessation or non-existence of an express condition or state of things, going to the root of the contract, and essential to its performance'. It was true that in their letters the parties had not expressly referred to the purpose of the hiring (watching the coronation procession), but the court could look at the attendant circumstances in order to discover what the 'foundation of the contract' might be.—There was, however, another 'coronation case' in which it was held that the contract was not invalidated by the cancellation of the festivities (*Herne Bay Steamboat* v. *Hutton*, [1903] 2 KB 683). Here the defendant had hired the plaintiff's ship for the day on which King Edward VII was to review the fleet, since he wanted to watch the review and also to see the English fleet anchored at Spithead. The review was cancelled but the court held the defendant to the contract. The distinction between this case and *Krell* v. *Henry* may be that the person hiring the ship could still make the trip and show his guests the fleet, so that despite the cancellation of the naval review the contractual purpose could still be achieved in part. Furthermore, the plaintiff was in the business of letting out his ships throughout the year for all manner of purposes: he had no interest in the defendant's particular aim in engaging the ship, which therefore constituted only a unilateral motive in the defendant and not the common basis of the contract between the parties. The cases are discussed in detail in MCELROY/WILLIAMS above p. 555.

The other root of the present English doctrine is a line of cases in maritime law. These are cases in which a shipowner was unable to provide the chartered ship at the right time and place because without any fault on his part the ship had been damaged or requisitioned or because the port nominated by the charterer had been closed by war. The question in these cases is whether the delay attributable to such events is such that reasonable businessmen would regard the charterparty as at an end.

See *Geipel* v. *Smith*, (1872) LR 7 QB 404; *Jackson* v. *Union Marine Ins. Co.*, (1873) LR 8 CP 572; *Dahl* v. *Nelson, Donkin & Co.*, (1881) 6 App. Cas. 38.

Since the First World War the English courts have fused these two lines of decisions into the 'doctrine of frustration of contract'. It is applied today in cases of factual or legal *impossibility*, in cases of *frustration of purpose* (as in *Krell* v. *Henry*) and finally in cases where the change of circumstances has so delayed performance or altered its nature that performance rendered thereafter would be something 'radically different' from what was envisaged by the parties at the time of the contract.

See *Davis Contractors Ltd.* v. *Fareham U.D.C.*, [1956] AC 696, 727 ff.; *F. A. Tamplin Steamship Co.* v. *Anglo-Mexican Petroleum Products Co.*, [1916] 2 AC 397.

There is some dispute in England whether the judge should decide cases of this sort by construing the contract or simply by laying down what seems to him to be reasonable and fair in the circumstances of the individual case. The first view, called the 'implied term theory', goes back to *Taylor* v. *Caldwell* and has been endorsed in a long line of later decisions. Under this theory the judge must ask what agreement reasonable parties would have reached if at the time of making the contract they had foreseen the subsequent events and made some provision for them. Thus in *Hirji Mulji* v. *Cheong Yue S. S. Co.*, [1926] AC 497, 510, LORD SUMNER said: 'Frustration . . . is explained in theory as a condition or term of the contract, implied by the law ab initio, in order to supply what the parties would have inserted had the matter occurred to them, on the basis of what is fair and reasonable, having regard to the mutual interests concerned, and of the main objects of the contract'. Other decisions speak of the 'presumed common intention of the paties'; see *Bank Line Ltd.* v. *Arthur Capel & Co.*, [1919] AC 435, 455, and the other decisions cited by McNair (above p. 555) 143 ff.

According to the other view, the courts have power to adapt or undo contracts on the basis of equity: 'The court imposes upon the parties the just and reasonable solution that the new situation demands'.

See CHESHIRE/FIFOOT pp. 514 ff. Among the judges who have shared this view are LORD WRIGHT (see *Denny, Mott & Dickson Ltd.* v. *Fraser*, [1944] AC 265, 274 ff.) and LORD DENNING (see *Ocean Tramp Tankers Corp.* v. *V/O Sovfracht*, [1964] 2 QB 226, 238: 'If it should happen, in the course of carrying out a contract, that a fundamentally different situation arises for which the parties made no provision—so much so that it would not be just in the new situation to hold them bound to its terms—then the contract is at an end'.)—Other judges prefer to use the metaphor of the collapse of the 'foundation of the contract': thus in the *Tamplin* case [1916] 2 AC 397, 406), LORD HALDANE asked whether 'the occurrence ... may be of a character and extent so sweeping that the foundation of what the parties are deemed to have had in contemplation has disappeared, and the contract itself has vanished with that foundation'.

As English writers recognize (see TRAKMAN, above p. 555), it does not make much difference which of these views is adopted. A judge who avoids a contract on the ground of supervening events because he finds this 'just and reasonable' could and would reach the same result if he had to do so on the basis of 'construction of the contract'. In either case the critical consideration is whether the event which has brought about the change of circumstances is one of the risks which reasonable businessmen would put on the contractor seeking to avoid the contract. Two decisions on sale and charter contracts, both concerned with the effect of the closure of the Suez Canal in 1956/7, show how carefully English courts consider and evaluate all the relevant facts, regardless of the legal concepts in which they proceed to clothe the resulting decisions.

In *Tsakiroglou & Co.* v. *Noblee Thörl GmbH*, [1962] AC 93, 300 tons of Sudanese groundnuts were sold by contract dated 4 October 1956 at a price of £50 per ton c.i.f. Hamburg, and the vendor undertook to ship the goods in Port Sudan in November/December 1956. On 2 November 1956 the Suez Canal was blocked owing to the war between Israel and Egypt. Although the vendor could still have had the goods delivered to Hamburg via the Cape of Good Hope, the freight would have amounted to £15 per ton as opposed to £7 10s. by way of the Suez Canal. Accordingly the vendor refused to load the goods and declared the contract at an end. An arbitrator, appointed pursuant to contract, held that the vendor was in breach and must pay damages amounting to £5,600; this award was upheld by the courts, and by the House of Lords on final appeal. The dominant consideration was that this was a contract of sale in which it was indifferent to the purchaser by what route the vendor delivered the goods to Hamburg: the date of arrival in Hamburg, which was not fixed in the contact, was not material to him and carriage round the Cape would not have affected the condition of the goods. The doubling of the freight, on the other hand, was regarded as unimportant.

The same result was reached in the American decision of *Transatlantic Financing Corp.* v. *United States*, 363 F. 2d 312 (DC Cir. 1966), but not in *Carapanayoti & Co.* v. *E. T. Green*, [1959] 1 QB 131 where in a similar case, though more immediately in the shadow of the recent war, MCNAIR, J. came to the opposite conclusion.

The case of *Ocean Tramp Tankers Corp.* v. *V/O Sovfracht*, [1964] 2 QB 226, was rather more complicated. In September 1956 the defendant chartered a ship from the plaintiff for a voyage from Genoa to India via a Black Sea port at a fixed hire per month of the voyage. At the time the charter was concluded it was obvious to the parties that the Suez Canal might well be closed, but even so they included no term to cover this eventuality, meaning to 'leave it to the lawyers to sort out'. The Court of Appeal had to decide, *inter alia*, whether the charterparty was avoided by the fact that after loading in Odessa the ship could no longer proceed to India by way of the Suez Canal. In his very interesting opinion, LORD DENNING first gave the lie to the widespread belief that the 'doctrine of frustration' was applicable only if the events in question had been *unforeseen*. Then he asked whether the situation produced by the closure of the Canal entitled the defendant to throw up the charter, and held that this would only be so if the need to sail round the Cape put the defendant in a position 'fundamentally different' from that envisaged at the time of the contract. This was not the case: the voyage from Genoa to the port of discharge in India would have taken 138 days instead of 108 and would therefore have been relatively more expensive for the defendant, but the ship and its crew were such that the cargo would be perfectly safe on the voyage round the Cape. Accordingly, the increase in time and expense of the voyage did not entitle the defendant to terminate the contract. In other cases, however, first instance judges have reached a different conclusion: see *Société Franco-Tunisienne d'Armement* v. *Sidermar S.p.A.*, [1961] 2 QB 278.

In the *United States* distinctions are drawn according to whether the change in circumstances renders the performance impossible (impossibility) or very much more difficult (impracticability) or futile and pointless (frustration).

The first class of case includes not only situations in which performance is rendered absolutely impossible for the debtor—as when the concert hall which he has leased out burns down or where the specific thing he has sold is destroyed before the risk in it passes—but also situations in which the change in circumstances has rendered performance by the debtor very much more onerous or costly. In Restatement (Second) of Contracts (1981) §261 we find that the debtor is freed from his obligation to perform if after the formation of the contract his performance.

'is made impracticable without his fault by the occurrence of an event the non-occurrence of which was a basic assumption on which the contract was made'. This is very like the provision for sales contracts in §2-615 UCC, that delay in delivery or non-delivery of the goods does not constitute a breach of contract 'if performance as agreed has been made impracticable by the occurrence of a contingency the non-occurrence of which was a basic assumption on which the contract was made'.

It will be obvious that these are empty formulas without effective content; only by a close study of decided cases can one learn when a debtor will be released by a change in circumstances. It is accepted that the mere fact that performance has become more expensive does not of itself make it a case of 'impracticability'; much more important are the *facts* which have rendered performance more costly, and, further, which of the parties bore the risk that these facts might occur. In general, changes in the price of raw materials are at the risk of the party bound to obtain them in order to perform the contract; so, too, when owing to unexpected circumstances materials cease to be available from the anticipated source of supply, but are to be had from elsewhere, though more expensively. The person who has promised to deliver goods to a particular place is not released just because unforeseen circumstances make it impossible to deliver except by a longer and more costly route, though it may be different if it is an entirely unexpected event, such as the outbreak of war, the imposition of an embargo, or a disastrous crop failure which renders performance much more difficult and expensive.

Full details are in FARNSWORTH, *Contracts* (1982) 670 ff., with extensive references to the decisions of state courts.

American lawyers, unlike the English, restrict the notion of 'frustration' to cases where the promised performance can still be tendered (and paid for) but has, by reason of unforeseen circumstances, become very largely worthless or pointless (see Restatement (Second) of Contracts (1981) §265). Typical cases include those in which some administrative measure, serious civil unrest, or natural events have prevented the party from using the leased property as he had planned, or from exporting the purchased goods to the intended destination.

In *Lloyd* v. *Murphy*, 25 Cal. 2d 48, 153 P. 2d 47 (1947) a person rented a property shortly before the Second World War for use as an automobile dealership. When the US government imposed strict limitations on the sale of new motor vehicles, he refused to honour the contract, but was held bound by it. The court noted that the premises lay on a main thoroughfare and could be used for other purposes, perhaps by a sub-tenant, that an experienced businessman might have foreseen such wartime restrictions, and that the sale of automobiles had not been completely banned but only curtailed. 'The doctrine of frustration has been limited to cases of extreme hardship so that businessmen, who must make their arrangements in advance, can rely with certainty on their contracts ... The sale of automobilies was ... merely restricted and if governmental regulation does not entirely prohibit business to be carried on in the leased premises but only limits or restricts it, thereby making it less profitable and more difficult to continue, the lease is not terminated or the lessee excused from further performance.' See also CHAPMAN, 59 *Mich. L. Rev.* 98 (1960); HAY (above p. 208); and FARNSWORTH, *Contracts* (1982) 689 ff.

V

Our comparative survey shows that all the legal systems under consideration have had to face the problem of contracts affected by supervening events, but have used rather different methods and formulas to solve it. The stance of French law is very distinctive, for it continues to reject the doctrine of 'imprévision', except where it would be incompatible with the immediate public interest to require the contractor to perform in the new situation and so force him out of business in the long run. This restrictive position of the French courts has compelled the legislator expressly to recognize the need to adapt or modify transactions affected by war, which is in practice the most important cause of contracts being rendered impossible or nearly impossible to perform. Businessmen have reacted to this judicial attitude by making an express allocation of risks in their contracts and by taking to arbitration, but it is hard to judge the precise extent.

The German and Anglo-American legal families, on the other hand, accept the principle that courts have power within narrow bounds to release parties from their contractual obligations, not only where the equilibrium of the transaction has been distorted but also where its purpose had been frustrated. The practical results reached by the courts are not easy to compare, partly because rather different types of case have arisen in the different countries and partly because in such cases ancillary attendant factors play an unusually important but imponderable role. Even the rule that price rises can never justify rescission of a contract is sometimes qualified: in the 'reservoir case' the Swiss Bundesgericht rescinded a 90-year-old contract because of a price rise attributable to a gradual and sustained loss of the purchasing power of currency over many decades, while the German Bundesgerichtshof held the parties to a similar contract which had run for sixty years. An important factor in the Swiss case was perhaps the fact that the party in difficulties was a charitable institution which faced liquidation if the contract were upheld without modification. In decisions regarding the revalorization of mortgages and the consequent claim for contribution, the German courts themselves have adapted contracts to a devaluation of the currency, but it must be noted that this was in a situation where, owing to a fairly sudden change in the economy, the purchasing power of the legal currency was tending towards zero at great speed.

English and American courts have not yet had to cope with such catastrophes. It is true that the First World War caused great price rises in England and the courts had to consider whether such price rises could rank as a ground of release. In a series of cases the courts held not, repeating the simple formula that 'a person was not entitled to be excused from the performance of the contract merely because it had become more costly to perform it' (*Bolckow Vaughan & Co.* v. *Companāia Minera*, (1916) 33 TLR 111) but this was surely because these price rises were simply the consequence of wartime shortages of certain raw materials rather than a symptom of a general economic collapse, as in Germany at the time. As we have seen, the German courts in similar circumstances held the parties to their contract despite price rises. It is impossible to say how English courts would react in the face of galloping inflation but one might refer to an observation of VISCOUNT SIMON in *British Movietonews Ltd.* v. *London Cinemas*,

[1952] AC 166, 185 that 'a wholly abnormal rise or fall in prices, sudden depreciation of currency, an unexpected obstacle to execution' might be circumstances whose occurrence, on a proper construction of a contract, could free the parties from their obligations under it. Quite recently LORD DENNING held that a contract concluded for an unlimited period of time can be terminated if prolonged inflation, even at current levels, has seriously distorted the relation between performance and counterperformance. The defendant water company had contracted in 1929 to provide the plaintiff's hospital 'at all times hereafter' with water at a price of 2.9 p. per unit. When the price of water in the open market had risen to 45 p. per unit the water company terminated the contract and the Court of Appeal held that it was entitled to do so (*Staffordshire Area Health Auth'y* v. *South Staffordshire Waterworks*, [1978] 1 WLR 1387). The other two judges founded on the special facts of the case, but LORD DENNING stated that 'the time has come when we may have to revise our views about the principle of nominalism': seeing that the price of water had risen by a factor of twenty and would rise further, 'The situation has changed so radically since the contract was made fifty years ago that the term of the contract "at all times hereafter" ceases to bind: and it is open to the court to hold that the contract is determined by reasonable notice.' This is sharply criticized by CHESHIRE/FIFOOT p. 250.

While the dominant German cases on the effect of altered circumstances on contracts are those which sought to deal with the 'mass calamities', to use WIEACKER's apt phrase, after the two World Wars, the English cases get their special flavour from the strong mercantile and maritime element which emerges in the judgments. Not only are cases of 'frustration of charterparties' historically a source of the modern English doctrine but they still come before the courts in large numbers. What impresses the foreign observer is not only the careful analysis of the facts of the individual case, as one would expect of English judges practised in the art of distinguishing, but also the clear deference to the views and needs of commerce. If our very summary investigation of the question has suggested that English courts are less ready than German courts to hold that altered circumstances have brought a contract to an end, this is certainly attributable to the fact that the English courts are readier to meet the demands of international trade, for in the cases under discussion commercial men incline to keeping the contract on foot. This is shown, for example, by the fact that in the Suez Canal decisions we have mentioned, the commercial arbitrators were all in favour of maintaining the contract; such a view in relevant commercial circles is obviously adopted as law by the English courts more readily than is usual in Germany.

The general tests and standards applied in these cases by courts in different countries also differ. The German Bundesgerichtshof still uses the time-honoured language of the doctrine of the collapse of the 'foundation of the transaction', as it did in the 'pneumatic drill case', emphasizing that it is always a matter of 'evaluating the circumstances of the individual case in good faith and equity' and garnishing the dish with the assertion that release from a contract is only justifiable if there is no other way to avoid an 'intolerable result incompatible with law and justice'. The *Swiss* courts stress that when subsequent events have caused a disequilibrium between performance and counterperformance the judge may modify the contract if the creditor's insistence on his rights would constitute 'usurious exploitation' of the debtor. The *English* courts ask whether, if the debtor were required to perform in the altered circumstances, this would be something 'fundamentally different' from what was envisaged at the time of the contract.

The very vagueness of these formulas may lead the reader to conclude that any attempt to discover concrete standards of solution will be fruitless and, since in the last resort the courts are led by considerations which are hardly susceptible of rationalization, futile as well. There may be some truth in this, but a word of warning is in place. The tendency to decide these cases solely by the use of general formulas and the standards of 'Treu und Glauben', 'justice', or what is 'just and reasonable' should be resisted. The English courts may be relatively immune to the dangers inherent in such formulas, but this is less clear of the German courts. Reliance on these general formulas makes it too easy to overlook the fact that the rights of the parties must in the first instance be judged by the *contract* they have made, for it might well have contained an express allocation of the risk of the supervening events. The task for the courts is therefore to fill a gap in the contract which exists because the parties did not foresee a subsequent change of circumstances which has now occurred, or failed to make provision for it if they did foresee it. The means of filling this gap in German law is called 'ergänzende Vertragsauslegung' (suppletive construction). The aim of the exercise is not to discover the 'hypothetical intention of the parties', that is, how the parties would have dealt with the point at issue if during the contractual negotiations some third party had drawn their attention to it, nor is it to discover the 'basis of the transaction' in OERTMANN's sense, namely the actual view of the future development of events consciously entertained by one party at the time of the contract to the knowledge and with the acquiescence of the other party. The aim is to find out what the relevant commercial interests would regard as the normal and appropriate allocation of risks in contracts of the type in question (correctly so held in BGHZ 74, 370). The provision on release from liability in art. 74 in ULIS rests on this view, and so does the 'implied term theory' of English law which, properly understood, is sound in point of legal policy, for it constantly reminds the judge that he must not simply decide the case in accordance with what seems just and equitable to him at the time of his decision. The *contract* is the law adopted by the parties, and it is the contract which the judge must use as a starting-point for his deliberations; if it has a gap, he must fill it in accordance with the standards developed by reputable commercial men for contracts of that type. No doubt this investigation leaves the judge a great deal of room for play, but it remains true that he must take functional and equitable considerations into account only to the extent necessary for the performance of his proper task, namely the discovery of the allocation of risks typical of contracts of the same type.

B. Unjustified Enrichment

45

Unjustified Enrichment in General

V. CAEMMERER, 'Bereicherung und unerlaubte Handlung', *Festschrift für Ernst Rabel*, vol. I (1954) 333.

——, 'Problèmes fondamentaux de l'enrichissement sans cause', *Rev. int. dr. comp.* 18 (1966) 573.

CASAD, 'Unjust Enrichment in Argentina, Common Law in a Civil Law System', 22 *Am. J. Comp. L.* 757 (1974).

DAVID/GUTTERIDGE, 'The Doctrine of Unjustified Enrichment', 5 *Camb. LJ* 204 (1935).

DAWSON, *Unjust Enrichment, A Comparative Analysis* (1951).

——, 'Indirect Enrichment', *Festschrift für Max Rheinstein* II (1969) 789.

DRAKIDIS, 'La "Subsidiarité", caractère spécifique et international de l'action d'enrichissement sans cause', *Rev. trim. dr. civ.* 59 (1961) 577.

ELMAN, 'Unjust Enrichment in Israel Law', 3 *Israel L. Rev.* 526 (1968).

D. FRIEDMANN, 'Some Trends in the Development of the Law of Unjust Enrichment', in *Beiträge zum deutschen und israelischen Privatrecht* (Neue Kölner rechtswissenschaftliche Abhandlungen no. 81, 1977) 155.

W. FRIEDMANN, *Die Bereicherungshaftung im angloamerikanischen Rechtskreis* (1930).

——, 'The Principle of Unjust Enrichment in English Law, A Study in Comparative Law', 16 *Can. Bar Rev.* 243, 365 (1938).

GOFF/JONES, *The Law of Restitution* (3rd edn., 1987).

GORÉ, *L'Enrichissement aux dépens d'autrui* (1949).

GRAUER, *Die ungerechtfertigte Bereicherung im französischen Privatrecht* (1930).

HAKULINEN, 'Die ungerechtfertigte Bereicherung im finnischen Recht', *Vom deutschen zum europäischen Recht, Festschrift für Hans Dölle* I (1963) 401.

KELLMANN, *Grundsätze der Gewinnhaftung, Rechtsvergleichender Beitrag zum Recht der ungerechtfertigten Bereicherung* (1969).

KLIPPERT, 'The Juridical Nature of Unjust Enrichment', 30 *U. Tor. LJ* 356 (1980).

KNAPP, 'Die ungerechtfertigte Bereicherung in den Rechten der europäischen sozialistischen Länder', *Festschrift Zweigert* (1981) 465.

KÖNIG, *Der Bereicherungsanspruch gegen den Drittempfänger einer Vertragsleistung nach französischem Recht* (1967).

KUPISCH, *Die Versionsklage, Ihre Entwicklung von der gemeinrechtlichen Theorie des 17. Jahrhunderts bis zum österreichischen ABGB* (1965).

MARTINEK, 'Der Weg des Common Law zur allgemeinen Bereicherungsklage: Ein später Sieg des Pomponius?', *RabelsZ* 47 (1983) 284.

MAUDSLEY, 'Restitution in England', 19 *Vand. L. Rev.* 1123 (1966).

MOSOIU, *De l'enrichissement injuste, Étude de droit comparé* (1932).

MUNKMAN, *Quasi-Contracts* (1949).

NICHOLAS, 'Unjustified Enrichment in the Civil Law and Louisiana Law', 36 *Tul. L. Rev.* 605 (1962), 37 *Tul. L. Rev.* 49 (1962).

O'CONNELL, 'Unjust Enrichment', 5 *Am. J. Comp. L.* 1 (1956).

PALMER, *The Law of Restitution* (1978).

ROUAST, 'L'Enrichissement sans cause et la jurisprudence civile', *Rev. trim. dr. civ.* 21 (1922) 35.

STOLJAR, *The Law of Quasi-Contract* (1964).

TRIMARCHI, *L'arricchimento senza causa* (1962).

WACKE, 'Vorteile und Nachteile des deutschen Bereicherungsrechts,' in: *Beiträge zum deutschen und israelischen Privatrecht* (Neue Kölner rechtswissenschaftliche Abhandlungen no. 81, 1977) 131.

WAHL, *Vertragsansprüche Dritter im französischen Recht* (1935) 133 ff.

WILBURG, *Die Lehre von der ungerechtfertigten Bereicherung nach österreichischem und deutschem Recht* (1934).

WINFIELD, *The Law of Quasi-Contracts* (1952).

ZIMMERMANN, 'A Road Through the Enrichment Forest?, Experience with a General Enrichment Action', 18 *Comp. Int. LJS Afr.* 1 (1985).

I

MOST rights in all advanced systems of private law arise either from a *contract* or a *tort*. Even a layman has no difficulty in understanding the sort of situations covered by these areas of law. When one points out that there is also an important place for claims which rest neither on contract nor on tort but on 'unjustified enrichment', or, as the French say, 'enrichissement sans cause', the situation is different. The layman can make nothing of the expressions, and can hardly be blamed for it. Indeed, if the jurist asked himself why the expression 'unjustified enrichment' is so colourless, he might well find that it was because he crams under it a whole series of very disparate situations whose only common feature is a negative one, namely that they are neither contract nor tort. This is a view with which many Anglo-American lawyers would sympathize. They would unhesitatingly accept that a person who had received a payment made in error must give it back and that a person who has unwittingly used material copyrighted by another must hand over any profits even though there was no contract between the parties nor any real tort. Yet if one said that both cases rested on a unitary principle, a 'principle of unjust enrichment', they would either demur or regard the observation as mere speculation. German lawyers, for example, are readier to accept that claims for 'unjustified enrichment' have a unitary basis. This is probably attributable to an invention of the fertile jurists of ancient Rome, the 'condicto', whose significance for modern Civil Law only becomes evident if one understands how very differently the Common Law has developed in this area.

The Roman *condictio* was an *actio in personam* designed to enforce an obligation with a specific content. It was 'abstract' in the sense that the formula made no mention of the *basis* of the defendant's obligation. The *condictio* could therefore be used wherever a specific sum of money or a specific chattel had to be handed over to the plaintiff, regardless of the ground of the obligation: the creditor could use it to recover a sum of money whether he had lent it or been promised it by document or by stipulation. The Roman jurists went further, for they soon realized that the 'abstractness' of the *condictio* made it capable of use in situations where the defendant was withholding something from the plaintiff without any justification and ought to give it up. The normal case was where the plaintiff had handed over a sum of money or chattel to the defendant for some specified purpose which remained unfulfilled because of initial or subsequent impossibility. If a person handed over money to pay off a debt, to constitute a dowry, or to execute a legacy, and in reality there was no debt, the marriage did not take place or the will was invalid, the recipient could not retain what he had no title to receive (*sine causa*). In all these cases the action granted by the Roman lawyers to undo the effects of the transaction was the *condictio*.

This action did not, in classical times, rest on vague considerations of equity or as DAWSON (above p. 575, p. 59) says, 'the conscious appeal . . . to the principle of unjust enrichment and the moral ideas with which it was connected'. Admittedly the Corpus Iuris often links the *condictio* with the *jus naturae*, the *bonum et aequum*, or the *ius gentium*, especially in the famous fragment of POMPONIUS in D. 50, 17, 206: 'Iure naturae aequum est neminem cum alterius detrimento et iniuria fieri locupletiorem' (it is naturally unjust for one person to be wrongfully enriched at the expense of another), but the dominant view now has it that these are post-classical generalizations abstracted by schoolmen for pedagogical purposes. Classical Roman lawyers proceeded less on the basis of such general formulas than on a practical consideration of the individual case, and they extended the *condictio* to an increasing number of well-defined situations whose common element was not that 'the plaintiff had a special ground for claiming but that the defendant had no adequate grounds for retaining' (RABEL, *Grundzüge des römischen Privatrechts* (1955) 119). It is worth noting that although the classical condictio was used in many different areas it remained a single action with a unitary formula; the categorization of the *condictio* into various types is as post-classical as its affiliation to the principle of *aequitas* (on the whole matter see KASER, *Das römische Privatrecht* I (1955) §139, II (1959) §270, SCHWARZ, *Die Grundlage der condictio im klassischen römischen Recht* (1952)).

The different types of *condictio* developed under JUSTINIAN (*condictio causa data causa non secuta, ob turpem vel iniustam causam, indebiti*, and *sine causa*; see the titles to D. 12, 4–7) still survive more or less clearly in the Continental codes and form the heart of enrichment claims. Only in one respect has later development moved right away from Roman law: under the influence of natural lawyers who found a few handholds in the Roman sources, a general claim for useful expenditures has been developed which entitles 'him at whose expense something useful has been done for another' to reclaim it in specie or its value (see ALR 13 I §§262 ff., §1041 ABGB).

This is a generalization of the Roman *actio de in rem verso*. The *actio de in rem verso* was one of the claims, called 'actiones adjecticiae qualitatis' by the Glossators, which could under certain circumstances be brought directly against a superior by a person who had transacted with his slave, *filius in potestate*, or employee; it thereby served in some measure as a substitute for the institution of direct representation otherwise unknown in Rome. If the inferior had used any gain from his transaction with the third party for the benefit of his master, the third party could sue the master direct by means of the *actio de in rem verso* (see KASER, *Das römische Privatrecht* I (1955) §§62, 141).

In many books on the *Gemeines Recht*, Prussian and Austrian law this general claim for the repayment of useful expenditures was treated in close proximity with the *condictio*, and in France the lawyers adopted the *actio de in rem verso* of the *Gemeines Recht* as the basis for a general claim for unjustified enrichment for which the Code civil itself made no provision (for the details, see KUPISCH, above p. 576). By contrast, the German BGB did not adopt the *actio de in rem verso*, and in the countries where it is in principle admissible, as in Austria and France, its area of application has been severely curtailed by judicial decision.

II

Like the *Swiss* Code of Obligations, the *German* BGB devotes a special chapter to rights arising from 'unjustified enrichment' and starts out with a comprehensive general clause. §812 par. 1 BGB lays down that 'A person who without legal justification (*ohne rechtlichen Grund*) obtains anything from a person at his expense, whether by transfer or otherwise, is bound to give it up to him. This obligation also arises if the legal justification subsequently ceases to exist or if the transfer does not have the effect envisaged in the transaction.'

According to art. 62 OR, 'A person who is unjustifiably enriched at the expense of another must return the enrichment. This obligation arises in particular if a person has received a benefit without any valid ground or on a ground which did not come about or subsequently ceased to exist.'

§812 BGB distinguishes according to whether the uncovenanted benefit arises 'by transfer' or 'otherwise'. In the first group, the so-called 'Leistungs-kondiktionen', fall cases where the claim is brought to recover a benefit which the plaintiff conferred on the defendant consciously and intentionally, but which he now wants back because the transfer was 'without legal justification'. The most important instance of such a transfer ('Leistung') is the transfer of money or other things, but a *Leistung* may take the form of the assignment of a right, the delivery of possession, the surrender of a receipt, document of indebtedness, or negotiable instrument, or even the performance of services of one kind or another which the person receiving them would otherwise have paid for. A 'Leistung' also occurs if one person is released at the expense of another from an obligation owed to a third party. In all these cases the critical question is whether the benefit so transferred is 'without legal ground', that is, whether the recipient can point to any valid agreement or relationship with the transferor which entitled him to retain what he has received. Thus there is a 'justification' for a payment of 1,000 DM if it is made by purchaser to vendor in payment of the price or by bank to customer as a credit advance or by prospective father-in-law to son-in-law. But if the sales contract, being illegal, was void *ab initio* or if the loan was induced by fraud and the bank rescinds it or if the intended wedding never takes place, there is no longer any legal ground, if there ever was one, to justify the recipient's retention of the money.

One may find in §812 par. 1 sent. 2 BGB, art. 62 par. 2 OR and §1431 ff. ABGB the distinction between the various types of *condictio* known to Justinian, but this is of no practical importance since they are all instances of a transfer made 'sine causa'. What is worth noticing, however, is that the provisions regarding the restitution of an 'unjustified enrichment' pay no attention to the reason for the original or subsequent invalidity of the obligation. For example, it is immaterial whether the underlying obligation is illegal or immoral (see above Ch. 35), void for 'initial impossibility' (see above Ch. 43 II), or subject to rescission *ab initio* for error, duress, or deceit (see above Ch. 38); these questions all concern the validity of the contract and are therefore dealt with in the relevant section of the Code. The law of unjustified enrichment only moves in when the invalidity of the underlying transaction has been determined by reference to *other* provisions.—Nor is it a matter for the law of unjust enrichment to determine how contracts are to be unravelled which were valid to begin with but were later rescinded on the ground of a breach of contract (see above Ch. 43) or of a fundamental change of circumstances (see above Ch. 44): here it is the law of contract which controls not only the question whether the contract is rescindible but also how benefits conferred under the contract have to be given back (see §§323 ff., 346 ff. BGB, art. 109 OR, §921 ABGB), though on this matter German law calls in aid some provisions of the law of unjustified enrichment (§§323 par. 3, 327 sent. 2, 557*a*, 628 par. 1 sent. 3 BGB).

§814 BGB provides that a person cannot reclaim a benefit he has conferred if he knew that he was not bound to confer it. Swiss and Austrian law put the same idea more positively by prescribing that a person who has made a transfer he was not bound to make may only reclaim it if he was in 'error' about his obligation (art. 63 OR, §1431 ABGB). Of course the error in question here is quite different from the error required to justify the rescission of a contract: even a grossly negligent error, an immaterial error, or an error of law is sufficient to ground a restitutionary claim (see BGE 64 II 127; 70 II 271; BG St. Gallen SJZ 63 (1967) 110; OGH 20 June 1922, ZBl. 1922 no. 259).

This difference in the formulation of these codal provisions makes for a difference in the burden of proof: in Germany it is the *defendant* who must prove that at the time of the transfer the plaintiff knew he was not bound to make it (RGZ 133, 277), while in Switzerland and Austria it is for the *plaintiff* to establish that he made the transfer because he wrongly supposed he was bound to (see BGE 24 II 182; OGH 20 June 1894, GlU XXXII no. 15158).

A claim for restitution is also excluded if the transfer satisfied a moral obligation or an obligation which was time-barred or subject to some other defence: in such cases a debtor who could not be *sued* for performance cannot reclaim if he performs *voluntarily* (§§813, 814 BGB, art. 63 OR, §1432 ABGB).

A restitutionary claim is needed to solve a special class of case which arises only in Germany; these are the cases in which, thanks to the 'principle of abstraction' (see above p. 474), a person becomes vested with ownership or some other right as the result of a conveyance or assignment based on an invalid contract. Suppose that a person sells a painting and delivers it to the purchaser and that it later appears that the contract of sale was void for want of agreement or is rescinded for error. In that case the purchaser will nevertheless have become owner of it since German law makes a clear distinction between the contract of sale and the actual conveyance. At this point §812 BGB steps in and empowers the vendor to demand the restitution of the benefit conferred, namely the ownership in the painting. In Swiss law, by contrast, a conveyance of immoveables (art. 974 par. 2 ZGB) or chattels (BGE 55 II 302) is valid only if the underlying transaction is valid, so the vendor retains his ownership of the picture and therefore has a claim based on *ownership* which, unlike the claim based on *enrichment*, will procure the retransfer of the picture even if the purchaser is bankrupt. Of course the purchaser may already have resold the painting to a third party; if so, the third party, if in good faith, will have become owner of it (art. 714, 933 ZGB) and the original vendor will have only an enrichment claim with which to sue his purchaser for what he received from the third party.

In Germany, claims for the restitution of benefits conferred by the plaintiff's own act *sine causa* lie only against the party on whom the plaintiff conferred the benefit and not against third parties indirectly benefited by the transfer. Thus if a person uses borrowed money to reconstruct his wife's house, and the loan contract is invalid, the lender cannot claim restitution from the wife, even if the borrower is insolvent. The same rule applies if a building subcontractor under contract with the builder puts bricks and mortar into the house of a third party: he can only sue the main contractor, on the contract if it is valid or in unjustified enrichment if it is not; he cannot sue the third party for any increase in the value of the house attributable to his work and materials. The German courts here speak of the need for 'directness of transfer' (*Unmittelbarkeit der Vermögensverschiebung*): the loss of the plaintiff and the benefit to the defendant must result from one and the same transaction. The purpose of this restriction is obvious. The transferor should only be able to sue the transferee with whom he had a contract and should not acquire an additional debtor just because the object transferred happens to have ended up among the assets of a third party. It is also perfectly fair that the transferor's suit, in contract or restitution, should lie only against his contractor: he made the contract in reliance on his contractor's capacity to pay, and should bear the loss himself if this reliance was misplaced and the transferee gets into financial difficulties which prevent his paying the contract price or, should the contract fail, the value of the enrichment.

In other words, German law today refuses to recognize the *actio de in rem verso* as accepted in the *Gemeines Recht* and in Prussian law (see RGZ 1, 143; 1, 159; ROHG 3, 377; the negative attitude of the German legislator may be seen in Motive II p. 872).— *Swiss* law adopts the same position. In BGE 42 II 467 a farmer was placed under interdiction and his sons took on the management of the farm. They bought two cows from the plaintiff in their own name and added them to the herd. The vendor claimed the price from the father, and the Bundesgericht rejected the claim: the defendant became owner of the cows not at the plaintiff's expense but at the expense of his sons to whom the cows belonged after they had bought them from the plaintiff in their own name.—By contrast, §1041 of the *Austrian* ABGB admits the *actio de in rem verso* in very wide terms: the owner whose property 'has been used for the benefit of another . . . without any agency' is entitled to demand its return or reimbursement from that other. Despite this, the Austrian courts have always held that the *actio de in rem verso* of §1041 ABGB is simply 'a supplementary remedy which is only to be used in the case where there is no contract or analogous relationship between the plaintiff and the third party which could be used for the decision of the case' (OGH 16 Jan. 1952, SZ XXV 13). Thus a building contractor retained by a tenant to improve the rented house had no claim against the landlord for payment of the amount by which his labours had improved the value of the house (OGH 7 Jan. 1930, SZ XII 7; to the same effect OGH 1 June 1955, JBl. 1956, 17, with an exhaustive review of the cases and a critical note by GSCHNITZER); nor can a building contractor retained by the owner of a house to instal central heating claim payment from the person who subsequently buys the house (OGH 11 April 1934, SZ XVI 73). The courts do, however, reserve the power to allow the *actio de in rem verso* where the third party has contracted with the plaintiff in his own name but 'had no independent economic role to play, was dealing in the interest of the defendant in suit and was economically nothing more than a conduit' (OGH 16 Jan. 1952, SZ XXV 13). The only known case which allows the *actio de in rem verso* on this ground arose during the German occupation of Austria: a building contractor was engaged by an administrative unit of the German Reich to reconstruct a hospital belonging to the Austrian province of Carinthia, and after the war the province of

Carinthia was held bound to pay (OGH 22 Nov. 1950, JBl. 1951. 339; see also OGH 24 Jan. 1948, SZ XXI 60 and OGH 8 March 1950, SZ XXIII 53).

It follows from what has been said that a tradesman who improves or repairs an object which does not belong to his contractor cannot, if his contractor becomes insolvent, use §812 BGB to claim the value of the improvement from the *owner* of the thing. This rule is, however, qualified in cases where the tradesman is still in *possession* of the thing he has repaired: here all systems agree that the tradesman may hold on to the thing, even against its owner, until he has been paid for his work.

The method of protecting the repairman is different in the different systems: in *Germany* he is given claims for improvement under §§994 ff. BGB (see BGHZ 34, 122), in *Switzerland* he has a lien under art. 895 ZBG, and in *Austria* he is allowed to withhold the thing under §471 ABGB (see OGH 1 April 1959, ZVR 1960 no. 45).

So far we have been considering the *Leistungskondiktion*, or claim for the restitution of a benefit conferred by the plaintiff's own act, where the essential element is always a transfer, performance, or payment, that is, a benefit deliberately conferred by the plaintiff which cannot be retained because the underlying obligation was either invalid *ab initio* or has subsequently been rescinded. We must now turn to enrichments 'arising otherwise', of which the most important instance occurs when a person uses or profits from property or rights vested in another without his authorization. A defendant who was *at fault* in interfering with the rights of others will be liable to pay damages in tort, but even if his interference is perfectly innocent he is bound under §812 BGB to restore to the owner of the right the value of the use he has made of it. In such cases German lawyers speak of 'Eingriffskondiktion' (*condictio* based on interference).

For example, if a person lets his cattle graze in someone else's meadow or unwittingly consumes fuel belonging to another or utilizes a stranger's railway track (RGZ 97, 310), he must restore the value of the use which he thereby appropriated to himself, regardless of whether he was at fault in so doing. This is also the best way of solving a problem which has been much discussed in Germany, where a person without any contractual relationship uses the parking place of another: a person who drives into a parking place on the highway and states that he does not intend to pay any parking fee since he thinks there is no right to charge such fees is bound, should he be wrong, to pay the value of using the parking place. The reason is not that his driving into a parking place for which fees are charged constitutes a 'de facto contract' (*faktisches Vertragsverhältnis*), though it was so held in BGHZ 21, 319, 333 ff., but because he has unjustifiably interfered with someone else's right to charge for parking.

The person who makes unauthorized use of the right of another must reimburse that person up to the value of such use even if he can show that the other would not or could not have used the right himself. The purpose of the restitutionary claim is not to compensate for a *diminution* in the assets of the plaintiff—that would be damages for loss suffered—but to transfer to the party with the better right an *accretion* to the assets of the defendant. The owner is the person with the better right, for it is to the owner alone that the legal system accords the power to use his property as he thinks fit, or to allow others to do so, for a fee, should he so choose.

Another instance of the '*condictio* based on interference' arises when a person sells the property of another in such circumstances that his purchaser becomes owner of it. The previous owner can require the vendor to hand over what he received from the third party purchaser.

See §816 par. 1 BGB. This is also the position of *Austrian* and *Swiss* law EHRENZWEIG, *System des österreichischen allgemeinen Privatrechts* II (2nd edn., 1928) 726; BUCHER, *Schweizerisches Obligationenrecht, Allgemeiner Teil* (1979) 618 f. and BGE 87 II 20.—If the *third party* acquires the thing *gratuitously*, §816 par. 1 sent. 2 BGB exceptionally provides that the enrichment claim may be directed against him as well: whether this is true in Swiss law as well is not clear (see v. BÜREN, *Schweizerisches Obligationenrecht* (1964) 310).—There is some dispute about how to solve the case where the third party does not acquire ownership in the thing, as happens if it is stolen property (§935 BGB, art. 934 ZGB). If the third party is unknown or for some reason not practically amenable to a suit based on ownership, should the owner be able instead to make the vendor disgorge what he received from the third party? This is allowed in Germany, provided the owner recognizes the transfer of title to the third party as valid and thereby forfeits his ownership (see RGZ 105, 84; 106, 44; 150, 31, where the reasons given differ somewhat). The Swiss Bundesgericht apparently decides otherwise (see BGE 71 II 90).

The *condictio* based on interference is also very important where absolute rights other than ownership have been infringed. Thus when there is even an innocent infringement of a *copyright* vested in another, the German courts apply the general provisions regarding restitution of unjustified enrichment. For example, if a person makes a commercial publication of an actor's picture without his consent, he must pay a sum of money on the basis of unjustified enrichment, the sum to be determined in accordance with the honorarium which an actor would normally charge for his consent to such publication (BGHZ 20, 345, 354 ff.; see also RGZ 121, 258; BGHZ 5, 116, 123).

With respect to an innocent infringement of *patent* or *design* rights, the courts used to hold that no enrichment claim lay: as the special laws provided for damages only when the infringer had been *at fault*, there was no room for the application of the general rules of private law. This was an error, and it has now been corrected: the innocent infringer of another's patent or design right must now disgorge his enrichment (BGHZ 68, 90). There is some dispute over the quantum of recovery, but the better view is that the infringer should pay what he would have had to pay for a licence, had he known that a licence was required (see BGH NJW 1982, 1154).

III

The Civil Code in *France*, unlike those of Germany and Switzerland, has no general provision regarding the restitution of unjustified enrichment. This is because POTHIER, whose writings dominate the law of obligations in the Code civil, concentrated on the *condictio indebiti* at the expense of other forms of liability in unjust enrichment, to which he accorded no comprehensive treatment. Furthermore POTHIER gave a great deal of scope to the institution of *negotiorum gestio*, which consequently became applicable, at a pinch, in cases where a transfer had to be undone because the purpose for which it was made could not be fulfilled. Thus of the many rules related to unjustified enrichment which are strewn throughout the Code civil, the most important are those concerning the payment of a thing not due (paiement de l'indu) and *negotiorum gestio* (*gestion d'affaires*). These two institutions are brought together in the Code civil under the title 'Des Quasi-contrats' (arts. 1371 ff.).

After the Code civil came into force in 1804 the French courts attempted to solve cases on enrichment on the basis of the codal provisions, and they followed POTHIER in holding that there might be *negotiorum gestio* although the gestor was acting only in his *own* interests and for his own purposes (the so-called 'gestion d'affaires anormale').

See Req. 19 Dec. 1877, DP 1878. 1. 204. The plaintiff had delivered police uniforms to the City of Bordeaux, but the contract under which he did so later turned out to be invalid. His claim for payment was allowed on the basis of *negotiorum gestio*. See also Req. 16 July 1890, DP 1891. 1. 49, noted by PLANIOL; KÖNIG (above p. 575) 17 ff.

In the second half of the nineteenth century, however, the French courts began to realize that the rules contained in the code and especially those regarding *gestion d'affaires* were inadequate to deal with cases of unjustified enrichment. The development of a *general* claim for enrichment owes much to the textbook of private law by AUBRY and RAU which was the first to treat the enrichment claim quite separately from *negotiorum gestio*.

The views of AUBRY and RAU were followed by the Court of Cassation in the famous *Boudier* case, but before turning to that landmark decision we shall deal briefly with the case of unjustified enrichment which is expressly regulated in arts. 1376 ff. Code civil, namely *répétition de l'indu* or the restoration of payments made pursuant to a supposed debt. The Italian Codice civile also has special rules concerning the payment of a thing not due (*pagamento dell'indebito*, arts. 2033 ff. Codice civile), although it has general provisions regarding unjustified enrichment.

In the chapter devoted to the performance of obligations, the Code civil already states that 'tout paiement suppose une dette: ce qui a été payé sans être dû, est sujet à répétition (art. 1235: 'payment presupposes a debt: what has been paid without being due may be reclaimed'). This claim for restitution is laid down in greater detail in arts. 1376 ff. Code civil as one of the claims based on quasi-contract.

The first requisite is that the recipient have been enriched by a 'payment'. This includes the payment of money, the transfer of things, and analogous transactions such as having one's account credited, but not the rendering of *services*, which therefore has to be dealt with by the *general* enrichment claim.

Next, the transfer must have been made pursuant to a debt which did not exist at the time. This includes the case where a debt is owed *by a third party* and the transferor pays it in the supposition that it is owed by himself: the transferor can claim restitution from the creditor unless the latter, thinking the debt has been paid off, has destroyed the document of indebtedness (art. 1377 par. 2 Code civil) or released securities (see Civ. 27 Nov. 1912, DP 1913. 1. 96; see also art. 2036 Codice civile). However, if one pays off a time-barred debt one cannot claim back what one has paid even if one was unware of the time bar (Req. 17 Jan. 1938, DP 1940. 1. 57, noted by CHEVALLIER; art. 2940 Codice civile).

The final requirement for this type of restitutionary claim is that the transfer have been made in the erroneous supposition that there was a duty to make it. The burden of proving such an error rests on the transferor (Civ. 1 May 1938, Gaz. Pal. 1938. 1. 667). If the error is the payer's own fault, he cannot recover if the payee was owed that sum by someone else (Com. 23 April 1976, DS 1977, 562, noted by VERMELLE; Com. 22 Nov. 1977, JCP 1978. II. 18997, noted by GÉGOUT). It is different if the money was not due from anyone: for example, if a person receives from his insurer a sum of money to which he was not entitled and it was the insurer's own fault that it supposed the money to be due, the payee must repay it, unless the insurer's fault was a gross one. If repayment would be prejudicial to the insured, however, the amount to be repaid will be reduced (Soc. 3 Nov. 1972, JCP 1974. II. 17692, noted by GHESTIN). A person who knows he is not bound to pay but is forced to do so against his will by the pressure of circumstances may also be able to claim restitution: the debtor who has paid his debt but lost the receipt and pays a second time under threat of suit can claim restitution on finding the receipt again (see Civ. 2 April 1890, DP 1891. 1. 182).

Italian law has one very odd rule: if a person thinks he owes money which in fact is owed by *someone else* and he pays it, he can only claim restitution if he proves not only that he made this mistake *but also* that the mistake was an excusable one to make (art. 2036 Codice civile), whereas if *no one* owed the money he thought he owed, he need not prove any mistake at all (Cass. 3 Jan. 1950, no. 8, Foro it. Mass. 1950, 4)!

No claim lies in either French or Italian law for the restitution of what has been voluntarily transferred in pursuance of a duty of honour or morals. This follows from the general provisions regarding obligations, performance of which, once rendered, cannot be reclaimed (art. 1235 par. 2 Code civil, 2034 Codice civile).

It will be seen that these rules regarding the *répétition de l'indu* in French law cover most of the cases dealt with in German law by the *Leistungskondiktion*, but there remain many situations which they cannot, under present French doctrine, adequately solve. These include the claims for reimbursement for *services* rendered without legal ground, the restitution of property transferred for a purpose which fails, cases of 'interference', and, above all, those cases suited to the *actio de in rem verso* where the thing reclaimed only came into the defendant's hands through the intermediacy of a third party who received it directly from the plaintiff. Here use is made of the *general* enrichment claim as established by the Court of Cassation in the *Boudier* case (Req. 15 June 1892, DP 1892. 1. 596, S. 1893. 1. 281, noted by LABBÉ).

The facts of the case were as follows. The plaintiff Boudier had supplied fertilizer to the tenant of a farm. The fertilizer was delivered and used by the tenant, but then the lease was terminated. Landlord and tenant agreed that the unharvested (and fertilized) crop should be taken over by the landlord at a valuation made by experts and set off against the outstanding rent. When the plaintiff learnt of this agreement, he did not sue the insolvent tenant but brought an action directly against the landlord for the value of the fertilizer. The Court of Cassation allowed the claim. This is not remarkable in itself, since the same result had been reached in several previous cases with the help of the institution of *gestion d'affaires anormale*. It is the *reasoning* of the judgment which is striking, for it recognizes a general enrichment claim under the name of 'action de in rem verso', resting directly on considerations of equity and not on any codal provisions: '. . . on the third ground of appeal, that the principles of the action de in rem verso have been misapplied: given that there are no fixed conditions for the exercise of this action which derives from the principle of equity that one must not enrich oneself at the expense of another and which is not covered by any text in our laws; given that it is enough to render the claim admissible that the plaintiff allege and offer to prove that a benefit has accrued to the defendant at his expense or by his own act . . .'.

It soon became apparent that the terms of the *Boudier* decision were far too wide and that a claim for enrichment requires more than that the defendant should have received some benefit at the expense of the plaintiff. AUBRY and RAU had insisted on a further requirement, namely that the enrichment of the defendant occur 'sans cause légitime' and that in addition the plaintiff should have at his disposal no other action, contractual or delictual, for the recuperation of his loss. In the following years the Court of Cassation accepted these requirements in slightly modified form. It was then seen that the expression 'action de in rem verso' applied to only one part of the area covered by the general claim for unjustified enrichment, so nowadays writers bring it under the concept of 'enrichissement sans cause', which SALEILLES borrowed from German law.

According to the principles developed by the courts for the general enrichment claim, the first requirement today is that the plaintiff should have suffered an impoverishment ('appauvrissement') and that, in consequence, the defendant should have gained an enrichment ('enrichissement'). On this point French law makes no distinction according to whether the impoverishment/enrichment occurs as the result of a 'transfer' by the plaintiff or 'arises otherwise'. Most cases of 'Leistungskondiktionen' will fall under the rules of the Code civil regarding 'répétition de l'indu', but where this is not so, as in the case of services rendered, the action *de in rem verso* takes its place: a person who works in her fiancé's business in view of a forthcoming marriage which does not take place may claim the value of her services unless it was the intention of the parties that the services should be gratuitous (Dijon 7 Feb. 1928, Gaz. Pal. 1928. 1. 501). Cases of 'interference' are also covered: for example, if a person unaware of his relationship to a decedent is informed by a genealogist of his rights of inheritance and vindicates those rights without paying the genealogist the requested fee, the genealogist may claim the value of the information by means of the action *de in rem verso* (Poitiers 2 Dec. 1907, DP 1908. 2. 332; Riom 20 June 1950, Gaz. Pal. 1950. 2. 221). So also if a waterworks uses the plaintiff's pipes for distributing water to its consumers it must pay for this use; in its characteristic lapidary way the Court of Cassation bases this claim directly on the 'principe d'équité que nul ne peut sans juste cause s'enrichir aux dépens d'autrui' (Req. 11 Dec. 1928, DH 1929, 18). If a music publisher exercises the copyright of an opera beyond the period permitted by its contract with the composer, it must disgorge the extra profits (Civ. 6 July 1927, S. 1928. 1. 19). However, the courts seem to be unwilling to extend this idea to cases of infringement of patent rights: the Court of Appeal of Paris rejected an enrichment claim brought by the patentee on the ground that it was subsidiary to the claim for patent infringement ('contrefaçon') which was specially regulated by statute and was in the case before it already time-barred (8 March 1922, Gaz. Trib. 1922. 2. 344).

The Court of Cassation has also refused to allow the owner of stolen goods to bring an enrichment claim against a person who resold them at a profit after buying them in good faith from the thief (Civ. 11 Feb. 1931, DP 1931. 1. 129, noted by SAVATIER, S. 1931. 1. 273, noted by GÉGOUT). In another case, however, a trustee in bankruptcy had collected on a claim which had vested in the plaintiff before the bankruptcy, and the plaintiff was allowed to claim the amount collected as being an unjustified enrichment to the mass (Civ. 18 Jan. 1937, DH 1937, 145). It thus appears to be the law in France that if a person collects on a claim which is vested in another he must disgorge the enrichment (compare §816 par. 2 BGB), while if a person sells another's chattel he need not do so (contrast §816 par. 1 BGB and RGZ 106, 44).

A further essential ingredient of an enrichment claim is that the enrichment be 'sans cause légitime'. As in German law, this is the case when there is no valid underlying contract. The French judge does not ask whether the *plaintiff's transfer* was made pursuant to a valid contract, but only whether the *defendant's benefit was received* pursuant to such a contract. This would be a distinction without a difference if the enrichment claim only lay where the benefit comes to the defendant directly from the plaintiff, as it does in Germany owing to the principle of directness, but as the *Boudier* case itself shows, French law also allows an enrichment claim where the benefit to the defendant is merely indirect, that is, where it comes to him only after passing through the assets of a third party. In these instances of the *actio de in rem verso*, the French view is that the plaintiff's enrichment claim is excluded if the defendant received the benefit in question pursuant to either a *contract* or a *statutory duty* between himself and the third party. If there is no such contract or statutory duty between the defendant and the third party, there will be no 'cause légitime' to justify the defendant's benefit, and the defendant will have to disgorge the value of the benefit even if the plaintiff had a valid contract with the third party on which he could sue.

The Court of Cassation has affirmed these principles in many decisions, never more clearly than in Req. 22 Feb. 1939 and Civ. 28 Feb. 1939, DP 1940. 1. 5, noted by RIPERT. The plaintiff was retained by the tenant of commercial premises to do repair work on them. The tenant became insolvent, and the plaintiff brought a claim for the value of his work against the landlord–owner. In both cases the Court of Cassation decided that the claim must fail if the tenancy agreement required the tenant to return the premises *in good repair* at the end of the tenancy: it was true that the plaintiff's repairs had increased the value of the lessor's premises but this benefit found 'sa juste cause' in the contract with the tenant. To the same effect Civ. 7 July 1896, DP 1898. 1. 18; Civ. 18 Oct. 1898 DP 1899. 1. 105; Civ. 9 Nov. 1909, DP 1911. 1. 169; Req. 12 Feb. 1923, DP 1923, 1. 64. The whole question is excellently dealt with by KÖNIG (above p. 575) 31 ff. with further references to judicial decision and legal literature.—The outcome is different in cases where the defendant *cannot* show that he has a contract with the third party which entitles him to retain the benefit. In Req. 11 Sep. 1940, S. 1941. 1. 121, noted by ESMEIN, the defendant had sold land to a purchaser who then retained the plaintiff to do certain building works. After the building works had been completed the purchaser became insolvent, so the defendant rescinded the sale contract and sought to repossess the property. On this, the plaintiff, instead of suing the insolvent purchaser on the building contract, brought an *actio de in rem verso* directly against the defendant, and his action succeeded with the approval of the Court of Cassation. Here the benefit to the defendant was not justified by any 'cause légitime', since he had no contractual right against the purchaser to receive back his property improved by the building works. See also Req. 20 Dec. 1910, DP 1911. 1. 377, and the further decisions cited and well discussed in KÖNIG (above p. 575) 90 ff.

These principles were only clarified in the course of the twentieth century and French writers have asked whether the decision of the Court of Cassation in the *Boudier* case itself is compatible with them. It is generally held that it is. Of course the landlord and tenant in that case had agreed that the value of the crop should be set against the outstanding rent, which makes it seem as if the landlord, sued in an *actio de in rem verso* by the supplier of the fertilizer, would have a 'cause légitime' for retaining the benefit of the crop, namely the agreement to take it over from the tenant. However, in his note on the case in S. 1893. 1. 281, LABBÉ observed that in valuing the crop the experts had deducted the price of the fertilizer on the ground that the landlord would make a special payment to the tenant in respect of it. If so, the enrichment of having the crop fertilized would not be justified by any 'cause légitime', that is, by any valid contract with the tenant. On these facts the plaintiff would win even today.

In addition to the requirement of 'cause légitime', the French courts have worked out a whole series of other requirements which restrict the area of application of the general enrichment claim. Scholars put these restrictions, or some of them, under the heading 'subsidiarité de l'action de in rem verso', meaning that the enrichment claim must give way if there is any other legal basis on which the plaintiff can ground his claim.

See the details in DRAKIDIS, *Rev. trim. dr. civ.* 59 (1961) 577.—The Italian Codice civile makes this explicit in art. 2042 which lays down that an enrichment claim may not be brought if the plaintiff has any other way of claiming compensation for his impoverishment.—As to French law, one might think that this principle of subsidiarity would defeat an enrichment claim in all the most typical cases of the *actio de in rem verso*, since where the benefit has passed to the defendant through the assets of a third party the plaintiff normally has a valid contract with that third party on which he could sue. The Court of Cassation has not accepted this implication, for it has expressly decided that the existence of such a contractual claim against a third party does not affect the 'caractère subsidiaire de l'action de in rem verso', at any rate if the contractual claim cannot be *realized* because of the insolvency of the third party, which is nearly always the case (Req. 11 Sep. 1940, S. 1941. 1. 121 and KÖNIG (above p. 575) 78 ff.). The Italian courts have adopted the same position (see Cass. 26 March 1953, no. 782, Foro it. 1953 I c. 1467).

The principle of subsidiarity is of practical importance in cases where the plaintiff has a claim against the defendant on a contract or some other legal ground which is now unenforceable because of prescription or time-bar or some other reason; in such cases the plaintiff may well try to have recourse to the action *de in rem verso*, but he will try in vain. Thus if a plaintiff suing on a loan contract finds that he cannot adduce the documentary proof required by art. 1341 Code civil he is not allowed to seek recovery on the same facts on the basis of unjustified enrichment (the *Clayette* case, Civ. 12 May 1914, S. 1918. 1. 41). The same is true if, owing to a miscalculation, a builder quotes too low a price for building a house; he cannot use the *actio de in rem verso* in order to claim the shortfall, for this would be to circumvent the provisions of art. 1793 Code civil which puts the risk of such excess expenditure on the builder (Civ. 2 March 1915, DP 1920. 1. 102). When the Order of Jesuits was disbanded by the state, donors were given a set period in which to bring restitutionary claims against the liquidator; a donor of land who had allowed that period to expire was not allowed to bring a claim for unjustified enrichment (Civ. 22 Feb. 1922,

S. 1923. 1. 153). To give another example, already mentioned, a patentee cannot bring an action *de in rem verso* against an infringer of his patent if the special statutory claim for infringement has prescribed (Paris 8 March 1922, Gaz. Trib. 1922. 2. 344).

The result of these cases would be much the same in the German courts.—It is true that the *Clayette* case could never arise in the same form, since in Germany the non-observance of the required written form makes the contract invalid while in France art. 1341 Code civil simply makes the contract unenforceable for want of proof, while remaining valid in itself (see above Ch. 34 II). But if a German court was faced with a contract which was valid but for some reason unenforceable, it would refuse to allow an enrichment claim against the contractor just as the Court of Cassation did, though its reason would be that the transfer was made pursuant to a contract and therefore was not 'sine causa'.—The same applies where a person seeks to prove in a liquidation after the expiry of the statutory period, as is shown by a very similar case heard by the Reichsgericht (RGZ 124, 204). The creditor of a company in liquidation instituted his claim only after the year provided by §73 of the Companies Act (GmbHG) had expired and the assets had been distributed to the other creditors. He brought an action against one of these other creditors, asserting that the defendant had been enriched at his expense by receiving too high a dividend. The Reichsgericht rejected the claim on the ground that the transfer was justified by the statutory provisions of the Companies Act, whose aim was to make the distribution of assets conclusive after the expiry of the year laid down.

IV

Unlike the Continental European legal systems, England has no general claim for the restitution of unjustified enrichment, statutory or judicial. English law certainly allows a plaintiff to sue in most of the situations where he would have a claim for enrichment on the Continent, but instead of asking whether all the ingredients of a general comprehensive enrichment claim are present in the particular case it asks whether the case falls within any of the various heterogeneous types of claim which exist. Some of these were developed in the Courts of Equity, but mostly they arose 'at law' and are usually referred to in England by the term 'quasi-contracts'. It was the procedural forms of action with their compartmentalizing effect which prevented common lawyers seeing that unjustified enrichment called for analysis as a unitary problem: English law as a whole grew up within the bounds of the various forms of action and this is especially true of that part of private law which on the Continent is called the law of unjustified enrichment. Only now that the modes of thought characteristic of the forms of action are on the wane is the notion that a unitary principle, namely that of 'restitution of unjust enrichment', underlies these various forms of action beginning to emerge, much more clearly in the United States than in England.

As in Rome, the first forms of action to serve restitutionary purposes in

English law had the concurrent function of enforcing contracts. Just as the *condictio* was directed to procuring the transfer of a certain thing, whether the obligation to transfer it stemmed from a loan, a stipulation, or the receipt of an *indebitum*, so in England in the fourteenth and fifteenth centuries the action of debt served to recover liquidated sums of money whether owed as money borrowed, as a monetary penalty, or under a judgment, as well as in the case where the sum of money in question had been paid by the plaintiff to the defendant in performance of a contract and was now being reclaimed on a 'failure of consideration' after the collapse of the contract. The action of account also provided a method of solving unjust enrichment problems; this was primarily a means of adjusting accounts between the parties, but it could also be used by plaintiffs who had transferred something to the defendant by mistake or pursuant to a contract invalid for want of consideration. Unfortunately the actions of debt and account had an extremely cumbrous and expensive procedure, in which the defendant could even obtain judgment if he 'waged his law' by swearing with oath-helpers that he was not liable. This made the English courts in the course of the sixteenth and seventeenth centuries ready to use the more flexible action of *assumpsit* in cases previously triable by debt or account. *Assumpsit*, after emerging from the law of tort, originally lay only where one party had expressly undertaken ('assumpsit') by contract to do a particular thing; if the defendant performed badly or failed to perform altogether the plaintiff could bring the action of *assumpsit* and claim damages. Gradually this action was also allowed in cases where the defendant owed a specific sum of money which could have been claimed in an action of debt. It was enough if after the debt had arisen the debtor expressly undertook to pay it; the creditor's claim was then called 'indebitatus assumpsit'. After a path-breaking decision of 1602, *Slade's* case, it was admitted that any debt, regardless of its legal source, could be claimed by an action of *assumpsit*, even if the promise to pay had not actually been made but had to be inferred, as a mere fiction, from the circumstances. This opened the way to proving claims for unjust enrichment in the form of 'indebitatus assumpsit', but it was still based on the fiction that the debtor had 'undertaken' to pay the debt which had already arisen on some other legal ground. Consistently with the characteristic English lawyer's habit of thinking in types of case, several distinct types of case gradually separated out within the form of *indebitatus assumpsit*. The action *for money had and received* lay for the recovery of money which the plaintiff had paid to the defendant by mistake or under duress or in performance of an invalid contract. The action for *quantum meruit* or *quantum valebat* lay when the defendant had accepted goods or services from the plaintiff without any particular price being agreed. Finally the action for *money paid* (laid out and expended for the use of another) lay if the plaintiff had paid money to a third party for the benefit of the defendant. 'By 1750, defendants had been forced in individual cases to give back gains on substantially all the grounds we have recognized in modern law' (DAWSON (above p. 575) 11).

No effort had yet been made in England to put these various types of case on a unitary foundation. LORD MANSFIELD was the first to make such an attempt, in the famous case of *Moses* v. *Macferlan*, (1760) 2 Burr. 1005, 97 Eng. Rep. 676. The plaintiff had endorsed a negotiable instrument upon the defendant's agreeing in writing not to take recourse against him. The defendant proceeded to sue on the instrument and obtained judgment against the plaintiff from a court which professed itself unable to take account of the collateral agreement. The plaintiff paid off the judgment against him and raised an action for repayment before another court, the Court of King's Bench. LORD MANSFIELD granted the plaintiff's claim for money had and received, and stated the ground of the claim as follows: 'If the defendant be under an obligation, from the ties of natural justice, to refund, the law implies a debt, and gives this action, founded in the equity of the plaintiff's case, as it were upon a contract (quasi ex contractu, as the Roman law expresses it) . . . the gist of this kind of action is that the defendant, upon the circumstances of the case, is obliged by the ties of natural justice and equity to refund the money.'

This decision of LORD MANSFIELD certainly made it possible to sever the historical connection between the existing enrichment claims and the law of contract. However, the development took a different, indeed an opposite direction. Until then the supposition of the fictive contractual promise to repay had been seen as a procedural device which made it possible to use *assumpsit* to enforce enrichment claims, but from the middle of the nineteenth century the courts began to treat the fictive promise, called 'implied contract', as being the very foundation of the enrichment claim. To derive these claims from 'natural justice and equity' as LORD MANSFIELD had proposed, not only appeared to trespass over the border of equity jurisprudence in the technical sense but also ran counter to the positivism and concern with precedent typical of the English judiciary at the turn of the century.

LORD MANSFIELD's theory therefore came in for much criticism. It was described as 'vague jurisprudence which is sometimes attractively styled as "justice as between man and man" ' (LORD SUMNER, in *Baylis* v. *Bishop of London* [1913] 1 Ch. 127, 140) and as 'well-meaning sloppiness of thought' (SCRUTTON, LJ in *Holt* v. *Markham*, [1923] 1 KB 504, 513). HANBURY observed that LORD MANSFIELD in *Moses* v. *Macferlan* had crossed the very narrow bridge 'which leads from the sound soil of implied contract to the shifting quicksands of natural equity' (40 *LQ Rev.* 31, 35 (1924)).—This trend reached its apogee in the House of Lords decision of *Sinclair* v. *Brougham*, [1914] AC 398. A building society had acted as a bank, *ultra vires*, that is, outside the objects of the society stipulated in its rules. When the building society went into liquidation, the depositors claimed the amount standing to their credit and, *ultra vires* contracts being void in English law, did so by means of an action for money had and received. The House of Lords held that no claim for money had and received could be allowed, since such a claim was based on a promise to repay implied by the law, and in the instant case any such promise, had it been given expressly, would also have been *ultra vires* and invalid: 'The law cannot de jure impute promises to repay, whether for money had and received or otherwise, which, if made de facto, it would inexorably avoid' ([1914] AC 398, 452). A similar decision had already been made in *Cowern* v. *Nield*, [1912] 2 KB 419. In that case an infant who promised to deliver specific goods received the purchase price in advance. The purchaser rejected a part which was unsatisfactory and the infant did not deliver the remainder so the purchaser brought a claim for repayment of the price. So far as the claim was based on breach of contract it was unsuccessful, since the contract was invalid by reason of the defendant's infancy, but the claim for money had and received was equally unsuccessful, for, according to the court, this claim also arose *ex contractu* and therefore foundered on the defendant's infancy. To the same effect was *R. Leslie Ltd.* v. *Sheill*, [1914] 3 KB 607. These decisions are much criticized by English writers today, and they do indeed apply the theory that enrichment claims are based on quasi-contract with a rigour which demonstrates that even England has its own forms of *Begriffsjurisprudenz*. The true question, namely how to balance the interest of the creditor in recovering moneys unjustly withheld and the interests underlying the doctrines of *ultra vires* and infancy was not raised by the courts in either case (on this see the excellent treatment by GOFF/JONES (above p. 575) 10 f., 349 ff., 360 ff.).

The view is now gaining ground in England that cases of 'quasi-contract' should no longer be seen as depending on an imputed promise. 'In our view, the concept of implied contract is, in this context, a meaningless, irrelevant and misleading anachronism' (GOFF/JONES (above p. 575) 10). Writers and courts alike are increasingly coming to realize that the great range of restitutionary claims afforded by English case-law all rest on the principle that a benefit which the defendant has acquired at the expense of the plaintiff must be restored, so far as the defendant's retention of this benefit would rank as an 'unjust enrichment'. 'The principle of unjust enrichment', as GOFF/JONES say in their recent English work, 'presupposes three things: first, that the defendant has been enriched by the receipt of a benefit; secondly, that he has been so enriched at the plaintiff's expense; and thirdly, that it would be unjust to allow him to retain the benefit' (above p. 575, pp. 16 f.).

The law of restitution in the *United States* started to develop from the point reached in England under LORD MANSFIELD, but it did not follow the English attempt to make the duty of restitution rest on an 'implied contract'. As early as 1893 KEENER published a work on the law of 'Quasi-Contracts' and it was followed in 1913 by a work of the same title by WOODWARD. WOODWARD emphatically denied that 'quasi-contractual' claims rested on any 'contract implied in law'; he defined these claims as 'legal obligations arising, without reference to the assent of the obligor, from the receipt of a benefit the retention of which is unjust, and requiring the obligor to make restitution' (above p. 576, p. 4).

In 1937 a great step forward was taken by the Restatement of the Law of

Restitution (hereafter called Restatement), produced by the American professors SEAVEY and SCOTT. It brought together all the rules developed by the courts for the restitution of unjustified enrichment, including for the first time the restitutionary claims developed in the Courts of Equity (on this see SEAVEY/SCOTT, 54 *LQ Rev.* 29 (1938); WINFIELD, 54 *LQ Rev.* 529 (1938), and MARTINEK (above p. 576) 294 ff.), and set out the general proposition that 'a person who has been unjustly enriched at the expense of another is required to make restitution' (§1).

On considering the most important types of case which give rise to restitutionary claims in Anglo-American law, we discover that the distinction between 'Leistungskondiktion' and 'Eingriffskondiktion' which is drawn in the German legal family is also useful for the presentation of the Common Law. Thus GOFF/JONES organize the material according to whether the defendant acquired the benefit 'from or by the act of the plaintiff'—which approximates to the 'Leistungskondiktion'—or whether he obtained it 'by his own wrongful conduct', which approximates to the 'Eingriffskondiktion'.

GOFF/JONES make a further group of the cases where the claim is for the restitution of a benefit which the defendant acquired *from a third party* ('where the defendant has acquired from a third party a benefit for which he must account to the plaintiff'). It may surprise civilian readers to find that this section includes rules which entitle a person who has paid off a debt owed by a third party to exercise all the rights against the third party which were vested in the creditor before the payment ('doctrine of subrogation'; see also Restatement §162). Thus the surety who pays off the debt may take recourse against the debtor by using the claims vested in the creditor before the payment and may exercise any securities the creditor may have had. The same is true of the insurer who has paid the insured, for he may exercise the latter's claims against the party responsible for the occurrence of the insured event. On the Continent there are special statutory rules for most of these cases, making the claims of the recipient against the third party vest in the person making the payment by means of a *cessio legis* (see §§774, 1143, 1225 BGB, 67 German Law on Insurance Contracts (VVG), art. 1251, 2029 Code civil, 36 French Law on Insurance Contracts (13 July 1930)). It is easy to forget that this statutory assignment in reality only serves to secure the plaintiff's recourse claim on paying the debt of another and that this claim is based on principles of unjust enrichment, for the idea of 'prohibition of enrichment' does not normally appear except in connection with insurance and §67 of the German VVG. In the Common Law, by contrast, the invariable justification for the doctrine of subrogation is that without it the third party would be unjustifiably enriched, and this is why the rules developed for this purpose are treated as manifestations of the principle of enrichment, not only in the Restatement but also in GOFF/JONES (on this see also v. CAEMMERER, *Festschrift Rabel*, 360 ff.).

(*a*) We now turn to the cases where the plaintiff is claiming the restitution of benefits acquired by the defendant *'from or by the act of the plaintiff'*. These are classified in the Common Law in accordance with the circumstances which render it unjustifiable for the defendant to retain the benefit he has received.

One important group consists of those cases where payment was made in the erroneous supposition that there was a debt ('payment under mistake', §§6–69 Restatement). Another large group consists of transfers made under 'compulsion' or 'coercion': a person is entitled to reclaim what he has transferred under 'duress' or under circumstances which show that 'undue influence' has been brought to bear on him by the recipient, commonly by exploiting a close family relationship. Like GOFF/JONES, the Restatement finds a case of 'performance under compulsion' in the situation where one of several common debtors has paid off the creditor, under compulsion by him, as it were; his payment frees the other common debtors from their liability and he may seek payment from them under the 'doctrine of contribution'. These contribution claims are a judicial creation in the Common Law and rest directly on 'principles of justice' rather than on the *contract* which normally exists between the common debtors. Characteristically, the development in this area of English law was gradual; contribution was first recognized in cases of joint suretyship and extended only later to other forms of joint liability. Even today GOFF/JONES make a careful distinction between contribution claims lying between partners, sureties, insurers, trustees of the same property, and so on, and the special rules of contribution applicable to any of these relationships may not apply to others. Nevertheless, GOFF and JONES have been successful in their attempt to work out general principles in this area (above p. 575, p. 272; see also the Restatement §§81–5), thereby repeating the process of gradual generalization of the rules which took place in Germany in the eighteenth and nineteenth centuries and led to the unsurpassably abstract provisions on common debts contained in the BGB (§§421 ff.).

Another important group is composed of cases where the debtor has conferred a benefit in pursuance of a contract which was void or has been avoided for some reason such as mistake, incapacity, altered circumstances, breach of contract, or illegality or immorality. Not all these cases are yet treated by the Common Law as instances of a common type, namely the claim for restoration of benefits conferred under a defective contract. There are no general rules which apply to all such cases. What matters is the *kind of defect* which renders the contract invalid, even when it comes to undoing the effects of the invalid contract. Where the plaintiff claims from the defendant the return of some thing transferred pursuant to an invalid contract, English and American judges look to the precedents on incapacity, illegality, or whatever particular fault rendered the contract invalid, with the result that the Common Law rules regarding the restitution of benefits transferred pursuant to a defective contract differ quite widely depending on the ground of invalidity involved. This manner of proceeding has its advantages and disadvantages, as the comparative lawyer can see. On the one hand, the Common Law can regulate the effects of invalid contracts in accordance with the relevant interests, which differ depending on the type of defect. On the other hand, this adaptability is purchased at the price of a very considerable casuistical diversity which makes it bewildering to the Continental observer, since it is almost impossible to state any general rules at all.

This bewilderment stems from a fact already noted above (Ch. 45 II), namely that in the Germanic systems and, to a lesser degree, the Romanistic systems as well, the law of enrichment is not troubled with the question whether the underlying contract is valid or not (on this also v. CAEMMERER, *Festschrift Rabel* 343 ff., and DAWSON (above p. 575) 113 f.). That is a matter for the law of contract. Only when the question of the validity of the contract has been determined does the law of enrichment step in: it then asks whether any benefit has been transferred under this contract, already held invalid, and concludes that, if it has, the defendant acquired it 'without legal ground' and must therefore give it up. Of course even the Continental law of enrichment cannot be wholly indifferent to the question *for what reason* the contract was invalid. Thus in the Germanic systems there are special provisions in the law of enrichment which apply only in cases where it is *illegality* or *immorality* which renders the underlying contract invalid (see §§817, 819 par. 2 BGB, 1174 ABGB, art. 66 OR, and, in detail, below Ch. 46 III). The reason for the invalidity of the contract may also affect the extent of the defendant's liability in unjust enrichment: under §§818 par. 3, 819 BGB the defendant who no longer has what he received is not liable unless he *knew* at the time of receiving it that there was no ground for his doing so. In practice this means that the recipient cannot escape on the ground that his enrichment has ceased to exist if the underlying contract was tainted by his *deceit* or *duress*: conversely, a *minor* may raise this defence even if he knew of the invalidity of the contract at the time he received the benefit, since the courts, in order to protect him, do not hold this knowledge against him (on this, see also below Ch. 46 IV 3b).

(*b*) Great practical importance attaches in the Common Law to the class of case where the defendant has acquired a benefit not as the result of an act of the plaintiff but '*by his own wrongful conduct*', that is, as one would say in Germany, by making unauthorized use of a thing or right vested in another. Starting from the fact that this interference with the right of another constitutes a tort, the Common Law then allows the victim 'to waive the tort', that is, to ignore the tort claim for damages and to sue the interferer instead for the return of the economic benefits he gained from his tort. For example, if a person sells or does work on a moveable which does not belong to him, he is guilty, even if he is in good faith, of the tort of conversion or trespass to chattels (see below Ch. 47 III); it is a 'trespass to land' if a person allows his cattle to graze on someone else's land or builds on it, withdraws minerals from it, or allows gases or liquids to flow over it, or in any other way disturbs another in his possession. In all these cases the victim may refrain from exercising his tort claim for damages and require the other to pay the value of the chattels he has used up or the proceeds of the sale he has made or the value of the use he has had of them. No final answer has yet been given to the question whether a person who has infringed the rights of another without causing him any loss must pay for simply making use of it. In *Phillips* v. *Homfray*, (1883) 24 Ch. D. 439 a person used roads and passages under the plaintiff's land in order to carry away minerals extracted from his own mine. He died shortly thereafter, with the result, according to the old principle 'actio personalis moritur cum persona' then in force, that the tort claims for damages based on his trespass to land also came to an end. The plaintiff therefore sued his heirs, not for damages, but for the value of the benefit which the estate had gained from the decedent's use of the plaintiff's roads and passages. The claim was rejected since the plaintiff had not suffered any proveable harm ('the damages which have been done to him are unliquidated and uncertain') and because the decedent had not converted any property into assets of his own but had simply saved himself expense.

The decision is criticized by GOFF/JONES (above p. 575) 607 ff. and STREET, *Principles of the Law of Damages* (1962) 25 ff. In the United States opinions differ. With regard to the unauthorized use of *moveables*, the Restatement says in §128 (i): 'A person who has tortiously used the chattel of another is under a duty of restitution to the owner for the value of the use, although the owner would not have used the chattel and although it was not harmed by the use.' A similar result was reached in *Olwell* v. *Nye & Nissen Co.*, 26 Wash. 2d 282, 173 P. 2d 652 (1946), where the defendant had made unauthorized use of a machine left unused by the plaintiff in a warehouse.—The Restatement is not unequivocal concerning the unauthorized use of *land* (see §129). Several decisions have already departed from *Phillips* v. *Homfray* and have allowed the plaintiff to claim even though the value of the property was not lessened by the use and although in making the use the defendant simply saved himself expenditure; see *Raven Red Ash Coal Co.* v. *Ball*, 185 Va. 534, 39 SE 2d 231 (1946); *Edwards* v. *Lee's Administrator*, 265 Ky. 418, 96 SW 2d 1028 (1936); *De Camp* v. *Bullard*, 159 NY 450, 54 NE 26 (1899), and the other decisions cited in DAWSON/PALMER, *Cases on Restitution* (1958) 25 ff. and in PALMER (above p. 576) §2.5.

The Common Law also uses the notion of 'waiver of tort' where, rather than interfering with another's ownership of things, the defendant has infringed intangible rights vested in the plaintiff, such as patents, copyrights, trade marks, trade secrets, and so on. In such cases the courts allow the plaintiff to claim restitution of the profits made by the infringement.

See *Peter Pan Mfg. Corp* v. *Corsets Silhouette, Ltd.*, [1964] 1 WLR 96; *Matarese* v. *Moore-McCormack Lines*, 158 F. 2d 631 (2d Cir. 1946); *Eckert* v. *Braun*, 155 F. 2d 517 (7th Cir. 1946); *Reynolds* v. *Whitin Mach. Works*, 167 F. 2d 78 (4th Cir. 1948). Where the infringement is *innocent*, it is not so clear that the plaintiff may claim restitution of profits. See GOFF/JONES (above p. 575) p. 618). Nor is it clear what the relationship is between the special statutory claims for the infringement of patents and so on and the general legal remedies (see PALMER (above p. 576) §§2.7 and 8). There have been occasional attempts in the United States, so far without success, to waive the tort in cases of interference with *rights of personality* and to claim restitution of the benefits which the infringer acquired through the commercial use of the plaintiff's picture or of false or injurious statements about him; see *Hart* v. *E. P. Dutton & Co.*, 197 Misc. 274, 93 NYS 2d 871 (1949) and the exhaustive treatment with further references in YORK, 'Extension of Restitutional Remedies in the Tort Field', 4 *UCLAL Rev.* 499 (1957) and PALMER (above p. 576) §2.9.

(c) The rules of Anglo-American restitution law so far portrayed are principally the product of decisions of Common Law courts, but the *Courts of Equity* also developed useful remedies in this field, which are incorporated in both the Restatement and the textbook of GOFF/JONES. Apart from the 'doctrine of subrogation', which has already been mentioned, the most important are the 'constructive trust' and the 'equitable lien'.

A trust exists when a person in whom a right is vested is bound to exercise this right on behalf of specified beneficiaries according to rules developed by the Courts of Equity (on this see the treatment in Ch. 21). Normally such a trust arises as the result of a transaction between the parties and is called an 'express trust', but a 'constructive trust' arises when the law itself treats a person as trustee of a particular object for the benefit of another. Under both an express and a constructive trust the beneficiaries' right to the trust property is *quasi in rem*; this right, also developed by the Courts of Equity, enables them, *inter alia*, to claim the object or its proceeds should the trustee go bankrupt.

While such a real right can only exist if the object in question can be identified and distinguished from the trustee's other property, the Common Law has produced a series of fictions in the interest of beneficiaries which permit a real claim to survive even if trust moneys are mixed in the trustee's bank account with money of his own, or are used by the trustee along with money of his own for the purchase of land. In such a case an 'equitable lien' in the amount of the beneficiaries' entitlement is imposed on the bank account or on the land, and this lien is privileged should the trustee go bankrupt ('doctrine of tracing'; for the details see GOFF/JONES (above p. 575) 63 ff.; *In re Tilley's Will Trusts*, [1967] Ch. 1179; Restatement §§202 ff.). If the trustee has conveyed the trust property to a third party in breach of trust, this third party may be treated as constructive trustee and made to disgorge as such unless he acquired the property as a 'bona fide purchaser for value', that is, for consideration and without knowledge that the disposition to him was in breach of trust (see KÖTZ, *Trust und Treuhand* (1963), with further references).

It is therefore very material, especially if the defendant is insolvent, to discover whether the plaintiff's restitutionary claim can be based on a constructive trust, that is, whether the defendant was a constructive trustee for the plaintiff of the property in issue. This critical question is answered differently in English and American law. In *England* the view is that a constructive trust can arise only if there is a 'fiduciary relationship', that is, a relationship of special trust and reliance; only then is there any analogy with an express trust created by legal act which would justify applying the rules of trust to the fiduciary so as to require him to give up the property belonging in equity to the other. Thus, for example, a solicitor may be constructive trustee for his client (*Re Hallett's Estate*, (1880) 13 Ch. D. 696), an executor for the next of kin (*Re Diplock*, [1948] Ch. 465), a company director for the company (*Sinclair* v. *Brougham*, [1914] AC 398), and under certain circumstances an agent for his principal (*Burdick* v. *Garrick*, (1870) LR 5 Ch. App. 233).

Continental lawyers may not immediately appreciate why both GOFF/JONES (above p. 575, p. 632) and the Restatement (§§190 ff.) treat these cases as involving the restitution of an *unjustified enrichment*. If a lawyer retains funds collected for his client from a third party, there is a sense in which the lawyer is unjustifiably enriched by those funds at the expense of his client, but to emphasize this point would be to abandon a principle which Continental jurists regard as fundamental, namely that a plaintiff cannot have any claim based on enrichment if the defendant is already bound *by contract* to hand over what is in issue. On the other hand, Continental lawyers are perfectly familiar with the urge to 'reify' the principal's claim so as to give it priority in bankruptcy, a matter on which the constructive trust allows the Common Law to go very much further than the Continental legal systems can (see KÖTZ (above p. 598) 144 ff.).

In the *United States* it is *not* a requirement for a constructive trust that there be any special fiduciary relationship between the parties. The American courts treat the constructive trust as a legal device capable of use wherever the defendant has in his possession identifiable property which he should hand over on the ground that he would be unjustifiably enriched at the plaintiff's expense if he were allowed to keep it.

See SCOTT, 71 *LQ Rev.* 39 (1955) and §160 Restatement: 'Where a person holding title to property is subject to an equitable duty to convey it to another on the ground that he would be unjustly enriched if he were permitted to retain it, a constructive trust arises.' Similar phrases may be found in the cases: see *Beatty* v. *Guggenheim Exploration Co.*, 225 NY 380, 122 NE 378 (1919); *Knight Newspapers* v. *Commissioners of Internal Revenue*, 143 F. 2d 1007 (6th Cir. 1944).—In England, too, it has been proposed that instead of treating the constructive trust as a 'substantive institution' requiring a special fiduciary relationship between the parties, it should be treated, as in American law, as a 'remedial institution' to be invoked wherever the court finds that the defendant is unjustifiably withholding identifiable property from the plaintiff. In particular the proposal has been made by WATERS, *The Constructive Trust* (1964) and 'The English Constructive Trust: A Look into the Future,' 19 *Vand L. Rev. 1215* (1966).

The types of case in which the American courts hold a defendant 'unjustly enriched' at the expense of the plaintiff with regard to a particular item of property are quite familiar. If the plaintiff has transferred the object to the defendant by *mistake* and the object is still ascertainable in the hands of the defendant, the defendant is treated as a constructive trustee of this property for the benefit of the plaintiff (see §163 Restatement). The same is true when the plaintiff made the transfer because he was deceived, coerced, or unduly influenced by the recipient or by a third party (see §§116 f. Restatement). In these cases the constructive trust is being used to undo defective dispositions of property, the same function as is performed in Romanistic systems by the 'répétition de l'indu' and in the Germanic systems by the right to reclaim the performance of a supposed obligation. The result of imposing a constructive trust, however, differs from the result on the Continent, for it accords the plaintiff a *real* claim of considerable effectiveness.

In *Re Berry*, 147 F. 208 (2d Cir. 1906) the plaintiffs had erroneously sent the defendant a cheque for $1,500 in payment of a non-existent debt. The defendant gave the cheque to his bank for collection and was credited with its value. He then became bankrupt. Withdrawals had been made from the defendant's account after it had been credited with the proceeds of the cheque, but it never fell below $1,500. The court held that the defendant and his trustee in bankruptcy held $1,500 of his bank account 'on constructive trust' for the plaintiffs, which they could claim in priority to the general creditors.—In *General Motors Acceptance Corp.* v. *Larson*, 110 NJ Eq. 305, 159 A. 819 (1932) the defendant falsely represented, with the aid of forged contract documents, that he was entitled to receive the price under certain contracts of sale and thus induced the plaintiff bank to pay him $34,000 or so for an assignment of those rights. He paid this sum into his bank account, which was subsequently reduced by withdrawals to about $10,000. This amount the defendant lent to a third party on the security of certain mortgages, and then became bankrupt. The court decided that the defendant had become constructive trustee of the whole $34,000 which he had acquired by fraud but that this sum had been reduced to $10,000 by his bank withdrawals. This was represented by the mortgages, so the plaintiff was entitled to demand them out of the bankrupt's property. See also *Southern Coal Co.* v. *McAlpine*, 176 Okla. 492, 56 P. 2d 413 (1936) and the many further decisions cited in SCOTT, *The Law of Trusts* (1956) §§465 ff. and PALMER (above p. 576) §11.5.

V

It has often been stated in Germany that claims for enrichment are based in the last resort on considerations of equity and justice. These claims are granted, so the argument runs, if the acquisition of benefits 'appears on some special ground to be unjustified, that is, to conflict with justice and equity' (ENNECCERUS/LEHMANN, *Recht der Schuldverhältnisse* (4th edn., 1954) §220 I), especially when, thanks to formal rules of law and the 'principle of abstraction' in particular (see above Ch. 40 II), the recipient acquires ownership in things which it would run counter to the goal of a just and equitable ordering of economic relations to allow him to retain; the law must then afford a claim for adjustment, 'in order, so far as possible, to heal the wounds which it itself inflicts' (DERNBURG, *Bürgerliches Recht* II 2 (3rd edn., 1906) 677 f.). The Reichsgericht itself once spoke of 'considerations of equity . . . which are the basis of the adjustment of benefit and detriment which the law seeks to achieve by means of the claim for enrichment' (RGZ 86, 343, 348).

Today these observations should be treated with some reservation. The law of unjust enrichment is alive and well, as a comparative survey shows, in places which do not recognize the principle of the abstract nature of conveyances at all. This can be seen from the judicial decisions we have mentioned in the very common situations where the principle of abstraction has no role to play, as where enrichment claims are directed to the restitution of money paid or the value of services performed by the plaintiff *sine causa* or the profits of an unjustified interference with his rights. It is correct enough to say that the law of unjust enrichment is founded on equity and justice, but so are the law of contract and the law of tort, and to no lesser degree. Historically speaking, claims for enrichment may always have been traced to *aequitas* or the law of nature, perhaps because this was necessary at a time when these claims still had to fight for recognition alongside those resting on contract or tort. Today, however, they have an unquestioned place in all legal systems, and as compared with other areas of private law the law of unjust enrichment is neither higher nor lower in rank. As v. CAEMMERER rightly says, 'if a person has delivered something to the wrong person or has paid his creditor twice or has made a down payment on a contract which never eventuates, his right to restitution . . . is of the same order of dignity as a claim for the repayment of a loan or on the cancellation of a contract' (*Festschrift Rabel*, 339; see also the apt observations of WILBERG (above p. 576) 18 ff.).

French writers have also attributed the *actio de in rem verso* to consider-ations of equity. Thus ESMEIN writes: 'The action de in rem verso has entered our law simply as a means of filling gaps which makes it possible to award an indemnity in cases where justice absolutely requires it' (S. 1941. 1. 122).—DAVID said likewise: 'The doctrine has always been applied in practice with due regard to the requirements of natural justice. It is consequently impossible to state the doctrine in a form which is absolutely systematic, dominated as it is by the subjective and paramount notions of morality and fair play' (5 *Camb. LJ* 222 f. (1935)).—So also ROUAST: 'Underlying the cases concerning unjustified enrichment we find a principle of natural law, the principle of the equilibrium of performance and counterperformance' (*Rev. trim. dr. civ.* 21 (1922) 93).

This viewpoint is somewhat more plausible in French law, for it must be remembered that the general claim for enrichment is not laid down in the Code civil, and it was easy to justify its judicial creation in the *Boudier* case by the consideration that the gap in the Code civil had to be filled in accordance with the requirements of equity. As DAVID's observation shows, French writers have not been entirely successful in fixing the limits of the action *de in rem verso* with sufficient precision; until this is done, linking the claim to equity may mitigate the lack of a satisfactory systematic structure.

The striking feature of French law is its principled acceptance of the *actio de in rem verso*, which allows a claim for enrichment where the benefit was acquired by the defendant only *indirectly* from the plaintiff as a result of the plaintiff's having transferred it to a third party who then conferred it on the defendant. The Court of Cassation has certainly admitted that it went too far in giving unlimited admission to the *actio de in rem verso* in the *Boudier* case. It has therefore worked out a series of restrictive conditions which the theorists have sought to sum up in two requirements: first, the enrichment of the defendant must not be justified by an 'cause légitime', which in cases of the *actio de in rem verso* means that the benefit must not have come to the defendant as a result of any contract between him and the third party; secondly, the plaintiff must not have a claim based on any other legal ground ('principe de la subsidiarité), which, in cases of the *actio de in rem verso*, means only that the plaintiff must not have any contractual claim against a *solvent* third party. The practical difference between German and French law in such cases may be summed up as follows: if the plaintiff confers a benefit on a third party pursuant to a valid contract and the third party transfers this benefit to the defendant, the plaintiff will never have an enrichment claim in Germany, while in France he will have one provided that the third party is insolvent and that the defendant cannot point to any valid contract with the third party which justifies his retaining the benefit as against the third party.

One must not be too quick to take issue with these decisions of the Cour de Cassation. The *actio de in rem verso* was well known to the *Gemeines Recht* and to the Prussian Land Law, and it is a tenable view that the German courts succeeded in setting proper limits to it, even if the draftsmen of the BGB found it 'an extremely confused and complicated matter' (Motive II 872) and refused to adopt it.

The restrictive conditions worked out by the Reichsgericht at that time are, not surprisingly, more or less congruent with those recognized by the Court of Cassation. Thus in RGZ 1, 143 the Reichsgericht had to deal with a case in which the father-in-law of the defendant, acting in his own name, bought machines from the plaintiff in order to instal them in the defendant's mill. Shortly after the machines had been installed, the father-in-law died without leaving any appreciable property, and the supplier sued the miller for the value of the machines. The Reichsgericht had to apply Prussian law and decided that the claim should be allowed unless the miller could show that he received the machines pursuant to a contract of sale with his father-in-law.—Now if the father-in-law, in purchasing the machines, had been acting as the miller's agent or as a *negotiorum gestor*, the supplier could have obtained a judgment against his heirs and then garnished his indemnity claim against the miller (§§670, 683, 257 BGB) and so finally have been able to bring a claim for payment against the latter. But is this not unnecessarily circuitous? Take the case that the father-in-law's estate is insolvent and in liquidation. Is it fair that his claim for indemnity from his son-in-law should be used to satisfy the other creditors of the estate when the purchase of the machines was a transaction in which the father-in-law, as the Austrian courts would say, 'had no independent economic role to play, was acting in the interest of the defendant in suit and was economically nothing more than a conduit'?

Nevertheless, there are some considerations which suggest that it was perhaps a good thing for the present German law to reject the *actio de in rem verso*. It seems a sound principle of legal policy even in the law of contract that a man should seek his reward where he has placed his trust, and that he should look to the contractor on whose capacity to pay he relied in making the contract. Furthermore, the *actio de in rem verso* can expose the defendant to an undesirable double liability, though doubtless in different amounts, first to the plaintiff in the *actio de in rem verso* and secondly to the third party. Finally, there is a risk that if a direct claim by means of the *actio de in rem verso* is allowed, defences which the third party might justifiably raise against the plaintiff may be ignored (see WAHL (above p. 576) 142). The rejection of the *actio de in rem verso* may lead to inequitable results in a few cases where the third party acted solely in the interests of the defendant without any view to personal gain, as often happens if there is a close family relationship. The courts may sometimes be able to help by finding that the third party acted as the defendant's representative or for 'those whom it may concern', but rather than extend these institutions unduly, the courts should be prepared in exceptional cases to allow a direct claim quite openly, provided that the interests of neither the third party nor the defendant are infringed in the individual case.

When one moves from the enrichment law of the Continental systems to what is now called the 'law of restitution', even in England, namely that area of the Common Law which contains all the rules which seem to Anglo-American lawyers to rest on the idea of preventing unjust enrichment, one might be entering another world. We have seen that the basic function of the 'law of restitution' in the Common Law can be described in much the same terms as that of the law of enrichment on the Continent. Thus a German lawyer would accept the concept of unjustified enrichment as defined by GOFF/ JONES, who require 'first, that the defendant has been enriched by the receipt of a benefit; secondly, that he has been so enriched at the plaintiff's expense; and thirdly, that it would be unjust to allow him to retain the benefit'. And the words of art. 62 par. 1 OR that a person 'who has unjustifiably been enriched out of the assets of another' must give up the enrichment are perfectly in tune with §1 of the American Restatement which says that 'a person who has been unjustly enriched at the expense of another is required to make restitution to the other'. But we must remember, as the Restatement expressly says (Introductory Note to §1), that these propositions of Anglo-American theory are simply 'general guides for the conduct of courts'; they are 'principles', not 'rules' susceptible of direct application to the individual case. Instead they simply give the courts an idea of the direction in which they should apply and develop the specific rules worked out in the case-law. In German law it is different: when §812 BGB lays down that the defendant must have obtained 'something' 'through the act of another' 'at his expense' 'without legal ground', it is using these phrases to specify the essential ingredients of an enrichment claim which the courts apply directly to the individual case after concretizing them and equipping them with specific technical meaning. Too much should not be made of these differences. As we have seen, the Common Law has been making efforts in the last few years to distil the general princples from the ferment of different types of liability in unjust enrichment exemplified in the case-law. Contrariwise, no German or Swiss lawyer would deny that a judge will learn very little from the abstract statutory requirements for an enrichment claim until he ascertains how other judges and writers have given them shape and content. v. CAEMMERER, who has produced a 'typology of enrichment claims', quite rightly emphasizes that 'the enrichment claim can be given form and limits . . . only with such a typology, not with general criteria' (*Festschrift Rabel*, 337). Despite the differences between the law of enrichment in Germany and the law of restitution in the Common Law, it is manifest that an approximation will take place in the theoretical treatment of these areas of law. The unduly *abstract* detail of the German code will be loosened by a typology of enrichment claims and in the Common Law general rules will be developed to give form and structure to the unduly *concrete* details of the case-law. Each system has a great deal to learn from the other.

46

Unjustified Enrichment—Specific Topics

In addition to the works cited above pp. 575–6:

Aubert, *La Répétition des prestations illicites ou immorales en droit français, en droit suisse et dans la jurisprudence belge* (1954).

Bolgár, 'The Present Function of the Maxim Ignorantia Iuris Neminem Excusat—A Comparative Study', 52 *Iowa L. Rev.* 626 (1967).

v. Büren, 'Bemerkungen zu Art. 66 OR', *SJZ* 58 (1962) 225.

v. Caemmerer, 'Preisverstöße und §817 Satz 2 BGB', *Süddt. JZ* 1950, 646.

Dawson, 'Restitution without Enrichment', 61 *BUL Rev.* 563 (1981).

Flessner, *Wegfall der Bereicherung, Eine rechtsvergleichende Untersuchung* (1970).

Flume, 'Der Wegfall der Bereicherung in der Entwicklung vom römischen zum deutschen Recht', *Festschrift Niedermeyer* (1953) 160.

Friedmann, 'Consequences of Illegality Under the Israeli Contract Law (General Part) 1973', 33 *ICLQ* 81 (1984).

Gooderson, 'Turpitude and Title in England and India', 1958 *Camb. LJ* 199.

Grodecki, 'In pari delicto potior est conditio defendentis', 71 *LQ Rev.* 254 (1955).

Hackbarth, 'In pari turpitudine melior est conditio possidentis, Ein Vergleich zwischen dem anglo-amerikanischen und dem deutschen Recht', (Diss. Hamburg, 1967).

Honsell, *Die Rückabwicklung sittenwidriger oder verbotener Geschäfte, Eine rechtsgeschichtliche und rechtsvergleichende Untersuchung zu §817 BGB* (1974).

Lloyd, *Public Policy, A Comparative Study in English and French Law* (1953) 97 ff.

New York Law Revision Commission, Restitution of Money Paid Under Mistake of Law: Report of the Law Revision Commission of the State of New York (1942) No. 65 (B).

Niederländer, 'Nemo turpitudinem suam allegans auditur', *Ius et Lex, Festgabe für Gutzwiller* (1959) 621.

Ripert, *La Règle morale dans les obligations civiles* (4th edn., 1949) 183 ff.

Rittner, 'Rechtswissen und Rechtsirrtum im Zivilrecht', *Festschrift für Fritz von Hippel* (1967) 391.

Rummel, 'Kondiktion bei verbotenen und sittenwidrigen Rechtsgeschäften', *ÖJZ* 1978, 253.

Rusch, 'Art. 66 OR im Lichte der bundesgerichtlichen Praxis', *SJZ* 47 (1951) 369.

Sabbath, 'Denial of Restitution in Unlawful Transactions—A Study in Comparative Law', 8 *ICLQ* 486, 689 (1959).

Savey-Casard, *Le Refus d'action pour cause d'indignité, Étude sur la maxime Nemo auditur propriam turpitudinem allegans* (1930).

Stadden, 'Error of Law', 7 *Colum. L. Rev.* 476 (1907).

Sutton, '*Kelly* v. *Solari*: The Justification of the Ignorantia Iuris Rule', 2 *NZULR* 173 (1966).

TRIMARCHI, *L'arrichimento senza causa* (1962).

v. TUHR, 'Zur Lehre von der ungerechtfertigten Bereicherung', *Festschrift für E. I. Bekker* (1907) 293.

TZARANO, *Étude sur la règle: 'Nemo auditur propriam turpitudinem allegans'* (1926).

WADE, 'Benefits Obtained Under Illegal Transactions—Reasons for and Against Allowing Restitution', 25 *Tex. L. Rev.* 31 (1946).

——, 'Restitution of Benefits Acquired Through Illegal Transactions', 95 *U. Pa. L. Rev.* 261 (1947).

WINFIELD, 'Mistake of Law', 59 *LQ Rev.* 327 (1943).

WOODWARD, 'Recovery of Money Paid Under Mistake of Law', 5 *Colum. L. Rev.* 366 (1905).

I

IN the previous chapter our rather compressed survey of the rules of unjustified enrichment in the German, Romanistic, and Anglo-American legal families focused more on their systematic structure than on the typical function of individual enrichment claims. It was consequently impossible to make any detailed observations of a comparative legal nature. This we shall now try to do within the limits of available space, by considering a few special topics in the law of enrichment more closely. We shall ask what happens when a plaintiff seeks restitution of a benefit he has conferred on the defendant pursuant to an illegal or immoral agreement, or for an illegal or immoral purpose (below III). We shall ask what happens when a defendant who has received an unjustified benefit seeks to raise the defence that he has lost or disposed of this benefit or otherwise altered his position in reliance on his right to keep it (below IV). But we shall start with a comparative investigation of a remarkable rule of the Common Law to the effect that restitution of money paid by mistake will be denied if the plaintiff made the payment by reason of a mistake *of law*.

II

The Common Law rule that a plaintiff cannot reclaim money he paid under a mistake of law goes back to the old English decision of *Bilbie* v. *Lumley* (1802) 2 East 469, 102 Eng. Rep. 448. Here the plaintiff was an insurer who had paid the insured sum to the defendant policy-holder and sought its repayment on the ground that the defendant had no right to the insured sum because at the time of the contract he had concealed circumstances which increased the risk. It was nevertheless clear that at the time he paid the insured sum the plaintiff knew or could have known all the facts which entitled him to withhold payment. During the course of the trial LORD ELLENBROUGH asked the plaintiff's counsel if he could cite any precedent in which a claim for restitution of money had been allowed to a person who had paid in full knowledge of all the facts relating to his liability but in ignorance of the legal position. Although there were in fact several such decisions (see in particular *Bize* v. *Dickason*, (1786) 1 TR 285, 99 Eng. Rep. 1097), counsel was unable to name one. LORD ELLENBOROUGH thereupon declared that 'every man must be taken to be cognisant of the law; otherwise there is no saying to what extent the excuse of ignorance might not be carried' and dismissed the claim. Since that time it is a recognized principle of the Common Law that the restitution of money paid when not due is excluded if the defendant believed he was entitled to it and the plaintiff, though aware of all the relevant facts, believed himself bound to pay because he drew the wrong legal conclusions from them.

In the United States also the courts have by and large accepted the principle that there can be no restitution of benefits conferred under a mistake of law. The New York Law Revision Commission recommended that the distinction between mistake of law and mistake of fact be abolished (see Report 1942 no. 65 B), and this recommendation was enacted in §3005 NY Civil Practice Law.—Writers also disapprove of the distinction, see WOODWARD (above p. 606); STADDEN (above p. 605); PALMER (above p. 576) §§14.27 and 16.4.—§45 of the Restatement of the Law of Restitution states the principle that restitution of benefits conferred under a mistake of law is excluded, but in §§46 ff. lays down a series of exceptions so far-reaching and so well supported in the case-law that in CORBIN's view 'it would be a poor judge who cannot find sufficient authority for deciding contrary to *Bilbie* v. *Lumley*' (§617).

No comparable rule is to be found in Continental legal systems. This is obvious for *German* law since the plaintiff in an enrichment claim is not required to show that he was *in error* in conferring the benefit: a benefit may be reclaimed whenever as a matter of objective law there was no obligation to confer it, the only exceptions being if the plaintiff was positively aware that he was not bound to confer the benefit, or was so bound, but by a duty of morality or honour rather than law (§814 BGB). But even in countries such as Austria, Switzerland, and France, where the civil code expressly makes the claim for restitution dependent on the plaintiff's having been in error about his duty to perform, there is no further requirement that his error be an error *of fact* and not simply an error *of law*. Indeed, §1431 ABGB expressly allows a claim for the restitution of benefits which the plaintiff conferred 'by mistake, even a mistake of law'. After some initial doubts, resolved in BGE 40 II 249, the courts in Switzerland have adopted the same position. The same is true in France (Req. 4 Aug. 1859, DP 1859. 1. 362; Req. 21 July 1908, DP 1909. 1. 175).

If the answer given by modern German law is clear, we should not forget that until the BGB came into force courts and writers were divided on it. WINDSCHEID found in the Roman sources 'an indubitable axiom very clearly stated' that if the error were one of law the *condictio indebiti* was inadmissible unless it could exceptionally be shown that the error of law was excusable (*Lehrbuch des Pandektenrechts* (1865) §426 n. 14). In the past 70 years researches in Roman law have benefited from the results of the critical school of interpolationists, and it now seems that in classical times an error of law only barred the *condictio* if the performance induced by the error was nevertheless required by a moral duty or by good faith. The prime example of this is the case where a testator had burdened his heir with a *fideicommissum* requiring him to transfer the estate to a subsequent heir. The *senatusconsultum Pegasianum* permitted the heir under certain conditions to retain one-quarter of the estate (the *quarta falcidia*) for himself, but if, in ignorance of the law, he failed to do so, could not reclaim as an *indebitum* the excess he had transferred. Modern scholars think that JUSTINIAN was the first to generalize the thought that an error of law was fatal (see the details in SCHWARZ, *SavZ/Rom.* 68 (1951) 266; SCHWARZ, *Die Grundlage der condictio im klassischen römischen Recht* (1952) 101 ff.)—Under the *Gemeines Recht* the dominant view was that an error of law excluded the *condictio* unless, exceptionally, it was an excusable error (an exhaustive list of views is given in SAVIGNY, *System des heutigen römischen Rechts* III (1840) 447 ff.) and this position was adopted by the courts as well (see for example Oberappellationsgericht Lübeck 29 Nov. 1856, SeuffA 13 no. 254 with further references).—By contrast, the General Land Law of Prussia had no comparable provision, and the Prussian Obertribunal allowed a *condictio* even if the plaintiff's error were one of law (29 Feb. 1840, ObTr. 6, 8) or an inexcusable error (22 Feb. 1855, ObTr. 30, 76).

This shows that English and German law take different views of the relevance of errors of law in enrichment cases, but that does not mean that similar cases will necessarily be decided differently in the courts. It could well be that English courts use the doctrine of 'mistake of law' to answer needs and interests which are equally well recognized in Germany but answered there by using other doctrinal concepts. In order to see whether this is so, we shall consider some of the types of case where the English courts reject a claim for restitution on the ground that the plaintiff's mistake was one of law.

First there are the cases where the plaintiff's view of the law *only later* proves to be incorrect, normally by reason of a supreme court decision. Taxpayers have often tried to reclaim from the treasury money paid on a construction of a taxing statute which is later shown to be erroneous. The normal reason given for rejecting such claims in England is 'mistake of law'. In *National Pari-Mutuel Ass. Ltd.* v. *The King*, (1930) 47 TLR 110, the plaintiff was a club which set up a betting office for members only and supposed that this made it liable to pay gambling taxes as a 'bookmaker' under the Finance Act, 1926. In 1929 the House of Lords held that a club which ran a betting shop for members only was not a 'bookmaker' under the Finance Act, and the club reclaimed the taxes it had paid in the intervening years. The claim was rejected because the plaintiff's error consisted of a misconstruction of a statute and was therefore a mistake of law which was fatal to the claim.

To the same effect: *Whiteley, Ltd.* v. *The King*, (1909) 101 LT 741; *Sawyer & Vincent* v. *Window Brace Ltd.*, [1943] 1 KB 32; *Campbell* v. *Rainey*, 127 Cal. App. 747, 17 P. 2d

310 (1932); *O'Malley* v. *Sims*, 51 Ariz. 155, 75 P. 2d 50 (1938); *Glasgow Corp.* v. *Inland Revenue*, 1959 SLT 230; *Werrin* v. *The Commonwealth*, (1937/1938) 59 CLR 150; *Kelly* v. *The King*, (1902) 27 VLR 522.—The defendant in *Henderson* v. *Folkestone Waterworks Co.*, (1885) 1 TLR 329 was a water company entitled by private Act of Parliament to charge its consumers water rates up to a certain amount. A decision of the House of Lords in another case (*Dobbs* v. *Grand Junction Waterworks Co.*, (1883) 49 LTR 541) made it clear that the defendant, having misconstrued the statute, had charged water rates in excess of its powers. The plaintiff claimed restitution. He was unsuccessful. After suggesting that the decision of the House of Lords might have altered the law only *pro futoro*, LORD COLERIDGE held that in any case it was highly undesirable that a decision of the highest tribunal at variance with the view of the law previously entertained should set off a whole chain of restitutionary claims.—The French Cour de Cassation also regularly holds that a firm cannot reclaim social security payments just because a subsequent decision *inter alios* shows that the charges were improperly raised. The cases have so far involved firms which knew at the time of payment that the construction of the relevant rules was in doubt (see Soc. 24 May 1973, Bull. civ. 1973. V. 306; 28 Nov. 1973, Bull. civ. 1973. V. 567). In the case last cited the Cour de Cassation left open the question whether the result might not be different if the subsequent decision represented 'une évolution de la jurisprudence' rather than simply 'une interprétation nouvelle des textes en vigueur'.

The result of these cases would have been just the same in Germany but the reasoning would have been entirely different. In Germany taxes and levies are demanded of the citizen by means of a special administrative act (tax assessments and so on). Special methods are provided for questioning administrative acts and they must be exercised within certain set periods (see §§44 ff. Law on Procedure in Tax Matters (FGO), 58 ff. Law of Administrative Procedure (VwGO)). If the citizen fails to exercise his rights in the proper way and at the proper time he cannot recover what he has paid even if it later appears that it was wrongly demanded. An administrative act now immune from attack provides a legal basis which justifies the state in retaining what it received. Even if the rule authorizing the levy is later held to be unconstitutional by the Bundesverfassungsgericht, payments made cannot be reclaimed from the state on the ground of unjustified enrichment if the administrative act is no longer subject to question (expressly laid down in §79 par. 2 Law on the Federal Constitutional Court (BVerfGG)).

The New York case of *Doll* v. *Earle*, 59 NY 638 (1874) presents the problem in a different guise. Mortgagor and mortgagee could not agree whether under existing law the mortgage was to be paid off in paper money or in gold; if in gold, the mortgagor would have had to pay an extra $895. They agreed that the mortgagor would put $895 in escrow, to be returned to him or paid to the creditor depending on the law laid down by the United States Supreme Court. The Supreme Court first gave several decisions to the effect that payment should be made in gold (see *Hepburn* v. *Griswold*, 75 US 603 (1869)) and the mortgagor released the money to the mortgagee. A year later, however, the

Supreme Court reversed itself (*Knox* v. *Lee*, 79 US 457 (1870)) and the mortgagor claimed the money back. His claim was rejected because it was a mistake of law which induced him to release the money: 'Every man is to be charged, at his peril, with a knowledge of the law. There is no other principle which is safe and practical in the common business of mankind. And to permit a subsequent judicial decision in any one given case, on a point of law, to open or annul everything that has been done in other cases of the like kind, for years before, under a different understanding of the law would lead to the most mischievous consequences . . .' (cited in the New York Law Revision Commission Report (1942) no. 65 (B) p. 17).—To the same effect is *Cooley* v. *Calaveras County*, 121 Cal. 482, 53 P. 1075 (1898) where the court said: 'The agreement was in exact accordance with the general understanding of the law at the time it was made. Two years afterwards the court of appeals, in another case, gave a different construction. The community would be in a miserable condition if at every change of opinion upon questions of law all their previous contracts and settlements were to be overturned. Men could never know the end of their controversies.' *Bagby* v. *Martin*, 118 Okla. 244, 247 P. 404 (1926) is to the same effect.

It will be clear that it is not the plaintiff's 'mistake of law' which is the true ground for excluding the claim for restitution in the decisions just mentioned. The claim is rejected because legal security would be gravely imperilled if transactions which were wholly executed on the basis of a particular view of the law could be reopened simply because that view of the law has been seen in the light of a later decision to be incorrect.

A similar case has been decided in Switzerland. The plaintiff had drawn a negotiable instrument which was protested for non-payment, and an endorser took recourse against him which the plaintiff satisfied in return for the protested instrument. Four years later the Bundesgericht handed down a judgment which condemned the standard practice of notaries of allowing a subordinate to make the protest at the place of payment after the notary himself had signed the document of protestation (BGE 27 II 74). After this judgment was rendered, the plaintiff discovered that the instrument he had paid off had not been validly protested, and that he had not been bound to satisfy the recourse claim against him. The Bundesgericht rejected his claim for repayment, flirting with the notion that a claim for enrichment is excluded by a mistake of law before going on to say: 'But even if one does not want to go so far as to hold that a mistake of law is insufficient in enrichment claims generally, still a mistake of the kind before us cannot ground a claim for restitution . . . not until more than eight years after the payment did the plaintiff have the idea that he might claim back what he had paid, induced so to believe through the decision of the Bundesgericht which has been cited . . . But if one allowed restitution claims in such cases because the view of the law taken by the Bundesgericht was different from that of the person making the payment, it would endanger legal security and open the door to endless lawsuits. In a case like this, at any rate, the error as to the obligation by no means satisfies the requirement of art. 72 par 1' [now art. 63 par. 1 OR] (BGE 31 II 291, 295).

The Swiss Bundesgericht here was making the same appropriate value judgments as one finds in the decisions of the Common Law courts. Admittedly it would be more candid to say that a supreme court decision which controverts a view of the law generally entertained or a practice in common use should have effect only as to the future. Such a decision often has more in common with the creation of a new legal rule or the enactment of a new statute than with the discovery and correction of a mistake long concealed (see BGH NJW 1957, 263; BVerwGE 17, 256, 260 f.). If this is so, then the reason for denying the enrichment claim in such cases cannot be that the plaintiff has conferred the benefit under a mistake of law, since in fact he made no mistake at all about his obligation, but rather simply did what, under the existing law, he was bound to do.

It is not always a subsequent judicial decision which brings to light the mistake of law pursuant to which the plaintiff conferred the benefit. It often happens that after making the payment the plaintiff realizes by himself or is told by someone else that he was in error in making it. If the plaintiff was in possession of all the relevant facts at the time he made the payment his claim for repayment will be denied for 'mistake of law', but when we look at the cases more closely we see that in many of them the denial of the claim can be based on much more cogent grounds, well known to the German lawyer.

This is well illustrated by the decision in *Derrick* v. *Williams*, [1939] 2 All ER 559. The defendant had caused fatal injuries to the plaintiff's son in a traffic accident, and the son died a few days later. The defendant denied liability but made a 'payment into court' (for the details see COHN, *JZ* 1959, 463) of some £50. The plaintiff accepted this sum and went no further with the proceedings. There was no reference in the agreement to any damages for loss of expectation of life since the Court of Appeal in *Rose* v. *Ford*, [1936] 1 KB 90 had held that no such claim descended to the victim's estate. The House of Lords reversed the Court of Appeal on this point (see *Rose* v. *Ford*, [1937] AC 826) and the plaintiff sought to continue his suit in order to obtain compensation for the items of loss not taken into account. The court held that this was inadmissible. First it stated that the plaintiff's error was a 'mistake of law' and then it founded on the argument, which we have already noted, that legal security would be imperilled if executed transactions could be reopened because the courts had changed their minds: 'It was a mistake of law, and consisted of the fact that the plaintiff was under the belief that the law as laid down by this court in *Rose* v. *Ford* was correctly laid down. In that he was wrong, and he is asking the court to say that, having acted upon the basis of a mistaken view of the law, now that the law has been enunciated by the highest tribunal, he is entitled to make another attempt. That is a thing which, it seems to me, cannot be permitted on principle. It appears to me to be completely indefensible . . . It would be an intolerable hardship on successful litigants if, in circumstances such as these, their opponents were entitled to harass them with further litigation because their view of the law had turned out to be wrong . . .' ([1939] 2 All ER 559, 565).

A judge in Germany would certainly have decided the case the same way, for the reason that in accepting the sum offered the plaintiff had concluded a *compromise* (Vergleich, §779 BGB): in cases of compromise the risk of being wrong in law is placed on the party in error.

On this see, for example, RG JW 1938, 1722.—Both in France and in Italy it is expressly laid down that compromises may not be reopened by reason of error of law (art. 2052 Code civil, art. 1969 Codice civile).

In other cases the plaintiff has, to the recipient's knowledge, been in doubt about his liability to pay, but has overcome his doubts and made the payment. In such a case the recipient should be protected in his reliance on the supposition that the payment is conclusive, and the additional ground that the person paying was labouring under a 'mistake of law' simply conceals the real reasons for denying the claim.

See *Rogers* v. *Ingham*, (1876) 3 Ch. D. 353; *Monroe National Bank* v. *Catlin*, 82 Conn. 227, 73 A. 3 (1909); *Keazer* v. *Colebrook National Bank*, 75 NH 278, 73 A. 170 (1909).

Judges in Germany are familiar with such cases as well. It is true that according to the wording of §814 BGB restitution of a benefit is only excluded if the transferor 'knew' that he was not bound to make it, but independently of §814 BGB the courts have held that the general principle of good faith in legal dealings requires restitution to be excluded even if the transferor was *merely in doubt* about his obligation, 'that is to say, when the transferor has made it clear to the recipient that he intends to make the transfer even should he not be obliged to make it, when his behaviour is such that the recipient is entitled to conclude that he will let the transfer stand whatever the true position as to the underlying obligation may turn out to be' (BGHZ 32, 273, 278; RGZ 144, 89, 91).

'Mistake of law' is given as the reason for denying a restitution claim in yet another class of case where the decision would be better based, as it is in Germany, on the ground that the recipient has used up the money in good faith or has otherwise made irreversible dispositions, that is, when German lawyers would use the technical term of 'disappearance of the enrichment' (*Wegfall der Bereicherung*, §818 par. 3 BGB; see the details below Ch. 46 IV).

This can be seen in an old English decision which is still used today as authority for the proposition that restitution is excluded if the mistake was one of law. In *Brisbane* v. *Dacres* (1813), 5 Taunt. 143, 128 Eng. Rep. 641, the captain of an English warship paid the admiral, his superior officer, part of the freight he had received for the carriage of goods. This was in line with a practice recently current, but neither the captain nor the admiral knew that this practice had been brought to an end shortly before the payment was made. Nearly six years later the captain demanded the money back, without success. To a large extent the judgment was based on precedents supporting the rule that no one may reclaim money paid in full knowledge of the facts but in ignorance of the law, but SIR JAMES MANSFIELD asked the direct question whether in the circumstances it was fair and equitable to reclaim the money from the admiral. He said that it was not: 'For see how it is! If the sum be large it probably alters the habits of his life, he increases his expenses, he has spent it over and over again, perhaps he cannot repay it all or not without great distress: is he then, five years and eleven months after, to be called on to repay it?' See also *Re Hatch*, [1919] 1 Ch. 351; *Holt* v. *Markham*, [1923] 1 KB 512; and *Traweek* v. *Hagler*, 199 Ala. 664, 75 So. 152 (1917): in the last of these cases the court rejected the claim for restitution because the plaintiff had conferred the benefit under a 'mistake of law', but even if the plaintiff's mistake had been a 'mistake of fact', the judgment proceeded to say, the claim must be rejected 'where, as here, the payment has furnished the specific inducement to some affirmative action by the payee . . . whereby his situation has been unfavorably altered'.

Perhaps enough has been said to support the suggestion that the general rule of the Common Law which denies the restitution of money paid by mistake of law very often serves to answer needs and interests which are not only recognized in German law but are openly and specifically referred to in statutes and judicial decisions. This may well be true in other types of case than those mentioned here. Thus on the Continent there is no right to reclaim payment of a debt which is already prescribed, or restitution of benefits conferred pursuant to a duty binding in honour and ethics only (see, for example, §§222 par. 2, 814 BGB; art. 63 par. 2 OR; Req. 17 Jan. 1938, DP 1940. 1. 57; art. 2034, 2940 Codice civile). If one analysed the cases in Anglo-American law, one would probably find that here too the claim for repayment would be rejected on the ground that the payment was made under a 'mistake of law'. But the truth of the matter is that the notion of 'mistake of law' is quite out of place in cases concerning the restitution of benefits conferred without legal ground. 'Error iuris neminem excusat' is a brocard which may in times past have been useful enough, especially in criminal law, but in modern times there are so many regulations of every kind that the citizen cannot be expected to know them, and the principle that everyone must bear the consequences of his ignorance of the law has lost much of its force even in criminal law, not to mention private law (on this see RITTNER, above p. 605). The English courts know this perfectly well. Indeed, in a few decisions they have gone in for a kind of tactical withdrawal by saying that a 'mistake of law' means only an error relating to certain fundamental legal rules, to 'the general law, the ordinary law of the country' (*Cooper* v. *Phibbs*, (1867) LR 2 HL 149, on which see GOFF/ JONES (above p. 605, p. 149). This distinction is artificial and quite impractical. Here as elsewhere it would be much better to avoid taking refuge in legal jargon and to seek to discover and to reconcile the relevant interests and needs in a perfectly open manner.

III

A person who receives a benefit without having any contract or other legal title to justify his retention of it must return it to the person from whom he received it. This is the basic principle of the *Leistungskondiktion*, but if the reason for the absence of 'causa' is the illegality or immorality of the underlying agreement the principle has to be qualified. If the plaintiff knew the transaction was illegal or immoral the legal system will have to decide whether to deny him the redress of an action for restitution. Many such cases were discussed in the Roman sources. A person could not reclaim a bribe paid to a judge or witnesses (D. 12, 5, 3) or hush-money paid to the person who caught him *in flagranti* (D. 12, 5, 4 pr.) or the price paid for immoral acts (D. 12, 5, 4, 3): 'dixi cum ob turpem causam dantis et accipientis pecunia numeretur, cessare condictionem et in delicto pari potiorem esse possessorem' (PAPINIAN, D. 12, 7, 5, pr.).

   This rule is still in force everywhere, often laid down expressly in the civil codes (see §817 sent. 2 BGB, art 66 OR. §1174 ABGB, art. 2035 Codice civile), often simply applied by the courts (as in France, not to mention the Common Law countries), but its practical application has become increasingly difficult under modern conditions. In Rome during the classical period 'turpitudo' consisted of behaviour in breach of traditional ethical canons, especially of offences against the integrity of family life or the age-old conventions of proper behaviour (see KASER, *SavZ/Rom.* 60 (1940) 95), and it is still obvious that a person guilty of scandalous behaviour which contravenes these elementary rules cannot claim the assistance of the law to undo his dealings. But legal systems today increasingly invalidate transactions for simply running counter to the aims of social and economic policy endorsed by the state for the time being, and it may be doubtful whether it is completely fair to deny all restitutionary claims to the parties to such transactions, forbidden though they are. Even if all legal systems in principle accept the traditional rule that benefits transferred so as to procure an illegal or offensive result cannot be reclaimed, the real problem is to discover what precise form this rather amorphous principle should take in modern circumstances and how precisely the different systems apply it in different types of case. This is a question on which we can do no more than give a few pointers.

   1. There are many different views about the legal policy underlying the

denial of restitution claims in this area. The commonest consideration is that the state must deny its aid to a plaintiff who invokes it to help with the execution of his shady plans: 'no court will lend its aid to a man who founds his cause of action upon an immoral or illegal act' (LORD MANSFIELD in his classical opinion in *Holman* v. *Johnson*, (1775) 1 Cowp. 341, 98 Eng. Rep. 1120). There are many variants of this opinion, some emphasizing the moral obliquity of the plaintiff, many laying more stress on the thought that a court would soil its hands 'by adjusting among dishonest men the results of their unholy speculations' (*Gravier* v. *Carraby*, 17 La. 118, 36 Am. Dec. 608 (1841)). Even in Germany the safeguarding of the court's dignity is often put forward as the critical consideration: restitution should be denied 'in order to protect the state from having its courts improperly invoked by deliberate criminals' (OGHZ 4, 60; so also v. CAEMMERER (above p. 605) and RAISER, *JZ* 1951, 719). High-minded though this position is, easy generalization should be avoided. Granted that the plaintiff consciously broke the law in entering the contract, the court should still make a careful investigation of the facts to see whether in the particular case the purpose of the law broken by the parties or some other public interest may not be better advanced by allowing rather than rejecting the claim for restitution.

Similar criticisms can also be brought to bear on another view, according to which the denial of restitution is justified by the infamy of the plaintiff: he should be 'punished', and there is no better way of deterring the public from improper transactions than by making it very clear that in such a case they will forfeit the protection of the law. Even the Reichsgericht has designated the denial of restitution 'as a punishment for the active manifestation of an evil disposition' (RGZ 105, 270, 271; see also RGZ 161, 52, 60), and the Bundesgerichtshof has stated that §817 sent. 2 BGB, which denies restitution in such cases, 'can at least be justified on the ground that the claimant should be punished by the loss of his claim for behaving contrary to law' (BGHZ 39, 87, 91). But it is odd to 'punish' people without asking whether there is any reasonable relationship between the penalty imposed and the gravity of the offence, and a 'punishment' which leads to the enrichment of the *accomplice*, by allowing him to keep the money he has received even if he is more despicable than the transferor and therefore much more 'punishable', is very peculiar indeed.

The punishment theory becomes less objectionable if *neither* of the parties gets to keep the benefit which it was forbidden to give and receive but it is transferred instead to the state or to some charity. THOMAS AQUINAS, speaking of simony (the illicit traffic in holy property), said: 'Since in this case the recipient acted improperly in accepting the benefit, he must not be allowed to keep it, but must use it for pious purposes' (Book II Part II *quaestio* 62, 5; see now Can. 729, 1435 §1 Cod. Iur. Can.).—This solution may also be found in the General Land Law of Prussia: a transferor may not reclaim what he transferred in execution of an illicit transaction, 'but the treasury has the right to take the forbidden gain from the recipient' (§§172 f. I 16). This solution is perhaps a little unrealistic since one can hardly expect plaintiffs to sue for the benefit of the treasury, but the civil codes of the socialist states have all adopted it with simple idealism: see, for example, art. 412 Polish Civil Code, 361 par. 3 Hungarian Civil Code, 473 par. 4 Civil code of the RSFSR.—A modified form of this idea has been discussed in the United States: WIGMORE proposed that the plaintiff should be allowed to reclaim the benefit, on the condition that he pay a penalty to be fixed by the court in accordance with 'the degree of moral turpitude involved, the relative guilt of the parties and the plaintiff's motive in bringing the suit' (25 *Am. L. Rev.* 695, 712 (1891); so also WADE, 95 *U. Pa. L. Rev.* 304 f. (1947)).

2. These attempts to find a single basic idea which explains the widespread refusal of restitutionary claims are not very satisfactory. One would do better to ask whether any concrete rules and standards are used to decide whether restitution should be granted in a particular case or not. This is an area in which the Common Law in particular has produced some interesting notions. There the courts hold that a claim for restitution should only be denied if the parties are 'in pari delicto'; if it was primarily the defendant who was guilty of the illegality or immorality, the relatively innocent plaintiff should be allowed to reclaim. This principle is used in several different type of case. For example, a plaintiff is not 'in pari delicto' with the defendant if he was induced to enter the agreement by the defendant's representation that it was lawful, nor if the defendant has exploited his difficulty, simplicity, or inexperience, and the same is true if the prohibitory law which renders the contract invalid was designed to protect a special class of persons which includes the plaintiff.

See the summary of the cases in GOFF/JONES (above p. 575) 406 f. and PALMER (above p. 576) §8.6.—Similar considerations have often been used by the German courts as well. The general view is that §817 sent. 2 BGB only excludes a claim for restitution if the plaintiff's offence against law or morals was *'intentional'*. According to the courts, a plaintiff's behaviour is not 'intentionally immoral' if he reluctantly complied with the compelling demand of an economically stronger party or if he was in a necessitous condition (see RGZ 97, 82, 84; BGH LM §817 BGB no. 12). These are the very cases in which the Anglo-American courts would allow restitution on the ground that the plaintiff was not 'in pari delicto'.

The Common Law also allows a restitution claim to succeed if it is brought before the objectionable transaction has been completely executed. If a person makes a gambling contract forbidden by the law, he can claim back what he transferred as long as it remains uncertain whether the event on which the bet turns will occur or not; if the amount of the wager has been deposited with a third party as trustee, restitution is allowed even *after* the occurrence or non-occurrence of the critical event, provided that the trustee is still in possession of the money, for then the forbidden transaction is not yet fully executed. Behind this rule is the idea that it is good to give the plaintiff an incentive to timely regret or, as the courts say, a 'locus poenitentiae' which encourages him to abandon the objectionable transaction before it is fulfilled. Many critics admittedly think that this rule has precisely the opposite effect, for if the defendant, for one reason or another, is unwilling to execute the transaction, the plaintiff can induce him to fulfil it, objectionable though it is, by threatening that he will otherwise invoke the doctrine of 'locus poenitentiae' and claim back what he has transferred. The practical application of this doctrine has led to many borderline difficulties. In particular it is not clear how far the implementation of the forbidden transaction must have gone, nor is it clear whether the plaintiff must have been genuinely repentant or whether it is enough if the execution of the transaction was prevented or hindered by the defendant's refusal to perform or by some other cause.

See the cases in GOFF/JONES (above p. 575) 413; WADE, 95 *U. Pa. L. Rev.* 282 ff. (1947); and PALMER (above p. 576) §8.7.

In another line of decisions one finds the rule that the plaintiff should be allowed to bring a claim if he can formulate it successfully without mentioning the forbidden transaction. This rule is applied in cases where pursuant to an objectionable agreement the plaintiff has pledged, leased, bailed, or made a conditional sale of his goods. In such a case the plaintiff can base his claim on his ownership or, if the defendant has already sold or altered the goods, on a tort of the 'conversion' type (see below Ch. 47 III). Here it is normally the *defendant* who raises the immorality or illegality of the contract as a defence, and the courts are tempted to think the plaintiff relatively 'innocent' and to give him judgment. There is much dispute about the propriety of applying this idea in practice, for it was quickly realized that 'permitting the plaintiff adroitly to frame his declaration so as to omit any illegal aspect and make it necessary for the defendant to call attention to the illegality involved means that the whole decision is based not upon the merits of the plaintiff's claim but upon his attorney's skill in drafting a declaration' (WADE, 95 *U. Pa. L. Rev.* 268 (1947)).—See also the decisions cited in GOFF/JONES (above p. 575) 402 f., particularly *Taylor* v. *Chester*, (1869) LR 4 QB 309 and *Bowmakers Ltd.* v. *Barnet Instruments, Ltd.*, [1945] KB 65, noted by HAMSON, 10 *Camb. LJ* 249 (1948/1950).

The German courts have a doctrine analogous to this Common Law rule, that §817 sent. 2 BGB only applies to claims based on §812 and not to claims based on ownership (§985) or on tort (§§823 ff. BGB). The Bundesgerichtshof has sought to justify this rule by saying that 'when the claim can be based on §§823 or 985 ff. BGB . . . the plaintiff has on his side a right which receives stronger protection from the legal order than the right of a plaintiff with only a restitutionary claim' (BGH JZ, 1951, 716 with a critical note by RAISER). This principle is highly suspect, since it bypasses the critical question whether the purpose of the prohibitory statute or the public interest in the repression of immoral transactions will be better advanced by allowing or by denying the claim, whatever its legal basis. v. CAEMMERER (above p. 605) and RAISER (above p. 615) have shown that there are certain circumstances in which §817 sent. 2 BGB must apply even to a claim based on *ownership*: according to courts and writers alike in Germany, a transfer of property pursuant to an objectionable contract is generally valid, and is only invalid if it constitutes an especially gross breach of law or morals; accordingly only in the case of the most shocking offences will the transferor remain owner of the thing he has transferred in execution of an illegal or immoral agreement; but if the principle mentioned were to be applied, this is precisely the case in which the return of the thing must always be decreed, since the plaintiff can rely on §985 BGB as well as on §812.

3. In France also there are certain circumstances in which the courts reject claims for the restitution of benefits conferred pursuant to an illegal or immoral contract. The Code civil contains no relevant provision, so the courts rely on the traditional formula 'Nemo auditur propriam turpitudinem allegans'. It is particularly difficult to discover what factors move the courts to allow or reject the claim for restitution, for the criteria mentioned in the judgments are sometimes repetitious, contradictory, and unspecific. One common view is that restitution should be denied if the agreement is immoral (*convention immorale*) but generally allowed if the agreement is simply illegal (*convention seulement illicite*). Accordingly a claim for restitution is usually granted in the case of offences against price regulations or other prohibitory laws of economic policy. Thus a person who has knowingly bought food without the requisite licence may claim back the price: 'although the courts refuse a right of suit to a person relying on a contract which is void as being immoral or contrary to good custom, this is not so if the contract is simply prohibited by statute and contrary to public order without being contrary to good customs and morals' (Aix 28 March 1945, Gaz. Pal. 1945. 2.12, noted by H. & L. MAZEAUD, *Rev. trim. dr. civ. 44* (1946) 30).—On the other hand there was a dispute about the treatment of black market transactions; often the restitutionary claim was allowed (for example, Trib. com. Seine 23 Dec. 1948, Gaz. Pal. 1949. 1. 22), often not (for example, Trib. com. Seine 2 Nov. 1945, Gaz. Pal. 1946, 1. 21).

But if the transaction contravenes fundamental unwritten rules of behaviour, especially those of sexual morality, restitution is excluded: 'the courts of justice will not settle accounts of this nature'.

See PLANIOL/RIPERT/ESMEIN VII no. 750, and Civ. 25 Jan. 1972, D. 1972, 413; Com. 27 Apr. 1981, D. 1982, 51, noted by LE TOURNEAU. It is not surprising that the distinction between contracts which are 'immoral' and those which are 'simply forbidden' has led to the gravest borderline disputes in practice. (On this see AUBERT (above p. 605) 95 ff.) Even so, this distinction has been adopted in Italy: art. 2035 Codice civile provides that restitution is only to be denied if the transaction represents an 'offesa al buon costume' on the part of the transferor. Thus if goods are sold in defiance of a statutory prohibition, or a higher price is demanded than is allowed by law, the purchase price or the excess can be reclaimed (for example, Cass. 15 Dec. 1955 no. 3883, Giust. civ. Mass. 1955, 1457; Cass. 10 July 1958 no. 2501, Giust. civ. Mass. 1958, 889). But a person who invests in a partnership to run a forbidden gambling club cannot claim back his investment (Cass. 17 June 1950 no. 1555, Foro it. Mass. 1950, 326).

French writers have tried to explain and reconcile the decisions by saying that they allow restitution wherever this best conduces to 'ordre public'. It is true that the courts have often allowed a claim if it would be contrary to the public interest to permit the situation brought about by the objectionable transfer to continue. In such a case the plaintiff gets back what he conferred, despite his conscious participation in an illegal or immoral transaction. This may be unsatisfactory. But what is more important is the consideration that it would be contrary to the general interest to endorse and confirm the economic situation which the performance has brought about contrary to law.

It is for this reason that public or semi-public officials must disgorge the bribes they have accepted (see Civ. 5 Dec. 1911, S. 1913. 1. 497). If the price of a purchase is understated in a notarized land transaction, the purchaser may demand back the excess paid (Req. 24 Oct. 1928, Gaz. Pal. 1928. 2. 747; the German courts reach the same result, but only because the application of §817 sent. 2 BGB was specially excluded in such cases (see BGHZ 11, 90)). Further French decisions are cited by AUBERT (above p. 605) 108 ff.

4. The legal systems we have looked at adopt very different standpoints for the solution of the question whether the plaintiff should or should not be allowed to reclaim what he has transferred pursuant to an illegal or immoral contract. Our discussion has been far too brief to permit a critical appraisal of the criteria employed; for that, one would require a careful comparative investigation directed to the solutions in the different types of case. Such an investigation would probably show that similar cases are decided in very much the same way, though by different methods, and that any difference in the actual results is attributable less to any difference in methods than to divergences in value judgments. The comparative lawyer is forced to the conclusion that the really interesting question here is basically whether the *purpose* of the provision which renders the contract invalid is best answered by allowing the recipient to keep what was transferred under that contract or by making him restore it to the transferor. We should consider the *purpose* of the prohibitory statute not only to discover whether a contract which conflicts with it is *invalid* or not, as is always done, but also to see whether it excludes the restitution of transfers made in breach of its provisions. It is much the same when the contract is invalid for immorality rather than illegality. Here too the judge must openly ask whether the public interest in the repression of immorality of the type in question will best be answered by allowing or

denying the claim for restitution. Allowing the plaintiff to recover the benefit or the defendant to retain it may seem wrong when both have consciously participated in the objectionable transaction, but the solution of having the state confiscate the objectionable benefit and thereby take it away from both parties can only be considered in the most unusual cases, and so giving the benefit to an unworthy party is the price that must be paid in the pursuit of advancing general interests of a higher order.

The judge's task, then, is openly to ask the question whether in the type of case before him the public interest would be best advanced by allowing or dismissing the restitutionary claim. With characteristic deftness, the Common Law has concretized this general rule in its doctrines of 'locus poenitentiae' and 'in pari delicto'. If the public has an interest in the prevention of the execution of objectionable transactions, then in certain types of case it may well be sound to give the transferor an incentive to make prompt disclosure of the transaction by allowing him the right of restitution if he does so. Equally it is legitimate to ask whether the plaintiff belongs to the group of persons whom the statute in question was designed to protect. If so, one may allow him a restitutionary claim on the ground that he is not 'in pari delicto'. By contrast, it is quite unsound to hold that restitution must always be allowed if the plaintiff can base his claim on ownership or on tort and can thus state his claim without disclosing the objectionable transaction: this is to use formal criteria unconnected with the vital interests involved.

For the same reason one cannot accept the doctrine which keeps appearing in German decisions, that restitution must always be allowed if the recipient was not to keep the benefit for himself but only obtained it 'for temporary purposes', simply as a 'conduit'. The Bundesgerichtshof has decided that an attorney who offered to exchange German money into foreign currency in breach of exchange control regulations was bound, notwithstanding §817 sent. 2 BGBZ, to return to his client the money he received for this purpose (BGH 28, 225). This is certainly correct, not because the attorney received the money only 'for temporary purposes' and was to return it to the client after making the exchange, but because the public interest in repressing currency speculation is best served by requiring restitution of a person who used his knowledge and connections to solicit such shady dealings and who would, were he allowed to retain the money, be able in the future to offer himself with impunity for similar services. By contrast, the Bundesgerichtshof gave the right reasons for allowing the owner of premises let as a brothel to reclaim them before the expiry of the lease (BGHZ 41, 341): the court eschewed the unhappy doctrine that §817 sent. 2 BGB does not bar a claim based on ownership, and decided quite rightly that the effect of allowing the lessee to use §817 sent. 2 BGB as a defence to claim for repossession of the premises during the period of the lease would be to legalize the brothel in a manner inconsistent with the 'purpose of §138 BGB'.

IV

1. According to §818 par. 3 BGB, a person who has received a benefit without legal cause is released from the obligation to make restitution to the extent that he 'has ceased to be enriched'. Though it is questioned nowadays (see above Ch. 45 IV), the underlying legislative idea is that the enrichment claim, being based simply on equity, should not cause any loss to the defendant (see Protokolle II, pp. 706 f.). For this reason, 'enrichment' in German law traditionally means an economic increment, the amount by which all the advantages accruing to the recipient from the transaction which enriches him outweigh the associated disadvantages. It is inferred from this that the recipient may set off against the enrichment any disadvantages he suffered in connection with the acquisition of the benefit or which he would suffer in consequence of making restitution, up to the time when the claim for restitution was brought or he realized that he was not entitled to retain the benefit. Thus the recipient's duty is terminated or diminished if what he received is destroyed, embezzled, or confiscated (see RGZ 65, 292; 79, 285 (embezzlement); RG BankArch. 26 (1926/1927) 123 ff.; OGHZ 1, 98 (confiscation)); if he lends the money he receives to a trickster or invests it in an industrial enterprise which is dismantled after the war (see BGH JZ 1961, 699 (trickster); BGH MDR 1957, 598 (investment)); if he makes a gift of the goods he received or sells them at a loss (see RG WarnRspr. 1917 no. 140 (gift); RGZ 75, 361; RG JW 1915, 711 (sale at a loss)); if he spends money on what he received in the belief that he was entitled to keep it (RGZ 117, 112; RG WarnRspr. 1919 no. 196); if he increases his standard of living (RGZ 83, 159; 83, 161), allows claims to prescribe (RGZ 70, 350), surrenders claims (RG JW 1909, 274), or assumes obligations from which he cannot free himself without loss (RG JW 1914, 302; RG JW 1928, 2444). He may also set off the costs of acquisition and restitution (RGZ 72, 1 (brokerage charges); BGHZ 32, 240, 244; OLG Hamburg MDR 1953, 103 (costs of unsuccessful execution); RGZ 96, 345, 347; OGHZ 4, 81, 86 f. (expense and risk of return)). In brief, the plaintiff must bear the risk of all the events which negative or neutralize the economic benefit accruing to the defendant. This is the 'weakness' of the enrichment claim which is so often referred to (as by v.TUHR (above p. 606) 305). For German lawyers, indeed, it is the characteristic feature of enrichment liability.

2. Other legal systems are not so generous towards the defendant, but the rules vary a good deal in the different countries.

(*a*) All Continental codes apparently grant certain privileges to the good faith recipient, but they do not all draw the dividing line between good and bad faith in the same place. Apart from the case where a claim has already been instituted, the BGB imposes the stricter liability for bad faith only where the defendant was fully aware that there was no legal justification for his receipt (§819 par. 1), and the courts do not regard mere knowledge of the facts which destroy the justification for the transfer as sufficient (see RG WarnRspr. 1918 no. 224; RG JW 1931, 529). The Austrian and Swiss codes remove the privilege if the recipient 'should have reckoned on restitution' (art. 64 OR) or 'should in the circumstances have suspected . . . that the transferor was in error' (§1437 ABGB).

(*b*) The extent of the liability of the bona fide recipient is often linked in the codes to the extent of liability of a good faith possessor when sued by the owner in a *vindicatio*. Thus in dealing with the liability of the recipient of a thing paid when not due, §1437 ABGB refers to the claim of the owner against the possessor, and while arts. 1376 ff. Code civil lay down specific rules for the liability of the recipient of a thing not due, the rules themselves are very like those laid down by the other Continental codes for the relationship between owner and possessor. In Swiss law, a set-off for expenses incurred by the recipient in improving the property received is allowed in the same way as in the case of an unauthorized possessor (art. 65 OR). Frequently, the *vindicatio* itself is used, because in Swiss law, in deviation from the principle of abstraction (see above p. 575) property does not pass unless the underlying transaction is valid.

In these countries, as under §§987 ff. BGB, a person sued by the *vindicatio* has a defence if the object originally received has been lost, destroyed, or unprofitably consumed, but the only losses he gets credit for are expenditures on the very thing he received, necessary expenditures being admitted without limitation, useful expenditures only to the extent that the object is rendered more valuable at the time of restitution (§§331, 323 ABGB; art. 65 par. 1 OR: art. 1381 Code civil; PLANIOL/RIPERT/ESMEIN VII no. 746 *ad fin.*).

(*c*) In some Continental countries the recipient of *money* transferred without justification is treated very severely. In Roman law the payee remained absolutely liable whatever happened, being bound to repay the same sum just as if he had borrowed it (see v. TUHR (above p. 606) 297 ff.; SIBER, *Römisches Recht* II (1928) 218 f.). This doctrine survived in the legal literature of Europe from the time of the Glossa Magna until the time of codification. It was followed by the Prussian General Land Law (§193 16 I), and although WINDSCHEID dissented from it, a vocal minority of the nineteenth century pandectists supported it (on the whole development from the time of the Glossa Magna, see FLUME, above p. 605).

This time-honoured rule is still adhered to in Austria, France, and Italy, not just out of loyalty to tradition but with some empirical justification. Stress is laid on the fact that the extreme fungibility of money makes it practically impossible to trace the money received through all its metamorphoses in the assets of the recipient, or on the view that since money may be used in so many different ways the recipient must be taken to have benefited from the mere fact that he once had the money to dispose of as he thought fit.

See KLANG/GSCHNITZER, *Kommentar zum ABGB* IV (2nd edn., 1951/1963) §877 n. III 2 *a*(p. 158); KLANG/WILBURG, *Kommentar zum ABGB* VI (2nd edn., 1951) §§1431 ff. n. X B 2 (p. 480); EHRENZWEIG, *System des österreichischen allgemeinen Privatrechts* II 1 (2nd edn., 1928) 740; PLANIOL/RIPERT/ESMEIN VII no. 746; BEUDANT/LEREBOURS-PIGEONNIÈRE/RODIÈRE, *Cours de droit civil français* IX 2 (2nd edn., 1952) no. 1751; TRIMARCHI (above p. 606) 160 f.

The rule is also applied if the recipient's original duty to make restitution of a specific chattel ever takes the form of a money debt, as happens if the recipient consumes the chattel for his own purposes. In this case, further developments of the recipient's financial situation do not affect the creditor.

In Austria this is treated as implicit in §1041 ABGB; for France, see DEMOGUE, *Traité des obligations* III (1923) nos. 81, 111, 171.

(*d*) Given the conceptual form in which enrichment claims have been clothed, it is difficult to take account of disappearance of the enrichment in England. If an 'implied contract' is found to exist when a person has received a thing he should not be allowed to retain (see above pp. 591 ff.), the claim for restitution rests on the contractual promise to repay, fictional though it may be, and not so much on the continuing retention of the benefit (MAUDSLEY (above p. 576) 1132 ff.). On the other hand, where as a result of a 'constructive trust' a quasi-real right to trace is granted (see above p. 598) a certain limitation of the defendant's liability arises from the fact that the object in question or its substitute must still be capable of identification in the defendent's hands. The constructive trust will therefore fail if the object has been disposed of gratuitously or used up unprofitably. Some effect is thereby given to the notion of 'disappearance of the enrichment', but this is because the constructive trust is closely allied to concepts in property law, rather than because of a conscious appreciation of the fact that the recipient's economic position has altered for the worse in the meanwhile.

However, the defence of 'estoppel', as developed in the law of equity, makes it possible for English law to take explicit account of factors which reduce the enrichment where the defendant was justified in the circumstances in relying on the propriety of the payment. A person who represents to another, by words or unequivocal behaviour, that a particular state of affairs exists is prevented or 'estopped' from later asserting the contrary if the representee in reliance on the situation as represented has engaged in dispositions which would now prove disadvantageous to him if he had to make restitution. This defence naturally turns on the conduct and posture of the parties at the time of the unjustified acquisition of the benefit which is now being reclaimed. For this reason it is said that the mere fact that the transfer was made does not act as an 'estoppel' against the transferor: 'A mere mistaken payment in itself cannot give rise to an estoppel' (GOFF/JONES (above p. 575) 704). In cases of payment by mistake English judges tend to ask which of the parties was responsible for the error in the particular case and which of them should bear the loss in view of the underlying relationship. Another relevant factor is whether either party was guilty of any breach of duty to the other.

The defence of estoppel allows the courts a good deal of room for play. For example, they are very favourable to defendants who are asked to restore excess personal income paid by mistake. The simple facts of the much-cited case of *Skyring* v. *Greenwood*, (1825) 4 B. & C. 281, 107 Eng. Rep. 1064 were that a major of artillery had for several years been drawing too much pay because the paymaster has overlooked a Board of Ordnance directive. The judges felt able to reject the claim, on the ground that 'It is of great importance to any man that he should not be led to suppose that his annual income is greater than it really is. Every prudent man accommodates his mode of living to what he supposes to be his income. It therefore works a great prejudice to any man, if . . . he may be called upon to pay [the sums] back' (id., at 289). It was added that the paymaster was guilty not only of an error in computing the defendant's income but also of a breach of duty towards him.

The case of *Holt* v. *Markham*, [1923] 1 KB 504 was rather similar. The army paymaster omitted to take account of a relevant regulation and paid the defendant officer, who was retiring from the service, too large a gratuity. Eighteen months later, when the error was discovered, a request for repayment was made, but on an erroneous view of the facts which the defendant corrected in a long letter. Two months later the demand was renewed, this time on the right grounds. Meanwhile the defendant had invested what was left of the money and had lost it. The claim for restitution was unsuccessful. Two judges were of opinion that after receiving no reply to his letter to the plaintiff the defendant was entitled after such a lapse of time to suppose that the doubts as to the correctness of the amount of the gratuity has been resolved in his favour (BANKES and WARRINGTON LJJ, at pp. 511–12). SCRUTTON LJ was prepared to hold that the plaintiff was estopped by the payment and the expiry of eighteen months (p. 514).

Favour is also shown to the defendant if the unjustified benefit arose between parties who were already in a duty relationship with each other. Thus in the case of *Deutsche Bank* v. *Beriro*, (1895) 73 LT 669 an importer asked his bank to collect on a negotiable instrument. The bank mistakenly reported that the instrument had been met and paid him its value. It later appeared that in fact the instrument had not been honoured, but by then the importer had irrevocably credited the amount to his foreign business partner. The judge held that the bank was 'estopped' by its behaviour from reclaiming the payment; it was also, through the oversight of one of its staff, in breach of its duties towards its principal in giving him false information regarding the collection on the instrument. This error did not affect the defendant: 'Upon what ground of law or of equity can they say that they can get rid of the consequences of their breach of duty because they had made a mistake?' (MATHEW J., 670 f.).

If there is no special duty of care between the parties the courts are less tender to the interests of the party enriched. Thus in *Weld-Blundell* v. *Synott*, [1940] 2 KB 107 the first mortgagee, having foreclosed on the property, mistakenly retained too little of the proceeds for himself and sent too much to the second mortgagee. When the first mortgagee reclaimed the excess, the second mortgagee objected that the payment had made him delay taking timely action against the owner of the property on his own account. To this the judge said: 'I do not think an estoppel arises unless it can be shown that there was neglect or misconduct on the plaintiff's part in making the misrepresentation' (p. 114), and since a first mortgagee owes a second mortgagee no particular duty of care when he is calculating the distribution of the proceeds, no estoppel arose against the plaintiff.

A defendant who has himself caused or actually demanded the mistaken payment will not be heard to say that he made irrevocable dispositions on the faith of it. The leading case of *Durrant* v. *The Ecclesiastical Commissioners*, (1880) 6 QBD 234 is an example. The plaintiff was charged a sum for tithes because he was erroneously entered in the tithe-book as occupant of certain property. When he reclaimed the money it was too late for the church to make demand on the person truly liable, but the judge declined to take this fact into account in favour of the defendant church. The church's position had certainly altered to its disadvantage in the meanwhile, but there was no conduct on the part of the plaintiff such as disentitled him from recovering.

(*e*) American law, having accepted LORD MANSFIELD's view that the duty of restitution imposed on the party enriched rests on 'natural justice and equity' (see above Ch. 45 IV), found it easy, when weighing up the 'equities' in the individual case, to take account of the fact that no benefit remained to the defendant out of what he had acquired. In 1875 the New York Court of Appeals held that restitution should not be granted 'if payment has caused such a change in the position of the other party it would be unjust to require him to refund' (*Mayer* v. *New York*, 63 NY 455 (1875)). Nowadays the Restatement of the Law of Restitution makes 'change of circumstances' a good defence to all restitutionary claims (§142).

A 'change of circumstances' (or 'change of position') is found in those situations where German law would find that the enrichment had disappeared: destruction, loss or theft of the object received; unprofitable use or sale at a loss; expenses incurred on the property received; the assumption of legal obligations which are unavoidable or avoidable only at a loss; the surrender of rights or securities; the omission to exercise one's rights in due time; unprofitable investment of money received; gifts made out of what was received; peculation by staff. See the cases cited by PALMER (above p. 576) §16.8.

Since the defence rests on equitable considerations, the mere fact that the benefit has disappeared does not of itself extinguish the liability: the defence is successful only if the change in the situation makes it inequitable to order restitution. Here American lawyers see a problem of loss-shifting: if the situation is such that the defendant would be worse off after making restitution than he was before acquiring the benefit in the first place, then the question is whether this loss should be borne by the plaintiff by leaving his original loss uncompensated, or by the defendant by requiring him to make restitution despite the loss this will cause him. The outcome depends on a weighing of the 'equities' on both sides: the loss will be put upon the party who in view of all the facts is principally responsible. In making this judgment the behaviour and position of the parties is investigated in detail, both as of the time of the transaction which procured the transfer and later. Other circumstances also, such as the social and financial situation of the parties, may have a role to play.

The following cases illustrate the method of decision.

In *Behring* v. *Somerville*, 44 A. 641 (NJ 1899) a mortgage was assigned to B who did not know that it had already been assigned to A. B thus acquired only a secondary right, but the owner paid B the amount of the mortgage in ignorance of the first assignment, and claimed the money back when he discovered his error. Meanwhile B had surrendered the mortgage. The court rejected the claim for repayment. Both parties had made the same error, and both had the same means of checking the truth of the matter in the mortgage register. In such a case neither party had more claim to redress than the other, so they were 'to be left in the position in which they placed themselves'. In *Jefferson County Bank* v. *Hansen Lumber Co.*, 246 Ky. 384, 55 SW 2d 54 (1932) a person bought a cargo of wood under an agreement providing for payment to the defendant bank against documents. On hearing from the vendor that the goods had been shipped, the purchaser paid forthwith, without seeing the documents. In fact the goods were never shipped, and the vendor went bankrupt after the bank had remitted the purchase price to him. Nine months later the plaintiff reclaimed the purchase price from the bank, but in vain. The court stated at the outset that it was a matter for regret that in the circumstances the payment must represent a loss for one or other of the parties, but this loss must be borne by the person 'whose fault or negligence this loss is most fairly attributable to'. The court then held that since the plaintiff was entitled to withhold payment until the documents arrived, he acted with undue haste in making the payment and with undue sloth in reclaiming it. In practical terms the plaintiff was not so much asking for the restitution of an unjustified enrichment as seeking to put on the defendant a loss for which he himself was responsible. *Moritz* v. *Horsman*, 9 NW 2d 868 (Mich. 1943) shows that this equitable liability may be affected not only by the conduct of the parties in the transaction which conferred the benefit but also by other circumstances. The plaintiff, an adopted child, received part of the estate of his adoptive father on the assumption that he was a statutory heir. Later it appeared that the relevant legislation gave adopted children no right to inherit. The natural children thereupon demanded back the $13,000 which the defendant had received. He still possessed $5,000 in government bonds, but he had spent $3,000 on a house and furniture, and could give no precise information about the rest. The court noted in his favour that he had only $5,000 left in his hands, that he had been out of work for some time, that his wife's illness over a year had caused him great medical expenses, and finally that all the parties had laboured under the same excusable error of law. The court then said that it would be harsh and inequitable to make the defendant liable in these circumstances for the full amount he had received. It decided that he could afford $2,500 over and above the $5,000 he still had, and should pay two-thirds of this total of $7,500, namely $5,000, which he still had in liquid form.

3. Our sketch of the way foreign systems set about solving these problems shows that there is nothing necessary or self-evident about the principle of liability adopted in Germany, but that despite all the differences in their theoretical starting-points, the various legal systems very often reach the same results. In the space at our disposal we can illustrate this in only two cases: (*a*) the erroneous overpayment of allowances, pensions, and other personal emoluments, and (*b*) the enrichment of minors.

(*a*) According to §818 par. 3 BGB a person who receives money paid in error ceases to be liable if he spends the money without saving himself other expense. On general principles this fact has to be proved by the recipient, but where the sum overpaid was in respect of earnings and allowances the German courts assume from experience that a recipient does not save up the increments in his earnings but uses them immediately to improve his standard of living, with the result that he no longer retains the amount of the overpayment when it is reclaimed. The courts therefore allow those who receive such sums to rely on §818 par. 3 BGB on a mere showing that all the money has been used up (see RGZ 83, 159 and 161; BVerwGE 8, 261, 270; 13, 107, 110). At first this was accepted only where the money had been spent on transient items such as food and travel and so on, but more recently the courts have been ready to allow the set-off even to a recipient who still retains the equivalent of what he spent, provided that he would nevertheless suffer loss if he had to repay it, as happens in the case of furniture, whose resale produces only a fraction of its true value (BGH MDR 1959, 109).

To give further help to the recipient of extra personal income, the courts have recently been making great play with another rule which within proper limits is a well-established implication of §818 par. 3 BGB: this is the rule that a benefit is not diminished if it is used to pay off debts, since paying the creditor reduces the debt in an equal amount (see STAUDINGER/LORENZ, *Kommentar zum BGB* (12th edn., 1979) §818 n. 38). The Bundesverwaltungsgericht allows the defence of cessation of enrichment in such a case since even if he pays off some debts the official is still adjusting his standard of living to the amount he actually receives (BVerwGE 15, 15, 17 f.).

Such decisions rest on social considerations which arise in other countries as well. In Austria the rule that the exact amount of money received must always be repaid really ought to make such considerations inadmissible but in the case of overpayment of earnings the courts are ready to make an exception. The Oberste Gerichtshof once said in a case where the pension of a railway official had been miscalculated in his favour: 'This affects a great many people; the railways have their own office for calculating retirement pensions, for which the administration of the railways is responsible; it might even be thought that the railways were at fault in misleading people by paying them too much. It is true that retirement pensions take the form of money payments, but their purpose is to maintain the recipient. This is the purpose for which the recipient receives and uses the money, as both parties must obviously realize each time payment is made; furthermore, as has already been said, the overpayment normally causes the extra expenditure. In most cases therefore a claim for repayment is grossly inequitable since the official can be in no position to keep funds on hand to meet it' (OGH 23 April 1929, SZ XI 86 (p. 265)).

The same problem arises in France. The codal provisions regarding the payment of a thing not due do not permit any set-off for consequent disadvantages, but the courts allow the recipient a counterclaim for damages based on delictual liability for negligence or fault in the state administration. It is easier for French law to do this than for German law, since liability for tort in France may arise in respect of 'pure' economic loss whereas in Germany this is impossible because of the restrictive list of compensable heads of damage adopted in §823 par. 1 BGB (see below Ch. 47 II and IV). The normal case to cite as an example of a claim for repayment being met by a claim for damages is a fairly old decision by the Conseil d'État (1 July 1904, S. 1904. 3. 121). For fifteen years a pensioner received overpayments which he spent on living expenses. The Conseil d'État rejected the claim for repayment. To persist in an error for so many years must necessarily constitute a 'faute de service qui engage la responsibilité de l'État'.

In England an 'estoppel' only arises when there is some special fact which induced the recipient's reliance, so one would not expect the defence of expenditure to succeed very often. Nevertheless it appears that judges in cases of this sort are especially generous in allowing the mere fact of the mistaken payment to suffice, a holding they can reinforce, if they choose, by invoking the rule about mistake of law (see above Ch. 46 II) and by treating any internal regulations about emoluments as 'law', disregard of which excludes any claim for restitution.

(*b*) All legal systems protect *minors* in one way or another from the harm they might suffer from entering into binding contracts. For this protection to be effective, it must not only limit the contractual capacity of minors but also attach some qualification to their duty to make restitution of benefits received through the execution of contracts or otherwise.

In German law the general formula of §818 par. 3 BGB protects minors like everyone else: one is liable in restitution only up to the amount of the economic benefit still remaining in his hands. The special protection of the minor only becomes evident when one turns to the rules which determine the stricter liability of the bad faith recipient (§819 par. 1 BGB). According to the courts and writers alike, a minor's bad faith is not held against him, provided that his statutory representative was unaware of the acquisition and its want of legal justification (RG JW 1917, 465); it is also accepted that a minor is only liable if he could be held liable in delict (§§828, 829 BGB; see BGHZ 55, 128 at 135 f.).

In other countries the special protection afforded to minors is more marked since the *general* rule of liability is not sufficient to protect them. For example, minors might be put at risk by the rule in Austria and France that there is absolute liability to repay money unjustifiably received, were it not that an exception is made to this rule in their interest. In both countries minors are liable only if what they received was in fact used for their benefit, a fact which must, apparently, be proved by the plaintiff.

Austria: OGH 22 Aug. 1951, SZ XXIV 204; OGH 13 Dec. 1905, GlUNF VIII no. 3246; OGH 2 July 1913, GlUNF XVI no 6514.—France: art. 1241, 1312 Code civil.— Italy: art. 2039 Codice civile.—But French lawyers are so attached to the rule of absolute liability for the repayment of money that it reappears even if the recipient lacks contractual capacity; he remains liable for any benefit in kind procured by the money transferred even if he does not succeed in retaining it. If he uses the money for making purchases, he remains liable for the whole sum even if what he buys is later destroyed or depreciates. It is said that the plaintiff in restitution 'n'est pas responsable de l'avenir et des causes étrangères, mais seulement de la dissipation' (PLANIOL/RIPERT/ ESMEIN VI no. 323).

In English law there is no need to refer to rules about the extent of liability or the retention of the enrichment since minors are exempt *ab initio* from any duty to repay. If what the minor received or its substitute is still identifiable in his hands then equitable rules may be applied to require the minor to disgorge, as in a constructive trust (see *Stocks* v. *Wilson*, [1913] 2 KB 235; GOFF/JONES (above p. 575) 434), but the other party cannot by rescinding acquire a purely personal money claim, for fear that this would come close to enforcing the invalid contract. 'Restitution stops where repayment begins' (ANSON/GUEST, *Principles of the English Law of Contract* (26th edn., 1984) 200). The minor therefore goes free if what he received or its substitute is not there to hand over, whether it is just lost or has been consumed by use, usefully or not. In addition, he is never under any liability consisting of an obligation to pay money, as happens if the benefit took the form of services or of money which has been mixed with his own assets.

These results are based essentially on two decisions at the beginning of the century. *Cowern* v. *Nield*, [1912] 2 KB 419 involved a prepayment which a minor tradesman received under a contract which he failed to perform, and *Leslie* v. *Sheill*, [1914] 3 KB 607 involved a loan of money to an infant. In both cases it was categorically held that there was no duty to repay, partly on purely conceptual grounds (see above p. 593), but partly also because 'this would be nothing but enforcing a void contract' (LORD

SUMNER, in *Leslie* v. *Sheill*, [1914] 3 KB 607, 619).—American law by and large follows the English pattern. The Restatement starts by saying that the defence of 'change of circumstances' is at least as available to infants as to adults (Restatement §139 Comment *d*). In fact the protection of minors goes well beyond the general defences. Most courts still apply the traditional rule that unless what he originally received or its substitute is still identifiably present in his hands, an infant party to a void contract is under no duty to make restitution to the other party. According to many decisions, the same is true if restitution in kind was impossible *ab initio* (on the whole matter see WILLISTON §238; SIMPSON, *Handbook of the Law of Contracts* (2nd edn., 1965) 228 ff.).

4. The examples we have given show that in all legal systems liability depends on considerations appropriate to the particular type of case, and that these considerations, which are much the same everywhere, oust or temper the abstract rules of liability preformulated in general terms. Social factors are taken into account when the overpayment is of personal income, and minors who receive benefits are accorded special protection in line with the aim of the legal order as manifested in the law of contract.

The solutions in these cases seem to impose themselves automatically in the various systems, and they call for no further discussion, but several points emerge from the *general* solutions adopted by the different legal systems (see 2 above) which might be used with profit elsewhere. Even if one does not accept the theory that remedies in unjust enrichment are purely equitable (see above Ch. 45 IV), it still seems a good idea, particularly prominent in American law, to make the outcome depend on the conduct and posture of both parties during and after the relevant transaction; there is also merit in the view that the party who receives the benefit is responsible for any decisions he makes in the management of his own assets, even if the doctrine it is sometimes used to justify, namely that the liability to repay is absolute, is itself too rigid.

These points are rather obscured by the accepted German law that enrichment is simply an economic imbalance. Traditionally, a decision about liability in unjustified enrichment is the result of pure mathematics in which value-judgments have little part to play, but one immediately sees how relevant they are if one puts the question asked by the American lawyer, namely, who should properly bear the *loss* resulting from the disappearance of the enrichment. On this view, the continuing liability of the defendant depends on whether the *events* which cause the loss should be *imputed* to him or to the other party.

(*a*) It seems right that the conduct and position of *both* parties should play a part in any such decision. A. V. TUHR complained that the rules as to liability accepted by the dominant German view took no account of the differences in the position of the parties in the various types of enrichment claim. With regard to the *Leistungskondiktion*, where the plaintiff confers the benefit on the defendant in the first instance, he was in favour of a generous relaxation of the defendant's liability; a person who wants to undo a transfer he has made because he was mistaken as to his obligations should only be allowed to rely on his error and so be 'disruptive of commerce' if, like the mistaken party under §122 BGB, he accepts the loss which restitution will cause to the other party. On the other hand, where the enrichment has come not from a giving by the plaintiff but from a taking by the defendant as, for instance, in cases covered by §816 par. 1 sent. 1 BGB, the party benefiting deserves no protection if he makes bad investments, omits to use his rights and opportunities, or enters new obligations, for harm of this sort is incurred by all those who overestimate the assets at their disposal: he should not be able to shift them to the person entitled to restitution (v. TUHR (above p. 606) 314 ff.; adumbrated by HEINRICH SIBER, *Schuldrecht* (1931) 445 f.).

But one can safely go a step further, as some other writers (especially WILBERG (above p. 576) 138 ff.; so also, with cautious agreement, RABEL in *RabelsZ* 10 (1936) 426 f.) and American lawyers do, and ask within the different types of claim which of the parties was principally responsible for the enrichment or its disappearance, as having *caused* it or been *at fault* with regard to it. If a creditor destroys a document of indebtedness after receiving payment from a third party in error, the question whether the loss attributable to the consequent difficulty of proof should be borne by the creditor or by the third party who wants to reclaim the sum may be eased by the consideration, *inter alia*, whether the creditor peremptorily and cogently demanded the sum from the third party or whether the third party, believing himself to be the debtor, spontaneously made the payment or even whether the payment was intended for someone else and was made to the creditor only through the oversight of a bank. In the latter situation one must also, in order to solve the situation satisfactorily, ask which of the parties should be responsible for the errors of the bank in question.

(*b*) When it comes to deciding which of the parties should bear the loss attributable to events which diminish the enrichment, it is useful to bear in mind that the recipient should be responsible for economic decisions within his own sphere. In Germany, §818 par. 3 BGB puts on the plaintiff any economic misfortunes suffered by the recipient as a result of his dealings with what he received; the plaintiff in restitution must bear the loss if the purchaser of land resells it at too low a price, if the vendor of land invests the purchase price foolishly (RGZ 75, 361; RG JW 1931, 529), if the recipient of a payment not due makes a loan of it to a third party who then goes bankrupt (RG WarnRspr. 1912 no. 360; BGHZ 26, 185, 194 ff.), or if the vendor invests the deposit received under an invalid contract in his own business which is later dismantled or destroyed by bombs (BGH MDR 1957, 598).

But it would be more realistic to hold that in general everyone should bear the normal risks of the conduct of his affairs; as RABEL once said, 'the way the recipient deals with the property he has received is . . . exclusively his own affair' (RABEL (above p. 531) 427). There is therefore a valid point in the doctrine which still obtains in many countries that the recipient of money must always pay back the same amount: money is so easily used that it is particularly easy to say that what the recipient does with it is his own responsibility.

The idea that in general a person must take responsibility for the consequences of his own 'economic conduct' (FLUME (above p. 605) 157) only loses its force in a case where the receipt of the benefit induces the recipient to be prejudicially feckless, generous, or foolhardy; such behaviour is a true type of reliance damage which should be dealt with in terms of causation and fault rather than in relation to the question within whose economic sphere the dispositions took place. Nor can the idea be applied in cases where the law makes it clear, as it does in cases of minority, that it intends so far as possible to protect special groups of people from the disadvantageous consequences of managing their affairs.

(c) The example of the liability of minors suggests a further ground for the allocation of loss which has not yet been consciously applied in the law of restitution. Even where the law of restitution is in general less favourable to the defendant than it is in Germany we have seen that the arguments of legal policy which protect minors are so powerful that their liability for the losses which would result if restitution were required is either excluded or heavily limited. In other words, the rule which decrees the invalidity of a minor's contract and permits its rescission can usefully be referred to when the question is which party should suffer losses arising from the disappearance of the benefit transferred.

In the law of tort German courts and writers are coming increasingly to accept RABEL's view that the 'purpose of the law' may be at least as important in the allocation of loss as the traditional theory of adequacy (see below p. 642). The example of the liability of minors suggests that the problem of imputing loss may be approached from this standpoint in the law of *enrichment* as well: in proper cases the extent of liability in restitution may be affected by the purpose and power of the rule which justifies the claim. Of course this is not possible where restitution claims are based directly on a general rule of enrichment law, for the general idea of justice that assets which have gone astray should be channelled back to those who deserve them (see RGZ 120, 299 f. and 351) can give no useful answer to the question of how to impute the loss in a particular case. But where, for example, the rules which make the contract void (formal requirements, statutory prohibitions, and so on) and by so doing trigger the restitution claim have a clearly discernible policy goal, the purpose of the rules which make a restitution claim possible may offer a valuable ground for determining the extent of the ensuing liability in restitution.

Similar considerations may be of use in certain cases where the enrichment arises as a result of the defendant's own act, provided the cases are sufficiently clearly circumscribed. For instance, there is a rule in Germany that a person who sells or consumes someone else's goods and is sued in a *condictio* by the previous owner cannot set off the price he paid the third party for them. The reason for this, *inter alia*, is that such a set-off would not have been possible in the vindication to which he would have been liable before he disposed of the goods (BGHZ 14, 7, 9 f.; v. CAEMMERER, *Festschrift Rabel* I (1954) 385 f.). This shows that ownership not only forms the basis of the *condictio* but also has the further effect of determining the extent of liability.

C. TORT

47

Tort in General

ATIYAH, 'Negligence and Economic Loss'. 83 *LQ Rev.* 248 (1967).

V. BAR/MARKESINIS, *Richterliche Rechtspolitik im Haftungsrecht* (1981).

BLEY, *Schadenersatz im Zivilrecht* (1963).

——, 'Über rechtswidrige Schadenszufügung und zivilrechtliche Verantwortlichkeit bei der Schadensverhütung und beim Schadensausgleich', *Probleme des sozialistischen Zivilrechts* (1963) 224.

V. CAEMMERER, 'Wandlungen des Deliktsrechts,' *Hundert Jahre deutsches Rechtsleben, Festschrift zum 100jährigen Bestehen des Deutschen Juristentages II* (1960) 49.

CATALA/WEIR, 'Delict and Torts: A Study in Parallel', 37 *Tul. L. Rev.* 573 (1963), 38 *Tul. L. Rev.* 221, 663 (1964), 39 *Tul. L. Rev.* 701 (1965).

DIAS/MARKESINIS, *The English Law of Torts, A Comparative Introduction* (1976).

DRESTLER, *Haftungsbegrenzung im anglo-amerikanischen Negligence-Recht* (1967).

EÖRSI, 'Die zivilrechtliche Verantwortlichkeit im ungarischen Zivilgesetzbuch', *Das ungarische Zivilgesetzbuch in fünf Studien* (ed. Eörsi, 1963) 261.

ESMEIN, 'Le Nez de Cléopatre ou les affres de la causalité', D. 1964 *Chron.* 205.

FLEMING, 'Remoteness and Duty: The Control Devices in Liability for Negligence', 31 *Can. Bar Rev.* 471 (1953).

GEORGIADES, 'Standpunkt und Entwicklung des griechischen Deliktsrechts', *Festschrift Larenz* (1983) 175.

GIOVANNONI, 'Le Dommage indirect en droit suisse de la responsabilité civile, comparé aux droits allemand et français', *ZSR* 96 (1977) 31.

GRAY, 'Soviet Tort Law: The New Principles Annotated', *Law in Soviet Society* (ed. La Fave, 1965) 180.

GREEN, 'The Duty Problem in Negligence Cases', 28 *Colum. L. Rev.* 1014 (1928), 29 *Colum. L. Rev.* 250 (1929).

GREGORY, 'Trespass to Negligence to Absolute Liability', 37 *Va. L. Rev.* 359 (1951).

HELLNER, 'Développement et rôle de la responsabilité civile délictuelle dans les pays scandinaves', *Rev. int. dr. comp.* 19 (1967) 779.

HOLMES, *The Common Law* (1881), Lecture III (Torts—Trespass and Negligence).

HONORÉ, 'Causation and Remoteness of Damage'. XI *Int. Enc. Compl. L.* 'Torts' (1971) Ch. 7.

HORSTERS, *Die materielle Verantwortlichkeit im sozialistischen Recht* (1967).

JAMES, 'Scope of Duty in Negligence Cases', 47 *NWUL Rev.* 778 (1953).

KESSLER, *Fahrlässigkeit im nordamerikanischen Deliktsrecht* (1932).

KRUSE, 'The Scandinavian Law of Torts', 18 *Am. J. Comp. L.* 58 (1970).

LANG, *Normzweck und Duty of Care, Eine Untersuchung über die Grenzen der Zurechnung im deutschen und anglo-amerikanischen Deliktsrecht* (1983).

LAWSON/MARKESINIS, *Tortious Liability for Unintentional Harm in the Common Law and the Civil Law*, 2 vols. (1982).

LIMPENS/KRUITHOF/MEINERTZHAGEN-LIMPENS, 'Liability for One's Own Act' XI *Int. Enc. Comp. L.* 'Torts' (1972) Ch. 2.

LIPSTEIN, 'Protected Interests in the Law of Torts', 1963 *Camb. LJ* 85.

LÜER, *Die Begrenzung der Haftung bei fahrlässig begangenen unerlaubten Handlungen, Eine rechtsvergleichende Studie zum deutschen, englischen und amerikanischen Zivilrecht* (1969).

MARKESINIS, 'The Not So Dissimilar Tort and Delict', 93 *LQ Rev.* 78 (1977).

——, 'La Perversion des notions de responsabilité civile délictuelle par la pratique de l'assurance', *Rev. int. dr. comp.* 35 (1983) 301.

——, 'La politique jurisprudentielle et la réparation du préjudice économique en Angleterre, Une approche comparative', *Rev. int. dr. comp.* 35 (1983) 31.

MARSHALL, 'Liability for Pure Economic Loss Negligently Caused, French and English Law Compared', 24 *ICLQ* 748 (1975).

MARTY, 'L'Expérience française en matière de responsabilité civile et les enseignements du droit comparé', *Mélanges Maury* II (1961) 173.

——, 'La Relation de cause à effet comme condition de la responsabilité civile', *Rev. trim. dr. civ.* 38 (1939) 685.

McGREGOR, 'Personal Injury and Death', XI *Int. Enc. Comp. L.* 'Torts' (1972) Ch. 9.

MOTULSKY, 'Die Zurechenbarkeit des Kausalzusammenhanges im französischen Schadenersatzrecht', *RabelsZ* 25 (1960) 242.

OSAKWE, 'An Examination of Modern Soviet Tort Law', 54 *Tul. L. Rev.* 1 (1979).

POSNER, 'A Theory of Negligence,' 1 *J. Leg. Stud.* 29 (1972).

PREUSS, *Vertragsbruch als Delikt im anglo-amerikanischen Recht* (1977).

RODIÈRE/PÉDAMON (ed.), *Faute et lien de causalité, Étude comparative dans les pays du Marché commun* (1983).

RUDDEN, 'Soviet Tort Law', 42 *NYUL Rev.* 583 (1967).

SMITH/BURNS, 'Donoghue v. Stevenson, The Not So Golden Anniversary', 46 *Mod. L. Rev.* 147 (1983).

SÓLYOM, *The Decline of Civil Law Liability* (1980).

STOLL, 'Consequences of Liability: Remedies', XI *Int. Enc. Comp. L.* 'Torts' (1972) Ch. 9.

——, *Kausalzusammenhang und Normzweck im Deliktsrecht* (1968).

——, ' "The Wagon Mound"—Eine neue Grundsatzentscheidung zum Kausalproblem im englischen Recht', *Vom deutschen zum europäischen Recht, Festschrift für Hans Dölle* I (1963) 371.

STREET, 'The Twentieth Century Development and Function of the Law of Tort in England', 14 *ICLQ* 862 (1965).

SYMMONS, 'The Duty of Care in Negligence, Recently Expressed Policy Elements', 34 *Mod. L. Rev.* 394, 528 (1971).

SZPUNAR, 'The Law of Tort in the Polish Civil Code', 16 *ICLQ* 86 (1967).

TERCIER, 'Cent ans de responsabilité civile en droit suisse', in: *Hundert Jahre Schweizerisches Obligationenrecht* (ed. Peter/Start/Tercier 1982) 203.

TUNC, 'Les Problèmes contemporains de la responsabilité civile délictuelle', *Rev. int. dr. comp.* 16 (1967) 757.

——, 'The Twentieth Century Development and Function of the Law of Torts in France', 14 *ICLQ* 1089 (1965).

——, *La responsabilité civile* (1981).

——, 'Torts, Introduction', XI *Int. Enc. Comp. L.* 'Torts' (1983). Ch. 1.

VINEY, La Responsabilité: conditions (Traité de droit civil (ed. Ghestin) vol. IV 1982).

WILLIAMS, 'The Foundation of Tortious Liability', 7 *Camb. LJ* 111 (1939–41).

WHITE, *Tort Law in America, An Intellectual History* (1980).

WINFIELD, 'The History of Negligence in the Law of Torts', 42 *LQ Rev.* 184 (1926).

——, 'Duty in Tortious Negligence', 34 *Colum. L. Rev.* 41 (1934).

I

BOTH the law of contract and the law of tort entitle people to claim compensation for harm they have suffered. The law of contract does so only in a rather limited area, where the plaintiff has been disappointed in his justifiable expectation that the defendant would honour his promise. But citizens have many other interests and the law of tort deals with the cases where they have been infringed, where the plaintiff's health has been impaired, his reputation besmirched, his land adversely affected, his goods damaged, or where he has suffered some other economic loss. There is an enormous range of such harmful occurrences, and it is the function of the law of tort to determine when the victim ought to be able to shift on to the shoulders of another the harm to which he has been exposed.

In its early stages the law of tort normally comprises several concurrent types of liability, imposed in situations where a defined tangible interest has been invaded by specified physical conduct. Thus in Roman law the most important types of such tort liability arose from *injuria, furtum,* and the *lex Aquilia. Injuria* was an offence to another's person or personality; in pre-classical Rome the prime instances were murder, assault, and forcible housebreaking, but *injuria* came to include all outrages against a man's honour. *Furtum* at first covered only theft proper, but it was later much extended and became a comprehensive tort to property; the scholars of the *Gemeines Recht* were following the Romans when they included embezzlement, the unjustified use of another person's property, and even the conscious acceptance of something not due and the destruction of a document of indebtedness. Most interesting of all is the development of liability under the *lex Aquilia*; as we shall see, it bears a most striking resemblance to the development of the English tort of trespass.

At the outset the *lex Aquilia* only imposed liability on those who killed someone else's slave or farm animal or damaged someone else's property by 'urere, frangere, rumpere'. The act had to be done 'injuria'; originally this required consciousness of the doing of the harm, that is, a deliberate act, but even in the pre-classical period the lawyers started to treat mere *culpa* as sufficient, and the *lex Aquilia* gradually came to embrace negligent homicide and property damage. The harm had originally to be caused by a positive act which damaged the property by direct corporeal means, but this requirement was also relaxed and in the late classical period *actiones utiles* and *actiones in factum* were granted where the harm to person or propety was only an indirect consequence; for example, liability was imposed not only for setting fire to a ship but also for damaging it more cunningly by cutting the hawser (see ULPIAN, D. 9, 2, 29, 5 and on the whole matter KASER, *Das römische Privatrecht* I (1955) §§41, 118 II, 142 ff.).

Roman lawyers, however, never arrived at the general principle that everyone is responsible for the harm he is to blame for causing. This principle had to wait until the seventeenth and eighteenth centuries for its promulgation by the great natural lawyers, especially GROTIUS and DOMAT. Thereafter it made its way into many of the codes of Europe.

II

The law of tort in *Germany* before the BGB came into force presented a very variegated picture. The *Gemeines Recht* was still based on the traditional types of liability inherited from Rome. Efforts had been made to adapt them to the needs of the time, and the coverage of the *lex Aquilia* in particular had been greatly extended. The requirement of damage to some physical thing was not, however, abandoned, and purely economic harm was compensable only under the *actio doli*, which required proof of deliberate wrongdoing on the part of the defendant. When it was suggested that at least *gross* negligence should generally lead to tort liability, JHERING objected: 'Just think what it would lead to if everyone could be sued in tort for gross negligence as well as fraud! Anything and everything—an unwitting utterance, carrying a tale, making a false report, giving bad advice, speaking an unconsidered judgment, recommending an undeserving serving-maid one used to employ, answering a traveller's question about the way or the time or whatever—all this, if grossly negligent, would make one liable for the harm it caused even if one was in perfect good faith; if the actio de dolo were so extended, it would become the veritable scourge of social and commercial intercourse, conversation would be gravely inhibited, and the most innocent language would become a snare' (*JherJb*. 4 (1861) 12 f.; see also Oberappellationsgericht Lübeck, 13 Oct. 1838. SeuffA 8 no. 137).

Elsewhere in Germany legislators, influenced by the idea of a purely rational law, had broken with the traditional special types of liability, and had adopted a general clause of liability in tort. We shall soon be discussing the famous example in the French Code civil which was in force in Baden and West of the Rhine. The Prussian General Land Law also laid down in §§1 ff. I 6 that 'a person who injures another intentionally or by gross negligence must pay full compensation to that other', while 'the person who injures . . . another by only moderate carelessness' need only pay for 'the palpable harm caused thereby'; according to §8 I 6, 'injury' (*Beleidigung*) means the unlawful causing of harm, and 'harm' according to §1 I 6 means 'every impairment of a man's condition with regard to his body, his freedom, his honour or his wealth'. The Austrian ABGB also has a general clause: 'Everyone is entitled to demand compensation for harm from the person who causes it by his fault, whether the harm arises from breach of a contractual duty or quite apart from any contract' (§1295).

The men behind the German BGB were much tempted to follow the great model of the Code civil and to include a general clause which would impose liability in damages whenever harm was unlawfully and culpably caused. The first draftsmen believed that it would be impossible to secure sufficient protection against unlawful acts by attaching liability to particular types of tortious behaviour, since they might not cover all proper cases. After discussion a compromise solution was arrived at which avoided the casuistry of the special types of tort recognized by the *Gemeines Recht* yet stopped short of taking the crucial step to the great general clause. Such a general clause, it was felt, would simply conceal the difficulties; it would empower the judge to resolve them, and this would be inconsistent with the current German view of the judicial function. It was also feared that unless the statute laid down fixed standards the German courts might 'produce outgrowths such as one finds in many French decisions' (Protokolle II, p. 571). As a result, the BGB has no general rule covering liability for harm caused by unlawful acts. Instead, it lays down three heads of tortious liability in the two paragraphs of §823 BGB and in §826 BGB.

1. Under *§823 par. 1 BGB* liability for causing injury in an unlawful and culpable manner only arises if the injury affects the victim in one of the legal interests enumerated in the text; these legal interests are life, body, health, freedom, ownership and any 'other right'.

The requirement of *unlawfulness*, according to most writers, is satisfied by any invasion of one of the legal interests specified in §823 par. 1 BGB which is not justified by any of the few special privileges such as self-defence, necessity, and so on. The requirement of *culpability* or fault is satisfied if the harmful conduct is either intentional, that is, accompanied by the intention of invading the protected legal interest, or negligent. Negligence connotes a want of that degree of care which is generally regarded as necessary in society (§276 BGB); for this purpose one must consider how a conscientious and considerate man would have behaved in the same situation. If the harm was caused in the course of some specialist activity, the courts ask whether the defendant showed the degree of care to be looked for in the average member of the specialist group in question, professional or not.

In the last few years there has been some dispute among German lawyers concerning the meaning and scope of the concepts of 'unlawfulness' and 'culpability'. According to one modern view, harmful behaviour should only be qualified as 'unlawful' if it is discountenanced by law as contravening some legal prohibition or command addressed to the citizen. On this view, behaviour does not become unlawful under §823 par. 1 BGB simply because it causes an infringment of one of the legal interests there specified; it is unlawful only if the person causing the harm behaved either deliberately or without the care generally required in society. This leaves the futher question when behaviour which is unlawful in this sense is also *culpable*. Here the new doctrine simply asks whether the defendant, on the ground of his minority (§§827, 828 BGB), was unable to realize that his conduct was unlawful and that he might have to answer for the resulting damages, or whether the defendant's culpability was excluded by such individual factors as his inability to appreciate the objective circumstances which rendered the situation dangerous. There are still many points of dissension between the adherents of this new doctrine, but in fact these borderline disputes are not of much practical significance; given that a person who causes harm despite observing all the requisite precautions is not liable, it is normally quite immaterial whether his non-liability is attributed to want of *unlawfulness* or want of *culpability*.

Then it must be shown that the culpably unlawful behaviour caused harm to one of the legal interests specified in §823 par. 1 BGB. According to the terms of this section, these include, apart from the integrity of the victim's person and property, those of his interests to which the courts have accorded the status of an 'other right'. These include all the interests which the legal order protects *erga omnes*—real rights such as servitudes and rent charges, the possessory right to acquire a thing such as is enjoyed by a conditional buyer, the right to a name, patent rights, and other industrial property rights regulated in special statutes. One's estate as a whole is, however, not an 'other right' in the sense of §823 par. 1 BGB. Economic loss can be compensated under §823 par. 1 BGB only if it flows from an injury to one of the legal interests specified in that provision: a person who suffers personal injury and damage to his car in a traffic accident can claim damages for all the economic loss consequent on the personal injury, such as medical expenses, or on the property damage, such as the cost of hiring a substitute car, but if culpable behaviour causes the victim only 'pure' economic harm unconnected with any personal injury or damage to his property or the invasion of any 'other right', no claim arises under §823 par. 1 BGB.

If an excavator at work on a piece of land culpably damages a power cable with the result of cutting off the power to a factory some way away, his liability to the factory under §823 par. 1 BGB depends essentially on the nature of the harm caused by the interruption of the power supply. If all that happens is that the machines are brought to a halt and that the output is diminished the owner of the factory cannot claim damages since the carelessness of the excavator has only caused him an economic loss (see BGHZ 29, 65, and BGH NJW 1977, 2208), but if the power interruption causes the incubators in a poultry farm to cool off, the spoiling of the eggs is an injury to property and the excavator must pay not only the value of the eggs but also all other economic loss which the poultry farm suffers in consequence of their being spoilt (see BGHZ 41, 123). The Oberster Gerichtshof in Austria decides likewise (see OGH 6 Sept. 1972, *JBl* 1973, 579; 18 June 1975, *JBl* 1976, 210). The Swiss Bundesgericht, on the other hand, holds that economic harm due to the stoppage of the business is compensable, emphasizing that negligently to interrupt a power cable operated by a public utility is a punishable offence under art. 239 of the Swiss Criminal Code (BGE 101 Ib 252, 102 II 85). See also BÜRGE, *JBl* 1981, 57, and below Ch. 47 V.

The person whose unlawful and culpable behaviour infringes one of the legal interests listed in §823 par. 1 BGB must pay for all the harm which the victim suffers in consequence of the invasion. The only limit to the extent of the harm for which compensation must be paid is that there be a legally relevant causal connection between the behaviour which renders the defendant liable and the consequential harm. The Reichsgericht laid down that such a causal connection exists whenever the conduct of the defendant was such that 'it was apt to lead to the result which occurred, taking things as they normally happen and ignoring very peculiar and improbable situations which men of the world would not take into account' (the doctrine of 'adequate causal connection'; for example, see RGZ 158, 38; 170, 136). This view has been adopted by the courts of Austria and Switzerland as well.

This formula has been used, for example, to support a decision that the party responsible for personal injuries is also liable for their aggravation by faulty medical treatment, at any rate if the doctor's mistake was a medical error which might be expected by those in the know, and not a flagrant breach of basic and elementary rules of the art (RGZ 102, 230; RG JW 1937, 990). Similarly a defendant is liable if his victim dies in a flu epidemic which breaks out in the hospital to which he is taken (RGZ 105, 264). By contrast a defendant responsible for causing the plaintiff to lose a leg was not liable for his inability eight years later to hurry to his air-raid shelter when there was a sudden burst of artillery fire (BGH NJW 1952, 1010), although liability was imposed on a defendant responsible for an accident which caused the plaintiff to have an artificial leg when, twenty two years later, the victim, still unsteady on his feet, fell in his his room and hurt himself again (RGZ 119, 204). Medical conditions triggered off by an accident to an unusually susceptible victim are always 'adequately' caused (RGZ 155, 37; 169, 117; but see also BGE 66 II 165, where it is said that the risk of extreme susceptibility to harm may be allocated in part to the victim under art. 43 and 44 OR).

Recent court decisions in Germany show an increasing appreciation of the fact that questions of causation in law cannot be answered by applying purely logical and abstract standards but depend essentially on a value-judgment (see BGHZ 3, 261, 267; 18, 286, 288). This is connected with the acceptance not only by many writers but also by the courts of a teleological theory propounded by RABEL, according to which one must take account of the protective function of the rule which imposes the duty to make compensation: if a person causes harm by neglecting a particular rule of conduct, he should pay for such consequences as it was the meaning and purpose of the rule of conduct infringed to guard against.

See the extensive treatment in RABEL, *Recht des Warenkaufs* I (1936) 473 ff.; v. CAEMMERER, *Das Problem des Kausalzusammenhangs im Privatrecht* (1956); and STOLL, *Kausalzusammenhang und Normzweck im Deliktsrecht* (1968).—The Bundes-gerichtshof applied this doctrine in its decision that a person who was to blame for a traffic accident, while bound to pay the victim's medical expenses, was not bound to pay the legal expenses he incurred in retaining an attorney to defend him, and defend him successfully, in the ensuing criminal proceedings: 'the risk of being involved in criminal proceedings and incurring the expense of one's defence therein is a risk to which everyone is exposed; it does not figure among the dangers which the law seeks to guard against by bringing the integrity of health and property under the protection of §823 par. 1 BGB' (BGHZ 27, 137, 141f.).

2. Liability under *§823 par. 2 BGB* arises when a 'statute designed to protect another' is culpably contravened. Protective statutes in this sense include all the rules of private and public law, especially criminal law, which are substantially designed to protect an individual or a group of individuals rather than the public as a whole. Here too it is of some importance what form the harm takes, whether injury to health, damage to property, or merely economic harm, for harm is only compensable if it results from the very danger which it was the purpose of the protective statute to diminish or eliminate. If the protective statute is directed to the prevention of personal injury and property damage only, a claim for the compensation of pure economic loss based on §823 par. 2 BGB will fail.

For example, the federal railways, after being held strictly liable to the victim of an accident under the Imperial Law of Liability (*Reichshaftpflichtgesetz*), could not claim damages for its expenses from the person responsible for the accident on the ground that he was guilty of a breach of §315 Criminal Code (negligent imperilling of rail traffic) and that he was therefore liable to them under §823 par. 2 BGB. §315 Criminal Code is certainly a protective statute, but its purpose is only to afford protection against personal injury and property damage, not to safeguard the general resources of the railways (BGHZ 19, 114, 125 f.; see also BGHZ 39, 367).—But if a director of a limited company culpably fails to start liquidation proceedings when the company becomes insolvent and so commits an offence under §64 GmbHG (Companies Act), the corporate creditors who thereby suffer economic loss can claim damages from the director personally under §823 par. 2 BGB in connection with §64 GmbHG: the very purpose of §64 of the Companies Act is to guard against this type of harm suffered by creditors as a result of delay in bringing the liquidation proceedings (see BGHZ 29, 100).

3. The third head of general tort liability in the BGB is *§826*. A person is liable under this section if he 'intentionally causes harm to another in a manner which offends *contra bonos mores*'. The courts have used this provision to impose liability in a whole range of types of case where one party has caused harm to another by behaviour so offensive and improper as to incur strong disapprobation from the average person in the relevant section of society. It is not necessary to show that the defendant actually intended to cause the harm; it is enough if he was conscious of the possibility that harm might occur and acquiesced in its doing so. Liability is thus incurred by a person who knowingly persuades a vendor of goods already sold but not delivered to make them over to him, or by a partner who goes behind another partner's back and indulges in private transactions of a type reserved for the partnership, or by a person who markets goods which are a 'servile imitation' of another person's unprotected wares, knowing that the public may well be deceived about their provenance, or by an employer who lures away the employee of another knowing and accepting that this will cause harm, or by a person who recklessly gives false information about the creditworthiness of another party, conscious that the person seeking information could suffer harm thereby.

A person who acts *contra bonos mores* 'for purposes of competition in business' incurs liability under the general clause of §1 of the Law of Unfair competition (UWG). Many special instances of unfair competition are dealt with in detail elsewhere in this statute.

4. Barely eighty years have passed since the BGB came into force, but this has been long enough to show that the three heads of tortious liability just enumerated leave considerable areas uncovered. One gap was in the protection afforded to rights of personality. Other statutes apart from the BGB admittedly have provisions which cover tortious invasions of particular aspects of one's personality, such as one's name or the right to one's picture or one's rights as artistic creator, and it was often possible to grant the victim a claim under §823 par. 2 BGB on the ground that the texts which make it an offence to insult or defame people are protective statutes. Furthermore §826 BGB could be applied if the defendant's behaviour was outrageous and it could be shown that he intended to produce the harm. But these grounds of liability sometimes proved inadequate and sometimes they forced the courts into very strained reasoning. In 1954, therefore, the Bundesgerichtshof for the first time handed down a judgment which recognized as an 'other right' under §823 par. 1 BGB a person's right to his personality: as we shall see later (below

Ch. 50), this makes it easy to deploy the law of tort against conduct injurious to the dignity of the human being such as the unauthorized publication of the details of a person's private life.

Experience has also shown that the three heads of liability in tort often do not give sufficient protection in respect of *pure economic harm* negligently caused. Modern conditions require that some economic interests be protected against merely negligent invasion, or, to put it the other way round, there are now certain situations where it seems fair to impose on the citizen special duties to take care to avoid causing mere financial injury. One legal technique to meet this new need is for the courts to recognize, as the Reichsgericht did in the first instance, a so-called 'right to an established and operative business' and rank it as an 'other right' in the sense of §823 par. I BGB. Whenever it is necessary on legal or practical grounds to impose liability on a person who has culpably injured interests worth protection, the defendant's behaviour has been treated as an invasion of that 'right to an established and operative business' and liability has been imposed if he was at fault. The need was first felt in cases where the defendant had caused the plaintiff to stop some productive activity by claiming that he himself had an exclusive patent, licence, or other right. If it subsequently transpired that the defendant had no such right, he was held liable for the economic loss he had thereby caused even if he had made his claim without knowledge of its baselessness, provided he had acted unreasonably after inadequate investigation (RGZ 58, 24; 94, 248; 141, 336). This type of case led the Reichsgericht to say at the outset that the 'right to an established and operative business' was only infringed if the very stock, components, or constituents of the business were adversely affected, but it became necessary to extend the protection afforded by the law of tort to other forms of harm, and the Bundesgerichtshof has now reached the view that all aspects of a business, and not just its stock, are protected, provided 'one is dealing with the intrinsic and characteristic manifestations and connections of the business in its economic and productive functioning'. The defendant's invasions must always be 'business-connected'; this they are if they 'are in some way directed against the business as such . . . and do not simply affect rights or interests which are separable from the business as a functioning unit' (BGHZ 29, 65). Such formulas are not very informative. The real question, as the types of liability set down in the BGB are extended, is to decide what types of case of negligent causation of economic harm should lead to such liability. This problem can only be solved by an open discussion which takes account of whether the parties need protection and whether the interests of the plaintiff are such as to justify imposing on others a duty to behave with care to prevent the harm in issue.

The 'right to an established and operative business' is still used by the courts in cases where the defendant has unjustifiably and culpably restrained the plaintiff's business activity by claiming an exclusive right, but cases increasingly come up where protection is sought against negative criticisms which adversely affect the plaintiff's business.

For example, in BGHZ 3, 270 a church periodical described a woman's magazine as 'an outgrowth of the cultural sump of dubious journalism'.

In other cases the defendant has published true *facts* about the plaintiff damaging to his business, and published them in an impermissible manner not justified by any genuine or pressing interest and obviously entailing serious consequences for the plaintiff.

See BGHZ 8, 142, where a trade association sent out lists to its members which, *inter alia*, described the plaintiff as a 'slow payer'.

To invite the public to boycott a business may constitute an invasion of the 'right to an established and operative business' and so lead to liability in damages, if the invitation was culpable and not made in pursuit of justifiable interests (see, for example, BGHZ 24, 200). The same question is raised where economic harm is due to other forms of disapproabtion, where, for instance, a newspaper is impugned as a 'confession hound' or 'fool bait' (see BGHZ 45, 296), or products are unfairly decried in a consumer magazine or television broadcast (compare BGHZ 65, 325, and NJW 1970, 187, 189). In deciding whether there has been an invasion of the 'right to an established and operative business' in such cases, a balance must be struck between the protected business activity of the plaintiff and the equally protected freedom of expression on important economic issues, including matters of interest to consumers, which should be freely and openly discussed.

III

The *Common Law* of torts started out by having specific types of liability just like Roman law, but whereas on the Continent legal scholars ironed out the old distinctions between the several delicts to the point where a general principle of delictual liability became not only a possibility but an actuality in most legal systems, Anglo-American lawyers have largely adhered to the separate types of case and separate torts which developed under the writ system. Since the great reforms of 1875 English plaintiffs are no longer penalized for not mentioning the right tort in their statement of claim, but Anglo-American lawyers, judges and attorneys alike, still habitually and automatically tend to classify the case before them as falling within one of the traditional types of tort and to ask whether it satisfies the requirements of, say, conversion, nusiance, defamation, negligence, deceit, or the rule in *Rylands* v. *Fletcher*. Each of these separate torts is regarded as independent, each has its own constituent elements and its appropriate defences, and each protects a particular interest of the citizen against a specified form of invasion. As late as the end of the nineteenth century the question was raised in England and the United States whether in view of the number of independent causes of action in tort it made any sense at all to have a course of lectures or write a book on the 'Law of Torts'. When the first important book on the law of torts appeared in 1860, ADDISON's *Wrongs and Their Remedies, being a Treatise on the Law of Torts*, it elicited from O. W. HOLMES, who was reviewing it, the remark that 'Torts is not a proper subject for a law book' (5 *Am. L. Rev.* 340 (1871)). But only ten years later HOLMES himself wrote a masterly chapter on the law of tort in his famous book *The Common Law* and thereby did more than anyone else to disclose the common roots and lines of development in this area of law.

No one today doubts that the 'law of torts' constitutes a coherent body of law which can be lectured on or written about, but a great deal of ink has been spilt on both sides of the Atlantic over another controversy, namely whether any general principle of liability for improper harmful conduct is to be found underlying the various specific torts. In 1910 SALMOND strongly denied it:

'Does the law of torts consist of a fundamental general principle that it is wrongful to cause harm to other persons in the absence of some specific ground of justification or excuse, or does it consist of a number of specific rules prohibiting certain kinds of harmful activity, and leaving all the residue outside the sphere of legal responsibility? It is submitted that the second of these alternatives is that which has been accepted by our law. Just as the criminal law consists of a body of rules establishing specific offences, so the law of torts consists of a body of rules establishing specific injuries. Neither in the one case nor in the other is there any general principle of liability' (*Law of Torts*, 2nd edn., 1910) 8 f.).

The contrary view was adopted by POLLOCK and WINFIELD.

See POLLOCK, *Law of Torts* (12th edn., 1923) 20 ff.; WINFIELD, 27 *Colum. L. Rev.* 1 (1927); in between, WILLIAMS (7 *Camb. L.J* 111 (1939/1941) with further references).

It is a purely academic question which of these views is to be preferred. Everyone agrees that Anglo-American lawyers do in fact start from the specific torts, and no one denies that the courts have power to adapt the rules of tort to changes in social and economic conditions by imposing liability to make compensation where previously there was none. It is futile to ask whether in so doing the courts are simply stretching the specific torts which already exist or are finding a new area for the expression of a latent general principle of tort liability. Whether we prefer specific torts or general principle, the actual problems remain the same.

One of the oldest tort claims in the Common Law is trespass. The writ of trespass originally led to a penalty as well as to compensatory damages and was issued wherever a person forcibly and in breach of the peace—*vi et armis contra pacem domini regis*—invaded another's quiet possession of land or moveables (trespass to land or to chattels) or affected his physical integrity (trespass to the person). Just like the *actio legis Aquiliae*, trespass required a direct attack on the person or thing against the will of the plaintiff. If the harm to the plaintiff occurred only as the indirect result of the defendant's conduct or, even directly, from an omission to act, the trespass claim was unavailable; by contrast very little attention was paid in earlier times to the question whether the defendant's behaviour must have been deliberate or negligent. During the fourteenth century an action of trespass on the case, later called simply 'action on the case', was introduced to cover areas where trespass did not apply, where the plaintiff's injury was an indirect consequence of the defendant's conduct, positive or negative. The distinction was clearly drawn by BLACKSTONE J. in *Scott* v. *Shepherd*, (1773) 2 Wm. Bl. 892, 96 Eng. Rep. 525. 'If I throw a log of timber into the highway (which is an unlawful act) and another man tumbles over it and is hurt, an action on the case only lies, it being a consequential damage; but if in throwing it I hit another man, he may bring trespass because it is an immediate wrong.'

The distinction between causing harm intentionally and negligently was not clearly made in the Common Law to begin with. In the example just given, provided that the log hit the plaintiff during its flight, the trespass claim lay whether the defendant intended to cause the harm or merely acted negligently in throwing the log into the highway. As time went on, however, the trespass claim was gradually limited to cases of intentional harm, and today intentional conduct is required for those specific torts which developed out of the writ of trespass to the person, namely *assault* (the direct threat of immediate corporeal contact), *battery* (personal injury), and *false imprisonment*. The same is true for trespass to land, the unauthorized entry on premises occupied by another.

Liability in trespass is incurred by a person who enters the land of another without his consent, whether on, above or below the surface, or causes anyone else or any thing (for example rocks, refuse, water) to do so. Liability in damages only arises if the act which constitutes or causes the invasion is intentional, though the defendant need not have known that the land in question belonged to another. If a person conducts activities on his own land which unintentionally lead to damage on a neighbouring property, the modern view is that trespass only lies if he was negligent in causing the damage. For example, if bricks fall on to the plaintiff's land or harmful vibrations are caused by the defendant's explosions, the defendant is not liable in trespass if he observed the requisite precautions, though he is generally liable regardless of fault, at least in the United States, on the principle of *Rylands* v. *Fletcher* (on this see below Ch. 49 IV). If smoke, vapours, smells, and so on unduly affect a person's land, the person causing them is liable, again regardless of fault, in the tort of *nuisance*, whose pedigree is as long as that of trespass. The distinction between liability in trespass to land, nuisance, and *Rylands* v. *Fletcher* is extremely fine and varies from jurisdiction to jurisdiction within the Common Law.

Much the same is true of the tort remedies which protect a person's *moveable property* against improper invasions of his rights. Here the Common Law offers three torts which partially overlap: trespass to chattels, detinue, and conversion. Conversion, the most important of these in practice, is applicable when the defendant has done something in relation to the plaintiff's moveable property which is inconsistent with the plaintiff's ownership. The thief who takes the thing away from the owner is liable in conversion, but so also is a person who consumes the goods of others or destroys or alters them or who sells or pledges them with a third party.

In certain circumstances, indeed, liability in conversion may be incurred by a defendant when the thing is taken away from him against his will by a third party. In one case the plaintiff let a motor car on hire-purchase and the hire-purchaser lent it to the defendant. The defendant used the car for smuggling and the car was confiscated by customs officers. The plaintiff withdrew from the hire-purchase transaction for non-payment of instalments, sued the defendant for conversion of the vehicle, and succeeded. It was true that the defendant had not himself disposed of the vehicle, but he had so used it that its confiscation was the 'natural and probable consequence of his acts' (*Moorgate Mercantile Co.* v. *Finch and Read*, [1962] 2 QB 701).

The sole requirement for liability in conversion is that the defendant should consciously and intentionally have dealt with the goods. The defendant need not have been at fault: he will be liable in damages even if he believed in good faith that the thing he consumed or used was his own or reasonably thought he was entitled to consume or use it. Thus the tort of conversion covers an area which in German law is uneasily divided between three fields of law: unjustified enrichment, the law relating to the relationship between owner and possessor, and the law of tort based on culpable interference with property.

So far we have been dealing mainly with torts which generally involve an intentional interference with the integrity of person and property and which normally appear in books under the heading 'Intentional Interference with Persons or Property'. But the Common Law has a number of other torts which give protection against *economic loss* intentionally caused. These torts correspond to some of the types of case in Germany where liability is imposed under §826 BGB for causing harm intentionally and immorally. A person who knowingly deceives another by means of a false statement of fact is liable for *fraud* or *deceit* and must pay for the consequent harm (*Derry* v. *Peek*, (1889) 14 App. Cas. 377). A person who knowingly induces another to break a contract with the plaintiff is liable to the plaintiff for the tort of *inducing breach of contract* (see *Lumley* v. *Gye*, (1853) 2 El. & Bl. 216, 118 Eng. Rep. 749). A person is liable for *passing off*, in the absence of any special statute regarding trade-marks, design patterns, and so on, if he sells goods so like those of another manufacturer in name, construction, or packaging that consumers cannot easily distinguish their origins. If a person in bad faith makes false, but not necessarily defamatory or offensive, statements about the plaintiff which cause him harm in his trade or profession, the plaintiff may recover for this economic loss by the tort of *malicious falsehood*. If two or more people agree to restrain trade by an improper boycott or an impermissible limitation of competition, they are liable to the injured third party in the tort of *conspiracy*. If a person threatens another with violence or other serious harm so as to cause that person to harm a third party, the third party may sue for *intimidation*, supposing he can satisfy the other requirements laid down by a series of cases.

This tort occurs most frequently in labour law, where there is an improper threat of a strike. In *Rookes* v. *Barnard*, [1964] AC 1129, the defendant trade unionists threatened their employer with a strike unless he forthwith gave notice to an employee who had just left the union after repeated disputes. The employer yielded to this threat and the employee who had lost his job brought a direct claim for intimidation against the trade unionists for compensation for the loss caused to him by his dismissal. The House of Lords allowed the claim on appeal.

Other important Common Law torts are concerned with the protection of honour, professional reputation, and privacy against attack. We shall deal with these, and also with cases of strict liability, below (see Ch. 49 f.).

In order to complete our survey of the Anglo-American law of tort, we must now turn to the tort which is the most important in practice, namely *negligence*.

Negligence as a tort, like many other torts in the modern Common Law, developed out of the action of trespass on the case and was not recognized as an independent ground of tortious liability until the nineteenth century. The external stimulus for this development was the great growth in the use of machinery in industry and transport and the large increase in accidents which this led to. Such accidents were normally not caused intentionally, and their proliferation brought people to see that their typical feature was the reprehensible neglect of the requisite care and that *this* fact was the real ground for holding the defendant liable. This line of thought was decisively advanced by the fact that the principle of 'no liability with fault' answered the extreme liberalism of the time and served the interests of early entrepreneurial capitalism; this became the key idea of the law of tort and its approprite legal form was the tort of negligence which now became more and more independent. Trespass itself quite soon came under the influence of the doctrine of fault for the first time. Even here the plaintiff who could not show that the invasion was intentional was gradually required to prove that the defendant had omitted to take the requisite care.

The first English decision to point in this direction was *Stanley* v. *Powell*, [1891] 1 QB 86 (which was further extended by *Fowler* v. *Lanning*, [1959] 1 QB 426); in the United States it was *Brown* v. *Kendall*, 60 Mass. 292 (1850), printed in GREGORY/KALVEN/EPSTEIN, *Cases and Materials on Torts* (3rd edn., 1977) 64.

'Negligence' literally means absence of care, neglect, or inattention. The word 'negligence' is used in this general sense to describe careless conduct in all manner of different contexts throughout the law of tort, but the use of 'negligence' to denote the tort of that name must be sharply distinguished. Here the word acquires a quite precise technical meaning as a shorthand description for the conditions under which a person can be made liable for harm he did not intend to cause. The first of these conditions is that the defendant should have been under a *duty of care* owed to the group of persons of which the victim was one. In addition the defendant must have been in *breach* of this duty of care. Finally, in order to be imputable to the defendant, the *damage* (or *injury*) for which compensation is claimed must be a reasonably relevant consequence of his careless behaviour. The three most important requirements for negligence liability are thus *duty*, *breach*, and *damage* (or *injury*): 'In order to support an action for damages for negligence the complainant has to show that he has been injured by the breach of a duty owed to him in the circumstances by the defendant to take reasonable care to avoid such injury' (*Donoghue* v. *Stevenson*, [1932] AC 562, 579, *per* LORD ATKIN).

We may give a simple example. If a driver runs into a pedestrian and injures him, his liability, which in the Common Law still rests on the tort of negligence rather than on any special strict statutory liability, depends first of all on whether the driver was under any *duty of care* towards the victim. In this case there is no doubt that this requirement is satisfied: every driver owes a duty to all other persons on the highway to drive his vehicle with care so as to avoid causing them personal injury. Then the victim must prove that the driver was in *breach* of his duty of care, that is, that he did not behave as a 'reasonable man of ordinary prudence' would have done in the situation to avoid the impending harm. Finally, the harm of which the victim complains must be a proper consequence of the breach of the duty of care. Such a causal connection undoubtedly exists if the car collides with the pedestrian and breaks his leg, but it is more doubtful whether the pedestrian could recover for any aggravation of his injuries through the error of a doctor or its prolongation through some additional infection contracted at the hospital or if, while he was hobbling around on crutches as a convalescent, he fell over again and broke the other leg. The question for the Common Law here is whether the careless behaviour is still to be seen as a 'proximate cause' of the harm or whether the harm for which compensation is claimed is not too distant or 'too remote' a consequence to be imputed to the defendant. One of the most disputed questions in the Anglo-American law of tort is what criterion to apply here. In England the problem was ventilated once again in a fairly recent decision of principle by the Privy Council, *Overseas Tankship (U.K.) Ltd.* v. *Morts Dock & Engineering Co. (The Wagon Mound)*, [1961] AC 388.

The defendant's tanker (*The Wagon Mound*) was being refuelled in Sydney Harbour when a large quantity of oil was spilt into the harbour by the carelessness of the defendant's employees. The oil spread over the surface of the water until it reached the plaintiff's wharf about 600 yards away. The plaintiff took advice and learnt that in normal circumstances fuel oil floating on water could not be ignited, so he continued repairing a ship tied up to his wharf. During these operations molten metal occasionally fell into the water, and two days later a couple of drops unfortunatley fell on a rag or a piece of waste floating on the water and set it alight. This acted as a kind of wick in the oil and started a conflagration which caused very extensive damage to the ship and the wharf. The question was whether the defendant was responsible for this harm. Theretofore the Court of Appeal decision *In re Polemis and Furness Withy & Co.*, [1921] 3 KB 560 had been authority for the rule that a careless defendant was answerable for all 'direct' harm, even if it was not foreseeable, but in *The Wagon Mound* this rule was abandoned. It was laid down that a defendant was liable for all harm 'of such a kind as the reasonable man should have foreseen'. Here it could reasonably have been foreseen that the plaintiff's wharf might be fouled by the fuel oil, but not that it might be set alight in the manner which occurred. On this decision see STOLL (above p. 636), with extensive references to periodical literature and subsequent English decisions.

In the United States there is no single approach to this question. The courts use many different phrases to describe the consequential harm for which the defendant must pay: it must be the 'direct', the 'foreseeable' or the 'natural and probable' consequence of the defendant's careless conduct. Subtle technical distinctions and general theories have not been adopted in the United States, since most people there have the sceptical view that phrases such as 'proximate cause' or 'remoteness of damage' simply conceal the fact that in determining whether a particular harmful consequence should or should not be attributed to the defendant in the case there is a constant battle between the various 'policies' of purposiveness, equity, legal certainty, and social justice. Thus PROSSER (p. 279) quotes with approval the following observation by STREET on the problem of 'proximate cause': 'It is always to be determined on the facts of each case upon mixed considerations of logic, common sense, justice, policy and precedent . . . The best use that can be made of the authorities on proximate cause is merely to furnish illustrations of situations which judicious men upon careful consideration have adjudged to be on one side of the line or the other'.—See also the observation of JUDGE ANDREWS in *Palsgraf* v. *Long Island Railroad Co.*, 248 NY 339, 352, 162 NE 99, 103 (1928): 'What we do mean by the word "proximate" is that because of convenience, of public policy, of a rough sense of justice, the law arbitrarily declines to trace a series of events beyond a certain point. This is not logic. It is practical politics.'

Of these ingredients of liability in negligence, two are perfectly familiar to German tort lawyers, namely, failure to exercise the requisite care and adequate causal connection between the careless conduct and the harmful consequence. But the further precondition of liability for causing unintentional harm in the Common Law must be stressed: not only must the defendant have been careless but his carelessness must also be in breach of a particular duty of care owed by him to the victim. Thus until well into the twentieth century the Common Law had great difficulty in making the manufacturer of defective products liable to the consumer, since it was thought that whereas a person who manufactured or repaired goods of any kind was under a duty of care towards his purchaser or customer, he owed no such duty to any third party with whom he had no contract. Such a third party, therefore, if injured by the faulty manufacture of the goods, could not claim damages for breach of contract, since he had none with the manufacturer, or for negligence, since he was owed no duty of care. It did not do the victim any good to prove the manufacturer had been careless if he was under no duty of care: 'A man is entitled to be as negligent as he pleases towards the whole world if he owes no duty to them' (*Le Lievre* v. *Gould*, [1893] 1 QB 491, 497, *per* LORD ESHER).

There was a gradual relaxation of the severe rule that even the proven carelessness of a manufacturer did not expose him to any tort liability towards third parties who had no contract with him. It was not applied where the defective goods were inherently dangerous (poisons, explosives, firearms), and the decision of the New York Court of Appeals in *MacPherson* v. *Buick Motor Co.*, 217 NY 382, 111 NE 1050 (1916) created a further important restriction of the principle. In a judgment written by CARDOZO the court accepted that even a motor car was 'dangerous' and that the manufacturer therefore owed a duty of care not only to the person who bought it from him but also to any user of the car, with the result that he was liable in damages if the user was injured by his negligence. A step forward was taken sixteen years later by the House of Lords in the celebrated decision of *Donoghue* v. *Stevenson*, [1932] AC 562. This case held that the manufacturer owes the consumer a duty of care at least when, through the intermediacy of a dealer, he delivers to the consumer goods whose freedom from defect neither the dealer nor the consumer was in any position to ascertain. The facts of the case were as follows.

The plaintiff went into a cafe with a friend who bought her a bottle of ginger-beer. When her friend refilled her glass the remains of a decomposed snail unexpectedly floated out of the bottle. The plaintiff, shocked at the sight and at the thought that she had already drunk a whole glass of this remarkable beverage, fell victim to gastritis and sued the manufacturer of the ginger-beer. At first instance the judge decided that her statement of claim disclosed a 'good cause of action' and that she should be permitted to bring evidence that the manufacturer had been at fault. The Inner House of the Court of Session vacated this judgment and rejected the plaintiff's claim, but the House of Lords restored the decision of the trial judge by a majority of three to two.

In his speech, LORD ATKIN attempted to formulate a general definition of the relationship which must exist between two persons before the law will impose on one of them a duty of care towards the other. He said: 'The liability for negligence, whether you style it such or treat it as in other systems as a species of "culpa", is no doubt based upon a general public sentiment of moral wrongdoing for which the offender must pay. But acts or omissions which any moral code would censure cannot in a practical world be treated so as to give a right to every person injured by them to demand relief. In this way rules of law arise which limit the range of complainants and the extent of their remedy. The rule that you are to love your neighbour becomes in law, you must not injure your neighbour; and the lawyer's question, Who is my neighbour? receives a restricted reply. You must take reasonable care to avoid acts or omissions which you can reasonably foresee would be likely to injure your neighbour. Who, then, in law is my neighbour? The answer seems to be—persons who are so closely and directly affected by my act that I ought reasonably to have them in contemplation as being so affected when I am directing my mind to the acts or omissions which are called in question' ([1932] AC 562, 580; see also *Grant* v. *Australian Knitting Mills*, [1936] AC 85).

There have been further developments, at least in the United States, since *Donoghue* v. *Stevenson* and *McPherson* v. *Buick Motor Co*. Those decisions still made the outcome of a negligence suit depend on the consumer's being able to prove some want of care in the manufacturer. Today, however, the manufacturer of defective goods whose defect causes harm to the consumer may be liable even if he was not at fault at all (on this see also below Ch. 49 V).

Anglo-American courts also employ the notion of 'duty of care' in cases where Continental courts would see only a question of causal relationship. Suppose that someone, not himself at physical risk, witnesses a traffic accident and suffers a nervous shock, whether because he was closely involved or because a member of his family was actually or supposedly injured. The Common Law approaches the question whether the person who caused the accident must compensate the shock victim, who may well have been some distance away from the scene, by asking whether the defendant owed the victim a duty of care.

See *Hambrook* v. *Stokes Bros.*, [1925] 1 KB 141; *Chester* v. *Waverley Corp.*, (1939) 62 CLR 1; *Bourhill* v. *Young*, [1943] AC 92; *King* v. *Phillips*, [1953] 1 KB 429; *Chadwick* v. *British Railways Board*, [1967] 1 WLR 912, and the important recent decision of the House of Lords in *McLoughlin* v. *O'Brian*, [1893] 1 AC 410.

The so-called 'rescue cases' are also treated in a like manner. If a person negligently causes a dangerous situation, he can be sued by one who is injured in attempting a rescue: he owes a duty of care to those of whom he should reasonably foresee that they might in the circumstances feel called upon to undertake a rescue with all the risks involved. This also applies when someone is to blame for endangering *himself*: the passenger who leaps on to a moving train at the last moment may be liable to the guard who is injured in attempting to rescue him (*Harrison* v. *British Railways Board*, [1981] 3 All ER 679).

Claims for damages for negligence are almost always brought where the plaintiff has suffered *personal injury* or *property* damage. There is no general principle in the Common Law which excludes negligence liability in cases of pure *economic* harm, but here again the duty doctrine helps the courts to prevent negligence liability going overboard. This is clearly seen in the cases where a person suffers economic harm from relying on information which his informant ought to have known was false. If the information was given pursuant to a contract for reward, the informant is liable on the basis of the contract. But if the person who receives the information transmits it to a third party who then relies on the information and suffers harm, there are no contractual links between that victim and the original informant. This is true even when the informant knew that the information was going to be passed on to that particular third party. It might be possible, at a pinch, to construe the provision of information *for* a third party as an offer to form a contract *with* him, but even this would not impose any contractual responsibility on the informant in the Common Law, as no consideration has been promised or provided by the third party (see above Ch. 36 II). The injured third party is thus forced back on to the law of tort, and indeed to a suit in negligence, since in the absence of any intention to deceive on the part of the informant, the prerequisites for an action of decit are unsatisfied. Of course the informant will not be liable to the third party in negligence unless he owed him a duty of care.

For a long time the courts refused to hold that any such duty existed, even when the informant knew that the third party would incur expenditure on the faith of the accuracy of his report. This rule was applied again in *Candler* v. *Crane Christmas & Co.* [1951] 2 KB 164, but its instability is indicated by the powerful dissenting opinion of LORD DENNING (ibid. at 179 ff.). Twelve years later his opinion was endorsed by the House of Lords in *Hedley Byrne & Co.* v. *Heller & Partners*, [1964] AC 465: a person who, in a business situation, gives information, advice, or an opinion, apparently based on special skill or knowledge, incurs a duty of care towards those who, as he knows or should reasonably foresee, will take specific action in reliance on the soundness of what he said. See now *JEB Fasteners Ltd.* v. *Marks, Bloom & Co.*, [1983] 1 All ER 583 (CA), and *Yianni* v. *Edwin Evans & Sons*, [1982] QB 438.

Courts in *Germany* have often held the informant liable to third parties in such situations. Sometimes they invoke §826 BGB and hold that an accountant who wantonly issues a false statement as to the creditworthiness of a firm is acting *contra bonos mores* and is liable to a third party if he recognized and acquiesced in the risk that the statement would be transmitted to the third party and relied on by him (see BGH WM 1956, 1229). More often the informant is held liable under the law of contract, on the basis that there is a contractual or near-contractual relationship between him and the third party. German courts decide whether there is a contract on factors very like those which the House of Lords in *Hedley Byrne* held relevant to the finding of a duty: (for example, see BGHZ 7, 371; BG WM 1965, 287; WM 1966, 1148).—English law also uses the law of tort when a solicitor instructed by a client to draw up a will leaving a bequest to a named third party is so negligent that the legacy is invalid and the third party loses the intended bequest: the lawyer must pay for the designated legatee's financial loss, for he is under a duty of care to him and is liable in negligence for his breach of it; see *Ross* v. *Caunters*, [1980] 1 Ch. 297, and the Californian cases *Biakanja* v. *Irving*, 49 Cal. 2d 647, 320 P. 2d 16 (1958); *Lucas* v. *Hamm*, 56 Cal. 2d 583, 364 P. 2d 685 (1961); *Heyer* v. *Flaig*, 70 Cal. 2d 223, 449 P. 2d 161 (1969). German lawyers say that the contract between the lawyer and client is one with protective effects for the intended legatee (see BGH JZ 1966, 141, noted by W. LORENZ).

Liability for negligently causing mere economic loss has been imposed in other types of case in England recently. Thus a local authority which carelessly approves the foundations of a privately built house as meeting the legal requirements when they do not may be liable to the person who owns the house when the defect becomes apparent, however many intervening sales there may have been: its duty of care in the exercise of its statutory powers extends not only to personal injury or property damage but also to the cost of putting the foundations right so as to prevent the occurrence of any such damage.

See *Anns* v. *Merton London Borough Council*, [1978] AC 728. The paragraph in which LORD WILBERFORCE formulated the conditions under which a duty of care will be held to exist has been constantly cited ever since: ' . . . the position has now been reached that in order to establish that a duty of care arises in a particular situation, it is not necessary to bring the facts of that situation within those of previous situations in which a duty of care has been held to exist. Rather the question has to be approached in two stages. First one has to ask whether, as between the alleged wrongdoer and the person who has suffered damage there is a sufficient relationship of proximity or neighbourhood such that, in the reasonable contemplation for the former, carelessness on his part may be likely to cause damage to the latter—in which case a prima facie duty of care arises. Secondly, if the first question is answered affirmatively, it is necessary to consider whether there are any considerations which ought to negative, or to reduce or limit the scope of the duty or the class of person to whom it is owed or the damages to which a breach of it may give rise'. (ibid. at pp. 751–2).

This formula makes it possible to limit the scope of a duty of care with regard either to persons or subject-matters as the requirements of the case seem to require, but for a time it seemed that liability in negligence might be extended very far.

Thus in *Junior Books* v. *Veitchi Co.*, [1983] 1 AC 520, the plaintiff site-owner had required his main contractor to employ the defendant as subcontractor to put the floor in a factory which was being built. The floor which the defendant negligently installed was not dangerous to person or property but it was badly defective and had to be replaced. The defendant was held liable in the tort of negligence for the plaintiff's extra expenditure and business loss during the replacement. The decision was properly criticized (see the dissenting opinion of LORD BRANDON, at p. 547; JAFFEY, 1983 *Camb. LJ* 37, and W. LORENZ, *Essays in Memory of Professor Lawson* (1986) 86), and it has since been very much limited by the courts, so that fears that liability in tort would become very extensive have been allayed. Thus the manufacturer of a defective chattel is not liable for the merely economic loss suffered by a sub-purchaser (*Muirhead* v.

Indus. Tank Specialities, [1985] 3 All ER 705 (CA)), and the person who carelessly damages goods is liable only to their owner or possessor at the time, not to the others who may foreseeably suffer financial loss in consequence (*Leigh & Sillivan* v. *Aliakmon Shipping Co. (The Aliakmon),* [1986] 2 All ER 145 (HL); *Candlewood Nav. Corp.* v. *Mitsui OSK Lines,* [1985] 2 All ER 935 (PC)). LORD WILBERFORCE's observations in *Anns* are now to be read subject to the overriding consideration that it must be reasonable to impose a duty in the circumstances, and the actual decision in *Anns* has been limited to cases where the claimant is an actual occupier endangered by the defect in the building (*Peabody Donation Fund* v. *Sir Lindsay Parkinson,* [1985] AC 210). But see also *J'Aire Corp.* v. *Gregory,* 157 Cal. Rptr. 407, 598 P. 2d 60 (1979), in which a lessee was awarded damages against a building contractor for the business loss due to the contractor's negligent failure to perform his contract with the lessor.

IV

Almost the whole of the *French* law of delict rests on a mere five articles in the Code civil which have remained in force virtually unchanged for 180 years. The first of these texts is the famous general clause of art. 1382, which is amplified in art. 1383. These provisions are as follows. Art. 1382: 'Every act whatever of man which causes damage to another obliges him by whose fault the damage occurred to repair it.' Art. 1383: 'Everyone is responsible not only for the damage which he has caused by his own act but also for that which he causes by his negligence or imprudence.'

These propositions are based on the idea that the whole of the law of delict can be traced to a unitary fundamental principle, an idea which first appears in the works of the great natural lawyers of the seventeenth century. Believing that a legal order could be inferred from reason alone, they were brave enough to go behind the traditional specific torts and seek out and formulate a general principle of delictual liability. As early as GROTIUS's *De jure belli ac pacis libri tres* (1625) we find the following: 'We have said above that there are three sources of our legal claims, pact, wrong and statute. Enough has been said about contracts. Let us come now to what is due by the law of nature in consequence of a wrong. By a wrong we here mean every fault, whether of commission or of omission, which is in conflict with what men ought to do, either from their common interest or by reason of a special quality. From such a fault, if damage has been caused, by the law of nature an obligation arises, namely, that the damage should be made good.' (tr. Kelsey.)

The formulation of the texts on delict in the code civil is mainly attributable to the great French scholar JEAN DOMAT, whose influential work *Les Loix civiles dans leur ordre naturel* (1689) made a great contribution to the intellectual basis of the Code civil with its systematic exposition of Roman law, adapted to the needs of the time and spiced with French legal ideas in the light of the new doctrines of natural law. He already employed the notion of 'faute' and erected the general principle that compensation must be made not only for harm caused intentionally but also where the actor was guilty of want of care. On this basis POTHER distinguished into 'délits' and 'quasi-délits' the conduct which involved liability in damages; the former comprised conduct marked by 'dol ou malignité', and the latter included behaviour which caused harm 'sans malignité, mais par une imprudence qui n'est pas excusable'. Following on this, the Code civil places its texts on the law of delict in a special chapter entitled 'Des délits et quasi-délits', and modern French writers likewise distinguish between 'responsabilité délictuelle' and 'responsabilité quasi-délictuelle'.

A general clause in delict appears in other great codes of the Age of Enlightenment, such as the Prussian Land Law (see above p. 293) and the Austrian ABGB of 1811 (§1295), and it has proved very successful in the twentieth century as well: the Swiss OR of 1911 (art. 41), the Greek Civil Code of 1940 (art. 914), the Italian Codice civile of 1942 (art. 2043), the new Portuguese Civil Code of 1966 (art. 483), and the civil codes of the socialist countries all control delictual liability by means of a general clause. These codes, however, unlike the French Code civil, also have many special provisions to deal with important collateral questions, such as the delictual liability of minors, the relevance of the victim's fault and the compensability of moral harm.

It is clear enough that if a legislator is content with the stately enactment of texts as terse as arts. 1382 f. Code civil, the courts must perform the real task of creating comprehensive rules and standards to determine the substance and limits of a tort claim so outlined. The Code civil never explains at all what is meant by 'dommage' in art. 1382: whether moral harm is included, whether only personal injury and property damage are to be compensated or mere economic loss as well, whether ricochet victims can rely on art. 1382 Code civil, these and many other questions the legislator has left to the courts. It should therefore come as no surprise to learn that the modern French law of tort is basically pure judge-made law and that its rules have often only a very tenuous connection with the text of the Code itself. This judge-made law is superbly laid out in the great textbooks on 'responsabilité civile', especially the three-volume work of HENRI MAZEAUD, LÉON MAZEAUD, and ANDRÉ TUNC. Here we can only indicate the most important lines of development taken by the courts in relation to arts. 1382 f. Code civil.

The first requirement of a successful claim for damages in delict is that the victim should have suffered harm (*dommage*). From the very beginning French lawyers have taken this to include so-called 'dommage moral', that is, non-pecuniary harm including harm to human feelings, as we shall see later when we deal with the protection of personality and privacy.

Here we may point out that the French courts have gone suprisingly far in granting a personal claim for compensation to *dependants* of a person tortiously killed, for the moral harm they suffer through 'perte d'affection'. Originally the Cour de Cassation was inclined to grant such a claim only to those who were related to the decedent by blood or marriage (see Req. 2 Feb. 1931, S. 1931. 1, 123), but it has since been accepted that a foster-child (Caen 4 July 1935, DH 1935, 514), a fiancée (Crim. 5 Jan. 1956, D. 1956, 216), and even the concubine of a married man (Ch. mixte 27 Feb. 1970, D. 1970, 205; Crim. 19 June 1975, D. 1975, 679, noted by TUNC) may claim compensation for their grief, provided they can prove that they were very close to the decedent and seriously affected by his death. Damages for pain and suffering are also given when severe injuries rather than death result from the accident 'car les soins et les chagrins que cause l'infirmité d'un être cher ne sont pas moins réels' (Civ. 22 Oct. 1946, JCP 1946. II. 3365). The Cour de Cassation has gone a step further: the owner of a horse killed by the defendant's fault was granted damages not only for the cost of replacing it but also for the pain and suffering 'que lui causait la perte d'un animal auquel il était attaché' (Civ. 16 Jan. 1962, D. 1962, 199). On this see MAZEAUD/TUNC nos. 320 ff. and VINEY (above p. 637) no. 266.

It is of no importance what particular *legal interest* has been prejudicially affected; a person who by 'faute quasi-délictuelle' or mere negligence causes pure economic loss is in principle liable for it. This gives rise to serious borderline problems, especially in cases where the death or injury of a primary victim causes economic loss to a third party. Naturally the descendants and widow may claim damages for this loss, as may all other persons who by statute were entitled to support, but while many legal systems deny a claim to any other 'indirect victim' (see §§844 f. BGB, 1327 ABGB, art. 928 Greek Civil Code), or only grant title to sue to specified groups of persons carefully identified by statute (as in the 'Wrongful Death Statutes' in the Common Law), the French courts, lacking any legislative guidance, had to feel their way from allowing a claim to the brother, the foster-mother, and the illegitimate unrecognized children to the fiancée, the *de facto* spouse, and even, though here the courts vacillated a good deal, the concubine of a lawfully married decedent, provided that they can prove that they were being maintained by the decedent until the time of his death.

See the details of the cases in VINEY (above p. 637) nn. 271 ff.—Swiss law has also adopted a flexible approach here. Art. 45 par. 3 OR lays down that compensation must be paid to those whose 'provider' (*Versorger*) has been killed. 'Provider' in the sense of this text is taken to mean a person who has in fact provided support for the plaintiff or who would in the normal course of events so provide it. In consequence the Swiss courts have on several occasions given damages to the fiancée of the victim on the ground that her future right to support has been lost: see BGE 44 II 66; 57 II 53; 66 II 206 (the German courts decide otherwise under §§844 f. BGB and the Austrian courts under §1327 ABGB: see KG NJW 1967, 1089 and OGH 3 Oct. 1935, SZ XVII 132).

The French courts have gone even further and in some decisions have even allowed a claim for damages by the employer of the person killed.

Thus a football club was able to claim damages from the person who carelessly killed one of their professional players. The court found that the club's need to pay a high transfer fee for a substitute player constituted special damage (Colmar 27 April 1955, D. 1956, 723, noted by SAVATIER; the Italian courts have come to the same conclusion:

Cass. 26 Jan. 1971, n. 174, Foro it. 1971 I 342 and 1285). The Court of Appeal of Lyons granted the claim of an impresario who lost takings as a result of the death of an actor (26 Jan. 1956, D. 1958, 253) but this decision was quashed (see Civ. 14 Nov. 1958, Gaz. Pal. 1959. 1. 31, noted by MAZEAUD in *Rev. trim. dr. civ.* 57 (1959) 92). MARSCHALL V. BIEBERSTEIN, *Reflexschäden und Regressrechte* (1967) 39 ff. contains an extensive discussion of the question whether and how far an employer can claim compensation for the 'ricochet damage' which he suffers as the result of the death or injury caused to his employee. There is some uncertainty in the law here. In one case the plaintiff's debtor was killed in a traffic accident for which the defendant was responsible, and the plaintiff was unable to collect his debt because the heirs refused to accept the inheritance. The case went all the way to the Cour de Cassation and the plaintiff creditor's claim was ultimately dismissed, but only on the ground that the causal connection between the tortfeasor's fault and the creditor's harm was insufficiently close (Civ. 21 Feb. 1979, Bull. civ. 1979. II. 42).

A further requirement for liability in delict under art. 1382 Code civil is that the harm must be attributable to a 'faute', that is, culpable behaviour on the part of the defendant. The Code civil offers no definition of 'faute', but writers have produced many different theories, most of which treat 'faute' as a failure to observe a precept of behaviour which the defendant should have respected. The doctrine presented by MAZEAUD/TUNC best fits the decisions of the courts. Relying on art. 1383 Code civil it distinguishes between 'faute délictuelle' and 'faute quasi-délictuelle', the former being characterized by the defendant's intention to cause the harm, while the latter is constituted 'by criticable conduct which a responsible person similarly circumstanced would not have committed' (MAZEAUD/TUNC, nos. 380 ff.). Accordingly, so far as undeliberate harm is concerned, all systems agree in testing the behaviour of the defendant against that of the 'reasonable man of ordinary prudence' or the 'homme avisé' or the conduct of a person who exercises 'the care requisite in social intercourse' (§276 BGB).

There are, however, significant differences with regard to the conditions of liability of children or other persons who are not fully responsible for the harm they cause. For a comparative survey, see STONE, *Festschrift für Ernst Rabel* I (1954) 403.

French lawyers draw no clear distinction between unlawfulness and fault. Both are contained in the concept of 'faute'. If the defendant acted in self-defence or in a state of necessity, or if there were other 'faits justificatifs', to use the expression of MAZEAUD/TUNC, nos. 488 ff., or if the court finds that the boycott or strike called by the defendant was justifiable or that the defendant behaved just like an 'homme avisé' in the same situation, the defendant's liability is excluded for want of 'faute'; neither the French courts nor the French writers draw any subtle doctrinal distinctions or even enter the lists on the 'concept of unlawfulness' so familiar to German controversialists.

Of particular interest are those types of case where the French courts hold that the fault of the defendant lies in an 'abus d'un droit' or abuse of a right. First there are the cases where the right was exercised with the intention of doing harm.

These are mainly cases of landowners exercising the rights in an abusive manner. For examples, see the famous *Clément-Bayard* case before the Cour de Cassation, where the defendant had erected on his land an enormous wooden tower topped with metal spikes in order to prevent his neighbour from using his land as an airfield for dirigibles (Req. 3 Aug. 1915, S. 1920. 1. 300). See also Civ. 20 Jan. 1964, D. 1964, 518, where the defendant maliciously and capriciously grew giant ferns to darken the plaintiff's land.

But the French courts also award damages under art. 1382 Code civil where the defendant had no intention of causing harm by the exercise of his right but simply acted without the care called for in the circumstance. Most writers, too, including MAZEAUD/TUNC, accept that a person may be liable for abuse of right even if he is guilty only of a 'faute quasi-délictuelle'. Thus the courts grant a claim for damages in delict if a contractor exercises a right under the contract in a unreasonable manner and thereby causes unintended harm. There is a well-developed line of cases in labour law which grant the employee damages for 'rupture abusive du contrat' against the employer, even if the latter did not intend to cause harm but was simply guilty of 'légèreté blâmable' (see Soc. 11 May 1964, D. 1964, 520), and the same is true if a contract of partnership or agency is prematurely determined in such a way as to prejudice the other party. But even outside contract law there are cases where liability is imposed on a person for abuse of right although he had no intention of causing harm. Thus a court may hold that it was wrong in the circumstances of the case for a party to an industrial dispute to call a strike or lock-out, or that it was improper of a tradesman to boycott or blacklist a competitor. So, too, a person may be liable if he breaks off an engagement or non-marital relationship in a brutal way, or improperly abandons precontractual negotiations, an 'abus du droit de rompre la négociation'. In German law this last situation is covered by the rules of *culpa in contrahendo*. Details of the French law can be found in VINEY (above p. 637) nos. 197 and 475.

There is one large class of case where the doctrine of 'negligent' abuse of right gets into difficulties, and this is where procedural rights in litigation are being exercised. 'Le droit d'ester en justice'—the right to bring a claim, to make an appeal, to call witnesses, to execute judgments, and to take other steps in connection with a lawsuit—may only be exercised within certain limits and the abuse of this right leads to liability under art. 1382 Code civil. There is no difficulty in the rare case where the defendant takes procedural steps simply out of malevolence towards the other party, but if a person in good faith makes an appeal from a first instance judgment which it is grossly unreasonable of him to suppose ill-founded, what is to happen? If his appeal is dismissed is he to be liable to the other party not only for the costs of the appeal, but also for any further harm he may have suffered? Here the courts are extremely cautious and only find that a person was guilty of a 'faute' in making an appeal or raising a defence if it must have been perfectly evident to the appellant or defendant that the step he was taking was bound to be futile. On the other hand, the courts have no hesitation at all in imposing liability on a person who prematurely executes a judgment which is later quashed (see, for example, Civ. 10 Jan. 1949, S. 1950. 1. 71 and MAZEAUD/TUNC no. 591). In all these cases the claim is based on art. 1382 Code civil, but behind the façade of this general clause the different types of case clearly have a life of their own, for a finding of 'faute' results from the application of very different factual tests, designed to produce the right results in the different types of case.

For full details of liability for abuse of procedural rights, see HOPT, *Schadenersatz aus unberechtigter Verfahrenseinleitung, Eine rechtsvergleichende Untersuchung* (1968).—Similar doctrinal difficulties arise with the liability of a landowner for causing undue disturbance to his neighbour (*trouble de voisinage*). For cases of this type French law has no special test like §§906 BGB, 364 *a* ABGB, art. 679 Swiss Civil Code, and the tort of nuisance in the Common Law, so here too liability must be based on art. 1382 Code civil. Now it is perfectly clear that a person is not really at fault at all if he has administrative approval for his business and it is not reasonably possible from a technological point of view to prevent the undue effect it has on neighbouring land. Art. 1382 Code civil is applied all the same, and HENRI and LÉON MAZEAUD justify this by saying that since the owner could close down his business his failure to do so constitutes a 'faute' to the extent that it unduly interfered with the neighbour. For TUNC the justification for imposing liability is that a landowner who is running a business of some use to the public must alleviate any special hardship it entails for his neighbours. This is a very apt explanation, but it is very difficult to reconcile it with the principle of fault which underlies art. 1382 Code civil. See the details in MAZEAUD/TUNC nos. 593 ff., and VINEY (above p. 637) n. 243.

The third essential precondition of delictual liability in French private law, after 'dommage' and 'faute', is a 'lien de causalité': there must be a causal link between the faulty behaviour of the defendant and the harm suffered by the plaintiff. In the French view no such link exists if the harm is traceable to a 'cause étrangère' rather than to the defendant's conduct. *Force majeure*, defined as an irresistible and unforeseeable event outside the control of the defendant, constitutes such a 'cause étrangère', as do the fault of the victim himself and behaviour of a third party which could not normally be foreseen by the defendant. If the judge finds that the *force majeure*, the fault of the victim, or the behaviour of a third party contributed to the occurrence of the harm but was not sufficiently a 'cause étrangère' to snap the causal link, he may reduce the amount of damages by an appropriate amount. So far as remoteness of harm is concerned, the French courts take the view that harm calls for compensation only if it is a direct and immediate consequence (*une suite immédiate et directe*) of the event in question. This is inferred from art. 1151 Code civil, which by its terms applies to the law of contract.

On the whole matter see MOTULSKY (above p. 636), MAZEAUD/TUNC nos. 1417 ff., and VINEY (above p. 637) n. 332 ff. The French courts have not produced any fixed criteria for limiting compensable consequences: 'In France, as elsewhere, it is the good sense of the judge and not the application of a precise criterion which determines whether the occurrence of the harm was so unforeseeable or extraordinary that the defendant should not be made responsible for it' (PLANIOL/RIPERT VI no. 541).

V

The chief task of the law of delict is to select out of the enormous range of daily occasions when harm is caused those where, in accordance with the sentiment of justice and equity prevailing in the society at the time, the victim should be allowed to transfer the loss to the defendant. The legal techniques which are used for this purpsoe seem to vary considerably. A legal system may progressively identify particular interests as worthy of protection and give them that protection against a particular kind of behaviour by setting up a special kind of tort. Such a process of developing specific torts is historically the older method everywhere, and very clear traces of this tradition may be seen in all those legal systems, such as the Common Law, where the law of tort has not been smoothed out by thorough legislative alteration. This is in stark contrast with the solemn and formal elegance of the general clause in delict in the French Code civil, which goes back to DOMAT and POTHIER. Under the influence of natural law thinking they made extrapolations from the casuistical Roman law of delict and arrived at idealistic, if somewhat literary, formulas which were enacted into law when the enlightened zeal of the French Revolution made the time ripe. The German BGB did not follow the grand model of the Code civil but took a more cautious and intermediate position. This decision also bears the mark of its time, for in nineteenth century Germany the natural law movement had been brought to a virtual halt by the influence of SAVIGNY and his Historical School of Law. Furthermore, as is well known, it was not idealists but officials, not revolutionaries but professors, who attended the birth of the BGB.

If we leave the history and attend to the practicalities of the law of tort, we quickly see that underneath the doctrinal variations the groups and types of case which appear problematical owing to the exigencies of actual life are much the same in all the legal orders under consideration, even if they are dealt with in different portions of the legal system and even, occasionally, with divergent results. This may be demonstrated in the area of harm intentionally caused in competition and industrial disputes. Here the Common Law operates with a whole series of special torts, such as fraud, malicious falsehood, conspiracy, intimidation, and so on, while German law has only the provisions of §826 BGB and §1 UWG (Law against Unfair Competition) in addition to the general rule developed by the judges concerning the 'right to an established and operative business', and French law gets by with only a single provision, namely art. 1382 Code civil. But in Continental legal systems these general clauses only take on significance when concretized in particular types of situation which are subsumed under them. To give an example, every legal system is familiar with cases where one person induces another to break his contract with a third party. Here the Common Law has the special tort of inducing breach of contract. For the Geman lawyer such a case falls under the general clause of §826 BGB but when he goes to the commentaries on this section he immediately looks under the key-word 'Inducement of Breach of Contract' (*Verleitung zum Vertragsbruch*) to find a careful collection of all the judicial decisions and asks whether the case before him satisfies the conditions laid down in those decisions. French lawyers and judges operate in exactly the same way.

For example, see the collection of relevant decisions in PALANDT/THOMAS, *Bürgerliches Gesetzbuch* (43rd edn., 1984) §826 note 8*q*, with the heading 'Verletzung von Vertragsrechten Dritter, insbensondere Verleitung zum Vertragsbruch' (invasion of contractual rights of third parties, including inducement of breach of contract). See also MERTENS in *Münchener Kommentar* (1980) §826 BGB, marginal notes 123 ff., under the heading 'Participation in Another's Breach of Contract'; see, too, Juris-Classeur civil, arts. 1382–3 Code civil, Responsabilité du fait personnel, La faute (Applications) nos. 47–58 with the heading 'Fault of a Third Party in Relation to a Contractor', and so on.—For a comparative study see H. C. FICKER, 'Interference with contractual relations und deliktsrechtlicher Schutz der Forderung', *Festschrift für Hans G. Ficker* (1967) 152.—It would be easy to give further examples of different systematic treatments of the same situation. Whenever a businessman suffers loss because a trade union has called a stoppage of work, the basic question is how to accommodate the right to strike with the right to conduct one's business unhindered. Different legal methods are adopted to deal with the problem, since the French lawyer asks if there was a 'faute' in the form of an abuse of right (see MAZEAUD /TUNC no. 590) while the common lawyer inquires whether the tort of conspiracy has been committed (see, for example, *Crofter Hand Woven Harris Tweed Co. Ltd.* v. *Veitch*, [1942] AC 435), and the German lawyer asks if there has been an improper invasion of the 'right to an established and operative business' (see BAGE 15, 211, 215 f.).

Nevertheless, one must not forget the difference between the Common Law's method of having specific torts and the way in which Continental legal systems deal in particular groups of case under a general clause. The common lawyer regards the specific torts as pretty independent, only tenuously and invisibly connected with each other. In Continental law it is different, for although Continental lawyers subcategorize the cases which fall under the general clauses of §826 BGB and art. 1382 Code civil, they nevertheless realize that despite the differences beween these groups of cases the imposition of liability in damages ultimately depends on the same statutory text and on the fulfilment of its requirements. This remains true even if it may be intellectually difficult to reconcile a particular type of case with the general clause, as French lawyers have found with liability for undue 'troubles de voisinage' and art. 1382 Code civil. The Common Law tends to the independence of casuistry while the Continental law tends to the coherence of a system; both methods of approach doubtless have their good and their bad points. The strength of the Common Law probably resides in the careful way it weighs and works out the specific characteristics of each individual tort and of the type of case to which it is applied; this may well conduce to more appropriate solutions but there is undoubtedly a risk that if each separate tort has its own preconditions, defences, and legal consequences, the system may become unduly complex from the technical point of view.

When we come to the important area of liability for unintentional harm, even Common Law systems virtually have a general clause in the form of the tort of negligence. All legal systems agree in principle that the defendant's liability depends first of all on whether he has fallen short of the 'care requisite in social intercourse' or has behaved otherwise than a 'reasonable man' or an 'homme avisé' would have acted in the same situation. But the satisfaction of this test does not necessarily render the defendant liable, for even if it has been established that the defendant was at fault and that the victim would not have suffered the harm but for that fault, there are still many cases in which on one ground or another the liability of the defendant is brought into question or excluded. If a restaurateur keeps rat poison in an unmarked container above the stove, this is certainly negligent in view of the risk that his patrons may be poisoned. But suppose that the rat poison *explodes* through overheating, and that the restaurateur had no idea that poison could explode at all. Should he be liable for the harm caused by the explosion? (See *Larrimore* v. *American National Insurance Co.*, 184 Okla. 614, 89 P. 2d 340 (1939).) If a person carelessly causes a traffic accident, is he also to be liable for the nervous shock sustained by someone miles away from the accident? What if the plaintiff was not even born at the time of the accident, but was injured in the womb when his mother was injured by the defendant? What is to happen if after a traffic accident a citizen is injured during the pursuit of the escaping tortfeasor or suffers harm while attempting to look after the primary victim? What if the defendant was responsible for causing the death of a third party and the death causes harm to the plaintiff, either because the decedent would have supported him, whether bound to or not, or was under contract to do something for the plaintiff which would have saved the plaintiff expense or brought him a profit? Many more such cases could be instanced. In all of them there has undoubtedly been careless behaviour on the part of the defendant, and in all of them it can also be said that the harm for which compensation is sought would not have occurred but for that behaviour. Yet these considerations do not by themselves produce any appropriate means of limiting liability for negligence. Accordingly, all legal systems have a supply of further doctrines which permit the judge to balance the interests involved in that type of case and so to decide whether compensation should be paid or not. The comparative lawyer is not surprised to find that this same process of evaluation takes place in very different systematic contexts. Whether a defendant who is responsible for injuring a person is also liable to a third party who voluntarily undertakes to rescue the victim and is himself injured in the process is a question which in England and the United States is technically answered by asking whether the defendant owed a 'duty of care' towards the rescuer; in Germany and France, on the other hand, one asks whether there is a sufficient causal connection or 'lien de causalité' between the defendant's carelessness and the rescuer's injury.

See the 'rescue cases' cited above p. 653 and RGZ 50, 219, 223; BGHZ 56, 163; Grenoble 7 Dec. 1959, D. 1960. J. 213, and the extended treatment by RIOU, *Rev. trim. dr. civ.* 55 (1957) 221.

In Germany the question of liability for nervous shock is also treated as a problem of 'adequate causal connection', while in the Common Law it is dealt with either as a problem of 'remoteness of damage' or as a 'duty' problem. Whatever doctrine is mobilized in these cases, the crucial question remains: if a person witnesses or learns of an accident and suffers shock because of his particular sensitivity, must he bear the consequent loss himself as a misfortune built into his constitution or can he shift it to the person who caused the accident? This is a matter for evaluation and judgment involving many very different factors (on this see E. V. HIPPEL, *NJW* 1965, 1890, and the speech of LORD WILBERFORCE in *McLoughlin* v. *O'Brian*, [1982] 1 AC 410). The difficulties are not resolved by asking whether such damage was 'outside the probabilities of life' and consequently not 'adequately caused', or whether the shock victim was one of those to whom the person responsible for the accident owed a duty of care because such harm was 'reasonably foreseeable'. As FLEMING writes (above p. 635, p. 486), 'Recognition of a duty of care is the outcome of a value judgement that the plaintiff's interest, which has been invaded, is deemed worthy of legal protection against negligent interference by conduct of the kind alleged against the defendant.' The same is true for the doctrine of causal connection. As V. CAEMMERER has emphasized, this also involves 'a wide variety of normative problems' and in fact there is 'nothing for it but to determine the range of compensable harm by setting up a typology of critical cases and so developing the meaning of the rule which imposes liability' (V. CAEMMERER, *NJW* 1956, 569, 570).

One situation where there is a particular need to limit the liability of negligent persons is where their negligence causes merely *economic harm*. The different legal systems have very different systematic and technical devices for answering this need. As we have already seen, German law in principle denies any liability in tort for purely economic harm negligently caused, unless the defendant was in breach of a relevant protective statute or it is one of those cases in which the courts have held that the 'right to an established and operative business' has been infringed. The need to limit liability for economic loss negligently caused is answered in the Common Law by the 'duty' device once again; where the defendant's behaviour has infringed the merely 'pecuniary interests' of another the courts are very reluctant to find the duty of care which is a precondition of liability in damages for negligence.

The problem is especially clear in cases in which a builder negligently breaks a cable or pipe and interrupts the supply of electricity, water, or gas. If a third party's property is damaged or destroyed, the courts in Germany grant him a claim for the consequent economic harm (see above p. 641), since §823 par. 1 BGB protects 'ownership' against negligent damage; but if the third party's complaint is simply that his business has been brought to a standstill so that he cannot continue production but must still pay his employees, this is 'pure economic loss' and there is no liability. §823 par. 1 BGB does not apply, even in the form of an invasion of the 'right to an established and operative business', and the defendant is not liable under §823 par. 2 BGB because he is not in breach of any protective law designed to protect people from pure economic loss (BGHZ 66, 388). English courts decide likewise, sometimes on the ground that this is outside the scope of the builder's duty of care (as in *Weller & Co.* v. *Foot & Mouth Disease Research Institute*, [1966] 1 QB 569), sometimes on the ground that pure economic loss is 'too remote' and therefore not compensable (*S.C.M. Ltd.* v. *Whittall & Son Ltd.*, [1971] 1 QB 337; *Spartan Steel & Alloys Ltd.* v. *Martin & Co.*, [1973] QB 27). But English judges naturally realize that this is a question of public policy and that the arguments should be openly canvassed rather than hidden behind a smokescreen of legal jargon. Thus LORD DENNING in the *Spartan Steel* case said after reviewing the cases: 'The more I think about these cases, the more difficult I find it to put each into its proper pigeon-hole. Sometimes I say: "There was no duty." In others I say: "The damage was too remote." So much so that I think the time has come to discard those tests which have proved so elusive. It seems to me better to consider the particular relationship in hand, and see whether or not, as a matter of policy, economic loss should be recoverable, or not' (ibid. p. 37).

If one considers which party can more easily prevent the harm or insure against loss of production due to interference with the energy supply—the user of the energy by business interruption insurance or the building contractor by liability insurance—the position of the German and English courts is quite justifiable. Cover by business interruption insurance is suggested by the fact that the risk in question is *invariably* covered by the manufacturer's policy, since the energy supply may be interrupted by other events, such as act of God, and the liability of the suppliers of the energy is almost always excluded by their general terms of business. Furthermore, policies always have a monetary limit to their cover, and it is easier for the manufacturer than for the building contractor to say how much harm is likely to result from business interruption and so to fix an appropriate limit. Finally, business interruption insurance operates more smoothly, in that the liability of the insurer does not depend on the tort liability of the insured—often quite a complex legal question—and the manufacturer seeking compensation will be dealing with 'his own' insurer rather than with a liability insurer he has never met before. It is true that it is the builder who can, by taking care, avoid damaging the means of supply, so he must be given an incentive to take all appropriate precautions by making it expensive for him if he fails to do so. People tend to say nowadays that if the tortfeasor can insure against liability so that he does not have to put his hand in his own pocket, the threat of liability is no deterrent, but they are wrong: careful conduct still pays dividends, for a tortfeasor with a bad claims experience may lose his no-claims bonus and have to pay higher premiums or meet his insurer's safety requirements. This incentive is maintained by the rule which the German and English courts have adopted, for the builder is held liable if any property is damaged or destroyed by his negligence.

It must be admitted that the distinction between property damage and pure economic loss may seem somewhat capricious and arbitrary, and that it may not always be easy to draw the dividing line between them. In one famous decision the High Court of Australia ignored it (*Caltex Oil Ltd.* v. *The Dredge 'Willemstad'*, 51 AJLR 270 (1976)). Caltex, the well-known oil company, used to deliver oil by means of a pipeline belonging to a third party. During dredging operations the defendant negligently damaged the pipeline and Caltex had to get the oil delivered by more expensive means. Caltex sued for the extra expense and won. Note, however, that most of the judgments turned on the fact that Caltex was the sole user of the pipeline, as the defendant dredger-owner could have known; and that the Privy Council, unable to discover a single *ratio decidendi*, has declined to follow the decision (*Candlewood Navigation Co.* v. *Mitsui OSK Lines (The Mineral Transporter)*, [1985] 2 All ER 935 (PC)).

The literature on the question of liability in tort for 'pure economic loss' in England and the United States is now immense: see ATIYAH, MARSHALL, SYMMONS (above p. 635), and LAWSON/MARKESINIS (above p. 636) 80 ff., MARKESINIS, 35 *Rev. int. dr. comp.* 31 (1983); HARVEY, 'Economic Losses and Negligence', 50 *Can. Bar Rev.* 580 (1972); JAMES and JOLOWICZ, 'The Tort Law and Non-Physical Loss', 12 *JSPTL* 91, 104 (1972); PARTLETT, 'Recovery of Economic Loss for Negligence in Australia', 9 *Sydney L. Rev.* 121 (1980); RIZZO, 'A Theory of Economic Loss in the Law of Torts', 11 *J. Leg. Stud.* 281 (1982); STEPHENS, 'Negligent Acts Causing Pure Economic Loss', 23 *U. Tor. LJ* 431 (1973); BISHOP, 'Economic Loss in Tort', 2 *Oxf. J. Leg. Stud.* 1 (1982).

The French Civil Code makes no distinction between 'pure economic loss' and harm, physical or non-physical, to a person's health, property, or other things to which he has a right: under arts. 1382 and 1384 whoever causes 'dommage' of any kind is bound to make compensation if the manner by which he caused it renders him liable. But, as one might expect, the courts have other devices for imposing the necessary limits on liability for pure economic loss. For harm to be compensable, it must be 'certain' (and not simply 'hypothétique' or 'éventuel'), and it must be 'une suite immédiate et directe' of the defendant's conduct. The courts have a great deal of room for play here and can invoke these formulas to reject or allow claims as they think fit. The cryptic style of judgments in the Cour de Cassation makes it very difficult to discover the true grounds on which claims for damages are accepted or rejected (see Ch. 9 I). Thus in a case where the plaintiff had suffered pure economic loss as a result of the defendant builder's negligence in interrupting the supply of energy, the Cour de Cassation allowed him to recover for it as a 'conséquence directe du fait de l'entrepreneur' (8 May 1970, Bull. civ. 1970. II. 122), without making any allusion to the problems which similar cases have caused to the courts in other countries. Again the Cour de Cassation has held that when a municipal bus company lost fares because its buses were delayed owing to a traffic accident due to the defendant's fault, its loss was 'ni hypothétique ni indirect' and was consequently recoverable (Civ. 28 Apr. 1965, D. 1965, 777, noted by ESMEIN). Finally the courts can reject liability for pure economic loss by refusing to qualify the defendant's behaviour as 'faute', even if by standards normally applied the negligence would be clearly established. One can find some support for this in the cases relating to the abuse of procedural rights. A person may be very unreasonable in supposing that he has a good claim; nevertheless he may safely sue without fear that if he loses the action he may have to compensate the other party for all his loss on the ground of an 'abus du droit d'ester en justice'. German and French law may appear to have adopted fundamentally opposing starting points, since the BGB by its terms is unwilling to admit tort liability for pure economic loss whereas the Code civil does so quite readily, but in both countries the practice of the courts seems to adopt an intermediate position.

48

Liability for Others

ATIYAH, *Vicarious Liability in the Law of Torts* (1967).
BARAK, 'The Nature of Vicarious Liability in English Law', *Ann. dir. comp.* 40 (1966) 1.
BATY, *Vicarious Liability* (1916).
BYDLINSKI, 'Zur Haftung für Verrichtungsgehilfen', *ZVR* 1980, 354.
V. CAEMMERER, 'Wandlungen des Deliktsrechts', *Hundert Jahre deutsches Rechtsleben, Festschrift zum 100jährigen Bestehen des Deutschen Juristentages* II (1960) 56 ff., 115 ff.
——, 'Reformprobleme der Haftung für Verrichtungsgehilfen', *ZfRV* 14 (1973) 241.
CHAPMAN, 'Liability for the Negligence of Independent Contractors', 50 *LQ Rev.* 71 (1934).
DOUGLAS, 'Vicarious Liability and Administration of Risk', 38 *Yale LJ* 584, 720 (1929).
EÖRSI, 'Private and Governmental Liability for the Torts of Employees and Organs', XI *Int. Enc. Comp. L.* 'Torts' (1975) Ch. 4.
ERDSIEK, 'Die Problematik des §831 BGB und seine Einwirkung auf unsere Vertrags- und Amtshaftung, Ein Beitrag zur Reform des Haftungsrechts', *JurJb.* 8 (1967/68) 36.
FLOUR, *Les Rapports de commettant à préposé dans l'article 1384 du Code civil* (1933).
JAMES, 'Vicarious Liability', 28 *Tul. L. Rev.* 161 (1954).
JOLOWICZ, 'Liability for Independent Contractors in the English Common Law—A Suggestion', 9 *Stan. L. Rev.* 690 (1957).
KRÜGER, *Haftung des Dienstherrn für Gelegenheitsdelikte seiner Hilfspersonen nach deutschem und französischem Recht* (1980).
LASKI, 'The Basis of Vicarious Liability', 26 *Yale LJ* 105 (1916).
NEUNER, 'Respondeat Superior in the Light of Comparative Law', 4 *La. L. Rev.* 1 (1941).
SCHLINK, 'Die Haftung für selbständige Unternehmer nach deutschem bürgerlichen Recht im Vergleich mit der Haftung für independent contractors nach dem Recht der Vereinigten Staaten von Amerika' (Diss. Freiburg, 1977).
SEAVEY, 'Speculations as to "Respondeat Superior" ', *Harvard Legal Essays* (1934) 433.
SEILER, 'Die deliktische Gehilfenhaftung in historischer Sicht', *JZ* 1967, 530.
SMITH, 'Frolic and Detour', 23 *Colum. L. Rev.* 444, 716 (1923).
STOLJAR, 'The Servant's Course of Employment', 12 *Mod. L. Rev.* 44 (1949).
TENDLER, 'Le Rapprochement des droits français et suisse en matière de responsabilité des commettants du fait de leur préposé', *Rev. int. dr. comp.* 24 (1972) 677.
VERNESCO, *La Notion de préposé et l'idée de fonction* (1933).

VINEY, *La Responsabilité: conditions* (Traité de droit civil, ed. Ghestin vol. IV 1982).

WALD, 'La responsabilidad civil del patrón por actos de sus dependientes en el derecho brasileno y en el derecho comparado', *Bol. Inst. Méx.* 9 (1956) 31.

WILLIAMS, 'Liability for Independent Contractors', 1956 *Camb. LJ* 180.

——, 'Vicarious Liability and the Master's Indemnity', 20 *Mod. L. Rev.* 220, 437 (1957).

WOELLERT, 'Die außervertragliche Gehilfenhaftung im nordischen Recht', *RabelsZ* 39 (1975) 304.

ZANDER, 'Die Haftung für Verrichtungsgehilfen, Ein Vergleich des deutschen, schweizerischen und österreichischen Rechts' (Diss. Tübingen, 1966).

I

THE idea underlying the principle of no liability without fault, as we have seen, is that only when the defendant may be charged with careless behaviour is there sufficient reason to make him bear the loss caused to the victim. This is not to say that the careless conduct need be that of the defendant *personally*: as against the victim the defendant might be responsible for the conduct of a *third party* as well, on the ground that he has used the third party's services in some activity in the course of which the third party injured the plaintiff by malice or negligence. If a person is run over by a taxi, the principle of no liability without fault entails that the consequent loss may only be shifted to the taxi-owner if he was driving the taxi carelessly or in disregard of the rules of the road. The plaintiff's legal position should perhaps not be any different if the taxi was being driven by an employee of the taxi-owner rather than by the owner himself. Even in this case one might infer from the principle of no liability without fault that the taxi-owner should not be liable unless he personally was at fault: then instead of concentrating on whether the taxi was being driven properly and in accordance with the rules of the road one would ask whether the owner could be blamed for having a driver he should have known was incompetent or for not paying enough attention to the driver's manner of driving or perhaps for not sufficiently emphasizing the importance of obeying the rules of the road. The other view would be to make the owner liable if the *driver* had been careless, regardless of any personal fault in the owner. Whether this solution is consistent with the principle of no liability without fault is an idle question, but it may be suggested that it is, since fault, though not necessarily the personal fault of the defendant, remains a precondition of liability, unlike the cases of strict liability which will be dealt with in Chapter 49.

II

In the *Germanic* legal family, the liability of a superior for the harm caused by his staff always depends on whether any *personal* fault of his contributed to the harm. This rule is attributable to the scholars of the *Gemeines Recht* who thought that the principle of no liability without fault must apply without any qualification to vicarious liability as well, and believed Roman law to support their view. They argued that to make an entrepreneur liable for the harm caused by his workers whether he was personally at fault or not would be to impose on him a liability for mere accidents, contrary to the principle of fault which was the moral basis of the law of delict: as JHERING said, 'It is not the occurrence of harm which obliges one to make compensation, but fault. This is as simple as the chemical fact that what burns is not the light but the oxygen in the air' (*Das Schuldmoment im römischen Privatrecht* (1867) 40).

It is an invention of the pandectists that there was no liability for others in Roman law unless the superior was himself at fault. In fact the Romans never considered the problem of liability for others as a whole at all; much less did they arrive at any general solution. There were many individual types of case where they made certain superiors liable, normally without reference to their personal fault, for the consequences of the faults of their inferiors, and a different policy reason for imposing such liability underlay each type of case. Certainly the principle of the *Gemeines Recht* did not apply in the most important cases of liability for others, for most of the people whose services free Romans used were slaves and members of the family, and if any of them committed a delict, the person with power over them was unconditionally and inescapably liable, subjet to this, that he could avoid his obligation to pay compensation by handing over to the victim the person who injured him (*noxae datio*).

For the development of liability for others in the *Gemeines Recht*, see SEILER (above p. 669); for Roman law see KASER, *Das römische Privatrecht* I (1955) 527 ff.

The view of the *Gemeines Recht* met with some opposition in the second half of the nineteenth century. It had to be restricted in the important area of industrial accidents, and also where a business activity was so dangerous as to create a specially great risk of harm. So obvious was it that a mistake on the part of an employee might cause grave damage that it would have been very shocking if the entrepreneur had been permitted to escape liability by proving that he himself was free from fault. Accordingly, the Imperial Law of Liability of 1871 imposed strict liability on railway companies and so made it unnecessary to prove fault in either the employer or his employees, and it also laid down that owners of mines, quarries, and factories should be liable although they themselves were not at fault if their *managerial* employees caused harm to third parties in the faulty execution of their tasks. It was sought to extend vicarious liability to all business employers in respect of all employees who were at fault, and a rule to this effect was endorsed by the Eighteenth Deutsche Juristentag in 1886.

Nevertheless the draftsmen of the BGB adhered to the conservative view that the head of a business should not be liable for the harm caused by his staff unless he himself was at fault. It was admitted that the contrary opinions had 'an element of justification in as much as they are based on the idea that a person who enjoys the benefits of an enterprise should have to make good the harm which it causes to third parties', but it was thought that this idea could best be implemented by special legislation applying it to specified types of business and imposing at the same time an obligation to insure. Otherwise the burden would possibly be too great for 'smallholdings and many branches of industry which need protection' (MUGDAN II p. 1094). The only concession made to the opponents was that §831 enacted in favour of the victim a presumption that the employer was at fault and the onus of rebutting this presumption was placed on the defendant employer. A similar rule is to be found in Swiss law (art. 55 OR).

Austrian law differs from German and Swiss law in important respects, though the rule in §1315 ABGB is not very clear. In Austria also it is the basic principle that an employer is liable only if he himself was at fault, but, contrary to the rule in §831 BGB and art. 55 OR, it is for the victim to prove this. Only when the victim can establish that the tortfeasor was 'incompetent' (*untüchtig*) is the employer liable in the absence of personal fault. On the positive law in Austria and the efforts to reform it, see EDLBACHER, *VersR* 1962 (Karlsruher Forum) 17 f.—In *Switzerland* art. 55 OR is drafted very much like §831 BGB. The Swiss courts, like those in Germany, as we shall see, have contrived to make it very difficult for the employer to exculpate himself. On this see KELLER, *Haftpflicht im Privatrecht* (3rd edn., 1978) 119 ff.; TENDLER (above p. 669). In *Sweden* and *Finland* it used to be the law that the employer was liable only when he himself was at fault (see ANDRESEN, *RabelsZ* 27 (1962/1963) 252), but the legislature in both countries has abolished the employer's right to exculpate himself. For the details see WOELLERT (above p. 718).

The first precondition for the liability of a head of a business under §831 BGB for harm caused by a third party is that the third party be a person he has 'appointed to perform a function'. In the view of the German courts a person qualifies as a servant ('Verrichtungsgehilfe') if he is subject to the orders of his superior and works under his supervision and control. The largest class of these are salaried and wage-earning employees. If a doctor chooses a nurse to operate his radiological apparatus, she is his 'servant', but if apparatus and nurse are provided by the hospital and the doctor is not empowered to give her instructions about how to operate the apparatus, he is not responsible for her. Independent craftsmen, carriers, and building contractors are not 'servants' in the sense of §831 BGB unless they are dependent on those who retain them. Difficulties arise in cases where one employer lends his employees to another on the terms that they must follow the latter's instructions. Here again the question is whether the first employer retains any right and duty to supervise and control the 'borrowed servants' (see BGH VersR 1956, 322; BGE 42 II 617).

A further requirement for the liability of the superior is that the harm be caused by the assistant 'in the exercise of the function assigned to him'. The assistant need not have been employed to do the very act which directly caused the harm: it is enough that his act fell within the steps normally incidental to the execution of his functions. For example, if a scaffolding erector throws a piece of wood into the highway and injures someone, it is relevant whether he threw it in order to deter children from endangering themselves by playing with scaffolding materials on the sidewalk, or whether he saw an acquaintance coming along the road and wanted to make him jump; in the former case alone is there a sufficient internal connection between the damaging act and the duties of the workman (see BGH VersR 1955, 205). The distinction may be difficult to draw. If an employer sends a man to do construction work on a site some distance away, say, in the factory of a client, and the employee causes an accident on his way there, §831 BGB only applies if the employer specified the means of transport and the route (see RG DR 1942, 1280, and contrast OLG Munich MDR 1959, 391). If a truck-driver carrying goods deviates from the prescribed route and runs over a third party, the internal connection between the accident and the course of his employment may continue to subsist if the deviation is relatively trivial, but not if he goes off on a trip of his own (see RG LZ 1930, 589). If the same driver, in disregard of an express prohibition, takes a companion on the trip and causes him an injury, his flouting his superior's instructions is so flagrant that the accident can be treated as having occurred only 'on the occasion of' his employment (BGH NJW 1965, 391), but it may be different if the reason the driver contravened his instructions was to deliver the goods more swiftly (see BGH NJW 1965, 391 and NJW 1971, 31). Of course one should bear in mind that in such cases the employer is strictly liable under the Road Traffic Act (§7 par. 3 StVG) even when the requirements of §831 are not satisfied.

Once it is established that the assistant caused the harm in the 'execution of the function assigned to him', the defendant principal is liable unless he can prove that he took all the generally requisite precautions in selecting, training, and supervising the assistant, and thereby satisfy the *Entlastungsbeweis* or exculpatory proof. To go by the terms of §831 BGB, it is not actually necessary that the assistant should have been at *fault*: even where the assistant was not careless at all it would appear that his superior must bring the exculpatory proof. However, as STOLL (JZ 1958, 137) and V. CAEMMERER (above p. 669) have shown, exculpatory proof can only be required in such cases if the reason that the assistant was not at fault was delictual incapacity, unsuitability for the employment in question, or inadequacy of instruction or equipment. In such cases it may be appropriate to make the presumption under §831 BGB that some fault of the principal underlay the appointment of the unsuitable assistant or the inadequate instruction or equipment, but if the assistant is free from fault and no such want of care on the part of the principal can have contributed to the accident, §831 BGB does not apply: if a driver injures a pedestrian because he skidded on an invisible pool of oil on a dark street, his employer is not liable and there is no occasion to adduce §831 BGB and ask whether he was careful in selecting and supervising the driver.

In the normal case where the employee was at fault or where fault on the part of the principal in the circumstances of the case cannot be ruled out in advance, the principal must seek to satisfy the requirements of the exculpatory proof under §831 BGB. The courts are extremely strict with regard to this proof, especially in the very important cases where the plaintiff has been injured by a transport employee such as a train-driver, truck-driver, tram-driver, level-crossing keeper, or station attendant. Large transport undertakings are required to supervise their drivers by having regular and secret tests in which an examiner follows behind the driver and satisfies himself as to the carefulness of the driving. In the case of young drivers and recently appointed or inexperienced truck-drivers this is of general application. One might think that the circumstances of the accident itself were the central issue, but in suits based on §831 BGB it is rather lost sight of. If a person is injured in a train crash, the claim for damages under §831 BGB depends not on the fault of the train-driver, which is normally perfectly clear, but on whether the defendant railway exercised sufficient supervision and control over the driver; the requisite degree of control and supervision depends on how well the driver passed his driving test, how much experience he had at the time of the accident, and whether he had been guilty of similar errors before, to the knowledge or constructive knowledge of his employer (see BGH VRS 16, 164). These are matters of which the plaintiff can have no cognizance before the trial and neither he nor his counsel can make any reasonable prediction about the outcome of the suit; in cases of this sort, therefore, he must either take the risk of bringing a suit in the hope that the proof turns out favourably for him or content himself with the lower sums accorded to him regardless of fault on the part of the transport undertaking or its personnel under the strict liability laid down by the Road Traffic Act or the Law of Liability (see below Ch. 49 II).

§831 BGB is thoroughly unsound in policy and the only reason it has remained in the BGB so long is that the judges have done much to undermine its effect. Legal institutions which allow the courts to grant *contractual* claims for damages have proved especially useful although since the harm to the plaintiff is caused by breach of a general duty owed to everyone it should properly be dealt with by the law of tort (see above p. 492) and v. CAEMMERER (above p. 669) 56). If the case is moved into the law of contract and defendant is deprived of the exculpatory proof under §831 BGB and is rendered unconditionally liable to the plaintiff 'contractor' for the fault of his personnel (§278 BGB). If a car salesman omits to display a notice in the showroom warning of the freshly polished floor, a customer who slips and falls on it can always claim damages from the firm on a 'contractual' basis. If he came to discuss the details of a purchase already concluded, the contract, on the

German view, would oblige the dealer not only to deliver the automobile but to see to the safety of his sales premises, and the failure to observe this duty of care, which would otherwise constitute a tort, is here concurrently a 'positive breach of contract'. The same is true if there is no contract between the parties and the customer visits the premises simply to look at the new models with a view to possible purchase. The courts give a contractual flavour to this situation by holding that as soon as negotiations start and before any contract is ever concluded there arises a mutual duty of care, breach of which makes the dealer contractually liable for 'culpa in contrahendo'. And if the customer's wife happens to accompany him and she is injured, she also has a contractual claim since it is constant German practice to extend to her the protective effects of her husband's legal relations. Accordingly, wherever an accident which should really be covered by the law of delict is sufficiently closely connected with a business matter, the party whose servant causes the harm is barred from resorting to the exculpatory proof under §831 BGB. Many people are of the view that for this purpose a mere 'social' contact is as good as a business relationship and would give a contractual claim for damages not only to injured purchasers and potential purchasers but also, for example, to a bailiff who came to the showroom not to *buy* an automobilie but to *seize* one (on this see Dölle; *ZgesStW* 103 (1943) 67). The English jurist Pollock stated that the strict liability of a master for the torts of his servants, such as exists at Common Law, was justified by the consideration that if it did not exist a 'huge expansion of implied, i.e. fictitious, contracts, to no great advantage of either law or conscience, would ensue; the development of German law has vindicated this prediction to the hilt.

See *Holmes–Pollock Letters* (ed. DeWolfe Howe, 1961) 234.—There are many other legal devices which render it impossible for an employer to resort to the exculpatory proof under §831 BGB and make him strictly liable for harm caused by employees at fault. They may all be found in Erdsiek (above p. 669), but here we may mention one of them, developed by the courts, namely the principle of the employer's duty to indemnify the employee. If an employee is charged with a 'dangerous' job and injures a third party in the course of it, he is entitled, unless he intended to cause the harm or was grossly negligent in causing it, to demand that his employer indemnify him against the damages claim brought by the third party. This is justified by the view that whereas no single error of an employee is inevitable, the chance of the occurrence of such errors has proved to be intrinsic to all human activity, and should be borne by the employer as part of the risk of the business (for example, see BAGE 5, 1). If a third party is injured by the carelessness of an employee and sues the employee and the employer in the same suit, it will do the employer no good to bring successful exculpatory proof under §831 BGB, for although the claim against him would have to be dismissed, the principle we have just mentioned requires him to indemnify the third party on behalf of his employee: §831 is effectively avoided. Obviously enough, an employer who fails to bring the exculpatory proof and is held liable to the third party personally can not bring any claim for indemnity against the employee: §840 par. 2

BGB expressly provides for such an indemnity (as does art. 55 par. 2 OR), but the courts refuse to take any notice of these provisions, so they have largely become obsolete.

In the circumstances it is not surprising that §831 BGB has been heavily criticized in the Federal Republic and the efforts to reform it have culminated in a draft statute from the Ministry of Justice. The proposed new text is as follows: 'A person who appoints another to perform a function is bound along with that other to indemnify a third party for the harm caused by an intentional or negligent tort committed by that other in the execution of his task.'

In East Germany the *courts* have pushed the development in the same direction. In a leading case (NJ 1965, 125) the Oberster Gerichtshof decided that if an employee causes harm to a third party by breach of the duties of his employment, the business is liable under §831 BGB and cannot free itself by proof of care in the selection an supervision of the worker. The court also held that in such a case *only* the business could be sued. The new East German Civil Code of 1975 now lays down in §331: 'If a worker in a business in the execution of his duties as such causes harm, the business must make the harm good. The worker is not himself liable to the party injured. The worker's liability to the business under labour law and other provisions remains unaffected.' The last sentence is a reference to §§260 ff. Labour Code (1977): the business can claim indemnification for the full amount of the damages paid to the injured party only where the worker caused the injury intentionally, while negligent workmen only pay for the harm up to the amount of their monthly pay.

III

The French Code civil lays down in art. 1384 par. 1 that one must pay for the harm 'which is caused by the act of persons for whom one is answerable'. The subsequent paragraphs of art. 1384 list the persons for whom one is so answerable. These include the employee or *préposé*: if the employee injures a third party in the exercise of the functions assigned to him, his employer or *commettant* is bound to compensate the third party (art. 1384 par. 5).

This provision, like art. 2049 Codice civile, which is essentially the same, has always been understood to impose on the employer an unconditional liability to respond for the delicts of his employees. All that is required to render the employer liable is that the person who caused the harm be his assistant, that the assistant have caused the harm in the exercise of his functions, and that the assistant himself, he had been sued, would have been liable to the victim in tort. If these conditions are satisfied, the liability of the employer is established; he cannot escape liability by proving that he was very careful in selecting and supervising his assistant.

1. The French courts apply the same standards as the German courts in deciding whether the person who caused the harm was a 'servant' of the defendant employer in the sense of §831 BGB. For this purpose one asks whether the assistant was in a relation of dependence on the employer, that is, whether he was bound to follow the orders and instruction given to him with regard to the execution of the work assigned to him. Independent craftsmen, building contractors, forwarders, and carriers are thus generally not the *préposés* of their clients, and the same is true even of doctors in a hospital or in the state health service since, according to the courts, they are not subject to the control of their employers in the exercise of their profession (see the critique by VINEY (above p. 670) 879 f.). In earlier days the courts often held that the employer must not only have the power to instruct but also the freedom to choose his assistant. Recent decisions, however, hold that a person may be an assistant under art. 1384 even if his employer is forced to employ him, provided that he must follow the instructions and orders which the employer is empowered to give: examples would be an army training officer seconded to a shooting club or a convict assigned to work in a business (see Paris 9 Dec. 1938, DH 1939, 136; Req. 21 Oct. 1942, Gaz. Pal. 1942. 2. 243).

The same test is applied in cases where an employee is 'lent' to another business for a period of time; here too the question is which of the parties in the case had the power to give the 'borrowed' servant instruction about how to do the work. On occasion the courts have tried the interesting experiment of dividing the activity of the employee into two parts, making the superiors liable respectively for the part controlled by each, and deciding to which part the harmful act appertained. If a transport firm supplies a building contractor with a truck and driver for a few days' excavations it may be relevant whether the accident is caused by bad driving or by faulty loading; the transport company would be liable for the driving and the building contractor for the loading, provided that the loading was under his control and instructions (on this see Civ. 20 July 1955, JCP 1956. II. 9052, noted by SAVATIER; Civ. 17 July 1962, Gaz. Pal. 1962. 2. 309; and VINEY (above p. 670) 880 ff.).

2. Once it is determined that the person who caused the harm was a *préposé* of the defendant employer, one aks whether he caused the harm in the execution of the tasks assigned to him. As art. 1384 par. 5 Code civil expressly says, employers are only liable for the harm which their staff cause in 'the tasks for which they are employed'. The courts frequently paraphrase this requirement in terms at least as vague as art. 1384 par. 5 itself. The employer is liable not only when the assistant is executing the tasks assigned to him, but also when he is using the materials put at his disposal for other purposes, provided 'that the harmful act is related to the exercise of his functions by a link of connection or causality, and that the employee can be supposed to have acted on behalf of the employer' (Civ. 1 July 1954, D. 1954, 628 and constantly thereafter).

A look at the cases shows that the courts are very generous in attributing delicts to the employer. For example, a person who sends an agricultural worker to fetch a tool from a neighbour is liable if on the way the labourer is careless in filling his petrol lighter and causes a fire (Civ. 19 Dec. 1950, JCP 1951. II. 6577, noted by RODIÈRE). The same is true if a farmer sends his lad to help out a neighbour for the day: if, while riding back on an unlighted bicycle, the lad runs into a pedestrian, the farmer is liable for the harm without regard to the question, which German courts would ask, whether the farmer stipulated the route or means of transport (Soc. 7 Jan. 1965, Bull. civ. 1965. IV. 5). If the employee is on the way between his *home* and place of work, however, the employer is not liable for any accidents he may cause (Crim. 28 Nov. 1956, JCP 1957. IV. 2). Employers are often held liable for intentional torts as well. On several occasions the courts have decided that a transport company is liable for assaults committed by its driver on other road users who objected to his mode of driving (Paris 8 July 1954, Gaz. Pal. 1954. 2. 280; Crim. 16 Feb. 1965, Gaz. Pal. 1965. 2. 24; *contra*, Montpellier 22 April 1964, JCP 1964. II. 13766, noted by MAURY). It might be possible to justify these decisions on the ground that truck-drivers whose mode of driving is questioned are not unlikely to resort to fisticuffs, and that their employers should be able to foresee it, but in other decisions this factor is lacking. Thus an employer has been held liable for a driver who spied a pheasant on the plaintiff's land, stopped the truck, shot the bird with a handy gun, and bore it off (Crim. 23 Nov. 1928, Gaz. Pal. 1928. 2. 900). The proprietor of a cinema has even been held liable for an usher who took a client who asked him for information down to the cellars and murdered her (Crim. 5 Nov. 1953, Gaz. Pal. 1953. 2. 383). Very controversial are the cases in which a person uses an employer's vehicle without his knowledge or consent and injures a third party. The older cases always made the employer liable for such accidents (see, for example, Civ. 18 Dec. 1933, S. 1934. 1. 107; Crim. 18 Oct. 1946, S. 1947. 1. 39), but the civil chambers of the Court of Cassation started to adopt a more cautious approach (see Civ. 1 July 1954, D. 1954, 628). But the criminal chambers of the court, which very frequently have to deal with the civil consequences of criminal acts when there is a *partie civile* to the prosecution, adhered to the traditional view, and even refused to follow a decision of the Chambres Réunies which had held an employer not liable where an employee with no driving licence had caused an accident while using a company vehicle for personal purposes (Ch. réun. 9 March 1960, D. 1960. 329, noted by SAVATIER). So in 1977 the Chambres Réunies handed down another decision in a case where a driver had used the vehicle put at his disposal to go on a joy-ride with five fellow workers, one of whom was killed and the four others injured owing to his negligence (Ch. Réun. 10 June 1977, JCP 1977. II. 18730, with conclusions by Avocat-Géneral GULPHE). Even this decision has failed to procure harmony, so that, to use the words of Geneviève VINEY, we still have to cope with a 'jurisprudence pléthorique et contradictoire que la Cour de Cassation n'a pas, jusqu'à présent, réussi à discipliner' (above p. 670, at 891; see also HASSLER, D. 1980. Chr. 125).

3. Although art. 1384 par. 5 Code civil does not make this clear, there is generally agreed to be a further requirement for the employer's liability, namely that the employee himself should have been guilty of a tort under arts. 1382 ff. Code civil. If the employee has no delictual capacity the employer is only liable if he knew or should have known of this incapacity when he was appointing or supervising him (Paris 23 June 1950, Gaz. Pal. 1950. 2. 209; Civ. 15 March 1956, JCP 1956. II. 9297, noted by ESMEIN). It is for the victim to prove the fault of the employee.

If the employer is liable to the victim under art. 1384 par. 5 Code civil, the question arises whether he may claim an indemnity from the employee. It has been generally accepted in France that he can; indeed, the Cour de Cassation so decided (Civ. 13 Nov. 1964, JCP 1965. II. 14110, noted by BIZIÈRE; Civ. 20 March 1979, D. 1980, 29, noted by LARROUMET). The Chambre Sociale of the Cour de Cassation, which deals with labour law, however, never holds the employee contractually liable except in cases of gross negligence (see, for example, Soc. 27 nov. 1958, D. 1959, 20, noted by LINDON), and it would be only logical to apply the same rule where the employer is suing on the basis of having paid the third party whom the employee injured. (See the details in VINEY (above p. 670) 903 ff.)

IV

Liability for third parties in the *Common Law* rests on much the same principles as in French law. In both systems there are essentially two conditions which must be satisfied before a defendant has to pay for the harm caused by the tort of another: the other must be the servant of the defendant, and he must have caused the harm in the course of his employment. This liability is quite independent of any fault in the master.

1. In order to decide whether the tortfeasor was a 'servant' of the defendant or an 'independent contractor', the Common Law courts ask if the defendant had sufficient power of direction and control over his activities. Whether this is so or not depends on a great variety of factors: it speaks against a person's being a servant if he has special expertise and experience or can decide how or where or when the work is to be done or if he uses his own tools or if he is paid by results rather than by time, and so on. In earlier days the English courts adhered to the 'control test', and doubts arose whether people such as doctors or ships-captains could be classed as servants, since such experts could not be controlled in their professional spheres even by those who employed them. Today, however, it is generally recognized that the control test is of limited application to specialists and experts, and one now tends to ask whether the third party formed an integral part of the defendant's business organization.

See *Cassidy* v. *Ministry of Health*, [1951] 2 KB 343, and the comment of KAHN-FREUND, 14 *Mod. L. Rev.* 504 (1951).—Cases of 'borrowed servants' also cause difficulty in the Common Law, for they raise the question which of two persons is the master. There are many reported cases in England, and in the United States they are innumerable: see ATIYAH (above p. 669) 152 ff.; SMITH, 'Scope of Business: The Borrowed Servant Problem', 38 *Mich. L. Rev.* 1222 (1940); and the interesting Comment in 76 *Yale LJ* 807 (1967), all of which have extensive references to the cases.

2. If a plaintiff has been injured by a tort committed by a servant, the liability of the defendant employer depends on whether the servant committed the tort in the course of his employment. Not very much can be gleaned from the general formulas which seek to refine on this requirement. Thus PROSSER (p. 502; see p. 503 ff.) states that a servant acts 'in the course of his employment' if his acts 'are so closely connected with what the servant is employed to do, and so fairly and reasonably incidental to it, that they may be regarded as methods, even though quite improper ones, of carrying out the objectives of the employment'. See also Restatement (Second) of Agency (1958) §§228 ff.

It would be quite impossible to tackle here the immense number of relevant cases in Anglo-American law, so we shall attend only to a few topics we have referred to in our discussions of German and French law.

When an employee goes to and from his place of work, he is not in the course of his employment and his employer is not liable for accidents he causes *en route*. The situation is different if after he has finished his work an employee collects his pay on the way home and carelessly injures a fellow-employee on the employer's premises. Here the tortfeasor is still in the course of his employment and his employer is liable to damages.

See *Staton* v. *National Coal Board*, [1957] 2 All ER 667; *Bell* v. *Blackwood Morton & Sons Ltd.*, 1960 SLT 145. In such cases, since the victim is himself an employee, he has a claim to social insurance benefits, but in English law, unlike German law (§636 RVO), he also retains his more extensive rights under the general rules of tort law, subject to certain qualifications.

If an employee is directed by his employer to go and work on another site, the employer is liable if he causes a traffic accident *en route*. This is true even if the employee disregards any instructions the employer may have given on the matter unless the employee's choice of route increased the risk of accident to an extent which the employer could not reasonably have foreseen. If the employer tells an employee to go in a company car and leave a message somewhere, he is liable for an accident caused *en route* even if the worker ignores his instructions and takes his own vehicle.

See *McKean* v. *Raynor Bros. Ltd.*, [1942] 2 All ER 650; other English cases may be found in ATIYAH (above p. 669) 225 ff., and American cases in JAMES (above p. 669) 174 f.—Similar rules are applied if at the time of the accident the employee had left the prescribed route; on this see ATIYAH (above p. 669) 251 ff.; SMITH (above p. 669); DOUGLAS (above p. 669), all of which contain a mass of case-law.

As in Germany, an 'inner connection' is required between the harmful act of the servant and the task he was employed to do. This is exemplified in cases where an employee on duty starts smoking and carelessly causes a fire. If the job involves the carriage of inflammable materials or otherwise calls for special care because of the intrinsic fire hazard the employer is liable, but not if a truck driver lights a cigarette, throws the match out of the window, and thereby sets alight a pile of cuttings by the side of the highway. In the first case it seems fair that an employer who has men perform tasks which carry a high risk of fire should bear the inherent and foreseeable risk of fires carelessly caused.

See *Jefferson* v. *Derbyshire Farmers Ltd.*, [1921] 2 KB 281; *Herr* v. *Simplex Box Corp.*, 330 Pa. 129, 198 A. 309 (1938); *George* v. *Bekins Van & Storage Co.*, 33 Cal. 2d 834, 205 P. 2d 1037 (1949); ATIYAH (above p. 323) 259 ff.; Restatement (Second) of Agency (1958) §235.

3. A further precondition of the liability of the employer is that the employee should have caused the harm by means of a *tort*. One constantly speaks of the employer's 'liability for the *torts* of his servant' (see, for example, Restatement (Second) of Agency (1958) §219 and *passim*). This is not a requirement whch has attracted much attention, and it does not seem to have led to any problems in practice.

In principle if liability is imposed on the employer as a result of the employee's injuring a third party the employee is bound to indemnify the employer. The Common Law seems not to accept any qualification of this duty to indemnify, such as a limitation to cases of particularly gross negligence; see the striking, not to say shocking, decision of the House of Lords in *Lister* v. *Romford Ice & Cold Storage Co.*, [1957] AC 555, and the comment by WILLIAMS, 20 *Mod. L. Rev.* 220, 437 (1957); JOLOWICZ, 1957 *Camb. LJ* 21; STEFFEN, 25 *U. Chi. L. Rev.* 465 (1958); GARDINER, 22 *Mod. L. Rev.* 652 (1959), and ATIYAH (above p. 669) 422 ff.

4. If a third party is injured by the negligence of someone who is not a servant but an 'independent contractor', he can in principle claim damages only from the independent contractor himself, and not also from the person who paid him. This principle of the Common Law is, however, subject to important exceptions, when it is usually said that the duty of care owed to the public by the employer is 'non-delegable ', that is, that it cannot be delegated to an independent contractor in such a way that the employer is freed from liability to the injured party and only the independent contractor remains liable to him. In such cases it is occasionally said that the employer owes not just the normal 'duty to take care' but the higher 'duty that care is taken'. The result is that the employer must answer for the fault of the independent contractor as he does for that of a servant.

It is difficult to find any common thread running through the cases in which the Common Law adopts this position. Many of them smack of 'neighbour law', as German lawyers would say. *Bower* v. *Peate* (1876), 1 QBD 321 is an example. Here a builder was employed to make an excavation and the neighbouring land was damaged by the withdrawal of support. Although it was clear that the defendant landowner was not personally at fault at all and that the builder was an independent contractor, the neighbour's claim was granted. There are a great number of these cases both in England and in the United States (Restatement (Second) of Torts (1965) §422 A), and they also arise in Germany, though in a different technical guise. In Germany the question is whether the liability of the landowner for the acts of his building contractor should be judged by §831 BGB or rather, since neighbours are in a 'community relationship' analogous to contract, by §278 BGB. The Bundesgerichtshof has held that the owner is liable only under §831 BGB (BGHZ 42, 374). §831 BGB does not help the plaintiff at all, since the building contractor is normally independent and therefore not a 'functional assistant'. It would be otherwise if §278 were held applicable, since an independent contractor may very well be a 'assistant for performance' (*Erfüllungsgehilfe*) and the result would be the same as in the Common Law. The German courts try to get round their self-denying ordinance by holding the owner to extreme care in his supervision of the building contractor and in this way, if it seems desirable, they can make the owner liable, though for his *own* fault (see, for example, RGZ 132, 51, 58 f.; BGH NJW 1960, 335).

Common Law and German law reach the same result, though again with different doctrinal methods, in another group of cases as well. By granting the plaintiff a contractual claim for damages the German courts can use §278 BGB to make the defendant liable even for an independent contractor; the Common Law uses the law of tort, but exceptionally renders the defendant liable for the fault of his independent contractor. If a tenant is injured by the defective condition of premises which the landlord has promised to keep in proper condition, the landlord will be liable in damages even if he entrusted the work of maintenance and repair to independent contractors rather than to his own employees, provided that the independent contractors were at fault. The same is true if as a matter of business a person allows the public to enter or use his property. If the property is dangerous owing to the fault of an independent contractor and someone is injured in consequence, the proprietor will be liable if the victim was one of those who could be expected to enter the land or use the property for business purposes (on this see Restatement (Second) of Torts (1965) §§419–22, 425). In such cases the German courts would unhesitatingly treat the relationship of the parties as contractual or semi-contractual and hold the defendant liable under §278 for the fault of his contractor as an 'assistant for performance'.

Finally, liability for the fault of an independent contractor has been extended to cases where there is no contractual or semi-contractual or even neighbourly relationship between the parties. For example, a person who procures building operations to be done must take proper safety precautions to prevent risk to passing public traffic. This duty is also 'non-delegable'. A person subject to such a duty, very commonly a local authority, will therefore be liable if anyone on the public highway falls into an open pit or an unguarded trench or is injured by falling scaffolding owing to the fault of an independent contractor to whom he entrusted the requisite security precautions (see ATIYAH (above p. 669) 352 ff.; *Salsbury* v. *Woodland*, [1970] 1 QB 324; Restatement (Second) of Torts (1965) §§417 ff.). This overlaps with another class of case where the defendant is held liable for the fault of an independent contractor engaged on 'ultrahazardous activities' which call for special security arrangements. Here too the duty to take proper precautions is regarded as 'non-delegable'. A person who engages in building, demolition, or scaffolding operations, sprays pesticides from planes, sets up high tension electricity cables, or lays pipes close to highways will be liable for the fault of anyone to whom he entrusts these 'ultrahazardous activities' and it makes no difference that these persons are independent contactors (see *Honeywill and Stein* v. *Larkin Bros. Ltd.*, [1934] 1 KB 191 and Restatement (Second) of Torts (1965) §§416, 427).

V

Our comparative survey has shown that in the Romanistic and Anglo-American legal families the rules of vicarious liability are essentially in agreement. The questions are whether the party causing the harm was the defendant's assistant, '*préposé*' or 'servant', and whether he caused the harm to the victim by means of a tort committed in connection with the functions for which he was employed or 'in the course of his employment'. If these conditions are satisfied, the liability of the superior is established even if he took all necessary care in the selection and supervision of his employees.

The new draft version of §831 BGB in Germany is in line with these rules, since it would deprive the employer of the possibility of proving that he was not personally at fault and would make his liability depend simply on the employee's having caused the harm to a third party by means of a tort. Accordingly, the enactment of the draft would achieve a large measure of legal unity in an important area of the law of tort.

But there are grounds other than those of legal unification for endorsing the proposed amendment of §831 BGB. It gives the right result. As has already been indicated, the German courts have already gone far to introduce it into the positive law, by construing situations as contractual, by making exculpatory proof extremely difficult, and by requiring the employer in many cases to indemnify his employees against tort claims by third parties, regardless of his own care in selecting and supervising them. Indeed, it is now generally admitted that the proposed version of §831 BGB provides the right solution and justifies the actual results, at least for the defendant employer who is in business and can accordingly count up the risk of harm being done by his staff and distribute to his customers the cost of insuring against it. But it has been objected that the new rule might be burdensome for *private* employers. The only significant cases in practice arise out of *traffic accidents* caused by employees. Is it really fair that a private citizen should be made liable if his chauffeur negligently causes an accident or if his housemaid goes to fetch the milk, crosses the road when the lights are red, and causes a truck to swerve into the ditch? In fact it would only be if the private employer had to pay for the resulting loss out of his own pocket that §831 BGB as proposed would lead to unsatisfactory results. But this is generally not the case so far as traffic accidents are concerned. Everyone is bound by law to take out insurance against liability for the harm caused by the person he has drive his automobile. The fear that such a person may be shortsighted enough to take out inadequate cover may be met by raising the statutory minimum. It is true that if his housemaid causes a traffic accident when cycling or on foot the employer will not be covered by the compulsory liability insurance, but here too the problems should be solved in the proper place, namely in the law of traffic accidents. One might even follow up the suggestion of E. v. HIPPEL (*NJW* 1967, 1729, 1735) that traffic accident insurance covering accidents caused by pedestrians and cyclists as well should be made compulsory. It must be said, too, that both in the Common Law and in French law private employers are liable for the faults of their employees and this has caused no problems or movements for reform; the only cases which actually arise are those where the private employer is made liable for a traffic accident caused by his employees, and the same would be true in Germany.

In France and in the Common Law countries it has often been asked what the true justification for the principle of vicarious liability may be, and many different answers have been given. For example, it has been said that a legal system which affords the employer the liberty of extending the range of his activity and the amount of his profit by employing others should make him accept the increased risk that third parties may be harmed : *qui sentit commodum debet sentire et onus.* This proves too much, for the positive law does not put on the employer the risk of the harm his employees may cause *without* any fault. This objection is met by the explanation that responsibility is imposed on the employer because the employee is his *alter ego*, his 'long arm', and the legal system treats the fault of the employee in his employment as being that of the master: *qui facit per alium facit per se.* For others, the liability of the employer for the fault of his staff is justified on the ground that it gives the employer an added incentive to take precautions to avoid harm being caused to third parties and that it has the added advantage of avoiding tiresome disputes about the internal organization of his business. Another doctrine, favoured by American authors in particular, has it that the cost of accidents should be borne by the person who can most easily distribute it to the whole community by means of insurance at the smallest social cost and with the minimum waste; it is normally the employer rather than the employee, much less the victim, who is the best 'risk-absorber' and therefore he must answer for the torts of his employees. The same result is reached by another and more recently developed American theory that the principal task of the law of damages is to procure that all the costs of the production of goods and services should be reflected in their price so that people wondering whether to pay for them or not should be able to decide whether they are important and useful enough to be worth a price which includes the cost of the accidents involved in their production.

The theories adduced to justify vicarious liability in France are listed in MAZEAUD/ TUNC I nos. 928 ff.; Anglo-American views are collected and evaluated in WILLIAMS, 20 Mod. L. Rev. 220, 228 ff. (1957) and ATIYAH (above p. 669) 12 ff. But see also the writings of LASKI, SMITH, DOUGLAS, SEAVEY, and JANES (all cited above p. 669), and note the rather cool reception given by Judge FRIENDLY to the 'economic' justification of the rule of respondeat superior (*Ira S. Bushey & Sons* v. *United States*, 398 F. 2d 167 (1968)).

No single one of these 'theories' gives a satisfactory explanation of the institution of vicarious liabilty since each of them emphasizes one of the underlying value-judgments at the expense of the others. Nevertheless, taken together, they indicate the policy considerations which one should bear in mind in deciding what the rules of vicarious liability should be. None of them suggests that the liability of the employer should depend on his personal fault in selecting and supervising his men: on this ground also the new version of §831 BGB is a step forward.

49

Strict Liability

ANCEL, 'La Responsabilité sans faute en droit français', *Travaux de l'Association Henri Capitant* II (1947) 249.

ATIYAH, *Accidents, Compensation and the Law* (3rd edn., 1980).

——, 'No-Fault Compensation: A Question That Will Not Go Away', 54 *Tul. L. Rev.* 271 (1980).

CORNELIS, *De buitencontractuele aansprakelijkheid voor schade veroorzakt door zaken* (1982).

EDLBACHER, 'Wandel und Krise des Haftungsgrundes des Verschuldens', *Festschrift Wilburg* (1965) 81.

EHRENZWEIG, 'Assurance Oblige—A Comparative Study', 15 *L. Contemp. Probl.* 445 (1950).

——, *Negligence without Fault, Trends toward an Enterprise Liability for Insurable Loss* (1951), reprinted in 54 *Calif. L. Rev.* 1422 (1966).

EÖRSI, 'The Adaptation of Civil Liability to Modern Needs', *Rev. Contemp. L.* 10 (1963) no. 2, p. 11.

ESSER, *Grundlagen und Entwicklung der Gefährdungshaftung* (1941).

——, 'Die Zweispurigkeit unseres Haftpflichtrechts', *JZ* 1953, 129.

FLEMING/HELLNER/V. HIPPEL, *Haftungsersetzung durch Versicherungsschutz* (1980).

FRIDMAN, 'The Rise and Fall of Rylands v. Fletcher', 34 *Can. Bar Rev.* 810 (1956).

FRIEDMANN, 'Social Insurance and the Principles of Tort Liability', 63 *Harv. L. Rev.* 241 (1950).

GILLARD, 'Vers l'unification du droit de la responsabilité', *ZSR* 86 (1967) 193.

GROSSFELD, 'Haftungsverschärfung, Haftungsbeschränkung, Versicherung, Umverteilung', *Festschrift Coing* II (1982) 111.

HANNAK, *Die Verteilung der Schäden aus gefährlicher Kraft, Grundsätze einer Schadensordnung für die Gefahren der modernen Technik* (1960).

HELLNER, 'Tort Liability and Liability Insurance', *Scand. Stud. L.* 6 (1962) 129.

V. HIPPEL, *Schadensausgleich bei Verkehrsunfällen, Haftungsersetzung durch Versicherungsschutz, Eine rechtsvergleichende Studie* (1968).

HÜBNER, *Die Haftung des Gardien im französischen Zivilrecht* (1972).

ISON, *The Forensic Lottery, A Critique on Tort Liability as a System of Personal Injury Compensation* (1967).

JAMES, 'Accident Liability Reconsidered: The Impact of Liability Insurance', 57 *Yale LJ* 549 (1948).

JØRGENSEN, 'Towards Strict Liability in Tort', *Scand. Stud. L.* 7 (1963) 27.

KLEIN (ed.), *Deutsch-französisch-schweizerisches Colloquium über die Grundlagen und Funktionen des Haftpflichtrechts* (1973).

KÖTZ, *Sozialer Wandel im Unfallrecht* (1976).

MILLER, 'Compensation for Personal Injury: Social Insurance in Comparative Perspective', *Comp. L. Yb.* 4 (1980) 221.

MORRIS, 'Hazardous Enterprises and Risk Bearing Capacity', 61 *Yale LJ* 1172 (1952).

OFTINGER, 'Der soziale Gedanke im Schadenersatzrecht und in der Haftpflichtversicherung', *SJZ* 39 (1942/43) 545, 561.

——, 'L'Évolution récente de la responsabilité sans faute en droit suisse', *Travaux de l'Association Henri Capitant* II (1947) 263.

——, 'L'Évolution de la responsabilité civile et de son assurance dans la législation suisse la plus récente', *Mélanges Savatier* (1965) 723.

PROSSER, 'The Principle of Rylands v. Fletcher', *Selected Essays on the Law of Torts* (1953) 135.

RINCK, *Gefährdungshaftung* (1959).

SAVATIER, *Comment repenser la conception française actuelle de la responsabilité civile?* (1967).

SCHILCHER, *Theorie der sozialen Schadensverteilung* (1977).

SPENCER, 'Motor-Cars and the Rule in Rylands v. Fletcher: A Chapter of Accidents in the History of Law and Motoring', 1983 *Camb. LJ* 65.

STARCK, 'Les Cas de responsabilité sans faute', *Rev. trim. dr. civ.* 56 (1958) 475.

STARK, 'Probleme der Vereinheitlichung des Haftpflichtrechts', *ZSR* 86 (1967) 1.

——, 'Entschädigungsrecht am Scheideweg: Haftpflichtrecht mit Haftpflichtversicherung oder Personen- und Sachversicherung', *VersR* 1981, 1.

STONE, 'Liability for Damage Caused by Things', XI *Int. Enc. Comp. L.* 'Torts' (1983) Ch. 5.

STRAHL, 'Tort Liability and Insurance', *Scand. Stud. L.* 3 (1959) 199.

SZPUNAR, 'La Responsabilité sans faute dans le droit civil polonais', *Rev. int. dr. comp.* 11 (1959) 28.

TERCIER, 'Quelques Considérations sur les fondements de la responsabilité civile', *ZSR* 95 (1976) 1.

TUNC, *La Responsabilité civile* (1981).

——, (ed.), *Pour une loi sur les accidents de la circulation* (1981).

——, 'Traffic Accident Compensation: Law and Proposals', XI *Int. Enc. Comp. L.* 'Torts' (1971) Ch. 14.

USSING, 'The Scandinavian Law of Torts, Impact of Insurance on Tort Law', 1 *Am. J. Comp. L.* 359 (1952).

——, 'Evolution et transformation du droit de la responsabilité civile', *Rev. int. dr. comp.* 7 (1955) 485.

VINEY, *Le Déclin de la responsabilité individuelle* (1964)

——, *La Responsabilité: conditions* (Traité de droit civil (ed. Ghestin) vol. IV 1982).

VOIRIN, 'De la responsabilité civile à la sécurité sociale pour la réparation des dommages corporels, Extension ou disparition de la branche accidents du travail', *Rev. int. dr. comp.* 31 (1979) 541.

VAN DER WALT, 'Strict Liability in the South African Law of Delict', 1 *Comp. Int. LJS Afr.* 49 (1968).

WEYERS, *Unfallschäden, Praxis und Ziele von Haftpflicht- und Vorsorgesystemen* (1972).

WILL, *Quellen erhöhter Gefahr, Rechtsvergleichende Untersuchungen zur Weiterent-*

wicklung der deutschen Gefährdungshaftung durch richterliche Analogie oder durch gesetzliche Generalklausel (1980).

ZACHERT, *Gefährdungshaftung und Haftung aus vermutetem Verschulden im deutschen und französischen Recht* (1971).

ZWEIGERT/KÖTZ, *Die Haftung für gefährliche Anlagen in den EWG-Ländern sowie in England und den Vereinigten Staaten von Amerika* (1966).

I

IN all the legal systems considered in the previous chapter the law of tort is basically founded on the principle that the only sufficient reason for shifting a victim's loss to the person who caused it is if the latter was guilty of reprehensible or careless behaviour in causing it. This principle of no liability without fault prevailed in Germany and France apparently unchallenged until the end of the nineteenth century, as it did also in the countries of the Common Law, where its influence helped to make the tort of negligence into an independent ground of liability. As a matter of intellectual and social history, the principle of no liability without fault has its roots in the liberal individualism of a century ago: a responsible individual's freedom of movement should only be limited by the imposition of liability in damages if he culpably failed to conduct himself in accordance with the general duty to act carefully. Along with this there went, especially in England and the United States, the fear that extensive liability might inhibit nascent industries and so delay general progress. This meant that even the most serious industrial accidents had to be borne by the worker and his family unless they were attributable to the fault of the employer, but this was perfectly acceptable to the social Darwinism in English-speaking countries: 'Sound policy lets losses lie where they fall, except where a special reason can be shown for interference' (HOLMES, *The Common Law* (1881) 50). Germany was the first country to deviate from the principle of fault, originally for the benefit of a strictly limited group of victims: in the eighteen-eighties, when capitalism still had a patriarchal streak, there was enacted under BISMARCK a system of workmen's compensation for *industrial accidents*. This removed the most acute problem concerning accidents from the law of tort and took it into the law of social insurance; private lawyers no longer had to worry about it and the rest of the law of tort could remain quietly in thrall to the traditional notion of the primacy of the fault principle, subject to the strict liability introduced for railway *accidents* by special statutes in Prussia (1838) and in the German Empire (1871). Efforts were made to introduce stricter liabilities when the BGB was being prepared but they were unavailing. The general principle that liability for harm arose only as the result of a 'fault' was thought to be intrinsically sound, as being 'the product of a high state of cultural development. It is of central importance for the delineation of the spheres of rights within which individuals can develop their individuality. In determining whether or how to act one should have to take account of the legal interests of others only if the requisite forethought suggests that they may be affected. If after careful reflection an act seems to present no danger for others one should be free to do it, and if it nevertheless causes harm to someone else's legal rights that person must put up with it just as if it were an accident' (Motive II p. 1074).

In modern conditions a law of damages which rested on these principles would be hard to accept. A great many factors have led industrial states in the West and in the East to limit, restrict, or evade the pure principle of fault in tort law, or even to abandon it quite openly for certain types of accident. These factors include the growing use of machines and technical devices of all kinds in industry, manufacture, and transport, the increased risk they present of causing damage to person or property so severe as to exceed the victim's capacity to bear it, the victim's consequent need for protection, the possibility of spreading the risk of loss through the community as a whole by means of insurance, and the great change in people's view of the degree of social security which a legal system should guarantee to its members. It seems obvious to us today that a person who suffers an accident at his *place of work* should obtain compensation whether his employer was at fault or not, but we should not forget that in many countries until quite recently this principle was regarded as positively revolutionary because it was irreconcilable with the principle of fault. Even in 1911 the Court of Appeals in New York declared a statute unconstitutional for making employers in certain dangerous industries strictly liable for industrial accidents. The argument that the statute simply removed the obsolete Common Law rule that a worker entering employment consciously accepted the risk of accidents met with a dry answer from JUDGE WERNER: 'It would be quite as logical and effective to argue that this legislation only reverses the laws of nature, for in everything within the sphere of human activity the risks which are inherent and unavoidable must fall upon those who are exposed to them . . . The Constitution, in substance and effect, forbids that a citizen shall be penalized or subjected to liability unless he has violated some law or has been guilty of some fault.' *Ives* v. *South Buffalo Railway Co.*, 201 NY 271, 94 NE 431, 444 (1911).

Attempts to justify supposedly immutable postulates of justice by invoking the law of nature have often failed, and in this matter too the feeling gradually prevailed that it was socially unacceptable to make the worker himself bear the consequences of an accident at work. In all legal systems today the cost of industrial accidents is, by one legal mechanism or another, imposed on employers who can add it as an item of cost to the price of their products and services and so spread it throughout society: 'The cost of the product should bear the blood of the workman' (LLOYD GEORGE).

Industrial accidents are the clearest instance of open abandonment of the principle of no liability without fault but there are many rules of the law of tort which weaken the principle considerably, if more surreptitiously. It would be an error to suppose that this is an Either–Or situtation, that a legal system must either accept or reject the principle of no liability without fault as a whole. What happens in practice is that liability for fault imperceptibly shades into strict liability, and it is often a meaningless question whether a particular legal system, with regard to accidents of a particular type, adopts the principle of fault or of causal liability.

As is well known, the first qualification of fault liability in its pure form arose when courts in the legal systems under discussion ceased to be satisfied with the degree of care which it was possible to expect the defendant personally to show, and look instead to the *typical* abilities of the professional or trade group to which he belonged. No one can now escape liability on the ground that he was too old or infirm or slow to avoid the harm. It is the same when courts exact a degree of care proportional to the magnitude of the risk. Thus in England and the United States a duty of 'high care', the 'highest care', or the 'utmost care' is imposed on businesses which deal in dangerous and potent substances (see ZWEIGERT/KÖTZ (above p. 688) 32, 42 f.), and the same is true in Germany (see RGZ 147, 353, 356; BGH NJW 1965, 197, 199). The degree of 'care' demanded of the defendant is often so extreme as to be barely distinguishable from liability without fault. In general, whenever it seems necessary in order to achieve a socially acceptable distribution of the accident risks peculiar to modern life, the courts tend to insist on precautions which it is virtually impossible to satisfy, and they can do this because, judging a case *ex post facto*, they can always discover some precaution or other which, had the defendant adopted it in time, would have prevented the occurrence of the harm.

The results of cases of harm caused by electric power cables in the United States, where liability depends on negligence, are quite comparable with those in Germany, where the courts have at their disposal a claim based on the strict liability imposed by §2 of the Law of Liability; see, for example, *Jones* v. *Southern Utah Power Co.*, 106 Utah 482, 150 P. 2d 376 (1944); *Ottertail Power Co.* v. *Duncan*, 137 F. 2d 187 (8th Cir. 1943); *Chase* v. *Washington Power Co.*, 62 Idaho 298, 111 P. 2d 872 (1941). Even before this special statutory liability was introduced in Germany, the courts were able to assist plaintiffs by stretching the notion of fault; see RGZ 147, 353. An instructive slection of similar cases may be found in ESSER, *Grundlagen* 7 ff. and JZ 1953, 129.

One may also weaken the principle of fault by means of rules concerning the burden of proof. As a general principle it is for the victim to prove facts which show that the defendant was at fault in causing the harm, but in many cases this burden of proof has been reversed. The courts have been able to do this in Germany and France by adopting various methods of giving the victim a *contractual* claim for damages, with the benefit of the more favourable rules regarding burden of proof (see above Ch. 41 II, 43 III 2). But even within the law of tort there is a presumption that the defendant was at fault in certain types of accident; in proportion as the means of rebutting this presumption are restricted, liability for presumed fault assumes the character of strict liability. Thus, for example, the German courts have developed a principle that in a tort suit for injuries due to a defective product the plaintiff need only prove that the product was defective when it left the defendant's factory, and it is then for the manufacturer to show that neither he nor any of the employees involved in the manufacture was guilty of any want of care (BGHZ 51, 91; and see below V). Again, once it is shown that a doctor has committed a 'serious' error in treatment the burden will be on him to dispel any doubt about its causal contribution (BGH NJW 1968, 1185, and constantly thereafter). In applying art. 1384 Code civil, which we shall soon be discussing at length, the French courts speak of a 'presumption of liability', but this presumption is so difficult to rebut that it is almost identical with the special statutory torts in Germany based on strict liability ('Gefährdungshaftung'). A milder form of liability for presumed fault can be found, for example, in §§836 ff. BGB and §1319 ABGB, which require a proprietor of landed property to pay for the harm occasioned to persons or property by the collapse, in whole or in part, of a defective building or construction affixed to the land. In the Swiss OR (art. 58) liability for constructions (*Werkhaftung*) is rather stricter: 'construction' includes not only highways, squares, passageways, scaffolds, and ski-lifts but also stairlights and faulty floors, and if they are defective or badly maintained their owner can only escape liability if he proves that a third party or the victim himself was responsible or that the defect was attributable to an accident which he could not have foreseen (see BGE 63 II 95); Swiss writers describe this as a 'causal liability' (see OFTINGER, *Schweizerisches Haftpflichtrecht* I (4th edn., 1975) 26 ff.). Liability for damage done by an animal is treated as liability for presumed fault in Austria and Switzerland (see the terms of §1320 ABGB and art. 56 OR), but here too it is made so difficult to rebut the presumption that in Switzerland this liability also is described as causal liability (see OFTINGER, ibid.).

The Austrian Oberster Gerichtshof was once faced with a case in which the plaintiff motor-cyclist had collided with a dog which the defendant had taken on a country road without a lead. The defendant was held liable. 'The qualities of a dog are well-known and so the defendant ought to have realized that this dog, especially in view of its ear infection, might not notice a motor-cycle coming up behind it and might run out into the highway'. The court also dealt sharply with the point that it would not have helped to call the dog to heel. 'If the defendant had had the dog at heel, a well-timed call or whistle would have stopped it from endangering the motor-cyclist. If she did not have the dog at heel she was in no position to control it, and that is a ground of liability.' (OGH 27 Oct. 1954, SZ XXVII 267; see also OGH 28 Sept. 1938, SZ XX 198; BGE 67 II 26 and 77 II 43.)—In German law the keeper of an animal is allowed to exculpate himself if the animal is domesticated and useful, such as a guard-dog, a draught horse, or a milk cow, but the keeper of 'luxury animals' is liable for the damage they do even if he can prove that he exercised every conceivable care in looking after them (see §833 BGB).

Even where the onus of proof remains with the victim in accordance with general principle, there are many ways of making the requisite proof easier. An important instance in Germany is the 'Anscheinsbeweis' or 'prima-facie-Beweis': a victim who cannot prove facts which are direct evidence of the defendant's fault may still succeed if he proves other facts which, given one's general experience of the way things occur, justify the conclusion that the defendant failed to exercise the care called for in the circumstances. For example, if on a straight highway under normal weather conditions a motorist on the wrong side of the road collides with an oncoming car, one's immediate impression is that the motorist was not driving properly. According to the German courts this does not make for a reversal of the burden of proof; the defendant motorist need not bring positive proof that he behaved carefully but it is up to him to show that there was something untypical and extraordinary in the situation—perhaps that the stretch of road was unusually susceptible to black ice or strong side-winds—so as to suggest an alternative explanation of the accident. If the defendant fails to satisfy this requirement, as he usually does, the judge may proceed on the basis that the fault which 'normally' inheres in such a situation is proved in the case before him (invariable holding: for example, see BGHZ 8, 239).

Common Law courts do likewise with the 'doctrine of res ipsa loquitur'. The leading case is *Scott* v. *London & St. Katherine Docks Co.*, (1865) 3 H. & C. 596, 159 Eng. Rep. 665. The plaintiff was walking past a warehouse when sacks of sugar inexplicably fell on his head. The court said 'There must be reasonable evidence of negligence. But where the thing is shown to be under the management of the defendant or his servants, and the accident is such as in the ordinary course of things does not happen if those who have the management use proper care, it affords reasonable evidence, in the absence of explanation by the defendant, that the accident arose from want of care.'

It is not entirely agreed in England what constitutes a satisfactory 'explanation by the defendant'. Many decisions apparently require the defendant to negate the possibility that the harm was caused by his fault, by proving that he was not negligent (see *Moore* v. *Fox*, [1956] I QB 596); other decisions apparently treat it as sufficient if the defendant shows that it is *possible* that the harm was caused without his fault (as in *The Kite*, [1933] P. 154), and this is the dominant view in the United States and in the Commonwealth countries.

In the United States there is another important factor which makes negligence liability approach a liability independent of fault, namely that tort suits are almost always tried before a jury (see Ch. 20 V). In such a suit the sole function of the judge is to control the oral proceedings, to decide how the parties may prove their allegations, and finally to lay down the rules of law for the jury to apply to the facts. The jury alone evaluates the evidence and applies the rules of law laid down by the judge to the facts; above all it decides whether the defendant was at fault or not. Only in exceptional cases can the judge require the jury to give judgment for the plaintiff or for the defendant, or vacate a verdict rendered by the jury: he may do so only if the evidence led by the parties is unquestionably inadequate to sustain the claim or ground the defence, or if the jury's verdict is in flagrant contradiction with the matters proved in evidence. It will be plain that laymen will always tend to give judgment for the plaintiff and to hold that the defendant's behaviour was negligent, especially if the defendant is a large and obviously solvent corporation or if the accident is clearly covered by the defendant's liability insurance.

II

We have seen that liability for fault may be more or less covertly made to *approximate* to strict liability: an 'objective' standard of negligence may be applied, the requisite degree of care may be raised, the burden of proof may be reversed, and doctrines such as *res ipsa loquitur* may be invoked. We must now consider the types of accident for which the legislator or the courts have *openly* broken with the principle of fault. In *German* law, apart from liability for 'luxury animals', strict liability has been introduced exclusively by the legislator in a long series of special statutes not incorporated in the BGB. The reason for this is presumably that the German legislator still regards the principle of fault as the essence of the law of delict, and considers strict liability as anomalous and exceptional, meriting the less exalted status of enactment in special detailed statutes. There is also a long tradition behind this tendency to use special statutes: in 1838 §25 of the Prussian Law of Railway Undertakings imposed strict liability on railways for all harm to persons or property occurring 'through carriage on the railway' unless the defendant could prove 'that the harm was caused by the fault of the victim or by an external and unavoidable event'. This statute was adopted in similar form by other states in Germany and in 1869 by Austria as well. 1871 saw the enactment of the Imperial Law of Liability, which is still in force today, though it has been amended frequently and is now called simply the Law of Liability. It lays down strict liability for harm to *persons* arising 'through the operation' of railways.

Harm is caused 'through the operation' of the railway if it is caused or contributed to by sudden braking, collapse of the track, sparks from the trains, signal failure, or other incidents of the technical operation of running a railway. Accidents to persons mounting or dismounting from trains or using railway stations are also included if they are due to the specific dangers of railway travel such as the height of the running-boards, the haste of passengers, or the crowd on the platform, but a person who falls on a stairway in a station simply because the steps are defective can claim damages only under §823 par. 1 BGB. The railway is not liable for accidents caused by *force majeure* (*höhere Gewalt*). This is understood by the courts to mean external and elemental forces of nature or the conduct of third parties whose effects could not have been prevented even by the most extreme precautions. The railway will even be liable for flash floods, heavy snowstorms, or avalanches unless no conceivable precautions, such as a warning system or a reduction of speed, could have forestalled the accident. Nor is it a case of *force majeure* if the event which caused the harm is of such frequent occurrence that the railway should take account of it even if it can do nothing about it.

A passenger injured by sudden braking may sue the railway even if it is due to the quite unforeseeable appearance on the track of children or cattle which have broken through the protective fence. See RGZ 54, 404; BGH VersR 1955, 346.

If a victim contributes to the accident by his own fault, the courts weigh up the extent to which the dangerousness of the railway and the fault of the victim contributed to the harm and apportion the damages accordingly (see BGHZ 2, 355).

In 1943 and 1977 the Law of Liability was extended by special statutes to cover cases in which death or personal injury is caused 'by the effects of electricity, gases, vapours, or liquids' coming from 'an installation for their transmission or supply by cable, pipe, or otherwise'. Included in particular are high tension cables, gasholders, steam conduits, and waterpipes. Once again liability is in principle excluded only in cases of *force majeure*. In a case where an 11-year-old child was injured when his kite, attached by wire rather than thread, came in contact with a high tension cable the Bundesgerichtshof held the defendant liable (BGHZ 7, 338); such an accident was very unusual but it did not have that extraordinary, 'almost elemental quality' required before one could speak of *force majeure*. In such a case, however, the damages may be reduced on the ground of the plaintiff's contributory fault.

The liability of the custodian of a *motor vehicle* is less strict. It was introduced in 1908 and is now contained in the Road Traffic Act of 1952 (StVG). §7 StVG makes the custodian of a motor vehicle ('Halter'—normally, but not necessarily, the owner) liable for damage to person or property which arises 'through the operation' of the vehicle. Liability is excluded 'if the accident is caused by an unavoidable event attributable neither to a defect in the construction of the vehicle nor to a failure of any of its functional parts. In particular an event is unavoidable when it is attributable to the behaviour of the victim or of a third party not involved in the operation or of an animal, and both the custodian and the driver of the vehicle have taken all the care called for in the circumstances of the case.'

This means that even unforeseeable and unavoidable failure of the components of the vehicle—such as a tyre defect, axle fracture through metal fatigue, brake failure, or the steering seizing up—makes the custodian liable, but if the accident is due to an 'external' event such as the occurrence of black ice or an animal running in front of the vehicle or faulty driving on the part of other motorists, the custodian is not liable if he can prove that both the driver and he himself observed 'all the care called for in the circumstances'. Such care is defined by the courts as 'care going beyond what is usually required, extreme and thoughtful concentration and circumspection' (BGH VersR 1962, 164; and repeatedly thereafter). In practice such proof is hardly ever forthcoming, and only in very few cases—such as when a car leaves the road because of entirely unpredictable black ice or a small child darts out on to the street from between two parked cars, or a car projects a stone which strikes a pedestrian—has it been accepted that the accident was one which an 'ideally careful' driver could not have avoided. If any fault on the part of the victim contributed to the occurrence of the harm, damages are reduced as under the Law of Liability. Passengers in a vehicle can only sue the custodian under the Road Traffic Act if they were being carried by way of business and for reward, as in a taxi or bus; injured passengers in other cases must use the general provisions of the law of delict (§§823 ff. BGB).

The Air Traffic Law of 1922 lays down an especially strict liability for harm caused to persons and things other than those being carried in the airplane pursuant to contract. In practice this means harm caused on the surface of the earth, whether by flight noise or by crashing or crash-landing: the custodian of an airplane is liable even if he can show that the harm was caused by *force majeure* (see §§33 ff. Air Traffic Law).

A characteristic feature of all the statutes mentioned so far is that they strictly limit the amount of damages payable. Claims in respect of immaterial harm are wholly excluded, and an upper monetary limit is also fixed for the liability of the defendant. In the case of death or personal injury the custodian of a motor vehicle is liable only up to 500,000 DM, and if damages are payable in the form of an annuity, it may not exceed 30,000 DM per year. These limits are increased by statutory amendment from time to time in order to take inflation and other factors into account. If several people are injured or killed in the same accident, the applicable limits are 750,000 DM and 45,000 DM; if the total damage exceeds these limits, the victims' claims are scaled down. This is why almost all damages suits for personal injuries sustained in traffic accidents are based on §§823 ff. BGB as well as the Road Traffic Act. Indeed, only so can one obtain damages for pain and suffering. This means that even if liability under the Road Traffic Act is clear there is often a long and tiresome dispute about the proof of fault.

Since 1939 the custodian of a motor vehicle has been required by law to have insurance covering his liability for the harm caused by the use of the vehicle. A licence to use the vehicle will only be issued if a certificate of insurance is produced. An analogous duty to insure is imposed on the custodian of an airplane but not on the enterprises rendered liable by the Law of Liability.

Strict liability also arises under the Atomic Energy Act of 1959. A distinction is drawn between the liability of the operator of an *installation* for the production or fission of nuclear materials and the liability of any other possessor of radioactive *materials*. The first is liable for personal injury and property damage caused by the effects of nuclear operations within the installation, even if those effects are due to *force majeure*, with an upper limit of 15,000 DM payable per year as annuity for the harm caused to an individual and of 500 million DM for the aggregate harm (including property damage) caused by a single accident. The possessor of radioactive materials is less strictly liable: like the custodian of a motor vehicle, he may escape liability by proving that he observed 'all the care called for in the circumstances', but this does not apply if the harm is due to a failure of safety devices, even if this could not have been known or avoided by the defendant. Here also there is a duty to take out insurance, but in view of the enormous risks appertaining to the operation of nuclear installations, further cover is mandatorily provided by the state.

Finally there is the important liability laid down by the Water Maintenance Act of 1957 (§22) for *pollution of water*. Water for this purpose includes all ponds, lakes, rivers, and streams as well as the water-table, and anyone who introduces into such water substances which alter its composition is liable to pay damages for the harm thereby caused to others, including pure economic loss. The same liability, with the exception of *force majeure*, attaches to the operator of an installation for the manufacture, storage, or carriage of materials: if any materials are introduced into water as defined, the operator of the installation is liable in damages. 'Installation' for the purpose of the statute includes not only storage-tanks for oil and paraffin, tanker vessels, and oil pipelines, but also the sort of petrol tankers which supply gas-stations (so BGH VersR 1967, 374). Considering that the pollution of a river or the water-table itself may cause enormous harm, especially of the pure economic variety, it is all the more surprising to find that the Water Maintenance Act diverges from the usual practice of imposing an upper monetary limit to the strict liability of the defendant. The statute does not introduce any obligation to insure, although one may be confident that practically all the operators of installations which carry a risk of water pollution will have taken out suitable insurance policies. All such policies, however, will contain an upper limit and beyond that limit the risk must be borne by the operator himself.

Given this variety in the grounds of statutory liability, it is not surprising that the German courts have always held that the imposition of strict liability is a matter for the legislature and not for the judiciary. This view may already be found in a judgment of the Reichsgericht in 1912. GRAF ZEPPELIN, whose airship had had to make a forced landing, was sued by a spectator who was struck and injured by the anchor chain when a sudden gust of wind tore the airship loose from its anchors. The question for the Reichsgericht was whether it were possible to apply by analogy the texts which laid down strict liability, such as §833 BGB, the Imperial Law of Liability, and the very recent statute which imposed liability on the custodian of a motor car. The Reichsgericht held that no such application by analogy was possible, even although the operation of an airship was an act of bravado entailing risks much less under control than those of railways or motor cars; the provisions laying down strict liability were 'by reason of their exceptional character not applicable even to the unusual circumstances of travel by airship' (RGZ 78, 171, 172). In a case in which a person was killed by a high tension cable the Reichsgericht decided likewise before the enactment of the special liability for electricity installations. It held that liability without fault could only be imposed by the legislator: 'if the legislator has not done so, it must be concluded that the legislator rejects such far-reaching liability'. Fortunately the court was able to help the widow in the case by reversing the burden of proof and by holding that the duty of care called for very remarkable precautions (see RGZ 147, 353).

In *Austria* the types of strict liability are very like those in Germany, though there is no strict liability for water pollution and there is the peculiarity that in 1959 the liabilities of the custodian of a motor vehicle and the operator of a railway were put in the same statute, with differing limits of liability. In this statute liability is generally excluded if the accident was caused by an 'unavoidable event'. 'Unavoidable event' is defined in the same way as in §7 of the German Road Traffic Act, with the difference that an event is not treated as unavoidable if it is due to an 'extraordinary operational hazard' caused by a third party. This seems to offer the possibility of holding the custodian of a motor vehicle liable if in an attempt to avoid a child who suddenly rushes on to the highway he quite innocently collides with a pedestrian. On this see EDLBACHER, *ÖJZ* 1959, 310.

It is to be observed that unlike the Reichsgericht the Austrian Oberste Gerichtshof has felt able to go in for *analogy* and to apply the provisions of statutes imposing strict liability to other 'dangerous' undertakings. Even before the introduction of the special statutory liability for electric installations, the running of high tension cables counted as a 'dangerous undertaking' (OGH 10 Sept. 1947, SZ XXI 46; *contra* RGZ 147, 353). Strict liability was also imposed by analogy on a chemical factory whose emissions quickly destroyed a circus marquee (OGH 20 Feb. 1958, SZ XXXI 26; see also OGH 18 March 1953, SZ XXVI 75 *ad fin.*, and OGH 30 Aug. 1961. SZ XXXIV 111; see WILL (above p. 687) 80 ff.), where these cases are carefully analysed.

Although *Switzerland* also adheres to the view that strict liability can only
be imposed by special statutes, it has taken a very different path from
Germany and has imposed strict liability in different cases or in cases
differently delineated. A comparison with German law clearly demonstrates
that element of chance and caprice which is inseparable from any legislative
nomination of 'dangerous' operations. Thus the Swiss Law of Railway
Liability of 1905 attaches strict liability not only to the operation of railways
but also to their construction. This leads to strange distinctions. If an innocent
stranger is injured during quarrying operations, the general provisions of the
law of tort apply unless the stone from the quarry was to be carried away by
rail and used for the construction of a railway, in which case strict liability
applies, as it does for the construction or repair of railway tunnels, bridges,
and stations (see BGE 36 II 242). It is immaterial whether the building
operations are being executed by the railway itself or by an independent
contractor, but strict liability applies only in respect of personal injuries. In
respect of property damage one must always prove that the railway was at
fault, unless the owner of the property was himself personally injured. Thus if
a person's motor vehicle is totally destroyed at a level crossing, the strictness of
the railway's liability depends on whether the car-owner was bruised or not (!).
Swiss law also imposes strict liability on the concessionaire of a shipping
route, and it seems perfectly reasonable to treat a passenger who is hurt while
embarking on a steamer on Lake Constance at least as well as a passenger who
is hurt while getting on a train, which is rather less dangerous (see BGE 36 II
89). A statute of 1902 deals with liability for harm caused by the operation of
low or high tension cables, but does so in a manner very different from the
Imperial Law of Liability in Germany. As in Germany there is a special statute
covering the liability of the custodian of motor vehicles or airplanes and the
operator of nuclear installations, but in marked distinction to German law
only the last two statutes, for airplanes and nuclear installations, contain any
monetary limitation on the amount of compensation. The Swiss Pipeline Law
of 1963 imposes strict liability on the operator of a pipeline 'for the
transmission of mineral oil, natural gas or other fluid or gaseous material for
combustion or fuel, as specified by the Bundesrat'; a Law of 1971 imposes
liability on a person who pollutes water 'by his plant, installation, or acts or
omissions'; and finally the Law on Explosives of 1977 imposes liability on the
occupiers of business premises 'in which explosives or fireworks are produced,
stored, or used'. On all these enactments see KELLER, *Haftpflicht im
Privatrecht* (3rd edn., 1978).

A glance at the patchwork of special instances of strict liability imposed by
statutes in Germany, Austria, and Switzerland makes it clear that they leave
uncovered many businesses, installations, and activities which pose at least as
great a risk of harm. It is far from obvious why a person should be strictly
liable if he decides to move earth by means of a light railway while he is liable

only for negligence if he uses heavy bulldozers for the job. And why should an injured person's right to damages depend on whether the accident took place on board a steamer or a train? And if a motorized conveyance causes injury, why should liability turn on whether it is a chairlift, a motor car, a motorboat, a light railway, a hoist, a funicular, or an escalator? It may be said that the legislator can always deal with novel needs by introducing new instances of strict liability, as Switzerland did most recently in 1977 with its Law of Explosives, but even so the law will inevitably limp along behind technology; in any case, is it not perhaps unreasonable to take up the time and energy of the legislative machinery, already very stretched, on the amendment of the law on matters which, even in the context of the law of tort, are fairly interstitial?

The enactment of a general principle to amplify or replace the specific instances of the present law has often been proposed not only in Germany, but in Switzerland and Austria as well. The factual preconditions of strict liability would be stated in such a way that the courts could introduce strict liability wherever advancing technology produced a serious risk of danger. The exact wording of such a law has been a matter of debate, but the problem hardly seems insoluble. See the proposals in KÖTZ, 'Haftung fur besondere Gefahr, Generalklausel fur die Gefährdungshaftung', *AcP* 170 (1970) 1; v. CAEMMERER, *Reform der Gefährdungshaftung* (1971); DEUTSCH, *Haftungsrecht* I (1976) 382 ff.; WILL (above p. 687); KÖTZ, 'Empfiehlt sich eine Vereinheitlichung und Zusammenfassung der gesetzlichen Vorschriften über die Gefährdungshaftung?' *Gutachten und Vorschläge zur Überarbeitung des Schuldrechts* (W. German Ministry of Justice, 1981) 1779. There is a similar proposal in Switzerland; see STARK, 'Einige Gedanken zur Entwicklung des Haftpflichtrechts', *25 Jahre Karlsruher Forum* (Suppt. to VersR., 1983) 66. Two other reforms of strict liability in German law are urged: to abandon the monetary ceilings and to introduce damages for pain and suffering. See KÖTZ in the *Gutachten* mentioned above, pp. 1923 ff. Then the situation would in this respect be like that which now prevails in Switzerland as well as in all countries in which strict liability has been developed by the courts.

III

Until the end of the nineteenth century it was accepted without question by *French* courts and writers that all the delictual provisions of the Code civil rested on the principle of fault. This was clear from the very words of art. 1382 and 1383, but art. 1384 was also understood in this sense, par. 1 of which enacts that 'One is responsible not only for the damage which one causes by one's own act but also for the damage which is caused by the act of persons for whom one is answerable or of things which one has under one's control.'

So far as this provision laid down liability for *other people*, it was taken to presume some fault in the choice or supervision of one's assistants. The reference to liability for *things* was taken to be simply a preliminary indication of the liabilities imposed by art. 1385 and 1386 on the guardian of an *animal* and the owner of a *building*; according to the view then current, such persons could also exonerate themselves by proving that they were not at fault in watching over the animal or that the ruinous building was properly constructed and adequately maintained.

The growing number of industrial accidents due to the increased use of machines in industry and transport led the French Cour de Cassation in 1896 to adopt a view which had occasionally been expressed by writers and was now to become the starting-point for a revolutionary change in the law of delict. The proposition was that in ordaining liability for the things 'which one has under one's control' art. 1384 par. 1 was not simply making a preliminary announcement that arts. 1385 and 1386 were about to impose liabilities for animals and ruinous buildings, but had an independent force of its own and was applicable in all cases in which any thing under the defendant's control had caused harm in any form. At the outset, this view simply led to a reversal of the burden of proof: the victim no longer had to prove that the defendant was at fault under arts. 1382 f., but could rely on the presumption of liability enacted by art. 1384 par. 1, now that it was no longer thought to be restricted to animals and ruinous buildings. Admittedly this was not to abandon the principle of fault: the Court of Cassation on several occasions allowed the defendant to exonerate himself by proving that his control over the thing was impeccable (see, for example, Req. 30 March 1897, D. 1897. 1. 43).

In 1898 the enactment of a statute which gave workers injured in industrial accidents a claim for damages against their employer whether he was at fault or not did away with the principal reason for an extensive construction of art. 1384 par. 1, but the Court of Cassation carried it a stage further in a decision of 19 January 1914: the Court laid down that a custodian of a thing could escape liability in damages under art. 1384 par. 1 only by proving that the damaging occurrence was due (*a*) to *force majeure*, (*b*) to the fault of the victim, or (*c*) to the fault of a third party (Req. 19 Jan. 1914, S. 1914. 1. 128, and constantly thereafter).

Thenceforth it was clear that proof by the defendant custodian that he was not to blame for the occurrence of the harm was not enough to free him from liability.

These decisions regarding the liability of a custodian for harm done by the thing were affirmed and a few doubtful questions resolved by the celebrated *Jand'heur* decision of the Chambres Réunies of the Cour de Cassation. The cardinal parts of the judgment, which are still echoed by the courts today and have themselves become the object of exercises in construction, are as follows: 'The presumption of liability laid down in art. 1384 par. 1 against the person with control over an inanimate object which has caused harm to another can only be rebutted by proof of accident or *force majeure* or of some external cause not attributable to the custodian, and it is not sufficient to free the custodian from liability that he prove that he was not at fault or that the cause of the harmful event has remained unexplained. This presumption is applicable whether the thing which caused the harm was impelled by human hand or not; nor is it necessary that the thing have any defect in its construction which made it apt to cause the harm, since art. 1384 attaches liability to the custody of the thing and not to the thing itself.' (Ch. réun. 13 Feb. 1930, S. 1930, 1. 121.)

The *Jand'heur* decision brought the French law of liability essentially to its modern position, to which we must now turn, remembering that this extensive construction of art. 1384 par. 1 has made it virtually unnecessary for French law to have special statutes to introduce strict liability for defined types of accident. The liability of railways and tramways, and of operators of installations for the production, storage, or transmission of electricity, gas, or dangerous substances are all covered by art. 1384 par. 1 and the cases which construe it.

Special strict liability statutes affect only the operator of a cable car (1941), the custodian of an airplane with regard to damage done on the surface of the earth (1955), and the operator of a nuclear installation (1965). The liability of custodians of motor vehicles was based exclusively on art. 1384 par. 1 until recently, but has now been rendered even stricter by a statute of 1985 (see below p. 686).

1. The first precondition for liability under art. 1384 is that the harm must have been caused by a *thing*. 'Thing' here includes every corporeal object. The composite form of the object is immaterial: fluids and gases are included, as are radioactive materials and electrically energized wires.

See Trib. civ. Marseilles 8 June 1950, Gaz. Pal. 1950. 2. 137; Civ. 17 Dec. 1946, Gaz. Pal. 1947. 1. 129 and ALIBERT, *Obligations et responsabilités des distributeurs d'énergie électrique* (1937) 336 ff.—Animals and, under certain circumstances, buildings are not, however, 'things' in the sense of art. 1384 par. 1. To them the special provisions of art. 1385 and 1386 apply, which the courts construe as meaning that the custodian of an animal is liable regardless of fault, while the owner of a building is only liable if there was an objective defect in the construction of maintenance of the building (see MAZEAUD/TUNC II nos. 1054 ff., 1073).

It is irrelevant whether the thing caused the harm as a result of being impelled or not. Motor cars, trains, ships, and elevators are 'things' in the sense of art. 1384 par. 1 just as much as a board with a protruding nail (Civ. 17 Jan. 1962, D. 1962, 533) or a trapdoor on a dark stairway (Civ. 14 May 1956, JCP 1956. II. 9446). Nor is it necessary that the thing be intrinsically or potentially dangerous so as to require delicate handling or constant supervision. For a time the courts accepted this distinction as a means of limiting what might otherwise seem the boundless area of application of art. 1384 par. 1, but the *Jand'heur* decision made it clear that nothing turns on the dangerousness of the harmful object.

For the details of the development by the courts see MAZEAUD/TUNC II nos. 1209 f., 1216 ff.—Today a pedal cycle which collides with a pedestrian (Paris 8 March 1934,

Gaz. Pal. 1934. 1. 943), a ski which comes off the skier's boot (Chambèry 15 Feb. 1944, Gaz. Pal. 1944. 1. 134), or a chair that a passer-by stumbles over (Civ. 24 Feb. 1941, S. 1941. 1. 201) are all agreed to be 'things' under art. 1384 par. 1 although clearly none of them is particularly dangerous.

Liability for physical harm caused by *fire* is pure fault liability, thanks to a special law of 1922, incorporated into the Code civil as art. 1384 par. 2. The victim must show that the fire was attributable to the fault of the defendant from whose premises or moveable property it arose, by proving, for example, that he stored inflammable material without adequate security precautions or that he failed to obey the instructions of the fire brigade.

See, for example, Civ. 5 May 1926, Gaz. Pal. 1926, 218; Civ. 23 March 1926, DP 1926. 1. 129 and the full details in Mazeaud/Tunc II nos. 1329 ff. and Brochet, Gaz. Pal. 1961. 1. Doctr. 55.

2. If a vehicle leaves the highway and crashes into a wall, it would be absurd to say that the wall is a 'thing' which causes harm under art. 1384 par. 1. In order to prevent its application in such cases, the French courts have laid down a further condition for liability under art. 1384 par. 1, namely that the thing should not have played a 'purely passive role' in the production of the harm but that it must have been a 'productive cause of the damage'. Thanks to this limiting criterion, art. 1384 par. 1 does not apply to cases in which one cannot speak, as art. 1384 par. 1 itself does, of the harm being caused by the 'act' of the thing, because the thing, though participating in the occurrence of the harm, was in its normal place and normal condition at the time.

Thus if there is a collision between a moving vehicle and a properly parked car, the presumption of responsibility enacted by art. 1384 par. 1 does not attach to the custodian of the car. But if the collision takes place at night and the car was inadequately lit or was parked in a place of poor visibility, even the stationary car can be seen as a 'productive cause of the harm'. If the motor vehicle was in motion at the time of the accident, this is almost always the case, but even here one can imagine exceptions: a cyclist injured in a collision with a truck cannot sue the *gardien* of the truck if at the time of the accident it was travelling at a proper speed on the correct side of the road (see, for example, Civ. 26 Oct. 1949, Gaz. Pal. 1950. 1. 79). Art. 1384 par. 1 is not applicable if a person falls unconscious against a central heating radiator of standard temperature and burns himself on it (Civ. 19 Feb. 1941, S. 1941. 1. 49), or falls on a perfectly safe stairway (Civ. 18 July 1939, Gaz. Pal. 1940. 1. 54), or slips on a properly maintained marble floor in a hotel (Req. 28 July 1941, S. 1941. 1. 206) or stumbles over a basket of wine-bottles set out on the sidewalk by the vintner for normal display purposes (Paris 14 Jan. 1935, Gaz. Pal. 1935. 2. 157): the radiator, the stairway, the marble floor, and the basket of wine bottles played a 'purely passive' role in the occurrence of the harm. It is different, however, if a customer entering a restaurant in the dark falls over a chair outside it and injures himself (Civ. 24 Feb. 1941, S. 1941. 1. 201); in this case the chair can be regarded as a cause of the harm because it was in an unusual position. It must be admitted that the courts have hereby introduced the fault notion to a certain extent into liability under art. 1384 par. 1, for proof that the thing was in a normal condition at the time of the harm is often tantamount to proof that the custodian was not at fault.

3. A further requirement for liability under art. 1384 par. 1 is that the person being sued for damages be the custodian ('gardien') of the thing which caused the harm.

According to the decision of the Chambres Réunies of the Cour de Cassation of 2 Dec. 1941 (DC 1942, J. 25) a person is 'gardien' of a thing if on the facts he has the use, management, and control of it ('usage, direction et contrôle'), that is, if he has the power of physical disposition over it. Generally this is the owner, but the owner may be able to show that he transferred the custody ('garde') of the thing to someone else, either pursuant to a contract of lease or services or by some purely factual act. Thus an owner who allows his employee to use a vehicle retains custody as long as the employee is using the vehicle in the scope of his employment, but if the employee takes it on an unpermitted trip, the custody of the vehicle passes from the employer (see Req. 8 Oct. 1940, Gaz. Pal. 1940. 2. 65); the owner also loses custody of a vehicle if it is stolen (Ch. réun. 2 Dec. 1941, DC 1942. J. 25) or if he takes it to a garage for repair (Civ. 8 May 1964, Gaz. Pal. 1964. 2. 362).

The French courts have difficulties with cases in which a thing causes damage during transportation. The 'liquid oxygen' case is a famous instance. Here the defendant company had filled a number of its bottles with liquid oxygen under pressure and had handed them to a carrier for delivery to a customer. When the bottles were being unloaded in the customer's factory one of them exploded and injured two workmen, who now claimed damages.

The Court of Appeal at Poitiers originally held that the carrier was the custodian of the bottles (29 Oct. 1952, JCP 1952. II. 7410), but this decision was quashed by the Court of Cassation and remained to the Court of Appeal of Angers, with an instruction to find out 'if the person to whom the custody of the thing was said to have been transferred had not only the use of the thing which caused the harm but also the power to look after it and to check all its components' (Civ. 5 Jan. 1956, D. 1957, 261). The Angers Court of Appeal again decided against the carrier (15 May 1957, JCP 1957. II. 10058) and the case came before the Court of Cassation once more, which finally declared that the defendant owner was the custodian (Civ. 10 June 1960, D. 1960, 609).

The Court of Cassation's position therefore seems to be that the owner of a bottle of gas which explodes while being carried by an independent contractor is still its 'gardien' and is liable on that basis if, as in this case, the explosion was caused not by the handling or unloading of the bottle but by an undiscovered fault in its construction. Many people think that a distinction must be drawn between control of the *handling* of the thing (*garde du comportement de la chose*) and control over the *construction* of the thing (*garde de la structure de la chose*); the first attached to the carrier, the latter to the owner of the bottle. In each case the judge must decide whether the damage was due to the handling of the thing or to a fault in its construction.

The following writers in particular have espoused this view: GOLDMAN, *Mélanges Roubier* II (1961) 51; TUNC, *JCP* 1957. I. 384, *JCP* 1960. I. 1952 and *Rev. trim. dr. civ.* 59 (1961) 125 ff., and MAZEAUD, *Rev. trim. dr. civ.* 55 (1957) 529.—ESMEIN, JCP 1960. II. 11824, also approves of the decision of the Court of Cassation on the ground, *inter alia*, that it makes good sense from the insurance point of view, since the premiums are much easier to work out if liability insurance is taken out not by the carrier but by the person who normally uses such bottles as containers for his products. The courts sometimes use the distinction between 'garde du comportement' and 'garde de la structure' in cases of products liability. A person who is injured when a bottle of mineral water explodes can use art. 1384 par. 1 against the manufacturer who bottled the water: certainly the manufacturer has relinquished possession of the bottle, but he remains its *gardien* so far as its internal structure goes, especially for faults in the material. See Poitiers, 23 Dec. 1969, Gaz. Pal. 1970. 2. 13; Civ. 12 Nov. 1975, JCP 1976. II. 18479, noted by VINEY.

4. Liability under art. 1384 par. 1 is excluded if the custodian of the thing can prove that the harm was due to *cas fortuit* or *force majeure*, these expressions being synonymous in the view of the French courts.

According to the cases, an event constitutes *cas fortuit* or *force majeure* if it is external to the thing which does the harm and is both unforeseeable and unavoidable in its consequences. (Civ. 2 July 1946, D. 1946, 392.)

One important effect of the rule that the cause must be 'external' or 'outside' the thing which does the harm is that a latent defect in the thing, such as a defect in the way it is made or the material it is made of, does not release the defendant even if it was quite impossible for him to discover and remove the defect. This rule is applied in cases in which an automobile accident is caused by something internal which the custodian could not have foreseen such as a sudden failure of brakes or steering or by the blowout of a tyre.

See for example, Paris 18 July 1930, DH 1930, 530; Req. 22 Jan. 1945, S. 1945. 1. 57; Civ. 6 March 1959, Gaz. Pal. 1959. 2. 12. Liability is also imposed if without any fault on his part a driver loses consciousness at the wheel (see Civ. 18 Dec. 1964, D. 1965, 191).

If the cause of the harm is 'external' to the thing in this sense, a further requirement is that the custodian should not have been able to foresee it even if he was exercising all the requisite care. Most decisions deal with cases in which the custodian of a motor vehicle argued that the unexpected occurrence of a patch of oil on a highway (Civ. 28 Oct. 1965, D. 1966, 137, noted by TUNC) or of black ice (Civ. 7 Mar. 1957, D. 1957, 394) constituted *force majeure*. It was only rarely that the courts admitted this defence, and it has now been completely abolished by the Law on Traffic Accidents of 5 July 1985 (see below).

Natural events are only regarded as *force majeure* if they occur with unforeseeable suddenness and irresistible violence and the custodian in the case could not possibly or reasonably have taken the steps required to prevent the harm (see MAZEAUD/TUNC II nos. 1607 f., citing many decisions). In such a case the custodian is freed from liability entirely, but if the 'fait de la chose' contributed to the harm, courts have been known to make the *gardien* liable for an appropriate *part* of the harm only (Com. 19 June 1951, D. 1951, 717, noted by RIPERT).

It follows from the *Jand'heur* decision that liability under art. 1384 par. 1 is excluded if the cause of the harm is the *faulty conduct of the victim*, though only when the fault of the victim was so serious as to constitute, from the point of view of the *gardien*, 'force majeure', rendering the accident 'imprévisible et irrésistible'. But the courts soon held that even when the fault of the victim did not constitute 'force majeure', it might lead to a *reduction* of his claim for damages, rather than an exclusion of it. The courts therefore examined the extent to which in the circumstances of the individual case the harm was due to the fault of the victim on the one hand and the 'conduct' of the thing on the other. Indeed some cases have held that the victim's claim can be reduced even when, as in the case of a minor, the conduct was not negligent at all. Writers were very critical of this, and pointed out that if, as is usually the case, the defendant is the *gardien* of a motor vehicle, he is required to be covered by liability insurance. (See Civ. 17 Dec. 1963, D. 1964, I. 158, noted by TUNC; criticized with further references by VINEY (above p. 687) 508 ff., DURRY, *Études dédiées à Alex Weill* (1983) 217.)

All these rules have since been scattered to the winds by a decision of the Cour de Cassation followed by legislation. In the *Desmares* case (Civ. 21 July 1982, D. 1982, 449, with conclusions by Avocat-général CHARBONNIER) the plaintiffs were struck by an automobile when they were crossing a road. The defendant insurer, held liable below, complained to the Cour de Cassation that the lower court had failed to inquire whether the plaintiffs' behaviour had been negligent, for in that case the amount of their claim should be reduced. The Cour de Cassation declared that the question was irrelevant: the *gardien* is not liable at all if the victim's conduct was 'imprévisible et irrésistible', but otherwise, as in the case at hand, he is liable *in full*. The decision, the full story of which is given by TUNC, *Essays in Memory of Professor Lawson* (1986) 71, was like a legal earthquake. About half of the courts of appeal in France simply refused to follow it. Some writers welcomed it as giving better protection to victims of traffic accidents, while others considered it a clear instance of legislation by judicial fiat, and all criticized it for failing to clarify its range of application. It was imperative that Parliament intervene. Building on the work done by various governmental commissions set up for the reform of traffic accident compensation since the mid-sixties, mainly at the instance of ANDRÉ TUNC, the Law 85–677 of 5 July 1985 was passed with near unanimity. Its main thrust was drastically to limit the extent to which the negligence of a traffic accident victim may reduce his claim for bodily injury or death. No such reduction is admissible if the victim is under 16 or over 70 years old, or if he is disabled as to 80 per cent or more. Other victims' claims are affected only if their conduct amounts to a 'faute inexcusable' which is also the 'cause exclusive de l'accident'. If the victim is a driver, however, the Law does not protect him. This gap has been very successfully filled by the insurance industry which has marketed a new type of accident insurance covering drivers and their families. TUNC (ibid.) estimates that as a result of the legislation and the new type of accident insurance, compensation in 85 per cent or even 90 per cent of all accident cases will now be independent of the negligence of tortfeasor and victim. It is still technically correct to speak of a system of tort 'liability' for traffic accidents. In substance, however, tort liability has been largely replaced by a system of insurance protection. On this see below VI.

5. Whether liability under art. 1384 par. 1 is still an instance of liability for fault is a question which is much debated by commentators in France even today. A number of older writers, especially SALEILLES and JOSSERAND, held that it was not. In their view the cardinal reason for transferring a loss to the person who caused it was not the fact that he was at fault but the fact that society had an objective social interest in requiring compensation for the harm: such an interest normally existed if the conduct of a perfectly permissible business created a risk of harm to third parties uninvolved in it, and the operator who sought to profit from his enterprise must accept the risks of harm intrinsic to it regardless of whether he or any of his assistants might be to blame in a particular instance. These writers called this doctrine the 'théorie du risque créé' and held that it underlay act. 1384 par. 1 Code civil.

This view has not prevailed in France. The great modern writers on the law of delict, especially the MAZEAUD brothers and ANDRÉ TUNC, think that the French law of liability still rests on the pricinple of fault. This is admittedly not easy to reconcile with the liability for things imposed by art. 1384 par. 1. They argue that the provision imposes an 'obligation de résultat' on the custodian of a thing, a duty to prevent the thing escaping from his control ('que la chose échappe au contrôle matériel de son gardien'). If the thing does escape from the control of the custodian this *ipso facto* constitutes a 'faute dans la garde' even if in the particular case there is no evidence of any reprehensible conduct on the custodian's part (see MAZEAUD/TUNC II nos. 1312 ff., 1318).

Turning from this doctrinal dispute among French writers, we have to say that liability under art. 1384 par. 1 Code civil is truly strict liability in so far as the harm is due to a defect in the construction of the thing or to some failure of its components, but if the thing behaved properly and there was no malfunction, the custodian of the thing is only liable on the basis of a presumption: if he can prove that no fault attached to him or those for whom he was responsible and that every possible precaution in the circumstances was taken, then the cause of the harm, whether it be the behaviour of the victim or of a third party or *force majeure*, is 'normally unforeseeable' and he is released from liability (see MAZEAUD/TUNC II nos. 1328–4 f., 1653, 1665).

As construed by the French courts, therefore, art. 1384 par. 1 Code civil contains elements of fault liability and elements of strict liability. Liability is imposed regardless of fault if the harm was caused by a defect in the thing or a failure to operate properly or if the cause of the harm remains unexplained; in other cases the custodian may succeed by proving that he was not at fault, though this proof is extremely difficult to establish, and has recently been abolished altogether in traffic accidents.

6. Of the other legal systems which have been influenced by the French Code civil we can here take a quick look only at *Italy* and, because of an interesting legislative proposal, *Holland* (for more detail with further references, see ZWEIGERT/KÖTZ (above p. 688) 20 ff., 54 f.).

The Italian Codice civile, apart from imposing liability on the custodian of an animal and the owner of a building (arts. 2052 f.), makes the driver and custodian of a motor vehicle strictly liable, in a manner akin to §7 St VG: it is impossible to escape liability for harm caused by a fault in construction or maintenance but in other cases exoneration is possible if the defendant did everything possible ('tutto il possibile') to avoid the accident (see art. 2054). Furthermore, if harm is caused by a thing art. 2051 Codice civile imposes liability on the person who had control of it: this provision is the direct descendant of art. 1384 par. 1 Code civil and is construed and applied in much the same manner. The Code civile strikes out on a path of its own by imposing liability under art. 2050 on a person who conducts an activity which is *dangerous* either in itself or by reason of the materials it uses: if harm is caused in the execution of such an 'attività pericolosa' the operator is liable in damages unless he can prove that he took all the precautions which might have avoided the harm. Although this might appear to be a liability for presumed fault, the courts in fact apply the same standards to this exculpatory proof as they do in a case of liability for things. There is therefore no practical difference between liability for things under art. 2051 and liability for dangerous activities under art. 2050, but having an alternative ground of liability does allow the Italian courts to adopt a more flexible approach, for if the harm is caused by the fall of a high tension electric cable, they can say that this harm was caused by the dangerous *activity* of transmitting electricity and are not forced to say, as the French courts rather animistically do, that the harm was caused by a *thing*, namely the falling cable.

IV

1. In *English* law a person can hardly ever claim damages for personal injury or property damage without having to prove breach of a duty of care, though there are a few instances where Parliament has imposed strict liability: on the owner of an airplane for damage caused by it on the surface of the earth (Civil Aviation Act 1982), on the producer or user of atomic energy (Nuclear Installations Act 1965), and on a person who stores gas underground (Gas Act 1965). Under certain circumstances the keeper of an animal may be liable without fault for damage done by it (Animals Act 1971).

Britain has no special law imposing strict liability on the custodian of a *motor vehicle*. But while the French courts have improved the rights of the traffic victim by developing the strict liability of the *gardien* of a chattel under art. 1384 par. 1 Code civil, England still applies the general rules of negligence at Common Law. It is true that after 1930, when owners of motor vehicles were required to have liability insurance, the courts began 'in cases where the plaintiff excited their compassion . . . to twist the law of negligence to make a defendant liable for negligence when he was really not negligent at all, to make his insurers pay' (SPENCER (above p. 687) 80). So a learner driver who had just obtained a provisional licence has been held to be acting negligently in not displaying the care of an experienced driver (*Nettleship* v. *Weston*, [1971] 2 QB 691), and a truck-owner has been held liable for a defect in the brakes which no layman could ever have discovered (*Henderson* v. *Jenkins & Sons*, [1970] AC 282). Even so, cases constantly crop up such that with the best will in the world one cannot find any negligence. Many people find this unsatisfactory. LORD DENNING has written:

'In the present state of motor traffic, I am persuaded that any civilised system of law should require, as a matter of principle, that the person who uses this dangerous instrument on the roads—dealing death and destruction all around—should be liable to make compensation to anyone who is killed or injured in consequence of the use of it. There should be liability without proof of fault. To require an injured person to prove fault results in the gravest injustice to many innocent persons who have not the wherewithal to prove it' (*What Next in the Law?* (1982) 128). The Royal [Pearson] Commission on Civil Liability and Compensation for Personal Injury agreed that reform was urgently required, but instead of simply proposing that vehicle-owners be made strictly liable in tort, it advocated the abandonment of tort law altogether and its replacement by a system of compensation run by the state (see below VI). This may be right, but it is so radical a step that it is most unlikely to be taken in England for a long time yet, so the situation where there is no liability unless there is negligence is likely to continue for some time. On this see the critical comments by SPENCER (above p. 687).

Only one case of strict liability has been developed by the English courts. This arises under the celebrated decision of *Rylands* v. *Fletcher* in 1868. Here the defendant was having a reservoir constructed on his land in order to power his mill. On the chosen site there were disused mine shafts, filled with earth, and they were connected with the underground mineworkings operated by the plaintiff on the neighbouring land, though the defendant had no means of knowing this. When the reservoir was filled, water flowed down the mine shafts and flooded the mine-workings next door. It could not be shown that the defendant was at fault at all, but he had to pay damages. The rule formulated by BLACKBURN, J. on appeal has since become classical: 'We think that the true rule of law is, that the person who for his own purposes brings on his lands and collects and keeps there anything likely to do mischief if it escapes, must keep it in at his peril, and, if he does not do so, is prima facie answerable for all the damage which is the natural consequence of its escape' (*Fletcher* v. *Rylands*, (1866) LR 1 Ex. 265).

This decision was upheld by the House of Lords in *Rylands* v. *Fletcher* (1868), LR 3 HL 330, with the addition of the further requirement that the storage of the thing must constitute a 'non-natural user' of the land.

This precedent became the source of many different lines of cases which can only be presented in outline here.

The rule in *Rylands* v. *Fletcher* applies not only to the escape of water but also to the escape of gas or electricity stored in bulk, normally for industrial purposes, on the defendant's land, and even to the escape of water or gas from pipes in which the defendant is conveying it over the land of others. The courts have also applied *Rylands* v. *Fletcher* in cases where harm was caused by detonations in a quarry, or by the explosion of dinitrophenol in an explosives factory or of petrol vapours in the empty tank of a parked bus. The rule may also be applied to *continuing* situations, as where poisonous gases are emitted from a factory.

See, for example, *Northwestern Utilities Ltd.* v. *London Guarantee and Accident Co.*, [1936] AC 108 (fracture of subterranean gas-pipes); *Rainham Chemical Works Ltd.* v. *Belvedere Fish Guano Co.*, [1921] 2 AC 465 (explosives); *Halsey* v. *Esso Petroleum Co. Ltd.*, [1961] 2 All ER 145 (sulphurous soot).

Liability does not arise unless the bringing of the damaging thing on to the defendant's land constitutes a 'non-natural user' of the land. As was said in *Rickards* v. *Lothian*, [1913] AC 263, 280, 'It must be some special use bringing with it increased danger to others, and must not merely be the ordinary use of the land or such a use as is proper for the general benefit of the community' (see the extended treatment in STALLYBRASS, 3 *Camb. LJ* 376 ff. (1929) and GOODHART, 4 *Camb. LJ* 13 ff. (1930)).

A claim under *Rylands* v. *Fletcher* will consequently fail if water or gas escapes from standard domestic piping or if harm is caused by defective electric wiring in a house or business premises or by a fault of a theatre's sprinkler system. An additional ground for the dismissal of a claim under *Rylands* v. *Fletcher* in such cases may be that the tenant consented to the risk of accidental defects in the utilities in the leased premises and must therefore base any claim on 'negligence'.

Another requirement for liability under *Rylands* v. *Fletcher* is that the harm must have been caused by an 'escape' of the thing: the harmful thing must have left the area under the defendant's control and have caused the harm outside it. This criterion used to be very loosely applied by courts of first instance.

When a hotel suffered from vibrations caused by pile-driving in the vicinity, no fault needed to be proved: *Hoare* v. *McAlpine*, [1923] 1 Ch. 167.—In *Attorney-General v. Corke*, [1933] Ch. 89 a landowner had allowed gypsies to live in their caravans on his land and was held liable to his neighbours for the harm they caused by 'swarming' over their land.—Liability was also imposed on the operator of a fair-ground when a seat flew off a spinning carrousel and injured a person standing nearby (*Hale* v. *Jennings Bros.*, [1938] 1 All ER 579).

The breadth of such decisions was critized by commentators and a subsequent decision by the House of Lords considerably limited their scope as precedents.

In 1942 when the plaintiff was working in the defendant's munitions factory she was injured in an explosion which occurred in the factory during working hours. She claimed damages from her employer. It was no bar to the claim that the harm was caused by an accident at work, since under the English law then in force the workman might elect between suing the employer for damages under the general law of tort or claiming social security benefits (Workmen's Compensation Act, 1925, ss. 29 f., now repealed). The plaintiff based her claim exclusively on liability under *Rylands* v. *Fletcher* and neither alleged nor offered to prove that the defendant was at fault in any way. The trial judge gave judgment for the plaintiff, but the Court of Appeal reversed (*Read* v. *J. Lyons & Co. Ltd.*, [1945] KB 216). In a judgment of principle the House of Lords confirmed the dismissal of the plaintiff's claim (*Read* v. *J. Lyons & Co. Ltd.*, [1947] AC 156), on the ground that the harm did not result from any 'escape' from the defendant's land but occurred entirely within his factory. The House of Lords was not impressed by the obvious objection that it could hardly make any difference whether the plaintiff was hurt just before or just after she entered the factory gates ([1947] AC 156, 177 f.).

No claim arises under *Rylands* v. *Fletcher* if the harm was caused by an Act of God. By this the courts understand an exceptional event caused by natural powers which is quite unforeseeable and whose effects cannot be prevented. The courts have often said that even an unusually severe storm or a remarkably heavy fall of rain or snow does not amount to an 'Act of God': apparently the only case in which liability under *Rylands* v. *Fletcher* has been negatived on the ground of Act of God involved rainfall 'greater and more violent than any within the memory of witnesses' (*Nichols* v. *Marsland*, (1876) 2 Ex. D. 1).

In its Report the Royal [Pearson] Commission on Civil Liability and Compensation for Personal Injury (Cmnd. 7054 (1978)) recommended that new instances of strict liability be introduced by statute and imposed on railway undertakings, manufacturers of defective products, and those giving experimental treatment or drugs to 'human guinea-pigs'. In addition, strict liability should be imposed on the controllers of things or operations in two categories, those which are of an unusually hazardous nature and those which, though normally safe, are likely, if they go wrong, to cause serious and extensive harm. It would be for the relevant Minister, acting by statutory instrument, to decide which installations and activities should attract this strict liability, as the 'process of judical legislation' would inevitably be tedious.

2. The principle underlying *Rylands* v. *Fletcher* is generally accepted in the *United States* as well: indeed, the American courts seem to be in the process of freeing it from the restrictive conditions of liability laid down in the leading decision and expanding it into a general strict liability for particularly hazardous activities. Many courts still cite *Rylands* v. *Fletcher*, but others establish an identical or similar principle without mentioning the case by name. For this purpose some of the several states have used the tort of 'nuisance', which mainly covers cases of continuing harm caused by gases, steam, smells, and so on, though it is occasionally applicable to sudden and isolated occurrences such as explosions (see PROSSER, 'Nuisance without Fault', 20 *Texas L. Rev.* 399 (1942)). Finally the courts have occasionally invoked the Restatement. Restatement (Second) of Torts (1977) §519 contains a general rule imposing strict liability on a person who causes harm through an 'abnormally dangerous' activity: 'One who carries on an abnormally dangerous activity is subject to liability for harm to the person, land or chattels of another resulting from the activity, although he has exercised the utmost care to prevent the harm'.

Whether an activity is 'abnormally dangerous' or not depends on factors listed in §520: whether it involves a high risk of some harm or some risk of great harm, whether such risk could be eliminated with reasonable care, and whether the activity is one of common usage, or appropriate to the locality, or of sufficient social utility.

The cases in which American defendants have been held liable on such grounds are very much like those in England. They involve storing large quantities of water in tanks or reservoirs, keeping explosives or inflammable liquids in bulk, operating drilling devices in built-up areas, and using poisonous chemicals as pesticides. Strict liability is also imposed if explosions project fragments of stone on to the land of third parties or cause vibration damage to their buildings. By contract, suppliers of gas or electricity are not normally subject to strict liability; the custodian of a motor car and the operator of a railway are also usually liable only for negligence, and this is true in most states even of the owner of an airplane which causes damage on the surface of the earth.

Even towards his passengers the owner of an airplane is liable only for negligence unless it is 'international carriage' under the Warsaw Convention of 1929 (to which the United States has now acceded) when liability is virtually strict, though limited in amount.

In deciding whether or not to impose strict liability for the harm done by an activity, business, or situation, the American courts always take account of any special circumstances in the locality which may have rendered it especially dangerous. This is the same idea as leads English courts to deny liability under *Rylands* v. *Fletcher* for 'natural' uses of land, but it seems to have particular importance in the United States because of the vast differences between different localities in terms of population and degree of industrialization. The consideration that the defendant was in an industry of special economic importance may also affect the courts, though they do not always admit it.

Thus in *Turner* v. *Big Lake Oil Co.*, 128 Tex. 115, 96 SW. 2d 222 (1936) the defendant oil company had on its land great basins for the reception of salt water from their wells. The edge of one of these basins gave way, and the escaping water caused serious harm to the plaintiffs. The defendant, who was not shown to have been guilty of any fault, was held not liable, because the court found that the rule of *Rylands* v. *Fletcher* was not applicable. One of the principal reasons given for this by the court was that in Texas, where the extraction of oil was one of the most important industries and there were thousands of oilwells, there was nothing non-natural about keeping salt water in basins, since that was an unavoidable incident of drilling for oil.—Further examples are given by PROSSER, 'The Principle of Rylands v. Fletcher' (above p. 687) 163, 170 ff., 186 ff.

Strict liability does not attach if the harm is due to an act of God or the unforeseeable intervention of a third party for whose behaviour the defendant is not answerable.

V

It emerges from our comparative survey that the tendency of the law of tort in all the legal systems investigated has been to improve the position of victims by restricting or even abandoning the principle of 'no liability without fault'. This tendency is stronger and more marked in certain types of accident than in others. Various reasons can be given: that the victims of certain types of accident deserve particular protection, that certain unusual risks are acceptable only if liability is particularly strict, that in certain types of case fault is especially difficult to prove, that the risk of certain accidents is especially easy to insure against, and that the premiums paid by the party at risk can very easily be disseminated. Industrial accidents provide the best-known example: here the long-standing practice has been not to increase liability in favour of the victim but rather to do away with it entirely and replace it with a system of social insurance. For *traffic accidents* also most countries have a specially strict liability, and many legislatures, appalled by the thalidomide tragedy, have enacted special rules for compensating those injured by *defective drugs* (see the comparative study by FLEMING, 'Drug Injury Compensation Plans', 30 *Am. J. Comp. L.* 297 (1982)). For accidents arising from the operation of a *nuclear installation* traditional rules of liability for fault have been abandoned everywhere (comparative treatment by OLLIER, XI *Int. Enc. Comp. L.* 'Torts' (1983) Ch. 5 §§214–25). But we turn now to an interesting and important type of case which attracts a particularly strict regime of liability, the case where a person suffers personal injury in consequence of a *defective product*.

What is of special importance is whether the victim has any claim *against the manufacturer*. To have such a claim is of very considerable interest to the victim, for while he may well have an action against the seller if the product was one that he had purchased, his rights will be determined by the contract of sale, and the terms of that contract may exclude or qualify any right to compensation, or subject it to a monetary limit, a short period of limitation, or a requirement of notice. Furthermore in many legal systems the liability of a seller depends on his being at fault with regard to the defect in the goods, and if the seller is merely a cog in the manufacturer's distributive system it may not be easy to establish any such fault on his part, especially as sellers often lack the technical expertise required to test the safety of complex pieces of apparatus before delivering them to the customer. But there is another reason for making the manufacturer directly liable, namely that the defect may cause harm to someone other than the purchaser, perhaps a member of his family or even a complete stranger in the vicinity. A pedestrian on the sidewalk who is injured when a car leaves the road because of a defective axle or a patron in a pub who is struck by flying glass when a defective bottle of mineral water explodes at the next table will be interested in suing the manufacturer of the car and the bottle which they have not themselves bought.

Policy reasons for imposing strict liability on the manufacturer of defective goods are not far to seek. Today as never before, thanks to the modern division of labour, people need and want to use products whose safety they themselves are in no position to check. This being so, the public must be able to rely on being able to use such products without injury to themselves or their property, all the more so as manufacturers deliberately and for commercial gain direct their advertising so as to induce consumers to count on the excellence of their wares. It is accordingly unacceptable that the consumer who without any fault on his own part is injured by a defect in the goods should be left uncompensated just because he cannot prove any lack of care on the part of the manufacturer, as normally he cannot when production is automated. But if such a victim is to have a claim for damages at all, it is only right that it should lie against the manufacturer: not only because he controls the manufacturing process and, usually, the advertisement of the product on the market, but also because he can insure against this risk most cheaply and pass on the cost to all his consumers by taking the premiums into account when he is pricing his goods.

It was the courts in the United States that led the field in developing products liability. Ever since the decision in *MacPherson* v. *Buick* (above p. 652) it has been agreed that the manufacturer of goods owes a duty of care not only to the person to whom he sells them but also to any third party injured by their use. The victim thus had a claim in negligence. But such a claim only succeeds if the victim can prove that the manufacturer was at fault, in breach of his duty of care. With the help of the courts this obstacle has been overcome. First the courts went to the law of contract and enlisted the aid of the warranty from the law of sales. Now in the Common Law a claim for breach of warranty is one of strict liability and it entitles the purchaser to full damages and not simply, as is normally the rule in German law, to a diminution or the return of the price he has paid. On the other hand, a claim for breach of warranty in principle lies only against the person with whom the injured buyer contracted, that is, the retailer, and it can be brought only by the buyer himself and not by members of his family, guests, or other persons who may be injured by the defective goods. The courts therefore sought to extend the protection of the manufacturer's contractual guarantee so as to include the final consumer, his family, and others close to him. Sometimes they spoke of 'warranties running with the goods'; sometimes they found it unduly formalistic to restrict the claim for breach of warranty to adjacent parties when there was a chain of sales and gave the final consumer a direct claim against the manufacturer as a 'permissible short-cut' which saved time and money. Such ideas were first used in cases of bad food, then in cases of products designed for intimate bodily use such as soap, hair-dyes, clothes, cigarettes, vaccines, and so on, and finally wherever the goods would be dangerous to the user if defective, such as cars, car-tyres, domestic appliances, heating appliances, and so on. The Uniform Commercial Code has adopted this position (§2-318). But a contractual claim for breach of warranty had the further drawback that it could be affected by the terms of the contract of sale. Here too the courts used all the weapons at their command, deploying the device of restrictive construction *contra proferentem* and sometimes even holding that the exemption clause in issue was contrary to public policy and void (see *Henningsen* v. *Bloomfield Motors Inc.*, 32 NJ 358, 161 A. 2d 69 (1960)).

Contractual principles are still occasionally used in the United States, but the general view now is that when a consumer is injured by an objectively defective product, the strict liability of the manufacturer should be cut free from the law of contract and based openly on tort. It is now a '*strict liability in tort*'.

First pointers in this direction were *Escola* v. *Coca-Cola Bottling Co.*, 24 Cal. 2d 453, 150 P. 2d 436 (1944; see especially the opinion of JUDGE TRAYNOR); *Greenman* v. *Yuba Power Products Inc.*, 59 Cal. 2d 57, 377 P. 2d 897 (1963).

The breakthrough occurred in 1965 when Restatement (Second) of Torts was published, with the following §402 A:

(1) One who sells any product in a defective condition unreasonably dangerous to the user or consumer or to his property is subject to liability for physical harm thereby caused to the ultimate user or consumer, or to his property, if
  (*a*) the seller is engaged in the business of selling such a product, and
  (*b*) it is expected to and does reach the user or consumer without substantial change in the condition in which it is sold.
(2) The rule stated in Subsection (1) applies although
  (*a*) the seller has exercised all possible care in the preparation and sale of his product, and
  (*b*) the user or consumer has not bought the product from or entered into any contractual relation with the seller.

Courts in most of the states have adopted this rule in one form or another. The component elements have been more closely specified and in many respects the protection afforded to the victim has been improved. In particular it is agreed that 'innocent bystanders', that is persons who are not part of the distributive chain but who find themselves by mishap in proximity to the defective product, can base a claim on products liability. Furthermore the courts allow suits against not only the manufacturer but also wholesale and retail distributors, suppliers of defective components for incorporation into an end-product by a manufacturer, those who lease or hire out defective products (*Price* v. *Shell Oil Co.*, 2 Cal. 3d 245, 466 P. 2d 722 (1970)), and finally those who purchase the actual manufacturer's business and then engage in the manufacture of similar products (*Ray* v. *Alad Corp.*, 19 Cal. 3d 22, 560 P. 2d 3 (1977)). In exceptional cases, indeed, the plaintiff may win even although it is not established *who* produced the defective product.

The plaintiff in *Sindell* v. *Abbott Laboratories*, 26 Cal. 3d 588, 607 P. 2d 924 (1980) had suffered physical injury because her mother, while pregnant with her, had taken the drug DES which is harmful to the foetus. Claim was brought against a few of the 200-odd firms which produced DES at the time and used it in their products. The plaintiff was unable to prove which of the defendants had produced the pills her mother had taken years before, and it was quite possible that none of the defendants had made them; nevertheless the court decided in the plaintiff's favour and held that the defendants must pay damages in proportion to their share of the DES market at the time.

The central question in products liability cases is whether the goods were *defective* at the time the defendant put them into circulation; it is no longer relevant whether or not the defendant was guilty of any negligence. Thus the plaintiff's position is better than in a negligence case, but not so much better as one might at first suppose. Certainly the plaintiff's position is better when there is a *manufacturing defect*, where a defective example of an otherwise sound product has somehow slipped through, for liability is established simply by proof of the defect. Such cases are, however, fairly uncommon. More often the case involves a *design defect*, where the plaintiff alleges that the entire output of a particular product of the defendant's, be it a car, a lawnmower, a heater, or whatever, has a defective design or that the entire batch of a particular drug or food product has noxious side-effects.

Is it a defect in a caterpillar tractor if the rear-view mirror is so placed in relation to the driver's seat that when he sits back there is a 'blind spot' (*Pike* v. *Frank G. Hough & Co.*, 2 Cal. 3d 465, 467 P. 2d 229 (1970))? Is it a defect in an automobile if the petrol tank is not in the best place to minimize the risk of getting damaged and letting out petrol which may catch fire? Is there a design defect in a truck if it has no grid at the rear to prevent a car sliding under it in a rear-end collision (*Mieher* v. *Brown*, 54 Ill. 2d 539, 301 NE 2d 307 (1974))? The critical question here is whether, given the state of technical knowledge at the time, some safer method of construction was possible and should have been adopted. It will be seen that many of the relevant facts and considerations are the same as in a claim based on negligence. It is undecided whether the relevant state of the art is to be judged as of the time the product was manufactured or whether the manufacturer is liable for 'development risks' as well, that is, is liable if safer methods of construction are devised after the harm has occurred. The same question arises where liability is based on a *fault of instruction*. Is the manufacturer liable if he fails to draw the customer's attention to dangers in the product which, although evident today, were quite unknown when the product was put into circulation? The practice of the courts varies here. Cases where the court applied the state of the art at the time of the judgment are *Bailey* v. *Boatland of Houston Inc.*, 585 SW 2d 805 (Tex. Civ. App. 1979; fault of construction); and *Beshada* v. *Johns-Manville Products Corp.*, 19 NJ 191, 447 A. 2d 539 (1982; fault of instruction).

The number of 'products liability' cases decided by American courts is now stupendous, and the number of publications and multi-volume loose-leaf services on the subject testify to the enormous interest of practising lawyers in this area. Vertiginous sums are often awarded to successful plaintiffs, and European observers are also surprised when the manufacturer of a single product which has been used with apparent safety for many years is faced with thousands of claims when its adverse effects are finally discovered.

According to a Report in 1983, there were about 5,000 claims outstanding against the manufacturers of DES and about 16,000 claims against manufacturers of asbestos, two of which, both well-known and flourishing firms, have gone into liquidation after discovering that their probable liabilities exceeded their assets: see DWORKIN, 'Federal Reform of Product Liability Law', 57 *Tul. L. Rev.* 602, 627 ff. (1983), and now RUBIN, Mass Torts and Litigation Disasters, 20 *Ga. L Rev.* 429 (1986). The size of the damages awards is explicable in part by the fact that in American courts, which take personal injury claims very seriously, the damages are awarded by a jury, which favours the plaintiff in a case of doubt (see vol. I, Ch. 20 V). Furthermore, punitive damages may be awarded in cases where the manufacturer has been particularly careless. One should add that, as the jury well knows, the plaintiff's attorney handles the case on a contingent fee basis, normally taking at least 30 per cent of the damages. Circumstances are clearly quite different in the United States, but even there thought has been given to introducing legislation in order to curb the excesses. See DWORKIN (above p. 340).

Special rules for the liability of the manufacturer of products have been developed by courts in Europe as well. *France* shows that to a large extent one can achieve the desirable sharpening of liability by extending claims in contract. Under art. 1645 Code civil the seller of defective goods must compensate the buyer for all harm due to the defect if he *knew* of the defect in the object sold. The French courts have repeatedly laid down 'que doit être assimilé au vendeur qui connaissait les vices de la chose celui qui par sa profession ne pouvait les ignorer' (Civ. 17 Feb. 1965, Bull. civ. 1965. III. 112). This means that anyone who has sold defective wares in the course of his business, whether as manufacturer, wholesaler, or retailer, is treated as if he had been aware of the defect. From this it follows not only that he is liable to the purchaser for all the harm resulting therefrom, but also that he is barred by art. 1643 Code civil from excluding this strict liability by any term he may put in the contract. Now this being a contractual liability, the ultimate consumer can in principle sue only the retailer from whom he bought the thing, but of course the retailer, if sued, can immediately bring an 'appel en garantie' against the wholesaler for an indemnity in respect of any liability to the consumer, for the wholesaler's liability is equally strict, and the wholesaler in his turn can sue the manufacturer on the same basis, with the result that the chain of purchasers is 'wound in' and at the end of the day the manufacturer pays and the consumer is paid without any fault being proved. 'Pour éviter cette cascade de recours' the courts have allowed the final purchaser to leapfrog over his predecessor in title, who may be insolvent or out of the jurisdiction, and sue the first seller, normally the manufacturer, directly. (See Civ. 5 Jan. 1972, JCP 1973. II. 17340, noted by MALINVAUD; 9 Oct. 1979, Bull. civ. 1979. I. 192.)

The only victims in France who need to sue in *tort* are 'innocent bystanders' who stand outside the chain of purchasers. The courts have been very helpful to these plaintiffs as well. Often the courts rely on arts. 1382 f. Code civil, on the assumption that the manufacturer is *ipso facto* at fault if he puts a defective product into commerce or fails to give proper instructions about its use. In other cases they use art. 1384 Code civil; of course the manufacturer no longer has the defective thing in his actual control, but he can still be regarded as the 'gardien' of its construction, that is its being free from hidden defects (see Civ. 12 Nov. 1975, JCP 1976. II. 18479, noted by VINEY, and above p. 703). Alternatively, if the victim thinks fit, he may sue the owner of the thing as *gardien* under art. 1384, and since the owner is normally the last purchaser he can, as we have already seen, 'wind in' the chain of purchasers and see to it that liability ends up with the manufacturer.

In *Germany* there was a long period of doubt whether to base the manufacturer's liability on the tort provisions of the BGB or on the manufacturer's special, nearly contractual relationship with the consumer, one argument in favour of the latter being that by advertising his wares with brand names, trade marks, or indications of quality and by devising a distribution system which reduces the intermediary to a mere conduit, the manufacturer gives the impression, even a guarantee, that the consumer can rely on the quality of the product.

The Oberster Gerichtshof in *Austria* took the contractual route, and held that the contract of sale between the manufacturer and the first buyer was 'a contract with protective effect for anyone who draws his entitlement from a chain of further contracts, whether of sale or service'. This is because the manufacturer must know that after passing along the chain of sales his product 'finally reaches a consumer who in reliance on there being no defect in the thing he has bought allows his legal interests to be affected by it'. (OGH 4 Feb. 1976, *JBl.* 1977, 146, noted by RUMMEL, and OGH 28 Nov. 1978, *JBl.* 1979, 483; 8 May 1979, *JBl.* 1979, 653.) This contractual solution had the advantage of rendering the manufacturer liable for the fault of his employees as if it were his own (§1313 *a* ABGB), a stricter liability than existed in a mere tort claim (see §1315 ABGB), but it had the disadvantages that an exclusion of liability in the contract between the manufacturer and the first purchaser excluded claims brought by the last purchaser (so held in OGH 28 Nov. 1978, *JBl.* 1979, 483) and that a victim who was no part of the chain of purchasers had to resort to the general principles of tort liability. See the criticisms by POSCH, *Verhandlungen des 8. österreichischen Juristentages* (1982) with further references.

In contrast, the Bundesgerichtshof in Germany has now put it beyond doubt that if the injured person is in no direct contractual relationship with the manufacturer his claim has to lie in tort. The claim must be based on §§823 ff. BGB, which means that in principle the plaintiff must prove that the defendant manufacturer was guilty of some want of care. The BGH has nevertheless made an exception to this principle in the area of products liability. The plaintiff only has to prove that the goods were in an objectively defective condition when they left the factory and that his injury was due to that defect. Once this proof has been led the liability of the manufacturer is established, unless he can prove that he and all those who were involved with the product during its manufacture took all the necessary care.

This important principle was first laid down by the Bundesgerichtshof in the so-called 'fowl-pest' decision (BGHZ 51, 91). The plaintiff was a chicken-farmer who decided to have his chickens vaccinated against fowl-pest. The veterinary surgeon used a vaccine which he had obtained from the defendant manufacturer. A few days later fowl-pest broke out in the plaintiff's farm and more than 4,000 chickens died of it. It was established that there were impurities in the vaccine because of some mistake in the manufacture and that the outbreak of fowl-pest on the plaintiff's farm was attributable to this. The Bundesgerichtshof found that this was sufficient to make the defendant liable, for once it had been shown that the vaccine had left the factory in a defective condition it was for the defendant to prove how the defect arose and that no blame attached to the firm or its staff. Such proof the defendant was unable to adduce.

This is the only means of escape for the manufacturer, a *probatio diabolica* which can hardly ever be, and never has been, successful, for there must be no gap in the manufacturer's evidence that in designing the process of manufacture, in selecting the machinery for quality control and in issuing instructions to his staff he took all the necessary and requisite precautions to be expected of a proper manufacturer of products of that kind. In addition he must prove that he was careful in choosing and supervising all the personnel who might have been at fault in causing the defect or failing to discover it (BGH NJW 1973, 1602). The same rules of proof apply in cases of *design defects* (BGHZ 67, 359, 362), but in cases of *inadequate instructions* it is normally for the plaintiff to prove that the defendant was obliged to give appropriate instructions (see BGHZ 80, 186). No one, however, suggests that §823 BGB can render the manufacturer liable for *development risks*.

Liability for development risks does exist in one area, namely in the manufacture of medicaments, under §§84 ff. of the Medicaments Law of 1978. Under this law the manufacturer is liable if injury or death is caused by the use of a medicament 'if, by reason of the manner of its development or manufacture the medicament, being used as prescribed, has adverse effects beyond what medical science regards as acceptable'. Such liability is limited in amount and does not extend to damages for pain and suffering.

There have been repeated demands for a law which imposes liability without fault on the manufacturer of products. This thought underlies the draft 'European Treaty on Products Liability' emanating from the Council of Europe in 1977 (see FLEMING, 23 *Am. J. Comp. L.* 729 (1975)), and now the Directive of 25 July 1985 of the Council of the European Economic Community 'on the approximation of the laws, regulations and administrative provisions of the Member States concerning liability for defective products'. The Directive provides that the producer should be liable independently of any fault for the harm caused by a defect in goods produced by him; goods are defective when they do 'not provide the safety which a person is entitled to expect, taking all circumstances into account'. Member States have the option of imposing a monetary ceiling (of not less than 70 million ECUs) on the producer's liability.

VI

Tort law turns on the concept of *liability*, on the view that a person has to pay for harm suffered by another only if for some specified reason he can be made 'liable' for that harm. Tort law specifies the reasons which justify making people liable for harm; as we know, reasons generally accepted are that he caused the harm by breach of some duty of care owed to another or that he had created a source of special risk and the harm was due to such a risk. If the victim cannot find anyone on whom to fix liability, he obtains no compensation for his harm, at any rate not through the law of tort: 'Sound policy lets losses lie where they fall except where a special reason can be shown for interference' (O. W. HOLMES, *The Common Law* 50 (1881)).

But can the law of tort, with such concepts, provide a proper solution to the problem of compensation for harm, especially for personal injury suffered in accidents? The question is being discussed all over the world. People's views of the extent to which the law must provide social security for the individual citizen have altered profoundly. As more and more people are being protected against more of the risks inherent in living, such as the economic consequences of deprivation, sickness, and unemployment, it is consistent to urge that the citizen be freed from the risks of *accident* as well, even if he cannot satisfy the traditional tests of tort law and establish a sufficiently close relationship to a 'responsible' cause of the injury. For this reason many countries have proposed, and some have enacted, schemes to replace the law of tort for certain types of accident or indeed for accidents of all kinds, so as to enable a victim to claim compensation for his personal injury regardless of any particular person's liability, or from an insurer who can spread the cost through the whole community of persons exposed to that risk. This by no means entails that the individual whom the law of tort would have held 'liable' always gets off scot-free, for he may be rendered liable to the insurer whenever indicated by considerations of accident prevention or loss distribution, for example, in cases of gross negligence. In practice the law of tort would simply be replaced for certain types or all types of accident by a system similar to that for industrial accidents, such as was introduced in Germany over a century ago and is now in force in most countries of the world.

The area of *traffic accidents* is eminently suitable for 'insurance protection rather than tort liability', because despite ubiquitous improvements in the law of tort by legislatures and courts, there are still a number of gaps in its protection of the victim.

Thus German law is criticized for reducing the victim's claim whenever his own fault or the dangerous propensity of his vehicle contributed to the accident; other grounds of criticism are that a gratuitous passenger in the vehicle involved in the accident cannot recover against its custodian unless he proves fault under §§823 ff. BGB; so, too, if the accident was caused by a pedestrian or pedal-cyclist; again, the victim gets nothing if no third party is involved—sudden black ice, for example—or where the involvement of another vehicle constituted an 'unavoidable event' for its driver and custodian (see above p. 694).—A comprehensive criticism of tort law as a mechanism for compensating accident victims, with exhaustive references to the literature, may be found in TUNC, XI *Int. Enc. Comp. L.* 'Torts' (1983) 63 ff.; TUNC, *La Responsabilité civile* (1981) 97 ff.; ATIYAH, *Accidents* 468 ff.; ISON (above p. 686).

Another objection to the law of tort is that, operated as it is by courts and liability insurers, it takes more time and money than a system of accident insurance.

It has been estimated in Britain that of every £100 paid in premiums by motorists only £55 goes to victims; the rest is eaten up in court and lawyers' fees, the administration costs of insurers, and the sums paid to their agents. Under the industrial accident insurance scheme, by contrast, about £90 out of every £100 goes to victims (see the Report of the Royal [Pearson] Commission on Civil Liability and Compensation for Personal Injury (1978) (Cmnd. 7054) nos. 83, 121, 261, and also ATIYAH, *Accidents* 511 ff.). The difference is mainly due to the fact that every single case requires a finding on questions of fault, contributory fault, and the other components of liability at law, as well as over the extent of the victim's property damage, personal injury, and pain and suffering. These questions are often disputed, and have to be taken to court by lawyers. If an accident insurance system replaced the law of tort it would be easy to specify precise prerequisites to compensation, avoiding, in particular, the problem of establishing fault, just as is done for industrial accidents. Further administrative savings can be achieved by removing property damage from the scheme, and paying for personal injury in accordance with a fixed tariff.

Accident insurance has already wholly or partially replaced the law of tort as regards traffic accidents in many countries: Sweden, Norway and Finland, Israel and Poland, and in many states and provinces in Canada, Australia, and the USA.

Detailed references may be found in v. HIPPEL, in FLEMING/HELLNER/v. HIPPEL, 48 ff. Note that in the United States the 'no-fault' systems retain the law of tort if the harm exceeds a certain limit ($50,000 in Michigan and New York).—In Germany a system of traffic accident insurance has long been advocated by v. HIPPEL. In Great Britain the Pearson Commission proposed in 1978 that compensation for victims of traffic accidents should be provided by the state, much as for victims of industrial accidents, the costs to be funded by a tax on fuel oils. On this see FLEMING, 42 *Mod. L. Rev.* 249 (1979); MARSH, 95 *LQ Rev.* 513 (1979); KÖTZ, *VersR* 1979, 585.—Similar plans for other instances of damage to health have been proposed and sometimes implemented, for example, for harm suffered in medical treatment (see WEYERS, 'Empfiehlt es sich, im Interesse der Patienten und Ärzte ergänzende Regelungen für das ärztliche Vertrags- (Standes-) und Haftungsrecht einzuführen?', *Verh. DJT* 52 (1978) A 1.

But the introduction of a system of insurance for traffic accidents does not solve the whole problem of serious and fatal accidents. After all, the needs of the victim and his family are exactly the same whether the accident occurs at work, on the way to work, on the way somewhere else, in the home, at school, or in some sporting activity. Is there any good reason for selecting certain types of accident for privileged treatment and giving them a special compensation system, especially when any distinction between 'insured' and 'uninsured' accidents is bound to lead to artificial distinctions, as the law of industrial accidents clearly shows? If this is admittedly unavoidable when certain specified types of accidents are selected for specially favourable treatment, would it not be logical, if one is to replace the law of tort by a system of insurance, to protect the citizen against *all accidents whatever*? Such systems have been discussed all over the world, and such a system was introduced in New Zealand in 1972.

The Accident Compensation Act of 1974 in New Zealand, based on the recommendations of a Government Commission chaired by Mr Justice WOODHOUSE, does away with the law of tort for all 'personal injury by accident' and confers special rights against the Accident Compensation Board, a state organ, on the victim or his dependants. To meet the expenditures of the Board, two funds were created: victims of *traffic accidents* are paid from a fund supported by taxes on owners of motor vehicles, while a different fund, fuelled by levies on employers, meets claims by employees for industrial diseases or personal injuries caused by accidents (other than traffic accidents) whether occurring at work or not. Other payments made by the Accident Compensation Board are met from general tax revenues. See BLAIR, *Accident Compensation in New Zealand* (1978); PALMER, *Compensation for Incapacity, A Study of Law and Social Change in New Zealand and Australia* (1979); ISON, *Accident Compensation, A Commentary on the New Zealand Scheme* (1980); FLEMING and v. HIPPEL, in FLEMING/HELLER/v. HIPPEL (above p. 686) 11 ff., 51 ff., all with further references. Of course people have asked why the person whose health has been injured by an *accident* (or an industrial disease) should be any better off than the person who suffers similar harm from a non-industrial disease or some congenital ailment. Voices have been raised in favour of 'equal treatment for all victims', for the creation of a system of compensation which would in principle give the same compensation for the same injury; for example, see ATIYAH *Accidents* (above p. 686) 498 ff.; ISON (above p. 686) 55 ff.; v. HIPPEL in FLEMING/HELLNER/v. HIPPEL (above p. 686) 59 f.

All the present indications are that the role of tort liability in the compensation of personal injury will get smaller and smaller: the future belongs to systems of compensation where the nature and extent of compensation depends on the nature and extent of the harm and not on the way the harm arose or on whether it can be 'attributed' to any particular person. The goal can admittedly be achieved in different ways. One way is to go straight for comprehensive reform and create a system of 'people's accident insurance' on the New Zealand pattern. This way is most unlikely to be adopted in countries with traditional and complex rules of compensation. These rules may not always function in a satisfactory manner, there may be some regrettable lacunae, and they may not always be well integrated, but they often cover so much of the ground already that the need for total, radical, and immediate reform seems less urgent; furthermore, the lawyers and insurance men in these countries have a vested interest in the work and income generated by the existing system of accident compensation, so it is unrealistic to expect its conversion into a 'people's accident insurance' system overnight. In such countries, therefore, it makes more sense to go in for gradual development of the existing institutions in the direction indicated, by extending the *social security system* which is already independent of the law of tort, and on the other hand modifying the *law of tort* so as to make it function more like a system of accident insurance.

Social security systems are better developed in some countries than others, but in most industrial states today most citizens who have an accident are covered not only for medical costs, but also for loss of income, at any rate for a period. Where the accident causes permanent disability protection tends to be adequate only if the victim is an employee and the accident is an accident at work, but an accident suffered on the way to or from work is treated as an industrial accident in many countries, and some countries, such as Switzerland and the Netherlands, have gone further and include all accidents suffered by a worker, including 'accidents off work'. In Germany it has long been agreed that the same rules should in principle apply to accidents suffered by a housewife doing the housework, and only lack of funds has prevented actual implementation, but since 1971 the same protection as is given to victims of industrial accidents has been afforded to school-children and students who have an accident at, or on the way to or from, kindergarten, school, or college; indeed, the Federal Government is considering extending this protection to all accidents, and not just 'educational accidents'. All this goes to show that there is a constant increase in the number of accident victims who need only resort to the private law of tort for those items of harm, such as pain and suffering, which are not covered by the welfare and social insurance systems (see KÖTZ pp. 8 ff.).

But even in the law of tort, as it applies to accidents, developments in the last few decades strongly suggest that one day it will really be functioning very much like a system of accident insurance, though in legal disguise. This is especially true for traffic accidents. The custodian of a motor vehicle must take out liability insurance today everywhere, and his victim is given a direct claim against the insurer, being more or less protected even if the insured has failed to pay the premium or broken a term of the policy or even if he has not insured the vehicle at all, or if the insurer is unidentifiable (as in a hit-and-run case) or insolvent. Gaps remain, but it has long been demanded that they be closed and the liability of the custodian extended.

In Germany people want damages for pain and suffering allowed and the monetary ceilings removed in cases of strict liability. Strict liability should cover passengers in the vehicle and should be excluded only in a case of true *force majeure*, not whenever there is an 'unavoidable event'. Above all the defence of contributory negligence should be excluded except where the victim was guilty of intentional fault or gross negligence, as is the case in Sweden (see Ch. 6 §1 of the Law of Liability 1975) and France (Act no. 85-677 of 5 July 1985, see above p. 706). If all those proposals were implemented, the result would be very much like a system of traffic accident insurance.

50

Invasions of the Right of Personality

BADINTER, 'Le Droit au respect de la vie privée', *JCP* 1968. I. 2136.

BLOUSTEIN, 'Privacy as an Aspect of Human Dignity: An Answer to Dean Prosser', 39 *NYUL Rev.* 962 (1964).

BRITTAN, 'The Right of Privacy in England and the United States', 37 *Tul. L. Rev.* 235 (1963).

V. CAEMMERER, 'Privatrechtlicher Persönlichkeitsschutz im deutschen Recht', *Festschrift F. v. Hippel* (1967) 27.

COING/LAWSON/GRÖNFORS, *Das subjektive Recht und der Rechtsschutz der Persönlichkeit* (1959).

CONSTANTINESCO, 'Die Persönlichkeitsrechte und ihr Schutz im französischen Recht', *AcP* 159 (1960/61) 320.

DE CUPIS, *I diritti della personalità* (2nd edn., 1982).

DWORKIN/FLEMING/HUBRECHT/STROMHOLM/FINŽGAR/KÜBLER, *Die Haftung der Massenmedien, insbesondere der Presse, bei Eingriffen in persönliche oder gewerbliche Rechtspositionen im englischen, amerikanischen, französischen, schwedischen, jugoslawischen und deutschen Recht* (1972).

EHLERS/BAUMANN, 'Verletzungen des Persönlichkeitsrechts in der französischen Rechtsprechung, Ein Vergleich mit dem deutschen Recht', *ZvglRW* 77 (1978) 241.

EDLBACHER, 'Der Stand der Persönlichkeitsrechte in Österreich', *ÖJZ* 1983, 423.

FRANK, 'Der Schutz der Persönlichkeit in der Rechtsordnung der Schweiz', *AcP* 172 (1972) 56.

FRITSCHE/POSCH, 'Der zivilrechtliche Schutz der Persönlichkeitsrechte der Bürger', *NJ* 1982, 224.

GATLEY/LEWIS, *On Libel and Slander* (8th edn., 1981).

GRÜNHUT, 'Der Schutz der Persönlichkeitssphäre im englischen und amerikanischen Recht', *ZStW* 74 (1962) 319.

GURRY, *Breach of Confidence* (1984).

GUTTERIDGE/WALTON, 'The Comparative Law of the Right to Privacy', 47 *LQ Rev.* 203, 219 (1931).

HAUSHEER, 'Verstärkter Persönlichkeitsschutz: Der Kampf ums Recht an verschiedenen Fronten', *Festgabe Deschenaux* (1977) 381.

V. HIPPEL, 'Persönlichkeitsschutz und Pressefreiheit im amerikanischen und deutschen Recht', *RabelsZ* 33 (1969) 276.

HOTZ, *Zum Problem der Abgrenzung des Persönlichkeitsschutzes nach Art. 28 ZGB* (1967).

JÄGGI, 'Fragen des privatrechtlichen Schutzes der Persönlichkeit', *ZSR* 79 (1960) 133 a.

KAYSER, 'Les Droits de la personnalité, Aspects théoriques et pratiques', *Rev. trim. dr. civ.* 69 (1971) 445.

——, 'Le Secret de la vie privée et la jurisprudence civile', *Mélanges Savatier* (1965) 405.

KRAUSE, 'The Right to Privacy in Germany: Pointers for American Legislation?', 1965 *Duke LJ* 481.

LEUZE, *Die Entwicklung des Persönlichkeitsrechts im 19. Jahrhundert* (1962).

LINDON, *Les Droits de la personnalité* (1974).

LOBEDANZ, 'Persönlichkeitsschutz und Ersatz immaterieller Schäden im spanischen Recht', *AcP* 164 (1964) 78.

LÜCHINGER, 'Der privatrechtliche Schutz der Persönlichkeit und die Massenmedien', *SJZ* 70 (1974) 321.

MAX-PLANCK-INSTITUT FÜR AUSLÄNDISCHES UND INTERNATIONALES PRIVATRECHT, *Der zivilrechtliche Persönlichkeits- und Ehrenschutz in Frankreich, der Schweiz, England und den Vereinigten Staaten von Amerika* (1960).

PROSSER, 'Das Recht auf die Privatsphäre in Amerika', *RabelsZ* 21 (1956) 401.

——, 'Privacy', 48 *Calif. L. Rev.* 383 (1960).

PÜSCHEL, 'Persönlichkeitsrechte unter dem Schutz des künftigen Zivilrechts', *NJ* 1967, 726, 758.

RAVANAS, *La Protection des personnes contre la réalisation et la publication de leur image* (1978).

REDMOND-COOPER, 'The Press and the Law of Privacy', 34 *ICLQ* 769 (1985).

RIGAUX, 'L'Élaboration d'un "Right of Privacy" par la jurisprudence américaine', *Rev. int. dr. comp.* 32 (1980) 701.

RUPP, 'Zur Pressefreiheit in den Vereinigten Staaten von Amerika, Anmerkungen zu einigen neueren Entscheidungen', *Festschrift Zweigert* (1981) 763.

SCHMIDT-DAHLENBURG, *Der zivilrechtliche Ehrenschutz in England im Hinblick auf den gegenwärtigen und künftigen Ehrenschutz im deutschen Bürgerlichen Recht* (1962).

SCHWENK, 'Das allgemeine Persönlichkeitsrecht in amerikanischer Sicht', *Rechtsvergleichung und Rechtsvereinheitlichung, Festschrift zum 50jährigen Bestehen des Instituts für ausländisches und internationales Privat- und Wirtschaftsrecht der Universität Heidelberg* (1967) 233.

SCHWERDTNER, *Das Persönlichkeitsrecht in der deutschen Zivilrechtsordnung* (1977).

SIEPP, 'English Judicial Recognition of a Right to Privacy', 3 *Oxf. J. Leg. Stud.* 325 (1983).

STOLJAR, 'A Re-Examination of Privacy', 4 *LS* 67 (1984).

HANS STOLL, 'Empfiehlt sich eine Neuregelung der Verpflichtung zum Geldersatz für immaterielle Schäden?', *Verh. DJT* 45 (1964) I/1 S. 51.

STOUFFLET, 'Le Droit de la personne sur son image', *JCP* 1957. I. 1374.

STRÖMHOLM, 'Right of Privacy and Rights of the Personality, A Comparative Survey', *Acta Instituti Upsaliensis Iurisprudentiae Comparativae*, vol. VIII (1967).

WACKS, *The Protection of Privacy* (1980).

WADE, 'Defamation and the Right of Privacy' 15 *Vand. L. Rev.* 1093 (1962).

WAGNER, 'Le "Droit à l'intimité" aux États-Unis', *Rev. int. dr. comp.* 17 (1965) 365.

WARREN/BRANDEIS, 'The Right to Privacy', 4 *Harv. L. Rev.* 193 (1890).

WESTEN, 'Der zivilrechtliche Persönlichkeitsschutz im sozialistischen Recht', *ROW* 11 (1967) 145.

WESTIN, 'Science, Privacy and Freedom: Issues and Proposals for the 1970s', 66 *Colum. L. Rev.* 1003, 1205 (1966).

——, *Privacy and Freedom* (1967).

WINFIELD, 'Privacy', 47 *LQ Rev.* 23 (1931).

YANG, 'Privacy: A Comparative Study of English and American Law', 15 *ICLQ* 175 (1966).

ZEPOS, 'Der Schutz der Persönlichkeit nach dem griechischen ZGB', *Festschrift v. Caemmerer* (1978) 1129.

I

OUR discussion of the law of delict hitherto has mainly been concerned with rules which protect the body and health of human beings or their ownership and other economic interests. But every legal system must also decide how and how far to protect its citizens against invasions directed against their personality as such. Of course rules which provide compensation for personal injury and property damage ultimately safeguard the personality by rendering the right to life, physical integrity, and property meaningful by protecting them against attack by third parties, but private law must protect a man's personality not only where it is indirectly infringed in its physical manifestations but also where it is attacked directly by outrages against his honour, by the publication of his private affairs, by the unauthorized recording of his confidential utterances, or suchlike unpermitted trespasses into the area of his privacy. German lawyers here speak of 'invasions of the right of personality' (*Verletzungen des Persönlichkeitsrechts*).

The need for protection against invasions of the right of personality, now universally manifest, has become most strikingly evident in the course of the twentieth century. The reasons for this are not difficult to discern. While it is agreed on all hands that the press, radio, and television not only satisfy the perfectly legitimate desire to be entertained but also make a substantial contribution to informing and educating the public by means of report, commentary, and criticism and so permit the formation of public opinion in a manner essential for the functioning of a modern democratic state, it is no less indubitable that the public need for amusement and information may come into conflict with the equally deserving interests of a person who finds that his private affairs are being published, his name bandied about, and his picture broadcast, or who realizes that the incorrect or incomplete information given about him is defaming him or putting him in a false light. Modern advertising methods also endanger the right of personality for in their campaigns they notoriously tend to use the name and picture of persons known and unknown without always obtaining the necessary permission from the persons named or portrayed. Before long, also, a special need for confidentiality will arise as individuals increasingly resort to state organs for benefits and to private undertakings for services, since 'dossiers' will then be drawn up on them and as modern methods of documentation facilitate the storage and retrieval of data there will be an increasing danger that the state, the press, employers, or other interested persons may obtain such information and so be able to acquire full knowledge of every individual's life down to the last detail. Finally it should be remembered that modern technology has produced devices which offer untold possibilities of trespass into the individual's privacy, such as telephoto lenses, concealed recording machines, and tiny microphones which let one listen in to telephone conversations or even personal conversations behind four walls. All these devices are available today to government departments and private individuals alike and are constantly being improved upon (for the details see WESTIN (above p. 726)). It is not enough to mobilize the *criminal* law: private law must also contain rules which an individual may effectively use to counter such invasions of his privacy and so prevent the degradation of his personal dignity.

II

No rule in the *German* BGB protects the human personality as such against injurious invasion. It is true that §823 par. 1 BGB allows a claim for damages to be brought if one's body, health, life, or freedom are culpably affected, but this only protects the physical aspects of individual existence and does not offer any protection against invasions of one's honour or privacy. It is true that even during the nineteenth century eminent scholars asserted that the law of tort should protect 'the general human right of personality', especially the 'right to honour' and the 'right to one's private sphere'.

For example, see v. GIERKE, *Deutsches Privatrecht* I (1895) 707 and KOHLER, *ArchbürgR* 7 (1893) 94; for the history of the matter see LEUZE (above p. 725) and SCHEYHING, *AcP* 158 (1959/60) 503.

But the BGB contains no echo of these views, apart from providing in §12 that a person whose *name* is used by another without permission may demand the cessation of such use; this right to one's name is also treated as an 'other right' under §823 par. 1 BGB so that the person affected can also claim damages from any person who culpably uses his name for any loss he suffers. The courts were also quick to give legal protection against invasions of the *'right to one's own picture'*. In 1889 the Reichsgericht was faced with the question whether the heirs of Bismarck could insist on the destruction of flashlight photographs of Bismarck's corpse taken by the defendant photographers after stealing by night into the room where he died. The Reichsgericht held that such a claim was good: the defendants had obtained these pictures by the unlawful act of trespassing on the property of others and were therefore bound to destroy the pictures under the rules of the *condictio ob iniustam causam* (RGZ 45, 170). The sense of public outrage at this incident led to the inclusion in the Law of Artistic Creations of 1907 (*Kunsturheber-gesetz*) of §§22 ff. which provide that 'pictures' may only be circulated or displayed with the consent of their subject, if alive, or of his relatives. A special exception was made for figures of contemporary history, the publication of whose pictures is generally permissible without consent unless it infringes a 'justified interest' of the subject, as would be the case if he were photographed against his will in his private surroundings and there was no justifiable public interest in having such information (BGHZ 24, 200). When the statute was enacted 'picture' was understood to signify only a portrayal embodied in some physical thing but in a famous decision in 1920 the Kammergericht held that Kaiser Wilhelm II had been 'pictured' by an actor on the stage who wore a facial mask and aped his clothing, hairstyle, deportment, and accent. The Kaiser's suit for an injunction succeeded; he was certainly a figure of contemporary history, but his portrayal on the stage was 'one-sided and tendentious' (KG JW 1928, 363). Although KOHLER had emphatically insisted that everyone should be able to enjoin the 'publication of confidential letters' as a 'grave invasion of his private life', the courts were very hesitant to give any legal redress. The Reichsgericht would only afford such protection to letters which were 'an original artistic creation' so as to fall under the concept of 'literary work' in the sense of the Law of Literary Creations: NIETZSCHE's letters qualified since he showed himself to be an 'artist in correspondence' (RGZ 69, 401) but WAGNER's letters did not, as they were simply 'business letters' (RGZ 41, 43). One could hardly deny, however, that the publication of 'business letters' may also constitute an invasion of the writer's right of personality.

The courts had other means at their disposal of satisfying the need to protect the individual's personality apart from the law regarding names, the right to one's own picture, and the law of artistic and literary creations. A person whose honour or reputation was besmirched by statements about him could claim damages if he could show that the defendant was guilty of the crime of insult or slander (§§185 ff. Criminal Code), for the defendant would then be in breach of a protective statute in the sense of §823 par. 2 BGB. After much hesitation the courts also issued injunctions to prevent the future publication of such offensive statements (RGZ 156, 372). Again, §824 BGB renders a person liable in damages if he publishes facts which he knew or should have known to be untrue and which might prejudice another person's credit or cause him other harm in his trade or profession. §826 BGB is also of great importance here, since behaviour which would now constitute an invasion of the right of personality might very easily be seen as an offence *contra bonos mores*.

In RGZ 115, 416 for example, it was held to be an offence *contra bonos mores* for an information bureau to publish the details of the defendant's conviction twenty years previously: there is a general social duty not to hound a person for the whole of his life with an offence long since past; he should rather be helped to make good his lapse by creating a new life for himself and winning back his social reputation by impeccable conduct. Accordingly the most that could properly be said in the situation was that 'in his youth' the plaintiff had allowed himself to be embroiled in matters which brought him into conflict with the criminal law.

That in all these cases one and the same legal interest, namely the human personality in all its manifestations, was under different forms of attack and should be afforded protection, is a view the Reichsgericht never accepted. It resolutely declined to hold that the *general* right of personality deserved protection as much as the right to one's name or picture or artistic or literary creations.

Nor did the Reichsgericht allow its view to be affected by the fact that many years before the BGB came into force Switzerland had adopted a model rule which allowed a person who had been injured 'in his personal affairs' to enjoin the guilty party and claim damages from him if he were at fault (see art. 55 OR (1881), now art. 28 ZGB, 49 OR). The objection which the Reichsgericht raised against the proposal to recognize the general right of personality, namely that such a right is a 'concept unamenable to precise definition' (see KG JW 1928, 363) could also be levelled against the Swiss rule, but the way the Swiss courts have dealt with it shows that lawyers on the Continent too often underestimate the capacity of the courts to concretize a suggestive general clause. The Swiss Bundesgericht has gone carefully from case to case, weighing and balancing the interests on both sides, and giving protection against defamatory statements, embarrassing disclosures, invasions of family life (in particular by requiring an adulterer to pay damages: see BGE 84 II 329), and invasions of privacy. It is worth noting that art. 28 ZGB also gives protection against the 'economic side' of the right of personality, with the result that blacklists, boycotts, and other impermissible economic weapons can be dealt with under art. 28 ZGB as an invasion of the personal freedom to engage in trade or profession without interference (see, for example, BGE 82 II 292), whereas in Germany they would be dealt with under §826 BGB as an offence *contra bonos mores* (see, for example, RGZ 130, 89) or under §823 par. 1 BGB as an invasion of the 'right to an established and operative business' (see, for example, BGHZ 24, 200 and above pp. 644 ff.).

Only after the Second World War did Germany take the crucial step. The need for effective protection of human dignity and personal freedom had become abundantly manifest during the Nazi dictatorship, and the Basic Law, unlike any previous German constitution, gave these values a prominent and important position in arts. 1 and 2. In addition, technological advances had greatly increased the possibilities of unpermitted invasions of the private sphere and secret surveillance devices of all kinds had emerged from the pages of science fiction. It had also been shown that sensational press reports on the private life of individuals might constitute an invasion of their personality even if the circumstances reported were true in fact and not defamatory in effect. But in these cases no effective protection was afforded by the rules developed by the Reichsgericht. The ground was thus prepared for the path-breaking decision of the Bundesgerichtshof in 1954 in which for the first time it recognized the general right of personality as an 'other right' under §823 par. 1 BGB.

The defendant was a weekly periodical which had published an article taking exception to the foundation of a bank by Dr Schacht, an Economics Minister under Hitler. The plaintiff was retained by Dr Schacht as his attorney and in that capacity, pursuant to his client's instruction and expressly on his behalf, wrote to the defendant and demanded that certain corrections be made in the article. The defendant published this letter in its 'Readers' Letters' column with omissions which made it appear as if the plaintiff had acted spontaneously and as a private individual in making these demands in the interests of Dr Schacht. The plaintiff claimed that the defendant should be made to correct this misrepresentation by a suitable retraction, and the claim succeeded at first instance, for reasons which were in line with the decisions of the Reichsgericht: by the manner in which the defendant had published the plaintiff's letter it had brought him into disrepute and lowered him in public estimation; the defendant was therefore guilty of defamation (§187 Criminal Code) and accordingly liable under §823 par. 2 BGB. On appeal the higher court was unable to find that the publication of the letter was defamatory of the plaintiff and dismissed the claim. For the Bundesgerichtshof it was immaterial whether the defendant were guilty of a crime or not since, in reliance on arts. 1 and 2 of the Basic Law, it held that private law protected the general right of personality as such: to publish the letter in mangled form as was done here constituted an invasion of the 'private sphere of the author as protected by the right of personality' since it presented a false picture of his personality (BGHZ 13, 334).

In a quick succession of other decisions the law of tort was used to protect other manifestations of the general right of personality. The courts held it actionable to use the name of a famous artiste in an advertisement, to publish a picture under circumstances which gave the impression that the person portrayed was a murderer, and to publish a factitious interview with Princess Soraya, a well known figure of international society; making a secret recording and communicating a confidential medical certificate to a third party were also tortious, subject to the qualification that an overwhelming interest such as the discovery of a serious crime by means of the recording or medical certificate might serve as a justification. Where newspaper reports are inaccurate, incomplete, biassed, or defamatory it is particularly difficult to weigh up the values of the right of personality on the one hand and the freedom of the press on the other, but it has always been recognized that in addressing itself to politicians, publicists, or other persons in the public eye or in dealing with 'questions of public importance', the press is entitled to go in for very severe and even one-sided criticism, whereas if it publishes private and family affairs with names attached for no good reason, much sterner standards will be applied.

Once an invasion of the right of personality has been established the plaintiff is entitled to have it undone, as by the retraction of a defamatory statement, and to demand that it not be repeated. Furthermore, if the defendant was at fault, the plaintiff may claim damages for the economic harm which he suffered in consequence of the invasion of his personality. For a long time the plaintiff could obtain no compensation for any moral or non-economic harm since §253 BGB unequivocally lays down that damages in respect of such harm may not be ordained except in the cases prescribed by law, mainly for corporeal injuries. Since a decision in 1958, however, the Bundesgerichtshof has disregarded the terms of this provision (BGHZ 26, 349), on the ground that the protection of the right of personality by private law would be 'patchy and inadequate' unless the defendant had to reckon on a sanction which properly reflected the seriousness of his behaviour and its consequences (see BGHZ 35, 363). It is now standard practice for the court to award damages for moral harm if the invasion of the plaintiff's right of personality is 'grave'; here the motive of the defendant, the seriousness of his fault, and the mode and extent of the harmful invasion are relevant considerations. In so deciding, the Bundesgerichtshof has brought German law into line with Swiss law on this point: art. 49 OR allowed a claim for such damages only where the infringer had been negligent and damages were 'justified by the gravity of the invasion and the fault'.

By an amendment in force since 1 July 1985, art. 49 OR has been altered so as to allow monetary compensation when necessary in view of the 'gravity of the invasion': 'grave fault' on the part of the infringer is no longer required, since it is not clear 'why Swiss law should give less protection to the personality as such than to economic interests' (to quote from the reasons in BBl. 1982 II 681).—STOLL (above p. 725) has made an exhaustive comparative study of the question of monetary compensation for infringements of the right of personality. This shows that Germany stands almost alone in having a rule as unfortunate as §253 BGB, though it is true that the courts in *Austria*, despite increasing criticism from writers, hold that money damages are payable for infringement of the right of personality only in the few cases specified by statute (see EDLBACHER (above p. 724) 429; BYDLINSKI, *Festschrift v. Caemmerer* (1978) 785).—The *socialist* countries, on the other hand, were until recently almost unanimous in refusing damages for invasions of the right of personality, on the ground that an award of damages would 'amount in the last analysis to a materialization of the right of personality and run contrary to the basic principles of the protection of the right of personality in socialist law' (PÜSCHEL (above p. 725) 760). The new Civil Code of East Germany of 1975 recognizes the citizen's right to respect for his personality (§§7 and 324 ZGB), but the victim of a breach can claim damages only for the resulting economic harm ((§336); on this see FRITSCHE/POSCH (above p. 724). The *Polish* Civil Code (1964) makes an exception when the infringement takes the form of deprivation of liberty or, in the case of a woman, of sexual abuse (art. 445). *Hungary*, on the other hand, now recognizes money claims for immaterial harm across the board: under art. 354 of the Hungarian Civil Code damages are payable when the victim has suffered in his ability to take part in social life or there has been some other serious and lasting effect on his life-style (on this see BÁRD/KISS *VersR* 1981, 911). The *Yugoslav* Law of Obligations of 1978 is to the same effect (arts. 200 ff.; see STANCOVIC, *Rev. int. dr. comp.* 31 (1979) 765).

In a country like Germany, where the Civil Code is only eighty years old, emphasis is still on the Code and not on the courts, and if the courts openly deviate from the terms of the Code and invent their own rules of law as the German courts have done in the area of the protection of the right of personality many people will greet the development with some unease. Accordingly, the Federal Ministry of Justice soon started to articulate the basic ideas laid down by the Bundesgerichtshof, with the addition of a few collateral provisions. This draft 'Law for the Reformation of the Protection of Personality and Honour in Private Law' was very carefully prepared and took account of the special interests of the press throughout, to the extent of expressly stating that reports even on the shameful details of private and family life were permissible if they served 'the reasonable vindication of a justifiable public or private interest'. The criticism aroused by the Ministry's proposals was so furious that they were shortly afterwards dropped. When the draft was being discussed the press itself was regrettably far from fair in the way it informed the public; in particular it did not make it clear that the draft was really nothing more than a codification of existing judicial law. Of course this furore did not make the courts deviate an inch from the direction they had chosen, though new cases have led them to make some new distinctions and develop new points. The latest legislative proposals limit themselves to including 'personality' among the specified protected legal interests in §823 par. 1 BGB and supplementing §847 BGB by adding that a claim for compensation for moral harm is allowable in the case of an invasion of personality which 'can be regarded as grave in the circumstances'. All that is proposed is to fit the BGB to the existing situation; the rules of German law regarding the protection of the personality remain a pure judicial creation.

III

In 1970 the *French* Code civil adopted a terse provision: 'Chacun a droit au respect de sa vie privée' (art. 9), but the actual effect of this enactment was slight, given that the courts had already protected the right of personality in private law by using the general clauses in arts. 1382 and 1383 Code civil, according to which everyone must pay for the harm he causes by his 'faute'. These articles of the Code civil make no overt distinction between material and moral damage. While some older authors held that damages could not be awarded for immaterial harm, and others restricted it to cases of criminal behaviour and yet others to particular types of immaterial harm, such restrictive views have now been abandoned; even the courts today treat both types of harm in the same way and see no need to indicate in their decisions which part of the damages awarded to the plaintiff appertains to the material and which to the moral harm.

See MAZEAUD/TUNC I nos. 301 ff. and STOLL (above p. 725) 75 ff.—The quantum of damages awarded for moral harm depends on the circumstances of the case, and may even be purely symbolic. In a case where the plaintiff's wife had committed adultery and he claimed damages for his moral harm from her and her lover, the court awarded damages of only one franc ('franc symbolique') against the wife in view of the 'extenuating circumstances', on which the court did not expatiate. (Agen 18 July 1902, DP 1903. 2. 344; see also Paris 10 July 1957, D. 1957, 622.)—Similarly the Conseil d'État awarded only one franc to a woman who had been stopped on the street by a policeman in the defendant city and asked, for no apparent reason, whether she were registered with the health police (21 Feb. 1936, Gaz. Pal. 1936. 1. 605). This hesitancy on the part of the Conseil d'État may be referable to its earlier refusal to grant damages for immaterial harm at all, though more recently it has become more generous; on this see MORANGE, D. 1962. Chron. 15 and LUCE, JCP 1962. I. 1685.

It will be obvious that a legal system can adopt a very flexible approach to the problem of protecting the human personality if its law of tort applies whatever legal interests have been affected (*contra* §823 par. 1 BGB) and it can give damages quite freely for immaterial harm (*contra* §§253, 847 BGB). Accordingly, the French courts have never hesitated to characterize as 'faute' the publication of confidential letters, the dissemination of facts about a person's private life, or the unauthorized use of a person's name, and to award the plaintiff damages for the moral harm as well as the economic harm. French law has therefore not had to develop the concept of a 'general right of personality' and NERSON, one of the leading authorities in this area of law, has observed that 'no one in France today still believes in the existence, as a matter of technical law, of a general right of personality' (above p. 724, p. 84; accord AMIAUD (above p. 724, 297 f.)). French writers have simply sought to distinguish the various 'rights of personality', not without disputes whether a particular personality interest should theoretically rank as a 'right' or not, and French legal literature is replete with expressions like 'right to the confidentiality of one's correspondence', 'right to one's picture' and 'right to the privacy of one's domestic life'.

Perhaps it is because French lawyers have not had to establish the right of personality in the teeth of specific and narrow legislative texts that they include under the heading of 'protection de la personnalité' some types of case which the German lawyer would not. Decisions nullifying a testamentary condition that a legacy should determine if the legatee marries a Jew (Trib. civ.

Seine 22 Jan. 1947, D. 1947, 126) or avoiding as being contrary to public policy
a prohibition on competition contained in a contract of employment are
justified by French writers on the ground that they vindicate the important
personal freedoms to marry and choose one's place of work and so ultimately
safeguard the human personality. This is also the point of view from which
they observe the many judicial decisions on damages claims for breach of
family duties, especially where an innocent spouse claims compensation for
the moral damage caused by the other's adultery (see Crim. 17 Oct. 1956, DH
1957, 245, noted by BRETON).

The standards applied by the French courts to the 'classical' forms of the
protection of the personality, such as the protection of one's picture or name,
one's honour or privacy, are very like those in positive German law. *Pictures*,
in general, may only be published with the agreement of the person portrayed,
but the courts limit this principle, much as does §23 of the German Law of
Artistic Creations, by holding that pictures of persons caught in the limelight
of publicity may be published without permission. The same is true of people
who appear simply as figures in a landscape or beside a monument, but even in
these cases the publication should not be permitted to infringe justifiable
interests of the persons portrayed. Two decisions of the Court of Appeal in
Paris show how these interests are weighed up.

In Paris 24 March 1965, JCP 1965. II. 14305 the plaintiffs, a married couple, were
photographed while posing for someone else in extremely scanty holiday dress in front
of the Tower of Pisa, and the defendant periodical used this photograph to illustrate a
satirical article on Italian tourist attire. The court held that the defendant should have
rendered the faces of the plaintiffs unrecognizable, but that by displaying themselves in
such garb in front of the Tower of Pisa the plaintiffs had been at fault and had
contributed to the misadventure. The Court of Appeal therefore reduced to 500 NF the
damages of 2,000 NF awarded by the trial court.—In Paris 14 March 1965, JCP 1965.
II. 14223, *France Dimanche*, the defendant, published a sentimental article about the
family of GÉRARD PHILIPPE, the famous actor, giving details of his 9-year-old son's
illness, embellished with a photograph taken by reporters who had forced their way
into hospital and photographed the child in bed. PHILIPPE's family was the object of
great public interest and the boy's illness had already been mentioned in the
newspapers, but the trial court ordered the temporary confiscation of the article and
the Court of Appeal upheld this judgment with the observation that this was an
'intolerable invasion of private life'.

When details of a person's *private life* are published, similar considerations
apply.

Paris 16 March 1955, D. 1955, 295 is an interesting case on the facts. *France
Dimanche* published a series of articles entitled 'My Life, by Marlene Dietrich' which
purported to give the actress's reminiscences in the form of an interview, although
MARLENE DIETRICH had neither given any interview nor permitted the defendant to
make any such publication. The reported facts were essentially true and were probably

more or less well known, but the defendant was held liable to pay 1,200,000 francs, principally because the defendant's conduct had effectively thwarted the actress's intention to write and publish her own memoirs.—The Italian cases point in the same direction: see TRIMARCHI, *RabelsZ* 25 (1960) 261.

Many French cases involve the question whether an unflattering resemblance between a person and a character in a *novel* may constitute an invasion of his personality. The author of a war story in which a French officer betrays his companion's plan of escape from a German prisoner-of-war camp must do his research thoroughly and take every care not to attribute to such a reprobate the name of any living French officer who was ever a prisoner-of-war (Paris 10 July 1957, D. 1957, 622; see also Trib. civ. Seine 24 Oct. 1936, Gaz. Pal. 1936. 2. 794). The writer of a *roman-à-clef* may also make himself liable if he gives his characters unattractive traits.

See Paris 24 April 1936, DH 1936, 319; Amiens 6 July 1932, S. 1932, 2. 233; Rennes 31 May 1951, DH 1951, 484.—The Court of Cassation in another interesting decision imposed liability on a historian of wireless telegraphy who omitted all reference to a man who, according to MARCONI himself and other leading physicists, had made a great contribution to the discovery (Civ. 27 Feb. 1951, D. 1951, 329, noted by DESBOIS; but see also Paris 23 Jan. 1965, Gaz. Pal. 1965. 1. 361).

Confidential letters have been well protected against publication by the French courts since the eighteen-eighties. Here too the principle is that the recipient of a confidential letter has no right to publish it without the consent of its writer. This used to be based on an 'implied contract' between the correspondents, but today it is recognized that the right to the confidentiality of one's letters is a right of personality.

See, for example, Trib. civ. Seine 27 Nov. 1928, DH 1928, 616. In this case some letters which ROMAIN ROLLAND had written to a well-known author had somehow come into the hands of the defendant dealer who was proposing to auction them and who had, for this purpose, published extracts from them in his catalogue. The court held that only *one* of these letters was confidential and could not be sold; the others only contained views which ROLLAND had publicly expressed in books and articles, so they could be sold, but it was wrongful to publish extracts from *any* of the letters, and the defendant had to pay damages of 2,000 francs.

The writer's consent is not required if there is a very good reason for publication, such as the disclosure of the letter in court

See the decisions cited in the Report of the Max Planck Institute.—The interest in confidentiality must yield if the publication of the letter is necessary for the conviction of a defendant in a criminal trial, but the decision of Toulouse 2 March 1933, DP 1935. 2. 55, noted by APPLETON, probably goes too far. After studying the decision of a court in a case involving his client, an attorney wrote to her saying that in his view the court had made itself into an accessory to the crime, and, with his permission, the client produced this letter in the cassation proceedings. The state prosecutor, thus alerted, brought disciplinary proceedings against the attorney and used the letter to secure his conviction.

The Court of Cassation also holds that the agreement of the parties is required for the recording and reproduction of confidential *telephone conversations.*

In one case the judicial police had authorized the defendant to install a listening device so as to catch the unknown person who was constantly bothering her with insulting telephone calls. The defendant did so and discovered that the plaintiff was the anonymous caller, but the plaintiff then turned the tables on the defendant by suing her for damages under art. 1382 Code civil for breach of the secrecy of telephone conversations. The Court of Cassation upheld the plaintiff's claim (see Civ. 18 March 1955, D. 1955, 573, noted by SAVATIER; JCP 1955. II. 8909, noted by ESMEIN).

Private law also gives protection against invasions of *honour* and *reputation* under art. 1382 Code civil, but in practice this is intimately linked with art. 29 of the Law of the Press of 29 July 1881, which makes it a crime to insult a person in public (injure) or to publish defamatory statements of fact about him (detamination). Claims for damages are normally brought in the *criminal* trial, with which the injured party associates himself as *partie civile*; if a court, an official, or a soldier is defamed, this procedure *must* be used (art. 46). Although in general a person cannot be convicted of defamation if he can prove that what he said was true, no such proof is admissible if the dishonourable facts relate to the *private life* of the person attacked (art. 35). If the defendant cannot prove the truth of what he said, it is presumed under art. 35 bis that he was acting in bad faith; this presumption may be rebutted, not by mere proof of the defendant's good faith belief in the truth of what he said, but by the additional proof that he carefully investigated the information, that he acted with due regard for the interests involved, and that he chose the least offensive manner of publication in the circumstances.

IV

The *Common Law* rules which protect the human personality are best approached by making a distinction between attacks on a person's honour and all other forms of invasion of his personality. Reflections on honour and reputation in England the United States are mainly sanctioned by the tort of *libel* and *slander*, which together comprise *defamation*. Other invasions of personality are sanctioned in the United States as being invasions of the *right of privacy*, but the English courts have not yet recognized any such general right to the protection of one's privacy although, as will be seen shortly, they can often help in such cases by a wide application of the torts of libel and slander or by allowing a claim for breach of copyright or 'passing-off' (see above p. 648) or some other cause of action.

1. *Defamation* occurs if a person's honour, reputation, or esteem is adversely affected by someone's expressing himself to a third party in a manner calculated to bring the plaintiff into 'hatred, ridicule or contempt' or otherwise to lower him in the estimation of reasonable persons. Protection is afforded only if the plaintiff's public reputation has been affected: it is not enough, as it is in Germany, for a person's dignity or self-esteem to be wounded by objectionable remarks made *inter partes*. If the defamatory statement is made in a permanent form, especially in written or printed words or pictures or caricatures, this will be *libel*; broadcasting by radio or television is also treated as libel in England under s. 1 of the Defamation Act, 1952. It is a case of *slander* if a person's reputation is affected by oral expression, insulting mime, or derisive gesture. The practical importance of the distinction between libel and slander is that in a libel suit no special damage need be alleged or proved: the court can fix the quantum of damages in relation to the gravity of the defamation without requiring proof of any particular loss. In slander cases it is different, for the plaintiff is normally required to prove that he suffered some material loss as a result of the slander, such as a loss of promotion or custom or employment. There are certain narrow categories of case, however, where this rule does not apply: if the defendant accuses the plaintiff of a serious crime or imputes to him some loathsome disease which would exclude him from society or makes statements calculated to affect the plaintiff's trade or profession, or finally if he accuses a woman of unchastity or adultery, the slander is exceptionally said to be 'actionable per se', which means that the plaintiff need not prove any special economic harm. It need hardly be said that these rules are quite irrational. A person defamed on a postcard which only one other person ever reads can claim damages without proof of any loss, while a person slandered before an audience of 10,000 people in a manner which affects him in his private capacity and causes him no provable pecuniary or professional harm will have no claim for damages at all unless he is credited with criminality or contagion.

The explanation for these artificial distinctions, for which no one has a good word to say in the Common Law today, is to be found in English legal history. Slander, the older tort, fell within the jurisdiction of the ecclesiastical courts in the Middle Ages; the royal courts intervened only when the defamation had secular consequences in the form of some temporal loss. Defamation in print, once it was invented, should have attached itself to slander, but instead the infamous Star Chamber Court assumed jurisdiction over the press, and the special rules it developed were retained when jurisdiction in such cases passed to the regular courts.

A person may perfectly well be liable for defamation even if no blame at all attaches to his publication or transmission of the defamatory statement. If a plaintiff's reputation has objectively been affected by what a newspaper has printed about him, the newspaper will be liable in damages even if its management was unaware of the plaintiff's existence and had no intention of defaming him; indeed, the newspaper will be liable even if the publication was defamatory of the plaintiff only by reason of circumstances which the publisher did not know and could not have known.

The leading decision in England is *Hulton and Co.* v. *Jones*, [1910] AC 20. The defendant published in the *Sunday Chronicle* an article on a popular French seaside resort which made great fun of the fact that Englishmen who were perfectly decorous on their own side of the Channel immediately turned into lounge lizards and Lotharios on the other. Passing mention was made of a certain Artemus Jones, said to be a church-warden when at home in Peckham: 'here, in the atmosphere of Dieppe, on the French side of the Channel, he is the life and soul of a gay little band that haunts the Casino and turns night into day, besides betraying a most unholy delight in the society of female butterflies'. There then emerged from the provincial backwoods of England a person who astonished the defendant by announcing himself as Artemus Jones and ready to prove that his acquaintances had identified him with the hero of the article. The defendant, though in perfect good faith, was held liable in all courts to the tune of £1,750.—See also *Cassidy* v. *Daily Mirror*, [1929] 2 KB 331. In this case the defendant newspaper published a picture of Mr Cassidy in the company of a young woman whom the caption described as his fiancée. The defendant must have supposed that this was acceptable since Cassidy himself had approved the publication of the picture and the caption, but Mrs Cassidy nevertheless sued them for damages and proved that acquaintances had inferred from the caption that she was not in fact married to Mr Cassidy.—In another case a newspaper published a true fact about the person named; another person of the same name to whom the fact as reported could be attributed was allowed to sue the newspaper regardless of whether it could have foreseen or prevented such false attribution (*Newstead* v. *London Express*, [1940] 1 KB 377).

It follows from these remarkably strict rules that the risk of paying damages attaches to everyone who says anything which might injure another's reputation even if he was not at all negligent in not realizing that it might do so. On one or two points the courts have been able to relax these rules. If a defamatory statement comes to the notice of a third party without the knowledge and consent of the defendant, he can escape liability if he shows that he was not at fault. Thus if the defendant says something defamatory in a communication to the plaintiff and a third party overhears the conversation or opens the injurious letter this would normally be a case of libel or slander, but the defendant will not be liable if he can prove that it was not careless of him not to foresee that the third party might learn what was said. The courts also allow a defendant to exculpate himself if he was involved in the publication of the defamatory statement, but only in a subsidiary capacity: a lending-library, bookshop, or news-stand, unlike the author, publisher, or printer, will not be liable if despite all care on their part they were unaware of the defamatory nature of the publications they lent or sold.

In other cases, however, it is not necessary for the defendant to have been at fault. In particular the press is liable in damages for libel even if the publisher, editor, and author could not possibly have known that the statement was false or that it might defame the plaintiff. For such cases of 'innocent defamation' an alleviation has been made by s. 4 of the Defamation Act 1952, whereby liability may be avoided if the periodical immediately publishes an apology and a correction. Liability for defamation is also avoided if the defendant can rely on some 'privilege' attaching to the misrepresentation or critical comments. Such a privilege arises out of the interests involved, and it may be 'absolute privilege' or 'qualified privilege'. 'Absolute privilege' attaches to defamatory statements made by judges, jurymen, advocates, witnesses, or parties in litigation or similar proceedings, to statements made by officials in the course of their duties and by Members of Parliament in the legislative chamber. In these cases the motive behind the statement and the manner of its publication are quite irrelevant. This is not so where the privilege is only 'qualified': a person may rely on qualified privilege if he spoke in advancement of some legitimate private or public interest, but he must go on to prove that he believed in the truth of what he said, that he chose the least injurious mode of publication, and that he did not act with the intention of causing harm. If a defamatory observation is by way of opinion, the defence of 'fair comment' applies in like circumstances.

The details of the whole matter and a wealth of references to the case-law may be found in GATLEY/LEWIS (above p. 724, p. 290 ff.); OHLGART, 'Wahrnehmung berechtigter Interessen durch die Presse, Ein rechtsvergleichender Beitrag zur Neuordnung des zivilrechtlichen Ehrenschutzes' (Diss. Hamburg, 1963), as well as the Report of the Max-Planck-Institut.

2. A man's personality may be impaired in other ways than by besmirching his reputation or aspersing his honour. We must now very briefly turn to the rules which have been developed in the Common Law to deal with *other invasions of personality*, and we must start with a famous law review article published in 1890 by a well-known Boston lawyer, WARREN, in conjunction with BRANDEIS, who was later to be appointed to the United States Supreme Court (4 *Harv. L. Rev.* 193 (1890)). The authors of this, 'perhaps the most famous and certainly the most influential law review article ever written.' (HENSON (ed.), *Landmarks of Law, Highlights of Legal Opinion* (1960)) sought to prove that many precedents, apparently based on defamation, invasion of property, breach of contract, and other familiar grounds of claims were in substance sanctioning the invasion of a general right, the so-called 'right of privacy', in an individual's domestic life. The authors came to the quite novel conclusion that the positive law contained a general principle 'which may be invoked to protect the privacy of the individual from invasion either by the too enterprising press, the photographer, or the possessor of any other modern

device for recording or reproducing scenes or sounds' (4 *Harv. L. Rev.* 193, 206 (1890)).

The immediate consequences of this article were meagre. A few courts seemed ready to follow the views of WARREN and BRANDEIS while others rejected them out of hand, in particular the New York Court of Appeals in a case where the picture of a pretty girl was used in a flour advertisement without her consent (*Roberson* v. *Rochester Folding Box Co.*, 171 NY 538, 64 NE 442 (1902)). This decision evoked a storm of protest in New York which promptly resulted in the enactment of a law which is still in force: §§50–1 of the New York Civil Rights Law make it actionable to use the name or picture of a person 'for advertising purposes or for the purposes of trade' without the written consent of that person. A few years later the Supreme Court of Georgia in a similar case adopted the conclusions of WARREN and BRANDEIS and supported them with cogent reasoning (*Pavesich* v. *New England Ins. Co.*, 122 Ga. 190, 50 SE 68 (1905)). Since then one jurisdiction after another has recognized the 'right of privacy' as worthy of protection until today almost all of the United States accept this view.

PROSSER had sought to distinguish the extremely copious case-law into various types of case (48 *Calif. L. Rev.* 383 (1960); criticized by BLOUSTEIN, 39 *NYUL Rev.* 962 (1964)). Within the 'law of privacy' he finds four different types of case in each of which a different interest is protected against different forms of invasion. In the first group he puts cases where there has been an unpermitted invasion of the plaintiff's private territory or a meddling in his private affairs, such as listening in to private conversations with the aid of microphones and telephone taps, surveillance of the plaintiff's dwelling, unpermitted entry into hotel rooms, and rummaging through handbags. The second group of cases deals with the unauthorized publication of facts from a person's private life which, though true in substance, are painful or embarrassing. In these cases it is often very difficult to balance the individual's interest in maintaining secrecy concerning his private life with the public interest in instruction, information, and entertainment. Two well-known cases, out of a great many, may be mentioned: both of them deal with the question whether the press or the cinema is entitled to expose a person involuntarily to public attention many years after the public first became interested in him.

In *Melvin* v. *Reid*, 112 Cal. App. 285, 297 P. 91 (1931) the plaintiff, then a prostitute, had been the accused in a sensational murder trial. On acquittal, she gave up her unfortunate mode of life, married an excellent man, and earned the respect of her neighbours and friends who were quite ignorant of her past. Seven years after the marriage the defendant destroyed her newly won social position by producing a film about the murder trial which used the plaintiff's maiden name and gave an accurate picture of her previous mode of life. The court held that the plaintiff's claim for damages must succeed.—In *Sidis* v. *F-R Publishing Corp.*, 113 F. 2d 806 (2d Cir. 1940) the federal courts in New York came to the opposite conclusion. The plaintiff here was born with extraordinary mathematical gifts and became a famous wunderkind. At 11 he could teach experts about four-dimensional bodies and at 16 he graduated *summa cum laude* from Harvard University. He later became nauseated with mathematics and repelled by life in the limelight, so he sought to obliterate all traces of his existence and disappeared into obscurity as an accountant, collecting tram tickets in his spare time and studying a very minor tribe of Indians. More than twenty years later the defendant published an article about him, not at all unfriendly in tone, which gave a faithful portrayal of his whole life story. The plaintiff had a breakdown and died shortly thereafter. The court rejected the plaintiff's claim on the ground that in cases of this sort the legal system could only protect the average man and intervene where the normal citizen of customary phlegm would have felt himself injured by the publication and not where, as here, the plaintiff found the publication intolerable only by reason of his exceptional sensitivity and reclusiveness.

The third class of PROSSER's cases includes those where the defendant has placed the plaintiff in a false light in the eyes of others. If a person, without any authority, signs the plaintiff's name to a telegram to a politician lobbying him on behalf of some proposed law, or if a person illustrates an article on drugs or juvenile delinquency with a picture of someone not involved at all, or if a person ascribes to the plaintiff in a make-believe interview opinions which in fact he does not hold, he will be liable for invasion of the 'right of privacy'; such cases almost always satisfy the requirements of the tort of defamation as well, since the plaintiff's honour and reputation are usually adversely affected. Finally, in his fourth group PROSSER puts the cases in which a person uses the name or picture of the plaintiff without his consent in a written or filmed advertisement or in the name of a firm or on his goods or in a similar context.

The *English* courts have not yet accepted that the invasion of the 'right of privacy' constitutes an independent tort. In relevant cases they continue the practice observed by WARREN and BRANDEIS of using other grounds of liability, especially defamation.

The case of *Tolley* v. *J. S. Fry & Sons Ltd.*, [1930] 1 KB 467 is typical. The defendant candy manufacturer used a picture of the plaintiff, a well-known amateur golfer, in public advertisements without his consent; an accompanying lyric equated the quality of the defendant's chocolate with the excellence of the plaintiff's golf. All the courts agreed that the claim for damages could only succeed if libel were established, that is, if the plaintiff's reputation or honour had been prejudiced by the content and form of the advertisement. Since the advertisement represented the plaintiff as a golfer of great merit, it was difficult to see that his honour had been besmirched, but it was held, at least in the House of Lords ([1931] AC 333), that the public could have made the defamatory inference that the plaintiff, although an amateur, had accepted payment for his consent to the publication. That this was not the true ground for granting the plaintiff damages may be seen by asking what the result would have been had he been a professional player. In other cases, too (*Dockrell* v. *Dougal*, (1899) 80 LT 551; *Corelli* v. *Wall*, (1906) 22 TLR 532; *Monson* v. *Tussauds Ltd.*, [1894] 1 QB 641) the emphasis is laid on the tort of libel although what is really involved is an unpermitted invasion of the plaintiff's privacy rather than an attack on his reputation.—The courts also have other grounds of liability which they can use in such cases. For example, if a person who contracted to take photographs of the plaintiff disseminates them to third parties without his consent, he will be liable in damages, either because the distribution of the photographs constitutes a breach of his 'implied contract' with the plaintiff (see *Pollard* v. *Photographic Co.*, (1888) 40 Ch. D. 354) or because it constitutes an infringement of the plaintiff's copyright in the photographs (*Williams* v. *Settle*, [1960] 1 WLR 1072).— See also *Sim* v. *H. J. Heinz Co. Ltd.*, [1959] 1 WLR 313. To speak the words in one of their television advertisements the defendants retained an actor known for his ability to mimic the voice of the plaintiff, a well-know film star. The plaintiff argued that the public would suppose that he was doing the speaking in the advertisements and he sought an injunction on the basis of defamation since it would prejudice his reputation as a filmstar if he were thought to be taking part in television commercials. Subsidiarily he relied on the tort of passing-off, which applies where one person passes off his own goods as those of another (see above p. 648), and the court held that as an actor he had a commercial interest in his voice analogous to that of a tradesman in his wares.—All this only goes to show how strained the law can become if invasions of personality have to be remedied under the traditional categories of tort law. See also the critical observations by WACKS (above p. 725) 166 ff.

Even in England there have been many attempts to procure general protection for the right of privacy. In 1931 WINFIELD proposed that the 'offensive invasion of the personal privacy of another' should be recognized as an independent tort (above p. 380, p. 41). In 1961 LORD MANCROFT introduced into the House of Lords a Right of Privacy Bill (printed in STRÖMHOLM (above p. 725) 220 f.; see also NEILL (above p. 725); BRITTAN (above p. 724) 261 ff.)). The Bill provided that a person should be entitled to claim damages if details of his personal life or affairs were published in the press, in films, on the radio, or on television, unless the defendant could prove that the publication was justified by one of the 'privileges' known to the law of defamation or by some 'reasonable public interest'. The Bill obtained a majority in the House of Lords, including the votes of well-known judges like LORD GODDARD and LORD DENNING, but it was not proceeded with. The reason seems to have been the fear, much emphasized by the press, that the concept of 'reasonable public interest' would in practice be extremely difficult to apply. Even so, the House of Commons saw further attempts in the 1960s to promote legislation to protect the right of privacy (see WACKS (above p. 725) 6 ff.). Finally a governmental [Younger] Commission was set up. It proposed several specific measures, but decided that it would be pointless to enact a general right of privacy:

'the best way to ensure regard for privacy is to provide specific and effective sanctions against clearly defined activities which unreasonably frustrate the individual in his search for privacy' (see Cmnd. 5012 (1972) no. 633, and WACKS (above p. 725)

8 f.). Since Parliament has not even taken the specific steps proposed, it still falls to the courts to develop rules to protect the right of privacy, defamation apart. They have held that information regarding a person's private life or intimate area may not be published if it was obtained through a breach of confidence. Thus a woman may enjoin her divorced husband from publishing in a magazine intimate details about her which he learnt during the subsistence of the marriage and in the confidence engendered by it (*Duchess of Argyll* v. *Duke of Argyll*, [1967] 1 Ch. 302; see also *Fraser* v. *Evans*, [1969] 1 QB 349; *Woodward* v. *Hutchins*, [1977] 1 WLR 760, and WACKS (above p. 725) 15 f., 83 ff.). No such claim lies if the plaintiff's private secrets were not 'confided' in anyone but were were brought to light by independent research; information obtained by illegal telephone tapping, however, is obtained in breach of confidence; see *Francome* v. *Mirror Group Newspapers*, [1984] 1 WLR 892.

V

Our comparative survey of the ways in which the private law sanctions invasions of the human personality has been far too short to serve as the basis of a critical judgment. In particular we have been able only to hint at two difficult problems: first, the question of the quantum of damages (for the details see STOLL (above p. 725)), and secondly the central question how the different legal systems weigh up the public interest in information and entertainment with the individual's need to be protected from invasions of his private sphere.

The great relevance of constitutional law to this balancing process may be seen from decisions in Gemany and the United States. In recognizing the 'general right of personality' the Bundesgerichtshof emphasized the entrenched position accorded to human dignity and the fundamental right freely to develop one's personality by arts. 1 and 2 of the Basic Law, but it has also stated that this is not an unqualified right but is limited by another constitutionally protected right, namely the right to free expression of one's opinions in speech, picture, and writing. Especially when an individual is publicly criticized, all the circumstances of the case must be considered in balancing the interests involved and deciding whether priority is to be given to the citizen's right of personality or the freedom of the press, both of which are constitutionally guaranteed. In performing such a balancing operation the Supreme Court of the United States has accorded the freedom of the press a higher standing than elsewhere, making it a characteristic feature of American public life. In many recent decisions it has specified the circumstances under which it is constitutionally permissible to hold an organ of the press liable in damages for 'defamation' or for infringement of the 'right of privacy'. The leading case is *New York Times Co.* v. *Sullivan*, 376 US 254 (1964). The defendant newspaper published a report which was sharply critical of the conduct of the local police chief during racial unrest in Alabama. The report was in certain respects inaccurate, and the Supreme Court of Alabama held that the newspaper must pay damages of $500,000. The Supreme Court of the United States quashed this decision as unconstitutional: if liability were imposed on an organ of the press simply because it had got the facts wrong, the press would seek to avoid liability by 'self-censorship', which was incompatible with the 'profound national commitment that debate on public issues should be uninhibited, robust and wide open' (ibid. p. 270). Thus a 'public official' complaining of criticism must also prove that the defendant newspaper publisher had published the false report 'with knowledge of its falsity or in reckless disregard of the truth'. The Supreme Court has subsequently applied the same principle to cases in which the plaintiff was not a 'public official' at all, but simply a 'public figure' who had acquired some notoriety. For example, see *Curtis Publishing Co.* v. *Butts*, 388 US 130 (1967). The press has the same privilege regarding invasion of privacy (see *Time Inc.* v. *Hill*, 385 US 374 (1967)). This was even extended to cases where the plaintiff was a private individual who had had the misfortune to be involved in a situation of sufficient public interest to attract media coverage (*Rosenbloom* v. *Metromedia Inc.*, 403 US 29 (1971)). But this was to go too far, and since *Gertz* v. *Robert Welch Inc.*, 418 US 323 (1974) the pendulum has begun to swing back. 'Private' plaintiffs no longer have to prove that the false report was published intentionally or with gross negligence, but some fault is still required (in contrast with England (see above p. 737)) before the press can constitutionally he held liable for an inaccurate factual report.

The most important cases in which protection has always been afforded against invasions of personality involve attacks on a man's honour and reputation. What is striking here is the difference between legal systems in the degree of connection between private law and criminal law. At one end of the scale we find Franch law, where not only are civil and criminal proceedings procedurally connected through the *partie civile* device but where there is also a substantial link between the determination of criminal liability and the determination of 'faute' under art. 1382 Code civil. In the Common Law, on the other hand, criminal law has virtually no importance at all with regard to defamation; indeed, it may well be that the explanation of the very high damages which are awarded in defamation suits, much to the surprise of the Continental jurist, lies in the fact that in this area private law is performing the functions of criminal law. On this point German law has undergone an interesting development. Since honour is not one of the interests legally protected by §823 par. 1 BGB, the courts originally had to refer to the criminal law in order to ask whether the defendant had committed the offence of insult or slander and so broken a protective statute under §823 par. 2 BGB. Once the courts established the 'general right of personality' this link between private law and criminal law in protecting honour was loosened, and the courts can now hold that the defendant's behaviour is an unpermitted invasion of the 'general right of personality' and give damages to the plaintiff under §823 par. 1 BGB without asking whether that behaviour also constituted the crime of insult or slander.

The English courts have not yet recognized the 'right of privacy' and in consequence can only afford the protection of the law in cases where the defendant's conduct satisfies the requirements of the tort of defamation, of breach of copyright, breach of contract, or some other head of liability. In the United States the development has rather been in the reverse direction: the courts tend more and more to treat cases where facts concerning the private life of the plaintiff have been published without his consent or where he has publicly been placed in a false light as invasions of the 'right to privacy' although the tort of defamation has been committed as well. PROSSER has warned that this development runs the risk of evading the defences which have been very carefully worked out in defamation suits (48 *Calif. L. Rev.* 401 (1960)). WADE (15 *Vand. L. Rev.* 1093 (1962)) welcomes the merger of the tort of defamation in the general claim for invasion of the right of privacy as being the best way to get rid of the 'anomalies and absurdities' in the law of libel.

Only *French* private law has been able to give protection to the human personality without any doctrinal difficulties: whereas the United States courts had to follow WARREN and BRANDEIS in extending the number of traditional types of tort, and the *German* courts had to deviate from §823 par. 1 BGB, which was too narrowly drafted, and from §253 BGB, which was wholly misconceived in limiting the duty to pay damages for immaterial harm, France had no need to make comparable efforts. It is much easier for a legal system to adapt itself to rapid movements in an area of law and to afford effective and necessary protection against novel, unexpected, and sophisticated forms of invasion of the human personality if it does not have a traditional law of actions such as the Common Law has nor narrow texts like those of German tort law. It is true that the adaptability of French law is bought at the price of the boundless unspecificity of art. 1382 Code civil, which simply lays down that every 'faute' entails liability in damages. For this reason the solution of Swiss law seems to us to be the best. Art. 28 of the Swiss Civil Code and 49 of the Swiss Law of Obligations provide that a person who is injured 'in his personal affairs' has legal protection but that monetary damages may be ordained only in cases of 'particular gravity of the invasion'. These rules are as specific as is possible and as general as is necessary. If only the fathers of the BGB had had the courage to draft similar provisions, the courts and legal scholars in Germany would have been spared a great deal of trouble.

Index